Short Story Criticism

Guide to Gale Literary Criticism Series

When you need to review criticism of literary works, these are the Gale series to use:

If the author's death date is:	You should turn to:
After Dec. 31, 1959 (or author is still living)	***CONTEMPORARY LITERARY CRITICISM*** for example: Jorge Luis Borges, Anthony Burgess, William Faulkner, Mary Gordon, Ernest Hemingway, Iris Murdoch
1900 through 1959	***TWENTIETH-CENTURY LITERARY CRITICISM*** for example: Willa Cather, F. Scott Fitzgerald, Henry James, Mark Twain, Virginia Woolf
1800 through 1899	***NINETEENTH-CENTURY LITERATURE CRITICISM*** for example: Fyodor Dostoevski, Nathaniel Hawthorne, George Sand, William Wordsworth
1400 through 1799	***LITERATURE CRITICISM FROM 1400 TO 1800*** ***(excluding Shakespeare)*** for example: Anne Bradstreet, Daniel Defoe, Alexander Pope, François Rabelais, Jonathan Swift, Phillis Wheatley ***SHAKESPEAREAN CRITICISM*** Shakespeare's plays and poetry
Antiquity through 1399	***CLASSICAL AND MEDIEVAL LITERATURE CRITICISM*** for example: Dante, Homer, Plato, Sophocles, Vergil, the Beowulf Poet

---

Gale also publishes related criticism series:

BLACK LITERATURE CRITICISM
Covers the most significant Black authors of the past 200 years.

CHILDREN'S LITERATURE REVIEW
This series covers authors of all eras who have written for the preschool through high school audience.

SHORT STORY CRITICISM
This series covers the major short fiction writers of all nationalities and periods of literary history.

POETRY CRITICISM
This series covers poets of all nationalities and periods of literary history.

DRAMA CRITICISM
This series covers playwrights of all nationalities and periods of literary history.

ISSN 0895-9439

Volume 11

Short Story Criticism

Excerpts from Criticism of the
Works of Short Fiction Writers

8920

David Segal
Editor

Laurie DiMauro
Marie Lazzari
Thomas Ligotti
Janet M. Witalec
Associate Editors

Gale Research Inc. • *DETROIT* • *WASHINGTON, D.C.* • *LONDON*

STAFF

David Segal, *Editor*

Laurie DiMauro, Marie Lazzari, Thomas Ligotti, Janet M. Witalec,
Associate Editors

Rogene M. Fisher, Christopher Giroux, Brigham Narins, James
Poniewozik, Debra A. Wells, Lynn M. Zott, *Assistant Editors*

Jeanne A. Gough, *Permissions & Production Manager*

Linda M. Pugliese, *Production Supervisor*

Paul Lewon, Maureen Puhl, Camille Robinson, Jennifer VanSickle,
Editorial Associates

Donna Craft, Rosita D'Souza, Sheila Walencewicz, *Editorial Assistants*

Sandra C. Davis, *Permissions Supervisor (Text)*

Maria L. Franklin, Josephine M. Keene, Michele M. Lonoconus, Denise
M. Singleton, Kimberly F. Smilay, *Permissions Associates*

Brandy C. Merritt, Shalice Shah, *Permissions Assistants*

Margaret A. Chamberlain, *Permissions Supervisor (Pictures)*

Pamela A. Hayes, *Permissions Associate*

Karla Kulkis, Nancy Rattenbury, Keith Reed, *Permissions Assistants*

Victoria B. Cariappa, *Research Manager*

Maureen Richards, *Research Supervisor*

Robert S. Lazich, Mary Beth McElmeel, Tamara C. Nott, *Editorial
Associates*

Andrea Ghorai, Daniel J. Jankowski, Julie K. Karmazin, *Editorial
Assistants*

Mary Beth Trimper, *Production Director*

Catherine Kemp, *Production Assistant*

Cynthia Baldwin, *Art Director*

Nicholas Jakubiak, C. J. Jonik, Yolanda Y. Latham, *Keyliner*

Since this page cannot legibly accommodate all the copyright notices, the Acknowledgments constitute an extension of the copyright page.

The paper used in this publication meets the minimum requirements of American National Standard for Information Sciences—Permanence Paper for Printed Library Materials, ANSI Z39.48-1984

Library of Congress Catalog Card Number 88-641014
ISBN 0-8103-7953-8
ISSN 0895-9439
Printed in the United States of America
Published simultaneously in the United Kingdom
by Gale Research International Limited
(An affiliated company of Gale Research Inc.)

Contents

Preface   vii

Acknowledgments   ix

Preface

Short Story Criticism (SSC) presents significant passages from criticism of the world's greatest short story writers and provides supplementary biographical and bibliographical materials to guide the interested reader to a greater understanding of the authors of short fiction. This series was developed in response to suggestions from librarians serving high school, college, and public library patrons, who had noted a considerable number of requests for critical material on short story writers. Although major short story writers are covered in such Gale series as *Contemporary Literary Criticism (CLC), Twentieth-Century Literary Criticism (TCLC), Nineteenth-Century Literature Criticism (NCLC),* and *Literature Criticism from 1400 to 1800 (LC),* librarians perceived the need for a series devoted solely to writers of the short story genre.

Scope of the Work

SSC is designed to serve as an introduction to major short story writers of all eras and nationalities. Since these authors have inspired a great deal of relevant critical material, *SSC* is necessarily selective, and the editors have chosen the most important published criticism to aid readers and students in their research.

Approximately ten to fifteen authors are included in each volume, and each entry presents a historical survey of the critical response to that author's work. The length of an entry is intended to reflect the amount of critical attention the author has received from critics writing in English and from foreign critics in translation. Every attempt has been made to identify and include excerpts from the most significant essays on each author's work. In order to provide these important critical pieces, the editors will sometimes reprint essays that have appeared in previous volumes of Gale's Literary Criticism Series. Such duplication, however, never exceeds twenty percent of an *SSC* volume.

Organization of the Book

An *SSC* author entry consists of the following elements:

- The **author heading** cites the name under which the author most commonly wrote, followed by birth and death dates. If the author wrote consistently under a pseudonym, the pseudonym will be listed in the author heading and the author's actual name given in parentheses on the first line of the biographical and critical introduction.

- The **biographical and critical introduction** contains background information designed to introduce a reader to the author and the critical debates surrounding his or her work. Parenthetical material following the introduction provides references to other biographical and critical series published by Gale, including *CLC, TCLC, NCLC, Contemporary Authors,* and *Dictionary of Literary Biography.*

- A **portrait of the author** is included when available. Many entries also contain illustrations of materials pertinent to an author's career, including holographs of manuscript pages, title pages, dust jackets, letters, or representations of important people, places, and events in the author's life.

- The list of **principal works** is chronological by date of first publication and lists the most important works by the author. The first section comprises short story collections, novellas, and novella collections. The second section gives information on other major works by the author. For foreign authors, the editors have provided original foreign-language publication information and have selected what are considered the best and most complete English-language editions of their works.

- **Criticism** is arranged chronologically in each author entry to provide a useful perspective on changes in critical evaluation over the years. All short story, novella, and collection titles by the author featured in the entry are printed in boldface type to enable a reader to ascertain without difficulty the works discussed. Also for purposes of easier identification, the critic's name and the publication date of the essay are given at the beginning of each piece of criticism. Unsigned criticism is preceded by the title of the journal in which it appeared.

- Critical essays are prefaced with **explanatory notes** as an additional aid to students and readers using *SSC.* The explanatory notes provide several types of useful information, including: the reputation of a critic, the importance of a work of criticism, and the specific type of criticism (biographical, psychoanalytic, structuralist, etc.).

- A complete **bibliographical citation,** designed to help the interested reader locate the original essay or book, follows each piece of criticism.

- The **further reading list** appearing at the end of each author entry suggests additional materials on the author. In some cases it includes essays for which the editors could not obtain reprint rights.

Beginning with volume six, *SSC* contains two additional features designed to enhance the reader's understanding of short fiction writers and their works:

- Each *SSC* entry now includes, when available, **comments by the author** that illuminate his or her own works or the short story genre in general. These statements are set within boxes or bold rules to distinguish them from the criticism.

- A **select bibliography of general sources on short fiction** is included as an appendix. Updated and amended with each new *SSC* volume, this listing of materials for further research provides readers with a selection of the best available general studies of the short story genre.

Other Features

A **cumulative author index** lists all the authors who have appeared in *SSC, CLC, TCLC, NCLC, LC,* and *Classical and Medieval Literature Criticism (CMLC),* as well as cross-references to other Gale series. Users will welcome this cumulated index as a useful tool for locating an author within the Literary Criticism Series.

A **cumulative nationality index** lists all authors featured in *SSC* by nationality, followed by the number of the *SSC* volume in which their entry appears.

A **cumulative title index** lists in alphabetical order all short story, novella, and collection titles contained in the *SSC* series. Titles of short story collections, separately published novellas, and novella collections are printed in italics, while titles of individual short stories are printed in roman type with quotation marks. Each title is followed by the author's name and the corresponding volume and page numbers where commentary on the work may be located. English-language translations of original foreign-language titles are cross-referenced to the foreign titles so that all references to discussion of a work are combined in one listing.

A Note to the Reader

When writing papers, students who quote directly from any volume in the Literary Criticism Series may use the following general forms to footnote reprinted criticism. The first example pertains to material drawn from periodicals, the second to material reprinted from books:

[1] Henry James, Jr., "Honoré de Balzac," *The Galaxy* 20 (December 1875), 814-36; excerpted and reprinted in *Short Story Criticism,* Vol. 5, ed. Thomas Votteler (Detroit: Gale Research, 1990), pp. 8-11.

[2] F. R. Leavis, *D. H. Lawrence: Novelist* (Alfred A. Knopf, 1956); excerpted and reprinted in *Short Story Criticism,* Vol. 4, ed. Thomas Votteler (Detroit: Gale Research, 1990), pp. 202-06.

Suggestions Are Welcome

Readers who wish to suggest authors to appear in future volumes, or who have other suggestions, are invited to contact the editors by writing to Gale Research, Inc., Literary Criticism Division, 835 Penobscot Building, Detroit, MI., 48226-4094.

ACKNOWLEDGMENTS

The editors wish to thank the copyright holders of the excerpted criticism included in this volume, the permissions managers of many book and magazine publishing companies for assisting us in securing reprint rights, and Anthony Bogucki for assistance with copyright research. We are also grateful to the staffs of the Detroit Public Library, the Library of Congress, the University of Detroit Library, Wayne State University Purdy/Kresge Library Complex, and the University of Michigan Libraries for making their resources available to us. Following is a list of the copyright holders who have granted us permission to reprint material in this volume of *SSC*. Every effort has been made to trace copyright, but if omissions have been made, please let us know.

COPYRIGHT EXCERPTS IN *SSC,* VOLUME 11, WERE REPRINTED FROM THE FOLLOWING PERIODICALS:

Anglo-Irish and Irish Literature—Aspects of Language and Culture: Proceedings of the Ninth International Congress of the International Association for the Study of Anglo-Irish Literature, v. II, eds., B. Bramsbäck and M. Croghan, Uppsala 1988. Acta Univ. Ups.: *Studia Anglistica Upsaliensia.* © Birgit Bramsbäck, with the authors of articles, in so far as their respective contributions are concerned, 1988. Reprinted by permission of Birgit Bramsbäck and Maria Edelson.—*Arizona Quarterly,* v. 38, Autumn, 1982 for " 'Dr. Jekyll and Mr. Hyde': Anatomy of Misperception" by Daniel V. Fraustino. Copyright © 1982 by Arizona Board of Regents. Reprinted by permission of the publisher and the author.—*Book World—The Washington Post,* September 19, 1982; May 12, 1991. © 1982, 1991, *The Washington Post.* Both reprinted with permission of the publisher.—*Boston Review,* v. XI, December, 1986 for "The Beattietudes" by Mark Silk. Copyright © 1986 by the Boston Critic, Inc. Reprinted by permission of the author.—*Canadian American Slavic Studies,* v. 19, Fall, 1985. Copyright © 1985 by Charles Schlacks, Jr., Publisher. All rights reserved. Reprinted by permission of the publisher.—*CLA Journal,* v. XXI, September, 1977. Copyright, 1977 by The College Language Association. Used by permission of The College Language Association.—*College English,* v. 26, February, 1965 for "Thematic Rhythm in 'The Red Pony' " by Arnold L. Goldsmith. Copyright © 1965 by the National Council of Teachers of English. Reprinted by permission of the publisher and the author.—*Commentary,* v. 63, February, 1977 for "Ann Beattie & the 60's" by John Romano; v. 75, March, 1983 for Ann Beattie and the Hippoisie" by Joseph Epstein. Copyright © 1977, 1983 by the American Jewish Committee. All rights reserved. Both reprinted by permission of the publisher and the respective authors.—*The Commonweal,* v. LXXV, December 8, 1961. Copyright © 1961, renewed 1989 Commonweal Publishing Co., Inc. Reprinted by permission of Commonweal Foundation.—*The Denver Quarterly,* v. 15, Summer, 1980 for "Ann Beattie: Still with the Sixties" by Karla M. Hammond. Copyright © 1980 by the University of Denver. Reprinted by permission of the author.—*English Studies in Africa,* v. 31, 1988 for "The Marvellous Rose: Christ and the Meaning of Art in 'The Nightingale and the Rose' " by Guy Willoughby. Reprinted by permission of the publisher and the author.—*Essays by Divers Hands,* v. XXXVIII, 1975 for "Flaubert and the Art of the Short Story" by A. W. Raitt. © A. W. Raitt 1975. Reprinted by permission of the author.—*Études Anglaises,* v. XXXVII, April-June, 1984. Reprinted by permission of the publisher.—*French Studies,* v. XXIX, July, 1975. Reprinted by permission of the publisher.—*The Hollins Critic,* v. XIII, April, 1976. Copyright 1976 by Hollins College. Reprinted by permission of the publisher.—*The Hudson Review,* v. XXX, Autumn, 1977; v. XL, Winter, 1988. Copyright © 1977, 1988 by The Hudson Review, Inc. Both reprinted by permission of the publisher.—*The Humanities Association Bulletin,* v. XXI, Winter, 1970. Reprinted by permission of the publisher.—*The Journal of Religion,* v. 69, July, 1989. © 1989 by The University of Chicago. All rights reserved. Reprinted by permission of The University of Chicago Press.—*London Magazine,* n.s., v. 22, March, 1983. © *London Magazine* 1983. Reprinted by permission of the publisher.—*Los Angeles Times Book Review,* October 12, 1986. Copyright, 1986, *Los Angeles Times.* Reprinted by permission of the publisher.—*MELUS,* v. 12, Fall, 1985. Copyright, MELUS, The Society for the Study of Multi-Ethnic Literature of the United States, 1985. Reprinted by permission of the publisher.—*Midstream,* v. XXI, January, 1975 for "The Riddle of Tillie Olsen" by Elenore Lester. Copyright © 1975 by The Theodor Herzl Foundation, Inc. Reprinted by permission of the publisher and the author.—*Modern Fiction Studies,* v. XIV, Winter, 1968-69. Copyright © 1969 by Purdue Research Foundation, West Lafayette, IN 47907. All rights reserved. Reprinted with permission.—*The Modern Language Review,* v. 76, July, 1981 for "The Problem of Truth in 'San Manuel Bueno, Mártir' " by C. A. Longhurst; v. 80, October, 1985 for "Spatiality and Structure in Flaubert's 'Hérodias' " by R. B. Leal. © Modern Humanities Research Association 1981, 1985. Both reprinted by permission of the publisher and the respective authors.—*The Nation,* New York, v. 214, April 10, 1972. Copyright 1972 *The Nation* magazine/The Nation Company, Inc. Reprinted by permission of the publisher.—*National Review,* New York, v. XXV, August 31, 1973. © 1973 by National Review, Inc., 150 East 35th Street, New York, NY 10016. Reprinted with permission of the publisher.—*Neophilologus,* v. LXXI, January, 1987 for "Unamuno's Impostors:

son.—Lisca, Peter. From *The Wide World of John Steinbeck*. Rutgers University Press, 1958. Copyright © 1958 by Rutgers, The State University. Renewed 1986 by Peter Lisca. Reprinted by permission of the publisher.—Marías, Julián. From *Miguel de Unamuno*. Translated by Frances M. López-Morillas. Cambridge, Mass.: Harvard University Press, 1966. Copyright © 1966 by the Presidents and Fellows of Harvard College. All rights reserved. Excerpted by permission of the publishers and the author.—Meyers, Jeffrey. From an introduction to *The Body Snatcher and Other Stories: Robert Louis Stevenson*. Edited by Jeffrey Meyers. New American Library, 1988. Introduction and bibliography copyright © 1988 by Jeffrey Meyers. Used by permission of New American Library, a Division of Penguin Books USA Inc., New York, NY.—Nabokov, Vladimir. From *Nabokov's Dozen: A Collection of Thirteen Stories*. Doubleday & Company, Inc. 1958. Copyright © 1958 by Vladimir Nabokov. All rights reserved.— Nadeau, Maurice. From *The Greatness of Flaubert*. Translated by Barbara Bray. The Library Press, 1972. Copyright © 1972 by The Library Press. Reprinted by permission of Open Court Publishing Company, La Salle, Illinois.—Nassaar, Christopher S. From *Into the Demon Universe: A Literary Exploration of Oscar Wilde*. Yale University Press, 1974. Copyright © 1974 by Yale University. All rights reserved. Reprinted by permission of the publisher.—Neider, Charles. From an introduction to *The Complete Short Stories of Robert Louis Stevenson*. Edited by Charles Neider. Doubleday & Company, Inc., 1969. Copyright © 1969 by Charles Neider. All rights reserved. Used by permission of Doubleday, a division of Bantam Doubleday Dell Publishing Group, Inc.—Orr, Elaine Neil. From *Tillie Olsen and a Feminist Spiritual Vision*. University Press of Mississippi, 1987. Copyright © 1987 by the University Press of Mississippi. All rights reserved. Reprinted by permission of the publisher.— Ouimette, Victor. From *Reason Aflame: Unamuno and the Heroic Will*. Yale University Press, 1974. Copyright © 1974 by Yale University. All rights reserved. Reprinted by permission of the publisher.—Owens, Louis. From *John Steinbeck's Re-Vision of America*. University of Georgia Press, 1985. © 1985 by the University of Georgia Press. All rights reserved. Reprinted by permission of the publisher.—Perrone-Moisés, Leyla. From " 'Quidquid volueris': The Scriptural Education," translated by Robert Riger, in *Flaubert and Postmodernism*. Edited by Naomi Schor and Henry F. Majewski. University of Nebraska Press, 1984. Copyright © Éditions du Seuil. Translation copyright © 1984 by the University of Nebraska Press. All rights reserved. Reprinted by permission of Georges Borchardt, Inc. for Éditions du Seuil.—Porter, Carolyn. From "Ann Beattie: The Art of the Missing," in *Contemporary American Women Writers: Narrative Strategies*. Edited by Catherine Rainwater and William J. Scheick. The University Press of Kentucky, 1985. Copyright © 1985 by The University Press of Kentucky. Reprinted by permission of the publisher.—Roe, David. From *Gustave Flaubert*. Macmillan Education Ltd., 1989. St. Martin's Press, 1989. © David Roe 1989. All rights reserved. Used by permission of St. Martin's Press, Inc. In Canada by Macmillan, London and Basingstoke.—Steinbeck, John. From a letter to Edith Mirrielees, dated March 8, 1962. © by Elaine A. Steinbeck. Reprinted by permission of Elaine A. Steinbeck and McIntosh & Otis, Inc.—Timmerman, John H. From *The Dramatic Landscape of Steinbeck's Short Stories*. University of Oklahoma Press, 1990. Copyright © 1990 by the University of Oklahoma Press, Norman, Publishing Division of the University. All rights reserved. Reprinted by permission of the publisher.—Twitchell, James B. From *Dreadful Pleasures: An Anatomy of Modern Horror*. Oxford University Press, 1985. Copyright © 1985 by Oxford University Press, Inc. All rights reserved. Reprinted by permission of the publisher.—Valdés, Mario J. From *Death in the Literature of Unamuno*. University of Illinois Press, 1964. © 1964 by the Board of Trustees of the University of Illinois. Reprinted by permission of the publisher and the author.—Van Buren, Jane Silverman. From *The Modernist Madonna: Semiotics of the Maternal Metaphor*. Indiana University Press, 1989. Copyright © 1989 by Jane Silverman Van Buren. All rights reserved. Reprinted by permission of the publisher.—Wyers, Frances. From *Miguel De Unamuno: The Contrary Self*. Tamesis Books Limited, 1976. © by Tamesis Books Limited, London, 1976. Reprinted by permission of the publisher.

PHOTOGRAPHS AND ILLUSTRATIONS APPEARING IN *SSC*, VOLUME 11, WERE RECEIVED FROM THE FOLLOWING SOURCES:

© Jerry Bauer: p. 1; Copyright © Philippe Halsman 1968: p. 118; Courtesy of Mrs. Vera Nabokov: p. 131; Jacket of *Nabokov's Dozen*, by Vladimir Nabokov. Copyright. Used by permission of Doubleday, a division of Bantam Doubleday Dell Publishing Group, Inc.: p. 146; Photograph by Leonda Fiske: p. 162; Erich Auerbach Collection, FRPS: p. 201; © 1983 Richard L. Allman: p. 216; Photograph by Sonya Noskowiak, courtesy of Arthur F. Noskowiak, The John Steinbeck Collection, Stanford University Libraries: p. 244; Courtesy of Mrs. E.G. Ainsworth, John Steinbeck Library, Salinas, Steinbeck Archives: p. 255; The Bettmann Archive: pp. 310, 405; Reprinted by permission of the Estate of Miguel de Unamuno: p. 341.

Ann Beattie

1947-

American short story writer, novelist, nonfiction writer, and author of children's books.

INTRODUCTION

Beattie's fiction focuses on individuals whose passivity and inability to comprehend themselves or others trap them in dissatisfactory situations. Beattie employs a prose style composed of flat, declarative sentences and detached observations that parallel her characters' listlessness. Her protagonists are typically well-educated people of the "baby boom" generation who experience a sense of loss as they attempt to reconcile the idealistic convictions of their youth with their present lifestyles. Refusing to resolve the dilemmas posed in her fiction, Beattie rarely explores the desires that motivate her characters. She focuses instead on their external environment, providing idiosyncratic and telling details, including frequent references to popular culture. While some critics object to her characters' lack of psychological and historical backgrounds, others praise Beattie for the photographic accuracy of her descriptions, and most agree that her stories realistically reflect the disjointed and haphazard nature of contemporary life.

Beattie's first three volumes of short fiction focus on characters who lack permanent emotional ties—individuals who experience a pervasive, vague despair with their present lifestyle and the future. With *Distortions,* her first collection of stories, Beattie earned a reputation for realistic depictions of passive people stranded in unfulfilling situations as a result of their adventures in the hedonistic 1960s. For example, "Fancy Flights" includes a much-lauded description of a man high on marijuana. "Wally Whistles Dixie," also from this volume, concerns a thirty-year-old ballerina who marries a man half her age. *Secrets and Surprises* portrays similar characters in the increasingly conservative 1970s. Many of the characters in this collection are involved in ungratifying relationships they seem unable to leave, or still mourn the loss of a lover years after the end of the affair. *The Burning House,* Beattie's third volume of short stories, includes "Learning to Fall," in which a woman takes the son of her friend on a weekly outing to New York. They are accompanied by her lover, to whom she can neither commit herself nor completely relinquish. Critics often found the stark, crystalline quality of Beattie's prose coupled with an absence of commentary upon her characters' actions or inability to act unsettling.

Where You'll Find Me, and Other Stories contains pieces in which the past helps illuminate, if not relieve, Beattie's characters' present dissatisfaction. Beattie depicts middle-aged people who have never achieved the success or happi-

ness for which they seemed destined in their youth. The most celebrated story in this collection, "Janus," concerns a woman's obsession with a bowl given to her by a former lover. Critics note that the determining factor in the protagonist's life is loss; thus the beautiful bowl, perpetually empty, is symbolic of the woman herself. While generally praised, *Where You'll Find Me, and Other Stories* was regarded by some as lacking the emotional and technical range of Beattie's earlier volumes.

In *What Was Mine, and Other Stories,* Beattie also introduces characters whose past informs their present, but in this collection memory serves as a coping device and a source of growth. The mood of "In Amalfi" is one of serenity and enchantment as a divorced couple use their vacation in Italy as an occasion to reflect upon the past and escape the realities of the present. The collection's title story is marked by the narrator's feelings of loss and abandonment as photographs of the father he never knew spark memories of the childhood he spent with his mother and her boyfriend. It is through his reminiscing that the narrator comes to understand the profound effect both the boyfriend and absent father have had upon his life. Applauded by critics for its more introspective and sympathetic tone,

What Was Mine, and Other Stories is widely acclaimed as Beattie's most fully realized work of short fiction.

PRINCIPAL WORKS

SHORT FICTION

Distortions   1976
Secrets and Surprises   1978
The Burning House   1982
Where You'll Find Me, and Other Stories   1986
What Was Mine, and Other Stories   1991

OTHER MAJOR WORKS

Chilly Scenes of Winter   (novel)   1976
Falling in Place   (novel)   1980
Love Always   (novel)   1985
Spectacles   (juvenilia)   1985
Alex Katz   (art criticism)   1987
Picturing Will   (novel)   1989

CRITICISM

John Romano   (essay date 1977)

[*In the excerpt below, Romano praises Beattie's sympathy for her characters and her attention to detail in* Distortions.]

Ann Beattie's stories have been appearing in the *New Yorker* for the past few years, and have now been collected in a volume called *Distortions,* published simultaneously with the author's *Chilly Scenes of Winter,* a novel. It is unusual, of course, for a new author to appear with two books at once, but evidently Ann Beattie has been able to compel special treatment from her publisher as well as from reviewers and readers. It is the uniqueness of her talent that compels. Her best fiction renders a distinctive subject matter in a distinctive tone, and the note she sounds is powerfully her own.

Her subject matter is a certain shiftlessness and lack of self-apprehension besetting people in their twenties and thirties: a former Phi Beta Kappa guiltily resigned to living on welfare checks, young wives rejecting husbands and lovers in desultory and emotionless gestures of independence, a lesbian feminist whose only friends are male. She conveys the drabness of these lives by her tone and by an almost hallucinatory particularity of detail. We are taken on that round of grocery shopping, walking the dog, getting the worthless car fixed, which Auden had in mind when he said that "in headaches and in worry, / Vaguely life leaks away." But Beattie's writing is not tedious; there is, instead, something graceful and painstaking about her fidelity to the ordinary.

The story, **"Imagined Scenes,"** presents a young woman who works nights sitting up with an old man who has insomnia, while her husband, a graduate student, is busy studying for his oral exams. Or so she assumes. The daily schedules of the couple barely overlap. They do not inhabit the same hours, and there is something chilling and mysterious about the gap between them. When she returns home in the mornings, there are frequent signs of inexplicable activity: three coffee cups on the table, or a favorite plant missing. Once when she calls home at four in the morning there is no answer. Her husband's explanations are plausible—a couple she has never met came to visit, he was asleep when the phone rang—but they are oddly insufficient, too, and seem slightly sinister in the haze of mutual incomprehension. The glimpses, the physical data, which the woman has of her husband's life in her absence tell her nothing, though they hint at guilty secrets. They cannot be either ignored or interpreted. Scattered among them are the monologues of her patient, the old man, which are very skillfully made to seem only accidentally relevant to the woman's puzzling home life. We are given nothing more. However, a suggestion of the peculiar way in which Beattie makes such material her own lurks in the title: **"Imagined Scenes."** We do not realize, or not all at once, that what the young woman has "imagined" is not her husband's private or guilty activity. She has accepted not the explanations but the sufficiency unto themselves of the physical facts. She "imagines" only that she is in Greece, or someplace warm, by the sea, while the scene of her actual present life is snowy. It is the reader who has been seduced into guessing at the husband's hidden life.

I dwell on this short story because it seems to me emblematic of Beattie's skill in this genre. But one thing more should be said about it, which goes rather beyond skill. We guess at the "real facts" of the woman's life because we care about her, her sadness has been made significant. It follows that the author has cared about her in the making. But then it is more astonishing to perceive that the woman cares so little, so indistinctly, for herself. She is not suspicious, she has no imagination; the mark of Beattie's respect for this creation is not to have slipped her some healthy suspicion, as it were, under the counter. In this forbearance the writer resembles some impossible ideal of a loving parent who succeeds in not interfering in her children's lives. To love one's characters—Tolstoy is the presiding genius here—is to allow them to be who they are.

A risk of a particular kind attends this achievement and Beattie is not immune to it. The style of much "serious fiction" in recent years has tended to be cool, to attend scrupulously to the surface of events, with a language pruned and polished in respect of its own surface. Now Beattie's writing has something in common with this style: her sentences are often plain, flat, their grammar exposed like the lighting fixtures in avant-garde furniture boutiques, and the effect is at first wearying. Only later does the sympathetic center of her work betray itself. We may feel misled by the outward reserve, but, again, her willingness to distort when necessary, her passion for the particular, is ultimately an index of her concern for the integrity of things and people in themselves.

Many of the people in these books verge on the grotesque—dwarfs, a cleaning woman hulking in mind and body who believes she was a cat in a former life. Here, too, Beattie risks a convergence with her slicker contemporaries, whose fascination with the grotesque is full of smugness about what is "normal." (Beattie herself invokes the photographs of Diane Arbus in several places, but I for one have never quite decided what Arbus's relation to her subjects really was.) There is a dog in *Chilly Scenes of Winter* who is a good example of Beattie's success with the grotesque. The dog is purchased to replace an entirely admirable dog who has died of old age, much mourned. But the new dog is ugly—part dachshund, part cocker spaniel—as well as hapless and insomniac. And yet, the people around him feel the dog must be fed and must not be compared to his predecessor; at night, his audible perambulations must be endured. Because, "terrible genetic mistake" that he is, the dog, named "Dog," is real and undeniable. He is part of that world of fact that Beattie honors almost compulsively, whatever its unwelcomeness or distortion. (pp. 62-3)

John Romano, "Ann Beattie & the 60's," in Commentary, *Vol. 63, No. 2, February, 1977, pp. 62-4.*

Peter Glassman   (essay date 1977)

[*Glassman is an American educator and critic. In the following excerpted review of* Distortions, *he hails Beattie as a "new and important talent," lauding her awareness of her characters' humanity and her clear, economic prose style.*]

[Regarding Ann Beattie], I can think of no other American writer save Thomas Pynchon who has found so wide and respectful an audience so early in her career. No one who has a serious interest in contemporary fiction can fail to be aware of Beattie's abrupt and alarming stories. Their publication in [*Distortions*] marks, I believe, a genuine event in the national life.

I suppose that one first feels struck by Beattie's consummate technical virtuosity. Her frigid prose, the shocking inexorableness of her humor and narrative designs, the macabre and spare efficiency of her thought, conspire to project her tales as actual—if rather awful—occurrences of modernist existence. I have called Beattie's prose cold: but one must read this most wicked and witty writer very closely indeed. It is true that she assembles as subjects a grotesque community of dwarfs, fats, gargoyles, and sluts, a bizarre collection of the lonely, the disoriented, and the dispossessed. Never, though, does she permit her figures to seem merely apathetic or aimlessly malcontent. Nor does she ever dismiss them as freaks. Beattie constructs her stories from within a soft and subtle sensibility of sympathy, participation, and hopefulness. She understands that, however capricious or queer, her characters' pains have their origin less in the morasses of individual neurosis than in the insipidity of the culture at large, the withering vapidity of the historical processes which envelop one and with which one must manage to coexist in some sort of emotional relation. It is the sign of her extraordinary intelligence and gentleness that Beattie considers her fictionalized people to be as human as their author; that she regards her own suffering as conterminous with that of her roughly satirized characters.

I suppose that one first feels struck by Beattie's consummate technical virtuosity. Her frigid prose, the shocking inexorableness of her humor and narrative designs, the macabre and spare efficiency of her thought, conspire to project her tales as actual—if rather awful—occurrences of modernist existence.

—*Peter Glassman*

Beattie comprehends, this is to say, that we are driven into our misery and peculiarity because, appropriately, we cannot accommodate the abstraction and absurdity which surround us. Her characters fervently want to feel; especially they long to love. But the rapidity and monstrousness of contemporary history, the dearth of external supports for even the minimal impulses of human life, seem to the stories' people to invalidate the very possibility of achieving affective experience. A woman called Cynthia wonders, "What am I trying to think about? . . . It is cold in the kitchen, and she is not hungry so much as empty. . . . She shivers with the coldness of it." A man named David's "feelings were so clichéd that he couldn't go through with them." "Ah, Wanda," says Ray. "You know that the world always dumps on you." Cynthia "begins to think that it's Nixon's fault—all of it . . . Damn you Nixon, she thinks. Damn you." "Death. Death everywhere," mourns another poor soul. "Japan, Viet Nam. Mortuary Science." Although they know that "death is everywhere," Beattie's characters insist that their lives become fruitful. Their humane and courageous hunger for the sensation at least of fellowship leads the stories' people to contrive strained and desperate terms of association with one another. In *Distortions* marriages become desiccated and collapse. Affairs terminate. Families disintegrate. Connected persons wantonly wrench and devastate one another. Couples eat junk food, smoke marijuana, drink liquor, listen to music, or listlessly sleep together rather than talk to one another. Particularly these molested and minified people try to anthropomorphize animals: Beattie's narratives almost invariably involve distorted emotional uses of cats and dogs, extreme and more than vaguely psychotic interactions with perplexed domestic beasts. Yet, none of this symptomatology of disjunction diminishes the fact that Beattie's characters do try to engage one another. However contorted, however abused, the experiment of partnership proposes itself in these rich and yearning tales as a bright and beckoning, if a haphazard, imaginative necessity. In this sense Beattie's characters are larger than the world which they occupy and more noble than their actual biographies. Like figures in cartoons they pop up whole and breathing and anxious for further knowledge no matter how often they get themselves squashed by their intransigent urge to discover the undiscoverable.

Beattie's master, no doubt too masterfully before her in **Distortions,** of course is Samuel Beckett (she names characters "Sam" with teasing frequency). Like Beckett, Beattie often is somewhat locked by her vision. Her judgments and her art are so defined, as it were so preconceived, that she does not always leave room for herself, her characters, or her readers to create independent responses to the circumstances which she invents. But Beattie also is as brave, and for that matter as funny, as Beckett. She sets no limits to the implications of her thought: she is willing to insist that things are exactly as they appear to be. Too, Beattie's powers grow considerably more sophisticated as her work progresses. Her most recently published piece, a story called **"Shifting,"** suggests that she already begins to release herself from her closed and in some measure overly convinced world view. The publication of **"Shifting,"** taken together with the simultaneous appearance of *Distortions* and *Chilly Scenes of Winter,* makes it vividly apparent that a new and important talent has come into being in our country. I feel the greatest trust in the health of Ann Beattie's talent, and the greatest sense of excitement about the body of work which she is producing. (pp. 447-48)

> *Peter Glassman, "American Romances: Fiction Chronicle," in* The Hudson Review, *Vol. XXX, No. 3, Autumn, 1977, pp. 437-50.*

Gail Godwin   (essay date 1979)

[*Godwin is a prolific American novelist, short story writer and essayist. In the following review, she faults some of the stories in* Secrets and Surprises *for their abundance of detached characters but illustrates how other stories become meaningful when characters are involved in their surroundings.*]

The characters who populate [*Secrets and Surprises*], Ann Beattie's second short-story collection, came of age during the 1960's. They are, on the whole, a nice-looking bunch of people who have never suffered from any of the basic wants. Most of them, for reasons often unexplained, share a mistrust of passion and conversation. If a man and woman get together, it is because of a shared car or animal, or because each has a famous parent, or maybe simply because one of them has run out of other people to live with; and, even when they live together, they speak in cool little ironies or deadpan non sequiturs. They live in student apartments in Boston or New Haven, or young-married or young-career quarters in Philadelphia or Manhattan, or sometimes a group of them share a house in Vermont; but they exist mainly in a stateless realm of indecision and—all too often—rather smug despair.

Penelope, in the story **"Colorado,"** we are told, "simply would not argue. She thought it took too much energy." She has "flunked out of Bard and dropped out of Antioch and the University of Connecticut, and now she knew that all colleges were the same . . . She had traded her Ford

for a Toyota, and Toyotas were no better than Fords." Penelope wants to go to Colorado. "Why Colorado?" her boyfriend asks. She says they can ski, "Or we could just ride the lift all day . . . " They go, because, in all but one of these stories, the woman is stronger than the man. When they get there, the house of the couple they are staying with looks exactly like a house in the East. The boyfriend, disoriented, smokes a joint and asks his host, "What state is this?"

In **"Friends,"** the longest piece in the volume, an endless marijuana party is going on at Francie's Vermont house; finally the real world intrudes and someone's car is stolen; then nothing happens again for a while, except people call their parents or discuss the dancing lessons they had to take; eventually the car thief returns to be reimbursed because the car wasn't worth anything. "I know your brother," he tells Francie, as conversationally as if they were meeting at dancing class, but also taking her money at knifepoint. At some later point in this meandering tale, Francie has "made it" as a painter and someone from *The Village Voice* has just arrived to interview her. We are left holding the door with Francie's platonic lover, who lets the journalist in.

In **"A Vintage Thunderbird,"** Karen lends her old lover the keys to her Thunderbird when she takes up with her new lover. And this seems to assuage his pain: "Every time he drove the car, he admired it more. She owned many things that he admired: a squirrel coat with a black taffeta lining, a pair of carved soapstone bookends that held some books of poetry on her night table, her collection of Louis Armstrong 78's." Frequently, in these stories, things are substitutes for the chancier commitment to people; things people buy or live with or give one another are asked to bear the responsibility of objective correlatives, but too often they become a mere catalogue of trends. The reader is left holding an armful of objects and wondering what emotional responses they were meant to connect him with.

Perhaps the best level on which to enjoy these stories is as a narrative form of social history. Miss Beattie has a coolly accurate eye for the *moeurs* of her generation. ("His daughter from his first marriage . . . sent him an Irish country hat. The present made him irritable . . . 'She wants to make me a laughable old man,' he said.") A young woman whose brother has just died in Vietnam sits on her family's dock and awaits her own response: "I was smoking grass, as usual—staring out at the water . . . I was thinking about how often my friends and I thought ironically, and how irony had been absent from my childhood . . . I was wondering if children miss a lot of ironies, or whether that had been a different world and everything in it really hadn't been ironic." But a sharp eye for *moeurs* doesn't add up to a full fiction any more than the attitude of irony can be said to represent a full human response.

The story that, to my taste, best weds feeling with artistic control is **"Distant Music,"** in which an office girl and a graduate-school dropout are brought together by a mongrel puppy named Sam. They take the dog because they fear for its life. They order their lives around it and for a time, consequently, they protect and nourish each other, the thriving puppy their evidence that survival is possible even in huge cities. Each of them grows, but, as is frequently the case, in opposite directions. When Jack leaves for California, where his songs soon catch on (there is a good one about "a dog named Sam") the dog left behind turns vicious. A bad mix, says the veterinarian, and Sharon must put Sam away. But when we last see Sharon, she has taken a man "new to the city" over to New Jersey to show him that, from the proper perspective, New York can be scaled to human possibility. The form of the story and the experiences of its characters have added up to something meaningful.

> *Gail Godwin, "Sufferers from Smug Despair," in* The New York Times Book Review, *January 14, 1979, p. 14.*

Ann Hulbert   (essay date 1979)

[*In the review below, Hulbert commends the power and poignancy of* Secrets and Surprises *and discusses Beattie's emphasis on descriptive details over structured plots.*]

Secrets and surprises might seem like unexpected specialties for Ann Beattie. In the pages of *The New Yorker* and of her two previous books—*Distortions,* a collection of short stories, and *Chilly Scenes of Winter,* a novel—she anatomizes the everyday lives of characters who are headed nowhere in particular and are unfamiliar with the usual literary kind of secrets and surprises—the kind associated with epiphanies. But as Beattie has hinted all along and emphasizes in this new collection of short stories [*Secrets and Surprises*], hidden knowledge and unexpected discoveries are also staples of ordinary, undramatic life. They don't just belong to rare moments, and they don't necessarily irradiate life with significance. Her characters are lonely and can't help having secrets; they are used to being taken aback by the unexpected because they foresee little and control less. Their lives don't really change after they acknowledge their secrets to themselves or partially reveal them to others. Instead, another disorderly day dawns. In the appropriately uninflected prose and loosely structured stories of *Secrets and Surprises* Beattie makes the days and characters come to life—almost paradoxically—more powerfully and poignantly than she has before.

The days Beattie depicts, however nondescript they are, are not the 9-5 mainstream kind. She writes about her own contemporaries, who turned 20 and lethargically offbeat as the 1960s came to an end. They lead marginal lives out in the country or on the fringe of cities. A character in *Chilly Scenes of Winter* articulates the feeling that pervades almost every story: " 'Everybody's so pathetic,' Sam says. 'What is it? Is it just the end of the sixties?' "

It's not that the 1960s have left Beattie's characters bitterly disillusioned about politics or society; the decade has simply drained them. They aren't motivated by any ambitions of their own, or by external goals or expectations. Instead of looking out for number one or trying to be respectable, they look to friends, with whom they often share a kind of communal esprit, although nothing as concrete as a commune. In her stories, Beattie shows from up close how ambiguous these friendships can be, how many secrets and surprises they can hold.

In fact, her longest story is entitled **"Friends."** There Beattie evokes in rich detail the amorphous scene of drifting friends—and lovers, since that is what many of the friends have been or wish they were—that sets the tone for the whole collection. Perry, the protagonist, has abandoned the lonely project of winterizing his Vermont house to join a crowd of old friends—gathered from various outposts in New England—for a partying weekend at Francie's house in New Hampshire. The first night there, when all the guests are sprawled drunkenly about the house, Perry retreats to the attic mattress he has appropriated after countless weekend visits.

> Waiting to fall asleep he thought about what Francie had told him recently: that he was her best friend. 'A woman should have another woman for her best friend,' Francie said and shrugged, 'but you're it.' 'Why would you have to have a woman for a best friend?' he said. She shrugged again. 'It's hard for men and women to be best friends,' she said. He nodded and she thought he understood, but all he meant to acknowledge was that they were close, but that there was also something hard about that. What it was, was that it had never been the right time to go to bed with her, and if he did it after all this time, he would have been self-conscious.

In any case, there is barely a moment for unassertive Perry to divulge his secret love in the confusion of friends—a band of rock musicians, a "spacy" woman and her baby daughter, a neurotically hypersensitive teacher, and an array of other flaky types—dropping in and out, breaking up and making up. But there is no place for frustration or resentment to mount in Beattie's diffuse atmosphere; ambivalence prevails. "Sometimes it bothered him that he was just one of the people she liked to have around all the time, although it meant a lot to him that they had all been friends for so long." Beattie unobtrusively displays truly remarkable imaginative insight and accomplished control in her evocation of Perry's low-key preoccupation. As she showed in *Chilly Scenes of Winter* in her exhaustive portrayal of her lovelorn protagonist, Charles, she is at home in the emotional life of men—attuned to their hopes, reveries and romantic longings, which interest her more than their lusts.

Beattie's central theme is one that calls for variations; for the relationships she describes are distinguished by seeming—at least to those involved in them—*not* to follow any standard pattern. Commitments are unclear, expectations unformulated and communications faulty. Beattie imagines variations in all their minute particularity in her stories; and this collection of them conveys an often dispiriting sense of the common underlying muddle.

The general outline of **"Friends"** reappears in **"A Vintage Thunderbird"** and **"Colorado,"** and Beattie comes the closest she ever does to suggesting a representative predicament. Nick and Robert, the protagonists of these stories, are best friends with Penelope and Karen respectively, but secretly wish they were more. The women, enigmatic themselves and not very understanding of others, meanwhile move in with and out on other men. Neither Robert nor Nick makes the move to surprise his friend with an admission of his love; but each is always there to deal with the surprises visited upon him by that friend. The surprises—even those that directly affect the friendship, as when Penelope suddenly proposes to Robert that the two of them leave "stifling" New Haven and head for Colorado—are not decisive turning points; they are barely registered as ripples in the general drifting course of their lives. It's details, however, more than situation outlines (there really are no plots) that count for Beattie and that she makes weigh with us. She describes the nondescript, accounts for moments that usually slip away between eventful hours, notes unconnected thoughts that pass through her characters' minds, records minute details—"the little crust of salt on her bottom lip." The ineluctable but unpredictable daily progress of lives on her pages seems familiar, in a depressing yet also reassuring and even enlightening way; days in real life have the same mixture of commonplace outline and mysterious detail.

Beattie adds familial relations to other of her stories, and she shows that blood ties don't clarify or secure matters between characters. In **"La Petite Danceuse de Quatorze Ans"** the famous artist fathers of Griffin and Diana are part of the cause of their having a relationship in the first place and all of the cause of the complications of it. (In fact, the father fixation so dominates that we miss the disparate array of minor preoccupations Beattie usually gathers about her characters and apparently artlessly arranges.) The ironic narrator of **"The Lawn Party,"** one of the best stories in the collection, returns to his parents' house for the Fourth of July with his daughter, without his wife, and without his arm, which he has lost in a car accident with his wife's sister, the woman he really loved. He refuses to join his relatives on the lawn but does not really escape them. Instead he distracts himself from serious solitary brooding with sardonic banter with emissaries sent to rouse him—and even with his student/friend who might be a real companion. Beattie explores the claims of siblings in **"Deer Season,"** where two sisters try to rearrange their stultifying life together when a past common lover returns, and in **"A Clever Kids Story,"** which depicts a sister's effort to come to terms with her memory of her youthful adoration of her brother. As usual, there is no final reckoning for Beattie's characters, just a trying process of reacting—usually with an unsettling lack of feeling or energy—to demands and events they don't control and can't neatly reconcile.

Other stories are about stranger human contacts—about relationships that emphasize the root sense of isolation and enigmatic detachment latent in all her stories. In **"Distant Music"** Sharon and Jack, who share a hatred of laundromats, guilt about not sending presents to relatives on birthdays and Christmas, and a dog—part Weimaraner, part German Shepherd—named Sam," meet in Washington Square on Friday to spend the weekend together and trade Sam for the next week. Sharon is silent and not used to being loved; and she seems strangely unperturbed when Jack leaves her and when Sam, grown vicious, is put away. In **"Octascope,"** a less successful story, another passive woman and her baby move in with a mari-

onette-maker, sight unseen. She longs, almost desperately, for facts about him, words from him: "I have to know if we are to stay always, or for a long time, or a short time," she says. Instead, the two of them talk of eggs and beehives. There is a lot of disquieting, empty space in these stories—in the characters' heads and hearts and in the holes between characters.

But Beattie sees more than blankness. The secret she shares with us in acutely captured moments and carefully recorded details is of the unobtrusive but crucial presence of generous impulses and good intentions in lives that are lonely and undirected, in friendships that are full of ignorance and confusion. And at a time when hopelessness and bleak isolation are assumed in much fiction—and are never very far from her own—that is a surprise. (pp. 34-6)

Ann Hulbert, in a review of "Secrets and Surprises," in The New Republic, *Vol. 180, No. 3, January 20, 1979, pp. 34-6.*

Karla M. Hammond   (essay date 1980)

[*In the following excerpt, Hammond discusses Beattie's preoccupation with the 1960s in* Secrets and Surprises *and how her bare prose style reflects the despondency of her characters.*]

Secrets & Surprises is a strange title for this, Ann Beattie's second collection of short stories, third work of fiction. The lives of Beattie's various characters are inevitable and predictable given the nihilistic environments in which they find themselves. While there are undoubtedly secrets these people keep from one another, in their characteristic silences and cryptic non sequiturs, there are few surprises. There is a feeling of entrapment, whether it is the result of bad weather (as in **"Weekend"**) forcing people together or the mere fact that they have run out of places to live and people with whom to take up residence. Concurrently, there is a sense of desperation entailed in choice: where to live, with whom to live, who to leave, what occupation to follow. Beattie's characters continually allude to their depression as though it were a personal credo or esthetic, the admitting of which might liberate them.

Having reviewed Beattie's earlier work, I am no stranger to her storyline or the familiar strain of pessimism that runs its course in her narrations. What prevents the pessimism in all this from degenerating into unrelenting gloom and fatalism is her crisp, blunt style (reminiscent of Hemingway), her way of observing at a distance and presenting facts through sparse but graphically detailed remarks and flat statements. Her expertise in this makes even the most incredible event believable and at times frighteningly foreseeable.

In the late seventies, Beattie is still writing about the sixties in that she concerns herself with people who came of age on maria Muldair, birth control pills, and 1966 Mustang convertibles. In those rare instances when Beattie speaks of younger men and women, they seem spellbound by some delusive nostalgia which might attract them, for example, to the house of an aging ex-English professor

("Weekend") or the values of the generation directly preceding them. There are remnants of the communes of the sixties and the futile attempts to nourish and protect each other. The end result is, however, the aimlessness of those who are incapable of seeing anything through: "She had flunked out of Bard and dropped out of Antioch and the University of Connecticut, and now she knew that all colleges were the same—there was no point in trying one after another. She had traded her Ford for a Toyota, and Toyotas were no better than Fords" ("Colorado"). Similarly, Beattie's characters drift in and out of each others' lives with little sense of purpose, direction, or union. What affections they form are for vintage Thunderbirds and dogs rather than each other. Those who are married have formalized their relationship(s) more from habit, familiarity, or loneliness than love, mutual respect, or a sense of responsibility. And what understanding they derive from their marriages is never made clear.

Frequently the characters themselves are reduced to "he," "she," or nicknames without any last name. Identification is infrequent and neither group encounters nor phone calls change this. Perhaps part of the dilemma rests in the surface level of the story. While the events of the story are horrifying on occasion, on the surface there is little self-analysis. People who may seem serious on first encounter are really despondent ("Distant Music").

The phone is a central image in Beattie's work in that it speaks to two issues: uncertainty and a lack of communication. People in Beattie's stories are often waiting for the phone to ring, waiting for that magical instrument to weld a conversation out of silence, to bring about some change in their life; one story, "Friends," ends with a telephone ringing. But there is little stay against the displacement of these characters' lives. As in Samuel Beckett's *Waiting for Godot,* one finds the anticipation without any logical resolution. Beattie's people, too, are caught up in the absurd—the more terrifying here though because it's not a dream world but chilling reality.

Beattie's people are all too frequently *shellshocked*—stunned, stoned, emotionally disturbed, or in mourning—from loss or inertia. They're symptomatic of an age whose implications far transcend the Vietnam War, although that's part of the cause, as Beattie shows in several stories—among them **"Shifting"** and **"The Lawn Party."** In the former, Andy has been wounded and Natalie, the female protagonist, envisions his leg being blown sky high by a land mine. The latter story ironically opens on the Fourth of July in the midst of a lawn party where the guests / relatives wear "little American flags pinned somewhere on their shirts or blouses or hanging from their cars. A patriotic group. . . My father loves this day better than his own birthday." Meanwhile, the anti-hero of the story, the wounded presence, observes the festivities with disdain and reluctance from an upstairs bedroom window. Beattie, in her typically candid if somewhat ironically offhand manner, reports that his refusal to join the party is a statement that might be:

> dismissed with a wave of the hand, but I have none. No right arm, either. I have a left hand and a left arm, but I have stopped valuing them.

It's the right one I want. In the hospital, I rejected suggestions of a plastic arm or a claw. "Well, then, what do you envision?" the doctor said, "Air," I told him. This needed amplification. "Air where my arm used to be," I said. He gave a little "Ah, so" bow of the head and left the room.

The final irony exists in the source of the injury—not Vietnam as one might have surmised, but the result of a car accident in which his wife's sister (with whom he may have been having an affair) was trying to kill herself (and succeeded).

But it is not Beattie's strategy for us to feel sympathy so much as annoyance with her characters for their refusal to take charge of their lives. They are caught in the wake of the sixties, prisoners of low paying jobs, no jobs at all, limited skills, divorce, and death. Perhaps nuclear warfare and economic recession have made any positive planning for a future painful if not prohibitive. They live in the present not so much passionately as *obsessively* as one man who dreams of consummating a hopeless relationship: "He felt sorry for her, and sorry for himself that he wasn't what she wanted" ("Friends").

If Beattie has any gift or genius, it is her ability to closely chronicle the time in which she lives. Thus, it is not surprising that her characters, while living transient lives, are aware of even the most minute details—what in other situations might be trivial. In the course of creating a social history, Beattie does not pretend that her people are larger than life. She allows them to be weak, confused, and irresolute. However, for the most part they are survivors. Beattie has gone to the heart of her own generation and lets that perfectly timed beat and rhythm tell its own story in a manner that is at once compelling and thoroughly convincing. (pp. 115-17)

> *Karla M. Hammond, "Ann Beattie: Still with the Sixties," in* The Denver Quarterly, *Vol. 15, No. 2, Summer, 1980, pp. 115-17.*

Jonathan Yardley (essay date 1982)

[*Yardley is an American critic and editor. In the review below, he suggests that* The Burning House's *narrow scope results in empty narratives about uninvolving characters.*]

Ann Beattie is a writer of formidable, scary talents, and she is in rare form in several of the 16 stories collected in *The Burning House.* Her prose is as uncluttered as a cupboard in a vacant house. She sees with a clarity that admits compassion but not sentimentality. Her eye for detail is penetrating and selective, and she is as up-to-date as next week's Top-40 list. Her work affords me enormous pleasure and, from time to time, a welcome sense of unexpected discovery.

Further, Beattie is especially comfortable and accomplished with the short story. Notwithstanding the excesses of critical applause that greeted her recent novel, *Falling in Place,* she hasn't quite figured out how to sustain an extended story; in its final hundred pages or so, *Falling in*

Place collapses of its own weight into what is for Beattie a most uncharacteristically contrived conclusion. Beattie is a miniaturist—or, as some reviewers have described her, a "minimalist"—whose strength is brevity and who seems most sure of herself when loose ends are left untied; as a result she is more suited to the form of the story than that of the novel. A few of her stories—my favorites are **"Shifting,"** from *Secrets and Surprises,* and **"The Cinderella Waltz,"** from the current collection—nudge right up to the borders of real artistry.

So here we have this brilliant writer—yes, brilliant—who though only in her early thirties has already produced five praiseworthy books. Yet this body of work suggests nothing so much as that she is all dressed up with nowhere to go. Over and again, she uses her fine talents to write the same story about the same people: privileged children of the '60s who have failed to grow up and who stumble through life certain only that "what will happen can't be stopped." With occasional gratifying exceptions, the emptiness of Beattie's fiction is astonishing; her prose may be as uncluttered as a cupboard in a vacant house, but it remains that the house of her fiction *is* vacant.

Though Beattie is widely regarded as a "spokesperson" for the generation that came of age during the '60s, her strongest literary influence appears to be that chronicler of '50s suburban angst, John Cheever. Literally and figuratively, Cheever's people are the parents of Beattie's. Her settings are much the same as his—the wealthier precincts of suburban Connecticut, Manhattan, Los Angeles, Charlottesville—and so are her subjects: domestic entanglements and disappointments from marriage to divorce, with pregnancies and affairs and separations as way stations between them. Where Cheever's people fled into martinis and Chivas Regal, hers find escape routes in white wine (gallons and gallons of it) and Valium. Just as Cheever knew all the brand-name signposts of his time and place, so she has identified those of hers: L. L. Bean, Dylan, Godiva, Coltrane, LSD. Like Cheever, she would argue that an upper-middle-class existence is no barrier to universal meaning; unlike Cheever, she has failed to prove the point.

The narrowness of her fiction is quite remarkable. It conveys no awareness that there is a larger world than that inhabited by these bored, haphazardly educated, half-stoned post-collegians named Justin and Jason and Amy and Holly who lie around in sparsely furnished houses or apartments and indulge themselves in empty fatalism; her typical female character "had a breech birth and a Caesarean and she's seeing a shrink twice a week and she still has a problem with drugs" and Daddy probably is picking up the tab. The most these superannuated adolescents can come up with, apart from "what will happen can't be stopped," is: "Hey. . . . Everything's cool, O.K.? No right and no wrong. People do what they do. . . ." *Que sera, sera:*

> They were married in the living room of this house, while it was still being built, with Elvis Presley on the screen singing "As Long as I Have You." Holly carried a bouquet of cobra lilies. Then I sang 'Some Day Soon'—Audrey's fa-

vorite Judy Collins song. The dog was there, and a visiting Afghan. The stonemason forgot that he wasn't supposed to work that day and came just as the ceremony was about to begin, and decided to stay. He turned out to know how to foxtrot, so we were all glad he'd stayed. We had champagne and danced, and Martin and I fixed crepes.

That passage is acute in its observed detail, but Beattie's own point of view toward what she depicts is wholly elusive. Does she see Judy Collins and cobra lilies and large shaggy dogs and crepes merely as details, or as the cliches of a certain time and place that in point of fact they are? Is she aware that dancing with the stonemason is simple slumming, or does she romanticize it as a triumph of the worker-student alliance, or is it only another part of the landscape to be conscientiously and accurately recorded? Who knows? Beyond her own apparent complicity in the fatalism she describes, she disappears from her own fiction as a moral force.

But it is impossible to dismiss her. When she takes the trouble to infuse a story with genuine energy, the results can be eye-opening. In the aforementioned **"The Cinderella Waltz,"** she produces four real people who have real problems that are resolved, or left unresolved, in an entirely real way. The narrator is a woman who is divorced from her husband, who left her after acknowledging his homosexuality. Their daughter, who is nine years old and precociously worldly-wise ("Children seem older now"), is the tie that keeps them bound together and leads to the woman's close friendship with her ex-husband's male lover: "It seems perfectly logical that he should come alone to talk—perfectly logical until I actually see him coming up the walk. I can't entirely believe it. A year after my husband left me, I am sitting with his lover—a man, a person I like quite well—and trying to cheer him up because he is out of work." Beattie understands that the situation is in more or less equal measures funny and sad; her accomplishment is that she also makes it believable and true.

It is therefore more than slightly ironic that **"The Cinderella Waltz,"** one of the few stories in which Beattie's characters behave in a demonstrably adult manner, should end with the narrator wondering "if Milo and Bradley and I haven't been playing house, too—pretending to be adults." Certainly that is applicable, though, to most of the others who slouch through these pages. Their fondest memories are those from childhood, when life was less complicated and demanding, and their fondest desire is to return to that easy innocence; failing that, they complacently continue their childish ways—avoiding commitment, responsibility and challenge, consoling themselves with the morally bankrupt cop out that "what will happen can't be stopped." They are unlikely to find a more observant or perceptive chronicler than Ann Beattie, but there is precious little in what she writes to persuade us that they are worth such attention. It is difficult to avoid the unpleasant conclusion that a marvelous writer is simply wasting much, if not all, of her time.

Jonathan Yardley, "Days of Wine and Vali-

um," in Book World—The Washington Post, *September 19, 1982, p. 3.*

To say that Ann Beattie is a good writer would be an understatement. Her ear for the banalities and petty verbal cruelties of the late '70s middle-American domestic idiom is faultless, her eye for the telling detail ruthless as a hawk's. She knows her characters inside out, down to the very last nastiness and sniveling sentiment, and she spares us nothing.

—*Margaret Atwood, in* **The Washington Post Book World,** *1980.*

Anatole Broyard   (essay date 1982)

[*Broyard was an American critic, essayist, and short story writer. In the following review, he lauds Beattie for her fully developed characters and dynamic prose style in* The Burning House.]

When I was a child, I got lost at Coney Island one day and ended up in a pound—like a dog pound—for lost children. What was curious about the place, as I remember it, was the fact that most of the children were not crying, but sitting and staring into space, waiting to be rescued.

This is how the people in Ann Beattie's first two volumes of stories struck me. They were lost in a Coney Island world, waiting for something to happen. But in *The Burning House,* her third collection, Miss Beattie seems to be changing—in my opinion, for the better. Most of her characters now have recognizable desires, color in their cheeks, energy in their movements. Sometimes they even cry.

In one piece, a young woman actually asks her husband, in italics, mind you, *"You don't love me?"* Another story ends with the sentence: "I am really at some out-of-the-way beach house, with a man I am not married to and people I do not love, in labor." In her earlier stories, the first two clauses of that last sentence would almost have gone without saying.

"Tell me why you love me so much," a man says to a woman, and adds, "Don't make analogies." Another couple sleeps in a bed "as wide as the ocean." Still another man says to another woman, "You know all my secrets and when we're apart I feel like they're dead inside you." Like Miss Beattie, perhaps, looking back on herself, a woman remarks that "I was fooled into thinking I knew these people because I knew the small things, the personal things."

What she means by this last reference is what they smoke or drink, what kind of whimsical birthday presents they give one another, what sort of fruit they carry off planes (pineapples), or what they laugh at most easily. Now, in

The Burning House, a man says to a weeping woman. "Just tell me what you've done." Not what's been done to you, but what you've done, as if to suggest that she is at least partly responsible for her own unhappiness. A husband urges his wife to say "I have a nice life."

After she's divorced, one of these women of Ann Beattie's goes to the house of another unhappy divorced woman and they take turns holding and kicking a tambourine, as if it's the only thing left in this world for them to do. There's pathos in these stories, in the characters themselves, rather than in the sadness of what's missing in their makeup.

There's one long story, **"Winter: 1978,"** that strikes me as a regression. The actions of the characters are determinedly, even implacably gratuitous, and to obscure them even further they are buried in the paraphernalia of verisimilitude. At times, I wondered whether there might not be a wild laugh echoing through this story, but this is just a guess, probably a wrong one, for writers are never so serious as when they are bad.

Miss Beattie used to have a reticence about language that seemed to be the trauma of her generation, but she now allows herself an occasional pretty or rhythmical sentence. She doesn't take refuge any longer in a deadpan style. In the whole book, I noticed only three bad sentences. Writing about a dog chewing a clothesline, Miss Beattie says, "His involvement is quite erotic." In another place, she writes, "There's no difference between the way the air looks and the noncolor of my drink." The third sentence is too long to quote.

Still, Miss Beattie has come so close to the normal in this book that when I found six people cheering a sponge as it expanded in the water of a bathtub, I wasn't sure whether she was cheering with them or mocking them. I wish she had not made two other people drive through the night to Brattleboro, Vt., just because a friend called and said he was besieged by wasps—but no reader can have it all his own way.

There's a lovely scene of a baby sitter named Inez reading a bedtime story in Spanish to a contented child who doesn't understand a word. And another moment in which a young mother imagines her son and his dubious father ascending in a glass elevator somewhere in California. Perhaps my favorite image is the one in which a divorced woman goes to a dance class and "learns to fall."

I think Miss Beattie is learning to fall, too. She may even be falling for us—her all-too-human readers. While it may be a risky thing to do, it's more fun than kicking a tambourine.

Anatole Broyard, *"Kicking and Falling," in*
The New York Times, *September 25, 1982, p.
16.*

Margaret Atwood   (essay date 1982)

[*A Canadian novelist, poet, critic, and short story writer, Atwood is the author of the acclaimed novel* The Handmaid's Tale *(1985). In the review below, she commends*

Beattie's use of a deadpan prose style in The Burning House *to capture her characters' fear of freedom and instability.*]

[*The Burning House*] is Ann Beattie's third collection of stories in eight years; it follows two novels, *Chilly Scenes of Winter* and the recent *Falling in Place.* By anybody's standards, this is a huge output, but Miss Beattie shows no signs of slackening.

A new Beattie is almost like a fresh bulletin from the front: We snatch it up, eager to know what's happening out there on the edge of that shifting and dubious no man's land known as interpersonal relations. How goes the fray, at least in the area roughly defined as New York, with Vermont on the upper perimeter and Virginia on the lower one? (Sometimes people in these stories have moved to California, but they secretly long for the East, where the snow doesn't come in tiny expensive packets.) Whatever happened to all those people who grew up really believing that all you need is love? Are they any better off than the generations of Elvis and green hair and heavy metal that flank them? In the war between men and women, is anybody winning, or is it even a war? How are life, liberty and the pursuit of happiness getting along these days?

Not too well, going by the evidence of these 16 stories. Happiness is still being pursued, sort of; at least, the characters in these stories can remember what it was like when they were pursuing it. By now, many have flagged and are substituting Valium. Even the more harrowing forms of tripping out are things of the past: These people are on maintenance doses, getting from one day to the next, one lover to the next, like a climber seizing the next rung on the ladder without having any idea of where he's going or wants to go.

What ails them? (For there are none who are not ailed, with the possible exception of two dead young men whose absences form the centers of two of the longer and more important stories here.) Life is too easy an answer. It seems to be more a matter, strangely enough, of liberty. There are no longer any ties that bind, not securely, not definitively: jobs, marriages, the commitments of love, even the status of parent or child—all are in a state of flux. Thus everything is provisional, to be re-invented tomorrow, and no one can depend on anyone else. The characters watch each other with preternatural, Magic Realism intensity; a gesture or chance remark may signal the beginning of the end, a shrug may spell doom.

Freedom, that catchword of sixties America, has translated into free fall, or a condition of weightlessness, and the most repeated motifs in the book are variants of this. **"Learning to Fall," "Gravity," "Afloat"** and **"Running Dreams"** are titles of stories. "Space cadet" is a phrase used by one character of another, but in some ways all the protagonists, both men and women, are defined by their relationship to this label. Zipped in, petrified, like the little boy in a beekeeper's suit in **"Sunshine and Shadow,"** they peer out through Plexiglas at the dangerous collisions around them, at the fatal stars. "I float between them," says one woman, "knowing . . . that desire can be more overwhelming than love—the desire, for one brief moment, simply to get off the earth." And in **"The Burning House,"** a husband tells his wife, "Men think they're Spider-Man and Buck Rogers and Superman. You know what we all feel inside that you don't feel? That we're going to the stars. . . . I'm looking down on all of this from space. . . . I'm looking down on all of this from space. . . . I'm already gone." These are stories not of suspense but of suspension.

Freedom is the freedom to take off, but when you're being taken off from, as happens to most of the people in these stories, it doesn't feel quite the same. What many of these characters want is to be grounded. Like spies on the run, they're searching for a safe house, and houses and their furnishings loom large. But the houses tend to be booby-trapped: Home is no longer a comfy fortress, as the book title more than hints. Even the most domestic of activities—cooking dinner, fun with the dog—are fraught with a jittery sense of wrongness. Sometimes the characters, nostalgic for Christmas trees the way they used to be, return to their own pasts, but the lovely Pennsylvania farmhouse of **"Sunshine and Shadows,"** which lulls us into security with its patchwork quilts and golden oldie records, is indicative of what is likely to happen to anyone who gets sucked in by the décor: "When he moved his head nose-close to the window he could see the cement driveway . . . where his mother had run a hose into the car and killed herself with carbon monoxide."

This is also a good example of Ann Beattie's method. The detail is casually dropped on the reader's head in passing, not treated with special rhetoric, just *there,* like a vase or a clock; and it is the evenness of tone used to describe both horrific event and trivial observation alike that accounts perhaps for the eerie, shell-shocked effect of Miss Beattie's prose. By now this is a technique she wields with absolute control. Compared to the earlier stories, these are less grotesque, more narrowly and intensely focused, more accomplished; they are also less outrageous and less outraged and more sympathetic to their characters. The mood is not bloody-minded; rather it is sorrowful. Most of the stories are about the process of separating, but there are no causes proposed, only affects, and thus no one is seen as responsible for the pain. The result is a certain moral attenuation. This is not hell but limbo, which some writers have located on the moon: That's where the space cadets end up.

No one is better at the plangent detail, at evoking the floating, unreal ambiance of grief. I would say Ann Beattie is at her best here, except that I think she can do even better. One admires, while becoming nonetheless slightly impatient at the sheer passivity of these remarkably sensitive instruments. When that formidable technique is used on a subject large enough for it, the results will be extraordinary indeed. Still, that's like caviling because Wayne Gretzky misses one shot. If Miss Beattie were a ballerina you could sell tickets to the warm-ups. (pp. 1, 34)

Margaret Atwood, "Stories from the American Front," in The New York Times Book Review, *September 26, 1982, pp. 1, 34.*

Joseph Epstein   (essay date 1983)

[An American editor and critic, Epstein has served as fiction critic for Commentary *and is the author of* Plausible Prejudices: Essays on American Writing *(1985). In the following overview of Beattie's works through* The Burning House, *he faults the prevalence of passive, hopeless characters and the lack of purpose in her stories and accuses her of being "the chief purveyor of her own generation's leading clichés."]*

I have now read Ann Beattie, her two novels and the three volumes of short stories that comprise her collected work to date. This is no small output for a writer of thirty-four. There are fifty of these stories. I believe I may have read some of them earlier when they first appeared in the *New Yorker.* I say "I believe" because I am not always certain. Reading them in her books I experienced a sense of *déja lu.* Have I read them before, or have I instead read stories like them, for I am told that Ann Beattie already has a number of imitators? (One line of dialogue I do clearly remember having read earlier. It runs, "Name me one thing more pathetic than a fag with a cold," and is uttered by a homosexual.) Ann Beattie's novels and stories do make an effect: they depress, even when they have what ought to be happy endings. Yet they somehow do not stay with one; they seem to seem to slide off the page; one story melts into another, and the whole finally dissolves in the mind, like one of those small blue pills some of Ann Beattie's characters require to get through the day, a downer.

As I read through story after story of Miss Beattie's, I asked myself why these stories—stories written by a writer with a true command of prose style and a deadly eye for right details—were at once vaguely depressing and distinctly forgettable? I have, for example, been reading Miss Beattie's latest collection of stories, *The Burning House,* and turning back to the book's table of contents I notice that I cannot connect stories to titles. Was **"Afloat"** about the woman about to have a child with a man to whom she is not married? Is **"Playback"** about the young man who works for an advertising agency? Is **"Desire"** the story in which everyone gets stoned, or in which the woman's husband leaves her for another man? Beats me.

As for the depression, well, one is used to depression in modern fiction, which provides many laughs but very few smiles. One is used to it in traditional literature, too. *Anna Karenina* comes down with a bump. But however depressed that great book leaves you, you do feel you have got something for your sadness. The depression that comes with reading Ann Beattie is of a different order, and not just because she isn't Tolstoy. It is depression at reading about the sheer hopelessness of her characters' lives; from these lives, they learn nothing and neither do we. Nor, by design, are we supposed to. In one of the stories in *The Burning House* it is said of a six-year-old girl: "She used to like stories to end with a moral, like fairy tales, but now she thinks that's kid's stuff."

Miss Beattie has a real subject, and a highly interesting one. Her subject is the fate of her own generation, the generation that was in college and graduate school in the late 60's and early 70's. This generation, as everyone knows, grew up in the shadow of the Vietnam war, and it was the first to have a free hand with sex and drugs, to know splendor both in and on the grass. I recall, in the middle 60's, a *Partisan Review* symposium, those occasions on which intellectuals are invited to say things they are sure to regret later, in which nearly all the participants had a good word for the young. Everyone agreed that this was to be a generation of great promise. The members of this generation felt that they were promising, too, but they also felt that they were, in some odd and never quite defined way, promised. Promised what? Because of their own intrinsic superiority, moral and intellectual, they felt they were promised a freer and richer and happier life than any known before here in America and possibly on earth.

But the world of the 60's ended neither with a bang nor with a whimper but, it would seem from Ann Beattie's fiction, with an album. "Rachel cried when she heard Dylan's *Self-Portrait* album, because, to her, that meant everything was over." in the story **"The Lawn Party"** from the collection *Secrets and Surprises* (1979) we read: "When Janis Joplin died Elizabeth cried for six days." (p. 55)

About all of Ann Beattie's fiction there is something of an after-party atmosphere. Her stories begin after the 60's binge is done and gone. No mention is made of the Democratic convention of 1968, of the marches and protests, of any other of the momentous happenings of those years. In one of her stories a maimed Vietnam veteran appears, in another a woman's brother is mentioned as having been killed in Vietnam, and in yet another a veteran is said to be unable to stop talking about Vietnam. Yet Miss Beattie does not hammer away at Vietnam or speak of politics except obliquely, though a foul air of things gone wrong hovers about her characters and their world. Anxiety, disappointment, despair, these are the pollutants in the Beattie atmosphere, and both characters and readers are made to choke on them.

Already in *Distortions* (1976), her first book of stories, the general pattern of Ann Beattie's fiction is set. *Distortions* is very much a young writer's book, and hence rather more experimental than the more mature Ann Beattie's fiction will be. The book's opening story is about a marriage of dwarfs. Another story is done in short takes, rather like blackout sketches. "Wesley has gaps between his teeth," one such take begins; "Janie Regis' hair is all different colors," the next one picks up. Another experimental story is entitled **"It's Just Another Day in Big Bear City, California,"** a title which is almost a story in itself. But the less experimental Ann Beattie's stories are, the better. Taken by themselves, some of the straighter stories are quite impressive—**"Wolf Dreams,"** for example, written when Miss Beattie was only twenty-six. Nearly all the stories show a high degree of professional polish. The dialogue always feels right; the interior monologue, too, seems on target. The flat style, a Beattie trademark, is already in use in *Distortions,* as in this opening passage from a not very good story entitled **"Hale Hardy and the Amazing Animal Woman"**:

> Hale Hardy went to college because he couldn't think of anything better to do, and he quit because he couldn't see any reason to stay. He last-

ed one and a half years. He did not exactly quit; he was thrown out. When that happened he went to visit his sister Mary, who was living with another girl, Paula, who was being supported by some dude. Hale didn't know the dude's name, or why he was supporting her, or why his sister was living there. He just went.

That passage reveals more than the style of Miss Beattie's fiction; it reveals the peculiar will-lessness of her characters. Passive agents, they do not act but are acted upon. "The important thing," one character in a story in *Distortions* advises another, "was to know when to give up." Here is a note Ann Beattie has held through all her books. The first story in *The Burning House* ends thus: "What Ruth had known all along: what will happen can't be stopped. Aim for grace."

Amazing grace. If grace is what Ann Beattie's characters aim for, very few achieve it. But then they don't aim very carefully. Not much in life interests them. Politics doesn't—though they are all convinced that America is hopeless—neither conventional politics nor emotional politics. "There aren't any answers," says a Beattie character. "That's what I've got against woman's liberation. Nothing personal." Although people have love affairs, once a couple moves in together, the end is in sight. Sex is no big deal. Miss Beattie rarely describes it. Detailed description tends to be reserved for getting stoned. Few relationships endure. Work is pointless. Things fall apart; the center, hell, in Ann Beattie's fiction not even the fringes seem to hold.

In a diary entry of 1945 Noël Coward wrote: "Read Elizabeth Bowen's new short stories; exquisite writing but a trifle too inconclusive." Perhaps it is well that Coward did not live to read Ann Beattie's stories. Miss Beattie specializes in the inconclusive; inconclusiveness, in her fiction, is quite deliberate. It is part of her method. E. M. Forster once wrote that the king died and then the queen died is a story, but the kind died and then the queen died of grief is a plot. Miss Beattie does not go in much for plot. Her work is, in some respects, anti-plot. In the story **"Greenwich Time"** in *The Burning House* a man is at the house of his former wife and her current husband; the house was one he once lived in with his wife. Now he is alone in it with his young son and the maid. His ex-wife and her husband are late—unusually late. Generally they are home long before now. It is worrisome. Yet why they are late, whether they will eventually arrive home safely, these are things we never learn. Instead, **"Greenwich Time"** ends with the maid telling the man that, though he may have been dispossessed from this house, she is still his friend. "Then they stood there, still and quiet, as if the walls of the room were mountains and their words might fly against them." That's it. End of story. Cut and print that (the *New Yorker* did, originally).

Chekhov instructed that if a gun appears on the wall in a scene in the first act of a play, before the play is over the gun will be fired. Not in Ann Beattie's stories; more likely the wall will disappear. This is again by way of saying how little interested she is in plot in the conventional sense. What her fiction strives to achieve is not development of character, accounts of motivation, or moral resolution—

no, what she strives to achieve are states of feeling. This she often succeeds in doing. Thus in a story such as **"A Reasonable Man,"** from the collection *Secrets and Surprises,* she can show what a woman feels who is mismarried and on the edge of nervous breakdown—loneliness, frustration, anxiety, quiet terror—and you will feel it, too. Attempting to capture states of feeling, as opposed to doing so within the construction of careful plots, is of course a great aid to composition, which helps explain why Miss Beattie has been so prolific. What is less clear is why the states of feeling her stories reveal are always those connected with sadness and loss. (pp. 55-6)

Philosophy resides in composition, and the method by which Miss Beattie creates her stories and novels tells much about their author's view of the world. There is, to begin with, the causelessness in her fiction. Her characters are seldom allowed to know why things happen as they do, and without such knowledge there cannot be any deliberate action. It is for this reason that almost every Ann Beattie character is so passive and, finally, so depressing. What, after all, can be more depressing than to be certain that one has no control whatsoever over one's destiny? Destiny, in the grand sense, simply does not exist in Miss Beattie's fiction. Her characters neither know about it nor seem to care about it. All that they do know is that they are living in the shade of a malaise; since this malaise is rather vague, so are the reasons for their unhappiness. Can it be, one sometimes wonders, that the reason they are so unhappy is that they do not feel happy enough—that they feel life has reneged on its promises?

What is more, as they grow older, it continues to do so. Certainly, Miss Beattie's fiction grows more and more cheerless. The first two stories in her latest collection, *The Burning House,* bring forth a brain-damaged child and a brain-damaged adult. The word cancer pops into the discussion fairly regularly. The intake of pills seems greater: yellow Valium, blue Valium, green Donnatal, reds. In one story a child is read to from the works of R. D. Laing, and in another a woman thinks, "Children seem older now." Many is the miscarriage and no fewer the abortions. Meanwhile, the 60's themselves begin to fade: Dennis Hopper—the usual prizes for readers who remember that name—puts in a cameo appearance in one story in *The Burning House,* and in another, set in Virginia, it is said that "Art Garfunkel used to have a place out there." People sit around and tell where they were when John F. Kennedy was shot. But I had better stop—this is beginning to get me down.

What does Ann Beattie think of all this? I happened to note that *The Burning House* is copyright under the name Pity & Irony, Inc. I don't know if that denotes a tax shelter or a self-regarding literary criticism. Miss Beattie pities her characters, true, but in the end her irony does not go very far. In her fiction it is not always easy to distinguish author from subject, dancer from dance. Her identification with her characters is nearly complete. In the biographical note to *The Burning House* she is made to sound like nothing so much as one of them: "She occasionally teaches writing at the University of Virginia and lives, with her dog, in New York City." Ann Beattie is a generation writer, and that is a severe limitation. Milan Kundera, in his novel *The Joke,* has one of his characters say: "The very thought of a generation mentality (the pride of the herd) has always repelled me." But a more severe limitation is that, while she knows a good deal about life's phenomena, she chooses to deny life's significance. In so doing, she ends by denying significance to her own work, for literature is finally about the significance and not the phenomena of life. At this point in her career, Ann Beattie is the chief purveyor of her own generation's leading clichés—the L. L. Bean of what passes for 60's existentialism. (p. 58)

Joseph Epstein, "Ann Beattie and the Hippoisie," in Commentary, *Vol. 75, No. 3, March, 1983, pp. 54-8.*

Pico Iyer   (essay date 1983)

[*In the review below, Iyer characterizes Beattie's prose style as suffering the same uncertainty and lack of direction as her characters in* The Burning House.]

The *New Yorker* has long seemed to be written for, by and about those who lead lives of quiet desperation. In its discreet, fearfully subdued stories the usual milieu is peripheral suburbia, the usual mood penumbral regret. Indeed, many of the magazine's most celebrated contributors—Salinger, Cheever and Updike among them—have distinguished themselves by coolly chronicling the sad eccentricities, plaintive longings and quiet frustrations of their generation. The newest inheritor of this tradition, speaking for a new and peculiarly displaced generation, is Ann Beattie.

The surface details of Ann Beattie's stories [in *The Burning House*] so strikingly resemble Cheever's that one can almost read them as a sequel. For although her characters swallow pills instead of booze; although they flee to California instead of Europe; although their hassles are those of cohabitation instead of marriage—they might well be the offspring of Cheever's well-heeled lonelyhearts, raised on expectations they frequently let down. Like their literary forefathers, Beattie's well-educated vagrants often reside in Connecticut and pursue moderately successful careers. In truth, they could almost be mistaken for the charmed, witty bright young things who inhabit beer ads on TV, but their urbanity ensures that their lives, like their words, sidestep all the obvious clichés. Most of them are haunted by a cool sorrow and a listless despair.

For Ann Beattie is perhaps the first and the finest laureate of that generation of Americans born to a society built on quicksand and doomed to a life in the long, ambiguous shadow of the 'sixties. The characters in her stories are left-overs from that abandoned decade, hung over with its legacy, saddled with hand-me-down customs that have gone out of style. Usually in their early thirties, they stand for all those who were neither incapacitated by Vietnam nor unhinged by drugs, but unsettled only by their innocence of both extremes. Sprung loose from certainties without being swept up by revolution, old enough to have witnessed turmoil, yet too young to have beaten or joined it, they find themselves stranded in that famous space be-

tween one world that is dying and another that is powerless to be born. They routinely—if not religiously—smoke dope, crash on sofas, sing along to Dylan, shack up and hang out; but they also think of ardour, passion, change itself as cobwebbed anachronisms. For there is resolution in revolution; and if the 'sixties were a time of decisiveness, however reckless, wayward or violent, the 'seventies recoiled into hedged bets and hesitations. In this fictional world conviction has followed convention into premature retirement; commitment is a dirty word.

The natural element of these drop-outs *manqués* is therefore a kind of limbo, a no-man's land. Their scruffily hip dwellings are not in the city, but not entirely out of it. They are always moving, but rarely going anywhere, in flight—from reality, responsibility, normality—without a destination. Their secession from the world is more a silence than a statement. All of them are, in every sense, between engagements, forever commuting between one another's homes and lives, both of which they enter and leave with casual frequency. As one nameless figure remarks, 'Everybody who doesn't take hold of something has something take hold of them'. And Ann Beattie evokes this atmosphere of dangling conversations between people deaf to one another's griefs with characteristic compression: her characters are constantly calling each other up, being answered by machines and left to whisper their secrets and endearments into thin air.

Ann Beattie has always crafted metaphors that precisely reflect off-balanced lives slipping out of control. Her last novel was titled *Falling in Place;* stories in [*The Burning House*] are called **'Learning to Fall'**, **'Gravity'**, **'Waiting'**, **'Afloat'** and **'Like Glass'**. They are preoccupied with weightlessness and drifting, with water and air. Characters do not sink or swim; they float or—as the modish phrase has it—they go with the flow. It is the unspoken irony of [**"The Burning House"**] that nothing seems to be 'burning'; on the contrary, Beattie's frosty and fragmented terrain was marked out by the title of her first novel—*Chilly Scenes of Winter.* Beattie stories are archetypally set in winter, when snow eradicates colour, contour, and contrast, when fingers and lives seem numbed, when people, shuddering, can claim to be cool. Here is not, to be sure, the anorexic pallor of Joan Didion's cardiograms of stunned or shattered nerves. Nor is it the over-heated whiteness of Emily Dickinson, staring so intensely at a single spot that she grows dizzy. Beattie's is the white of hospital sheets and muffled December fields: not neurosis, but paralysis.

Numbness pervades the parched, exhausted mood of her stories. Utterly toneless, she reads them herself into a plain, flat voice that suggests deadened feelings or, on occasion, a determined attempt to fight back tears. Her wan sentences and neutral cadences follow one upon another with sharp, chill clarity. Wandering like their protagonists' days, her stories have no resolution—in part because their people cannot make sense of life, in part because nothing ends in any case. As if to invert the eventful frenzy and clamourous manic swings of the world according to television, a Beattie story is naked of explosions or alarums. It has no strain, and no looseness; no lyricism or radiance or rhythm or hope. Reading it is like driving for mile after mile down a straight road through a snow-covered desert.

One of Beattie's deftest narrative tricks is to catch the blur of personal relations in today's America by plunging her reader without any introduction or reference into a chaos of first names (uninterested in the public world, she rarely mentions surnames). Upon beginning one of her stories, it always takes a while to determine the relations between the floating soap-bubbles: a child can easily be mistaken for a boy friend, a gay lover for a brother, or a son. For the family structure of middle-class America has imploded, and domestic structures have been grotesquely distorted and distended. People seem to change spouses, disguises, even sexual preferences at random: thus children do not know their uncles, girls are older than their step-mothers and many need calculators to count their siblings or parents. Everybody cares about 'relating' to everybody else in part, perhaps, because relatives are unknown. Nothing is quite as it seems or as it should be: in one Beattie story, a woman shares roller-coaster rides, confidences and a joint with her husband's gay brother; in another, the narrator must try to win over her lover's teen-age daughter; and in a third, a woman commiserates with her husband's live-in male lover as all three try to cope with separation.

Elsewhere, again and again we see men boyishly wooing their children. For it is the dark and perverse paradox of modern America's broken families that adults and children have effectively exchanged places. . . . While all too many adults lust after adolescence, all too many kids are thrust into a precocious maturity. Forced to fend for themselves, to confront both the sins of their fathers and the vices of their peers, more and more children are hustled by privilege and negligence into a hard wisdom they must reluctantly assume. . . . In Beattie's stories, children are knowing before they are discriminating: a six-year-old refuses stories with morals, dismissing them as 'kid's stuff'; parents read their children R. D. Laing instead of fairy tales; one nine-year-old carries around Samuel Beckett. Even as these children are turning into tough little realists, their parents are tumbling into stolen romances and irresponsible rites, belatedly courting an innocence they had earlier squandered. We see them dressing up as bears, playing with frisbees, devising quirky surprises for their lovers and running with dogs. And we come to see that their prankish charm is part of their affliction, a refuge and a mask. 'If the birds could talk,' announces one nonchalant narrator, 'they'd say that they didn't enjoy flying.' It is sad that the children of Beattie's world are afraid, confused, disenchanted; it may be sadder that their elders are no wiser and no better off.

It cannot be denied that Ann Beattie's stories are perfect mirror-images of the protagonists and predicaments they describe. But because her theme so rarely varies or evolves (save for one gay and giddy interlude called **'Happy'**, an exception to prove the rule), her tales seem almost mass-produced. All the off-beat tunes she plays are in the same (minor) key: after reading a few, one feels that one could write a few. Collect some characters, and name them Jason, say, or Barrett or Hilary. Give them trendy occupations and some engaging idiosyncrasies. Place their homes in the woods, and supply them with shaggy dogs, coffee and conversation around the kitchen table. Make it a grey day in winter. Let there be a phone call to a former lover, a child from a sometime marriage. Ensure that someone takes Valium and someone refers to a gynecological operation. Write in a withered present tense and end before the conclusion (it was once noted that a *New Yorker* story is a regular story with the final paragraph lopped off to give the impression of restrained subtlety and truthful complexity).

This is not entirely to disparage Ann Beattie's commanding talents. Her spare, soft-spoken prose is singularly observant: she can conjure up a dog without a single physical detail, so keen is her sense of gesture. She clearly knows the very pulse and heartbeat of her dreamless drifters—indeed, with her long fair hair, air of seraphic funkiness, and apparently itinerant, make-shift life-style she seems to belong in their midst. She performs many tasks with unrivalled skill: conveying the weary braveness of children and their secret wish to be children again, or the poignancy of the grown men who try to entertain them, equally eager and equally desperate; pinning down voguish tastes, brand-name allusions and aimless dialogue; sketching pale, lead-coloured skies. The harsh transparency of her unblinking, unstinting realism seems almost photographic.

And ultimately these stories may be best regarded as a collection of photos in an album: each records a situation, revives a memory and redeems nothing. Reading them is like consulting a doctor's X-ray of contemporary America. But just as a doctor is vulnerable to the very disease he treats, the closeness of Beattie's manner to her matter can be suffocating. Privy to anomie, her stories become party to it; faithful to the details of the world, they seem treacherous to the energy and heroic idealism that are America's saving grace. (pp. 87-91)

Pico Iyer, "Shadows of the 'Sixties," in London Magazine, *n.s. Vol. 22, No. 12, March, 1983, pp. 87-91.*

Blanche H. Gelfant   (essay date 1984)

[*In the excerpt below, Gelfant praises Beattie's keen ear for dialogue in* Distortions *and* Secrets and Surprises *and discusses her treatment of death, anxiety, and breakdown in both works.*]

Entering Ann Beattie's fictional world through her collection of stories, ***Secrets and Surprises,*** I drift through desolate landscapes with numb aimless characters who are nowhere wherever they are, and wherever they are is where I do not want to be. For them, the climate of all seasons is adversary and the same. "We are thinking about spring," she says in **"Octascope,"** but it is "the dead of winter"—"It will rain, or snow." Rain shrouds the New England countryside and the tomblike house where "they are trapped together by rain" in **"Weekend."** Traps can cripple before they kill. The trap of **"Tuesday Night"** gets a mouse by its paw; then it must be beaten to death with a screwdriver. I do not want to be trapped—not again. I still feel the exquisite pain of being trapped by Hemingway, Salinger, and Didion, writers whose nihilism gives Beattie inspiration. I do not want to wander—as I have with Kerouac—in a pointless world, or to come to rest in the *dead* of winter. I want to get out of fantasized landscapes of nothingness.

At the moment, reality offers no escape. Outside the snow falls as thickly, as pallingly, as in the stories. Soon I shall see nothing. The streets and mountains of New Hampshire are disappearing under lowering skies. It is two o'clock of a December afternoon. The storm has begun. Soon the driving will turn hazardous. Cars will swerve and skid, and death will strike of a sudden as it does in **"Starley,"** killing a young man who crosses the snowy street for a bag of ice cubes.

Sudden pointless death stalks Beattie's world, a world of the young in perpetual mourning. The walking dead—the numbed, or stunned, or stoned, or mad—mourn the buried and check their calendars by the dates of their dying. "In 1969 Joseph died in Vietnam," his sister recounts in **"A Clever-Kids Story,"** and at the end of every summery day in 1969 she sits on the dock and smokes grass, and never recovers from her loss. Beattie's stories are elegiac, but no ceremony, not even that of writing a formal lament for the dead, can lay to rest persons and purposes gone with the end of the sixties. (p. 33)

In *Secrets and Surprises,* references to Vietnam are infrequent but overt and predictable. Jane warned Joseph in **"A Clever-Kids Story"** not to go—to run away to Canada. Now his life is ended. In **"Shifting,"** Natalie told Andy "not to go to Vietnam." Now he tells her, "You were right"—and he has lost a leg and the use of his arms to prove it. Now he is listening, but "she had nothing to say." The achievement of Beattie's stories is the way they fill the silence that remains when the song is over, the way they say *nothing* when there is nothing to say.

Some people find trivia interesting; they can make up stories through an accumulation of the insignificant. When meaning or purpose has been erased, trivia can fill the leftover blanks—those visible on a page of writing, those suspended elusively in time. In daily life, trivia often fill the voids in time, and for a while keep us from confronting their meaninglessness and menace. The events that fill the time of Beattie's fictions are random, disjointed, brief, often idiosyncratic, and marked by an inconsequentiality that displaces attention from silence, death, and nothingness to daily attempts to stay confusion. "I'm mad because you just add to the confusion," Estelle tells her little boy in **"It's Just Another Day in Big Bear City, California"**— the day that spacemen Donald and Fred (retarded) appear to take pictures of Estelle and her husband, Big Bear (no relation to the city or the story's title). "This is a random landing. . . . We found you by accident," the spacemen explain to the drunk and disconcerted couple. As disconcerting as spacemen to Estelle is a Coke machine that won't work, part of the general disorder of everyday details—of hors d'oeuvres in which liver is "hidden," of broken plastic milk glasses, blue velvet birds on a birthday card, a valentine's quilted taffeta heart, a La-Z-Boy reclin-

er, human intestines used as a jumping rope at mortuary school, and a 1965 Peugeot. The Peugeot is the last thing Estelle's brother thinks of, wondering why he is not thinking of his mother or father or sister rather than his car, as he lies dying in Vietnam. The background for the day's confusion—"just another day"—is the sixties, thrust visibly before us as the pictures of Estelle's album. Estelle's snapshots of the sixties "really kill" Bobby, who begins to laugh "uncontrollably." Loss of control comes easily to Beattie's characters, always on the edge of hysteria, panic, or madness. Clutching at trivia is their way of steadying themselves. You try not to go crazy by making glazed pots in **"A Reasonable Man,"** or by listening ritualistically, obsessively, for a phone call; or by writing down an account of the routine moments of your day in **"Victor Blue,"** a story in *Distortions.*

Mr. Edway's "secret book" in **"Victor Blue"** gives us a code for reading Beattie. Like her story, the book keeps a meticulous record of inconsequential progress, that of a violet, a kitten, a library book (when borrowed, read or not read, and returned). It lists recipes, TV programs, meals (eaten or not eaten), weather forecasts and actual weather, all of which Mr. Edway epitomizes in one word—"Trivia." So thoroughly do trivia displace attention, his and our own, that we hardly realize that Mrs. Edway is in agony with terminal cancer and deliberately oversedating herself until she dies.

Such displacement suggests that the true subject of Beattie's stories may be too painful to confront directly. The pain of living for a useless death must be camouflaged. This is the function of massing trivial details, comic or grotesque in *Distortions,* and in *Secrets and Surprises* so utterly mundane that they begin to seem in Beattie as they are in Barthelme, self-parodic. The short story will be sustained by trivia; a sudden revelation of the significance they have hidden, as a hostess hides liver in a hors d'oeuvre, will surprise and satisfy. But the novel becomes monotonous when insignificant details multiply and recur. (pp. 34-5)

In **"Dwarf House,"** the first story of *Distortions,* Beattie shows men and women literally diminished. James is only "four feet, six and three-quarters inches tall"; but a little man, especially when he reaches the age of thirty-eight, can want what any man wants, though his dimension seems to distort normal values and make them questionable. At the end of the story, against his mother's wishes, James marries the little woman he loves—and the wedding sets the world against a perspective described by his mother's bitter aphorism: "Real love comes to naught. I loved your father and we had a dwarf." MacDonald echoes his mother as he listens to Tammy Wynette sing "D-I-V-O-R-C-E": "Everything is for nothing." At the wedding, MacDonald sees the dwarfs "swarm" around the happy couple, and he is reminded of ants he saw converge upon a piece of Hershey bar. Everything sweet in life is devoured; we are left with nothing. Still, the bride is radiant at the wedding, and MacDonald kneels to her and to all beautiful brides and happy marriages. The story ends with his ambiguous gesture, and with the tension between marriage as a strangely diminished ritual and yet one beautifully if precariously sustained.

Secrets and Surprises contains fewer surprises than ***Distortions***—no spacemen or dwarfs appear, no child prodigies like Wally living in a tree in **"Wally Whistles Dixie."** The muting of surprise entails a loss of humor, idiosyncrasy, and tension, and of the quirky charm that I admired for just missing cuteness. Clarity and craft compensate for these losses. The new stories evoke a less ambiguous view of aimlessness than **"Dwarf House"** and other earlier stories, like a favorite of mine called **"Wanda's"**; and none matches the story I consider Beattie's consummate achievement, one which merges the typical elements of her art into an original, striking, and haunting work—**"The Lifeguard."**

In ***Secrets and Surprises,*** the trivia are more minute and unattractive than in ***Distortions,*** the characters in greater bondage to them—like the nameless obsessed *She* of **"A Reasonable Man,"** for whom going to the cleaners is an event, and the typically "depressed" *I* of **"Tuesday Night,"** for whom "some time to do just what I want to do" is excruciatingly eventless. Beattie seems merciless to women trying to "liberate" themselves, like this *I* of **"Tuesday Night"** (or that screwy lesbian of *Chilly Scenes of Winter*). Such women become aimless once they aim to discover, assert, or free themselves, because they have a self only in relationship to a man. Divorced from Henry and about to be dumped by Dan, the Tuesday Night woman exists in limbo, like the mouse in her apartment, caught in a trap by one paw. To the partially trapped, freedom seems possible, but Beattie is as brutal to the Tuesday Night woman as Dan to the mouse he bludgeons to death. Time is the woman's trap. Released into time—one night a week, like the maid's night off—the woman chooses trivia, lacking energy, imagination, or experience for significant action (she does not know, as we already do, that significant actions—like those of the sixties—also end in nothing). Here are some of the things the woman does on her Tuesday nights: she reads "a dirty magazine," calls long-distance and discusses varicose veins, bakes four loaves of bread, burns a pie crust, gets "depressed" and drinks Drambuie, browses through *Vogue,* tries yoga, sees a movie, sips a milk shake, and reminisces about necking with a high-school date. Surface and depths in the story exist on the same plane, which is to say the story is all surface with nothing more implied, nothing more at stake, than what appears as trivia. In Hemingway's understated stories, surface and depths were as distinct and inseparable as in the two-hearted river where Nick went fishing. In Flannery O'Connor's stories, women acted vacuously, but their actions were implicated in the eternal drama of good and evil, significant to the damning or salvation of the soul. I am not suggesting conversion to Catholicism for Beattie. I am indicating the aesthetic problem—Hemingway's problem in his finest and most understated stories—of creating interesting and significant stories out of the trivia that surface in our time—that become merely surface without depths, except for the empty abyss of nothingness. (pp. 36-7)

In **"A Clever-Kids Story,"** Joseph the storyteller who

thought himself "indestructible" is killed in Vietnam. Because he could order his stories, he could not imagine chaos beyond his control, though his sister tries to warn him, to prevent him from going: "He didn't understand how bad, and how pointless, things were in Vietnam. No matter what I said, his attention didn't focus on it, and I couldn't make him understand." Though Joseph is "a clever kid," clever enough to make the impossible sound "reasonable," he does not understand that life is different from art and eludes the artist's shaping. He can imagine kindness and miraculous rescue in his stories, but he cannot imagine the disorder and the destruction of the world whose violence awaits him. Disorder envelops Joseph and Janet as children—their mother has an abortion, their father bums around, their houseguest cries and is not entirely recovered from his breakdown. As Janet remembers the summers in New Hampshire and tries to understand what happened and why she could not save Joseph from Vietnam, she sees that the divorce between storytelling and life was already there in childhood, just as the beginnings of her parents' divorce were there, but neither she nor Joseph understood: "As Joseph was fabricating stories that spring, strange things were happening that we didn't know about." Years later her lover sleeps in Joseph's bed; he offers her sex, but she wants a story, such as a child tells, such as she tells when she speaks of her brother: "As I got older, if I told people about my brother, the stories would always be about my brother as a child—I got older, but Joseph was still frozen in childhood."

"A Clever-Kids Story" shows J. D. Salinger's abiding influence upon Beattie and upon the art and function of her storytelling. Like Salinger, she values childlike innocence, precociousness, and whimsy. At her best, she tells stories that embody these qualities while she shows them imperiled. Whatever anxieties of her own her stories master, they show no way for the reader to control the world or his or her self. Characters break down or die as they do in Salinger; when they live, they often seem "frozen in childhood" like Holden Caulfield and Phoebe. (pp. 38-9)

Storytellers often retell stories, their own and others'. It is a way of demonstrating the "indestructibility" that Joseph unwisely took for granted—showing that a good story and a good storyteller never die. It may be a sign of depletion, or of impatience—the rush to write another story before you have another story to tell; or an urge to perfectibility, the desire to say what you said, but perfectly this time. One story might be called "on the road," and of course has been called that by Jack Kerouac in the famous novel of the fifties which looms over Beattie's aimless wanderers. They are not wild, like Kerouac's Dean Moriarty, not inspired like him with a mad sense of America, of the West, not driven toward "It," the center of Time that only a Holy Goof, a modern Saint, can penetrate. But they are as circular and futile in their movements, and as obsessive. In **"Hale Hardy and the Amazing Animal Woman,"** Hale Hardy, a college dropout (naturally), becomes obsessed with seeing the Grand Canyon because he has read a book, *Lolita.* "That book put women in his mind. He thought it might be a good idea to pick up some woman and drive across the country with her. . . . Eat ice cream with some woman, peering into the Grand Canyon." How listless and unprovoked this desire is compared to Humbert Humbert's obsessive passion for Lolita. The attenuation and diminution of desire show again that everything comes to nothing, even stories of inordinate passion. "What state is this," Robert asks, confused by pot and life, when he arrives finally in Colorado, driven both by aimlessness and obsession, but without the frantic joy that was the companion to Kerouac's Dean Moriarty and Sal Paradise—at least at times, at the beginning of the road. When Hale Hardy gets to the Grand Canyon, he gazes into a "vast pit," the familiar abyss of nothingness; when Robert gets to Colorado in the story **"Colorado,"** he is where he has always been, in the state of confusion.

These are typical men, dropouts of the fifties who have let twenty years slip by without affecting their consciousness. The women also are reenacting a story already told, most effectively and economically in Joan Didion's novel *Play It As It Lays,* to which there is an indirect but unmistakable allusion in Beattie's current story **"A Reasonable Man."** Like Salinger's characters and Kerouac's, Didion's woman is trying to maintain her tenuous control, though she has slipped into certifiable madness. So has Beattie's nameless *She* in a story that recapitulates the state of obsession and paralysis of women in earlier Beattie stories, **"The Parking Lot," "Four Stories About Lovers,"** and most notably, **"Downhill."** *She* is obsessed with a telephone that remains "inexplicably silent," becoming the symbol (as it was for Maria in *Play It As It Lays*) for breakdown in communication, solipsism, and nothingness—a world annihilated by disorder cannot generate meaningful messages. Nihilism lapses into silence. Women can achieve a delicate equilibrium in Beattie's world if they are "simple," like Lenore in **"Weekend."** That means they love to cook, care for children, and nurture Peruvian ivy and shattered but arrogant men. . . . In **"Starley,"** life picks up for Donald in the summer of 1976: "He had a girl friend, Marilyn, who was excessively kind. She made a lobster stew that made his eyes water with pleasure." That was 1976 when, the story implies, you had better be "simple," an object of comfort and desire; or else you might go mad. In your madness, you might dream as *She* does (as does Didion's Maria) of domestic bliss, the only thing that can save you—your child, your husband, your home—all that you would preserve from the devastations of time (as Maria would preserve "Damsom plums, apricot preserves, Sweet India relish and pickled peaches"). In **"Shifting,"** Natalie makes what Marge Piercy has called "small changes." She learns how to drive a shift car, though her husband does not teach her, and she learns that "isolation" can be beautiful if it is captured as a gesture in art. "This was in 1972, in Philadelphia," the last line of the story informs us—still a long way to go. Like Natalie, Diana in **"La Petite Danseuse de Quatorze Ans"** admires a statue, this time of a young dancer "poised for a moment before she moves." The most modern of Beattie's women are arrested in such a moment, not yet moving, but poised—uncertainly poised—before they might make a gesture which could advance them into the world that came into being when the sixties ended. Maybe that world gives women only the illusion that they might assume control and become the tellers of their own story. In **"Distant Music,"** Sharon hears the incidents of her life retold in a hit song that her former lover Jack has written. That is his version, lacking the ironic twist she knows but is not telling.

The snow has stopped. Soon the snowplows will come. The roads will clear, and I shall get out. This essay will come to an end and leave me thinking about the sense of ending in Ann Beattie's stories—stories that end in irresolution, suspension, irony, or erasure. As though scenes were etched upon a magic slate, they disappear quickly after they make themselves visible because they lack consequence. They describe the trivia left around after the end of the sixties; they deny importance to the trivia; they leave us with *nothing.* They leave us in the *dead* of winter, though we know the snow has stopped; and even if it comes again, we know that winter must yield to another season. Is it entirely delusory to think summer will be different?

Beattie's vision of the sixties is by no means unique. That the decade left us with a daily expectation of loss—the TV becoming our magic slate where people and promises were shown and erased—becomes an explicit statement in a novel as radically different from Beattie's fiction as Walker Percy's *Lancelot,* published in 1977: "We were wondering who was going to get assassinated next. Sure enough, the next one did get killed. There it was, the sweet horrid dread we had been waiting for. It was the late sixties and by then you had got used to a certain rhythm of violence." The effect of this violence is inertia, symptomatic of a sense of helplessness and futility. This sense is by no means unique to Beattie's fiction. I find it permeating a fine Canadian novel that has an almost uncanny resemblance to *Chilly Scenes of Winter*—Richard B. Wright's *The Weekend Man,* published in 1970. The weekend man and Beattie's Charles would understand each other.

So much for the erasure. Now for the magic—all the wonderful, indelible aspects of Ann Beattie's secrets and surprises. She has the secret of exact infallible perfectly timed dialogue and of smooth transitions at difficult junctures. Her stories turn into surprises because their aimlessness is leading nowhere and any twist or turning is unexpected and turns adventitiousness into inevitability. I like the moments of violence that intrude suddenly upon apathetic characters. Nick's two muggings in **"A Vintage Thunderbird"** are the best things that happen to him—sudden, simple, weird, frightening, evoked as if by magic through Beattie's language. The sudden manic madness with which *She* runs on the beach at the end of **"A Reasonable Man"** breaks though the story's inertia and creates excitement and tension and fear. The authority of Beattie's detail is indisputable and shocks us into a gasp of pleasure at recognizing the familiar as inevitable. Most of all the magic is in sentences.

> If she were the piece of sculpture and if she could feel, she would like her sense of isolation. She could remember how light, how buoyant, she had felt being tossed high in the air, and thought that perhaps being powerless was nice, in a way. Behind the house is a ruined birdhouse, and some strings hang from a branch, with bits of suet tied on. The strings stir in the wind. I stare

at her and imagine her dress disappearing, her shoes kicked off, beautiful Danielle dancing naked in the dusk. She stood amid the scattered clothes, wondering if it could be true. "Wait a minute," he said. "Wait." "Wait for what?" she whispered.

(pp. 40-3)

Blanche H. Gelfant, "Ann Beattie's Magic Slate or The End of the Sixties," in her Women Writing in America: Voices in Collage, *University Press of New England, 1984, pp. 31-43.*

Carolyn Porter   (essay date 1985)

[*Porter is an American critic and educator. In the following essay, she attempts to go beyond the common critical view that Beattie's writing conforms to traits stereotypical of fiction published in the* New Yorker *in order to examine the diversity and experimental qualities of her stories.*]

Ann Beattie is known for a certain kind of story. It is, notably, a *New Yorker* story, one marked by understatement, caustic dialogue, and an unsentimental view of social relations. These relations are found, or more often fail to be found, among members of the baby-boom generation, now in their twenties and early thirties. If they have children, they are necessarily unsentimental creatures, already wise in the ways of a world in which their parents are alienated, their homes unsettled, their futures unsure. The stereotype can be further refined. There are a dog, for example, indoor plants, and a lot of snow; the first two absorb an inordinate amount of the characters' emotional energy, and the last encloses them as if they were trapped inside one of those glass balls in which the snow flies when the ball is shaken or turned over.

While this stereotype is by no means inaccurate, it can easily blind us to the variety and the experimental energy of Beattie's work. Her characters, for example, are not exclusively young to middle-aged. **"Victor Blue"** is focused on one week in the life of an aged couple, the last week, as it turns out, for one of them. **"Imagined Scenes"** and **"Marshall's Dog"** include old people as crucial, if not central, characters in the picture being drawn. More important than the range of characters in her work, from babies to the dying generations, is a set of narrative techniques whose developing suppleness reflects an intense narrative imagination, one always at work at the task of finding the means to write the novel of manners in a period during which manners have lost the ground charted for them by even so recent an explorer as John Updike. If we look beneath the stereotype at a few of Beattie's narrative techniques, perhaps we can begin to account for the peculiar quality of her fictive, yet familiar world—the sense that something has been lost, although no one can quite remember what.

But first, let me clear the ground a little. It is fashionable these days, especially perhaps on the West Coast, to express a superior disdain for Beattie. Of the several people to whom I mentioned that I was writing this essay, not one expressed admiration for her work. They disliked her per-

spective, her style, her characters, or what they seemed collectively to regard as her snobbery. I confess to having shared this attitude, if in a milder version; I did not like the world she portrayed, but I could never manage to stop reading her. Rereading the five volumes of hers that have been published, I find that every one of these denigrators, myself included, could figure as a character in one of her books. Such an ironic tribute may mean nothing, or it may mean that Beattie has caught us out, revealed us in a light that is not merely unflattering, but disturbing—much as an old photograph of a group of friends can, in retrospect, disturb us by uncannily exposing the concealed facts, such as who loved whom, who was deceiving or being deceived by whom, even who was doomed.

The analogy with photography is apt in more ways than one, but it is most obviously apt for what the photograph leaves out—*why* X is deceiving Y, for example, or *why* Z is doomed. Beattie's recent stories are beginning to address the why, but in her first collection, **Distortions,** the characters and their relations are exposed without being explained. In effect, the hidden is revealed but not redeemed from what Henry James called life's "splendid waste." Indeed, it is often the waste itself that is portrayed. A reader may complain that the picture lacks depth, but it remains disturbing. Further, if Beattie's techniques worked initially to represent the surfaces of a world perceived as surface, as I think they did, they have now begun to serve as a ground on which to build a more complex narrative.

A more formidable complaint is that such pictures lack breadth. Needless to say, the colleagues to whom I have referred as possible characters in Beattie's stories all come from and inhabit the same social stratum on which Beattie focuses her lens—the white, upper middle class. Here James's example is congruent, and one of his critical principles is apt: the author must be granted her subject. What does not figure in Beattie's fictive world would, and does, fill many people's lives—poverty, say, or hunger, or discrimination, to mention only the bluntest abstractions for all that remains unrepresented. James's point, of course, was to insist upon measuring a wrier's worth, not by her subject, but by what she does with it. On the face of it a conservative principle, this rule applies as well from a certain time-honored perspective of the left. That is, if, as Lukacs argued, the artist's subject and perspective are dictated by her historical period and class, and if, as Sartre insisted, an individual's project is to make something of what time and place have made her, then a writer's subject is circumscribed by socially and historically determined conditions, and the great writer is the one whose art makes the most of those conditions by representing them accurately. There are some problems with this line of reasoning, of course, not least of which is that it minimizes the question of an author's choice of subject. But this is not a troublesome issue for the kind of leftist to whom these remarks are addressed in order to remind him or her that the white upper middle-class world of Beattie's stories and novels is theoretically capable of displaying social truth.

Finally, in regard to the question of breadth, it is worth recalling the doubtful ground on which critics once compared Jane Austen's miniature art invidiously with Tolstoy's panorama. Fortunately the sexist bias that informs such views has in recent years given way, at least partially, in the face of feminist readings of Austen and other writers whose "merely" domestic or gothic or popular art has begun to reveal the narrative wealth that such labels served to repress. James's principle may have emerged from the most haut bourgeois critical mind in English letters, but it remains in force for any critic who values his or her own integrity.

This said, we can proceed to the integrity of Beattie's art, specifically to the narrative techniques she has developed toward a contemporary novel of manners. I should emphasize *toward,* since Beattie's two novels, *Chilly Scenes of Winter* and *Falling in Place,* are not altogether successful as novels. In what follows, I will focus on her first short-story collection, ***Distortions,*** then on her more recent one, ***The Burning House,*** because in these works we can see Beattie's techniques take shape and develop. It is not only, however, that her techniques are more clearly visible in the stories, but also that they work more effectively in this short form, which leads me to concentrate on these volumes and to claim that they are superior to Beattie's novels. It remains to be seen whether Beattie can write a fully successful novel, but it is already clear that her mastery of the short story derives from the sensibility of a novelist of manners. Nor do I think such mastery worth any less than that of the novelist. The short story collection in the modern era has roots in a tradition that goes back to *Dubliners* and *Winesburg, Ohio,* a tradition that has come to fulfill many of the same functions as the novel of manners. While none of Beattie's collections is unified around a town or a central character, each is focused—as the stereotype indicates—on certain social groups and on the present, the tense used by Beattie in almost all her stories and even in her first novel. Further, one of the social marks of the generation and the period she is primarily concerned with portraying is its mobility. These people's lives do not adhere to a city or town. Instead, they are attached to cars, plants, dogs—that is, not only to objects, but to transitory ones. In short, the narrative means of capturing the manners of contemporary life are not easy to come by, and the short-story collection may well have some advantages over the novel. It may also be meeting the demands of a reading public not only dwindling in size, but one becoming more responsive to synecdoche. That is, just as cartoons have been simplified, reduced from detailed visual plentiude to spare line drawings as we have become attuned to the comic strip, perhaps readers—at least readers of the *New Yorker*—have grown accustomed to an analogous economy of exposition in narration, an economy of which Beattie's stories are exemplary.

Having hovered over the affective fallacy, I now return to hover again over the mimetic one by claiming that Beattie's techniques, even while producing results that often seem highly artificial, are informed by a clean aim at the real, the here and now, and that those techniques, so far, have worked better at portraying contemporary life in her short stories than in her novels. The central reason for this is that Beattie's most marked talent is for eliminating dis-

crete chunks of exposition, that laying out of background information which the short story must find a way of minimizing. One way of occulting exposition and at the same time exploiting the limits of the short story is to develop a symbolic context and meaning for the events being portrayed, as both Joyce and Anderson did. Beattie's solution is strikingly different. By using the present tense, she not only removes any temptation to lapse into straight exposition, forcing it to emerge either through a character's consciousness or through dialogue, but also limits the consciousness in question severely. At the same time, she refuses the rewards of the symbolic; that is, her narratives are supported, not by metaphor, but by metonymy. Not all this is necessarily apparent in any one story, but it becomes clear in the course of ***Distortions*** as a whole.

The simplest of Beattie's stories in this volume are those that are focused on a single character whose experience is represented in a series of frames, as in a cartoon strip. **"The Parking Lot,"** for example, follows an unnamed woman through a week in which she begins an affair. The affair itself is not represented, but the parking lot is. It serves not merely as visual background but as thematic center. The routine of her life is punctuated by her departure from the parking lot each day, the only time she seems to become conscious of herself or of her surroundings. The parking lot serves, not as symbol, but merely as link—virtually the only link in the woman's life. The story represents the cognitive dissonance endemic to the clerical worker's life, in which the cycle of work, exhaustion, eating, and sleeping repeats itself until "she finds herself in the parking lot, a whole day gone," wondering "what happened in the period between sitting at the dining table and now when she is walking across the parking lot?"

Despite the enlightened arrangement by which she and her husband work alternate years, her life is utterly conventional, as are her attitudes. She cannot see why other people's marriages fail, why they too cannot make arrangements. Despite the fact that she is treated with a sustained, if muted irony, this woman's story is curiously humorless. She would be an easy target for satire, if it were not for the pity her case evokes. By staying just inside the rim of her consciousness, the narrative voice never allows us the distance necessary for satire, but by clinging to that rim, the voice prohibits any view of a genuine interior and indeed suggests that there is no such interior. What is missing is any self-consciousness, any awareness of the dissatisfactions that lead her to start the affair.

Not all these stories are so humorless or so affectless, however. **"Wolf Dreams,"** like **"The Parking Lot,"** portrays a woman lost to herself, but its heroine, Cynthia, is painfully conscious of her own unhappiness, though just as painfully unable to understand it. Cynthia's life is a caricature of a story from *Bride* magazine. She marries Ewell W. G. Peterson at seventeen, then Lincoln Divine at twenty-nine, and is now planning to marry Charlie Pinehurst as soon as she loses twenty pounds and her hair has grown long enough for her to have curls falling to her shoulders on her wedding day. She has a recurring nightmare in which she is standing at the altar with Charlie in a wedding dress not quite long enough to hide the fact that she is standing on a scale. It may be no wonder to us that she finally rejects Charlie—and his rejection of her—but it remains a wonder to her.

While **"The Parking Lot"** is one monotonous series of days fused by a seamless present tense, **"Wolf Dreams"** almost produces a plot, a developing sequence of events ending in Cynthia's rejection by Charlie. Like Lily Bart in Edith Wharton's *House of Mirth,* when she inexplicably fails to show up in time for church with Percy Gryce, Cynthia strikes up a drunken conversation with a stranger on the train while Charlie has gone to the bar, as a result of which Charlie refuses to accompany her when they reach her home town and her waiting parents. Whereas the roots of Lily's ambivalence are not only revealed, but are made to serve as the basis of a social critique, Cynthia's ambivalence remains a mystery to herself and little more than a caricature of confusion to the reader. While she is a step ahead of the wife in **"The Parking Lot"** in the path toward self-consciousness, Cynthia will clearly never arrive even at the point reached by Jake Barnes in *The Sun Also Rises* when he says, "I did not care what it was all about. All I wanted to know was how to live in it." Such a statement draws its force from the very possibility of meaning it denies, just as Hemingway's understated prose is fueled by the energy required to repress all those romantic desires to which it ironically refers, even clings. In the world of *Distortions,* however, the possibility of meaning is not even there to be denied. At the end of **"Wolf Dreams,"** Cynthia sits alone at her parents' kitchen table and asks herself, "What am I trying to think about?" When she closes her eyes, all she can see is a picture of a "high white mountain. She isn't on it, or in the picture at all."

In the end, neither of these characters amounts to much more than a sketched figure that provides a focal point on which what might be called the idiocy of married life comes into view, in one as lived, in the other as both desired and spurned. Beattie's method here resembles that of the boy Bryce in the later story **"Desire,"** when he cuts out a picture from a coloring book: "Bryce wasn't interested in coloring; he just wanted to cut out pictures so he could see what they looked like outside the book." Like Bryce, whose efforts may well represent Beattie parodying herself, Beattie is here trying out oblique methods for gaining narrative access to lives that seem already flattened out, unreal. They remained flattened, but in **"Marshall's Dog,"** she can be seen putting the cut-out pictures together in ways that begin to make them seem real.

"Marshall's Dog" is built out of segments arranged without apparent regard for chronology, plot sequence, or thematic development. The story opens with a segment describing Marshall's eighty-two-year-old mother. This is followed by a scene at Sam's cafe, where some teenage girls are being teased by a couple of boys. It turns out that one of them, Mary, is Marshall's niece. Marshall and his sister Edna live with their mother. Their brother, George, is Mary's father. George has had an affair with Beverly, a waitress in Sam's cafe. Marshall and Edna drive a snowmobile. Marshall's dog shows up occasionally at the cafe.

As these facts emerge, we get a peculiar family portrait, peculiar because of the way the portrait is composed. One

segment is often linked to the next by the most arbitrary verbal association. At the end of one section, Mary's mother offers to drive Mary to school and "looks at the car through the frosty window." The next section opens, "It is cold in the house," but this is Marshall's house, and this segment deals with Marshall's mother. Or again, this segment ends with "the dog is barking. The soup is boiling over," a statement that seems, but actually is not, continuous with the opening line of the next segment, "What a mess." This "mess," it turns out, refers to the pizza smeared on Mary's shirt at Sam's cafe one summer when Mary is fifteen. Such metonymic associations serve not only to connect segments, but also to generate them. The opening segment, for example, begins:

> She was eighty-two when she died. She had the usual old-lady fears—Democratic Presidents, broken bones. When the spaghetti was snapped in half and dropped into the boiling water she heard the sound of her own bones cracking. She loved spaghetti. They had to eat so much spaghetti. She wouldn't eat the sauce. She had butter with her spaghetti. She used to knit for her son, Marshall. She loved her son, she knitted all the time. Once she knitted him a bathrobe and he broke out in a rash all over, an allergy to wool.

Even when metaphors appear, they refuse to function normally—that is, to create and develop symbolic meanings. Instead, they act as metonymy does in Roman Jakobson's theory, returning to the relations of contiguity which generate narrative movement. Here, "old-lady fears" lead to "broken bones." "Broken bones" are like "spaghetti . . . snapped in half," but rather than building on this metaphor, the narrator goes on to what accompanies the spaghetti—sauce or butter. Spaghetti is, again, like yarn. But no sooner is that similarity functioning than it collapses once more into metonymic roaming until it reaches its end in the memory of Marshall's rash.

In a sense, the whole of **"Marshall's Dog"** is generated by this metonymic association, as if Beattie simply picked up one thread and then another in a piece of fabric, pulling each until it would not give any more, but meanwhile gathering the cloth into a pattern that highlights its textures. The technique resembles smocking. Such a conceit, however, fails to capture what is most elusive and disturbing about Beattie's metonymic method here—its capacity to substitute for the closure of a conventional plot development, a closure that feels like the expiration of a breath or of a life. The story opens with an announcement of the old lady's death but ends with the death of Marshall's dog, which serves as the referent for the title. But these deaths do not stand in any resonant symbolic relation to each other. Rather, when Marshall's dog is run over in the snow, it is simply that all the metonymic lines have been played out. They do not meet on some symbolic note; there is no epiphany, either about dogs or death. They simply exhaust themselves. Such a technique has the curious effect of making the arbitrary seem real, or perhaps of revealing how arbitrary is the real.

If, however, this world is real in some sense, it remains off balance, leaving us hoping that we have missed something.

The title of the story underscores this quality. Marshall's dog is given pride of place even though its death evokes no great pathos. Unlike some of Beattie's dogs, it is genuinely peripheral to the lives of the characters. The dog is not there, throughout, and at the end it is not there for good. Perhaps, after all, it is the missing center, what is not there, that throws the metonymic engine into gear.

A similar technique is used to comic effect in **"It's Just Another Day in Big Bear City, California."** This story opens with a paragraph worth quoting in full:

> Spaceship, flying saucer, an hallucination . . . they don't know yet. They don't even notice it until it is almost over their car. Estelle, who has recently gone back to college, is studying Mortuary Science. Her husband, Alvin William "Big Bear" Benton, is so drunk from the party they have just left that he wouldn't notice if it were Estelle, risen from the passenger seat, up in the sky. Maybe that's where she'd like to be—floating in the sky. Or in the morgue with bodies. Big Bear Benton thinks she is completely nuts, and people who are nuts can do anything. *Will* do anything. Will go back to school after ten years and study Mortuary Science. It's enough to make him get drunk at parties. They used to ask his wife about the children at these parties, but now they ask, subtly, about the bodies. They are more interested in dead bodies than his two children. So is Estelle. He is not interested in anything, according to his wife, except going to parties and getting drunk.

Like the opening of **"Marshall's Dog,"** this paragraph moves from one idea to another along a metonymic axis, but instead of repeatedly running down, the chain circles back on itself, and the next paragraph starts over from the same point: "Spaceship, flying saucer, an hallucination. . . ."

At the center of this paragraph is the logical circularity: Estelle is studying mortuary science and therefore she is "nuts"; Estelle is "nuts" and therefore she is studying mortuary science. This, we learn, is why Big Bear gets drunk at parties, although it is also clear from the final sentence that it is because Big Bear is not interested in anything except going to parties and getting drunk that Estelle has gone back to school. One is reminded of R. D. Laing's knots. Big Bear and Estelle constitute a double bind, both sides of which the story proceeds to elaborate. Beattie builds the story out of segments, pieces of dialogue, and narration that represent both the past (this party, other parties, Estelle's brother's death in Vietnam) and the future (Estelle's and Big Bear's interaction with the spacemen, Donald, Fred, and Bobby). The illusion of moving forward in time, however, is undermined, not only by the use of the present tense, but also by the fact that the development of the story is actually organized around the drive to expand the implications of the opening paragraph metonymically.

Thus, for example, because Big Bear's son learns that there is a Big Bear City in California, we are eventually shown a scene in Big Bear City in which a child and his mother try to get a soft drink out of a broken dispensing machine in a gas station. Because Estelle lets the spaceman Bobby take a picture of her "mooning," Bobby is later depicted showing the picture to his friend on Mars. Because Estelle and Big Bear drive her dead brother's Peugeot, Estelle's brother is seen dying on a field in Vietnam, wondering "what will happen to his Peugeot." The story expands across space and time as if it were pursuing its associative links at random, until it can find a reasonable place to stop. Like **"Marshall's Dog,"** though even more pointedly, the story comes to rest on a purely arbitrary close, ending with the line that becomes its title, "It's just another day in Big Bear City, California."

Unlike **"Marshall's Dog,"** however, this story is propelled by metonymic associations that are fueled by an impulse we can see at work in other Beattie stories, such as **"Imagined Scenes"** or **"Fancy Flights"**—the desire for a fantasy that will prove different, better, richer than the reality in which the characters are caught. If you began with a hallucination that proved to be real, you would expect this desire to be fulfilled. Yet the scenes on Mars are virtually indistinguishable from those on earth. Little boys want goldfish or soft drinks; the goldfish die and the machines fail to deliver. Mothers are frustrated. Estelle's "hands roam around in dead bodies the way coyotes roam around the desert," Big Bear thinks, "just for something to do." In many of the segments, moreover, the same circular dialogue repeats itself, not only between Big Bear and Estelle, but also between the card saleswoman and her husband and between the spaceman Bobby and his son. As the fantasy expands, it not only repeats itself in different settings, but also grows more familiar, more real. It's just another day in Big Bear City, California. It is as if something like free association led in a circle back to the quotidian.

Whether comic or somber, these early stories produce a vision of a world in a state of lack. Henry James would have called Beattie's a scenic method, and would have been right up to the point at which he would have despaired at the lack of a center. But it is that lack of a center which distinguishes Beattie's narrative method. Beginning with a set of characters in situation and bringing them into focus only gradually—and then obliquely—Beattie exposes and develops them as if they were a piece of film. This is both the virtue and the defect of her early work, and it is signaled, I think, by the title she gave her first collection. For *Distortions* refers not only to the distorted forms of human life portrayed in the stories, but also to the distortion implicit in her method of representation. Beattie's various means of telling-it-slant tell a certain truth, perhaps, but a limited one.

As I have indicated, the most significant advantage of Beattie's method is the remarkable economy that it facilitates. Exposition is always deftly woven into narration. Sometimes this technique leaves the reader in doubt about the relations that the narration develops. **"Victor Blue,"** for instance, obscures the gender of the narrative voice, destabilizing the reader's perspective for much of the story. Here, the lack of discrete exposition is exploited to provoke sudden, retrospective enlightenment; the narrator is not, we discover, a sister or companion to Ms. Edway, but is *Mr.* Edway. More often, however, the exposition spun out along with the narration has no such dramatic function, but serves rather to represent characters as fused with their contexts—geographical, familial, social—from the outset. While the result is striking in its capacity to encompass character and background in one narrative motion, the price paid for such economy is high. Characters so fused to their contexts cannot stand out from them, much less alter them. This sense of characters fused to a frame, of course, is most marked in such stories as **"The Parking Lot,"** but even in **"Marshall's Dog"** or **"Big Bear"** it is less the development of characters than the deft manipulation of the frames by which the illusion of motion and change is created. The metonymic associations expand the frame, elaborating a larger picture, but the characters remain fixed within it.

It would be possible to argue, of course, that such limits are built into the genre of the short story itself, the art of which is that of revelation rather than of complex development. But the advance marked by *The Burning House* suggests that Beattie is more than capable of expanding these limits. (I pass over *Secrets and Surprises,* Beattie's intervening and transitional volume of stories, for the sake of economy.) The same techniques we have seen her use in *Distortions* are recognizable in *The Burning House*—story construction by segment, simultaneous narration and exposition, reliance on metonymy and the present tense—but here they produce a far more resonant result.

The economy mastered in *Distortions,* for example, is now put to more ambitious uses. In **"Learning to Fall,"** Beattie tells one story, at the same time using it to tell another. One story is Ruth's. Ruth is the mother of Andrew, an eight-year-old who has suffered slight brain damage and facial paralysis as a result of a mangled forceps delivery. Andrew's father left Ruth six months before Andrew was born. Ruth teaches at a community college, where she earns hardly any money. Once or twice a month, her lover, Brandon, comes to spend the day with her. "Like many people," Brandon envies Ruth. "He would like to be her, but he does not want to take her on. Or Andrew." When Brandon visits Ruth, Andrew goes to the city with Ruth's friend, who tells the story and whose own story eventually emerges in the course of her narration. She is married to one man, Arthur, and in love with another, Ray. Although she has broken up with Ray, she meets him in the city when she takes Andrew there. Indeed, it was when she quit being Ray's lover that she began taking Andrew to the city. By the third page her story begins to creep out around the edges of Ruth's and eventually encircles it. In effect, one narrative serves as exposition for the other, and then they change places, Ruth's story providing context for the narrator's.

By the end of the day in New York, where events form the actual narrative line, the unnamed narrator has given up trying to resist loving Ray. Taking her cue from Ruth, whose dance instructor has been teaching her to fall and is her model of valor in the face of an unjust fate, the narrator recognizes "what Ruth has known all along: what will happen can't be stopped. Aim for grace." Here the associations by which the story unfolds are far more controlled than those in *Distortions.* One source of control is

Beattie's use of a first-person narrator, a choice she makes far more often in *The Burning House* than in *Distortions.* As a consequence, what the narrator sees and does is circumscribed and guided by her own preoccupations. Further, while they seem to unroll metonymically as before, the associations turn out to be partially metaphorical, to build a loose structure of meaning. The pool of blue water at the bottom of the Guggenheim is related to Hall's Pond, where Ruth swam the day before Andrew was born; it is related in terms made explicit by the narrator when she hears herself admonishing Andrew not to drop pennies into the pool from the walkway because he might hurt somebody. Realizing the irony of protecting others from a child himself mangled at birth by an impatient doctor, she feels guilty, a feeling later made specific by her recognition that she has been using Andrew as an excuse to meet Ray. Meanwhile, Hall's Pond, introduced in the preceding segment in a scene remembered merely because it preceded Andrew's birth, has begun to function as the basis for a set of images in which birth, pain, pools, and drowning prefigure the narrator's own fears of letting go, losing control. Consequently, when the story lands on the line "Aim for grace," its almost onomatopoeic resonance derives from a whole train of moments of which this line is the echo and the culmination.

If such a reading seems strained, it is—at least in the sense that such images are never allowed by Beattie to sit around festering with symbolic meaning in the way such a reading might imply. The story unfolds with an easy grace, moving from one scene to the next until the day's end, and it does so by means of the techniques that I have described—apparently random associations recorded in the present tense, incorporating exposition seamlessly along the way. What is new here is that when the reader reaches the end, something has changed. The narrator has reached a turning point toward which the story has been driving all along. She has learned to fall, a phrase whose verbal origin may seem arbitrary, but whose meaning is enriched by its appropriateness to Ruth's entire life.

Beattie's stories now end, then, with more than arbitrary closes because their associations are no longer purely arbitrary. And whether it is cause or effect of Beattie's technical control in *The Burning House,* her characters have also changed. They are more likable, and their relationships with each other are stronger, whether for good or bad. The women, particularly, move out of their frames and come alive, whether with love and envy, as in **"Playback,"** or with lonely terror, as in **"Waiting."** There is the same sense of something lost, something missing, but Beattie is now zeroing in on it, sometimes even naming it. In the title story, **"The Burning House,"** a woman wonders why, though she has "known everybody in the house for years," she knows them "all less and less" as time goes by, and then she finds out. "Your whole life you've made one mistake," her husband tells her at the end, "you've surrounded yourself with men." He continues: "Let me tell you something. All men—if they're crazy, like Tucker, if they're gay as the Queen of the May, like Reddy Fox, even if they're just six years old—I'm going to tell you something about them. Men think they're Spider-Man and Buck Rogers and Superman. You know what we all feel inside that you don't feel? That we're going to the stars." A comic epiphany, this, but with a punch, since it accounts perfectly for the behavior of every man in the story.

The power of Beattie's endings is even more evident in **"Running Dreams."** Here again, the first person enables Beattie to exploit old techniques to a more ambitious end. A series of discontinuous scenes delivered in the present tense portrays two couples, both estranged, but for different reasons, spending a weekend together and just barely keeping their building anger, fear, and hostility from exploding. This is a common enough situation for Beattie, but here the peripheral, dissociated qualities of these people's lives, emblematized by the David Hockney drawing they discuss at one point, is both set in relief and blown away—almost literally—by the final paragraph, in which the narrator, Lynn, recounts a memory of her dying father:

> I didn't know my father was dying. I knew that something was wrong, but I didn't know what dying was. I've always known simple things: how to read the letter a stranger hands me and nod, how to do someone a favor when they don't have my strength. I remember that my father was bending over—stooped with pain, I now realize—and that he was winter-pale, though he died before cold weather came. I remember standing with him in a room that seemed immense to me at the time, in sunlight as intense as the explosion from a flashbulb. If someone had taken that photograph, it would have been a picture of a little girl and her father about to go on a walk. I held my hands out to him, and he pushed the fingers of the gloves tightly down each of my fingers, patiently, pretending to have all the time in the world, saying, "This is the way we get ready for winter."

This description does more than reveal why Lynn is the strongest person in the group, although that is one of its purposes. By placing the present in context with the past, it shakes the present to its roots, exposing its emotional poverty when seen in relation to a scene of poignant plenitude. Finally, it is noteworthy that Beattie uses the photograph as an image here. The "picture of a little girl" imagined would resemble a host of pictures drawn from Beattie's earlier stories. It is as if she were placing an example of her earlier work into a new context, where it comes alive.

In *Distortions,* Beattie was spinning a net of words with which to catch life in motion almost at random. Her means were often extravagant, and extravagantly displayed, as in **"Big Bear City"** or in other stories such as **"Wally Whistles Dixie,"** a parody of J. D. Salinger. In *The Burning House,* no such display is made of the artist's artistry, and there is nothing random about her aim. Yet the techniques developed in *Distortions* clearly served as necessary apprentice work for the lucid perfection of many of the stories in *The Burning House.* **"Winter: 1978,"** the most ambitious story in the volume and arguably the finest piece of work Beattie has done so far, presupposes stories such as **"Marshall's Dog,"** but leaves them far behind in its mastery of a similar subject—a group of people whose relations are captured in an emotional nexus in time.

The advance marked by **"Winter: 1978"** seems partly the result of a technique of juxtaposition. Just as in **"Learning to Fall"** two narrative planes operate in relation to each other and in **"Running Dreams"** the past suddenly stands over against the present, in **"Winter: 1978"** two settings, California and Connecticut, serve to enforce the story's move from a hollowed-out now to a then that proves almost as empty. Like many of the characters in *The Burning House,* Nick and Benton in **"Winter: 1978"** are the now successful members of the baby-boom generation. Benton's art sells well in L.A., through the agency of one Allen Tompkins, whose library in Beverly Hills is "illuminated by lamps with bases in the shape of upright fish that supported huge Plexiglass conch shell globes in their mouths." Nick has made money in the record industry and spends his time making sure that such bands as "Barometric Pressure" are provided with chicken tacos. Both Nick and Benton come from wealthy families, but their own successes are personal, although accidental. Benton's work was discovered by Tompkins one night in the framing shop where Benton worked. Nick's entrance into the record industry is the result of his getting a job in exchange for making a dope connection with the former supplier of a philosophy professor's daughter.

"Winter: 1978" portrays these characters as they confront death, specifically the death of Benton's younger brother, Wesley, and generally the death of their youth. The story is constructed, as usual, out of segments, but because the past tense is used, the segments are ordered almost conventionally. They depict events that proceed chronologically in a single sequence, beginning in Los Angeles, where Nick lives and where Benton has come with his girl friend, Olivia, to sell his latest pictures to Tompkins, and ending in Connecticut, where Wesley has drowned and has been buried before Benton could be reached. That Nick should accompany Benton and Olivia back to Connecticut almost as if he were along for the ride is made entirely plausible by the portrait of life in L.A. with which the story opens. Once in Connecticut, however, Nick serves as a center of consciousness, sufficiently out of the picture to see it whole, yet sufficiently involved by his own common history with Wesley and Benton to take it personally.

For Nick, the East is home. As soon as he is headed there, he remembers "what Thanksgiving used to be like, and the good feeling he got as a child when the holidays came and it snowed." He wishes for snow throughout his visit. In a passage that echoes Nick Carraway's famous description of his Midwest, Nick drives past "houses that stood close to the road. There was nothing in California that corresponded to the lights burning in big old New England houses at night." Nick's sentimental longing for the New England winters of his youth, is undercut by the scene he confronts in Connecticut. Wesley's mother, Ena, presides over a parody of the "big old New England houses" of Nick's memories. She has assembled the fragments of her family at Wesley's house as a "tribute to Wesley—no matter that in the six months he'd lived there he never invited the family to his house." She relentlessly invokes a rural

New England tradition, ordering wood, for instance, from Hanley Paulson whom she seems to regard as a trusted servant of the gentry. It is not Paulson, however, who shows up with the wood, but his son, who steals all Wesley's pumpkins. The entire scene at Wesley's house testifies to the gap between Nick's sentimental image of New England and the reality of a world all too reminiscent of California. Uncle Cal, for example, has recently moved to East Hampton and hired a vegetarian decorator named Morris, "who paints the walls the color of carrots and turnips."

Similarly, Nick's romantic memories of his own youth are undercut once his discrete images come unraveled. A snowy Christmas scene turns into a revelation of family disorder when Nick recalls his father's drunken impersonation of William Tell. The image of a large red stocking his uncle had hung for him during another Christmas turns into another scene of conflict between his uncle and his father. The only images that resist such disintegration are those Wesley saw and photographed.

Wesley's photographs—of wind chimes hanging on a broomstick in a graveyard, of a "tombstone with a larger-than-life dog stretched on top," of Nick's hands folded on top of the *New York Times*—provided the only clues to a puzzle that no one save Nick is really concerned to solve: who Wesley was. Recalling Wesley's photographs becomes for Nick a means of mourning, although primarily a mourning for the loss of his own youth. Looking at his hands, Nick realizes that "what Wesley had seen about them had never come true." Wesley himself remains an enigma whose death is appropriately imagined in the form of a photograph of two bright orange life vests floating beside a boat in water "gray and deep," a photograph Nick captions "Lake Champlain: 1978." Such captions suggest why these images retain their force. As Nick remarks, "Photographer gets a shot of a dwarf running out of a burning hotel and it's labeled 'New York: 1968.'" The caption refuses to refer to the people or events photographed. It refers only to when and where the photographer was when he took the picture. This, the caption suggests, is what he saw at that time and in that place. No comment. No explanation. Even to inquire how the effect of a picture was achieved is a vain endeavor. When Nick asks Wesley how he got the "softness" in the picture of his hands, Wesley replies, "I developed it in acufine."

Such photographs resemble Beattie's earlier stories in their insistence on simply portraying a scene without comment or interpretation. What and where take such precedence over why as almost to annihilate it. But here, such photographic images serve a larger narrative interest. "Lake Champlain: 1978" cannot be explicated. It cannot be read as a symbolic construct. But because it is situated within a narrative about time and loss, it can function not merely as an image, but as an experience of time and loss, as it manifestly does for Nick: "He had to catch his breath when the image formed. He was as shocked as if he had been there when they recovered the body." The imagined photograph becomes an event in the story, specifically the event of Wesley's death as witnessed by Nick, and the story, in turn, becomes **"Winter: 1978"** because it re-counts an equally resonant moment. On the one hand, Nick's images of New England unravel, as Connecticut and the past are exposed as the same world as California and the present, a world in which parents try to get rid of their children only to pretend to themselves later that they always cared. But his is not merely the ironic loss of something that never existed, for on the other hand, he experiences a real loss, one described perfectly in Benton's closing speech to his son, Jason: "Benton told him this fact of evolution: that one day dinosaurs shook off their scales and sucked in their breath until they became much smaller. This caused the dinosaurs' brains to pop through their skulls. The brains were called antlers, and the dinosaurs deer. That was why deer had such sad eyes, Benton told Jason—because they were once something else." The cryptic copyright notice in *The Burning House,* "Irony & Pity, Inc.," is ironic in its self-reflectiveness, but it speaks as well to Beattie's larger capacity for pity.

If, as I have argued, Beattie's narrative method works by a metonymic unraveling, a movement from one detail to the next, her advances in *The Burning House* derive from a new focus on and control of that method. Her more frequent use of the first person, her willingness to let metaphors grow from and give resonance to the train of associations on which her stories ride, her use of the past tense—all these are marks of an author still experimenting, but with tools now refined and proven. The distance she has crossed could also be measured by comparing *Chilly Scenes of Winter* with *Falling in Place,* but her second novel fails, in my judgment, to live up to the promise of **"Winter: 1978."** It remains to be seen whether Beattie's techniques can be made to work for the novel, but they have already made something new of the short story, enabling it to cut into contemporary life where it hurts. (pp. 9-25)

Beattie on the 1960s and her works:

Am I a product of [the 1960s]? I suppose to some extent everybody is a product of their time. But I don't think that I know anything more about that period than anyone else does. And I'm rather surprised that so many people have found what I write to be conspicuous. I didn't go about it in a calculated way at all. I'm surprised people have put all these labels on me. . . . I don't invent these headlines and I don't work for these magazines. I think I'm writing about a specific group of people whom I do presume to know something about. I'd be the first to admit they are upper-middle-class WASPs. But again, if their concerns don't transcend that, it's fair to criticize me. You're not going to categorically criticize Malamud for writing about Jews, or Joyce for writing only about Dublin. Very often, when the argument stops there, I throw up my hands and wonder what these people do expect from literature. It doesn't seem unfair to me to ground something in the present day if you can also transcend that.

Ann Beattie, in an interview in the San Francisco Review of Books, *1985.*

Carolyn Porter, "Ann Beattie: The Art of the Missing," in Contemporary American Women Writers: Narrative Strategies, *edited by Catherine Rainwater and William J. Scheick, The University Press of Kentucky, 1985, pp. 9-25.*

Michiko Kakutani   (essay date 1986)

[*In the review below, Kakutani faults Beattie's detached prose style in* Where You'll Find Me, and Other Stories *but lauds her sympathy for her characters and her ability to create moving scenes.*]

"The middle of the target was this blue star," says a character in one of Ann Beattie's new stories [in *Where You'll Find Me, and Other Stories*]. "I was such a great shot that I was trying to win by shooting out the star, and the guy finally said to me, 'Man, you're trying to blast that star away. What you do is shoot *around* it, and the star falls out.' "

For readers of her previous novels and short stories, the foregoing could serve as a succinct description of Ms. Beattie's narrative method—a method that works through omission and understatement, irony and indirection. There tends to be little authorial comment in her fiction—few attempts to interpret behavior or conversations and almost no effort at all to situate her characters within some larger frame of reference, moral or historical. Instead, things simply happen—someone drifts out of one relationship and into another or moves from one house to the next.

In Ms. Beattie's finest work, this method has resulted in widely imitated narratives that mirror in their very structure the fragmented, fragmentary nature of their characters' lives, narratives that capture the strobe-light effect of contemporary life through their pointillist detail and fractured observation. Unfortunately, it's also a technique with decided limitations—the author's deadpan delivery can devolve into a pose of anomic detachment that's as irritating (and ultimately as ineffectual) as her characters' relentless passivity; and her gift for external description can be used to avoid looking at more elusive emotions. We may end up knowing what her people listen to on the radio, what they keep on their end tables and what they say to their dogs—all without having the faintest idea of who they really are.

Certainly *Where You'll Find Me*—Ms. Beattie's fourth volume of stories—includes several tales that suffer from such weaknesses. **"Snow"** is a mannered prose poem about lost love that reads like a random collection of notebook jottings. **"The Big Outside World"** becomes a labored attempt to draw some sort of analogy between an upsetting incident—some street people ambush a package of clothes meant as a Goodwill donation—and an anxious woman's state of mind. And **"Coney Island"** seems like a formulaic exercise in the depiction of our inability to connect: we're told that the two old pals sitting around the kitchen table both have problems—one has a wife in the hospital, the other is thinking about an old love affair—but a sense of their personalities and friendship is telegraphed by only

the broadest, most obvious details. We know, for instance, that they're both distracted and worried because Drew is playing with the salt and pepper shakers (which happen to be in the shape of penguins) and Chester is fiddling with a radio that needs batteries; and we also know that they're not doing a great job of cheering each other up because they keep missing each other's jokes. In the end, it's simply not enough to make us care.

Happily, many of the stories in this volume are more substantial—more sympathetic toward their characters as well as denser and most satisfying as fictions. Ms. Beattie's people—the battered emotional casualties of the 1960's and the hip survivors of the Me Generation—are teetering now on the margins of middle age, and the aging process has made them somewhat less careless about their lives. Like their predecessors, they're still afflicted by a sense of aimlessness and uncertainty, but now the stakes are higher—cancer, infertility, the death of a child—and they're a little more concerned about the consequences of their actions, a little more appreciative of the connections they do maintain with family and friends.

A sense of sadness hangs over many of these characters— in part, it's a nostalgic yearning for their receding youth ("We'll put on some Fifties music and play high school," says one); and in part, an apprehension of the terrible precariousness of life. Memories of a summer in Vermont prompt a man to re-examine the emotional losses he's incurred (**"Summer People"**); and a desultory chat in the kitchen jars a housekeeper and her now grown charges into a mood of melancholy recollection. The heroine of **"In the White Night"** remembers the time their Christmas tree caught fire and their little girl, Sharon, tried to rush toward the flames; and she also remembers the night in the hospital when they learned that Sharon had leukemia.

Whereas many of Ms. Beattie's earlier stories tended to take a random, almost improvisatory shape, several of the ones in *Where You'll Find Me* evince a pointed interest in sustained narrative form. **"Janus"**—which portrays a woman's obsession with a bowl given to her by a former lover—becomes a highly crafted, almost surreal meditation on the intrusion of time past into time present and on the perils of everyday life. And **"Spiritus"** grows from a stream-of-consciousness riff into a portrait of a man torn between his devotion to his wife and his passion for another woman.

As ever, the stories in this volume attest to Ms. Beattie's gift for weird analogies, her ability to grab cheap, glittering bits of dialogue out of the air. What's new about these stories is their intermittent lyricism, combined with a shift of voice that signals a willingness on the part of the author to risk subjectivity. A man is transfixed at the moment his car crashes by a glimpse of an old friend going trick-or-treating with her children—dressed, absurdly enough, as a skeleton. And a woman whose daughter has recently died imagines as she drifts off to sleep beside her husband that "in the white night world outside, their daughter might be drifting past like an angel." With such passages, Ms. Beattie's cameralike accuracy with detail gives way to something a little more personal and poetic, and the result is stories that have the capacity to move as well as persuade us.

Michiko Kakutani, in a review of "Where You'll Find Me, and Other Stories," in The New York Times, *October 1, 1986, p. C23.*

Amy Hempel   (essay date 1986)

[*Hempel is an American short story writer, critic, and editor. In the following review, she applauds Beattie's precise, economical dialogue in* Where You'll Find Me, and Other Stories *but faults the stories' lack of resolution.*]

"Any life will seem dramatic if you omit mention of most of it," says a character in Ann Beattie's short story, **"Snow."** And two paragraphs later, "People forget years and remember moments."

These two statements are clues to Beattie's program in **Where You'll Find Me,** her seventh book of fiction and fourth collection of stories since **Distortions** was published 10 years ago.

These 15 stories represent a scaling down of situations and lives recognizable from Beattie's earlier work. There are families who "argued with each other and made pronouncements instead of having conversations." There are lovers who don't connect—exhausted city women and lonely, touchy men—and a woman who is embarrassed to learn that she's fallen in love with her husband at the same time he was beginning to have an affair.

Passengers in cars listen to the Eurythmics and Hall & Oates. Reference is made to the recent films, *Agnes of God* and *Paris, Texas.* (As a shortcut to establishing mood and signaling an audience, or as a means to place a story in the moment, this device dates a story.)

Now hitting 40, those who flowered in the '60s still smoke the occasional joint; now it helps them transform the baseboards of a Victorian house into *faux marbre.*

Social behavior is simplified—"If people did not argue in front of their friends, they were not having problems . . . " thinks a character in **"In the White Night."** Or behavior remains as baffling as ever—"How do people make small talk when they've shared a world?"

Many of the characters here are interchangeable with those of Beattie's early *New Yorker* stories. The names are new, but it's still Drew and Kyle and Cammy and Renee and why their lives are falling apart.

At a deeper level, **"In the White Night"** shows a husband and wife making the "necessary small adjustments" to their daughter's death from leukemia. The father in **"Summer People"** sees menace to his vacationing family from an envious, inquisitive salesman and from the woman next door. In fundamental ways, he feels himself excluded from the workings of his own family.

The title story [**"Where You'll Find Me"**] is the best in the book. A woman of 38, her arm a "broken wing," out of work and unsure of her standing with her lover, visits her brother and his family at Christmas. With charm, range

and insight, Beattie gives us intimacy and uneasy confessions, and a wonderfully sardonic 11-year-old girl.

As before, when Beattie's characters say something, it is not dialogue, but *speech*—the way people really sound. And, as in all of her work, there are precise images and associations. The woman who broke her arm had first slipped on ice after trying to stop a bus by "shaking (her) shopping bags like maracas in the air."

In **"High School,"** a woman observes her dinner partner: He eats only raw food, and has brought his own. He crunches a bud of cauliflower. If a certain kind of pain had sound, the noise of teeth crunching through cauliflower might represent it.

"Janus" is a fable-like story about a Realtor who attributes her success in selling houses to a cream-colored bowl that she places in each house before she shows it. This is new territory for Beattie, who is on more familiar ground in **"Coney Island"** and **"Cards,"** where she writes about the complexity of friendship.

"Cards," first published in *Esquire,* is two savvy women at lunch. They note the flirtation of a man at the next table as Josie reveals an awkward development—her lover has become friends with the ex-lover of her luncheon companion (one thing these stories have plenty of is *lovers*). Difficult to explain, Josie says, but she would be traitorous not to try.

Drew, in **"Coney Island,"** visits his friend Chester hours before going to meet an old girlfriend, now married. With Chester's wife in the hospital for exploratory surgery (she can't get pregnant), Drew rhapsodizes about his former lover.

"Charlotte's elbows were pointy, like a hard lemon. I used to hold onto her elbows when I made love to her," he tells his friend. "What a thing to be sitting here remembering."

If these remarks have so far leaned heavily on quotes from the stories, it is the same mechanism by which we forget years and remember moments.

There are memorable lines in **Where You'll Find Me,** but for memorable *stories,* a better choice is Beattie's peak performance, **The Burning House.** In those remarkable stories, the perfect, shivery endings called for a decent interval before going on to the next. In this new collection, more often than not, all that happens when you finish reading a story is—you finish reading a story. (pp. 2, 11)

Amy Hempel, in a review of "Where You'll Find Me, and Other Stories," in Los Angeles Times Book Review, *October 12, 1986, pp. 2, 11.*

Thomas R. Edwards   (essay date 1986)

[*In the review below, Edwards commends Beattie's sparse language in* Where You'll Find Me, and Other Stories *for communicating the shallow nature of her characters but notes that this same economy narrows the scope displayed in her earlier volumes of short stories to the exclusion of humor and feeling.*]

Though most of the stories in Ann Beattie's new collection, *Where You'll Find Me,* are pretty terse, one of them, called **"Janus,"** is sufficiently open and worked out to give convenient access to the materials from which they all are made. In **"Janus,"** Andrea, a successful suburban real-estate agent of a certain age, uses a glazed bowl of her own to provide a special touch of elegance to the houses she shows for sale. It is "both subtle and noticeable—a paradox of a bowl," and Andrea is sure that it brings her professional luck. Once, when she forgot to remove it when she left a house, she felt as if she'd forgotten a friend, or a child (though she has no child). Her husband, a stockbroker, thinks it "pretty" but pays it no special attention, since he no longer takes particular pleasure in the possessions they have acquired "to make up for all the lean years when they were graduate students."

Yet for Andrea the bowl *is* special. She sometimes dreams about it coming "into sharp focus," she imagines a "deeper connection" between it and herself, her use of it becomes more deliberate, possessive, anxious about damage. It emerges that it was a gift from her lover, who later left her because she would not give up her "two-faced" life and commit herself to him alone. The story ends with her continuing in her undemonstrative but acceptable marriage, often looking at the bowl, "still and safe, unilluminated," an image of feeling made esthetic and thus endurable: "In its way, it was perfect: the world cut in half, deep and smoothly empty. Near the rim, even in dim light, the eye moved toward one small flash of blue, a vanishing point on the horizon."

If the story is perhaps a little diagrammatic, this ending is fine, especially since Andrea is not allowed fully to recognize how aptly the bowl reflects her own condition. And her condition, with due allowance for individual circumstances, is essentially that of most of the women, and some of the men, in these stories. The recurrent motive is loss, and diminished replacement. Divorce, the loss of lovers and friends and expected futures, childlessness or the death of children, departures from former homes—Ms. Beattie's people suffer emotional and moral disconnection in a world that has yet been rather generous to them in material ways. They live comfortably enough in New York, the suburbs, the country; they work at business, finance, editing, modeling, writing, the law; they have been to college and sometimes graduate school, and now, as they approach 40, they miss what they remember as the innocence and intimacy of student community, "all those people" (as one character wistfully reflects) "who took themselves so seriously that everything they felt was a fact."

The belief that feelings are facts is what has been lost, or safely displaced onto objects like Andrea's lucky bowl. Estranged from their own emotional centers, these people experience their lives as revisable hypotheses, stories, sources of metaphors that they can never quite accept as literal connections between people or things. And yet they are not free—people, places and objects, present or remembered, continue to ask for the directness of response that can't now be given. "People and things never really got left behind," one character discovers after a humiliating attempt to give her old clothes to Goodwill, and the imperishability of relations that can no longer be enjoyed or used is the painful figure in the carpet.

Ms. Beattie is a pre-eminent writer of her generation, and it's easy enough to think it a second "lost generation," but simply to call hers post-Vietnam fiction or whatever is a crude and deceptive historicizing at best. (The striking thing about Hemingway, Fitzgerald and Faulkner is not what the war did to their imaginations but how quickly and naturally they found in their experience new forms of what American literature, literature generally, had always been concerned with.)

Ms. Beattie contemplates life through the sensibilities of educated, upper-middle-class people born soon enough to have been marked and directed by the 1960's and 70's but also late enough not to have suffered the sharpest personal consequences of those times. They are drawn to the country but are not counterculturalists (nor indeed anything else—no articulate political or social passions stir in them at all). If they occasionally smoke a little pot, they seem in no danger of involvement with any worse substance. Traditional work and its rewards do not deeply engage them, but they have no trouble amassing money and property. Their marriages and relationships often fail, but whose don't these days? On the analogy of "yuppies" they might be called "nummies"—not-so-young urban malcontents—but it's greatly to Ms. Beattie's credit that she concerns herself not with the supposed public sources of their numbness but with the insight it provides into the desires of people thwarted by their immediate culture, as human desires so commonly are.

A few of the stories in *Where You'll Find Me* pursue economy to the point of inconclusiveness, but most of them have the sensitive elegance one hopes for from this remarkably gifted writer. The cultivation of brevity, however, makes it hard to read as a book—only two of the stories run to more than 11 pages, and a kind of vertigo sets in as one struggles to adjust to rapid changes of characters, settings and issues.

Ms. Beattie's earlier story collections—*Distortions* (1976), *Secrets and Surprises* (1978) and *The Burning House* (1982)—were considerably more ample in scale and mood. I assume that she has been trying to pare things down, to minimize explanatory and connective matters, to distill significance into moments of speech, gesture, image. If so, a purer art is achieved at some cost. Those earlier stories that are longer are sometimes rough and wasteful, but they are full of energy, exuberance and daring, what I can only call *life*. So too is Ms. Beattie's most recent novel, *Love Always* (1985), whose impressive gravity of outlook has plenty of room for a large, outrageous comic inventiveness that many of the earlier stories also draw on. But there are few laughs or even smiles to be had in *Where You'll Find Me,* and few venturings beyond a rather buttoned-down obliquity and economy of means that make even more evident how narrow Ms. Beattie's social theater now is. I kept wishing for some poor people, some important characters much older, or younger, than these nummies, someone whose name weren't Garrett, or Gaye, or Kyle, or Renee, or Drew. Certainly I wish that the one older and poorer character who does appear weren't called Mrs. Camp.

Like Ms. Beattie's recent books, *Where You'll Find Me* is copyrighted by Irony and Pity Inc., which is presumably one of those legal fictions sometimes recommended to successful writers by their tax accountants. But while the new volume has enough irony and pity in it to satisfy anyone, the touch of jaunty self-mockery in the corporate name seems less appropriate here. For all their subtlety of feeling and technique, these stories left me wondering, however churlishly, if Ms. Beattie isn't in some danger of taking her materials, and possibly herself, a little too seriously.

Thomas R. Edwards, "A Glazed Bowl of One's Own," in The New York Times Book Review, *October 12, 1986, p. 10.*

Mark Silk   (essay date 1986)

[*In the following excerpt, Silk compares* Distortions *and* Where You'll Find Me, and Other Stories *and notes that the latter collection displays an increased development in characterization and plot and a greater sense of optimism.*]

'Don't think about a cow,' Matt Brinkley said. 'Don't think about a river, don't think about a car, don't think about snow. . . .' "

So begins [*Where You'll Find Me, and Other Stories*], Ann Beattie's latest collection of short stories, and a fitting beginning it is. For a dozen years now, Beattie has been the mistress of what might be called the tale of impaired consciousness, through which the characters move in a cloud of unknowing, not thinking about, hardly sensible of, what ails them. Non cogito, ergo what?

What ails Vernon and Carol, the middle-aged couple Matt Brinkley is talking to in **"In the White Night,"** is the death of their daughter from leukemia years before. But something new is going on here. Vernon may try hard to think "positively," but he is "never impervious to real pain." Carol is feeling the pain, and she knows whence it comes. After the two have driven home through a thickly falling snow, they lie down in the living room, he on the sofa, she on the floor below. "In the white night world outside, their daughter might be drifting past like an angel, and she would see this tableau, for the second that she hovered, as a necessary small adjustment." Have the inhabitants of Beattieland finally grown up, become aware of themselves, figured out how to cope with the feelings? If so, they've come a long way.

Consider Michael—unemployed, separated from his wife and small daughter, and stoned on hash—in the following passage from **"Fancy Flights,"** one of the first stories Beattie published in the *New Yorker* (in 1974), reprinted in her first collection, *Distortions.*

He turns the record off and then is depressed that there is no music playing. He looks over the records, trying to decide. It is hard to decide. He lights his pipe again. Finally, he decides—not on a record but what to eat: Chunky Pecans. He has

no Chunky Pecans, but he can just walk down the road to the store and buy some. He counts his change: eighty cents, including the dime he found in Prudence's underwear drawer. He can buy five Chunky Pecans for that. He feels better when he realizes he can have the Chunky Pecans and he relaxes, lighting his pipe. All his clothes are dirty, so he has begun wearing things that Richard left behind. Today he has on a black shirt that is too tight for him, with a rhinestone-studded peacock on the front. He looks at his sparkling chest and dozes off. When he awakens, he decides to go look for Silas. He sprays deodorant under his arms without taking off the shirt and walks outside, carrying his pipe. A big mistake. If the police stopped to question him and found him with that . . . He goes back to the house, puts the pipe on the table, and goes out again.

A more exquisite rendering of drugged-out inanition can scarcely be imagined, and it is as if cannabis had extended its influence over all the stories in the collection: *distortions* indeed, and not in the benign sense of dopey bliss. There is the slovenly woman in **"Downhill"** who is so disoriented that she cannot keep track of how long her husband has been gone, and imagines she is spending her birthday alone. There is the college dropout in **"Hale Hardy and the Amazing Animal Woman"** for whom getting to the Grand Canyon becomes an *idée fixe* (comparable to those munchies for the Chunky Pecans).

These characters inhabit a dimly lit present; the past is something they don't wish to be reminded of. "What an amazing life David has had," begins **"Wally Whistles Dixie."** Married to a thirty-year-old ballerina at the age of sixteen, David is musical, literate, and capable of catching a mosquito wherever it may noiselessly be hiding in a room. He is left a lot of money, and makes a success of a restaurant ("sushi being then very hard to find in that part of Vermont"). Happy, however, he is not. One night his alienated son Wally comes upon him lying on his back on the front lawn (being eaten up by the mosquitos), and asks whether the family can take a trip to Reno, where "it all began." David balks. " 'Why do you sound so depressed?' 'I'm not in a very good mood, Wally. And I don't really like to be reminded of how your mother picked me up in Reno, Nevada.' 'Do you think there's something awful about it?' 'I just don't like to think about it.' " From amazement to catatonia.

Did Beattie mean to condemn these numbed-out lives? Certainly she did no moralizing, and her carefully wrought endings always quivered enigmatically, as if to say, you're not going to catch me making any judgments. What made her so hard to pin down, though, was the shiftiness of her narrative voice. Towards the end of **"Wally Whistles Dixie,"** for example, the third-person narrator bluntly announces "what will happen" to David and his family: "Sheila [the wife] has one breast cut off, then the other. It becomes her new excuse for not dancing. If you don't believe this is at all logical, try taking a few leaps without your breasts and see how hard it is to keep your balance." Two sentences of dry declaration, then the reader is handed something very like the excuse itself, as

Sheila would have made it: "*You* try taking a few leaps without your breasts." Who is telling this story anyway?

From the fag end of "the sixties," Beattie proceeded in her second collection, *Secrets and Surprises,* into that cultural Thermidor known as the Me Decade. The characters give the impression not so much of being stoned as of having washed up on shore—human flotsam miserable about where the tide has deposited them but powerless to move.

"**Weekend,**" a hair-raising story about a philandering, alcoholic professor turned down for tenure, concludes with the female protagonist, the long-suffering woman with whom he lives, leaning her head on his shoulder, "as if he could protect her from the awful things he has wished into being." Nick, in "**A Vintage Thunderbird,**" is a monument to fecklessness—the kind of person who gets mugged in public, who expects his telephone calls to end with people hanging up on him. He remains obsessed with his old girlfriend Karen, and the talisman of his obsession is the Thunderbird convertible she bought when they were in love. In the end it turns out that she, who had appeared to be merely tolerating him out of pity, is no more able to get on with her life than he is with his. The car, however, has been sold, and the best they can do is to think of how to get it back.

If *Secrets and Surprises* was filled with longing for relationships that have fallen apart, Beattie's next collection, *The Burning House,* seemed to abandon all hope. ["**The Burning House**"] ends with the husband taking his wife's hand. " 'I'm looking down on all of this from space,' he whispers. 'I'm already gone.' " At the end of "**Afloat,**" the first-person narrator is overwhelmed by "the desire, for one brief minute, simply to get off the earth." The key story may be "**Learning to Fall,**" about an outing to New York City taken by a nameless first-person narrator and the mildly retarded son of her friend Ruth. The boy, Andrew, "likes to do things in private. You can see the disappointment on his face that other people are in the world." Like many another Beattie character, the narrator is in a similar condition. She can't stop herself from calling her sometime lover Ray, but sounds "disappointed, far away" when he says hello. When he shows up she won't take his hand, so he puts it around her shoulder: "No handswinging like children—the proper gentleman and the lady out for a stroll. What Ruth has known all along: what will happen can't be stopped. Aim for grace." Grace? The theological resonance is hard to miss. In a predestinarian world where what will be will be, how *can* one aim for such a thing?

That is the question to which Beattie, in [*Where You'll Find Me, and Other Stories*], seems to be seeking an affirmative answer. Where else to go but up? In "**Snow,**" a woman looks back fondly on a love affair; longing has softened into nostalgia. "**Skeletons**" ends with one of those hapless Beattie males thinking back to a woman who had been his ideal. In "**Times,**" a woman manages to recapture her childhood love of Christmas at her parents' house. "**Heaven on a Summer Night**" recalls an elderly housekeeper's "life she loved so much." The timeless present of *Distortions* has now given way to the discovery of a usable past. But it is not only the past which holds moments of grace.

In "**Lofty,**" a woman climbs a tree and gazes down at the place where she had lived with her former lover, then descends and—with no hint of ambivalence—throws her arms around her husband. In "**Coney Island,**" a man musters the strength to see his former girlfriend. "Ches," he asks his drinking buddy, "Have you ever been in love?" The "objective" situations of these characters have not changed; there are still the broken marriages, the lost relationships that Beattie's readers have come to expect of her. What is missing is the resignation and despair. At the end of "**High School,**" one friend says to another, "Come on—you can't quit on me now." In "**Spiritus**" and "**Where You'll Find Me,**" flirtations offer the promise that somewhere love is possible, if only over the rainbow.

The results are decidedly uneven. "**Cards,**" a slight account of a pick-up at a fashionable restaurant, is barely a cut above women's magazine fiction. "**Janus,**" an "*idée fixe*" story about a woman's attachment to the ceramic bowl given to her by a former lover, is dull and unconvincing. And the writing at times displays an unaccustomed sloppiness—wasted words, an excessive reliance on abstractions, inept images. "She went to sleep with no more interest in her surroundings than she would have had in an anonymous motel room." The sentence is deflated by that "anonymous." "She was right; parks of any real size rarely had a discernible shape any more." *Any more?*

The broader problem is, in a sense, existential. In her earlier bleakness, Beattie had a way of twisting a knife in the guts of her stories; a grim finality was almost always achieved. But putting across a happier or more openended message is trickier business, and she still seems to be struggling to figure out how to manage it. In one case, however, she unquestionably succeeds.

"**Summer People**" may or may not refer to Hemingway's posthumously published "Nick Adams" story of the same name. Besides sharing a title, both use images of a seal, and both are about Sex and the Man. The Hemingway story recounts how Adams, the young would-be writer, and his beloved Kate make love for the first time (at her insistence) on a blanket in the Michigan woods. Beattie's tale is more complicated. Tom and Jo are vacationing in Vermont with his son by his first marriage. Where Nick is bursting with his limitless future, Tom is disquieted—by an odd stranger who wants to buy his property, by Jo's continual hunger for sex. He can't "imagine caring for anyone more than he cared for her," but is he still in love? If only an author would step in and tell him "what would happen, if he had to try, another time, to love somebody."

The story ends with a pool attendant whistling as he makes "an adjustment to the white metal pole that would hold an umbrella the next day." Just so. Beattie's new world is one where the necessary small adjustments are starting to be made. (pp. 22-3)

Mark Silk, "The Beattietudes," in Boston Review, *Vol. XI, No. 6, December, 1986, pp. 22-3.*

> I think because I was attuned visually, it kind of figures that I would marry a painter. He's a narrative painter, and I think in terms of our working method he and I are extremely similar. He often will do a multipaneled canvas, with a central panel and side panels that comment on it. I do the same in the stories, with characters commenting from the sides.
>
> —*Ann Beattie, in* The New York Times Book Review, *1991.*

Michiko Kakutani   (essay date 1991)

[*In the review below, Kakutani characterizes Beattie's prose style in* What Was Mine, and Other Stories *as mature and substantial and applauds her increased emotional and moral depth.*]

Since the mid-70's, when her stories first began appearing in *The New Yorker,* Ann Beattie has written four novels and five collections of short stories, including her latest, *What Was Mine.* They are books that chronicle the shifting landscape of her characters' lives as they exit the post-counterculture years and enter the 80's and 90's, books that attest to the continuing evolution of Ms. Beattie's literary style.

Her early fiction was populated by an assortment of young people, suffering from passivity, alienation and an unnamed sense of dread. They tended to sit around one another's houses or apartments, smoking dope, listening to music and trading jokes and non sequiturs. There was little direction to their lives, and Ms. Beattie's narratives often felt similarly shapeless and random. People seemed to relate better to their pets than to one another, and they drifted from place to place, relationship to relationship, without apparent motive or reason.

In her more recent work, Ms. Beattie's characters are older. They've exchanged grubby apartments in Boston and New Haven for suburban homes and country houses; many of them are married, with children and real jobs. Although Ms. Beattie still uses her magnetic eye for detail to delineate these people's domestic routines, her highly developed sense of irony is no longer omnipresent, and she now tends to shape her characters' lives into densely patterned tales, full of recurrent images and motifs.

Her obsession with missed connections has also developed into something sadder and wiser. Her people no longer suffer from a nonspecific anomie; rather, they are contending with the more intractable problems of grown-up life: divorce, illness, death, the loss of love, hope and desire.

Certainly this is true of her vibrant new collection, *What Was Mine.* Most of the tales in this volume deal with fragmenting marriages, and many of them circle, nervously, around the subject of death. [**"What Was Mine"**] is a nos-talgic monologue in which the narrator reminisces about the two men who shaped his youth: his father, who was killed in a freak accident, and his mother's boyfriend, who recently died of a heart attack.

"Imagine a Day at the End of Your Life" is another elegiac monologue by an aging man, who reminisces about his family and tries to imagine the moment of his death. **"You Know What"** describes a father's attempt to soften the impact on his daughter of her teacher's sudden death. And **"Windy Day at the Reservoir"** uses the drowning of a retarded man as a kind of metaphor for the sense of loss and disillusionment sustained by all its characters.

Both **"You Know What"** which focuses on a single family and **"Windy Day,"** which focuses on two couples, are really novellas, rather than short stories, and their capacious length allows Ms. Beattie to develop the many filaments of experience that define her characters' lives. We see how these people relate to one another within the confines of a family, and we see how their familial ties affect their interaction with the friends, neighbors and strangers who pass through their lives.

Unlike Ms. Beattie's early stories, these novellas leave the reader with a sense of the characters' pasts, how shifting circumstances affect their feelings for one another, and how past actions impinge upon the present. As a result, there is a new moral density to these tales, and awareness of consequences and time. This deepening of focus can also be detected in several of the shorter stories: **"In Amalfi"** creates a melancholy portrait of a couple who have fallen in love, separated and reconciled many times over the years, and **"Horatio's Trick"** depicts the bonds of affection and irritation that bind a mother and her grown-up son through the years.

To be sure, some of the other stories in this volume lack this emotional depth; they're delicate, brittle collections of random details and clever apercus that feel like a throwback to the author's earlier and less successful fictions.

"The Longest Day of the Year" is a clumsily ironic tale about a divorcing couple who are visited by an irritable Welcome Wagon lady, who happens to be married to a marriage counselor. **"Home to Marie"** is a one-joke story about a woman who stages a fake party in order to exact revenge on her husband. And **"Installation #6"** is a slim monologue about a disabled handyman who helps his younger brother with an art exhibition. Just why these stories have been included in this collection is a mystery. Perhaps they were meant to pad out the volume; perhaps they were meant to throw the achievement of the other tales into relief.

In any case, they fail to diminish the overall effect of this volume, so accomplished are the other stories and novellas. In the best of these fictions, the reader can watch Ms. Beattie put her natural gifts—for dialogue, for social detail, for describing the incongruous effluvia of contemporary life—at the service of an evolving authorial vision. These stories are not simply Polaroid pictures of the passing parade of life, but finely orchestrated paintings created by an artist, who has continued to grow and mature over the years.

Michiko Kakutani, "Tales of the Intractable in a Grown-Up World," in The New York Times, *April 23, 1991, p. C16.*

Donna Rifkind   (essay date 1991)

[*In the following review, Rifkind commends Beattie's use of suggestive description in* What Was Mine, and Other Stories *to establish mood and character but faults some stories for lacking depth and plot unity.*]

Ann Beattie has made a career of looking deeply into surfaces. In story collections such as **Where You'll Find Me** and **Distortions,** and in such novels as *Chilly Scenes of Winter, Love Always* and, most recently, the highly praised *Picturing Will* (1989), she uses the countless superficial details that proliferate in the lives of everyday Americans—brand names, television shows, song lyrics, current events and the latest slang—to measure the quality of her characters' existence.

Instead of explaining, for example, why a person's life is empty, Beattie will leave us to guess at the emptiness by mentioning that this person has Captain Crunch and bourbon for dinner and drives a Pinto. Emotions in Beattie's fiction are rarely defined or interpreted; they are submerged under a smooth layer of minutiae instead. Hers is an arresting technique, much imitated by scores of fiction-workshop alumni. Yet how far can an author keep skimming surfaces before readers start wishing for a bit more depth?

Beattie's new book of short fiction [**What Was Mine, and Other Stories**], provides some answers. In the collection's best stories, the quotidian details are cleverly arranged to form a suitable backdrop for the characters' lightheartedness.

"In Amalfi," for instance, manages to capture some of the shimmering qualities of an Impressionist painting. The protagonist here is Christine, who finds the serene, eternal-summer ambience of Amalfi perfect for musing about her life and that of her ex-husband, Andrew, with whom she has been vacationing. It seems they are the only Americans on the island: the recent bombing of Libya and the Chernobyl disaster have chased other tourists away. Because these hints of calamitous world events make the resort atmosphere of Amalfi more enchantingly remote than it actually is, the story has a lovely, almost magical mood.

In the title story, **"What Was Mine,"** Beattie again uses atmosphere to great effect. The story's flavor this time is bitter rather than pleasing, as the narrator, Ethan, looks back on his dreary Washington childhood. On Saturday nights he used to accompany his mother to a bar off Pennsylvania Avenue called the Merry Mariner, where they would listen to her lover play piano and tenor sax.

In the shadows of the story Ethan's dead father keeps haunting him, so that the entire reminiscence is infused with feelings of loss and abandonment. Beattie's depiction of the lonely, bewildered young boy, sitting in a murky bar decorated with nets and conch shells and listening to "Let Me Call You Sweetheart" and "As Time Goes By," is as effectively melancholy as **"In Amalfi"** is light and breezy.

Other stories in the collection have their moments, but are not quite so forceful. The premise of **"Home to Marie"** is interesting—the narrator's aggrieved wife sets up the house for an elaborate cocktail party, then, in a nasty surprise, announces that there is no party, and she is leaving for good—but the story fizzles out after the initial shock is revealed. **"Horatio's Trick,"** about a forlorn alcoholic divorcee whose 19-year-old son comes to visit for Christmas, is serious and thorough, but a bit dull.

Then there are selections in the book that are all surface, with little or no connection to any underlying reality. Among these are **"Television,"** a silly sketch about a couple who take their lawyer to lunch; **"Installation #6,"** in which a museum lighting designer complains disjointedly about his dreadful childhood; and **"Windy Day at the Reservoir,"** a tedious, rambling narrative about a husband and wife who are housesitting in Vermont.

Random House is now labeling the advance copies of its books "Random Writers," and it is hard not to sneer at the pertinence of the campaign's title. For at her worst Beattie is the most random of writers, throwing together a jumble of unconnected details in an attempt to work up to some profound unifying message that never quite materializes. **"Windy Day at the Reservoir"** alone is brimming with such mundane artifacts as Yard Guard and Deep Woods Off, Teenage Mutant Ninja Turtles, a cookbook called *Mastering the Art of French Cooking* and a perfume called Graffiti.

Yet all these facts, presented shallowly and indiscriminately, add up to nothing more than bits and pieces of the way we live now. While several stories in Beattie's uneven new book manage to dig below the surface, most of them show her to be an archeologist of modern-day America whose random shards and remnants do not even begin to recreate a city.

Donna Rifkind, in a review of "What Was Mine, and Other Stories," in Book World— The Washington Post, *May 12, 1991, p. 8.*

Ron Hansen   (essay date 1991)

[*Hansen is an American novelist, critic, and educator. In the review below, he lauds Beattie's greater sympathy and compassion in* What Was Mine, and Other Stories *in comparison to her previous collections.*]

Ann Beattie is justly famous for fictions that freshly and insightfully portray those Americans in their 30's and 40's who have little to complain about—but little to care deeply about either. She is the geographer of an East Coast limbo where all is out of kilter, disjunctive, feckless and fractional, a harried country of brand names and infidelities where, as William Faulkner once said, "It all tastes the same."

The characters in the 12 fine stories in **What Was Mine** are too haunted by their fully reasonable fears and forebodings to do more than hang on or hide out. Emotional bunkers have been built, marriages and jobs have been abandoned; for these people, the lofty pursuits of the

1960's have given way to transient pleasures, anxious retrenchment and tentative accommodation.

In a fascinating Christmas story, **"Horatio's Trick,"** a half-drunk mother receives some painful criticism from her son, a junior at Notre Dame. She never asks him anything, he says, because she's "afraid of what every answer might be." And she has to concede that he has scored his point: "She was just sitting there, scared to death." It's a posture that wouldn't be unfamiliar to the househusband in **"You Know What,"** who hears that his child's teacher has been killed by a truck in a hit-and-run accident as she went out for groceries and thinks "that that is so often the way. That in some very inconspicuous moment, a person can be overwhelmed."

This kind of fragility also informs one of the collection's briefest entries, **"Installation #6,"** the first-person account of a highly dysfunctional family told by a handyman who has retired on disability while still in his 40's. Now he fills a few of his hours by putting in the gallery lighting over a piece of his kid brother's conceptual art: a manhole cover with a hidden recording of Irene Dunne and Allan Jones singing "Only Make Believe."

One of the most poignant and accomplished stories in *What Was Mine* is the title piece. Narrated by a man named Ethan, ["What Was Mine"] looks back to the days of his youth, after World War II, when the boy's father died in a freak accident and his mother chose to stay true to her husband's memory by refusing to marry her boyfriend, a musician whom she asked her son to call Uncle Herb—and who lived, for appearance's sake, in their dining room. As Ethan grew older, his mother grew increasingly angry with Herb, despite the fact that he and the boy were as close as father and son. Finally, she forced Herb to leave: "He said that he himself found it unbelievable. Then, suddenly, he began to urge me to listen to Billie Holiday's original recordings, to pay close attention to the paintings of Vermeer, to look around me and to listen. To believe that what to some people might seem the silliest sort of place might be, to those truly observant, a temporary substitute for heaven."

Ann Beattie has always been unusually good at handling a masculine perspective, as she proved in her funny and affecting first novel, *Chilly Scenes of Winter*. Here, as in her earlier fiction, the men are faithful, forlorn, frequently bewildered, frankly sentimental and completely genuine.

On the other hand, Ms. Beattie's women often seem harder to figure—ill-defined and passive one moment, fiercely irrational and pitiless the next. Each seems primed to explode. Early in **"Windy Day at the Reservoir,"** for example, a husband reflects that "when something stopped being fun, Fran usually found a way to stop doing it"—and so we are not surprised to learn, later on, that she has left him for another man. In **"Home to Marie,"** a husband tells how his wife hired a caterer and set up a party at their house but failed to invite any guests; instead she fled, leaving him alone with all the trays and platters in order to punish him for the occasions, years and years ago, when she had prepared food and helplessly waited alone for him to come home.

Another of these unpredictable women, Christine, sits in a hotel bar **"In Amalfi"** and remembers,

> vaguely, reading a story in college about an American woman in Italy, at the end of the war. The woman was sad and refused to be made happy—or at least that was probably what happened. She could remember a great sense of frustration in the story—a frustration on the character's part that carried over into frustrating the reader.

At times, Ms. Beattie frustrates her own readers in just this way. She prefers inference over illustration, summary over causality, a formless accretion of details over formulas of plot and trenchant dramatic action. And yet she's never predictable, simpleminded or slick. She seems truly interested in and mystified by the people she writes about. And she's wonderful at finding the telling image, as when she writes that two troubled characters are "as close as two fingers in a splint," or when she has a housewife unashamedly describe the "hand-colored engravings of trout" that her husband bought "for a dollar each, from people who didn't know any better," as "the nicest things we had."

What Was Mine is Ann Beattie's ninth book and fifth collection of stories, following *Distortions* (1976), *Secrets and Surprises* (1978), *The Burning House* (1982) and *Where You'll Find Me* (1986). Those earlier collections were praised for their inventiveness, their humor and eccentricities, their almost photojournalistic chronicling of our worldly disconnections. *What Was Mine* may be even better, for here Ms. Beattie has forsaken irony for honest introspection, and her famous detachment has given way to greater sympathy and tenderness. "All my life," confesses a man in one of these stories, "I've felt like I was just making things up, improvising as I went along. I don't mean telling lies, I mean inventing a life. It's something I've never wanted to admit."

We all do that, and we seldom admit it. Ann Beattie has the insight to see it and to know just what we mean. (pp. 3, 14)

> *Ron Hansen, "Just Sitting There, Scared to Death," in* The New York Times Book Review, *May 26, 1991, pp. 3, 14.*

Patricia Storace   (essay date 1991)

[*In the following excerpt, Storace notes that while Beattie skillfully presents minute details in* What Was Mine, and Other Stories, *her writing is sometimes shallow and insubstantial due to her "radical economies" in language, plot, and character.*]

Ann Beattie appears to be living a double life as a writer. As a writer, she may be married to literature, but she seems to be having an affair with television. There is a strain of Beattie story that can be read in a state something like the kind of sensuous amnesia that television often provokes. In this kind of Beattie story, character, decor, and language are smoothly recognizable without being truly specific, as if they were the results of casting instead of writing. We know details about the characters that are establishing instead of revealing; as in the story **"Honey,"** [in *What Was Mine, and Other Stories*], we know that Elizabeth is forty-five, drinks Courvoisier, owns wind chimes, but not what her personal history or passions are. Some of Beattie's characters and settings have at best the life of images; there can be something oddly interchangeable about them, as if they were not quite important to their own stories, and could be shifted to other stories with the right cosmetic changes.

Since 1976, Beattie has been known for her bittersweet, intelligent, and suave stories of the confusions and fears of prosperous, most often youthful, Americans. Her new collection, *What Was Mine,* with its catered parties in Charlottesville, vacations in Amalfi, and Vermont farmhouses crammed with folk art, is rooted firmly in the territory she has made her own, for good and ill. Beattie's characters are emotional drifters, unstable in the midst of their tasteful houses, barely able to sustain connections with each other; they wish they could burrow in their luxuries like sleepers under covers. It is a fresh source of wonder for them that death is present even on the most idyllic afternoon.

In **"In Amalfi,"** on an afternoon of chilled white wine and Mediterranean views, the main character waits for the return of someone boating: "She reminded herself that it was a calm sea, and that the woman could not possibly be dead." In **"You Know What,"** a father is told that his daughter's teacher has been hit by a truck: "She was struck from behind. . . . She was out getting groceries. It seems clear that that is so often the way. That in some very inconspicuous moment, a person can be overwhelmed." There is no escape either for people who have given up trying to placate death by offering it a cocktail and an hors d'oeuvre.

In her opening story, **"Imagine a Day at the End of Your Life,"** Beattie suggests that there is something tragic even in the simple act of perception; perception, which is supposed to join us to the world, also separates us from it, since what is perceived fully will include an ominous consciousness of coming death. The father of a family goes for a rare walk in the woods:

> That day in the woods, I thought: Don't run away from the thought of death. Imagine a day at the end of your life. . . . You're not decrepit, you're not in pain, nothing dramatic is happening. . . . You're going along and suddenly your feet *feel* the ground. . . . Clouds elongate and stretch thinly across a silvery sky. . . . Then imagine that you aren't there. . . .

Seven out of the twelve stories concern themselves with the consequences of divorce, and all are shadowed by the allusion to a violence underlying American domestic life. Working within a narrow range of class and setting and emotional preoccupation can sharply expose a writer's mannerisms and technical preferences, and means that within close confines, even within the same story, good and bad variations on the same material will be played out.

Beattie achieves her pervasive atmosphere of threat and disorientation through radical economies. She often truncates her characters, emphasizing what is peripheral about them instead of what is central. In **"The Longest Day of the Year,"** the narrator, a woman whose third marriage is failing, describes a trying visit from a neurotic neighbor. We never learn the narrator's name or background; we learn little about her marriage, and we never find out where she is living, though most of the story is taken up with a discussion of the community. What is local and distinctive, in both characters and setting—history, class, education, region—goes unaccounted for. As in a conventional television series, the episode itself is supreme, and the complexity of social detail is diluted.

In **"What Was Mine,"** although the widowing of the narrator's mother is a crucial event in both their lives, the mother tells her son nothing about his father. She doesn't reminisce or talk about his gestures or how they met; nor does the son ever ask her to talk about his dead father. Without context, their behavior seems inexplicable. Beattie's stories sometimes seem less narratives than assemblages; she pares away a character's history and what it may contribute to his motivations, foreshortening her people into a permanent present tense, while lavishing her most detailed descriptions on the objects surrounding them, telling her story through props. **"The Working Girl"** even reads like a treatment, since Beattie is openly giving the characters and settings the traits that will quickly establish them for the reader: "Details. Make the place seem real. In the winter, when the light disappears early, the office has a very strange aura. The ficus trees cast shadows on the desks." We are never told what the working girl's work is; there is no explanation of why her lover leaves his wife for her, no clue to what draws them together. We know that "her future husband had two dogs in his life, and one cat," but not where he comes from, or what he does. The omissions create the unnerving distortion that is the hallmark of Beattie's world; Beattie achieves the illusion of alienation and unknowability between character and character by limiting severely what the reader can know about them. In **"Honey,"** a story about a group of suburbanites seen at leisure and again during a moment of common crisis when a swarm of bees attacks their Sunday brunch, we know little about the past of the main character, her occupation, or her strained marriage, but the meals she makes are exhaustively described:

> One tray was oval, painted to look like a cantaloupe. The other was in the shape of a bull. She had bought them years ago in Mexico. Deviled eggs were spread out on the bull. The cantaloupe held a bottle of gin and a bottle of tonic. A lime was in Z's breast pocket. A knife was nestled among the eggs.

The trays are given what almost amounts to a biography; the characters are not.

There is a disturbing undertone in some of Beattie's work, a kind of American equivalent of the state of mind that in Britain is called "twee." In Britain, "twee" involves the sentimentalization of the past, all thatched cottages and Devon cream teas on flowered china. Its tougher transatlantic cousin is the sentimentalization of pop culture, its adorable bad taste, its sly celebration of the menace hiding beneath the facades of ordinary lives. It is the twee of

David Lynch movies or *Twin Peaks,* in which the perversities and evil that go unacknowledged under their suburban marquetry give those lives a sentimentally heroic dimension, in which pop culture and suburban trappings are invested with a precious malice. Many Beattie stories are riddled with this tone.

In **"Honey"** an undercurrent of drunken flirtation between an older married woman and a younger man is given an infusion of queasy charm:

> Inside, Len went to the basement door. . . . She followed him . . . there was a rather large cage with MR. MUSIC DUCK stenciled across the top. . . . The duck . . . hurried to a small piano. . . . After five or six notes, the duck hurried to a feed dish and ate its reward.
>
> "They were closing some amusement park," Len said. "My brother bought the duck. The guy who lives two houses over bought the dancing chicken."

This is adorable Americana, its very innocence a self-loving decadence, cherishing and superior to its own expert bad taste. Piano-playing ducks accompanying bizarre erotic transactions are America's equivalent of the thatched cottage, as are menacing lawn sprinklers: "The lawn sprinkler revolved with the quick regularity of a madman pivoting, spraying shots from a machine gun." And "Welcome Wagon" ladies, as in **"The Longest Day of the Year,"** cracking up during the course of their hospitality visits to neighbors, revealing their awful secrets and the awful secrets of their seemingly placid small towns. When the wife in **"Home to Marie"** puts her husband through an elaborate charade of preparing for a catered cocktail party, and tells him that there is no party, and that she is leaving him, you can practically hear the laugh track, except that this time the laughter sounds sinister.

Beattie's characters tend to behave with a solitary theatricality, as if they were living in front of invisible cameras, like Charlotte, the divorcée of **"Horatio's Trick,"** who on receiving a Christmas present of chocolates from her ex-husband, "dumped the contents out onto the kitchen floor and played a game of marbles, pinging one nut into another and watching them roll in different directions." And when this variety of Beattie character has a conversation, the dialogue has a calculating quality, as if the character were talking for publication or being filmed. Charlotte speaks to her son with precisely calibrated, mannered pauses: " 'No,' she said quietly. 'You're entirely right. He didn't even notice that we left.' " The final speech of **"You Know What"** spoken between two men, strangers brought together by an accidental death, has just this tailored-for-an-audience quality: " 'McKee,' Stefan says, walking beside him, 'all my life I've felt like I was just making things up, improvising as I went along. I don't mean telling lies, I mean inventing a life. It's something I've never wanted to admit.' "

Paradoxically, Beattie's best writing is concerned with wordlessness. She is a marvelous witness of how behavior, rather than words, carries coded messages of love and hate. At a family reunion in **"Imagine a Day at the End of Your Life,"** "The TV ran night and day, and no one

could keep on top of the chaos in the kitchen. Allison and Joan had even given friends the phone number, as if they were going into exile instead of visiting their parents for the weekend. The phone rang off the hook." And in **"Honey"** it is in a moment of wordless panic, when bees invade an elegant outdoor meal that the characters show what they are; the arrival of the bees is like a testing in wartime:

> Max became in an instant the coward, chair tipped back, colliding almost head-on with Margie Ferella; . . . as a bee flew past Ellen's nose, she screamed, shooting up from the chair, knocking over her glass of wine. . . . Louise snatched the baby back from Ellen, hate in her eyes because Ellen had been concerned only with her own safety, and it had seemed certain that she would simply drop the baby and run.

In the last and best story of the collection, **"Windy Day at the Reservoir,"** Beattie's brilliant observation of the inarticulate governs the story. Here she gives a virtuoso account of the relationship between a single mother and her twenty-six-year-old retarded son, done entirely without a moment of conversation between them.

In describing the boy's infancy, Beattie gets across the sheer murderousness obligation can take on:

> His screaming when he was two years old had brought his mother to tears, daily. . . . She had a lock on one small closet that contained clothes she would wear when she took him into Boston to see doctors. Except for those clothes she would often stay, all day, in her nightgown. Even after his teeth came through, she rubbed his gums with whiskey, hoping he might fall asleep earlier. She would smash delicate things that fascinated him before he had a chance.

Through the action alone, Beattie conveys devastatingly the nakedness of the mother's love and hate, her impulse both to kill and to sustain her son.

Beattie succeeds remarkably in her portrait of the boy himself, with his incommunicable resentment over the inexplicable restraints of his life, and the eerie coherence of his view of the world, far more coherent than his mother's. "Royce, after promising he wouldn't go out, had left a note for his mother (he had whirled the yellow crayon around and around in a circle, so she would know he was taking a walk around the neighborhood)." The mother's world is one of desperate fidelity, the boy's one of omnipotent appetite.

The passages describing the boy's walk outdoors are commandingly alive:

> He took off one shoe and sock and left them by a tree, because the little piggy that cried "Wee-wee-wee" all the way home was also telling him it wanted to walk barefoot on the grass. When he took off the shoe, he made a mental note of where to find it again. He had left it at tree number fifty. There were exactly four thousand four hundred and ninety-six trees on this road to the reservoir.

The boy is made up of components, and each component has its own desire.

It is this story in particular that shows how much better than Ann Beattie Ann Beattie can write. Like her most interesting characters, her work is a mixture of weaknesses and strengths. She is in the exceptional position of a writer whose powers may guide her into unknown territory, and whose weaknesses are marked by an easy glamour and appeal that can undermine the reality of her gifts. (pp. 10-11)

Patricia Storace, "Seeing Double," in The New York Review of Books, *Vol. XXXVIII, No. 14, August 15, 1991, pp. 9-11.*

FURTHER READING

Bibliography

Opperman, Harry and Murphy, Christina. "Ann Beattie (1947-): A Checklist." *Bulletin of Bibliography* 44, No. 2 (June 1987): 111-18.
    Lists both primary and secondary materials.

Criticism

Bell, Pearl K. "Literary Waifs." *Commentary* 67, No. 2 (February 1979): 67-71.
    Review of *Secrets and Surprises* in which Bell compares Beattie to John Cheever as a chronicler of a generation and faults her writing style as unimaginative and tedious.

Dezure, Deborah. "Images of Void in Beattie's 'Shifting'." *Studies in Short Fiction* 26, No. 1 (Winter 1989): 11-15.
    Examines Beattie's treatment of loss and void in the short story "Shifting."

Gerlach, John. "Through 'The Octascope': A View of Ann Beattie." *Studies in Short Fiction* 17, No. 4 (Fall 1980): 489-94.
    Analyzes the short story "The Octascope" as representative of Beattie's fictional style and content.

Hill, Jane Bowers. "Ann Beattie's Children as Redeemers." *Critique: Studies in Modern Fiction* XXVII, No. 4 (Summer 1986): 197-212.
    Chronicles Beattie's treatment of children as positive influences in her works through *The Burning House.*

McCaffery, Larry and Gregory, Sinda. "An Interview with Ann Beattie." *The Literary Review* 27, No. 2 (Winter 1984): 165-77.
    Interview in which Beattie discusses her writing habits and reveals the ideas that inform her minimalist prose style and characterizations.

McKinstry, Susan Jaret. "The Speaking Silence of Ann Beattie's Voice." *Studies in Short Fiction* 24, No. 2 (Spring 1987): 111-17.
    Examines Beattie's "open" narrative style and compares it with a traditional "closed" style.

Miller, Philip. "Beattie's 'Janus'." *The Explicator* 46, No. 1 (Fall 1987): 48-9.
    Analyzes Beattie's use of myth and tragedy in the short story "Janus."

Murphy, Christina. *Ann Beattie.* Boston: G. K. Hall, 1986, 138 p.
    Only book-length critical overview of Beattie's works.

Additional coverage of Beattie's life and career is contained in the following sources published by Gale Research: *Contemporary Authors,* Volumes 81-84; *Contemporary Literary Criticism,* Volumes 8, 13, 18, 40, 63; *Dictionary of Literary Biography Yearbook: 1982;* and *Major 20th-Century Writers.*

Gustave Flaubert

1821-1880

French novelist, short story writer, and playwright.

INTRODUCTION

Frequently associated with the realist and naturalist schools of fiction, Flaubert is best known for *Madame Bovary; mouers de province* (*Madame Bovary*) and is often considered the most influential novelist of the nineteenth century. He is, however, also recognized as a master of the short story form, and his only short fiction collection, *Trois contes* (*Three Tales*), is often praised as the fullest expression of his mature genius. A meticulous craftsman, Flaubert diligently researched his subjects, infused his works with psychological realism, and aimed for an objective prose style "as rhythmical as verse and as precise as the language of science."

After receiving his early education in Rouen, where he was born, Flaubert studied law in Paris at his father's request but also wrote prodigiously during this period. In 1844 he suffered the first attack of a nervous disorder resembling epilepsy which plagued him throughout his life and which many critics feel partially explains the pessimistic tone of his fiction. The malady disrupted his studies, and Flaubert consequently devoted himself wholly to literature. In the next decade he published *Madame Bovary,* which became the subject of an obscenity trial due to its sexual themes, and his subsequent acquittal in 1857 brought him international notoriety. Flaubert continued to write novels but began work on "La légende de Saint-Julien l'Hospitalier" ("The Legend of Saint Julien Hospitaller") in 1875. Troubled by bankruptcy, poor health, and lack of progress on the novel *Bouvard et Pécuchet* (*Bouvard and Pécuchet*), Flaubert used this exercise in short story writing "to pass the time and see if I can still write a sentence." Upon completion of two more tales—"Un coeur simple" ("A Simple Heart") and "Hérodias"— Flaubert published *Three Tales* two years later to positive reviews. He died in 1880 of cerebral hemorrhaging.

Three Tales concerns saintly figures living in widely separated historical periods: contemporary France, the Middle Ages, and classical antiquity. In the first story, "A Simple Heart," Flaubert traces the life of Félicité, a simpleminded servant who loses everything that matters to her: loved ones, health, and home. Nonetheless, Félicité never questions her belief in a merciful and loving god and, just before her death, sees what she believes is the Holy Spirit. Critics often assert that this work attacks organized religion of nineteenth-century France and, specifically, the Roman Catholic church, but they acknowledge that Félicité is never presented unsympathetically. Modeled on a beloved servant from Flaubert's youth, she remains "a simple heart" in a wholly positive sense. Flaubert confided

to Madame Roger des Genettes that his aim in this story was "to move, to bring tears to the eyes of the tenderhearted" and called the work "just an account of an obscure life, the life of a poor country girl who is pious but mystical, faithful without fuss, and tender as new bread."

Flaubert learned of the legend of Saint Julien as a child in Rouen, where the local cathedral had a stained-glass window honoring the saint. Many years later Flaubert drew on medieval manuscripts and works by Jacobus de Varagine and E. H. Langlois in an attempt to document Julien's childhood, obsession with killing, and ultimate salvation. Set in the Middle Ages, the story is endowed with such supernatural phenomena as a talking stag and the saint's ascension into heaven. The tale ends with Flaubert interrupting the narrative to state: "And that is the story of St. Julien . . . , more or less as it is depicted on a stained-glass window in a church in my part of the world." Early reviewers were initially puzzled by this disclaimer, but later critics viewed it as an invitation to reread the tale as an examination of the relationship between art, artist, and audience.

"Hérodias," which also deals with religious figures and was similarly inspired by a mural in the Rouen cathedral, examines sexual warfare, decadence, and political ambition and treachery. Unlike the protagonists of "A Simple Heart" and "The Legend of Saint Julien Hospitaller," the title character in this story is not a role model, but the spiteful, manipulative, and power-hungry wife of the tetrarch of Galilee and the personal enemy of Iaokanann, better known as John the Baptist. Set in ancient Judea, "Hérodias" unfolds during a period of twenty-four hours and culminates in the prophet's beheading at the request of Hérodias's daughter, the seductress Salomé. Maurice Nadeau has argued that "Hérodias" isolates that "moment when history ceased to be the history of Mediterranean antiquity and became the history of the modern world."

Noting that *Three Tales* emphasizes sainthood and aspects of the Christian concept of the trinity, many critics have categorized these stories as exercises in moralistic writing, but the collection has produced additional interpretations. Some assert that the volume demonstrates Flaubert's belief that history can be divided into three distinct phases: paganism, Christianity, and *muflisme,* the last of which refers to Flaubert's conception of the nineteenth century as an era marked by the petty values and lifestyles of the bourgeoisie. Others argue that the collection concerns individuals struggling against the repressive dictates of patriarchal society. Scholars have also studied this volume from a post-structuralist viewpoint and as an exercise in form, noting that Flaubert's use of spatial imagery functions as a thematic device which is repeated throughout the collection. Almost all critics agree, however, that although realism and naturalism, by definition, exclude moralization, *Three Tales* does not represent a departure from Flaubert's aesthetic belief in realism. Because divine and supernatural intervention are both possible and probable for Félicité, Julien, and Iaokanann, Flaubert required that the reader also accept them as realities within the context of the stories. Consequently, critics consider "A Simple Heart," "The Legend of Saint Julien Hospitaller," and "Hérodias" as realistic and psychologically accurate as Flaubert's masterpiece, *Madame Bovary.* Nadeau has asserted that *Three Tales* gives "us the opportunity of studying an example of perfect art, an art which consists in the extraordinary economy of the narrative and the vivid evocation of the characters and the very special worlds they live in, all expressed in a style which the author can modulate at will between dazzling and tense, dramatic and dreamy, sober and subtle."

PRINCIPAL WORKS

SHORT FICTION

Trois contes: Un coeur simple; La légende de Saint-Julien l'Hospitalier; Hérodias　1877
　[*Three Tales,*　1903]

OTHER MAJOR WORKS

Madame Bovary; moeurs de province　(novel)　1857
　[*Madame Bovary,*　1881]

Salammbô　(novel)　1862
　[*Salammbô,*　1886]
L'éducation sentimentale: Histoire d'un jeune homme　(novel)　1869
　[*Sentimental Education; A Young Man's History,* 1898]
Le candidat　(drama)　1874
La tentation de Saint Antoine　(novel)　1874
　[*The Temptation of Saint Anthony,*　1895]
Bouvard et Pécuchet　(novel)　1881
　[*Bouvard and Pécuchet,* 1896]
Correspondence. 4 vols.　(letters)　1887-93
Oeuvres complètes. 28 vols.　(novels, short stories, essays, letters)　1910-54
Selected Letters　(letters)　1953

CRITICISM

George Saintsbury　(essay date 1878)

[*Saintsbury was a late-nineteenth and early-twentieth-century English literary historian and critic. Hugely prolific, he composed histories of English and European literature as well as numerous critical works on individual authors, styles, and periods. In the following excerpt, Saintsbury offers a positive review of* Three Tales.]

[*Trois Contes*] has the curious merit of giving in little examples, and very perfect examples, of all the styles which have made [M. Flaubert] famous. **"Un Coeur Simple"** displays exactly the same qualities of minute and exact observation, the same unlimited fidelity of draughtsmanship, which distinguish *Madame Bovary* and *L'Education Sentimentale.* **"La Légende de Saint Julien l'Hospitalier"** shows the same power over the mystical and the vague which is shown in *La Tentation de Saint Antoine.* **"Hérodias**" has the gorgeousness, the barbaric colours, and the horror of *Salammbô.* Of the three I have no hesitation in preferring **"La Légende de Saint Julien."** The history of the Norman *bonne* Félicité, her fidelity, her narrow brain, her large heart, the way in which employers, relations, and all connected with her make use of her and owe her no thanks, is a wonderful *tour de force,* but it has the defects of its quality. One feels that the author is in effect saying, "I am going to make you, whether you will or no, take an interest in this commonplace picture of humble life"; and though he is successful, there is a certain sense of effort and of disproportion. **"Hérodias,"** again, has much the same defects as its prototype. The sketch of Aulus Vitellius is faithfully loathsome, and the scenery of the sketch is as a piece of scene-painting unsurpassable. The breath of the Dead Sea and the desert, the atmosphere of Jewish, Idumaean, and Arab savagery, is all over it; but the "nervous impression" still stands in the way. In **"Saint Julien"** this is no longer the case, and the effect is admirable. (p. 590)

[The] importance of this writer is very much greater as a

maker of literature than as a maker of novels, though I am far from inferring that in the latter capacity he must not be allowed very high rank. His observation of the types of human nature which he selects for study is astonishingly close and complete; his attention to unity of character never sleeps, and he has to a very remarkable degree the art of chaining the attention even when the subject is a distasteful one to the reader. He has been denied imagination, but I cannot suppose that the denial was the result of a full perusal of his work. . . . [His imagination] is poetic rather than fictitious; it does not supply him with a rush of lively creations like the imaginations of the Scotts and the Sands, but with fantastic and monstrous figures, which his admirable writing power enables his readers to perceive likewise, and that not dimly, nor through a misty and hazy atmosphere. There are few things more curious than the combination of such an imagination with the photographic clearness of observation and reproduction. . . . (pp. 593-94)

> *George Saintsbury, "Gustave Flaubert," in* The Fortnightly Review, *Vol. 29, April 1, 1878, pp. 575-95.*

Benjamin F. Bart   (essay date 1947)

[*An American educator, editor, and critic, Bart specializes in French studies; his work on Flaubert includes* Madame Bovary and the Critics: A Collection of Essays *(1966) and the biography* Flaubert *(1967). In the following excerpt, Bart acknowledges that Realism traditionally precludes moralization, but argues that "The Legend of Saint Julien Hospitaller," a moral tale, can still be categorized as a realistic work.*]

The proper interpretation of **"La Légende de Saint-Julien l'Hospitalier"** of Flaubert has been a matter for such dispute that it is worthwhile to re-examine it. The core of the problem is whether the work has a moral significance or is merely the "petite bêtise moyenâgeuse" that Flaubert terms it in a letter to George Sand. Is there a moral element in Realism as Flaubert practised it? His longer works present so much material that equivocation is possible: **"Saint-Julien"** is of sufficiently brief compass to permit a clear answer. And fruitful discussion of Realism, or of any other literary doctrine, must be based upon such textual examination rather than upon abstract reasoning taking as its point of departure words like "impassivity" or "impartiality."

The traditional understanding of Realism excludes moralization: the author may not intervene to draw conclusions. It was, however, obvious to the Realists themselves that by their very choice of subject, they were often moral in their intent. Thus, Zola, in the Preface to *L'Assommoir*, characterizes his work as "de la morale en action." But this type of approach Flaubert deliberately denies himself when he says: "La morale de l'art consiste dans sa beauté même, et j'estime par-dessus tout *le style d'abord* et ensuite le vrai." Beauty, then Truth, these are to be the only criteria. One misses the familiar third element, the Good.

In regard to **"Saint-Julien,"** Descharmes is categorical:

> Il me semble qu'il n'y a aucune moralité à tirer de *Saint-Julien* . . . parce que Flaubert . . . n'a jamais pensé que l'œuvre d'art dût avoir une signification ou une moralité quelconque. C'est la base de toutes ses théories esthétiques et littéraires.

And this would appear to be the consensus of critics. Flaubert has sought Beauty, and only Beauty. He did not wish a moral implication in his works; therefore there is none. And if one reads it in, one is falsifying the story, deliberately doing violence to Flaubert. But the problem is not so simple as this.

An analysis of **"Saint-Julien"** demonstrates that in the case of so conscientious an artist as Flaubert the resolution of the problem of morality in the work of art lies in the thesis as old as Socrates that the Beautiful is the True and is the Good, a formula which Flaubert would not have challenged. For he himself said: "Est-ce qu'il n'est pas temps de faire entrer la Justice dans l'Art? L'impartialité de la peinture atteindrait alors à la majesté de la loi—et à la précision de la science." Or again, and even more clearly: "Non, ce qui me soutient, *c'est la conviction que je suis dans le vrai,* et si je suis dans le vrai, je suis dans le bien, j'accomplis un devoir, j'exécute la justice." If the work of art be truly beautiful, it will also be good; that is, it will join the stream of human life in terms of its meaning. Flaubert, in seeking beauty and truth in his tale, is led to morality.

One aspect of the question must be disposed of at the outset: in what form did Flaubert find the tale originally, what moral elements are there in his sources? The sources of **"Saint-Julien"** have been examined in detail several times. The several medieval versions all gave Flaubert essentially the same legend, differing only in detail. But the story as Flaubert tells it departs considerably from the sources; and the points of difference are illuminating.

Let us consider the legend as Flaubert found it in the version of Jacobus de Voragine in the *Legenda Aurea*. Julian, a young noble, is out hunting one day, following a deer. Suddenly, the deer, inspired by God, turns and asks: "Tu me insequeris, qui patris et matris tue occisor eris?" Julian flees to avoid the accomplishment of this dire prediction. After serving a foreign prince, he is rewarded by being married to the widow of a rich lord. His parents, after long search, find his dwelling place and are received by his wife in his absence. She has them sleep in her own bed. Julian returns on the following morning while his wife is out at church. He comes to the bed to awaken her and finds his parents there but mistakes them for his wife and a lover. Without a word, he draws his sword and kills them. Leaving the house, he meets his wife and understands what he has done. Realizing that the prediction has been accomplished, he informs his wife of his decision to flee and then acquiesces in her desire to accompany him. They go off and, coming to a dangerous river, they spend their lives ferrying people across it. One night, he hears a voice, goes out, and finds a stranger half-dead from cold. He brings him in to warm before the fire, but this is not enough; he must put him in his own bed. (pp. 23-4)

From his friend [L. F.-Alfred] Maury, Flaubert learned

additional details of Julien's childhood and, more important, an expansion of the final scene. Concerning the leper, there are simply more details:

> Julien le prit sur ses bras, l'appuya contre as poitrine, et le front rongé d'ulcères du lépreux retomba sur le front de son hôte, et le sang livide des plaies du pauvre retomba sur les joues et sur la bouche de Julien, qui le souffrit de joie. . . .

For the most part, however, one is struck by the differences between the sources and the work of Flaubert. Some of these I shall want to consider in the analysis of Flaubert's text. But one or two may be cited here. In the sources, through no fault of his own, a man commits a crime; for that crime, he does penance and is pardoned by the Lord. If moral there be, it is only that the ways of the Lord are inscrutable and that we may be absolved by our good deeds. The legend is eminently a part of popular folklore. It has been given a religious flavor; but fundamentally it is only an inversion of the "grateful animal theme." Flaubert could have eliminated the moral element without doing serious injury to the value of the story considered from the esthetic point of view. Giraud sums up his study of the problem of the sources by quoting from Flaubert's correspondence:

> Je désirais mettre à la suite de **"Saint-Julien"** le vitrail de la cathédrale de Rouen . . . et cette illustration me plaisait *précisément* parce que ce n'était pas une illustration, mais un *document* historique. En comparant l'image au texte, on se serait dit: Je n'y comprends rien. Comment a-t-il tiré ceci de cela?

What transformation does this material undergo in the hands of Flaubert?

Broadly speaking, Flaubert divides his story into The Predictions, The Preparation for the Crimes, The Crimes, The Effort to Expiate, The Expiation, The Absolution. So described, the fundamental symmetry of the structure is apparent. But the development of this harmony has led Flaubert to a moral structure as well: in his hands, the harmonious is the good. By deliberately recasting the original legend in this balanced form, Flaubert has given it an inherent moral structure. With *Madame Bovary,* it would be extremely difficult to untangle these threads; but on a small scale and with a clear example like **"Saint-Julien"** this demonstration may be undertaken.

Let us turn to the detail of the story. The opening pages describe rapidly the château, Julien's parents, and the birth of Julien himself. There follows, with equal rapidity, the double prediction: Julien will be holy but will shed criminal blood. The dual nature thus expressed carries through the childhood of Julien, which Flaubert passes over quickly.

Then, as Julien is growing up, we come to the fatal obsession that will mark the whole first half of the tale, as Julien fulfills the evil destiny predicted for him. The story under Flaubert's touch becomes a study of bloodlust, of the development of a mania, an obsession with killing. It has been said [by De Lastic]:

> **"La Légende de Saint-Julien l'Hospitalier"** est

une œuvre absolument complète au point de vue psychiatrique . . . On y trouve l'observation d'un obsédé impulsif, avec son étiologie, l'origine de son idée, son développement, son exécution et la terminaison de la maladie; et tout cela est décrit dans des termes qui collent si bien au sujet, suivant une expression chère à l'auteur, que le lecteur sent défiler en lui les états d'âme du malade.

The early appearances of Julien's criminal nature are handled by Flaubert with delicacy, yet power. The first clear indication is the mouse which comes out during mass and attracts the interest of the boy. This interest rapidly develops into an obsession as Julien watches and wonders if the mouse will reappear: "Elle revint; et, chaque dimanche il l'attendait, en était importuné, fut pris de haine contre elle, et résolut de s'en défaire." The tense usage is worth noting as the hatred becomes a fact, an event which took place against the background of his being irritated. There is no moral issue stated here. We are dealing only with a psychological phenomenon, the genesis of an obsession. Julien strikes the mouse, "et demeura stupéfait devant ce petit corps qui ne bougeait plus."

Without more ado, we move to the second stage, this one requiring a more conscious desire for blood: "Toutes sortes d'oisillons picoraient les graines du jardin." Julien kills them, "et les bestioles lui pleuvaient sur les épaules si abondamment qu'il ne pouvait s'empêcher de rire, heureux de sa malice." Killing no longer leaves him stupefied; he enjoys it. Soon he will need it. But what is the precise force of "heureux de sa malice?" Is Julien consciously enjoying evil? Yes, of course, but enjoying it as would a madman: insanity, not moral responsibility.

The third stage comes at once: the killing of the pigeon. But Julien's stone only wounds the bird:

> La persistance de sa vie irrita l'enfant. Il se mit à l'étrangler; et les convulsions de l'oiseau faisaient battre son cœur, l'emplissaient d'une volupté sauvage et tumultueuse. Au dernier roidissement, il se sentit défaillir.

A love of killing, a fury when his will is crossed here, a "défaillance" when the obsession is satisfied: Julien is now psychopathic.

It is his misfortune that everything concurs to force him deeper into the toils of his malady. His father teaches him to hunt, urges him on. And we watch Julien grow in his love of the chase, in his love of the kill. His preoccupation with wild animals is such that: "Il devint comme elles. Quand sa mère l'embrassait, il acceptait froidement son étreinte, paraissant rêver à des choses profondes." Finally, we come to the supreme satisfaction of his obsession: the great hunt. Here, everything is handled with consummate art. Nature seems to adapt herself: she is cold and hard. A cock is killed, two wild goats are massacred. Gradually, the air of mystery grows stronger; the animals, even, are of strange and unknown species: "Au milieu du lac, il y avait une bête que Julien ne connaissait pas, un castor à museau noir. Malgré la distance, une flèche l'abattit; et il fut chagrin de ne pouvoir emporter la peau." And we are in the midst of a land of miracles: endless animals swarm about and Julien can kill at will. The beasts

> . . . tournaient autour de lui, tremblantes, avec un regard plein de douceur et de supplication. Mais Julien ne se fatiguait pas de tuer, tour à tour bandant son arbalète, dégafnant l'épée, pointant du coutelas, et ne pensait à rien, n'avait souvenir de quoi que ce fût. Il était en chasse dans un pays quelconque, depuis un temps indéterminé, par le fait seul de sa propre existence, tout s'accomplissant avec la facilité que l'on éprouve dans les rêves.

And then the deer! Hundreds of them backed up in a valley: "L'espoir d'un pareil carnage, pendant quelques minutes, le suffoqua de plaisir." Completely under the domination of his mania, no longer in any way master of himself, Julien has lost all sense of time, of place. And the troubled brain is reflected in the rest of his body; suffocation overcomes him. At this moment, nothing but a tremendous and soul-stirring shock can release him from the domination of his mania. The great deer provides it. Julien's last arrow remains planted in the deer's forehead:

> Le grand cerf n'eut pas l'air de la sentir; en enjambant par-dessus les morts, il avançait toujours, allait fondre sur lui, l'éventrer; et Julien reculait dans une épouvante indicible. Le prodigieux animal s'arrêta; et les yeux flamboyants, solennel comme un patriarche et comme un justicier, pendant qu'une cloche au loin tintait, il répéta trois fois:
>
> —"Maudit! maudit! maudit! Un jour, cœur féroce, tu assassineras ton père et ta mère!"

Julien, "stupéfait, puis accablé d'une fatigue soudaine," weeps, is overcome.

Julien's shock is moral in character. Weeping, he realizes at last that he has committed a crime. And here a study of the sources is most important, for this element is wholly absent in them. In the medieval form, Julien is not cursed by the deer; the deer does no more than refer to the crime to come. For in the original, Julien is not felt to have sinned yet. Flaubert, by a calculated addition, has deliberately altered the story as he found it; it is of the utmost significance that it is this key incident which gives the moral meaning to the whole work.

One or two phases in the passage merit our closer attention: the deer has appeared "comme un patriarche et comme un justicier." Julien, after being under the spell of an obsession with blood, with killing, will now struggle with a guilt complex. Does not harmony, balance, require just this? The picture has been completely one-sided until now: Julien has been the wrong-doer, has progressed from crime to crime, each adding to the horror of the preceding. Now, following the rigorous structure which Flaubert has established for his tale, Julien must fulfill the other aspect of his destiny. Impelled by a desire for balance and harmony, Flaubert will now reduplicate the steps that have led to the crime. But in this case they will be the steps leading to the expiation. Its character, the precise way in which Flaubert paints the picture will be of the highest importance to us. Will he point the moral explicitly? Will it be

there implicitly, for all to see if they wish? Or must we read it in?

Julien began his crime in early childhood and by little stages. Balance requires then that the expiation be of the same character: it may come only slowly. Here, Flaubert shows great insight: Julien is frightened by his experience and fears the fulfillment of the curse. But the consciousness of guilt is not yet complete. He is ill, physically, psychologically: he cannot shake off the terror of the curse. In fact, in his diseased brain, a new idea, a grander killing, begins almost to take hold. Julien is meditating on the prediction of the murder of his parents:

> Puis il songeait:
> —Si je le voulais, pourtant?
> Et il avait peur que le Diable ne lui en inspirât l'envie.

So, ultimately, he flees. Does Flaubert call this an evasion of guilt? Does he ask us to see a moral problem here? Leading up to the flight, the text reads, "Quand il fut rétabli complètement, il s'obstina à ne point chasser." There is nothing here but a quiet statement of fact. Later, Julien lets a sword slip, cutting his father's cloak:

> Julien crut avoir tué son père, et s'évanouit.
>
> Dès lors, il redouta les armes. L'aspect d'un fer nu le faisait pâlir. Cette faiblesse était une désolation pour sa famille.

Shortly thereafter, his javelin narrowly misses his mother. Flaubert continues at once: "Julien s'enfuit du château et ne reparut plus." He is faithful to his method. The facts of the case are there. We may interpret them in psychological fashion—or moral—if we care to. But we cannot claim that Flaubert has invited us to do so.

Part One was the development of the mania and the commission of a crime leading to a prediction of a countercrime whose force Julien would feel. Part Two is the murder of his parents. Julien's exploits in foreign lands recall the medieval epics; but we learn that he is mortally afraid of killing old people. Evasion is the key-note. And the *merveilleux* element enters again in his miraculous ability to free people.

Julien marries and is happy; but he is unoccupied. Hence, his mania can slowly come to the fore again. He begins to dream of the chase and is temporarily satisfied by fantasy. But ultimately the temptation is too much for him and he goes out upon the last fateful hunt.

The second hunt is an obvious parallel of the first. Indeed artistically, it must be so, if any principle of balance or harmony is to be observed. But this is also what ethics would demand. If sin and retribution are to have any meaning, they must be parallel, their relation must be manifest. Julien's sin has taken the form of abuse of animals: retributive justice demands that it be by animals that he suffer. And it is of the utmost significance that this return to hunting does not occur in the sources! Flaubert has added it to meet the requirements of his vision of the tale.

Where, in the first hunt, nature seemed to bend her every effort to concur in Julien's desires, here, we find the very reverse. The light is deceptive; there is silence, loneliness, a vague uneasiness. And then we meet the specific terrors of the woods: deep shadow, the crackling of leaves.

In the first hunt, all of Julien's efforts were crowned with success. Balance requires the opposite here; Flaubert offers it. None of Julien's weapons seem to have any effect upon the beasts. There are signs of death and decay everywhere: bones, crosses, hyenas. And at last, all of the animals that he has hunted crowd around him:

> Il restait au milieu, glacé de terreur, incapable du moindre mouvement. Par un effort suprême de sa volonté, il fit un pas; ceux qui perchaient sur les arbres ouvrirent leurs ailes, ceux qui foulaient le sol déplacèrent leurs membres; et tous l'accompagnaient.

Julien is returning, helpless, furious. Not even this experience has made him fully realize the character of his mania, has made him see it in its true light. It does not seem strained to say that he is evading the issue. Our feeling of justice demands that he face it. Our artistic sense also requires that more come. It does.

Julien, back in the grounds of his own château, comes upon three pheasants and captures them. But he finds them changed into a single dead and rotting body. Note the character of his reaction, again an addition by Flaubert to the sources: "Cette déception l'exaspéra plus que toutes les autres. Sa soif de carnage le reprenait; les bêtes manquant, il aurait voulu massacrer des hommes." There can be few more dire punishments than those received as a result of being allowed to commit the crime we wish to: it is artistic balance and terrible moral justice. It is justice in this awful majesty which Julien must face. For he returns to kill his parents.

Artistically, we must have here, as it were, a gathering of the threads that have gone to make the story. Flaubert has revived the element of the hunt. He has reintroduced Julien's parents. It remains only to bring in his wife and the great deer who had cursed him. After driving the dagger into the bodies of his parents, Julien "écoutait attentivement leurs deux râles presque égaux, et, à mesure qu'ils s'affaiblissaient, un autre, tout au loin, les continuait. Incertaine d'abord, cette voix plaintive longuement poussée, se rapprochait, s'enfla, devint cruelle; et il reconnut, terrifié, le bramement du grand cerf noir." Note that this critical incident, too, giving especial point and meaning to the murder, is absent in the sources. Julien's wife enters; he knows and understands his crime. A fleeting hope that it is not true leads him to look closely at his parents. Then, in his own words, "désormais il n'existait plus." He flees again, as Part Two comes to its tremendous close.

What do artistic balance and harmony now require? A crime has been committed; a second one was required to bring the guilty man to a full realization of his state. That realization has been accomplished. Amends, expiation are the only possible sequence. A moral issue is here involved, categorically. But it has been claimed that Flaubert refuses to allow such an issue in a work of art. Only beauty, truth, can be involved. Perfect beauty, however, will require the moral issue to be present now, far nearer to the surface than in the earlier sections: the two have coincided.

For convenience's sake, we may take as our guide the division adopted by the Catholic Church for repentance and expiation: Contrition, Confession, Satisfaction must precede and validate Absolution. Julien goes off, to beg his living. Flaubert states: "et son visage était si triste que jamais on ne lui refusait l'aumône." Esthetics, ethics demand this; and Flaubert, following the dictates of the one, offers us the other as well. The work has a moral character in this passage at least, extending even to the choice of words.

Confession must follow Contrition: "Par esprit d'humilité, il racontait son histoire." Flaubert may have had no moral thought in mind in writing these two sentences, the one following directly upon the other. But if their resemblance to Catholic doctrine (and here we are using Catholic terminology only because it is concise and clear) is only coincidence, then that coincidence is the inevitable result of the esthetic demands of the story. Retributive justice is an esthetic demand now; any other turn to the story would be unacceptable.

Satisfaction for the crime committed is the next requirement before Expiation is complete and Absolution can follow. It would not be emotionally complete were Julien to be allowed to stop here; morality and esthetics continue in close alliance. Julien tries to offer the required satisfaction by his way of life. He is rejected by all, even by the animals. He is haunted by the death rattle. He macerates his flesh; he hopes for death.

But the tone of the story thus far has been heroic. All has been of epic dimensions from the first descriptions of the riches of the castle. Were the tone to change now, were lesser acts to complete the tale, there would be a serious change in character, a disparateness between the first two parts and the Third. Esthetics demands heroics in the Third Part. So does morality, for the crime was great. Julien can find atonement only in a sacrifice of heroic character, in something which by its nature partakes of the ultimate as much as did his submission to his mania. Again, ethics and esthetics are at one. By living a life of sacrifice for others, he may offer up his life as satisfaction for his crime. Note, however, that Flaubert does no more than state the facts. Julien has come to a river:

> Une vieille barque, enfouie à l'arrière, dressait sa proue dans les roseaux. Julien en l'examinant découvrit une paire d'avirons; et l'idée lui vint d'employer son existence au service des autres.

How casually Flaubert states this! The second half of a sentence suffices! But Flaubert would feel it inartistic to hammer the point: it must develop naturally from the story. And the master has succeeded here.

Julien has at last found the way to absolution and the story moves rapidly to its conclusion. All the necessary data have been established. Julien finds his labor a torture, extremely difficult to accomplish; but he accepts it "avec douceur." And then, as we enter the final scene of the leper, the miraculous appears once again: the three calls, the voice heard across the river despite its width, the storm, the sudden quieting of the waters. The leper, if he is properly to sum up the whole story, must include the two elements of the original predictions for Julien. He must be both wonderful and dreadful:

> En approchant de lui la lanterne, Julien s'aperçut qu'une lèpre hideuse le recouvrait; cependant, il avait dans son attitude comme une majesté de roi.

Given the role that the leper is to play in the story, these are the two attributes that he must also have from the moral point of view. Similarly, Julien must mortify every sense, just as his gratification of his passion has been complete: harmonious balance and ethics are again in accord. Julien must give up food, drink, fire, his bed, even his body to the leper. And in return—Heaven.

The facts seem to have spoken for themselves. In Part One, an esthetic sense established the data for the story. A moral could be read into it; but it was in no way required and may be rejected as superimposed. But by Part Two, the two elements are present and working toward the same goal. In Part Three, the two become inseparable, can no longer be distinguished, as they are both necessary. It would appear that in his effort to create the true and the beautiful, Flaubert was inevitably writing a moral tale.

But to what extent is consciousness of the import of one's acts a necessary part of morality? And to what extent is Julien conscious of this import? In our view, Julien could perhaps be dismissed as an amoral person throughout all of Part One, were it not that in Parts Two and Three, he shows himself capable of realizing his state. After the murder of his mother and father, he comes to a full realization of what has been only a dim and somewhat obscure idea until then. At this time, we can no longer speak of him as dominated by his insanity. This other side of his character, by showing its presence even after his deeds, establishes the responsibility for his acts. He was repeatedly warned; yet he persisted. Then, being responsible, what attitude does he have toward his sacrifice? To determine this, we must examine in detail Flaubert's method of presentation of the scene with the leper.

Julien, in the story as Flaubert tells it, has almost no reactions to his experience with the leper. Let us note the few that there are. Julien is having a terrible struggle to get the boat back across the river: "Mais comprenant qu'il s'agissait d'une chose considérable, d'un ordre auquel il ne fallait pas désobéir, il reprit ses avirons . . . " This categorical imperative belongs solely to the domain of ethics; it would seem to imply a consciousness on the part of Flaubert, if not of Julien. But it does not state—and the omission is vital—that Julien realizes that he is expiating his sins.

Flaubert commits a serious sin against good taste after having Julien find that his water has been turned to wine. The numerous biblical connotations, the Marriage at Cana, the Eucharist, make this quite permissible. But Flaubert adds, "Quelle trouvaille!" Julien might have had many reactions to the wine; this one is startlingly crude. It would be easier simply to reject it as bad taste, but it is in the heart of what is perhaps the most crucial section of

the tale from our point of view and as such must be considered. We must take it to be a total failure of Julien to realize that there is any meaning to the discovery. The leper extends his hand and drinks the pitcher at a draft. For Julien, it is only one more humiliation of the flesh. This he accepts without protest. From there to the ultimate elevation to heaven, there are no comments on the reactions of Julien to his expiation.

Is Julien then conscious of his acts, conscious of their moral implications? It is never stated in so many words. That, certainly, would have been contrary to the doctrine of Flaubert. Then are we reading it in if we find it there? The phrase is unjust. It is not read in: it is implicit. We have seen, throughout the whole tale, the gradual convergence and fusion of the moral with the esthetic element. The two senses in us have been satisfied by the presentation of the facts: we look to these last few moments to complete that satisfaction. And we find it there.

This is the implication of the method which Flaubert uses. He is not amoral; he is not rejecting a moral element. He is saying, rather, that the moral must be inherent in the tale if it is to be present at all. He will write his story with only the goal of truth and of beauty in view. But if he succeeds, he will also have an inherent moral arising out of the beauty: Justice will have entered Art. Flaubert himself states this thought with a clarity beyond cavil in a letter to George Sand. As it was written as he was finishing this tale, we may fairly apply the statements to **"Saint-Julien":**

> Quant à laisser voir mon opinion personnelle sur les gens que je mets en scène, non, non, mille fois non! Je ne m'en reconnais pas le droit. Si le lecteur ne tire pas d'un livre la moralité qui doit s'y trouver, c'est que le lecteur est un imbécile ou que le livre est *faux* au point de vue de l'exactitude. Car, du moment qu'une chose est vraie, elle est bonne. . . . Et notez que j'exècre ce qu'on est convenu d'appeler le réalisme, bien qu'on m'en fasse un des pontifes. Arrangez tout cela.

Perhaps the conciliation lies in esthetics!

Fundamentally, Flaubert asks that his reader be alert. The appreciation of a work of art is, and must be, an interplay, an exchange between the creator and his public. In music, the composer has the right to demand that the listener permit himself to be carried with the music to the extent that it will bear him. In painting, the spectator must penetrate into the picture, must have some degree of *Einfühlung* if he is properly to appreciate it; this, the painter may demand as a right. And in literature, Flaubert insists that the reader must also take an active part. The artist will place before him, in a skillful arrangement, all the materials; but the artist must not break the spell by intervening to point the moral. The reader must actively participate in the experience, must draw the conclusions. It is in this sense that I interpret Flaubert's doctrine of impassibility. And in this understanding of the doctrine, there is inherent in **"La Légende de Saint-Julien l'Hospitalier"** a profound morality. (pp. 25-33)

Benjamin F. Bart, "The Moral of Flaubert's

'Saint-Julien'," in The Romanic Review, *Vol. XXXVIII, No. 1, February, 1947, pp. 23-33.*

Ben Stoltzfus   (essay date 1961)

[*Stoltzfus is an American educator, critic, and fiction writer. In the following excerpt, he discusses how Flaubert's point of view and use of irony in "A Simple Heart" culminate in a critique of organized religion.*]

In spite of Flaubert's statement [that **"Un Cœur simple"** is simply the story of a poor country woman's life], readers and critics frequently see an ironic level in this story. Brunetière said that **"Un Cœur simple"** was but another example of Flaubert's attack on human stupidity and the bourgeois mentality, while [Anthony] Thorlby says [in his *Gustave Flaubert and the Art of Realism*] that the Holy Ghost parrot ambiguity sums up the irony of Flaubert's realism. On the other hand, [Albert] Thibaudet maintains [in his *Gustave Flaubert, sa vie, ses romans, son style*] that the story, as a turning point in Flaubert's career, marks a decisive change of attitude and indicates a shift towards human pity. [In an introduction to *Three Tales,* Harry] Levin stresses the intense bond of personal sympathy which drew Flaubert to Félicité. [In her *Gustave Flaubert et le principe d'impassibilité,* Marianne] Bonwit also underlines Flaubert's tenderness towards Félicité. If, as Flaubert and many distinguished critics maintain, the mood of the story is one of sympathy towards Félicité, are we justified in searching for the irony which people like Brunetière and Thorlby see in it? I think we are, but we must not look for it on the realistic level. The irony comes from the story's symbolic meaning which is hidden beneath its realism. **"Un Cœur simple"** has two levels: a realistic and a symbolic one, and consequently, two points of view, both of which are Flaubert's. If we accept Flaubert's own statement that the story is very serious and very sad, and the fact that Félicité was fashioned in part after a cherished old servant, "la chère Julie," we can state with Thibaudet and Levin that on the realistic level, Flaubert's attitude towards Félicité is a sympathetic rather than a critical one. On the other hand, critics like Brunetière, though limiting themselves to an analysis of the story's realism, have sensed a hidden irony, but have misinterpreted its meaning, since the irony is not to be found in the *realistic* handling of Félicité and Loulou. It is an "ironie à rebours," an operative irony as Henry James would call it. This hidden irony, which seems to run counter to the sympathetic realism of the story is, nevertheless, consistent with Flaubert's hostility towards human incompetence, and derives its impact, though it is not evident, from the skilful handling of Félicité and Loulou as a combined symbol. Beneath the detailed realism of Félicité's mysticism lurks Flaubert's attack on organized religion and the church. It is not an attack on Félicité. Félicité is merely the dupe of religious faith. It is the veiled attack on religion which gives the story its irony and its point of view.

Why veiled? George Sand, in her correspondence with Flaubert, had counselled him to be less impersonal in his writing. In his answers Flaubert defended his position by saying that the artist must not express his opinions in a work of art: "l'artiste ne doit pas plus apparaître dans son œuvre que Dieu dans la nature." Though Flaubert's treatment of Félicité does represent an increasing sympathy and tolerance towards man, he consciously and artistically had to use symbolism in order to inject his criticism of the church. This criticism is not Félicité's but his. Flaubert, therefore, is the hidden speaker in the story.

"Un Cœur simple," in its mastery of form and content, is an example of his maturest writing. The work itself is a skilful creation of a void, the absence of God; and Flaubert sets out to recreate in the reader the emotional void of a world from which God is absent. Félicité, in her devotion, represents Christian charity, Christian virtue, and Christian self-abnegation, and she dies "happy" in the vision of a Holy Parrot. And, by Christian standards, Félicité should inherit the "kingdom of earth." On the symbolic level, however, and in a godless universe, Félicité's self-abnegation appears meaningless and it is this "non sense" which Flaubert recreates as an emotional undercurrent.

When T. S. Eliot said that "the only way of expressing emotion in the form of art is by finding an 'objective correlative'," he was describing an artistic equation which had been in use for a long time. When Flaubert uses a set of objects, or a situation, or a chain of events as the formula for a *particular* emotion, he is communicating sensory impressions. This is why the symbolic content of **"Un Cœur simple"** is not immediately evident. *Gulliver's Travels* is a lucid reasoned transposition of reality. At no point, however, in Flaubert's narrative can verisimilitude be questioned. In fact, the symbolic meaning of Flaubert's story is at first only vaguely apprehended. It is felt. It is communicated as sensory experience rather than as reasoned perception. It is the chain of Félicité's experiences and her final hallucination which communicate the void and the particular malaise which readers so often complain about. Flaubert's symbolism and his objective correlatives not only infuse his novels and stories with the "silence" of poetry (to use Bremond's expression), they frequently are the objectification of his point of view. These visual correspondences, unlike *Gulliver's Travels,* are real, they are what they seem to be, *i.e.* as *Madame Bovary*'s title suggests, "mœurs de province." But they are also much more. Thus, Loulou is a parrot, and at the same time a symbol of psittacism, that malady of so many of Flaubert's characters who either parrot banalities without thought or meaning, or are the victims of this psittacism. If Loulou is the archetype of the Flaubertian hero, then this marvelous parrot, this winged ape, plays an interesting and important symbolic role. Félicité is the owner of the parrot, but since she worships it, she is also the victim of this psittacism. Félicité's subsequent illness and "madness" present themselves as a case of psittacosis, that disease of parrots easily communicable to man and known more commonly as parrot fever. Is not Flaubert saying that this is the disease of religious faith?

How and why is Félicité affected? She is not very bright. Even though she does have an animal capacity for survival, her intellectual achievements are slight and all her literary education derives from Paul's geography picture book. Later, much to the amusement of M. Bourais, Félicité, who has been shown where Havana is, asks to see a picture of the house in which her nephew is living. Her comprehension of abstracts (like maps) is incomplete. Yet, in the presence of danger (the episode of the bull), she acts quickly and effectively and keeps the bull at bay by throwing clods of turf in his eyes. Félicité's intelligence, however, is so limited, that Flaubert, though caustic, remains kind to her. Unlike Charles Bovary, she is in no position to harm others, for she does not have even the rudiments of knowledge. Her stupidity is not only congenital, but derives also from the animal complacency and silence of the cows she tended as a young girl. Flaubert is less patient with Charles' stupidity. But he is certainly more tolerant of Charles' inadequacy than he is of Homais', as the vitriolic attack which he directs against Homais indicates. Flaubert excuses Félicité for the vicarious manner in which she derives her pleasures. He even excuses her self-abnegation, her sacrifices, and her devotion to others, be they Mme. Aubain, Virginie, her nephew, the soldiers, the sick, the Poles, father Colmiche, or even Loulou. But if Loulou is a symbol of psittacism, as M. [Luc] Dariosecq demonstrates [in his "A propos de Loulou," *French Review*, (1958)], and if Flaubert's irony is a condemnation of characters like Homais, Bournisien, and Charles Bovary, why is he less biting with Félicité who, in her religious fervor, is as guilty of psittacism as they are? If he spares her, it is perhaps because she is so full of "bonne volonté," because she is "un cœur simple," and because she doesn't know any better. She is, as Levin says, one of Flaubert's few women of good will. The guilty one is not Félicité but organized religion, and it is the church which, on the symbolic level, will bear the brunt of Flaubert's attack. Félicité's faithfulness and obedience are total and Flaubert is tolerant of her insufficiencies. His attitude, however, changes perceptibly the moment she acquires Loulou. Félicité's frantic search for the lost parrot prompts Mme. Aubain to say that she is mad. Is there irony in this "madness"? Has Félicité already been contaminated by a religious psittacosis? Is she not symbolically suffering from parrot fever and does she not die of pulmonary congestion (high fever and pulmonary involvement being the symptoms of psittacosis)? Does she not confuse the parrot with the dove, and in her final delirium does she not imagine, instead of the Holy Ghost, "un perroquet gigantesque, planant au-dessus de sa tête"? Flaubert's hostility to religion is, of course, well known, but to have Loulou represent the spiritual comforts of faith is the supreme mockery. Loulou, who represents the psittacism of the church, does in fact, seem to have infected Félicité. This is no doubt what the critics, who speak of irony, sense in the story. Félicié's blindness, which prevents her from seeing that Loulou has a broken wing (the Holy Ghost is no longer airborne), and is being eaten by worms, seems to represent, from Flaubert's point of view, the blindness of man who cannot understand that religion is a delusion. Thus, Félicité, who embodies the very simplest qualities of life, and who is, and always has been, a simple servant, and who must explain to herself the resemblance between the dove and the parrot, reasons that "le Père, pour s'énoncer, n'avait pu choisir une colombe, puisque ces bêtes-là n'ont pas de voix, mais plutôt un des ancêtres de Loulou." Typical of the lack of insight into Loulou's psittacism and Félicité's psittacosis is the opinion of Fourcaud who would

eliminate Félicité's attempt at an explanation and limit the description to its purely realistic elements.

Loulou is the symbol of Flaubert's *particular* emotion. Félicité eventually identifies the parrot with the Holy Ghost, and we accept this confusion as a "normal" manifestation of her simplicity, age, and sickness. It is less obvious, I believe, that Loulou is Flaubert's symbol rather than Félicité's. Félicité is in the chain of events and she, like Loulou, becomes a symbol. It is this interaction which is Flaubert's emotional formula and which communicates his point of view. This point of view is not expressed overtly, but is communicated as sensory experience. On the symbolic level, as we might expect, Flaubert is not expressing Félicité's point of view but his own.

Félicité's trip to Le Havre to have Loulou stuffed reinforces the religious hostility expressed in the story. The description of Félicité on foot, in the middle of road, is perhaps significant. Is the road life itself? Does the galloping mail-coach, bearing down upon her like a whirlwind, symbolise the aging process? Does the coachman who cannot stop the galloping horses represent the inexorable flow of life down hill? Does the wound which the coachman inflicts on Félicité, as she is hurtled to the ground, represent a statement by Flaubert about man's metaphysical suffering? If this wound is man's existential "angoisse," and if Loulou is the symbol of religious fever, then Flaubert is expressing his attitude towards religion and its inability to fill the void of man's existence: Félicité "se consolait de sa blessure en regardant l'oiseau" (simultaneous irony and symbolism here). Thus Félicité's state of mind has been communicated by a skilful accumulation of symbolic events whose meaning is automatically released by the recapitulation of her past life:

> Alors une faiblesse l'arrêta; et la misère de son enfance, la déception du premier amour, le départ de son neveu, la mort de Virginie, comme les flots d'une marée, revinrent à la fois, et, lui montant à la gorge l'étouffaient.

This is the wound of her life which prompts the stifled cry of suffering. Her religion is her consolation; her room soon becomes a small chapel full of all the bric-a-brac and bits of ribbon, "toutes les vieilleries dont ne voulait plus Mme Aubain," while Loulou, stuffed full of the Holy Ghost, dominates her improvised altar. This then, Flaubert seems to be saying, is Félicité's "madness." For prayer, according to such a point of view, is the meaningless repetition of words by those who are not intelligent enough to see that there is no comfort for the wound of existence. Flaubert is stating obliquely therefore that people who parrot the teaching of the church are suffering from psittacosis, a more acute form of psittacism. Those suffering from psittacism are mere automatons, wooden creatures, but those suffering from psittacosis are even more deranged, for they are the victims of a disease.

Thus, Loulou's and Félicité's union represents Flaubert's distaste for religion. At no point in the story, however, does he openly deride it. Félicité's hallucination, as she dies, is apparently her own, as have apparently been all her previous reactions. Yet, even on her death-bed, Flaubert will not relinquish her or her thought processes: "elle *crut* [my underlining] voir, . . . un perroquet gigantesque," obliquely injects Flaubert's final negation of her most cherished vision. This negation creates the void, the very absence of comfort which her religion is expected to provide. She did not see, she only *thought* she saw. This is Flaubert's concluding statement.

Flaubert, therefore, in **"Un Cœur simple,"** skillfully blends form and content in such a way as to obscure his strong attack on religion which, as we might expect from him, is but one of the manifestations of the "stupidité humaine," less commonly known as parrot fever. If the reader of **"Un Cœur simple"** is left with an aftertaste of futility which is perhaps not readily explainable, it is due to the formula which subliminally expresses Flaubert's point of view. He evokes the desired emotion through the objectification of sensory experience. It is Flaubert's state of mind, not Félicité's, which is communicated to us. While on the realistic level Flaubert remains sympathetic to Félicité, on the symbolic level, she becomes the victim of her own religious psittacism. Flaubert therefore seems to be deliberately hiding the ironic content when he says that the story is exclusively "serious" and "sad."

It is this dual point of view which makes **"Un Cœur simple"** so successful. On the realistic level, Félicité is the devoted, hard working servant, who stoically accepts all of life's hardships and dies, with a smile on her lips, and a sympathetic pat on the head by Flaubert. On the symbolic level however, the story reverses its meaning. It recreates the ambiguity and complexity of life itself, so that the gradations between white and black, night and day, good and evil, merge into a cosmic shade of gray, a dimension in which contradictory values and reality blend imperceptibly into a final resolution which affirms and at the same time negates the reality of experience. Thus Flaubert's simultaneous blend of two contradictory points of view, the sympathetic and the ironic, the realistic and the symbolic, represents some of his best writing artistically and his maturest metaphysical expression of life's complexity. (pp. 19-25)

Ben Stoltzfus, "Point of View in 'Un Coeur simple'," in The French Review, *Vol. XXXV, No. 1, October, 1961, pp. 19-25.*

Victor Brombert **(essay date 1966)**

[*Brombert is an American critic who specializes in modern French literature. In the following excerpt, taken from his* The Novels of Flaubert: A Study of Themes and Techniques, *he analyzes the themes and imagery of "Hérodias" and "The Legend of Saint Julien Hospitalier." In discussing the second story, Brombert examines Flaubert's sources and the similarities between Flaubert and St. Julien.*]

[**"La Légende de Saint Julien l'Hospitalier"**], which Flaubert claims to have composed as a relaxing exercise, but which he himself termed "effervescent," is in fact, in its very craftsmanlike perfection, one of his most turbulent texts. Cruelty, spirituality, pathology—the most disturbing aspects of his temperament as well as the most paradoxical interplay of themes make of this reworking of a minor saint's legend one of Flaubert's most "personal" works. No text of Flaubert's appears on the surface more impassive and more liberated from any element that is not under the strictest esthetic control. The aloofness of an almost inhuman hero, the historical and mythical distance, the utilization of an already existing legend, the display of quaint erudition—all suggest a totally impersonal relation between the author and his literary material.

Yet **"Saint Julien"** could serve as a point of departure for a study of Flaubert's most intimate motifs. Above all, the pervasive theme of unwitting and yet deeply wished-for parricide assumes such a haunting and even nightmarish quality that it is difficult not to relate it in depth to Flaubert's own involved guilt feelings. And around this central obsession, a cluster of other themes casts a light which, in esthetic as well as in psychological importance, extends far beyond the miraculous and obscure existence of the saint. No literary subject is ever chosen altogether fortuitously. Flaubert himself might have thought that all he wished to do was to rival in words the images of a stained-glass window—a tempting enterprise, no doubt, for one who, like Flaubert, enjoyed the challenges of art. In fact, however, **"Saint Julien"** yields to the careful reader a rich repertory of the most revealing Flaubertian themes which are here interwoven in a particularly interesting manner: the fascination of the bestiary, the monastic urge, the image of the alienated saint, the temptation of despair, self-abnegation as a form of self-disgust ("Sa propre personne lui faisait tellement horreur . . . "), the dream of possible regeneration through copulation with Horror ("Julien s'étala dessus complètement . . . "). The very structure and rhythm of the tale, with its apparent lack of psychological determinism, sum up the climate of Flaubert's work. A crisis of the human will is at its center. The guilelessness of Ju-

---

On Flaubert's aims and inspirations:

Whatever [Flaubert] was, he was no slapdash writer carried away by the fire of inspiration; he was above all a perfectionist who knew what he wanted and had the patience to work on until he had reached the final form which he was pursuing. His guiding thread was the search for the unique expression, 'la forme', which ought to embody the idea which he wished to express. His method could not be reduced to a formula or mathematical proposition which could be unfailingly applied and unfailingly successful; it was the pragmatic search of the dedicated craftsman who tries various parts, polishes them up and replaces them until he has succeeded in making a whole. The word 'craftsman' would certainly have horrified some of Flaubert's contemporaries who believed that the artist could only create in moments of exaltation, with the Muse in his arms. Flaubert was having no love-affair with the Muse, he was married to her; she was always with him, she was, to borrow the expression from Ezra Pound, his Penelope; and he had the sustained inspiration of the men who carved the stones of cathedrals.

Joyce Cannon, in her "Flaubert's Search for a Form in 'Hérodias'," in The Modern Language Review, *April, 1962.*

lien, the ineluctability of his situations, which succeed each other in paratactic fashion, while stressing the mystery of the human potential, confirm a sense of impotence and surrender which characterize the over-all vision of Flaubert. The vocation of sainthood, much like the artist's vocation, is a retreat from oneself.

It was in the fall of 1875, during a leisurely stay in Brittany, that the idea of the tale crystallized in Flaubert's mind. A letter to Mme Roger des Genettes informs us about his frame of mind: he wants to verify whether he "can still write a sentence"; he assures his friend that the project amounts to nothing at all, that it is devoid of any importance. A therapeutic exercise, one gathers! To be sure, Flaubert was in need of some distraction. The endless task of *Bouvard et Pécuchet,* the failure of his play *Le Candidat,* the death of his friend George Sand in 1876, made this a disheartening period in his life. But neither the idea of a literary "distraction," nor the later claim to compose a triptych covering three different historic periods (**"Hérodias"** and **"Un Coeur simple"** were to represent antiquity and the modern world) can be taken at face value. In fact, the genesis of **"Saint Julien"** goes back to about thirty years earlier when, in the spring of 1846, during an excursion to Caudebec-en-Caux in the company of Maxime Du Camp, Flaubert saw a little statue of the saint which unquestionably brought back to his mind the well-known stained-glass window of the Rouen cathedral. Moreover, it is very likely that, as early as 1846, he was already familiar with the work of E. H. Langlois entitled *Mémoire sur la peinture sur verre et quelques vitraux remarquables des églises de Rouen,* which gave an account as well as reproductions of this work.

The literary sources of Flaubert's tale are well known; they have been discussed with much finesse by Marcel Schwob in *Spicilège.* The life of the saint as gathered by Jacques de Voragine in the *Légende Dorée,* and as reproduced in Vincent de Beauvais' *Speculum historiale,* constitutes the fundamental text. But influences other than those suggested by Schwob are possible. In 1825, a Scottish ballad, *Lord Kenneth et la Belle Ellinour,* in which a huntsman aiming at a swan kills his beloved, appeared in *Ballades, légendes et chants populaires.* A few years later, a story on a related theme appeared in *La France littéraire.* It is not unlikely that Flaubert was acquainted with both. At any rate, the hunting motif coupled with that of the murder of a loved one was certainly not alien to the Romantic imagination.

The mythical context of the legend is banal enough. Behind the story of hunting, suffering animals, and a sinner's existence which, through a mortification of the flesh, leads to sainthood, it is easy to recognize some archetypal themes: the human soul imprisoned in an animal, the oracle in the form of a nonhuman, the long expiation of a much-feared crime. The basic legend is unquestionably endowed with a strong poetic potential: the hunting motif and fairy-tale atmosphere, the image of the wide river and of the difficult crossing, the miraculous element and the strong dose of naïveté. Flaubert was no doubt drawn to this basic simplicity of a folk story which preserves and communicates a whole range of undefinable and some-

what mysterious affective values with the strength of an indisputable evidence. Flaubert adheres to the poetic spirit of the legend. He preserves and exploits the forest and the hunting scenes, the feeling of the miraculous and the sense of violence tamed by magic.

There is, however, much poetry that is distinctly his own. A temporal unreality achieved through the rapid succession of tableaux such as occurs commonly in dreams is one of the characteristic features of this tale. Movement is here most often the quick transition from one form of immobility to another. The very landscape seems transfixed ("Il vit reluire tout au loin un lac figé, qui ressemblait à du plomb"), and the characters appear like plastic figures, like statues in slow motion. But the most masterful Flaubertian touches are those which communicate an uncanny poetry of darkness and of silence. The rooms of the palace are "filled with twilight." The shadows of the trees cover the moss; and in the heart of the woods the obscurity becomes "profound." As for the silence, it amounts almost to an unheard music. In the white marble palace, the silence is such that one can hear the rustle of a scarf or the echo of a sigh.

Although Flaubert claimed to have recaptured the imaginative world of medieval legends and of iconography, there are some differences which point to a total departure from the spirit of the sources. I refer not only to the concern for structure, rhythm and symmetry, nor to the taste for the somewhat artificial picturesque detail (archaic forms, terms of venery, epic enumerations, lists of sonorous names of dogs and falcons), but to Julien's choice to remain utterly alone in penitence. For according to the folkloric tradition, his wife accompanies him on the hard road toward salvation. Marcel Schwob very astutely comments that the Julien of the legend, submissive to his destiny, is a man who does not know guilt. He is apparently not in need of that solitude sought by the anguished soul. And this is the significant difference—a difference which makes of this work something of a fascinating, disturbing and unwitting confession: Flaubert's Julien feels secretly and irremediably *guilty.*

To insist almost exclusively on the technical features of the tale—as so many critics have done—represents therefore a very limited reading of the text. Some go so far as to banish any "meaning" whatsoever from **"Saint Julien."** René Descharmes, for instance, not only refuses to read any psychology into the work, but categorically denies that there is any significance to be derived from it. According to him—and this seems to be the prevailing view—**"Saint Julien"** is nothing more than a fully satisfying *esthetic* construction.

It is true that Flaubert himself, in his conversations as well as in his letters, repeatedly denounced "moral" preoccupations in art as a sure source of boredom and inauthenticity (though the didactic heresy was not always absent from his literary enterprises: *Bouvard et Pécuchet* is a most ambiguous work in this respect). But granted that **"Saint Julien"** is pure of any such intention, it is obvious that a work can be deeply meaningful, in personal as well as in artistic and thematic terms, without any clearly formulated moral or conceptual preoccupations on the part of the author. To a careful reader, aware moreover of the many threads which bind this unassuming tale to the rest of Flaubert's writing, **"Saint Julien"** is undeniably a most rewarding text for close scrutiny. It offers some searching insights into the author's own tormented psyche.

Perhaps the most significant departure from the sources is Flaubert's insistence on Julien's family situation. Whereas traditional accounts—for instance that of Saint Antonin, which proceeds immediately to the hunt—do not deal with the world of his parents, Flaubert devotes a relatively great amount of space to the future saint's relations with his father and mother, and to his "home"-atmosphere. "Father" and "mother" are the very first words of his text. And the opening paragraphs are exclusively devoted to the evocation of family values: order, peace and security. The family castle is a solid establishment. Solidity is, as it were, the central motif of these first pages. The four towers are covered with plates of lead, the heavy walls are supported by massive rocks. And with solidity goes self-sufficiency, opulence and a sense of protection. Several enclosures enfold this world on itself. The castle has its own bakery, wine presses, stables and granary. Nothing seems to be lacking in this well-provided, well-ordered, well-administered little universe. The shiny locks, the rich tapestries, the closets filled with linens, the cellars filled with wine, and the coffers filled with bags of silver symbolize a sense of property and of propriety which—if translated into "bourgeois" terms—is reminiscent of Flaubert's own prosperous, well-established, respected and respectable family. And yet this peace and order the young Julien feels somehow compelled to disrupt. The tale is first of all the account of a moral and psychological explosion.

The paternal house—or castle—is indeed a place of security; it is also one of enclosure. Walls protect, but they also imprison. This world of towers, hedges and enclosures is a private world, an inner world—but it is also a contained world from which one may need to burst out, even if the price be the very loss of the much-needed security. This ambivalence (one of the aspects of the dialectics of immurement and freedom) is further stressed by the dual and contradictory values represented by the father and the mother. The very prophecies concerning Julien's future seem mutually exclusive. The mother is told by the old hermit that Julien will become a saint; the father is promised by the old gypsy that his son will become a glorious warrior. That Julien, despite the apparent incompatibility, will in fact be both warrior and saint only stresses the fundamental tension between thought and action, between the life of the spirit and the life of material exigencies and worldly success. There is little doubt that in Flaubert's own private universe, the father—an energetic and successful physician—represented activity, responsibility and practical achievement, whereas his mother, soon to become a widow, stood for the monastic values of retirement, serenity, meditation and passivity. This polarization of the parents is quite obvious in the tale. The mother, who is modest, serious and thoughtful, has organized her household "like the interior of a convent." The father, on the other hand, appears in the triple rôle of warrior, initiator and judge. He is the arbiter of his vassals' quarrels, he

advises the peasants (Flaubert's father was revered by the simple folk of Rouen), he teaches Julien the art of venery, presents him with a pack of dogs, and entertains his old war companions. Ironically, it is with the very sword which his own father gave him that Julien by accident almost kills him before even leaving the castle.

Surely the figure of this competent and materially minded, benevolent father, husband and justicer suffices to give some relevance to the Sartrean analysis of the relations of Gustave with the grave Dr. Flaubert, médecin-chef of the Hôtel-Dieu in Rouen. According to Sartre, the "terrible docteur" was a heavy presence: he dominated his son, he destroyed his spiritual longings toward faith, he was responsible for his monastic writer-vocation and even for his dose of femininity. Even after allowing for much sophisticated exaggeration and dogmatic prejudice, Sartre's diagnosis of Flaubert's father-fixation and father-contempt comes much closer to the truth than the traditional view—for which Flaubert himself is in large part responsible—of an admiring son, filled with affection and with esteem for his meritorious father. In reality, the philistine limitations of Dr. Flaubert were only too evident to the sensitive Gustave, and on such occasions as the family voyage to Italy, during Caroline's honeymoon, these limitations appeared almost as a caricature of the bourgeois. To be sure, when convenient, Flaubert derived considerable pride from his family's status in Rouen (at the time of his trial, for instance, he considered this status as a weighty argument in his favor); but it is clear also that he derived considerable satisfaction from indirect, and perhaps only partly conscious, debunking of his father's values and professional abilities. The clubfoot incident in *Madame Bovary* (it would seem that Flaubert read a treatise which mentions an unsuccessful treatment of a clubfoot by his very father), and even more the relevant pages in *Bouvard et Pécuchet,* should be read in this light. It is also significant that the father and the mother, in **"Saint Julien,"** hide from each other the contradictory prophecies they have heard: the secret they do not want to share is symbolic of a fundamental disharmony.

The Oedipal situation in **"Saint Julien"** is bound up with the theme of escape and liberation. The young man, having discovered death, discovers also a basic rift and a latent chaos in the apparent order. He not only desires to elude his destiny, but feels positively ill at ease in an oppressive and confining family atmosphere. Symbolically, he now wants to hunt "loin du monde"—alone and far from everyone. Symbolically also, he is attracted to vast forests and interminable plains. He develops a taste for the absolute and appears to be absorbed by deep meditation. Most significant, even his mother's kisses are now met with reluctance ("il acceptait froidement son étreinte"). Flaubert's tale is in part the account of a rebellion weakened by scruples and by infinite regrets. Nothing is more pitiful than Julien's ultimate nostalgia for family life. The hermit, living alone near the big river, occasionally feels the yearning to plunge into the life of a community just to feel human contact. And as he glimpses through ground-floor windows old men holding infants on their knees, he feels "choked with sobs." Similarly Flaubert, the Croisset hermit, occasionally visited the capital, only to seek refuge once more in the house near the "big river." And nothing is more pathetic—and also more relevant to Julien's situation—than Flaubert's confession to George Sand, written only a short time before composing the tale: "I adore children, and I was born to be an excellent daddy. . . . It is one of the melancholies of my old age not to have a little being to love and to caress."

But more significant than these affinities between the medieval and the nineteenth-century hermits is the deep-rooted obsession with parricide which pervades the entire tale. For parricide in **"Saint Julien"** is not merely a fact, it is a permanent and haunting terror. Uncanny incidents announce a fate that cannot be eluded: the sword which Julien clumsily lets fall almost wounds his father; the javelin which he aims at what he takes to be a stork almost kills his mother; animals lead him to the place where he will murder his parents. And the outraged and accusing glance of these animals is like a parental reproach. The huge stag he has mortally wounded looks at him like a solemn "patriarch," or better still, like a "justicer." A strong sense of guilt darkens the entire work, a guilt which preëxists to the actual fact of the crime. For Julien, long before his dreadful deed, is terrorized by his own potential, by his inner temptation. "Si je le voulais, pourtant? . . . " he asks himself in anguish, aware of a personal demon (the word "diable" is actually used) that propels him to criminal action. And when the parricide is consummated, Julien's memory assumes a nightmarish turn, as it constantly reënacts the deed which he both needed and hated to commit: "chaque nuit, en rêve, son parricide recommençait."

The association of the animals, his parents and the murder is particularly interesting. Animals and the hunt are of course an important element in the folk legend concerning Julien. But not only is there an extraordinary concentration of animals in Flaubert's tale, it is also quite obvious that he has tried more consciously to establish a correspondence between the beasts and the theme of parricide. The weird invulnerability of the animals in the surrealistic sequence that precedes the murder is symbolic of a conscience that refuses to be silenced. The beasts and the motif of bestiality are deeply bound up with the father and the mother images. (Does he not mistake his mother for an animal?) In one of the most curious sentences of **"Saint Julien,"** this relationship is explicitly stated: "il lui semblait que du meurtre des animaux dépendait le sort de ses parents" ("it seemed to him that his parents' fate depended on the murder of the animals"). Finally, the impassioned killing of his parents, in bed and in a blind spell of sexual jealousy, adds further weight to this important theme.

The violence and indulgence in cruelty which characterize **"Saint Julien"** are another "personal" Flaubertian element. In this short work, as much if not more so than in *Salammbô,* Sainte-Beuve might have detected a "pointe d'imagination sadique." When Julien, as a boy, discovers the reality of death, he discovers at the same time his own destructive urges. The hunt becomes for him a mere pretext for murder and gratuitous savagery. But it is not a simple exercise in brutality. His surprise when he watches the bleeding mouse, his delight when his dogs break the

rabbits' backs, the zest with which he lops off the rooster's feet, the joy with which he plunges his dagger into the goat, the skillful thoroughness with which he kills cranes with his whip—all this sanguineous enthusiasm points to an infantile sadism and to a savagely voluptuous imagination which links agony and guilt with the earliest manifestations of sex. Flaubert's vocabulary is here of the utmost interest. The convulsions of the pigeon Julien strangles fill him with a "volupté sauvage et tumultueuse." At the bird's ultimate spasm of life he almost swoons ("il se sentit défaillir"). Similarly, at the thought of real carnage, "il suffoqua de plaisir." His arrows produce "enfonçures" in the mass of the animals. Dreams and acts of slaughter soon assume orgiastic proportions. There is no end to his murderous appetite: "Julien did not tire of killing." After the massacre, he contemplates with an "oeil béant" the enormities he has committed. Then, as after an orgy, an "immense sadness" overcomes him. The taste for blood grows into a real addiction: his very notion of Paradise is a place where he sees himself surrounded by animals he can kill. The murder of his parents in his own bed is characteristically gory: splashes and "pools" of blood cover their white bodies, the bedsheet, the ground; they stain an ivory figure of Christ hanging in the alcove. This taste for physical horror comes to a climax in the final scene, when the leper with the running sores and nauseous breath penetrates into Julien's bed.

What immeasurably increases the interest of these themes of the hunt and of cruelty is that they are here clearly coupled with the theme of failure—not to say impotence. The heaviness of the atmosphere is oppressive, at times paralyzing. The "lac figé"—that immobilized, imprisoned body of water, almost Mallarmean in its sterile nature—is an objective correlative of an inner landscape that becomes increasingly static and demoralizing. Even the amazing energy that goes into killing becomes ineffectual in the face of a quantitative massiveness. The proliferation of phenomena is such that the human will and the human deed turn out to be derisory: "cela n'en finissait pas." The hunt ultimately appears like a desperate and futile effort in a noxious dream.

The oneiric oppression and sense of frustration become the central motif in the second hunt, when invulnerable animals seem to mock and defy the ineffectual huntsman. But it is not so much the animals who are endowed with invulnerability, as it is Julien's own weapons which prove to be inoffensive. His arrows, aimed at the wild animals, land like gentle white butterflies. His lance, as it reaches the bull, bursts into fragments. Freudian exegetes and symbol hunters could hardly hope to find a more rewarding document.

What develops is a sense of entrapment. From the beginning of the tale, the paternal castle, with its enclosures and walls, suggests confinement and constriction. No real liberation occurs. The departure, the crime, the penance, and even the eventual sainthood—the elements of the basic folk story—do not free Julien from the obsession with immurement and ensnarement, so central also in *Madame Bovary,* and again in *Salammbô,* where an entire army is trapped. In **"Saint Julien,"** the animals who at the beginning were trapped by the protagonist (there is a parallel between the "cirque" and the "défilé de la Hache" in *Salammbô*), later, during the second hunt, form "a narrow circle" around the powerless huntsman. The cluttered forest, through which he has to cut his way, is similarly a confining element from which he feels the need to extricate himself. And the peering eyes of the animals staring at him are like an exteriorization of his own ensnaring conscience. A chronic and inescapable sense of guilt is indeed one of the most fundamental traits of the Flaubertian psychology: not a Christian guilt, but a deep-rooted sense of the *péché d'exister,* almost Sartrean in nature, and which explains perhaps why Sartre has been for so long fascinated and at the same time repelled by Flaubert.

It is easy to see by what logic the frenzy of destruction ultimately results in an urge to self-destruction. An oppressive sense of guilt leads to dreams of annihilation which, echoing similar dreams in other works of Flaubert, constitute a recurrent and major theme. Julien, the torturer, becomes the self-torturer. His own person inspires him with an invincible aversion. The temptation of suicide compels him to expose himself to countless perils. But salvation, he learns, cannot be achieved through the simple refusal to live. Saintly abnegation is for him the only death in this life—which is also a form of reconquest and repossession. Sainthood, in Flaubertian terms, is of course a concept which, together with monasticism, can easily be related to the artist's self-abnegation. "I live like a Carthusian friar"—"I live like a monk"—these expressions occur repeatedly in his correspondence, and they are always related to his dedication to the mystique of Art. The need to abhor his flesh is certainly not a religious reaction with Flaubert, but it is a manifestation of a deep-seated hate of life on the one hand (". . . moi je la déteste, la vie"), and on the other a permanent spiritual quest. Flaubert, who did not strictly speaking write a "novel of the artist," is nonetheless an outstanding illustration of the modern writer's tendency to make of the artist—himself—the hero of his own creation. In the nineteenth century, Art becomes the subject of art, and Thought the subject of thought. The artist, even when he feels saved by Art, is caught in his own private drama, in the mirror-disease of his own mind.

Thus, despite the artistic "distance" the author establishes between himself and the subject of his tales, despite the apparent quest for a formal perfection, there is much in this short work that is extremely self-revealing. The theme of isolation is perhaps nowhere more bitter in Flaubert. Of all his characters, Julien is probably the most "alone." Emma at least had her lovers, Mathô has Spendius as a companion, and Frédéric has his childhood friend Deslauriers. Even Saint Antoine, the hermit, has the company of the loquacious Hilarion. In fact, the notion of the "couple" seems quite basic to the structure of many of Flaubert's novels, culminating in the caricatures of Bouvard and Pécuchet, who in turn seem to prefigure the pathetic couples of Samuel Beckett. Only Julien, and to some extent Félicité (who is also a manner of saint), are deprived of companionship. The weird silence which reigns throughout the story stresses the saint's alienation.

This aloneness is of course only one aspect of the work. A latent fear of life is another of Flaubert's basic themes. Did he not, at the age of twenty-five, advise a friend never to marry, never to have any children, to have as few sentimental attachments as possible so as to remain least vulnerable (" . . . offre le moins de prise à l'ennemi")? The enemy, of course, was life itself. This fear of life he later freely confessed. To George Sand he admitted that he had been a "coward" in his youth: *"j'ai eu peur* de la vie." The statement, in Flaubert's case, must be taken quite literally. His fear is really a form of horror and revulsion: "Life is such a hideous thing that the only way to bear it is to avoid it." This escapism explains in part Flaubert's ambiguous attitude toward "reality": a mixture of fascination and repugnance. For quite surely Flaubert was not merely trying to justify an esthetic aberration when he wrote to Laurent Pichat, the director of the *Revue de Paris,* which was publishing *Madame Bovary,* that the "ignoble reality" described in the novel made him sick, that he abhorred "la vie ordinaire."

Flaubert's chronic attraction to unreality and "surreality," the recurrent motifs of metamorphosis and undoing, have no doubt much to do with this need for escape. The very structure of **"Saint Julien"** produces the effect of a succession of tableaux which rapidly glide by and fade into each other. Flaubert's conscious desire was evidently to reproduce, in literary terms, the rhythm and the atmosphere produced by a sequence of frescoes or a series of stained glass windows. But the technique goes in depth, and represents more than a literary exercise. The very articulations of the narrative ("Puis," "Cependant," "Bientôt"), the fading and melting of forms, the movement of dark shapes—all this suggests a constant alteration. The world of Flaubert is indeed a strange combination of sameness and undoing, of immobility and violence, of stasis and destruction. Are creation and destruction "sisters," as Marcel Schwob suggests? Certainly the very blending in one single character of a potential for annihilation and a potential for sainthood is highly revealing.

Finally, this very theme of sainthood is an important key to the understanding of Flaubert's work. Whether it is Saint Antoine, Saint Julien or the saintly provincial virgin who was to develop into the conception of Madame Bovary, the central figure remains that of a human being tormented by his own inherence, dreaming of an impossible escape and an unattainable absolute. It is this dissatisfaction and this longing, this condemnation to the self and this desire to transcend it which bring out in Flaubert's work this "aspiration vers l'infini" which, according to Baudelaire, is one of the most significant characteristics of Romanticism. There is little doubt that his obsession with the theme of sainthood marks, in its various disguises and avatars, a definite crisis of faith. Sartre makes Flaubert's father directly responsible for this crisis: ". . . this crushing father who did not cease, even once dead, to destroy God." Sartre's blunt emphasis on the nefarious influence of one of the parents is thoroughly dogmatic and fails to take into account the role of the mother. But if indeed, as is very possible, the materialistic Doctor was an impediment to his son's idealistic aspirations—if indeed, to use Sartre's image, he partly succeeded in killing "God" in him—then the theme of parricide, related to the theme of sainthood, takes on a renewed meaning. (pp. 217-32)

. . . . .

> They served bull kidneys, dormice, nightingales, minced meat in vine leaves; and the priests discussed the question of resurrection. Ammonius, disciple of Philo the Platonist, thought them stupid, and said so to some Greeks who were making fun of oracles. Marcellus and Jakob had met. The first was telling the second of the happiness he had experienced on being baptized into Mithras, and Jakob was urging him to follow Jesus. Palm and tamarisk wines, the wines of Safet and Byblos, flowed from jars into bowls, from bowls into cups, from cups into gullets; there was much talking and all were in an expansive mood. Jacim, although a Jew, no longer concealed his worship of the planets. A merchant from Aphaka was dazzling the nomads by detailing the wonders of the temple of Hierapolis, and they were asking how much a pilgrimage there would cost. Others held fast to the religion of their birth. A German who was almost blind sang a hymn of praise to that promontory of Scandinavia where the gods appeared with their radiant faces; and people from Sichem refused to eat turtledoves, out of deference for the dove Azima.

This passage, so typical in its effects of variety, confusion and counterpoint, fulfills both a dramatic and a thematic function preceding the climax in Section III of **"Hérodias."** Coming soon after the description of the lavish banquet hall where the tetrarch Herod is entertaining priests, Roman officers and notables of various faiths and regions, it suggests the mounting frenzy of mind and body, and sets the stage for Salome's dance and Saint John the Baptist's decollation. The episode is based on accounts in the gospels of Saint Matthew and Saint Mark, as well as on a large iconography with which Flaubert was obviously familiar. The elaboration of details and the interpretation of psychological relationships and of events are, however, Flaubert's own.

The story, in Flaubert's version, is set against a background of political tension. Herod, worried by the situation at home and by military danger, anxiously awaits the arrival of the Roman proconsul Vitellius and his legions—though he is full of apprehension about them also. The feast in celebration of his birthday is to have political as well as diplomatic value. But when Vitellius and his decadent son Aulus arrive, it becomes increasingly clear that Herod's worries are not exclusively political and military. Symbolically locked up in a cistern like an underground guilt, John the Baptist, known to the Jews as Iaokanann, and reputed to be a resurrected Elias, continues to bellow forth prophetic denunciations of the tetrarch's adultery and incest, and to invoke eschatological punishment upon the sinful Pharisees and Sadducees.

The gastronomic orgy and heated conversations thus take place against a background of intrigue and fanaticism, in a climate of latent guilt, suspicion, religious antagonisms and racial hatreds. The appearance of rare dishes such as bull kidneys and nightingales is preceded by agitated con-

troversy on resurrection, and followed by explosions of bigotry and clear signs of a rebellious mood. Very skillfully Flaubert thus prepares the stage for Salome's dance. Almost without transitions, and with great naturalness, the political and religious turbulence is transmuted into sexual fever. The dance itself progresses from a mood of youthful expectation, to funereal despondency, to languid surrender, to brutal quest of satisfaction, and finally to a frenzy which mimes the female's lascivious ecstasy. This crescendo in turn builds up to the backstage execution of Iaokanann and to the lurid display, at the banquet table, of his decapitated head.

The beginning of the quoted paragraph reveals Flaubert's perennial fascination with eccentric feasts. His obsession with appetite and digestion comes to the fore in the figure of Aulus, who spends most of his time stuffing himself and vomiting. Aulus' capacity for gulping and guzzling is truly impressive. Once again, *goinfrerie* is the physical equivalent of a craving which betrays a fundamental lack of balance. Decadentism is here not merely a metaphor: Aulus, "this flower from the mud of Capri," has participated in the debauches of Tiberius' imperial court, and was later to gain the favor of Caligula, Claudius and Nero. It would be a mistake, however, to attribute such decadent motifs to a simple desire to *épater le bourgeois*. The taste for truculence and exotic flight of fancy Flaubert carried deeply and permanently in himself. This, more so than any similarity of sources and setting, explains why he was so concerned with the danger of imitating *Salammbô*. He knew that the same fondness for the *gueulade* animated his Biblical tale. " . . . ça se présente sous les apparences d'un fort gueuloir . . . " he writes to Turgenev; and to Maupassant a few days later: "ça se gueule."

The banquet, in addition to representing one of the set elements of the legend, is thus far from gratuitous. The personal and dramatic values of the episode are obvious. But its thematic function should not be overlooked. For this prelude to violence and death takes the form of a false communion. The guests partake of the same meats and wines, but nothing breaks down the barriers between them. Carnality is thus once again linked to the theme of incommunicability. On numerous other occasions the sharing of food, in Flaubert's novels, brings out a sense of distance and divorce. Emma Bovary feels most exasperated and lonely at mealtimes; the entire bitterness of her conjugal life seems served to her on her plate. Similarly, though in a different register, the dinner at the Café Anglais, in *L'éducation sentimentale,* stresses the gap between Frédéric's desire and Rosanette's whorish perfidy. And after the supper he offers in his new apartment, the saddened young man feels as though a "large ditch filled with darkness" separates him from his friends. An almost deathlike sterility is often associated, in Flaubert's work, with moments seemingly given over to sensuous provocation or satisfaction. Salome appropriately dances to the "funereal sound" of pipes. Death, of course, reigns in the very landscape of **"Hérodias."** The hot wind seems to carry the stench of the accursed cities of Sodom and Gomorrah, buried under the heavy waters of the Red Sea. As for the mountains Herod surveys from the top of his citadel in Machaerus, they appear like tiers of huge petrified waves.

The opening sentence of the quoted paragraph is of further interest because of a characteristic construction repeated three times in the same passage. Its two parts are divided by a semicolon and by the conjunction *et,* which Flaubert here preferred to the more obvious temporal conjunctions *pendant que* or *tandis que.* The result is a total absence of subordination, and a leveling or equalization of all experience. The author subversively refuses to establish any hierarchy among the elements of the description or the events. Eating dormice and nightingales thus appears exactly as important, or unimportant, as discussing the question of resurrection. This juxtaposition of dissimilar elements is among Flaubert's favorite instruments of irony and intervention, one which he has inherited from the eighteenth-century ironists, in particular from Voltaire, whom he admired immensely. The paratactic *et* of course also helps establish an atmosphere of confusion, and suggests the din in the banquet hall; it does serve a function here not of consecutiveness but of simultaneity. Above all, it tends to discredit the manner and subject of the priests' discussion.

This equalization of values, leading to a pervasive relativism, is brought out even more sharply in the following sentence. A disciple of Philo the Platonist expresses his opinions about the stupidity of the priests to some Greeks, who in turn make known their contempt for oracles. The multiplicity of points of view is intensified by the fact that Philo was born a Jew (he represents Alexandrine Judaism) and that the Greeks, on the other hand, have become skeptical about their own traditions. This parallel and antithetic construction is carried on as we learn that Marcellus tells Jakob of the beauty of Mithraic initiation, while Jakob urges him to become a follower of Jesus. The syncretic tendencies of the conversations are neutralized by the fact that nobody seems really to listen. We witness a frantic bazaar of ideas, as Flaubert succeeds simultaneously in evoking the clash of beliefs and in establishing a climate of absurdity. Interest in the distant past and especially in the history of religions usually corresponds in him to his most pessimistic moods.

As the paragraph progresses, there is a crescendo of confusion and meaninglessness. The wines do not add to the lucidity of the guests. Flaubert insists on the variety and the flow of wines (from jars to bowls, from bowls to cups, from cups to gullets), and this variety and flow provoke and symbolize the nature of the conversation. Ebriety corresponds to ideological intemperance, to muddled talking and thinking. "Iaçim, bien que Juif, ne cachait plus son adoration des planètes." The sentence is loaded with the irony dear to the Encyclopedists. The "bien que Juif" stresses religious relativism; the adverb "plus" points simultaneously to the usual prudence of Iaçim and to the effects of alcohol. At the same time, religious beliefs are reduced to the level of personal preferences and passing fads, as erratic and eccentric as human temperaments under the effect of excessive libation.

Even more humorously degrading is the next sentence. A merchant flabbergasts the nomads by describing the marvels of the temple in Aphaka. *Merveilles* has an appropri-

ate double sense: religion is here entrusted to the rhetoric of traveling salesmen. Religious pilgrimages are talked about as though they were visits to special fairs that should not be missed. Once again the sentence is divided by a semicolon followed by the conjunction *et,* thus establishing an ironic equality between the first part, in which the temple is extolled, and the second part, in which the listeners and putative converts inquire about the cost of the journey. A not so faint suggestion of charlatanism creeps into the account. Spirituality is replaced by pedestrian material concerns.

The last part of the paragraph completes the relativistic subversion. Flaubert utilizes the biblical historical moment to stress not revelation, but the absence of a unique Truth. "D'autres tenaient à leur religion natale." At first sight, the sentence seems to emphasize spiritual allegiance. But the very word "others" implies precisely that no experience is universal; it is a reminder of the fragmentary nature of experience. The allegiance is, moreover, of a very limited kind. The word "native" is brought into a critical, and potentially derogatory, association with the word "religion." The entire Voltairean heritage is felt in this sentence.

The climax occurs when the mystic song of a German praising the Northern gods is opposed antithetically to the superstitious refusal of the people of Sichem to eat turtle-doves. Once again the semicolon followed by the conjunction *et* is the instrument of oblique irony. The evoked vision of divine figures appearing in all their radiance is brought into perfidious juxtaposition with some meaningless tribal taboo. The end of the sentence might have come straight out of the *Lettres persanes* or *Candide.* The sentence is doubly insidious, for the dove Azima is unmistakably an allusion to the Holy Ghost.

The paragraph which has been under discussion is an excellent example of Flaubert's passionate impartiality. For his apparent impassiveness is not to be taken as a sign of aloofness, but rather as the very method whereby he imposes his personal vision. It would be as wrong, however, to consider this style a proof of the author's archeological distance as it would to interpret such a passage as a blunt attack on religion. The critique goes deeper. Values, beliefs, truths, experiences—all these are thrust here, as elsewhere in Flaubert's work, into a hopeless juxtaposition. Coexistence brings about neither ultimate peace nor resolute war, but a latent frustration from which there is no cure. It makes of living and believing a chronic "impossibility." From contradictions arise neither a purifying conflict nor a definitive debate, but dizziness and surrender. Torn between incompatible imperatives, worn-out Herod gives up Iaokanann's head.

Although there is nothing in Flaubert's correspondence to indicate that he was interested in the mystic possibilities of the story (he claimed to be fascinated by the political and psychological elements), the tale suggests a nostalgia for that precisely which seems to be *absent.* If Flaubert can be said to "associate" with any of the characters in **"Hérodias,"** it is surely with the life-weary tetrarch. He was indeed very taken with this personage. "La vacherie d'Hérode pour Hérodias m'excite." And again: "What tempts me here is the official expression of Herod (who was a true perfect).'' But it is clear that the fascination, at least as it developed during the process of writing, had more to do with his sadness and his lethal fatigue. All hope seems to escape from the fortress of Machaerus as the three men carry Iaokanann's heavy head toward Galilee. The end of **"Hérodias,"** appropriately ambiguous, reminds us that the spiritual theme is never absent in the *Trois contes.*

As usual, Flaubert reveals far more of himself than would at first be suspected. Personal memories are transmuted into a special form of poetry: the legend or historical fact "overdetermines" preëxisting experiences or velleities. This is especially obvious in the case of Salome's dance. The performance of Hérodias' daughter is indeed at the heart of the tale; it is that focal point in the genesis toward which all attitudes and events seem to converge. But its intimate significance is that it rehearses, after an interval of twenty-five years, the dances of the Near Eastern prostitutes Flaubert and his friend Bouilhet had witnessed in the house of the courtesan Kuchiouk Hanem during their journey through Egypt. It is clear that the dance of Salome was for Flaubert the culminating point of his tale. "I am sick with fear at the thought of Salome's dance. I'm afraid to spoil it," he writes to his niece Caroline. The *Notes de voyages* of 1850 contained details which, from the point of view of 1876, present an undeniable proleptic interest. Aziza's motionless face as she dances with her neck sliding back and forth on her vertebrae ("terrifying effect of decapitation") prefigures the expressionless face of Salome (" . . . et son visage demeurait immobile"). The performance of Kuchiouk Hanem, who during her dance gradually lowers the head until she reaches with her teeth a cup of coffee on the ground, prefigures Salome's feat of leaning over so low, with her legs spread apart, that her chin touches the floor. But far more interesting still is Flaubert's remark, in his 1850 travel notes, that while lying beside Kuchiouk, with his fingers passed through her necklace, he was reminded of Judith and Holofernes. It is significant that from the outset the experience of the Near Eastern dance is associated with a biblical image, and more specifically with the decapitation of a man by a woman's will, in an atmosphere heavy with sexuality. The entire memory is further charged with a special melancholy, as Flaubert wonders whether Kuchiouk Hanem will think of him more than of the many others who have been there. The exercise of the senses leaves behind an acrid taste—an experience that was to become familiar in the fictional work of Flaubert.

Nothing is thus more deceptive than the apparent dryness and impartiality of the tone in **"Hérodias."** The colors of the "Orient" and the tensions of the human drama are suggested in condensed, muscular, almost elliptic sentences. These sentences are often remarkable for their impeccable sobriety, which only stresses the latent violence of the atmosphere.

> Il fouilla d'un regard aigu toutes les routes. Elles étaient vides. Des aigles volaient au-dessus de sa tête; les soldats, le long du rempart, dormaient contre les murs; rien ne bougeait dans le château.

It is truly a historian's style, exploiting in particular the resources of the indirect discourse:

> Vitellius demanda pourquoi tant de monde. Antipas en dit la cause: le festin de son anniversaire . . .

At times the condensation is almost baffling:

> Les Sadducéens feignirent un grand émoi;—le lendemain, la sacrificature leur fut rendue;—Antipas était du désespoir; Vitellius demeurait impassible.

or even more so in the following paragraph, which could come straight from the pen of the tersest memorialist:

> L'exaltation du peuple grandit. Ils s'abandonnèrent à des projets d'indépendance. On rappelait la gloire d'Israël. Tous les conquérants avaient été châtiés: Antigone, Crassus, Varus. . . .

The lapidary quality of sentences such as these is clearly the result of a conscious effort. Shortly before writing **"Hérodias,"** Flaubert confided to George Sand his boundless admiration for the rhythmical achievements of Montesquieu's prose. He cited the following as an example: "Les vices d'Alexandre étaient extrêmes comme ses vertus. Il était terrible dans sa colère. Elle le rendait cruel." The pattern is obvious: one could adduce endless examples of Flaubertian sentences modeled along these lines, in apparent contradiction to his turbulent lyricism.

This interplay of a chiseled prose and an eruptive physical and psychological setting, though it underscores the occult ferment and prepares the paroxystic effect, does bring about some needless obscurity. In his desire to streamline his tale, Flaubert was determined to avoid lengthy explanations. He tried to leave out what he himself, in a letter to Maupassant, calls the "explications indispensables." No wonder that Taine, despite his admiration, reproached Flaubert for some needless obscurities. A number of passages indeed require elucidations: the genealogy of Herodias, the identity of the two Vitelliuses, the reasons for the Roman general's dislike of Herod are not made translucid to the unprepared reader. The verbal denseness, characteristic of Flaubert's art, is brought in **"Hérodias"** almost to the danger point. It has been said that Flaubert would tear down a forest in order to construct a matchbox. The documentation, even for his shortest works, is impressive and eclectic. The efficacy of his prose is in large part dependent on this wasteful and at the same time astringent economy. "It seems to me that French prose can achieve a beauty inconceivable so far," he writes to his friend Turgenev. This obsessive struggle with the demon of language shows no sign of relenting. Neither *Madame Bovary,* nor *Salammbô,* nor *L'Éducation sentimentale,* nor even *La Tentation de saint Antoine* has satisfied his dream. He continues to yearn for that impossible beauty. He continues to search for that "bon motif," as he puts it, which will be just right for his "voice." The artist's personal struggle remains to the very end at the center of his work.

Finally, the immobility of the moral and physical setting can be as deceptive as the apparent neutrality of the style. Stasis is in part the result of a repeated substitution of description for narration. As Geneviève Bollème puts it, with Flaubert "description is narrative." It does seem to cancel the event. Moreover, in **"Hérodias"**—just as in *Salammbô*—Flaubert insists on the plastic and terrifying fixity of landscape and architecture, and toys with geometric patterns. The very first sentence describes a rocklike formation in the shape of a geometric figure:

> La citadelle de Machaerous se dressait à l'orient de la mer Morte, sur un pic de basalte ayant la forme d'un cône.

The geometric imagery is further developed as Flaubert describes the houses at the "base" of the rock, surrounded by the "circle" of a wall, and the wall of the fortress with its numerous "angles." Nor is this imagery reserved for military installations. The region of Engedi draws a black line ("barre noire") across the landscape; Hebron rises in the shape of a "dome"; and, dominating Jerusalem, appears the huge "cube"-shaped tower of Antonia. But this choreography of forms which seem immobilized (much like the hills which appear like petrified waves) conveys the impression of an eruptive terrain. Silence, in **"Hérodias,"** is oppressive; it announces the cry of terror or agony. And it is significant that the most "silent" paragraph in the entire tale—the one that describes the empty roads, the sleeping soldiers and the ominous tranquillity in the castle—immediately precedes the outburst of the cavernous voice of Iaokanann rising as from the bowels of the earth. This disquieting irruption is symbolic of Flaubert's relation to his artistic material. From behind the apparently unperturbed surface and wall of controlled craftsmanship, a pressing, at times anguished voice can be heard. It belongs to one who is also a manner of prophet. (pp. 246-56)

> *Victor Brombert, in his* The Novels of Flaubert: A Study of Themes and Techniques, *Princeton University Press, 1966, 301 p.*

Flaubert on the role of the artist:

What one does is not for oneself, but for others. Art is not interested in the personality of the artist. So much the worse for him if he doesn't like red or green or yellow: all colors are beautiful, and his task is to use them.

> *Gustave Flaubert, in a letter to Louise Colet, in* The Letters of Gustave Flaubert: 1830-1857, *edited and translated by Frances Steegmuller, Belknap Press, 1980.*

Maurice Nadeau   (essay date 1969)

[*Nadeau is a French educator, critic, and editor who has written extensively on Flaubert. In the following essay taken from Barbara Bray's 1972 translation of his* Gustave Flaubert écrivain, *for which Nadeau was awarded the Grand Prix de la critique litteraire in 1969, he examines the stylistic features and themes of* Three

Tales *as well as the events surrounding its composition, publication, and reception.*]

"Un Cœur simple," "La Légende de Saint Julien l'Hospitalier," and **"Hérodias"** were composed in the intervals of writing *Bouvard et Pécuchet,* the major work to which Flaubert devoted the last ten years of his life, dying before it was finished. Bereavements, ruin, attacks of depression and despair deprived him of strength and energy to work unremittingly at the novel itself. So to give himself a breathing-space and prove to himself that his genius was intact, he undertook shorter works on different subjects and in different styles, requiring a less massive effort. They emerge as products of a professionalism, experience, and aesthetic which have become part and parcel of the author himself, so that he need no longer suffer all the "throes of style."

Whereas in each of his major works up till then Flaubert had gone into the attack with a new vision and a new method, in the *Trois Contes* he trusted himself to his talent, and allowed himself to exploit the riches he had accumulated in the course of years of research. There was no question of just letting his pen run away with him. The sort of second nature he had attained to was made up of rigor and meticulousness and a feeling for beauty which allowed no half-measures. He researched, organized, corrected, and relied on his skill. But at least he did not despair of doing something worth while, or doubt of his success. He was like a virtuoso who after long practice and having overcome countless difficulties is completely master of his art, and can play the most difficult scores from memory.

And like a virtuoso, Flaubert entered into possession of worlds he had already explored and long inhabited, performed new variations on his own well-known themes, and thus allowed himself a pleasure he had almost always denied himself before. Different as they are from one another, the *Trois Contes* give the impression of an act of creation in which inspiration, theme, and writing all combine to form a single object, marked unmistakably with the stamp of Flaubert's genius.

First, chronologically, comes **"La Légende de Saint Julien l'Hospitalier."** Flaubert had already thought of writing it several times, ever since he had studied the native images illustrating the life of the saint in a stained-glass window in Rouen Cathedral. That was in 1846. Ten years later, in 1856, he returned to the project, then abandoned it. In 1875, after the Commanvilles' and his own ruin, when he had taken refuge at Concarneau with his friend Georges Pouchet, Flaubert, worn out and looking back over his life and the memories of his youth, thought he might kill time and distract his mind from his woes by at last putting this old project into effect.

In 1874, on the visit to Rigi-Kaltbad with his friend Laporte, he had made notes on the subject and done a good deal of reading, ranging from *La Légende Dorée*, written by Jacques de Voragine in the 13th century, through various treatises on hunting, falconry and painting on glass to contemporary works by Lavallée and Blase.

The story was to be broadly drawn, its general tone that

of medieval legend such as it might be handed down by popular and religious folklore. Flaubert wanted to show a simple man a prey to human instinct, and subject, like Oedipus or Orestes, to a terrible fatality, from which he is ultimately saved by Grace. He had to steer a middle course between fairy-tale and hagiography, between plausibility of character and social and historical background and a certain atmosphere of magic. This magical element would give a deeper meaning to Julian's murderous sadism, and allow the whole of Creation to become active and vocal. Flaubert aimed at creating an effect of wonder, not through unbridled imagination or inordinate use of symbol, but by placing everything within a single consistent universe which lent its own values to men, events, and the world. Divine intervention itself would seem quite natural against a long tradition of the lives of saints and martyrs.

Flaubert had not taken on any difficulties which he could not overcome in a few months, and in February 1876 the story was finished.

The meaning he had wished to impart to "the story of Saint Julien such, more or less, as it is to be found in a church window in my country" is transmitted so clearly through the richest, most dense and beautiful prose Flaubert ever wrote that it placed Taine among the foremost of Flaubert's contemporary admirers. He wrote to the author: "It is not the Middle Ages itself, but the world as imagined by the Middle Ages. What you were aiming at when you tried to produce the effect of a stained-glass window is achieved: the pursuit of Julian by the animals, the leper—all this is the authentic mentality of the year 1200."

Men of letters as well as philosophers and historians gave their approval. From the time the story first appeared in serial form in *Le Bien Public* in April 1877 right up to the present day, everyone used the word *"chef-d'œuvre."* In 1893 Marcel Schwob exclaimed how hard it was "to imagine the miraculous transformation which decked in purple and gold" the simple figures of the legend as transmitted by tradition; he pointed out the skill with which the author had made Julian's soul human and the setting of the story vivid. Gustave Flaubert had succeeded in fusing into "one miraculous literary enamel all the trappings of chivalry, together with the simplest of popular religious tales."

In 1922, Albert Thibaudet was also struck by the "dazzling fusion," which, as Schwob said, enabled us to know "a soul very close to our own." Thibaudet went on: "Julian is caught up in the vortex of fate, a vortex which will not release him because it is his very nature, because it is our very nature." Flaubert seemed to have written this masterpiece of French prose "in a state of grace in which human affairs took on an absolute symbolic value, and in which everything, including style, unfolded with a kind of fluid necessity." Thus, by a paradox which has few parallels, the story Flaubert wrote by way of a "rest" from pressing anxiety turned out to be one of the greatest achievements of literary art.

Flaubert was still in his "state of grace" when, with **"Saint Julien"** only just finished, he began to write **"Un Cœur simple."** This story, too, was quickly written: he finished it in August 1876.

This time Flaubert plunged into his own legend, into the memories of his childhood and youth, among the people he had known in a world now vanished.

George Sand had criticized his earlier works for lack of feeling, harshness towards his characters, too critical an attitude towards life and the world, deliberate and systematic cantankerousness, and inhuman objectivity. **"Un Cœur simple"** was intended to show her that a novelist did not have to appear in his work and bedew it with tears in order to show the qualities prized by the *"chère maître,"* and that the milk of human kindness could flow from the author to his characters through the simplest, most naive, and most "realist" of stories. After George Sand's death Flaubert wrote to her son: "I began **"Un Cœur simple"** just for her, with the sole object of pleasing her. She died while I was in the middle of it. Thus is it with all our dreams."

While he was still "in the middle of it," in June 1876, he wrote to Mme Roger des Genettes: "I want to move, to bring tears to the eyes of the tender-hearted; I am tender-hearted myself." He summarized the work itself as follows: "The story of **"Un Cœur simple"** is just an account of an obscure life, the life of a poor country girl who is pious but mystical, faithful without fuss, and tender as new bread. She loves in turn a man, her mistress's children, her nephew, an old man she looks after, and then her parrot. When the parrot dies she has it stuffed, and when she too dies she confuses the parrot with the Holy Ghost." Then, anticipating Edma's smile, he added: "This is not at all ironical, as you suppose. On the contrary, it is very serious and very sad."

Life continued to rain blows on him, snatching away family and friends: Louise Colet's death in 1876 meant the loss of another part of his youth. He was haunted by the thought that by withdrawing from life in order to represent it better he might have made a fool's bargain. "I was a coward when I was young," he wrote to George Sand, "I was afraid of life. But everything has to be paid for." So he plunged more and more, as he grew older, into the nostalgic world of childhood, of his uncles and aunts, of his connections and acquaintances in Honfleur and Pont-l'Évêque. He saw again the lush water-meadows by the Touques, and the sunny landscapes of Trouville. And then, as Thibaudet says, he "cast a net over his former life," in order to dredge up the treasures hidden there. In the guise of the harsh and touching story of a loyal servant-girl—partly the Léonie of his friends the Barbeys at Trouville, partly his own old Julie—he brought to life again, sometimes under their real names, people he had known in the old days, and, in their real colors, places he had recently revisited, his heart full of sensations from the past.

Mme Aubain in the story is great-aunt Allais. Paul and Virginie, himself and his sister Caroline when they were young. Félicité's nephew, Victor, who dies of yellow fever in Havana, was really the nephew of Captain Barbey, who had already figured in the same way in the first *Education*.

The Marquis of Gremanville was great-great-uncle Charles-François Fouet, better known to all his relations as "Councillor" de Crémanville from his post under the *ancien régime* as councillor-auditor to the Cour des comptes at Rouen. Even the parrot Loulou had a model in a stuffed bird Flaubert obtained from the Rouen Natural History Museum and kept in his work-room. The places in which the story was set were still unchanged when Gérard-Gailly visited them half-a-century later. "I went to Gefosses," he writes. "I walked up the sloping courtyard and saw the house in the middle, and the pond where Paul skimmed stones; and, from the highest point in the meadow, I made out, beyond a beautiful landscape, the 'grey patch' of the sea."

The sources have a special importance here. Flaubert, by making a dramatic transposition of his memories and composing the story of Félicité, intended to revive in himself, as accurately as possible, real episodes of his childhood, and to see the people and places concerned in their light. This was a substitute for the memoirs he had wanted to write but had abandoned; and he did not mean to have the story of his old servant found ridiculous. Into his account of this existence buffeted by all life's cruelties, he put all his heart, his regrets, and his nostalgia; he did so without departing from his aesthetic, thus accomplishing a *tour de force* from which all tension and effort seem absent. In this masterpiece of naturalness, noble sentiments do make excellent literature, in spite of Gide, and no one but Flaubert has the right to joke about this unexpected aspect of his talent. *"Cette fois-ci, on ne dira plus que je suis inhumain. Loin de là, je passerai pour un homme sensible, et l'on aura une plus belle idée de mon caractère,"* he wrote, when he had brought his story to a successful conclusion. ("This time they won't say I'm inhuman. On the contrary, I shall be considered a man of feeling, and people will take a nobler view of my character.")

This is not to say his philosophy had become gentle and optimistic. Though in the case of Félicité he was operating at the level of very elementary feelings, once again he was depicting the injustice of fate and the emptiness of all hopes. Whether one asked little or much of life, it always gave the same tragic and disillusioning answer.

Flaubert started **"Un Cœur simple"** in March 1876. Already, in April, while he was still writing it, he was thinking of a tale in a completely different vein which in color, atmosphere, and characters would form a contrast with the "humble reality" he was now in the midst of. On August 17, immediately after finishing the story of Félicité, he wrote to his niece: "Herodias presents herself, and I *see* (clearly, as I *see* the Seine) the surface of the Dead Sea shimmering in the sun. Herod and his wife are on a balcony from which you can see the gilded tiles of the temple."

He had been caught up again in his dream of the East, this time linked to another image from Rouen Cathedral, where in a tympanum over one of the side doors Salome was sculpted dancing on her hands before Herod, with the executioner brandishing his sword nearby, preparatory to decapitating John the Baptist. The story was in the line of *Salammbô* rather than of the Scriptures, a tale full of ferocity and lust, in which Flaubert meant to wrest a morsel of living flesh from a confused history of Jews, Romans, Arabs, pagans, and sectaries of a faith in the process of being born. He also wanted it to be a significant episode, in the course of which, in a medley of races and religions, amidst the rebellions of subject peoples against Rome and their wars among themselves, Judaea, still awaiting a Messiah, became the true Promised Land. Flaubert isolated the moment of Salome's dance and the beheading of John the Baptist, the moment when history ceased to be the history of Mediterranean antiquity and became the history of the modern world.

He made use of the legend of Herodias. But what the Gospels of Saint Matthew and Saint Mark could not give him were the characters of the historical figures he wanted to portray, the psychological explanations of Herodias's victory over her husband, what lay behind the bold stratagem by which she extorted the monstrous promise from the Tetrarch. If *Salammbô* is like a fresco, **"Hérodias"** resembles one of those antique jewels engraved with some legendary or symbolic story, in which the infinite diversity of human feeling is expressed in myth.

Herod Antipas, a weak ruler whose power may be snatched away at any moment either by those above him or by those below, represents the craven cruelty of man governed by his appetites and in a chronic state of fear. Herodias, a mixture of "Cleopatra and de Maintenon," embodies the restless hatred of an ambitious woman who has backed the wrong horse and shrinks at nothing to rectify matters. Salome, so charming and innocently shameless, is a girl who is not unaware of the strange effect she has on men, and lets herself be used to pull other people's chestnuts out of the fire. Flaubert's other characters, while not drawn in depth, are vividly depicted: they are either borrowed from history or legend, or defined by their part in the action. Around them is a vast cacophonous choir of different races, bands, crowds and armies. And over and above all this, East and West meet in uncertain battle.

Flaubert condenses this prodigious panorama of political and religious history into a few pages, and shapes it with a few strokes. He did not achieve his object with the same facility as in the other two stories. He undertook harassing bibliographical and archaeological research for it; he got friends and acquaintances to help him with the vast documentation necessary; the worst worry of all was the fear that he might repeat the effects of *Salammbô*, when what he needed was an entirely different human and material climate. He exploited his own recollections of the Holy Land, and made Salome dance with the same wanton movement of the hips as Kuschiuk Hanem. It was only by a series of adjustments and readjustments that he finally managed to hold the balance between history and psychological truth. He was walking a tightrope and performing balancing acts at the same time. And yet sometime she himself was astonished at the speed with which his pen raced across the paper; he said he was prey to *"une effrayante exaltation."* He finished **"Hérodias"** in three months, at the end of January 1877.

In March he sold **"Hérodias"** and **"Un Cœur simple"** to *Le Moniteur* and **"La Légende de Saint Julien l'Hospitalier"** to *Le Bien public.* At the end of the month

Charpentier sent him the proofs of the book, which came out at the end of April. For these various publications Flaubert received what he considered enough to live on for a year, and his state of euphoria was the more pronounced because, for once, the critical reception was almost unanimously cordial.

Edouard Drumont talked of "marvels"; Saint-Valry, in *La Patrie,* of "an excellent combination of accuracy and poetry"; Charles Bigot, in *Le XIXe siècle,* spoke of "perfection"; even old enemies like Sarcey at last paid homage. Naturally, Flaubert's friends and admirers from the beginning were not to be outdone. Once again Théodore de Banville used his theater column to salute "three absolute and perfect masterpieces, created with the power of a poet sure of his art, who should only be spoken of with the respectful admiration due to genius." Karl Steen (Mme Alphonse Daudet) and Guy de Valmont (Maupassant) gladly joined in the raptures. Only Brunetière, espousing the old quarrels of *La Revue des Deux Mondes,* considered the *Trois Contes* "certainly the weakest thing Flaubert has done"; he alone saw in them "the sign of an imagination that is drying up." But this sour small voice was drowned by the acclamations of the "young men"—Paul Alexis, Henry Céard, Léon Hennique, J.-K. Huysmans, Octave Mirbeau, and Maupassant—who on April 16 gave a dinner in Flaubert's honor. Goncourt and Zola were also invited, and this caused the papers to announce the birth of the *"l'école naturaliste."*

The public reception was more reserved; or rather, the public's curiosity was soon satisfied. Their attention was distracted by a political crisis which led to the government of May 16, and this affected sales. At the beginning of the month Charpentier was selling three hundred copies a day, but this dwindled to a half-dozen or so. Flaubert changed his tune. "As for my poor book, it's completely flattened. All I can do is rub my belly." He returned to Croisset, "sick to death of Paris" and disillusioned once more. "To the dreariness of my private affairs is added the disintegration of public ones. My whole horizon is black." So he bravely set to again on *Bouvard et Pécuchet.*

[*Trois Contes* gives] us the opportunity of studying an example of perfect art, an art which consists in the extraordinary economy of the narrative and the vivid evocation of the characters and the very special worlds they live in, all expressed in a style which the author can modulate at will between dazzling and tense, dramatic and dreamy, sober and subtle.

—*Maurice Nadeau*

While *Trois Contes* served as a distraction for Flaubert during the more ambitious work he had in progress, and while it has not the weight of *Madame Bovary* or

L'Education sentimentale, it does not deserve to be put in the shade by the books he took longer to write. These three short narratives are more like shoots off the main plant which take only a few weeks to flower. They bear witness to the vigor and potential of the tree itself. The *Trois Contes* also showed that Flaubert was not the mere plodder ill-informed criticism had made him out to be, but that he could mobilize his resources without undue time or trouble.

But the comparison must not be pushed too far. The usual view is that **"Un Cœur simple"** belongs to the same world of everyday reality as *Madame Bovary,* the description of which caused Flaubert to be dubbed a "realist." Still according to this view, **"Saint Julien"** derives straight from the religious and legendary world of *La Tentation,* while **"Hérodias"** comes from the highly-colored and barbaric world of *Salammbô.* All this would make the book a sort of synthetic summary of the author's talents, containing the three complementary aspects of his inspiration. But this is a very rough and ready account of the matter. In each case the story is not so much the issue of the novel concerned as a distant relation. But if Flaubert included them all in a single volume, he did so for good reasons.

Although he was hard up, he was too scrupulous to indulge in just putting a book together. And his usual indifference to publication absolves him of the suspicion of wanting to give his audience something to keep it going. It was after **"Saint Julien,"** while he was writing **"Un Cœur simple"** and thinking of **"Hérodias,"** that he spoke of publishing *un livre assez drôle",* that is, a book that would probably surprise people because of the obvious contrasts of subject and style, but which would in fact be an original and independent work, not intended to be too closely associated with his previous books. He did not see Félicité as Emma Bovary, and he does not make us enter into her consciousness. Saint Julien, unlike Saint Anthony, is not a man always asking himself questions, usually insoluble ones. And the Judaea of A.D. 30 bears no resemblance to Carthage. Nor are the mechanics of creation the same in *Trois Contes.* Flaubert had turned aside from the novel and from the "fundamentally impossible" book he was working at, the exact nature of which he was not sure about. He wanted to try a new register he had felt he had a gift for when he was young—as if he wished to prove to himself he had not been wrong.

In his previous works Flaubert had tried to fill a void in himself, though he never entirely succeeded in doing so, and each book, once finished, left him still unsatisfied. In *Trois Contes,* though he did not make this attempt, he did make use of the same live substance, made up of different combinations of reality and dream, observation and vision, myth and symbol, intuition and deduction. This substance took form in accordance with an internal logic which resolved each problem on a different level of the past. For convenience, these levels may be labelled historical, legendary, and personal; but Flaubert's material in fact constituted a single imaginary world, subject to Fate and sometimes to Grace, a world in which human resolves are undone by life, and which is full of signs, premonitions, and myths. The past invoked by Flaubert had in fact been remade by men, as if to give it a meaning and prevent it falling into oblivion.

Flaubert did the same with his own past. The story of Féli-cité, like that of Hérodias and Julian, resembles a stained-glass window or rough-cut image in stone.

Flaubert made this past actual by preserving its colors. Whereas in *Madame Bovary* and *L'Education sentimen-tale* he wrote from a present which unfolds before the reader's eyes, producing in him the illusion of finding out what happens at the same time as the author, in *Trois Contes* he retraces in each case a history already over. For a greater or less time it has already been consigned to the annals of history or memory, and Flaubert sets his charac-ters in motion against a framework given in advance by public or private events. Instead of evolving freely, as in the novel, and conducting the author towards new discov-eries about themselves, life, and himself, the characters obey a destiny already sealed for ever.

The story-teller describes lives which are ended for good and all, and he has no power to intervene. He simply de-scribes them, with art, accuracy, and verisimilitude.

This is perhaps why *Trois Contes* is not the first book of Flaubert's one turns to for excitement, surprise, and a les-son on life. But it does give us the opportunity of studying an example of perfect art, an art which consists in the ex-traordinary economy of the narrative and the vivid evoca-tion of the characters and the very special worlds they live in, all expressed in a style which the author can modulate at will between dazzling and tense, dramatic and dreamy, sober and subtle. His only object is to enjoy, and to make us enjoy, his talents and his mastery of them. If it were anyone else but Flaubert one might think the creator had been given a holiday to leave scope for the artist. What *Candide* is to the 18th century, *Trois Contes* is to the 19th—one of the great triumphs of French prose. (pp. 249-60)

> *Maurice Nadeau, in his* The Greatness of Flaubert, *translated by Barbara Bray, The Li-brary Press, 1972, 306 p.*

Robert T. Denommé (essay date 1970)

[*Denommé is an American critic and educator who spe-cializes in French literature. In the following excerpt, he examines the stylistic features of "A Simple Heart," claiming that Flaubert's use of irony allowed him to cri-tique organized religion and still present Félicité as a sympathetic figure.*]

Despite Flaubert's vigorous disclaimer to the contrary, a number of critics of recent vintage have been prompted to interpret **"Un Coeur simple"** as an ironic commentary on human stupidity and on stultifying bourgeois attitudes. Flaubert's writings prior to 1876, to be sure, virtually re-sound with pages of biting satire and bitter irony; *Madame Bovary, Salammbô* and *L'Education sentimentale* all at-tack virulently, at strategic intervals, the vacuity of many social, political and religious institutions. What distin-guishes **"Un Coeur simple"** from the previously completed stories, however, is the discernible shift of tone and mood

that the narrative assumes. Indeed, the remarkable fusion of tenderness with what Victor Brombert so aptly terms "refined irony" produces an effect hitherto alien to the ma-jority of the novelist's better-known interpretations of hu-manity [*The Novels of Flaubert: A Study of Themes and Techniques*]. This notable shift of emphasis may be at least partially explained by the series of unfortunate incidents that befell Flaubert from 1870 to 1876. The critical fail-ures of *La Tentation de Saint-Antoine* and *Le Candidat,* the deaths of his mother and of such friends as Louis Boui-hlet, Sainte-Beuve, Louise Colet, and George Sand, and the serious financial difficulties he encountered all doubt-lessly contributed in some manner in altering his literary vision and modifying his personal attitude. The resulting attenuation in mood and tone, far from emerging as the fitful and short-lived personal reaction to unfavorable cir-cumstances, resulted rather from Flaubert's scrupulous attention to relevant details and his painstaking effort to obtain specific effects; he wrote to his niece, Caroline, on 1 July 1876: "Je lutte comme un forcené contre les diffi-cultés de mon *Coeur simple,* qui augmentent de jour en jour." Flaubert's modified vision of humanity reaches its culminating point in the unfinished *Bouvard et Pécuchet,* which illustrates, ironically, the intellectual pursuits and failures of two friends without ruthlessly exploiting or condemning them for their folly. Like the two male pro-tagonists, Bouvard and Pécuchet, Félicité in **"Un Coeur simple"** ironically unveils the futility and fatuousness of specific bourgeois practices while enlisting at the same time the undeniable sympathy of the reader.

"Un Coeur simple" deliberately refrains from unleashing any direct assault upon the ineffectiveness of organized re-ligion or the narrowness of intellect and attitude that char-acterizes the typical provincial bourgeois. That any such overt critical confrontation is avoided in the story is attrib-utable to the fact that Flaubert abstains from resorting to his favorite technical device, the *style indirect libre,* in order to fashion the portrait of his main character. The *style indirect libre,* a type of indirect discourse obtained through the momentary association between the con-sciousness of the character involved and the directing in-telligence of the narrator, would have endowed the narra-tive with a tone radically different than the one achieved in **"Un Coeur simple."** It is more than likely that Flaubert, intent on portraying Félicité with sympathy and even ten-derness, realized that such a technique, in this instance, would impair him in achieving the desired effects. Félicité, unlike Emma Bovary, is incapable of formulating her thoughts or impressions on any appreciably precise or so-phisticated level. The collaboration entered upon by Flau-bert and Emma Bovary through the *style indirect libre* un-derscores with particular acuity the consciousness of his protagonist's state of mind, thus mercilessly exposing her to the reader's ridicule as the stupidly ironic victim of her own carefully contrived delusions. . . . (pp. 573-74)

Flaubert's heroine in **"Un Coeur simple"** escapes the igno-miny of such exposure primarily because she never experi-ences such complicated consciousness of her predicament. Moreover, her aspirations are too indelibly imprinted with simplicity and innocence for them to become so easily the brunt of the author's exploitation. Yet Félicité, the main focal point in the story, differs radically from her likely predecessor, Catherine Leroux, in the chapter on the *comices agricoles* in *Madame Bovary*. The brief but memorable sketch of Catherine Leroux at the awards ceremony is noticeably tinged by the intrusion of Homais' sarcastic comment so as to make it virtually impossible for the reader to view the old woman's plight with wholly sympathetic eyes. Flaubert's apparently neutral statement—"Dans la fréquentation des animaux, elle avait pris leur mutisme et leur placidité"—is to a significant degree colored by Homais' strident and gratuitous exclamation to the notary: "Quel fanatisme!" The author of **"Un Coeur simple"** chooses to look at Félicité with discreet omniscience and withholds editorial comment, content to portray his protagonist by listing details that characterize her outlook: "Son visage était maigre et sa voix aiguë. A vingt-cinq ans, on lui en donnait quarante. Dès la cinquantaine, elle ne marqua plus aucun âge;—et, toujours silencieuse, la taille droite et les gestes mesurés, semblait une femme en bois, fonctionnant d'une manière automatique."

There is no evidence of any compulsion to make of his simple-minded heroine an object for derision. To have exploited Félicité's simplicity in the manner that Catherine Leroux's stupidity was singled out in *Madame Bovary* would have reduced **"Un Coeur simple"** to a cynical commentary on fanaticism and ignorance. Such a single-minded interpretation robs Flaubert's story of its richer dimension.

Flaubert endows the heroine of his short story with the kind of homogeneous vision of reality that enables her to retain a remarkably even sense of composure in the face of tragedy and adversity. Félicité's simple view of life contrasts sharply with Flaubert's complex interpretation of reality. The latter's acute awareness of the complications and contradictions inherent in the world that he sought to comprehend inspired him with the voracious desire for understanding that is discernible in all his fiction. The confusion of change and movement, however, prevented him from pursuing such a goal with the kind of detachment he desired; the much-sought collaboration between his imagination and his practical intelligence never successfully took place, and the final homogeneity or synthesis failed to materialize to the extent that he had wished. . . . To a significant degree, *Madame Bovary* remains perhaps the author's most cogent statement on the sense of inadequacy resulting from the failure to fashion successfully a homogeneous world from an essentially heterogeneous one. Emma Bovary never succeeds in sustaining her illusory existence for any great length of time because she continually submits her somewhat deficient imaginative powers to the scrutiny of a sordid external reality. She repeatedly becomes aware of her self-deception until she is finally driven to her destruction. Ironically, Félicité, much more ignorant and certainly much less articulate than Emma, achieves a satisfying homogeneity of vision by transforming ordinary reality through her imagination alone.

Félicité's instinctive retreat into the more predictable world of her private imagination is in fact prompted by the overwhelming confusion and bewilderment she experiences when compelled to face the jarring complexities of

The Saint Julien Window in the Rouen Cathedral, which inspired Flaubert's "La legende de Saint Julien l'Hospitalier."

external reality. Flaubert records the incident at Colleville with apt vividness: "Tout de suite elle fut étourdie, stupéfaite par le tapage des ménétriers, les lumières dans les arbres, la bigarrure des costumes, les dentelles, les croix d'or, cette masse de monde sautant à la fois. Elle se tenait à l'écart modestement, quand un jeune homme d'apparence cossue, et qui fumait sa pipe les deux coudes sur le timon d'un banneau, vint l'inviter à la danse." In her insecurity, Félicité accepts Théodore's invitation to dance with him but is rudely shaken when she must resist his crude overtures. Thus, her subsequent withdrawal from the pressing requirements of a complex external reality appears as a defensive reaction to which she has recourse when she intuitively realizes that she is ill-equipped to function effectively under such circumstances. Henceforth, Félicité gazes at reality through her imagination and with her innate common sense. The real irony, of course, is that, despite her ignorance and simple-mindedness, she not only manages to function adequately but she is able, unconsciously, to project her own world outwardly to the point of touching and affecting the lives of others.

Félicité's daily existence, like that of Emma Bovary, is defined by the same kind of boredom, disappointment, and discouragement that mar the security and serenity of an ordered life. Unlike Emma, however, Félicité preserves her equanimity: she proceeds with remarkable resilience to repair whatever havoc may have been wrought by personal tragedy, indifference, and even cruelty. Condemned to perform the simplest chores, she escapes from most of the ravages of boredom by lavishing her attention on others: Mme Aubain, Paul and Virginie, Victor, the *père* Colmiche and Loulou, the parrot. Of all the characters in **"Un Coeur simple,"** it is Félicité who emerges most successfully in the battle against frustration through positive and durable activity. Flaubert counterpoints Félicité's response to Paul's departure for Caën with those of Mme Aubain and Virginie: "Mme Aubain se résigna à l'éloignement de son fils, parce qu'il était indispensable. Virginie y songea de moins en moins. Félicité regrettait son tapage. Mais une occupation vint la distraire; à partir de Noël, elle mena tous les jours la petite fille au catéchisme." Ultimately, it is Félicité's constructive attitude that allows her to escape the stultifying effects of an uninteresting existence, for like Emma Bovary and Mme Aubain, she is exposed to the same monotonous routine of provincial life. The protagonist of **"Un Coeur simple"** is exposed to the cruel indifference and callousness of society that in one instance nearly succeeds in unnerving her to the point of imbalance. Having suffered the ignominy of the mailcoach driver's whiplash, Félicité makes her way painfully to a summit that commands a view of Honfleur, and momentarily yields to Emma's temptation: "Arrivé au sommet d'Ecquemauville, elle aperçut les lumières de Honfleur qui scintillaient dans la nuit comme une quantité d'étoiles; la mer, plus loin, s'étalait confusément. Alors une faiblesse l'arrêta; et la misère de son enfance, la déception du premier amour, le départ de son neveu, la mort de Virginie, comme les flots d'une marée, revinrent à la fois, et, lui montant à la gorge, l'étouffaient." Fortunately, Félicité's nostalgia is short-lived; the gnawing memory of her mis-

fortune doubtlessly is allowed to surface because of her semi-conscious physical and mental state at the time.

What is frequently conveyed in almost antithetical terms is the fact that Flaubert's heroine in **"Un Coeur simple"** differs so radically in attitude from his earlier protagonist, Emma Bovary. Flaubert shows Félicité actively resisting the stultification caused by monotony and by the slow, tragic passage of time. While it remains undeniable that the theme is established from the beginning and sustained throughout the narrative, it is interesting to note the coded and even somewhat ambiguous language in which it is cloaked. In Madame Bovary, the novelist's intended criticism of the deficient romantic personality and of the mechanized gentry is spelled out in more direct and explicit terms. Flaubert's novels understandably allow more importance to dialogue than do the short stories. In *Madame Bovary,* for example, the spoken language of the characters plays an important role in establishing the kind of private world in which they function. In such stories as **"Un Coeur simple,"** where dialogue is reduced to a strict minimum, Flaubert has recourse rather to symbols in order to evoke or suggest the various attitudes that he intends to portray. It is no small irony that the older, and consequently more mature artist resorts in his later fiction to the utilization of an outwardly more subjective technique of presentation. The highly suggestive passages describing the rooms inhabited by Mme Aubain and the servant convey with effective symbolism the opposing attitudes of immobility and activity, passive resignation and active resistance. . . . After alluding to the faded, flowering wallpaper in Mme Aubain's bedroom, the mattressless beds of the children, Paul and Virginie, the closed living room with the covered furniture, Flaubert continues his description in the following vein: "Un lucarne au second tageé éclairait la chambre de Félicité, ayant vue sur les prairies." Strategically inserted in the opening pages of **"Un Coeur simple,"** such descriptive passages set the tone and mood for the tale.

The progressive shrinkage of Félicité's recognizable universe, brought about through the deaths of those she has loved, the eventual loss of part of the Aubain property and the subsequent impairment of her hearing and seeing faculties apparently condemn her to a life of virtually absolute isolation. Yet the opposite effect takes place. The isolation she experiences in a sense enables her to proceed unhampered and uninhibited by external forces to fashion the kind of private, homogeneous world that brings about the solace and security that she seeks. As her solitude increases, the powers of her creative imagination also increase. What Victor Brombert calls "the perversion of the Logos" resembles in many ways the nature of the child-poet's vision. Like the child-poet, Félicité creates through her imagination a simplified universe in which the jarring dissonances of a complex external world are conspicuously absent. Félicité's hallucinations or willful distortions of reality are in no way identifiable with the complicated *malaise* endured by Emma Bovary, Frédéric Moreau, and Mâtho. Flaubert's servant in **"Un Coeur simple"** succeeds in inducing the transformations that allow her to rectify the inequities of reality. This is how, for example, she is permitted to take part with Virginie in the first communion ceremonies. In similar fashion, Flaubert invites the reader to penetrate Félicité's imagination at Virginie's funeral procession. The faithful servant rectifies what she considers to be the arbitrary injustice of reality by her decision to mourn both Mme Aubain's deceased daughter and her own nephew, Victor. . . . For the most part, Félicité emerges unscathed from her highly imaginative excursions precisely because she does not seek the corroboration of external reality in her experiences. Since she successfully maintains her own sense of equilibrium in the illusory world that she evolves, she never exposes herself to the destructive consciousness of self-deception and ridicule.

When deafness and virtual blindness finally condemn Félicité to the seclusion of the single room she occupies in the Aubain household, attended only by the mère Simon, she escapes progressively from the requirements of the heterogeneous external reality in which all individuals must learn to function. Old age and eventually illness free her from maintaining any kind of relationship with the harsh world of fact. Her mistaking Loulou for the Holy Spirit, indulgently dismissed as the ranting of delirium, conserves intact the illusions nourished by her imagination in more lucid intervals. Thus Félicité's spiritualization of Loulou achieves the status of a poetic metaphor for the Holy Spirit; as such, it emerges as one of the most exalted expressions of Hugo's romantic synthesis: the sublime residing in the grotesque.

What understandably disturbs the critics who persist in placing **"Un Coeur simple"** in the same ironic tradition established by Flaubert in his completed novels is that one might suspect a double viewpoint: Félicité grossly misinterprets religious dogma and so, logically, she should be victimized by her own delusions. Yet Félicité's illusory world, as limited as it may appear, provides her with experiences that are as rich and personally satisfying as those of Emma Bovary are flimsy and ultimately corrosive. A comparison of Félicité's and Emma's death scenes verifies the positive value that is unfolded in the short story and the negation that is underscored in the novel. Emma's final agony is counterpointed by the ominous song of the blind man, whose words recall and comment on the dying woman's adulterous life:

> —'L'Aveugle!' s'écria-t-elle.
>
> Et Emma se mit à rire, d'un rire atroce, frénétique, désespéré, croyant voir la hideuse face du misérable, qui se dressait dans les ténèbres éternelles comme un épouvantement.

In striking contrast, Félicité's dying moments are depicted as literally enshrined in the brilliant rays of a golden sun and, if anything, are counterpointed by the joyous religious ceremony of the Fête-Dieu, suggesting the triumphal apotheosis of the faithful servant and of her parrot. Among the variegated objects that magnetically attract the attention of the worshippers is the stuffed parrot, Loulou, transformed by his relationship to the expensive vases and colorful flowers that bedeck the altar on which they are placed: "Un sucrier de vermeil avait une couronne de violettes, des pendeloques en pierre d'Alençon brillaient sur la mousse, deux écrans chinois montraient leurs

paysages. Loulou, caché sous des roses, ne laissait voir que son front bleu, pareil à une plaque de lapis." The very rhyming of the ceremony—the slow marching, the silence of the crowd, and the kneeling in reverent gesture—acts as a parallel to the slowing beat of Félicité's dying heart. From her bed, she participates in the festivities: "Une vapeur d'azur monta dans la chambre de Félicité. Elle avança les narines, en la humant avec une sensualité mystique; puis ferma les paupières. Ses lèvres souriaient." When juxtaposed to the fatuous, pointless dialogue entered into by Homais and Bournisien in the room where Emma lies in state, the death scene of Félicité suggests a striking impression of harmony and respect.

If it is true that on the ironical level **"Un Coeur simple"** conveys the sense of void without God, it may also be held that through the power of Félicité's poetic imagination, that void is in a sense eliminated. Moreover, the names of Félicité, Paul and Virginie, Théodore, and Mme Aubain need not necessarily be interpreted on an exclusively ironic level; they are also used iconically since they contribute in fashioning the illusion or idealized reality that Félicité strives to obtain. For her, the child-poet, these characters have been all that their names signify. Whatever irony emerges from **"Un Coeur simple"** stems from the respective positions and attitudes of Flaubert and his readers who will evaluate both Félicité and the environment in which she has been compelled to function. (pp. 575-81)

> *Robert T. Denommé, "Félicité's View of Reality and the Nature of Flaubert's Irony in 'Un Coeur simple,'"* in Studies in Short Fiction, *Vol. VII, No. 4, Fall, 1970, pp. 573-81.*

A. W. Raitt (essay date 1973)

[*An English critic, educator, and editor, Raitt has published studies of Balzac, Mérimée, and other French writers. In the following excerpt, originally presented to the Royal Society of Literature in 1973, Raitt examines the circumstances surrounding the composition of* Three Tales, *the uniqueness of Flaubert's short fiction—a "near-miracle"—and Flaubert's views on the genre.*]

Paradoxical as it may seem, it is by no means self-evident that the greatest novelists make the greatest short-story writers, still less that the greatest short-story writers can convert themselves into even moderately successful novelists. H. E. Bates has said of the short stories produced by eminent nineteenth-century novelists like Thackeray and Meredith that 'they recall too often the dish hashed up from the left-overs of the joint'; while on the other side, novels composed by masters of the short story such as Hoffmann, Mérimée and Maupassant tend to give the impression of an imperfectly joined mosaic of independent episodes. Indeed, many expert practitioners of the short-story form either never attempted to write a novel or never managed to complete one—one thinks of Poe, Nerval, Chekhov or Katherine Mansfield. The broad vision, the grand design, the gift for synthesis required by the novel are not often combined in the one mind with that ability for terse concentration, for the selection of significant detail, for the distillation of meaning and emotion from a single action which are essential for excellence in the shorter form. Only a handful of the outstanding composers of narrative fiction have attained equal mastery of both genres: Balzac, Turgeniev, Joyce and, perhaps supreme among them, Gustave Flaubert.

Flaubert's case is moreover unusual in that, unlike the other authors who have demonstrated comparable adeptness in handling the two forms, he came to the short story through the novel rather than the other way round. Balzac, Turgeniev and Joyce had all established their reputation as short-story writers before winning even greater fame as novelists. Flaubert on the other hand, though as a schoolboy he wrote many tales in imitation of the Romantics (borrowing not only the subject but even the title of Mérimée's *Mateo Falcone*), began his public career with *Madame Bovary* and thereafter, apart from occasional misguided forays into the theatre, wrote nothing but novels until he was in his fifties. There is no evidence that in the intervening period he ever contemplated turning his hand to the short story, and in the end it was largely accident that caused him to take it up in the 1870s and to produce that incomparable set of three masterpieces, his last completed work, which appeared under the title *Trois Contes* in 1877. The sequence of events is plain: half-way through the composition of his fascinating but impossibly ambitious *Bouvard et Pécuchet*, Flaubert's world was shattered when he had to sacrifice the whole of his fortune to save his niece and her husband from bankruptcy. Already exhausted by the almost unbelievable efforts he had expended on *Bouvard et Pécuchet*, saddened by a series of bereavements, discouraged by the invariably hostile and uncomprehending reception given to his novels, he so far lost confidence in himself that he despaired of ever being able to write again. It was in those unpromising circumstances that after several weeks of impotence he finally decided to experiment with the shorter form, 'to pass the time and to see if I can still write a sentence—which I doubt.' The result was **'La Légende de Saint Julien l'Hospitalier,'** a subject he had had at the back of his mind for many years and which he now managed to put on paper. The success of this exercise encouraged him to go on to **'Un Coeur simple,'** the story of a simple Norman serving-woman which he had likewise first conceived long before, and then to add **'Hérodias,'** his account of the beheading of St. John the Baptist, in order to make a volume of respectable size. That short stories written in conditions of such depression and discouragement by a man in his late fifties who had never hitherto taken seriously any narrative form other than the full-scale novel should turn out to be among the supreme examples of their kind seems little short of miraculous. It is the circumstances which made this near-miracle possible that I propose to look at today.

Perhaps the first point to be made is that in many ways Flaubert's three tales are unique, and that their aims and methods are quite unlike those of the vast majority of short stories. Traditionally, at least until writers like Chekhov proved that a short story does not necessarily consist of a complete and well-rounded plot, the short story has been the favourite vehicle of the *raconteur,* of the man adept at retailing anecdotes. Flaubert on the other hand was singularly impatient, in his maturity, with the whole idea of story-telling. His disdain for narration as such

gives him a hankering after the unrealizable ideal of 'a book about nothing,' and inspired an extraordinary tirade noted in the Goncourt journals:

> I don't give a damn about the story, the plot of a novel. When I am writing a novel, my idea is to render a colour, a tonality. For instance, in my novel about Carthage, I want to do something purple. In *Madame Bovary*, my one thought was to produce a grey coloration, the damp, rotting colour of the existence of woodlice. I was so little concerned with the story that had to be put in it that a few days before I began writing the book, I had imagined *Madame Bovary* quite differently.

Plot for Flaubert is then subservient to the need to produce a particular impression, definable in terms of colour as here, but perhaps also as a shape, as a texture, or as a rhythmic experience (whence, at least in part, the primordial importance he accorded to style).

This is as true of his short stories as it is of his novels. There is in them no hint of that dramatic and suspenseful unfolding of a striking anecdote which characterizes so many nineteenth-century short stories; no unexpected twist in the action, no surprise ending, not even the single salient incident around which most writers like to construct their tales. **'Un Coeur simple'** indeed relates the life-story of a humble maidservant to whom nothing exciting ever happens, and though the events of **'Hérodias'** are intensely dramatic, one may wonder how far Flaubert really is concerned with giving his version of the execution of John the Baptist when one realizes that the work appears to have originated with the idea of writing a novel of political life under the Second Empire entitled *Monsieur le Préfet*. Even with **'Saint Julien l'Hospitalier,'** which has the strongest and clearest story-line of any of the three tales, it is difficult to avoid the feeling that Flaubert's real preoccupation is less with the medieval hagiographical legend for its own sake than for the unspoken themes that lie behind it and that first attracted him to it. Of course, this is not to deny the meticulous attention which Flaubert pays to the mechanism of plot or the art with which he organizes and gradates dramatic effects. But he does stand alone among the writers of his time in regarding anecdote not as the essential object of a short story but as one element among many which combine to form a finished artefact the value and significance of which far transcend the sequence of events which it recounts.

One reason why anecdote in Flaubert's short stories loses the primacy it tends to have elsewhere lies no doubt in the remarkable process of maturation which the subjects of all three tales underwent. In the nineteenth century, the short story was closely associated with journalism, and there is no doubt that pressure to meet newspaper deadlines or desire to exploit a highly profitable vein sometimes led even the most conscientious artists to make use of subjects which had not properly ripened in their minds—some of Maupassant's greatest tales only acquired their ultimate quality when he had reworked at leisure ideas first published in almost skeletal form and had added to them the flesh and blood of human reality. Likewise, necessity often forced Villiers de l'Isle-Adam hurriedly to write up a story that he would have preferred to mull over much longer. With Flaubert, not only is such haste unthinkable, but when he did decide to write his tales, he chose subjects which had begun to take shape in his imagination years and even decades before. The story of St. Julien had probably first come to his notice in 1835; in 1846 he had talked of one day writing his own version of it; he had done some desultory reading for it in 1856; but it was only in 1875 that he eventually committed it to paper. Adumbrations of **'Un Coeur simple'** likewise go back to his childhood: a character much like Félicité figures in a tale he wrote at the age of fifteen, and, strange as it seems, was almost taken as the heroine of *Madame Bovary:* 'the first idea I had was to make her into a virgin, living in the depths of the country, growing old in misery, and ending in the last stages of mysticism and imagined passion.' Only **'Hérodias'** seems to be a relatively new subject, but even there he had been taking notes for it five years previously, as well as reflecting on *Monsieur le Préfet* from which its underlying theme derives. The result is that the subjects had all acquired an extraordinary richness of texture and resonance through this long process of evolution: the alluvial deposits left by years of meditation, experience and feeling have given them a depth of fertility almost unequalled in the short story.

This quality of complex profundity is enhanced by the fact that Flaubert never makes explicit—perhaps not even to himself—precisely what significance he attaches to the subjects. Whereas many short-story writers either deliberately underline what sense the reader is meant to extract from a tale, or else so arrange its elements that the intended effect is clear and unambiguous, in the *Trois Contes* Flaubert points no morals, drops no hints, suggests no interpretations. Events are related with detachment; comment is eschewed. This is not only a function of that celebrated impersonality on which Flaubert laid such stress, and which is perhaps more perfectly realized in these tales than in any of his other works. It arises also from the singularly concrete quality of his imagination, which leads him from the outset to conceive a narrative in the uniquely individual terms of material reality, of particular people in a particular setting and in a particular light. Unlike for instance Zola, who for the most part worked by defining a general idea or plan and then constructing characters and incidents to flesh it out, Flaubert sees plot, character and structure as an indivisible unity, endowed from the start with a presence and an individuality of its own, from which all abstract and generalizing elements are rigorously banished. Thus it is that before writing a word of **'Hérodias'** he exclaimed to a friend: 'I can *see* (clearly, as I can see the Seine) the surface of the Dead Sea, sparkling in the sun. Herod and his wife are on a balcony from which one looks out over the golden tiles of the Temple.' So too with Félicité, whose existence and surroundings are visualized with a meticulous and single-minded intensity that immerses us in the very stuff of her being. In the notes and drafts for **'Un Cœur simple'** one can see Flaubert living Félicité's life with a passionate empathy that makes every detail, every incident vividly present for him. Many of the details and incidents in the end are sacrificed and do not appear in the finished text, but both those that survive and those that are removed help to convey a rare sense of a

unique, irreplaceable personality, as strongly individuated as any living being. One is struck too, even in the manuscripts, by Flaubert's absolute refusal to identify Félicité's characteristics in the vocabulary of psychological typology or emotional analysis, which would detract from the uniqueness of her experience. The stories thus acquire a three-dimensional quality extremely rare in works so short, and at the same time provide the reader with the sense of a reality which, like that of life itself, is meaningful, but with a meaning that cannot be circumscribed in abstract formulas or precise definitions.

A consequence of this mode of creation is that an entirely new role devolves upon description. In most short stories, as in most pre-Flaubert novels, descriptive passages serve essentially as background, as the stage setting in which the characters will appear to act out their parts. For Flaubert description serves a different purpose. It is an integral part of the whole experience of the figures whom he writes about and into whose lives we enter. Flaubert sees that no feeling and no event can exist in the abstract; it is always inseparably associated with the physical circumstances in which it occurred and can only be evoked by reference to them. Look for instance at the scene where Félicité arrives at the convent after the death of her beloved Virginie:

> Félicité went up to the second floor. From the doorway of the room, she could see Virginie lying on her back, her hands clasped together, her mouth open, her head tilted back under a black crucifix that leant over her, her face whiter than the curtains that hung motionless on either side. Mme Aubain was clinging to the foot of the bed and sobbing desperately. The Mother Superior stood to the right. Three candlesticks on the chest of drawers added touches of red to the scene, and fog was whitening the windows. Some nuns led Mme Aubain away.

Though this is one of the emotive climaxes of the tale, Flaubert says nothing at all about Félicité's feelings; instead, he puts us in her position so that we see the picture as she saw it and would recall it. The moment in time is fixed indelibly by visual means; the emotions are implied, not stated in what would inevitably have tended to be undifferentiated abstractions—grief, sorrow or whatever. The same technique, adapted to suit the aesthetic and technical postulates of each tale, is used throughout the book. It is perhaps most apparent in **'Un Cœur simple'** because the point of view is almost always Félicité's and because the simple-minded Félicité, devoid of any capacity for intellectual abstraction, lives above all in her physical contacts with the outside world (that is what motivates and justifies her consoling deathbed vision, in which she *sees* her parrot as the Holy Ghost receiving her into heaven). But it is also strongly and vitally present in **'St. Julien,'** where the whole narration of the saint's life is an implicit allusion to a stained glass window, as is made clear by the last sentence: 'And that is the story of St. Julian Hospitator, more or less as it is depicted on a stained-glass window in a church in my part of the world.' As for **'Hérodias,'** it contains a wealth of descriptive writing which communicates a stifling sense of the remorseless pressure of a physical milieu. Each tale thus creates its own imaginative world which the reader can move into and inhabit as with perhaps no other short stories.

All this implies that, just as Flaubert assigns a special and unusual function to description in his stories, so he does with detail. It is customary for short-story writers to impose unity on their works by focusing the reader's attention on one or two significant details, carefully selected for their evocative power or their symbolic overtones—one thinks of the vase in Mérimée's *Le Vase étrusque,* which acts as both the cause and the emblem of Saint-Clair's jealousy, or in Vigny's *Laurette,* of the sinister red seal on the letter which is the hero's death warrant. Flaubert does not operate in that way in the ***Trois Contes.*** Even where a particular object is given especial prominence and fulfils a central function in the tale, as with Félicité's parrot, it remains only one among a whole variety of similar objects—in the remarkable passage in which he catalogues the contents of Félicité's room, Flaubert only arrives at the parrot after having listed scores of other possessions, many of them known to us from previous episodes in the story. Likewise in **'Hérodias,'** though the last sentence narrows the focus right down to the severed head borne by the disciples—'as it was very heavy, they each carried it in turn'—the preceding scene, in which the head is passed around the various guests at the feast, has already reduced it to the status of only one object among the many depicted in the story. This relative fullness of detail gives the tales a texture more akin to that of novels than is usual in short stories, and obviates that feeling of somewhat contrived bareness that lesser authors may inadvertently convey to their desire for concision.

It is indeed noteworthy that each of the ***Trois Contes*** contains much more material, and material of a much more diverse kind, than authors usually think it wise to include in works of such brevity. **'Un Cœur simple'** and **'La Légende de Saint Julien, l'Hospitalier'** both consist of biographies which follow their protagonists through from birth to death, instead of relying on the much more common short-story technique of using a single incident to illuminate a whole life, as Maupassant so frequently and so brilliantly does. **'Hérodios,'** it is true, compresses its events into twenty-four hours, but they form a pattern of such intricate complexity, involving so many different named characters, that many readers, from Flaubert's time to the present day, have found it confused, difficult, and obscure. It may well be that it was Flaubert's long and undivided preoccupation with the novel that led him to take such apparently unwieldy subjects when he eventually turned to the shorter form; but the fact remains that, with the possible exception of **'Hérodias,'** the challenge is magnificently met and overcome. How has Flaubert carried off this exceptional feat?

Here it becomes necessary to differentiate between the three stories and to analyse each of them separately to see how in each case Flaubert has solved the problems posed by his choice of material. In **'Un Cœur simple,'** the main difficulty arises from the necessity of providing a sense of unity and a forward-moving impetus in the long and uneventful time-span of Félicité's existence, a difficulty increased by the obstacles in the way of involving the reader

in the experiences of an illiterate and inarticulate serving-woman who communicates with nobody and who never reflects on her own situation. The key to Flaubert's resolution of the difficulty is to be found above all in his astonishingly subtle use of *style indirect libre,* the free use of the imperfect tense to convey the thoughts and feelings of a character without resorting either to direct quotation or to accurately reported speech. It is of course one of the outstanding features of Flaubert's style throughout his prose fiction, but nowhere is it put to better or more consistent use than in **'Un Cœur simple,'** where its peculiar advantage is that it enables the author, almost from one end of the story to the other, to be simultaneously within his character and outside her. The unity of point of view is thus more rigorously preserved than anywhere else in Flaubert's fiction, yet without limiting his expressive resources to the exiguous vocabulary and rudimentary mental equipment of his heroine. Consider for instance the sentence describing the end of Félicité's long and anxious wait for the return of her stuffed parrot: 'At last he arrived—looking quite magnificent, perched on a branch screwed into a mahogany base, one foot in the air, his head cocked to one side, and biting a nut which the taxidermist, out of a love of the grandiose, had gilded.' The perceptions contained in the sentence are not explicitly referred to Félicité, but one notices that the supposed magnificence of the bird must represent her reaction to it while the absurdity of the golden nut stuck in its beak, implied only by the exaggeratedly climactic rhythm of the phrase, cannot be. The repeated use of this technique throughout the tale entails very careful handling of language so as to prevent the reader sensing any dichotomy between author and character: the sentences are relatively short and simple in structure, the images are few, unobtrusive and mostly culled from the world of nature and domesticity with which Félicité was familiar, the vocabulary is restrained and homely. A delicate balance is thus consistently maintained which enables Flaubert to crate a unified work of art out of what at first blush might have seemed diffuse and unpromising material.

The *Trois Contes,* by their complexity, their density, the subtlety and power of their themes, the sense they convey of a depth and breadth of life extending far beyond their apparently restricted confines, stand alone among French and even among world short stories.

—*A. W. Raitt*

The problems of **'La Légende de Saint Julien l'Hospitalier'** are different. The legend with its contrasting scenes of hunting, parricide, expiation and apotheosis, has a dramatic energy of its own, which Flaubert exploits to the full. But he has added a further, unexpected dimension to it by viewing it not only as a story to be told in its own right, but also as a re-creation of medieval art. Hippolyte Taine perceptively remarked to him: **"Julien"** is very true, but it is the world *imagined* by the Middle Ages, and not the Middle Ages themselves; which is what you intended, since you wanted to produce the effect of a stained glass window; that effect is there; the pursuit of Julien by the animals, the leper, it's all the pure ideal of the twelfth century.' The effect is created from the start by all manner of barely perceptible touches: an almost fairy-tale vagueness in the setting ('Julian's father and mother lived in a castle in the middle of a forest, on the slope of a hill'), a naïve exaggeration in the descriptions ('lands so hot that men's hair caught fire like torches in the burning sun'), a discreet use of archaic terms and old-fashioned constructions, a matter-of-fact acceptance of the supernatural, more ornate and colourful imagery, a deliberate stylization of the secondary characters. Avoiding the pitfalls of pastiche on the one hand and incongruity on the other, Flaubert has produced a highly original and successful medieval tonality in the language and presentation of **'Saint Julien.'** This achievement is all the more striking in that, despite appearances, the legend is more than an artificially ingenious aesthetic exercise. Running through it is not only a carefully and convincingly motivated study of a man in the grip of an uncontrollable blood lust, but also a disturbing complex of underlying themes interrelating cruelty, eroticism, guilt, and atonement through self-immolation. These undertones are all the more effective for remaining unspoken. The **'Légende'** is not only one of Flaubert's most elusively enigmatic works; it is also, in its very detachment and distance, one of his most personal.

In **'Hérodias,'** Flaubert himself was painfully aware of the intractability of the material on which he had decided to work. Repeated complaints in his letters bear witness to the struggle he had to render it artistically viable: 'the problem is, so far as possible to do without indispensable explanations'; . . . 'I have landed myself with a little piece that is anything but easy, because of the explanations the French reader needs. To produce something clear and lively out of such complex elements presents gigantic difficulties.' With his customary scrupulousness, he had spent two months reading everything he could find on the death of John the Baptist and its historical, political, religious, social, and racial background—at least thirty books and articles zealously studied and annotated—and Taine claimed that **'Hérodias'** had taught him more about the origins of Christianity than the whole of Renan's vast work on the subject. But it is undeniable that Flaubert has sought to include in the story more information than the average reader could reasonably be expected to assimilate—even Taine himself misread one passage where concision had led to ambiguity.

But one should beware of the facile assumption that in **'Hérodias'** Flaubert is simply a historian who knows too much to make himself comprehensible to the profane. **'Hérodias'** is not a historical reconstruction, though it may look like one. As Flaubert once declared, 'I consider technical details, precise information, in short the historical and exact side of things, to be very secondary. Above all else, I am seeking for beauty, which my fellow-writers don't much care about.' That this principle is applied here

is shown by the numerous historical anachronisms and mis-statements in **'Hérodias,'** which arise not from carelessness but from a conscious decision to sacrifice factual accuracy to a higher truth. This means that ultimately the reader has no need to remember the mass of detail about people, places, sects, parties, beliefs, politics and so forth which is so profusely supplied in the first part of the story. What Flaubert wants to do is to build up a vast network of pressures bearing down on the Tetrarch Herod and weighing on the administrative decision, fraught with consequences, that he has to take about the life or death of his prisoner Iaokanann (John the Baptist). It is of little moment if the reader cannot follow the daunting complexity of the factors involved, since Herod cannot either; and in the end, when Salome dances, everyone forgets them, united only in the lust for the girl: 'And the nomads inured to abstinence, the Roman soldiers skilled in debauchery, the avaricious publicans, and the old priests soured by controversy all sat there with their nostrils distended, quivering with desire.' The decision to execute Iaokanann is wrung from Herod by a frenzy of animal desire, not by a rational consideration of the rights and wrongs of the case. It is in this that as Flaubert says in a letter, Herod 'was a real prefect' and that **'Hérodias'** is revealed as the projected novel *Monsieur le Préfet* in another guise. And the totally unforeseen ironic consequence of Herod's decision, as we realize from the concluding tableau of the disciples bearing away the prophet's head, symbol of his message, is the spread of Christianity.

Once one reads the story in that light, it becomes clear that the detail in it, the multiplicity of characters, the constantly shifting point of view are essentially subservient to an impressionistic purpose, and the sensitive reader will understand that, implicitly, **'Hérodias'** constitutes a devastatingly misanthropic and pessimistic comment on the way humanity conducts its affairs. There is, in other words, a hidden design which justifies and binds together the apparently multifarious threads of which the story is composed. The unity of focus in **'Hérodias'** is less easy to grasp than in the other two tales; perhaps even it is less perfectly realized, at least on the surface. But its presence gives the tale its real strength and originality.

It appears then evident that, however belated and unorthodox Flaubert's cultivation of the short-story form may have been, he was intensely alive to the peculiar problems it posed and enormously skilful in solving them. That he did succeed so magnificently is in no small measure due to the seriousness with which he set about his task. He may have started **'Saint Julien'** as a less demanding enterprise than the crushing burden of *Bouvard et Pécuchet*, but that was above all a matter of scale. Once he had decided to write these tales, he treated them with precisely the same scrupulous conscientiousness, precisely the same attention to detail, precisely the same fanatical care over style as he brought to his novels. It has been calculated that, proportionately to their length, *Trois Contes* were written just as slowly and with just as much difficulty as *Madame Bovary*, and the piles of manuscript material in Paris and Rouen, recently published in full for the first time, demonstrate how meticulously he documented himself (even for **'Un Cœur simple,'** on parrots, on pneumonia, on religious processions), how thoroughly he thought out the plan of each tale, how many times he was prepared to draft and redraft their expression. There is no hint of that slightly supercilious attitude to the short-story genre one occasionally detects in great novelists, and which may be responsible for the casualness with which someone like Zola tossed off the most disastrously inept little tales. Whether Flaubert ever in so many words tried to distinguish the principles of short-story writing from those of the novelist's art is open to doubt, but it is certain that in practice he did not make the mistake of treating the tale as a truncated or embryo novel. Formally, the *Trois Contes* have an unmistakable identity of their own—or perhaps it would be fairer to say three separate identities, since there is no question of a threefold application of the same formula—and though they could certainly not have been written without the years of meditation and experience Flaubert had devoted to the novel, they show that the lessons of those years had been used flexibly and sensitively to fit in with the conditions of a different form.

It remains to ask what the *Trois Contes* add to the corpus of Flaubert's works. Would our image of the writer be the same if he had never written them, or do they contain something new and irreplaceable, not to be found elsewhere in his writings? It is as well first of all to dissipate one possible misunderstanding, namely that each of the *Trois Contes* is a pendant to a major work of which it repeats the effects in miniature. In this way, '**Un Cœur simple**' has been claimed to follow *Madame Bovary;* '**La Légende de Saint Julien l'Hospitalier**,' *La Tentation de Saint Antoine;* and '**Hérodias**,' *Salammbô*. It is true enough that, as we have already seen, there is a close relation between the genesis of the subject of '**Un Cœur simple**' and that of *Madame Bovary*. It is true too that Flaubert himself was worried about the resemblance between '**Hérodias**' and *Salammbô:* 'I'm afraid of reverting to the effects produced by *Salammbô,* since my characters belong to the same race, and it's more or less the same setting.' But apart from the theme of sainthood and asceticism, there is little to connect '**Saint Julien**' with *Saint Antoine*, the one intimately dependent on its medieval atmosphere, the other set in a desert in the ancient world. Even with the other two tales, the similarity with the novels is more apparent than real. After expressing his fears about '**Hérodias**' and *Salammbô*, Flaubert goes on: 'however, I trust that this criticism, which people will no doubt level at me, will be unjustified', and so indeed it proves to be. *Salammbô* is basically concerned with dark and mysterious themes linking mysticism and carnality, eroticism and death; '**Hérodias**' is a bitterly ironic comment on human frailty and animality. Indeed, one might be tempted to argue that *Salammbô* in that respect is closer to '**Saint Julien**,' and that the pessimism of '**Hérodias**' relates it more cogently to *La Tentation* or even to *Bouvard et Pécuchet*. As for '**Un Cœur simple**,' despite the unmistakable features which it has in common with *Madame Bovary*, especially in its evocation of the Norman countryside and the humdrum monotony of provincial life, Flaubert was in no doubt that it marked a new departure in his art, and it is worth considering in what ways this is so.

Though the idea of the story is old, '**Un Cœur simple**' was in the end committed to paper in response to a sort of challenge from George Sand. For years, she and Flaubert had been conducting a running argument about impersonality in literature, and in 1875 she had finally got under his skin by accusing him of wilfully depressing his readers: 'you create desolation', she said. Flaubert defended himself by claiming that he had no desire to desolate people but that he could not change his eyes: he had to tell the truth about life as he saw it. But clearly the reproach rankled, and '**Un Cœur simple**' was begun as an attempt to show George Sand that, without departing from his canons of impersonality or falsifying his view of the world, he could nevertheless write a work the effect of which would be consoling. 'You will see from my story of '**Un Cœur simple**,' where you will recognize your direct influence, that I'm not as stubborn as you think. I believe you'll approve of the moral tendency of the work, or rather of its human undertones.' Unfortunately, George Sand never read it, as she died before it was finished, so we do not know how she would have reacted to it. But it is clear that, to please her, Flaubert was trying to do something he had never done before, and this is what gives '**Un Cœur simple**' its unique quality and makes it for many readers Flaubert's greatest work.

In order to achieve his end, Flaubert has centred the work on a character who is wholly admirable and who leads her life in a way that renders her proof against the buffetings of fate. Félicité's whole existence is dominated by the selfless love she feels for others—her suitor Théodore, the children, Paul and Virginie, her haughty employer Mme Aubain, marching soldiers, cholera victims, a dying old man, and finally her parrot. Each of these objects of her love is successively taken from her, and the progression is one of ever-diminishing human contact, from people close to her to strangers, then to an animal, and finally, after Loulou the parrot's death, to a stuffed relic, a thing. But because she never expects anything in return, this apparently catastrophic decline into total solitude does not destroy her as a similar decline destroys Emma Bovary. On the contrary, her virtue is rewarded by the tranquillity of her soul (to use the words noted by Flaubert in the margin of one of the manuscripts), and she dies in peace with the beatific vision of the parrot receiving her into heaven. The contrast with Emma's hideous death-bed vision of the blind beggar looming up over her is exemplary. Emma has lived only for herself and the result is disaster: Félicité (so aptly named, and without irony) has lived entirely for and in others, and the result is the only life-story in Flaubert's works, with the possible exception of '**Saint Julien**,' that carries its own justification within itself and that provides its protagonist with an unshakable inner equilibrium. It is as if she had heeded the advice proffered by Flaubert to his niece while he was working on the story: 'so far as possible, one should always concentrate on things outside oneself; otherwise one drowns in a sea of sadness. Take the word of an old man rich in experience.' This is the solution momentarily and accidentally adopted by Frédéric Moreau, the hero of *L'Éducation sentimentale,* when with amateurish enthusiasm he studies to become a historical writer; in the most revealing aside in the book, Flaubert says: 'As he immersed himself in the personality of others, he forgot his own, which is perhaps the only way not to suffer from it.'

'Un Cœur simple' thus reverses the customary pattern of the world depicted in Flaubert's fiction, where idealism is trampled underfoot and mediocrity triumphs. Here, without commentary or sentimentality, we are shown a character who finds serenity and equilibrium amid adversity, and who dies happy, as the work moves to a soberly majestic conclusion. Here lies the 'consolation' Flaubert wished to demonstrate to George Sand; but here too is the same harshly clear-sighted vision of life everywhere present in his works. Viewed objectively, Félicité's life is a long succession of disappointments, hardships, misunderstandings, and the world in which she moves is as grim and bleak as any Flaubert depicts. But because he constantly refuses to step outside her and judge her situation from above, and because she has none of the introspective intelligence which would enable her to see it for herself, as Emma Bovary eventually sees the reality of her position, she keeps her faith undimmed to the end. The vision of the celestial parrot may be an illusion, but it is an illusion which remains intact, and the reader is induced to acquiesce in it and to share in the sense of beatitude which descends on her. This tenderness towards Félicité and the extraordinary tact of feeling which permits Flaubert to preserve his customary pessimistic outlook while producing a work which is morally uplifting, make 'Un Cœur simple' fundamentally different from everything else he wrote.

The *Trois Contes* do then in their different ways add something of their own to the greatness of Flaubert, not least because he has used the short narrative form to say some of the things most important to him. In both theme and technique he has treated the short story as of equal stature with the novel. This is indeed what gives these tales their peculiar and lonely eminence in the history of the nineteenth-century short story. For they do not fit easily into the story of the evolution of the genre, since Flaubert has largely ignored the lessons of great predecessors like Mérimée and has developed his own concept of the form from his experience as a novelist. Likewise, subsequent practitioners, even his disciple and close friend Maupassant, have not seen fit to follow his example in this field. The *Trois Contes,* by their complexity, their density, the subtlety and power of their themes, the sense they convey of a depth and breadth of life extending far beyond their apparently restricted confines, stand alone among French and even among world short stories. (pp. 112-26)

A. W. Raitt, "Flaubert and the Art of the Short Story," in Essays by Divers Hands, *n.s. Vol. XXXVIII, 1975, pp. 112-26.*

A. E. Pilkington   (essay date 1975)

[*In the following excerpt, Pilkington argues that Flaubert's narrative stance and references to medievalism in "The Legend of Saint Julien Hospitaller" provide a rational explanation for the supernatural and mythic aspects of the tale and classify it as a work of realist fiction.*]

A basic problem in Flaubert's **"Saint Julien"** is that of the respective roles of divine Providence and personal responsibility in the working-out of the fate of the hero. How far should Julien's behaviour be seen strictly in terms of a supernaturally ordained pattern, and how far can it be seen in the purely rational terms of moral responsibility and individual psychology? Stress has been laid on [what G. Michaut has termed in an introduction to *Trois contes*] 'cette fatalité qui doit faire de Julien un parricide malgré lui', as well as on [what C. Digeon calls in his *Le dernier visage de Flaubert*] the total absence of psychology in a story where it is the 'croissance continue de la fatalité divine qui assure le développement de l'action'; more recently it has been argued that Flaubert was here writing at such a distance from his subject-matter that Julien ceases to be a character at all and becomes simply an element in the formal rhythm of the story. These three views represent an extreme position; criticism has more commonly stressed a 'balance' or a 'fusion' between the supernatural and psychological elements of the story. This paper will try to suggest a third approach, by showing how, throughout **"Saint Julien,"** Flaubert is careful to create at least the *possibility* of a purely rational explanation of whatever appears to be miraculous or supernatural; and that in the repeated juxtaposition of the 'mediæval' view of the ubiquity of Providence—made explicit throughout the story—and the rationalistic nineteenth-century view—which is implicitly present, and which was Flaubert's own—lies much of the fascination of the work.

Supernatural intervention is seemingly first evinced by the prophecies vouchsafed to Julien's parents. In both cases it can be argued that perfectly ordinary phenomena take on a special meaning in terms of the mentality and situation of the individual who perceives them. Before the prophecies occur, Flaubert is careful to tell us enough about the parents to enable us to interpret them in this way: the various details given about life in the castle make clear the concern of the mother with religion, and of the father with fighting, so that it will be clear that each prediction is very much in line with the mentality, and presumably the expectations, of each parent.

The shift from objective reality to the subjective perception of that reality is apparent in the description of the prophecy to the mother:

> Un soir, elle se réveilla, et elle aperçut, sous un rayon de lune qui entrait par la fenêtre, comme une ombre mouvante. C'était un vieillard en froc de bure . . .

The objective reality, which anyone in the room would have seen, is that of the play of shadow caused by moonlight, but the affirmation 'c'était un vieillard' is no longer Flaubert describing what was there but simply a rendering in free indirect style of what the mother thought was there. The transition from authorial statement to individual point of view is as unobtrusive as in the many cases in the novels where this stylistic device is used. The same contrast between objective fact and the subjective vision is played upon also with regard to what the mother hears:

> Les chants du banquet éclatèrent plus fort. Elle entendit la voix des anges . . .

The absence of a linking conjunction, or of comment from Flaubert, leaves the reader to draw the conclusion that the angelic voices were no more than the 'chants du banquet' perceived in a subjective and distorted way. The following day, the servants are questioned; they claim to have seen no hermit and the conclusion ('Songe ou réalité, cela devait être une communication du ciel') is again plainly not Flaubert's own, but only that of the mother herself, again rendered in free indirect style.

The prophecy to the father can be interpreted along similar lines. Just as the mother's perception is modified by her deep piety and by the emotional effect of childbirth, so is that of the father by his devotion to martial values and by the fact of his having been celebrating for three days and four nights. It is early morning, mist is swirling about and the wind is whistling. In these exceptional circumstances, it is natural that he should take a swirl of fog for a human figure, and the sound of the wind for that of words. There is then in both episodes a suggestion that the perception of ordinary phenomena is deformed by the character and situation of each parent. The theme is taken further by the account of Julien's childhood; the boy is thrilled by stories of fighting, and this confirms the father in his belief that Julien will be a conqueror; when he gives alms, however, he does it with such grace that his mother is reassured in her belief that he will lead a life of piety and become an archbishop. Flaubert again uses the technique of juxtaposition without comment, in order to suggest that both parents see only the evidence which suits them, and simply ignore or fail to perceive altogether whatever conflicts with the hopes which they have for their son.

This same theme acquires a broader importance in the course of the story, where it becomes plain that Julien's fate—whatever other forces may be at work—is at least in part a consequence of the failure of other people, either from ignorance or prejudice, to judge his situation objectively. There are three instances of this failure. The first occurs immediately after Julien for the first time experiences a swoon of sadistic delight in killing the pigeon. He feels a 'volupté sauvage et tumultueuse', and the next paragraph states abruptly:

> Le soir, pendant le souper, son père déclara que l'on devait à son âge apprendre la vénerie;

The father assumes automatically that a boy of this rank will take up hunting, and this is cruelly ironical, since it is plain to the reader that someone who derives the excitement from killing which Julien has just discovered should be kept away from weapons. Secondly, Julien renounces the use of weapons after nearly killing his father by letting slip a heavy sword; his family are saddened by this decision, as it is felt to be dishonourable and unworthy of his ancestors, and it is the old monk who orders him to take up again his 'exercices de gentilhomme' and this 'au nom de Dieu, de l'honneur et des ancêtres'. The third instance occurs when Julien's wife encourages him to take up hunting again, after he has told her of his fear of becoming a parricide. In these three cases, the hand of Providence is not unambiguously apparent, but the hand of other people certainly is—people who from ignorance or from an imperfect appreciation of Julien's character encourage him

in exactly those pursuits which do eventually lead, through the frustrations of the second hunt episode, to his becoming a parricide.

B. F. Bart has pointed out how time and space are manipulated in the first hunt episode to suggest a dream-like quality about Julien's experience. Julien carries out acts of slaughter 'dans un pays quelconque, depuis un temps indéterminé' and with 'la facilité que l'on éprouve dans les rêves'. The hallucinatory nature of the whole episode is further suggested by the fact that the vast tract of country in which Julien hunts is unknown to him, and yet near enough to the castle to enable him to return there immediately. The psychological element in the hallucination is brought out also by the description of the stag as 'solennel comme un patriarche et comme un justicier', since Julien's father is described earlier in terms of these two qualities— 'il se promenait dans sa maison, rendait la justice à ses vassaux'. The prediction makes it clear that it is Julien's 'cœur féroce' which will end by making him a parricide (rather than accident or fate); and the effect on Julien is to inspire the fear not so much of accidentally killing his parents as of experiencing a conscious desire to do so:

> Sa prédiction l'obsédait; il se débattait contre elle. "Non! non! non! je ne peux pas les tuer!" puis il songeait: "Si je le voulais, pourtant? . . ." et il avait peur que le Diable ne lui en inspirât l'envie.

The identification of the stag with the father is psychologically suggestive and is possibly taken up later when the description of Julien's father arriving at his son's palace singles out 'sa taille haute et sa grande barbe', which looks back in what would be a characteristically Flaubertian manner to the description of the stag as being 'monstrueux de taille' and wearing a 'barbe blanche'. Julien's fear that he might actually wish to kill his parents is presented in the terms in which it would be natural for a mediæval mind to see it—as an urge inspired by the Devil; and this obscure fear is suggested by the metaphorical identification of the stag with the figure of the patriarchal justicer that is Julien's father. Julien's later conviction that 'du meurtre des animaux dépendait le sort de ses parents' shows his half-formed awareness that a man who is driven by blood-lust to slaughter animals might well come to slaughter people as well, and this is exactly what does happen after the abortive second hunt:

> Cette déception l'exaspéra plus que toutes les autres. Sa soif de carnage le reprenait; les bêtes manquant, il aurait voulu massacrer des hommes.

At the outset of the episode of the second hunt, Flaubert is careful to point out that Julien's perception of reality is erratic and uncertain: he confuses patches of moonlight with pools of water, and takes pools of water to be patches of grass, and this blurring of objective reality prepares the way for the hallucinatory events which follow. Among these is the shattering of Julien's lance in the encounter with the bull:

> Alors son âme s'affaissa de honte. Un pouvoir supérieur détruisait sa force.

The explanation in terms of 'higher power' is that of Julien, rendered in free indirect style, and framed naturally in terms of the mediæval view of the ubiquity of 'higher powers'. The two statements here are not formally linked, so that it is left to the reader to supply the connection and to see in the conclusion about the 'pouvoir supérieur' a product of the state of moral collapse described in the first sentence. This technique of juxtaposition works in an essentially suggestive way, and through its economy is admirably suited to the formal limits of the *conte*. The ending of the second hunt episode parallels that of the first, in that it ends equally abruptly: the cock calls, and Julien recognizes his palace. The sudden transition in both cases from the nightmarish to the familiar suggests that the hunt has taken place in a country of the mind through hallucination brought on by blood-lust and guilt.

The reappearance of the stag immediately after the murder of the parents again raises the question of the forces acting on Julien. His furious slaughter ('il trépignait, écumait, avec des hurlements de bête fauve') is a product of the frustration of his desire to kill, and of the final deception of his mistaking a dead bird lying in the grass for three live birds—an error comprehensible in the mental state of a man desperate to find something alive so that he can kill it, and which looks back moreover to Julien's erratic perception of reality at the beginning of the expedition. The appearance of the stag might then be taken as an instance of a 'balance' between the psychological and the supernatural; in fact the stag does not actually appear at all—it is Julien who thinks that he can *hear* it:

> Il écoutait attentivement leurs deux râles presque égaux, et, à mesure qu'ils s'affaiblissaient, un autre, tout au loin, les continuait. Incertaine d'abord, cette voix plaintive longuement poussée, se rapprochait, s'enfla, devint cruelle; et il reconnut, terrifié, le bramement du grand cerf noir.

There is here at least the possibility of seeing the same exploitation on Flaubert's part of the gap between objective fact and subjective response as in the prophecies to the parents. Just as the parents really do see and hear *something,* which anyone would have heard and seen but which they perceive in a subjective way according to their mentality and situation, so here Julien really does hear something, namely the death-groan of his parents. We are free to suppose that it is only in Julien's mind that this 'becomes' the belling of of the stag through a hallucinatory association. The *point de départ* is as much a part of the world of facts as in the case of the prophecies, but it is from the world of objective fact that what appears to be supernatural does spring. Although the belling of the stag is described as long-drawn and piercing, when Julien's wife enters it is because 'le tapage du meurtre l'avait attirée'; the absence of any mention of the stag, even though this had followed the 'tapage du meurtre' which she *did* hear, suggests that it had never been there for anyone else to hear, since it had no reality outside the mind of Julien.

The unobtrusive use of Julien's viewpoint is apparent in the description of his wanderings in Part III:

> Il contemplait avec des élancements d'amour les

> poulains dans les herbages, les oiseaux dans leurs nids, les insectes sur les fleurs; tous, à son approche, couraient plus loin, se cachaient effarés, s'envolaient bien vite.

These lines could be taken to imply that Julien is now an outcast from the world of living things, and that the animals are providentially fated to flee from him; the episode would then be a further instance of the intervention of Providence in Julien's life. It should be noted, however, that the behaviour of the animals and birds is perfectly normal, since these creatures tend to be frightened away by *anybody* who approaches them, and it would therefore be surprising if they did *not* behave in this instinctive way with regard to Julien as well. Here in short it is Julien's guilty mind which reads a special meaning into ordinary facts: a process which recurs in the following paragraph:

> Il rechercha les solitudes. Mais le vent apportait à son oreille comme des râles d'agonie; les larmes de la rosée tombant par terre lui rappelaient d'autres gouttes d'un poids plus lourd. Le soleil, tous les soirs, étalait du sang dans les nuages.

It is plainly only to Julien that the wind would sound like a dying gasp, and the falling dew be reminiscent of drops of blood. Flaubert gives both the objective reality and Julien's subjective response to it, so that when we are told that the sun covered the clouds with blood each evening, it is clear that this reads only at first sight as if it were an objective statement by the author, but that it is in fact simply the special way in which Julien would see what to anyone else would be a perfectly ordinary sunset. In lines such as these, Flaubert gradually allows Julien's point of view to take over completely, but without of course actually saying that this is what he is doing. The same point could be made about a sentence which describes Julien's reaction to his crime:

> Il ne se révoltait pas contre Dieu qui lui avait infligé cette action, et pourtant se désespérait de l'avoir pu commettre.

[In *On Reading Flaubert* Margaret G. Tillett has] said that this single sentence contains 'volumes of thought and speculation', hinging on the paradox of a man feeling desperate remorse for a crime which had been inflicted on him by God. It might equally be argued that this sentence is not so much suggestive as marked by an inconsistency resulting from an uneasy marriage of the mediæval and the modern, the providential and the psychological. It could, however, be maintained more plausibly perhaps that the qualification 'qui lui avait infligé cette action' is no more than an expression of Julien's own very natural belief in a guiding Providence, since it is obvious that he would share the mediæval view of a God who intervenes in human life. This is indeed in line with what Julien had said to his wife shortly after the murder:

> Elle avait obéi à la volonté de Dieu, en occasionnant son crime . . .

which is plainly Julien's own view expressed in free indirect style and not a view to which Flaubert commits himself, any more than he commits himself to the view that 'Dieu [. . .] lui avait infligé cette action'.

Flaubert suggests in two ways that the final episode with the leper should be seen as an extreme form of hallucination on Julien's part. Firstly, he has now resolved to 'employer son existence au service des autres', and seeks to live according to the ideals of complete charity and total self-abnegation. The leper provides an opportunity for an act of self-sacrifice which could scarcely go further—an act the possibility of which is created by the saint's consuming urge to perform it, in a hallucinatory way. Secondly, and linked to this, we are told explicitly, just before the final episode, of hallucinations suffered by Julien, in which he sees scenes of his youth and then the murdered bodies of his parents, and this section ends with a reference to his falling habitually into 'un assoupissement où les visions funèbres continuaient'. The account of Julien's life as a hermit is reminiscent in one important respect of *La Tentation de saint Antoine*, where it is suggested that the extreme physical privations and hardships undergone by the saint may account at least in part for what in the final version of the work are presented as hallucinations and distorted perceptions of reality rather than more 'objectively' allegorical figures and events. Similarly in **"Saint Julien"** Flaubert is careful to lay stress on the extremely unpleasant conditions in which Julien lives as a hermit and which precede the final episode with the leper. The starting-point again consists in a gap between objective reality and what Julien takes to be real:

> Il tendit l'oreille et ne distingua que le mugissement des flots.

Anyone else would have heard only the sound of the river; but a man in Julien's physical and mental state might naturally take this for a voice, and this is the beginning of a subjective process which comes to displace completely the initial objective reality. In his study of the role of hallucination in Flaubert [in *French Studies,* (1956)], J. C. Lapp has shown how, in the case of the hallucinatory experiences of Charles and Emma, the subject retains a 'sensorial anchor to the real world'. In the case of Julien, the 'sensorial anchor' is present as the starting-point of a form of experience which in its dynamic development comes to displace the real world altogether: the sound of the river 'becomes' a voice, just as the death-gasp of the parents 'became' the belling of the stag. The process is akin to what Flaubert, drawing on his own experience, described to Taine as follows:

> ça commence par une seule image qui se développe et finit par couvrir la réalité objective.

The displacement of objective reality by a subjective image was something that Flaubert was familiar with from his own experiences of having hallucinations initially 'dans la tête' and then actually 'devant les yeux'. It is known that Flaubert deliberately exploited his own experience of hallucinations, since he felt that he had thereby come to know 'de curieux phénomènes psychologiques'. More immediately relevant is his claim:

> Tout ce qu'il y a dans sainte Thérèse, dans Hoffmann et dans Edgar Poe, je l'ai senti, je l'ai *vu,* les hallucinés me sont fort compréhensibles.

Flaubert might well have added Saint Anthony and Saint

Julian to his list of 'hallucinés', since he appears to have seen in both saints instances of the deformation of objective reality in an essentially hallucinatory way.

If it is the case, then, that for each supernatural event in **"Saint Julien"** there is left open the possibility of a rational explanation in terms of psychology (which may take the form of simple point of view or of actual hallucination) or physiology, one may conclude that the story is not so much an escape into the world of the Middle Ages but very much the work of a nineteenth-century rationalistic mind. **"Saint Julien"** presents not perhaps so much an 'amalgam' of the two idioms of the mediæval and the modern, as an invitation to the reader to keep these quite separate and to see in the 'mediæval' dimension a product of Flaubert's presentation of certain episodes in terms of the subjective viewpoint and understanding of the characters, while being always careful to allow the possibility of an explanation of the 'supernatural' along rational lines and of Julien's whole fate along psychological lines. This would not be very different from what Flaubert had already done in the final version of *La Tentation de saint Antoine;* and it would mean that the reader should be alive to [what R. J. Sherrington calls] the same 'contrast between reality as the reader knows it to be, and reality as the characters conceive it', as in *Madame Bovary* and *L'Education sentimentale.*

There is, however, one important difference in the degree of irony which accompanies the realization of this contrast: the conceptions of reality entertained by Emma and Frédéric are continually ironized, in that they spring from a refusal to see things as they are and depend ultimately on a more or less deliberately dishonest attitude to life. The irony in **"Saint Julien"** works in a much more neutral way, since the conflict is not between the private and self-regarding delusions of the hero and a wider reality within the work, but between two essentially different world-views: the mediæval with its belief in fate and the supernatural, the modern with its belief in rational explanation and moral responsibility. Frédéric's delusions are criticized as wilful and perverse; those of Julien, like those of his parents, are a natural expression of the collectively shared beliefs of the period in which he lives. The critical sense is here tempered by the historical sense, the 'sens historique', the discovery of which seemed to Flaubert to be one of the few redeeming features of the nineteenth century. It may be that in **"Saint Julien"** Flaubert has gone some way towards realizing the future programme of this historical sense as he defined it in 1859:

> Le *sens historique* est tout nouveau dans ce monde. On va se mettre à étudier les idées comme des faits, et à disséquer les croyances comme des organismes.

[A. W. Raitt writes that the] 'croyances' of mediæval men are presented 'historically' and naturally in the story, but Flaubert is careful to ensure that the reader is put into a position to be able to 'dissect' them sufficiently well to see the work as essentially 'a serious study of a man uncontrollably lusting for blood', and where fatality is exactly what it is in the novels—a matter of character and human agency. (pp. 266-75)

A. E. Pilkington, "Point of View in Flaubert's 'La Légende de Saint Julien'," in French Studies, *Vol. XXIX, No. 3, July, 1975, pp. 266-79.*

Flaubert on art and emotion:

The less you feel a thing, *the more capable you are of expressing it as it is* (as it *always* is, in itself, in its universality, freed from all ephemeral contingencies). But one must be able to *make oneself feel it.* This faculty is, simply, genius: the ability to *see,* to have the model posing there before you.

That is why I abhor rhetorical poetry, pompous poetry. To express things that are beyond words, a look is enough. Exhalations of the soul, lyricism, descriptions—I want all that to be in the *style.* Elsewhere, it is a prostitution of art and of feeling itself.

Gustave Flaubert, in a letter to Louise Colet, in The Letters of Gustave Flaubert: 1830-1857, *edited and translated by Frances Steegmuller, Belknap Press, 1980.*

William J. Beck (essay date 1977)

[In the following essay, Beck examines how Three Tales *reflects Flaubert's view of history.]*

Just as Julius Caesar had declared that all of Gaul was divided into three parts, so Flaubert was fond of saying that the history of the world comprised three stages. There is a neat parallel between this concept of world history and each of the tales in Flaubert's trilogy, **Trois Contes.** While this striking similarity has not been pointed out heretofore by critics, it may well be that Flaubert, perhaps only unconsciously, was illustrating his theory of the steady deterioration of western civilization by each of his short stories, **"La Légende de Saint Julien l'hospitalier," "Hérodias,"** and **"Un Coeur Simple."**

Most readers of Flaubert are familiar with his personal identification with Saint Polycarp. For many years, he had the habit of referring to himself as the reincarnation of this Saint, who had been a bishop of Smyrna, early in the Christian era. What appealed particularly to Flaubert was the Saint's reiterated exclamation, "My God, my God, what a century you have placed me in." Often, "century" was changed to "country" depending on which dimension, time or place, was particularly more oppressive to Flaubert at the moment. In any event, the author, like Saint Polycarp, felt that he too had been born at the wrong time, and toward the end of his life, this sentiment became increasingly unbearable. Splenetic by temperament, Flaubert became more and more irritated with his personal situation, not solely because he was becoming old and ill, because his closest friends were dying one by one, and because his financial situation was precarious, but principally because of the defeat of France at the hands of the Germans, coupled with the fall of Louis Napoleon and the advent of the Commune. Added to all of this was the pain of the realization that he was fated to live in the most bourgeois of times, with all ideals and values, particularly in the arts, on the sharp decline, or even nonexistent.

Perhaps less familiar to Flaubert's readers is his observation that the history of western civilization consisted of three stages, *paganisme, christianisme, muflisme.* While his characterizations of antiquity and of the Middle Ages are acceptably innocuous or unprovocative, his term for the modern period is acerbic and not readily translatable for the uninitiated. "Mufle" means simply an animal's muzzle or snout; as slang, however, it refers to a disagreeable or crude person, in popular parlance, a louse or a stinker. "Muflisme," therefore, is Flaubert's description of his contemporary period, the epitome of boorishness, utilitarian, bourgeois, and without ideals.

It is noteworthy that Flaubert's historical delineations are also accurate one-word descriptions of each of his three tales, and the reader cannot help but be persuaded that this parallel has more significance than mere coincidence. **"Hérodias,"** the last written of his stories, is perhaps the least disconnected and the most rapidly moving of the **Three Tales.** More important, however, it was a milieu, a subject, and a period that for a long time had fascinated Flaubert. Essentially an archeological description of Judeo-Roman society just prior to the advent of Christ, **"Hérodias"** is filled with the color, the movement, the sultry climate, and the sensuality of the pre-Christian era. While it is true that the story seemingly prepares the reader for a religious theme, Flaubert himself declared in a letter to a friend that the tale " . . . n'a aucun rapport avec la religion." The theme, the action, and the background are thoroughly pagan, and the entire story is a perfect exemplification of what was surely Flaubert's favorite time in world history, the period of *paganisme.*

In **"La Légende de saint Julien l'hospitalier,"** Flaubert evokes another exotic world of the past, the Middle Ages. Once again, the odor, color, and violent passions of a bygone era come to life, but the sobering note of the Christian message is emphasized. The earliest and perhaps the most conventional of the three tales, **"Saint Julien"** is transitional, since initially the hero seems to have his roots in the pagan world. Early in his life he comports himself in a rash and brutal manner, enough to remind the reader of the ambience of **"Hérodias."** This pagan sinner, however, eventually becomes a saint, and his story can be found eternalized in the stained glass window in the Rouen Cathedral. With its rich decorations, its religious symbolism, and its varied bestiary, the tale resembles a medieval tapestry, the entire work evoking an idealized medieval society, patriarchal, chivalrous, supernatural, the consummate illustration of *christianisme.*

Speaking of **"Un Coeur Simple,"** Flaubert wrote in a letter to Mme Roger des Genettes, "Cela n'est nullement ironique comme vous le supposez . . . " The fundamental meaning of the tale is to be derived in large measure from the tone of tenderness and compassion that is all-pervasive; to deny the genuiness of this mood would be a serious misreading of the story. Indeed, Flaubert has given the sympathetic account of a saintly person, of an uncomplaining figure who has surpassed all earthly suffering through humility and love. His representation of Félicité, the bourgeois saint, is not itself ironic; we have the novelist's assurance for this and we know that he was sincere.

Notwithstanding Flaubert's sympathy for Félicité, indeed, several critics have gone so far as to see his personal identification with her, there is in fact an ironic dimension in the short story. The tale is Flaubert's satiric comment on the reduced possibility for heroic actions in his contemporary society. The character of Félicité is an illustration of the impossibility of the exotic, Flaubert's artistic expression of his utter disdain for the modern world, in which there is very little color or ideals, much boredom and monotony, a world of quiet abnegation and of little risk. Félicité herself, however, is clearly not the object of Flaubert's antipathy; toward her he feels only tenderness and sympathy. How diminished, however, how colorless is Félicité's world when compared to the grandeur and even to the nobility of the pagan and Christian eras! Her world and times, and indeed Flaubert's, are a period of abject *muflisme*.

While it is true that these three tales were written in the following order: **"Saint Julien," "Un Coeur Simple,"** and **"Hérodias,"** it is significant that when they were first published in 1877, in Paris, by Georges Charpentier, the new order was **"Un Coeur Simple," "Saint Julien,"** and **"Hérodias."** Although the reader would have expected the publication to follow either the sequence in which they were written or, perhaps more logically, the historical order from ancient to modern, Flaubert chose otherwise. Always oriented toward the ideal, the novelist, in *Trois Contes,* flees backward in time from his bourgeois present, peregrinates through the Middle Anges, and finally sauntering through antiquity, is able to enjoy the delights of the epitome of civilization, the pagan latin world. Earlier, Flaubert had declared on a number of occasions that his contemporary period of *muflisme* would witness " . . . la fin du monde latin," and to him this would be the final destruction of a civilization which had been long in dying.

Trois Contes symbolizes the esthetic, and perhaps the religious, inner conflict of Gustave Flaubert. During most of his life, while he harbored a hatred for the bourgeoisie, the idealist in him yearned for past epochs, for more exotic eras and civilizations. Flaubert's mortal enemy was the times, which he characterized as a 'barbarie" and a "reculade," and in which, he declared, "il est désagréable de se trouver . . . ," because . . . "toute délicatesse d'esprit sera impossible." Contemporary man, Flaubert felt, had a morbid desire to flee from the narrowness of daily living and from the monotony of modern industrial civilization.

One method of deliverance from the age of *muflisme* is by self-abnegation, by a complete withdrawal from the crassness of modern society. This was the route chosen by Félicité, whose final years resembled strikingly those of Flaubert. In the pursuit of dreams and ideals, however, the best escape from reality, from the ennui of bourgeois existence, is via a pilgrimage, whether real or imaginary, into exotic climes, into heroic epochs of the past. As is demonstrated by his almost religious pursuit of the mystique of Art, by his devotion to the past, and by his successive journeys into the beyond, the latter route, it is clear, was chosen by

the monk of Croisset. *Muflisme, christianisme, paganisme.* (pp. 74-8)

William J. Beck, "Flaubert's Tripartite Concept of History and 'Trois Contes'," in CLA Journal, *Vol. XXI, No. 1, September, 1977, pp. 74-8.*

Leyla Perrone-Moisés   (essay date 1980)

[*In the following essay, Perrone-Moisés analyzes one of Flaubert's early short stories, "Quidquid voleuris," from a "nonevolutionist" approach, comparing it to Flaubert's later works.*]

The signs of a future perfection are often looked for in Flaubert's juvenilia. Using the works of his mature years as the model and telos, the imperfections in his early works have been disclosed and pardoned, and only that which sheds light on the great works to come has been valorized. According to this evolutionist reasoning, in **"Rêve d'enfer"** (1837) Flaubert reveals his promise and talent, in **"Mémoires d'un fou"** (1838) he is doing better, with **"Novembre"** (1842) he has progressed further, and so on. In literature, as in life, the adolescent must be surpassed by the mature man, the apprentice must give way to the master; it is all a question of education, whether sentimental or stylistic.

In this way the works of the adolescent Flaubert have been seen as rough outlines in which we can read the precursive signs of his geniality and of his neuroses. In his early works critics have noted Flaubert's first literary influences and the traces of his first traumas; in them they have observed imperfections of style and composition— exaggeration, repetition, a declamatory tone, a lack of taste and proportion—and have attributed these to the immaturity of his character. All of this is progressively rectified; and if the critics are not in agreement when it comes to the "first important work" by Flaubert, they all agree that in 1857 his education was complete.

Meanwhile, in spite of their assertion of Flaubert's evolution, numerous critics have arrived at the conclusion that he never changed. Flaubert always takes up the same subjects, often the same scenes, the same comparisons. The temptations are never overcome, the educations are never finished; the *garçon* survives, aged and incorrigible, in Bouvard and Pécuchet. Thus the work of Flaubert is the perfect place to study at once evolution and permanence. Already in 1909 [in his *Flaubert: Sa vie, son caractère et ses idees avant 1857*], René Descharmes sees in the juvenilia "the seeds of his future masterpieces." In following the evolution of the young Flaubert, he says, "I watched a transformation of his character and of his aesthetic . . . but at the same time I found throughout the survival of primitive tendencies."

That Flaubert could have developed over the years and that nonetheless he could have remained always the same is not an inextricable paradox. It is what happens to most writers, to most people. What is particularly interesting in Flaubert's case is that he could have changed in such a radical, voluntary manner and at the same time could have stayed so thoroughly and obsessively the same to the end.

What I propose to do here is to look at one work from Flaubert's juvenilia from a nonevolutionist point of view; to highlight in it what is not only *already* but *always* there, to expose not only that which is to endure but also that which was silenced, that which was killed in Flaubert so that the great works could be written. This silence and this death, which are the basis for the evolution of Flaubert, command our attention, not because they came to fruition, but, on the contrary, because they were never perfected: the howling remains audible over the measured thoughts and phrases, the corpse has always been the active fertilizer of their flowering. I propose to examine this other Flaubert, the adolescent, not as the potential, yet imperfect one, but as a writer already mature after a fashion.

"Quidquid volueris," the psychological tale written in 1837, has always been seen by the critics as an adolescent's extravagance. Even after 1931, when D. L. Demorest showed the richness and the subtlety of the images in this tale, the last two decades of criticism have turned a deaf ear to the poetic *gueuloir* of the adolescent Flaubert. This text has been used as a document of biographic interest; it has been analyzed as a failure. It has been consigned to romantic sources, easily interpreted by psychoanalysis, accused of referential or stylistic unseemliness; in it the critics have seen, each in his turn, *lacks* or *excesses*.

Djalioh, the sentimentally ineducable ape-man, first monster of the temptation of Saint Flaubert, shrieks like a hysterical woman. It has been said that he shrieks too much to be taken seriously, and rightly so. The defenders of style do not like hyperbole. **"Quidquid volueris"** is thus nothing but a curiosity, the flawed beginnings of the extremely educated prose to come or the first sign of a neurosis which was to evolve also.

If, on the contrary, one were to read this tale outside the evolutionist perspective, Djalioh might be understood differently. Let us for a moment take ourselves out of the context of Flaubert's great repertory, by asking a hypothetical question: if Flaubert had died young, like a Lautréamont, would a work like **"Quidquid volueris"** still be readable? And how?

Djalioh, the hero of this ultra-Romantic short story is not a René or an Adolphe, nor is he a Quasimodo, while he owes more than one trait to all of them. René and Adolphe are socially inept characters who ask themselves psychological questions and answer with metaphysical ones. Quasimodo's maladjustment is accentuated more strongly, but this "monster" is still an error of human genetics. Djalioh is a complete mistake, an aberration, the impossible: the ape-man, son of an orangutan and a black woman.

The ape-man comes from a much vaster mythology than the personal phantasms of our young romantic author. While the subject is fascinating and has been the object of numerous studies, I am going to concentrate here on only a few. According to André Leroi-Gourhan [in his *Legeste et la parole: Technique et largage*], this myth, common to several prescientific peoples, is the result of a spatial merger, the result of an ethnocentric point of view: "The presci-entific thinker considers as an essential people those who constitute his ethnic nucleus, beyond which, in increasingly distant aureoles, less human beings appear with stranger and stranger hybrids."

Among the hybrids imagined by man, the ape-man is one of the most constant and most perturbing, in so much as it represents the limit between the fantastic and the probable. In our culture this being appears among the monsters of medieval architecture and in the navigational maps of the fifteenth and sixteenth centuries. These maps confirm the ethnocentrism noted by contemporary anthropology: the unknown seas were inhabited by hybrid peoples, less and less human the further one got from Europe. The more recent discovery of the great apes in Africa and Asia seemed to confirm at least one of the medieval fantasies; to the eyes of the travelers, these apes were hardly more shocking than the American Indians, and if they admitted the humanity of these beings, then they could easily speculate about the humanity of the animals as well.

By the eighteenth century, in the West, the myth of the ape-man was fixed as a possibility which should be examined by science. [Jean-Jacques] Rousseau discusses this question at length in the tenth note of his *Discours sur l'inégalité* and shows himself strongly inclined to admit the humanity of the great apes:

> All of these observations about the variety that thousands of causes can produce, and have, in fact, produced in the human species, make me doubt whether various animals that resemble men—taken by travelers for beasts through a lack of investigation or because of some differences which they noticed in their exterior conformation, or only because the animals did not speak—are not in effect veritable savage peoples, a race dispersed long ago in the woods, that has not had the occasion to develop any of its faculties, has not attained any degree of perfection, and which finds itself still in the primitive state of nature.

By the nineteenth century the discovery of prehistoric remains, such as those of the Grotto of Engis in 1833, had suggested other similarities between men and apes. These fossils were still anthropologically illegible, but they invited a more disturbing reading than the previous spatial one. It is not until 1859, some twenty years after Flaubert's tale, that Darwin cleared up this mystery with his theory of evolution, which met with no small resistance. Meanwhile, the phantasmatic force of myth continues to exert itself alongside science. The myth of the ape-man has persisted to this day, passing through Tarzan (whose animal side, as Leroi-Gourhan observes, is assumed by his companion Cheeta), it is reincarnated in King Kong and the inhabitants of the *Planet of the Apes*.

Flaubert's character appeared at this time of uncertainty, when the presence of the animal in man was beginning to be suspected, no longer as the symbolic existence of evil in a foreign body, but as an essential coexistence. At the time of **"Quidquid volueris,"** large monkeys were first exhibited at European fairs and circuses, provoking extravagant commentary in the press. While the human appearance of the apes was shocking people, interest grew in cases of the reverse like Victor de l'Aveyron and Kasper Hauser.

Flaubert, like Rousseau, is firmly on the side of the apes. The narrator of **"Quidquid volueris"** puts all of his sympathies in the character of Djalioh, with whom he identifies. "That which is best in me is poetry, is the beast," Flaubert will say later. Opposed to the narrator are the "civilized men" of the tale, who, in an exemplary incarnation of the ethnocentric attitude, make fun of Djalioh. The monster comes from far away; he is born in Brazil. What is more, he is born of an inferior, ethnically and socially: his mother is black and a slave, "a silly little Negro woman," according to Paul de Monville, the tale's civilized character. This relation to the other, whom one would like to keep totally distinct but whom one finds to be a part of oneself, raises the whole question of racism. Thrice removed from men by his foreign, animal, and black origins, Djalioh is kept at a distance by this society. Paul de Monville and his friends test the ape-man by their criteria for humanity and conclude, relieved, that "it is an inert animal without intelligence." What are these criteria of humanity?

Whereas contemporary anthropologists define mankind by its vertical posture, the presence of a shortened face, freedom of the hands during locomotion, and the use of interchangeable tools, in M. Paul's circle the conditions for humanity are as follows: the ability to smoke cigarettes, to hunt, work, read, write, and to love horses and women. Now since Djalioh does not satisfy these conditions, they can affirm that "decidedly he is an idiot." M. Paul and his friends' ethnocentrism is even more deeply rooted than that of the prescientific peoples: their criteria for humanity came from the habits of an extremely closed circle inside a given social group.

Like Rousseau, who ends his note on the apes by remarking on the almost inhuman stupidity of the observers who described them, Flaubert emphasizes the brutishness of men in relation to Djalioh. As we all know, the sympathy of the Romantics for primitives and savages is proportional to their aversion to a society in which their aspirations were unrealizable. For Flaubert, and like Flaubert, Djalioh is the antibourgeois par excellence.

Gustave was the idiot of the family, Flaubert was the idiot of the salons, according to Théophile Gautier. As an adolescent he felt like an ape: wild, clumsy, he managed poorly with language; in short, he was monstrous. **"Quidquid volueris"** is thus the story of an ape told by another ape. Even the subject of the tale is that of a failed education. Raised by the Frenchman who is his adoptive father, Djalioh ends up by raping and killing this man's wife, after having murdered his child and before eliminating himself. Djalioh is not a "noble savage." His sentimental education will have been a resounding failure. The amorous initiation proves to be radically antisocial: instead of an apprenticeship, we witness a rite of passage so bloody that the hero dies from it. The subjective is revealed here as not assimilable to the social: Djalioh, the excessive individual, must die so that society can continue to live by its preconceived ideas. The adolescent's social and sexual conflict is resolved through the elimination of his alterity.

The evolutionary side of the question is what interests us here: the fact that this backward little boy *became* a great writer, the fact that this child was *transformed* into a master of style. It is about this that we marvel ceaselessly, just as we are unendingly moved by the fact that a species of monkey could become the human wonder that we are. As Jacques Lacan puts it [in *Ecrits* (1960)], "It is not because of Darwin that people think themselves any less on the top of the heap of creatures, since that is precisely what he convinces us of."

Two questions are then worth asking: At what price this evolution for Flaubert? And, what do we eliminate, we critics, in order to maintain this vision of an evolving Flaubert, who progressively corrected the excesses (faults) of his juvenilia to arrive at the perfection of *Madame Bovary?*

By approaching the savage discourse of **"Quidquid volueris"** like salon critics, we react to the young Flaubert like M. Paul's friends confronted with Djalioh: according to the criteria of (Jean de la Varende in *Flaubert par lvi-même*] . . . we will be surprised by certain "invocatory exaggerations, certain religious obsecrations," by "the excessive romanticism of comparisons," we will ask that "the plot remain full and sustained," and we will perhaps conclude like Anatole France, who says of Flaubert: "That man who had the secret of infinite words was not intelligent." We will wait for him to evolve in order to recognize in him a master of literature, underestimating the adolescent-ape-writer on behalf of the mature civilized writer.

Djalioh is aphasic, but he has verbal and even oratorical thoughts, organized according to grammatical rules and decorated by rhetorical ornaments. Of all the implausibilities in the tale, this is certainly among the least implausible, and like all the rest it requires no explication.

Nevertheless, Djalioh's aphasia is psychoanalytically plausible. I am not invoking a clinical psychoanalysis of Flaubert the man, but a general psychoanalytic knowledge which this text, like all great literary works, possesses and makes explicit. Djalioh does not speak, because he lacks an *imago.* His relation to his own image is blocked, he does not arrive at a spatial auto-identification which would facilitate his access to language. When he looks at people, he does not see himself in them: they seem too animallike, a fact which the narrator ceaselessly emphasizes throughout the ball sequence. On this occasion, Djalioh appears extremely civilized in his sullen reserve, in contrast to the beelike women who "buzz," the carp-men who "jump about," and the couples who "gallop."

On the other hand, when he looks at Madame de Lansac's monkeys, he feels "drawn toward them by a strange sympathy." But here also, there is an irreducible difference: the monkeys look too much like people, they act like "kings," "lawyers," "women of pleasure." Faced with his half-brothers and sisters, Djalioh awaits an impossible "birth," immobilized in the fetal position, that of the newborn before speech: "seated on the ground, his knees drawn up to his head, his arms on his legs, and his half-dead eyes fixed on a single spot."

M. Paul tells us that when he had taken Djalioh to a brothel, he fled carrying a "rose and a mirror." Placed in a sexual situation, Djalioh reveals his double nature. As an animal, his sexual instinct is a need, which, like all needs, can be satisfied. As a man, Djalioh invests this instinct with desire which, as we know, is by definition without object and thus doomed to frustration. His escape from the brothel is due to his inability to decide between need and desire. At the first level of interpretation, rose and mirror correspond to nature and culture. But a subtle network of associations which runs throughout the tale invites us to read many other things: in the rose, woman, inaccessible but perishable; in the mirror, the lure of identity, vanity, which in this tale is mainly masculine. In the final scene of the tale flowers and mirrors are again present. The frustration of the animal, thwarted in his need, leads him to kill; that of the man frustrated in his desire leads him to kill himself. On the symbolic level the rose is crushed and the mirror is broken. Suicide is the definitive proof of Djalioh's humanity.

During the whole tale Djalioh never looks at himself in a mirror; his aspiration for an *imago* remains unsatisfied. The mirror is the attribute of humans: M. Paul "looks at himself in the mirror" and finds himself handsome; Adèle (his wife), in the last sequence of the story, "seeing herself nude in the mirror in the arms of Djalioh, let out a scream of horror and prayed to God." Djalioh, seen in the mirror, concretizes the specular fascination that the ape holds for mankind.

Djalioh remains at an intermediary stage between the absence and presence of an *imago,* between need and desire. He remains on the verge of speech, and he very nearly speaks at his most human moments, which are his moments of desire. It is for this reason that the simple opposition between nature and culture, evoked by several critics, is not sufficient here. At the moment of Paul and Adèle's marriage, "his fat lips, cracked by fever, and covered with pimples, moved actively like someone speaking fast"; and the moment he approaches the young woman: "Djalioh did not answer; he only stammered and hit his head in anger." According to Lacan, "The moment when desire is humanized is also the moment when the child is born to language." Djalioh remains on the edge of desire, of language, of humanity. Deprived of speech and humanity, he is at the same time preserved from the social indignity of men, and he possesses that language of the heart which the Romantics dreamed of; he expresses himself by purer means than verbal language, as, for example, in the strange music that he draws from the violin.

For Djalioh every being is the irreducible other: half identified with people, half identified with apes, he cannot but desire, in distress and aphasia, this mixture of identity and alterity which he discerns in the other.

For M. Paul, the other is Djalioh. This "son" produced by "unusual means" is the perverse result of his white man's desire. Paul bought Djalioh's father, the orangutan Bell, from a black; with this ape as intermediary he impregnates a black woman. Paul's virility and paternity pass through the relay of the animal and the black race. The birth of Djalioh, he says, filled him with joy, an ambiguous joy which resembles that of a father but which is

given a scientific alibi (as a successful experiment): "I was certainly very happy, the question was resolved." Perhaps the real question resolved here is that of his virility.

Not only does Paul see his virility confirmed by the production of a child, but this exploit also gets him a supplementary penis: the Cross of Honor, awarded by the Institute of Sciences. Of this cross, he says to his friends: "It pleases women; they look at it smilingly when you talk to them." The impregnation of a black woman by an ape bought from a black is for Paul the realization of a racist phantasm: "In the wildness of our *jouissance,*" says Lacan on the subject of racism [in *Télévision*] "there is nothing but the Other that situates it, but only in so much as we are separated from it."

Djalioh's very name marks this distance, this alterity: "That? That's Djalioh." "What is Djalioh?" "Oh! It's a long story." J. Piaget Shanks observed that Esmeralda's goat in *Notre-Dame de Paris* is called Djali, as is Emma Bovary's greyhound. All one has to do is to add to the name Djali the exclamation "Oh!" as Flaubert emphasizes in this dialogue, to obtain the shocking name, the name of the monster. Djalioh is born "in Janeiro." This designation of the city of Rio de Janeiro by its last word, contrary to French and Portuguese usages, must be due to the homophony of Djalioh-Janeiro, which associates the two words in the same linguistic oddity. Even by its phonetics this name designates someone who is radically foreign.

The essence of the other is topographic: everyone is the other of his or her other, it is a question of one's point of view. In this way Djalioh is a monster for Paul and his friends, and the handsome Paul is a monster for the black woman who rejected him: "The stupid thing never wanted me; she probably found me uglier than a savage." Flaubert himself voluntarily hesitates: "Here is the monstrous aberration of nature who was in contact with M. Paul, that other monster, or, rather, that wonder of civilization who had all the right symbols: grandeur of spirit and hardness of heart."

Remember that Djalioh's father was named Bell and "that it was the most handsome [*bel*] orangutan ever." By naming and designating it in this way the narrator makes fun of Paul, the handsome (*bel*) man, "who was conceited enough to believe that all the women were in love with him." A subtle reversal of esthetic categories is under way here, unsettling the ethnic hierarchy at the same time.

If Djalioh, animal and black, is M. Paul's other, for Djalioh and for M. Paul, as males, the other is Adèle. Woman simultaneously awakens in them sexual desire and the death instinct that accompanies the consciousness of the other. For the narrator, himself male, woman is that attractive and repellent other, fixed in the vegetative metaphor, throughout the whole story: woman as a wilted flower, always close to decomposition, a metaphor that achieves two objectives at once: it dehumanizes woman by giving her another nature and then kills her. Woman is at one time a flower, at another she is an animal (bee, mare), but most frequently she is a thing. M. Paul includes her in his inventory among his furniture, paintings, and property, and she imagines herself as "a Lady, that is to say, something which bears a big shawl and walks alone in the streets."

The tale also poses the question of the otherness of childhood. As a backward adolescent, Djalioh is in the way of the adults. "Stop it, little monster!" the adult says to the child. Flaubert, himself having matured and progressed beyond literary aphasia, represses the little monster that he was; and we, the others, the readers, regard his juvenile compositions with an adult condescension.

For the narrator and the reader, Djalioh, as an ape, is the closest other to a person, equipped with all the attractions that derive from this resemblance-difference: "I never liked apes, says the young Flaubert, but perhaps that's wrong because they seem to me a perfect imitation of human nature. When I see one of these animals—I'm not speaking here of people—I think I am seeing myself in a magnifying mirror." It is not by chance that Lacan's text about the mirror stage [in *Ecríts*] is full of references to apes: "an operation which, though carried out within nose-shot, so to speak, would be almost the quality of this *aha!* which enlightens us about the chimpanzee's intelligence, amazed as we are to sense this miracle on the face of our equals, it does not fail to bring about a deplorable result."

In the end, Djalioh's alterity is seen as demonic. As a "demon," Djalioh is the other "within" us. "What in those days," writes Freud, "were thought to be evil spirits to us are base and evil wishes, the derivatives of impulses which have been rejected and repressed. In one respect only do we not subscribe to the explanation of these phenomena current in medieval times; we have abandoned the projection of them into the outer world, attributing their origin instead to the inner life of the patient in whom they manifest themselves."

The way the name *Djalioh* is introduced into the text is enlightening about his nature as creature of the psyche. At the start of the tale, the narrator presents three characters—Paul, Adèle, and her mother Madame de Lansac—when suddenly at the tail end of a paragraph, this strange name jumps out like a jack in a box: "Madame de Lansac left to give some orders for the next day and to close all the doors, to lock all the locks, leaving only Paul and Djalioh." Appearing so soon after the locking of the locks, this name, in a sense, enters by the keyhole, like the little devils (Diablotins) of the prologue: "Come to me dreams of a poor fool! Come one and all, my good friends the Diablotins. . . . Come one and all, children of my brain, give me for a moment one of your follies, one of your strange laughs. . . . You will arrive by my keyhole."

To the questions already asked, let me add one last one: by eliminating this young, diabolical, crazy, excessive Flaubert for the sake of a more civilized Flaubert, are we not, in effect, exorcising some of our very own literary demons? In the name of a certain civilized image that we have of literature, we refuse its savage and impure manifestations.

"I am an old raving romantic," Flaubert tells Sainte-Beuve and the critics of the future. We all know that Djalioh, like Madame Bovary, is Flaubert himself. But the didactic simplification of the Romantic disciplined by realism persists till the end. It must be said that not only was Flaubert always a Romantic, as everyone knows, but also that he was *never* a naïve Romantic, a dyed-in-the-wool Romantic.

Flaubert was Romantic to the end, but prematurely, precociously, he belonged to that species of Romantics which was rotten from the start, perhaps even the most radical among the Romantics, gnawed at by irony to such a degree that their Romanticism begins at a point beyond Romanticism itself. Like Lautréamont, and thirty years before him, Flaubert felt, beginning with **"Quidquid volueris"** that Romanticism was not viable, that "literature" was no longer viable; their works are at the same time the death and the funereal celebration of literature in its last glorious form. Disappointment, regret, and derisive laughter are already there, from the start and forever.

The kinship between the young Flaubert and Lautréamont becomes apparent in the reaction of the critics. What has been said about **"Quidquid volueris"** is what has been said for a long time about *Les Chants de Maldoror:* that it is exaggerated ("I exaggerated a little," Ducasse admits with false modesty in a letter), insane, in bad taste, spottily successful, ends badly, too much like oratory, melodramatic, unbelievable, and so on.

The parallel can be extended even further. Lautréamont went from the *roman noir* to the *platitudes* of the *Poésies.* Flaubert also begins with the *roman noir* and ends up with *Bouvard et Pécuchet.* In the interval, however, he was the author of masterpieces. Imagine for a moment that we bypassed this great interlude and we read Flaubert like Lautréamont, detecting in his work the sudden change, the replacement of the wild Romantic by the caricaturist implicated in *bêtise,* without the possibility of assimilation and without the indication of a resolution to the literary crisis or the general crisis.

"Quidquid volueris" and *Bouvard et Pécuchet,* when thought of as the two key chronological points in Flaubert's work, are not assimilable on the level of plot or on the level of style: they are unbelievable stories, enunciated in an uncertain tone for the listener, who does not know how to hear them. These two works do not permit us to speak *reasonably* of them, except if we regard the first as a rough outline and the second as a long shot. The first is too much (hyperbole), the second is too little (platitude); nothing can be said about them if we remain attached to traditional literary categories, because the first will bog down our discourse in its pathetic eloquence, and the last, as Flaubert hoped, will lead us into the quicksand of generalized *bêtise.* This is exactly like *Les Chants de Maldoror* and the *Poésies.* What Flaubert and Lautréamont are saying is this: "Since it is insane to be Djalioh / Maldoror, I will be "sane" and "scientific" like M. Homais or the school manuals." Evidently, however, Bouvard and Pécuchet, like Ducasse in *Poésies,* finally prove to be the subverters of reason and science. Ineducable, in short.

The narrator's discourse in **"Quidquid volueris,"** like Count Lautréamont's, already shows the traces of the wound from which literature suffers, through the introduction of self-criticism and differences in level of the enunciation:

> . . . the moon, through the tall elms, shown limpid and calm across their interconnecting branches. Again the moon! Of course, she must necessarily play a big role, it is the sine qua non of any gloomy work, like the rattling of teeth and bristling of hair; but, anyway, that day there was a moon. Why take her away from me, my poor moon? Oh! my moon, I love you! You shine well on the steep roof of the château, of the lake you make a wide belt of silver, and in your pale glimmer each drop of rainwater that falls, I say each drop, suspended from the edge of a rose leaf, seems a pearl on a beautiful woman's breast. This is old enough! But let's stop there and come back to the subject at hand.

In the same way as Lautréamont, young Flaubert subverts his own romantic style; he lets himself slip into comparisons and shows that the word *like* can engender an automatic and infinite discourse: "His soul took to what was beautiful and sublime, like ivy to debris, flowers to springtime, the tomb to the corpse, and unhappiness to people."

The Romantic is assassinated by the most exacerbated of the Romantics, on the level of the story (*récit*), and on the level of discourse (*discours*). The character of Djalioh dies at the end of the story, and his internal discourse, of an inspired lyricism, is definitively recuperated by the discourse of the grocers who comment on the action on the last page of the tale. The grocers' discourse prevails over that of the ape-man, just as that of Homais is to prevail over that of Emma, at the end of *Madame Bovary*. Is not Homais the perfect example of a Homo sapiens, he who believes in evolution and progress? "Fabricando fiat faber, age quod agis," cites Homais.

Djalioh disappears, but in Flaubert's later works the traces of this murder remain visible. While M. Paul continues his social life and the fresh young Adèle is transformed into stinking carrion, Djalioh is assigned a special fate: he is, in a certain sense, immortalized: "Oh! He is superb, varnished, polished, well groomed, magnificent, since, as you know, the zoological society took possession of him and has made him into a fine skeleton."

Like Djalioh, the Romantic will remain fossilized in the archeological strata of the Flaubert domain. The Goncourts understood it well, when they said to their friend: "He's a man with something that's been killed underneath." "With me nothing has been erased," Flaubert himself confirmed in a letter to Louise Colet. Djalioh's skeleton has its symbolic counterpart in the stuffed parrot which Flaubert kept on his table. They are the two trophies of this suicidal hunt, lyricism and eloquence reduced to the condition of fetishes. The ape and the parrot are complementary: the one appears human but is without a voice, the other has the voice without the appearance. They are both exotic, both Brazilian (the parrot is from the Amazon) and, as such, they commemorate the loss of a paradise where the heart spoke its true language.

In the process of repression, the corpse does not disappear: "As for the memory of Rodolphe, it had descended to the very bottom of her heart, and there it remained, more solemn and immobile than a king's mummy in a crypt." All one has to do, in this extract from *Madame Bovary,* is replace Rodolphe with Djalioh, and Emma with Flaubert to give **"Quidquid volueris"** its proper place in the monument that is Flaubert's oeuvre.

Flaubert keeps on killing Djalioh, and the paradox is the same as that which produced *Maldoror-Poésies*. What his age offered him as the antidote to madness, as the alternative to delirium, was *bêtise*. And, with Flaubert's pen, *bêtise* itself goes mad, the remedy becomes poison, and his submission to the grocers' discourse becomes the sharpest form of revolt: Romanticism is triumphant and agonizing in its own denial and derision.

A great author's early works are not only the beginning and the source; since, if there is such a thing as stylistic progress, writing (*l'écriture*) knows no progress, it is nothing but change spiraling around the same. The ape-man is not only the idiot who will be surpassed by the masterful writer; Romanticism is not merely a movement that is supplanted by another; barbarism, clichés, *bêtise* are not the others of literature, but integrate its very matter; the Other is not the only beast, and we cannot rid ourselves of it unless we abstain from desire.

Writing feeds on the dead zones of individuality and on the debris of that superb mummy, literature. (pp. 139-53)

Leyla Perrone-Moisés, " 'Quidquid volueris': The Scriptural Education," translated by Robert Riger, in Flaubert and Postmodernism, *edited by Naomi Schor and Henry F. Majewski, University of Nebraska Press, 1984, pp. 139-59.*

Flaubert on objectivity:

An author in his book must be like God in the universe, present everywhere and visible nowhere. Art being a second Nature, the creator of that Nature must behave similarly. In all its atoms, in all its aspects, let there be sensed a hidden, infinite impassivity. The effect for the spectator must be a kind of amazement. "How is all that done?" one must ask; and one must feel overwhelmed without knowing why.

Gustave Flaubert, in a letter to Louise Colet, in The Letters of Gustave Flaubert: 1830-1857, *edited and translated by Frances Steegmuller, Belknap Press, 1980.*

Susan Cauley Selvin (essay date 1983)

[*In the following excerpt, Selvin examines Flaubert's use of spatial form in* Three Tales.]

Flaubert came late to the genre of the short story—turning from the novel to this form only near the end of his career in 1875—and undertook the project of his *Trois Contes* as a source of recreation and consolation during the difficult period of the composition of *Bouvard et l'écuchet.* Yet even in these tales, written primarily "to pass the time and to see if I can still write a sentence—which I doubt," Flaubert maintained his innovative approach to literary form and, indeed, perfected narrative techniques with which he had experimented in the novel. *Trois Contes* presents a striking departure from the established narrative code of the short story. Traditionally, this form relied heavily on temporal motifs, on the linear succession of events in a pattern of cause and effect, in order to recount the unfolding of a dramatic anecdote; emphasis was placed on plot and the development in time of a central suspenseful action. Flaubert, however, abandons this anecdotal linear narrative; the flow of time in *Trois Contes* is subordinated to the creation of an overall impression or tableau which emerges from the inherently spatial plan of the text.

It has often been noted that Flaubert's late works depart from the traditional temporal scheme of nineteenth century narrative; Georges Poulet, in *Les Métamorphoses du cercle,* contends that while other novelists "se contentaient de suivre le héros, d'action en action, le long de sa ligne temporelle. . . . Flaubert est le premier qui, abandonnant cette conception unilinéaire ou monocentrique, construise son roman comme une série de foyers à partir desquels, en avant, en arrière, de tous côtés, il y a un déploiement et un rayonnement à la fois temporel et spatial." Critical discussions like Poulet's tend to emphasize Flaubert's stylistic innovation in the novel without seriously considering the ostensibly casual texts of *Trois Contes.* Yet it is precisely in these short tales that Flaubert achieves the fullest expression of a formal technique which had developed throughout his career as a novelist; in *Trois Contes,* Flaubert arrives at what Joseph Frank has called "spatial form" in literature. A brief summary of Frank's ideas will serve as a vehicle for discussion of Flaubert's innovative technique in *Trois Contes.*

Joseph Frank characterizes the concept of spatial form in literature as a modern rejection of classical aesthetic principles such as those defined in the eighteenth century by Lessing's *Laokoon.* Lessing systematically formulated the distinction between painting and poetry in terms of the spatial or temporal elements proper to each medium. "Form in the plastic arts, according to Lessing, is necessarily spatial, because the visible aspect of objects can best be presented juxtaposed in an instant of time. Literature, on the other hand, makes use of language, composed of a succession of words proceeding through time; and it follows that literary form, to harmonize with the essential quality of its medium, must be based primarily on some form of narrative sequence." But modern literature, according to Frank, is in the process of abandonning narrative sequence and "is moving in the direction of spatial form." This narrative form appears most often in twentieth century poetry such as that of Pound or Eliot. Frank defines spatial form in poetry in these terms: "Syntactical sequence is given up for a structure depending on the perception of relationships between disconnected word-groups. To be properly understood, these word-groups must be juxtaposed with one another and perceived simultaneously; only when this is done can they be adequately understood; for while they follow one another in time, their meaning does not depend on this temporal relationship."

Although this "space-logic" of modern aesthetic form is most readily perceived in poetic language, Frank skillfully applies his idea of spatial form to the narrative discourse of the novel as well. Clearly, textual space in the novel, or in the short story, must be based on units of meaning larger than the word-groups of a poem; here, it is the interplay of relationships among scenes or among levels of action within a particular scene which accomplishes the "spatialization" of form. Modern novelists, in their handling of plot and action, "exhibit a tendency to counteract time by 'spatializing' its flow, that is, to create relations of meaning detached from pure succession." According to Frank, this weakening of the chronological order of the text and the resultant growth of intemporality—or spatiality—in literature began to develop in prose narrative during the second half of the nineteenth century.

The predominance of such a spatial form in Flaubert's *Trois Contes* has not been overlooked by contemporary literary critics. A.W. Raitt, in his essay "Flaubert and the Art of the Short Story," notes that in *Trois Contes,* "plot for Flaubert . . . is subservient to the need to produce a particular impression, definable in terms of colour . . . but perhaps also as a shape, as a texture, or as a rhythmic experience." But having suggested such provocative textual characteristics as "shape," "texture," and "rhythmic experience," Raitt limits his comments on Flaubert's narrative technique to the new role played by description in the short story and fails to address himself to the problems of structure and style inherent in the practice of spatial form. As William Holtz has aptly remarked in an article elaborating Frank's theory: "Spatial form is not, as we might guess, necessarily 'descriptive' writing aimed at the mind's eye but rather a form that grows out of the writer's attempt to negate the temporal principle inherent in language and to force apprehension of his work as a total 'thing' in a moment of time rather than as a sequence of things."

The study of spatial form in *Trois Contes* undertaken by Michael Issacharoff in his recent work, *L'Espace et la nouvelle,* corresponds more closely to Joseph Frank's aesthetic principles. Issacharoff goes beyond the role of description in Flaubert's texts to suggest the possibility of a "symbolique combinatoire" in *Trois Contes,* a reflexive structure of symbols and narrative techniques which resembles "une mosaïque, une juxtaposition d'éléments dans le temps et dans l'espace, et non une série d'unités intégrales consécutives." Yet Issacharoff discusses the combination of symbols and the non-linear structure of *Trois Contes* only in terms of the work as a whole; by superimposing the three tales on each other, he demonstrates the intertextuality, the "jeu de relations des trois textes" which makes of *Trois Contes* more a narrative space than a linear sequence of scenes and events.

But if Flaubert truly initiated a new spatial form for the short story, an adequate reading of *Trois Contes* must lead to an appreciation not only of the architectural qualities of the work as a whole but also of the structural and stylistic elements within the individual tale which serve to spatialize a traditionally dynamic narrative mode. Indeed, William Holtz has suggested that such close textual analysis is essential to any discussion of spatial form in literature; for Holtz, the negation of the temporal principle and the emphasis on spatial relationships within the text is based on two distinct components: "the disruption (or disappearance) of the sequential principle of 'action' or 'plot'" and "the corresponding distortion of sequential principles of syntax and expository discourse." Following Holtz's guidelines, this study will attempt to define Flaubert's techniques of spatialization through an investigation of the ways in which the sequential principles of plot and expository discourse are disrupted or undermined in each of the three tales. The analysis will follow the chronological order of composition of the texts.

A consideration of the three tales in the order of their composition is especially important for an examination of Flaubert's transformation of the short story from a linear, anecdotal narrative to a more spatially organized, poetic text. The first of the *Trois Contes*—"**La Légende de saint Julien l'Hospitalier,**" written in 1875-76—was inspired by two artistic sources which lend themselves to, and indeed require, a narrative form consisting of large tableaux or interwoven blocks of text. In an epilogue to his first tale, Flaubert states: "Et voilà l'histoire de saint Julien l'Hospitalier, telle à peu près qu'on la trouve, sur un vitrail d'église, dans mon pays." If Flaubert's tale reproduces in language the legend of Julian as it appears in visual art, its organization must approximate that spatial structure which Schiller attributed to the latter medium.

Moreover, this initial tale is identified not as a "conte" but rather as the legend of Saint Julian. As legend, the text participates in a traditional generic code which, according to Benjamin Bart and Robert F. Cook, prescribes an architectural type of narrative structure. In their study *The Legendary Sources of Flaubert's Saint Julien,* Bart and Cook describe the gradual growth of the hagiographical legend as a process of accretion and expansion based on an initial image of the saint's life. The legend of Julian most likely began with the simple image of Julian hospitator and ferryman. Later elaborations upon his story added the motifs of parricide, forewarnings, hunting, and marriage. Through the participation of many creators, the definitive form of the legend gradually emerged from the "embroidering upon successful narrative structures drawn . . . from tradition." The composition of the legend, therefore, "is not linear, since in its most common form, it is put together from demonstrably independent and no doubt discrete elements."

Flaubert, in order to maintain the form and meaning of his legendary sources, was obliged to construct his tale around the traditionally juxtaposed images of Julian as parricide, hunter, hospitator, and ferryman. Remaining faithful to the embroidered texture of the legend described by Bart and Cook, Flaubert depicts the life of Julian not through the dynamic unfolding of sequentially related events but rather as a series of fixed images which must be combined by the reader in order to arrive at a full impression of the saint. Thematically, the temporal flow of Flaubert's narrative is arrested by the division of Julian's life into a limited number of discrete incidents and by the evocation of his personality in terms of a series of fixed

identifies all of which ultimately contribute to our understanding of Julian. Moreover, the structure of the tale serves to undermine any linear, dynamic progression and sets up a kind of textual mosaic in three parts which emphasizes the spatial potential of the linguistic medium.

Just as the triptych serves as the basis for the overall structure of *Trois Contes,* so too does this figure dictate the composition of the Julian legend. The three chapter divisions in the text correspond to three distinct periods in the life of the saint; and the relationship established among these three parts of the tale depends less on a cause and effect, temporal unraveling of the plot than on structural similarities and reflexive correspondances among the various episodes. Each chapter of Flaubert's legend consists of two clearly discernible elements: a long passage in the imperfect tense which broadly paints an extended period of Julian's life and a shorter evocation, in the perfect tense, of a single important incident. In the first chapter, the passage in the imperfect tense describes Julian's early years of life at his father's castle and, most notably, his youthful hunting experiences. Many pages of text similar to the following offer a condensation or resumé of Julian's childhood:

> Souvent on menait dans la campagne des chiens d'oysel, qui tombaient bien vite en arrêt. Alors des piqueurs, s'avançant pas à pas, étendaient avec précaution sur leurs corps impassibles un immense filet. Un commandement les faisait aboyer; des cailles s'envolaient; et les dames des alentours conviées avec leurs maris, les enfants, les camérières, tout le monde se jetait dessus et les prenait facilement.
>
> D'autres fois, pour débûcher les lièvres, on battait du tambour; des renards tombaient dans des fosses, ou bien un ressort, se débandant, attrapait un loup par le pied.

Near the end of the first chapter, the tone and verbal tense change, however, as the narrative suddenly focuses on a single event in Julian's life: "Un matin d'hiver, il partit avant le jour. . . ." Nearly as many lines of text as were devoted to the whole of Julian's childhood are now supplied to recount his meeting with "le grand cerf" and the mysterious animal's prediction of Julian's inevitable parricide: "Maudit! Maudit! Maudit! Un jour, tu assassineras ton père et ta mère!"

Similarly, the second chapter of Flaubert's legend begins with a descriptive passage covering many years of Julian's life first as a wandering adventurer and later as the husband of an emperor's daughter. At the conclusion of this chapter, however, the descriptive mode is again interrupted by the account of a decisive moment in Julian's life—the murder of his father and mother. In the third chapter of the legend, Julian's subsequent roles of beggar and ferryman are evoked through a descriptive resume; and again at the end of this chapter the narration of a single event—that of Julian's encounter with the leper-Christ—interrupts the description to isolate an important scene from the saint's life: "Alors le lépreux l'étreignit; et ses yeux tout à coup prirent une clarté d'étoiles; ses cheveux s'allongèrent comme les rais du soleil; le souffle de ses narìnes avait la douceur des roses; un nuage d'encens s'éleva du foyer, les flots chantaient. . . . Le toit s'envola, le firmament se déployait;—et Julien monta vers les espaces bleus, face à face avec Notre-Seigneur Jesus, qui l'emportait dans le ciel."

Both the extended narration of habitual activities in the imperfect tense and the selective concentration on decisive moments in Julian's life disrupt the traditional temporal flow of the short story and substitute for sequential plot development a series of isolated, static tableaux reminiscent of the portrayal of the legend in the windows of the church at Rouen. The descriptive passages compress many years of the saint's life into a relatively small textual space; they constitute a kind of generalized frieze which characterizes a whole period of Julian's life. In such passages we clearly see the operation of what Georges Poulet calls "la durée répétitive" of Flaubert's texts: "Par l'idée de suite et d'identité, le passé s'unit au présent, et le présent à l'avenir, pour constituer une même trame uniforme. En avant, en arrière, à perte de vue, la durée s'étend comme une masse temporelle homogène. . . . Le temps est un vide à l'intérieur duquel existe un seul moment toujours pareil . . . "

The three passages in the perfect tense which depict individual incidents in Julian's life also serve to arrest the time flow of the narrative. Rather than combining many separate moments into a homogeneous block of repeated activities, these texts immobilize the character in an instant of time and confront the reader with snapshot-like images of singularly important events. The elaboration and juxtapo-

sition of such discontinuous, independent fragments of the saint's life allow us to isolate and grasp a moment of time, to achieve that pure time which, for Joseph Frank, "is not time at all—it is perception in a moment of time, that is to say, space."

Each of the six principal passages which we have isolated in the Julian legend serves, therefore, to undermine the traditional temporality and linearity of the short story plot. Moreover, the individual passages of each narrative mode—description in the imperfect, momentary action in the perfect tense—combine in two important ways to create an overall spatial pattern in Flaubert's text. Thematic similarity unites the three descriptive passages which present Julian as hunter, adventurer and ferryman; all of these texts provide a background impression of Julian as wanderer and evoke the general pattern of his life. The three moments of isolated activity, on the other hand, embody in their frozen snapshot images the whole of Julian's exceptional story, the motifs of forewarning, parricide and salvation in sainthood. The juxtaposition of these six tableaux renders, therefore, a complete view of the life of Saint Julian.

Another important factor in the creation of this textual mosaic is Flaubert's use of predictions in the first chapter of the legend. Here, three separate prophecies—of Julian's worldly success and riches, of his religious importance and of his inevitable parricide—embody the whole of the following legend. Suspense is minimized and subsequent passages only fulfill and reiterate the truth of the initial predictions. Each moment of the text, therefore, reflects forward and backward to another corresponding moment; and only when the entire tale has been read can all of the intricate interweavings and interrelationships be fully appreciated. Flaubert's **"Légende de saint Julien l'Hospitalier"** presents one of those spatial forms in prose narrative which, according to Joseph Frank, "the reader is forced to read . . . in exactly the same manner as he reads modern poetry—continually fitting fragments together and keeping allusions in mind until, by reflexive reference, he can link them to their complements."

The motif of prophecy in the Julian legend also has important repercussions for the stylistic aspect of this tale. The introduction of a supernatural mode of perception allows Flaubert to temporarily abandon normal syntactical structures and to reiterate, on the level of language itself, the spatial pattern of the entire tale. The great stag's prediction of Julian's parricide consists of the repeated refrain "Maudit! Maudit! Maudit!"—a linguistic structure which arrests the temporal flow of the narrative and undermines the sequential principles of literary discourse.

In its overall structure, then, as well as in such specific stylistic devices, Flaubert's **"Légende de saint Julien l'Hospitalier"** adapts the conventions of the short story to the more spatial, embroidered quality of the legend. This process transforms the linear anecdotal form of the short story in ways which reappear in the two other tales of *Trois Contes.* Before considering the application of this narrative technique to the other tales, however, we must note one additional way in which the motif of space is foregrounded in the Julian legend. Throughout the series of

Caricature of Flaubert by Roland Gerards.

tableaux which constitute Julian's story, the saint's physical environment undergoes a gradual compression or constriction. Julian begins his life in the seemingly unlimited fields and forests surrounding his father's castle; later, having renounced the practice of hunting, he restricts his living space to the confines of the emperor's castle; after his crime of parricide, Julian isolates himself in a tiny cabin on a river bank. The tale ends with a descriptive concentration on one point in space—the embrace of Julian and the leper—which, finally, opens onto the transcendent glory of Julian's assumption into heaven. Georges Poulet finds this motif of the gradually shrinking space—or of the contracting circle—in all of Flaubert's later works: "De fait, toutes les oeuvres de la vieillesse de Flaubert ont pour thème l'existence rétrécie ou circonscrite." This emphasis on spatial relationships and description of the character's physical environment clearly reinforces the mosaic quality of Flaubert's text and disrupts the traditional development of the short story plot.

With the composition of **"Un Coeur simple"**—chronologically the second of his *Trois Contes*—Flaubert applied these spatial techniques drawn from the legend to the creation of a modern prose fiction. Félicité's story, like that of Julian, emerges from the mosaic-like juxtaposition of fixed tableaux rather than from a dynamic, cause and effect narration of the events comprising her life. The division of the text between moments of description summarizing long periods of time—Poulet's "durée répétitive"—and more succinct accounts of significant individual incidents recurs in this second tale. Félicité's daily life in the home of Madame Aubain is characterized by passages offering a generalized evocation of habitual activities: "Elle se levait dès l'aube, pour ne pas manquer la messe, et travaillait jusqu'au soir sans interruption; puis, le dîner étant fini, la vaisselle en ordre et la porte bien close, elle enfouissait la bûche sous les cendres et s'endormait devant l'âtre, son rosaire à la main." The passage of time is also frequently undermined by explicit omission of long periods devoid of significant events: "Puis des années s'écoulèrent, toutes pareilles et sans autres épisodes que le retour des grandes fêtes: Pêques, l'Assomption, la Toussaint." Against this homogeneous background in which time's flow is subordinated to the repetitious nature of her daily existence, important moments in Félicité's life appear as snapshot images reminiscent of the Julian legend. The accounts of her youthful "histoire d'amour," of the death of Virginie and Madame Aubain, and of the arrival, death and subsequent preservation of the parakeet Loulou expand a moment of time in order to fully explore its contours and texture.

Although **"Un Coeur simple,"** maintains the basic mosaic structure of the Julian legend, its spatial form relies more heavily on another technique also present in the first tale, that of the constriction or compression of the environment surrounding the central character. The entire narration of Félicité's existence can be understood in terms of the gradual shrinking of the physical space in which the character moves. Initially, Félicité interacts with a large number of friends and relatives who visit Madame Aubain and she frequently leaves Madame Aubain's home to travel to Trouville, Honfleur or Le Havre. As the story proceeds, however, family and friends disappear and Félicité is left with only the parakeet Loulou as a constant companion. Félicité's excursions outside the walls of Madame Aubain's house become increasingly rare until, finally, she no longer emerges from her own room. As in the Julian legend, the final scene of **"Un Coeur simple"** reduces the external environment to a single point in space through the concentration on the figure of Loulou. That this physical compression results in the symbolic transcendence of the story's conclusion further attests to the negation of linear time and to the emphasis on spatial relationships which dominates the text of **"Un Coeur simple."**

Yet considered only in terms of the entire tale, the gradual spatial compression which occurs in **"Un Coeur simple"** appears to follow a linear, sequential development in time. Another aspect of Flaubert's use of this motif must be examined in order to fully illustrate the way in which temporal flow is undermined in **"Un Coeur simple."** Not only the tale as a whole, but also each individual incident or descriptive passage fully depicts the telescoping space in which Félicité lives. The formal similarity which exists among the discrete tableaux of this tale makes of each passage a kind of mise-en-abîme of the whole and establishes a pattern of repetition which disrupts temporal progression in the text. A brief investigation of two selections from **"Un Coeur simple"**, will illustrate this structural principle.

In the second chapter of his tale, Flaubert recounts at length the simple "histoire d'amour" of Félicité. Her relationship with Théodore begins in an exterior setting which remains imprecise and seemingly unlimited; returning home from Colleville together, Félicité and Théodore first embrace "au bord d'un champ d'avoine." Their second meeting takes place in a more precise location: "sur la route de Beaumont." Subsequently, Théodore receives permission to visit Félicité privately and the setting of their rendez-vous becomes more defined and enclosed: "ils se rencontraient au fond des cours, derrière un mur, sous un arbre isolé." The affair ends at the local "Préfecture" where Félicité's solitude and disappointment are concentrated in the single image of Théodore's friend who greets her with news of her lover's betrayal. In this account of Félicité's love story, the reader passes from an exterior setting without specific limitations through a series of more precise locations to a final solitary figure which summarizes the entire passage.

Perhaps the most striking embodiment of this microstructure of constricting space occurs at the end of **"Un Coeur simple"** with the death scene of Félicité. In this passage, too, the external world appears as a circular form whose circumference becomes gradually more constricted until the narrative concentrates on a single point in space. The scene begins with the depiction of "les fabriciens, les chantres, les enfants [qui] se rangèrent sur les trois côtés de la cour." But the description soon focuses on a single element in that environment: "les encensoirs, allant à pleine volée, glissaient sur leurs chaînettes." This initial compression of the external world permits the transition to an even more enclosed space, that of Félicité's room, and to a description of Félicité herself. "Une vapeur d'azur monta dans la chambre de Félicité. Elle avança les narines, en la humant avec une sensualite mystique. . . . ." The implied passage to the perspective of Félicité then permits the evocation of her final, concentrated vision of "un perroquet gigantesque, planant au-dessus de sa tête."

It is appropriate that the tale should end with this isolated image of Loulou, because the parakeet plays an important role in **"Un Coeur simple":** through the discourse of Loulou, Flaubert here achieves that spatial form in language which we found in the great stag's repetition of "Maudit!" in the Julian legend. The very name of this bird, who is so ironically sanctified in Félicité's vision, embodies the principle of repetition and circularity which serves to arrest dynamic movement even on the syntactical level of the narrative. Loulou's limited vocabulary, moreover, consists of a simple trio of expressions: "Charmant garçon! Serviteur, Monsieur! Je vous salue, Marie!" As Luc Dariosecq has noted [in "A propos de Loulou," *French Review* (1958)], these three phrases offer a complete summary of Félicité's universe; the fact that Loulou chants these words in a kind of non-communicative babble further reinforces the static, circumscribed nature of Félicité's existence.

"Un Coeur simple," therefore, like the legend of Julian, presents, both in its structural and stylistic elements, that spatial form initially described by Joseph Frank. **"Un Coeur simple,"** principally through the motif of circumscribed space, and **"La Légende de saint Julien l'Hospitalier"** through its symmetrical mosaic construction disrupt the linear progress of the traditional short story form. Yet both of these tales embody an implicit temporal movement in that they present an account of a complete human life; their scope remains tied to the dramatic plot development of the conventional short story.

In the last of the *Trois Contes*—**"Hérodias"**—the temporal element is reduced to a minimum by the limitation of the story's action to a period of twenty-four hours. This text successfully combines the narrative techniques of the Julian legend and **"Un Coeur simple"** to achieve the fullest elaboration of that spatial form which had fascinated Flaubert since his first encounter with the legend form. The structure of **"Hérodias"** embodies both the architectural layering of the legend form and the motif of compressed narrative space evident in **"Un Coeur simple."** The technique of creating a textual mosaic built up from discrete tableaux or blocks of narrative operates in two directions in **"Hérodias."** The setting of the tale is divided into three vertically juxtaposed areas: the subterranean cell of Saint John which haunts the characters throughout the story; the intermediate setting of Herod's palace—a larger space than that of John's cell but which resembles the latter in its circular, enclosed form of a "couronne de pierres" within "le cercle d'un mur"; and, finally, suspended above these earthly *milieux,* the sky itself which plays an important role in the prophecies of the tale and offers also the image of the rising sun so essential to the theme of Christ's imminent arrival. The entire "plot" of this tale consists in the reciprocal action among these three interwoven spaces. John's presence poses political problems for Herod and inspires lengthy debates with his wife Hérodias. Similarly, John's life depends completely on Herod's pronouncements and his monologues shouted from the cell window refer repeatedly to the sinful lifestyle of Hérodias. The celestial setting dominates and controls all of these human lives; the stars foretell Herod's destiny while the anticipated sunrise of Christ's appearance dictates John's behavior and sanctifies his death.

In terms of the narrative structure of this text, the architectural technique operates horizontally to set up a series of distinct segments of description and action reminiscent of the divisions of the Julian legend. **"Hérodias,"** like the legend, is divided into three chapters, each of which comprises a descriptive moment followed by a dramatic scene. The first chapter consists of a lengthy description of the area surrounding Herod's palace followed by a dialogue between Herod and Hérodias; the second chapter presents a description of the interior of the palace and John's vehement monologue; in the third chapter, the descriptive mode is resumed in the evocation of the banquet hall, and Salomé's dance embodies a kind of non-verbal communication calling for the death of John. Just as in the Julian legend, each part of the text is completed and enriched in meaning by other narrative moments; the textual segments interrelate in a reflexive pattern more complex than the linear unfolding inherent in all literary discourse. The reader of **"Hérodias"** must combine the three descriptive passages in order to visualize the whole setting of the tale. Moreover, the three moments of communication intertwine to effect the only real "action" of the tale—the death of John. The hatred expressed by Hérodias in her conversation with Herod finds its complement in John's reproaches launched from his underground cell: "Ah! c'est toi, Jézabel!" Salomé's dance incarnates the desires of both characters; in retrospect, it fulfills the angry wishes of Hérodias but, in demanding John's death, this dance also makes way for the prophesied savior: "Pour qu'il croisse, il faut que je diminue."

A complex architectural structure is thus established in **"Hérodias"** through the interrelationship of the vertically layered levels of the setting and the horizontally juxtaposed moments of narration. In order to further disrupt the sequential principles of literary form and achieve full expression of spatial organization, **"Hérodias"** also relies on the theme of the gradually constricting narrative space already seen in **"Un Coeur simple."** The tale begins with the description of a vast exterior setting and a dialogue which takes place on the terrace of Herod's palace; in the second chapter the description is restricted to the interior of the palace and John's monologue emerges from the confined space of the underground cell; in the concluding chapter, a more limited setting—that of the banquet hall—is described in detail and action is limited to Salomé's erotic dance; and this tale, like its predecessors, ultimately focuses on a single point in space: here, John's head exhibited to the banquet guests.

Not only in the structure of the tale as a whole but also within individual passages these techniques drawn from the **"Légende de saint Julien l'Hospitalier"** and **"Un Coeur simple"** unite to achieve a crowning elaboration of spatial form in **"Hérodias."** A text chosen from the third chapter of this tale will serve to illustrate spatial form in the microstructure of **"Hérodias"**:

> On servit des rognons de taureau, des loirs, des rossignols, des hachis dans des feuilles de pampre; et les prêtres discutaient sur la résurrection. Ammonius, élève de Philon le Platonicien, les jugeait stupides, et le disait à des Grecs qui se moquaient des oracles. Marcellus et Jacob s'étaient joints. Le premier narrait au second le bonheur qu'il avait ressentí sous le baptême de Mithra, et Jacob l'engageait à suivre Jésus. Les vins de palme et de tamaris, ceux de Safet et de Bybios, coulaient des amphores dans les cratères, des cratères dans les coupes, des coupes dans les gosiers; on bavardait, les coeurs s'épanchaient. Iaçim, bien que Juil, ne cachait plus son adoration des planètes. . . . et des gens de Sichem ne mangèrent pas de tourterelles, par déférence pour la colombe Azima.

This passage sets up an ironic contrast between two thematic elements: the physical description of the activities of eating and drinking and a theological discussion conducted by the priests during the meal. These two textual components recall the juxtaposed layers of scene and description present in the tale as a whole. Through an intricate play of reflection and repetition, Flaubert gradually weaves these two narrative threads into a complex verbal tapestry; and as the composition progresses, the distance between the two diminishes until the text concludes with their union in a single emphatic image. In the first sentence of this text, the extended enumeration of foods served at the banquet is abruptly interrupted by the introduction of a religious vocabulary: "et les prêtres discutaient sur la résurrection." In the following sentences, this religious terminology is displayed in much the same way as were the food items of the first clause; a fragmented list based on key theological terms—"oracles," "baptême," "Jésus"—recalls the initial enumeration of "des rognons de taureau, des loirs, des rossignols . . . " The structural similarity of these thematically contrasting sentences establishes a reflexive play between the two elements and prepares their ultimate fusion in the "colombe Azima."

The mention of "les vins de palme et de tamaris, ceux de Safet et de Byblos" suggests a return to the alimentary list of the first clause; but the choice of wine as the subject of this list corresponds as well to the religious nature of the priests' discussion. Moreover, as the wine flows "des amphores dans les cratères, des cratères dans les coupes, des coupes dans les gosiers," the accompanying conversation becomes increasingly animated: "on bavardait, les coeurs s'épanchaient." This close relationship between the nourishment which enters the mouths of the priests and the words which leave their mouths leads finally to the complete fusion of food and theology in the image of "la colombe Azima." The figure of this sacred animal embodies both the alimentary and religious motifs of the passage; its significance can only be fully appreciated in its interrelationship with each of the preceding elements. Moreover, as the culminating focus of this passage, the "colombe Azima" presents a single point in space—reminiscent of Félicité's parakeet or Julian's embrace with the leper—

which summarizes the movement of the entire text. In this passage, then, as in the tale as a whole, the motifs of spatial juxtaposition and compression combine to create a linguistic structure which must be perceived not sequentially in time but as a single tableau, an intricately woven fabric or, perhaps most appropriately, a non-linear movement through space like the dance of Salomé.

The spatialization of form which occurs throughout Flaubert's **Trois Contes** serves, as we have seen, to disrupt the linear temporal progression traditionally associated with the linguistic medium. More specifically, the static, mosaic-like composition of **Trois Contes** represents a significant departure from the dominant narrative modes of the nineteenth century. Since the beginning of the century, the influence of a powerful bourgeoisie with its "new, historical defence of progress" [as Georg Lukács has argued in his *The Historical Novel*] had contributed to the rise of the historical novel and the anecdotal short story. This spirit of progress and the accompanying view of experience [which Richard Terdiman has termed] as "sequential, progressive, analyzable" clearly informs the dynamic action in the novels of Balzac and Stendhal or the short stories of Maupassant. But the spatial form initiated by Flaubert in **Trois Contes** implies a rejection of historical time and chronologically ordered experience; indeed, Joseph Frank characterizes this artistic mode as the expression of "an existence wrenched free from all submission to the flux of the temporal." With the development of spatial form, "the objective historical imagination, on which man has prided himself, and which he has cultivated so carefully since the Renaissance, is transformed . . . into the mythical imagination for which historical time does not exist—the imagination which sees the actions and events of a particular time merely as the bodying forth of eternal prototypes." Spatialization of literary form consists, therefore, in the transmutation of the "time world of history into the timeless world of myth."

The importance of Flaubert's narrative innovation in **Trois Contes** must be understood in terms of this relationship between spatial form and myth. The return to the Julian legend as a source for his first tale suggests that Flaubert himself was aware of the link between spatially organized narration and archaic forms; moreover, as Raymonde Debray-Genette has discovered, the initial plan for **"Hérodias"** ended with the following indications: "La tête apportée sur un plat. Soleil levant. Mythe." Thematically, as well, Flaubert's **Trois Contes** seem closely tied to the world of myth; the sacred nature of these stories, the saintly heroes who represent prototypes of human behavior, the ritual quality of the characters' lives all correspond to the mythic realm. Even the subject matter of this trilogy of traditional legend, popular folk tale and biblical story is related to myth. Francis Ferguson, in " 'Myth' and the Literary Scruple" [in John B. Vickery's *Myth and Literature: Contemporary Theory and Practice*] defines three varieties of mythic expression found among primitive peoples: "Legends, . . . stories about the past which were believed to be true of the past . . . ; Folk or Fairytales, told only for fun, without reference to truth . . . ; and Religious Myths, which represented basic elements in the creed, the morals, and the social structure of that people."

Yet even more striking than these thematic similarities between *Trois Contes* and myth are the structural and formal qualities shared by Flaubert's tales and archaic modes of expression. The very spatial motifs employed by Flaubert to arrest linear time in *Trois Contes*—the mosaic-like juxtaposition of interrelated tableaux, the emphasis on habitual, repeated activities, and the motif of the constricting circle—correspond to qualities inherent in myth. According to Mircea Eliade—*The Myth of the Eternal Return*— "neither the objects of the external world nor human acts, properly speaking, have any autonomous intrinsic value" for archaic man. Since reality "is a function of the imitation of a celestial archetype" any individual object or event acquires meaning only when juxtaposed with another, similar entity among mythical prototypes. Discrete elements of human existence must, therefore, be removed from life's temporal sequence in order to attain full significance. Much the same process operates in the mosaic composition of *Trois Contes;* individual moments in each of the three tales combine in a pattern of mutually reflexive relationships to undermine the relevance of chronological sequence in the hero's life.

Another important structural aspect of myth is found in the cyclical representation of reality and in the function of ritual and paradigmatic activity. Because, in myth, "an object or act becomes real only insofar as it imitates or repeats an archetype, . . . reality is acquired solely through repetition or participation." Existence is ordered not along a linear, chronological continuum as in modern history, but rather according to recurring periodic cycles such as the end of the old year and the beginning of the new, the passage of seasons, or, in human terms, the movement from life through death to rebirth. Rituals and ceremonies commemorating these mythical movements are designed to "suspend the flow of profane time, of duration, and project the celebrant into a mythical time" devoid of the sequential properties of history. In *Trois Contes,* Flaubert, too, draws upon motifs of repetition and cyclical movement to achieve the spatialization of literary form. Each of the three tales traces the hero's life through the cycle of life, death and rebirth and embodies the circular mythic motif of fall and ascension. In addition, the ultimate passage of the central character from a place of darkness and isolation to the luminous glory of sainthood or heaven recalls the play of light and darkness characteristic of the solar cycle so essential to mythic movement. Throughout *Trois Contes,* emphasis on the characters' habitual—almost ritualistic—activities and even the linguistic repetition of key phrases (the great stag's "Maudit," Loulou's trilogy of expressions, John's "Pour qu'il croisse il faut que je diminue") again suggest a close relationship between Flaubert's narrative techniques and the ceremonial structure of myth.

The third important spatial technique in *Trois Contes*— the recurring motif of the constricting circle and the final concentration on a single intense image—derives from another aspect of mythical form which Mircea Eliade calls the "symbolism of the center." Coupled with the archaic reliance on archetypes and ritual repetition, Eliade finds a series of beliefs which betray the prestige of the center for the mythopoeic mind. The Sacred Mountain, where

heaven and earth meet, is perceived as the center of the world; by extension, the temple or palace becomes a Sacred Mountain, the meeting place of earth, heaven and hell. In myth, "the center . . . is pre-eminently the zone of the sacred, the zone of absolute reality." Flaubert's evocation of his characters' lives in terms of the contracting circle and his choice of the single point in space—the center—as the site of their final transcendence represent yet another link between spatial form and myth in *Trois Contes.*

The close relationship between spatial techniques in *Trois Contes* and the structures of myth further suggests that spatialization of form, for Flaubert, derives from an artistic need to negate or transcend historical time. As T.S. Eliot remarked (with reference to the work of James Joyce), the use of myth in literature "is simply a way of controlling, of ordering, of giving a shape and a significance of the immense panorama of futility and anarchy which is contemporary history." The rejection of historical time and the resultant exploitation of archaic themes and structures in *Trois Contes* do not, however, represent an abrupt chance in Flaubert's creative program. Although his early works betray an acute interest in history, the development of Flaubert's oeuvre demonstrates a gradual disillusionment with the idea of historical progress and with the significance of history for aesthetic form. The bulk of Flaubert's mature works were written after the Revolution of 1848, an event which, (as we know from his account of it in *Éducation sentimentale*) thoroughly shattered his faith in history. Flaubert was not alone in his disappointment; Richard Terdiman characterizes this revolution as "the historical event which finally made it impossible for writers to believe in history;" and Georg Lukács, tracing the development of the historical novel in France, must admit that after 1848 "history as a total process disappears; in its place there remains a chaos to be or-

---

On Flaubert's religious beliefs:

"A Simple Heart" is, in symbolic terms, Flaubert's personal summing up. It is also his religious statement. Flaubert was actually religious, although he shunned doctrine and belief; religious as Kafka was, as anyone is whose life is consecrated to selfless ends of truth and beauty. Félicité's life is a devoted one, despite the coldness of her employer, that sourhearted mistress of the simple heart. She is capable of infinite sympathy. She merges her destiny wholly with those she loves and serves. Her name characterizes her: she made of her miserable existence something worth while after all, by sheer faith and selflessness. Compared with the vanitarianism of his bourgeois contemporaries and with what he called in disgust their *muflisme,* their muckery, Félicité's selfless devotion, her adjustment to nature's ways, her ready acceptance of death, must have seemed to Flaubert to comprise a life comparable to his own, with its monastic elements—suffering without self-pity, surrender to an ideal.

Charles Neider, in his Short Novels of the Masters, Holt, *Rinehart and Winston, 1967.*

dered as one likes." That Flaubert felt deeply the collapse of the bourgeois concept of history is evident from passages of his *Correspondance* such as the following: "J'ai le sentiment de la Fin d'un monde. Quoi qu'il advienne, tout ce que j'aimais est perdu. Nous allons tomber, quand la guerre sera finie, dans un ordre de choses exécrable . . . " (pp. 202-18)

> *Susan Cauley Selvin, "Spatial Form in Flaubert's 'Trois Contes'," in* The Romanic Review, *Vol. LXXIV, No. 2, March, 1983, pp. 202-20.*

R. B. Leal (essay date 1985)

[*In the following essay, Leal examines how Flaubert's use of architecture, landscape, space, and vertical and horizontal imagery makes a cross the predominant structural feature of "Hérodias."*]

Numerous Flaubert critics have been struck by the vocabulary of geometry that appears in **'Hérodias',** the third of the *Trois contes.* [In *The Novels of Flaubert*] Victor Brombert, for example, notes 'the geometric imagery of **"Hérodias"**' and [in Claudine Gothot-Mersch's *La Production du sens chez Flaubert*] Raymonde Debray-Genette speaks of 'la géométrisation du paysage'. This feature of Flaubert's style is in fact evident in the very first paragraph where one encounters all the terms 'cône', 'cercle', and 'angles' in the space of a few lines.

Such vocabulary stands as an open invitation to structuralists with a mathematical bent to seek to express the structural patterns of **'Hérodias'** in terms of geometrical figures. The invitation has been accepted, notably by Raymonde Debray-Genette, Michael Issacharoff, and most recently by John O'Connor, all of whom tend to develop the earlier seminal work of Georges Poulet.

In his article entitled 'La pensée circulaire de Flaubert', [*Nouvelle Revue Française* (1955)] in which he focuses on *Madame Bovary* but claims wide application for his theories, Georges Poulet introduces not only the figure of the circle but also that of the spiral to represent Flaubert's normal manner of establishing the relationship between a subject and its environment. In this structural method he sees an important contribution to the development of the novel in France: 'Flaubert est le premier qui, abandonnant cette conception unilinéaire [de Balzac et de Stendhal], construise son roman comme une série de foyers à partir desquels, en avant, en arrière, de tous côtés, il y a un déploiement d'objets et un rayonnement à la fois temporel et spatial'. In discussing the circle and the spiral with their corresponding centre or point of origin, Poulet is also led to introduce ideas of 'dedans' and 'dehors', as the subject (Emma Bovary in Poulet's article) successively withdraws into her own consciousness and then, 'se laissant pénétrer par les choses, [devient] elle-même une quasi-chose, une réalité objective'.

In her analysis of **'Hérodias'** Raymonde Debray-Genette opts for the circle, discovering among the different characters a circular structure of dependence, in which strength depends upon weakness: 'La force ne peut vivre que du recours à la faiblesse, qui devient donc une force. Le conte

ne présente pas une analyse historique, c'est une structure circulaire à la fois narrative et symbolique'. Such a pattern does indeed appear to be present in **'Hérodias'** but, as a comprehensive representation of the narrative structure of the story, it lacks the dynamic features of Poulet's spiral or constantly-changing concentric circles.

In his article **"Hérodias"** et la symbolique combinatoire des *Trois contes*' [*Langages de Flaubert* (1976)], Michael Issacharoff exploits the spatial concepts of 'dedans' and 'dehors' evoked by Poulet. Issacharoff's thesis is expressed in these terms: 'Une seule dialectique, me semble-t-il, domine le système symbolique de **"Hérodias"**: *celle du dedans et du dehors. Le dedans (espace clos, contrainte) et le dehors (ouverture, évasion) est l'axe principal de la nouvelle.*' After examining **'Hérodias'** from this perspective, Issacharoff claims to find the same spatial dialectic in the other two *contes* and sees in it the principal unifying element of the *Trois contes.* The theory works well for **'Hérodias'** but is less obviously valid for the other two.

One interesting but ultimately unsatisfactory structural approach to *Trois contes* is that recently proposed by John R. O'Connor, who in 1980 treated '*Trois contes* and the Figure of the Double Cone' [*PMLA*]. Acknowledging his debt to Poulet, O'Connor adapts Poulet's 'spiral' or series of 'contracting and expanding concentric circles' and relates it in linear and temporal (though not causal) fashion to the geometrical figure of two similar but interpenetrating cones having the apex of each vortex in the middle of the other's base. It is a figure that he takes from Book I of W. B. Yeats's *A Vision*. Establishing this as a structural pattern or 'geometrical matrix' for each of the three *contes,* O'Connor proceeds to show how in each case empirical or objective reality (cone A) declines in importance as spiritual or subjective reality (cone B) increases.

Despite its appearance of relative complexity, this attempt to find a structural pattern common to the three *contes* in fact suffers from excessive simplification. O'Connor seeks to cast into the same essentially linear structure three stories by a writer who, as Poulet points out in the passage quoted above, proceeds by 'une série de foyers' rather than by following a more traditional 'conception unilinéaire'. It is significant that, on O'Connor's own admission, ' **"Un Cœur Simple"** is . . . more clearly and completely illustrative of the figure of the double cone as a motive form than **"La Légende de Saint Julien l'Hospitalier"** ', and he posits the expanding cone as only implicitly realized in **'Hérodias'** by a 'form of absence'. Although few would question that at least in the first two stories there is a general tendency to stress the spiritual element at the end of each story, the figure of the double cone is inappropriate as a unifying structure for all three and is of very doubtful validity for **'Hérodias'**.

In an *intervention* following the paper of Michael Issacharoff at the colloquium on Flaubert held in London (Ontario) in 1973, Raymonde Debraye-Genette suggested that in the spatiality of *Trois contes* there is stress on both a horizontal dimension and a vertical dimension. The suggestion is a fruitful one, since particularly in **'Hérodias'** terms suggesting verticality and horizontality not only abound but form a clear underlying structural pattern that is not accounted for by the patterns that have so far been surveyed. . . . [Here] I shall not only demonstrate the presence of this formal pattern but also highlight some of its significant psychological and theological ramifications. It will be seen that ultimately the vertical and the horizontal meet to form the figure of the cross, a fact which tends to add further weight to Per Nykrog's contention about Flaubert that 'le Christianisme, compris d'une façon non-dogmatique et séparée de l'Église, occupe une place de tout premier ordre dans son interprétation de l'histoire mentale de l'humanité' ['Les *Trois contes* dans l'évolution de la structure thématique chez Flaubert', *Romantisme* (1973)].

'Hérodias' opens with a description of Herod Antipas looking out from the terrace of his palace in the citadel of Machaerous. Below him are the waters of the Dead Sea, with Jericho to the north and the brown tents of hostile Nabataean Arabs to the south. In front of him are the mountains of Judaea, with Jerusalem and its dominating Tower of Antonia clearly visible. Behind him other mountains rise into the clear sky where he is conscious of the presence of eagles. Antipas's psychological state at this moment is described in terms of this rugged countryside and specifically in terms of height and depth: 'Tous ces monts autour de lui, comme des étages de grands flots pétrifiés, les gouffres noirs sur le flanc des falaises, l'immensité du ciel bleu, l'éclat violent du jour, la profondeur des abîmes le troublaient'. Antipas is disturbed not only by the depths beneath him but also by the mountains and by the endless blue sky above. The depths of the Dead Sea do in fact suggest a link with the heights, since below its waters lie the cities of Sodom and Gomorrah destroyed by divine intervention from above. Such divine intervention by the vertical forces of divinity terrify him: 'Ces marques d'une colère immortelle effrayaient sa pensée'. Precariously perched between heaven and the valley's depths, 'suspendue au-dessus de l'abîme' Antipas's citadel of Machaerous, like its master, already seems threatened by vertical forces above and below.

Antipas's disquiet is further increased by the sound of John the Baptist's voice, coming, it seems to him, from the 'depths of the earth'. Antipas both respects and fears John. While not wanting him killed, he is anxious that his existence should not be known and that he should be kept muted below ground level so that his voice and influence will not rise to penetrate and threaten the area of the tetrarch's worldly concerns. As the waters of the Dead Sea conceal the reality of divine intervention in human affairs, so Antipas hopes to suppress John's words of judgement, which he nevertheless suspects to be inspired from on high.

Despite her intense hatred of John, Herodias also sees him as situated in the tradition of the Jewish prophets, providing a vertical link with the One whom Phanuel the Essenian refers to as 'le Très-Haut'. In explaining her hatred to Herod, she recalls the occasion when John had hurled at her 'toutes les malédictions des prophètes', which fell around her like storm rain. Raising his arms to the heavens, he had appeared to call down thunder from above like the Elijah he is reputed to be. On this occasion the reality

of the threat that he presents to her way of life is given symbolic expression by her chariot becoming bogged down in sand up to the axles. John represents for her the vertical moral and spiritual dimension that threatens to impede her 'horizontal' progress, that is to say, her worldly ambition to create an extensive empire for Antipas. In seeking to destroy John, Herodias is consequently provoking a definitive conflict between his values and the worldly values that she espouses. This is a conflict that Antipas would prefer simply to avoid. Because she provokes such a fundamental crisis, Herodias comes to occupy a central place in the *conte* and indeed merits the choice of her name as its title.

The first half of the central Part II of 'Hérodias' is given over to an elaboration of the worldly, horizontal emphasis Herodias introduces in Part I. The arrival of the Roman proconsul Lucius Vitellius and his profligate but influential son Aulus provides an opportunity for a description of the temporal might of Rome spread throughout the world. The worldly concerns of the principal Jewish sects are also described in some detail. This is the world in which Antipas considers himself to be forced to live, a corrupt, decadent world of personal aggrandizement and quest for power. It is a world on which he is forced to rely since, despite his extensive armoury, he has been obliged to call in Vitellius's aid to repel the threat against him of the Nabataean Arabs.

The coherence and unity of Antipas's corrupt world are shattered in the second half of Part II by the denunciation of John, whose dungeon is revealed at the midpoint of this central chapter. In the description of John and his outburst, there are the same two clear spatial emphases that recur in this story: the horizontal and the vertical.

The horizontal receives the more obvious initial emphasis. John's prison is situated beneath the paving stones and bronze 'rondelles' of the courtyard, so that he is denied access to Herod's world of political activity and to the freedom of the air above. The horizontal impediments to John's ascension from his depths are multiplied in the description that Flaubert gives of his prison. Beneath the 'couvercle doublé de bois, s'étendait une trappe de même dimension'. Further down, and obvious when John tries to stand, is 'une grille horizontalement scellée'. The effect of these horizontal impediments is given dramatic emphasis when John catches sight of Herodias: 'L'homme effroyable se renversa la tête; et, empoignant les barreaux, y colla son visage'. Following John's bitter denunciation of Herodias's morals, the trapdoor is slammed shut, the covering is replaced, and John's voice and presence are once again shut out of consideration below ground level. But before John's voice is silenced, the links between this prophet-prisoner and a transcendent spiritual world are clearly established. The appearance of doves at the moment when John's dungeon is revealed not only evokes the third Person of the Trinity but recalls John's baptism of the one who came to be seen as representing the entry of the deity into the 'horizontal world' of man's activity. As it castigates Herodias, John's prophetic voice escapes to the mountains, associates itself with thunder and returns to blast the citadel from on high: 'La voix grossissait, se développait, roulait avec des déchirements de tonnerre, et, l'écho dans la montagne la répétant, elle foudroyait Machaerous d'éclats multipliés'. The association of John in his depths with the transcendent figures of Holy Spirit, Son, and Yahweh of the Old Testament is quite clear. He does in fact refer at different times to 'le Fils de David', to 'l'Éternel' and to 'le Seigneur'. But such an association, creative of a vertical moral and spiritual dimension, is not allowed to establish itself and to cut through Antipas's corrupt world. The dungeon sealed, John's moral pronouncements are lost as the various groups of his hearers learnedly debate the possible justifications of Antipas's association with Herodias.

The final two pages of Part II provide another example of the conflict within Antipas's mind between respect for the spiritual and the temptation of the worldly. As he looks towards the setting sun the vertical asserts itself: 'Sur la rougeur du ciel, qui enflammait l'horizon, les moindres objets perpendiculaires se détachaient en noir'. Shortly afterwards he accepts without question the astrological deductions of Phanuel who, from the beginning of the month, has been studying the heavens and has concluded that a great man is about to die. Concluding that he is the man in question, Antipas turns from this dimension, first to seek courage from Herodias, then to find assurance in a medal of the emperor which Herodias gives him, and finally to be distracted by a glimpse of a beautiful young girl whom he takes to be her slave. By the end of Part II Antipas has clearly returned to the lascivious, political world of his time and repressed once again the world that John represents.

In the opening description of Part III the spatiality of the banqueting-hall is given particular stress. It is described as having three naves 'comme une basilique' (a fact which already suggests a religious, vertical dimension), and the eye is immediately led up the columns, past the bronze capitals, and on to the clerestory galleries above. By contrast, the tables, weighed down with food, extend the full length of the main nave and emphasize the horizontal, this-worldly aspect of the celebration. The candelabra on the tables, however, burning like 'buissons de feu' (perhaps a reference to Moses at Horeb) lead the eye, and, it would seem, the whole person into the heights of the ceiling, from where the candle lights appear 'comme des étoiles'. Thus at the outset of this final climactic chapter there are alternating emphases on height and length, on the vertical and the horizontal, together with several indirect references to a purified form of religion. The scene is set for the dual emphasis on a worldly celebration and on the significant religious and spiritual event with which the chapter concludes.

Religion figures largely in the conversation that takes place during the feast, and in particular there is discussion on the significance of 'un certain Jésus' and John the Baptist. However, the discussion remains on an intellectual level until mid-chapter, when the question of John's fate is raised by the arrival of a group of his supporters clamouring for his release. Mirroring John's own imminent 'ascension', they emerge from the depths of the ravine to make their presence felt at the castle gate. From this mo-

ment the verbal and physical violence of Antipas's guests grows until it is channelled by Salome's dance into a request for John's head. Indeed Flaubert takes considerable pains to present Salome's dance as focusing and expressing the attitudes not just of those present but of the whole known world. She dances 'comme les prêtresses des Indes, comme les Nubiennes des cataractes, comme les bacchantes de Lydie', and she holds fascinated in sensual ecstasy 'les nomades habitués à l'abstinence, les soldats de Rome experts en débauches, les avares publicains, les vieux prêtres aigris par les disputes'. Salome's dance is the extreme case of the horizontal, worldly emphasis in '**Hérodias'**, since it becomes in Flaubert's story a privileged expression of the attitudes and desires common to all mankind. The situation gives point to Phanuel's statement earlier in the story that John's work must penetrate to the limits of the earth.

Salome's dance and its sequel, the beheading of John, are consequently presented not just as the culmination of a politico-religious struggle between Herodias and John, or between Herodias and Antipas. They also constitute the violent point of intersection between, on the one hand, the forces of politics and worldly religion—the horizontal—and, on the other hand, the spiritual and moral message of John—the vertical. The banqueting-hall at Machaerous has become a spiritual battlefield of considerable importance.

That John's death constitutes such a significant point of conflict is indicated partly by the vision Mannaei has of 'le Grand Ange des Samaritains, tout couvert d'yeux et brandissant un immense glaive, rouge et dentelé comme une flamme'. Terrified, he is at first unable to despatch John, and it is only the combined fury of Herodias, Antipas, the priests, the soldiers, and the Pharisees that drives him back to his task, this time successfully accomplished.

In this context the elevation of John's head in the feasting-hall has considerable symbolic value. It represents the dramatic entry into the horizontal world of Antipas and his guests of the vertical world that John represents. No longer is he kept in the depths, shut under by horizontal restrictions. His head pierces the horizontal world above and manifests the link with the divine that Antipas has always suspected. Indeed, we may go further and see in this intersection of the vertical and the horizontal the figure of a cross, which foreshadows, and which for Flaubert is causally connected with, the even more theologically significant cross of Jesus Christ.

The link between John's death and Jesus Christ is established by Flaubert in many ways. In the first place, it is significant that Phanuel receives the long-awaited news that Jesus is indeed the Christ immediately after the decollation, and only then does he come to understand the statement attributed by Flaubert to John: 'Pour qu'il croisse, il faut que je diminue'. These words are unbiblical and theologically unacceptable (since they suggest Jesus's total dependence on John), so that their presence in the text is particularly significant. Through them the link between John's death on the one hand and Jesus's elevation and recognition as the Christ on the other is presented by Flaubert as not accidental but necessary. In death as in life

John is the precursor of Jesus, the circumstances of his death forming the symbol of the Cross and allowing the significance of Jesus to appear.

In the second place, as the time of John's death approaches, the figure of Jesus becomes progressively more dominant. Initially he is referred to by John in unspecific fashion as 'il', and then as 'Fils de David'. Later, Antipas's guests discuss him at length by name and finally he is recognized as the Christ by John's disciples at the end of the story.

A third link is to be found in the way in which Flaubert draws numerous parallels between John's death and elevation and Jesus's. Associated with both is an angelic vision; priests, soldiers, and Pharisees all play a part; the chief Roman official tries not to soil his hands in the affair; death is associated with darkness, spiritual victory with dawn; an apparent victory for the forces of the world is transformed by the disciples into an immense spiritual victory; and there is a parallel between the tradition of 'the harrowing of hell' by the Christ and the announcement that John 'est descendu chez les morts annoncer le Christ!'. Antipas, moreover, appears as something of a Judas figure. His reluctance to hand over John to the executioner is tempered by the hope that this act will force John to reveal whether he is the prophet Elijah or not; at the end of the story Antipas is pictured as alone and a prey to sorrow and despair; and finally, though he becomes the instrument of the death of a divine messenger, his action unwittingly advances the divine plan of salvation. The final scene, with Antipas pondering the sacrifice of John and Phanuel praying, arms extended, in the middle of the main nave, transforms the banqueting-hall into the basilica to which it was likened at the outset.

A number of students of 'Hérodias' have recognized that there are elements of allegory and myth in the historically-based tale. Raymonde Debray-Genette, for example, remarks that '[la mort de Jean] est un fait historique, mais elle est traitée aussi comme un fait mythique', while C. H. Wake states: 'Flaubert uses symbolism in "Hérodias" in such a way that it virtually transforms the story, beneath the exterior realism, into an allegory'. My analysis has shown that these elements are present and that they are most clearly manifested by a study of the way in which Flaubert uses horizontal and vertical space ultimately to suggest the symbol of the Cross. [In 'La Mort et la rédemption dans *Les trois contes* de Flaubert', *Neophilologus*, 1972] Frederic J. Shepler sees the thematic pattern of death and redemption as constituting the unity of *Trois contes* as a whole. '**Un Coeur Simple**' does not obviously fit this pattern but it is clear that the Western and the Christian readers of '**Hérodias**' become progressively more aware of these themes and of the cross that they evoke as the story proceeds and the figure of Jesus Christ becomes more dominant. In '**Hérodias**' Flaubert, while not treating a religious subject directly, has used themes and symbols from Christian history and tradition. In so doing he gives greater depth and resonance to a story in which at one stage he was afraid that the exotic elements would unduly dominate. (pp. 810-16)

R. B. Leal, "Spatiality and Structure in Flau-bert's 'Hérodias'," in The Modern Language Review, *Vol. 80, No. 4, October, 1985, pp. 810-16.*

Leonard Marsh   (essay date 1986)

[*In the following excerpt, Marsh examines the role of vision in "A Simple Heart" and its religious implications for the protagonist.*]

Flaubert was a master practitioner of free indirect discourse enabling the reader to slip easily from the narrated text to the mind of his character. Thus, a reading of *Madame Bovary* lets us in a sense enter into Emma's psyche, her boredom, emotions and machinations. Yet, as Victor Brombert has noted [in his *The Novels of Flaubert: A Study of Themes and Techniques*], Flaubert hardly uses this stylistic device in "**Un Coeur simple**" to let the reader into the mind of the tale's central character, Félicité. Perhaps this is so because Flaubert wanted to underline the absence of normal conceptive powers in this character who was to be by her very nature so simple, the very antithesis of Emma, willing to accept life's routine, uncomplicated and uncontriving. Instead, Flaubert lets the readers know Félicité by letting them participate in her limited powers, not of conception but of sense perception. As Brombert has pointed out, it is Flaubert's masterstroke that he can present a central character who is basically inarticulate and yet let the reader participate in the way she perceives the world.

Like her powers of intellection, Félicité's powers of sense perception are limited. At many junctures in the text the narrative voice makes obvious that Félicité is hard of hearing. This is so to highlight by paradox her own sensitivity to the gospel Logos. She instinctively lives the gospel message albeit incomprehensible and oftentimes unheard. But Félicité is also afflicted with defective vision and this is not so obvious in the text. In fact, Flaubert leads the reader very subtly into Félicité's mode of visual perception, a mode which is marked by an initial focussing on an object followed by its dissipation and loss in a vague expanse of space and confusion. It is my purpose to explore this mode of visual perception in the text and to consider its import in the tale's last scene of Félicité's agony and mysterious final vision.

Light enters Félicité's upstairs room through a small dormer window, only to lead the reader's field of vision back out to the vastness of a prairie plain: "Une lucarne au second Étage éclairait la chambre de Félicité, ayant vue sur les prairies." This brief, hardly substantial visit to the faithful servant's living quarters at the beginning of the *conte* has no narrative value other than to let the reader know that the room exists. It does, however, have an important subtextual value. It sets the stage for the reader to get a glimpse of the world as it is perceived by the room's occupant, and even more importantly it lets the reader into that process of perception by training his eye first on a fine ray of light, a point in space, and then on spatial expanse.

Félicité, Mme Aubain, Paul, and Virginie would picnic from time to time at the old, memory-filled farmhouse in

Geffosses. Flaubert neatly slips in a detail letting the reader know that these trips were made "Quand le temps était clair." On a clear day long-distance sight is easy but not for Félicité, and this we are skillfully led to perceive as we follow Félicité's line of sight to a near focal point and then off to some vague distance: "La cour est en pente, la maison dans le milieu; et la mer, au loin, apparaît comme une tache grise." Félicité has defective vision, but does not suffer because of it for she is unaware of it. Is not this the way all the world sees? Even the reader is unaware of it for the skillful narrative voice lets the reader "see" through Félicité's eyes and does not demonstrate this defect as it does Félicité's defective hearing when it recounts her failure to hear the carriages on the road to Honfleur.

Félicité's senses may be defective, her intellect may not be keen, but her heart does move her to a noble and heroic act. One fall evening the family was returning from Geffosses through pasture lands. Once again the scene is characterized as a clear focal point, a limited portion of the sky illuminated by moonlight, and then a hazy, unclear expanse of space: "La lune à son premier quartier éclairait une partie du ciel, et un brouillard flottait comme une écharpe sur les sinuosités de la Toucques." This above ground scene set, Flaubert then takes us along with Félicité and the Aubain family on the textually rich path through the pastures. As the moonlight beams through a portion of the dark sky, so do the eyes of immobile steer roam the pasture lands and follow these four as they tread their way home. By the time they reach the third pasture some steers get up and surround them but retreat after being calmed by Félicité. In the next pasture a bull, "que cachait le brouillard," approaches and is sensed only by the sound of its bellowing and galoping. Now it closes in. Moonlight shining, steers' eyes roaming, bull's eyes coming out of the fog to defy Félicité! Confronted, the faithful servant incapacitates the focal circle of light, the bull's eye, rendering its vision blurred by throwing dirt and grass at it. Sight captured, then thwarted; clarity, then obscurity; focal point, then broad expanse—such is Félicité's experience of visual perception, an experience Flaubert has stylized by having Félicité unwittingly inflict that experience on her assailant.

Félicité's life is filled with short-lived relationships, short like the time span during which she can savor the object of her cares or grasp a particular object in sight. One such relationship is that which she has with her nephew Victor. She had asked permission to receive Victor's visits "pour 'se dissiper' " and Victor would come to visit bringing his clothes to be sewn. Both were satisfied with this symbiotic ritual. When Victor breaks the ritual by telling her that he will be leaving by boat the day after next for a long-term employment, Félicité makes it her business to see the boat off, only to get lost on the way and miss it as it separates from the quai. She even yells Victor's name to some young sailor on the boat she doesn't even recognize. Immediately, the narrative has the boat focused and then lost on the large:

> La voile avait tourné, on ne vit plus personne;—
> et, sur la mer argentée par la lune, il faisait une
> tache noire qui pâlissait toujours, s'enfonça et
> disparut.

Months pass with no word from Victor. An apothecary tells Félicité he has heard that Victor's boat arrived at Havana. Victor and Havana, Victor and cigars, Victor and smoke—a string of associations leads Félicité to visualize her Victor as a point lost in smoke:

> A cause des cigares, elle imaginait la Havane un
> pays où l'on ne fait pas autre chose que de fumer,
> et Victor circulait parmi les nègres dans un
> nuage de tabac.

The pity is that the boat she saw, the sailor she waved to and the Havana scene she visualized have only possible connections to Victor. She never saw him leave and never did hear from him in Havana. Even in her imagination Félicité's powers of concretizing are limited.

What was at the beginning of the *conte* hardly a glimpse of Félicité's room becomes at the end a detailed setting. Suffering from symptoms of pneumonia, Félicité is confined to this small and crowded room. In her dormer window Félicité had hung a popular characterization of Jesus' baptism featuring the Holy Spirit in the form of a dove. Curiously, the dove resembles her stuffed parrot Loulou in its plasticity ("ses ailes de pourpre et son corps d'émeraude." So alike were the dove and the parrot that she placed them together enabling her to see them both at the same time, perhaps because her narrow field of vision required it. Both dove and parrot, bathed in the same light of the dormer window seen by the reader at the beginning, mesh into a single focal point of religious devotion, a focus which Félicité will hold on to but momentarily, only to be lost in old memories and the vague expanse of sleepy ecstasy:

> Chaque matin, en s'éveillant, elle l'apercevait [le
> perroquet] à la clarté de l'aube, et se rappelait
> alors les jours disparus, et d'insignifiantes actions jusqu'en leurs moindres détails, sans
> douleur, pleine de tranquillité.
>
> . . . . .
>
> En l'enveloppant [le perroquet] d'un regard
> d'angoisse, elle implorait le Saint-Esprit, et contracta l'habitude idolâtre de dire ses oraisons
> agenouillée devant le perroquet. Quelquefois, le
> soleil entrant par la lucarne frappait son oeil de
> verre [du perroquet], et en faisait jaillir un grand
> rayon lumineux qui la mettait en extase.

Another source of light for Félicité's small room is an oeil-de-boeuf which looks onto the yard. Outside, beneath the circular light source, has been set up one of the three traditional Corpus Christi altar stations at which the priest will place for adoration and benediction the sunburst golden monstrance containing at its center the sacred host. Félicité in her infirmity is unable to participate in the religious services and even to view them through the oeil-de-boeuf. But her companion, "la mère Simon," climbs up on a chair and thus "dominait le reposoir." The reader is led to infer that it is from this standpoint and only through the eyes of "la Simonne" that Félicité "sees" the altar. Thus, Félicité must bypass the oeil-de-boeuf for she now perceives not through her own eyes but with the eye of imagination. Even what she sees in her mind's eye is characterized by her familiar ritual of perception: a spot, a circle, lost in expansive space or smothered by clutter. The stuffed parrot which had been the center of her life and which she had had placed at the altar as her contribution to the festive decor now meshes as focal point of light with the oeil-de-boeuf and the host in the sunburst monstrance. Yet, once again identified by its plasticity with the Holy Spirit, the parrot is lost from sight and, "caché sous des roses, ne laissait voir que son front bleu, pareil à une plaque de lapis." Even the monstrance, with the host at its center, focal point of the religious ceremony, gets lost in a cloud of incense: "Le prêtre gravit lentement les marches, et posa sur la dentelle son grand soleil d'or qui rayonnait. . . . Et les encensoirs, allant à pleine volée, glissaient sur leurs chaînettes."

Flaubert immediately transports the reader back into Félicité's room via a rising "vapeur d'azur," which functions as a vehicle simultaneously uniting the incensed host, the plasticity and "souffle" of the Holy Spirit, and the blue-beaked parrot. Inhaling the fumes, Félicité "sees" no more with a focused eye but now, "blinded" by the misty fog of incense, she perceives entirely through the sense of smell. Here, where one sense fails, another takes over. Sight yields to smell and smell quickly yields to taste. Her inhalation of the incense is but a metaphor for her reception of the sacrament on this feast of Corpus Christi:

> Une vapeur d'azur monta dans la chambre de Félicité. Elle avança les narines, en la humant avec une sensualité mystique; puis ferma les paupières. Ses lèvres souriaient.

In fact Félicité delights in this reception of communion in the same way she had delighted in her vicarious reception of the sacrament the day of Virginie's first communion. Only on that day Félicité had advanced not her nostrils but her eyes to see the child and imitate her; "Quand ce fut le tour de Virginie, Félicité se pencha pour la voir; . . . au moment d'ouvrir la bouche, en fermant les paupières elle manqua s'évanouir."

At the moment of her agony Félicité's senses are slowly exhausted. Sight and hearing have gone. The touch of her heartbeat slowly disappears like the running of fountain water and the sound of an echo: "Les mouvements de son coeur se ralentirent un à un, plus vagues chaque fois, plus doux, comme une fontaine s'épuise, comme un écho disparaît . . . ". With her last breath goes that sense of smell which had brought her communion with God. It is at this level of perception, after the senses have been exhausted and when the mind or soul experiences that final expanse of transcendence, that we finally meet Félicité on the noetic level. Here it is that ironically Félicité both grasps an object of focus existing in her imagination, holds on to it, and does not lose it in expanse. In fact, her point of focus coincides with expansive space. The object is conceived as a gigantic parrot—so enormous she could hardly miss it—which is presumably her Loulou, the guise of God in the person of the Holy Spirit: " . . . et quand elle exhala son dernier souffle, elle crut voir, dans les cieux entr'ouverts, un perroquet gigantesque, planant au-dessus de sa tête." The "perroquet gigantesque" figures by virtue of its hyperbole as the embodiment of a focal point of certitude, form incarnate, occupying the totality of an amor-

phous expansive space of doubt implied by "souffle," "crut," "cieux entr'ouverts," and "planant." It is the point where the axes of certitude and doubt intersect, where reason is illuminated by faith, where the physical and spiritual intertwine. Clearly hallucinatory but nonetheless illuminative, here is where Flaubert redeems Félicité's simplicity, justifies her defective vision, and lets her experience in almost a mystical way the puzzling God she knew only as the Spirit in the form of Loulou. (pp. 185-89)

Leonard Marsh, "Visual Perception in Flaubert's 'Un Coeur simple'," in Studies in Short Fiction, *Vol. 23, No. 2, Spring, 1986, pp. 185-89.*

Jane E. Marston (essay date 1986)

[*In the following essay on "The Legend of Saint Julien Hospitaller," Marston examines the relationship between Flaubert's tale, the art of story-telling, and his inspiration for the tale, the stained-glass window of the Rouen cathedral, which is, in itself, a work of art.*]

In [**"La Legend de Saint Julien l'Hospitalier"**], Flaubert depicts a romance-world of archetypal actions and supernatural events, a world removed from time by its static pictorial quality and its aura of mysticism. However, he abruptly returns the reader to the world of historical time when, at the end of the story, he introduces a first person narrator: "Et voilà l'histoire de saint Julien l'Hospitalier, telle à peu près qu'on la trouve, sur un vitrail d'église, dans mon pays." Before reaching the final sentence, the reader does not know about either the narrator or the window, and he does not recognize that he is sharing, with the teller of the story, a moment of aesthetic contemplation. The narrator, in recalling the window, contemplates an art-object, and the central interpretive problem of the story becomes the one that Flaubert himself posed: "En comparant l'image au texte on se serait dit: 'Je n'y comprends rien. Comment a-t-il tiré ceci de cela?' " That is, what is the relation of one art-object (Flaubert's story) to the other (the stained-glass window of Rouen cathedral)?

Stylistically, Flaubert recreates the aesthetic attractiveness of the window through his own sensuous language, charged with the sense of religious mystery generated by the material of the legend. His narrative thus approximates, as closely as it can, a static art-form. But the last line destroys the illusion of exact correspondence between the window and the text, which never can attain the status of an object. Not only does the speaker's phrase "à peu près" deny his reliability as an objective observer, but the reader becomes aware of a mediating, distancing consciousness that has, without his knowledge, come between himself and the object of contemplation.

As the reader is plunged into the mundane, historical world of the narrator, the legendary world recedes, coming to rest, finally, in the image of a static, perfect form (the window) untroubled by the temporality of narrative and inaccessible except through the narrator's memory. The effect of this unexpected shift in point of view is to draw attention away from the story of Saint Julian and to direct it toward the first person speaker's sense of pleasure in his own recitation (as well as Flaubert's pleasure in his own method of storytelling). Drawing upon the critical terminology of Roland Barthes, Dennis Porter discusses the pleasure of reading as a subject of *Madame Bovary* and makes a general point relevant to **"La Légende de Saint Julien":** "In a *texte de jouissance* the reading aim is diverted from taking pleasure in the parts of a text in the anticipation of an end to a total absorption in those parts. . . ." The total absorption of narrator and reader in the parts of Flaubert's story is made dramatically clear by the release of attention brought about in the reader through the distancing last line of the story.

Julian's experiences and the narrator's are not unrelated, however, for the narrator's self-effacement through storytelling parallels Julian's self-effacement through religious mysticism. **"La Légende de Saint Julien l'Hospitalier"** therefore develops a correspondence, present in Flaubert's works as early as *Madame Bovary,* between aesthetic and religious pleasure (Emma expects to find in religion the annihilation of self and possession of ideality that she experiences through reading and also seeks through physical passion).

To become a saint, Julian must act out a process of sin and expiation, a process beginning with his killing the white mouse on the altar of his parents' castle, reaching its culmination in violence with his slaying of his parents, and completing itself in his union with the leper. Psychologically, in acting out this process, he integrates opposing facets of his personality.

Division in Julian's psychic life results from contradictory prophecies concerning his future, the one spoken to his mother averring that he will become a saint, and the one spoken to his father, that he will become a great warrior (at least, Julian's father associates the "sang" and "gloire" of his ambiguously worded prophecy with the activity of warfare). Each parent keeps his prophecy a secret and educates Julian according to his own expectations: "Quand il eut sept ans, sa mère lui apprit à chanter. Pour le rendre courageux, son père le hissa sur un gros cheval." Julian therefore feels an internal conflict between the pursuit of spiritual contentment and the pursuit of worldly pleasure. (Early in the story this conflict takes the form of a contest for Julian's attention between the attractions of the cloistered tower where he studies with a monk and the attractions of hunting.)

However, far from being incompatible, the prophecies and the activities issuing from them actually are strikingly similar. Julian's slaying the mouse first brings to light both the superficial dualism and the underlying unity of Julian's psychic life: "Il frappa un coup léger, et demeura stupéfait devant ce petit corps qui ne bougeait plus. Une goutte de sang tachait la dalle." The killing of the mouse seems at first to confirm the father's prophecy. The killing, preparing Julian for the bloodshed of warfare, stains the altar and violates the purity of the religious life. However, precisely because it takes place on an altar, the action also replicates ritual sacrifice and fulfills the prophecy spoken to Julian's mother. Religious ritual, associated with bloodshed, provides the sensuous satisfaction of hunting, while

hunting, a masculine activity, appeals to the ascetic disposition of the monk.

Secular and sacred experience have an inverse relationship to each other in the story because, as Flaubert shows us, they are sublimations of Julian's instinctive life. Sainthood and warfare have the same psychological underpinnings in eroticism (the blood of the mouse staining the white altar has clear sexual overtones), and the guilt and repression which attend Julian's killing of animals provide a psychological basis for his dualistic nature. Julian's hunting, in particular, is fraught with suggestions of sexual pleasure, as in the instance of his killing a pigeon: "La persistance de sa vie irrita l'enfant. Il se mit à l'étrangler; et les convulsions de l'oiseau faisaient battre son cœur, l'emplissaient d'une volupté sauvage et tumultueuse."

However, the sexual basis of Julian's actions leads beyond the conclusion that human desire for spiritual and secular power grows out of our natures as sexual beings. The unconscious, from which these desires come, forms a principle of unity underlying the antithetical social roles of saint and warrior, and the guilt that Julian suffers because of the opposition between these roles affirms the value of the unconscious as a source of wholeness of self. Julian in fact has internalized the prophecies as conflicting ethical systems, and his own internal struggle shows the destructiveness of sublimated emotions that have become reified as social codes. In Jungian terms, Julian fails to integrate *anima* with *animus* in his own psyche, with the result that he is at odds with his own instinctive life.

Julian symbolically attempts recovery of psychological coherence through his episodes of hunting and also through his final encounter with the leper. His killing of a mountain goat supplies an image of both copulation and crucifixion, an image signifying his need to be cleansed of guilt: "Julien s'élança pour le frapper, et, glissant du pied droit, tomba sur le cadavre de l'autre, la face au-dessus de l'abîme et les deux bras écartés." This image is repeated in Julian's final embrace of the leper: "Julien s'étala dessus complètement, bouche contre bouche, poitrine contre poitrine." Images of spiritual cleansing and sexual release occur simultaneously as Julian is granted a beatific vision. His union with the leper represents absolute self-surrender, the perfect humility that is the condition of his sainthood.

Similarly, the narrator achieves paradoxical liberation through self-effacement as he creates a story from a series of pictures. His ego disappears during his vicarious immersion in the pictures of the glass window and, at the end of his meditation, it reappears, as is signalled by the possessive adjective "mon" that gives the speaker individual identity.

The stained glass window, serving as an object of both religious and aesthetic contemplation, itself embodies the opposition between spirit and flesh found in the legend. One connection between "image" and "texte," therefore, is that both artifacts express the paradoxical role of sin and guilt in the process of salvation. The colors of the window bring to mind references to stains in the Julian legend, especially in Flaubert's description of the parents' deathbed, where light shining through a bloodstained window falls upon the corpses. Just as bloodstains signify Julian's guilt and imply his need for expiation, the stains of the window signify the human sense of sinfulness that has produced religious art.

Julian's slaying of his parents truly is a *felix culpa,* for it leads him to a life of humility and eventual union with Christ. Similarly, human sinfulness has produced the window, a vehicle of praise, mediating between man and God as it leads the eye heavenward. However, it is the importance of the window as art-object that Flaubert emphasizes. The creation of the art-work is what has supplied the artist with release from guilt and the psychic incoherence it brings, just as the creation of a narrative has allowed the story's narrator to achieve the serenity that sets the tone of the last line. Sublimated into art, guilt takes on the static beauty of the Rouen window.

In part, Flaubert suggests that art replaces religion in the modern world as a way of satisfying human yearning for the ideal and eternal and of providing psychological relief from guilt. In so doing, he relies upon what one source calls the "familiar idea that literature and the arts, as well as religion, are transmutations of the biological instincts." Even Flaubert's style suggests this substitution, for violence and carnality assume spiritual qualities as they are transmuted into art.

However, Flaubert sees a more complex relationship between art and religion than this idea expresses. That relationship emerges when, at the end of the story, the legend is placed in a cultural context by the speaker's reference to a church in his native country. The window is part of the speaker's heritage, part of the past that he shares with worshippers at Rouen cathedral. By constructing a legend—a story combining historical and imaginative facts, including the "facts" of the window and his own additions to them—the first person narrator reveals the function of narrative art as a preserver of cultural identity. Religion remains vital as part of personal and communal memory, and art and religion in fact sustain one another in the life of the community.

The speaker's reconstruction of the life of Saint Julian restores to him the sacramental vision of medieval man, and memory performs the sacramental function of restoring to him the experience of communal worship. More importantly, the cyclic nature of legend recapitulates the cyclic nature of durational time, the eternal "moment" experienced during the telling of a single story. Therefore, in **"La Légende de Saint Julien l'Hospitalier,"** narrative form itself stands as an archetype, an abstract symbol of deep consciousness, through which the individual self transcends time and recovers wholeness of personality. (pp. 341-45)

> *Jane E. Marston, "Narration as Subject in Flaubert's 'La Legende de Saint Julien l'Hospitalier,'" in* Nineteenth-Century French Studies, *Vol. XIV, No. 3 and 4, Spring-Summer, 1986, pp. 341-45.*

Flaubert on "pure Art":

What seems beautiful to me, what I should like to write, is a book about nothing, a book dependent on nothing external, which would be held together by the internal strength of its style, just as the earth, suspended in the void, depends on nothing external for its support; a book which would have almost no subject, or at least in which the subject would be almost invisible, if such a thing is possible. The finest works are those that contain the least matter; the closer expression comes to thought, the closer language comes to coinciding and merging with it, the finer the result. I believe the future of Art lies in this direction. I see it, as it has developed from its beginnings, growing progressively more ethereal, from Egyptian pylons to Gothic lancets, from the 20,000-line Hindu poems to the effusions of Byron. Form, in becoming more skillful, becomes attenuated; it leaves behind all liturgy, rule, measure; the epic is discarded in favor of the novel, verse in favor of prose; there is no longer any orthodoxy, and form is as free as the will of its creator. . . .

It is for this reason that there are no noble subjects or ignoble subjects; from the standpoint of pure Art one might almost establish the axiom that there is no such thing as subject—style in itself being an absolute manner of seeing things.

> *Gustave Flaubert, in a letter to Louise Colet, in* The Letters of Gustave Flaubert: 1830-1857, *edited and translated by Frances Steegmuller, Belknap Press, 1980.*

David Roe   (essay date 1989)

[*In the following excerpt, Roe provides a thematic analysis of* Three Tales, *arguing that each story concerns itself with martyrdom or sainthood.*]

Although Flaubert occasionally nurtured projects for short fictional works—in particular for an Oriental tale—he wrote none for some thirty years after his youthful experiments. Only frustration with the slow progress made on *Bouvard et Pécuchet* drove him back to the form in the autumn of 1875, as an exercise in style, a relaxing therapy and a way of proving that he had not lost the capacity to write. On holiday in Brittany he began a *conte* retelling the life of St Julian the Hospitaller (originally planned in 1856). Its brevity and the legendary quality of the subject had no effect on his method. He made no attempt to finish his text from his memory and imagination while on holiday: he must first consult the sources, examine his dossiers on the background. By the time he completed the text, in February 1876, he had planned two more: the life of a servant woman in Normandy, spanning the nineteenth century (**'Un Coeur simple'**) and the last day of John the Baptist (**'Hérodias'**). Completed by February 1877, the three stories were published together as, simply, ***Trois Contes,*** in April.

Not only did this volume represent a new formal departure, after a series of long and complex novels, it seemed to aim at the widest possible variety within the short stories' compass: in setting (biblical, medieval, modern), in timescale (from twenty-four hours to seventy years) and in structure (from the single strand of a biography to the multiple interrelation of a dozen significant characters). The collection also neatly summarises Flaubert's three great literary preoccupations: modern France, hagiography, and the ancient history of the Mediterranean civilisations. But in each case the story marks a new departure. The modern work focuses for the first time on a plebeian protagonist; the saint's legend is set in medieval Europe, while the ancient history is that of Palestine at the time of Christ.

Despite this wide variety, the stories' themes have much in common, and it is tempting to see them almost as a single work illustrating three main phases in the history of Christianity. The origins are treated in John's prophecy; **'La Légende de St. Julien l'Hospitalier'** evokes a golden age of belief and mystery, of God's power active in the world; while the naïve faith of the servant Félicité, set against the empty outward show and ritual of modern Catholicism, represents a late stage of decline and decay, which is given greater emphasis by appearing first in the volume. Looked at in another way, the great difference in period between the stories is less important than the close similarities between three central characters, who are all in their different ways martyrs and saints. Certainly one of their great merits, in Flaubert's eyes, must have been their total detachment from the middle-class world of *Bouvard et Pécuchet* and its fundamental mediocrity. The stories, indeed, contain none of the comic tonality of the bourgeois novels.

'Hérodias', curiously, is the story least concerned with the theme of sainthood. Flaubert himself, commenting in 1876 that he was writing a lot about saints, insisted that at least his 'John the Baptist' would not be an edifying tale: his main themes were race and politics. As his title indicates, the story does not concentrate either on the figure of Christ (though the brief mention, by invoking miracles, links this text to the other two) or that of John, who is heard more in his role of angry, Jewish prophet of Israel's doom than as the definitive voice announcing the coming Messiah. The body of the story contains a remarkable compression of the politics, passions and ambitions in conflict in Palestine around the time of Christ's preaching, the secular background to the beginnings of Christianity, for which Flaubert leaned heavily on Greek and Roman historians. His reader, more familiar with the Gospel narrative, thus gains an entirely new perspective on the events. At the same time, he has the sense that lesser conflicts occupy centre stage: the major issue, historically, the coming of Christ, being kept in the wings like the Punic Wars in *Salammbô*.

This effect of extratextual perspective is weakened, for the modern reader of **'Hérodias',** by the fact that history since 1877 has assured a painful relevance for Flaubert's picture of the region as a battlefield of sectional, racial and religious interests exacerbated by the involvement of foreign superpowers. Many readers find that the sheer complexity of the political and ideological issues finally defeats Flaubert's art in the limited compass of the 'tale'. Certainly he has room for only the briefest of signposts to situate the

numerous conflicts symbolically brought together, at considerable cost to strict chronological accuracy, on a single day in Herod's palace at Machaerous. It may, however, be argued that the sense of obscurity and confusion created is probably just the effect that the ever sceptical Flaubert sought in the first place.

Apart from this suggestive and thought-provoking historical perspective, Flaubert also adds to the bald Gospel narrative the dimension of psychology and motivation, painting Herod as fearful and mediocre, Hérodias as ambitious, strong-willed and passionate, driven not only by political expediency but also the shame and insecurity of being Herod's queen by a marriage of dubious legality. Her plan, hidden like many of the stratagems in *Salammbô,* can be guessed at by the reader, who picks up clues which Herod, self-absorbed and blind as Frédéric Moreau, fails to understand. Indeed the story is full of characteristic features of Flaubert's vision of human nature. The great and powerful are devalued systematically. Vitellius, the Roman governor feared by Herod, trembles for his own job, which depends on the Emperor's perverted interest in his son, who is no Adonis but a fat adolescent, a compulsive eater (one of Flaubert's favourite devices for showing up the animality of man). Any crowd is implicitly denigrated, from the common people to a clutch of high-ranking officials. Female sexuality is a redoubtable destabiliser; while marriage is unsuccessful, entered for selfish reasons and disappointing even those.

The characteristic 'apparition' of the ideal woman is reduced to an erotic impulse, though it still results in Herod, on contemplating Salome, surrendering his independence, like Charles, Mâtho and Frédéric before him. The metaphysical dimension is presented ambiguously, through a clash of opinions. A full-scale argument about resurrection—again accompanied by a feast—ends inconclusively; Phanuel's astrologically-inspired prophecy is juxtaposed to the divinely-inspired words of John (carefully 'distanced' by being saddled with the barbarously unfamiliar name Iaokanann). The executioner's claim to have seen an angel protecting John is contradicted by the pragmatic Romans, who not only saw, but killed, 'a Jewish captain', making any possible miracle a question of point of view, as will happen with Félicité's deathbed religious vision. But whereas the executioner eventually carries out his task, Phanuel, in the final lines of the story, leaves his post and sets off 'towards Galilee', with John's followers, prefiguring the faith of the apostles, who leave everything to follow Jesus.

The theme of language itself is treated no less ambiguously. Communication is frequently a problem for the characters, whether in the context of allusive and obscure prophecies or of interlocutors speaking through interpreters. But there are hints of the power of the word. It is John's word, 'this force more pernicious than the sword', that drives Hérodias to fury; echoing Flaubert's conviction that the hostility of censorship, authority, society or critics to some writers reflected a similar fear of the truth-telling power of their language.

Flaubert certainly displayed his own technical powers, fusing erudition with spectacle and sometimes disturbing psychology, as he had in *Salammbô*. His topographic descriptions are again evocative and symbolic, while in the rather gratuitous inventory of Herod's secret armoury he seems to be unleashing the forces of his own unconscious, first in a spiral of sadism inspired by the weaponry, then in a mysterious description of the king's prized horses, which some critics have interpreted as projections of the novelist's own repressed energy and violence.

The interplay of characters' words and silences, prominent here, recurs in the other tales, and has perhaps contributed to a whole school of interpretation which seeks to 'read' the saint figures as projections of Flaubert's severe and ascetic concept of how the artist should relate to himself and to others. The analogy cannot be denied; but it should not be forgotten that as in all the other analogies between Flaubert and his main characters, there remains the central difference that none of the characters is a creative artist. Even Bouvard and Pécuchet, though they wield pens, will get no farther than copying, shoring up fragments, not constructing a work, and doing it for themselves, not for others.

If Flaubert's aim was to put religion in a secondary place in **'Hérodias'**, he could hardly do the same with the life of St Julian. However, his approach to the legend resembles his use of the Gospels in that he grafts on additions and explanations, bringing to bear his erudition, his concept of human nature and his sceptical view of religious interpretations of the world. He adds first a great deal of colour, notably in descriptions of costumes, buildings and hunting scenes, though avoiding the precise localisation which is such a feature of **'Hérodias'**. Secondly he develops the personality of Julien to help explain events. Thirdly, he redraws the lines which in the legend restrict the field of divine intervention. Given the long timespan, he is able to adopt some of the techniques of the novels to fix the psychology.

Julien's mother and father are briefly characterised as representatives of the complementary religious and military attitudes to life of the Middle Ages, with Julien inheriting something from each. Education develops both innate traits, and the narrative structure itself repeatedly underlines their interrelations: Julien's first experience of killing takes place in Church. The doctor's son then carefully traces the escalation of this syndrome and of the accompanying emotional responses. Julien's father innocently conspires by having him equipped and taught to hunt. But the fantasy of legend is not forgotten: the whole animal kingdom is exposed to Julien's bloodlust, which culminates in a solitary expedition of hallucinatory destructiveness.

The often hyperbolic feelings and desires of Flaubert's modern, 'realistic' characters may be carried into action in the legend. When a magic stag resists his weapons long enough to deliver a terrible curse-cum-prophecy that he will kill his parents, it is explicitly related to his given character as a 'savage heart'. Julien, weighed down by this, falls ill, communicating his secret to no-one, partly because he is not sure that he would be incapable of such a deed, especially if the Devil took a hand. The typical Flaubertian oscillation between two possible responsibilities, that of the human individual and that of a higher

power, will continue throughout the text. Thus his parents and the castle priest between them help to generate the circumstances where unintentionally, but responding to the promptings of his 'savage heart', he almost fulfils the prophecy. Julien's parents have been given different prophecies about his future, his mother being told categorically that he will be a saint, his father more confusingly hearing:

> Ah! ah! your son! . . . much blood! . . . much glory! . . . always happy! . . . the family of an emperor!

Although he flees his parents' castle and lands, he cannot escape his personality, and his new career as a soldier combines his savage heart with a desire to escape the curse by dying in battle; to which is added a new feature, the defence of what is right. Winning the hand of a Princess whose Oriental milieu is one of Flaubert's devices for avoiding too 'local' a colour, Julien finds himself back at peace, able to listen again to the temptations of his nature and the regret for his lost parents. His wife tries to overcome his sadness, urging him to return to hunting. Though he reveals the prophecy, she argues it away. But when Julien does succumb, it is not to the lure of her arguments, but to mysteriously attractive shapes and sounds of animals. This time he pursues a sequence of predator animals, neither harming, nor being harmed by them. Their vengeance, like the menace of the magic stag, will be indirect, for they merely build up his frustrated bloodlust so that when he returns home to find a male head on his wife's pillow in the darkness his response will be swift and violent. Like the rest of the story, the scene is a delicate balance of modern realism—in the attendant circumstances—legendary magic and religious mystery, with a cruelly ironic overall effect.

Julien's parents, with good reason to believe that the prophecies made to them are being realised, are killed as they peacefully await his return. It is tempting to see the role of Julien's wife as a misplaced example of Flaubert's misogyny. Certainly she influences events no less than three times, and Flaubert's most striking deviation from his medieval sources is to send Julien out alone on his penitential road, rejecting the positive view of marriage presented by the legend, where the wife shares and comforts. But to say, as Duckworth does, that 'it is because he cannot forgive her that he goes off alone', is to ignore the text. For while the legends seem to dissociate entirely the early phases of Julien's life from any divine intervention, Flaubert's Julien exculpates his wife precisely by invoking God's role. The narrator reports his words:

> She had obeyed the will of God in causing his crime and must pray for his soul, since from this day on he no longer existed.

Julien then begins a second purgatory on earth, separated from his fellow-men by his crime. The paradox of Julien's attitude is neatly summed up:

> He did not revolt against God who had inflicted this action upon him, and yet he despaired at having committed it.

Flaubert does not tell us whether it is from God that 'the

idea came to him to use his life in the service of others'. The noble Julien becomes a servant, struggling at thankless tasks like Félicité. The relentless realism of these paragraphs gives way gradually to the marvellous, which will dominate the final episode. First comes a voice, unbelievably audible through a storm and 'with the intonation of a church bell', then the waters are instantaneously calmed. Yet the reader loses contact neither with concrete reality in all its ugliness (the caller is a leper), nor with the evolution of Julien's character. He is now all tenderness in the face of danger or horror, and his total forgetfulness of self has its reward, for he is at last carried skywards, the miracle happening this time in full view of the reader. But the text does not end on this paragraph of full-blown lyricism. Flaubert, who had already introduced the word *Legend* into the title of his story, distances himself twice more with a last sentence which brings the reader back to a modern perspective and presents the author as no more than a translator:

> And that is the story of St Julian the Hospitaller, more or less as it is found on a stained glass window in a church near my home.

The text had, of course, made no real effort to respect precisely the nature and limitations of either the medieval story or the purely visual medium of the glass. Indeed, planning a later edition, Flaubert tried to persuade his publisher to include a reproduction of Rouen's St Julian window; not as an illustration—he abhorred illustrations of literary texts—but as a document:

> Comparing the image to the text, people would have said: 'I can't understand it. How did he get this from that?'

The mystificatory intent is not confined to this trick. Flaubert in the story itself walks one of his customary 'tightropes', this time between the past and the present. He seeks to satisfy both the modern demand for verisimilitude and human motivations, and the medieval belief in mystery, in the power of the divinity, and in that coexistence of the ordinary and the marvellous which is such a feature of its thought as of its visual arts.

Yet while providing both a context and motivations, he is careful not to conclude, and leaves the story doubly open-ended. The final 'cutaway' refuses to endorse the miraculous, while the whole complex account leaves unresolved the dialectic of individual responsibility v. divinely controlled determinism. Unlike his sources, Flaubert offers no explicit reason why Christ comes to save Julien, so that his God, finally, moves in a more mysterious way than that of medieval hagiographers. It has always been the artist's privilege to refuse to answer the questions he puts. Flaubert wrote in 1879:

> The people who surprise me are not those who try to explain the incomprehensible, but those who think they have found the explanation, those who have 'le bon Dieu' (or 'le non Dieu') in their pocket. Yes indeed! any dogmatism exasperates me. In a word, materialism and spiritualism seem to me to be two impertinences.

(pp. 87-94)

With '**Un Coeur simple**' there is no game of hide-and-seek between ancient sources and modern interpretations. The story is entirely Flaubert's, indeed intimately so, for it is steeped in his own memories of the region in which it is set, and uses for partial model Julie, an old family servant who was still alive in the 1870s, growing blind and infirm. Yet the story's structure contains a curious echo of the way the other two retell and expand a pre-existing narrative.

It begins with a brief, schematic outline of Félicité's adult life, seen from the outside, which is then elaborated in greater detail. The first chapter presents the ideal servant, reliable, hardworking, conscientious, undemanding. As she grows old in the job, she becomes completely dehumanised, and the chapter ends with this strong image:

> . . . she seemed to be a woman made of wood functioning in an automatic way.

The other chapters, going beyond this appearance, demolish the implications of the image. Though a creature of limited intelligence, driven by basic instincts, Félicité is never a woman of wood. The sufferings to which her real sensibility will repeatedly expose her, while recalling the sadistic undercurrent present in the two other tales, seem mainly to illustrate Flaubert's own warnings, throughout his correspondence, of the danger one runs by allowing oneself to have feelings. Sign of superiority over the bourgeois, it is also one's Achilles heel. The greater importance of the theme of feeling here, compared with the other tales, is stressed in Flaubert's own comments on it. He insisted that his aim this time was not to be cold and inhuman, but to appear 'a sensitive man', and to generate pity in his readers for Félicité.

Chapter II thus announces itself the story of her love and observes from the outside the feeling as it is transferred from an unworthy youth who leaves her in the lurch to the children of her mistress and thence to a long-lost nephew. All take her for granted, and though active and surrounded by colour and life, Félicité is already basically alone, like the saints in the other tales. In Chapter III, the reader is installed inside Félicité's consciousness and the theme of religion is grafted onto that of feeling. The choice of her viewpoint allows the author to conceal narratorial opinions on the validity both of what she is taught and what she makes of it, though he has no difficulty in indicating such opinions by his customary tactics of juxtaposition or *reduction ad absurdum,* to which he is able to add the naïve questions of Félicité herself, briefly adopting the role of *Candide* (or Bouvard or Pécuchet).

The description of Virginie's first communion, however, reminds us that for Flaubert the object of a feeling matters less than the intensity and authenticity of the feeling itself. Félicité is never closer to her middle-class predecessors in his fiction than when she is identifying intensely with the communion of Virginie, never, that is, except when experiencing a typical disappointment with the concrete reality of her own communion the next day. In this brief story, Flaubert has almost achieved his goal of narratorial non-intervention; but one of the two explicit generalisations accompanies Félicité's identification with Virginie, which is attributed to 'the imagination that true feelings of tenderness bring'. The same imagination is stirred later by her unworthy and unappreciative nephew Victor, to whom she transfers her tenderness when Virginie has been sent off to school.

Her 'simple heart', in contrast to Julien's, will always be a tender one. In other ways there are curious parallels between the two, scaled down to fit Félicité's modest social reality. Her courage, for example, is shown in the face of the somewhat domestic challenge of a bull. She makes, on foot, several painful journeys which, pilgrimages of affection in intent, become Calvaries in miniature as she suffers all kinds of disappointments and indignities. Ironies abound in them, as when she commends the departing Victor to God, only for him to die some time later in the West Indies. Soon after, Virginie, seeming to improve in health, has a sudden relapse and dies. Félicité watches the body, like Flaubert with his sister or Le Poittevin, or Charles with Emma; and the narrator's second aside pinpoints the nature of the mysterious or miraculous dimension in this modern story:

> She kissed (Virginie's eyes) several times; and would not have felt any great surprise if Virginie had opened them again; for such souls the supernatural is quite simple.

When Félicité's tenderness broadens to embrace a wider world than her 'family', the effect is almost to parody **'St Julien'**: her final object of devotion, le père Colmiche, is more or less an outcast, suffering notably from a prominent tumour on his arm. But there is an extra episode in Félicité's life, after her 'leper'. A parrot gradually becomes the focus first of her emotional, then of her religious preoccupations. The few joys and many sufferings of Félicité's earlier life are repeated with the usual ironic twists. Thus one of the parrot's escapades, by involving her in a long hunt, undermines her robust health; while the desire to keep it, after its death, precipitates the most brutally painful of her pilgrimages to Honfleur.

The gradual fusion of the parrot with her image of the Holy Spirit is as carefully plotted and motivated as the development of St Julian's bloodlust or his progress to selflessness. Félicité has never had much communication with others, and old age and deafness intensify this typical Flaubertian situation. It is noticeable that even her brief communion in grief and memory with her mistress, the momentary abolition of so many barriers, is wordless:

> they embraced, satisfying their suffering in a kiss which made them equal.

The stripping down of a life to its bare essentials had, in the cases of John and Julien, given them lucidity and heroic stature in the face of a cruel world. The modern parallels are unheroic, involving the thoughtless indifference of Madame Aubin's son and daughter-in-law (the sale of furniture, the deterioration of the fabric of the house) and Félicité's own realistically-portrayed decline into invalidity, some senile mental confusion, blindness and finally pneumonia. The pathos of the situation is underlined by repeated references to her thoughts and feelings as well as by external description. The last scene rhythms together the solemnity and spectacle of the Corpus Christi procession with Félicité's death throes, alternating poetry and medical realism until in the final lines it is the realism which gives way to the poetry, transferred now to the evocation of Félicité as she dies content and confident in her simple belief:

> Her lips were smiling. The movements of her heart slowed one by one, each more vague, more gentle, like a spring drying up, like an echo disappearing; and, when she breathed out her last breath, she thought she saw, in the heavens as they opened, a huge parrot, gliding over her head.

There is no miracle, only an individual vision, and it is tempting to detach the parrot from its place in Félicité's mental processes and see it as another parodic distortion of the religious theme. But the poetic text is not, this time, undercut by a deliberate distancing device. On the contrary, Flaubert is trying to draw his reader in, to identify with the 'simple' character and her perspective: hence the careful rhythms, the brief similes, creating an atmosphere of peace so different from the deaths of Emma or Salammbô. This of course does not mean that Flaubert shares Félicité's faith, though he may well envy its way of resolving the problem of living—and dying—in a cruel, unfeeling and even absurd world.

Since Edgar Allan Poe's early essays on the short story, the genre has frequently been compared more to lyric poetry than to the longer narrative forms. It is often argued that to succeed, it must suggest, opening up new perspectives as it resonates in the reader's mind. Though he was neither a theoretician of the form nor an assiduous practitioner of it, Flaubert did in *Trois Contes* produce texts of concentrated power and extraordinary suggestivity. The stories have occasional weak points, in the clarity of narration, of continuity or even of style. But their ambiguous, enigmatic quality is on the whole deliberate, and an important factor in the hold they have taken on generations of readers, who will no doubt continue to disagree about their basic meaning. At once Romantic and Realist, objective in their narrative techniques yet deeply personal in their links to Flaubert's most abiding intellectual preoccupations and deepest-rooted impulses, they manage to incarnate many of the qualities of his established art as a novelist and show him mastering, in late middle age, the skills required of a demanding new literary form. (pp. 95-8)

> *David Roe, in his* Gustave Flaubert, *Macmillan Education Ltd., 1989, 128 p.*

Aimée Israel-Pelletier   (essay date 1991)

[*In the following excerpt, taken from her* Flaubert's Straight and Suspect Saints: The Unity of "Trois Contes," *Israel-Pelletier examines the similarities between the stories in* Three Tales, *particularly their conclusions, asserting that each story focuses on an individual engaged in a power struggle with the ruling class.*]

There is in Flaubert a predilection for images and states of fullness, totality, and completion. As if these were the signs of a superior sensibility, of moral and intellectual integrity and perfection. For Flaubert, the role of good readers, like the role of good writers, is to work slowly to unearth the rich deposits which are alluded to in the depths, and at the surface, of a given text or of a given experience. If conclusions are undesirable, for Flaubert, it is because they seem to simplify the complex reality of things.

Flaubert's view on conclusions is not informed by an ontological questioning of the possibility of concluding, of knowing. After all, conclusions are a sign of "stupidity" only "most of the time." His remarks on the subject betray an elitist bias. They imply that only an enlightened few are justified in this practice; all others he suspects of superficiality and dogmatism. Flaubert's attitude stems from a fear that conclusions, regardless of who makes them and regardless of how they are arrived at, are likely to be accepted at face value as truth by most men. Underlying this fear is an uneasiness about what he suspected was a dangerous democratizing of knowledge and of intellectual authority. Much of what informs Flaubert's responses to social and aesthetic issues can be linked to a disillusionment with what he felt to be the leveling of moral, aesthetic, and political values brought about by democratic principles and ideals. Though, as Sartre has remarked, Flaubert shared many of the values of the bourgeoisie, a class to which he belonged, he could only envisage this class as mindless, deficient, and morally bankrupt. Moreover, he could only imagine it as a victorious, socially and politically dominant class. In the works prior to the *Trois contes,* the victory of the bourgeoisie, or of the dominant class, over the individual is a common theme. In the *Trois contes,* however, Flaubert emphasizes the victory of the individual over the class in power. (pp. 110-11)

Conclusions in Flaubert's work are highly thought out and carefully executed passages. Generally speaking, Flaubert conceived and wrote his concluding passages before he had developed other important features of the work. Once written, they were rarely altered. When he did change them, the changes were for the most part minor. They nearly always involved stylistic refinements, attempts to make the flow of images and sounds more harmonious or, in the case of **"Hérodias,"** more rhythmical. Flaubert's conclusions are not primarily aimed at befuddling the reader, as is often argued. Rather, they are meant to put the reader in awe of Flaubert's mastery of orchestration, style, effect; equally important, they are meant to make the reader think about the meaning of the work. If Flaubert's conclusions strike us as open ended, undetermined by explicit authorial intention, it is because this is the best way to make us think about what we have been reading. The endings of *Le Père Goriot* and *Le Rouge et le noir,* for example, are not less enigmatic. How is the reader meant to interpret Rastignac's challenge or Julien Sorel's shooting? Balzac and Stendhal are not more helpful to us in determining the meaning of their conclusions than is Flaubert.

The relative lack of changes which conclusions underwent in Flaubert is all the more striking since he worked and reworked his material obsessively. **"Un Cœur simple"** is a case in point. The ending changed little, while the conception of the characters, especially that of Félicité herself, experienced significant alterations. . . . [In] the earlier drafts, for example, Félicité's stupidity is more awkward, more dense. She is an opinionated person. She can be openly angry and hateful toward others. She expresses herself far more forcefully and more directly than in the final text. On the whole, her character is more bold than in the final text, where the description is far more nuanced and the character, enigmatic. Flaubert's conception of Félicité goes through changes not only throughout the drafts but, also, in the final text itself. For example, it has to strike the reader as quite odd that this sensitive and emotional woman who is capable of so much love and suffering throughout the story is described at the beginning as "une femme en bois, fonctionnant d'une manière automatique." If we find this characterization so misleading, it is not because the character of Félicité unfolds slowly. It is not, moreover, because Flaubert wants, somehow, to motivate us to regard her differently at the end from the way we regarded her at the beginning. There is a conceptual flaw and an obvious incongruence in this description of Félicité which others have noted as well. However, I think that it is justified given the exigencies of Flaubert's imaginary. If Flaubert missed this particular incongruence in his characterization of Félicité and neglected to correct it during numerous subsequent revisions, it is because this detail plays a fundamental role in the economy of Flaubertian desire. Félicité, like Saint Julien and Iaokanann, must follow the itinerary of the Flaubertian model for transcendence and fulfillment. This seemingly "wooden" woman will have to give up her, so to speak, hardness in order to be transformed into pure desire in the union with the parrot/Holy Spirit. The disintegration or dissolution of form as a sign of the progress of Flaubertian desire toward transcendence is a central model and metaphor in his work. It is a movement that can be traced in all three of the stories as well as elsewhere in Flaubert's work. . . . It can be traced cogently in **"Un Cœur simple,"** where Félicité's faculties are slowly eroded, and in **"Hérodias,"** where Iaokanann's decapitation becomes an emblem and a figure of this process.

René Girard may not be right in suggesting that *all* conclusions are the "axle" around which novels turn. But it is certainly true that for Flaubert, endings and the effects he wanted these endings to produce were often the clearest and, to his mind, the most meaning-ful parts of his projects. From *Madame Bovary* on, they serve to give the reader a clue for interpreting the meaning of the characters' lives, the meaning of the work.

It has been suggested that the conclusion of **"Un Cœur simple"** is not a true conclusion, that is to say, it does not recall the beginning and it fails to put the elements of the story together in a meaningful way for the reader; it opens rather than closes the text of Félicité's life to interpretation. It has been further suggested that the famous incipit of the story, "Pendant un demi-siècle, les bourgeoises de Pont-l'Evêque envièrent à Mme Aubain sa servante Félicité," is a phrase one expects to find at the end of the story and not, where it is, in the beginning; placing it at the beginning suggests that the narrative of Félicité's life will not be developed further, that her life is presented as a closed case. This may be so. But the reason we might feel this way is that, for Flaubert, though conclusions are the end of the character's itinerary they, just as surely, are meant to offer the reader an opening for interpreting the life of that character, to give it and the work itself meaning. The conclusion of **"Un Cœur simple"** is a conclusion in the sense that it is the culmination of the character's itinerary, the end of the narrative of her life. The incipit, on the other hand, like the characterization of Félicité as an inanimate or "wooden" creature, must necessarily limit and fix the identity of the character. It must do so because, as I have suggested above, it is in the nature of Flaubert's imaginary to depict the itinerary of a character and the progress of a narrative as the slow unfolding and transfiguration of form into something more amorphous, more rarefied and idealized. The movement of writing is always for Flaubert a kind of opening, an "épanouissement." Thus incipits close and limit in order that the rest of the work can more dramatically open and expand.

This expansive movement serves to reinforce the narrative unity of the *Trois contes.* Each of the three stories ends on a victorious note which is accompanied by an image of expansion and dilation. In **"Un Cœur simple,"** Flaubert ends the narrative of the character's life with an evocative image of enormous proportions; the skies open and reveal Loulou as a "perroquet gigantesque." In **"Saint Julien,"** though the story itself concludes with an evocation of the narrator/scribe with both feet planted on the ground of his native town contemplating the stained-glass window depicting the saint, the character's itinerary culminates with the leper and Julien embracing and expanding together, "et celui dont les bras le serraient toujours grandissait, grandissait, touchant de sa tête et de ses pieds les deux murs de la cabane. Le toit s'envola, le firmament se déployait." Both endings represent a union of the character with the desired or idealized other (Félicité and Loulou, and Julien and the leper). That other is itself represented as a union of two figures (Loulou-Holy Spirit and leper-Christ). The identification of these two figures with one another is the end result of the characters' effort, their strategy, for making reality (Loulou and the leper) coincide with illusion, with its idealized and desired double (the Holy Spirit and Christ). In the process, the particular and the personal are legitimized and the universal and abstract are made more personal and more effective, thus allowing the characters to fulfill their desires and fantasies.

What about the conclusion of **Hérodias?** On the surface, it would seem to be different from the other two stories. But, like **"Un Cœur simple"** and **"Saint Julien,"** **"Hérodias,"** too, ends with an image of expansion and dilation. Only, here, the expansion is not, as in the two previous tales, ascending and vertical; it is descending and horizontal. **Hérodias** . . . starts on an elevation (as opposed to the other two tales, which end on an elevation). It starts where the itineraries of the two others end (in the skies) and it carries through these last two movements to their conclusion; the conclusion of **"Hérodias"** descends or lands, so to speak, the narrative of the *Trois contes.* This movement had been already sketched in the conclusion of **"Saint Julien"** where Flaubert, the writer/scribe, brings the narrative down to where he and his readers stand.

The ending of **"Hérodias"** is not only the conclusion of **"Hérodias"** itself, as it most surely is. But it is also the conclusion of the *Trois contes.* The theatrical conclusion of **"Hérodias,"** we might call it the last act of **"Hérodias,"** opens with an illumination, "A l'instant où se levait le soleil." The light which spills over in the concluding scene symbolizes the moment of revelation; the meaning of the prophet's message becomes clear. Its breadth overwhelms those who understand it. Christ's potential for the future is acknowledged. By the same token, the implication, here, is that the meaning of the *Trois contes* ought to be, by now, clear as well. Expansion and dilation are represented as enlightenment and dissemination. "Console-toi! Il est descendu chez les morts annoncer le Christ!" Thus, Iaokanann continues his descent (and the narrative's topographic descent from the citadel of Machærous) below the surface to disseminate the message to the dead, while at the surface, his head, this head heavy with disseminating potential, spreads horizontally, to the living on earth, the message of the coming of Christ and of hope.

Not only does the conclusion of **"Hérodias"** serve as a conclusion to the *Trois contes.* The story as a whole represents a dramatic conclusion to the work. **"Hérodias"** completes the previous tales by repeating their main themes and, most dramatically, by making more explicit what had been only implicit in the two narratives. This last story is a revelation or an unraveling on the surface of the secrets which **"Un Cœur simple"** and **"Saint Julien"** keep hidden both from the power system they target and from the reader who keeps only to the straight text.

What is the "revealed" meaning of the *Trois contes* which the ending of **"Hérodias"** refers to? The *Trois contes* is distinguished from all of Flaubert's previous works, as I have claimed throughout this book, by the way each of the three stories dramatizes the victory of the individual over the system in power. The characters find ways of undermining this system and of triumphing over it by imposing their own interpretations, their own values, over those values and interpretations the system has imposed as law. Thus, Félicité finds a way of achieving salvation through a mis-reading and a mis-representation of the Holy Spirit. Julien, in turn, uses the text of sainthood (the hagiographic model) to act out his hostility toward society. In **"Saint Julien,"** much as in **"Hérodias,"** the parental couple, the king and the queen, represents the law, the root of civilization and of corruption. Julien's parricide is an attempt to reverse the process of civilization and return to a primitive and ideal state. Julien's repressed oedipal struggle is reflected and amplified in Iaokanann's voice decrying the incestuous relationship of Herod and Hérodias and calling upon the destruction of the civilization they celebrate.

Both Félicité's and Julien's subversive plans are personal and secretive. However, no one can doubt that Iaokanann is expressing, and loudly at that, the same hostility and the same subversive message that Félicité and Julien do privately and on the sly. Iaokanann, quite literally, gives voice to Félicité and Julien's grievances against civilization. When Félicité struggles against the oppressive and repressive male-dominated system, she is struggling against her gender-biased, bourgeois-dominated civilization. Julien may not be motivated by the same injustice; he is twice privileged by birth, being both male and rich. Yet, he is moved even more strongly than she is to undermine civilization. In a manner, Julien's answer to Félicité is that civilization itself is the cause of the individual's suffering and not the specific injustices (be it poverty or sexual domination) through which it might express itself; civilization is, by its very nature, repressive.

In **"Saint Julien,"** the repudiation of civilization and the violence against it are more total than in **"Un Cœur simple."** We can note a progression; this repudiation and this violence become even more pronounced in **"Hérodias."** In the *Trois contes,* men (or the father) are the signifiers of the "law" of civilization. In **"Hérodias,"** the father as the signifier of the law is impotent. He is in fact absent as person, as character. Conceptually, standing as he is in the oedipal scenario, as the representative of the primary social taboo that founds society, the interdiction of incest, his impotence and his failure to uphold the law are obvious in the incestuous relationship (incestuous in Iokanann's eyes) between Herod and Hérodias. Furthermore, the fact that the father is absent from **"Hérodias"** and that thematically **"Hérodias"** underscores the end of a civilization dominated by the Father (the Judaic God) confirms the positive and optimistic ending of the *Trois contes* as a whole. In **"Un Cœur simple,"** Félicité finds a way to exclude men from her world; in **"Saint Julien,"** Julien tries to kill the father and, in an important sense, succeeds; **"Hérodias"** marks the end of his rule and the triumph of the son. Like Félicité and Julien, Iaokanann wins in the end; in winning, he confirms the successes of Félicité and Julien in subverting the system in power. (pp. 111-16)

The *Trois contes* suggests that the way to triumph over the power structure is to work from within it. This is suggested, one would say, literally and graphically in **"Hérodias"** (Iaokanann is most literally or topographically inside the power structure). To understand is to be inside; similarly, to destroy one must also be inside, like a virus in an organism. Understanding the system is, then, a necessary first step in the process of subversion (Bouvard and Pécuchet are engaged in trying to understand the system and its values). This is the reason why the system in power tries to limit access to key texts by making these texts too abstract for the likes of Félicité. Those in power are in charge of administering and communicating these texts. Power slips from one group to another when the group in power can no longer control the meaning and the interpretations of these texts. Texts that are likely to slip the control of the dominant group and serve to encourage subversive behavior and thought are, Flaubert tells us, texts that appeal to the imagination and to sentiment (the Gospels for Félicité, hagiography for Julien). This is why literature, art, is feared by governments and by the moral bourgeois majority; it is "insurrectionnel aux gouvernements et immoral aux bourgeois"; "La littérature n'est pas une chose abstraite; elle s'adresse à l'homme tout entier." Thus, in **"Un Cœur simple,"** the language of the dogma is too abstract and too obscure to be understood and used by Félicité. The Gospels, on the other hand, are more accessible. Though we would undoubtedly consider her understanding of the Gospels a faulty one, it remains true that Flaubert presents her as willfully, perhaps by some superior intuition, misunderstanding and misrepresenting these texts. The Gospels offer her the working model for subverting the system. Similarly, it is because Julien understands the workings of both the worldly and the religious ethics of his father and his mother that he is able to subvert both and define himself as a being apart. It is not important how Félicité and Julien receive this knowledge; what is important is that they use it *systematically* to plot against their oppressors. Both Julien and Félicité succeed because they are able to penetrate the system and, using its own values and its own language, undermine it and, ultimately, destroy it.

If Herod fails miserably, it is because, unlike Félicité, Julien, and Iaokanann, he is unable to understand (on any level) either the magical power of Hérodias (his oppressor) or the meaning of the prophet's message (his only chance to be saved). And he does not understand mainly because he seems to lack the desire to understand; he shows little desire to penetrate the mysteries which surround him. Thus, he is often presented gazing at the surface and from a distance. He is indifferent to everything save aesthetic and sensual pleasures. Of all the characters in the *Trois contes,* he is the most passive; even Madame Aubain responds more decisively to situations that concern her family. Herod's ignorance of the meaning of things which touch his life is shown as a factor of his unwillingness to be involved, his reluctance to make decisions and to take responsibilities for his choices. For this reason, he would postpone indefinitely the decision to kill Iaokanann. For this reason, too, he loses the only chance he has of escaping the tyranny of Hérodias. Herod is the most (anachronistically) Sartrian of Flaubert's characters. Before Iaokanann's decapitation, and throughout the story, Herod has a vague sense that the prophet's words carry an important message. Yet he fails to pierce the meaning of this message because, as Hérodias shows too well, he can be distracted by easy pleasures. In the end, Herod follows his nature and opts for aesthetic and sensual pleasures over meaning and hope—exemplified in Iaokanann's message. Meaning, on the contrary, is precisely what both Félicité and Julien vigorously and surreptitiously seek. Meaning (salvation and union with the idealized other) is what they find; to be more accurate, meaning is what they, by dint of effort and design, forge for themselves. (pp. 116-18)

There is a temptation to identify Herod the aesthete with Flaubert; this position would not be wholly unjustified. But . . . Flaubert is only partly reflected in the lame and troubled figure of Herod. He is more fully represented by the figure of Herod's alter ego, Iaokanann, who embodies the meaning and the message of Christ. Flaubert, in **"Hérodias,"** fantasizes sharing in the glory of the character who overcomes pessimism and sterility and brings hope to mankind. He identifies with that part of Iaokanann (whom I have read as a figure for the writer and the writing process) that holds that a work of art as a purely aesthetic object is doomed to the kind of sterility that Herod symbolizes. In Herod, Flaubert might indeed be seeing himself, but only a certain aspect of himself; namely, the aesthete, the one responsible for the dead end he had reached in *Bouvard et Pécuchet.*

To undermine the optimistic ending of both **"Hérodias"** and the *Trois contes* on the assumption that the conclusion of **"Hérodias"** is an ironical statement based on the similarities we can point to between Herod's decadent civilization and Flaubert's own—thus suggesting Christ's (the Son's) failure to bring about change—is both unfruitful and incorrect. Flaubert may not have been optimistic about the state of affairs of his time; and he may not have been optimistic about the turn his own life had taken, both professionally and personally. But in the *Trois contes,* Flaubert draws up a scenario in which he comes to terms with illusion (hence fiction) as the only way to confront reality and win. Forging new and creative strategies by which to negotiate with society, not on its own terms but on his own, seems to have offered Flaubert what he needed at this point in his career; namely, the sense that art was indeed supreme and redemptive both for the individual in his most private self and for the individual in his interaction with society.

Illusion in the *Trois contes* is not, as elsewhere in Flaubert, tested by circumstances and, in the process, found to fall short of fulfilling the character's desires. Rather, it is shown to be a legitimate form of action. The *Trois contes* represents an example, perhaps the sole example in Flaubert's work, which considers fiction as a productive way of dealing with the world. Just as the historical Christ changed Western culture through his visions, so might the artist change perceptions of the world and, ultimately, change the world itself. Flaubert inserted in the margins of the drafts of **"Un Cœur simple"** a phrase concerning Félicité: "il faut que l'on veuille l'imiter." This is a telling phrase. Though he did not say the same of Julien and Iaokanann, it is obvious that, despite their overbearing nature, the three characters are meant to strike the reader (of both the straight and the subversive interpretations) as exemplary, thus, as worthy of imitation. Here, Flaubert may have felt especially good about his faithfulness to the classical principle of "plaire et enseigner." Flaubert's fantasy about the potential of fiction may have been more than a fantasy; writing with a sense of optimism may have convinced Flaubert of the power of fiction to change the world.

In the *Trois contes,* Flaubert fantasizes, as I said, he might have even believed, as did his friend George Sand, that through literature one can empower those who have been estranged and silenced by the system. By giving them a voice, as Iaokanann gives voice to Félicité's and Julien's grievances, and by providing them with a space where their desires might be reflected, the writer can claim a community with whom to undermine and, eventually, reshape society in view of accommodating the singular and the disenfranchised. Rimbaud believed in the "verb," and perhaps to a certain extent so, too, did Flaubert. If illusion had the power to alter states of mind (Saint Antoine would be the most dramatic example of that), perhaps it had the power to alter the world. Indeed it may well be that one of the things Flaubert learned about writing fiction through writing the *Trois contes* is that in order to revitalize fiction and to revitalize himself as a writer, he had to convince himself that literature mattered, that it could offer hope to readers who felt alienated from the system.

Just as Flaubert reevaluates his relationship to the characters and uses them to express a fantasy of power over the dominant culture, Flaubert in the *Trois contes* rethinks the place and the role of the reader in his work.

> Quaint à laisser voir mon opinion personnelle sur les gens que je mets en scène, non, non, mille fois non! Je ne m'en reconnais pas le droit. Si le lecteur ne tire pas d'un livre la moralité qui doit s'y trouver, c'est que le lecteur est un imbécile ou que le livre est *faux* au point de vue de l'exactitude.

By refraining from offering explicit indications about a work's meaning and by refusing to volunteer his views on the characters and the way the reader is meant to perceive them, Flaubert had opened the way for the reader to participate in the interpretation of the work to a larger and more significant extent than ever before in the novel. The reader in Flaubert holds a key role in the formulation of the work's meaning. This is due in large part to Flaubert's deliberate effort to keep out of the work explicit references concerning his intentions, references which might bias the interpretation of the work and discourage the reader from questioning the text and questioning his or her own values with regards to subjects treated in the text. It is also because Flaubert's aesthetic sense demanded that his style be allusive and that his meaning be suggested rather than stated. (pp. 118-20)

Flaubert's reluctance to validate certain narrative facts, some trivial and some not so trivial (say, the color of Emma's eyes or the question of whether Julien's parricide is determined by his psychology or by supernatural causes), leaves the reader with the impression that he or she is alone with the work, that he or she alone is responsible for its meaning. To a certain extent, this is true. But to a much greater extent, it is not. Depersonalization of the narrative may give the impression that the author is absent; but Flaubert's presence in his narrative is, on a certain level, even more pervasive and insidious than Balzac's or Stendhal's presence in their works precisely because it is not as obvious. Flaubert's text offers the reader the sense of the autonomy of the narrative; what it does not offer is explicit guidance; the key word here being explicit. It is, therefore, inevitable that some readers will misread; and this is not at all undesirable, as Félicité's and Julien's examples suggest.

Thus by minimizing the explicit presence of the author in his work, Flaubert gives the reader an important function in the interpretation of the work. The reader is perceived in a special relationship to the writer; he or she is responsible for framing and formulating the work's meaning. The reader is, so to speak, an author-ity. But by the same token, and perhaps because the role has become so important, the reader becomes for Flaubert a source of ambivalent feelings. In Flaubert's mind, the reader is an accomplice, but an accomplice who cannot be trusted to share the same values as Flaubert himself. Though in the *Correspondance* Flaubert, at times, speaks of the "public" as intuitively enlightened, far more often he refers to it as severely handicapped in matters of art. Flaubert was convinced that only a few readers would understand the enormity of the task he had assigned himself in a given work.

Only a few could be expected to follow the complexities of its designs, the "ruses" of style and the "profondes combinaisons" necessary for expressing his complex intentions. Thus, by opening the text to the reader's interpretation by his own reticence to explain, interpret, and judge character and event, Flaubert had also opened the way for an unreliable and an undesirable alliance. Flaubert's work as a whole, from *Madame Bovary* to *Bouvard et Pécuchet,* is built on his tacit acknowledgment that he is not alone in fathering his texts, but that they are likely to be fathered, mostly, by incompetent readers.

Why does Flaubert place the reader in this position? Why does he give the reader responsibility for formulating the meaning of the work when he was convinced that most readers are incapable of seeing its value, its artistic merit? There is in this gesture a form of masochism or, more specifically, an impulse toward self-sacrifice in the name of art. This attitude serves a special need. This complicity with the reader is, in point of fact, what redeems Flaubert's literary vocation; it is what helps him to distinguish himself from that despised yet important other, the "common" man, the utilitarian bourgeois. Because the alliance with a despised reader is so difficult to accept and because an aesthete like Flaubert could not imagine, and thus could only be obsessed by, such an alliance, Flaubert

could experience literature as his ultimate suffering, his ultimate sacrifice, and, by the same token, his ultimate contribution to humanity. "Saint Flaubert," as Valéry rightly called him, must seek and must accept (or must imagine) the indifference and the abuse of those he serves, namely, the general reader, just as Saint Julien, assisting travelers to cross the dangerous river, accepts and, also, invites their abuse. Flaubert in his text, once again like Saint Julien ferrying travelers, does not conceal well his contempt and his desire for violence against the people he so clearly seeks out. These feelings of contempt and hostility toward the reader motivate Flaubert to make the reader's task of interpreting, of finding meaning, a frustrating and thankless task for most readers. Flaubert's strategies are not intended to undermine interpretation or meaning itself; after all, he expected that a "few" would understand, and he wrote for them. What appears to be a deliberate sabotage of this search for meaning is the result of trying to manage a complex and ambivalent attitude toward the reader as an active factor in the interpretation of the work. The result is a work whose meaning must not be easily seen. Rather, it must be uncovered by sheer effort, desire, by aesthetic sensibility. Thus, much in Flaubert's revisions are meant to make the work enigmatic. Psychologically, Flaubert needed to find a style and a structure that would

Flaubert's birthplace, the Hotel Dieu, Rouen, France.

raise the hostility of some of his readers while inviting others to read him differently from the way they had read novels before.

Even though in the *Trois contes* Flaubert works to make the meaning of his narratives more difficult to decipher, his attitude toward his reader becomes somewhat more accommodating and more tolerant than in previous works. In fact, more so than anywhere else in Flaubert, one cannot speak of reader and text in the singular. Flaubert no longer seems to be writing and counting on only the "few" to understand and appreciate his work. He writes a work that is accessible to them and to a more general readership—not necessarily the bourgeoisie, but not excluding them. What is especially striking in the *Trois contes,* what gives the work such power, is that Flaubert does not undermine the common reader's interpretation; in other words, he does not undermine the surface and literal reading of the three stories—as accounts of the lives of three exemplary individuals who can be related easily to a model, namely sainthood or the process of sacrificing worldly pleasures and happiness for a transcendent goal. Neither does he valorize, as he often does in his letters and elsewhere, the importance of reading in depth to understand the characters' psychology, as the reader does in the reading of the subversive text. In the *Trois contes,* Flaubert creates a narrative structure able to support what is, essentially, two contradictory readings with neither one standing as more legitimate than the other. In this lies the brilliance of Flaubert's conception. At all moments, we are presented with a surface and a depth which run concurrently and yet independently of one another. Alongside the techniques of multiple points of view and free indirect discourse, this narrative structure, which we also find in *Bouvard et Pécuchet,* must count as one of Flaubert's more successful strategies for expanding and enriching prose, Flaubert's ultimate design and ambition. By allowing form ("la plastique") to support more substance ("la matière"), Flaubert expands the space of representation. (pp. 120-23)

[The] stories in the *Trois contes* can be read as allegorical narratives of writing. In writing the three stories, Flaubert was trying to understand how he wrote and, even more basically, what is writing. I consider the *Trois contes,* in part, as Flaubert's attempt to recover his own past, both his personal past (in **"Un Cœur simple,"** for example) and his own literary past (in the way the three stories relate stylistically and thematically to the larger works). More importantly for me, I see the work as Flaubert's attempt to recover a lost sense of wonder and optimism about the capacity of language to express being and to transform the self, to reflect the world and to transfigure that world. In the passage quoted above, Flaubert compares himself to a cathedral whose stained-glass window reflects on his soul the beauty of the universe. The stained-glass window, however, does more than reflect; it transforms the universe. Similarly, the narrator/scribe at the end of **"Saint Julien"** has not simply recorded the life of the saint as it is represented in the stained-glass window; he has transfigured it. In the passage cited above, Flaubert expresses the fantasy of a language that would be (like the stained-glass window which is between himself and the world) transpar-

ent and yet, paradoxically, "transfiguring" (the stained-glass window, language, makes the world more beautiful).

What Flaubert sought to recover in the *Trois contes,* what he thought he once possessed—and which he, perhaps, never really possessed—was the sense that language is all powerful and magical. The dramatization of this ideal is especially striking in **"Un Cœur simple"** and **"Hérodias."** **"Saint Julien,"** the first of the three stories to have been written, and written specifically, Flaubert tells us, to find out if he still knew how to write, is the story in which Flaubert acts out in most elemental terms the workings of language and the problems he encountered when writing. In writing this story, he discovered something important. It is only with the conclusion of **"Saint Julien"** that he finds, fantasizes, a solution; and this solution enables him to continue with the *Trois contes* and to return with enthusiasm and optimism to *Bouvard et Pécuchet.*

Flaubert's problems with language and the resolution of these problems are in **"Saint Julien,"** as in each of the stories, dramatized through the character's attempt to act out his desires on the world. I [suggest that in] . . . **"Saint Julien"** that hunting is a metaphor for writing, that Julien's arrows represent the writer's pen and that the animals stand for the world. At first, things seem relatively simple for the hunter. Julien aims at his prey and kills it. He succeeds at hunting because he does not realize the implication of his act. He does not realize that this violence touches not only the animals he kills but his own parents. His passion, in other words, becomes a crime. When Julien realizes the consequences of his passion for hunting, he stops hunting and suffers from melancholy and impotence. He is debilitated by the realization that to hunt is, in fact, to kill. In terms of the linguistic analogy, the writer becomes aware that language in the process of naming necessarily destroys the object the writer aims to represent; language, in other words, substitutes itself for the world. This act of substitution and appropriation makes the writer feel responsible for violating the integrity of the world he wants to represent. The dilemma is clear; on one hand, writing abolishes the world, on the other, not writing destroys the writer (Julien suffers when he cannot go hunting).

The writer's problem stems from having once believed, and expected, that words stood for things and from having discovered, subsequently, to his anguish, that they do not, really. The writer discovers that in the process of representing, language deforms and destroys the world. To put it another way, for Flaubert, language, through style, "ought" to reflect the world; it ought to be as simple as aiming your arrow and striking your prey. His experience as a writer, however, assures him that this is not the case; language is in a troubled relationship to the world. In his desire and expectation that words communicate in as direct a way as possible, Flaubert remains true to the classical ideal he defended throughout his career.

When he speaks about classical principles of representation, Flaubert nearly always speaks in a lofty tone which can only put us on guard against taking these remarks as anything more than fantasy, the fantasy of simplicity, of perfect word to world fit. But, for being a fantasy, this ideal is not less a preoccupation, a goal, and a problem to work out. In his *Hommage à Louis Bouilhet,* Flaubert praises his friend for a style where words reflect thought in a most direct way: "Voilà un style qui va droit au but, où l'on ne sent pas l'auteur; le mot disparaît dans la clarté même de l'idée, *ou plutôt, se collant dessus, ne l'embarasse dans aucun de ses mouvements, et se prête à l'action*" (my italics). Indeed, Flaubert's fantasy is for the writer to disappear from his writing and for words to stick like glue to ideas and then to vanish. The fundamental problem facing Flaubert in the moment of writing is what degree of tolerance, or distortion, can he accept before he considers that the system has broken down—before the relationship between words and world becomes too tenuous for him to support? The question posed implicitly in **"Saint Julien"** is will the writer continue to seek a language that is transparent and reflecting or will he acknowledge the impossibility of this task and accept that the gap between sign and signifier is inevitable, that words do not "stick" to things because there is interference from the perceiving and desiring subject (the writer)? In other words, to what extent do point of view and desire distort the world and is this distortion (or violence) acceptable for a writer who insisted on impersonality and on the classical notion of word to world fit? Until he has answered this question, writing remains problematic.

I pointed out in **"Saint Julien"** that to write, for Flaubert, is to write against the father. This is a difficult task, since the father is the signifier of the law and of language. To write against the father would be, then, to write against language. How can one write with language and against it? This not only means that language as a theme will be undermined (as is the case in so many of Flaubert's novels—Flaubert has a way of undercutting characters who use language well). More seriously, it will mean that the writer cannot write. But Flaubert must write, just as Julien must hunt. In the chapter on Julien, I remarked that the answer lies in an alternate language, one which does not perceive a difference between the concepts and the metaphors of "reflection" and of "transformation." To continue writing, Flaubert will have to imagine a language that is not governed by the father, by difference and by violence, by interference and by distortion. Julien can only be the happy man his name implies and Flaubert can only be happy writing if a way can be found to kill the father (suppressing violence and difference) without, by the same stroke, giving up their passions, without giving up hunting and writing. Flaubert finds the answer when he realizes, through Julien's oedipal struggle for individuation at the end, that the son can be victorious over the father if he can appropriate for himself the father's authority (recall the fountain episode) and if he can take the mother as a model for a kind of writing against the father. This realization on the part of Flaubert regarding the mother's contribution in the formulation of the ideal language might explain why Flaubert comes to terms with his mother's death during the composition of the *Trois contes.* Four years after her death, he finds himself consoled. "Faut-il te dire mon opinion?" he writes Caroline. "Je crois que (sans le savoir) j'avais été malade profondément et secrètement depuis la mort de notre pauvre vieille. Si je me trompe, d'où vient cette espèce d'éclaircissement qui s'est fait en moi, depuis

quelque temps! C'est comme si des brouillards se dissipaient. Physiquement, je me sens rajeuni."

The mother offers Julien a model for a language which, like the "dialogues" between Félicité and Loulou, has no recourse to violence and to difference. The mother is a figure of abjection, the figure of identity, of the dissolution of difference. She represents the ideal of a pre-oedipal paradise, a space where the son can rethink (re-write) himself a new without reference to the father. The language the mother suggests to the son is dramatized in all the scenes of fusion and union we find in the *Trois contes.* We find it first in the conclusion of **"Saint Julien,"** where Julien lying atop the leper merges with him and expands until he dissolves into the firmament, having been transfigured into Christ. The fusion of the bodies of the leper, of Julien, and of Christ recalls the passage quoted earlier from Flaubert's homage to Bouilhet, where he expresses the ideal style as one in which words stick to thought, become invisible, and follow thought to action. These images or metaphors for writing as the process by which the world is reflected and, at the same time, transfigured are expressed, as I have shown earlier, in the very last sentence of **"Saint Julien,"** where the narrator/scribe informs the reader that he (the narrator/scribe) had been the vehicle of this process, of this translation (reflection and transformation). It is also expressed in the drama of Julien's metamorphosis into Christ through the leper (a figure for the abject/mother). It is further expressed in the image of Loulou as one and the same as the Holy Spirit through Félicité's desire for this union. The example of Iaokanann is an even more dramatic expression of the process of reflection and transformation; Flaubert presents a character who is one with his words through his powerful voice. His words are, indeed, his body; Iaokanann is the message (and the message itself is about messages). But this message will have meaning only when it is embodied and transfigured in Christ; it will only have a meaning through his presence: "Pour qu'il [for Christ, for Christ's message] grandisse il faut que je [my voice, my body, my person] diminue." Iaokanann's example highlights Flaubert's desire for a perfect fit between words and their referents. It highlights, as well, the importance of the writer's voice (his point of view and his desires) in shaping (transfiguring) the message. Having shaped the message, the writer's voice must then be suppressed or buried in order to allow the message, the idea, the word to appear as the perfect reflection of the world.

Flaubert's ideal language is an erotic language, a language of sameness and identity that excludes difference and violence. It is a language that could only achieve its goal by gliding from one signifier to the other, by sliding from one domain ("reality") to the other ("dream/desire"). It does not proceed by difference and reason. Masculine discourse by its valuation of difference as a means of producing meaning cannot serve to reflect the world or to reflect being and makes way for the erotic feminine. Flaubert, in the *Trois contes,* conceives of discourse as a transparent and unresisting medium (less a "body" than a glass, a filter where the world/text is figured). It is a language which, at once, reflects and, magically, transfigures. It is in these terms that Flaubert describes poetic language, as we see, for example, in his description of the style of Leconte de Lisle: "La poésie n'est qu'une manière de percevoir les objets extérieurs, un organe spécial qui tamise la matière et qui, sans la changer, la transfigure. . . . Il faut pour bien faire une chose, que cette chose-là rentre dans votre constitution." Flaubert's fantasy of writing a language that is both reflecting and transfiguring finds expression in the *Trois contes* as a discourse and an aesthetics of pleasure, of eroticism, of the feminine. A style that is both reflecting and transfiguring might just be what Flaubert envisaged when he spoke of "poetic prose." This would be a style where suggestion, identity, union, and harmony would take the place of declaration, definition, difference, and violence.

Both **"Un Cœur simple"** and **"Hérodias"** are informed by the conclusion of **"Saint Julien."** **"Un Cœur simple"** offers a striking example of continuity. The repudiation of the masculine, of the father, is carried through with a vengeance. **"Un Cœur simple"** is a feminine world, the reverse in many ways of **"Saint Julien."** Instead of a male protagonist, Flaubert chooses a woman; Julien's violence is converted into tenderness and compassion in the character of Félicité. Julien had already, in Part 3 of the story, tried to substitute love for violence—and he succeeded in reaching his goal better through love than through violence. In **"Un Cœur simple,"** Félicité can be said to have benefited by the resolution of **"Saint Julien."** Realizing that one cannot eliminate the masculine head-on, that to kill the father means to steal his authority, undermine it and make it slip to a more desirable order, Félicité uses (mis-uses) the male-dominated linguistic system to bring about the desired results. The Gospel's imaginative discourse furnishes her with the model. Flaubert's fantasy of a sign that is only minimally distanced from the signifier, already dramatized in the conclusion of **"Saint Julien,"** translates into the union of Loulou and the Holy Spirit. The distance between sign and signifier is made even closer, as I have indicated, in the case of Iaokanann. There is a certain pleasure expressed on the part of Flaubert in showing that imagination (Félicité) and eloquence (Iaokanann) can communicate desire and satisfy both the mind and sentiment. Flaubert in the *Trois contes* does not accept the linguistic fact that words are inevitable distortions of the world they represent and that the voice is not closer to truth than are words on a page. Instead, he fantasizes a kind of erotic feminine language that signifies (reflects and transfigures) by eliminating difference, by abolishing distances.

Thus, from **"Saint Julien"** to **"Hérodias,"** there is a consistent attempt to excise the masculine and the violent from issues that reflect Flaubert's attitude to language and signification. **"Hérodias"** with its strong dramatization of the evil character of Hérodias, a woman, is no exception. She may be, literally speaking, a woman. But, more importantly, she represents the power of masculine rule, civilization. Flaubert wrote: "La femme est un produit de l'homme. *Dieu a créé la femelle, et l'homme a fait la femme;* elle est le résultat de la civilisation, une œuvre factice. Dans les pays où toute culture intellectuelle est nulle, elle n'existe pas (car c'est une œuvre d'art, au sens humanitaire; est-ce pour cela que toutes les grandes idées générales se sont symbolisées au féminin?" Indeed, Hérodias is not a "femelle"; she is anything but "natural."

Moreover, her relationship with Herod brings no offspring. This is a criticism that Iaokanann levels at her; and she is sensitive to it. True, she is a woman and a mother. But, as I pointed out in the last chapter, she has brought to the world a perversion of nature; Salomé, like herself, is a figure for artifice, for art and deception. Iaokanann, however, is the figure for the feminine, and his violent vituperations against Hérodias are meant to taunt her and make her envy him. Just as Loulou represents feminine discourse, and yet is for Félicité both a "son" and a "lover," so, too, is Iaokanann an androgynous figure for writing. As Charles Berheimer has argued in *Flaubert and Kafka,* Flaubert, as a writer, identifies with the feminine.

Flaubert, like the stained-glass window of a cathedral (he often compared himself to a cathedral), sees the artist as the medium through which reality is reflected but, also, through which it is transfigured and redefined. He wrote: "Une âme se mesure à la dimension de son désir, comme l'on juge d'avance des cathédrales à la hauteur de leurs clochers." Flaubert's desire to reconcile within himself the paradox of a language that he wanted so much to believe reflected being and yet that he suspected, desired, and tried so hard to make more magical, more responsive to desire, leads him in the *Trois contes* to imagine a wonderful structure whereby the text of the *Trois contes* opens itself and makes available a narrative that both reflects (the straight text) and magically transfigures (the suspect text) his and his characters' desires. This structure of optimism, doubly optimistic in that we find it so clearly in both the straight and the suspect readings, is the backbone of the *Trois contes.* The promise this work holds of a better future for illusion and for fiction makes the *Trois contes* unique in Flaubert. Flaubert's "swan song" is, ironically for a writer who has been so consistently characterized as a cynic and a hater of humanity, the most hopeful and, aesthetically, the most beautifully crafted of all his works. (pp. 124-30)

> *Aimée Israel-Pelletier, in her* Flaubert's Straight and Suspect Saints: The Unity of "Trois Contes," *John Benjamins Publishing Company, 1991, 165 p.*

FURTHER READING

Biography

Bart, Benjamin F. *Flaubert.* Syracuse, N.Y.: Syracuse University Press, 1967, 791 p.
    Comprehensive biography of Flaubert.

Lottman, Herbert. *Flaubert: A Biography.* Boston: Little, Brown and Company, 1989, 396 p.
    Biography that addresses popular preconceptions about Flaubert.

Sachs, Murray. "Flaubert's *Trois contes:* The Reconquest of Art." *L'Esprit Createur* X, No. 1 (Spring 1970): 62-74.

Discusses events surrounding the composition of *Trois contes.*

Sartre, Jean-Paul. *The Family Idiot: Gustave Flaubert, 1821-1957.* 4 vols. Translated by Carol Cosman. Chicago: University of Chicago Press, 1981.

> Biographical, psychological, and philosophical study of Flaubert that attempts to discover "the relationship of the man to [his] work."

Starkie, Enid. *Flaubert: The Making of a Master.* New York: Atheneum, 1967, 403 p.

> An extensive, well-documented portrait of Flaubert "the human being" as well as an informative analysis of Flaubert "the writer" through the publication and obscenity trial of *Madame Bovary* in 1856.

—————. *Flaubert the Master: A Critical and Biographical Study (1856-1880).* New York: Atheneum, 1971, 390 p.

> Treats Flaubert's personal life and career from 1856 until his death. This volume "is intended to show Flaubert in full possession of his art and craft, and how he used them in different ways, without repeating himself."

Williams, Roger L. "Gustave Flaubert." In his *The Horror of Life,* pp. 111-215. Chicago: University of Chicago Press, 1980.

> Attributes Flaubert's pessimism to his physical and emotional problems.

Criticism

Bart, B. F. "Flaubert and Hunting: 'La légende de Saint-Julien l'Hospitalier'." *Nineteenth-Century French Studies* IV, Nos. 1-2 (1975-76): 31-52.

> Examines the historical sources about hunting which Flaubert consulted and then incorporated in "La légende."

Bart, Benjamin F., and Cook, Robert Francis. *The Legendary Sources of Flaubert's "Saint-Julien."* Toronto: University of Toronto Press, 1977, 203 p.

Cross, Richard K. "Dead Selves: Epiphanies in *Trois contes* and *Dubliners.*" In his *Flaubert and Joyce: The Rite of Fiction,* pp. 17-32. Princeton, N.J.: Princeton University Press, 1971.

> Compares Flaubert's use of the epiphany in "Un coeur simple" to Joyce's in the short story collection *Dubliners.*

De Dobay-Rifelj, Carol. "Doors, Walls, and Barriers in Flaubert's 'Un coeur simple'." *Studies in Short Fiction* XI, No. 3 (Summer 1974): 291-95.

> Discusses Flaubert's use of barriers in "Un coeur simple" as "symbols of Félicité's growing isolation and rejection by the outside world."

Duncan, Phillip A. "The Equation of Theme and Spatial Form in Flaubert's 'Hérodias'." *Studies in Short Fiction* 14, No. 2 (Spring 1977): 129-36.

> Analyzes Flaubert's use of landscape, architecture, and movement as thematic devices in "Hérodias."

—————. "Another Ancestor of Emma Bovary: Julietta of 'Rêve d'enfer'." *Studies in Short Fiction* 15, No. 4 (Fall 1978): 454-56.

> Examines similarities between characters in *Madame Bovary* and "Rêve d'enfer," noting that this short story "anticipates the central role which the paradoxical po-

larity of matter and spirit will assume in [Flaubert's] mature work."

—————. "Paul and Virginie/Flaubert and Bernardin." *Studies in Short Fiction* 24, No. 4 (Fall 1987): 436-38.

> Argues that Paul and Virginie, characters in "Un coeur simple," allowed Flaubert to critique the "happy savage theme" advocated by Jacques Henri Bernardin de Saint-Pierre in his novel *Paul et Virginie.*

Gans, Eric Lawrence. *The Discovery of Illusion: Flaubert's Early Works, 1835-1837.* Berkeley: University of California Press, 1971, 169 p.

> Provides a psychostructural overview of the short stories which Flaubert wrote between 1835 and 1837, studying the "significance of each work in itself, both as a (synchronic) totality and as an element in a (diachronic) personal and literary evolution."

Ginsburg, Michal Peled. *Flaubert Writing: A Study in Narrative Strategies.* Stanford, Calif.: Stanford University Press, 1986, 207 p.

> Provides a textual analysis of Flaubert's narrative strategies, claiming that "it is the process of representation itself—the repetition or imitation in language of a lived experience and of a reality, physical or psychological—that is problematic in Flaubert."

Haig, Stirling. "History and Illusion in Flaubert's 'Un coeur simple'." In his *The Madame Bovary Blues: The Pursuit of Illusion in Nineteenth-Century French Fiction,* pp. 116-45. Baton Rouge: Louisiana State University Press, 1987.

> Analyzes Flaubert's view of history and objective reality as well as his use of color and light in an attempt to thematically relate "Un coeur simple" to the other stories in *Trois contes.*

Hubert, J. D. "Representations of Decapitation: Mallarmé's 'Hérodiade' and Flaubert's 'Hérodias'." *French Forum* 7, No. 3 (September 1982): 245-51.

> Explores similarities between Flaubert's and Stéphane Mallarmé's stories about John the Baptist, noting that in both works "poetic structure far outweighs all other considerations."

Killick, Rachel. "Family Likeness in Flaubert and Maupassant: 'La légende de Saint-Julien l'Hospitalier' and 'Le donneur d'eau bénite'." *Forum for Modern Language Studies* XXIV, No. 4 (October 1988): 346-58.

> Compares parent-child relationships, the quest, and the process of reintegration in Guy de Maupassant's "Le donneur d'eau bénite" and in his mentor's "La légende."

Lowe, Margaret. " 'Rendre Plastique . . . ': Flaubert's Treatment of the Female Principle in 'Hérodias'." *The Modern Language Review* 78, No. 3 (July 1983): 551-58.

> Argues that "Hérodias"'s plastic symbols—symbols having multiple meanings and historical significance—delineate connections between the Judeo-Christian tradition, Eastern religions, and French society and enabled Flaubert to critique organized religion of nineteenth-century France.

Lytle, Andrew. "Three Ways of Making a Saint: A Reading of *Three Tales* by Flaubert." *The Southern Review* 20, No. 3 (July 1984): 495-527.

> Analyzes how each story in *Trois contes* examines a different aspect of the Christian concept of the trinity.

Madsen, Börge Gedsö. "Realism, Irony, and Compassion in Flaubert's 'Un coeur simple'." *The French Review* XXVII, No. 4 (February 1954): 253-58.

> Discusses Flaubert's use of realism, irony, objectivity, and sympathy in "Un coeur simple."

Marsh, Leonard. "Félicité on the Road: A Synchronic Reading of a 'Un coeur simple'." *Romanic Review* LXXXI, No. 1 (January 1990): 56-65.

> Examines how Flaubert's use of time, tense, and the journey subverts "the traditional process of narrative and [generates] significance" in "Un coeur simple."

Neider, Charles, ed. "Gustave Flaubert (1821-1880)." In his *Short Novels of the Masters,* pp. 28-33. New York: Holt, Rinehart and Winston, 1967.

> Brief essay relating Flaubert's theory of art to "Un coeur simple."

Norman, Buford. " 'Un coeur simple' or 'Un coeur tendre'? A Comparison of Flaubert's Tale with Baudelaire's 'Harmonie du soir'." *Studies in Short Fiction* XIII, No. 1 (Winter 1976): 88-91.

> Explores similarities between Charles Baudelaire's poem "Harmonie du soir" and the ending of "Un coeur simple."

O'Connor, John R. "Flaubert: *Trois Contes* and the Figure of the Double Cone." *PMLA* 95, No. 5 (October 1980): 812-26.

> Analyzes the underlying structure of the stories in *Trois contes.*

Porter, Laurence M., ed. *Critical Essays on Gustave Flaubert.* Boston: G.K. Hall, 1986, 238 p.

> Contains critical essays on *Trois contes,* including Raymonde Debray-Genette's structuralist analysis of "Un Coeur simple" and Benjamin F. Bart's study of the psychological, sexual, and bestial elements of "La légende."

Purcell, Shelley. " 'Hérodias': A Key to Thematic Progression in *Trois contes.*" *Romanic Review* LXXX, No. 4 (November 1989): 541-47.

> Focuses on the order of the stories in *Trois contes,* noting that their interrelated themes culminate in "Hérodias."

Reid, Ian. "The Death of the Implied Author? Voice, Sequence and Control in Flaubert's *Trois contes.*" *Australian*

Journal of French Studies XXIII, No. 2 (May-August 1986): 195-211.

> Discusses how Flaubert establishes narrative authority in *Trois contes.*

Robertson, Jane. "The Structure of 'Hérodias'." In *Gustave Flaubert,* edited by Harold Bloom, pp. 161-85. New York: Chelsea House, 1989.

> Thematic and stylistic discussion of "Hérodias."

Schor, Naomi, and Majewski, Henry F. *Flaubert and Postmodernism.* Lincoln: University of Nebraska Press, 1984, 219 p.

> Collects papers from the Brown University Flaubert Symposium in 1980 that approach Flaubert's fiction from a postmodernist perspective, analyzing how Flaubert addresses the problems of the textual referent, marginality, and "the performative aspect of language."

Sherzer, Dina. "Narrative Figures in 'La légende de Saint-Julien l'Hospitalier'." *Genre* VII, No. 1 (March 1974): 54-70.

> Examines Flaubert's use of rhetorical figures and devices as a means of creating structure and theme in "La légende."

Thorlby, Anthony. *Gustave Flaubert and the Art of Realism.* New Haven, Conn.: Yale University Press, 1957, 64 p.

> A critical survey of Flaubert's major works, including *Trois contes,* as they relate to his theory of art.

Tillett, Margaret G. "An Approach to 'Hérodias'." *French Studies* XXI, No. 1 (January 1967): 24-31.

> Provides a thematic analysis of "Hérodias" that accounts for Flaubert's belief that art and religion are inseparable.

Woodhull, Winifred. "Configurations of the Family in 'Un coeur simple'." *Comparative Literature* 39, No. 2 (Spring 1987): 139-61.

> Explores the relationship between public duty, private life, and the power structure of nineteenth-century French society as depicted in "Un coeur simple."

Zants, Emily. "*Trois contes:* A New Dimension in Flaubert." *Nottingham French Studies* 18, No. 1 (May 1979): 37-44.

> Studies Flaubert's use of submission, domination, and the epiphany in his short story collection.

Additional coverage of Flaubert's life and career is contained in the following sources published by Gale Research: *Dictionary of Literary Biography,* Volume 119; *Nineteenth-Century Literature Criticism,* Volumes 2, 10, and 19; and *World Literature Criticism,* Volume 2.

Vladimir Nabokov

1899-1977

(Full name Vladimir Vladimirovich Nabokov; also wrote under the pseudonym V. Sirin) Russian-born American short story writer, novelist, poet, essayist, playwright, critic, translator, biographer, autobiographer, and scriptwriter.

INTRODUCTION

Nabokov is recognized as one of the great literary stylists of the twentieth century. His intricate, self-conscious novels and short stories are frequently concerned with the artist's relationship to his craft and the illusory nature of "reality"—a word Nabokov has said is meaningless without quotation marks. Although there are critics who find his work "icy," "precious," egotistically self-referential, and overly concerned with artifice, many maintain that such novels as *Lolita* and *Pale Fire,* as well as Nabokov's numerous collections of short stories, convey poignant regard for human feelings and are deeply moral. As the debate surrounding his short story "Signs and Symbols" exemplifies, Nabokov's linguistically refined body of work rewards both analytical and emotionally involved readings.

Nabokov's early short stories were written in Berlin, where Nabokov had settled along with other Russian émigrés who fled the 1917 Bolshevik revolution. These stories appeared in various Russian-language magazines and newspapers. Nabokov and his son Dmitri eventually translated most of his stories of this period into English; they have been collected in *Nabokov's Quartet, A Russian Beauty, and Other Stories, Tyrants Destroyed, and Other Stories,* and *Details of a Sunset, and Other Stories.* "The Potato Elf," from *A Russian Beauty,* is typical in its subtlety and sophistication. The story deals with the triangular relationship between Shock, ostensibly a stage magician, his wife Nora, and Shock's partner Fred Dobson, a dwarf known as the Potato Elf. On one level, the story appears to be a conventional tale of love, betrayal, and failed relationships. Critics note a second level, however, and point to Shock's suspiciously superior knowledge of events and situations, his ability to manipulate them, and the fact that Shock is refered to as a "conjurer" rather than a magician throughout the story. The added dimension of demonic powers focuses the reader's attention on the ways in which the plot consistently works out in favor of Shock. Ultimately, "The Potato Elf " is a story of manipulation, illusion, and the power of imagination over, in Walter Evans words, "a surfeit of reality."

After Nabokov emigrated to the United States in 1940, he attracted a narrow but enthusiastic readership with the stories he published in the *Atlantic Monthly, Esquire,* and the *New Yorker.* Written in English, some of these pieces

were collected in *Nine Stories;* others, including "Signs and Symbols" and stories composed in the 1950s, were collected in *Nabokov's Dozen.* "Signs and Symbols," his most famous story, has generated much debate. Written in 1948, the story concerns an elderly Russian woman and her husband living in the United States who try to visit their mentally disturbed son in the hospital on his birthday. The couple has carefully chosen a present, a set of ten small jars of fruit jelly. Care was taken because the young man suffers from what is called in the story "referential mania"; believing that everything in the world is essentially a veiled reference to him, he suffers from a paranoia so extensive that he suspects not only people but things—clothes, mountains, innocently offered gifts—communicate secret messages that he must decipher. His psychosis never abates, and the constant struggle to interpret his environment has led him periodically to try to kill himself. After being turned away by the hospital staff because their son has attempted suicide again, the man and woman vow to bring their son home and care for him themselves. The critical controversy centers on the details Nabokov entwined in the narrative. Commentators have concluded that the pattern of metaphors relating to death are either true "signs and symbols" indicating the meaning of the story, or are red herrings intended to frustrate and mislead readers accustomed to traditional narratives. While some critics have viewed "Signs and Symbols" as a moving story of an elderly couple coming to terms with the sense of duty they feel toward their son, others have seen it as a tour-de-force in which Nabokov, with enigmatic clues and suggestive ambiguity, causes the reader to experience "referential mania" in his perception of meaning where none exists. Critics agree, however, that the story contains the elegant language and attention to structure and detail that make all of Nabokov's work unique and challenging.

The reaction of émigré critics to Nabokov's fiction was mixed. According to Ludmila A. Foster, the majority view was "rather superficial"; many critics tended to "judge his work by extraliterary criteria" and generally came to the same conclusion, finding Nabokov to be "talented, brilliant stylistically and formally, but 'un-Russian.' " Alfred Appel, Jr. noted that the "un-Russian" epithet was based on a nineteenth-century view of Russian literature held by many émigré readers, critics, and publishers. According to this view, the writer bears definite social responsibilities and his work must be "relevant." Consequently, Nabokov's sophisticated and enigmatic stories were appreciated by a narrow segment of the émigré population. Later assessments consider these stories in the context of Nabokov's complete body of work and generally agree that they both anticipate many of the modernist themes characteristic of postwar literature and can be seen as studies or preliminary sketches for the more complex articulations Nabokov expressed in his novels.

PRINCIPAL WORKS

SHORT FICTION

Vozvrashchenie chorba   1930
Soglyadatay   1938
Nine Stories   1947
Vesna v Fialte i drugie rasskazy   1956
Nabokov's Dozen   1958
Nabokov's Quartet   1966
A Russian Beauty, and Other Stories   1975
Tyrants Destroyed, and Other Stories   1975
Details of a Sunset, and Other Stories   1976

OTHER MAJOR WORKS

The Empyrean Path   (poetry)   1923
Mashenka   (novel)   1926
   [*Mary,* 1970]
Karol', dama, valet   (novel)   1928
   [*King, Queen, Knave,* 1968]
Soglyadatay   (novel)   1930
   [*The Eye,* 1965]
Zashchita luzhina   (novel)   1930
   [*The Defense,* 1964]
Kamera obskura   (novel)   1932
   [*Laughter in the Dark,* 1938]
Podvig   (novel)   1932

   [*Glory,* 1971]
Otchayanie   (novel)   1934
Despair   (novel)   1937
Dar   (novel)   1938
   [*The Gift,* 1963]
Izobretenie val'sa   (play)   1938
   [*The Waltz Invention: A Play in Three Acts,* 1966]
Priglashenie na kazn'   (novel)   1938
   [*Invitation to a Beheading,* 1959]
Volshebnik   (novel)   1939
   [*The Enchanter,* 1986]
The Real Life of Sebastian Knight   (novel)   1941
Nikolai Gogol   (criticism)   1944
Bend Sinister   (novel)   1947
Conclusive Evidence   (autobiography)   1951
   [*Drugie berega,* 1954]
Poems: 1929-1951   (poetry)   1952
Lolita   (novel)   1955
Pnin   (novel)   1957
Poems   (poetry)   1959
Pale Fire   (novel)   1962
Speak, Memory: An Autobiography Revisited   (autobiography)   1966
Nabokov's Congeries   (novel, short stories, essay, and poetry)   1968
Ada; or, Ardor: A Family Chronicle   (novel)   1969
Poems and Problems   (poetry and chess problems)   1970
Transparent Things   (novel)   1972
Strong Opinions   (essays)   1973
Lolita: A Screenplay   (screenplay)   1974
Look at the Harlequins!   (novel)   1974
Lectures on Literature   (lectures)   1982
Lectures on Russian Literature   (lectures)   1982
Lectures on Don Quixote   (lectures)   1984
The Man from the U.S.S.R., and Other Plays   (dramas)   1984

CRITICISM

Richard Schickel   (essay date 1958)

[*Schickel is an American novelist, film and literary critic, and teleplay writer. In the following review, he examines the stories in* Nabokov's Dozen.]

Now that a couple hundred thousand Americans are feverishly thumbing through *Lolita* looking for the dirty parts (there aren't any), it might be well to take stock of the strange, brilliant talents of its author, Vladimir Nabokov.

He has been among us for years, his talents gaining increasing recognition from the small minority of literate readers—who will now, no doubt, summarily drop him for the sin of popularity. As those who picked up *Lolita* looking for a pornographic thrill have by now discovered, Nabokov's style is the very antithesis of that usually demanded in the cruel marts of best-sellerdom, as is his point of view.

For those who wish to test that point of view and that style, for those who are a little timid about the subject of *Lolita,* for those who shun literary controversy, there is, happily, an alternative. Doubleday has kindly provided us with *Nabokov's Dozen* a collection of 13 short stories by the master. Here you may test him on your literary palate without the intervention of hot pepper seeds.

The first thing to note about the stories is that most of them are more plotless than anything of Chekov's. They go far beyond—most of them—the *New Yorker* school of plotlessness. But don't think for a moment that "plotless" means pointless. Take, for example, **"Time and Ebb,"** a story which has absolutely no plot at all. It is merely the reminiscences of an old man written at the beginning of the Twenty-First Century. This device enables Nabokov to give an odd, brilliant insight into our own times:

> They had their meals at large tables around which they grouped themselves in a stiff, sitting position on hard wooden chairs . . . Clothes consisted of a number of parts, each of which, moreover, contained the reduced and useless remnants of this or that older fashion . . . In their letters they addressed perfect strangers by what was—insofar as words have sense—the equivalent of 'beloved master' and prefaced a theoretically immortal signature with a mumble expressing idiotic devotion to a person whose very existence was to the writer a matter of complete unconcern.

The quotations indicate another of Nabokov's characteristics—his preoccupation with the significance of minutiae. He does not note detail with the dull, dogged persistence of the realist. But when a bit of it strikes his fancy he worries it about, digging the last morsel of meaning (in terms of his characters and in relation to the aesthetic niceties of his story). Typical is **"Lance,"** in which he projects an as yet unborn descendant of the story's narrator into the position of being the first human to rocket to, and explore, another planet. But he is not concerned with the adventures of the explorer. No, his story is about the effect of the trip on the explorer's parents whose chief concern is, more or less, that their son remember to wear his rubbers. His adventure is, to them, simply too big to conceive in any other terms. Their reaction is a complex of simplicities, achingly human and sensitively rendered by Nabokov. He has a passionate desire for the right word, the right sound, the right rendering of color. Reading Nabokov is a marvelously creative experience, leading the receptive mind down dozens of delightful byways where, once the writer has pointed the way, it can find its own paths.

It is this quality in the work of Gogol which Nabokov admired so much in his fine little study of the Russian, published in 1944 by New Directions. It is obvious that Nabokov, in his own way, in a purely modern idiom, is following Gogol's lead. He too, as Turgenev once said of himself and his contemporaries, "crawled out from under Gogol's overcoat."

There is another, obvious quality in Nabokov's work which cannot go unremarked. That is its odd mingling of humor and sadness—something which is found in much Russian writing (Nabokov is a Russian emigre who now writes in English).

The other stories, all of them, deal with remembrances of things past. For example: **"Mademoiselle O"** is a sad, funny, oddly touching recollection of a grotesque governess Nabokov had in pre-revolutionary Russia. **"First Love"** is another autobiographical recollection of the sort the title describes. It is similar in mood to the section in *Lolita* dealing with the affair that first caused Humbert Humbert's passion for nymphets. **"That in Aleppo Once"** purports to be the letter of an emigre describing how his young wife went mad and was lost in the Nazi invasion (there is much mourning in Nabokov's work for people, places, things now lost forever). **"Cloud, Castle, Lake"** is the story of a sad, permanently displaced little Russian who wins a vacation hike with a group of Nazis and is made miserable by them for his inability to cope with the trip (so many of Nabokov's characters cannot cope with the people, places, things of the world) but who at last finds a scene of perfect beauty, a place he may recall from childhood, or, more likely, from the memories of childhood dreams. Of course, the Hitler youth forcibly drag him from his place of enchantment and it is lost.

Pnin, that delightful collection of short stories masquerading as a novel, is a quintessential Nabokovian piece. It is the story of an emigrant Russian professor teaching in America, funny in his ineffectual attempts to deal with the modern American world, sad in his wistfulness for times and places gone by. And *Lolita* is, in a sense, made up of the same ingredients. Humbert Humbert is obviously withdrawn from the world that threatens him. And his passion for little girls based on the aborted love of his childhood is obviously a bit of nostalgia carried to absurd lengths.

It is this recognition of nostalgia's absurdity which keeps Nabokov from falling into the bottomless pit of sentimentality. Behind every nostalgic reflection there is a sardonic laugh at the posturing involved in the recollection.

Above all, I believe, Nabokov is a poet of the absurd. He has written:

> The absurd has as many shades and degrees as the tragic has . . . You cannot place a man in an absurd situation if the whole world he lives in is absurd; you cannot do this if you mean by 'absurd' something provoking a chuckle or a shrug. But if you mean the pathetic, the human condition, if you mean all such things that in less weird worlds are linked up with the loftiest aspirations, the deepest sufferings, the strongest passions—then of course the necessary breach is there, and a pathetic human, lost in the midst of [a] nightmarish, irresponsible world would be "absurd" by a kind of secondary contrast.

This is what Nabokov does to his lost, bewildered, but somehow indomitable people. You can see it in *Pnin,* in *Lolita,* in the stories in *Nabokov's Dozen.*

Perhaps only an emigre like Nabokov, who has at least

twice had to flee the works of the madmen who inhabit our "nightmarish, irresponsible" world, can fully apprehend the full horror—and comedy—of the human condition's absurdity. Perhaps only he can know the full meaning of a nostalgia which is not merely, as I previously suggested, for times and places gone by, but for a world, and a place, which has never existed, and never can exist, in our world of men. Let me finally suggest that it is this vision of a higher reality which gives his work such importance, which transforms his memory-laden works into high art.

For, whatever the meaning of his work, his vision, we must always bear in mind the skill, the attention to meaning, the conscious skill with which he manipulates stubborn words. Many writers have had visions as sensitive as his. Many artists have had his word-skill without his vision. But high art is always a product of a combination of the two—vision and skill—in the mind of a genius. I risk that word with full consciousness of its dangers, with horrible examples of critics who have used it, and rued it, dancing before me. Vladimir Nabokov is a genius—one of the handful of major talents alive in our time. (pp. 46, 48-9)

> *Richard Schickel, "Nabokov's Artistry," in* The Progressive, *Vol. 22, No. 11, November, 1958, pp. 46, 48-50.*

As is well known (to employ a famous Russian phrase), my books are not only blessed by a total lack of social significance, but are also mythproof: Freudians flutter around them avidly, approach with itching oviducts, stop, sniff, and recoil.

—*Vladimir Nabokov, in his Foreword to* **The Eye, *1965.***

Howard Nemerov   (essay date 1959)

[*Nemerov was an American poet, novelist, and critic. A winner of the Pulitzer Prize and National Book award, he was appointed poet laureate of the United States for his distinguished body of works. In the following review of* Nabokov's Dozen, *originally published in 1959, Nemerov discusses loss, nostalgia, and the fluid identity of Nabokov's characters, offering one of the first assessments of "Signs and Symbols."*]

In trying to fix the quality of experience dominant over these stories I thought of some famous lines by William Empson:

It is the poems you have lost, the ills
From missing dates, at which the heart expires.

Thus Mr. Nabokov also; where are the poets, governesses, girl friends of yesteryear? he asks over and over. More precisely, *who* were they? People like Nina (**"Spring in**

Fialta"), Perov (**"A Forgotten Poet"**), or the wife of the narrator in **"That in Aleppo Once"** slip in and out of their stories as they slip in and out of their identities—identities for a long time nebulous, "historical," dependent upon the capriciousness of memory, then suddenly precise and unforgettable for an instant.

If that abused (and ordinarily abusive) word "experimental" may for once apply to something, these pieces exhibit Mr. Nabokov's experiments on the identities of his characters, on his relations with them, and on the questionably theatrical symbolisms, or styles of presentation, of Life, who is seen as "an assistant producer." These identities and relations are multiple, fluidly shifting; few of the persons involved are so simple as to be merely doubles, like the one in **"Conversation Piece"** ("a disreputable namesake of mine") or the poor, prize-winning traveler in **"Cloud, Castle, Lake,"** who is, says the author, "one of my representatives." The result is the depiction of a world by now familiar to Mr. Nabokov's readers, a world of objects fragmentary and allusive, elusive, illusive (all three will have to do), suggesting more or less fleetingly their relation to some lost whole; a world in which the possible immanence of meaning is either a stage trick on the part of the assistant producer, or else the disastrous visionary madness of the perceiver. For illustration, let one story stand for all, as by its title, **"Signs and Symbols,"** it seems to want to do. Here the sort of world I have ascribed to the author is compressed into eight pages which come as near the absolute of art as anything I have seen in the short story.

An old couple, refugees, are going to the sanitarium to take a birthday present to their incurably deranged son; they have chosen "a dainty and innocent trifle: a basket with ten different fruit jellies in ten little jars," and this choice has cost them much thought, since the young man's malady is such that almost any object in the world achieves for him a frightening, hostile significance, or else is simply meaningless and useless.

At the sanitarium they learn that their child has again attempted to kill himself; he is all right, but a visit is out of the question. They go home, they think about the past, they torture themselves, and, after midnight, decide they must bring the boy home, no matter what the inconvenience, what the danger, since until they do so life is impossible.

The decision makes them happier, and at this moment the telephone rings, frightening them; it is a wrong number, "a girl's dull little voice" wanting to speak to "Charlie." The telephone rings again, right away, and the old woman tells the girl "you are turning the letter O instead of the zero." The old people sit down to "their unexpected festive midnight tea," the man examines with pleasure the birthday present, the ten little jars; and the telephone rings again.

Readers who think first of "plot" will quite properly say, "but that isn't a story"; and so, in my description, it isn't. Yet in this simply articulated space a vast and tragic life works itself out, presenting the tension between meaning (which is madness) and the meaningless (which is the normal, or sane, condition of present life). The system of the young man's delusions has the high-sounding name of "referential mania," and might as well be called "Poet's Disease":

> In these very rare cases the patient imagines that everything happening around him is a veiled reference to his personality and existence. He excludes real people from the conspiracy—because he considers himself to be so much more intelligent than other men. Phenomenal nature shadows him wherever he goes. Clouds in the staring sky transmit to one another, by means of slow signs, incredibly detailed information regarding him. His inmost thoughts are discussed at nightfall, in manual alphabet, by darkly gesticulating trees. Pebbles or stains or sun flecks form patterns representing in some awful way messages which he must intercept. Everything is a cipher and of everything he is the theme. Some of the spies are detached observers, such are glass surfaces and still pools; others, such as coats in store windows, are prejudiced witnesses, lynchers at heart; others again (running water, storms) are hysterical to the point of insanity, have a distorted opinion of him and grotesquely misinterpret his actions. He must be always on his guard and devote every minute and module of life to the decoding of the undulation of things. The very air he exhales is indexed and filed away. If only the interest he provokes were limited to his immediate surroundings—but alas it is not! With distance the torrents of wild scandal increase in volume and volubility. The silhouettes of his blood corpuscles, magnified a million times, flit over vast plains; and still farther, great mountains of unbearable solidity and height sum up in terms of granite and groaning firs the ultimate truth of his being.

Over against this hostile and sinister truth (the universe does mean something, and if you are able to perceive it you will go insane and die) is set the life of the old couple, displaced persons with their hopes and memories (a pack of soiled cards and old photograph albums), with the near-absolute, meaningless chaos which twenty years of history have made of their lives. And the two halves into which the universe has thus split are mediated (not put back together) by those telephone calls. Just here, where the Satevepost reader waits for his satisfaction (it will be the doctor, announcing a sudden cure by miracle drug), and the reader of rather more artsy-crafty periodicals waits for *his* satisfaction (the young man has finally done away with himself), comes the exact metaphor for the situation, as the telephone, the huge, mechanical system whose buzz relates everyone to everyone else, has the last word: "you are turning the letter O instead of the zero."

Detail for detail there's a great deal more, but that is more or less how it goes. Not all the stories are that good (which would be asking a great deal), but this is a wonderful book. It is good that the (wildly improbable) success of *Lolita* could exert enough leverage to raise its author's short stories once more over the horizon, and all Mr. Nabokov's readers, the new ones and the others who will remember much of the present volume from the New Directions edi-

tion of *Nine Stories* (long out of print and hard or impossible to come by), ought to be grateful. (pp. 267-69)

Howard Nemerov, "The Ills from Missing Dates," in his Poetry and Fiction: Essays, Rutgers University Press, 1963, pp. 267-69.

L. L. Lee   (essay date 1965)

[*Lee is an American critic and educator. In the following essay, he focuses on the function of doubles and mirror images in five stories from* Nabokov's Dozen.]

To see an object as double is a defect of vision (diplopia), but to see it in the mind's eye as double is perhaps to see its other side, or, even, its reality, the ground of its being. Such seeing can be, paradoxically, the artist's method of proving the existence, and ambiguity, of the world he has created; it is the dialectic that gives meaning to the thing. And it can serve, too, to make the reader aware of his own ambiguity, of his possession or lack of self. But we can cite authority—James Joyce quoting S. T. Coleridge on Giordano Bruno: "Every power in nature or in spirit must evolve an opposite as the sole condition and means of its manifestation; and every opposition is, therefore, a tendency to reunion." Or, as in *Finnegans Wake,* "there being two sights for ever a picture," a phrase that nicely telescopes space and time, the world in which we live.

It is the concept of the double which is the Ariadne thread to lead us into and through the labyrinth of Vladimir Nabokov's short stories (in that wilderness of mirrors of the carnival maze, we see our bodies coming and going and are confused, but that is because we did not make the puzzle and are ourselves undefined). Nabokov is a conjuror, "a mirror maker of genius" like Sudarg of Bokay in *Pale Fire,* a writer in the manner of his own Sebastian Knight, of whom another character complains that he (Knight) seems "to be constantly playing some game of his own invention, without telling his partners its rules."

But Nabokov gives the rules; the only requirement is that the reader be the creative reader that he asks for. **Nabokov's Dozen** will include thirteen stories—what else should we expect? Yet, a title such as **"Scenes from the Life of a Double Monster,"** or the palpably living old man who may be the dead poet of **"A Forgotten Poet,"** or that the fact that **"Conversation Piece, 1945"** was originally called **"Double Talk"** must surely make us suspect some duplicity. But Nabokov's "duplicity" is not deceit, although deceit is a motif in almost all his stories; his doubling is an artistic realization of the unity of opposites which is always in precarious balance over the abyss, a demonstration that the anomalous is a ready and perpetual threat.

One more generalization: the Nabokovian story is rarely a story, *i.e.,* the chronological account of an action with a rise in intensity, a climax, and a resolution. Such a simple form allows no room for pattern, no room for the complexity and richness of language and image that reveal a world, a world of tension, not just a tension of action. [In "Vladimir Nabokov's Great Spiral of Being," *Western Humanities Review,* 1964] I have suggested . . . that the major pattern in Nabokov's novels is the spiral, a "dialectic" spiral [—in *Speak, Memory* Nabokov writes]: "Twirl follows twirl, and every synthesis is the thesis of the next series." The same pattern, the image of space and time in one, offers itself to the short stories—and gives us a base for our doublenesses.

The unity of opposites in a spiral demands metamorphoses, dream changes, if you like. And it is in the stories with the less obvious clues of title or situation that we must be most aware of this. **"That in Aleppo Once . . . "** looks, for instance, simple. The "story" is only a letter. A husband addresses it to a writer friend, relating how, as he (the husband) and his wife were trying to escape from a France being overrun by "gentle" Germans, they were accidentally separated. Reunited by apparent chance in Marseille, she confesses that she has been unfaithful; the husband, driven by his jealousy, hounds her until she says that what she had first admitted was untrue. But he cannot believe her. Now, just as he receives visas to leave for the United States, she disappears. Seeking her, he discovers that she has told their friends that she had fallen in love with another man but that the husband has refused her a divorce. The husband departs, alone, but on the ship he meets a physician who reports that he had seen the wife in Marseille a couple of days before sailing and that she had said that the husband would "presently join her with bag and tickets." And the letter ends with the "deceived" husband crying out, "Somewhere, somehow, I have made some fatal mistake. . . . It may all end in *Aleppo* if I am not careful. Spare me, V.: you would load your dice with an unbearable implication if you took that for a title." But that is the title.

The allusion to *Othello* is the apparent key to the story: the husband is another Othello, the dupe of his own jealousy. Instead of being betrayed, he has been blind, and, so, has betrayed. All this is true. But the reader must also understand that all this is not all the truth.

Let us begin with the address, "Dear V." One could pursue the suggestion that V. is an aspect, a double, of Nabokov—the same first initial, the penname V. Sirin that Nabokov signed to his Russian novels, the departure for the U. S. by both at almost the same time—but this is, here, of less import. Much more meaningful to the story is that V. is, in a strange manner, the man being written to and the man writing at the same time—he is, in other words, the author. The husband, who is also a writer, says that his wife's name "is the name of an illusion. Therefore, I am able to speak of her with as much detachment as I would of a character in a story (one of your stories, to be precise)." He does seem to ask that V. write the story: "I have a story for you," and he ends with the statement about the "unbearable implication." But the husband has already written, and entitled, the story. One may add that V. is the father of twins and his work is "diversified"; he is evidently a botanist as well as a writer (just as Nabokov is both a lepidopterist and a writer).

This is the requirement of dialectic: opposition gives meaning, identity, and, so, limitation to a character or situation; the left hand has no meaning unless there is a right hand, or at least the possibility of a right hand. But right and left hands have much in common, unlike right and left noses.

Still, there *is* a husband whose wife has betrayed him. This is true, if we accept the man's story, and if we do not accept it we seem to have just another psychological document, not a work of literature. However, despite the husband's plausible account of his wife's deception of him, he ends up by hinting that he may be wrong. Is he not, then, ill? He is if we come to the story expecting a realistic picture, a photograph, of our actuality.

The man is not ill; he is in a different world from ours, a world having the logic of the dream. [In his *The Expanded Moment*] Robert Gordon, in an otherwise perceptive comment on this story, appears to feel that its encompassing generalization is the "disintegration of European life in the age of Hitler." But this makes the story history, and it is larger than that. "Great literature," Nabokov says in his book on Gogol, "skirts the irrational." Such literature has a generalizing power beyond its moment; its function is to give us insight into the "absurd," which means the "pathetic, the human condition." The husband is V., perhaps he is Nabokov, he is Othello, and he is also Iago, the deceiver and the deceived; he is the "six subhuman doubles" of his passport photographs. He is not Man, however, for that would make him only the stick drawing of allegory (Nabokov, in the epilogue to *Lolita,* objects most strenuously to "symbols and allegories"). He is a betrayed husband first of all; he is not his doubles, they are he, the proof that he is absurd, *i.e.,* human.

And the wife exists too, even though the husband calls her an illusion. She also has a double existence: she is Desdemona but she is Iago (in the dream world, in Nabokov's worlds, gender is a shifty thing; one need only recall *Pale Fire.* And Shakespeare's Desdemona would have been played by a boy). She tells the husband that she has deceived him (Iago) and so she has deceived him; but she is also innocent (Desdemona). She who has no name is almost the same as the unnamed girl whom the detective insists is the husband's wife in an episode just moments before the husband actually does find his wife again.

Nevertheless, cannot one argue that she is the ill one? Her guilt exists only in her fantasy, and that is why the husband feels *his* guilt; he has abandoned a sick woman. But once more one must note that the Nabokovian work is not a psychological, etc., representation of our world, but a creation of another world and is only so much a representation as to tell us that human existence is complex, absurd, and illogical-logical. Nabokov's dialectic is not a dialectic of the actual world but a dialectic of the artist's mind, a dialectic that lets us peep into the *real* behind "the stage setting that screens it."

The shape of the story offers its evidence, too. It is a circle, perhaps, as Nabokov says of Gogol's *The Overcoat,* "a vicious circle," from which there is no escape for the characters, forever fading into one another. V. is still being asked to write a story which is already written; the future is the past. And we must remember that the figure of the circle is a common literary device by which to demonstrate the coincidence of opposites as well as the contrariety of opposites: consider Yeats along with Joyce.

It is structure, again, that is most important in a story like **"Spring In Fialta."** One can best describe it as a series of waves within a circle, although this time the circle is not quite closed: the story will not be repeated. This circle, or rather spiral, of time is the present, with which the story begins and with which it ends—there is a time passage of less than a day—and the waves are those memories, flashbacks, of the narrator that are interspersed within the present of the story, his re-creation of the whole fifteen-year relationship between the woman Nina and himself.

The narrator, this time with a name, Victor (one more V), has arrived in the little Italian town of Fialta on a rainy spring day (this Prospero's misty rain world will melt in a dream dissolution at the end of the story and he will find himself elsewhere). There he meets Nina, a chance meeting as all their meetings have been, and spends the day in her company.

Nina is the wife of the writer Ferdinand, another of those many writers, like V. and Sebastian Knight, who echo, shadow, double one another and their creator. Ferdinand, it is true, seems to have little in common with Nabokov except that he is a "weaver of words," a phrase that Nabokov also uses to describe the much more sympathetic writer-translator Ember of *Bend Sinister.* But when Victor objects to Ferdinand's puns and "art of verbal invention," and asks why one should write "things that had not really happened in some way or other," all qualities of Nabokov, we must see another mask of the author, even if a distorted mask. Victor himself thinks that only the heart should have imagination, and that the writer should "rely upon memory, that long-drawn sunset of one's personal truth." Yet this, too, is a Nabokovian quality, this use of his own memories in his fiction: "A mere string of figures will disclose the identity of the stringer as neatly as tame ciphers yielded their treasure to Poe." One has only to compare *Speak, Memory* with almost any other work to see a new form of an old memory.

But, once again, it is not Nabokov's duples that bear the meaning; we must come back to the story. The "waves" of memory evoke a Nina who is almost the same as she was when she was only a girl but who, in each memory, is also subtly different. In Victor's first memory, she is seventeen and looks twenty; in this last meeting, she is thirty-two and looks much younger. And Victor speaks of "the Fialta version of Nina," her present double, but he also recalls being "introduced" to her twice, and both times her body, as she sits on a couch, is folded into a "Z."

And thus memory, the past, gets involved with the future as well as the present. As Victor, Nina, Ferdinand, and Ferdinand's shady friend Segur pass the automobile that will carry Nina to her death, Victor looks back "and foresaw, in an almost optical sense," the three getting into that automobile for the death ride; Nina will never grow older.

It is not, however, only structure and character that give "doubleness" to the story, but the repetition of significant images and words. Fialta echoes Yalta, a town from Victor's Russian past, and both echo *fialka,* the Russian word

for *violet,* a color and a flower that dance through the story from the first page to the last. Then, too, there is the young Italian girl "of twelve or so, with a string of heavy beads around her dusky neck," whose double (or herself) reappears later as "a native child, a swarthy girl with beads around her pretty neck," to receive candy from Ferdinand. And, most expressive, since it is almost an image of death, the recurrent glimpses, poster, advertising parade, and final truck, of the circus that is coming to Fialta, the wave of the future cutting across the wave of the past— Nina is killed when the departing automobile crashes into the arriving circus truck.

With **"A Forgotten Poet,"** we come to those stories that are most obviously duplex, those stories that say plainly that human life is an absurd, ambiguous affair. In 1899, fifty years after his death at twenty-four, the poet Konstantin Perov is honored at a literary meeting. But an old man appears, claims he is Perov, and disrupts the proceedings. Perov had died by drowning but his body had never been found, only his "clothes and a half-eaten apple." Nobody quite believes the old man, but, on the other hand, some almost do. Imposter or true poet, there is no answer. The old man finally dies in the 1920's, a haunting, dubious figure.

And the story is several ways deceptive itself. It embodies some of Nabokov's explicit attitudes on the nature of art, *e.g.,* no great art work has a didactic function. Perov's best poems are his purest, the narrator says. Yet here, as elsewhere, it is the moral quality of the work that counts, the very attack upon the *idées reçues* of our Western culture, at least our artistic culture. Yet it is a subversive attack, an attack expressed only in the style, as Leslie Fiedler might say.

The story is, moreover, a deliberate echo of an episode in *The Gift.* There some boys pretend to the narrator's grandfather that Pushkin, instead of dying in a duel at thirty-seven, is still alive at sixty. The boy who makes up the hoax is suddenly frightened by this ghost, this double, that he himself has conjured up, by this breaking out of the irrational that he has permitted. But what we readers perceive is the multiplication of doubles.

Now, such a subject, the reputed dead man's return to life, is of course an old one—Pelops, Lazarus, Rip Van Winkle, Enoch Arden, Mattia Pascal, Lawrence's Man Who Died—but in these examples there is no doubt that the "dead" man is alive. Nabokov's story, told with a dark humor, indeed ends with the old man truly dead, but his ghost is still there—he might have been the young poet Perov; he may be, in short, himself. But the equivocation is not an evasion on the part of the artist; the equivocation is the very heart of Nabokov's world, where we find "shadows linking our state of existence to those other states and modes which we dimly apprehend in our rare moments of irrational perception." Perhaps one should wonder about that other half of the apple (Adam's apple with a *wyrm* in it?), rather than whether the old man is Perov.

In **"Conversation Piece, 1945,"** first published, as I have noted, as **"Double Talk,"** the narrator, still one more writer, has an actual double, "a disreputable namesake, complete from nickname to surname, a man whom I have never seen in the flesh . . . ," although once seen in a photograph. And the reader never sees the man either; once again we are not certain that the person has a physical existence. But not only do the two share names, they also share an acquaintance with Mrs. Sharp who, naturally-unnaturally, is not one but two Mrs. Sharps, the first of a leftist political persuasion, the second rightist.

Except perhaps for **"The Assistant Producer,"** which has the unreality of the film script that it is in part parodying, or **"First Love"** and **"Mademoiselle O,"** both of which are really sections of the memoir *Speak, Memory,* this tale of double talk and doubles is the most "social" of Nabokov's stories. That is, it is the one most patently concerned with an actual time and place and with the social attitudes and movements of the time. The double of the narrator is a "very White emigré, of the automatically reactionary type," whereas the unnamed narrator, although no leftist (if that word has any meaning any more), seems to share political beliefs with the husband of **"That in Aleppo Once . . ."** who had written in a book "that, with all her many black sins, Germany was still bound to remain for ever and ever the laughing stock of the world." He is, in other words, a liberal, an individual, opposed to the "Communazist state" that Nabokov himself excoriates in *Invitation to a Beheading* (see *Speak, Memory*). For example, one of the unpleasant characters of **"Conversation,"** a Colonel Melnikov or Malikov (even his name cannot be clear), is able to attack the "Jewish Bolsheviks," emphasizing the adjective, but/and, "although a White Russian," can happily admire the tyrannous Joseph Stalin, who figures for him as one of Russia's "three great leaders," along with Ivan the Terrible and Peter the Great. It is the totalitarian nationalism, the state and society that "save" us from our lonely singleness, that appeals to him. But the artistic image is that, if we continue the political circle, left and right join and become one.

The social, political commentary is not, however, the burden of the story, unless it is phrased as the ability of each of us to contain contradictions. For, although the apparent subject is the "conversation" among the group of Nazi sympathizers to which the narrator, mistaken for his double, is invited, we know that the real subject is the narrator and his double, the double talk. Each pursues and is pursued by the other, and both pursuits are unwitting and unwilling. A library demands that the narrator return a copy of the "Protocols of the Wise Men of Zion," that forged piece of anti-Semitic propaganda he would not think of having borrowed; he is arrested for breaking mirrors (in which his double no doubt saw him) which he did not break; and, at the end, he gets a letter from his double which begins, "Esteemed Sir. You have been pursuing me all my life." They, too, are two, and yet one, *Doppelgänger* obsessed despite their wishes. And once more Nabokov does not neatly resolve his situation—the two will continue to revolve around one another, moths for the other's firefly.

"Scenes from the Life of a Double Monster" will not let us doubt that the two are one even if not quite. The "double monster" is (are?) Siamese twins, the scandal of human

individuality. One of them, an "I," not a "we," speaks; but it is only in appearance that the other does not seem to be there. The reader must be conscious that he is.

Floyd, the I, the eye in Nabokov's pun, states that at the age of three or four, although their bodies objected to this biformity, their minds accepted it: "Linked Floyd and Lloyd were complete and normal." For the wise double it is the single shape that is abnormal; they-he have-has their-his permanent shadow and mirror reflection, the immediate proof of ambiguity.

And yet Floyd is fascinated by the thought of being single, of being, in a sense, free; he dreams of meeting his twin, Lloyd, who is still "hopelessly joined to a hobbling twin while I was free to dance around them and slap them on their humble backs." But he will not be free, either of Lloyd or of the world. To be cut off, literally and symbolically, a fate that once threatens him, would be death and not freedom. And when, as children, the two attempt to escape from the household, their world and *the* world, they are kidnaped by their uncle-by-marriage, a minor entrepreneur—minor devil in spectacles (not, mind you, a monocle): they will be for the rest of their lives nothing but carnival freaks, both the person in the maze and the person in the mirror.

Lloyd, then, is Floyd; Lloyd is the mask, the form that enables Floyd to realize himself. But Lloyd is also Floyd's jailer and prisoner. And both of them are imprisoned in the world of time and space.

One is tempted to say, "As we all are," little Platonic half-eggs both seeking and shunning our other halves, who do

---

Nabokov on good readers:

Of course, no matter how keenly, how admirably, a story, a piece of music, a picture is discussed and analyzed, there will be minds that remain blank and spines that remain unkindled. "To take upon us the mystery of things"—what King Lear so wistfully says for himself and for Cordelia—this is also my suggestion for everyone who takes art seriously. A poor man is robbed of his overcoat (Gogol's "The Greatcoat," or more correctly "The Carrick"); another poor fellow is turned into a beetle (Kafka's *The Metamorphosis*)—so what? There is no rational answer to "so what." We can take the story apart, we can find out how the bits fit, how one part of the pattern responds to the other; but you have to have in you some cell, some gene, some germ that will vibrate in answer to sensations that you can neither define, nor dismiss. *Beauty plus pity*—that is the closest we can get to a definition of art. Where there is beauty there is pity for the simple reason that beauty must die: beauty always dies, the manner dies with the matter, the world dies with the individual. If Kafka's *The Metamorphosis* strikes anyone as something more than an entomological fantasy, then I congratulate him on having joined the ranks of good and great readers.

Vladimir Nabokov, in his Lectures on Literature, *Harcourt Brace Jovanovich, 1982.*

---

exist: "the double, the gangrel, that accompanies each of us—you, and me, and him over there," Nabokov says in *Invitation to a Beheading*. But we are as confused as Pnin is with the double professor(s) Tristram W. Thomas-Thomas Wynn who are Pnin's "Twynn" or "Tvin" problem.

And so we all are, so far as we can take Nabokov's work as an instance of insight into our world. And it is an insight, at least into that in our world which is irrational, the perplexity which is our, and its, identity. (pp. 307-15)

L. L. Lee, "Duplexity in V. Nabokov's Short Stories," in Studies in Short Fiction, *Vol. II, No. 4, Summer, 1965, pp. 307-15.*

Barbara Heldt   (essay date 1970)

[*In the following essay, Heldt discusses the distinction between art and life in "Spring in Fialta."*]

"Spring in Fialta," dated Paris, 1938, became the title story of two collections of Nabokov's short stories published in the United States, one in Russian and the other a paperback version in English. The latter includes three stories written originally in Russian; **"Spring in Fialta"** is one of these. Nabokov mentions it twice in *Ada,* and indeed **"Spring in Fialta"** resembles Nabokov's latest book in its openness, in its description of memory's triumph over time and space. The period from 1937 to 1940 contains both the peak and the finale of Nabokov's achievement as a writer in Russian. During those years he produced two plays, *The Event* and *The Waltz Invention,* and published the book version of *Invitation to a Beheading, The Gift* (his greatest novel of this period), and *The Eye* (a collection of short stories). In 1941 Nabokov published his first novel in English, *The Real Life of Sebastian Knight,* after he had come to the United States—now no longer really an émigré, but a refugee. The period immediately following would be Nabokov's darkest and most sparse; *Bend Sinister* was published in 1947. Now that Nabokov has matched and surpassed his early peaks of creativity, we can note with delight in the story **"Spring in Fialta"** all the most important Nabokovian artistic preoccupations and stylistic traits packed into a mere score of pages. It is as clear a masterpiece among Nabokov's short stories as *Lolita* and *Pale Fire* among his novels.

The protagonist-narrator of the story undertakes a quest similar to that which forms the structure of so many works by Nabokov. It is a journey without direction, unplanned and with an uncertain goal. Movement—through the ever-diminishing space of Russia, European capitals and finally the one small town of Fialta, and through a time made magical by the past being forever repeated in a résumé and brought up short by the present—leads finally not to something found but to an awareness of loss, the loss of a woman scarcely loved. The story begins and ends in the present and concerns a man who takes a short respite from a business trip, meets a woman he has met casually on several distant occasions, in several equally distant places, a woman married, like him, and always surrounded by "friends." The woman, Nina, is consistently generous and casual in giving herself to the narrator and to oth-

ers. The chance meetings between Nina and the narrator recur outside of the continuity of their separate lives, which form an almost irrelevant background. The narrator has a premonition during their "seemingly carefree, but really hopeless meetings" that "something lovely, delicate, and unrepeatable was being wasted: something which I abused by snapping off poor bright bits in gross haste . . ." (Lolita is similarly "wasted"). Immediately after this last meeting in Fialta, Nina is killed in an automobile crash.

The author himself makes a signature appearance in the story as a big Englishman who at one point steps from chair to window-sill to capture a "compact furry moth," analogous in its finished perfection to the work of art itself. This is not a playful quirk but a serious warning for the reader not to mistake the narrator for the author. The Englishman-author is bent on capturing one precise thing; the narrator is less sure of the object of his quest. Even if we did not know that a moth or a butterfly is the sign of lepidopterist Nabokov's presence, we would be aware that the Englishman's detachment from the events of the story contrasts markedly with the narrator's increasing involvement with them.

The appearance of the Englishman is a small detail which serves a special purpose, in a story where no detail is irrelevant. With Nabokov, detail can be savored even before it begins to form the inevitable complicated pattern of the work. Virginia Woolf writes of how certain scenes in the novels of the great classical writers give a finality of effect and lie "apart from the story, beyond the reach of change." With Nabokov not scenes but smaller units—images, phrases, even isolated words—seem to have the completeness of, for instance, the scene of the wolf-hunt in *War and Peace.* If enjoyment of the separate details of fiction apart from the total fiction were immoral, Nabokov would be one of the most immoral writers ever.

When Nabokov changes some details from Russian into English, he of course makes the detail more appropriate to the particular language, but he often strengthens the thrust of the whole story. The opening paragraphs, heavy with descriptive detail, set down the bright pieces that will compose the mosaic of the story (the poster of a visiting circus into whose truck Nina will crash in the final sentence, or the yellow bit of unripe orange peel which is echoed by her yellow scarf and yellow car). The narrator is ready for understanding, for he walks with all his "senses wide open." For Nabokov visual perception especially reveals what the lower senses, touch or taste, reveal for Proust; they provide a key to memory and ultimately to understanding of past and present alike. From Russian to English, Nabokov changes none of these basic images, but he does heighten the intensity of some phrases, because English suggests new linguistic possibilities. Thus the "sea rococo of shells" becomes in English the "mantelpiece dreams of sea shells," the "frozen carousel" becomes a "sorry-go-round," the "eye" of the Russian becomes "all my senses." The name Fialta is toyed with even more lovingly in English. In Russian it reminds the narrator of violets (described, but not named) and of the sound of Yalta; in English violets become "violaceous syllables," a viola appears, and the real place name (too prosaic-sounding perhaps after the Conference) becomes a more suggestive "lovely Crimean town."

On the other hand, nothing in English can replace the grammatical contrasts which in Russian underline the interplay of past and present that constitutes the essence of the story. In Russian the imperfective and perfective aspects of the verb alternate, often within the same sentence. The imperfective is used whenever the narrator recalls a past repeated and enduring. In English the verb itself cannot carry these qualities ("Every time I *had met* her . . . , she *had not seemed to recognize* me at once . . . "). The perfective aspect is used for the more abrupt narrative or historical present ("and this time too she *remained* quite still *for a moment*"), briefer and less enduring. (All italics mine.)

The key device of all Nabokov's art, from his early Russian works to his latest English ones, is his calling attention to the difference between art and life. Thus the "life" of fiction is purposely made to appear artistic. At least once in translating from Russian to English Nabokov reinforces the idea that the meetings of the two protagonists are staged. Whereas the Russian text just states: "I met Nina very long ago," the English reads: "My introductory scene with Nina had been laid in Russia quite a long time ago." The narrator of this story thus becomes a kind of sub-creator with his awareness that his life is staged, just as Humbert Humbert is aware of McFate pursuing him. The narrator says: "This time we had met in warm and misty Fialta, and I could not have celebrated the occasion with greater art, could not have adorned with higher vignettes the list of fate's former services, even if I had known that this was to be the last one. . . . " Nabokov makes the reader laud both the artifices of the author and the wonderment of the narrator who strives to grasp the full pattern of the mosaic in which he himself is depicted. There is in this story a sense of finality, of "that final appointment" set by fate. It is the finality not of life, but of art. Only in the English version does Nabokov mention "a fading memory of ancient mosaic design" on the sidewalk, another clue to the design of the story itself.

Every work of art is based upon choice and coincidence, but authors deal variously with the problem of how much of it to reveal. In *War and Peace* meetings and partings are so long delayed, so prepared by lifelike detail that they often seem no more coincidental than those of life itself. In *Doctor Zhivago* the thick network of coincidence must be taken on faith, as part of the work's symbolism. In the works of Laurence Sterne coincidence is rhetorically marveled at. Nabokov is closest to Sterne. He knows that the hand of the author can never be totally disguised, so he uses it as part of the fiction itself. Not God, but the author creates the events of fiction. His protagonist is aware of being manipulated, but this fact only enhances the suspense of the quest and the blinding flash of recognition at the end. The reader is aware of the author's task not only because the latter appears in the guise of an Englishman, but also because he is contrasted with a briefly appearing "Franco-Hungarian writer," a man who only wanted to weave words inventively. The narrator objects: "Were I a writer, I should allow only my heart to have imagination, and for the rest rely upon memory, that long-drawn sunset shadow of one's personal truth." The two would-be writer-characters add up to the author, who does both. But why not let the story itself prove this? Why break in with a polemic on art? Why let the narrator himself be a sub-artist, using such metaphors as "again and again she hurriedly appeared in the margins of my life, without influencing in the least its basic text." One answer is that in any case we are aware that fiction is fiction, and it is a feat of authorial skill when we see the hand of the artist in the process of sketching the outline of human faces, bringing them to life. Nabokov lets us witness the process of creation and the creation itself simultaneously.

Ultimately, however, only the creation itself matters. With Nabokov the strategy of skill is appropriate to a story about the necessity for skill, for application, in unraveling the threads of one's own existence. To some extent, then, within the framework of Nabokov's total creation, the narrator himself strives to create, but on another level he is part of the author's creation. There exists in almost any reader a resistance to the fact that the sound of a word may determine its meaning and therefore its very existence, as in the name Fialta. It is perhaps the same resistance we feel when we see fate determining character, a character suddenly become aware that he is caught in the plot of a fiction. These things must be yielded to in Nabokov, not in some mysterious way as in Pasternak's novel, but in order that mere illusion of reality may never become a prop for the reader's emotion. Nabokov weaves a tougher web of illusion, an illusion of *unreality*.

Nabokov's sentences exist to be looked at as well as through. When each image has been seen, it must be connected, counterposed to its kindred images in order to complete the mosaic. Often similarities are neighbors: Nabokov is as fond of the catalogue (often a catalogue of grotesques, for instance that of the habitués of a café) as was Pushkin. The catalogue device brings objects from disparate fields into contrasting juxtaposition. Again, it lends a kind of blatant virtuosity to the narration itself. But more often the connections between details are not made, for the details of his world are taken by the narrator to be clues to the mystery that can be solved only by his own memory. As the reader makes sense of the story, so, in a parallel fashion, the narrator makes sense of the meaning of his meetings with Nina. The reader is ahead in one sense, for in spite of all his sophistication he always expects a love story, which this turns out to be. But the narrator who is aware of the nature of his love only at the end makes more use of the clues, and leads the reader in the knowledge of memory's power to create understanding of the present through a reenactment of the past.

In the story, as in a religious ritual, the repetition of events and gestures abolishes time. The protagonists meet repeatedly, always in different places and never twice in a single year. All the settings are "trite" and unworthy except for the first and the last. The first meeting occurred around 1917 in the whiteness of a mythical Russian winter at a country estate, where the narrator kissed Nina before knowing her name. At the other meetings they are both émigrés, in transit, "acting out . . . (their) own aimless destiny." With Nabokov, Russian émigrés are a metaphor for any men in search of their own personal truth, and Russia is his metaphor for the mythical past, never to be recaptured except by the arduous effort of memory. Their final meeting takes place in the story's immediate past, in Fialta where the old and new towns symbolize the interlacing of present and past. Fialta seems reluctant to reveal anything (the story opens with the words: "Spring in Fialta is cloudy and dull"), but soon bright pieces of color begin to form the mosaic of memory: "a yellow bit of unripe orange peel on the old, slate-blue sidewalk, which retained here and there a fading memory of ancient mosaic design." While most of the clues in the story are colored, memory itself is white, as in the flash of understanding at the end. The white snow of Russia becomes a white sky and sun, as the whole movement of the story turns into the crescendo-diminuendo of the long final sentence:

> But the stone was as warm as flesh, and suddenly I understood something I had been seeing without understanding—why a piece of tin foil had sparkled so on the pavement, why the gleam of a glass had trembled on a tablecloth, why the sea was ashimmer: somehow, by imperceptible degrees, the white sky above Fialta had got saturated with sunshine, and now it was sun-pervaded throughout, and this brimming white radiance grew broader and broader, all dissolved in it, all vanished, all passed, and I stood on the station platform of Mlech with a freshly bought newspaper, which told me that the yellow car I had seen under the plane trees had suffered a crash beyond Fialta, having run at full speed into the truck of a travelling circus entering the town, a crash from which Ferdinand and his friend, those invulnerable rogues, those salamanders of fate, those basilisks of good fortune, had escaped with local and temporary injury to their scales, while Nina, in spite of her long-standing, faithful imitation of them, had turned out after all to be mortal.

The tinfoil, the glass and the sea, all details which had appeared before, are all reflectors, reflecting two ways, back into the past and forward from the past into the present. Each present meeting with Nina had brought a summary of all their past meetings, but the reason for this and the understanding that memory always comes too late appears in a white radiance at the end. Seeing had not been understanding until then. The narrator had assumed Nina to be a chameleon personality, like the protagonists in *The Eye* and in *The Real Life of Sebastian Knight,* because of her seemingly infinite adaptability and acquiescence. But chameleons, salamanders and basilisks are invulnerable species because of their very lowness on the evolutionary scale. The highest forms of life are the most transitory, and Nina proved finally to be ephemeral. The narrator had had premonitions of disaster, ones always centered on Nina herself. His fears that "something lovely, delicate, and unrepeatable was being wasted" are separated, until the end, from any feeling of his own final loss. Only then is the mosaic complete.

Nabokov is more interested in mosaics than in natural scenes, so of course the flash of understanding is as pat-

terned as the "lives" preceding it. The reader of common sense again protests that life itself would not be structured thus, but Nabokov peers at precisely the kind of mimicry Nina displayed, in an effort to penetrate life's secrets. Like an eccentric librarian in one of his own later stories, **"The Vane Sisters,"** Nabokov seeks in life—in words and in lepidoptery—"the chance that mimics choice, the flaw that looks like a flower." The very expression of the idea, as in this phrase the very letters of the words, yields patterns of mimicry. But art, of course, is really the opposite; it is the *choice* that mimics *chance.* Few writers other than Nabokov have dazzled us more thoroughly into a permanent awareness of this double truth. (pp. 128-35)

> *Barbara Heldt, " 'Spring in Fialta': The Choice That Mimics Chance," in* TriQuarterly, *No. 17, Winter, 1970, pp. 128-35.*

Alexander Theroux (essay date 1973)

[*Theroux is an American novelist, dramatist, and critic. In the following review of* A Russian Beauty, and Other Stories, *he finds the collection uneven in quality, while singling out the story "Ultima Thule" as a literary masterpiece.*]

The 13 short stories in [*A Russian Beauty, and Other Stories*], composed between 1924 and 1940 for Russian emigré periodicals and now translated (by author and son, Dmitri), all rather dolorifically footnote—for here we have, generally, a psychograph of Russian expatriates in the Twenties and Thirties in Germany—a world of very Bad Luck.

It's a Berliner Ensemble. Nabokov's characters are cuckoo-eggs in a foreign nest: Mislaid, displaced, their sad little squawks and memories for the what-might-have-been in Mother Russia, when heard, are ludicrously out of sync with the heft and rumble of an increasingly dark Berlin, which looms before us in a box-set of overheated rooms, desperate fox-trotting, emigré meetings and lectures, moth-eaten plush, *Inflationszeit,* grey walls, smoking to distraction, and frank bullying up and down every street.

Predictably, the theme of nostalgia is strong in these tales. The title story, **"A Russian Beauty,"** typifies the bittersweet mood of the collection. The young, prerevolutionary heroine, Olga, had everything Tolstoy's Natasha had.

> Her childhood passed festively, securely, and gaily, as was the custom in our country since the days of old. A sunbeam falling on the cover of a *Bibliothèque Rose* volume at the family estate, the classical hoarfrost of the Saint Petersburg public gardens. . . . A supply of memories, such as these, comprised her sole dowry when she left Russia in the spring of 1919.

Nubile there, she remains, transplanted to Berlin, an unclaimed blessing to the age of thirty, sadly driven to mild cynicism and retreat, when, one can't think luckily, a German named Fortsmann appropriates her. And she dies in childbirth. As in so many of these miniatures, Nabokov opts for the ironic, aposiopetic ending that always snaps off quickly like a broken doorknob, leaving one to guess what's inside. But we can imagine, which is, of course, our job.

Russians, displaced, go to the dogs. We find a plethora of wistful bumblers and self-deceivers, cartoons à la *Ninotchka* which Nabokov does so well, so tragicomically: the writer, Ilya Borisovich Tal, in the story, **"Lips to Lips"** (the novel over which he's "polishing his phrasing"), snickered at by each and all; the befogged 19-year-old Romantic poet and Oblomovian, Grisha, in **"Torpid Smoke,"** living a dream life and writing "perishable poems"; Konstantin in **"A Dashing Fellow,"** the fat mustachioed ersatz with lilac braces and mahogany-red street shoes who, riding third-class in trains, picks up stray girls with his inflated rhetoric and lies; the deaf widow Mints ("her profile opened like a nutcracker . . . ") in **"Breaking the News,"** who, the whole emigré community golf-headedly acting out charades, learns of her son's death so grotesquely; and in the (I think) allegorical **"An Affair of Honor,"** the rouged, be-monocled Anton Petrovich, with his shabby respectability and out-of-date *duello* code, who, in an intentionally un-Pushkinian way, flings his challenge ("One of us must perish!") in the face of his wife's seducer, the Moabit Berg—the latter, even though a Jew, still paradoxically one of the several examples of *der blonden Mannesrechtler*-type we best see in **"The Leonardo,"** where an eccentric painter, poor Romantovski, who sits up all night reading ("old, old tales") and who, after finding glue on his toilet seat and potato flour in his bedclothes, is finally set upon and stabbed by two frog-eyed Berlin brutes, the brothers Gustav and Anton, "gigantic, imperiously reeking of sweat and beer . . . with fecal matter replacing the human brain."

Several of the stories have non-German settings. **"Terra Incognita"** is just that: a tiny nightmare, rendered in stark and primary colors, with an unknown land as backdrop for a multiple killing. **"The Visit to a Museum"** is a Kafkaesque vignette epiphanizing by a single detail the Russia of yesterday from that of today. Finally, **"The Potato Elf,"** with its British setting, is very early and immature Nabokov; this documents, unsentimentally, The Life and Hard Times of a sexually disturbed dwarf (wrinkled face, castrate voice, eight-year-old appearance) and, but for a few memorable things, reminds one of early Carson McCullers. But wait.

I've saved the best for last. In this volume of fascinating, though sporadically uneven, tales is to be found, to my mind, one of the greatest short stories—may I be cavalier?—in the English language. It is called **"Ultima Thule."** (It has a fine but infinitely less exciting sequel, actually independent of it, entitled **"Solus Rex,"** also included.)

How can one sum up something so majestic, so multiform, so irreducible? Briefly, the narrator Sineusov, a chiaroscuro painter, is backtracking, memory-wise, that he might come to terms with his wife's death; he is so unhinged that he creates, mentally, an imaginary country (he had been illustrating a Scandinavian epic poem, *Ultima Thule*), an escapist vision where he becomes king (as K) and his wife queen (as Queen Belinda). This all recalls Nabokov's masterpiece, *Pale Fire*. One of Nabokov's most supreme creations, however, is a character in **"Ultima Thule"** called Adam Falter: medium, professor, metaphysician, genius, seer. The scene where Falter sees into the heart of Truth and screams paroxysmally for a full 15 minutes is easily one of literature's greatest set-pieces and, alone, is worth $7.95. Read this story.

Vladimir Nabokov's recognizable themes are all here, *in nuce:* the dream, memory, double-identity, fictive countries, parables of art; and they come to us in his consistently breathtaking and magic prose—*styled,* in the parlance of the watch industry—which always reaches out for the sinuosities of thought and those uncannily accurate observations by which we already know and worshipfully respect Nabokov. The stories are all memorable. But **"Ultima Thule"**? "Most tall hyperboles," as Crashaw said in another context, "cannot descry it." (pp. 955-56)

Alexander Theroux, "Berliner Ensemble," in National Review, *New York, Vol. XXV, August 31, 1973, pp. 955-56.*

William Carroll   (essay date 1974)

[*In the following excerpt, Carroll analyzes the ways in which the narrative devices in "Signs and Symbols" lead the reader to assumptions regarding the conclusion of the story.*]

> My characters are galley slaves.
>
> The design of my novel is fixed in my imagination and every character follows the course I imagine for him. I am the perfect dictator in that private world insofar as I alone am responsible for its stability and truth.
>
> —*Vladimir Nabokov*

Being a character in one of Vladimir Nabokov's fictions is evidently not much fun. Arbitrarily created, the character leads a life inherently fragile; he is continually jostled, transported in space and time, forced into exile at the stroke of a pen, capriciously tortured, driven into madness at the last moment (*Bend Sinister*), or abruptly "cancelled." As William H. Gass puts it, Nabokov's characters "are his clowns. They blunder comically about. Clubbed by coincidence, they trip when most passionate. With rouge on their pates and wigs on their features, their fundaments honk and trousers tear. Brought eagerly, naively near, beauty in a boutonniere pees on their faces." As flies to wanton boys are we to our authors, they kill us for their plots. Or so it seems to a series of characters in Nabokov's novels and short-stories, characters whose very position as characters-in-a-story seems to be one of the subjects of the stories in which they appear, and one of their own preoccupations there. Labyrinths, receding concentric circles, vertigo: Nabokov's fiction spawns special critical vocabularies and diseases in those who attempt to account for its persistently odd effect.

One way to a clearer perception of the aims of these fictions is to look closely at a few instances—especially at Pnin and the deranged boy in the story **"Signs and Symbols"**—in which a Nabokovian character's self-consciousness resembles, though in a distorted manner, our own self-consciousness as readers. I am not invoking the term "identification"; the laughter from Montreux would sweep it away anyhow. But these situations, these carefully arranged structures of self-consciousness, do seem, in curious ways, to be "archetypal" (another word Nabokov would never use). That is, our own sense of our-selves—lapsed believers in order unable to embrace disor-der, dimly aware of coincidence and patterns in experience but trying to ignore their import—is often like these char-acters' self-awareness. (pp. 203-04)

A victim of incurable derangement apparently from birth ("As a baby he looked more surprised than most babies"), with "no desires," the boy [in **"Signs and Symbols"**] per-ceives in the world about him nothing but "malignant ac-tivity that he alone could perceive." His parents are dull, sad people who are merely oblivious where he is paranoid. The boy lives in a closed system of signs, all of which point, malevolently, toward him. He suffers from "refer-ential mania," as "Herman Brink" calls it. His situation thus resembles that of a character in an incredibly com-plex fiction, in which every single word, every image, every nuance, is carefully related to that character's life; existing only inside the system, the character cannot know what the signs are pointing to, can only dimly guess at the outside referents. Thus, in Nabokov's story, what the boy "really wanted to do was to tear a hole in his world and escape." Death is apparently the only way open to him; his parents, trying to visit him, learn instead of his latest suicide attempt, "a masterpiece of inventiveness." An en-vious fellow patient, seeing (apparently) the boy's desper-ate clawing motion, "thought he was learning to fly—and stopped him." It is inevitable that the boy's cousin is "a famous chess player," a participant in another closed sys-tem of signs. The chessmaster Luzhin, in *The Defense*, like the boy here, attempts to escape his world through suicide, but fails: an eternity of dark and pale squares, another chessboard, "obligingly and inexorably spread out before him." As a child, we are told, Luzhin, working through classic chess games, "gradually ceased to reconstruct actu-ally on the board and contented himself with perceiving their melody mentally through the sequence of symbols and signs." Nabokov clearly links the two cases together.

Referential mania is the ultimate, insane extension of the act of personification. Lunatics and poets are, as they say, of imagination all compact. The boy believes that

> Phenomenal nature shadows him wherever he goes. Clouds in the staring sky transmit to one another, by means of slow signs, incredibly de-tailed information regarding him. His inmost thoughts are discussed at nightfall, in manual al-phabet, by darkly gesticulating trees. Pebbles or stains or sun flecks form patterns representing in some awful way messages which he must inter-cept. Everything is a cipher and of everything he is the theme.

Signs, patterns, messages, cipher, theme: these are terms of literary analysis. The boy is the "theme" of all reality and of the story. The primary meaning of "cipher" here is "secret writing based on a system"; the system, the mas-ter writer, remains unknown. Bad literary criticism is a

Nabokov at work in Montreux. He often stood at a lectern while writing.

hunt for "keys" in this sense, making of literature some-thing arcane and elite. But "cipher" also means, of course, "the mathematical symbol (0) denoting absence of quanti-ty," or zero. This is the more frightening possibility; it sug-gests that everything is a zero, meaningless, without sub-stance. The boy does attribute meaning, and it is this need to make such an attribution, a need we all feel, which taken to an extreme results in insanity. The intercepted messages may be in a code that reveals nothing.

After the cipher-theme comment, the unknown narrator of the story tells us of the "spies" who are "staring" and "gesticulating" at the boy:

> Some of the spies are detached observers, such as glass surfaces and still pools; others, such as coats in store windows, are prejudiced witnesses, lynchers at heart; others again (running water, storms) are hysterical to the point of insanity, have a distorted opinion of him and grotesquely misinterpret his actions. He must be always on his guard and devote every minute and module of life to the decoding of the undulation of things. The very air he exhales is indexed and filed away.

The boy conceives of three different kinds of "spies" or "inventors," then, those who have created and who moni-tor the closed system in which he suffers. And these three correspond to the kinds of rhetorical narrators used most commonly in modern fiction since James; the boy's per-sonifications are the personae Nabokov himself uses throughout his fiction. The "detached observers" do not intrude into their stories in obvious ways; they simply hold the mirror up to nature, as formula has it, and their em-blems here are "glass surfaces and still pools," calm, neu-tral reflectors of the world around them. Nabokov's earli-est novels and stories, like *The Defense,* are written from this point of view. The second kind of "spies" are those "prejudiced witnesses," seen *through* the glass now, not content with passive reflection, taking some active part in the ordering of things. One thinks here of the narrators of *The Real Life of Sebastian Knight* (an ultimately beneficient "prejudice") and *Pnin* (a malevolent one). The third type of narrator is "hysterical to the point of insanity," completely unreliable, one who "grotesquely" misinterprets the subject's actions. Their emblem is not the calm reflective mirror of the "still pools" but the turbulence of "running water, storms"—a version of the pathetic fallacy. The insane narrator is Nabokov's own special province: Smurov of *The Eye,* Hermann of *Despair,* Humbert Humbert of *Lolita,* Kinbote (for the sake of argument) of *Pale Fire* [in a footnote, Carroll comments: "Discretion forbids entering the controversy over whether Shade, Kinbote, or Prof. Botkin is the 'primary' narrator of *Pale Fire*"]. Mad artists, deflected or warped imaginations, offer oblique but spectacular perspectives on the nature of art, on the idea of transformation and distortion of "realty" [in a footnote, Carroll quotes Nabokov's remark that "Reality" is "one of the few words which mean nothing without quotes"]. and Nabokov uses them with increasing frequency in his work. As avatars of the imagination, these figures are our only means of seeing the world about them. Few other narrators in modern fiction are so astonishingly, so interestingly, unreliable.

The narrator-spies represent sheer terror for the boy, however; he is another character attempting to escape from his authors. But there is no escape:

> If only the interest he provokes were limited to his immediate surroundings—but alas it is not! With distance the torrents of wild scandal increase in volume and volubility. The silhouettes ofh is blood corpuscles, magnified a million times, flit over vast plains; and still farther, great mountains of unbearable solidity and height sum up in terms of granite and groaning firs the ultimate truth of his being."

The "still pools," already given way to "running water, storms," are now "torrents of wild scandal." It is the extension, the completeness, of the system which is so terrifying: "a dense tangle of logically interacting illusions, making him totally inaccessible to normal minds." The boy is the ultimate solipsist, dying from an overdose of meaning. The existence of one object which did not seem to point to him would represent the necessary "hole in his world," through which he might now and then seek relief. But there is none.

The boy thus lives continually in a world which seems governed by an all-powerful deity disturbingly like Descartes's famous "evil genius":

> I shall then suppose, not that God who is supremely good and the fountain of truth, but some evil genius not less powerful than deceitful, has employed his whole energies in deceiving me: I shall consider that the heavens, the earth, colors, figures, sound, and all other external things are nought but illusions and dreams of which this genius has availed himself in order to lay traps for my credulity.

The casualness of the "availed," the ubiquity of the "traps," increase the horror. Pnin has known this kind of a world, too, not only because of the narrator's actions, but as a result of childhood illnesses as well. The wallpaper in his room possessed patterns of oak leaves and purple flowers which tormented young Timofey: "he could not find what system of inclusion and circumscription governed the horizontal recurrence of the pattern." This childhood fascination with pattern led Luzhin to the glories and terrors of chess, but for Pnin it leads only to terror:

> It stood to reason that if the evil designer—the destroyer of minds, the friend of fever—had concealed the key of the pattern with such monstrous care, that key must be as precious as life itself and, when found, would regain for Timofey Pnin his everyday health, his everyday world; and this lucid—alas, too lucid—thought forced him to persevere in the struggle."

"Evil genius," "dreadful inventor," "evil designer," "friend of fever": this is the artist seen from within his artifact, from within a world in which paranoia is normality and the *deus absconditus* is a vain dream. Descartes imagined such a world but turned away from it; Nabokov imagined it and found a way for us to experience it with him.

"Referential mania" is a critical disease all readers of fiction suffer from. Our duty as critics is to explicate and analyze the signs—which point to a single meaning outside the work itself, as in allegory, or to another world inside the work—and the symbols—which point to various meanings simultaneously, both inside and outside the work. Over-reading is another, milder form of referential mania, and Nabokov has insured, through his rhetorical strategy, that the reader will succumb to the same mania that afflicts the boy. The story is studded with apparent signs and symbols that the gullible reader—that is, any reader—will attempt to link together in a "meaningful" pattern. Most of these signs point to the probably successful suicide of the boy. On the way to the hospital, for example, the parents take the underground train; but it "lost its life current between two stations, and for a quarter of an hour one could hear nothing but the dutiful beating of one's heart and the rustling of newspapers." Other things lose their "life current" and fall into darkness that day. The parents go to a bus stop, after learning of their son's latest suicide attempt: "A few feet away, under a swaying and dripping tree, a tiny half-dead unfledged bird was helplessly twitching in a puddle." This seems inevitably to be a "foreshadowing" of the son's death, the sort of symbolist anticipatory detail found in traditional fiction. Confronted with a similar vision in *Ada,* though, Van Veen has a more skeptical attitude, one which we might well emulate: "A dead and dry hummingbird moth lay on the window ledge of the lavatory. Thank goodness, symbols did not exist either in dreams or in the life in between."

The rest of the parents' day is filled with similar omens. A picture of Aunt Rosa reminds the mother that "the Germans put her to death." She dimly senses a larger power behind such events; but her vagueness is the opposite of her son's hyper-sensitivity. She has no idea of any source: "she thought of the endless waves of pain that for some reason or other she and her husband had to endure; of the invisible giants hurting her boy in some unimaginable fasion; of the incalculable amount of tenderness contained in the world; of the fate of this tenderness . . . of neglected children . . . of beautiful weeds." The existence of cruelty and death are indeed without apparent "reason," they are "unimaginable." Yet they are here, in an imagined fiction, as in the world. Nabokov gives us all sorts of signs that death is near, and we learn next how it is the fate of the "beautiful weeds" that they helplessly have "to watch the shadow of [the farmer's] simian stoop leave mangled flowers in its wake, as the monstrous darkness approaches."

That "darkness" seems imminent in the third and final part of the story; it is "past midnight" when the parents resolve to bring the boy home from the mental hospital, to care for him themselves. Another symbol of death appears when the mother picks up from the floor some playing cards and photographs: "knave of hearts, nine of spades, ace of spades, Elsa and her bestial beau." The mother is oblivious to the ace of spades, a familiar harbinger of death, but she is startled than by the telephone, ringing at "an unusual hour." It is a wrong number. "It frightened me," the mother says. The telephone rings again, again a wrong number, asking for Charlie. The mother replies: "You have the incorrect number. I will tell you what you are doing: you are turning the letter O instead of the zero." Absorbing the implications of *this* idea will take a moment. While it is a plausible explanation of the wrong number, the fact remains that there is no hieroglyphic difference between the letter and the number. We may recall an earlier line in the story: "Everything is a cipher and of everything he is the theme." Nabokov has placed us in the position of the boy here—is the O a letter of a number? Does it matter? Is this confusion a cipher—a clue to a hidden meaning? Or is it just null, a nero, without substance? It could be either.

The moment for our decision arrives quickly. After the second call, the father looks over the gift for his son: the ten little jars, each containing a different fruit jelly. He "re-examined with pleasure the luminous yellow, green, red little jars. His clumsy moist lips spelled out their eloquent labels: apricot, grape, beech plum, quince. He had got to crab apple, when the telephone rang again." And so the story ends. What has happened? Who is calling? Surely most readers of the story will feel that the hospital is calling to tell them of their son's suicide, an event the mother anticipated at the first call. This is the *third* call, a most prophetic and ominous number. The sequence of "eloquent labels," from apricot to quince, has been broken by the flat, cramped sound of "crab apple," fruit which is tart or sour while the others are luscious and ripe; it is an easy step to conclude that the sequence of wrong numbers has also been broken, by the "right" number, bringing bad news. And surely short stories aren't supposed to end with something as inconclusive as a wrong number? It seems that Nabokov has engendered in the reader (who eagerly assists him) a serious case of referential mania. A "cipher" can be a nullity just as easily as it can be a key, but most readers will see it as a key; we will conclude that the third

call is from the hospital. In so doing, we will have assigned a meaning to the signs based on something outside the closed system; we will have, in effect, participated with Nabokov in killing the boy. The overdose of meaning is our own; we can't accept a third random phone number, but must see the "death-pattern" completed, because that is the way our minds work. Nabokov made use of the same fact when he seemingly broke Pnin's punch bowl; but the pattern there, as here, was completed only in the reader's mind, not in the work itself. Enough for Nabokov to have suggested the possibility.

This strikes to the very nature of a created, fictional world and the kind of relationship a reader has to it. We have felt pity for the boy, sympathized with the parents, but probably separated ourselves from the boy's mania. It is our very participation in that mania, however, the need to see a completed pattern, that has "killed" the boy. It is just as plausible to argue, though, that the signs and symbols of death have no logically inherent and inescapable conclusion, that they point to nothing finally, and are as "meaning"-less as a sequence of random numbers. It is this ambiguity which makes the story so profoundly eerie. The "cipher" is constructed so that we have to supply a key, constitutionally unable to admit the possibility that there is none. As in *Pnin,* we find ourselves as fully engaged readers, seemingly exemplifying what we would prefer to reject, and vice versa. Both fictions encourage a denial of the power that informs them. Where is the essential paradox to be located, then—in the reader or in the author?

Both (the coward's answer). There obviously *are* patterns in Nabokov's fictions. In *Speak, Memory,* Nabokov himself, moreover, after relating a coincidence involving a Russian general and a match, says that "the following of such thematic designs through one's life should be, I think, the true purpose of autobiography." We perceive similar themes in every novel, every story. As Joan Clements, speaking of an unknown author, pants in *Pnin:* "But don't you think—haw—that what he is trying to do—haw—practically in all his novels—haw—is—haw—to—express the fantastic recurrence of certain situations?" Undoubtedly, we answer, for we have seen them. The rhetorical strategy of **"Signs and Symbols"** and, less clearly, of *Pnin* is first to offer "meaning" and "theme," to give us signs and the "fantastic recurrence of certain situations," and then deny or limit the pattern, to refuse to complete it and ask, with the innocence of a child, what pattern? It is yours, not mine. So we not only are *not* put off by coincidence and fantastic recurrence, by a pattern of signs; we are instead implicated in the pattern more deeply than we ever thought possible. The author's self-consciousness in these cases does *not* distance us, as critics tell us it usually does; rather, it draws us into the web of esthetic responsibility, and our anger at the cruel fates which torment Pnin and the boy deflects from the author and redounds on ourselves, his co-authors. the most remarkable thing about the whole process is that, somehow, we participate in both worlds, in that of the character and the author, creature and creator.

Nabokov tells us in *Speak, Memory* that

competition in chess problems is not really between White and Black but betwen the composer and the hypothetical solver (just as in a first-
rate work of fiction the real clash is not between
the characters but between the author and the
world), so that a great part of a problem's value
is due to the number of 'tries'—delusive opening
moves, false scents, specious lines of play, astutely and lovingly prepared to lead the would-be
solver astray.

The metaphors Nabokov employs here—"competition,"
"clash,"—are, for once, misleading, for they suggest an
absolute barrier between author and reader, an offputting
haughtiness. Thus Gass misconstrues the distinction between game and problem: "it's ourselves the moves are
made against: we are the other player. Most of Nabokov's
novels . . . are attacks upon their readers." This is too
crude, I think. In a game, the competition is everything;
in a problem, the solver reenacts the creative process of the
composer, preferably in the same sequence of moves. The
solver must become, as far as is possible, the composer's
double, his co-author, in effect. The relationship established between solver and composer, reader and author,
is thus a bond of sharing, not an irreconcilable division.
The greater authority is still on the author's side, admittedly, but in *Pnin* and **"Signs and Symbols,"** at least, we
share with Nabokov, for a moment, the incomparable eminence of the view from on high. It is a complex, and
breathtaking, accomplishment. The nature of the trick is,
I think, impossible to achieve in more traditional forms of
fiction.

Through this labyrinthine process, finally, Nabokov has
shown us what it is like to live in his world, and simultaneously reminded us of our position in our own. Ada tells
Van of a similar feeling:

> In 'real' life we are creatures of chance in an ab-
> solute void—unless we be artists ourselves, natu-
> rally; but in a good play I feel authored, I feel
> passed by the board of censors, I feel secure,
> with only a breathing blackness before me (in-

An excerpt from "Signs and Symbols" (the third section)

It was past midnight when from the living room she heard
her husband moan; and presently he staggered in, wearing
over his nightgown the old overcoat with astrakhan collar
which he much preferred to the nice blue bathrobe he had.

"I can't sleep," he cried.

"Why," she asked, "why can't you sleep? You were so
tired."

"I can't sleep because I am dying," he said and lay down
on the couch.

"Is it your stomach? Do you want me to call Dr. Solov?"

"No doctors, no doctors," he moaned, "To the devil with
doctors! We must get him out of there quick. Otherwise
we'll be responsible. Responsible!" he repeated and hurled

himself into a sitting position, both feet on the floor, thumping his forehead with his clenched fist.

"All right," she said quietly, "we shall bring him home tomorrow morning."

"I would like some tea," said her husband and retired to the
bathroom.

Bending with difficulty, she retrieved some playing cards
and a photograph or two that had slipped from the couch
to the floor: knave of hearts, nine of spades, ace of spades,
Elsa and her bestial beau.

He returned in high spirits, saying in a loud voice:

"I have it all figured out. We will give him the bedroom.
Each of us will spend part of the night near him and the
other part on this couch. By turns. We will have the doctor
see him at least twice a week. It does not matter what the
Prince [the man's wealthy brother Isaac] says. He won't
have to say much anyway because it will come out
cheaper."

The telephone rang. It was an unusual hour for their telephone to ring. His left slipper had come off and he groped
for it with his heel and toe as he stood in the middle of the
room, and childishly, toothlessly, gaped at his wife. Having
more English than he did, it was she who attended to calls.

"Can I speak to Charlie," said a girl's dull little voice.

"What number you want? No. That is not the right number."

The receiver was gently cradled. Her hand went to her old
tired heart.

"It frightened me," she said.

He smiled a quick smile and immediately resumed his excited monologue. They would fetch him as soon as it was day.
Knives would have to be kept in a locked drawer. Even at
his worst he presented no danger to other people.

The telephone rang a second time. The same toneless anxious young voice asked for Charlie.

"You have the incorrect number. I will tell you what you
are doing: you are turning the letter O instead of the zero."

They sat down to their unexpected festive midnight tea. The
birthday present stood on the table. He sipped noisily; his
face was flushed; every now and then he imparted a circular
motion to his raised glass so as to make the sugar dissolve
more thoroughly. The vein on the side of his bald head
where there was a large birthmark stood out conspicuously
and, although he had shaved that morning, a silvery bristle
showed on his chin. While she poured him another glass of
tea, he put on his spectacles and re-examined with pleasure
the luminous yellow, green, red little jars. His clumsy moist
lips spelled out their eloquent labels: apricot, grape, beech
plum, quince. He had got to crab apple, when the telephone
rang again.

Vladimir Nabokov, in his "Signs and Sym-
bols," Nabokov's Dozen: A Collection of
Thirteen Stories, Doubleday and Co., Inc.,
1958.

stead of our Fourth-Wall Time), I feel cuddled in the embrace of puzzled Will (he thought I was you) or in that of the much more normal Anton Pavlovich, who was always passionately fond of long dark hair.

In **"Signs and Symbols"** or *Pnin*—in virtually all of Nabokov's fiction—we are required to become "artists ourselves," to assign and to be assigned meaning, with the result that the "monstrous darkness" the mother in **"Signs and Symbols"** fears is mitigated, at least, into a "breathing blackness," one which is not merely a "void," but a blackness which may also be a cipher that is a sign, a letter (and hence a meaning) instead of a zero. All of us, everything, is "authored" in one sense or another. It is the special achievement of Nabokov's fiction that it induces a confirmation of this in us, that it represents a confirmation in itself. Better to be a "galley slave," laboring in service of the printed word, than not to feel "authored" at all. It is a very small affirmation, to be sure, but we are grateful for all such things these days. (pp. 208-16)

William Carroll, "Nabokov's Signs and Symbols," in A Book of Things About Vladimir Nabokov, *edited by Carl R. Proffer, Ardis, 1974, pp. 203-17.*

Hugh Kenner (essay date 1975)

[*The foremost American critic and chronicler of literary Modernism, Kenner is best known for* The Pound Era *(1971), a massive study of the Modernist movement, and for his influential works on T. S. Eliot, James Joyce, Samuel Beckett, and Wyndham Lewis. In the following review of* Tyrants Destroyed, and Other Stories, *he finds the collection pretentious, empty, and ultimately nothing more than self-appreciation on Nabokov's part.*]

Like Oscar Wilde and Charles Kinbote, Nabokov plays—has been playing now for many decades—a game to which self-appreciation is intrinsic. His invented selves even appreciate one another. John Ray, Jr., Ph.D., in his foreword to *Lolita,* tells us how to admire what Humbert Humbert accomplished in the 69 chapters of the narrative proper: "How magically his singing violin can conjure up a tendresse, a compassion for Lolita that makes us entranced with the book while abhorring its author!" Then Vladimir Nabokov, closing the huge parenthesis, supplies for our retrospective delectation in an afterword an inventory of the more magical bits: not the "good parts" of a porn novel—that's the list he's parodying—but Lolita playing tennis, or "the tinkling sounds of the valley town coming up the mountain trail (on which I caught the first known female of *Lycaeides sublivens* Nabokov)."

Ada concludes with a lyrical blurb for itself. The introduction to a reprinted *Bend Sinister* lists allusions no one seems to have noticed the first time around. The introduction to a revised *Speak Memory* prompts us to turn up a sentence deep in the book—"The ranks of words I reviewed were again so glowing, with their puffed-out little chests and trim uniforms . . ."—and discern buried there "the name of a great cartoonist and a tribute to him."

All reviewers, it seems, missed that one. Reviewers—torpid folk, and with deadlines—don't pick up Nabokov

sentences one by one, as they're meant to be picked up, or marvel at their iridescences, tap them for false bottoms, check them for anagrams. His only fit reader is finally himself ("it is only the author's private satisfaction that counts"), and the rest of us should wait to speak until we're spoken to—as we are being, constantly, by all those notes and prefaces.

Now on with the motley: **Tyrants Destroyed,** 13 stories scooped out of the past, 12 of them out of his remote Russian-language past when he went as "V. Sirin"; and lo, a foreword apprises us that his *oeuvre* has been accorded a full-dress bibliography and reminds us (cryptically) that he also wrote *Lolita.* The bang-you're-dead reviewer will lower his cocked index and think twice before pronouncing stories so sponsored dismayingly empty, especially as Nabokov has more than once slipped in ahead of him, anticipating doubts but leaving them equivocal.

For instance, the fourth story, **"Music,"** is called in its headnote "a trifle singularly popular with translators." This phrase conceals several false bottoms. Translators fall for my trifles. You are about to read a story that has been—so to speak—around. You are about to see a *real* job of translating ("by Dmitri Nabokov in collaboration with the author"). And since I present **"Music"** here with a certain amount of circumstantial fuss, including the date of its Russian-language appearance in a Paris émigré daily, you will understand "trifle" correctly; I, who also wrote *Ada* and *Pale Fire,* am entitled to call this story a trifle.

The story? Some 2,000 words about an unmusical man at a concert who spots his former wife and, while they sit silent, 20 feet from each other, must let the music—formerly meaningless to him—shape his reliving of a past he had shut away. Phrases like "How long ago it all seemed!" and "What bliss it had been" and "We can't go on like this" suggest a trifle indeed, unworthy of the master illusionist. Then she slips away, and then the name of the piece of music is revealed: " 'What you will,' said Boke in the apprehensive whisper of a rank outsider. 'A Maiden's Prayer,* or the *Kreutzer Sonata.* Whatever you will.' "

Careful—Beethoven's sonata shares its title with a Tolstoy fiction. Check *that* out, O researcher of the twenty-first century. And Beware of the Labyrinth.

So it goes. These are, generally, trick stories with a twist at the end, of the old-fashioned magazine kind. One—**"The Vane Sisters,"** already several times printed—has an acrostic in the last paragraph, implanted there by two dead girls of whose collaboration the narrator is supposed to be unaware. The headnote apprises us to watch for it. "This particular trick can be tried only once in a thousand years of fiction. Whether it has come off is another question." (But by prompting us, the sly author has *made* it come off.)

In another, dating from 1926, a lady devil offers a timid voyeur all the girls he shall covet between noon and midnight, gathered and placed at his complete disposal, provided only that the total number be odd. (Trick ending: His tally is 13, but one girl got counted twice.) Nabokov, anticipating groans, passes this tale off as "a rather artificial affair, composed a little hastily, with more concern for the tricky plot than for imagery and good taste." Lest we hasten to agree, he also remarks that it therefore "required some revamping here and there in the English version," readers of which are being spooked into discerning imagery and good taste.

A readier way to profit from this story (**"A Nursery Tale"**) is to discern in its plot, albeit half a century old, the Nabokov Theme full-bodied, a theme that has sustained story after story, novel after novel. A way of stating it, almost but not quite too general to be of use, is this: *A man almost possesses what he seeks, but loses it because of a quirk in the conditions.* (The Tithonus story, or a fairy-tale plot; no wonder it can be made to seem Protean.)

In the story the quirk was simple: The Devil meant an odd number of girls; the man toted up an odd number of encounters. In the novels it is apt to be more complex. The quester changes, or his object (*Lolita*). He becomes enmeshed in a larger design of his quarry (*Pale Fire; The Real Life of Sebastian Knight*). Or the author has contrived an unthinkable exaction; the unpayable price of Pnin's tenure (*Pnin*) would have been service under a long-ago trifler with his fiancée.

The *Pnin* case is instructive. Since this parvenu is also the novel's narrator, unmasking his steely smile in the final chapter, there to dispose of Pnin's destiny much as the author does, he very nearly fuses with the author or with what the author has called elsewhere "an anthropomorphic deity impersonated by me." ("I have finished building a world," says the novelist Sebastian Knight, "and this is my Sabbath rest.")

Those beautiful involuted sentences, which are Nabokov's hallmark, are ways to build a world, not ways to describe one. "Without any wind blowing, the sheer weight of a raindrop, shining in parasitic luxury on a cordate leaf, caused its tip to dip, and what looked like a globule of quicksilver performed a sudden glissando down the center vein, and then, having shed its bright load, the relieved leaf unbent. Tip, leaf, dip, relief. . . ." Between book covers, there is no leaf and no raindrop until the creator has done all that.

And as a narrator who fuses with V. Nabokov effects the destiny of Pnin, so what *happens* in these big and little worlds is what V. Nabokov has decreed shall happen, right down to the passage of an "inquisitive butterfly" across a tennis court in "Champion, Colorado," between Humbert Humbert and Dolores Haze, in a paragraph all to itself.

It is he, Nabokov, who is Humbert's "McFate"; he (not a dead girl) who planted the acrostic in **"The Vane Sisters"**; he who arranged the arithmetical misfortune of the timid voyeur; he who has equipped such a roster of his creatures with faulty hearts and decreed that the heart of Ivanov in the story **"Perfection"** should fail when it did (for particulars, see the story). Grown bolder, he has re-created space and time: The spaces and times of *Ada,* where old Russia's hegemony includes the North American continent, and where *Anna Karenina,* as though written by a counter-Tolstoy, opens with a sentence exactly inverse in sense to the sentence the earthbound Tolstoy wrote. Meddling with the future also, it is he who gives instructions to a twenty-first-century scholar (who will surely obey them, if he shall happen to exist).

It is he: That is what all the self-appreciation is really about. It is also why the stories in **Tyrants Destroyed** are so empty: the slight amusements of "an anthropomorphic deity," arranging small systems, like chess problems, to suit himself.

This deity will allot himself, say, 3,500 words, and will contrive within that limit to place the lost wife whom Luzhin is seeking on the very train where Luzhin works as a waiter, and have them not meet, have him even not find the ring she lost in the diner, have him go through with his plan to kill himself while the train bears her away toward Cologne. **"A Matter of Chance,"** it's called. Chance is seldom so hollowly neat. No, a better title would be "The Whims of Nabokov," iron whims.

By a fraudulent deity's tricks, he contrives to keep patterns trim within narrow limits. To the deity responsible for your life and mine, the minimum intelligible system appears to be the universe itself, and excerpts have a certain random look. Sensing this principle, V. Nabokov now inclines to refer every excerpt to its universe, which is The Complete Works of V. Nabokov. That is what is really going on in **Tyrants Destroyed:** less the promotion of some negligible stories than their careful assignment to year and month and room and weather and journal, the reinvention of an aspect of the author's past, a pendant to *Speak Memory.*

For his chief work is finally himself, as it was Hemingway's, as it was Huysmans's. Joris-Karl Huysmans (1848-1907) is a *point de repère* Nabokov's appreciators seem to have shunned. Contemplators of *Ada*'s lush verbal jungle (now sleeps the nacreous petal, now the gules) might adduce with advantage the creator of Des Esseintes, whose tortoises were bejeweled, and who tired of flowers, and indulged in artificial flowers, and then tired of those and sought out real flowers so exotic they could pass for artificial. (pp. 21-2, 24)

Hugh Kenner, "Mockings of the Master Illusionist," in Saturday Review, *Vol. 2, No. 12, March 8, 1975, pp. 21-2, 24.*

Thomas Rogers   (essay date 1975)

[*Rogers is an American novelist and critic. In the following review of* Tyrants Destroyed, and Other Stories, *he finds these early stories provide insight into Nabokov's artistic development.*]

Middle-aged American readers have become familiar with Nabokov's writing in an unusual way. That is, they tuned in on him in the late forties and early fifties, when he was at the peak of his powers, producing *Speak, Memory, Pnin,* and most of all *Lolita.* He had the effect of a new writer, though he had been an established Russian novelist for more than 20 years. Since then his American admirers have been treated to the rather uncanny experience of following Nabokov's later career while at the same time discovering his early works as these were successively translated into English by Dmitri Nabokov in collaboration with his father. This process has now reached some sort of climax with the publication a few months ago of Nabokov's latest novel *Look at the Harlequins!* and the republication in this collection of one of his earliest tales, **"A Matter of Chance,"** now first appearing in English 51 years after it was published in the Riga Segodnya on June 22, 1924. It is like listening at the same time to both ends of an unknown piece of music whose middle is strangely familiar.

To my ears most of Nabokov's writing since *Lolita* will necessarily remain more or less unknown. I cannot reread *Pale Fire,* and I could not get through *Ada* the first time around. Something has gone wrong: Nabokov's fiction has become approximately as accessible as the Swiss mountain peaks which now surround him, but that is another story. The story, or stories (there are 13 of them) in **Tyrants Destroyed** are accessible enough, perhaps because they were originally written for the sort of liberal émigré intelligentsia which, of all Nabokov's various audiences, must be the one he was most directly connected with. **"Bachmann,"** for example, begins with a straightforward address several light years removed from the prefaces, genealogies and alembications of Nabokov's later fiction. A pianist named Bachmann has died, and the narrator says quite simply: "This brought to my mind the story about a woman who loved him. It was told to me by the impresario Sack. Here it is." *Here it is.* Most of the stories in this collection have that sort of ring to them, the satisfying ring of a confident artist in touch with his world.

There are other satisfactions in store for our hypothetical middle-aged reader devoted to *Pnin* and *Lolita* and disenchanted by what has followed. He will find, for instance, that the title character of **"In Memory of L. I. Shigaev"** is an early version of Tiomfoy Pnin himself. Both Shigaev and Pnin are unusual characters in the Nabokov repertoire. They are kind men. Most Nabokov characters are so chock-full of their own obsessions that they have no room in their hearts for anything else. Pnin and Shigaev are different. They are bald, childless men whose research (Shigaev appears to be an economist) is unlikely to be published. Because of their psychic infertility they have a sort of inner space amounting almost to emptiness, where they are willing to play kindly host to more self-absorbed people.

Shigaev takes in a poet named Victor with "a perpetually inflamed soul." Victor has drunk himself into the "most Russian of hallucinations" and begun to see sluggish little devils creeping around the carpet and squatting like toads among the papers on his writing desk. Shigaev feeds him beet soup, tells him dull stories and makes him feel better. Victor cannot understand his own or other people's response to Shigaev. "What did he do to be so well liked? I don't know." It seems to be a law in Nabokov's world that kindness, when it exists, is either not recognized or ruthlessly exploited, as in Pnin's relationship with his ex-wife. Self-absorbed but creative lunatics get more out of life than nice people.

Aside from the pleasure of connecting these stories with

Nabokov's longer and better known works, our hypothetical reader will find at least one almost perfect little story, **"The Admiralty Spire,"** which must be among the most completely funny things Nabokov has ever written. A middle-aged Russian is writing a long, abusive letter to Mr. Serge Solntsev, author of a trite romantic novel. First he accuses Solntsev of being a lady novelist: "Every sentence of yours buttons to the left." Next he unmasks the lady novelist. She is none other than Katya, his long lost love, who has used and distorted the facts of their love affair to produce this paraody of his most cherished memories: "Listen—stop writing books! At least let this flop serve as a lesson." Finally it occurs to him that Katya may not be Solntsev—that a real Solntsev by a "rare coincidence" may have invented "this tripe." So he ends with a curt apology: "In that case, please forgive me, colleague Solntsev." The more one meditates on the hypothetical case—that Solntsev *is* Solntsev and not Katya—the funnier that apology becomes.

Finally, and most interesting of all, reading these stories one begins to feel that Nabokov is not as strange and *sui generis* as he is sometimes made out to be. Take **"Terror,"** for instance, a tale told by a poet who begins by not recognizing his own reflection in the mirror and ends up not recognizing anything—houses, trees, automobiles, people, dogs. "My line of communication with the world snapped . . . I was no longer a man, but a naked eye, an aimless glance moving in an absurd world." What saves the narrator's sanity is a telegram informing him that his mistress is dying. "Her death saved me. . . . Plain human grief filled my life. . . . " But he goes on to inform us that he knows his terror will return and that his "brain is doomed."

In his author's note to **"Terror,"** Nabokov compares the story (favorably, of course) with Sartre's *Nausea,* "with which it shares certain shades of thought and none of that novel's fatal defects." But if **"Terror"** has some very slight connection with Sartre, its ending suggested to me that the spirit of Edgar Allan Poe was hovering not far away. Poe is the one native American writer who might conceivably have influenced Nabokov, and (influence aside) it seems obvious that Nabokov and Poe have a lot in common. I say this rather worriedly, since I think of Nabokov as a very fine artist, whereas I was educated with Ivor Winters's critical dooms echoing in my ears, and Winters, after all, found that Poe wrote poetry fit only "to delight the soul of a housemaid." Housemaids have largely disappeared by now, but such pronouncements tend to linger in the impressionable mind so that, coming across a doomed brain and lots of madness and some dead or lost loves in these stories, I felt a critical question rising to the surface of my own troubled brain. Is there not an element of claptrap in these stories, of good old 19th-century romantic flimflam? I think there is, and that indeed it is one of the charms and surprises of reading this collection, that it allows one to think of Nabokov not in his own terms, which have become progressively more solipsistic and self-referential, but as a startlingly fresh and beautifully talented practitioner of certain fairy tale 19th-century literary traditions. Aside from Poe, I found myself thinking of Maupassant as I read the very early **"A Matter of**

Chance," which is just the sort of toughly ironic concoction with a wistful center that most of us ate up in high school.

I say this not to disparage Nabokov but simply to suggest that we are much closer to understanding what sort of artist he is if we think of him as a really good and witty Poe rather than an artful Sartre or a flighty Joyce. Nabokov has never set up to be a wise man or a sound observer of the human scene and it does him no good at all to be treated as a philosophic or comprehensive novelist, especially since within his own terrain of slightly unreal poetic obsessions he is quite clearly a supreme master. Who else could have brought off *Lolita?* (pp. 4-5)

> *Thomas Rogers, "Early, Artful Nabokov," in* The New York Times Book Review, *March 9, 1975, pp. 4-5.*

Nabokov on the writer's way of punishing tyrants and other criminals:

There is . . . one improvement that quite unwittingly a real writer does bring to the world around him. Things that commonsense would dismiss as pointless trifles or grotesque exaggerations in an irrelevant direction are used by the creative mind in such a fashion as to make iniquity absurd. The turning of the villain into a buffoon is not a set purpose with your authentic writer: crime is a sorry farce no matter whether the stressing of this may help the community or not; it generally does, but that is not the author's direct purpose or duty. The twinkle in the author's eye as he notes the imbecile drooping of a murderer's underlip, or watches the stumpy forefinger of a professional tyrant exploring a profitable nostril in the solitude of his sumptuous bedroom, this twinkle is what punishes your man more surely than the pistol of a tiptoeing conspirator. And inversely, there is nothing dictators hate so much as that unassailable, eternally elusive, eternally provoking gleam. One of the main reasons why the very gallant Russian poet Gumilev was put to death by Lenin's ruffians thirty odd years ago was that during the whole ordeal, in the prosecutor's dim office, in the torture house, in the winding corridors that led to the truck, in the truck that took him to the place of execution, and at that place itself, full of the shuffling feet of the clumsy and gloomy shooting squad, the poet kept smiling.

> *Vladmir Nabokov, in his* "The Art of Literature and Commonsense," *From his* Lectures on Literature, *Harcourt Brace Jovanovich, 1982.*

Eric Korn   (essay date 1975)

[*In the following review of* Tyrants Destroyed, and Other Stories, *Korn discusses the themes and "word games" of some of the stories.*]

There is a Borges story about a man who sets himself the life-task of writing *Don Quixote* exactly as Cervantes wrote it. Although the words are identical, he produces a quite different text, simply because the world has been inescapably altered by the passage of time and events, not

least by the existence of a book called *Don Quixote,* and words are charged with new meanings. A similar epistemological hurdle bars our approach to this collection of a dozen of Nabokov's early short stories, first published in Russian émigré journals in Paris, Berlin and Riga. They are translated by the author and Dmitri Nabokov; **"A Nursery Tale"**, we are warned, is "revamped"; but even so, even without the surely very deliberate selection and arrangement, it would be impossible to see clearly the work of the unknown foreign writer behind the lineaments of the literary figure of world distinction. This book is a new construction by Nabokov-1975, whatever the geological history of the blocks of which it is composed. Each story has an introduction, perhaps to be seen as a linking narrative; they are generally limited to bibliographical fact, though there is the occasional devastating throwaway: "It ['**Terror**'] preceded Sartre's *La Nausee,* with which it shares certain shades of thought, and none of that novel's fatal defects, by at least a dozen years."

The inclusion of the thirteenth story, **"The Vane Sisters"**, is odd and full of suggestion. Written in English, two decades after the rest, already published in magazines and in a collection, it does not, at first sight, belong. It's a haunting piece that concerns two sisters, both dead, one a believer in a kind of spiritistic revenance. The last paragraph contains—I can't be certain I would have noticed without the author's direction—an acrostic which sends one back to the first page of the story and shows that what had seemed merely atmospheric description of a winter scene—but the decor in Nabokov is always part of the plot—is pervaded by the girls' shades.

Is the whole collection to be read as an acrostic? If so, I have not deciphered it: but certainly it is pervaded with ghosts, with memories and the reconstruction of memories. The Ghost of Nabokov Present (the present being 1924–1939) communes with the Ghosts of Nabokovs Past, the whole edited by Nabokov Yet-to-Come.

It works, of course. The collection is moving, both as a single utterance and as a framework for the ingenious and delicate mosaic elements. In **"Music"** a man catches sight of his ex-wife as they attend a piano recital at a party. The apparent cliché of his recollections is brilliantly and wittily refreshed by the device of making him a musical illiterate.

In another story, Lavrently Ivanovich Kruzhevnitsyn (acronymically Lik, which "means 'countenance' in Russian and Middle English"), an actor of no discernible talent and without any personality under the mask, lives only in performance, relates only to the other characters on stage:

> He liked to tell himself that only on the stage did she live her true life, being subject the rest of the time to periodic fits of insanity, during which she no longer recognized him and called herself by a different name.

His past, in all its repulsiveness, is recalled by the sudden reappearance of a childhood enemy with bogus memories of the happy long ago.

More complex is the wonderful **"Admiralty Spire"**, where

the narrator is thrown into an existential panic by the appearance of a novel describing his past:

> Imagine the following: suppose I once took a walk through a marvellous landscape, where turbulent waters tumble and bindweed chokes the columns of desolate ruins, and then, many years later, in a stranger's house, I come across a snapshot showing me in a swaggering pose in front of what is obviously a pasteboard pillar; in the background there is the whitish smear of a daubed-in-cascade, and somebody has inked a moustache on me. Where did the thing come from? Take away this horror! The dinning waters I remember were real, and, what is more, no one took a picture of me there.

Soon it is clear that we are hearing two rival accounts of the end of an affair:

> I would try to persuade myself that it was I who had stopped loving Katya, as I hastened to gather up all I could recall of her mendacity, her presumption, her vacuity, the pretty patch masking a pimple, the artificial *grasseyement* that would appear in her speech when she needlessly switched to French, her invulnerable weakness for titled poetasters, and the ill-tempered, dull expression of her eyes, when, for the hundredth time, I tried to make her tell me with whom she had spent the previous evening. And when it was all gathered and weighed in the balance, I would perceive with anguish that my love, burdened as it was with all that trash, had settled and lodged only deeper . . .

How admirable the phrasing, how mercilessly right the word "invulnerable".

"In Memory of L. I. Shigaev" (much to do with memory, little with Shigaev) shows the same concerns:

> This is but one of the conceivable versions of my parting with her; I had considered many of these impossible possibilities while still in the first heat of my drunken delirium, imagining now the gross gratification of a good slap; now the firing of an old Parabellum pistol, at her and at myself, at her and at the paterfamilias, only at her, only at myself; then, finally, a glacial irony, noble sadness, silence—oh, things can go in so many ways, and I have long since forgotten how they actually went.

Less besotted readers than myself may find this and similar passages "self-indulgent", a word which has never seemed to me to have any place in a critical vocabulary, given its extraordinary implication that a writer ought lently to abstain from the things he does well.

There is no such thing as early Nabokov, unless, by some Sirindipity, the lost 1914 *Stikhi* should be recovered. The earliest story here (**"A Matter of Chance"**, 1924) shows no unripeness of skill, as fate not once but with grotesque persistence blocks a lovers' meeting. And it presents a Nabokov already in possession of a full freight of memories to work "without sadness, for", like the princess in this story, he "knew that happy things can only be spoken of

in a happy way, without grieving because they have vanished".

Perhaps I should follow the hint of the acrostic and turn back to the beginning. In the first (title) story of this otherwise engaging collection the author is at his most grim, fronting the crucial historical determinant of his life. Nabokov is no politician, exile his single political act: "I am no good at distinguishing what is good or bad for a state, and why it is that blood runs off it like water off a goose." It is not the systems he hates, but a composite individual through whom "everything I love has been besmirched".

Pervading those multiple ghosts of friends and lovers, there is—or Nabokov would have us detect—the mephitic stench of unfreedom; as the dead Vane sisters haunt a snowy New England street, so Stalin haunts every story. But a way of liberation is suggested: the narrator in **"Tyrants Destroyed"** contemplates first assassination, then suicide, to rid his world of the gross incubus; eventually he sees that the mere act of narration is enough:

> This is an incantation, an exorcism, so that henceforth any man can exorcise bondage. I believe in miracles . . . I may be right not to rule out the thought that my chance labour may prove immortal, and may accompany the ages, now persecuted, now exalted, often dangerous, and always useful. While I, a "boneless shadow", *un fantâme sans os,* will be content if the fruit of my forgotten insomnious nights serves for a long time as a kind of secret remedy against future tyrants, tigroid monsters, half witted torturers of man.

Perhaps this is too pat a formula to contain the diversity of even one man's struggle against oblivion; but Nabokov can enact the miracle of freeing himself from bondage through an act of creation if anyone can.

Eric Korn, "Secret Remedies," in The Times Literary Supplement, *No. 3845, November 21, 1975, p. 1379.*

Carol T. Williams   (essay date 1975)

[*Williams is an American critic and educator. In the following essay, she describes the themes and plots of the stories in* Nabokov's Dozen.]

Out of print in paperback for several years, the short story collection *Nabokov's Dozen* has recently been reissued—a welcome edition for both the Nabokov and the general literature teacher. The former can welcome the *Dozen* for accessible entry into Nabokov's world, and the latter for both excellence in the short story form and insight into human nature and "our times." Nabokov's is a baker's dozen of thirteen stories dating from the 1930's through the early 1950's, which, whether they focus on individual misfit-heroes or mirror the crazed, cracked world of this century, are pieces in the pattern of their author's fictional world.

Nabokov scholarship reiterates that he is the "conjurer," whose omnipresent mirror reflects not-quite-opposites because it is rippled—his definition of art is "the necessary ripple." This ambiguous image—the Nabokov story—is of the imaginative human being's ennobling, destructive quest to unite this world with another, ideal "state of being where art (curiosity, tenderness, kindness, ecstasy) is the norm." It is not that his malcontent/aspirers would "escape into aesthetics," but that they would apply to this world the rules of the other. They would create and immortalize. For this audacity they pay—Nabokov's biographer, Andrew Field, is wrong; his "real artist" cannot "move freely between the two spheres" and "return unharmed and exhilarated" from his vision of Eternity [*Nabokov: His Life in Art*]. His overreachers bridge the abyss between this world and another state of being where " 'the only real number is one,' " [*The Real Life of Sebastian Knight*] but they can neither share what they know nor, ironically, can they escape into *this* world. The special Nabokov fillip is his own omnipresence in his irony: as creator of this fiction, he too is a visionary. When Humbert tells Lolita that "the only immortality" they may share is "the refuge of art," we cannot miss the irony that both share the refuge of Nabokov's art. He has created them, "captured them in print"; and thus they both must die, just as the butterflies of Nabokov the lepidopterist must be killed if their beauty is to be preserved.

All of the stories in **Nabokov's Dozen** are about this quest to unify the two worlds of the mundane and the ecstatic. (*Ecstasy,* with its paradoxical connotations of lunacy and transcendent joy, is the perfect word for Nabokov's realm of art, the mad, paradisial mortal approximation of ideal "bliss.") All thirteen, like all his novels, end with the failure of the quest; but all are rich with the beauty encountered along the way to the inevitable falling short. "The only son of a great khan lost his way during a hunt (thus begin the best fairy tales and thus end the best lives)," says Nabokov. No matter if they focus on the individual **"Lance"** (a properly "mod" form of "Lancelot"), or on this "era of Identification and Tabulation" (**"Time and Ebb"**), the subject and pattern are the same: a dialectic between two states of being, and a synthesis—properly Hegelian—in which neither the thetic nor the antithetic "arc" is eliminated, but "spirals" are *aufgehoben*": *put aside,* in the paradoxical sense of both *cast away* and *preserved* in artistic resolution.

A **Dozen** story that illuminates Nabokov's "dialectic" clearly is **"Conversation Piece, 1945"** (or **"Double Talk,"** its original title). The narrator is typically Nabokovian: a Russian émigré, unnamed (because the unnamed is the unknown), and seemingly an elitist, ineffectual intellectual. Like Hermann, the narrator of *Despair* (1937), he believes he has a "disreputable" double, but his obsession with this invisible *semblable* seems unrelated to the subject: an encounter in the present, 1945, in a genteel Boston home with a Fascist apologist whom the narrator tries stammeringly to best. Yet the denouement suggests that "Dr. Shoe" is in fact one of the double's "intrusions" into the narrator's life, not by "chance" as he says but because (like the double in *Despair*), "Dr. Shoe" is the narrator's *doppelgänger,* his darkly unwelcome antithetical side. At the end, as usual in his short stories, Nabokov reveals the antithetic spiral. A disarming "all that remains to be told" is followed by a letter, our first word from the scorned dou-

ble: " 'Esteemed Sir, . . . You have been pursuing me all my life,' " with " 'depraved, decadent writings' " and now " 'you have the arrogance to impersonate me and to appear in a drunken condition at the house of a highly respected person. . . . I suggest that by way of indemnity. . . . ' " And the narrator concludes, "The sum he demanded was really a modest one."

Here he disappears—an example of Nabokov's aloof rhetoric because now we are full of questions. If he can be blackmailed, who has intruded on whom? Is he Nabokov's ironic self-portrait? (Nabokov often characterizes himself as "decadent" in the eyes of the Bolsheviks, from whom his family fled in 1919.) And if the narrator was drunk, can we believe his characterization of "Dr. Shoe"? Perhaps he is the Fascist. Whom can we believe? What is real? And with this question we see the political "arc" of the tale. Here too it reflects *Despair* and foreshadows Nabokov's best political story *Bend Sinister,* in its exposure of the murderous fallacy of *oneness* on earth: " . . . history had never yet known . . . such faith in the impending sameness of us all. . . . Communism shall indeed create a beautifully square world of identical brawny fellows." Unity in this world means totalitarianism; the Jews, Dr. Shoe tells the (receptive) Bostonians, " 'forced [World War II] upon two nations that have so many things in common.' "

"Cloud, Castle, Lake" (1937, in Russian) also condemns Nazi Germany, our whole civilization of "Identification and Tabulation" as well, and specifically, the masses, those "bouquets of stupidity" (*Despair*) that beleaguer the imaginative man. The narrator is again insubstantial: "I cannot remember his name at the moment. I think it was Vasili Ivanovich." And again he is "my representative." He is another intellectual Russian émigré, this time, again like Nabokov, in Berlin in "1936 or 1937." He has won a pleasure trip with a group of Germans who reveal themselves as gross bullies easily led by their "leader" (sent by the "Bureau of Pleasantrips") to harass Vasili because he would rather be alone and finally, rather leave the "communal journey" for a "dream" he "discover[s]" on the group's hearty, mass tramp: an "ancient black castle" beside a "pure, blue lake," in the exact middle of which a "large cloud was reflected in its entirety." It is a dream for Vasili (in the artistic form of a living painting) because the "inexpressible and unique harmoniousness of its three principle parts . . . was something so unique, and so familiar, and so long-promised, and it so *understood* the beholder" that he longs to stay there forever.

Vasili is Nabokov's typical Lancelot, questing perfection because he sees it, and sees it in disparate, mundane "details," when they converge and hence transcend their insignificance. On "the configuration of some entirely insignificant objects—a smear on the platform, a cherry stone, a cigarette butt," he would grieve the loss of the dream in life, what Nabokov's *semblable* Borges, in "The Immortal" calls the "preciously precarious;" [Nabokov writes:] "Never, never would he remember these three little things here in that particular interrelation, this pattern, which he now could see with such deathless precision." What Vasili cannot do that Nabokov can is accept the loss. As the Germans drag him away from his dream, he cries, " 'Oh, but this is nothing less than an invitation to a beheading. . . .' " Cincinnatus C., protagonist of the Nabokov novel *Invitation To A Beheading* is another visionary imprisoned in the " 'dark dungeon of the "here" because he had " 'discovered the little crack in life where it broke off ' " from " 'something . . . genuinely alive.' " To signify the false unity of the German group in **"Cloud,"** Nabokov doubles their names (cf. Humbert) and their appearances and then pronounces their destiny and that of his dreamer: "all gradually melted together, merging together, forming one collective, wobbly, many-handed being, from which one could not escape."

In another *Dozen* tale, **"Scenes From the Life of a Double Monster,"** (1950), this monstrous truth about mortal unity is embodied in absolute form. Human that the narrator Floyd is, he cannot recognize the intimations of ideal unity in his Siamese twinship with Lloyd: " . . . the interrupted gesture of one twin would be swallowed and dissolved in the enriched ripple of the other's completed action. I say *enriched* because the ghost of the unpicked flower somehow seemed to be also there, pulsating between the fingers that closed upon the fruit." If even Siamese twins cannot appreciate what it means to be "enriched"—to be "swallowed and dissolved," but also "somehow . . . there, pulsating," what chance have Nabokov's lovers?

"First Love" (1948) illuminates how memory functions in artistic creation. Early in the tale the memorist (apparently Nabokov himself, for he calls this "true" autobiography) describes childhood dreams of a "glass marble." At the end, describing his farewell to Colette in a Paris park (they are both ten), he reflects the marble again, unifying the story and irradiating its meaning:

> . . . and [Colette] was off, tap-tapping her glinting hoop through light and shade, around and around a fountain choked with dead leaves near which I stood. The leaves mingle in my memory with . . . some detail in her attire (perhaps a ribbon on her Scottish cap . . .) that reminded me then of the rainbow spiral in a glass marble. I still seem to be holding that wisp of iridescence, not knowing exactly where to fit it, while she runs with her hoop ever faster around me and finally dissolves among the slender shadows cast on the graveled path by the interlaced arches of its low looped fence.

As we visualize all these arcs—the hoop, the arches of the looped fence, the fountain, and especially the marble—we may see this first love as a "spiral" enclosed, but within glass and "rainbow" color. In *Speak, Memory,* Nabokov describes his own life as "a colored spiral in a small ball of glass," with his years in Russia (1899-1919) the "thetic arc"; the "voluntary exile" in France, Germany and England (1919-1940) the "obvious antithesis"; and the years in his "adopted country," the "beginning of a synthetic envelopment." **"Mademoiselle O"** ("true" enough to be a chapter in *Speak, Memory* as well as a *Dozen* tale) is another reflection of her author's dialectic. Nabokov's governess is alien in two worlds: her homeland Switzerland and Russia, in which she was merely hired help and which

she loved only in memory after she had left. Nabokov compares her to an "uncouth" swan trying to hoist itself into a boat, "dodo-like" but "strange[ly] significan[t]," and recalling *"Cygne"* of one of his favorites, Baudelaire: *"Comme les exilés, ridicule et sublime."* Like **"First Love"** and all Nabokov's fiction, **"Mademoiselle O"** seems basically about its author's lost homeland.

"Spring in Fialta" (1938) is one of Nabokov's most delicate configurations of the details of a hopelessly imperfect human love. "Spring in Fialta is cloudy and dull," Victor begins. Yet at the end of his narrative of the fifteen years of Nina's and his sporadic meetings, he is telling us that as she left him in Fialta, "suddenly I understood something I had been seeing without understanding," and at this moment, Fialta becomes "saturated with sunshine." What is clarified for Victor (or V.; V. Nabokov's "representatives" are often called V.) is an "insignificant" detail: "why a piece of tin foil had sparkled so on a pavement." He had seen it earlier, irrelevantly. Listening to complaints about the weather from Nina's husband, touching her elbow immediately after the surprise chancing upon her, why should he notice a "bit of tin foil"? And why, after she leaves, is it part of his sudden understanding?

Why except that just before her leaving, for the first time in their "supposedly frivolous" affair, "apprehensive" about a "rational interpretation of my existence," he has said he loves her. A rational interpretation of his marriage and his "carefree" affair requires that he tabulate, or "pin" Nina. And for this, of course, she must die. V.'s synthetic passage, all one sentence, flows from "saturated with sunshine" into a "dissolve" of meaning, a literal translation of the film maker's dissolve from one scene to another. " . . . and now it was sun-pervaded throughout, and this brimming white radiance grew broader and broader, all dissolved in it, vanished, all passed, and I stood on the station platform of Mlech with a freshly bought newspaper, which told me that . . . Nina . . . had turned out after all to be mortal." [In a Footnote, Williams writes: "More is needed on Nabokov's use of film though Alfred Appel's new work *Dark Cinema,* is a good start. (**'First Love'** also ends as Colette 'dissolves among the . . . shadows'). One of Nabokov's cinematic devices is the visual motif—as in **'Fialta,'** the bit of tin foil, and also the violet, associated with Nina, and the train, a favorite Nabokov image, associated with our 'intricate route' through life. The reason why cinema fascinates Nabokov is revealed in **'The Assistant Producer'** (*Nabokov's Dozen*), in which the Russian émigrés hired as extras by a German film company are described as 'totally unreal people [hired] to represent "real" audiences in pictures. The dovetailing of one phantasm into another produced upon a sensitive person the impression of living in a Hall of Mirrors, or rather a prison of mirrors, and not ever knowing which was the glass and which was yourself.' For an artist who would suggest the slipperiness of reality, the world of film is an ideal metaphor."] Nabokov's lovers—mortals who would become one—can never live in this world. But why Nina's death instead of Victor's? (Why Lolita's before Humbert's?) After all, it was V. who suggested the fatal "state of being." Of course the answer is that it is *beauty* that must be immortalized, and the artist must live to do the pinning.

The "V." who controls " **'That in Aleppo Once . . .'** " (1943) is a Russian émigré writer in New York and a collector of "lichens," i.e., another Nabokov. He is only the recipient of the nameless narrator's letter, and the letter is the story; but at its end, in the synthetic moment, the narrator turns control of his story's title over to V., and in this choice lies V. Nabokov's message. As always, in " **'Aleppo'** " we cannot know what is real or who tells the truth. All we can know is that to label is to possess, and to possess is to kill love—a banal message, enriched by the "intricate route." The narrator of " **'Aleppo'** " and his wife (also unnamed) are separated while fleeing the Nazis in France in 1940. Now he writes to convince V. that his wife "never existed," that she is only a "character in . . . one of your stories." He says that after he found her in Nice, she confessed that she had deceived him, but then denied it: " 'You will think me crazy. . . . Perhaps I live several lives at once. Perhaps I wanted to test you. Perhaps this bench is a dream.' " Her contradictory confessions unnerve him, and he tortures them both by questing obsessively for The Truth. After their visas appear, she again disappears and, finally giving up, he sails alone. But on the fourth day out another passenger says he saw his wife a few days before the sailing, walking "aimlessly" and saying "I would presently join her."

"It was at that moment," he writes V., "that I suddenly knew for certain she had never existed at all," and safe now in America, he longs for "real" life. And then a haunting sentence and incisive finish: "Somewhere, somehow, I have made some fatal mistake. . . . It may all end in *Aleppo* if I am not careful. Spare me, V.: you would load your dice with an unbearable implication if you took that for a title" And of course V. Nabokov does take his title from Othello's final speech before killing himself, the lines in which the Moor justifies himself as a hero that in Aleppo once, smote thus the circumcised dog who had beat a Venetian (V.ii.352-356). To Nabokov's mind, Othello has no reason to murder the Moslem (he writes his " **'Aleppo'** " about Europe in 1943). Nor has he reason to pursue the truth about Desdemona, his possession—no reason, that is, but human nature. Pathetic Othello, and pathetic nameless refugee in real life, fatally tormented by a vision of the perfectly "rational," and skewered by the final unbearable implication of his creator.

Two of Nabokov's most subtle miniatures of human impenetrability in the *Dozen* have as their protagonists old people who appear to be insensitive under the blows of this world's inexplicable and inexorable laws and orders. In addition, **"Signs and Symbols"** (1948) defines the Nabokov dreamer in *extremis:* mad. This is the old couple's son, not an actor in the story but the object of its focus, as of his parents. Incarcerated in a mental hospital, a victim of " 'referential mania,' " he "imagines that everything happening around him is a veiled reference" to himself. Other people he excludes from the "conspiracy—because he considers himself to be so much more intelligent than other men." But all of "phenomenal nature shadows him," and he must "devote every minute and module of life to the decoding of the undulation of things."

Like Nabokov's other victims of " 'referential mania' "—

Humbert, Kinbote (*Pale Fire*), Cincinnatus, and particularly Luzhin, his chess master (*The Defense*), the young man would "tear a hole in his world and escape." (Note the self-directed irony in these creations of a writer devoted to the "decoding of the undulation of things.") The story takes place on a day when he has again tried suicide. Bringing his birthday present to the asylum "for the fourth time," the parents are delayed by some of fate's mundane signs and symbols: rain, a stalled subway train and a bus that is late and "crammed with garrulous high-school children." The "camera" narrator records details similar to the bit of tin foil in **"Fialta"**—an "unfledged bird . . . helplessly twitching in a puddle" by the bus stop, for example. The old couple may not notice these details—unlike Nabokov's "representatives," his "V.'s," a camera cannot look into minds—but they imprint themselves on our developing picture of their world.

At the asylum they respond to the "brightly explained" news about their son just as they responded to the delays en route and, we are sure, to every one of the griefs of their years. They are mute, silent in the way of those permanently defeated. But after they return home, "he kept clearing his throat in a special resonant way he had when he was upset" (ibid.), and "she felt the mounting pressure of tears," and finally, "past midnight," " 'No doctors, no doctors,' he moaned. . . . 'We must get him out of there quick. Otherwise we'll be responsible. Responsible!' "

Just then, "the telephone rang." Of course we expect that the boy has killed himself. But instead: " 'Can I speak to Charlie,' said a girl's dull little voice." The husband resumes his "excited monologue" on how they will care for their son at home. "The telephone rang again." *This* is the asylum; the first call, we say, represented the delusive moment of hope conventional to ironic tragedy. But no. "The same toneless anxious young voice asked for Charlie." The old man explains: " 'You are turning the letter O instead of the zero.' " Then, "flushed and excited," they sit down to an "unexpected festive midnight tea," and as with "clumsy moist lips" he spelled out the "eloquent labels" on the boy's birthday jellies ("apricot, grape . . . "), Nabokov concludes: "He had got to crab apple, when the telephone rang again."

Is it the young girl? That is, does the drab mundane world of disordered buses harass the old couple once again? Or this time is it the bright voice from the asylum? The "Lady and Tiger" ostentatiousness of Nabokov's trick forces us to fit it into the story, and then we see its irony: who the next caller is is irrelevant, for alive or dead, the young man cannot live in this world. Earlier in the story his mother told us this when she

> thought of the endless waves of pain that for some reason or other she and her husband had to endure; of the invisible giants hurting her boy in some unimaginable fashion; of the incalculable amount of tenderness contained in the world; of the fate of this tenderness, which is either crushed, or wasted, or transformed into madness; of neglected children humming to themselves in unswept corners; or beautiful weeds that cannot hide from the farmer and helplessly have to watch the shadow of his simian stoop

leave mangled flowers in its wake, as the monstrous darkness approaches.

It is Nabokov's typical irony that such sensitivity is part
of a drab, nameless woman—one of the beautiful, vulnerable weeds in a world apparently "brightly explained" but
in reality, "simian." And if she is beautiful, what of that
"anxious" young voice without a face, a name, a character, that entered the world of Nabokov's story by chance?
How lovely she might be.

In **"The Aurelian,"** too (1931, in Russian), a Nabokov artist, alien in this world, is camouflaged with its dull trappings. He looks like a "churlish" German shopkeeper, but
actually "Pilgram belonged, or rather was meant to belong
(something—the place, the time, the man—had been ill
chosen), to a special breed of dreamers, such dreamers as
used to be called in the old days, 'Aurelians'—perhaps on
account of those chrysalids, those 'jewels of nature,' which
they loved to find hanging on fences above the dusty net-
tles of country lanes.' Something—the place, the time, the
man—had been ill-chosen: like Nabokov's other voyeurs
in this world, Paul Pilgram is fated to duplicity.

Pilgram's obsession, unknown even to his wife, is *"himself*
to net the rarest butterflies of distant countries;" and finally, although he knows it is "madness" to leave Eleanor to
their debts, he sneaks off. As he leaves, he perceives his
happiness "leaning toward him like a mountain." We have
read of the stroke that cancelled one of his earlier dreams:
"(like a mountain falling upon him . . .)." So we know
what the recurrence of the mountain image means and are
insulted by the conclusion, in which Pilgram's death is
loudly announced. But like the end of **"Signs and Symbols,"** the obituary is only apparently Nabokov's rhetoric
of disdain. His persona, unmasking at the end as always,
judges that Eleanor's discovery of the body is "irrelevant"
because she has already found Pilgram's note: " 'Off to
Spain. . . . ' " The death of his body is irrelevant because
the note reveals his other, real life, and that revelation,
which makes a whole of Pilgram's life, makes his death in
this world inevitable. After death, Nabokov's narrator
gives Pilgram his dream: "one can hardly doubt that he
saw all the glorious bugs he had longed to see." But *bugs*
counters the the glory of this dream, just as earlier the narrator had described it with phrases like "the furious throbbing of wings" and "the black pin upon which [a] silky little creature was crucified." At the end, Pilgram is not only
a drab shopkeeper and an exotic "aurelian"; when the two
converge, we see a complex, enigmatic, very real synthesis
of lover and crucifier.

Perhaps the most provocative exploration in ***Nabokov's
Dozen*** of the play between our urge toward ideal bliss and
our mortal fear of "slipping into a different dimension,"
is the short story of the modern knight of the grail, the as-
tronaut **"Lance."** Written in 1952, it was a prescient, and
is a haunting judgment on our attempt to master space.
Typically, however, Nabokov denies it social import:
"Not for me are the artificial little satellites that the earth
is promised; . . . set up by terrestrial nations n a frenzy
of competitive confusion, . . . and savagely flapping
flags." And typically he deceives us. (His interest in this
world is clearest in the ***Dozen*** in **"Time and Ebb,"** the

21st-century memoir of a ninety year-old who characterizes the 20th century as "atavistically prone to endow the
community with qualities and rights which they refused
to the individual.")

Thus carefully cut off from the science fiction "business,"
Nabokov's tale of "Emery L. Boke, more or less remote
descendant of mine who is to be a member of the first in-
terplanetary expedition," is told by a Nabokov representative who is "fifty and terrified." The unimaginative and the
terrified still exist in Lance's era. When he returns from
his adventure in space, his parents tell him that Chilla, his
beloved chinchilla, is " 'with child.' " But Lance is indifferent. His parents leave the hospital room where he is
being kept from human "contacts,' " and in the elevator
they join others from a world Lance has left forever. The
story concludes: "Going back [into space] in November
(Lancelin). Going down (the old Bokes). There are, in that
elevator, two smiling women and, the object of their bright
sympathy, a girl with a baby, besides the gray-haired,
bent, sullen elevator man, who stands with his back to everybody."

Nabokov's persona, although terrified, is different from
Lance's parents or the sullen elevator operator. He understands that Lance is not "the ordinary hairless ape, who
takes everything in his stride," but rather, "the man of
imagination and science, whose courage is infinite because
his curiosity surpasses his courage. . . . He is the ancient
curieux, but of a hardier build, with a ruddier heart." The
narrator grasps Lance's "main problem," also our haunting question: "Will the mind of the explorer survive the
shock" of the "atavistic moment" in which he leaves this
world? "Deep in the human mind, the concept of dying
is synonymous with that of leaving the earth. To escape
its gravity means to transcend the grave, and a man upon
finding himself on another planet has really no way of
proving to himself that he is not dead—that the naive old
myth has not come true." And really, Lance has not sur-
vived. (Have our real astronauts?) Like all of Nabokov's
dreamers, he has not returned unharmed from another
sphere. On earth he can only talk about his experience, especially his partner Denny, who did die in space. He is
eager to return. And also, the narrator notes, he has a
nosebleed.

Thus, silently, the narrator unmasks. Through this mere
detail, a nosebleed, he recalls a reminiscence of his own
earlier in the story. Then, in what had seemed a digression
from Lance's story, he had recounted his "vaguely recurrent" childhood dream of a nosebleed he ignored in his
anxiety to shovel into a little pail the "mass of
something— . . . oppressively and quite meaninglessly
shaped," which infuriated him because he could not "walk
around the view to meet it on equal terms." The elements
in his dream were not conventionally mythic; his quest
was only to see a shadow's face, only to know the unknown. In other words, it was only the most atavistic
myth of all. And, he says, perhaps when "Lance and his
companions reached their planet, [they] felt something
akin to my dream."

Thus Nabokov's "Dozen" are like all his fictions: " 'web[s]
of sense' " (as John Shade describes life in his poem, 'Pale

Fire"), composed of startling configurations of images, dialectical in structure, and each a slowly unfolding pattern of paradoxical truths concluding with a synthesis that reveals final truth—certain, complete truth—to be unknowable. The message camouflaged by Nabokov's art is Keats's principle of *"Negative Capability"*: "When a man is capable of being in uncertainties, mysteries, doubts, without any irritable reaching after fact and reason." To be known—to be "captured in print"—is to be immortalized, but it is also to be mortally dead. To know, transcendentally, is to be God, but also doomed in this world. That is the artist Nabokov's essential, ironically autobiographical conundrum. He is generally called precious, an elitist. But insofar as we are all *curieux* like Lance, all lovers like V., and all prisoners like Vasili Ivanovich—insofar as we dream—then we can see that it is finally for this world and not another that Nabokov creates. (pp. 213-23)

Carol T. Williams, "Nabokov's Dozen Short Stories: His World in Microcosm," in Studies in Short Fiction, *Vol. XII, No. 3, Summer, 1975, pp. 213-22.*

Leonard Michaels (essay date 1976)

[*Michaels is an American novelist, short story writer, playwright, and critic. In the following favorable review of* Details of a Sunset, and Other Stories, *he comments on Nabokov's ability to imbue inanimate objects with consciousness which mirrors that of the human characters.*]

Vladimir Nabokov's new collection of his old stories, *Details of a Sunset* (1924-1935); is much concerned with different kinds of loss—exile, failure of romantic love and family love, the death of a wife, the death of a son, the death of one's self—and yet the effects of these stories are mainly exhilarating, even affirmative. In the last story, as if to comment on this paradox, Nabokov says, "human consciousness is an ominous and ludicrous luxury." In other words, if our world were a simple, rational place, then sad stories couldn't be exhilarating, "ominous" wouldn't rhyme with "ludicrous," and there would be no such thing as humor (certainly not black humor) and also no such thing as art. There might even be no consciousness, but only the sort of mental life as exists, for example, in Marxian utopias. (These considerations are more subtle and more elegant in Nabokov's stories.)

In one story, **"The Return of Chorb,"** a young, very lively

Nabokov with his wife Vera, whom Alfred Appel called "his ideal reader and only real editor," and their son Dmitri, his father's cotranslator.

woman is accidentally killed on her honeymoon when she takes hold of a live wire. This is ironical, if not exactly funny, but Nabokov doesn't make much of the incident. The story is about Chorb, her husband. Tortured by loneliness and grief, he neglects to tell her parents that she is dead, and it takes him three weeks to return to her hometown in Germany where, desperate for news about their daughter, they wait. During these weeks Chorb revisits the sights and occasions of his honeymoon, hoping, by virtue of memory, "her image would grow immortal and replace her forever." Finally he returns to the hotel where he spent his first, chaste night with his bride, and he hires a prostitute—not for a sexual purpose but to help him re-create, simply by being in the room with him, the memory of innocent, passionate, married love. The result is ghoulish and horrible.

The meaning of this story—if there is any—might be: (1) romantic imagination, which grows immortal images, must not use the medium of commercial flesh; (2) some experiences belong to life, not to art, especially if they are infected with guilt; (3) consciousness cannot be manipulated in fictional ways in life without seeming squalid and sick. One could propose variations forever, but it is sufficient to say this disturbing, extraordinary story, which twists human sympathies through an intricate plot and culminates in gothic grotesquerie, could only have been written by Nabokov. This in itself might suggest a political idea (despotism) not too popular these days, but there is something heroic in Nabokov's unique, self-conscious, brilliant art.

In a story called **"Christmas"** the hero also suffers abysmal grief—over the death of his son—but he pursues no self-indulgent, psychotic consolation. By chance, while lingering over a wooden case containing the son's possessions, he notices an Atticus moth—warmed by the proximity of a father's grief—emerge from its chrysalid. The emergence, described in precise, sensuous detail, ends this way: "And then those thick black wings, with a glazy eyespot on each and purplish bloom dusting the hooked foretips, took a full breath under the impulse of tender, ravishing, almost human happiness."

In this lovely, poignant climax the reader isn't obliged to participate in a sloppy transcendence of the father's pain, but privileged to witness, with him, a moment when the world seems to answer to human need in a beautiful, miraculous manifestation. Nabokov, a writer whose awesome wit can bludgeon his critics into silence, can demonstrate exquisite good manners in dealing with his fictional characters and his readers.

"A Bad Day," perhaps the most artfully triumphant story in the book, describes a boy's anxiety and boredom during a visit to relatives, and Nabokov renders the whole occasion as if it were an expressive property of consciousness, redeemable from the obscure, unhappy clutch of time. Here the boy is traveling to his relatives: "The sound of the hooves suddenly acquired a ringing, resilient tone—because of the boards of the bridge over which the carriage passed." Because of the anapestic boards of the bridge, the sentence bumps and pulls along to where the road resumes. This tiny moment, like many others in the story,

is not merely heard but listened to. That is to say, it is not merely remembered and saved from time, but also savored, so to speak, by consciousness.

Throughout the book Nabokov's descriptive genius makes the world—hooves, boards, Atticus moths, etc.—render itself up to us in delicious peculiarities. Sometimes he humanizes things. Sometimes he thingifies humans: " . . . presently his eyes focused on a distant desk from behind which, like a tree grown by the glance of a fakir, Shchukin was rising." More often, however, in Nabokov's fakir glance, things humanify: "A tall tin teapot bearing a large birthmark on its flank stood with the air of a victim." "A tall tin teapot" is the sound it would make, complaining, if it dropped on the kitchen floor.

Not only can Nabokov seize the voice in what is seen, he can even tease the name from a dull, silent object. "Otto," written by some passerby in the snow that covers a pipe, suggests: " . . . how beautifully that name, with its two soft o's flanking the pair of gentle consonants, suited the silent layer of snow upon that pipe with its two orifices and its tacit tunnel." Consciousness, exhibited here in wordplay, is merely a function of coincidence—Otto, snow, tunnel. It doesn't mean anything. Nevertheless, Nabokov seems to have discovered something—ominous, ludicrous, luxurious—operating in the objective world *and* in our minds, as if it flowed between the two and might as soon find residency in one as in the other. Indeed, how beautifully o meets o through the tacit (t) ministrations of a tunnel (t). One wants to echo the effect, not explicate it.

For another example of this strange, beautiful operation, in a story called **"A Letter That Never Reached Russia,"** the narrator says: "As I wander along some silent, dark street, I like to hear a man coming home. The man himself is not visible in the darkness, and you never know beforehand which front door will come alive to accept a key with grinding condescension . . . " Consciousness, ordinarily resident in men, has been discovered, through the mediation of a key, remarkably dynamic in a door. To put it another way: whatever the man feels or does is reciprocally and equivalently done or felt in the door.

Even if we don't consider the subjects or the events in Nabokov's stories, it must seem that his imagination—simply in what it sees and in the way it speaks—has demonic powers. Therein lies much of its pleasure for readers, a literary experience reminiscent of "Alice in Wonderland," another playfully verbal world where the perversities of plot, wittily qualified by lots of pain and apprehensions of death, full of exotic and subterranean perceptions, leave one thrilled and pleased. ***Details of a Sunset*** is a very intriguing and immensely delightful book.

Leonard Michaels, "Early Stories, Full of Human Grief and Literary Pleasure," in The New York Times Book Review, *April 25, 1976, p. 5.*

Helen Muchnic   (essay date 1976)

[*Muchnic is a Russian-born American critic who has written extensively on Russian literature. In the follow-*

ing excerpt from her review of Details of a Sunset, and Other Stories, *she discusses the themes of some of these early works.*]

"This collection," Mr. Nabokov announces in a foreword, "is the last batch of my Russian stories meriting to be Englished." There are thirteen of them. Written and published in émigré journals between 1924 and 1935, they belong to the outset of his career when he was leading in Berlin "an odd but by no means unpleasant existence," as he described it later in *Speak, Memory,* "in material indigence and intellectual luxury among perfectly unimportant strangers." Now, in collaboration with his son Dmitri, he has translated them and supplied brief introductory notes.

In one of these notes he imagines someone asking, "What was your purpose, sir, in penning this story, forty years ago in Berlin?" and answers, "Well, I did pen it (for I never learned to type . . .); but I had never any 'purpose' in mind when writing stories—for myself, my wife, and half a dozen dear dead chuckling friends." The "dear dead chuckling friends," Russian intellectuals living in "foreign communities" in "more or less illusory cities," whose "spectral" inhabitants were "to the mind's eye as flat and transparent as figures cut out of cellophane," could be counted on to relish the look, gestures, preoccupations, behavior, and idiom of the Russian characters about whom most of the stories were written, of these lonely, uprooted men, making the best of their precarious lives in shabby rooms that were like temporary camps on unplanned, unpredictable, enforced journeys. Poverty to them is not important but, driven as they have been from their country, abandoned by those they love or alienated from them by space and time, their pain of loss is keen indeed.

In **"The Doorbell,"** a youth, after years of separation from his mother, after fighting in the civil war and wandering over Russia, Italy, Africa, the Canary Islands, manages to trace her to an apartment in Berlin only to discover that she has changed both in herself and toward him, and realizing he is not wanted, leaves after a few embarrassed moments for heaven knows what new adventures.

In **"The Reunion,"** a well-established Soviet man, on business in Berlin, comes to see his émigré brother in his tiny room. Without anything to say to each other, they try to make conversation and finally fasten on the one point they have in common, the memory of a black poodle they used to play with in childhood. But they have forgotten its name and the pathetic urgency with which they struggle to call it back is a measure of their estrangement from each other and from their past. The émigré brother is "a needy but neat little man, in a black suit worn shiny and a turn-down collar that was too large for him." He wears "spats to hide the holes in his socks," and is too proud to mention his poverty, too bruised to speak of his solitude, and too courteous to hint at how exceptionally inopportune the unwelcome visit has been. An unpretentious, sensitive man, he prefigures in his gentleness, delicacy, considerateness, his innate nobility, the most affecting to my mind of all Nabokov's creations, Timofey Pnin, who is as memorable as Akakiy Akakievich, the hero of Gogol's "The Over-

coat," or Turgenev's Mumu, or any number of Chekhov's piteous creatures.

There are other stories that have little or nothing to do with exile, that might have happened anywhere at any time, though three of them are set in Russia: **"A Bad Day,"** in which a little boy is rejected by his playmates for reasons he cannot understand; **"Orache,"** concerning another child, who has heard that his father's life is in danger but has no one with whom to share his overwhelming anxiety; **"Christmas,"** the sketch of a father shattered by the death of his young son; **"The Return of Chorb,"** where the parents and the husband, stunned by the loss of their daughter and wife, confront each other in speechless grief. The last two are extremely poignant and subtly ironic, mute little tragedies of ineffable anguish.

In **"A Busy Man,"** a solitary, anxious individual, who for the whole of his thirty-third year has been fearfully expecting death, prophesied long ago in a dimly remembered dream, wakes up on the sunny morning after his thirty-fourth birthday to realize that the dreadfully appointed time has come and gone. This happy joke on premonitions is the last story of the collection, and it seems to balance the tale of unforeseen and unannounced death with which the volume opens, a neat frame of opposites, perhaps intentionally designed to set off Nabokov's undogmatic, unsymbolic, unmetaphysical view of life's fortuitousness and unpredictability.

The opening story, Nabokov tells us, was first called **"Katastrofa,"** an "odious" appellation for which he himself could not have been responsible. The new title, **"Details of a Sunset,"** "has the triple advantage of corresponding to the thematic background of the story, of being sure to puzzle such readers as 'skip descriptions,' and of infuriating reviewers." Naïvely, one might have seen it as the pitiful tale of a young fellow who, unaware that the girl he loves has rejected him for another man, dies, as the result of a stupid accident, ecstatically thinking that she is by his side. But this would be wrong. The story should be read, according to Nabokov, not for what happens in it but for the way it is told, not for the narrative itself but for the skillful weaving of details in the process of narration.

Art to Nabokov is entertainment and his characters are pieces he manipulates on a chess board, devising problems for the absorbing, challenging, clever game of which he is a master. So about **"Christmas,"** a heartbreaking story, he notes that it "oddly resembles the type of chess problem called 'selfmate,' " thus, characteristically, taking away with one hand what he has given with the other, holding the reader off at arm's length, retreating to the formidable barricade he sets up between himself and his subject, himself and the reader. He is not Tolstoy thinking vulgarly of art as a language of emotions uniting mankind in brotherly love. His fiction, he always insists, is not about life but about art, and his characters, if not chessmen, are "methods of composition," like those in the novels of his Sebastian Knight, "as if a painter said: look, here I'm going to show you not the painting of a landscape but the painting of different ways of painting a certain landscape." Nabokov is such a painter, and the whole of his work may be read as his painting different ways of painting the landscape that has always engrossed him.

This landscape is the recondite, impenetrable, inner life of men, or rather the visible manifestations of this life, which interests him precisely because it is unfathomable. The "real" life of Sebastian Knight, to the discovery of which his adoring half brother devotes himself, remains a mystery. *Pale Fire* is a satiric contrast between the hidden depths of inward life and the showy spectacle of public adventures. Pnin, with his strange ways and his misuse of English idioms—"I am grazing," he explains when found leafing through his landlord's books—is to his colleagues a figure of fun, his nobility unappreciated and his suffering known only to himself. Nabokov execrates the presumptions of "depth psychology"; he is less concerned with character than with circumstance and pattern; his work is a bright surface protecting the concealed, cherished core of individual passion. (p. 22)

A work of art has no "purpose," form and content are one, method and form are everything. And Nabokov, the most self-conscious of authors, never tires of insisting that his theme is not "reality" (the word is regularly imprisoned in derisive quotation marks), neither "real" people, nor events, nor ideas. Realism is a loose way of thinking and the "realistic" novelist—Balzac, Stendhal, Gorky, Goncharov, Pasternak, even Tolstoy of *War and Peace* though not of *Anna Karenina*—is "middle-brow," like the writer in his own story, **"The Passenger,"** who seems to think that Life is a model for him to copy or sees himself as somehow in competition with Life and is disappointed when it eludes him.

Once, traveling in a train, he was caught up in an incident that seemed to have all the makings of a detective story of the kind he was in the habit of writing. But as it turned out, the repulsive passenger in the upper berth was not, as he had hoped, the criminal the police were after, and he himself would never know why the man lay there sobbing. "The trouble is that we are in the dark," he concludes, "maybe Life had in mind something totally different, something much more subtle and deep." Nabokov is careful to point out that his "middle-brow" writer is not a self-portrait—quite unnecessarily, for there is nothing clearer than that however in the dark his characters may be, Nabokov himself is not, that he knows all he wants to know and creates whatever depth and subtleties he pleases.

His way of thought, in which scientific faithfulness is combined with a miniaturist's exactitude and the canny logic of an expert in chess, is stringent, restricted, sharply focused. His vision is intense, absorbed, almost fanatically concentrated. He is like John Shade, the poet of *Pale Fire*, whose "eyes were such that literally they / Took photographs," so that whatever he looked on "was printed on [his] eyelids' neither side," and all he "had to do was close [his eyes] to reproduce" what he had seen. Nabokov's eye, fixed on details, is reinforced by microscope or spyglass: "a half-open matchbox with one burnt match lay on the stove," "a horsefly with satiny eyes settled on his sleeve," "an arrow of bright copper struck the lacquered shoe of a fop jumping out of a car."

One is reminded of Tolstoy's celebrated precision. But Nabokov's is wholly different. Tolstoy recorded ordinary objects "as if they had never been seen before" with great satiric and emotional power to emphasize the falseness of habit, the distortions of stereotyped attitudes. His scrupulous attentiveness originated in the introspection demanded by a relentless conscience and served a moral purpose, and also the interests of realism. Nabokov, on the other hand, points to minutiae that the casual eye would surely miss, but, once alerted, would see in the usual way. His method is descriptive, neither analytic nor moralizing, and his effects are not realistic but hallucinatory and surrealist.

"Is not every writer precisely a person who bothers about trifles?" says the novelist in **"The Passenger."** And in **"A Guide to Berlin,"** which Nabokov calls "one of my trickiest pieces," trifles are shown to be tremendous. The gigantic black pipes by the sidewalk, waiting to be buried; the streetcar that "will vanish in twenty years or so"; the workmen "pounding an iron stake"; the men and vehicles transporting bread, meat, bottles, letters, a large tree; the animals locked up in the zoo—all will vanish, and some curious man in the distant future will haunt museums for vestiges of the familiar things that furnish the daily life of the present. This is why the narrator thinks that "here lies the sense of literary creation: to portray ordinary objects as they will be reflected in the kindly mirrors of future times," and why at the end of the story he watches intently the barkeeper's child gazing in the direction where he and his friend are talking over drinks. His friend is puzzled: "I can't understand what you see down there." "What indeed! How can I demonstrate to him that I have glimpsed somebody's future recollection?" History itself, Nabokov implies, lives in the evidence of observed and recorded trifles, the only knowledge a human being may rightly claim. (*Speak, Memory*, one recalls, first appeared as *Conclusive Evidence.*)

These are man's authentic records, these trifles preserved in private consciousness. Everything else—theories and arguments, mass movements and public disasters—is hearsay at second hand, gossip and clichés. The pages in which Nabokov most nearly approaches his ideal of perfection, such as the chapter on butterflies in *Speak, Memory;* the portrait of Godunov-Cherdintsev's father in *The Gift;* the train rides in *The Exploit, Speak, Memory, Pnin;* the father's excursion into the country with his small son in *Bend Sinister* are eloquent with a sense of keenly lived and accurately transcribed experience—polished, elegant, reserved even when they speak of passion. His best work might appropriately bear the title he has presented to Sebastian Knight, *The Prismatic Bezel*. It is jeweler's work, without vagueness or depth, other than the mirror-depth of its lovingly burnished facets, expertly engraved with poignant shadows on their dazzling surfaces.

But there is another, lurid, nightmarish, and sadistic side to his mind's coin, the grotesque counterpart of his elegant restraint and tenderness. It is exhibited when, turning from precise observation and specific experience to nonaesthetic generalizations, notably the upheavals and plagues of Bolshevism and Nazism, he gives them body and, from the background of his dramas, brings them forth to center stage. This is what happens in *Invitation to a Beheading* and *Bend Sinister.* They were provoked by his abhorrence of mind-boggling tyranny, which could be expressed, he felt, only in nightmares. But his rational gift is not right for nightmares, and his humane intent takes the form of gruesomely contrived fantasies that assault our sensibilities without enlightening our experience, trivialize our knowledge of tragedy, and seem a travesty on the universal horror of our times.

The moral qualities Nabokov most admires—independence, pride, resilience—are most effectively incarnated in those of his heroes who must grapple with private sorrows rather than the avalanche of outward force, in Timofey Pnin rather than Cincinnatus C. of *Invitation to a Beheading* or even Adam Krug of *Bend Sinister,* whose magnificence as an artistic creation is dissipated in the unbelievable savageries he is dragged through. This, in part, Nabokov himself realizes. "The main theme of *Bend Sinister,*" he writes in an introduction, "is the beating of Krug's loving heart, the torture an intense tenderness is subjected to—and it is for the sake of the pages about David and his father that the book was written and should be read. The two other themes [that] accompany the main one . . . are merely my whims and megrims."

One is bound to agree. The instruction is obvious and needless. But Nabokov has little respect for the intelligence of the general reader. He sees him as a niggling, stupid, unperceptive adversary and defends himself with mockery. In this instance, he supplements his gloss with a three-page list of his "delicate markers," riddles and allusions implanted in the text to abash the reader, and remarks: "Most people will not even mind having missed all this; . . . ironists will point out the fatal fatuity of my explications. . . . In the long run, however, it is only the author's private satisfaction that counts." True enough! But how often is the faithful reader trapped by Nabokov's private satisfaction into suffering his "whims and megrims" and enduring his contempt!

It may be that Nabokov does not have the courage of his arrogance and, therefore, feels compelled, time and again, to herald his pre-eminence. Or maybe he simply loves to mystify and humiliate. At any rate, addressing forty years ago a few dear chuckling friends, he did not need to sheathe himself in the daunting armor of spiked disdain. And this may be the reason that his early stories are less suspiciously watchful, posturing, and unkind than the later fiction, directed to the unknown thousands of a world-wide audience. (pp. 23-4)

> *Helen Muchnic, "Jeweler at Work," in* The New York Review of Books, *Vol. XXIII, No. 9, May 27, 1976, pp. 22-4.*

John V. Hagopian (essay date 1981)

[*Hagopian is an American critic and educator. In the following essay, he takes issue with William Carroll's reading of Nabokov's "Signs and Symbols" (see essay dated 1974.)*]

Displaced persons and madmen are recurrent themes in Nabokov's fiction, and both are central to his early—and best—short story, **"Signs and Symbols."** The nameless family, probably Russian Jews, have shuttled from "Minsk, the Revolution, Leipzig, Berlin, Leipzig" to America where the father, "who in the old country had been a fairly successful business man, was now wholly dependent on his brother Isaac, a real American of almost forty years standing." The geographic and socio-political displacement, however, is subsumed in a larger, cosmic displacement; these people have no place in life or in the universe. The straightforward, declarative style ("That Friday everything went wrong") barely mutes the sombre tone. Unlike the larger, grander treatments of this theme in *Pnin, Bend Sinister* and *Pale Fire,* there is no wit or levity here to relieve the intense sadness of the human experience. That sombre tone is most appropriate to the mother, of whom—or *for* whom—the narrator says, "all living did mean accepting the loss of one joy after another, not even joys in her case—mere possibilities of improvement."

Tone and point of view are closely related, because the external, objective narrator effaces himself and, though he tells the story in the third person, presents only the thoughts and perceptions in her mind. The only factor that prevents a conversion of the story into an I-narrative simply by changing the third-person pronouns into the first person (i.e., "she waited for her husband . . . " to "I waited for my husband . . . ") is that the mother, a poor emigre, cannot realistically have such a magnificent command of the English language. But even though the language is Nabokov's, the mind it manifests is the mother's. Hence, it cannot be as William Carroll maintains, in the only full-length commentary on the story in all of Nabokov criticism, that "Nabokov has ensured, through his rhetorical strategy, that the reader will succumb to the same mania." And that perspective is not at all, as W. W. Rowe maintains, "an almost paranoiac mode of perception" [W. W. Rowe, *Nabokov's Deceptive World*]. On the contrary, the narrative technique serves as an implicit endorsement of her perspective on things. Indeed, the central thematic question of the story is: Is it necessarily paranoid to feel that nature and the universe are enemies of man? to want to "tear a hole in [the] world and escape"? To put it another way, does the story depict a context for human experience so benign that it is obviously madness to want to escape? What do the "signs and symbols" indicate? Dr. Herman Brink, presumably a Freudian psychiatrist and forerunner of John Ray, Jr., in *Lolita* (a breed that Nabokov detested), had diagnosed the boy's condition as "referential mania," a form of paranoia which the *Psychiatric Dictionary* defines as a delusion in which a patient misinterprets everything around him as having "a personal reference of a derogatory character toward him." Dr. Brink used the boy as a subject of a professional paper in which he gave a vivid description of his symptoms and drew the conclusion that to him "everything is a cipher and of everything he is the theme. . . . [that is] the ultimate truth of his being." But is it a fact that the boy's interpretation is a delusion, an aberration inconsistent with the "real" world depicted in the story?

William Carroll endorses Dr. Brink with the comment, "The boy lives in a closed system of signs all of which point, malevolently, toward him." It may be that anyone who seeks to interpret the meaning of the signs and symbols betrays himself as one of another breed that Nabokov detested. In a reply to W. W. Rowe's book he expressed indignation at "the symbolism racket in schools [that] computerizes minds but destroys plain intelligence as well as poetical sense. . . . The various words planted by an idiotically sly novelist to keep schoolmen busy are not labels, not pointers, and certainly not the garbage cans of a Viennese tenement, but live fragments of specific description, rudiments of metaphor, and echoes of creative emotion." But the story is entitled **"Signs and Symbols"** and clearly depicts characters who are intensely aware of them. The signs are not, as Carroll maintains, merely a "closed system" of the deranged son; nor is it true that "his parents are dull, sad people who are merely oblivious where he is paranoid." The world presented by the narrator and observed by the parents is fully consistent with the boy's vision of it. The parents have suffered much and their greatest suffering issues from their compassion for their unfortunate son. They make great sacrifices for him, go to a great deal of trouble to visit him regularly in the sanatorium, worry about getting him an appropriate present for his birthday, and have poignant reminiscences about his childhood. Upon learning of his renewed attempt to commit suicide, they determine to bring him home and care for him themselves in their cramped two-room flat. Such concerns gainsay Douglas Fowler's bizarre observation that the parents "are allowed to come before us as without genius, beauty, comic vulgarity, or monstrousness because they are marked for extinction, too" [Fowler, *Reading Nabokov*]. To be sure, they lack comic vulgarity and monstrousness, but they have a genius for survival and a beautiful capacity for family love. If they are "marked for extinction," it is only because they are old and have suffered much, and not because they are to be classed with the losers in Nabokov's world.

With respect to the significance of the signs and symbols of the story, it is important to keep in mind that everything is presented from the point of view of the mother. She is fully aware that, unlike Mrs. Sol "whose face was all pink and mauve with paint and whose hat was a cluster of brookside flowers" (i.e., she cosmeticizes the malevolence of nature), she "presented a naked white countenance to the fault-finding light of spring days." It is a fact and not a paranoid fantasy that the world she lives in is not at all friendly or succoring: "the Underground train lost its life current between two stations," "a tiny half-dead unfledged bird was helplessly twitching in a puddle," another passenger, a girl, was weeping on the shoulder of an older woman, the sanatorium was "miserably understaffed and things got mislaid or mixed up so easily," the husband's "clasped and twitchy hands had swollen veins and brown spotted skin," the son's "poor face was blotched with acne." These are not the insane imaginings of the boy, but a hard-fact reality that undermines Dr. Brink's diagnosis. They depict a world from which the urge to escape is not at all a symptom of madness.

Carroll argues that "Nabokov has insured, through his rhetorical strategy, that the reader will succumb to the same mania that afflicts the boy. The story is studded with apparent signs and symbols that the gullible reader—that is, any reader—will attempt to link together in a meaningful pattern." Carroll is clearly a post-modernist who believes that the story does not have a closed form that crystallizes a specific meaning determined by the author and that a reader who feels a "need to see a completed pattern . . . will have, in effect, participated with Nabokov in killing the boy." But Nabokov once said to Alfred Appel, "the design of my novel is fixed in my imagination and every character follows the course I imagine for him. I am a perfect dictator in that private world." It would seem to follow that a reader is obliged to discover the author's fixed design and follow the course he has imagined for his characters. But Carroll would have it that a reader who sees the design as leading inexorably to the death of the boy is guilty of murder! That raises the most crucial plot question: does the boy in fact die in the end?

The story has three parts. Part I depicts the abortive attempt of the parents to deliver a birthday gift, abortive because the boy had attempted to commit suicide. Part II focuses on the mother's meditations after their return to the flat, and Part III on the post-midnight decision to bring the boy home, followed by the ringing of the telephone. In effect, these are (1) the immediate context of the boy's suicide attempt, already examined above; (2) the family's history of pain and death, obviously modeled on Nabokov's own family history; (3) the successful suicide. The principal signs and symbols of Part II are the photographs and playing cards. Apart from the boy, the figures in the photo album include Aunt Rosa, exterminated by the Germans; a famous chess player cousin (readers familiar with Nabokov's sly practice of using principal characters in some works as background figures in others will recognize Luzhin, another suicide); and some "ugly vicious, backward children he was with in that special school" (like those in the school where Adam Krug's own son was killed in *Bend Sinister*)—all symbols of death and violence. At four, the boy looked away from an eager squirrel (like Pnin, he did not consider nature friendly even then); at six, he drew birds with human hands and feet (later, an envious fellow patient thought he was learning to fly—and stopped him from committing suicide), and as a teen-ager he developed "those little phobias . . . the eccentricities of a prodigiously gifted child hardened as it were into a dense tangle of logically inter-acting illusions, making him totally inaccessible to normal minds" (perfect description of Nabokov's own fiction). These images evoke in the mother thoughts of "endless waves of pain . . . of individual giants hurting her boy . . . of beautiful weeds that cannot hide from the farmer and helplessly have to watch the shadow of his simian stoop leave mangled flowers in its wake as the monstrous darkness approaches." That last image in which human perceptions and emotions are projected upon helpless weeds suggests that the mother, too, suffers from what Herman Brink called "referential mania." But the family's history fully justifies the feeling that they live in a malevolent universe.

All this brooding on pain and death leads to Part III, which occurs in a period of "monstrous darkness." The father who cries, "I can't sleep because I am dying," insists that they bring the boy home. The mother readily agrees, stooping to pick up some photos and cards, including the ace of spades (a symbol of death). It is then that they are frightened by the ring of the telephone, a wrong number. When the telephone rings a second time, the mother (who obviously has acute perceptions and intelligence) patiently explains, "I will tell you what you are doing: you are turning the letter O instead of the zero." Carroll says of this, "while it is a plausible explanation of the wrong number, the fact remains that there is no hieroglyphic difference between the letter and the number." He is so determined to keep the story from having a necessary closure that he cites the irrelevant hieroglyphic similarity of O and zero. But in fact on a telephone dial there is a significant hieroglyphic difference: the letter O is a perfect circle, whereas the number zero is a vertical oval. Even more important is the fact that the O appears in the sixth hole on the dial and the zero appears in the tenth! These significant details and the lapse of time between the second and third rings of the telephone make it highly unlikely that the third call is simply another wrong number. Nabokov said, "I like composing riddles with elegant solutions" (see the ending of **"The Vane Sisters"**). The signs and symbols of the story inexorably accumulate to make that third ring a portent of death. The fears of the parents come true, and the reader experiences the chilling shock of recognition that the sanatorium is calling to report that the boy has at last torn a hole in his world and escaped.

Carroll is clearly wrong in asserting that

> it is just as plausible to argue, though, that the signs and symbols of death have no logically inherent and inescapable conclusion, that they point to nothing finally, and are as "meaning"-less as a sequence of random numbers. It is this ambiguity that makes the story so profoundly eerie. The "cipher" is constructed so that we have to supply the key, constitutionally unable to admit that there is none.

But no legitimate artist produces randomness. Such a reading assumes that the story does not have implicit lines of force shaping a gestalt and leading to the closure of a specific design. The post-modernists must not be allowed to kidnap Nabokov. He may revel in intricacies and labyrinthine complexities and he may relish topsi-turvical coincidences, but John Shade in *Pale Fire* nicely articulates Nabokov's aesthetic: "Not flimsy nonsense, but a web of sense./Yes! It sufficed that I in life could find/Some kind of link-and-bobolink, some kind/Of correlated pattern in the game." As Hagopian observes, "One might say of Nabokov that the more a particular novel engages his own passions, the more he controls and conceals them by converting them into games, puzzles, and various intricate patterns; clear and obvious plots emerge from his pen only when he contemplates the experience with a cool, dispassionate objectivity" [John V. Hagopian, "Vladimir Nabokov," in *Dictionary of Literary Biography,* ed., J. Helterman and R. Layman]. In the final analysis, **"Signs and Symbols,"** despite its pessimistic world-view, emerges as one of Nabokov's most beautifully made and poignant short stories. (pp. 115-19)

John V. Hagopian, "Decoding Nabokov's

'Signs and Symbols', " in Studies in Short Fiction, *Vol. 18, No. 2, Spring, 1981, pp. 115-19.*

Walter Evans   (essay date 1982)

[*In the following essay, Evans explains the significance of illusion in "The Potato Elf."*]

The first of Nabokov's stories published in an American magazine (*Esquire,* December 1939), **"The Potato Elf "** or **"Kartofel'nyy el'f "** was originally written in Russian in 1929. Andrew Field [in his *Nabokov: His Life in Art*] considers the story not merely a "masterpiece" but Nabokov's "greatest short story"; yet his description of the conjuror Shock as a "sorrowful and even tragic figure" suggests that Field misinterprets that character's role in the story, picturing him much more as a victim of fate or of the potato elf than Nabokov ever does. Marina Turkevich Naumann [in her *Blue Evenings in Berlin*] clearly errs in depicting Shock as a godlike presence exercising "supernatural" powers over life and death (even Shock's wife Nora never draws such a conclusion) and in treating the piece primarily as "a love story." William Woodin Rowe's treatment [in his *Nabokov's Deceptive World*] combines plot summary with sex-symbol-mongering and has been specifically discredited by Nabokov himself.

These critics respond with a proper enthusiasm for the story's bizarre power but finally give Nabokov and the story too little credit: a masterpiece by Nabokov, one featuring a magician or conjuror at that, could hardly be as superficial, as barren of interesting games and compelling manipulations as these critics imply. They not only seriously misunderstand the plot: they miss Nabokov's point. Fortunately, Nabokov reveals his intentions rather clearly in certain passages of the story and also in some details that distinguish the story's first translation (by Serge Bertenson and Irene Kosinska), which Nabokov felt "betrayed" him, from his own later Englished version: "retranslating it properly is a precious personal victory that seldom falls to a betrayed author's lot." For example, a native speaker of English would be tempted to use more or less synonymously the words "magician" (employed throughout the first translation) and "conjuror" (Nabokov's own consistent choice). But those careful of their diction—and non-native speakers who consult a dictionary—will be aware of a slight but crucial distinction. In addition to the general connotations of magic and legerdemain and sleight-of-hand, the word "conjure" means "to summon a demon, spirit, etc. by a magic spell" (Second College Edition of *Webster's New World Dictionary*). In substituting "conjuror" for "magician" in his own translation of the story, Nabokov deliberately emphasizes this mysterious character's creative power to "conjure up" rather than merely manipulate.

All this is essentially irrelevant to the interpretations of critics like Rowe and Field and Naumann; one infers that so far as they are concerned the conjuror might as well have been a milliner or beekeeper or librarian. They see him as a wronged husband, innocently betrayed by his wife and his friend, faking suicide (or in Naumann's remarkably naive reading, returning from death's threshold) for some sort of bizarre revenge on his wife, arranging—apparently out of sheer coincidence—to leave England for America immediately after the adultery. Nonsense. Nabokov develops his characters much more carefully than that.

Nabokov constantly represents the conjuror in this story as a figure of power and control. For example, he repeatedly compares Shock to a poet and his conjuring to poetry: "He resembled a poet more than a stage magician;" he is rumored to compose "lyrical poems" (Shock denies the rumor); and his wife understands that "conjuror Shock was, in his own way, a poet." For Nabokov, the artist is preeminently the one who orders or controls, who employs illusions intelligently to manipulate an audience for some purposeful effect. In the story Shock unambiguously earns his title of artist generally and of conjuror specifically.

Let us consider the story carefully before continuing to generalize about it. The brief first paragraph introduces the dwarf Fred Dobson, whose stage name is the Potato Elf, and his friend and partner, the conjuror Shock. The second paragraph foreshadows the story's central episode—in fact, it would seem, Dobson's monologue here provides the inspiration which Shock's fertile mind seizes on as the basis for his most successful bit of conjuring: " 'a few months before I was born, my gin-soaked dad rigged up one of those wax-work cherubs, you know—sailor suit, with a lad's first long trousers—and put it in my mother's bed. It's a wonder the poor thing did not have a miscarriage. . . . this is, apparently, the secret reason I am—'." Fred thus ascribes his dwarfishness to the trauma caused his pregnant mother by his father's trick with a dummy. The much more artful Shock conspires a similar trick, only the boy-sized creature he maneuvers into his wife's bed is alive and the result quite different.

Fred, "the virginal dwarf," is bedeviled by lust. In the second paragraph of the story's second section Shock tells him: "What you need is a female dwarf." Apparently none is immediately available, but in the following paragraph, as Fred passes by the door to the female acrobats' room, the two women "both half-undressed" teasingly invite him in. Moments later Fred, "empurpled with lust, rolled like a ball in the embrace of the bare-armed teases." The acrobats' male partner unexpectedly appears and "silently, without any resentment," throws Fred out. Whom does Fred encounter but "Shock, who happened to be wandering past"? Perhaps all this is coincidence, but the next step can hardly be. " 'Bad luck, old boy,' " Shock sighs. " 'I told you not to butt in. Now you got it. A dwarf woman is what you need.' " Wheels turn in Shock's head, and he immediately announces: " 'You'll sleep at my place tonight' "—a curious choice of words when we realize Fred does "sleep" in the conjuror's "place," that is, with Nora.

Shock's wife, Nora, is, if not physically dwarfish, certainly spiritually so. The daughter of a "respectable" hack artist of conventionally realistic paintings, Nora is "of uncertain age," skinny, untidy, lifeless, altogether the sort of woman who "could hardly attract many men." Shock presents Fred to Nora as if he were a child and tersely announces: "Must be adopted." Careless readers may assume this is Shock's practical joke, as Nora seems to: " 'I'm not so easy to fool,' she sneered." But the masterful conjuror Nabokov has created could hardly stoop to a trick so obvious, petty, unimaginative, and easily foiled. That evening Nora mothers Fred, picturing in him the son whom Shock, or God, or Nature, or Nabokov has denied her. The next morning: "With an abstract smile Mr. Shock left for an unknown destination." The conjuror, so alive to both Fred's needs and his wife's, abandons them to human nature, which follows its course.

That afternoon Fred visits a cafe "where all kinds of performers gathered" and there encounters Shock, "who never frequented taverns." Pure coincidence? That depends on one's frame of reference. Fred decides to confess everything, but before he can begin Shock announces to his partner, friend, "adoptee": "By the way, tonight I appear together with you for the last time. That chap is taking me to America. Things look pretty good."

Why should Shock, who has in the last few hours shown such a solicitous concern for his partner, at this point (he hasn't seen Nora since leaving that morning) abruptly announce his departure for America? Because Shock already knows what Dobson now incoherently tries to explain to him: "Be brave, Shock. I love your wife. This morning, after you left, she and I, we two, I mean, she—." Shock seems to pay absolutely no attention, wanders into anecdote, then back to the topic: "You were about to tell me something, my little friend?" Did Shock miss the point? That's hard to believe of one who elsewhere exercises such masterful control, one who even when "immersed in astral fancies" is always "keenly observing everything around him." It's much easier to believe that here as throughout the story Shock has anticipated the other's action, remains perfectly in control, and is carefully creating precisely the effect he desires.

The following scene opens with Nora alone. We learn first that she feels contempt for "the dwarf," next that she imagines the secret of her adultery will for the first time give her power over the superior husband she has begun to resent almost to the point of hatred. Shock arrives and she considers him, gloating: "With grim pleasure she thought, 'Ah, if you only knew. You'll never find out. That's my power!' " Here, incidentally, we clearly glimpse one of the story's and Nabokov's major themes—the awesome power residing in manipulation of illusion.

Shock's oneupmanship continues, however. He convinces the initially quite skeptical Nora that he's in the last throes of a suicide by poison, and this "shock" coincides with her "shock" of recognition that, after all, she profoundly loves her husband. After screaming into the telephone for a doctor, she discovers the immaculate Shock before a mirror, methodically arranging "the black ends of his silk bow." She's been tricked again.

Next we discover Fred, eight years later, having retired to rural England. The pain of unrequited love has finally numbed; he suffers a few heart attacks; he lives anonymously, unseen by the villagers except when disguised as a child in his occasional nighttime rambles. Suddenly Nora appears alone at the door, in a black gown, veiled.

His affection completely dissipated over the years, Fred regretfully believes she must have come to renew their affair, but she has appeared for a different purpose (ellipsis in original):

> It was then that she told him in a very soft voice:
>
> "The fact is I had a son from you."
>
> The dwarf froze, his gaze fixing a minuscule casement burning on the side of a dark blue cup. A timid smile of amazement flashed at the corners of his lips, then it spread and lit up his cheeks with a purplish flush.
>
> "My . . . son . . . "
>
> And all at once he understood everything, all the meaning of life, of his long anguish, of the little bright window upon the cup.

She tells him the child is normal. When he asks to see the boy, she agrees but abruptly insists she must catch a train, and leaves. Heart swelling, Fred tries to imagine his son, and solely by this act of imagining (his own conjuring), "by the act of transferring his own aspect onto his boy, he ceased to feel that he was a dwarf."

Abruptly realizing he's without Nora's new address, Fred quickly dresses to go out—for the first time in many years as a man, not as a mock boy—and, vainly "trying to forget the heart breaking his chest with a burning ram," runs after Nora, pursued by a swelling mob of mocking boys and townspeople:

> She looked back, she stopped. The dwarf reached her and clutched at the folds of her skirt.
>
> With a smile of happiness he glanced up at her, attempted to speak, but instead raised his eyebrows in surprise and collapsed in slow motion on the sidewalk.

Nora, however, regards his corpse almost indifferently: " 'Leave me alone,' said Nora in a toneless voice. 'I don't know anything. My son died a few days ago.' "

A masterful story—throughout it Nabokov impresses us with the fact that he himself as artist functions as the master conjuror, the final source of power (which Nora explicitly identifies with deception) and of "shock." The character Nabokov most closely associates with artfully controlled illusion and with the creative use of "fiction" is the conjuror, who at first appears intentionally cruel. He seems to show contempt for both the adult dwarf and the childless Nora in introducing Fred as a candidate for adoption, later pretends not to comprehend Fred's attempted confession of the adultery Shock himself manipulates, and with the fake suicide drives Nora to hysteria.

Yet, viewed from another perspective, the conjuror's imaginative, creative use of illusion results in enormous boons for those he manipulates. Apparently potent only in the world of imagination and appearances, Shock has not physically produced a child for his frustrated wife, but his tricks finally result in one. What is to be valued more than life? Love? The false suicide "shocks" Nora into

comprehending "that she loved him more than anything in the world."

Fred, quite as frustrated as Nora, benefits from Shock's manipulations in achieving the bliss life has so far denied him—not only sexual intercourse but also a love for Nora which "shocks" him out of a narrow, if understandable, egotism. What could be more important than such love? Perhaps a sense of human dignity. The conjuror's manipulations "shock" Fred out of his dehumanizing life as a sideshow freak. As he writes to Nora: "Now you understand why I cannot continue to live as before. What feelings would you experience knowing that every evening the common herd rocks with laughter at the sight of your chosen one?"

A longed-for child, love, human dignity—close analysis reveals the almost divine benevolence of Shock's manipulations of imagination, conjuring up for these characters what a comparatively sterile reality has denied them.

"The Potato Elf " celebrates the creative manipulation of the imagination, but Nabokov clearly denies that trickery is a panacea, deception a utopia. "Practice no hurtful deception," counseled Ben Franklin. Nabokov represents as ugly, and as properly frustrated, Nora's intention secretly to triumph over the conjuror through the power she gains in deceiving him with the potato elf ("You'll never find out. That's my power!"). We should condemn her here, but Nabokov leads us to judge otherwise of Nora's impulsive attempt (she arrives dressed in mourning) to deceive Fred into believing his son still lives. Nora's final conversion to creative and benevolent employment of illusion seems a great moral triumph.

What of Frederick Dobson, the potato elf himself? Fred too practices deception, hiding himself away in the daytime pretending to be a normally proportioned invalid, then occasionally donning a wig and child's clothes to circulate in the village in darkness. The conjuror has allowed Fred to leave a painful life in "reality," to dream, to retire to Drowse (the unsubtly chosen name of the village in which Fred locates), there to play games of chess with Dr. Knight. The conjuror's manipulations have lent Fred a courage and a sense of human dignity which enable him to avoid ridicule and to lead a life he has freely chosen. Admittedly, the illusion's success prevents him from penetrating his pervasive loneliness and forming meaningful human attachments, but Nabokov keeps reminding the reader of Fred's imperfect heart (angina pectoris). The inevitable stimulation of attachments in the "real" world must carry an enormous threat to his life.

Nabokov dramatically ascribes the potato elf's climactic death not to illusion but to a surfeit of reality—perhaps more precisely a final refusal to remain in the benevolent realm of imagination. Fred expires because of a fatal compulsion wholeheartedly to embrace reality. Illusion showers Fred with benefits life otherwise denies him. But Fred literally destroys himself in refusing to be satisfied, in attempting to "realize" (make real) his now purely illusory child. Heart and life both fail when he madly pursues the dark chimaera of reality—Nora suitably garbed in mourning—into alien daylit streets mobbed with ridicule and contempt.

So we have finally, in **"The Potato Elf,"** not a conventional fiction in which "the major theme is a love story" but a Nabokovian masterpiece in which the major themes are conjuring, illusion, imagination, and the distinction between sterile reality and fertile illusion. Nabokov is the ultimate conjuror, and the story brilliantly celebrates the creative virtue inherent in such conjuring. (pp. 75-81)

> *Walter Evans, "The Conjuror in 'The Potato Elf',"* in Nabokov's Fifth Arc: Nabokov and Others on His Life's Work, *edited by J. E. Rivers and Charles Nicol, University of Texas Press, 1982, pp. 75-81.*

Larry R. Andrews   (essay date 1982)

[*In the following essay on "Signs and Symbols," Andrews analyzes the pattern of paranoid conspiracy Nabokov creates with the careful use of seemingly neutral details: jars of jelly, references to trees and birds, and the subtle coding of the names of characters who do not actually appear in the story.*]

In his little story about a family of émigré Russian Jews called **"Signs and Symbols"** (1948), Vladimir Nabokov suggests that the son is destroyed by the very forces he fears in his "referential mania." At least he tantalizes us with this possibility, yet all the while he is chuckling at us, and particularly if we are symbol-hunting critics, for momentarily believing in it. It is the intention of this study to demonstrate how Nabokov foreshadows by hidden clues an ending he does not reveal explicitly—the mad son's suicide, perhaps by defenestration. It will conclude by exposing the irony that makes these clues ultimately false.

On a first reading we may find the story superficial, with its shameless exploitation of suspense and clichéd, indeterminate ending. Can the author be *serious?* Yet the tone is quiet and unsensational. The characters' situation is compelling. Something leaves us vaguely uneasy. Upon further examination we perceive the narrator's wayward, Gogolesque eye for seemingly trivial and insignificant details. We notice the odd focus at both the opening and close of the story on the parents' birthday present of jellies for their insane son.

In the first paragraph of the story, Nabokov emphasizes the difficulty of finding the son a "safe" birthday present in view of his "referential mania": "For the fourth time in as many years they were confronted with the problem of what birthday present to bring a young man who was incurably deranged in his mind. He had no desires. Man-made objects were to him either hives of evil, vibrant with a malignant activity that he alone could perceive, or gross comforts for which no use could be found in his abstract world." The parents, however, are confident that they have found a proper gift: "After eliminating a number of articles that might offend him or frighten him (anything in the gadget line for instance was taboo), his parents chose a dainty and innocent trifle: a basket with ten differ-

ent fruit jellies in ten little jars." The jellies will come to seem anything but innocent, as we shall see, and Nabokov's emphasis on them here (end of sentence, end of paragraph, repetition of number) helps to establish their important role in the story.

Nabokov slyly reminds us of the jellies twice again in the middle of the story. When the parents are turned away from the sanitarium after learning of their son's latest suicide attempt, they bring the present back with them to save for the next visit, because "the place was so miserably understaffed, and things got mislaid or mixed up so easily." And later, on the way home, the mother gives the father the basket of jellies to take home, while she stops to buy fish. Then in the last paragraph the jellies loom large again. At the couple's "festive midnight tea" celebrating their decision to take their son out of the institution and care for him at home, "the birthday present stood on the table." The father is in the act of fondling the jars and spelling out the names of the jellies, when the telephone rings for the third time. With the third ring of the telephone the story breaks off, raising the possibility—but leaving it only a possibility—that the call is from the sanitarium and brings the news that the son has finally succeeded in killing himself. At the same time that Nabokov seems to be treating the jellies as "innocent," he has carefully linked them in the structure of the story to the son's fears, to his unsuccessful suicide attempt, and to the possibility of a final, successful suicide.

We do not know whether the late phone call at the end will be a wrong number again, a death notice from the sanitarium, or some other call. It could be either trivial or ominous. Yet the parents are frightened by the first call: "it was an unusual hour for their telephone to ring," the husband gapes in suspense at his wife, and the wife clutches "her old tired heart" and says, "It frightened me." Clearly they fear that their son has succeeded in killing himself. When the second call comes, the wife is much more matter-of-fact about it. By the third call they are completely relaxed over the pleasure of the tea and the "luminous" little jars. Their confidence makes them ripe for disaster. Nabokov has emphasized this confidence in the opening and closing paragraphs in order to make the reader suspect dramatic irony and conclude that the final call will report the son's death. The proof is that in both scenes he links the *jellies* to the parents' feelings of self-assurance. He thus leads us to suspect that the jellies are not "innocent" but are in some mysterious way a *cause* of the supposed death. An overwhelming irony becomes apparent in what appeared to be a rather plotless and inconsequential story: the parents, who have tried to please their son with a birthday gift, and who have decided to bring him back home to *save* him from suicide, may in fact have helped to cause his death. They may have been used unwittingly as part of the conspiracy of mysterious forces which the son has long feared and attempted to escape by suicide. But suicide in this context would, of course, be a self-defeating gesture, less a liberation than an ultimate entrapment signaling the triumph of the hostile forces.

Other details of the story support this view. The jellies are part of an intricate system of images and symbols which add a second dimension to Nabokov's title. On one level, the signs and symbols of the title are those mysterious sources of apparent meaning that afflict the son in his referential mania. On another level, they are the literary signs and symbols which the reader or critic must interpret in order to find meaning in the story. One cluster of such signs—in both senses—is the tree images. Trees are among the elements of "phenomenal nature" which supposedly conspire against the son in his delusions: "His inmost thoughts are discussed at nightfall, in manual alphabet, by darkly gesticulating trees." "Groaning firs" on mountainsides also participate. The jellies are an indirect extension of this tree imagery—they come from fruit trees—and can be seen as insidiously infiltrating the relatively treeless city and sterile sanitarium walls in the hands of the well-meaning parents. The names of the jellies are singled out for special emphasis at the end, as the old man's "clumsy moist lips spelled out their eloquent labels: apricot, grape, beech plum, quince." The stress on "eloquent" and the focus on the words themselves recall the "manual alphabet" of the trees. The father's act of pronouncing the words may in fact signal the son's death. Certainly the emphasis on external forces as bearers of secret coded messages puts us on the alert as to Nabokov's own tricks of language and imagery in the story.

The imagery of sinister trees is echoed elsewhere in the story. Immediately after leaving the sanitarium, the parents encounter a "swaying and dripping tree" with "a tiny half-dead unfledged bird" under it (the bird image will also soon prove momentous). The "swaying" motion here recalls the "manual alphabet" of the "gesticulating trees" mentioned above as well as the general description of the hostile forces as an "undulation of things." An unpleasant tree also figures prominently in the exposition of the son's increasingly phobic childhood. At the age of eight, he was "afraid of a certain picture in a book which merely showed an idyllic landscape with rocks on a hillside and an old cart wheel hanging from the branch of a leafless tree." Since leaflessness suggests lifelessness, this tree is perhaps intended to foreshadow the son's death. The tree images may even be reflected in the metaphor of "a dense tangle of logically interacting illusions" (jungle?) and in the references to the "swollen veins" in the old man's hands and the prominent vein on his head (leaf venation? roots?). Several other key objects in the story with sinister overtones are also products ("man-made objects") of trees—the Russian newspaper, the playing cards, the album and photographs, the wallpaper, the picture book, the cart wheel, and even the labels on the jelly jars (not to mention the paper on which the story itself is printed). Finally, the only animal life mentioned in the story occurs in passages on the son's mania and consists, with perhaps the exception of the bees suggested in "hives of evil," of species that inhabit trees: the squirrel in the park which the four-year-old boy was "looking away from" in the photograph; the primate in the metaphor of the scything farmer's brutal "simian stoop"; and, most importantly, the numerous references to birds.

While the tree images tend to be negatively colored and to function as hostile forces, the bird images that pervade the story are ambivalent and may suggest either freedom

or entrapment. A bird image with the former connotation appears in the description of one of the son's recent suicide attempts. Nabokov tantalizingly refuses to elaborate on this attempt, saying only that it was a "masterpiece of inventiveness" and that an "envious" inmate interpreted it as an attempt to fly. That it was indeed an attempt to fly—to escape from persecution by emulating a bird's freedom—is suggested by the later reference to the son's drawings of "wonderful birds with human hands and feet." This image, combined with the "envious" inmate's interpretation of the suicide attempt, hints that the son's final, successful suicide, if it occurred, also took the form of some ingenious emulation of flight. (The father's concern to keep knives locked up after their son returns to them shows the parents' misunderstanding of him.)

A conspicuously negative bird image, suggesting death and entrapment, occurs in close conjunction with the sanitarium. After failing to see their distraught son, the old couple encounter the "tiny half-dead unfledged bird . . . helplessly twitching in a puddle" cited earlier. Clearly this bird is a symbol of the son himself, who has never properly grown up and who is at the mercy of the sinister forces represented by the "swaying and dripping tree" overhead and the inescapable puddle. It also refers to the recent suicide attempt and foreshadows the possibility of successful suicide at the end. The son does not have wings and cannot escape, yet he perhaps tries to fly out a window at the sanitarium and is destroyed in the attempt.

Still more bird references infiltrate the story in clever disguises. On the bus from the sanitarium the boy's mother notices "a girl with dark hair and grubby red toenails . . . weeping on the shoulder of an older woman. Whom did that woman resemble? She resembled Rebecca Borisovna, whose daughter had married one of the Soloveichiks—in Minsk, years ago." The name "Soloveichik" is a diminutive of the Russian word for nightingale, *solovey,* subject of many popular songs, poems, and legends, in which it connotes persecution and sorrow. This nightingale reference is echoed in the names of the doctor ("Solov," a truncated form of the same word) and next-door neighbor (Mrs. "Sol," a still further shortened form of the word which may refer simultaneously to "sun," as we shall see).

In addition to the tree and bird images there is a host of other "signs and symbols" seemingly at work in the story. The suggestion that the son in the sanitarium is like a caged bird is related to a whole series of claustral images, which in turn reinforce the idea of a sinister conspiracy directed against and enclosing the son. The sanitarium, the parents' flat, and the building that contains the flat are oppressive enclosures. The son has tried to flee the institution. The flat is small and will seem even smaller if the son moves in, and it has a "narrow yard." The power failure in the subway causes temporary enclosure and entrapment and is the first example following the foreboding statement, "That Friday everything went wrong." The crowded bus, the hard rain, the umbrella, the bus-stop shelter, the puddle with the struggling bird, the landing on which the old man waits ten minutes, and the "unswept corners" of neglected children also serve to circumscribe and hem in. Even the jellies are imprisoned in jars, which in turn are enclosed in a basket. All of these images, besides commenting on the stifling and dehumanizing atmosphere of the city, reflect the son's mania: to him the whole world is an enclosure he wants to "tear a hole in . . . and escape."

Death images form another branch of the conspiracy and also serve as foreshadowing devices in the plot. The mother wears "black dresses"; the stalled subway is described as having "lost its life current"; the bird in the puddle is "half-dead"; the anonymous neighbor seen through the window is a "black-trousered man," lying, in a deathlike posture, "supine on an untidy bed"; Aunt Rosa was obsessed with death and catastrophe and was herself put to death; and the old father comes out of the bedroom saying, "I can't sleep because I am dying." The midnight hour and the crucial zero of the telephone number also intimate death. And in general, the imminence of death and decay pervades the old people's lives, from her heavy "trudging" up the stairs to his swollen head vein and the "horrible masklike grimace" in the mirror when he removes his dentures.

Another persistent pattern in the complex conspiracy of the story is the parent-child relationship, stressing an element of parental responsibility for the offspring's unhappiness or death. Was it right to place the son in the caged institution that "was so miserably understaffed," where "things got mislaid or mixed up so easily"? This innocent language refers to the jellies but obliquely suggests that the son himself has become a "thing" that the parents have "mislaid" and is now even more "mixed up" than before. The father suddenly decides to bring the son home, because he feels guilty over the latter's suicide attempts: " 'We must get him out of there quick. Otherwise we'll be responsible. Responsible!' he repeated and hurled himself into a sitting position, both feet on the floor, thumping his forehead with his clenched fist." The parents *are* indirectly responsible for the son's condition, not just because they have put him in an asylum or have been unable to understand him but because the jellies and every other object they come into contact with seem to use them to persecute him. This responsibility is implicit in the distance between parents and son. They were unusually old when he was born, and now twenty years later they are aged. They are also physically separated from the son. No direct communication between them and their son occurs in the story or even in the snippets of exposition from the past (photographs mingled with reminiscence). The budding child prodigy had become not only "difficult to understand" at eight but "totally inaccessible to normal minds" in his teens. The sanitarium nurse turns the parents away for fear that their "visit might disturb him." Even their various migrations through Europe and America in flight from revolution, world war, and pogrom must have had a disturbing effect on the child.

Again there are concealed clues to reinforce the monstrous suspicion that the story's end portends a suicide for which the parents are responsible. The story is filled with images of parental distance and neglect. The "unfledged bird" that symbolizes the son has been neglected by its parents—neither guarded closely nor trained for survival in the world on its own. The raven-haired girl on the bus is weeping on an older woman's shoulder and reminds the mother of another mother and daughter from the past. The girl here is unhappy and unkempt, with "grubby red toenails." Earlier the "garrulous high-school children" on the bus exist in isolation from parents and are annoying to the old couple. Later the mother muses on the "neglected children" of the world with impotent sorrow. The reference to the father's prosperous brother Isaac recalls the similar prosperity of the Biblical Isaac and underscores two other parallels with that story: (1) the extreme age of Abraham and Sarah when Isaac was born is a parallel to the age of the father and mother in the story; (2) the divine test in which Abraham nearly slew his son as a sacrifice is a parallel to the parents' implicit responsibility for their son's condition and his attempted suicides. The son's tragic wish to fly also reminds us of the Icarus myth, in which the father, Daedalus, is responsible for his son's death, while the father survives.

Other, less conspicuous symbolic patterns arise through the use of doubling [in a Footnote, Andrews directs the reader to the essay by L. L. Lee, "Duplexity in Vladimir Nabokov's Short Stories," *Studies in Short Fiction* 2, No. 4 (Summer 1965): 307-15. Lee's essay is reprinted above.]. We have seen that the black-trousered man is the son's double, because he is used to foreshadow the son's death. The son's cousin also serves as a double. This cousin is a "famous chess player" and is perhaps a projection of Luzhin in Nabokov's *The Defense*, who is also a victim of referential mania and who commits suicide by defenestration. There are other doubles for the parents and son in addition to the parallel sets of parents and children mentioned in the preceding paragraph. The insensitive nurse at the sanitarium is yet another reflection of the "irresponsible" mother. And two pairs of details link the son with the father: (1) at age six the son is described as having "insomnia like a grown-up man," and in the last scene we see that the father is unable to sleep for anxiety over his son; (2) the son is referred to as "ill-shaven," and one of the last details in the story shows that "although [the father] had shaved that morning, a silvery bristle showed on his chin." Furthermore, both the father and the son are imprisoned and dying. These details suggest that the son's condition is partly due to his similarity to his father, thus again implying the father's responsibility for the son's possible death.

Doubling is not only applied to character: there is also a doubling of images, such as those of trees and birds discussed earlier. In fact, almost every hostile image in the long paragraph describing the son's referential mania is doubled elsewhere in the story. Below is a list of such images:

Description of mania	*References elsewhere*
"clouds in the staring sky"	the cloudy, rainy day, "rain tinkled in the dark," "monstrous darkness"
"pebbles," "granite," "mountains"	"rocks on a hillside"
"stains"	"blotched with acne," "brown-spotted skin," "soiled cards," "large birthmark"
"sun flecks"	"Mrs. Sol," "fault-finding light of spring days"
"glass surfaces"	the mirror the father uses, "his raised glass," "his spectacles," the jelly jars
"still pools"	the puddle, the tea
"coats"	"old overcoat"

"store windows"	"windows were blandly alight and in one of them a black-trousered man could be seen," allusion to window in description of son's suicide attempt
"lynchers at heart"	"cart wheel hanging from the branch of a leafless tree," "one could hear nothing but the dutiful beating of one's heart," "her hand went to her old tired heart," "knave of hearts"
"running water," "torrents"	"raining hard," "dripping," "circular motion" of the tea
"storms"	"raining hard," "thunder"
"undulation of things"	"swaying," "waves of pain"
"air he exhales is indexed and filed away"	"foul air of the subway,"
	"pneumonia"
"groaning"	"moan"

Other pairs of images include the newspapers rustling on the subway echoed in the father's Russian newspaper at home and the "twitching" of the bird echoed in the "twitching" of the father's old hands. The sinister implications here are again monstrous. The real world of the parents and even the language of the story seem to be infiltrated by the hostile elements of the son's mania. Furthermore, the extraordinary emphasis on images of language codes ("veiled reference," "transmit," "alphabet," "messages," "cipher," "decoding") invites us to consider the story itself as a code with a sinister meaning.

Another pattern emerges from the numerological symbolism of the story, which brings us to the deck of cards and the telephone number. The numbers that dominate the story tend to be even:

> 2—"two-room flat," "twice a week"
> 4—"fourth time in as many years," "quarter of an hour," "four years old"
> 6—"age six," father reading sixth label when phone rings at end
> 8—"aged about eight"
> 10—"ten different fruit jellies in ten little jars," "ten minutes later," "aged ten"
> 12—"scientific monthly," "midnight"
> 20—"a score of years," age of son
> 40—"American of almost forty years standing"

Yet a few odd numbers infiltrate with particular suspiciousness. The mystic number three shows in the three sections of the story, three landings on the stairs, three cards on the floor, three telephone calls at the end, and three suicide attempts specifically mentioned or suggested. The knave of hearts and the nine and ace of spades, the cards that accidentally fall to the floor with the picture of Elsa and her beau, are also suspicious, since Nabokov's careful eye selects them for naming. The nine is yet another mystic number, the square of the mystic number three, which occurs regularly in the story. The ace of spades is a traditional omen of death. The knave of hearts contains at least three allusions, all of them relevant to the concerns of the story: (1) an allusion to guilt, since the knave of hearts is the stealer of tarts in Lewis Carroll's *Alice's Adventures in Wonderland,* which Nabokov translated into Russian and published in Germany in 1923; (2) an allusion to conspiracy and death, since in Nabokov's early novel *King, Queen, Knave* the "knave" conspires to murder his lover's husband; (3) an allusion to the rainy, claustrophobic setting of Baudelaire's first "Spleen" poem and to its description of an old deck of cards with dirty odors:

> Héritage fatal d'une vieille hydropique,
> Le beau valet de coeur et la dame de pique
> Causent sinistrement de leurs amours défunts.

Fatal inheritance from a dropsical crone,
The handsome knave of hearts and the queen of spades
Chat sinisterly of their dead loves.

These lines echo the story's pervasive imagery of death and decay and also the son's fantasy that things are communicating with each other in sinister ways about him.

When we hear of the "wrong number" on the first two phone calls, we are suddenly convinced that the texture of numbers in the story is part of the conspiracy against the son. All we know about the wrong number is that the girl is "turning the letter O instead of the zero." On the third try, presumably the girl dials the correct number, the zero. If so, the third ring is not hers and is perhaps the sanitarium's. Zero is a death omen as well as a "veiled reference" to the "cipher" of the referential mania: "cipher" can mean "zero" as well as "code" and "symbolic image." The zero is thus a part of the son's mania, and all the numbers seem to be a part of the code used by the hostile forces. The telephone itself becomes a sinister threat because of the numbers on its dial, because of the prominence of zero among those numbers in the story's final episode, and also because it is the most obvious example in the story of the sort of man-made "gadget" mentioned in the first paragraph as "malignant" and hence "taboo" as a birthday gift.

Another important detail in the phone call is the mention of the name "Charlie." It seems strange that Nabokov refuses to name the three leading characters in the story but gladly offers up the names of minor characters who do not even appear (Mrs. Sol, Herman Brink) and finally names a seemingly irrelevant "Charlie," who is asked for by someone dialing a wrong number! The namelessness of the main characters has, however, at least two purposes: it suggests their lack of clear identity, especially in the case of the son; and it also suggests, when set in the context of the extensive naming of others, that the world outside is strong and threatening and that names are a part of its sinister code. As in the case of the numbers, however, the hostile significance of the names is not always clear. By now we have surely come to see the story as a gothic tale.

The images that have symbolic overtones in the story sometimes occur with similar overtones in Nabokov's other work: Humbert fears the conspiracies of poplar trees and lovebirds in a cage; and Pnin is paranoiac about his oak-leaved wallpaper. The conspiracy finally extends beyond the world of this particular story to include characters in earlier novels (such as Luzhin) and also, proleptically, characters in the later novels as well. We are implicitly invited to read those novels in terms of this story and this story in terms of those novels, so that Nabokov's entire career gradually takes on the appearance of an elaborate code with an intricate symbolic meaning.

As we perceive the intricate system of hidden clues in the story, apparently planted by Nabokov to convince us that the son's paranoia is justified and the conspiracy real, we momentarily suspend our disbelief and see the world through the son's eyes, the sane and insane visions now reversed. The dull, gray world of the parents now seems impossible, unreal, insane, and tainted by mortality, while the son's imaginary world is intensely alive. The fictive world viewed by the son has taken over the "real" world of the parents in our eyes and in the fabric of the story. Everything in the story seems to corroborate the son's feeling of total vulnerability. The world has become a projection of his self turned inside out ("The silhouettes of his blood corpuscles, magnified a million times, flit over vast plains"). It is astonishing how Nabokov has involved us in this vision in so short a space. Yet, in retrospect, such a paranoiac view of the world seems preposterous, no matter how plausibly the fiction justifies it. The suggestion that occult influences have affected even the linguistic texture of the story seems, in retrospect, particularly absurd. The idea is slightly more credible in **"The Vane Sisters"** and **"Scenes from the Life of a Double Monster,"** because of their first-person point of view. But here, after being momentarily mesmerized by Nabokov's skillful imagery, we emerge from the trance realizing that the sly author has played a joke on us again. Not only do we realize that the son is, after all, mad and the "conspiracy" his delusion, but we also realize that the question of which world (the son's or the parents') is real has become irrelevant, since both are equally unreal fictions of the author.

The artificiality of the ending, with its suggestive withholding of the story's climax, reminds us of the artificiality of the whole. Furthermore, there are many crucial elements of the plot that are either denied us by the artifice of the story or filtered through secondary, unreliable sources, thus calling further attention to the story's receding levels of artifice. The narrator seems objective, yet he withholds a great deal of straightforward information we are sure he possesses. Exactly what was the "masterpiece of inventiveness" of the son's recent suicide attempt? We are told only that "an envious fellow patient thought he was learning to fly—and stopped him." The son himself never appears in person. We go to visit him with the parents but are turned away. His childhood is glimpsed only in impressionistic fragments through the medium of photographs. Most of the details of the story are seen through the eyes of the parents: the jellies, sanitarium, rain, bird, people on the bus, neighbors, cards, photographs, and telephone (e.g., "she glanced at his old hands"; "she . . . examined the photographs"; "he put on his spectacles and re-examined . . . the . . . little jars"). The description of the son's mania, which is central to the image patterns, is itself of doubtful "reality." His symptoms and the term "referential mania" are not related directly by the narrator but through the medium of "an elaborate paper in a scientific monthly." Undercutting the seriousness with which we may take the article is the light mockery of its author as a comic stereotype of a German psychiatrist in the adjective "elaborate" and in the name Herman Brink, with its reminder of the thin borderline between sanity and madness, reasonable and arbitrary interpretations, fiction and "reality." Further undercutting the authority of the report is the fact that the parents had "puzzled it out for themselves" long before (but this puzzling out produces, of course, still another subjective view). Finally, much of the mania is described in imagery of art, making us aware of the artifice of the scientific paper and of the story itself ("reference," "alphabet," "patterns," "messages," "theme," "misinterpret," "indexed and filed," "silhou-

ettes," "sum up . . . the ultimate truth of his being," in addition to the similar terms cited earlier). Brink's scholarly article can be seen as a fiction about the son, just as Nabokov's story is a fiction about Brink and the son, and just as this essay is a fiction about Nabokov's story. Where lies "reality"?

In his essay on the story William Carroll argues that "a 'cipher' can be a nullity just as easily as it can be a key, but most readers will see it as a key; we will conclude that the third call is from the hospital. In so doing, we will have assigned a meaning to the signs based on something outside the closed system; we will have, in effect, participated with Nabokov in killing the boy." Carroll also points out that it is "just as plausible to argue . . . that the signs and symbols of death have no logically inherent and inescapable conclusion." He nonetheless insists that "most readers" (and this presumably includes Carroll himself) automatically complete the pattern of symbols, assume that the third call is from the sanitarium, and therefore "kill" the boy by mentally writing their own ending to the story. Such a view does not take full account of the story's aesthetic implications. As soon as we appreciate that the story is a fiction and that all its clues are therefore false, the "reality" of the boy and his mania is shattered, and it is no longer possible to speak of our participation in his "world." There is no ambiguity left at the end about the significance or meaninglessness of the symbols in the story, and speculation about the boy's possible suicide is irrelevant, since the world of the story has ceased to exist with the story's final punctuation mark. It has been translated, so to speak, from our perspective to the higher sphere of the artist's fictive world (in which we are characters too) and ultimately to a configuration of black marks on the page. The reliability of *all* the information about the boy is questionable. Carroll's argument to the contrary notwithstanding, we *are* ultimately distanced from the story and hence even from what Carroll calls an "esthetic responsibility" for the boy's death.

This is the final stage of deciphering **"Signs and Symbols,"** the stage that goes one step beyond Carroll's otherwise convincing interpretation. This stage reminds us of the "Hegelian syllogism of humor" practiced by Axel Rex in *Laughter in the Dark:*

> Uncle alone in the house with the children said he'd dress up to amuse them. After a long wait, as he did not appear, they went down and saw a masked man putting the table silver into a bag. "Oh, Uncle," they cried in delight. "Yes, isn't my make-up good?" said Uncle, taking his mask off. Thus goes the Hegelian syllogism of humor. Thesis: Uncle made himself up as a burglar (a laugh for the children); antithesis: it *was* a burglar (a laugh for the reader); synthesis: it still was Uncle (fooling the reader).

William Woodin Rowe uses this passage to illustrate his contention that in Nabokov's works "the reader is often subtly induced to draw premature, erroneous conclusions about *what* is taking place." In "Signs and Symbols" the parents at first seem innocent. Then they appear to be implicated in their son's condition and perhaps his death; finally, we sense the hoax: the story is a fiction, and nobody is responsible. Yet the joke is a serious one. Nabokov is not simply playing an empty game at our expense. He is affirming art as sacred play. In calling our attention to the artifice of his story, he reminds us of the superior vision of the artist. As a private world of the imagination the story shares something with the son's mania. But unlike the latter it is redeemed by an act of freedom—the artistic expression that consciously creates the fictive world of the story and the playful configuration of its language. Nabokov succeeds in capturing both our belief and our disbelief. We relish the irony after the terror of momentary belief. And in so doing we are rescued from the foul air of mortality by the pleasure and vivifying force of art. (pp. 139-51)

> *Larry R. Andrews, "Deciphering 'Signs and Symbols',"* in *Nabokov's Fifth Arc: Nabokov and Others on His Life's Work, edited by J. E. Rivers and Charles Nicol, University of Texas Press, 1982, pp. 139-52.*

Leszek Engelking   (essay date 1985)

[*In the following essay on "The Visit to the Museum," Engelking discusses the Eastern European and Slavic origins of the story's Devil imagery.*]

"The Visit to the Museum" (Poseshchenie muzeia), a short story first published in 1939, recounts a devilish trick in which the narrator is mysteriously removed from France to his native Russia, forbidden to him, an exile.

Let us recall the plot. The narrator plans an autumn visit to the town of Montisert in the south of France. A friend of his, a fellow émigré, wants to buy a portrait of his grandfather, which, he has heard, hangs in the Montisert museum, and asks for help in the affair. The narrator, not very eager to carry out the request, inadvertently finds himself at the modest museum, and sees the portrait. He tries to buy it from the museum director who maintains, however, that the picture is not in the museum but agrees to sell it if he is mistaken. Having found that he is wrong, the director tears up the hastily-made agreement and walks away. Wanting to insist on the bargain, the narrator follows him through a surprising number of museum halls, but the director disappears. After long roaming through gigantic halls, the narrator at last finds a way out of the museum only to ascertain the rather dreadful fact that he is in snow-covered Leningrad. At the end of the story there is a short account of later events: "I shall not recount how I was arrested, nor tell of my subsequent ordeals. Suffice it to say that it cost me incredible patience and effort to get back abroad and that, ever since, I have foresworn carrying out commissions entrusted to me by the insanity of others."

Now I am going to justify my expression "a devilish trick." The devil figures in a number of Nabokov's works and the subject has been treated by Irene and Omry Ronen in their interesting article "Diabolically Evocative: An Inquiry into the Meaning of a Metaphor" [in *Slavica Hierosolymitana,* (1981)]. The Ronens do not, however, mention **"The Visit to the Museum."** Nevertheless, one can, I think, also detect infernal smells in this story. The devil's presence, however, is suggested here with great subtlety

and is hard to discern. The perceptive reader is able to get on the devil's track only with the appearance of the museum director, a certain Monsieur Godard. Godard, we read, has "a face very much resembling a Russian wolfhound; as if that were not enough, he was licking his chops in a most doglike manner, while sticking a stamp on an envelope;" he then throws the letter into the wastebasket, an act that seems to the narrator rather unusual. It is suggestive that in the folk beliefs of various nations, both in Western Europe and in Slavic countries, the devil frequently assumes the form of a dog. According to legend, Faust had a black dog and in Goethe's drama, Mephistopheles first appears as a black poodle. It might be mentioned here that the only German literary work Nabokov translated was the "Prologue" to Goethe's *Faust.* Nabokov's interest is also attested by his rather unfavorable remark that "there is a dreadful streak of *poshlust* running through Goethe's *Faust.*" It is true that devilish animals are generally black while in the Russian original of the story (but not in the English) Monsieur Godard is likened to a white dog. Although black is the most typical color of demons, red and white are also connected with them. In the Jacobean drama, *The Witch of Edmonton,* by Thomas Dekker, John Ford, and William Rowley, the devil appears upon the stage in the form of a dog. The hellish dog at first is black but in the fifth act changes its color into white.

The color black appears in Nabokov's story a little later: " 'We do have one [painting by] Leroy,' said M. Godard when he had leafed through an oilcloth notebook and his black fingernail had stopped at the entry in question." Claws and talons are very characteristic of the devil when he makes his appearance in human form. In Nabokov's devil-populated short story **"In Memory of L. I. Shigaev,"** the drunken narrator describes how one of his toad-like demon visitors "might scratch behind his ear with his foot, the long claw making a coarse scraping sound. . . . " It seems justifiable to see in Godard's "black fingernail" a suggestion of his devilish proclivities.

Monsieur Godard wants the narrator's proposal concerning the picture in writing: if the portrait is indeed in the museum, it will be sold for a certain sum; if not, the sum will be paid anyway. His demand seems to be an echo of Mephistopheles in Goethe's *Faust:* "Nur eins!—Um Lebens oder Sterben willen Bitt ich mir ein paar Zeilen aus." The museum director urges the narrator to use the red part of a red-and-blue pencil. Red pencil is, without doubt, a substitute for blood with which compacts with the devil are always signed.

The last firm suggestion of Godard's relationship with hell that I was able to discern is his "feminine heel": "I steered Godard to the portrait; he froze before it, chest inflated, and then stepped back a bit, as if admiring it, and his feminine heel trod on somebody's foot." Devils are often characterized by a defective leg. Most often they are believed to be lame or to have a hoof in place of a foot. In Goethe's *Faust,* Siebel, observing Mephistopheles, asks: "Why is that fellow's one foot lame?" and Mephistopheles himself makes mention of his horse's hoof, *der Pferdefuss* (line

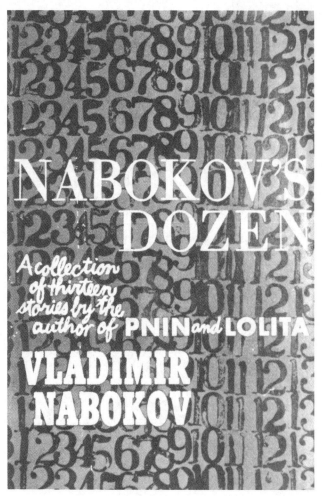

Dust jacket for the volume that includes "Spring in Fialta," "That in Aleppo Once . . . ," and "Signs and Symbols."

4065). Godard's "feminine heel," is in my opinion, a rather original equivalent of a horse or goat hoof.

In his book on Gogol, Nabokov observed that *Poshlust* "is one of the main attributes of the devil. . . ." In my view, the museum director epitomizes this trait. "Our Monsieur Godard," as the firm of Satan and Co. may be imagined calling their agent, insists the painting in question is not in the museum and tells the narrator: "I have been curator of our museum for almost twenty years now and know this catalogue [of its holdings] as well as I know the Lord's Prayer. It says here Return of the Herd and that means the herd is returning, and, unless perhaps your friend's grandfather is depicted as a shepherd, I cannot conceive of his portrait's existence in our museum." In view of Godard's probable infernal connections, his words may be true. His knowledge of both the Lord's Prayer and the museum catalogue may be insufficient.

Once on the devil's track, the reader may return to the very beginning of the story. Careful reading of the first pages will now enable him to discern the infernal aspect of various objects and secondary characters and to see their more obscure relationships with the devil's domain.

The narrator's friend, who wants to buy the portrait, is at the beginning of the story characterized as "a person with oddities, to put it mildly." Even more significantly, the story ends with the words: "ever since, I have foresworn carrying out commissions entrusted one by the insanity of others." The widespread belief that the insane are possessed by the devil is shared by the East Slavic peoples. The custodian of the museum also deserves notice. He is a cripple, having only one arm. In folk beliefs, various kinds of physical defects are ascribed to demons. The Belorussians believe not only in lame devils, but also in hunch-backed and twisted ones. Russians sometimes imagine devils to be crop-eared or to have only one ear. The famed Russian wood demon, the *leshii,* is often believed to have only one ear. It is quite possible that the custodian, "a banal pensioner with an empty sleeve," is an original devil—armless instead of being legless or lame. Perhaps his "vinegarish breath" is a Nabokovian transformation of the smell of brimstone.

Some of the objects exhibited in the first hall of the museum make one think of hell: "a pair of owls, Eagle Owl and Long-eared, with their French names reading 'Grand Duke' and 'Middle Duke' if translated." The Slavic people considered owls, especially the Eagle Owl, to be demonical birds, servants, and incarnations of the devil. The narrator's curiosity is aroused by "an assortment of strange black lumps of various sizes," over which there is "a photograph of an astonished gentleman with a pointed beard." The custodian cannot explain either what they are or who decided that they should be exhibited in the museum. The narrator thinks they bear "a great resemblance to frozen frass"—*podmorozhennyi navoz.* Folklore knows many tales about devils' gifts, precious objects or money, changed into manure. In a Russian folktale the devil wishes to deceive the tale's hero by giving him manure instead of precious coins—objects one might expect to find in a museum. One should also notice the *espan'olka* or "pointed beard" of the "astonished gentleman," whose photograph hangs over the strange objects. Although Nabokov uses neither the word "goatee" nor the Russian expression *kozlinaia borodka* "goat beard" (which differs slightly from an *espan'olka*), the gentleman's beard at least resembles a goatish one, which is a devilish attribute. There is another interesting exhibit in the museum: "a pale worm in clouded alcohol." Some Slavic peoples believe that worms are suffering souls.

As the narrator makes his way from the museum to Monsieur Godard's house, he barely escapes "the onrushing tires of a furious red bus." The color red, apart from its rather obvious political connotations, also has infernal ones. Red is probably the most frequent color of Slavic demons' dress. Shortly after the incident with the red bus, Monsieur Godard enters the story. After a short talk, the narrator and Godard go to the museum. Walking up the museum steps, the director doffs his hat as if entering a temple. Is the museum, therefore, a temple of Satan? The affirmative answer to this question would be a little precipitate but at least there is a possibility of such an interpretation of Godard's gesture. Another temple, the Montisert Cathedral, tries, perhaps, to prevent the narrator from meeting the museum director: " . . . the cathedral began

146

playing hide-and-seek with me but I outwitted it. . . . I crossed the asphalt thoroughfare and a minute later was ringing at the garden gate of M. Godard."

Putting people on the wrong path, misleading them, pulling them into swamps, bringing them on the brink of calamity, are all favorite sports of Slavic demons. Let me quote one example: "The devil once sat a peasant in a well. . . . 'My father-in-law invited me to come for tea and beer. I drank a mug of beer and saw that I was not a guest at my in-laws' but in a well, and that I wasn't drinking beer, but cold water. And I wasn't drinking it by the glass, but straight down the gullet.' " Is not this in a way similar to Nabokov's story? In **"The Visit to the Museum,"** however, the source of danger is different from that in folktales. It is the totalitarian state. Nabokov was, perhaps, like the father of Fyodor Godunov-Cherdyntsev, the hero of his novel *The Gift,* "uninterested in ethnography." Even without any special interest, however, some folk beliefs perhaps penetrated his consciousness. (I forego mention of the subconsciousness in order not to be taken for a member of "the Viennese delegation.") Therefore, I have decided that adducing the Slavic demonology would be both proper and useful in looking at his story **"The Visit to the Museum."** I am quite aware that, considering the variety of demonologic beliefs, some of the "devilish traces" might appear in the story by chance. There are, however, too many of them to think that all of the infernal associations are unintentioned.

Tradition does speak of proud noble demons such as Lermontov's "pechal'-nyi demon, dukh iznaniia" ("the sad demon, the spirit of exile"). It is not, however, Lermontov's noble demon who attends **"The Visit to the Museum,"** but it is rather the *besy,* the petty demons of *poshlust,* that same *poshlust* which Nabokov shows in *Invitation to a Beheading* (and elsewhere) as a typical attribute of the totalitarian state. (pp. 351-56)

Leszek Engelking, "Some Remarks on the Devil in Nabokov's 'The Visit to the Museum'," in Canadian American Slavic Studies, *Vol. 19, No. 3, Fall, 1985, pp. 351-56.*

John B. Lane   (essay date 1986)

[*In the following essay on "Signs and Symbols," Lane examines the narrative devices that produce both ambiguity and definite meaning in this story.*]

If Vladimir Nabokov ever entertained the notion that simple cause and effect provide an adequate explanation for the world in which human beings find themselves, he kept his moment of doubt to himself. All of his major fiction displays some kind of causal ambiguity, and in his short story **"Signs and Symbols,"** causal ambiguity is the physical world's most salient feature. The events of the story are simple: an elderly émigré couple attempts to take a basket of fruit jellies to their son who suffers from "referential mania" and is confined in a mental institution. When they arrive, they find that the young man has, for a second time, attempted suicide. His previous attempt was "a masterpiece of inventiveness," but both it and this subsequent effort were unsuccessful. He cannot be disturbed, so, with-

out seeing him or delivering their gift, the couple returns home. That night the old man cannot stop worrying about their son and is unable to sleep, consequently they are up later than usual. He is in the process of devising a plan to bring their son home, when the phone rings. It is a wrong number. He continues elaborating his plan and is again interrupted by the phone. The old woman explains to the girl who is calling, why she is getting the wrong number, and hangs up. Relieved at having formulated a plan for bringing their son home, the old man and his wife settle down to an unexpected, festive tea. The story ends with the phone ringing for a third time.

The natural world in Nabokov's story is filled with signs and symbols which both reflect the characters' lives and foretell coming events. The old woman, who is the narrational focus of the story, is an astute observer, but she gives no conscious credence to the nonrational portents in the story. Her son's perception of them, on the other hand, is sufficiently acute to make the world's malevolence intolerable for him. When the old couple walks by "a tiny half-dead unfledged bird . . . helplessly twitching in a puddle" that is "under a swaying and dripping tree," the incident is echoed in the description of the young man's illness, in which, the reader is told, "his inmost thoughts are discussed at nightfall, in manual alphabet, by darkly gesticulating trees." By means of such linkages of the world which the old couple inhabits with the world which the young man finds intolerable, Nabokov makes it clear both that it is a threatening world which the characters inhabit, and that the world's portentious nature is not just a product of the young man's deranged mind.

These different perceptions of the physical world, and the device of the final phone call are significant elements in the story, but Nabokov is seldom if ever content with limiting his fiction to the milieu of his characters and his tales invariably become a kind of literary chess problem (although an exception might be allowed for those in which a chess problem becomes a story). In writing on the composition of chess problems, Nabokov points out [in *Speak, Memory*] that "it should be understood that the competition in chess problems is not really between White and Black, but between the composer and the hypothetical solver (just as in a first rate work of fiction the real clash is not between the characters, but between the author and the world)." In **"Signs and Symbols"** the struggle between the author and the world is very much in evidence, but Nabokov takes the struggle a step further and forces the reader from his comfortable position as spectator, drawing him into the conflict.

A striking feature of most Nabokovian texts is authorial foregrounding, but in **"Signs and Symbols"** it is, while still present, uncharacteristically ambiguous and restrained. This restraint clearly helps the genre gimmick of the final phone call to function effectively, but more importantly, it provides a strong incentive for a crucial rereading, with its concomitant involvement of the reader in the story's more profound problems. Without this restraint the story might be too easily read as diverging from the trick-ending genre of popular magazine fiction only by the tinge of parody supplied by Nabokov's distinctive strain of narrative intrusion. Instead, the shifting, ambiguous, and finally mysterious character of the story's narrator points the way toward a fuller understanding of the story by leading the reader to search both for a clear picture of the author/narrator and for reassurance that his initial interpretation of the final phone call is justified. The authorial foregrounding is effected by two different means. The first and most noticeable is the overt manipulation of the language of the story, and the second is the presence of allusions to both personal biographical details and to literary subtexts. In **"Signs and Symbols"** there are none of the startling narrative intrusions which occur in some of Nabokov's writing, and the diction is less playful than is often the case, but nonetheless, the reader's attention is still drawn to an author lurking within the story.

In the foregrounding, based on language manipulation, the narrator's changes in diction and syntax are closely linked with the story's overall structure. The story consists of three, short, numbered sections. The first two sections are structurally very similar. They show a progressive development of literary style from a slow and highly objective beginning to a dramatic and subjective climax. The last section is uniform in style and deviates from literary transparency in only two minor ways [in a footnote, Lane explains: "One deviation from literary transparency is the 'Elsa and her bestial beau' reference which obtrudes from the rest of the text because of its ambiguity. The purpose is almost certainly to give extra emphasis to this important allusion. The other deviation in this section is: 'Having more English than he did' which is a syntactically structural link to the 'married already' and 'anyhow' of the first section. Both this and the 'bestial beau' allusion are discussed elsewhere in this paper"].

While both the first two sections begin in a highly objective tone, they are nonetheless distinctly different. In the opening of the first section, the word choice and grammatical structures are designed to remind the reader of the slightly awkward speech patterns which immigrants (like the old couple) often display. The opening of the second paragraph is a particularly good example:

> At the time of his birth they had been married already for a long time; a score of years had elapsed, and now they were quite old. Her drab grey hair was done anyhow. She wore cheap black dresses.

The word order of "been married already for a long time" and the nonstandard, literary use of "anyhow" are both calculated to link the narrator with the old couple. In the course of the first section the language gradually becomes subjective and highly lyrical. The diction, syntax, and imagery all differ dramatically from those which occur in the opening. The language ceases to be that of an elderly émigré couple and shows conscious "literary" artistry. The reader might be carried along by this gradual change and not notice the narrational change consciously, were it not for devices introduced to assure that the authorial presence is noted. The first such device is the extravagance of metaphor which creeps into a passage that begins as Doctor Herman Brink's strictly scientific description of the symptoms of referential mania. The second—an even

more consciously literary device—is the triple use of alliterative word pairs which appears in the last third of the concluding paragraph of the first section:

> He must be always on his guard and devote every *minute and module* of life to the decoding of the undulation of things. The very air he exhales is indexed and filed away. If only the interest he provokes were limited to his immediate surroundings—but alas it is not! With distance the torrents of wild scandal increase in *volume and volubility.* The silhouettes of his blood corpuscles, magnified a million times, flit over vast plains; and still farther, great mountains of unbearable solidity and height sum up in terms of *granite and groaning* firs the ultimate truth of his being. (emphases mine)

The lyricism of the close of the first section is emphasized by the abrupt return to a calm objective tone in the opening paragraph of the second section:

> When they emerged from the thunder and foul air of the subway, the last dregs of the day were mixed with the street lights. She wanted to buy some fish for supper, so she handed him the basket of jelly jars, telling him to go home. He walked up to the third landing and then remembered he had given her his keys earlier in the day.

While the tone of this paragraph has much in common with that of the beginning of the story, it is different in that the émigré speech patterns are not in evidence, and the narrator is of the standard, invisible, and omniscient variety. However, once again, the prose gradually changes, and the second section ends in a climax which is even more lyrical and syntactically complex than the close of the first section. Even without obtrusive devices like the alliterative word pairs of the first climax, the final sentence of section two makes it apparent that there is an author behind the chameleonic narrator:

> She thought of the endless waves of pain that for some reason or other she and her husband had to endure; of the invisible giants hurting her boy in some unimaginable fashion; of the incalculable amount of tenderness contained in the world; of the fate of this tenderness, which is either crushed or wasted, or transformed into madness; of neglected children humming to themselves in unswept corners; of beautiful weeds that cannot hide from the farmer and helplessly have to watch the shadow of his simian stoop leave mangled flowers in its wake, as the monstrous darkness approaches.

There is no such development in the third section. The narrator remains virtually invisible; there is no change in tone, syntax, or diction. But there is no need for a change. The reader reads the "signs" given by the first two sections and anticipates a third climax without the necessity of a change in style to help him along. The tension created by the interplay between the steady tone and the reader's expectation serves to heighten the impact of the final phone call. Although the tone is consistent throughout the third section, it contains several indications that a climax is coming. Two such indications occur in the final sentence.

The first is the "yellow, green, red" succession of jelly colours, which suggest the caution, go, and stop colours of a traffic light. However, the sequence of lights is different from that which occurs in traffic lights, and the change reflects the story's dramatic sequence: the series of portents and the unhappy recounting of the family's history (yellow), is broken only by the old man's brief moment of enthusiasm (green), which precedes the final call (red). The second indication in the final sentence has been described by William Carroll as "the sequence of 'eloquent labels' from apricot to quince . . . broken by the flat, cramped sound of 'crab apple,' fruit which is tart or sour while the others are sweet."

Other portents of the climax to come in the third section are the two allusions to mortality which occur there. The first comes in the opening of the section when the old woman hears her husband moan just before he staggers into the room—a description which would be more suitable for a heart attack than insomnia. This impression is supported by his statement: "I can't sleep because I am dying." The second occurs when the first phone call comes at "an unusual hour for their telephone to ring." After explaining to the caller that she has a wrong number, the old woman's "hand went to her old tired heart." These events serve as portents because they fit into a pattern of threes and twos anticipating a three which recurs throughout the story. Many of these are obvious and some have already been specifically referred to, such as the three sections of the story, the three phone calls, the three uses of alliterative pairs of words, the three jelly colors, and the two suicide attempts, but they extend to much more subtle references. One such is the mention of three names in the story—Sol, Soloveichik, and Solov—which share elements of a root that is the Russian word for nightingale, and thus are linked to the "half-dead unfledged bird" [in a footnote, Lane adds: "Actually, there may be an implied fourth use of the root 'sol' in the name Aunt Rosa. There is a small plant of wide distribution—now known as *drosera rotundifolia*—whose old European name was *rosa solis,* which means 'flower of the sun,' suggesting 'Mrs. Sol . . . whose face was all pink and mauve with paint and whose hat was a cluster of brookside flowers.' The plant lives in moist sunny areas and perhaps seems obscure, but in an earlier time when botanizing was a popular pastime, this plant was well known because it is insectivorous, and thus especially interesting. A naturalist of Nabokov's standing would almost certainly have known it well. The 'Aunt' of 'Aunt Rosa' suggests the homonym 'ant,' and thus the small insects it traps. The leaves are covered with long hairs which each have a single drop of sticky liquid on the end. A single plant will often have numerous victims adhering to it, which suggest Aunt Rosa and 'all the people she had worried about' trapped and killed by the Nazis. It is a difficult plant to describe, but the colors "pink and mauve" connected with Mrs. Sol, and the adjectives 'fussy,' 'wildeyed,' 'angular,' and 'tremulous' associated with Aunt Rosa all suit it. The fact that it would break the pattern of threes for the root Sol may seem a disadvantage, but as I attempt to demonstrate in this paper, this hidden deviation might actually suit Nabokov's larger purpose"]. Another (and, like the allusion to a heart attack, it also occurs in the third section) is founded on the

repetition of words by the old man. After he announces that he cannot sleep because he is dying, he says, "No doctors, no doctors . . . To the devil with doctors! We must get him out of there quick. Otherwise we'll be responsible. Responsible!" Aside from reinforcing the pattern of ominous threes and twos, this passage also lends credence to William Carroll's suggestion that the reader is himself at least partly "responsible" for killing the deranged young man by supplying meaning to the third ring.

While the foregrounding through literary and personal references is, like the language-based foregrounding, not as prominent as in some of Nabokov's other writing, it is still definitely present. The cryptic line in the description of "referential mania" ("Everything is a cipher and of everything he is the theme") has considerable relevance to the story—though it is far from clear in which sense it is to be taken: is it a code system? the key to such a code? a message in code? or a reference to the number 0 in the second phone call? Nonetheless it must have some foundation in the delight Nabokov took as a child in his monomaniacal Uncle, about whom he wrote "Uncle Ruka . . . prided himself on being an expert in decoding ciphered messages . . . we subjected him to a test one day, and in a twinkle [he] turned the sequence '5.13 24.11 13.16 9.13.5 5.13 24.11' into the opening words of a famous monologue in Shakespeare." Another glimpse of the author is given in the ironic treatment of the psychiatrist "Herman Brink," who writes an "elaborate paper in a scientific monthly" on the nature of the young man's illness, a problem which the old couple had puzzled out "long before." The disdain the narrator displays toward Herman Brink is perfectly in tune with Nabokov's many disparaging comments about Freudian psychology. His comment in *Speak Memory* is typical in tone:

> Let me say at once that I reject completely the vulgar, shabby fundamentally medieval world of Freud, with its crankish quest for sexual symbols (something like searching for Baconian acrostics in Shakespeare's works) and its bitter embryos spying from their natural nooks upon the love life of their parents.

The most concrete biographical detail comes in the climax of the story when the telephone rings for the third time, presumably signaling the young man's successful suicide. The concluding few lines bear more than a passing resemblance to Nabokov's account of his own father's death:

> On the night of March 28, 1922 around ten o'clock, in the living room where as usual my mother was reclining on the red-plush corner couch, I happened to be reading to her Blok's verse on Italy—had just got to the end of the little poem about Florence which Blok compares to the delicate smoky bloom of an iris, and she was saying over her knitting, "Yes, yes. Florence does look like a dimmy iris, how true! I remember—" when the telephone rang.

This telephone ringing ends the paragraph, and Nabokov gives no other description of the family's learning of his father's untimely death (he was killed while preventing the assassination of another speaker at a public meeting). The description provides a perfect reflection of the concluding paragraph of **"Signs and Symbols"** (the memoirs were written several years after the story), which is illuminating in that they both create ambiguities which are resolved only after some thought and rereading. In the memoirs, the specificity of the date and time seems incongruous when first read, falling as it does in a setting of apparently mundane reminiscence, but when the significance of the phone call dawns (somewhere in the following paragraph), the date and time suddenly make perfect sense. The same pattern occurs in the short story, but its resolution is considerably more difficult.

It seems clear in the story that there can be no happy resolution to the young man's difficulty. Paramount among the many indications is the methodical description of the course of his disease: "as a baby he looked more surprised than most" (indicating to the reader that he was abnormal from birth). An indication of the boy's early perception that the natural world is not benevolent is found in the comment: "Four years old, in a park: moodily, shyly, with a puckered forehead, looking away from an eager squirrel as he would from any other stranger." The information that at "age six . . . he drew wonderful birds with human hands and feet, and suffered from insomnia like a grown up man" suggests problems to come both through the physical symptom and through allusion to the "tiny half-dead unfledged bird." By age ten he is in a "special school" and causing his parents "shame, pity" and "humiliating difficulties." Finally, there "came a time in his life, coinciding with a long convalescence after pneumonia when those little phobias of his which his parents had stubbornly regarded as the excentricities of a prodigiously gifted child hardened into a dense tangle of logically interacting illusions, making him totally inaccessible to normal minds." [In a footnote, Lane adds: "One might also claim a biographical reference here, since Nabokov had prodigious mathematical abilities as a child, which disappeared following a long illness involving a high fever."]

That the young man's fate does not hold any pleasant surprises also seems to be indicated by several references to his parents, such as the comment about his mother that "this, and much more, she accepted—for after all, living did mean accepting the loss of one joy after another, not even joys in her case—mere possibilities of improvement" (72), or the pathetic description of his father's patently unworkable plan for bringing the boy home to their two room apartment: "I have it all figured out. We will give him the bedroom. Each of us will spend part of the night near him and the other part on this couch. By turns. We will have the doctor see him at least twice a week" (73). In fact the entire story is an agglomeration of signs and symbols pointing to the conclusion that there is no happy ending awaiting the characters. The indications seem to be unrelievedly bad, from the "cheap black dresses" of the first page to the succession of jellies which precedes the terminal phone call.

In addition to the several faint and one relatively strong autobiographical reference, there are also several faint allusions to Nabokov's own fiction and two strong references to external subtexts, including one to a classic of Russian literature. When the narrator mentions "the ugly,

vicious backward children, he was with in that special school," the description could apply just as well to the school for abnormal children where Adam Krug's son is killed in *Bend Sinister* and mention of the young man's "cousin, now a famous chess player" brings to mind Luzhin in *The Defense*. Aside from these allusions to his own literature, Nabokov includes an extensive reference to Puškin's short story, "The Queen of Spades." It occurs in the third section in a short paragraph concerning the old woman:

> Bending with difficulty, she retrieved some playing cards and a photograph or two that had slipped from the couch to the floor: Knave of hearts, nine of spades, ace of spades, Elsa and her bestial beau. (73)

The pervasive use of the number three in **"Signs and Symbols"** and the succession of three cards ending in an ace suggest the analogous pattern in Puškin's story. Elsa and her bestial beau suggest Lizaveta and her suitor Herman, and it is noteworthy that Nabokov also gives the name Herman to the psychiatrist in **"Signs and Symbols."** [In a footnote, Lane adds: "It is interesting that Nabokov chooses the name 'Brink' for his psychiatrist. It may be that he combined his disdain for Freudian psychology with another object of his scorn—detailed literary analysis (particularly of his own work)—in this choice. Bernhard ten Brink was a well-known literary scholar around the turn of the century whose most famous work was an extremely detailed analysis of the language and structure of Chaucer's writing. The distinctive 'ten' in his name also echoes the ten fruit jellies in ten little jars."] The "bestial beau" Herman in Puškin's story becomes obsessed with the three cards which seal his fate, and the description of his thoughts is a perfect example of "referential mania":

> Two fixed ideas can no more exist in one mind than, in the physical sense, two bodies can occupy one and the same place. "Three, seven, ace" soon eclipsed from Hermann's mind the form of the dead old lady. "Three, seven, ace" never left his thoughts, were constantly on his lips. At the sight of a young girl, he would say: "How shapely she is! Just like the three of hearts." When asked the time, he would reply: "About seven." Every pot-bellied man he saw reminded him of an ace. "Three, seven, ace," assuming all possible shapes, persecuted him in his sleep: the three bloomed before him in the shape of some luxuriant flower, the seven took on the appearance of a Gothic gateway, the ace—of an enormous spider. To the exclusion of all others, one thought alone occupied his mind—making use of the secret which had cost him so much.

The overwhelming impression of the signs and symbols in Nabokov's story is that the young man will die. There are, however, some less noticeable indications of the contrary, and the apparent time and date anomaly which Nabokov sets up and then resolves in his recounting of his father's death, has an interesting parallel in this short story. In the course of the litany of minor disasters which befall the old couple while they are trying to deliver their gift, we are told that "that Friday everything went wrong." A technically literal interpretation would seem to indicate that the final phone call must also fall into the category of "everything." However, the third section of the story opens: "It was past midnight . . . " and thus the phone call actually comes on Saturday morning. A close reading of the story reveals a plethora of symbolic premonitions, but a dearth of hard facts. Only the matter of time comes as a straightforward statement from the omniscient narrator, and it only indicates that the call cannot be interpreted *with certainty* as coming from the hospital, although this is the conclusion which the structure of the story seems to dictate. The two previous wrong numbers heighten our interest in the final call, but actually serve to make its interpretation less sure; without them, we could justify no other explanation for the call.

The ambiguity of the final phone call forces the reader—after an initial leap to a conclusion which is too obvious to be satisfying—to go back and examine the story for signs and symbols which will make everything clear. The subsequent discovery that there is virtually no additional information in the story, leads to a state of mind which the reader will sooner or later recognize as bearing an uncanny resemblance to the young man's "referential mania," a condition in which the sufferer:

> imagines that everything happening around him is a veiled reference to his personality and existence. He excludes real people from the conspiracy—because he considers himself to be so much more intelligent than other men. Phenomenal nature shadows him wherever he goes. Clouds in the staring sky transmit to one another, by means of slow signs, incredibly detailed information regarding him. His inmost thoughts are discussed at nightfall, in manual alphabet, by darkly gesticulating trees. Pebbles or stains or sun flecks, form patterns representing in some awful way messages which he must intercept. Everything is a cipher and of everything he is the theme.

Nabokov was very distrustful of what he referred to as the "symbolism racket" of standard literary criticism. No doubt his attitude can be attributed at least partly to protectiveness toward his own creations, however, his remarks in an interview with Alfred Appel, Jr. seem to have particular relevance to **"Signs and Symbols"**:

> My advice to the budding literary critic would be as follows. Remember that mediocrity thrives on "ideas." Beware the modish message. Ask yourself if the symbol you have detected is not your own footprint. Ignore allegories. By all means, place the "how" above the "what" but do not let it become confused with the "so what." Rely on the sudden erection of your dorsal hairs. Do not drag in Freud at this point.

There are footprints aplenty in **"Signs and Symbols."** Nevertheless, it eventually emerges that the story operates on three distinct levels: 1) the human story which the narrator describes, 2) a standard philosophical "second level" in which man's relation to the physical world is examined, and 3) a thoroughly Nabokovian object lesson for the *literati*.

The human story in **"Signs and Symbols"** is a simple, deft recounting of a day in the difficult life of an old émigré couple. With a few carefully detailed observations, Nabokov evokes a marital relationship in which the angularities of petty strife have long since been worn smooth. The old woman accepts her own suffering as being in the natural order of things, and she is solicitous of her husband, who cannot reconcile himself to the pain which their son's situation gives him. The old man's carefully structured plan reassures him, and formulating it allows him to relax, despite its obvious impracticality. The story is a beautifully drawn representation of that common condition among older couples, wherein the husband's assertiveness and orientation toward mechanical manipulation of the physical world has become a meaningless vestige of his productive years, while the wife's forebearance and compassion remain as the real foundation for their lives.

The story can also be read on a second level, which consists of a shift from the particulars of the characters' lives, to the universal that is evidenced in them. This theme in **"Signs and Symbols"** mines an apparently inexhaustible mother lode: the relationship between a fixed, discrete and causally determined physical world, and the mental construct of that world which is man's only means of perceiving it. The objective, scientific view is represented by Herman Brink's "elaborate scientific paper" and is given short shrift. His view that the young man's distrust of the physical is mere paranoia, is refuted both by the objective milieu of the young man's world and by his links to the unfledged bird, an unambiguous symbol of the casual cruelty of a nonteleological, mechanically unfolding world which is, if not antagonistic, at least totally indifferent to suffering. Nabokov expressed his personal reaction to this world in an interview given late in his life: "nature expects a full grown man to accept the two black voids fore and aft, as stolidly as he accepts the extraordinary visions in between . . . I feel the urge to take my rebellion outside and picket nature."

"Extraordinary visions" are prominent in **"Signs and Symbols,"** and the characters' responses to them vary considerably. Nabokov's years as a research entomologist probably left him more familiar than most writers with the world view that Herman Brink represents, but it can hardly be said to describe his own view of the natural world, which he presents in comments like: "I discovered in nature the nonutilitarian delights that I sought in art: Both were a form of magic, both were a game of intricate enchantment and deception." Both this comment and his unhappiness with the "voids fore and aft" seem to place him much less in sympathy with Herman Brink than with the young man who wants "to tear a hole in the world and escape." Though the natural world in **"Signs and Symbols"** is full of "enchantment and deception," there is very little of "delight," and the humor which is so characteristic of Nabokov's other writing is not readily apparent. The world in this short story is grim and full of ominous portents. The old woman's awareness of them is indicated both by the fright she displays at the first phone call and by descriptions which show her powers of observation, such as: "he kept clearing his throat in a special resonant way he had when he was upset," and "During the long ride to the subway station, she and her husband did not exchange a word . . . every time she glanced at his old hands (swollen veins, brown-spotted skin), clasped and twitching upon the handle of his umbrella, she felt the mounting pressure of tears." They are not spared the cruelty of the world surrounding them, and the only balance to it is the familial love which they have, part of the "incalculable amount of tenderness in the world" which is fated to be "crushed, or wasted, or transformed into madness."

Both as an entertaining narrative and as a fresh look at a standard literary/philosophical problem, the story is both readable and interesting, but it achieves its full stature through those elements which are directed specifically to the *literati*. Once the reader realizes that deciphering the signs and symbols is not going to yield the story's full meaning, and that he, as reader, is suffering from "referential mania," the story's meta-literary function begins to appear. Just as the old couple takes the young man "a dainty and innocent trifle" (the basket of jellies) which is calculated not to "frighten" or "offend," Nabokov presents a collection of discrete and multicolored literary devices for the reader's delectation. There is a broad array of literary devices in the story, which tend to fall into discrete portions of the text. The openings and closings of the first two sections (quoted and described above) are good examples, each being a small sample of a distinct type of prose, but there are many others. In fact, the reader conducting such a survey soon feels like the protagonist in Nabokov's story **"A Visit to the Museum,"** wandering from exhibit to evermore improbable exhibit, lost in an exposition hall of prose techniques.

Apart from the plentiful and readily apparent signs and symbols which contribute to "a dense tangle of logically interacting illusions" whose overall effect is to induce "referential mania," the story contains many other interacting references. These sometimes act as shaping devices, appearing at the beginning and end of paragraphs; in the opening of the story, for example, a phrase from the first sentence of the paragraph "for the fourth time in as many years," with its implied numerical repetition (reinforced by the homonym), is echoed by a phrase in the last sentence "ten different fruit jellies in ten little jars." The jelly jars themselves also serve to help tie the whole story together by appearing at the beginning of the first two sections and at the end of the third.

Pairs of linked references occur throughout the story. One such pair, for example, links father to son through similar parenthetical insertions. A description of the son—"(his poor face blotched with acne, ill-shaven, sullen and confused)"—is paralleled by that of the father: "his old hands (swollen veins, brown-spotted skin)." The first of a pair of catoptric images alludes to the reflective properties of "glass surfaces and still pools" in such a way as to make them seem like symptoms of madness. The second is a grotesque image of the old man at the mirror where, "straining the corners of his mouth apart by means of his thumbs, with a horrible masklike grimace, he removed his new hopelessly uncomfortable dental plate and severed the long tusks of saliva connecting him to it." In contrast to the first image, this one is readily acceptable as an objective description of reality despite the man/walrus meta-

morphosis which it describes. The man/walrus combination is in turn one of a pair of man/animal combinations in the story, the other being the bird/man combination found in the young man's drawings (quoted above). The photograph which introduces the "Queen of Spades" allusion also occurs twice in the story. Earlier, "from a fold in the album, a German maid they had had in Leipzig and her fat-faced fiancé fell out." Despite the fact that the two descriptions are of the same photograph, and both have alliterative descriptions of the fiance/beau, the reactions they evoke are very different: the first produces mild distaste, and the second loathing and apprehension. Such devices as these, and many others like them, are the structural units of the story, but alone they are only a collection of techniques. It is on the metaliterary level that they are given the coherence which makes them work as a literary unit.

Signs and symbols are the very stuff of language, both spoken and written, and they are so varied and complex a pair of ideas as to require fifty-eight separate entries in *The Oxford English Dictionary* [in a footnote, Lane adds: "In light of the prominence of the image of the basket of jellies, it is interesting that a now obsolete definition of 'symbol' is 'a contribution (properly to a feast or picnic)' (O. E. D., 1933, Vol. 10, 362)"]. No comprehensive definition will be attempted here, but a consideration of some of the underlying notions is useful in attempting to understand Nabokov's short story. The two concepts are closely related, but their essential difference is that signs tend to be *indications* of other things and act as messages, while symbols are *representations* of other things. The two functions are rarely clearly separated, and one of the central problems which the story poses for the reader is founded on the tension which occurs between the two functions when the usage is ambiguous. The "tiny half-dead unfledged bird . . . helplessly twitching in a puddle" is an image which is almost invariably alluded to in discussions of the story, but how is one to interpret it? As a representation, and therefore a symbol of the young man, as a symbol of the cruel indifference of nature, or as a portent of the young man's fate: a *sign* of things to come? When the old woman explains to the caller that she is confusing the letter O and the number zero—two very similar signs—is it a portent of the fatal call (third time's the charm), or is it a symbolic representation of the reader's difficulty in working out an interpretation of the story?

While such questions may have no definitive answer, they are central to the meaning of this story. All signs and symbols (and for that matter all perceptions) can be located somewhere between the two polarities which are referred to in such dichotomies as science/art, thinking/feeling, and rationality/intuition. When the reader tries to interpret one of the images in Nabokov's story (or any sign or symbol), he quickly discovers that it is not obviously one or the other, but seems to be a muddy mixture of the two, with which he feels more or less comfortable. The initial inclination may be to attribute this difficulty to intentional perversity, and this would probably be at least partly correct, but there is also a serious point being made about the nature of signs, symbols, and human perception: a point which concerns the paradox inherent in both language and knowledge. The more scientific, exact, and concrete a sign or symbol, the less meaning it can contain, and therefore with perfect exactness comes perfect meaninglessness. The corollary is also true. The more meaning something carries, the less exact it must become, hence a thing which encompasses all meaning is also perfectly inexact. It is this epistemological fact which can make discussion about the arts so frustratingly inexact, and it is the state of affairs to which Nabokov alludes through the timing of the final phone call ("that Friday everything went wrong . . . it was past midnight"): a precise description pertaining to an important event, but one which carries no relevant meaning. Nabokov causes the reader to compare this kind of information with such symbolic paradigms as the passage which speaks "of beautiful weeds that cannot hide from the farmer and helplessly have to watch the shadow of his simian stoop leave mangled flowers in its wake, as the monstrous darkness approaches," which has broad implications and clear relevance to the story, and yet can never be reduced to a precise meaning.

The intricately interconnected and diverse signs, symbols, devices, and references in Nabokov's story may well induce "referential mania" in the meticulous reader, but they are not just a diabolically contrived labyrinth, but rather a carefully elaborated statement about the nature of perception and interpretation: a statement which encompasses both literature and epistemology. The story is an effective trifle in a hackneyed genre, which simultaneously parodies that same genre, a philosophical trifle (in its evocation of the rational man/nonteleological nature conflict), and it is a leghold trap for heavy-footed symbolic racketeers. But it is ultimately founded on a thoughtful development of some of the basic concepts which underlie fiction and all language. While it abounds in those distinctively Nabokovian traits which result in amused delight or blind rage, according to individual temperament, it is at least as profound as it is playful.

The playfulness in the story is of an unusual flavor for Vladimir Nabokov, because it seems to smack more of grim cruelty than of the self-deprecating humor which one usually associates with his writing. Both this problem of the missing humor, and the more overt problem of the meaning of the final phone call may well have no final solution, but there are two references which I believe shed some light on them. First are the biblical allusions in the names of Isaac and Rebecca, and the pseudonym for Isaac's brother: "the Prince." Two fainter biblical allusions occur in the following line: "that Friday everything went wrong. The underground train lost its current between two stations." The stations of the cross are traditionally performed on Good Friday, the day on which Christ was crucified, and Rebecca's husband Isaac, son of Abraham and Sarah, was spared at the last moment when God—who had demanded that Abraham sacrifice his son as a demonstration of faith—struck the dagger from his hand.

The son spared at the last moment certainly seems to have a potential parallel in **"Signs and Symbols"** and it brings back to mind the allusion to "The Queen of Spades." The third card does not turn out to be the expected ace, and the description of Herman's shock in Pushkin's story may

well provide both the answer to the twin problems and the clearest glimpse of author and reader which **"Signs and Symbols"** contains:

> Herman started: indeed, instead of an ace, before him lay the queen of spades. He could not believe his eyes, could not understand how he could have slipped up.

> At that moment it seemed to him that the queen of spades winked at him and smiled. He was struck by an unusual likeness . . .

(pp. 147-59)

John B. Lane, "A Funny Thing About Nabokov's 'Signs and Symbols'," in Russian Language Journal, *Vol. XL, Nos. 136-37, Spring-Fall, 1986, pp. 147-60.*

Alfred Appel, Jr. on Professor Nabokov:

He was an immensely popular teacher . . . , particularly in his Literature 311-312 course, "Masterpieces of European Fiction." The course was unique in the smallest of ways (witness the "bonus system" employed in examinations, allowing students two extra points per effort whenever they could garnish an answer with a substantial and accurate quotation—"a gem"—drawn from the text in question).

Carefully handwritten and then typed out, an artist-scientist's anatomical examination of the books he admired and adored, Nabokov's lectures ranged widely and wildly in mood, from the most moving to the most farcical of moments. "You cannot understand a writer if you cannot pronounce his name," he would say, introducing Gogol ("Gaw-gol, not Gogal!"). He would then rehearse Gogol's death agonies, his head thrown back in pain and terror, nostrils distended, eyes shut, his beseechments filling the hushed lecture hall. Urging his students to become "creative readers," he would ask them to develop "the passion of the scientist and the precision of the artist"—double takes on the part of notetakers; didn't he mean the opposite?—and, digressing for the minute, Nabokov would toss brickbats at "Old Dusty" [Fyodor Dostoevsky] or "the Viennese quack" [Sigmund Freud], eliciting from the gallery as many gasps as laughs. He would conclude a lecture with a rhapsodic apostrophe to our writer's style: "Feel it in your spine; let us worship the spine—the upper spine, the vertebrae tipped at the head with a divine flame!" And then, as the hour ended, he would ask to see the students who had occupied seats 102 and 103 during the recent midterm examination. "I suspect mental telepathy!"

Alfred Appel, Jr. in his "Nabokov: A Portrait," Nabokov's Fifth Arc, edited by J. E. Rivers and Charles Nicol, University of Texas Press, 1982.

Leona Toker   (essay 1988)

[*In the following essay, Toker analyzes "Torpid Smoke."*]

Nabokov's short stories are polished self-contained works of art, yet they can also be profitably read in the light of their place in his general canon. This place is determined by the time when each story was written and by the way in which other works enrich and elucidate the significance of its images.

In the prefaces to his novels and short stories Nabokov usually notes the time when they were composed. The dates of composition are, indeed, more important than the dates of publication, because they provide glimpses, perhaps by way of deliberate yet coded leakage, into the workings of his imagination. These glimpses are particularly interesting in view of Nabokov's own concern with the different aspects of a writer's calling.

Nabokov's short stories are sometimes treated rather like studies that a painter makes in preparation for a major picture. In many cases, however, they may have served as repositories for what spilled over from longer works or as safety valves for the urgent material that had to be kept out of the novels lest it should interfere with their design. His 1935 story **"Torpid Smoke,"** written at the juncture of *Invitation to a Beheading* (composed in 1934) and *The Gift* (written during the years 1935-37) constitutes such a safety valve. The plight of the young poet Grisha, the protagonist, is a hybrid of the tendencies manifest in Cincinnatus of *Invitation* and Fyodor Godunov Cherdyntsev of *The Gift*. Yet unlike Fyodor, this young poet gets no encouragement from his environment for his wish to devote himself to literature; unlike Cincinnatus, he cannot reject his environment.

His father seems to be cultivated, well-meaning, and pathetically human—a far cry from the obnoxious "parodies" that surround Cincinnatus. Yet he has prevailed on Grisha to study political economy (for economic reasons, no doubt) rather than "something quite different." On the evening described in the story the father is sitting alone in the dining room, while Grisha's sister is entertaining her boy friend in the parlor and he himself is lying supine in his room. He is "drugged by the oppressive, protracted feeling so familiar to him," a feeling that follows upon some "gentle mysterious shock" and that will resolve itself in poetry. Nothing much happens on the surface of the story: Grisha has to remove a particle of food from between his teeth; his sister asks him to get cigarettes from their father, with whom she has had a quarrel; after the brief visit to the dining room Grisha's languor finds sudden release in a flow of verse.

The imagery of the story ostensibly serves to increase the density of the setting. However, as usual in Nabokov, the imagery is also functional: it forms a subtle network of parallels and nuances that both point to the genuineness of the young man's talent and suggest a reason for the "puerile" quality of his "perishable" production.

His languor set in when, while "trudging" on his father's errand after an ordinary day at the university and library, Grisha noticed the "wet roof of some pub on the edge of a vacant lot." The chimney smoke "hugged the roof, creeping low, heavy with damp, sated with it, sleepy, refusing to rise, refusing to detach itself from beloved decay." This synaesthetic image—visual, tactile, organic and empathetic—produced a "thrill" powerful enough to redeem the day. Grisha's evening is then spent under the influence of the torpor of the smoke.

Back in his room, he surrenders to a "languorous mist." The contours of his body seem to become indistinct, like those of the smoke: "the lane on the other side of the house might be his own arm, while the long skeletal cloud that [stretches] across the whole sky with a chill of stars in the east might be his backbone." In Nabokov's work a dissolution of identity suggests a closeness to the "involute abode" [*Pale Fire*], the abode of aesthetic objects and of "infinite consciousness" [*Bend Sinister*], something like Borges's Library of Babel. That is where Grisha is heading when his perception of the room yields to images of "a sea horizon or a strip of distant land," "a remote mirage enchanting in its graphic transparency and isolation: a stretch of water . . . and a black promontory with the minuscule silhouette of an araucaria"—the motif of a voyage is probably inspired by one of Grisha's favorite books, *Shatyor* (*Tent*), the collection of Gumilyov's "African" poems. Merging with the "involute abode," however, could be as lethal as the tropical swamps imagined by a dying man in Nabokov's **"Terra Incognita"** (1931). "One of the main characteristics of life," says the narrator of Nabokov's *Pnin,* "is discreteness. Unless a film of flesh envelops us, we die. Man exists only insofar as he is separated from his surroundings. The cranium is the space-traveler's helmet. Stay inside or you perish. Death is divestment, death is communion. It may be wonderful to mix with the landscape, but to do so is the end of the tender ego." The "waltwhitmanesque" [*Bend Sinister*] quasi-social "mixing" with the grasses of the landscape is physical death ("the dead are good mixers" [*Transparent Things*]); complete carnivalistic communion is loss of spiritual identity. The smoke of the chimney, a semi-transparent emblem of a mixture of matter and spirit, refuses "to detach itself from beloved decay," and seeks a quieting merger with the damp that has made it heavy. The young poet, however, resists that lure. Like Pnin, who extricates himself from his thoughts of death by (note the onomatopeia) "gently *ch*amping his den*tu*res, whi*ch*" [retain] the residue of lunch-time "co*tt*age *ch*eese," Grisha has a method of "measuring and marking himself off," that is, of regaining his discreteness, by palpa*t*ing, with "the *t*ac*t*ile *t*ip of his *t*ongue," "a shred of boiled beef firmly lodged in his *t*eeth"—note the alliteration as in "the *t*ip of the *t*ongue *t*aking a *t*rip" to say "Lolita" [*Lolita*]). He forces himself to get up and look for a "nice, poin*t*ed li*t*tle *t*ool, *t*o aid the soli*t*ary blind *t*oiler," his tongue. Having found such a tool, a safety pin, he removes the mote and swallows it—"be*tt*er than any dain*t*ies." In the hands of most other writers this episode might have been repelling, yet Nabokov knows how to salvage "average reality" (which might otherwise begin "to rot and stink") by endowing it with a quaint contextual meaning.

One must note that the corresponding passage in the Russian original of the story does not display the same richness of alliteration. In fact, the acoustic games pertaining to the image of the tongue in the English version seem to compensate the English reader for the loss of alliterations and assonances that exist in several other places of the Russian original and are impossible to reproduce in translation, for instance the *t, m,* and *n* interplay in "*tomnogo tumana*" ("of the languorous mist") or the evocative multiple sound patterns in the description of trudging on an errand, "Kogda s porucheniem otca prishlos' peret' *K* Osipovym," of the roof of the pub, "Po mokroj kryshe traktira na kraju pustyrja," and of the smoke, "stlalsja otjazhelevishij ot syrosti sytyj sonnyj dym iz truby." The translation runs as follows: "there was that wet roof of some pub on the edge of a vacant lot, and the chimney smoke hugged the roof, creeping low, heavy with damp, sated with it, sleepy." It might be interesting to compare the effect of the two passages in terms of the Nabokovian synaesthesia, his *audition colorée,* yet that is beyond the scope of the present paper.

The effect of the "pointed little tool" is re-enacted by Grisha's reluctant visit to the dining room on his sister's errand. He knows that his father secretly hopes for his company at evening tea, yet, impatient to regain his isolation and having "other things on [his] mind," Grisha does not oblige. He swallows his momentary remorse like the mote from his teeth:

> With terrifying clarity, as if my soul were lit up by a noiseless explosion, I glimpsed a future recollection; it dawned on me that exactly as I recalled such images of the past as the way my dead mother had of making a weepy face and clutching her temples when mealtime squabbles became too loud, so one day I would have to recall, with merciless, irreparable sharpness, the hurt look of my father's shoulder as he leaned over that torn map, morose, wearing his warm indoor jacket powdered with ashes and dandruff; and all this mingled creatively with the recent vision of blue smoke clinging to dead leaves on a wet roof.

The sting of conscience, soothingly distanced by the time-shift that turns it into a proleptic flashback (a "future recollection") in which the images mingle to form a synaesthetic complex (the aesthetic, the anaesthetic and the synaesthetic are interconnected throughout Nabokov's work), produces an outburst of verse as soon as Grisha regains his room. He knows that his poem will "wither" by the time the next one is printed, yet that does not matter. The story ends on a rhapsodic note:

> at this moment I trust the ravishing promises of the still breathing, still revolving verse, my face is wet with tears, my heart is bursting with happiness, and I know that this happiness is the greatest thing existing on earth.

The ravishing promise of poetry asserts the young poet's power, his "gift." It is on such exquisite moments rather than on the volume of completed production that the self-esteem of Fyodor Godunov-Cherdyntsev is based in Nabokov's *The Gift.*

Why, then, do Grisha's poems remain "puerile" and "perishable"? Is it merely youth or lack of experience that accounts for his obsolete, patly poetic diction ("modern *bereg* reverting to *breg,* a farther 'shore,' *holod* to *hlad,* a more classic 'chill,' *veter* to *vetr,* a better Boreas")? Youth is no explanation: among the books that had at one time or another "done his heart good," one finds an exquisite

novel, *Le Bal du comte d'Orgel,* written by Raymond Radiguet a short time before his death at the age of twenty.

Fictional bibliographies of "real" works are usually very important in Nabokov. If among Grisha's favorite volumes there is a book that can refute a reductive explanation of his artistic failure, there is also a book that can offer a more specific diagnosis instead. This is *The Defense,* a novel by Sirin (Sirin is, of course, Nabokov's pre-war pen-name), which, among other things, describes another writer's tragedy. Ivan Luzhin, the father of the protagonist of *The Defense,* is a novelist who cannot write his swan-song book because he insists on excluding from it all the "purely personal, unbidden recollections, of no use to him—starvation, arrest, and so forth." For Luzhin such uncouth lumps as the Russian revolution are "an encroachment upon creative freedom" because "the general opinion [is] that [it] had influenced the course of every Russian's life; an author could not have his hero go through it without getting scorched, and to dodge it was impossible." The significance of any event is, of course, relative, and one cannot dodge anything that exerts a pressure. Yet dodging issues is precisely what old Luzhin wishes to do when unable to come to terms with the world's refusal to accommodate his sentimental humanism. His didactic "oleographic tales for youngsters" used to offer wish-fulfilling compensation for the inadequacy of his system of values, yet evasion must have made itself felt in the artificiality of his novellas. To adapt the words of another fictional writer, Mr. R. of Nabokov's *Transparent Things,* the excluded lump would still "remain recognizable by the shape of the hole left in the texture of the tale."

It may seem that, unlike old Luzhin, the hero of **"Torpid Smoke"** does not fail to confront his plight. He knows that he is trapped between the happiness that accompanies creative experience and the price that he has to pay for it in personal relationships. He knows that the price is the touch of cruelty without which he cannot attain the self-isolation indispensable to poetic experience and production. Yet though Grisha can honestly face the conflict between aesthetic pursuits and human commitments there seem to be other issues that he is unwilling to process.

Indeed, the "pointed little tool" that Grisha uses at the beginning of the story is a *safety* pin. In the Russian original the pin is first referred to as "anglijskaja bulavka" (literally, "an English pin," which is the Russian for "safety pin") and then as bulavka, "a pin." In the English version, however, the word "safety" is not dropped on the second occasion. The translation thus activizes an undercurrent of significance: Grisha's painful recognition of his callousness to his father, the prick of remorse that transforms diffuse poetic experience into energetic creation, is also a *safety device,* a defense mechanism that takes his attention away from another matter. The sliding door to the parlor where Grisha's sister is, as they now say, "fooling around" with her boyfriend is closed. When Grisha is examining his table after the door has opened and the sister has thrust her head through it for a moment, "the shiny safety pin [has] disappeared:" the situation threatens to get out of control.

The image of doors, closed, open or ajar, has a specific significance in Nabokov's fiction. In the poem *"Vliublyon-nost'"* ("The Being in Love") in *Look at the Harlequins!*, this image is explicitly related to mystical experience. "Being in love" is not wide-awake reality, just as "a moon-striped ceiling" is "not the same kind of reality as a ceiling by day": when one is in love it is as if "the hereafter stands slightly ajar in the dark."

In *King, Queen, Knave* Martha Dreyer violently slams the doors on the possibility of any relationship that is not strictly carnal; in **"Torpid Smoke"** it is Grisha's sister who must have propped the door between the parlor and his room by a chair, lest the doorleaves should "crawl apart." Grisha, however, seems to welcome the precaution. The presence of Gazdanov's *Evening at Claire's* among his favorite books brings in associations with the dream of love in which sweetness has a touch of decadence (as in "beloved decay" of **"Torpid Smoke"**), with love in which purity is strangely mingled with the tolerance of the sordid. The text of **"Torpid Smoke"** does not make it clear whether Grisha is suppressing his sexual urges or is still waiting to find his Claire (no pun intended), or is irritated by the somewhat shameless courtship behind the translucent door. This does not really matter. What does matter is that he will not confront some aspect of his predicament.

Another sort of trouble that Grisha does not wish to face seems to be a cultural dilemma. A poet has his own access to extraordinary experience ("the hereafter standing slightly ajar"): he need not depend on falling in love. Grisha's evening is spent in an unlit room where "every object" has "shifted slightly under the influence of the outdoor rays," and "the noise of a car would curl up like a wispy column to be capitaled by a honk at the crossing:" the synaesthetic transformation of the familiar sound, which groups it with the images of the smoking chimney and, perhaps, the sister's cigarettes, is an experience of the kind that in *Speak, Memory* Nabokov describes as "leakings and drafts" that come, implicitly, from another dimension. Yet poetic experience alone does not turn one into a poet. "Beauty is momentary in the mind," says Peter Quince in Wallace Stevens's poem, "but in the flesh it is immortal." The hero of **"Torpid Smoke"** does not manage to capture beauty in the flesh of the linguistic medium. His tongue (*lingua, yazyk*) is but a "solitary blind toiler." The presence of Hoffmann and Hölderlin on his shelf suggests that he may be moving away from immediate contact with the living Russian language.

While her boy friend's "smart beige cap" and the bouquet of roses may suggest what attracts Grisha's sister in a suitor to whom her father objects, Hoffmann and, especially, Hölderlin may suggest the attraction that German culture holds for Grisha. (The legitimacy of this analogy may be supported by Nabokov's placing Pasternak's *Life, My Sister* on Grisha's favourite shelf—the title of Pasternak's collection connotes not an *Ada*-like incestuous romance but a sibling-like parallel between the lyrical hero and his somewhat estranged life.) In order to preserve the authentic life of one's own literary language during a permanent stay in a foreign country, one is well advised not to read books in the language of that country—Nabokov's own

case is instructive: he avoided reading German books while in Germany but then read extensively in English before and after his arrival in America. Symptomatically, though most books on Grisha's shelf are twentieth century poetry and fiction, after the German authors there come only a volume of early nineteenth-century poetry (Baratynskii) and an obsolete Baedeker tourist guide to the no longer existing precataclysmic Russia. Grisha's language, the "solitary blind toiler," is facing a blind alley. The young man, however, does not acknowledge the danger of a dead end. This is the second unconscious evasion that can lead the young poet to artistic dishonesty and thus further deprive his poems of the breath of authentic life.

The evasion that might have threatened the integrity of Nabokov's work is, however, the one of which Grisha is not guilty. What Nabokov had to face is, basically, the problem of realism in exploring the conflict between aesthetic pursuits and human commitments. The heroes of his novels are placed into circumstances that facilitate decision making. They are spared those moral ambiguities that arise when the claims of personal relationships drain or subvert creative energy. Cincinnatus of *Invitation to a Beheading* can make his way towards "beings akin to him" because everyone in his "hastily assembled and painted world" has failed him, freeing him from human commitments. Fyodor of *The Gift* is also free to pursue his course: the people to whom he is wholeheartedly committed do not interfere with his writing. Yet Nabokov knew that not every artist was so fortunate. Artistic honesty demanded attention to the conflict between creativity and personal commitments in the case when the commitments impede the artist yet cannot be rejected as cavalierly as at the end of *Invitation to a Beheading*. In the design of *The Gift* there is no place for this theme. Therefore, (in words of the Foreword to *Mary*) Nabokov got rid of it, for a time at least, through **"Torpid Smoke."** That left him free to show the satisfactory balance between communication and isolation maintained by the protagonist of *The Gift*.

The story of (and in) **"Torpid Smoke"** may shed some light on similar cases in literary history: Conrad, for instance, could not complete *Under Western Eyes* without interrupting his work on that novel in order to write "The Secret Sharer"; Dostoevski had to interrupt the work on *Crime and Punishment* in order to dash off *The Gambler*. There were, of course, financial considerations in Dostoevski's case, yet it is significant how carefully, how almost completely, the theme of gambling is excluded from *Crime and Punishment*.

"Torpid Smoke" is a story about the possible human price of poetic inspiration. Implicitly, however, it is also a story about the channelling of creative energies. These energies are drained, to some extent, by personal commitments, yet they seem to be drained to a much greater extent by conscious or unconscious efforts to repress a clamorous unprocessed inner turmoil. (pp. 239-46)

Leona Toker, "Nabokov's 'Torpid Smoke'," in Studies in Twentieth Century Literature, *Vol. 12, No. 2, Spring, 1988, pp. 239-46.*

David Field   (essay date 1988)

[*In the following essay, Field assesses the commentary on "Signs and Symbols" and distinguishes the "referential mania" of the insane son in the story from Nabokov's intricately self-referential narrative techniques.*]

Vladimir Nabokov began his lectures on literature by claiming that "the real writer, the fellow who sends planets spinning and models a man asleep and eagerly tampers with the sleeper's rib, that kind of author has no given values at his disposal: he must create them himself." Like the God of creation, the artist faces an amorphous world and must impose form on it: "The material of this world may be real enough (as far as reality goes) but does not exist at all as an accepted entirety: it is chaos, and to this chaos the author says 'go!' allowing the world to flicker and to fuse. It is now recombined in its very atoms, not merely in its visible and superficial parts." Nabokov thus seems to acknowledge that artists are supreme egotists who vie with Jehovah's power to create a world.

But that god-like creative act involves a tremendous risk because the artist may merely possess the insane notion that he or she is God. Such delusions of grandeur lead to a false sense of creation, for insane artists lack the power to recombine the world "in its very atoms" and must settle instead for an order that distorts reality, an order that they discern in the "visible and superficial parts" of the world. And that false order inevitably replicates the insane artists' imaginations because the chaos merely reflects elements of their own minds.

There is, nevertheless, a point of tangency between the hubris of the artist and the delusions of the insane, and Nabokov repeatedly acknowledged his sympathy for highly personalized and eccentric imaginations. In a lecture he gave his classes at Cornell, for example, Nabokov lashed out at "commonsense" (one word) and praised those who break from shared reality:

> It is instructive to think that there is not a single person in this room, or for that matter in any room in the world, who, at some nicely chosen point in historical space-time would not be put to death there and then, here and now, by a commonsensical majority in righteous rage. The color of one's creed, neckties, eyes, thoughts, manners, speech, is sure to meet somewhere in time or space with a fatal objection from a mob that hates that particular tone. And the more brilliant, the more unusual the man, the nearer he is to the stake. *Stranger* always rhymes with *danger*. The meek prophet, the enchanter in his cave, the indignant artist, the nonconforming little schoolboy, all share in the same sacred danger. And this being so, let us bless them, let us bless the freak; for in the natural evolution of things, the ape would perhaps never have become man had not a freak appeared in the family. (*Lectures on Literature*)

Because such freakish, insane-appearing minds may reach more sacred insight than those who accept society's shared reality, the only "real" worlds are highly personal imaginative creations: "What I feel to be the real modern world is the world the artist creates, his own mirage, which becomes a new *mir* ('world' in Russian) by the very act of his shedding, as it were, the age he lives in" [Nabokov, *Strong Opinions*].

Nabokov's short story **"Signs and Symbols"** illustrates this complex relationship between imagination and insanity. The story concerns an emigré family—an elderly woman, her husband, and their son, who is "incurably deranged in his mind" and confined to a sanitarium. Herman Brink, the psychologist in the story, had analyzed the "system of [the boy's] delusions" in "an elaborate paper in a scientific monthly:" the boy suffers from "referential mania," a disease which causes him to see messages to himself in all his surroundings. When the parents take the boy a carefully chosen birthday present, a basket with jars of fruit jellies, they learn that he has attempted suicide again—the doctor called his previous attempt "a masterpiece of inventiveness; he would have succeeded, had not an envious fellow patient thought he was learning to fly—and stopped him. What he really wanted to do was to tear a hole in his world and escape." The parents fear another attempt. When they get home, they decide to bring him there and care for him themselves since the hospital does not sufficiently attend to his needs. Late that evening, as the parents grow more convinced that their decision is sound, the phone rings, and "a girl's dull little voice" asks for "Charlie." The phone rings again, and "the same toneless anxious young voice asked for Charlie." The man explains to the young girl the nature of her dialing error. The story ends with the phone ringing for the third time, but we never learn the nature of the call.

Criticism has focused on the way that the reader's attempt to decipher the story's own signs and symbols—especially the reader's quest to determine whether or not the third phone call reports the boy's suicide—duplicates the very nature of the boy's insanity. William Carroll says that in the story "a Nabokovian character's self-consciousness resembles, though in a distorted manner, our own self-consciousness as readers." He claims that "referential mania," the disease from which the insane boy suffers, "is a critical disease all readers of fiction suffer from." Like Carroll, David H. Richter finds that **"Signs and Symbols"** engages the sensitive reader in a plight similar to that of the main character: "through Nabokov's device of narrative entrapment we become collaborators not only in crime but in creation."

Larry R. Andrews carries such reasoning further and, after arguing for a reading in which he deciphers the story's ending to show how signs point to the boy's suicide, he unravels his own and all other interpretations to reduce the story to "a configuration of black marks on the page," an abstract aesthetic pattern, "the higher sphere of the artist's fictive world (in which we are characters too)." And Paul J. Rosenzweig insists that "Nabokov undercuts the traditional distances among the realities of author, reader, and text by forcing the reader to become both a character in and author of the text.

Standing in stark contrast to such reader-response critics is John V. Hagopian, who argues that "no legitimate artist produces randomness." For Hagopian, the signs and symbols in the story all point to the boy's suicide; the story cannot metamorphose with each reader's interpretation, and a careful and scrupulous reading can yield its meaning. An example of the signs that alert us to the impending tragedy occurs in the story when the couple comes home: "The underground train lost its life current between two stations," and then, when they've left the subway to walk the rest of the way home, they see "a tiny half-dead unfledged bird" which is "helplessly twitching in a puddle." Their plan to bring the boy home puts him, in a sense, "between two stations." His childhood drawing of "wonderful birds with human hands and feet" and his effort to fly when attempting suicide both associate him with the helpless bird. Hagopian uses such evidence to infer that the boy does, in fact, commit suicide and that the third phone call conveys the bad news from the hospital.

But even Hagopian must grapple with the issue of meaning that inheres in details, and he must express faith in the order of the world of art. The other critics, in fact, acknowledge the evidence that Hagopian presents but refuse to believe in his conclusions. Nevertheless, all the interpretations move from the question of whether or not the boy commits suicide to a consideration of the very foundation of knowledge: can anyone know anything definitely? Are there any principles for determining reality? Are we not in fact all insane as we try to make order of the world? Or, as Nabokov's former student Thomas Pynchon puts it, "life's single lesson" may be that "there is more accident to it than a man can ever admit to in a lifetime and stay sane."

Is the boy in **"Signs and Symbols"** merely a misunderstood artist, a combination of all the freaks a commonsensical mob might put to death—prophet, enchanter, schoolboy, artist? His first attempt at suicide is "a masterpiece of inventiveness" and his desire to fly into a transcendent world through somehow connecting himself to nature links him with romantic poets. His active imagination, like all creative fancy, colors what he sees and performs a major transformation when it observes nature. According to Dr. Brink's diagnosis, in "referential mania,"

> the patient imagines that everything happening around him is a veiled reference to his personality and existence. . . . Phenomenal nature shadows him wherever he goes. Clouds in the staring sky transmit to one another, by means of slow signs, incredibly detailed information regarding him. . . . Everything is a cipher and of everything he is the theme. Some of the spies are detached observers, such as glass surfaces and still pools; others, such as coats in store windows, are prejudiced witnesses, lynchers at heart. . . . He must be always on his guard and devote every minute and module of life to the decoding of the undulation of things.

As the reader-response critics have pointed out, the boy's quest resembles critical and poetic inquiry as well as insanity. Carol T. Williams extends the argument and calls Nabokov's technique "self-directed irony" because he is "a writer devoted to the 'decoding of the undulation of things.' " Even Nabokov speaks explicitly about the importance of imaginatively connecting himself to "phenom-

enal nature." In *Speak, Memory,* after recounting the origin of his first poem, he relates that writing the poem was "a phenomenon of orientation" and explains that all poetry involves the attempt "to express one's position in regard to the universe embraced by consciousness." He goes on to say that "[t]he arms of consciousness reach out and grope, and the longer they are the better. Tentacles, not wings, are Apollo's natural members." Like the boy, Nabokov sends out his imaginative tentacles to the universe, enveloping "reality" with his own consciousness.

This similarity with the boy in **"Signs and Symbols"** goes even further, for Nabokov, too, saw messages to himself in the clouds. In Chapter Ten of *Speak, Memory,* he recalls a "particular sunset" and describes it as a "prodigious ovation in terms of color and form": "There it lay in wait, a family of serene clouds in miniature, an accumulation of brilliant convolutions, anachronistic in their creaminess and extremely remote; remote but perfect in every detail; fantastically reduced but faultlessly shaped; my marvelous tomorrow ready to be delivered to me." This, then, is almost an exact analogue to "referential mania," in which "clouds in the staring sky transmit to one another, by means of slow signs, incredibly detailed information" regarding the boy.

But, as Nabokov's John Shade acknowledges in *Pale Fire,* "resemblances are the shadows of differences," and, despite the similarities, there are several key differences between Nabokov and the boy in **"Signs and Symbols."** First, Nabokov repeatedly calls for the importance of scrupulously exact observation of nature. He is scathing toward those who do not recognize the differences between butterflies, trees, birds, and other creatures in nature. In *Speak, Memory* he lambastes his governess for not recognizing the difference between the butterflies which she accidentally destroyed by sitting on them and the completely different ones with which she tried to replace the rare originals.

Nabokov's character Fyodor in *The Gift* goes even further in praising scrupulous observation. He condemns the Russian materialist Chernyshevski, whose simple-minded materialism becomes the brunt of Fyodor's sharpest criticism: according to Chernyshevski, "We see a tree; another man looks at the same object. We see by the reflection in his eyes that his image of the tree looks exactly the same as our tree. Thus we all see objects as they really exist." Fyodor's summary of Chernyshevski's false materialism stands as Nabokov's own analysis of the defects of abstract thought: "All this wild rubbish has its own private hilarious twist: the 'materialists' ' constant appeal to trees is especially amusing because they are all so badly acquainted with nature, particularly with trees." Fyodor goes on to point out the ways that "materialism" leads to abstraction:

> Look what a terrible abstraction resulted, in the final analysis, from "materialism"! Chernyshevski did not know the difference between a plow and the wooden *soha;* he confused beer with Madeira; he was unable to name a single wild flower except the wild rose; and it is characteristic that this deficiency of botanical knowledge was immediately made up by a "generalization" when

Nabokov the lepidopterist at work at Harvard's Museum of Comparative Zoology in the mid-1940s. Several butterflies and a moth have been named for him.

he maintained with the conviction of an ignoramus that "they [the flowers of the Siberian taiga] are all just the same as those which bloom all over Russia!"

Chernyshevski becomes especially relevant for **"Signs and Symbols"** because his son suffered from an intense form of this inability to deal with the material world and contracted a mental illness requiring that he enter a nursing home. The son "was afraid of space, or more exactly, he was afraid of slipping into a different dimension," a fear realized by the boy in **"Signs and Symbols,"** who wants to tear a hole in his world and escape.

Nabokov stands in stark contrast to his governess and Chernyshevski because, when he infers messages from nature, he precisely describes what he sees and refuses to reduce nature to a beautiful garden or a transcendental message board. He claims that he permanently damaged his eyesight by spending long hours examining butterflies' organs under the microscope at Harvard's Museum of Comparative Zoology. Even when he does detect messages in nature, he alludes to the importance of scrupulous observation. He describes one cloud-filled sunset in which he "could pick out brightly stained structural details of celes-

tial organisms, or glowing slits in dark banks, or flat, ethereal beaches that looked like mirages of desert islands" (*Speak, Memory*). This description at once contains his future as a lepidopterist and implies the importance of meticulous observation of nature, for he describes the cloud as if it were a microscope slide with carefully stained and prepared butterfly organs on it. Even "the mirages of desert islands," his created artistic worlds, contain a paean to a reality principle, referring, as we have seen, to the Russian word for "world."

In analyzing paintings of insects, moreover, Nabokov criticizes artists who do not carefully scrutinize the world they paint:

> One simple conclusion I have come to is that no matter how precise an Old Master's brush can be it cannot vie in artistic magic with some of the colored plates drawn by the illustrators of certain scientific works in the nineteenth century. An Old Master did not know that in different species the venation is different and never bothered to examine its structure. It is like painting a hand without knowing anything about its bones or indeed without suspecting it has any.

Certain impressionists cannot afford to wear glasses. Only myopia condones the blurry generalizations of ignorance. In high art and pure science detail is everything. (*Strong Opinions*)

He insists that "the artist should *know* the given world" (his emphasis) and claims that "[i]magination without knowledge leads no farther than the back yard of primitive art, the child's scrawl on the fence, and the crank's message in the market place" (*Strong Opinions*). Criticizing John James Audubon's portraits of butterflies, he asks, "Can anyone draw something he knows nothing about? Does there not exist a high ridge where the mountainside of 'scientific' knowledge joins the opposite slope of 'artistic' imagination?" (*Strong Opinions*). Mountains convey a different message to the boy in **"Signs and Symbols"** because he sees his own form in them: "great mountains of unbearable solidity and height sum up in terms of granite and groaning firs the ultimate truth of his being." To Nabokov, on the contrary, mountains are a perilous challenge, for he must balance along their narrow ridges.

A second factor differentiating him from the boy in **"Signs and Symbols"** is Nabokov's self-awareness of the role of imagination. The fact that he could write a story like **"Signs and Symbols"** reveals his keen recognition of the perversions to which intellect is subject. He claims that "being aware of being aware of being" separates humans from animals (*Strong Opinions*). This self-consciousness also applies to the imaginative perception of all reality: as long as he is aware of being aware, as long as he knows that his imagination is at work, Nabokov protects himself from taking the messages in the clouds too literally. In the lecture on commonsense, Nabokov says, "A madman is reluctant to look at himself in a mirror because the face he sees is not his own: his personality is beheaded; that of the artist is increased" (*Lectures on Literature*). A sane artist may risk insanity, but he can put the world back together in an ordered fashion: "Lunatics are lunatics just because they have thoroughly and recklessly dismembered a familiar world but have not the power—or have lost the power—to create a new one as harmonious as the old. The artist on the other hand disconnects what he chooses and while doing so he is aware that something in him is aware of the final result." The very act of undercutting "reality" and making his art self-conscious about its technique qualifies Nabokov's deciphering of the world's signs and symbols. According to all our information—however tentative that information may be—the boy sees literal messages to himself in nature. And we don't need to depend on the shadowy Herman Brink, because the parents have figured out the boy's problems for themselves.

Finally, Nabokov differs radically from the boy because his own quest for an imaginative order originates in his love for his family. The very imaginative act which connects him to the universe also connects him to others in a deep and significant way. He makes explicit the fact that his desire for order and meaning in a world beyond this one comes from love, from a desire to believe in a world where seemingly immortal feelings can endure. Nabokov once claimed that the vividness of his memories "is all a matter of love: the more you love a memory, the stronger and stranger it is" (*Strong Opinions*). He says that his au-

tobiography originated with his love for his wife, his parents, and his son. This love created his desire to explore the universe with his poetic tentacles:

> Whenever I start thinking of my love for a person, I am in the habit of immediately drawing radii from my love—from my heart, from the tender nucleus of a personal matter—to monstrously remote points of the universe. Something impels me to measure the consciousness of my love against such unimaginable and incalculable things as the behavior of nebulae (whose very remoteness seems a form of insanity), the dreadful pitfalls of eternity, the unknowledgeable beyond the unknown, the helplessness, the cold, the sickening involutions and interpenetrations of space and time. (*Speak, Memory*)

In other words, Nabokov's love connects him to his family and others, just as surely as the boy's self-absorption in **"Signs and Symbols"** isolates him from his parents: the boy's "dense tangle of logically interacting illusions" makes him "totally inaccessible to normal minds." Nabokov recognizes the danger inherent in his own connection—the "very remoteness" of those distant regions "seems a form of insanity," and there is something dreadful about this quest, which forces him to face pitfalls and a sickening unknown. The threat of illness—and of insanity—lies close to the heart of his endeavor. The boy in **"Signs and Symbols"** falls prey to this threat, cuts himself off from his family, and becomes almost entirely solipsistic; Nabokov uses his aesthetic to achieve communication—not just with an abstract and anonymous audience but with those he loves most.

In short, **"Signs and Symbols"** shows how artistic imagination can become distorted and turn to insanity, preventing any communication. It shows the necessity for the artistic imagination to include an attention to natural reality, a scrupulous concern for detail. It also shows the importance for an artist of a keen awareness of his or her own limitations—Nabokov recognizes that his own imagination could become distorted or ill, that insanity lurks just beneath the surface of his artistic achievement. Focusing on the boy's possible suicide is a false trail that has misled critics—we cannot know whether he commits suicide or not, but we *can* know that he is insane. As Carol T. Williams has recognized, the identity of the final caller "is irrelevant, for alive or dead, the young man cannot live in this world." The boy may resemble Nabokov, but he also differs from him in deep and significant ways. Finally, just as Nabokov is not the boy in **"Signs and Symbols,"** so we readers need not be that boy. We need not suffer from "referential mania" so long as we remain meticulous in our attention to detail, so long as we recognize the imaginative nature of the inferences we draw, so long as we respect the quirkiness and individuality of artists and their art. (pp. 285-93)

David Field, "Sacred Dangers: Nabokov's Distorted Reflection in 'Signs and Symbols'," in Studies in Short Fiction, *Vol. 25, No. 3, Summer, 1988, pp. 285-93.*

FURTHER READING

Bibliography

Juliar, Michael. *Vladimir Nabokov: A Descriptive Bibliography.* New York: Garland, 1986, 780 p.
    Describes various editions of books by Nabokov.

Schuman, Samuel. *Vladimir Nabokov: A Reference Guide.* Boston: G. K. Hall, 1979, 214 p.
    Bibliography of secondary sources.

Biography

Boyd, Brian. *Vladimir Nabokov: The American Years.* Princeton: Princeton University Press, 1991, 783 p.
    Biography with bibliographical references.

————. *Vladimir Nabokov: The Russian Years.* Princeton: Princeton University Press, 1990, 607 p.
    Biography with bibliographical references.

Field, Andrew. *VN: The Life and Art of Vladimir Nabokov.* New York: Crown, 1986, 417 p.
    Biography with bibliographical references.

Criticism

Dole, Carol M. "Innocent Trifles, or 'Signs and Symbols'." *Studies in Short Fiction* Vol. 24, No. 3 (Summer 1987): 303-5.
    Assesses some of the critical readings of "Signs and Symbols" and offers interpretations of the story's troubling final phone calls and enigmatic jelly jars.

Naumann, Marina Turkevich. *Blue Evenings in Berlin: Nabokov's Short Stories of the 1920s.* New York: New York University Press, 1978, 254 p.
    Analyzes Nabokov's early short stories.

Proffer, Carl, ed. *A Book of Things About Vladimir Nabokov.* Ann Arbor: Ardis, 1974, 305 p.
    Includes critical and bibliographical essays on Nabokov's short stories and novels; see the essay by William Carroll above.

Richter, David H. "Narrative Entrapment in *Pnin* and 'Signs and Symbols'." *Papers on Language and Literature* Vol. 20, No. 4 (Fall 1984): 418-30.
    Discusses the ways in which Nabokov "entices the reader into a special mode of decoding the text" that results in false conclusions and the "ironic victimization" of the reader.

Rivers, J. E., Nicols, Charles, eds. *Nabokov's Fifth Arc: Nabokov and Others on His Life's Work.* Austin: University of Texas Press, 1982, 317 p.
    Essays on Nabokov's short stories and novels; see the essays by Walter Evans and Larry Andrews above.

Tookey, Mary. "Nabokov's 'Signs and Symbols'." *The Explicator* 46, No. 2 (Winter 1988): 34-6.
    Briefly summarizes the arguments of Carroll, Hagopian, and Williams (see essays above) on the meaning of the "cipher" in "Signs and Symbols."

Zweig, Paul. Review of *A Russian Beauty, and Other Stories* by Vladimir Nabokov. *The New York Times Book Review* (29 April 1973): 21.
    Finds that this collection of early Nabokov short stories "makes no major contribution to the Nabokovian opus"; however, within "the frozen brilliance of the stories" there is a trace of what makes Nabokov "our official literary stylist."

Tillie Olsen

1913-

(Born Tillie Lerner) American short story writer, novelist, critic, and essayist.

INTRODUCTION

Olsen is best known for fiction in which she explores feminist, labor, and social issues. Employing wordplay and such narrative devices as interior monologue, she voices the concerns of the powerless and underprivileged: women, the working class, and the victims of poverty and racism. Olsen asserts: "What matters to me is the kind of soil *out* of which people have to grow, and the kind of climate around them; circumstances are the primary key and not the personal quest for identity. . . . I want to write what will help change that which is harmful for human beings in our time."

Olsen was born in Omaha, Nebraska, to parents who had been political activists in Russia and who emigrated to the United States after the failed revolution of 1905. An avid reader, Olsen discovered Rebecca Harding Davis's short novel *Life in the Iron Mills; or, The Korl Woman* (1861) at age fifteen and later wrote that this book inspired her to become a writer, reinforcing her belief that "literature can be made out of the lives of despised people." After leaving high school and going to work to supplement her family's income, Olsen became active in leftist politics, eventually joining the Young People's Socialist League and the Young Communist League. In 1931 she went to Kansas City, where she was arrested for encouraging packinghouse employees to unionize. After serving her sentence, during which she developed pleurisy and incipient tuberculosis, Olsen went to Minnesota to recover from her illness and began the novel *Yonnondio: From the Thirties.* In 1933 she moved to California, where she married and had several children. She remained politically active, publishing articles about the San Francisco Maritime Strike of 1934 and poems about the plight of the working class in such socialist periodicals as the *Partisan,* the *Waterfront Worker,* and the *Daily Worker.* Olsen consequently won acclaim and encouragement from such prominent social commentators as Lincoln Steffens. The *Partisan's* 1934 publication of the short story "The Iron Throat," which became the first chapter of *Yonnondio,* earned Olsen a contract with Random House, and she gained national attention when the publisher was unable to reach her because she had been jailed for participating in the strike. Olsen published very little fiction in the 1940s and 1950s, concentrating instead on her family. In 1954 she enrolled in a writing class at San Francisco State University and won a Stanford University Creative Writing Fellowship. Another grant enabled her to finish *Tell Me a Riddle,* which was published in 1961.

Olsen's short stories, noted for their powerful and empathetic treatment of estranged characters, examine the effect of environment on the individual. "Hey Sailor, What Ship?," the only story in *Tell Me a Riddle* with a male protagonist, chronicles a sailor's reunion with Lennie, an old friend whose life he once saved and who has begun to settle down and raise a family. Although Lennie and his family remain indebted to Whitey and welcome him into their home, Whitey, an alcoholic, remains ill at ease, unaccustomed to being part of a family. Characters from "Hey Sailor" reappear in "O Yes," a tale documenting the effects that religion, race, and socioeconomic status exert on a friendship. Using the antagonist's baptism as its pivotal scene, "O Yes" focuses on the emotional distance that develops between a black girl and her white friend as the two enter adolescence. The remaining tales in *Tell Me a Riddle,* "I Stand Here Ironing" and the title work, employ stream-of-consciousness techniques and delineate some of the emotional and psychological burdens of motherhood. In "I Stand Here Ironing," a mother tries to convince herself and her daughter's guidance counselor that despite the demands that work, sickness, and other children have made of her time and money she has done her best for her child. Nevertheless, the mother resigns herself to her failure and her daughter's fate: "So all that is in her will not bloom—but in how many does it? There is still enough left to live by. Only help her to know—help make it so there is cause for her to know—that she is more than this dress on the ironing board, helpless before the iron." "Tell Me a Riddle," for which Olsen won the 1961 O. Henry Award for best American short story, recounts the final months of Eva, an elderly Jewish woman modeled on Olsen's mother. Eva was a political activist who came to America after the Russian revolution and, burdened by the responsibilities of marriage and childrearing, resigned herself to a life of housework and poverty. At the end of her life, Eva reevaluates the opportunities and pleasure she has denied herself as a mother, wife, and caretaker. In the process, she begins to put her desires before her family's and redefines herself as a woman and a human being. Another short story, "Requa," also examines the relationship between mother and child, but from a child's perspective; "Requa" relates fourteen-year-old Stevie's attempts to deal with his mother's death. Critics have praised Olsen's experiments with language—she often substitutes nouns for verbs—and use of what Elaine Neil Orr has termed a "collage effect" of texts and countertexts that mirror the protagonist's feelings.

Because Olsen has written widely about working-class individuals who have been "silenced" by the demands of family life, political activism, and financial hardship—forces that hampered Olsen's own career—she is often affiliated with leftist and feminist writers. Nevertheless, Olsen has remained popular with mainstream audiences, and Richard M. Elman has attributed this to Olsen's ability to accurately depict universal dilemmas: "In writing which is individualized but not eccentric, experimental but not obscure, [Olsen] has created imagined experience which has the authenticity of autobiography or memoir. With a faultless accuracy, her stories treat the very young, the mature, the dying—poor people without the means to buy or invent lies about their situations—and yet her writing never succumbs to mere naturalism."

PRINCIPAL WORKS

SHORT FICTION

Tell Me a Riddle   1961

OTHER MAJOR WORKS

Yonnondio: From the Thirties   (novel)   1974
Silences   (essays)   1978

CRITICISM

Richard M. Elman   (essay date 1961)

[*In the following essay, Elman examines the themes and narrative style of* Tell Me a Riddle.]

Four stories make up this first book [*Tell Me a Riddle*] by a gifted, mature artist with an uncanny sense of compassion. Rarely, at least in recent years, has the literature of alienation been engaged in such devout service of the imagination. In writing which is individualized but not eccentric, experimental but not obscure, Mrs. Olsen has created imagined experience which has the authenticity of autobiography or memoir. With a faultless accuracy, her stories treat the very young, the mature, the dying—poor people without the means to buy or invent lies about their situations—and yet her writing never succumbs to mere naturalism.

Some critics will persist in finding analogies to Mrs. Olsen's work in the socially conscious literature of the thirties. They are there, if one wishes to be blind to everything else, but the truth is that Mrs. Olsen has been more daring. Sometimes she is able to compress within the space of a single sentence or a brief paragraph the peculiar density of a career, a lifetime, in the manner of lyric poetry. It follows that the poverty which she describes never strikes one as formulary or anachronistic, but as an image for contemporary experience. Although addicted to metaphorical language, she uses it flexibly and unselfconsciously to record, to analyze, and then to judge, fusing it with thought and feeling in such a way that the prose becomes the central intelligence of these dramas. "For forty-seven years they had been married," she begins the title story of her collection. "How deep the quarrel reached, no one could say—but only now when tending to the needs of others no longer shackled them together, the roots swelled up visible, split the earth between them, and the tearing shook even to the children, long since grown."

Some of these stories have their faults, but they are faults of enthusiasm. Occasionally the prose will get out of hand, or, in choosing to be on such intimate terms with her characters, Mrs. Olsen will descend to a literal-mindedness which is her humanity unrestrained. Even so, there are stories in this collection which are perfectly realized works of art.

The foremost of these is a dramatic monologue entitled **"I Stand Here Ironing,"** in which an unnamed and physically nondescript woman (a voice really), after a lifetime of deprivation, explains as she does the day's ironing the growth of her estrangement from her homely, first-born daughter. As she describes the early slights and disasters which brought such a relationship about, one has revealed the many human forms which loss can take. Mrs. Olsen's woman is burdened with exhaustion, a victim of a world in which all the panaceas have been discredited. To say that she seems ordinary or without stature indicates only the costume she may be wearing, for her suffering is made extraordinarily vivid and historic.

At one point she ·eflects:

> In this and other ways she leaves her seal, I say
> aloud. And startle at my saying it. What do I
> mean? What did I start to gather together, to try
> and make coherent. I was at the terrible growing
> years. War years. I do not remember them well.
> I was working, there were four smaller ones
> now. She had to help to be a mother, and house-
> keeper, and shopper. She had to set her seal.
> Mornings of crisis and near hysteria trying to get
> lunches packed, haircomb, coats and shoes
> found; everyone to school or child care on time,
> the baby ready for transportation. And always
> the paper scribbled on by a smaller one, the book
> looked at by Susan and mislaid, the homework
> not done. Running out to that huge school
> where she was one, she was lost, she was a drop;
> suffering over the unpreparedness, stammering
> and unsure in her classes. . . .

"I Stand Here Ironing" is a catalogue of the failure of intimacy; yet it forces us to understand precisely because it
is so intimate.

The other stories in this remarkable collection have equally remarkable titles. One is called **"Hey Sailor, What
Ship"**; another, tersely, **"O Yes."** The title story is Mrs.
Olsen's longest and most ambitious work. Although she
had explored the possibility of multiple consciousnesses
functioning within the same dramatic situation in the earlier **"Hey Sailor, What Ship,"** one feels that in the final
story she has actually fleshed two protagonists of equal
vigor, enmeshing them in a marriage which seems as real
and as permanent as any one will encounter in recent fiction. **"Tell Me A Riddle"** is a modern day *Ivan Illych*. The
death of Mrs. Olsen's heroine is the death of social consciousness itself, gruesome, alienated, and without consolation. In the death-struggle of this old activist and her
mate (with both continually pitting their dignities against
the other), Mrs. Olsen has envisaged a true tragedy of
human mortality. In the last grim acts of a social protest
which sprang from love, not cant, she puts it more eloquently than I can, in the words of the desolated old man
who has been left behind, when he says: "Aaah, children
. . . how we believed, how we belonged." (pp. 295-96)

> *Richard M. Elman, "The Many Forms Which
> Loss Can Take," in* The Commonweal, *Vol.
> LXXV, No. 11, December 8, 1961, pp. 295-96.*

William Van O'Connor   (essay date 1963)

[*O'Connor was a practitioner of New Criticism, an influential movement in American criticism which paralleled
a similar movement in England led by I. A. Richards,
William Empson, and T. S. Eliot. Although the various
New Critics did not subscribe to a uniform set of principles, all believed that a work of literature must be examined as an object in itself through close analysis of symbol, image, and metaphor. In the following essay,
O'Connor explores the themes of anguish and despair
and the skillful construction of the stories in* Tell Me a
Riddle.]

Tillie Olsen writes about anguish. One character thinks:

"It is a long baptism into the seas of humankind, my
daughter. Better immersion and in pain than to live untouched. Yet how will you sustain?"

In one story a soft-hearted sailor has lived a boisterous,
rowdy, hard-drinking life. His world is empty, meaningless and in an eerie flux of days and nights at sea, transient
acquaintanceships at bars and brothels when he is very
drunk. His only refuge is a man whose life he had once
saved, and the man's family. He has given the wife and
children presents and much needed money. They have all
loved him, and welcomed his visits. But now that he can
tolerate his anguish only by constant drinking, during
which he uses foul language and is an embarrassment before their friends, they are torn between devotion to him,
or to what he once was, and their own respectability. Not
being able to tolerate their disapproval, he leaves. Drunk-
en, he looks back from a hill at their house, an island of
light and warmth. The image blurs, and the house becomes impersonal and anonymous. One knows the sailor
will find release from his pain only in the bottle, and finally
in death.

An early scene in a second story presents a white girl in
her early teens at a Negro church meeting. The singing,
shouting, and strange rhythmic movements terrify her,
and she faints. She has been very friendly with a colored
girl her own age, having shared dolls, parties, and secrets.
But white girls, in white society, eventually go their own
paths, and, reluctantly, the girls give each other up. The
white girl discovers she is filled with shame and guilt, and
wants her mother to explain why there is so much misery
and unhappiness. The mother embraces her, at the same
time wondering where she herself would find that "place
of strength" and "the gloved and loving hands" waiting
"to support and understand."

In a third story, a mother, standing over her ironing
board, ponders the life of her nineteen year old daughter.
Someone, presumably a principal or counselor, has asked
the mother "to come in and talk with me about your
daughter." As she irons, she thinks back over the girl's
life. The daughter was born in the depression. The father,
unable to endure their poverty, leaves them. The mother
works, puts the child in a nursery, then sends her to live
with her husband's family. The mother remarries. There
is never enough money, and they move frequently. The
girl is not good in school, even though she tries hard. She
has no close friends. She is small and dark, and not at all
out-going. She does have one talent—she can be a sad-
eyed clown, able to hold an audience enthralled; but a lack
of money prevents the mother from helping her develop
the talent. Eventually, the girl gives up in despair. The
bomb becomes her symbol of frustration, and she justifies
her passive opposition to society on the grounds that
"we'll all be atom-dead" soon and nothing will matter.
The mother believes that despite poverty and suffering
there is "still enough to live by." But she does not know
how to convince her daughter.

The story about the sailor is **"Hey Sailor, What Ship?"**
The story about the white and colored children is **"O
Yes,"** and the one about the mother and daughter is **"I
Stand Here Ironing."** The three stories have anguish and

despair as the antagonists. The protagonists hope, but with no real confidence. There appears to be no margin on the far side of despair for the sailor to reach. The children in **"O Yes"** find that friendship dissolves under economic, racial and social pressures. And the mother merely hopes that she can communicate her own sense of the value of life, even of lives lived in desperate circumstances.

A fourth story, **"Tell Me a Riddle,"** is about a Jewish couple who have been married for forty-seven years. The husband wants to retire to his lodge's Haven. He longs to be near other people, and to be free from economic worry. His wife wants to remain in her own house and to be free from all entanglements except the basic quarrel she has with her husband. Her quarrel with him has roots in the dim past. They have had many children, and were always poor. She resented his going out at night to visit with his cronies. She also had literary interests, but the pressure of work made it impossible for her to pursue them. Instead of reading, she sewed and scrubbed. Now in their old age they fight. Sometimes he cajoles her, hoping to win a victory; but she ridicules him, and soon he is calling her unpleasant names. Each gets a perverse joy out of their struggle, although he would be agreeable to a truce. Their children find all this distressing and unavailingly introduce many rational arguments about why it is foolish for their parents to quarrel.

She becomes ill, and after repeated refusals to visit a doctor she is examined. An operation follows, and the family learns she has cancer. She has about one year to live. A round of visits with their children follows. The grandchildren are noisy, and she is constantly tired. One child says, "Tell me a riddle, Grammy"; and she replies, "I know no riddles, child." In pain, she watches the activities of her children changing diapers; grandchildren climbing trees, hiding in closets; observes people in the streets, listens to sounds, and remembers. She relives her life, as a child in Europe, the birth of her children, the quarreling with her husband, and much else. Sometimes she sweats, sometimes she retches.

In California, they sit together on benches at the beach, watching other people playing, and looking out to sea. A grandchild who is a nurse lovingly attends her. He, the husband, feels death pursuing them, and refuses to take his wife home. These are the last two paragraphs:

> That last day the agony was perpetual. Time after time it lifted her almost off the bed, so they had to fight to hold her down. He could not endure and left the room; wept as if there never would be tears enough.

> Jeannie came to comfort him. In her light voice she said: Granddaddy, Granddaddy, don't cry. She is not there, she promised me. On the last day, she said she would go back to when she first heard music, a little girl on the road of the village where she was born. She promised me. It is a wedding and they dance, while the flutes so joyous and vibrant tremble in the air. Leave her there, Granddaddy, it is all right. She promised me. Come back, come back and help her poor body to die.

"Tell Me a Riddle" is as full of anguish as *The Death of Ivan Ilytch.* It is also as serene, with the distance and calm of tragedy. Miss Olsen shows the human being's capacity to endure his own suffering, his own irrationality, and his own despair. Only creatures capable of a great and transforming idealism could turn such suffering into peaceful acceptance. They are defeated, but they are not routed. Subjected to enormous indignities, they remain dignified. **"Tell Me a Riddle"** exhibits once again the classic tragic stance, and does it magnificently.

Miss Olsen's stories are quite skillfully put together. On occasion, San Francisco seems to be the locale of a story, but generally the setting is not specifically identified. There is a city, the ocean, or a poor neighborhood, and it could be any city, either ocean, and almost any poor neighborhood. The stories push away from the individual and the unique, toward the world of Everyman.

The sailor is any lonesome human being who hopes against hope that he can be free from his wretchedness. The white child is any child discovering ineradicable evil. The mother is any mother who has failed, or believes she has failed, in rearing her child. The Jewish couple are a man and a woman facing death.

Miss Olsen's method is reminiscent of Wilder's in *Our Town,* Thomas' in *Under Milk Wood,* and Hardy's in *The Dynasts.* She names characters, but usually one finds out very little about them. Sometimes they are only a voice. Conversations are universal rather than particularized. The voice of the Jewish husband—"You have important business, Mrs. Inahurry? The President wants to consult with you?"—is other Jewish voices one has heard, first generation immigrant, mocking, with ages of patience and suffering back of them. The sailor's language is any sailor's language: "She don't hafta be jealous. I got money for her." The young colored girl adopts jive talk: "Couple cats from Franklin Jr. chirp in the choir. No harm or alarm." The lonely child in the convalescent home writes an anguished letter: "I am fine. How is the baby. If I write my letter nicely I will have a star." And "There never was a star."

Characters are rendered only as much as is necessary to place them in a certain kind of environment. The homes of the children in **"Tell Me a Riddle"** are not described. One does not know much about their husbands or wives. The voices come in over one another. One is married to a doctor, whom she quotes. Another can't bear to see her mother suffer. A third needs more money. They are people. They breathe, suffer, wonder.

The chronology or sequence of events in the stories is ordered not as these occurred, but as they impinge on a character's memory. As in Faulkner's *Absalom, Absalom!* or *The Sound and the Fury,* Miss Olsen's stories seem gradually to "discover" themselves for the reader. She does, however, give the reader more assistance than Faulkner does. She does not immerse him so deeply in the dark recesses where events are happening but have not as yet been explained. She sets a scene quickly, usually with a few sentences. Then the characters take over, talking, remembering, laughing or crying. Occasionally the author intrudes with a refrain, such as *"Hey Sailor, what ship?"* or a rhetorical commentary, such as *"So it is that she sits in the wind of the singing, among the thousand various faces of age."* But mostly the action belongs to the characters.

When Miss Olsen is at her best, as in **"Tell Me a Riddle,"** she is a writer of tremendous skill and power. Her productivity has been small, but she would not have to write a great deal more than she has to earn a place among the eminent writers of short stories. (pp. 21-5)

William Van O'Connor, "The Short Stories of Tillie Olsen," in Studies in Short Fiction, *Vol. I, No. 1, Fall, 1963, pp. 21-5.*

Elizabeth Fisher (essay date 1972)

[*Fisher is the editor of* Aphra, The Feminist Literary Magazine. *In the following excerpt, she offers a positive assessment of* Tell Me a Riddle, *maintaining that Olsen's best stories concern feminist issues.*]

[Tillie Olsen's **"Tell Me a Riddle"**] is her masterpiece. My first reading of it was one of those shattering discoveries, an experience that, at first, reminded me of coming on Henry Roth's *Call It Sleep,* because that book, too, had been "buried," had a strong emotional impact, and dealt with poor immigrant Jews. However, Olsen's work has neither the particularity nor the special faults of Roth's; it has such compression and such scope that the analogy made by a friend of mine—her first reading of *The Death of Ivan Ilyitch*—seems to me a better one. With this difference: Tillie Olsen is not only a great writer, she is a feminist artist. Till the very end, we do not even know the name of the old woman whose long dying is the framework on which **"Tell Me a Riddle"** evolves. She is the mother, the wife, the grandmother. Only in the last 3 pages do we learn that she is Eva. But in the magic weaving of past and present which goes from Olshana in pre-revolutionary Russia to death in a strange impersonal Los Angeles, what comes out most strongly is the disadvantaging of woman, the denial of intellect and aspiration, the utter thanklessness of the mother's role. Seven children are brought up, through the vicissitudes of a working-class life during the past fifty years, and make the successful climb into the middle classes, but at what a cost, what a cost. The young girl steeped in 19th-century idealism gives way to the exigencies of 20th-century American materialism. Always "don't read, put your book away," and she dies shutting out her husband, babbling of the great world of books and culture, philosophy and music of which she has had only the most fleeting glimpses in her practical everyday life:

"The children's needings; that grocer's face or this merchant's wife she had to beg credit from when credit was a disgrace; the scenery of the long blocks walked around when she could not pay; school coming, and the desperate going over the old to see what yet could be remade; the soups of meat bones begged 'for the dog' one winter. . . ."

About Olsen's men it might be said, as of the husband in Beckett's *Happy Days,* how can they help others when they can't even help themselves? Her women can, but it is never enough, never right, never whole.

"The love—the passion of tending—had risen with the need like a torrent; and like a torrent drowned and immolated all else. . . . Only the thin pulsing left that could not quiet suffering over lives one felt but could no longer hold nor help." People have drawn on her, feeding, demanding more, more, so that, at last, drained without replenishment, she says, no, enough.

"Never again to be forced to move to the rhythms of others. Being at last able to live within, and not to move to the rhythms of others." This is the refrain of the tired old woman, battered by too much life, but free at last on her own limited terms. "If they would but leave her in the air now stilled of clamor, in the reconciled solitude to journey to her self." Hunched in the closet, she hides from the hurly-burly of family, from her daughter's "spilling memories," unable to touch the baby, "warm flesh like this that had claims and nuzzled away all else and with lovely mouths devoured . . . the drawing into needing and being needed." And later, "at the back of the great city" where her husband had brought her "to the dwelling places of the cast-off old," as she makes for "the far ruffle of the sea . . . though she leaned against him, it was she who led." What images and what economy, what a world is here compressed!

"I Stand Here Ironing" is the story told by a mother of how, wanting to do the best for her daughter, she was so often forced to do the worst, and it is one that every parent can recognize. In tight, economical prose she tears us with the parental experience, how we listen, wrongly, to other people, or are just imprisoned by events we could not foresee—desertion, poverty, expanding families; it is also a hopeful story of how children survive, sometimes even making strength, or talent, out of the deprivations they've endured. Tillie Olsen's is an unsparing but tender vision in which love is [a] need that is rarely answered, a vision of communication on strange, imperfect levels, and, above all, of resilience, a belief that human beings are not passive, that there is more in them "than this dress on the ironing board, helpless before the iron."

The two other stories in this volume, strong and well worked, would be accounted great if someone else had written them; they fade only beside the raw strength of the first-named ones. **"Hey Sailor, What Ship?"** tells of an alcoholic seaman who cannot survive ashore and who yet seeks the warmth of a family; it tells also of the limitations and cruelties and affections of the family trying to hold on to an earlier time's hope and community.

In **"O Yes"** there is a marvelous evocation of the black religious experience: "The crucified Christ embroidered on the starched white curtain leaps in the wind of the sudden singing"; "You not used to hearing what people keeps inside, Carol"; and a depiction of the snob and class pressures that drive apart two 12-year-old girls, one black, one white. The white girl doesn't want to be oppressed by life; "Why is it like this and why do I have to care?" Her mother knows, but is helpless with her own unassuaged needs, as she answers, inside to herself, "Caring asks doing. It is a long baptism into the seas of humanity."

Olsen's women alternatively reject and demand the full intensity of life. They are conscious, terrifyingly frighteningly conscious, and it is this that makes their pain and ours. Mortality presses on them with an awful weight, the finiteness of the human animal as opposed to the infinitude of the human spirit, or even to the possibilities of the human being. *"Humankind one has to believe."* And we feel with Lennie, Eva's son, "for that in her which never lived (for that which in him might never live) . . . *good-bye Mother who taught me to mother myself."*

What is wonderful is that, engaged, feminist, Olsen's work is also utterly transcendent—a contradiction of the art-for-art's sake purists. Though the subject matter may be autobiographical the author is everywhere and nowhere; this is indeed writing that consumes all impediments; incandescent, it glows and it burns. Read the stories; they will not be forgotten. (pp. 472, 474)

> *Elizabeth Fisher, "The Passion of Tillie Olsen," in* The Nation, *New York, Vol. 214, No. 15, April 10, 1972, pp. 472, 474.*

Ellen Cronan Rose on Olsen's creative aesthetic:

"Come to writing," a favorite phrase of Tillie Olsen's, expresses her vitalistic conception of the creative process. It means the inarticulate finding words, the dumbly sensed becoming sensible, the incipient meaning finding form. For the writer, it is breaking silence. For the actor in an Olsen fiction, it is a moment of perceiving, of knowing that there is shape and direction in the ceaseless flow of what must be. . . .

It is her plea, and her pledge: that the unobserved should be perceived, that the fleeting should be fixed, that the inarticulate should come to writing.

> *Ellen Cronan Rose, in her "Limning: Or Why Tillie Writes," in* The Hollins Critic, *1976.*

Elenore Lester   (essay date 1975)

[*Lester is an American critic and educator. In the following excerpt, she examines the elements of Jewish-American history in "Tell Me a Riddle."*]

The women's movement, like all political movements, has brought together strange bedfellows. Thus Tillie Olsen, a writer out of the poetic vein of the 30s literature of social consciousness, has been bundled into a bin with such Pop feminist writers as Erica Jong, Iris Owens, Anne Roiphe, Lois Gould, et al.

From one point of view Olsen should be the writer-laureate of the feminist movement for her masterwork, **"Tell Me a Riddle,"** a novella about a dying Jewish immigrant woman, was wrested out of her thwarted talent after a lifetime spent raising four children while working out-side the home at menial jobs and participating in radical causes. She published her first book at 50.

On the other hand, it seems fitting that she should stand outside the publicity spotlight of the woman's movement. Although her work is centrally concerned with women's lives it isn't glibly satirical like that of the feminist comedians named above, nor does it explode with hysteria and madness like that of Sylvia Plath. Nor does Olsen deal with bohemian women, their lovers and their nervous breakdowns like Anaïs Nin, Doris Lessing, Jean Rhys or Joan Didion.

The essential difference is that Olsen is not psychiatrically oriented like all of the others. Her somber portrayals of poor mothers grows out of a Marxist-Depression view of the uncolorful "little people," who despite the fact that they were victims of capitalism, seem to have little in common with the lively "oppressed people" of the 60s and 70s. Her brooding characters and "sensitive" writing are unfashionable. But **"Tell Me a Riddle"** won the O. Henry award for the best story of the year when it was published in New World Writing in 1961 and it was followed by a slim collection of short stories under the title of the novella. The three additional pieces in the collection are fragile, poignant sketches, all written in the 50s before **"Tell Me a Riddle"** and are distinctive for the almost biological closeness Olsen brings to her characters, seeming to draw breath with them. (pp. 75-6)

Olsen started writing in a period when Jewishness was not "in"—not in literature, nor the academic world and least of all in radical politics. Jews, eager to "make it" quickly in American life, changed their names and if possible their demeanor and memories. Ironically, one branch of idealistic radical writers, intent on bridging the gap between their heritage and grass roots America, also worked at expurgating Jewishness. Thus the blandness and cultural vacuity of the native scene that horrified such indigenous American writers as Edgar Lee Masters, Sinclair Lewis and Sherwood Anderson, was embraced by some Jewish writers as a mask for themselves and their characters. The American writers sought out misfits (we would call them freaks) to show that there was heart and soul and suffering somewhere in the country, but a good many Jewish writers kept their abundant resources under wraps.

The advent of Jewish writers like Bellow and Malamud expressing a specifically Jewish consciousness tuned to 50s existentialism rather than 30s radicalism apparently had no impact on Olsen. When she picked up her pen after the long hiatus of motherhood, she went right back to her proletarian "little people" as if the Popular Front, World War II, post-Marxist existentialism, postwar affluence and the popularity of the Jew-as-outsider had never left those drab Party-line pawns in the ashcan of history.

Interestingly, in one of her first stories of the 50s, **"O Yes,"** about a mother and little girl who visit a Negro (that's the word they used then) Baptist church, strange anonymous forebears again make a ghostly appearance. The child, frightened by the frenzy of the service, asks her mother why those people screamed so much.

"Emotion, Helen thought of explaining, characteristic of

the religion of all oppressed people, yes your very own great grandparents—thought of saying. And discarded."

What religion? The word and its associations are taboo. The author would probably say it didn't matter—that's the point. What mattered was the oppression, the emotion. Okay Huguenot.

The years of silence had surely weakened Olsen's muscles. In the sketches she takes a tiny area and sticks close to her intimate experience. There are no proud displays of writing prowess as in *Yonnondio*, but within their limitations those sad mothers throb with the author's own pulse.

And then comes **"Tell Me a Riddle."** The author emerges as from behind a veil. Writing with a technical originality, authority and subtle strength she has never before displayed, she relates the story of a Jewish woman's life. It is as if that grandmother, sick of being thrust out of the picture for so long, has finally seized Olsen's hand and forced it to "put down what I say." The Nebraska-born writer suddenly shows a complete familiarity with Jewish immigrant speech patterns and culture. In the rhythms of Yiddishized English she traces the ailing old woman's last months, *shlepping* with her husband over the country, visiting their children, and winding up at a dreary California seaside resort populated by the obsolesced aged taking advantage of the out-of-season rates. Details of the children's lives are sparse, given in elliptical vignettes, snatches of conversations, as if caught by a passerby or through the old woman's malfunctioning hearing aid and exhausted consciousness. Yet it is enough to convey the flatness and grossness of suburban life with its bustle of child-rearing. At one point the battered old woman hides in the closet to get away from the din and feel of it—only to find a fellow refugee there, her young granddaughter.

As her body dwindles, devoured by cancer, the old woman's past and inner life shine through with increasing intensity and we discover her essence—hiding as it were, in back of the closet. Memories of a tormented motherhood in which she was torn by the demands of eight children in an impoverished home and tried to slake her intellectual-spiritual thirst on Chekhov mingle with those of a dedicated girlhood in Czarist Russia where she was at one time imprisoned for revolutionary activities.

The old woman gets on with her dying and we move more deeply into her bitterness at the devouring of her life and aspirations. Her husband, driven to distraction by her agony and his glimpses into the dark corners of her heart, tries to comfort himself and her with thoughts of their grandchildren "who had never hungered, who lived unravaged by disease in warm houses of many rooms, had all the school for which they cared, could walk on any street, stood a head taller than their grandparents, towered above—beautiful skins, straight backs, clear straightforward eyes. 'Yes you in Olshana, he said to the town of 60 years ago, they would be nobility to you.' Their dream had after all come true in ways undreamed.

> *"And are there no other children in the world?* he answered as if in her own harsh voice.

> *"And the flame of freedom, the light of knowledge?*

> *"And the drop, to spill no drop of blood?"*

It becomes clear that although the old man has long made his relatively comfortable compromise with life, the old woman's gnarled stubborn spirit has weighed and measured everything against their highest ideals. She sings snatches of revolutionary songs to the end while the old man watches her die—"and with her their youth of belief, out of which her bright betrayed words foamed."

Betrayed words. Here is the heart of the story and it is a big story fraught with the reverberations of a long complex history. The old couple exemplifies those Jews whose geographical move out of the *shtetl* was accompanied with a philosophical journey from passionate belief in God to a religious belief in an international socialist Utopia. For them, coming out of a terror-ridden world, freedom, knowledge and the brotherhood of mankind were palpable holy words, not rhetoric. And the betrayal of both the couple and the words remains one of the tragic facts of our times. The story has an irresistible emotional momentum, moving from the old woman's outward eccentricities to the glowing core of her being. By anchoring the large subject to a woman's experience, Olsen has kept it immediate, personal and plain, its "Jewish heart" closer to the tradition of the Yiddish writer than that of the Jewish-American writer. And yet it is as universal in its implications as the old woman herself could desire.

Betrayed words. Only a writer who had traumatically experienced the last decades of radical history could have written such a story—and then only when the welling up of pressures within her corresponded with the break-up of old radical lines. Beside the old woman today's radicals are pseudo-radicals, born tainted with original sin, using words with easy cynicism.

Unfortunately, much of the rhetoric of the women's movement has taken this form. Simple-minded discussions of women as an oppressed class serves as a kind of Pop Marxism to keep the media buzzing. And when Olsen is advanced as an example of a woman hobbled by the "sexist society," it becomes clear that many factors in a writer's development are being swept under the rug (how many promising male writers have been silenced?). In Olsen's case one is tempted to wonder whether her totally absorbing motherhood was a way out of a trap for her, enabling her to stay emotionally alive when her writer's imagination was checkmated by her ideology. The Jewish issue is only a clue.

In any case, there is a cause for rejoicing that a writer of Olsen's special background and gifts was there to celebrate the old woman—the crystallization of a familiar enough type to American Jews, yet evidently long invisible to Jewish writers.

"Yonnondio! Yonnondio!—unlimn'd they disappear"; writes Olsen, quoting Walt Whitman on a lost tribe. Thanks to her that old couple and all they stand for will not be lost. (pp. 77-9)

> *Elenore Lester, "The Riddle of Tillie Olsen," in Midstream, Vol. XXI, No. 1, January, 1975, pp. 75-9.*

Ellen Cronan Rose   (essay date 1976)

[*In the following excerpt, Rose analyzes Olsen's creative aesthetic and aims as a writer.*]

Tillie Olsen was born in Nebraska. . . . [In 1961], she published her first book, a slim volume of short stories called ***Tell Me A Riddle.*** In 1974 she finally published a novel—*Yonnondio*—she had begun in 1932 and abandoned in 1937. To women in "the movement" she is a major literary figure, not so much despite as because of the paucity of her publications.

Since 1971 . . . Olsen has been stumping the country, speaking about women who have been prevented by their sex from utilizing their creative talents. These are her words:

> In the twenty years I bore and reared my children, usually had to work on the job as well, the simplest circumstances for creation did not exist. When the youngest of our four was in school, the beginnings struggled toward endings. . . . Bliss of movement. A full extended family life; the world of my job; and the writing, which I was somehow able to carry around with me through work, through home. Time on the bus, even when I had to stand, was enough; the stolen moments at work, enough; the deep night hours for as long as I could stay awake, after the kids were in bed, after the household tasks were done, sometimes during. It is no accident that the first work I considered publishable began: "I stand here ironing." In such snatches of time I wrote what I did in those years, but there came a time when this triple life was no longer possible. The fifteen hours of daily realities became too much distraction for the writing.
>
> As for myself, who did not publish a book until I was 50, who raised children without household help or the help of the 'technological sublime' . . . who worked outside the house on everyday jobs as well. . . . The years when I should have been writing, my hands and being were at other (inescapable) tasks. . . . The habits of a lifetime when everything else had to come before writing are not easily broken, even when circumstances now often make it possible for the writing to be first; habits of years: response to others, distractibility, responsibility for daily matters, stay with you, mark you, become you. I speak of myself to bring here the sense of those others to whom this is in the process of happening (unnecessarily happening, for it need not, must not continue to be) and to remind us of those (I so nearly was one) who never come to writing at all. We cannot speak of women writers in our century without speaking also of the invisible; the also capable; the born to the wrong circumstances, the diminished, the excluded, the lost, the silenced. We who write are survivors, 'onlys.' One—out of twelve.

I heard Olsen speak these words to a class at Dartmouth College last year, and I observed their galvanic effect on the students—mostly women—who heard them. My first exposure to Tillie Olsen was to Olsen the feminist. It was with this preparation that I first read ***Tell Me A Riddle***

and *Yonnondio*. I was thus unprepared for their impact on me.

For in her books, Olsen is no politician, but an artist. Her fictions evoke, move, haunt. They did not seem, when I read them, to belong to any movement, to support any cause.

And so I returned to Olsen's words about the situation of the woman writer to see if there was something I had missed, something the women's movement had missed.

In "Silences: When Writers Don't Write," originally delivered as a talk to the Radcliffe Institute for Independent Study in 1963, Olsen asks, "What are creation's needs for full functioning?" The answer *women* have heard is an echo of Virginia Woolf's "£500 a year and a room of one's own"—independence, freedom, escape from the restriction of traditional feminine roles. This is the answer Olsen herself gives on the lecture circuit. But in this early Radcliffe speech, her question seems not so much political as aesthetic.

Wondering what keeps writers from writing, Olsen turns to what writers—*men* writers—have themselves said about their unnatural silences, not periods of gestation and renewal, but of drought, "unnatural thwarting of what struggles to come into being, but cannot." She points to Hardy's sense of lost "vision," to Hopkins, "poet's eye," curbed by a priestly vow to refrain from writing, to Rimbaud who, after long silence, finally on his deathbed "spoke again like a poet-visionary." She then turns to writers who wrote continuously, in an effort to understand what preserved them from the unnatural silences that foreshortened the creativity of Hardy, Hopkins, Rimbaud, Melville, and Kafka. She cites James's assertion that creation demands "a depth and continuity of attention," and notes that Rilke cut himself off from his family to live in attentive isolation so that there would be "no limit to vision." Over and over in these opening paragraphs of "Silences," Olsen identifies the act of creation with an act of the eye.

In order to create, the artist must see. Margaret Howth, in Rebecca Harding Davis's novel of that name, is the type of the artist for Olsen, "her eyes quicker to see than ours." And one of the special handicaps of the woman writer, confined traditionally to her proper sphere in the drawing room or the kitchen, is that she is restricted to what Olsen calls "trespass vision" of the world beyond that sphere. But although she echoes Charlotte Brontë's lament that women are denied "facilities for observation . . . a knowledge of the world," Olsen does not equate the reportorial with the creative eye. Vision is not photography. Olsen quotes, approvingly, Sarah Orne Jewett's advice to the young Willa Cather: "If you don't keep and mature your force. . . . what might be insight is only observation. You will write about life, but never life itself."

In Rebecca Harding Davis's *Life in the Iron Mills*, to which Olsen has added an appreciative biographical afterword, the distinction between vision and mere seeing is dramatized in the reactions of two viewers to the statue Hugh Wolfe has sculpted out of slag. The mill owner's son has brought a party of gentlemen to see the mill. On their way back to the carriage, they stumble on Hugh's statue, the crouching figure of a nude woman, with outstretched arms. Moved by its crude power, the gentlemen ask Hugh, "But what did you mean by it?" "She be hungry," he answers. The Doctor condescendingly instructs the unschooled sculptor: "Oh-h! But what a mistake you have made, my fine fellow! You have given no sign of starvation to the body. It is strong,—terribly strong." To the realist, a portrait of starvation must count every rib. But Mitchell, who is portrayed as the dilettante and aesthete, a stranger to the mill town and of a different cut than the doctor, foreman, and newspaperman who round out the party, "flash[es] a look of disgust" at the doctor: " 'May,' he broke out impatiently, 'are you blind? Look at that woman's face! It asks questions of God, and says, "I have a right to know." Good God, how hungry it is!' "

So Olsen's vision is, in a sense, trespass vision. It is "insight, not observation," the eye's invasion of outward detail to the meaning and shape within. It is this creative trespassing that Rebecca Davis commends in Margaret Howth, whose eyes are "quicker to see than ours, delicate or grand lines in the homeliest things." And it is precisely that quality in Rebecca Davis herself that makes her so significant to Tillie Olsen, who says of her that "the noting of reality was transformed into comprehension, Vision."

Tillie Olsen's edition of *Life in the Iron Mills*, published by the Feminist Press, is central to an understanding of what she means by the creative act. It may or may not be one of the lost masterpieces of American fiction. Olsen herself admits that it is "botched." But it fascinates her because it is a parable of creation, a portrait of the artist. And significantly, that artist is a sculptor.

One of the unsilent writers Olsen quotes in "Silences" is the articulate Thomas Mann, who spoke of the act of creation as "the will, the self-control to shape a sentence or follow out a hard train of thought. From the first rhythmical urge of the inward creative force towards the material, towards casting in shape and form, from that to the thought, the image, the word, the line." Vision is perceptive seeing, which sees beneath and within the outward details the essential shape of the meaning of the thing perceived. Doctor May saw only the anatomy of Hugh's statue; Mitchell saw through to the woman's soul.

Sculpting is cutting away the exterior surface to come to the shape within the block of marble. Hugh spends months "hewing and hacking with his blunt knife," compelled by "a fierce thirst for beauty,—to know it, to create it." His struggle is first to see the beauty within and then to give it form, Mann's urge towards the material and then casting it in shape and form.

Olsen writes of Davis's art in similarly sculptural words: "It may have taken her years to embody her vision. 'Hewing and hacking' " like Hugh. The first pages of *Life in the Iron Mills* are the narrator's injunction to the reader to "look deeper" into the sordid lives of the mill workers, to ask whether there is "nothing beneath" the squalor. This preamble concludes with the artless confession that "I can paint nothing of this" inner reality, "only give you the outside outlines." But the strength of the tale is in Davis's

ability to sculpt that inner reality, to dissolve the outside outlines and uncover the moral shape of her simple tale. For Olsen it is "a stunning insight . . . as transcendent as any written in her century."

Vision is not photography. Sculpting is not cameo carving. Rebecca Harding Davis excoriated the Brahmins she met on her trip north from her native Wheeling, West Virginia. Emerson and Bronson Alcott, she wrote in her journal, "thought they were guiding the real world, [but] they stood quite outside of it, and never would see it as it was. . . . their views gave you the same sense of unreality, of having been taken, as Hawthorne said, at too long a range." In other words, they imposed their vision of the world on the world of fact, pasted their carvings on the surface of things. Davis criticized them for ignoring the "back-bone of fact." To see the inner shape, you have at least to acknowledge the contour of the surface.

In her own tale of the down-trodden, *Yonnondio*, Olsen addresses the Brahmins of our day:

> And could you not make a cameo of this and pin it onto your aesthetic hearts? So sharp it is, so clear, so classic. The shattered dusk, the mountain of culm, the tipple; clean lines, bare beauty—and carved against them dwarfed by the vastness of night and the towering tipple, these black figures with bowed heads, waiting, waiting.

The aesthetic eye sees "at too long a range." It abstracts from surface detail a pleasing pattern. But the creative eye, the visionary eye, apprehends the surface in order to comprehend the inner shape which gives it meaning.

Thus by accreted detail, Olsen's definition of the creative act comes into focus. The artist stands, always, in relation to a world of fact. He can record it or he can transform it. In the one case, the standard by which he measures his achievement is fidelity to fact. In the other, his standards are formal. Between these extremes, Tillie Olsen places the creative act. Fidelity to fact, but essential fact. Form and pattern, but exposed, not imposed. (pp. 1-6)

When I began this study of Tillie Olsen, I was motivated by my sense that beneath the polemic about the predicament of the woman writer lay something like this more comprehensive aesthetic. What gave me this sense, or suspicion, was Olsen's fiction, which transcends her oratory. But before I turn to an appreciation of that fiction, I want to examine briefly the source of the disparity between Olsen's real aesthetic and her current feminist articulation of it.

Throughout her non-fiction writing, as we have seen, Olsen uses the metaphor of sculpture to define the creative act. To be a writer, one must "be able to come to, cleave to, find the form for one's own life comprehensions." But in an article published in *College English* in 1972, "Women Who Are Writers in Our Century: One Out of Twelve," Olsen uses this sculptural imagery to describe, not the artist, but the situation of women, who are "estranged from their own experience and unable to perceive its shape and authenticity," prevented by social and sexual circumscription from the essential act of self-definition and affirmation. The paradox of female reality, as Olsen understands it, is that immersion in life means loss of perspective, or vision.

The artist-visionary can supply that perspective, can "find the form" which constitutes the "shape and authenticity" of what Olsen calls "common female realities."

Thus in "One Out of Twelve" and on the lecture circuit, Tillie Olsen exhorts women artists to take women's lives as their subject matter, finding a therapeutic link between the situation of women in our society and the peculiar kind of discovery implicit in the aesthetic creation. Accordingly she feels "it is no accident that the first work I considered publishable began: 'I stand here ironing'."

It is possible to read the first of the four stories that comprise *Tell Me A Riddle* as an exemplum of Olsen's feminist aesthetic. The mother-narrator of **"I Stand Here Ironing"** looks back over a life where there has been no "time to remember, to sift, to weigh, to estimate, to total." Caught in the mesh of paid work, unpaid work, typing, darning, ironing, she has suffered, but never had time and leisure to perceive and shape, to understand, the passionate arc of motherhood. Helplessly she looks back over her memories of her daughter's childhood and concludes, "I will never total it all."

What Olsen does, in **"I Stand Here Ironing,"** is to perceive and give form to the meaning of her narrator's motherhood, that "total" which the mother has no time to sum. As every female reader I have spoken to attests, this story movingly succeeds in articulating what Olsen calls "common female realities."

It is also possible to fit the title story of the collection into the Procrustean feminist aesthetic Olsen propounds in "One Out of Twelve." "Tell me a riddle, Grammy. I know no riddles, child." But the grandfather "knew how to tickle, chuck, lift, toss, do tricks, tell secrets, make jokes, match riddle for riddle." Why? Clearly because during all the years when she "had had to manage," to contend with poverty, to raise five children, to preserve domestic order, he "never scraped a carrot or knew a dish towel sops." The man is free, the woman bound. Women cannot "riddle" or form the experience they are utterly immersed in.

But **"Tell Me A Riddle"** is far more than a feminist document. In it, Olsen riddles the inscrutable by perceiving the meaning beneath and within the old woman's life and death. But this service is not rendered solely to the grandmother, but to all the characters in the story, and to the reader as well. Lennie, her son, suffered "not alone for her who was dying, but for that in her which never lived (for that which in him might never live)." And keeping his vigil by the dying woman's bedside, the grandfather achieves an epiphany, which the reader shares:

> The cards fell from his fingers. Without warning, the bereavement and betrayal he had sheltered—compounded through the years—hidden even from himself—revealed itself,
>
> > uncoiled,
> > released,
> > *sprung*

and with it the monstrous shapes of what had actually happened in the century.

"Tell Me A Riddle" is a story about "common female realities," but it is also a story about "common *human* realities." We are all bound slaves, all immured in immanence, pawns of economic and political forces we cannot comprehend. Stepping from moment to moment, we do not see that we are pacing out the steps of a "dance, while the flutes so joyous and vibrant tremble in the air."

Olsen has made the mistake, in her recent oratory, of confusing the general human situation and the particular plight of women in our society. What she empathically knows because she is an artist she thinks she knows because she is a woman, that our greatest need is to "be able to come to, cleave to, find the form for [our] own life comprehensions." In her fiction, if not in her rhetoric, Olsen does not reserve that need to the female half of the race. (pp. 6-9)

Ellen Cronan Rose, "Limning: Or Why Tillie Writes," in The Hollins Critic, *Vol. XIII, No. 2, April, 1976, pp. 1-13.*

William Peden on the veracity of Olsen's fiction:

Olsen unblinkingly confronts the most universal problem of the artist—that of suggesting the meaning that underlies the appearance, of embodying the ultimate reality that exists beyond the actions and thoughts of her characters. And she creates these characters with a feeling and understanding so deep as to be often literally painful, with at times an almost miraculous rendering of the rhythms of thought and speech patterns, with expert economy, with effective counterpointing of past and present, with judicious use of traditional and innovative narrative methods and technical devices.

William Peden, in his The American Short Story: Continuity and Change, 1940-1975, *Houghton Mifflin, 1975.*

Joanne S. Frye   (essay date 1981)

[*In the following essay, Frye asserts that motherhood is presented in Olsen's "I Stand Here Ironing" as a metaphor for the individual's search for selfhood and as a literary experience.*]

Motherhood as literary metaphor has long been a cliché for the creative process: the artist gives birth to a work of art which takes on a life of its own. Motherhood as literary experience has only rarely existed at all, except as perceived by a resentful or adoring son who is working through his own identity in separation from the power of a nurturant and/or threatening past. The uniqueness of Tillie Olsen's **"I Stand Here Ironing"** lies in its fusion of motherhood as both metaphor and experience: it shows us motherhood bared, stripped of romantic distortion, and reinfused with the power of genuine metaphorical insight into the problems of selfhood in the modern world.

The story seems at first to be a simple meditation of a

mother reconstructing her daughter's past in an attempt to explain present behavior. In its pretense of silent dialogue with the school's guidance counselor—a mental occupation to accompany the physical occupation of ironing—it creates the impression of literal transcription of a mother's thought processes in the isolation of performing household tasks: "I stand here ironing, and what you asked me moves tormented back and forth with the iron." Indeed, this surface level provides the narrative thread for our insights into both Emily and her mother. The mother's first person narrative moves chronologically through a personal past which is gauged and anchored by occasional intrusions of the present: "I put the iron down"; "Ronnie is calling. He is wet and I change him"; "She is coming. She runs up the stairs two at a time with her light graceful step, and I know she is happy tonight. Whatever it was that occasioned your call did not happen today."

As we read the story, then, we are drawn through a knowledge of the present reality and into participation in the narrative process of reconstructing and visualizing the past. With the narrator, we construct an image of the mother's own development: her difficulties as a young mother alone with her daughter and barely surviving during the early years of the depression; her painful months of enforced separation from her daughter; her gradual and partial relaxation in response to a new husband and a new family as more children follow; her increasingly complex anxieties about her first child; and finally her sense of family equilibrium which surrounds but does not quite encompass the early memories of herself and Emily in the grips of survival needs. We construct, too, an image of the stressful growth of the daughter from infancy through a troubled, lonely childhood, an alienating relationship to schools and friends, and an unsettled adolescence—and finally into the present nineteen-year-old, who "needs help," as the counselor insists, but who has also found a strong inner resource in her talent for mime and in her own sense of self.

The story is very fundamentally structured through the mother's present selfhood. It is her reality with which we are centrally concerned, her perception of the process of individuation to which the story gives us access. Her concerns with sorting through Emily's past are her concerns with defining the patterns of her own motherhood and of the limitations on her capacity to care for and support the growth of another human being. As she rethinks the past, she frames her perceptions through such interjections as "I did not know then what I know now" and "What in me demanded that goodness in her?"—gauges taken from the present self to try to assess her own past behavior. But throughout, she is assessing the larger pattern of interaction between her own needs and constraints and her daughter's needs and constraints. When she defines the hostilities between Emily and her sister Susan—"that terrible balancing of hurts and needs"—she asserts her own recognition not only of an extreme sibling rivalry but also of the inevitable conflict in the separate self-definitions of parent and child. Gauging the hurts and needs of one human being against the hurts and needs of another: this is the pattern of parenthood. But more, it is the pattern of a responsible self living in relationship.

The story's immediate reality continually opens onto such larger patterns of human awareness. Ostensibly an answer to the school counselor, the mother's interior monologue becomes a meditation on human existence, on the interplay among external contingencies, individual needs, and individual responsibilities. The narrative structure creates a powerful sense of immediacy and an unfamiliar literary experience. But it also generates a unique capacity for metaphorical insight into the knowledge that each individual—like both the mother and the daughter—can act only from the context of immediate personal limitations but must nonetheless act through a sense of individual responsibility.

The narrator sets the context for this general concern by first defining the separateness of mother and daughter: "You think because I am her mother I have a key, or that in some way you could use me as a key? She has lived for nineteen years. There is all that life that has happened outside of me, beyond me." Almost defensively, she cites too the difficulties of finding time and being always—as mothers are—susceptible to interruption. But in identifying an even greater difficulty in the focus of her parental responsibility, she highlights the thematic concern with guilt and responsibility: "Or I will become engulfed with all I did or did not do, with what should have been and what cannot be helped." She is, in other words, setting out to assess her own responsibility, her own failure, and finally her need to reaffirm her own autonomy as a separate human being who cannot be defined solely through her parental role.

When she identifies the patterns of isolation and alienation between herself and her daughter, she is further probing the awareness of her own separateness and the implicit separation between any two selfhoods. The convalescent home to which she sent Emily as a child is premised on establishing an "invisible wall" between visiting parents and their children on the balconies above. But, in fact, that wall is only an extreme instance of an inevitable separateness, of all the life that is lived "outside of me, beyond me." Even in her memory of deeply caring conversations with her daughter, the mother can only claim to provide an occasional external eye, a person who can begin to narrate for the daughter the continuity of the daughter's own past and emergent selfhood but who must stand outside that selfhood separated by her own experiences and her own needs.

In Emily's concern with her physical appearance we can see, distilled, the limitations of a parent's capacity to foster a child's growth in selfhood and finally of the possibilities of any full bridging of human separateness. Emily insists on being told "over and over how beautiful she had been—and would be, I would tell her—and was now, to the seeing eye. But the seeing eyes were few or non-existent. Including mine." The particular poignancy in Emily's own circumstances and needs does not lessen the power of the general insight: a human being cannot rely on the perpetual presence of external seeing eyes to validate her own authenticity as a separate self. Emily, feeling her isolation, and Emily's mother, feeling helpless to overcome her daughter's painful alienation, together give us a powerful lens on the vulnerability to external perceptions of self-hood: "the unsureness, the having to be conscious of words before you speak, the constant caring—what are they thinking of me? . . . ." Consequently, Emily's achievement of external validation as a gifted performer of pantomime cannot be expected to overcome her isolation: "Now suddenly she was Somebody, and as imprisoned in her difference as she had been in anonymity." And in watching her daughter's moving performance, the mother herself had confronted a new consciousness of separateness as she lost her sense of recognition for her own daughter: "Was this Emily?"

One of the central defining premises for the working out of separate personal identity for both mother and daughter is the power of cultural circumstances. The narrative is laced with references to the depression, the war, the survival needs which dictate unsatisfactory child care arrangements and equally unsatisfactory work circumstances. Even the dictates of pediatric treatises on breast-feeding by the decree of the clock become a part of the general cultural pressure which operates to define and limit the power of individual choice. Over and over, we are told of the limitations on choice—"it was the only way"; "They persuaded me"—and verbs of necessity recur for descriptions of both the mother's and Emily's behavior. In the attempt at summing up, the mother concludes: "She kept too much in herself, her life was such she had to keep too much in herself. My wisdom came too late. She has much to her and probably little will come of it. She is a child of her age, of depression, of war, of fear."

In such statements as "my wisdom came too late," the story verges on becoming an analysis of parental guilt. But though the mother expresses frequent regret for her own past limitations and failings, she is not at all insisting on guilty self-laceration. Rather she is searching for an honest assessment of past behavior and its consequences and for an accurate understanding of the role of cultural necessity which nonetheless allows for individual responsibility. She recognizes that there are some questions "for which there is no answer" and some causal relationships which cannot be deciphered: "Why do I put that first? I do not even know if it matters, or if it explains anything." At the same time, she insists upon the power and significance of her own actions within those limiting circumstances: that, of course, is the premise for the whole narrative reconstruction of the past through the self-awareness founded in present knowledge.

This claim to her own self-validation remains primarily a general premise of the story rather than a specific claim at points within the narrative. Her actual absolution—to the extent that she is seeking absolution from parental guilt—does not come in the particular recognition of past success or failure. Rather it comes in the growing emphasis upon Emily's separateness and Emily's right to make her own imprint upon the world in which she lives. The narrative's first interruption by immediate maternal necessity—the crying of the younger brother with wet diapers—marks the beginning of a clearer resistance to the forces of external necessities through this acceptance of Emily's separate selfhood. As Ronnie says "Shoogily," the

family word for comfort which originated with Emily, the mother recognizes the impact of Emily's presence and personhood: "In this and other ways she leaves her seal." The narrative then moves quickly into the identification of Emily's own special talent in pantomime and the balancing of external necessity, parental responsibility, and the assumption of Emily's own ultimate self-responsibility: "You ought to do something about her with a gift like that—but without money or knowing how, what does one do? We have left it all to her, and the gift has as often eddied inside, clogged and clotted, as been used and growing." Consequently, the second interruption—in Emily's own return from school—reaches toward the story's tenuous resolution in relinquishing the claim to controlling her daughter's destiny; the mother returns to her private monologue/dialogue, thinking: "She is so lovely. Why did you want me to come in at all? Why were you so concerned? She will find her way."

The tension in Emily's personality—which has continually been defined as light and glimmering yet rigid and withheld—comes to a final focus in the self-mocking humor of her allusion to the most powerful cultural constraint on human behavior: nothing individual matters because "in a couple years we'll all be atom-dead." But Emily does not, in fact, succumb to that despairing view; rather she is asserting her own right to choice as she lightly claims her wish to sleep late in the morning. Though the mother feels more heavily the horror of this judgment, she feels its weight most clearly in relation to the complexity of individual personhood and responsibility: "because I have been dredging the past, and all that compounds a human being is so heavy and meaningful in me, I cannot endure it tonight." And when she goes on from her despairing inability to "total it all" to the story's conclusion, she recenters her thoughts on the tenuous balance between the powerful cultural constraints and the need to affirm the autonomy of the self in the face of those constraints: "Let her be. So all that is in her will not bloom—but in how many does it? There is still enough left to live by. Only help her to know—help make it so there is cause for her to know—that she is more than this dress on the ironing board, helpless before the iron."

Her efforts, then, "to gather together, to try and make coherent" are both inevitably doomed to failure and finally successful. There cannot be—either for parent or for story-teller—a final coherence, a final access to defined personality, or a full sense of individual control. There is only the enriched understanding of the separateness of all people—even parents from children—and the necessity to perceive and foster the value of each person's autonomous selfhood. Though that selfhood is always limited by the forces of external constraints, it is nonetheless defined and activated by the recognition of the "seal" each person sets on surrounding people and the acceptance of responsibility for one's own actions and capacities. At best, we can share in the efforts to resist the fatalism of life lived helplessly "before the iron"—never denying the power of the iron but never yielding to the iron in final helplessness either. We must trust the power of each to "find her way" even in the face of powerful external constraints on individual control.

The metaphor of the iron and the rhythm of the ironing establish a tightly coherent framework for the narrative probing of a mother-daughter relationship. But the fuller metaphorical structure of the story lies in the expansion of the metaphorical power of that relationship itself. Without ever relinquishing the immediate reality of motherhood and the probing of parental responsibility, Tillie Olsen has taken that reality and developed its peculiar complexity into a powerful and complex statement on the experience of responsible selfhood in the modern world. In doing so she has neither trivialized nor romanticized the experience of motherhood; she has indicated the wealth of experience yet to be explored in the narrative possibilities of experiences, like motherhood, which have rarely been granted serious literary consideration. (pp. 287-92)

> *Joanne S. Frye, "'I Stand Here Ironing':*
> *Motherhood as Experience and Metaphor," in*
> Studies in Short Fiction, *Vol. 18, No. 3, Summer, 1981, pp. 287-92.*

Helge Normann Nilsen   (essay date 1984)

[In the following essay, Nilsen studies the political components of "Tell Me a Riddle."]

Tillie Olsen is a Jewish-American author, née Lerner, whose novel *Yonnondio: From the Thirties,* was written in 1932-33, but not published until 1974. In her short-story collection **Tell Me a Riddle** (1961), the title novella is about a dying Jewish woman, Eva, who looks back on her Russian childhood and emigration to America. Feminist as well as Jewish, or ethnic aspects, play a large role in the narrative, but there is also a strand of political idealism in it which constitutes a basic message. Among other things, **"Tell Me a Riddle"** is a story offering a strongly felt ideological and social vision to its readers. William Van O'Connor speaks aptly of the story's theme as "the human being's capacity to endure his own suffering" and praises Eva's "great and transforming idealism." However, he makes no reference to the political content of the idealism.

The utopian vision, or conviction, belongs to Eva, the ailing grandmother, and it has been a hidden, but essential part of her entire existence. She is brought back to it in spite of the fact that circumstances have prevented her from devoting herself actively to the realization of her youthful ideals. During their long married life together, Eva and her husband David have grown apart in many ways, and their children have become American Jews, assimilated and with little or no awareness of the ideas and the faith which their parents had been committed to in their younger days. Tillie Olsen's parents, Samuel and Ida Lerner, took an active part in the events leading to the abortive revolution in Russia in 1905 and left for America shortly after. There are obvious parallels between them and the ageing couple of **"Tell Me a Riddle,"** and in this story Olsen has erected a monument to those East European immigrants who fought for a better life for mankind as a whole, whether in Russia or the United States.

For Eva, life has been a struggle carried out in the utmost loneliness because she has been unable to share her deepest

convictions with anyone. She refuses to relinquish them, however, and feels that they are parts of an essential self or identity which she now, when the children are grown, has the opportunity to cultivate. The tragic irony of the tale is that she becomes mortally ill just when she has finally decided to do as she wishes. But in her stubborn insistence upon preserving an identity which transcends that of the mother and housewife, she represents a different kind of female character in Jewish-American fiction. The contrast is obvious if one compares her either with the self-sacrificing mother figures in Bellow's novels or the domineering Sophie Portnoy, Philip Roth's house tyrant in *Portnoy's Complaint* (1969). It is not that she has been slack in the execution of her household duties, but that she feels an obligation to something beyond this sphere. She delights in the fact it is so much easier now, when she and her husband are alone, to keep the house clean. It is "no longer an enemy" with whom she has been engaged in "endless defeating battle."

Bellow's saintly mothers, whether they are Sarah Herzog or Rebecca March, can think of nothing but the welfare of their families, even to the last breath of life. But Eva begins her rebellion when she is close to death and confounds the expectations of her husband and children. She signals her attitude of protest by refusing to accept David's suggestion of moving to a home for the elderly, and she cannot bear to handle and caress her daughter's baby. But most significantly, she talks incoherently, but intelligibly, about the radical ideas of her youth as she goes through the last stages of her illness.

The story of Eva's life as a mother of seven strongly suggests that she has paid a price that is too high, that traditional motherhood is a burden that stunts the development of a woman's talents and faculties. It is a harrowing tale of insufferable toil and anxiety during many years of economic hardship, of "humiliations and terrors" and "soups of meat bones begged 'for-the-dog' one winter." For her, the woman, the responsibility for home and children has been a total one and has created an imperative need in her psyche: *"Never again to be forced to move to the rhythms of others."* This resolution, so eloquently expressed, contains an ideological as well as a personal dimension. She will now return to the ideas of her youth and express them freely, reminding herself and others of the existence of ideals that she thinks are of vital importance. She no longer hesitates to admit that life in America has had a damaging influence on the Jewish immigrants. Thinking about her cousins, who want to see her, she dismisses them contemptuously as "pushers" and "hypocrites." The struggle for success has exacted a heavy price from all of them, and now she goes back, in her mind, to her roots, her youth in Russia, indulging in "old-country curses," but also singing, faintly, "A Russian love song of fifty years ago." The old couple have their disagreements, but they are still united by a bond of love and intimacy. After one of their quarrels, they sleep in separate beds, but they both suffer from the separation, being used to "old harmonies and dependencies deep in their bodies." However, Eva never agrees to David's decision to sell their house and move into a cooperative for the aged. But even at this late stage of her life she is powerless to prevent the sale or resist her husband and their children's suggestion that she and he should visit their daughter Vivi in Ohio.

For Eva, love, at least in theory, is a concept that goes beyond the personal and the familial; it has to be a part of a larger tradition or commitment. She reaffirms, however belatedly, that the meaning of love is ultimately a social one, that a common solidarity must unite all people, of both sexes and all ages. She herself, and women in particular, live *for* people instead of *with* them, as she points out to Vivi. In her she sees the same mistake repeated, the "lovely drunkenness" of motherhood which is not enough to make up for its curtailment of personal and intellectual growth. Her other daughter, Hanna, is another example, busy with her sons and with no time for herself.

Eva also rejects the Jewish heritage as it manifests itself in hospital visits by a rabbi and Hanna's lighting of Sabbath candles. Openly expressing the radical, Marxist-inspired convictions of her youth, she challenges what she regards as ethnic tribalisms and religious superstitions. When told that she is on the "Jewish list" of the hospital, she demands to be registered as "race, human; Religion, none." Eva is a universalist, a person who remains convinced that the human race can still become united by means of a set of rational and humanist values. "She is suggesting the failure of society, its lack of human understanding and caring for its fellow members—lack of understanding not just between individuals and families, but between different factions within a country and between countries and races as well." At the same time, it is clear that Eva herself has been the victim of a conflict between the demands of a revolutionary concept of love, which concerns mankind as a whole, and the love of husband and children that she has actually devoted her life to. She rejects the Jewish religion, but the Jewish code of ethics has lived on within her.

David tries to excuse Hanna and suggests that the lighting of the candles is a harmless custom. He has adapted himself to traditions which he does not seem to believe in any more than his wife. But she revives the views of their youth, passionately denouncing the old religion: "Superstition! From our ancestors, savages, afraid of the dark, of themselves: mumbo words and magic lights to scare away ghosts." For Eva, the view of religion as opium for the masses still holds good. Her experience as a mother in times of hardship has provided her with additional, tangible reasons for abandoning religion altogether. In the past ages, while children went hungry, candles were bought instead of bread, she argues, and goes on to attack the oppression of women that is also part of the scriptural view of the female role: "Religion that stifled and said: in Paradise, woman, you will be the footstool of your husband, and in life—poor chosen Jew—ground under, despised, trembling in cellars. And cremated. And cremated." As she sees it, their religion has mainly been an instrument of the destruction of the Jews themselves, and she refers both to the pogroms of the past and the recent Nazi holocaust. The Jewish religion and heritage may survive because they serve a need which seems to be ineradicable, but the point of the story is that someone like Eva, with her background and experience, has mainly been a victim

of this tradition. Her criticism of the religious heritage is entirely valid for her and points to essential limitations that have characterized it.

With gentle irony, David asks his wife if she thinks that she is "still an orator of the 1905 revolution." As far as Eva is concerned, the answer is yes, but he has lost faith in any idea or program which extends beyond the bonds of family and friends. Paradoxically, it is the woman, the housewife, who now, in her final stand, insists upon wider duties and responsibilities and feels an urgent need to draw attention to them as she observes her daughters making the same mistakes which the revolution wanted to prevent. Hanna gives her sons "superstition," and thus reason and progress are neglected.

Eva's faith is not defined in narrow terms, it is a general belief in the power of knowledge and education to transform the world. It has elements in common with Wells or Shaw as well as Marx or Bakunin. The essential thing is to work for the emancipation of mankind, to "learn what humanizes" and "smash all ghettos that divide us." The underlying assumption is a belief in the power of scientific knowledge and rational argument to improve and redeem the human race and unite it in convictions and pursuits that are commonly agreed upon. Ultimately, the survival of mankind will depend on the success or failure of the power of reason. Such is the conviction of Eva, passionately resurrected at the end of her life and amidst children who do not realize what she is trying to tell them and a husband who is made to realize how little he has known her.

There is no doubt about Eva's conviction or sincerity, but the circumstances of her life and death and the gap between the ideal and the real is a contrast, both tragic and ironic, to her message. In a century which has seen human cruelty perpetrated on an unprecedented scale, it seems naive to hold on to a nineteenth-century faith in progress. The ironic view is not only applied to the historic facts of our age, but also to Eva as a narrator. A certain distance is established between her and the implied author. There is very little in the text to support Eva's basically optimistic beliefs except her own fervour, and in David's gently ironic chiding of his dying wife, the implied author seems to speak. The poor woman's broken sentences and reminiscences express the pathos and convey the tender admiration in the story of a dead generation's naïve faith. This knowledge of a human frailty which limits and seems to defy any attempt to improve mankind links the work of Olsen to that of other Jewish-American writers, for example, Bellow. However, Eva herself is more credible as a humanist and idealist than a schlemiel figure like Moses Herzog, whose understanding of the need for love among men is purely theoretical.

Eva's vision of a better future for man not only derives from political tenets, but also includes elements of an older radicalism which may derive from American transcendentalism, the teachings of Emerson and Whitman. Her refusal to hold Vivi's baby is regarded as something unnatural by her daughter, and of this she is aware. But she has become seized by the urgency of other needs and preoccupations, a feeling that life must have more to offer than motherhood and family duties. There are "springs" in her that seek an outlet, "an older power that beat for life. Somewhere coherence, transport, meaning." What she craves is a "journey to her self." This does not only refer to the need for privacy. The self is the deeper reality, that aspect of her which is part of a larger, cosmic design. The wording of the text suggests parallels with the transcendentalist view of the universe as an organic whole created and upheld by a spiritual principle or being. There is no contradiction between such a world view and the rejection of established religion. Transcendentalism is radical in its insistence on self-reliance and individualism in matters of the spirit and of belief. Tillie Olsen's interest in Whitman is demonstrated in her novel *Yonnondio,* where lines from Whitman's poem, thus entitled, are quoted.

Eva's refusal to caress the baby is a symbolic gesture of defiance of the traditional sex roles that both she and her daughters have submitted to. She recognizes the force of the nurturing instinct in women, but she describes it negatively, as "the long drunkenness; the drowning into needing and being needed." She is no longer content to play the woman's role, now as a grandmother who is expected to take an active interest in her grandchildren's performances and activities. They want her to tell riddles, but she does not know any. The strength of her aversion towards the role of childminder is reflected in the fact that the story title derives from this request for riddles. In contrast, David croons over his daughter's baby and has plenty of time for him. The point is that he has never been overburdened with the raising of children and finds it easy to play the role of the affectionate granddaddy.

For Eva, the memory of the revolutionary period in Russia becomes increasingly significant, and she feels that the other Jews and their offspring have forgotten the lesson that was taught at that time. Vivi, for example, indulges in tearful recollections of her childhood which are devoid of any real historical awareness of the conditions the family had suffered from. Eva and David depart for California, and here they meet another old couple, Max and Rose, and their Russian background is referred to in a conversation about *"hunger; secret meetings; human rights; spies; betrayals; prison; escape."* But these are now "strange words" on the lips of people who have become oblivious of their real meaning and continued relevance. Their main interest is to live up to the American ideal of material success for themselves and their children. But Eva recalls that the revolution in Russia was fought for aims that are not limited to the material sphere, and she takes notice of a grandchild who much prefers watching television to hearing about the old days. Another such, a girl who drives her and David home, is proudly described by Max as "an American queen." The immigrant Jews' pride in their children's successful Americanization is evident in an early novel like *The Rise of David Levinsky* (1917), by Abraham Cahan, but in **"Tell Me a Riddle"** there is a highly critical perspective upon the development of the second and third generation of Jews in America.

The criticism is directed at the materialism and the betrayal of the old ideals. But Eva also laments the waste and neglect of human potential that she now observes more keenly in the modern, well-fed generation. The meaning of progress means above all personal growth, the full employment of talents and faculties which was the very meaning of the radical movement. But what she sees is "Everywhere unused the life," and she asks rhetorically if the idea of centuries of human life is not "to grow." This emphasis on the value and possibility of development and growth is endemic both in the radicals' belief in progress and the transcendentalist notion of a divine spark that is present in each soul and waits to be kindled. These ideas come to Eva when she and David visit the elderly Mrs. Mays, an acquaintance of Eva's who lives in a miserable room with only the pictures of her children to cheer her up. The young are careless and superficial, the old are cast off, abandoned to poverty, and Eva is stricken by fear for the future of a humanity that seems to have lost all moral and progressive guidelines. She seizes her husband's hand and utters her fearful question whether mankind is going to destroy itself. But his face reveals only his pity for her, and at this moment she realizes that she is dying, that it is her own end, or destruction, which is approaching. However, this knowledge only strengthens her sense of commitment to the values she was inspired by in her youth.

Jeannie, the granddaughter who nurses Eva during her last days, represents a suggestion, slight but discernible, that someone may be able to break out of the stultifying routines of American life. She plans to leave her job as a nurse because she realizes that she is unable to maintain the detachment that is required in this profession. She permits herself to feel the suffering that she witnesses, and this ability to empathize is related to Eva's insistence on solidarity and social responsibility. She thinks of enrolling in an art school, an indication that she intends to develop and grow. She is the only person in the story who seems to be willing to accept and understand Eva on her own terms, and the latter compares her to Lisa, a young woman whom Eva had admired in her youth. Lisa had been a martyr, a noble and courageous soul who was killed by the tsar's soldiers. She had been a follower of Tolstoy, the religious radical and idealist, and for her, life and knowledge had been "holy." The values that Eva is trying to express derive from various sources, Russian as well as American and European, but all her prophets share the view of human life as something infinitely precious and always capable of growth and change. She also recalls having found this attitude in a book which she once read and quotes this line from Chekhov's story *Three Years* (1895): "life may be hated or wearied of, but never despised." But she also feels lonely in a world where no one seems to share her convictions. Throughout the story she repeats her desire to go home several times, but finally she asks in exasperation: "Where *is* my home?" She is aware that David has sold their house, but her exclamation expresses an even deeper kind of alienation. In relation to Eva and her ideas, the strangeness of the Californian environment becomes a metaphor of the whole modern world. She refuses to enter the hospital, as the doctor and David suggest. The love that still exists between her and David is the only fragment left of the old values she has believed in, as she sees it, and she accuses him of being a traitor and coward who wants to run from their mutual commitment by leaving her in the hospital. Their children pay their last visits to the dying Eva, and now they begin to realize something of the hidden dimension in her that now is emerging. Clara, the eldest, hears her mother singing, brokenly, a song from her youth, and it dawns upon the daughter that she has never really known her mother. Lennie, the son, also perceives that something important, an unused capacity, is dying along with his mother and that he, too, has missed something because it was not possible for her to raise her children according to her ideals. Still, she has succeeded in instilling a certain independence in him: *"good-bye Mother who taught me to mother myself."*

Eva's devotion to the beliefs of her youth finds its climax in her quotations from a poem by Hugo. Here, a utopian vision of life in the twentieth century is presented, a promise that a new and lofty race shall arise and fulfil the dream of an ideal mankind. David remarks ironically that Hugo should be grateful for not having lived long enough to see how his twentieth century turned out to be. Obviously, the hopes of Hugo have turned out to be illusions, but Eva, who is now only partly conscious, continues to quote from the poem that had promised a glorious fate for mankind in this century. When contemplating his healthy American grandchildren, David can hear his wife's voice within him, asking if there are not other children in the world who, it is suggested, are less fortunate. She is his last link with "their youth of belief," and he begins to perceive the beauty of her idealism. He is also, unwillingly, reminded of the fact that he once had shared the same hopes for mankind and that he also has felt betrayed and bereaved because of the cruel disillusionments of the twentieth century. He has hidden these feelings even from himself, but his wife's suffering and reawakened devotion force him to a new insight into his own disappointment and how much of a loss it has been, also for him, to give up the beliefs of the past.

Hugo's words have become "stained" by history, but on Eva's lips they emerge "stainless." The idealism itself is always pure and perfect, even though it never corresponds with reality. David is struck by the wonder of what he observes, a woman dying in agony who reveals a simple and total faith in the idea of human progress and perfectibility. He thinks of the world of their youth and its many horrors and recalls, nostalgically, their capacity for belief in the midst of "filth, treachery, degradation." He is even carried away, just like Eva, by this memory and wants to recapture his own enthusiasm and bring the old message to the people in modern America. But he brings himself back to reality with his customary irony and gently accuses Eva of having momentarily deprived him of his senses.

At the end of the story, the social or political aspect recedes into the background, and Eva and David are brought together again, to the extent that one can speak of such a thing in these circumstances. Eva now utters words that relate to her childhood, and David accompanies her, as it were, back to the time when they met and fell in love. He finally falls asleep next to her, holding her hand, a gesture suggesting that their differences, however real, have not destroyed their love. Thus this story of suf-

fering ends on a note of reconciliation and peace. According to Jeannie, Eva's spirit has now gone back to her childhood, to the moment when she first heard music, watching a village wedding. Marriage, Tillie Olsen seems to say, is a valuable institution, the place where love lives long and survives in spite of everything. The political theme is a very important aspect of the narrative, but it does not dominate in the sense of constituting the last word of the story. Above all, the story conveys a sense of wonder, as well as of a certain piety, in the face of the strength and endurance of the idealism of the older generation. In the early part of the century, this idealism and these hopes shone brightly in all their glory, and it still survives here and there, as in the story of Eva. Olsen's nostalgic, gently ironic attitude to the visions of the past emerges eloquently in the dedication that is placed at the end of the narrative: "For two of that generation, Seevya and Genya. Infinite, dauntless, incorruptible. Death deepens the wonder." (pp. 163-69)

Helge Normann Nilsen, "Tillie Olsen's 'Tell Me a Riddle': The Political Theme," in Études Anglaises, *Vol. XXXVII, No. 2, April-June, 1984, pp. 163-69.*

Rose Kamel (essay date 1985)

[*In the following excerpt, Kamel observes that Olsen, like her literary predecessor Rebecca Harding Davis, writes about minorities, particularly women, whose potential for creativity, growth, and opportunity has been denied them due to their race, sex, religion, and socioeconomic status.*]

In 1954 . . . Olsen published the brilliant short story **"I Stand Here Ironing,"** having served a prolonged apprenticeship during which "there was a conscious storing, snatched reading, beginnings of writing" and always "the secret rootlets of reconnaisance." This reconnaisance involved not only obsessive reading but internalizing the lives of women writers, especially writers who were also mothers.

> Their emergence is evidence of changing circumstances making possible for them what (with rarest exception) was not possible in the generations of women before. I hope and I fear for what will result. I hope (and believe) that complex new richness will come into literature; I fear because almost certainly their work will be impeded, lessened, partial. For the fundamental situation remains unchanged. Unlike men writers who marry, most will not have the societal equivalent of a wife—nor (in a society hostile to growing life) anyone but themselves to mother their children.

Nowhere is Olsen's reading of another woman writer, her identification with this writer's concerns so elegiac, as in *Silences'* reprinting of Olsen's postscript to Rebecca Harding Davis' *Life in the Iron Mills,* a postscript longer than Harding's poignant novella. This postscript almost seamlessly blends critical analysis with self-scrutiny.

In particular, two patterns in Davis' life story parallel

Olsen's. The first is an awareness of working class hardship. . . .

The second was Davis' frustration as a woman. (p. 56)

Painstakingly, Olsen follows the twists and turns of her literary foremother's life. Feted by the transcendentalist pundits at Concord, Massachusetts, Davis found their ideals false to reality. Unmarried until the age of thirty-one, she was the object of pity, curiosity, sometimes scorn. When she finally married . . . , Davis discovered that wife-motherhood drained her of time and energy to write, even though she continued to do so. From her husband and literary critics she received little encouragement or recognition. At the age of seventy-nine she died in relative obscurity.

Davis' voice permeates at least two recurring themes in Olsen's autobiographical fiction: The tyranny of class struggle eroding the bodies and minds of workers and the children of workers; household drudgery and child care undermining a woman writer's creativity. But another still small voice, Olsen's own, is heard in her depiction of *Jewish* mothers and daughters struggling for selfhood in the promised land and of Jewish immigrant experience shored up in secular humanism. Characteristically, Olsen justifies her autobiographical focus by citing yet another woman writer, Ntozake Shange: "When women do begin to write . . . we write autobiography. So autobiographically in fact that it's very hard to find any sense of any other reality."

When still a young writer in the 1930s, having assimilated Davis as foremother, and long before she ever heard of Shange, Tillie Olsen wrote *Yonnondio,* a clumsy yet powerful depiction of a working class family driven from a rural village to a hog-slaughtering factory in the midwest where all succumb to grinding poverty and spiritual attrition.

Yonnondio's title is taken from Walt Whitman's poem. It undercuts the good grey poet's celebrating an America with limitless space, endless opportunity. Not that Olsen doesn't share Whitman's vision of collective human dignity; like Davis, Whitman's *contemporary,* she is outraged at an ideal being betrayed. . . . (pp. 57-8)

[In *Yonnondio*] Anna and her daughter Maisie respond as intensely as Whitman did to nature. The nature images suggest an extension of women's bodies—"the trees dipped and curtsied, the corn rippling like a girl's skirt"; the clouds are likened to Anna's belly big with child. But nature aligned with ruthless capitalism blights their lives, becomes a domesticity yoked to industrial waste: "Indeed they are in hell: indeed they are the damned, *steamed, boiled, broiled, fried, cooked,* geared, meshed."

Olsen's compiling of passive verbs links two spaces inhabited by working women. The first renders the stifling August air of a slaughter-house where at a temperature of 108° immigrant women swelter below in "casings," their task to dismember hog carcasses because men working on the floor above cannot endure the stench of pigs' blood and entrails. The second is Anna's kitchen, where she rhythmically stirs jam, tends a sick child while other chil-

dren tap her flagging energy. Anna also is "geared and meshed"; she thinks of drowned children while softly singing a childhood song, "I saw a ship a'sailing." In this context the sea fantasy obliquely evokes the pivotal immigrant experience Olsen will return to in **"Tell Me a Riddle."**

In *Yonnondio,* the plaintive immigrant voice only faintly infuses Anna's American dream:

> School for the kids Maisie and Willie Jim her Protestant husband working near her, . . . lovely things to keep, brass lamps, bright tablecloths, vines over doors, and roses twining. A memory unasked plunged into her mind—her grandmother bending in such a twilight over lit candles chanting in an unknown tongue, white-bread on the table over a shining white tablecloth and red wine—and she broke into song to tell Jim of it.

These occasional roses succumb to the struggle for bread. Linking factory and kitchen drudgery makes inevitable the reduction of iron-willed humans to scrap; in such an environment, analogous to Upton Sinclair's *The Jungle,* it is small wonder that Anna loses her baby, takes sick, and dies.

> Earth sucks you in, to spew out the coal, to make a few bellies fatter. Earth takes your dreams that a few may languidly lie on their couches and trill "How exquisite" to be paid dreamers.

Far more than her faint allusion to Jewish immigration, Anna suggests Davis' Korl Woman, the central metaphor in *Life in the Iron Mills.* Fashioned in pig iron by Hugh Wolfe, the wretched miner in Davis' story, this sculpture is "a nude woman's form, muscular, grown coarse with labor, the powerful limbs instinct with some one poignant longing. One idea: there it was in the tense muscles, the clutching hands, the wild, eager face. . . . " Hardly a Galatea, the Korl Woman symbolizes nearly all Olsen's narrator-personae, from Anna to Eva in **"Tell Me a Riddle,"** women of extraordinary potential wasted by capitalism and patriarchy. Whether pure or scrap, the iron image resonates throughout Olsen's texts.

"I Stand Here Ironing" depicts a nameless mother-narrator, who, having received a phone call from her daughter Emily's high-school guidance counselor that Emily is an underachiever, pushes an iron to and fro across the board on which Emily's dress lies shapeless and wrinkled. The narrator begins "dredging the past and all that compounds a human being." Her thoughts flow with the rhythm of the iron as she attempts to grasp the "rootlet of reconnaisance" to explain why it was that her oldest child was one "seldom smiled at." What would appear as understandable reasons—the Depression, the nineteen-year old mother, who at her daughter's present age worked at menial jobs during the day and at household chores at night, the iron necessity that made her place Emily in a series of foster homes, the desertion of her first husband, bearing and rearing four other children of a second marriage, all clamoring for attention—should account for Emily's chronic sorrow; but somehow they do not. Necessity dominating the mother's life could have tempered Emily, but the reader soon perceives that there may be another reason why Emily and the mother-narrator are silenced counterparts. The mother has remarried, but material comforts, an emotionally secure middle-class existence, cannot assuage her loneliness. Never having experienced the celebratory rituals of working-class communality, middle-class anomie distances her from other women. Her entire adult life has been interrupted by child care described by Olsen quoting [Sally Bingham in *Silences*]:

> My work "writing" is reduced to five or six hours a week, always subject to interruptions and cancellations . . . I don't believe there is a solution to the problem, or at least I don't believe there is one which recognizes the emotional complexities involved. A life without children is, I believe, an impoverished life for most women; yet life with children imposes demands that consume energy and imagination at the same time, cannot be delegated—even supposing there were a delegate available.

In **"I Stand Here Ironing,"** characteristic stylistic clues embedded in the occasionally inverted syntax, run-on sentences interspersed with fragments, repetitions, alliterative parallels, an incantatory rhythm evoke the narrator's longing not only for a lost child but for a lost language whereby she can order the chaotic dailiness of a working mother's experience.

> She was a beautiful baby. The first and only one of our five that was beautiful at birth. You do not guess how new and uneasy her tenancy in her now-loveliness. You did not know her all those years she was thought homely, or see her pouring over her baby pictures, making me tell her over and over how beautiful she had been—and would be, I would tell her—and was now to the seeing eye. But the seeing eyes were few or non-existent. Including mine.
>
> . . . . .
>
> Ronnie is calling. He is wet and I change him. It is rare there is such a cry now. That time of motherhood is almost behind me when the ear is not one's own but must always be racked and listening for the child to cry, the child call. We sit for awhile and I hold him, looking out over the city spread in charcoal with its soft aisles of light. "Shoogily," he breathes and curls closer. I carry him back to bed, asleep. *Shoogily.* A funny word, a family word, inherited from Emily, invented by her to say: *comfort.*

Emily's word play appears rooted in Yiddish (*shoogily—meshugah*) and there is something archetypically talmudic in her fascination with riddles (for which a younger sibling gets recognition) "that was *my* riddle, Mother, I told it to Susan . . . ," foreshadowing the leitmotif Olsen will orchestrate in **"Tell Me a Riddle."** When language inventiveness fails to mitigate against Emily's lack of achievement at school, when she tries and fails to authenticate herself, she escapes into another's role. Desperate for attention, identity, she responds to the mother's suggestion that she try out for a high school play—[Olsen notes in *Silences* that] "not to have an audience is a kind of death"—and becomes a comic crowd pleaser to the sound of thun-

derous applause. Thus, Emily finally commands some attention and affection and to a limited extent a control of life's randomness. Nonetheless, only articulation through language can free her from oppression. Silenced at home she lacks and will probably continue to lack centrality.

The story ends with the mother still ironing out the wrinkles in Emily's dress; like Emily she is "helpless before the iron," aware that this Sisyphus-like ritual cannot atone for the past, nor can she ultimately answer the riddle Emily poses within and without the family constellation. Certainly the chains of necessity should have justified the mother's past relationship with her eldest child.

> We were poor and could not afford for her the soil of easy growth. I was a young mother. I was a distracted mother. There were the other children pushing up, demanding. Her younger sister seemed all that she was not. There were many years that she did not want me to touch her. She kept too much to herself, . . . My wisdom came too late. She has much to her and probably nothing will come of it. She is a child of her age, of depression, of war, of fear.

Who speaks for the autobiographer? A nameless narrator once a poor Jewish parent, now part of a middle-class nuclear family. Emily, her silenced daughter, is in fact a disembodied dress pushed and pulled by her mother's iron. Shunted, stunted, despite her comic pandering to a mass audience at high school, Emily is a version of the narrator's atrophied self, a contemporary Korl Woman.

If not to have an audience is a kind of death, who listens to the autobiographer? Olsen has always sought a community of women readers identifying with her silences, carefully scrutinizing her self-censorship as she herself has done in the remarkable close reading of Rebecca Harding Davis' *Life in the Iron Mills*. It is this kind of imaginative scrutiny we must bring to a reading of **"O Yes,"** where once again working class communality is negated by middle-class distancing and silence defeats clamor on behalf of the poor.

Deceptively simple, this aforementioned theme emerges during a Black baptismal service for twelve year old *Pariahlee* Phillips (my italics). The only whites attending the all Black service are Pariah's closest friend Carol and Carol's mother, Helen, liberal, Jewish, middle class. The overheated, tumultuous service, enveloping one parishioner after another, pounds against Helen and Carol's class inhibitions. Terrified, Carol faints in church:

> And when Carol opens her eyes she closes them again, quick, but still can see the new known face from school . . . , the thrashing, writhing body struggling against the ushers with the look of grave and loving support on their faces, and hear the torn, tearing cry "Don't take me away."
>
> And now the rhinestones in Parry's hair glitter wicked, the white hands of the ushers, fanning, foam in the air; the blue-painted waters of Jordan swell and thunder; Christ spirals on his cross in the window, and she is drowned under the sluice of the slow singing and the sway.

The timeless sermon that recapitulates Old and New Testament suffering and redemption, serves two functions. The first is a subtle reminder to Helen and Carol of their de-facto segregation from the Black community, strongly personified by Alva, Parry's vital, resilient mother. The second underscores a Judaic-Christian patriarchal heritage that obscures women, but also makes them aware of how the power of the word mitigates against silence. The preacher arouses the congregation to feverish pitch:

> He was your mother's rock. Your father's
> mighty tower.
> And he gave us a little baby. A little baby to love.
>   *I am so glad*
> Yes, your friend when you are friendless. Your
> father
> when you are fatherless. Way maker. Door
> opener
>   *Yes*
> When it seems you can't go on any longer, he's
> there
> You can, he says you can
>   *Yes*
> And that burden you have been carrying—ohhh
> that
> burden—not for always will it be. No, not for al-
> ways.
>   *Stay with me, Lord.*
> I will put my *Word* in you and it is power
> I will put my *Truth* in you and it is power.
>   [Italics in the last two lines, mine]

Unfortunately, the frustration inherent in middle-class women's powerlessness censors Helen's need to voice passion and shape inchoate experience into language. In the hectic event following the service Helen's silence is especially telling. Heretofore, Carol and Parry have loved each other, but Carol's fainting at church marks the beginning of their estrangement:

> "How are you doing now, you littl ol' consola-
> tion prize?" It is Parry, but she does not come
> to the car or reach to Carol through the open
> window: "No need to cuss and fuss. You going
> to be sharp as a tack, jack." Carol answering au-
> tomatically: "as cool as a fool."
>
> Quick they look at each other.
>
> "Parry, we have to go home now, don't we
> mother?"

Not Helen but iron-willed Alva Phillips, seasoned in adversity, who unlike the mother in **"I Stand Here Ironing,"** chooses immersion into rather than withdrawal from life.

> *When I was carrying Parry and her father left,*
> *and I was fifteen years old, one thousand miles*
> *away from home, sinsick and never believing, as*
> *still I don't believe all, scorning, for what have it*
> *done to help, waiting there in the clinic and*
> *maybe sleeping, a voice called: Alva, Alva. So*
> *mournful and so sweet: Alva. Fear not, I have*
> *loved you from the foundation of the universe.*
> *And a little small child tugged on my dress.*

This passage suggests the similarity and difference between the white and Black mother. Both women have felt isolated, skeptical of religious orthodoxy. But whereas Helen internalizes this estrangement, distancing herself

from the immediacy of passion, and remains static and Korl-like, Alva allows communal celebration to temper her and thus sets her spirit free:

> *Eyes he* the small child *placed all around my*
> *head, and as I journeyed upward after him, it*
> *seemed I heard a mourning: "Mama, Mama, you*
> *must help carry the world." The rise and fall of*
> *nations I saw. And the voice called again Alva,*
> *Alva, and I flew into a world of light, multitudes*
> *singing, Free, free, I am so glad.*

Helen, who cannot even conceptualize this kind of force, feels divided not only from Alva but from herself. A dichotomy exists between Helen's (and by extension Carol's) head and heart, ultimately inhibiting the words she needs to comfort Carol and convey the meaning of Black communion.

> *Emotion,* Helen thought of explaining, *a charac-*
> *teristic of the religion of all oppressed peoples, yes*
> *your very own great-grandparents*—thought of
> saying. And discarded. *Aren't you now, haven't*
> *you had feelings in yourself so strong they had to*
> *come out some way?* ("What howls restrained by
> decorum")—thought of saying. And discarded.

Carol lives out the consequences of her mother's ambivalence. In the months to come, Carol and Parry seem as intertwined as they were before the baptism. But Jeannie, Carol's older sister, has warned her parents that the future holds little promise for that friendship. Both girls will shortly enter Junior High where a rigid hierarchy of social cliques divides academic performance/social conformity from the pariahhood of those who cannot or choose not to comply.

And what of Parry? If at the threshold of adolescence Carol seems to exemplify Helen's liberalism gone defensively rigid, Parry's uninhibited pride in her budding sexuality should affirm Alva's earthiness. But contradictions between the institutional racism of the school and the communality of the church have also damaged Parry. She must hurry home after school to look after younger siblings because Alva works the night shift. In the societal sorting process predicted by Jeannie, who has gone through it earlier, Parry falls behind the achievers, her dignity violated by a dress code incompatible with her exuberant sexuality. Carol's rejecting her eats away as Parry's breezy self-confidence. Visiting Carol, sick with the mumps, Parry brings over the assignments teachers have written down, not trusting Parry to remember what they were. Nervously Parry tries the old banter:

> Flicking the old read books on the shelf but not
> opening to mock declaim as once she used
> to. . . . Staring out the window as if the tree not
> there in which they had hid out and rocked so
> often . . . Got me a new pink top and lilac skirt.
> Look sharp with this purple? Cinching in the
> wide belt as if delighted with what newly swelled
> above and swelled below. Wear it Saturday night
> to Sweets . . . (Shake my baby, shake). Asking
> of Rembrandt's weary old face looking from the
> wall. How come (softly) you long-gone you.
>
> Touching her face to his quickly, lightly.

White culture denied her, Parry departs forever, announcing that from now on someone else would stop by with Carol's homework.

And yet Olsen never knots the complex strands of human experience. Years later, remembering the ecstasy of that church service, Helen and Carol discuss the bleak lives of Carol's Black high school mates whom, identifying with in some deep recess of her being, Carol cannot easily dislodge:

> "Mother, I want to forget about it all, and not care. . . . Why can't I forget? Oh why is it like it is and why do I have to care?"
>
> Caressing, quieting.
>
> Thinking: *caring asks doing. It is a long baptism into the seas of humankind, my daughter. Better immersion than to live untouched. . . . Yet how will you sustain?*
>
> Why is it like it is?
>
> Sheltering her daughter close, mourning the illusion of the embrace.
>
> *And why do I have to care?*
>
> While in her Helen, her own need leapt and plunged for the place of strength that was not-where one could scream or sorrow while all-knew and accepted, and gloved and loving hands waited to support and understand.

The seas of humankind, reminiscent of Anna's sailing song in *Yonnondio,* remind us as well how landlocked, trapped are the Annas and Parrys whose youth will erode under an exploitative system offering them little bread and no roses. Anna, Emily, and Parry, daughters; all three are young. Two are victims, the third possibly a survivor, for industrial violence and the depression are over and young Black women will eventually foment change. Their author's self-referential voice, decorous in *Silences,* becomes an extended wail in **"Tell Me a Riddle."** Her incantatory prose encapsulates Rebecca Davis' lament for the laboring poor, for women's souls reduced to scrap iron. Olsen's voice is an elegiac tribute to the Jewish immigrant experience gone sour in the promised land, adding a powerful dimension to the lives of Olsen's literary foremothers dead and Jewish mothers dying.

Not knowing she is dying, Eva, the grandmother in **"Tell Me a Riddle"** recognizes that for the better part of her existence she has lived "between" and "for" but "not with people." "Your sickness was in you, how you live," her husband Max tells her, recalling a penurious and cluttered past when she weighed each morsel of food and yet felt "hungry for the life of the mind." It would be simple enough to assume that Eva's cancer, like the one consuming Tolstoy's Ivan Ilytch becomes an extended metaphor for the unexamined life: marrying Max, bearing five children, conforming thereby to the iron tenets of Jewish patriarchy. Unlike Ivan Ilytch's marriage, however, one of chronic bad faith, Eva's relationship to Max is not loveless; he has been a union worker and has labored long for an earned retirement. And for too long Eva has surren-

dered, albeit uneasily, to the unspoken dictum that biology equals destiny.

After 47 years of living an unfulfilled life with Max, all the children grown and on their own, Eva's iron willpower undermines her gregarious husband's proposal that they move to a rest "Haven" he has chosen for them to live out their retirement. Accustomed to psychic privation, she intends to spend an old age on her own and private terms: "Let *him* wrack his head for how they would live. She would not exchange her solitude for anything. *Never again to be forced to move to the rhythms of others.*"

Bitterly the couple wrangle. Eva, wearing a hearing aid and turning on the vacuum cleaner in order to drown out Max's haranguing, rejects his plea that she owes them both an earned rest at the cooperative for the aged where others would do their chores and minister to their leisure needs. He enlists the aid of their adult children. Eva refuses point blank to hear these arguments.

> "Because I'm use't."
>
> "Because you're use't. This is a reason, *Mrs. Word Miser?* Used to can get unused!" "Enough unused I have to get used to already. . . . Not enough?" turning off the vacuum a moment to hear herself answer. "Because soon enough we'll need only a little closet, no windows, no furniture, nothing to make work, but for worms. Because now I want room. . . .
>
>   . . . . .
>
> Over the dishes coaxingly: "For once in your life to be free, to have everything done for you like a queen."
>
> "I never liked queens."
>
> "No dishes, no garbage, no towel to sop, no worry what to buy, what to eat."
>
> "And what else would I do with empty hands? Better to eat at my own table when I want and to cook how I want."

For Olsen, however, marriage signifies more than living falsely, acquiescing to the rhythms of others. Eva needs Max; they have become interdependent. Eva's ties to husband and children are a source of bonding as well as bondage. The symbiotic relationship unfolds early in the story before Eva's stomach pains and fatigue are diagnosed as symptoms of inoperable cancer. For example, during a heated quarrel on an unbearably humid evening, Max storms out, slamming the door despite his wife's uncharacteristic plea that he stay with her. The air is rent with Eva's cursing in Yiddish, a language she has not used in years:

> She was not in their bed when he came back. She lay on the cot on the sun porch. All week she did not speak or come near him; nor did he try to make peace or care for her. He slept badly, so used to her next to him. After all the years, old harmonies and dependencies deep in their bodies; she curled to him, or he coiled to her, each warmed, warming, turning as the other turned, the nights a long embrace.

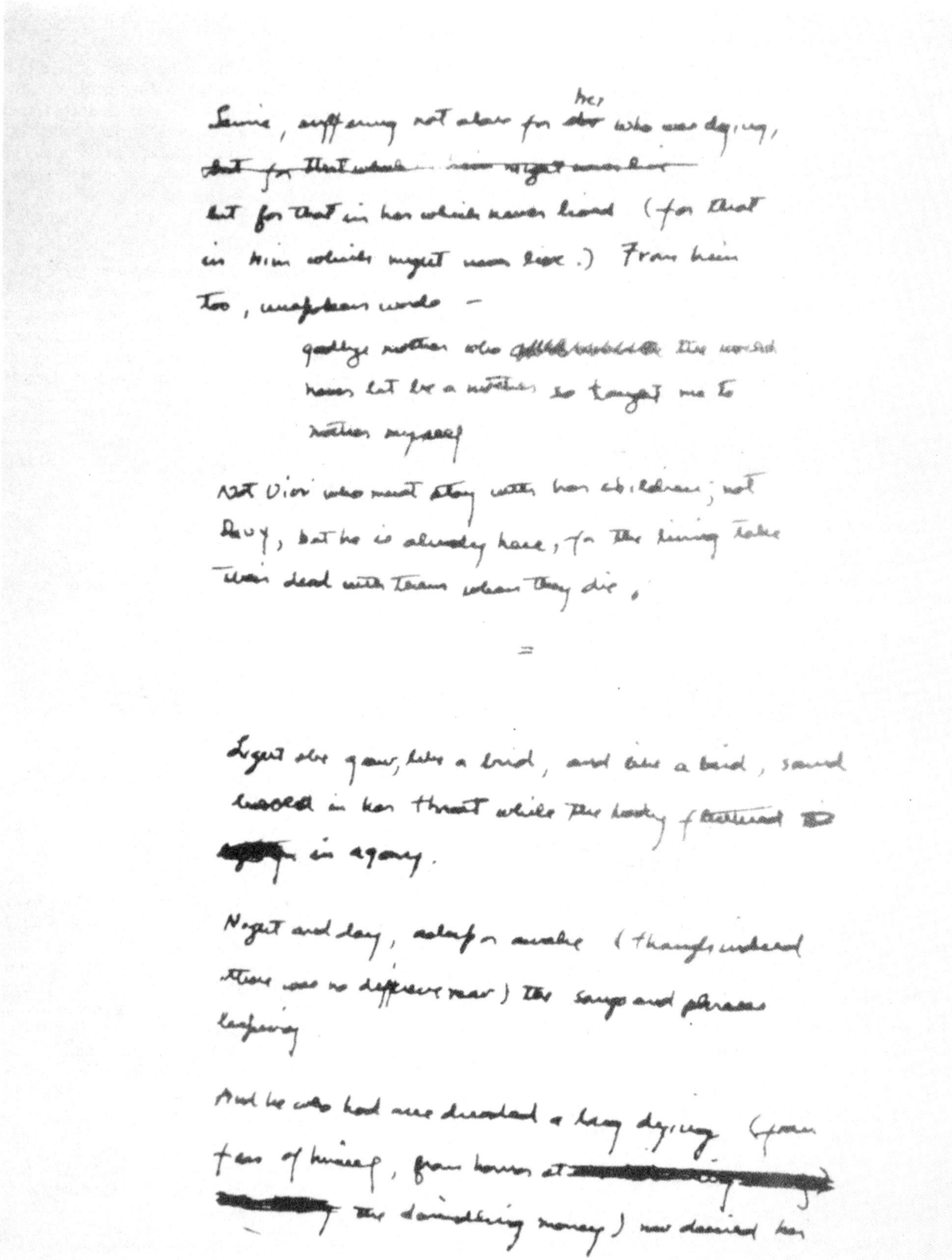

Original manuscript page from Tell Me a Riddle.

In the first passage Olsen's punning (used to it, uses) reveals the nuances of domestic drudgery. In the second a characteristic overflow of infinitives, gerundives, incantatory parallels underscores the reciprocity of a marriage that will not be reduced to bondage alone. Bonding, in fact, has always proved seductive to Eva:

> Immediacy to embrace, and the breath of that part; warm flesh like this a new grandchild placed on her lap that had claims and nuzzled away all else and with lovely mouths devoured; hot-living like an animal—intensely and now. . . .

And troubling:

> It is distraction, not meditation that becomes habitual; interruption, not continuity . . . work interrupted, deferred, relinquished makes blockage—at best lesser accomplishment. Unused capacities atrophy, cease to be. (*Silences*)

Her illness diagnosed, the information withheld from her, Eva is taken on a round of family visits she does not know are final. At Vivi's house, the younger daughter weeps nostalgically and when grandchildren clamor for attention, Eva withdraws in silence:

> It was not that she had not loved her babies, her children. The love—the passion of tending had risen with the need like a torrent; and like a torrent drowned and immolated all else. But when the need was done—oh the power that was lost in the painful damming back and drying up of what still surged, but had nowhere to go.

Nor is Eva's response bizarrely ungrandmotherly. It is honest, indicating a sub-rosa recalcitrance rejecting patriarchal categorizing (and Orthodox Jewish patriarchy codifying wife-mother behavior for thousands of years is unyielding, even today) of a grandmother's behavior according to Jewish custom. For the immigrant women transplanted to American soil the confluence of Jewish and Gentile patriarchy proved difficult to resist. Erika Dunkan writes [in *The Lost Tradition: Mothers and Daughters in Literature*]:

> In Jewish literature by *women,* mothers are the "bread givers" who try to make feeding into a replenishing ecstatic act. But the mothers are themselves starved in every way, sucked dry and withered from being asked almost from birth to give a nurturance they never receive. They are starved not only for the actual food they are forced to turn over to others, but for the stuff of self and soul, for love and song.

Thus, Eva, remembering her lost youth spent borrowing, scrimping, hoarding so that her brood could survive in America is the Korl woman grown old, resistive, being shaped in another image, fearful that she might drown in nurturing a grandchild, rather than immersing herself in the sea. Instead she bends her will to concentrate on what an older precocious grandson is exploring for his science project. To persistent queries—"Tell me a riddle, Grandma," she responds "I know no riddles," defining riddles as child's play that only Max, the fun loving grandfather can supply because his life has been freer. Alone, she holds a magnifying glass over young Richard's rock collection, laboriously repeating terminology—"trilobite fossil, 200 million years old, . . . obsidian, black glass,"—signifying Darwinian geology: "igneous, sedimentary, metamorphic."

If Eva's hearing aid drowns out the others claiming her attention, the magnifying glass represents an intense attraction for enlightenment, a rejection of ghetto irrationality she experienced at the turn of the century. She retains pre-atomic age optimism equating evolution with social progress. Lying in a hospital bed, her mind clouded in the aftermath of anesthesia, she is aroused by the chaplain:

> I think he prays. Go away please, I tell him. I am not a believer. Still he stands while my heart knocks with fright.

> You scared *him,* mother, he thought you were delirious [answers Paul, Eva's son-in-law].

> Who sent him? Why did he come to me?

> It is a custom. The men of God come to visit those of religion they might help. The hospital makes up the list for them—race—religion—and you are on the Jewish list. Not for rabbis. At once go and make them change. Tell them to write: Race, human. Religion, none.

In the same way she rejects Max's plea that for the sake of family harmony she shares in her daughter Hannah's benediction of the Sabbath candles: "Superstition! From the savages, afraid of the dark, of themselves: mumbo words and magic lights to scare away ghosts."

Eschewing the healing effect of ritual, Eva remembers too well the time when ghetto orthodoxy was "the opiate of the people," especially of women for whom the way out of dogma was through education. Thus, Olsen's use of Eva's magnifying glass is an inspired metaphor, allowing the old woman to peer through a glass clearly and see the world "steadily and whole."

Taking leave of her children, Eva allows Max to bring her to a frayed Los Angeles boarding house by the sea where she will spend the final weeks of her life. One afternoon, on the beach, feeling an upsurge of strength, Eva runs toward the ocean that brought her to America, followed by a stumbling Max who cannot stop her. Tripping over a rock, she puts it in a bag "to look at with a strong glass." The rock held against her cheek, Eva gazes at "the shore that nurtured life as it first crawled toward consciousness millions of years ago."

Although she affirms evolution, Eva, like Olsen and her foremothers, does *not* endorse the Social Darwinism that dominated turn of the century intellectual life, probably because such a belief would validate a nature "red in tooth and claw," a determinism: predatory, male, offering no hope of the progressive humanism she really worships. Eva's nurturing impulses have always included ministering to the wretched of the earth, from saving scraps of food and clothing for the poor to reading books that espouse doing away with outmoded social orders. Like Rebecca Harding Davis, whose mind Dr. Le Moyne opened to ethical radicalism, Eva remembers a girlhood mentor in the ghetto of Olshana, Lisa, a brilliant and artistic Russian revolutionary, who taught her to read. Despite beatings at home, Eva would sneak away to meet the idealistic Tolstoyan in much the same way Davis absorbed Le Moyne's subversive ideas in Wheeling, Pennsylvania, prior to the Civil War.

> At night past dogs that howled, terrible dogs,
> my son, in the snows of winter to the road, I to
> ride in her carriage like a lady, to books. To her,
> life was holy, knowledge was holy, and she
> taught me to read.

An informer having betrayed their underground cell, Lisa killed him in prison and was hanged.

> Everything that happens one must try to understand why. She killed one who betrayed many—betrayed all she lived and believed. In one minute she killed, before my eyes (there is so much blood in a human being, my son) in prison with me.

Lisa's revenge on those that would stultify ideas of human liberation live on in Eva's fading memory. To sustain what minuscule life she has, Eva must desperately reach out through time and space linking her selfhood with Lisa, a dead foremother, whom she must internalize before she can allow herself to die. Heartbreakingly for the husband and children who watch the agony of her final days, Eva turns from them to ideas, words, gleaned from books, recapitulated at the ultimate moment. Delirious she hears snatches of songs, sings, quotes: "Pain I answer with tears and cries, baseness with indignation, meanness with repulsion—for life may be hated or wearied of, but never despised." Captive to her fragmented utterances, Max, himself fearful of cancer, helpless before Eva's suffering, impoverished by the cost of her medical care, wearily tries to understand:

> "It helps, Mrs. Philosopher, words from books: It helps?" And it seemed to him that for seventy years she had hidden a tape recorder, infinitely microscopic, with her and that it had coiled infinite mile on mile trapping every song, every melody, every word read, heard, and spoken, and that maliciously she was playing back only what said nothing of him, of the children, of their intimate life together.

It is with a special intensity that Clara, Eva's eldest daughter, an "Emily" hardened to bitter middle age, listens to her mother's dying words. Old wounds throb anew as Clara recalls the deprived childhood in which she stood by helplessly as Eva begged storekeepers for extended credit, hoarded bits of meat and bone for soup, mended ragged clothing, drudged for others with no time to communicate with her first born:

> *Pay me back, Mother, pay me back for all you took from me. Those others you crowded into your heart. The hands I needed to be for you . . .*

> *Is this she? Noises the dying make, the crab-like hands crawling over the covers. The ethereal singing.*

> *She hears that music, the singing from childhood;*

> *forgotten sound—not heard since, since . . . And the hardness breaks like a cry: Where did we lose each other, first mother, singing mother?*

In silence Clara asks this profound Olsen riddle for which the answer would only exacerbate the wound. For Eva trusts only two women. The first was Lisa, her foremother, hanged in a Russian prison. The second is her granddaughter Jeannie, who understands Eva's starved soul and is reminiscent of Lisa in her dedication to alleviating human suffering. It is Jeannie who tries to bridge the gap between Eva and Max. A nurse and a talented artist, Jeannie not only moves into Eva's room to care for the dying woman, she paints her grandparents lying side by side, hands intertwined.

Perhaps Jeannie represents Olsen's attempt to affirm the artistic continuity transcending generations she experienced reading Rebecca Harding Davis. If so, this attempt is flawed. Jeannie's breathless buoyancy cannot unleash the suppressed creativity that adds up to an appalling waste of Eva's (and Clara's) potential.

Yet Olsen has given the closest reading possible to silenced writers, demonstrating two basic premises underlying their writing. The first, an ongoing tension between an artist (worker, Black, woman, Jew) in need of a voice, and a silence societally imposed, psychically internalized. The second, an imperative to find an audience for that energy, that authentic voice, an audience unlike the wealthy dilettantes in *Life in the Iron Mills,* fascinated by the Korl Woman while they allow its sculptor to rot in prison. If *not* to find an audience is always a kind of death, discovering the responsive reader valorizes the obscured artists' suffering and strength, giving them the power to formulate riddles we have never addressed, let alone redressed. As Harold Bloom has explained, literary forefathers have always influenced their writing sons, often causing them the "anxiety of 'this' influence." For Tillie Olsen, literary foremothers help engender and empower otherwise silenced women writers. (pp. 58-71)

Rose Kamel, "Literary Foremothers and Writers' Silences: Tillie Olsen's Autobiographical Fiction," in MELUS, *Vol. 12, No. 3, Fall, 1985, pp. 55-72.*

Margaret Atwood on Tillie Olsen:

Tillie Olsen's is a unique voice. Few writers have gained such wide respect based on such a small body of published work. . . . Among women writers in the United States, "respect" is too pale a word: "reverence" is more like it. This is presumably because women writers, even more than their male counterparts, recognize what a heroic feat it is to have held down a job, raised four children and still somehow managed to become and to remain a writer. The exactions of this multiple identity cost Tillie Olsen 20 years of her writing life. The applause that greets her is not only for the quality of her artistic performance but, as at a grueling obstacle race, for the near miracle of her survival.

Margaret Atwood, in her "Obstacle Course," in The New York Times Book Review, *30 July 1978.*

Naomi Jacobs   (essay date 1986)

[In the following essay, Jacobs examines Olsen's use of air, earth, fire, and water imagery to advance the plot of "Tell Me a Riddle."]

Tillie Olsen's novella, **"Tell Me a Riddle,"** is one of those stories that is passed on from teacher to student, from friend to friend, as a precious gift; often, the transmission is from woman to woman, for the story centers around the tragic diminishment of a woman by her life as wife and mother in a struggling working-class family. Because the depth of Eva's bitterness and the breadth of her losses speak so eloquently to readers who have felt equally diminished, discouraged, or betrayed by their circumstances, the critical response to the work has often focused on specifically feminist issues. One early reviewer, for example, stated that "what comes out most strongly is the disadvantaging of women, the denial of intellect and aspiration, the utter thanklessness of the mother's role"; another discussion of Olsen describes the quarrel between Eva and David as the "archetypal Male/Female fight." These issues are certainly crucial ones in the story. But to stop at Olsen's indictment of the ways in which traditional roles stifle women's selfhood is to understand only a part of this magnificent piece of fiction. Despite its unshrinking portrayal of all that goes unused in human beings, both male and female, the story's true plot is a profound spiritual rebirth, a plot presented not through action but through imagery based on the four pre-scientific elements: earth, air, fire and water. [The critic adds in a footnote: "This theory of elements was formulated by Empedocles, the fifth-century B.C. Greek philosopher; he postulated that all matter was composed of earth, air, fire, and water, which are brought together and separated by the forces of Love and Strife."] For Olsen, this imagery seems to have come from the words of J. A. Symonds, a song which Eva sings in her last delirium:

> These things shall be, a loftier race
> than e'er the world hath known shall rise
> with flame of freedom in their souls
> and light of knowledge in their eyes
>
> They shall be gentle, brave and strong
> to spill no drop of blood, but dare
> all . . .
>   on earth and fire and sea and air
> And every life shall be a song

In **"Tell Me a Riddle,"** these elements become metaphors for the spiritual states through which Eva passes in her journey from isolation to union, from a quarrel to an embrace, from silence to song—and ironically, from life to death.

The story opens in the realm of earth, that homely substance: the emphasis is on the dirt of life, the ugliness of strife between husband and wife and the grime of age, illness, and decay. A lifetime of tending children, mending clothes, and begging for bones at the grocer's has left Eva bitterly resentful and stone-hard. She feels robbed of the self she had been and the life she had imagined as a peasant girl and revolutionary orator in Russia, and she blames her husband for that loss though their poverty was to blame as well as he. Only through a terrible bartering of sensitivity for strength, of responsiveness for endurance, could she be the "rock" upon which her family relied. This process has cut her off from the very people for whom she sacrificed. Remembering how often she had been left alone with the children, she says to David, "You trained me well, I do not need others to enjoy"; she thinks "without softness" of the young wife she once was, and she now "would not exchange her solitude for anything." Her only wish is *"Never again to be forced to move to the rhythms of others"*—never again to be forced to *move,* but "at last to live within." The isolation and immobility that were once imposed have become familiar, comfortable; and so she sits "like a stone," static and wordless, half-blind, turning down her hearing aid until she is truly stone-deaf, so as to keep out the world that has battered and hardened her. A stone seems not to feel; it can, however, make itself felt, as Eva does through her cutting remarks to her husband. She is closed into herself, aware only of her own grievances and sorrows. She seeks a timelessness like that of stone, resists any move out of her peaceful present, whether to the past's "old terrors and humiliations" or to the future David wants at his lodge's Haven for the old. She dismisses her religious heritage as "mumbo words and magic lights to scare away ghosts"; and her admonition "not to go back, not to go back" to the superstitions of the past is also a refusal to go back to her personal past.

Eva's release from the realm of stone is precipitated by an operation which brings a temporary reprieve from physical pain. Though she has terminal cancer, she believes she has been cured, and flying across the continent to visit her children, she enters the realm of air: a lighter, freer version of her stony solitude. Clouds close beneath her, cutting her off from the human life below, "Vulnerable life, that could scar." Air is the invulnerable medium through which one may cut and leave no scar; Eva seeks to maintain such a hermetic stillness, to remain unmarked and to leave no mark. To her, the calm indifference that comes with distance gives her the air she needs to breathe; "remote above the dwindled earth, the concealed human life," she finds coherence and an emptiness that allows her to float. Yet air is also the realm of annihilation; as she will later recall, the millions who died in the Holocaust had "no graves—save air." Casting off encumbrances that would drag her down into that world of human struggle and suffering, Eva still rejects the possibility of connection and closeness. But the simple fact that she is moving again will inevitably bring an end to that airy detachment.

The voices of her grandchildren, the weight and warmth of a baby, call her, batter her defenses in "quick constant raps: let me in, let me in." Living again with a family of children, seeing her daughter Vivi "drowning into needing and being needed," she recalls her own time in the realm of water, the "passion of tending" that "had risen with the need like a torrent" and had been so painfully dammed back when the children left. Now, that "riverbed" is a "desert"; instead of love flowing freely, she has a "heart of ice." Yet the memory is strong enough to make her shudder and sweat, to melt that ice and force her to hear Vivi's "spilling memories" of the shared joy she has denied. Even stone will wear away under the constant pressure of water, and though Eva attempts to protect herself—she refuses to hold the baby and even hides in a closet to reinforce her hard-won indifference—her obduracy begins to soften and her obstinate self-absorption to give way to questioning. Despite all her efforts to "sheathe" herself, she cannot block out either the sight of her daughter's exhaustion, which brings back her own young motherhood, or the sounds of her daughter's reminiscing, which lets her know "the past was cherished, still lived" in Vivi. And so she begins to respond, to feel, and to seek again the springs of meaning, the streams of commitment, which seemed to have forever dried.

Hunched in her granddaughters' closet, she begins to sort out the meanings of her life as she recalls her grandson's recitation of a geology lesson:

> Of stones (repeating Richard) there are three kinds: earth's fire jetting; rock of layered centuries; crucibled new out of the old (*igneous, sedimentary, metamorphic*). But there was that other—frozen to black glass, never to transform or hold the fossil memory . . . (let not my seed fall on stone). There was an ancient man who fought to heights a great rock that crashed back down eternally—eternal labor, freedom, labor . . . (stone will perish, but the word remain). And you, David, who with a stone slew, screaming: Lord, take my heart of stone and give me flesh.

Eva herself is like that stone "frozen to black glass, never to transform or hold the fossil memory," or so she fears when she half-pleads to some unidentified spirit, "let not my seed fall on stone." Her seed has been her life, the loving and tending she gave her children, the struggle and the loss, and her plea now is for some meaning to this struggle, so that her life not remain outside of time and history, without ancestors or descendants. Like Sisyphus, she has endured a seemingly endless battle with crushing labor, yet perhaps her meaning is in that struggle; though stone will perish and all material things pass away, perhaps the word, the spirit of her life will endure, as the songs she used to sing still live in her daughter's singing. When she thinks of David killing Goliath with his stone, she must also think of herself and her fellow revolutionaries—her husband David among them—attempting to fell the giant of the monarchy, of the ways in which David wielded at least some of the "stones" that killed the life in her, and of her son Davy who killed and was killed in the war, and she desires a heart of flesh, a release from her heart of stone, to know and feel these things again. In this state she goes back at last to her long-denied past; when the children scream in play, she hears instead the screaming in the Russian prison where she was held long ago, and must remind herself "severely" of where in fact she is—another kind of prison, self-imposed.

Feeling the house, the memories, press too close, she must flee, and so goes with David to the "dwelling places of the cast-off old" on the California coast. Here she is drawn to the beach, where earth, water and air come together in

their simplest forms. She gathers sand—durable, impersonal, and inert as stone, but as multitudinous as human souls and human selves—to examine under her magnifying glass, and lies down where she can look "toward the shore that nurtured life as it first crawled toward consciousness the millions of years ago." In this landscape, the elements, though so clearly and broadly present, are fragmented and interpenetrating: the water breaks in the air, the sand absorbs the water, the air pulls water from the sand and returns it to the ocean. And this shift reflects the increasing integration in Eva of those elemental psychic qualities of endurance, solitude, and love which the physical elements represent. Eva moves toward and away from the truth she seeks, in an oceanic rhythm no stone could know; the life in her is drawn toward and repelled by the life outside her, and here, in a gentler mood, she seems to be trying to understand it all from the broad perspective of millions of years, millions of grains of sand. Life will not long allow for that—it is more complicated and more untidy—and Eva's stratagems to avoid facing the tragedy and the mystery of her own life and of the century are defeated by so common an event as a community sing.

Taken by an old friend to the auditorium where the elderly gather, Eva immediately turns down her hearing aid, but is unable to block out the music, which seems to her to be all the sounds of life: *"Yes, faces became sound, and the sound became faces; and faces and sound became weight—pushed, pressed,"* and she gasps for "Air," literally gasping for breath in the crowded room, figuratively gasping for the distanced calm she had achieved. Taken by the stench and coffin-like smallness of her friend's one room, she cries out to David her wrenching epiphany. She has seen these people rummaging for scraps in garbage cans, "Yet they sang like like Wondrous! . . . So strong for what? To rot not grow? . . . Singing. Unused——the life in them. She——in this poor room with her pictures——Max——You——The children Everywhere unused the life."

It is only after this strangling vision of the ways in which her youthful ideals failed not only herself but all, that Eva can find her way back to those ideals and to the realm of fire—"the flame of freedom, the light of knowledge"—in which her youthful self had burned. Idealism is born of pain; it is the shining phoenix rising from the fires of anger and of desire. Paradoxically, Eva's full comprehension of the universal waste of human potential also brings full comprehension of the value of the human spirit, which continues not only to endure but to hope and to sing. And so in her last weeks, she embarks on her final journey, which is in fact a return to her beginnings. She recaptures her past, speaking incessantly where she once had been silent, recalling scraps of books she had read, music she had heard, and she reaches out to the world she is about to leave: her radio is continually playing music—which combines order and struggle, and gives shape to human emotion—and her hand reaches across the bed at night for David's hand, though she accuses him of cowardice and betrayal during the day. "All that happens, one must try to understand," she says, and though it is unclear how much she does understand in her delirium, she now denies nothing of her past, reliving the exhaustion, the sordid needs of their poverty, recalling the greater horrors of the human past in the twentieth century, but also reconfirming the ideals for which she once lived. Fire appears here in the "lightness and brightness" of her granddaughter Jeannie, who seems to have inherited Eva's compassion and intensity; in Jeannie's description of the joyful candles at the Mexican feast for the dead, a ritual expressing a sense that the beloved dead are still present in some way and are cause for happiness rather than for grief; and in Eva's evocation of the Egyptian pole star, the seemingly unmoving distant fire upon which the doors of the death houses opened. This death room too opens upon a distant but steadily-burning light: the ideals to which Eva had held even in the darkest turns of the maze of her life. In a torment at once awful and beautiful, she burns with the knowledge of her own failure and with an undying desire for the better world she had envisioned. It is for this that Jeannie's face is "radiant" with tending her grandmother, whom she "incoherently" calls " 'My darling escape . . . my darling Granny'—as if that explained." In her last days, Eva grows light, "like a bird," a creature that rides the air and sings, and like a bird she sings, "bright, betrayed words . . . stained words, that on her working lips came stainless," words from their "youth of belief."

It is an excruciating irony that this rebirth should come only as Eva dies, but this irony intensifies rather than negates the meaning of her return. The very persistence of her beliefs in spite of all the denials and diminishments of her life—her capacity to retain yet rise above the enormity of her hurt and her loss—is a powerful affirmation of the strength of the human spirit, which can transcend both physical and emotional pain. In her last delirium, Eva returns to the moment in which she first heard music and experienced the delight which should be the birthright of every human being: "It is a wedding and they dance, while the flutes so joyous and vibrant tremble in the air." Her return to that moment of happiness in no way minimizes the tragedy of her life, but through this conscious decision to be somewhere else than in her suffering body, Eva affirms the value of her life and of her dreams. Like the two to whom the story is dedicated, Eva is "infinite, dauntless, incorruptible," and her death only "deepens the wonder" of her life. To Olsen, finally, the human being is not only an organism which needs soil, air, moisture and light for physical survival, but also a spirit which needs the nourishment of the parallel elements of strength, solitude, love, and the hope of knowledge and freedom. She demands, in the terms of the suffragists, not only bread but roses: not only survival but delight, the freedom to be fully oneself and fully human. (pp. 401-06)

> *Naomi Jacobs, "Earth, Air, Fire and Water in 'Tell Me a Riddle',"* in Studies in Short Fiction, *Vol. 23, No. 4, Fall, 1986, pp. 401-06.*

Elaine Neil Orr   (essay date 1987)

[*In the following essay, taken from her* Tillie Olsen and a Feminist Spiritual Vision, *Orr offers a thematic analysis of "Requa," Olsen's novella-in-progress.*]

In 1970, almost ten years after *Tell Me a Riddle* was pub-lished, **"Requa,"** the first part of a novella on which Olsen is still working, appeared in the *Iowa Review.* It was reprinted as one of the year's best short stories. As Olsen's latest and most complex fiction, the story illuminates her earlier periods by expanding the themes, motifs, and characterizations that have concerned her from the beginning. Moreover, in evoking a metaphorical pattern of the human journey and search for place (identity), **"Requa"** is paradigmatic of the evolving vision of redemptive hope that has inspired Olsen's career. The young protagonist negotiates a way through harms and brokenness that we now recognize as Olsen's way.

"Requa," or "Rekwoi," is an Indian name for a holy place, Olsen has said, where dances are performed to keep the floods away. The beauty of the sound is what attracted Olsen to it and the associations it evokes: requiem and reclamation. Both meanings hold important connotations . . . .

The story's complex and consistent use of paradox—healing comes through brokenness, wholeness issues from fragmentation, love is achieved as the main character comes face to face with loss and deprivation—is mirrored by the text itself. Sentences are unfinished, words—unconnected—dot the landscape of the page: the story ends without any final punctuation. At times one senses that the writer is at a loss as to *how* to create the feelings of brokeness except in this concrete way. Developing the theme of continuity, Olsen seems to insist rather pointedly that brokenness is the condition that elicits human bondedness. In fact, the story may await not so much Olsen's finishing of it as readers' response.

In ["After Long Silence," *Studies in American Fiction,* 1984], Blanche Gelfant offers a thematic connection between this and Olsen's second period: "In 'Requa' Stevie continues the quest of the Grandmother in **'Tell Me a Riddle.'** Different as they are, the resurrected boy and the dying woman are both searching for a transmittable human past that will give significance to their present struggle."

Gelfant's emphasis on the past in the story is in accord with our reading of the body of Olsen's work. She suggests as well the redemption that evolves through a recollection of history and the story's vision of relatedness. Thus, she suggests but does not fully develop the prophecy of Olsen's story, its pointing beyond itself to a future vision of human wholeness. In connecting not only Eva's and Stevie's quests but also Stevie's and the writer's search for voice, Gelfant provides a glimpse of the story's transcendence, its reflection of longings and hopes that inspire the narrative and lift our reading of it to an attitude of ultimate concern. Though the story dwells in territories of brokenness—the junkyard and the shattered human heart—it springs from the writer's longing for a different way—not, as Gelfant accurately notes, a pastoral past, but for a rebuilding, out of present technological waste, of a humane and creative world in which work and relationship sustain each member of the human community.

The metaphorical resonances that evolve in the narrative suggest a transcending vision of continuity and healing. At the same time, the use of a mother's love as the energy and power that infuses and directs the male characters points to the rootedness of Olsen's universally transforming vision in day-to-day maternal experience.

In the creative essay "The Coming of Lilith," Judith Plaskow proposes "telling a new story within the framework of an old one." Written during Olsen's most consciously feminist period, **"Requa"** tells the story of daily survival (a theme she has treated primarily in domestic contexts among women and children) in terms of a fourteen-year-old boy and his uncle. The effect is a narrative unique in subject, perspective, and style; I know of no other recent story to which it can be compared. In this last fiction, Olsen transforms male according to female and in so doing universalizes a feminist maternal spirituality, a vision of need and desire springing from the memory of a lost mother, perhaps like Eva, a "first mother, singing mother."

The gender change accomplishes a powerful expansion of Olsen's vision of care and nurture. Making a man responsible for a woman's child, Olsen envisions a conjoined male/female journey to wholeness through the depleting and agonizing realities of illness, waste, and loss. Though the woman is dead, her spirit is the grounding of the story, and her love seems reincarnated in the uncle, in other minor characters, and in the benevolent presence reflected in the narrator's voice.

"Requa" is the only one of Olsen's stories set in the thirties (1932), the years so crucial to her own development as a writer. It builds upon themes from all of her other writing: individual and community loss, impoverishment, and exhaustion; societal waste and destruction; and the indomitable human spirit, source and reflector of faith, hope, and love. As Gelfant notes, the story also continues Olsen's practice of giving voice to unnoted and muted people. These characters are more like the societally marginal Holbrooks than like the more culturally integrated characters of *Tell Me a Riddle.* Sharing the limited omniscient perspective, Stevie and Wes, nephew and uncle, recall for us the shared mother/daughter perspective in *Yonnondio.* The narrative situation is the death of the boy's mother, related through flashbacks, and his "adoption" by Wes, his mother's brother but a man he hardly knows. Taken from city to small town, Steve finds healing through working with his uncle in a junkyard.

Very likely, Olsen means for the characterization of this story to mirror the actual destruction brought to families by the Depression. The woman who emerges as Stevie's mother, through his almost incoherent remembrances, is probably in her thirties; she could even have been in her late twenties. What the boy remembers of her life and death is the ultimate exhaustion. In one flashback, he recalls this exchange with her: *"(Are you tired, Ma? Tired to death, love)."* While the brief conversation is extreme, it is not, in Olsen's world, uncommon. People are exhausted "to [spiritual and then physical] death" by overwork, by a world that will not, in any sustained way, aid the poor and the lame.

Embodying the absolute need for human continuity, Stevie's and Wes's relationship is paradigmatic of Olsen's vi-

sion of loss and recovery, brokenness and healing, which builds in force and clarity throughout her career. In reading of their experience, we are reminded of earlier characters, the children: Mazie, Emily, Carol, Parry; the men: Jim, Whitey, Lennie, David; and the women: Anna, Olsen herself in **"I Stand Here Ironing,"** Helen, Alva, Eva. The otherness or difference which we have met in these lives—their songs, giving power to the powerless; the miraculous, transforming hope of a mother; the musical sway of a church, which draws the time of redemption out of hearts and declares the day of the Lord—is even more striking in **"Requa."** The discards of humanity, the wastes of society, the barely reusable, are the sources in this world of redemption and hope. Not a pristine world, but the real world of abused and overlooked possibilities is the source of spiritual reclamation.

Stevie's journey for place and identity recalls journeys portrayed in the earlier work, and his tattered spirit reminds us of the need for healing so characteristic of Olsen's people. Learning of the human bonds that make life possible, the young protagonist glimpses the truth of the human situation as we, the readers, have come to see it in this canon of works. Picturing the boy's healing in terms of discarded objects and their potential remakings, Olsen gives expression to her faith: brokenness will not be the last word.

In **"Requa,"** Olsen continues the strategy of the *Tell Me a Riddle* stories, shifting back and forth between past and present and juxtaposing significant scenes. She experiments even more with interrupting the narrative by introducing countertexts. Earlier, she borrowed poems and songs from other historical contexts. Here, she creates her own poetry out of the story's context. She names machine parts, creating verbs drawn from mechanical work:

> sharping hauling sorting splicing
> burring chipping grinding cutting
> grooving drilling caulking sawing.

The collage effect of the writing parallels the reclamation theme, making do out of what is at hand. It also reminds us of Olsen's tendency to deny chronological time and to manipulate the text for the purpose of regaining lost time and opportunity. Even more is effected here, however. The careful aligning of words, chosen for sound as much as for sense, creates a kind of ritualistic chant. Olsen seems to employ these poetic enclosures as a new speech for an old purpose, as new images in a prayer for wholeness. One achievement of the style is its insistence upon the sounds of work as holy or redeeming. Like Jim Holbrook [in *Yonnondio*], Wes speaks with his hands.

Stevie undertakes two journeys in the story: the journey to his new home and an evening outing with Wes in search of good times. Beginning the first trip, Stevie feels confused: "He didn't understand how it was that he was sitting up or why he didn't have a bed to lie down in or why or where he was going." But a sign is offered to suggest that even in his alienation, Stevie is being offered a human connection. As uncle and nephew travel in the old truck, Stevie "sag[s] against his uncle who [doesn't] move away."

As the boy searches for some sense out of his situation, the narrator describes the annual journey of the salmon:

"(Underneath in the night, yearling salmon slipped through their last fresh waters, making it easy to the salt ocean years)." Later in the story, when Stevie in springtime joy runs down by the river, the same voice will remind us, *"And still the rippling, glancing, magnifying light. . . .* and flashing rainbow crescents he does not know are salmon leaping." The narrator's comprehension of the movement of all life toward maturation offers to the reader, if not directly to Stevie, a sense of the beneficent plan and pattern in the universe. The alliterative sway of the language—"underneath the night," "yearling salmon slipped," "flashing rainbow crescents"—offers a feeling of rhythm to the natural quest of all life toward fulfillment. We are reminded of Eva's "springs" and of Anna's need to be out in the world, in the wind.

Like theirs, Stevie's journey is undertaken in rupture and confusion; the human and earthly way of moving toward expression and fullness has been shattered. The mother's death, even the conditions of her life, leave the boy stunned and reeling. But the story's focus is upon the uncle's rescue of the boy and the healing of Stevie's brokenness. Thus the literal journey to a new home and work suggests metaphorically the greater spiritual journey toward wholeness and intactness. Set in a most desperate time in American history, **"Requa"** reminds us of the interconnection of physical and spiritual needs. Body and soul must be salvaged. Here as elsewhere in Olsen we find political voice disclosing artistic and religious meaning.

The story begins by depicting the physical disorientation Stevie feels: "Everything slid, moved, . . . Being places he had never been. Waiting moving sliding trying." At Wes's place, the boy transfers the truck's rocking inside his body: "And the round and round slipping sliding jolting moved to inside him, so he has to begin to rock his body: rock the cot gently, down and back." The truck's movement appears hazardous to Stevie's need for stability and security, yet when he rocks himself, we are reminded of his youth and his need for the lost mother, for her lap and arms.

Stopping the truck, Wes allows Stevie to rest on their way home. The boy pulls the tarp "down to [a] . . . stripe of sun" and "curl[s] till he [gets] all in a ball." When he wakes, he is warm; his uncle sleeps by the fire, and "across the creek, just like in the movie show or in a dream, a deer and two baby deers were drinking. When he lifted his head, they lifted theirs. For a long time he and the doe looked into each other's eyes. Then swift, beautiful, they were gone—but her eyes kept looking into his." Eyes become Stevie's link with his past. His most salient memory is his mother's face in death, especially her eyes, which he remembers as both "burning" and "gentle." The deer's eyes are a reflection of the second aspect: gentle, beautiful, but fleeting. At Wes's in bed his first night, the other visage appears: "blood dripping from where should be eyes Out in the hall swathed bodies floating like in bad movies." In understanding the dream and the deer, Stevie likens what he sees to the films of his former city life; they are his texts for interpreting the natural world that now flashes before him. This error in judgment, placing the cel-

luloid world before the real one, suggests Stevie's severing from his natural or whole self.

Fear of the burning eyes keeps Stevie from looking into faces, which are often, for Olsen, maps of the ways people have been. At the landlady's [Mrs. Ed's] table, he will not meet the eyes of those who speak to him. Later, pumping gas at Evans's fix-it shop, he rivets his eyes on the ground and refuses to look into the faces of the customers. But in moments of sympathy with Wes, Stevie's eyes become a means to searching out connection. One day, his uncle, Olsen's most sympathetically drawn workingman, comes home exhausted from work and slumps down in the chair in their room; "for a minute he let go, slept; snored, great sobbing snores." The narrator probes Stevie's sleeping consciousness: *"Something about the light, the radio, not being snapped on; the absence of the usual adopted pleasantries; some rhythm not right, roused the boy . . .* Was that his mother or his uncle sagged there in the weight of weariness." Blurry-eyed from first waking, the boy sees Wes as his mother. In weariness and weight, the bodies are the same, making male and female one. Even when Stevie, fully awake, knows the figure as Wes, he treats him as his mother, urging his uncle to put up his tired feet so Stevie can rub them. Through his own eyes, Stevie makes a connection between former life and new, using the memory of his mother to understand what is needed in the present.

But the memory of the terrible anguish in his mother's face overpowers that first connection, and in fierce determination he shelters himself from the loss she symbolizes, staying shut up in Wes's room, refusing to go to school, and continuing to avoid those who address him. In his helpless sleep, the look of death continues its visitation: "spectral shapes . . . out in the hall, swathed forms floated, wrung their hands."

Stevie cannot choose between the aspects of death and life that characterize his past. He must face both. The deer's face is the mediator. On the second journey with his uncle, to "celebrate," drink, and womanize, Stevie recognizes the deer's eyes. Amid the dancing and drinking and a feeling of sickness mixed with happiness, Stevie looks: "the fire? over the fireplace, branching antlers, sad deer eyes in the fire, branching antlers glowing eyes am going to be sick." The deer head above the fire is recreated in the burning flames. "Branching antlers" and "sad eyes" evoke majesty and utmost loss, a head severed from its body. The male recalls the female and the fawn: a family. Beauty and futility, life and death, are bound in Stevie's encounter with the deer. Human brutality is certainly suggested by the deer so that this more lyrical rendering of rupture and fragmentation recalls the societal sin evoked in the *Yonnondio* passage where machines mutilate, silence, and kill.

Stevie's understanding of death, gained through the deer's "sad" eyes, is followed by his second recognition of family continuity when again, after the long night of drinking, Wes comes home exhausted and despairing. Ordinarily a neat person, the uncle stumbles in, falling onto the bed with muddy shoes. Caring for him, Stevie acts like a mother tucking in a child:

> The blanket ends wouldn't lap to cover. He had
> to pile on his coat, Wes's mackinaw, and two

towels, patting them carefully around the sleeping form. *There now you'll be warm,* he said aloud, *sleep sweet, sweet dreams . . .*

His uncle moaned, whispered something; he leaned down to hear it, looked full on the sleeping face. Face of his mother. *His* face. Family face.

Stevie's journey for place, identity, and reclamation begins in his creative response to the pain of death. His quest is to chart a connection between himself and others, which will allow him to interact and to be a part of a community. Like a family of deer, Stevie and Wes are similar. What Stevie understands is their bond, something essentially the same connecting mother, self, and uncle. In his dreams that night, Stevie "hurtle[s] the fall over and over in a maggoty sieve where eyes glowed in rushing underground waters and fire branched antlers, fire needle after shining needle." The dream is a mosaic of earth's elements, suggesting both death and birth, harm and recognition. Whitey too saw fire and water and knew their power to destroy and to cleanse. The young boy, however, has greater opportunity for a new beginning.

Near the end of the story, Stevie recognizes Mrs. Ed's face in an old photograph; the incident suggests the triumph of "gentle" eyes in Stevie's quest, and of vision that sees similarity and leads to acts of care:

> [Stevie] sees that it is not shadows that hang on the wall around the bow, but Indian things: a feathered headdress, basket hats, shell necklace. Two faces dream in shell frames. One, for all the beard, Mrs. Ed's. *family face.*

The arrangement on the wall, a mosaic of human artistry, like Eva's mosaic of songs, stirs connections with the dream. Family pictures of Mrs. Ed's people [of white ancestry] are mixed with "Indian things." Unlike the dream, where death and life mix indiscriminately, and one is helpless before the spectral shapes of fear, this arrangement signifies human choice. Mrs. Ed chooses connection with the Indian past. She, of white descent, intertwines her life with Indian lives. The family face expands beyond mere facial resemblance to human likeness, so that Mrs. Ed's face is a map to the truly human/divine way of integration and bondedness. The difference or otherness of cultural distinctions is bound in the similarity of human need and possibility. Thus the family of humanity is evoked through Stevie's seeing, his recognition of Mrs. Ed in the context of Indian art, a human arrangement aligning race with race.

Stevie's journey is a journey through dream and waking, requiring a transformation of his mother's dying eyes into his own caring eyes. As Gelfant suggests, the way of his journey is similar to Eva's; he must go back through memory, recollecting for his present life the knowledge of love and original promise that can transform brokenness. Near the end, as he works through the past, making connection with the present, the narrator gives this description: "Miming Wes's face Sounding Evans dry ghost cough. Gentling his bruised shoulder. Sometimes stopping whatever he is doing, his mouth opening: fixed to the look on her dying face." Miming others, feeling as they do, Stevie's

journey weaves a family tapestry of human connections. Like the salmon and the deer, his journey is of death and rebirth, while the emblematic face of his mother is a reminder of pain and of the hope that may heal. Transposing the family order in **"I Stand Here Ironing,"** Olsen creates a child whose life inspirits the dead mother rather than a mother who hopes against the powers of death that threaten her daughter. By this latest story, then, we recognize in Olsen's world the spiraling journey of humanity, from child to parent to child.

Glimpsing the sustaining intergenerational vision that encompasses Olsen's world, we notice, however, that the setting is profoundly "unholy." The junkyard setting seems the most obvious contradiction to growth, beauty, and attainment. Yet, Wes promises Stevie: "I'll help you catch hold, . . . I promise I'll help," suggesting that he will offer Stevie a place to put down roots, to grow, and to blossom. The dump, then, becomes a context for recreation, for finding wholeness and holiness. Earlier, Wes declared in the presence of Mrs. Ed: "I'll tell you this, though, he's not goin through what me and Sis did: kicked round one place after another, not havin nobody. Nobody." Giving himself to the boy, even at work, in his impatience, Wes creates connection in an apparently hopeless place.

Even before the junkyard is introduced, the truck is an antagonistic setting, forcing the exhausted boy to wakefulness and sickness. Cold and weak, he hopes for a place to lie down and warm himself. But when he can leave the truck to rest, the outside world is a place of discomfort and distrust: "Everything slid, moved." The natural world is not always hospitable. Antagonists loom larger than life: "There might be snakes. The trees stretched up and up so you couldn't see if they had tops, and up there they leaned as if they were going to fall." These threatening places remind the boy of nights of staying up with his mother, afraid to sleep "cause he might . . . not hear her if she needed him." In his isolation, Stevie's world threatens life rather than feeding it. He finds no safe bed between heaven and earth.

Somnambulent, the boy seems suspended between consciousness and death. In his room at the end of a "cave"-like hall, he constructs a fort from the moving boxes. For days he sleeps, hardly getting out of bed, fighting desperately against Wes's prodding. When the uncle opens the door, he jumps from the bed to close it: *"Keep away you rememorings slipping slidings having to hold up my head Keep away you trying to get me's . . . I work so hard for this safety Let me a while Let me."*

On his first visit to the junkyard, the world rises up around Stevie, threatening him like the giant trees of the forest: "Too close: scaly, rapid river; too close: dwarfing, encircling: dark massive forest rise." But Wes's promise and his insistent caring begin to get through to the boy, and movement begins in Stevie's uneasy slumbering.

Having unpacked and distributed most of the belongings from Stevie's former life, Wes comes home one day and demands that they unpack "her" things. The box includes an array of cheap objects: "tiny Indian brass slipper ash tray," "Happy Joss/Hollywood California painted fringed pillow cover/kewpie doll green glass vase, cracked." Stevie cannot endure the exposure of his woundedness and the next day refuses to wake. But almost miraculously, he is up for the first time when Wes comes home that evening. "I did everything like you told," he offers, but when Wes tries to send him to school for the second time, he still refuses.

At work with Wes after begging for the chance, Stevie is at first only slightly more alert than at home. He does not listen: "Your ears need reaming?" Wes asks. Deaf and mute, Stevie shivers in fear and cold, hardly noticing Wes's careful instructions for sorting. Reverting to his former behavior of turning inward and fending off the world, the boy wraps himself in an old quilt, rocks himself, and sleeps. His behavior is like Eva's, though less self-conscious. He must turn off the outer sounds and sights to hear and see himself. First there is movement inward, then outward, though paradoxically his reconnections are also dependent upon the proddings of Wes and others' needs, to which Stevie slowly awakens.

The junkyard, like the earlier settings and like Whitey's bar, is at first only a place for Stevie to carve a moment of aloneness. But the sheer size and complexity of it insists upon the boy's attention. In moments of self-forgetfulness, Stevie meets the world, and remembrances—hunger, the excitement of doing something with hands, even the feeling of the bruise on his shoulder—bring awakening. The germinal feelings of warmth and anticipation slowly work in him, and he begins to respond to Wes's friendship, the job, and the coming spring:

> Afternoons, if the strong northwest winds of May have cleared the sky an hour or two, the coat distills, stores the sun about him as he moves through mound-sheltered warmth in and out of the blowing cold; or sits with Wes, poncho over the muddy ground, eating their baloney and bread lunch in the sun-hive the back of the scrapiron pile makes.

> Weeds, the yellow wild mustard and rank cow parsnip, are already waist high, blow between him and the river. Blue jays shrill, swoop for crumbs; chipmunks hover. Wes gabs, plays his harmonica. The boy lies face down in his pool of warmth. In him something keeps trembling out in the wind with the torn whirled papers, the bending weeds, the high tossed gulls.

A blossoming world is suggested, brought by the spring weather. The comfort and promise of rebirth, warmth, and beauty touch Stevie, calling him to join the celebration of returning life. Lying on the ground, he is like a seed close to the surface, lured from his slumber. He is called by the wind and Wes's music to break the boundary of isolation and join the living universe.

The body struggles to life; more difficult is sustaining and enhancing the boy's spirit. The outing with Wes is the context for Stevie's understanding of what nurturing is and how necessary for humans. The incident suggests that seeing life's beneficence in nature, Stevie may find his own way of blossoming.

Waiting for his uncle, who has left him in the woods when he goes to buy love from a prostitute, Stevie is outside when a rain comes up. He has never seen the rain in the country where it falls to the receptive earth. But he remembers another rain that caught him outside. Something about this rain and that memory culminates in Stevie's spiritual unfolding:

> Slap. On his face. Another slap. Great drops. *Rain.* Move, you dummy. Pushing himself up against a tree, giant umbrella in the mottled dark. Throb, sound in and around him (his own excited blood beat?) Rain, hushing, lapping

> City boy, he had only known rain striking hard on unyielding surface, . . . not this soft murmurous receiving: leaves, trees, earth. In wonder he lay and listened, . . .

>   . . . .

> Far down where Wes was, a branch shook silver into the light. Rain. *His mother's quick shiver as the rain traced her cheek. C'mon baby, we've got to run for it.*

> Laughing, one of her laughing times. . . . Tickling him, keeping him laughing while she dried his face.

The rain serves to move the passage from Wes's abandonment of Stevie to a remembered moment of joy. Stevie will "twist . . . away from the pain" of the memory, but the episode ultimately leads to Stevie's recognition of his uncle *as his mother.* Thus, in back-and-forth movement—toward memory and away from it—Stevie learns, from the rain and the receptive earth, something about human connection.

The meeting of earth and water is new to the boy, and he is intrigued. But unlike nature, Stevie needs a mediator, not only nutriment but *someone* to nurture him. Water is a symbol of sustenance; the mother is a symbol of sustainer.

Stevie's learning and healing become evident when he actively demonstrates his understanding at home. The text suggests that Stevie's blossoming, metaphorically germinated by the rain passage, is discernible in his learning to care for his uncle, whom he sees as a reflection of his mother. Reaching out to reciprocate the attention he has received, he begins to unfold, subverting the notion that the poor or the young cannot be nurturers or have little to give.

Thus the story portrays human caring as an act of beauty and as a fulfillment. Stevie's blossoming in **"Requa"** is precisely his learning to reach out to those around him and to recognize human likenesses. The lilting good-night wish: *"sleep sweet, sweet dreams"* suggests Olsen's poetic sense of small but essential deeds of care. Looking for a way to cover his uncle's ungainly body, Stevie fits together various garments and clothes. His actions suggest the human penchant to mime and mimic, to discover new ways of acting and responding, but for a significant purpose, to attend to someone's needs. Stevie's care of Wes symbolizes two central and interrelated human characteristics: human creativity—the ability to make, change, direct, connect, and discover; and human caring. The first makes the second possible, while the second is always the moral legislator of the first. Human wholeness and holiness are born in creative acts, moral and artistic, binding self's and other's identity and destiny. One's own creativity satisfies the self, who serves the other. In her latest story, Olsen portrays most successfully the absolute interrelatedness of morality and creativity by showing that it is when Stevie reaches beyond himself to others that his potential is tapped. Like her first communal "I," the voice of the people, Olsen uses Stevie's eyes as the eyes of the world, seeing need and hope as one. Thus, the perspective of the lowliest is the mirror, inner and outer, for knowing the truth and understanding the human heart.

If Stevie's journey for a vision of connectedness and his blossoming are shown in terms of his ability to care for someone else, the salvaging of junk is Olsen's metaphor for personal and universal integration and restoration. People, like the earth and her materials, are broken, used, discarded, and wasted. In sorting and fitting together—junkyard work—Olsen, who once worked in a junkyard herself, gives imagistic vision to a congruent and valued existence, where persons manipulate materials creatively and find a place for their contribution.

The piecing of spare parts is metaphoric of the human piecing or fitting together that takes place in the story at two levels. Stevie, the sickly protagonist, must piece together fragmented memories from his past in order to understand that his mother's love continues in the present. But Stevie's recovery happens communally. The nurture and care of the expanded family—Wes, Mrs. Ed, Yee (the cook), and Evans (his new boss)—make the story's theme of reconstruction a communal possibility. No one in the story, certainly not Stevie or Wes, is completely whole or self-sufficient. In fact, one becomes almost weary of the writer's insistence upon Stevie's sickliness; once he is described as "blowing out the biggest bubble of snot you ever saw."

The characters live in near poverty, with the uneasy knowledge that "half the grown men in the country's not working." Wes is an imperfect parent, and Stevie's near wellness at the end is tentative. But a community develops among the "family," composed of three races (Native American, Oriental, white). One cooks, one works a job, one remembers the dead. Working together, they create a holy, that is, a life-giving community of sojourners. We remember the intactness and bliss of the Holbrooks, for example, when they journeyed to the farm.

Stevie's brokenness is symbolized by the "broken" text, which lends to the reader a pictorial representation of the shifting and moving that the boy feels. The fragmentation of his only known world is represented by the distribution of his mother's worldly goods: "That one on top: left over groceries. Into the kitchen, Yee. . . . Bedding stuff, Bo; up to the attic. Pots and kitchen things, High. . . . [Lowered voice] Just her clothes, Mrs. Ed, you know anybody? Mrs. Ed's room. Lamps and little rugs, . . . Anyone for a lamp?" Afterward, Stevie thinks, "I don't know where anything is." The text suggests an association between the mother's death and material fragmentation. The boy

wants to bury the possessions and the hurt: *"Put it back," "all of it dead bury buried."* Like the mother in **"I Stand Here Ironing,"** he first attempts to stay or fix the memory.

At work, Stevie's job is to sort, to find a place for each thing, and to put it there so that when a customer comes, the sought piece can be found. Though he cannot face his mother's "junk," this sorting work is the means of the boy's personal recovery. Like the deer, it mediates the mother's presence. Discarded pieces from other homes remind him of some forgotten memory or feeling: "Wheat wreaths enamelled on a breadbox he is tipping to empty of rain Remembered pattern; forgotten hunger peanut butter, sour french bread Remembered face, hand, wavering through his face, reflected in the rusty agitated water." He destroys the breadbox, but the memories are too many and eventually, in the human reflected image—Wes/his mother—Stevie begins to let the past live. This reconnaissance in the junkyard is a striking and certainly "other" imagining for twentieth-century understandings. Olsen seems to point to the masses of broken and unheeded human lives, not to traditionally sacred texts and symbols and not to the glitter and polish of high technology, as harboring the divine promises of life for the future. If we read the story as disclosing political and spiritual truth, then we must consider the possibility that the historically abused are the source, and not simply the means, of the earth's renewal and hoped-for future.

The narrative voice has foreshadowed Stevie's recovery from brokenness:

> *But the known is reaching to him, stealthily, secretly, reclaiming.*

> Sharp wind breath, fresh from the sea. Skies that are all seasons in one day. Fog rain. *Known weather of his former life.*

> Disorder twining with order. The discarded, the broken, the torn from the whole: weathereaten weatherbeaten: mouldering, or waiting for use-need. *Broken existences that yet continue.*

The pieces of junk pass through Stevie's hands, "hard, defined, enduring," linking his new life to the city of his former existence. He uses the discards metaphorically to accomplish his own reclamation of body and spirit.

Wes offers a pattern for Stevie's work: "Singing—unconscious, forceful—to match the motor hum as he machines a new edge, rethreads a pipe. Capable, fumbling; exasperated, patient; demanding, easy; uncomprehending, quick; harsh, gentle; *concerned* with [Stevie]." Teaching the boy a skill, Wes illustrates his care for his nephew's whole self. The man's response to the child mirrors his work at the junkyard; in both he seeks to make something useful, functional, vital.

In Wes's work, Stevie sees *"the recognizable human bond"* reflected:

> accurately threaded, reamed and chamfered
>   Shim Imperial flared
>
>   cutters benders grinders beaders
>   shapers notchers splicers reamers

How many shapes and sizes,
how various, how cunning in

application.

The narrative summary: "How many shapes and sizes, /how various, how cunning in/ application" might describe humans, and the names of the parts might be human names. Olsen respects machinery, but only as a means: humanity is the beginning and the reason for its existence. Wes sees the parts of a whole, is able to break apart the useless old, and redeem it by reconstruction. The work itself is a bond, something man and boy do together. Yet this particular work of reclamation elicits the "more" of Stevie's personal healing and makes the bond between uncle and nephew a bond of spiritual redemption.

A brief closing scene takes place in a cemetery. On Memorial Day, Stevie accompanies Mrs. Ed to the graves of soldiers and of Indians. The boy separates himself, stumbling on an old jar, and coming upon the grave of an infant. He sits down by a small stone lamb: "How warm it felt down there in the weeds where nobody could see him and the wind didn't reach. The lamb was sun warm too. He put his arm around its stone neck and rested. Red ants threaded in and out; the smell was sweet like before they set the burn pile; even the crackling flags sounded far away." A sense of beneficence infuses Stevie's meditation and isolation. This solitude will be germinal, as Stevie, amid the disparate objects—the lamb, the weeds, the industrious ants, the crackling flags—is given a sense of safety and wholeness, the well-being he has sought since his mother's illness. Ultimately, Stevie's salvage comes from the grave, a human "junkyard." The mother's loss of her child is the obverse of Stevie's loss of his mother. Two halves remain. Together, Wes and Mrs. Ed can be the lost loved one (a mother) if Stevie (a child) will live and join them.

Like "I Stand Here Ironing," "Requa" closes on the edge of its beginning. Unlike the earlier story, however, this one is unfinished. Olsen intends more. One of the great paradoxes of Olsen's texts is the sympathy their incompleteness evokes in her readers. Considering her small canon, the never completed novel, and "Requa" (now over a decade since it was published as a work still in progress), one marvels at the way Olsen's vision seems to hover on the brink of expression. It is almost as if her art is a new form, as though she waits for an answer or echo. Even if "Requa" is completed, we can say that Olsen's words to us are brief, her style fragmentary, almost hesitant, her writing like a voice searching for itself and listening as much as—even more than—speaking.

Stevie's muteness, Eva's darkness, Carol's hibernation, Anna's inner ponderings, Jim's silent hands: these may be read as signs of desire for a new speech, a speech (as Nelle Morton says) that we must hear deeply to understand. Olsen's fictive vocabulary, concluding for now with an orphan whose life appears as tentative and unheeded as a dandelion, is both image and form. The images come primarily from maternal realities and hopes; they are of stooped mothers, of children in tears and laughter, of tables, beds, and wreaths of flowers. The form is listening, speaking, and waiting.

Olsen spent years listening, often against her will. Like the mother of "I Stand Here Ironing," and like Eva, she almost lost her voice. But miraculously she regained enough to give us these few stories. She ends them asking for beginnings, and the hope that is in them is her own waiting for an answer, for the echo of readers' voices. Thus is virtue made of necessity, as spirit rises from matter. The image of Stevie crouching in the cemetery is a word before words, a message whose form creates meaning. The unholy child ascends in our reading and meets the unholiness (the brokenness, loss, weariness) in ourselves. In our compassion for him, in our own crouching, we ourselves are cleansed and made new. (pp. 121-36)

Elaine Neil Orr, in her Tillie Olsen and a Feminist Spiritual Vision, *University Press of Mississippi, 1987, 193 p.*

My vision is very different from that of most writers. . . . I don't think in terms of quests for identity to explain human motivation and behavior, I feel that in a world where class, race, and sex are so determining, that that has little reality. What matters to me is the kind of soil *out* of which people have to grow, and the kind of climate around them; circumstances are the primary key and not the personal quest for identity. . . . I want to write what will help change that which is harmful for human beings in our time.

—*Tillie Olsen, in a speech at Emerson College, 1974.*

Blanche H. Gelfant   (essay date 1989)

[In the following essay, Gelfant discusses Olsen's themes and style in "Requa."]

No one has written so eloquently about silences as Tillie Olsen, or shown as poignantly that a writer can recover her voice. In her most recent fiction, a long story called "Requa," she reclaims once more a power of speech that has proved at times extremely difficult to exercise. Silence followed the publication, almost fifty years ago, of sections from her early and still unfinished novel *Yonnondio*. Then came *Tell Me a Riddle,* bringing Olsen fame but not the sustained power to write she needed, and for another long period her voice was stilled. In 1970 "Requa" appeared, an impressive work which received immediate recognition and was reprinted as one of the year's best stories [in *Best American Short Stories,* 1971]. For apparently fortuitous reasons, it is now little known, though as Olsen's most innovative and complex work of fiction, it deserves critical attention it has yet to receive. Complete but unfinished, "Requa" is still-to-be-continued story that develops the theme of human continuity in ways which seem almost subversive. Its form is discontinuous, as though to challenge its theme, and the text is broken visibly into fragments separated from each other by conspicuous blank spaces, gaps the eye must jump over and the mind fill with meaning. However, the story repudiates the meanings that might be inferred from its disintegrated form and from its imagery and setting, both influenced by literary traditions of the past that Olsen continues only to subvert. She draws obviously upon poetry of the twenties for her waste land motifs, and upon novels of the thirties for her realistic portrayal of America's great Depression. Waste and depression are Olsen's subjects in **"Requa,"** but Olsen's voice, resonant after long silence, is attuned to her vision of recovery.

In his poem "After Long Silence," Yeats had defined the "supreme theme" of recovered speech as "Art and Song." Patently, these are not the themes of Olsen's story. **"Requa"** is about uneducated, unsung working people struggling against depression, both the economic collapse of the thirties and the emotional depression of its protagonist, fourteen-year-old Stevie. The story begins with Stevie traumatized by his mother's death and the loss of everything familiar. Alone and estranged from the world, he is being taken by his Uncle Wes from his home in San Francisco to a small California town set by the Klamath River. Here men fish for salmon, hunt deer, and lead a life alien to a city boy. Stevie arrives at this town, named by the Urac tribe Rek-woi, or Requa, broken in body and spirit. A wreck of a child, still dizzy from the long bumpy truck ride, heaving until he "can't have 'ary a shred left to bring up," he seems utterly defeated, unable "to hold up." From the beginning, his obsessive deathwish leads to Stevie's withdrawal: "All he wanted was to lie down." He refuses to speak; he sees human faces dimly or not at all; he huddles in bed, hiding under his quilt and rocking. A "ghostboy" with dazed eyes and clammy green skin, he seems ready to lie down forever. But the story turns aside from death to describe a miraculous recovery, nothing less than Stevie's resurrection, for at the end the silent boy springs spectacularly to life. In the "newly tall, awkward body" he has grown into, he runs, "rassles," "frisks" about like a puppy; and when at last Stevie does lie down, he falls into a sweet sleep from which, it seems, he will awaken rested and restored.

Given the time and place, that recovery should become the pervasive action of the story seems as miraculous as a boy's resurrection. The time is 1932, and the setting a junkyard, the natural stopping-place for dispossessed people on the move during America's great Depression. "Half the grown men in the county's not working," Wes tells the boy, no jobs anywhere. Wes himself works in the junkyard, a realistic place described in encyclopedic detail and a symbolic setting suitable to the theme of loss and recovery. At the junkyard mounds of discarded and disjunct things represent tangibly a vision of disorder, disintegration, and waste. "U NAME IT—WE GOT IT," the yard sign boasts: tools, tees, machine parts, mugs, quilts, wing nuts, ropes, reamers, sewing machines, basket hats, "Indian things," baby buggies, beds, pipe fittings, five-and-dime souvenirs, stoves, victrolas. These wildly proliferating abandoned things form "Heaps piles glut accumulation," but the growing lists of material objects Olsen interjects into the story—or rather, makes its substance—undermine a common assumption that accumulation means wealth. On the contrary, things can reveal the poverty of a person's life. All the souvenirs that Stevie's mother had accumulated, now passed on to her son, are "junk." The more souvenirs the story mentions, the more it shows how little the mother had, though obviously she wished to possess something pretty even if it was only "a kewpie doll [or a] green glass vase, cracked" or a "coiled brass snake Plush candy box: sewing stuff: patches, buttons in jars, stork scissors, pin-cushion doll, taffeta bell skirt glistening with glass pinheads."

But things that at first seem worthless take on a strange incandescence in the story, initially perhaps because of the narrator's tone, a musing, mysterious, reverent tone that imbues isolated objects with emotional meaning. And the lives that seem wasted in the story also begin to glow. The dead mother's felt presence becomes stronger and brighter, shining through characters who help her son and through Stevie himself as he begins to recover. Even the junkyard changes. Piled with seemingly useless things, it gives promise of renewal, for the "human mastery, [the] human skill" which went into making machines, now broken and disassembled, can be applied again and the strewn parts made to function. Olsen's waste land inspires "wonder" at the technological genius that can rehabilitate as well as invent, though it has rampantly destroyed. Olsen expresses no nostalgia for a bygone pastoral past which many American writers wish recovered. She visualizes instead a reclamation in the modern world of the waste its technology has produced. In her story everything can be recycled, and anything broken and discarded put to new use. Nothing is beyond the human imagination that can create even out of waste, the "found" objects in a junkyard, a poetic text. Placed side by side, the names of these objects begin to form a concrete poem the story will interrupt, continue, and complete as it moves along. The first stanza, a listing of ingenious devices, implicitly extols human inventiveness and skill: "Hasps switches screws plugs faucets drills Valves pistons shears planes punchers sheaves Clamps sprockets coils bits braces dies." If these disconnected nouns form also a litany of waste, it is one that introduces the hope of redemption, for Olsen describes "disorder twining with order," a combination which qualifies chaos and may signify its arrest. Moreover, Olsen's final inchoate sentence traces a search through the "discarded, the broken, the torn from the whole; [the] weathereaten weatherbeaten: mouldering" for whatever can still be used or needed, for anything that can be redeemed.

At the junkyard, Stevie sees people as depleted as himself still hoping for redemption. The faceless, nameless migrant workers who stop to pick up a used transmission or discarded tire reflect widespread social disintegration, but like the migrant workers in John Steinbeck's *The Grapes of Wrath,* they persist in trying, struggling, moving. Battered as they are, they refuse the temptation to lie down, and they trade their last possession, a mattress or gun, for whatever will keep them going. "We got a used everything," Evans the yard-owner says, seeing to it that trashed and broken things are fixed and made usable again for people on the move. Evans is tough and wants the "do-re-mi," but whatever his motives, he is crucially involved in the process of recovery. His yard attracts people whose lives have been shattered, the dispossessed migratory workers and, in time, Stevie. The junkyard also sustains Wes, who keeps his self intact as he makes broken parts useful, working capably and even happily, "singing . . . to match the motor hum as he machines a new edge, re-threads a pipe." Meanwhile Wes is trying to make a new life for his nephew: "I'll help you to catch hold, Stevie," he says, "I promise I'll help." Other characters, barely identified, also help, and the story sketches in the outlines of people variously involved in the boy's recovery. Besides Evans, who gives Stevie a chance to work, the Chinese cook at the boardinghouse keeps him company, and the sympathetic landlady takes him on an outing that will complete his recovery.

As **"Requa"** describes the "concern" underprivileged or struggling characters show for each other, it raises Olsen's thematic questions about human responsibility and about the relationship between love and survival. Implicitly it asks why Wes, a lone workingman, should give his skill and energy to make trash useful to others and an alienated boy valuable to himself, and why anyone should care, as everyone does, whether a "ghostboy" recovers. The story thus restates Olsen's recurrent riddle, which is, essentially, the mystery of human survival as evidenced by people who continue to live and to care even though their lives seem broken and futile, and life itself full of pain. If human existence has meaning, as Olsen's fiction asserts, then suffering, bereavement, poverty, despair, all inseparable from day-to-day survival in a waste land, must be explained. So must the secret of recovery, which prevails against depression.

This is a complicated achievement already described in Olsen's earlier stories. In **"I Stand Here Ironing,"** a pock-marked girl becomes beautiful, her talent realized, her unhappy deprived childhood, never forgotten, transcended; and a mother, recalling this childhood, straightens out confused emotions and gains a sense of her own identity. Before the Grandmother dies in **"Tell Me a Riddle,"** she too searches through the past to see what of value she can retrieve; and as she becomes reconciled to her own painful life, now coming to an end, she finds meaning and continuity in all human existence. Olsen can describe such recoveries because she has a strong sense of history as both a personal past that gives one a continuous identity and a social legacy that links generations. This legacy, however, is neither whole nor complete, for history is a dump-heap strewn with broken promises and wrecked hopes, among which lie examples of human achievement. Someone must sort through the junk of history, redeem its waste, and salvage whatever can be useful for the next generation. This is the task of reclamation Olsen has assumed as a writer and assigns to her characters, often unnoted, unlikely, inarticulate people for whom she speaks. Indeed, this is why she must recover her own speech, no matter how long her silence, so that Wes, and Stevie, and the dying Grandmother can have a voice.

In **"Requa"** Stevie continues the quest of the Grandmother in **"Tell Me a Riddle."** Different as they are, the resurrected boy and the dying woman are both searching for a transmittable human past that will give significance to their present struggle. Both need a history as reusable as Wes's re-threaded pipes. The Grandmother finds hers in the record of humanity's continuous progress toward self-realization. She appropriates this history as a shared "Heritage": "How have we come from the savages, how no longer to be savages—this to teach. To look back and learn what humanizes man—this to teach." Young as he is, Stevie also looks back to learn from his past the secret of recovery, of how he might claim his rightful place as a human being. As the story begins he seems dehumanized, so broken and apathetic that he is unable to relate to anyone else or to himself, unable to see the people in the boarding-house or the beauty of the countryside that will in time shake him with "ecstasy." Described as a "ghostboy," he appears doomed to inanition, but the story struggles against this fate and insists in hushed portentous tones that something will save him: "The known is reaching to him, stealthily, secretly, reclaiming." Both mysterious and obvious, the *known* is Stevie's personal past, experiences from which he will in time draw the strength to live. This strength comes mainly from the remembered love of his mother, the person in his past who has provided him with a "recognizable human bond" which must sustain him and matter more than the losses that life makes inevitable. Even in his withdrawal, a quest for "safety" from the shocks he has suffered, Stevie recognizes that the bond is holding, that Wes is taking the place of his mother by showing "concern." Wes is in Stevie's "corner," willing to share whatever he knows. "I got so much to learn you," he says, looking to the future; and looking back at the past, he vows not to let Stevie "[go] through what me and Sis did." Though he is an orphan, Stevie belongs to a family bound together by ties Olsen insists can remain irrefragable, even in a landscape of waste. When Wes becomes helpless, falling on his bed in a drunken stupor, Stevie tends to his uncle as once he had been cared for by his mother. He takes off Wes's muddy shoes and covers his body with blankets: *"There now you'll be warm,* he said aloud, *sleep sweet, sweet dreams* (though he did not know he had said it, nor in whose inflections)." Then he stares at the sleeping face in a crucial moment of recognition: "Face of his mother. *His* face. Family face."

Once Stevie can see clearly the *"human bond"* created by the human family, he begins to see objects and people that had been vague: The windows in the dining room which had been "black mirrors where apparitions swam"; the Indian decorations on the wall; the bizarre family resemblance between a bearded face and the face of his landlady. The forces of reclamation are finally reaching Stevie, forces shaped by the care and concern that have linked generations together in an endless chain of human relationships. Thus, though **"Requa"** describes the fragmentation of a life disrupted by death, it creates in the end a vision of relatedness that gives the displaced person somewhere to belong. Wes's loyalty to his sister's child makes possible Stevie's recovery of the life he lost when his mother died; and Stevie's consciousness of recovery begins when he recognizes the face of his mother in any human being who cares for another, his uncle, his landlady, himself. In an unexpected way, Olsen speaks of the power of mother love as a basis for the continuity of one's self and of one's relationships with others. History keeps a record of these relationships, preserving and fostering the ties of one generation to another; and literature extends these ties as it creates a bond of sympathy between the reader and such unlikely characters as Stevie, whose experience of depression and death is universal.

As the story continues, work reinforces a recovery made possible by extended acts of love, and Stevie's apprenticeship period at the junkyard proves therapeutic. Understanding perhaps that he can learn from things as broken as he is, Stevie has begged to work with Wes rather than attend school. As he undertakes the task of sorting out the accumulated junk in the yard, the story begins to sort out its contents, separating order from disorder; and Stevie sorts out his life. He bungles and fails at his job in the junkyard, but he keeps trying because *"the tasks"* are there, *"coaxing."* Describing these tasks, ordinary daily labor, Olsen dignifies the menial worker and his work. Stevie sees Wes showing "concern" for a trashed car as "he machines a new edge, rethreads a pipe." A man's labor expresses his love; and a boy's tasks pull him "to attention, consciousness"; they teach him "trustworthiness, pliancy"; they force him "to hold up." The salvaging effect of work, even the work of salvaging, dramatizes the theme of **"Requa"** and shows Olsen's experience of the 1930s still shaping her social vision. During the Depression she had seen jobless men lose their self-respect, and she learned a simple tautological truth: economic recovery, as well as the recovery of a broken individual, comes with work. Even the most menial task, as she would show in **"Requa,"** can be redemptive. Instinctively, Stevie knows this and wants a job, "a learn job, Wes. By you." Work will bond him to another and teach him the secret of survival. At the junkyard Stevie slowly acquires skill and patience, which give him a sense of self-respect. He can put things together, including himself. As he sorts through heaps of waste, he finds a rhythm to his life: The incremental repetition of tasks produces a sense of pattern and continuity, of meaning. He is becoming someone who keeps working, making order, and making himself into an integrated person, like Wes. Slowly, "coaxed" by his tasks, he too is showing "concern."

The climactic moment of Stevie's return to life occurs, oddly enough, as he commemorates the dead. On Memorial Day, Mrs. Edler, the landlady, takes Stevie to church for a requiem celebration and then to several cemeteries. At church, encountering other "families, other young" who remember their dead, he realizes that loss, like love, constitutes a human bond. Moreover, as long as the dead are remembered they are never entirely lost, for the human community includes both mourners and the mourned. At the cemetery, Stevie embraces a stone lamb that may represent the ultimate inexplicability of death, the mystery of its arbitrariness as it claims an infant's life. The quaint consoling verse on the lamb tells that the baby is safely sleeping, and it seems to lull Stevie to rest: "The lamb was sun warm. . . . He put his arm around its stone neck and rested." Calmly embracing a figure of death, Ste-

vie at last finds peace at the Requiescat in Pace cemetery. His story, however, is not over, for the act of recovery is never entirely consummated. **"Requa"** concludes with the word "reclaiming," after which there is neither the end parenthesis the text requires nor a final period—as though the process of reclamation still goes on and will continue with no sign of ending.

In the last scene, Stevie's "newly tall" body suggests that time has effected recovery simply by letting the boy grow; but the natural gathering of strength that comes with the body's maturation needs the reinforcement of human relationship and love. A faceless woman, merely a name in the story, Mrs. Edler or Mrs. Ed, has taken Stevie in hand and acted as catalyst for his recovery. She does this, apparently, because she feels sorry for an orphan boy, though Olsen's characterization of Stevie raises questions of why she should mother him. Stevie is a silent, withdrawn, and ghostlike boy, if not sleeping then vomiting, and awake or asleep, dripping with snot. However, the characters in **"Requa"** have a clairvoyance that comes from caring, and they see beyond appearances, just as they communicate without words, or with curses and insults that express love. Throughout the story, Wes calls Stevie "dummy" and "loony" and swears the boy will end in the crazy house; but Wes's insults in no way affect his action nor show disaffection. Rather they express frustration as he waits for Stevie's recovery. Wes's happiest moment comes at the end of the story when he looks at the blissfully sleeping boy and says, "blowing out the biggest bubble of snot you ever saw. Just try and figger that loony kid."

Olsen's style in **"Requa"** is conspicuously varied. Lyrical passages are juxtaposed to crude dialectic speech, and stream of consciousness passages to objectively seen realistic details. Numerous lists of things represent a world of objects proliferating outside the self; but a mind encompasses these objects and tries to find in their disorder a way of ordering an inner tumult expressed by the roiling fragments of the story. Like the junkyard, the story is the repository of bits and pieces: sentences broken into phrases separated into words, words isolated by blank spaces. Single words on a line or simply sounds—"aaagh / aaagh"— mark the end of narrative sections, some introduced by titles such as *Rifts* and *Terrible Pumps*. Even the typography is discontinuous, so that the text seems a mosaic of oddly assorted fragments. In creating a visibly discontinuous text, in effect turning **"Requa"** into a design upon the page, Olsen attracts attention to her form, which always refers the reader to a social world that **"Requa"** presents as real, recognizable, and outside the fiction. Still **"Requa"** exists as an object: its varied typography creates truncated patterns of print that catch the eye; words placed together as lists or as fragmentary refrains form distinct visual units; blocks of nouns separated from the text produce concrete poems; intervening spaces turn into aesthetic entities. Mimetic of her theme, Olsen's form is enacting the story's crucial phrase: *"Broken existences that yet continue."* As a text, **"Requa"** is broken and yet continuous, its action extending beyond its open-ended ending. The story transforms a paradox into a promise as it turns the polarities of fragmentation and continuity into obverse aspects of each other. Merged together, the broken pieces of

"Requa" create an integrated self as well as an aesthetic entity. The story enacts a process of composition to show broken existences continuing, order emerging from disorder, art from images of waste, and speech from the void of silence.

Among the many reasons for silence that Tillie Olsen has enumerated, another may be added. Perhaps what the writer has to say is too painful to express: mothers die, children sorrow, working families are evicted from homes and left with nothing to trade for a gallon of gasoline. Olsen speaks of knowledge ordinarily repressed, and while she dignifies her characters and their work, her story denies the cherished illusion that childhood in America is a happy time of life. But "Requa" preaches no social doctrine; unlike the novel *Yonnondio,* which also describes a child caught in a period of depression, it preaches nothing at all, although a preacher's fragmentary phrases of consolation help restore the boy. Rather, the story contains a secret that must be pieced together from disconnected fragments, inferred from blank spaces on the page, melded out of poetic prose and vomit, snot, and violence. This secret, that broken existences can continue, is stated explicitly. Left unsaid is another truth that both affirms and subverts the view of the poet. Yeats had described speech after long silence as an extended discourse upon Art and Song, "we descant and yet again descant." In "Requa," Olsen has said nothing about art. Her speech, resumed after ten years of silence, simply *is* art. This is the secret inherent in Tillie Olsen's story of recovery, in which a child's renewed will to live becomes inseparable from an artist's recovered power to write. (pp. 61-8)

> *Blanche H. Gelfant, "After Long Silence: Tillie Olsen's 'Requa',"* in Studies in American Fiction, *Vol. 12, No. 1, Spring, 1989, pp. 61-9.*

Jane Silverman Van Buren   (essay date 1989)

[*In the following excerpt, Van Buren explores the treatment of motherhood in "Tell Me a Riddle."*]

Olsen argues that motherhood, as it is structured, prohibits the full flowering of the serious artist. As mother bears the major share of responsibility for child rearing, and children's needs may not be postponed, the priorities of the artist fall more and more into the background. Olsen adds that since society itself offers little protection and aid to families, the family (largely mother) must provide most of the needs of the next generation. [In *Silences* she] reveals that her own costs have been heavy.

> As for myself, who did not publish a book until I was 50, who raised children without household help or the help of the 'technological sublime,' (the atom bomb was manufactured before the first automatic washing machine); who worked outside the house on everyday jobs as well (as nearly half of all women do now, though a woman with a paid job except as a maid or a prostitute is still rarest of any in literature); who could not kill the essential angel (there was no one else to do their work) would not if I could have killed the caring part of the Woolf angel; as distant from the world of literature most of

my life as literature is distant (in content to) from my world.

In "Tell Me a Riddle," Olsen fashions an alter ego who shares the same dilemma. The main character Eva's intellectual life is made irreconcilable with her experience of motherhood as it is organized around the segregation of the sexual spheres. Eva, now a grandmother, bitterly accuses her husband David of robbing her of time to reflect, to think, and to read. Drawn in the style of Cassatt's self-respecting woman, she personifies women's individuality and mental strength and brings to us the history of many women. As a youngster in Russia, she gained her literacy and education through sacrifice and tragedy. A friend, an upper-class woman, defied authority and tradition to teach Eva to read. The woman was executed for her treason while Eva herself spent a year in prison. Thus, reading was a highly valued activity, a costly gift, and a means to her self-realization. Critical of traditional culture that crushes individuality, Eva vehemently rejects the lifeless shell of ritual and superstition. In response to religious practices, Eva says of her conventional daughter:

> Swindler. Does she look back on the dark centuries, candles bought instead of bread and stuck into a potato for a candlestick? Religion that stifled and said, 'In paradise, woman, you will be the footstool of your husband,' and in life poor chosen Jew ground under, despised, trembling in cellars and cremated heritage. How have we come from our savage past. How no longer to be savages, this to teach—to look back and learn what humanizes. This to teach—to smash all ghettos that divide us. Not to go back, not to go back. This to teach—learned books in the house. Will humankind live or die? And she gives her boys superstition.

Throughout the narrative and the long years of difficult child rearing, Eva maintains her freedom of mind, her conviction, and her anger. Despite the many obstacles she encounters and the pain she endures, her vitality and steadfastness are a legacy to her children. "Old scar tissues ruptured and the wounds festered anew. She thought without softness of that young life in the deep night hours while she nursed the current baby and perhaps held another in her lap or tried to stay awake for the only time to read."

Olsen, exploring the parameters of motherhood and female identity at mid-century faced the monster of urban industrial indifference rather than the old Victorian moral persecution. She found women and their children, particularly those of immigrants and working class origins lost and forgotten in the urban industrial culture, which she characterized as an extension of frontier values and manifest destiny and one in which actions and influence were to be realized largely in the possession of economic and military power. In one of Olsen's other pieces in the collection *Tell Me a Riddle* called "I Stand Here Ironing," she centers on the dangerous descent of a child reared on meager nurture. The working mother, like Harriet Beecher Stowe's earlier slave mothers, is forced to abandon her infant child to the blight of marasmus-like depression.

> She was a beautiful baby. She blew shining bub-

bles of sound. She loved motion, loved life, loved color and music and textures. She would lie on the floor in her blue overalls patting the surface so hard in ecstasy her hands and feet would blur. She was a miracle to me, but when she was eighteen months old I left her with a woman downstairs to whom she was no miracle at all, for I worked or looked for work.

As part of Olsen's rethinking family myths, she presents clearly the conflict between the mother self and the woman self or between the self and maternal obligation as well as the male/female tensions about women's mind and independence. Eva reminds her husband, the breadwinner father, of his indifference: "How cleverly you hid that you heard. Eighteen hours a day I ran and you never scraped a carrot or knew a dishtowel."

As Olsen presents the nuclear family structured on the painful and forced segregation of male and female, she connects the patterns to societal values which discount the plight of women and children who are without access to political and economic power, a culture of hard with an aversion to soft. "But for those years she had had to manage old humiliations and terrors rose up, lived again, and forced her to relive them. The children's needings, that grocer's face or the merchant's wife that she had had to beg credit from when credit was a disgrace. School coming and the desperate going over the old to see what could yet be remade; the soups from meatbones begged for the dog one winter."

Olsen reminds us of the importance of the experiences of reciprocity in their blissful as well as painful aspects. Despite the pain of her isolated situation, Eva has generously shared with her children her commitment to significance, awareness, and freedom of mind. The experience is wrenching and draining. Eva has given her mind and body to shelter her children from the searing edge of cultural indifference. Now, past the child-rearing tasks, she cherishes the vision of tranquility, of solace, of a time for herself. She says, "Never again to be forced to move to the rhythm of others, being able at last to live within and not move to the rhythm of others." She is painfully reminded by her grandchildren of the old experiences of attachment. "Now they put a baby in her lap. 'Do not ask me,' she would have liked to say, 'I cannot. Cannot. Cannot. Cannot.' What an unnatural grandmother not to be able to make herself embrace a baby."

Olsen turns her powerful lens on the demands of the maternal experience. Sex, power, and material reassurances fall away before the flood of these vivid memories. "It was not that she had not loved her babies, her children. The love, the passion of tending had risen with the need like a torrent, and like a torrent drowned and immolated all else." Olsen/Eva reminds us of the inevitability of the tearing weaning and the return to separate existence after intense reciprocity.

> But when the need was done, all the power that was lost and the painful damming back and drawing up of what still surged but had nowhere to go, only the thin pulsing left that could not quiet, suffering over lives one felt but could no longer hold or help.

On that torrent she had born them to their own lives and the river bed was desert long years now. Nor there would she dwell, a memoried waif; somewhere an older power that beat full of life, somewhere coherence, transport and meaning.

Olsen/Eva reminds us of the need for solitude as a time for rediscovery of the inner self. But they put a baby in her lap. The old claims of overflowing intimacy threatened to engulf her.

> Needlessly to embrace and the breath of that past: warm flesh like this that had claims and nuzzled away all else and with lovely mouths devoured; hot living like an animal intensely and now; the turning maze; the long drunkenness, the drowning into needing and being needed. Severely, she looked back, and the shudder seized her again, and the sweat. Not that way. Not there. Not now could she. Not yet. In all that visit she could not touch the baby.

Yet, Eva's generosity of spirit and maternal capacities radiate out into the next generation of mothers and children. Vivian, now grown, makes this connection with gratitude. "Nursing the baby my friends marvel, and I tell them, 'Oh, it's easy to be such a cow. I remember how beautiful my mother seemed nursing my brother and the milk just flows.'" The reciprocity moves over the generations.

As Olsen inherited the building blocks of a personal myth from her artist ancestors, her signs became filled with the released elements of their personal myths; and standing on the foundation of the work of Stowe, Alcott, and Cassatt, she rethinks cultural and personal themes of mothers and children from a less limited vertex. Her angry protests against the treatment imposed on women and children is not confined, but expands out into chains of meaning which reach backward and forward in time, across national barriers, generations, and overcomes biased oppositions. The semiotic chain of *Riddle* is made up of several relational structures. Eva, much like the signifiers Eva St. Clair/Cassie or Beth/Jo, or Irma/Freud, is not only at the center of the narrative, holding together many juxtapositions, but goes beyond the danger of sacrifice. Eva's experience as a young person in Russia contrasted with that of her old age in America illuminates her capacity to endure change and grow and influence the lives of three generations. As a woman escaped from tyranny, her life interfaces with her children and grandchildren, born and raised in a democracy. Eva's relationship to her husband David illuminates the contrast or juxtaposition between radical feminism and the traditional Jewish patriarchy. The most crucial juxtaposition of the piece, which provides a sign of the continuity of growth and bonding, is that of Eva's radicalism and devotion to revolutionary causes, with the commitment of her granddaughter Jeannie to work as a nurse for the poor and elderly. The emotional force of these juxtapositions breaks into the linear tidiness of the narrative and releases the meaning of Eva's life from saturated cultural preconceptions and from social customs and laws and from history and time. The significance and power of her feelings and attitude extend out for sixty years, sustained by her determination to survive.

At a still deeper level, the story finds its force in the processes of transformation of overflow, ecstasy, and being, which support and fill the symbolic juxtapositions. The transformations flow out of Eva's thoughts and images. A central image is of her grandchildren; their freshness, liveliness, and desire to know in contrast to her own difficult childhood and youth under tyranny and the hardship of raising her own children in a strange land without emotional and economic support. It is Eva's capacity for endurance and fidelity that has made their lives possible.

At the end of her life, Eva has only a few months to live, and she makes a last journey to visit her grandchildren, first at the house of her son, and then to her daughter's, and finally to her granddaughter's home. Her son's children are of latency age and enjoy grandmother immensely. They ask Eva to play, and to listen, and to tell them a riddle. Their excited love and appetite for companionship releases opposite images and circumstances in Eva's mind. She relives the conditions of her own education, the arrest and execution of her beloved mentor Lisa. Here, enthusiasm, love, and eager curiosity are counterposed to the conditions of tyranny in which love of knowledge is crushed. One side of this juxtaposition is the protection and nurture of children; the other, the hard container of tyranny which seeks to destroy authentic expressiveness and curiosity.

The second stop of Eva's last journey brings her to her daughter's family and a new baby. The snug, everyday family life laced with baby smells and sounds again evokes terrifying dreams and memories for Eva, not only the taxing experience of nursing and tending but of the insistent nightmare of the partial abortion of her own child self, of her creative thoughts, and of the death of the Lisa aspect of herself. How much of the authentic dreams had she been able to save for herself and for her children and their children?

The story also works throughout its course with the overflow between husband and wife. The turbulent relations between Eva and David are partly fed on the social prescriptions of what male and female must be. Eva, as the keeper of infantile life, and David, as the breadwinner father forced out of the mother-child sphere as she is kept out of the public sphere, antagonize each other from their oppositional priorities. Hard and soft, me and not-me, private and public clash and war in Eva and David's relationship. Another element of their dissension is Eva's private self. Eva as a talented intellectual and revolutionary fights for her privacy to think, read, and write. David cannot understand her interests and feels shut out. The needs of babies and husbands and the priority of intellectual and political commitment compete for Eva's attention.

Sitting loyally beside Eva as she lies dying, David reflects painfully on the gap between them. Prompted by the sound of her whimpers, death swallows, and pageant of halfdreamt memories, David realizes the jagged edge of their differences. Reflecting on her love for books, David says,

> "It helps, Mrs. Philosopher, words from books, it helps." But he felt pushed out—that for seventy years she had hidden a tape recorder infinitely microscopic within her, that it had coiled infinite mile on mile, trapping every song, every melody, every word heard and spoken and that maliciously she was playing back only what said nothing of him, of the children, and of their intimate life together.

Eva's nostalgic journey into her revolutionary activities and interests painfully reminds David of Eva's private self.

> The cards fell from his fingers without warning the bereavement and betrayal he had sheltered—compounded through the years—hidden even from himself—revealed itself,

> uncoiled
> released
> sprung

> And with it the monstrous shapes of what had actually happened in the century.

Olsen moves us from opposition to integration inside the male mind who loves his children and his wife. Continuing the death vigil with Eva, David views the enormity of her life. Empathetically responding to Eva's vivid parade of memories, David begins to journey with her:

> . . . and instantly he left the neat old woman poring over the Book of the Martyrs; went past the mother treading at the sewing machine; past the girl in her wrinkled prison dress, hiding her hair with scarred hands, lifting to him her awkward chain imploring eyes of love; and took her in his arms, dear, personal, fleshed, and all the heavy passion he had loved to rouse from her.

As Eva lies dying at Jeannie's Santa Monica apartment, the generational interface is explored in its final form. Olsen studies the mother-child feelings at the close of the parent's life. "Now one by one the children come, those that were able. Hannah, Paul, Sammy. Too late to ask; and what did you learn from your loving mother and what do you need to know."

The oldest child Clara, silent, reviews her bitterness. " 'Pay me back, mother. Pay me back for all you took from me. Those others you crowded into your heart. Is this she, noises the dying make, the crab-like hands crawling on the covers?' " Another child deplores the irrevocable rift between them. " 'I do not know you mother. Mother I never knew you.' " Still another experiences her death compassionately and mourns not only for himself but for that which never lived. For him, too, unspoken words, " 'Goodbye mother, who taught me to mother myself.' "

The surfacing and articulation of the feelings and attitudes that take place between the generations transform the nature and function of the familial myth. In this case, the myth instructs and offers reconciliation.

In the last days of Eva's life, her capacity to bond centers on the relationship to her granddaughter and to her husband David. She allows them to chaperone her to her death, and a new family group is created. Eva and Jeannie reveal themselves to each other in these painful last days. As Jeannie's anguish about her abortion is met by Eva's empathy (she too has lost children, one in Korea and one by abortion), Eva opens her life and mind to Jeannie to provide support and a sense of continuity, but also to pass on to Jean the values and history of her life. Later Jeannie tells her grandfather that Eva has the need to share her legacy and to pass on her knowledge. She particularly wants to pass on not only the legacy of attachment within the family but its implications in the social sphere. Her vision includes more than the politics of the Russian revolution; it extends to a personal politics of her own mind, a politics of freedom in which infantile mental life and its emotional forces as well as new ideas can survive without fear of the tyranny, torture, exile that stems from unintegrated hardness.

The Eva/David, Eva/Jean relationships are brought together powerfully by the imminence of Eva's death. Jean and her grandfather form a bond of solace to help Eva and him through the tearing separation. Jeannie accepts the legacy of Eva's political and social experiences and personal knowledge. In Eva's mythic odyssey within the Eva/Jean/David structure, all oppositions are brought together and integrated. Age and youth, male and female, weakness and strength, sickness and health, and of course finally life and death. Jeannie's mind takes on the responsibility that her grandmother's had held. She assumes the task of containing and integrating the powerful elements of her familial and personal myth. Similarly, Olsen takes on these tasks to create new cultural myths, meanings, and interpretations which value the female and child in all of us. Through this effort, no issue is hidden, nor disavowed. Eva as a white goddess, the mother of origin, provides us with the knowledge and the strength by which to make sense of the experience of the developmental journey of the self into individuated mental life. (pp. 161-67)

> *Jane Silverman Van Buren, "Other Madonnas," in her* The Modernist Madonna: Semiotics of the Maternal Metaphor, *Indiana University Press, 1989, pp. 161-67.*

FURTHER READING

Burkom, Selma, and Williams, Margaret. "De-Riddling Tillie Olsen's Writings." *San Jose Studies* 2, No. 1 (February 1976): 65-83.

> Asserts that Olsen's career through the mid-1970s can be broken down into three phases, in which she emphasizes the political sphere, private life, and feminist issues.

Cunneen, Sally. "Tillie Olsen: Storyteller of Working America." *The Christian Century* XCVII, No. 19 (21 May 1980): 570-74.

> Biographical sketch attributing the themes of Olsen's fiction to a combination of her skill at characterization and her ability to draw on her own experiences and family history.

Dunkan, Erika. "Coming of Age in the Thirties: A Portrait of Tillie Olsen." *Book Forum* VI, No. 2 (1982): 207-22.

> Examination of Olsen's incorporation of events from the 1930s into her own writing, particularly *Yonnondio*.

McNeil, Helen. "Speaking for the Speechless." *The Times Literary Supplement,* No. 4050 (14 November 1980): 1294.

> Favorable review of *Silences, Yonnondio,* and *Tell Me a Riddle.*

Niehus, Edward L., and Jackson, Teresa. "Polar Stars, Pyramids, and 'Tell Me a Riddle'." *American Notes and Queries* XXIV, Nos. 5-6 (January-February 1986): 77-83.

> Analysis of "Tell Me a Riddle" examining the process of association which leads the protagonist to refer to Thuban, the pole star of ancient Egypt.

Rosenfelt, Deborah. "From the Thirties: Tillie Olsen and the Radical Tradition." *Feminist Studies* 7, No. 3 (Fall 1981): 370-406.

> Emphasizes Olsen's involvement in radical politics and "contemporary feminist culture" and their impact on her writing.

Additional coverage of Olsen's life and career is contained in the following sources published by Gale Research: *Contemporary Authors,* **Volume 4, rev. ed.;** *Contemporary Authors New Revision Series,* **Volume 1;** *Contemporary Literary Criticism,* **Volumes 4, 13;** *Dictionary of Literary Biography,* **Volume 28;** *Dictionary of Literary Biography Yearbook, 1980;* **and** *Major 20th-Century Writers.*

John Steinbeck

1902-1968

(Full name John Ernst Steinbeck) American novelist, short story writer, nonfiction writer, playwright, journalist, and screenwriter.

INTRODUCTION

While Steinbeck is best known for his novel *The Grapes of Wrath* and is regarded as one of the most significant American novelists of the twentieth century, he first began to develop a distinct literary voice and to experiment with characterization, concision, and thematic unity in his short stories. Addressing the repercussions of social exploitation, puritanism, and materialistic values in his fiction, Steinbeck is noted for his sharp, forceful idiom, wry humor, and profound compassion for the poor, the inarticulate, and the politically oppressed. Stories such as "The Chrysanthemums," "Flight," "The Leader of the People," and "The White Quail" are considered among the world's best short fiction.

Many of Steinbeck's short stories are set in and around his birthplace, the Salinas Valley in California. It was here, after graduating from Salinas High School in 1919, that Steinbeck worked a variety of odd jobs, including store clerk, surveyor, and ranch hand, to pay for his college education. Steinbeck later incorporated these experiences and by extension his concerns about the working class into his writings. While intermittently taking biology and literature classes at Stanford University during the early 1920s, Steinbeck developed a "biological" view of humanity, a perspective that highly influenced his fiction. He believed that such evolutionary concepts as adaptation and natural selection apply to human society and that more profound observations could be gleaned from examining social groups rather than individuals. After a brief stint as a journalist in New York City, Steinbeck returned to California and completed his first novel, *Cup of Gold*. Despite the publication of this work in 1929, Steinbeck found it necessary to sell stories to magazines in order to support himself financially. These stories were later collected in the volumes *The Red Pony* and *The Long Valley*. Steinbeck continued to write short fiction throughout the 1930s, but after the success of his novels *Tortilla Flat* and *Of Mice and Men* he focused almost exclusively on writing novels until his death in 1968.

The Pastures of Heaven and *The Red Pony,* two volumes of thematically linked stories, are not generally considered short story collections in the traditional sense, but most critics deem them integral to Steinbeck's development as a short story writer. *The Pastures of Heaven* is a loosely related collection set in California's Corral de Tierra Valley. These stories concern a group of people who fail in their attempt to establish an idyllic farming community

free from restrictive urban pressures. Most critics agree that the characters in this volume—ordinary people whose illusions and self-deceptions prevent them from confronting life's realities—illustrate the frustration, despair, and isolation associated with contemporary American life. *The Red Pony* originally comprised three stories—"The Gift," "The Great Mountains," and "The Promise"—and the volume was expanded in 1945 to include "The Leader of the People." This collection details a boy's maturation and his acceptance of death when he loses his colt to pneumonia. Exploring such themes as the loss of innocence and faith, these stories evince Steinbeck's belief that suffering and grief are inevitable and must be experienced to live life fully.

The Long Valley, Steinbeck's most popular short story collection, contains all of Steinbeck's extant stories, including *The Red Pony,* the previously published *Saint Katy the Virgin,* and those stories set in the Long Valley. The volume also includes such widely anthologized stories as "The Chrysanthemums," "The Harness," and "The White Quail." While critics agree that the work suffers organizational problems because of its all-inclusive nature, they concede that Steinbeck's insightful treatment of such psychological concerns as repression, fear, violence, and suicide overshadows the volume's structural flaws. Throughout the collection, the majority of the characters are tormented people who are unable or unwilling to confront what Steinbeck has termed the "tragic miracle of consciousness." "The Chrysanthemums," for example, involves a woman who seeks love but is manipulated by a crafty vagrant, while "The Harness" focuses on a man who remains emotionally dependent on his domineering wife despite her recent death. Steinbeck further explores self-deception in "The White Quail," a story about a woman whose obsessive identification with a white quail reflects her inability to accept herself or others.

Early critical reaction to Steinbeck's short fiction was generally favorable, but following World War II his literary reputation began to decline. During the 1950s and 1960s commentators began to fault Steinbeck's stories for being sentimental, philosophically simplistic, and overly theatrical. Contemporary critics recognize, however, that Steinbeck's short fiction reflects the social and psychological concerns evident in his novels and that his stories often served as preparatory sketches for his longer, more celebrated works. Despite critical trends, Steinbeck's realistic yet sensitive portrayal of ordinary working-class people has consistently garnered praise and when Steinbeck was awarded the Nobel Prize in literature in 1962, the awards committee lauded his "sympathetic humor and sociological perception." Underscoring his aims as a writer in his acceptance speech, Steinbeck asserted: "The ancient commission of the writer has not changed. He is charged with exposing our many grievous faults and failures, with dredging up to the light our dark and dangerous dreams for the purpose of improvement. Furthermore, the writer is delegated to declare and to celebrate man's proven capacity for greatness of heart and spirit—for gallantry in defeat—for courage, compassion, and love. In the endless war against weakness and despair, these are the bright rally-flags of hope and emulation."

PRINCIPAL WORKS

SHORT FICTION

The Pastures of Heaven   1932
Nothing So Monstrous   1936
Saint Katy the Virgin   1936
The Red Pony   1937; also published as *The Red Pony* [enlarged edition], 1945
The Long Valley   1938; also published as *Thirteen Great Stories from the Long Valley* [revised edition], 1943; and *Fourteen Great Stories from the Long Valley* [revised edition], 1947
How Edith McGillicuddy Met R.L.S.   1943
The Crapshooter   1957

OTHER MAJOR WORKS

Cup of Gold   (novel)   1929
To a God Unknown   (novel)   1933
Tortilla Flat   (novel)   1935

In Dubious Battle   (novel)   1936
Of Mice and Men   (novel)   1937
*Of Mice and Men: A Play in Three Acts   (drama)   1937
The Grapes of Wrath   (novel)   1939
The Moon Is Down   (novel)   1942
†The Moon Is Down: A Play in Two Parts   (drama) 1942
Cannery Row   (novel)   1945
The Pearl   (novel)   1947
A Russian Journal   (travel essays)   1948
Burning Bright   (novel)   1950
East of Eden   (novel)   1952
Sweet Thursday   (novel)   1954
The Short Reign of Pippin IV: A Fabrication   (novel) 1957
Once There Was a War   (nonfiction)   1958
The Winter of Our Discontent   (novel)   1961
Speech Accepting the Nobel Prize for Literature   (speech) 1962
Travels with Charley: In Search of America   (nonfiction) 1962
America and Americans   (travel essays)   1966
Steinbeck: A Life in Letters   (letters)   1975
Working Days: The Journals of "The Grapes of Wrath" (journal)   1989

*This work is an adaptation of the novel *Of Mice and Men*.

†This work is an adaptation of the novel *The Moon Is Down*.

CRITICISM

Peter Lisca   (essay date 1958)

[*Lisca is an Italian-born American educator and critic who has written numerous works on Steinbeck, including* John Steinbeck: Nature and Myth *(1978). In the excerpt below, taken from his* The Wide World of John Steinbeck, *Lisca provides a thematic and stylistic analysis of* The Pastures of Heaven *and* The Long Valley. *While* The Pastures of Heaven *is not considered a short story collection in the traditional sense, Lisca considers the volume integral to Steinbeck's development as a short story writer.*]

In May of 1931 [Steinbeck wrote to his agents about *The Pastures of Heaven*]:

The present work interests me and perhaps falls in the "aspects" theme you mention. There is, about twelve miles from Monterey, a valley in the hills called Corral de Tierra. Because I am using its people I have named it Las Pasturas del Cielo. The valley was for years known as the happy valley because of the unique harmony which existed among its twenty families. About ten years ago a new family moved in on one of the ranches. They were ordinary people, ill educated but honest and as kindly as any. In fact, in their whole history I cannot find that they have committed a really malicious act nor an act which was not dictated by honorable expediency or out and out altruism. But about the M—s there was a flavor of evil. Everyone they came in contact with was injured. Every place they went dissension sprang up. There have been two murders, a suicide, many quarrels and a great deal of unhappiness in the Pastures of Heaven, and all of these things can be traced to the influence of the M—s. So much is true. I am using the following method. The manuscript is made up of stories each one complete in itself, having its rise, climax and ending. Each story deals with a family or individual. They are tied together only by the common locality and by the contact with the M—s. I am trying to show this peculiar evil cloud which follows the M—s. Some of the stories are very short and some as long as fifteen thousand words. I thought of combining them with that thirty-thousand ms called Dissonant Symphony to make one volume. . . . I think the plan at least falls very definitely into the aspects of American Life category. I have finished several and am working on others steadily. They should be done by this Fall.

Except for mentioning one more murder than appeared in *The Pastures of Heaven,* this letter is an accurate general sketch of the book's structure and content. Notations on the title sheet of the first draft (written in a 6 × 9 composition book) indicate, however, that earlier he had planned a slightly different scheme of organization. Steinbeck there noted that *"Pasturas"* would be "a curious story of which at least half—or one third—of the space is taken up with dramatis personae." His first plans called for a large portion of the book to deal with the various family histories *before* the Munroes arrive: "The first chapter will deal with the valley itself: and following that will be nine or ten chapters devoted to nine or ten families. Then will come the entrance of the M—s." The title page of this first draft also shows a different order for the stories; some, **"Howard and the Spinach"** and **"Blind Frank,"** do not appear in the final version. There are no titles in this first list which might suggest the book's last three sections: the stories about Pat Humbert, John Whiteside, and the group of bus passengers. Also absent is the story of the Lopez sisters, which Harry Thornton Moore says was originally part of *To a God Unknown,* although it would seem that the John Whiteside story, having many parallels to that book, fits better into its scheme.

This first draft abounds in deletions and additions. Steinbeck was having difficulties following his original plans, and in the margin opposite the third story, which introduced the Munroes, he wrote, "There are things so definitely wrong with this story that I think it had better be remade. A large part of it anyway." The eventual remaking was a great improvement because it brought together the two (pre- and post-Munroe) parts of each story into one unit. In some stories, for example the one about Pat Humbert and especially that about Shark Wicks (which was the first one he wrote), this splicing is still evident.

By the middle of August Steinbeck was well along, writing his agents that "The Pastures stories proceed rapidly. . . . They should be ready to submit by Christmas."

At that time he sent along the manuscript of "Dissonant Symphony," which he still thought might be included "under one cover with the Pastures of Heaven." It was *not* included with the stories, however, and after publication of *The Pastures of Heaven* in October, 1932, Steinbeck wrote, "The manuscript called Dissonant Symphony, I wish you would withdraw. I looked at it not long ago and I don't want it out. I may rewrite it sometime, but I certainly do not want that mess published under any circumstances, revised or not."

The Pastures of Heaven is not, strictly speaking, a novel, partly because the several stories are too autonomous structurally and aesthetically. Many of the episodes were based on stories Steinbeck's mother used to tell about her adventures when she, like Molly Morgan, taught school in rural communities. With one or two exceptions, there is no reason why one story must precede or follow another. The section dealing with Molly Morgan, for example, is not made more meaningful or effective by the role she played in two preceding stories—those of Tularecito and Junius Maltby. Although most critics have perceived that *The Pastures of Heaven* is not really a novel, most have missed the importance of the Munroe family and have tried to make too much of the stories' unity by pinning them together with some other theme: the contrast between dream and reality, the realization of life through illusion, and the suppression of the individual by society. Each of these themes may be made to apply to one or even two or three of the stories, but attempts to impose them on the book as a whole have only resulted in obscuring its real structure and distorting the emphasis of individual stories.

On the other hand, as Steinbeck indicated in his letter to his agents, the book has more unity than might be expected from a collection of short stories. In addition to the unity provided by a common locale and theme, the book is given a certain roundness by the two introductory stories about the valley's history, the penultimate story about the defeat of the valley's patriarch, John Whiteside, and the concluding story about the busload of tourists who look down on the valley and envy its apparent peace and tranquility. If it is kept in mind that although the Munroes are an "evil cloud," as Steinbeck put it, they never commit "a really malicious act nor an act . . . not dictated by honorable expediency or out and out altruism," it becomes obvious that these stories are given further unity by their common preoccupation with irony—the evil results of the Munroes' innocent actions.

This dominance of irony is established in the opening pages, which deal with the valley's history before the appearance of the Munroes. . . . The valley called the Pastures of Heaven is discovered and named by a Spaniard who recaptures there some converted Indians who had abandoned their new religion to avoid forced labor in the clay pits of the Carmelo Mission. And this Spaniard who had "whipped brown backs to tatters" and whose "rapacious manhood was building a new race for California," stands with his steel hat in his hand and whispers, "Holy Mother! Here are the green pastures of Heaven to which our Lord leadeth us."

The brief history of the first two families to settle in the Pastures of Heaven, on what will become the Munroe farm, also contributes to this ironic play on the valley's name. After building the big, square house in which the Munroes will live, George Battle sends back to New York for his mother, who dies in passage and is buried at sea; "and she had wanted the crowded company of her home graveyard." George Battle then marries an older spinster with a small fortune who, before being confined in an asylum, tries twice to burn the house down. The Battles' only son, John, turns out to be a religious fanatic who "covered his clothes and hat with tiny cross-stitches in white thread" and has a habit of charging into the underbrush and driving the devils from cover with a heavy stick. One evening he disturbs a rattlesnake. "He fell upon his knees and prayed for a moment. Suddenly he shouted, "This is the damned serpent. Out devil," and sprang forward with clutching fingers. The snake struck him three times in the throat where there were no crosses to protect him. He struggled very little and died in a few minutes." The next settlers, the Mustrovics, appear to be doing very well until one day they mysteriously disappear, so suddenly that they leave the kitchen table set with silver, saucers of porridge, and a plate of fried eggs.

After the entrance of the Munroes . . ., however, all the evils which overcome the people of the Pastures of Heaven seem to originate with some member of that family. Shark Wicks is undone, the whole tower of his hypothetical wealth crumbles, when he attempts to defend his daughter from the advances of young Jimmie Munroe. Tularecito, a strong, but usually harmless, idiot, is committed to an institution for the criminally insane after striking Bert Munroe with a shovel. When Helen Van Deventer and her mad daughter come to the Pastures of Heaven, Bert kindly tries to visit them and welcome them to the valley. He succeeds only in speaking to the mad Hilda through the bars of her prison room, and Hilda is shot by her mother when she escapes with the idea she is to marry the strange man who spoke to her. The idyllic existence of Junius Maltby and his son, Robbie, is ended when Mrs. Munroe, out of kindness, gives a bundle of clothes to the boy; Junius and Robbie had never before realized their poverty. The Lopez sisters can no longer give their favors to the men because Bert Munroe makes a suggestive joke to the wife of an innocent man whom Maria Lopez allows to ride in her wagon. Molly Morgan leaves town because the drunken tramp in Bert Munroe's car may be her father. Raymond Banks's pleasant visits to his friend, the warden at San Quentin, cease because Bert Munroe poisons his innocent mind. At first, Pat Humbert's desire to please Mae Munroe results in his opening the dreaded parlor where his parents died and from which their spirits still command him. However, when he goes to invite Mae to visit his expensive, remade "colonial room," he learns she is engaged to marry someone else. Whereas previously he had confined himself to the kitchen of the house, he now abandons the house altogether and goes to live in the barn. Finally, John Whiteside's ancestral home is destroyed by fire because Bert Munroe kindly suggests they burn the brush from around the house.

Each story revolves around this kind of irony, very remi-niscent of some of Hardy's poems. They are "satires of circumstance," in each case the circumstance originating with a member of the Munroe family. Some of the stories, for example the one concerning the Whitesides, are completely saturated with this technique. Old Richard Whiteside comes to the valley intending to found a dynasty and build a lasting home for that dynasty. His wife can bear only one heir, his son John. John, in turn, has only one son, Bill, on whom to place his hopes. Bill marries Mae Munroe, who does not like to live on a farm and who takes him to live in Monterey. The house itself is then inadvertently destroyed by the father of the young girl who is taking Bill away to the city. This irony, which is especially apparent in the stories dealing with social themes, helps to give the book a unity of tone and mood, though the theme which embodies this irony may vary from one story to another.

The Raymond Banks story is interesting for the light it throws on Steinbeck's much-touted addiction to the use of "violence" and "animality." Raymond Banks is a big, hearty, simple man who raises thousands of chickens on the best kept and most admired farm in the valley. Two or three times a year he receives an invitation from the warden at San Quentin, his old high school chum, to be a witness at an execution. These trips are the only vacations Raymond takes, and they provide him with some excitement and the opportunity to talk over old times. Hearing of Raymond's trips to San Quentin, Bert Munroe talks him into getting an extra invitation for him. When the time arrives, Bert not only refuses to go, but so firmly impresses Raymond with the gruesome possibilities of bungled hangings that he too gives up the trips. It would be wrong to see Bert Munroe as the normal man who pricks the bubble of Raymond Banks's naïve attitude, not only because Steinbeck consistently describes the Munroes as an "evil cloud," but because all Steinbeck's work, especially *The Red Pony,* denies this "unhealthy" view that violence and pain are necessary.

The complexity of the story and its real "meaning" lie in Steinbeck's portrayal of the two men. Bert Munroe's sensitivity and his dislike for fried chicken have their source in an incident of his youth, when he watched a man attempt to butcher a rooster and saw the badly mangled fowl running about in dying agonies. On the other hand, while Raymond likes hangings, he is not a cruel man nor a pervert. "The hanging itself was not the important part, it was the sharp, keen air of the whole proceeding that impressed him. . . . The whole thing made him feel a fullness of experience. . . . Raymond didn't think of the condemned any more than he thought of the chicken when he pressed the blade into its brain. No strain of cruelty nor any gloating over suffering took him to the gallows." Raymond butchers his chickens in the most painless, scientific way possible. Although he allows boys to watch him, he refuses to let them try it. " 'You might get excited and miss the brain,' he said. 'That would hurt the chicken, if you didn't stick him just right.' "

With Bert Munroe, however, it is clear that the attitude toward violence is morbid. He enjoys shivering at the horrible images of suffering which his mind readily conjures up. And it is obvious that he enjoys describing to Raymond in detail the incident from his youth and the possibility of a person's being strangled instead of having his neck broken, or of the head being pulled right off the body from the impact. He likes to horrify himself by imagining that it is he who is being hanged. Raymond listens painfully to his friend's elaborations and at the end cries, "I tell you, you don't think things like that. . . . If you think things like that you haven't got any right to go up with me." It is obvious that Steinbeck intends to show that Raymond has the healthy attitude and that it is Bert Munroe who has the sick one. Raymond's mind, however, has now been poisoned. He cannot go up to visit his friend, and some of his joy in the chicken ranch is also destroyed.

Like Hemingway, Steinbeck finds an important place for violence in his works; but whereas for Hemingway violence is part of a code, often to be sought as the final proof of manhood, Steinbeck merely accepts it as one of the facts of life which must be considered for a full understanding of man's nature and his place in the biological world of which he is a part. He once said about Ed Ricketts, whom he admired very much, "He hated pain inflicted without good reason. . . . When the infliction of pain was necessary, he had little feeling about it."

Except for the three stories about Raymond Banks, Pat Humbert, and John Whiteside, each of which serves its own purpose, the other stories in *The Pastures of Heaven* divide equally into two groups, each of which has a common theme. The stories concerning Shark Wicks, Helen Van Deventer, and Molly Morgan make up one of these groups. In each of the stories in this group the main theme is provided by a character who attempts to live happily by keeping up some illusion which is eventually destroyed.

Because his ambitions exceed his abilities and resources, Shark Wicks gradually builds for himself a dream world in which he figures as a financial tycoon. He keeps a ledger in which he periodically records imaginary purchases of stocks and real estate, always discovering that he has sold out just in time and turned tremendous profits. As the secret life of Shark Wicks takes up more and more of his attention, the valley people become more and more convinced that he actually has this wealth, and he becomes respected as a financial wizard.

Helen Van Deventer insists on caring for her mad daughter, refusing to place her in an institution although there is a possibility of curing her. Also, she refuses to forget about her husband Hubert, a sporting, superficial man to whom she was married for three months. For twelve years she enjoys bearing the cross of her daughter and tries to make more real and painful the memory of her husband, whom she hardly knew.

All her life Molly Morgan has nursed childhood memories of a gay, fun-loving father who used to return home at long intervals from "business trips," loaded down with fascinating presents and full of wonderful stories which delighted all the children of the neighborhood. One day he went off on a longer trip than usual and did not return; but she believes that someday he surely will, with new, fantastic stories and delightful presents.

None of these illusions has a basis in fact. Shark Wicks has neither wealth nor talent; Helen Van Deventer feels no real love for either her daughter or her dead husband; Molly Morgan's father is actually an alcoholic who used to go off on long periodic drunks. Yet at the end of each story, despite revelations through catastrophe, the characters persist in their illusions. Shark Wicks is convinced that he is a man of ability who has just never had a chance before but will henceforth really make good; Helen Van Deventer abandons the painful memory of her husband and takes up the guilt of having killed her daughter; Molly Morgan prefers to leave her happy valley rather than chance losing her romantic memory of her father. The three stories are variations on a theme.

The stories about Tularecito, Junius Maltby, and the Lopez sisters can be taken as forming another group. Whereas the stories in the first group present characters with an orientation to life which can be held only by ignoring facts, the characters in this second group fail, not because their orientation is untenable in an absolute sense, but because of society's intrusion into the individual's adjustment.

Tularecito, though of subnormal intelligence, is a gentle and useful person as long as he is not tampered with. Gomez, with whom Tularecito lives, says of him, "He can work; he can do marvelous things with his hands, but he cannot learn to do the simple little things of the school. He is not crazy; he is one of those whom God has not quite finished." Society insists that he go to school. Although he cannot understand the lessons, Tularecito has a great talent for drawing animals and is encouraged to cover the blackboards with his art. When they are erased to make room for something else, he literally wrecks the school. The teacher, Miss Martin, tells Gomez that Tularecito is dangerous, but he replies, "He is not dangerous. No one can make a garden as he can. No one can milk so swiftly nor so gently. He is a good boy. He can break a mad horse without riding it; he can train a dog without whipping it, but the law says he must sit in the first grade repeating C-A-T, cat' for seven years." Tularecito does become dangerous, however. The new schoolteacher, Molly Morgan, thinking that it would enrich the poor boy's life, encourages him to believe in gnomes and fairies. It is while digging for gnomes in the Munroes' orchard that he is interrupted and strikes Bert Munroe with a shovel. Tularecito is then confined in an institution for the criminally insane.

Junius Maltby, his young son, Robbie, and Jakob live together very happily on a run-down farm. Junius left his city job and came to the Pastures of Heaven for his health and has not done a bit of work since. He and Jakob, his "hired man," who also does nothing, throw a few seeds on the ground every spring, let nature take its course, and eat what they can get with least effort. "Often they went hungry because they failed to find a hen's nest in the grass when it came suppertime." They wear their ragged clothes, go barefoot, and spend their days reading and talking while they sit on a tree branch and cool their feet in the river. They discuss the battle of Trafalgar, the frieze on the Parthenon, Carthaginian warfare, the Spartan virtues, why large things seem good and small things evil, and many other erudite topics. "They didn't make conversation; rather they let a seedling of thought sprout by itself, and then watched with wonder while it sent out branching limbs. They were surprised at the strange fruit their conversations bore, for they didn't direct their thinking, nor trellis nor trim it the way so many people do."

This pleasant existence is first threatened when Robbie is forced to attend school. Society has waited patiently for this legal opportunity to interfere. As it turns out, however, Robbie's ability to tell interesting stories from Thucydides, Herodotus, and Homer, to discuss the practices of certain cannibal tribes and the conquests of Hengist and Horsa, make him a fascinating person both to the teacher and the other children. Robbie soon emerges as a natural leader.

The trouble comes when the school board decides that Robbie must have feelings of inferiority, since his clothes are not as good as those of the other children. Although Molly Morgan pleads against it, Robbie is called before the board and Mrs. Munroe presents him with a bundle of shirts and overalls, "trying not to look too pointedly at his ragged clothes." But Robbie notices the stare. "For a moment he looked about nervously like a trapped animal and then he bolted through the door, leaving the little heap of clothing behind him." The next time we see Robbie, he and his father are boarding a bus. Junius explains to Molly Morgan that he is going to try to get a job because his son has "lived like an animal too long, you see. Besides, Miss Morgan, he doesn't know how nice it will be in San Francisco." The irony of Junius' words indicates Steinbeck's own attitude.

This attitude was made even clearer when the story appeared as a monograph in 1936. Its title, **Nothing So Monstrous,** was taken from Robert Louis Stevenson, whom Robbie says his father knows by heart: "There is nothing so monstrous but we can believe it of ourselves." (*Virginibus Puerisque,* II) The context in which this sentence occurs is significant, for it lays stress on the "unfading boyishness of hope and its vigorous irrationality," which is one of Steinbeck's main points in the story. One of Stevenson's analogies applies directly to Junius Maltby:

> We advance in years somewhat in the manner of an invading army in a barren land; the age we have reached, as the phrase goes, we but hold with an outpost, and still keep open our communications with the extreme rear and first beginnings of the march. There is our true base; that is not only the beginning, but the perennial spring of our faculties; and grandfather William can retire upon occasion into the green enchanted forest of his boyhood.

The separate publication of this story included an epilogue which makes Steinbeck's sympathies even more obvious: "I've often wondered whether Junius got a job and whether he kept it. . . . I for one should find it difficult to believe he could go under. I think rather he might have broken away again. For all I know he may have come back to the Pastures of Heaven." There follows an imaginative reconstruction of Junius' return to the valley, and of the farmers coming in the evening to hear him tell his tales

about Herodotus, Delphi, and Solomon. The last words in the book are, "I don't know that this is true. I only hope to God it is."

The third story in this group dealing with "social" themes is that of the Lopez sisters. This is Steinbeck's first extended treatment of the *paisanos,* who appeared briefly in *To a God Unknown* and were to provide material for all of his next book—*Tortilla Flat.* The story carries further the tolerant attitude toward prostitution held by Coeur de Gris and "The Other Burgundian" in *Cup of Gold;* but while in the first novel this attitude seems, in part, to be exploited for its shock value, in *The Pastures of Heaven* it becomes the basis for serious social criticism.

Left no means of support by their dead parents, Rosa and Maria establish a restaurant in which they sell "TORTILLAS, ENCHILADAS, TAMALES AND SOME OTHER SPANISH COOKINGS". Although their cuisine is of the best, business is not sufficient to provide a living and they stimulate their trade by giving their favors to the male customers. As Rosa puts it, "Do not make a mistake, I did not take money. The man had eaten three *enchiladas*—three!" Three *enchiladas* becomes the standard rate of exchange and their business prospers. They are happy; the men are happy; no one suffers. The sisters' knees polish the floor where they confess before the Virgin each evening, and they never take "the money of shame." So guileless are they that when Maria returns from Monterey one evening and hears from Rosa that the sheriff has been there she says, "The sheriff, he came? Now we are on the road. Now we will be rich. How many *enchiladas,* Rosa? Tell me how many for the sheriff." The sheriff, however, has come to close the restaurant because Bert Munroe told a joke about Allen Huenker's riding to town in Maria's wagon and Allen's jealous wife insisted that the sheriff take action. Knowing that they cannot live without selling *enchiladas,* Maria and Rosa are forced to go to San Francisco and become whores. Whereas the sisters had taken their activities as amateurs lightly, their decision to go to San Francisco and accept "the money of shame" is a tragic blow to them.

When, after a dozen such episodes of frustration and ironic reversals of fortune, the author leaves the inhabitants of the Pastures of Heaven to take his perspective from a group of tourists on the valley's ridge, the reader is confronted with the book's final ironies. Each of the four tourists in turn looks down upon the beautiful valley: a successful businessman, a young bridegroom, a priest, and an old man. Each sees in the valley only a peaceful place, an ideal spot to which to retire someday, far from the violence and strife of the world. Steinbeck does not leave the irony there, for the motives of the tourists are ironies in themselves. The businessman would like to start a real estate development there; the bridegroom is reminded by the bride that he has too much to accomplish to hide away in such a retreat; the priest mentally scourges himself for thus wishing to escape from the travails of his calling; the old man wants to settle in the valley to escape the troubles which have prevented him from thinking his way through to some meaningful philosophy of life.

After the bus is again in motion, the bus driver adds his

bit: "I guess it sounds kind of funny to you folks, but I always like to look down there and think how quiet and easy a man could live on a little place."

The Pastures of Heaven marks an important point in Steinbeck's career. It reveals his disengagement from the romantic materials of *Cup of Gold* and the unwieldy mythical paraphernalia of *To a God Unknown;* and it announces his preoccupation with fresh materials much closer at hand—the ordinary people of his "long valley." At the same time, through its carefully patterned structure and pervasive irony, *The Pastures of Heaven* promises a writer who will be capable of subjecting his realistic materials to the demands of significant form. (pp. 56-71)

. . . . .

As the episodic structures of . . . *The Pastures of Heaven* attest, Steinbeck's talents at this stage in his career seemed inclined toward the short story form. And in fact he had been writing steadily in this genre even before *Cup of Gold,* but except for two stories printed in *The Stanford Spectator* and the *Stanford Lit,* none of his short stories was published until *North American* printed the first two parts of *The Red Pony* in November and December of 1933. This same periodical published "The Murder" and "The Raid" in April and October of 1934 and "The White Quail" in March of the following year.

Even this flurry of publication did not gain his stories entrance to other magazines. In July of 1935 Steinbeck wrote his agents that he had given "The Snake," which could find no other publisher, to a magazine "run in conjunction with a stable" [*The Monterey Beacon*] in return for six months' use of a big bay hunter. He humorously suggested that the agents could get their 10 per cent of the riding, but would have to come out to California for it. Later, this story was rejected by both *Atlantic* and *Harper's. Saint Katy the Virgin* is mentioned in the letters as early as May of 1932, when Steinbeck wrote, "As for St. Katy—I shall send you a copy, and this time keep her if you want her. She was a pleasant afternoon to me, when I was tired of trying to convince taxpayer and Old Subscriber that I could write the English language." Three years later it had still not found a publisher, and Steinbeck wrote that he "would like to make someone print St. Katy." Finally his publishers, Covici-Friede, issued it as a monograph in 1936. "Flight," rejected in 1937 by both *Scribner's* and *Saturday Evening Post,* was not published until it appeared in *The Long Valley.*

By this time *In Dubious Battle* and especially *Of Mice and Men* were making Steinbeck's reputation, and magazines which had turned him down earlier now vied for his short stories. "The Chrysanthemums" and a third part of *The Red Pony* ("The Promise") were published by *Harper's* in August and October of 1937. *Esquire* accepted "The Ears of Johnny Bear" in September of the same year, and in June of 1938 *Atlantic* printed "The Harness." "The Leader of the People" first appeared in *The Long Valley* and, while included in the 1945 edition of *The Red Pony,* was not a part of the 1937 edition, although it had probably been written by then. It is found in the same manuscript book with *Tortilla Flat,* "The Murder," and "The Chrysanthemums."

As may be suspected from the five books Steinbeck had published up to that time, these stories show a wide range of technique and subject matter. Two of the stories are studies of valley people such as might well have appeared in *The Pastures of Heaven.* In fact, "The Murder" has much in common with the stories in that earlier book. It will be recalled that while in a letter to his agents Steinbeck mentions two murders in the valley of Nuestra Señora, the book includes only one. Also, the story's basically ironic structure fits well in *The Pastures of Heaven.* One need only substitute a Munroe for the "George" who unexpectedly turns Jim back home to find his wife with her lover. There is one good reason why the story was not included in the earlier volume, however. Its happy ending would have jarred with the book's predominant tone. "The Harness" is similar in setting to the stories in *The Pastures of Heaven* and is similar in theme to the Pat Humbert section, but lacks both the ironic tone and "black cloud" which characterize all the stories in that book.

Another story, *St. Katy the Virgin,* illustrates Steinbeck's early versatility by being a goliardic farce in the best fabliau tradition. St. Katy is a pig who becomes converted from her sinful life, works miraculous cures, and, after her bones have become holy relics, is added to the "Calendar of the Elect." The story is rife with hilarious parodies of medieval arguments concerning the power of exorcism, the nobility of the lion ("a beast built for parables"), the power of the crucifix ("two great tears squeezed out of the eyes of Katy"), the true definition of virginity ("to differentiate between the Grace of God knocking it [the hymen] out from the inside or the wickedness of man from the outside"), and even the "usual scandal" about monks: "For a while it was thought that, because of her sex, she [Katy] should leave the monastery and enter a nunnery." *St. Katy the Virgin* is an altogether delightful tale that even Chaucer's Reeve or Miller would have been proud to present as his claim to the free dinner.

The dominant interest in many of these stories collected in *The Long Valley* is psychological, and in them, as in *To a God Unknown,* there is a certain resemblance to the preoccupations of D. H. Lawrence, for whom Steinbeck has expressed some admiration. Elisa Allen in "The Chrysanthemums," Mary Teller in "The White Quail," Amy Hawkins in "Johnny Bear," and the anonymous woman in "The Snake" are psychological portraits of frustrated females.

Elisa's silent rebellion against the passive role required of her as a woman (symbolized by her masculine manner of gardening) is triggered by the old pot-mender, who throws away the chrysanthemums she has given him. However, in rejecting her first impulse to violence (which is to witness a bloody boxing match), she lapses into frustration, and the story ends with her "crying weakly—like an old woman." This story was much admired by André Gide, who said it was "remarkable for its adroitness" and seemed "like a short story by Chekhov; one of the best by Chekhov."

In **"The White Quail"** Mary Teller's lack of sexual vigor is aptly symbolized by her prim garden and her self-identification with the single albino quail which comes to drink at its pool. The tangled thickets at the garden's edge and a prowling cat symbolize the rough, natural world which constantly endangers her ordered, artificial one of trimmed bushes and white quail. Although her cowed husband finds symbolic assertion in killing the white quail rather than the prowling cat she asked him to kill, this reaction, like Elisa Allen's desire to see violence, is a temporary one.

In **"The Snake"** a strange woman objectifies her frustration by watching a male rattlesnake eat a white rat; she first insists that she buy both. According to Steinbeck, the story is an accurate account of an incident which happened to Ricketts, his biologist friend.

"Johnny Bear" is a story about a cretin with a remarkable memory and mimetic talent. On one level, it is an exploration of the artist's role in society; for, like the artist, Johnny Bear holds the mirror up to mankind and reveals through his mimetic talent the hidden festers of society. He is described as "a kind of recording and reproducing device, only you use a glass of whiskey instead of a nickel." The central interest, however, is neither Johnny Bear nor the aristocratic spinster whose secret love affair with a Chinese laborer he so innocently divulges. Rather, it is the social group within which these characters exist, and the conflict between its innate curiosity and its desire to perpetuate the symbols of its decorum despite the further revelation by Johnny Bear that the spinster, aided by her sister, committed suicide—to hide her pregnancy. It is curious that such a story should, in narrative style and setting, be so reminiscent of O. Henry and Bret Harte: the atmosphere of the outpost saloon and boardinghouse; the stranger in town; the unexpected twist in the last sentence.

The psychological interest of these explorations of character is carried on into the two stories dealing with the current social scene, **"Vigilante"** and **"The Raid."** Dick and Root in **"The Raid"** are early studies for Mac and Jim of *In Dubious Battle;* they are party organizers coming into a small town. Whereas in the novel the action is physical and dramatic, in the short story the action takes place in the mind of the frightened neophyte. The story builds up its intensity through Root's struggles to conquer his growing fear of the beating they are in for at the hands of the raiding party. The narrative skilfully keeps the reader's sympathy with the two organizers without requiring approval of their cause. In fact, their Communism provides a fine ironical turn to the story. Dick, the more experienced one, is a veritable apostle of the class struggle. To strengthen his weak companion he points to a portrait they have hung on the wall and says, "He wasn't scared. Just remember what he did." Later he tells Root, "If someone busts you, it isn't him that's doing it, it's the System. And it isn't you he's busting. He's taking a crack at the Principle." In the hospital, when the neophyte tells Dick how he had felt during the beating, the latter says, "It wasn't them. It was the System. You don't want to hate them. They don't know no better." And Root replies, "You remember in the Bible, Dick, how it says something like 'Forgive them because they don't know what they're doing?'" Dick's reply is stern: "'You lay off that religion stuff, kid.' He quoted, 'Religion is the opium of the people.'"

Like **"The Raid,"** the story **"Vigilante"** avoids dramatic presentation of violence and focuses instead on the psychological action. Whereas **"The Raid"** depicts the victim of a mob before and after he is beaten up, **"Vigilante"** concerns itself with the psychological state of a man after he has helped lynch a Negro. The story explores the character's motivations, which become clear through his thoughts, and his conversations with a bartender and his own wife. As might be expected, the story has some development of Steinbeck's group-man theories. The vigilante, like the grandfather in **"The Leader of the People,"** fully lives only for that time when he is part of a group, and when that group disperses the single man is left a hull. "Half an hour before, when he had been hauling with the mob and fighting for a chance to help pull the rope, then his chest had been so full that he had found he was crying. But now everything was dead, everything unreal." A study of the several other passages describing the character's feelings makes clear that there is perhaps an even stronger drive than gregariousness. "He could feel the let down in himself. He was as heavily weary as though he had gone without sleep for several nights, but it was a dream-like weariness, a grey comfortable weariness." This and similar descriptions come sharply into focus when the vigilante is greeted by his wife as follows: "You been with a woman. . . . You think I can't tell by the look on your face that you been with a woman?" The story ends with the vigilante looking into a mirror and saying, "By God, she was right. . . . That's just exactly how I do feel."

One of the best stories in *The Long Valley* is **"Flight,"** whose firm prose style once again attests Steinbeck's debt to Hemingway. Everything which has been admired in such passages of Hemingway prose as the bus ride to Pamplona in *The Sun Also Rises* and the bullfighting scenes in "The Undefeated" can be found in this short story. Its style is a crisp rendering of factual details which, while staying always close to the actual object and action, avoids the myopic distortions of "realistic" writing. Take, for example, the scene in which Pepé, behind a rock on a high slope, is wounded in a duel with his pursuer far below:

> The rifle swung over. The frontsight nestled in the V of the rear sight. Pepé studied for a moment and then raised the rear sight a notch. The little movement in the brush came again. The sight settled on it. Pepé squeezed the trigger. The explosion crashed down the mountain and up the other side, and came rattling back. The whole side of the slope grew still. No more movement. And then a white streak cut into the granite of the slit and a bullet whined away and a crash sounded up from below. Pepé felt a sharp pain in his right hand. A sliver of granite was sticking out from between his first and second knuckles and the point protruded from his palm. Carefully he pulled out the sliver of stone. The wound bled evenly and gently. No vein nor artery was cut.

The surface story is a simple one. A young boy kills a man, takes flight, is pursued and shot. Through this uncomplicated plot, however, Steinbeck weaves a thread of moral allegory—the growth of a boy to manhood and the meaning of that manhood. When the boy Pepé throws his dead father's knife into a man as unerringly as he has been playfully throwing it into a wooden post, the cards are dealt. Sticking the post was a boy's game, but when he takes the stranger's insults as a man would and throws his knife, he has bid into a man's game and must play it to the end. Most of the story concerns itself with the time between Pepé's return home to prepare himself for flight into the desolate granite mountains and the time when, realizing there is no escape from the gangrene of his wound, he stands fully exposed on a high rock and receives the fatal bullet from his mysterious pursuer.

The flight itself has meaning on two planes. On the physical level, Pepé's penetration into the desert mountains is directly proportional to his increasing separation from civilized man and his reduction to the state of a wild animal. The extent to which this process has gone is measured by his encounters with a wildcat and later a mountain lion, both of whom regard Pepé with a calm curiosity, not yet having learned to fear man. The symbolic meaning of Pepé's flight moves in the opposite direction. On this level, the whole action of the story goes to show how man, even when stripped of all his civilized accouterments (like Ahab of his pipe, sextant, and hat), is still something more than an animal. This is the purpose of Pepé's losing consecutively his horse (escape), his hat (protection from nature), and his gun (physical defense), to face his inevitable death not with the headlong retreat or futile death struggle of an animal, but with the calm and stoicism required by the highest conception of manhood, forcing fate to give him a voice in the "how" if not the "what" of his destiny.

It is worth remarking that perhaps Steinbeck achieves this significant symbolic meaning of the story's ending at some expense of verisimilitude. The boy standing exposed on the high rock and taking his death is "theatrical" in the same way that the ending of almost every one of Steinbeck's novels is "theatrical"—not incredible or contrived so much as disjunctive, incongruous in realistic terms because of its too perfect symbolic congruity. This type of ending is one of Steinbeck's most consistent stylistic devices, and his persistent use of it in the face of almost unanimous adverse criticism must indicate that for him, at least, the important action to be terminated in his novels exists not on the physical plane, but on the symbolic. When these endings are examined in the light of the whole work, it becomes evident that their incongruity with the surface "realism" is overshadowed by their bringing into sharper focus the substrata of symbolism and allegory.

Although the four stories about Jody do not have plot continuity, they do have a continuity of theme—the education of a young boy. The three stories collected in the 1937 edition of *The Red Pony* show Jody's education through Nature, and **"The Leader of the People"** continues this education through Grandfather, who represents history, a sense of the past. Like **"Flight,"** these stories are remarkable for the lyric realism of their prose style, a style which

while coming to grips with the essentials of violence and death still retains a rhythm and tone more akin to the idyllic and pastoral than to the naturalistic. The result of this rhythm and tone is the creation of what Mr. T. K. Whipple has called "the middle distance." In this perspective the characters "cannot touch us, and yet we can see their performances with the greatest clarity and fullness. . . . We feel the appropriate emotions—pity, sympathy, terror and horror even—but with the delightful sense that we are apart, in the audience, and that anyhow nothing can be done or needs be done." This effect is very important in Steinbeck's work, and its presence is often a touchstone for his more successful works. It is through this technique of distance that the stories about Jody escape both the infantilism and the excessive psychological distortions which are the usual literary pitfalls of these stories' subject matter.

The central experience in each of the first three stories (**"The Gift," "The Great Mountains,"** and **"The Promise"**) is physical death: the red pony, Gitano, and the mare. Each shows death in a different perspective. The red pony comes from a broken-down "show," and its superficial prettiness is emphasized by the tinsel-hung, red morocco saddle that comes with it. " 'It's just a show saddle,' Billy Buck said disparagingly. 'It isn't practical for the brush. . . . ' " The red pony's death is in part the result of Jody's carelessness. Twice he falls asleep and allows the pony to escape into the storm, which aggravates the cold it caught from getting wet. Billy Buck has remarked, "—why a little rain don't hurt a horse." But it is fatal to the red pony. When Jody comes upon his red pony, already being devoured by the buzzards, anger seems a normal reaction. Carl Tiflin says, "Jody, the buzzards didn't kill the pony. Don't you know that?" The function of this incident in Jody's education becomes clear from Billy Buck's reprimand. " 'Course he knows it, Jesus Christ! man, can't you see how he'd feel about it?" It is important to note that he does not contradict the father's words, but merely relates Jody's action to its context of incomplete education. The reader may "feel" with Jody and "understand" with Carl, but he identifies himself with Billy Buck, the complete man whose perspective includes both the buzzards' place in the chain of being and their repulsiveness. And Billy Buck is the model on whom Jody is fashioning himself.

While the death of the red pony is associated with violence, pain, and disgust, the death of Gitano in **"The Great Mountains"** is as calm and peaceful as the title. Before the old Mexican comes "home" to the Tiflin ranch to die, Jody has already identified the western mountains, the "Great Ones," with death and the eastern ones, the Gabilans, with life. Symbolically, the Tiflin ranch lies in a valley cup formed by the two ranges. When Gitano disappears with the old horse, Easter, who is also waiting to die, Carl remarks, "They never get too old to steal. I guess he just stole old Easter." Jody, who has seen Gitano's old basket-hilted rapier (handed down from father to son since the conquistadores), who feels the significance of Gitano's journey into the symbolic "Great Ones," knows the truth. "Jody thought of the rapier and of Gitano. And he thought of the great mountains. A longing caressed him, and it was so sharp that he wanted to cry to get it out of his breast. He lay down in the green grass near the round tub [which Jody associates with life] at the brush line. He covered his eyes with his crossed arms and lay there a long time, and he was full of nameless sorrow." This sorrow comes not from grief for Gitano or the old horse, but rather from an emotional perception of that whole of which Gitano, Old Easter, the rapier, and the Great Mountains are parts, a recognition of the symbolic significance of their conjunction—"nameless" because intuitive and subconscious. Jody's sorrow is very much like that of the girl Margaret in Hopkins' poem "Spring and Fall: To a Young Child."

Like **"The Gift," "The Promise"** is a story about a pony. Whereas the first concerns itself with the pony's increasing sickness, ending in death, the second begins with a pony's conception and ends with its birth. And as Jody was spared no detail of the first pony's suffering and death, so he is spared no fact of life in the mare's pregnancy and the colt's birth. He is present at the violent copulation, cares for the mare during the progress of her pregnancy, sees the agonies of her labor pains, watches Billy Buck attempt to turn the colt in her uterus and, this failing, kill her with a hammer and cut the living colt from its dead mother. Jody's vital relation to this colt is as different from his relation to the red pony as the red pony's carnival background and useless red morocco saddle are different from the violence and suffering which bring the colt into the world. And the colt's birth provides Jody with a new insight into death. The red pony's suffering and terror had been the process of death, which meant life to the buzzards. Gitano had gone to his death calmly, of his own free will and accepting the inevitable. The mare's suffering and death are the price of life and give to Jody a new sense of his responsibility to that life.

In *Sea of Cortez* Steinbeck tells an anecdote, probably autobiographical, which further clarifies his attitude toward the natural processes of life in these Jody stories:

> A man we know once long ago worked for a wealthy family in a country place. One morning one of the cows had a calf. The children of the house went down with him to watch her. It was a good normal birth, a perfect presentation, and the cow needed no help. The children asked questions and he answered them. And when the emerged head cleared through the sac, the little black muzzle appeared, and the first breath was drawn, the children were fascinated and awed. And this was the time for their mother to come screaming down on the vulgarity of letting the children see the birth. This "vulgarity" had given them a sense of wonder at the structure of life, while the mother's propriety supplanted that feeling with dirtiness.

Because the style of the Jody stories is so perfectly suited to their theme and subject matter (as well suited, for example, as is the style of *The Pearl* to its own materials), the myriad specific details imbedded in these stories remain unobtrusive. Jody, however, is engaged in learning not only about such larger things as death, birth, and suffering, but also about the many particulars of ranch life and nature. The source for much of this information is Billy

Buck, who, along with other men of skill, occupies the place in the Steinbeck world that bullfighters do in that of Hemingway. Throughout his fiction Steinbeck pays tribute to the man who is skilled with his hands: the man who can, like Billy Buck and Slim, work with horses; the man who can, like Raymond Banks, kill chickens painlessly and with efficiency; the man who can, like Alec and Juan Chicoy, repair motors and gear assemblies. In *Cannery Row* Steinbeck refers to Gay, a self-made mechanic, as "the Saint Francis of all things that turn and twist and explode." This type of character is often depicted by Steinbeck, who thus expresses his admiration for the man who is close to life, whether that life be spent on a ranch, in a garage, or behind a lunch counter. In Doc of *Cannery Row* Steinbeck creates his ideal character by combining the man of skill with the man of contemplation.

While the boy Jody appears in **"The Leader of the People,"** it is not *about* him in the sense that the stories in *The Red Pony* are about him. This is why Steinbeck did not include this story in the first edition of *The Red Pony,* although he had probably written it by then since it is found in the same manuscript book as the earlier *Tortilla Flat,* **"The Murder,"** and **"The Chrysanthemums,"** where it is called "Grandfather." Although this story was later included in the 1945 edition of *The Red Pony,* in *The Long Valley* (1938) it appears under a separate title. The central character is Jody's grandfather, who was once "the leader of the people." It is Steinbeck's first explicit statement of his group-man theory, which was hinted at in the earlier stories and novels and which was to be developed at such great length in his next four books.

Through the garrulous grandfather Steinbeck poses the question of the meaning and place which the frontier spirit should have in our time. Through each character's attitude toward the grandfather, in whom the tradition is embodied, the author explores a distinct reaction to the American pioneer past. For Carl, it is something done with. The West Coast has been reached and the job now is one of consolidation. It is boring and pointless to dwell on the heroic deeds of our past; "Now it's finished. Nobody wants to hear about it over and over." In this dismissal there is perhaps an unconsciuos resentment of his own unheroic life. To Carl's wife, the daughter of Grandfather, the stories of the past are just as boring, but her attitude is more respectful. She listens out of loyalty, knowing what this past meant to her forebears. Billy Buck's attitude is a little more complicated. His own father was a mule packer under Grandfather's leadership, and he himself retains much of the self-reliant, able-handed spirit of the heroic past. He listens with respect born of understanding. For Jody, as for any other American youngster, this past was a time of excitement: Indians, wagon trains, scouts, crossing the plains.

Yet it is to Jody that the grandfather is finally able to communicate the double aspect of the meaning behind his tales of Indians and wagon trains:

> It wasn't Indians that were important, nor adventures, nor even getting out here. It was a whole bunch of people made into one big crawling beast. And I was the head. It was westering

and westering. Every man wanted something for himself, but the big beast that was all of them wanted only westering. I was the leader, but if I hadn't been there, someone else would have been the head. The thing had to have a head.

This is an important statement for an understanding of Steinbeck's group-man concept. The analogy of men to a "big crawling beast" was not intended to put, and in the context of Steinbeck's work does not put, men on the same moral basis as animals. Rather, it points out the energy that is released when the many desires of men can find expression in one unifying activity or aspiration. As the old man continues, it becomes evident that although "westering" may bear a superficial resemblance to animal migration, the impetus which drove his people had its roots not in the flesh but in the human spirit. "No place to go, Jody. Every place is taken. But that's not the worst—no, not the worst. Westering has died out of people. Westering isn't a hunger any more. It's all done."

Grandfather's statement is supported not only by Carl Tiflin and his wife, but by a continuum of symbols firmly imbedded in the story. The physical setting is alive not with Indians and buffaloes but with small and petty game—gophers, snakes, pigeons, crows, rabbits, squirrels, and mice. And these mice which Jody sets out to kill early in the story are, significantly, still alive at its end, fat and comfortable in a rotting haystack. Yet, the story is not a sentimental glorification of a heroic past set against a mean and complacent present. The frontier *is* gone; Jody's excitement about killing the mice is not, as Grandfather sees it, a symbol of a degenerating race; Carl Tiflin and his wife are not cruel and stupid, but competent for the tasks at hand; and their boredom with the old man's garrulousness is made understandable. Furthermore, in a very important sense it is Grandfather who has failed, in two ways. He has failed to adjust himself to the unavoidable fact that he could not go on being "the leader of the people" after the Pacific Ocean was reached. More important, despite his garrulousness he has failed to communicate to the new generation that "westering" was not just killing Indians and eating buffalo meat.

Perhaps the ultimate wisdom in the story belongs only to Billy Buck. When Jody remarks to him that the fat mice he intends to kill "don't know what's going to happen to them today," Billy Buck replies philosophically, "No, nor you either, nor me, nor anyone." Jody is "staggered" by this thought; he "knew it was true." This is Jody's lesson in history, the meaning of the past. Grandfather's frontier, like Frederick Jackson Turner's, was not so much a physical manifestation as an attitude of mind and a spirit which needs reviving in our time. Life is always a risk. The call for heroism is heard today as it was yesterday. The need for a leader of the people is still real, for we are all pioneers, forever crossing the dangerous and the unknown. (pp. 92-107)

Peter Lisca, in his The Wide World of John Steinbeck, *Rutgers University Press, 1958, 326 p.*

Steinbeck on the art of writing:

The craft or art of writing is the clumsy attempt to find symbols for the wordlessness. In utter loneliness a writer tries to explain the inexplicable. And sometimes if he is very fortunate and if the time is right, a very little of what he is trying to do trickles through—not ever much. And if he is a writer wise enough to know it can't be done, then he is not a writer at all. A good writer always works at the impossible. There is another kind who pulls in his horizons, drops his mind as one lowers rifle sights. And giving up the impossible he gives up writing. Whether fortunate or unfortunate, this has not happened to me. The same blind effort, the straining and puffing go on in me. And always I hope that a little trickles through. This urge dies hard.

Writing is a very silly business at best. There is a certain ridiculousness about putting down a picture of life. And to add to the joke—one must withdraw for a time from life in order to set down that picture. And third one must distort one's own way of life in order in some sense to stimulate the normal in other lives. Having gone through all this nonsense, what emerges may well be the palest of reflections. Oh! it's a real horse's ass business. The mountain labors and groans and strains and the tiniest of rodents come out. And the greatest foolishness of all lies in the fact that to do it at all, the writer must believe that what he is doing is the most important thing in the world. And he must hold to this illusion even when he knows it is not true. If he does not, the work is not worth even what it might otherwise have been.

John Steinbeck, in a diary entry later collected in The Paris Review, *1969.*

John Steinbeck   (letter date 1962)

[*In the following letter to his former Stanford University professor Edith Ronald Mirrielees, Steinbeck discusses the difficulties associated with writing short fiction.*]

Dear Edith Mirrielees:

Although it must be a thousand years ago that I sat in your class in story writing at Stanford, I remember the experience very clearly. I was bright-eyed and bushy-brained and prepared to absorb from you the secret formula for writing good short stories, even great short stories. You canceled this illusion very quickly. The only way to write a good short story, you said, is to write a good short story. Only after it is written can it be taken apart to see how it was done. It is a most difficult form, you told us, and the proof lies in how very few great short stories there are in the world.

The basic rule you gave us was simple and heartbreaking. A story to be effective had to convey something from writer to reader, and the power of its offering was the measure of its excellence. Outside of that, you said, there were no rules. A story could be about anything and could use any means and any technique at all—so long as it was effective. As a subhead to this rule, you maintained that it seemed to be necessary for the writer to know what he wanted to say, in short, what he was talking about. As an exercise we were to try reducing the meat of a story to one sentence, for only then could we know it well enough to enlarge it to three or six or ten thousand words.

So there went the magic formula, the secret ingredient. With no more than that you set us on the desolate, lonely path of the writer. And we must have turned in some abysmally bad stories. If I had expected to be discovered in a full bloom of excellence, the grades you gave my efforts quickly disillusioned me. And if I felt unjustly criticized, the judgments of editors for many years afterwards upheld your side, not mine. The low grades on my college stories were echoed in the rejection slips, in the hundreds of rejection slips.

It seemed unfair. I could read a fine story and could even know how it was done, thanks to your training. Why could I not then do it myself? Well, I couldn't, and maybe it's because no two stories dare be alike. Over the years I have written a great many stories and I still don't know how to go about it except to write it and take my chances.

If there is a magic in story writing, and I am convinced that there is, no one has ever been able to reduce it to a recipe that can be passed from one person to another. The formula seems to lie solely in the aching urge of the writer to convey something he feels important to the reader. If the writer has that urge, he may sometimes but by no means always find the way to do it. And if your book, Edith, does nothing more, it will teach many readers to perceive the excellence that makes a good story good or the errors that make a bad story. For a bad story is only an ineffective story.

It is not so very hard to judge a story after it is written, but, after many years, to start a story still scares me to death. I will go so far as to say that the writer who is not scared is happily unaware of the remote and tantalizing majesty of the medium.

I wonder whether you will remember one last piece of advice you gave me. It was during the exuberance of the rich and frantic 'twenties, and I was going out into that world to try to be a writer.

You said, "It's going to take a long time, and you haven't any money. Maybe it would be better if you could go to Europe."

"Why?" I asked.

"Because in Europe poverty is a misfortune, but in America it is shameful. I wonder whether or not you can stand the shame of being poor."

It wasn't too long afterward that the depression came down. Then everyone was poor and it was no shame any more. And so I will never know whether or not I could have stood it. But surely you were right about one thing, Edith. It took a long time—a very long time. And it is still going on, and it has never got easier. You told me it wouldn't. (pp. 136-37)

John Steinbeck, in a letter to Edith Mirrielees on March 8, 1962, in John Steinbeck: A Study of the Short Fiction *by R. S. Hughes, Twayne Publishers, 1989, pp. 136-37.*

Arnold L. Goldsmith   (essay date 1965)

[*Goldsmith is an American educator and critic. In the essay below, he examines the themes, symbols, and narrative structures that underlie and unify* The Red Pony.]

Underlying Steinbeck's four short stories which make up **The Red Pony** are thematic rhythms, structural balance, and a seasonal symbolism which skillfully integrate the whole work and relate it to his Emersonian mysticism found in later books such as *The Grapes of Wrath* (1939) and *Sea of Cortez* (1941). **"The Leader of the People,"** added by Steinbeck in 1938 to the three stories first published as **The Red Pony** in 1937, is an integral part of the whole work, but readers of college anthologies usually find one of the stories published separately or the first three as a unit, and thus miss a good opportunity to study Steinbeck's subtle extension of the themes expressed in **"The Gift," "The Great Mountains,"** and **"The Promise."**

The central figure unifying all four stories is Jody Tiflin. Like Hemingway's early hero Nick Adams, Jody is being initiated into a violent world where danger lurks everywhere, pain and death are imminent, and the best laid plans of mice and boys often go astray. In the first story Jody is ten, in the next apparently a year older, and in the third and fourth, probably twelve. The adventures of both youths are intended to teach them the need for stoic endurance in order to survive in an imperfect and cruel world. In this sense, Hemingway's stories and **The Red Pony** can be considered *bildungsromans,* but there are some significant differences. Because of Jody's age, sex plays much less a part of his initiation than it does in Nick's, whose experiences are not just vicarious. And violence, which explodes all around Nick and finally wounds him in the war, destroys only the things Jody loves, not harming him physically. Where Nick's wounds are both physical and psychic, Jody's are only psychic, and we do not know whether they have a permanent effect on him. The third story ends with Jody's thrill at the birth of his new colt, but even this thrill is dampened by pain: "He ached from his throat to his stomach. His legs were stiff and heavy. He tried to be glad because of the colt, but the bloody face, and the haunted, tired eyes of Billy Buck hung in the air ahead of him." The last story substitutes the tired face of Jody's grandfather for that of Billy Buck, but the optimism implied in the title as well as Jody's kindness to the old man are adequate evidence of the kind of adjustments Jody will make in life.

More important than the above contrasts is the fact that Steinbeck composed **The Red Pony** as an integrated whole, while Hemingway wrote the Nick Adams stories sporadically at different times during his literary career. All four stories in **The Red Pony** take place in the Salinas Valley, where Steinbeck himself grew up as a boy. The stories are filled with realistic and lyric descriptions of the Valley's flora and fauna (*e.g.,* horned toads, newts, blue snakes, lizards, buzzards, rabbits, hoot-owls, turkeys, coyotes, muskmelons, oakwoods, and black cypresses) which Steinbeck knew as intimately as Thoreau knew the woods, ponds, and fields around Concord.

The time sequence of the stories can be worked out as follows. **"The Gift"** begins in late summer and ends around Thanksgiving, the beginning of the winter with its rainy season in California. The reader of Hemingway's *A Farewell to Arms* is certainly familiar with the association of rain with disease, violence, and death, and such seasonal symbolism is most appropriate in the story about the death of Jody's pony suffering from pneumonia. **"The Great Mountains"** begins in the "heat of a mid-summer afternoon," probably a year after the first story began. It spans less than twenty-four hours, ending the next morning. **"The Promise"** begins that spring and ends eleven months later, in a January rain, once again an appropriate setting for the death of the mare Nellie and the birth of her colt. **"The Leader of the People"** takes place a couple of months later, in March, probably the same year that the mare died. The same unity of time and place found in the second story is evident here also. As in **"The Great Mountains,"** the story begins on an afternoon and ends the next morning.

This analysis of the time sequence helps illuminate the structural symmetry of the stories. Just as Hemingway in *A Farewell to Arms* alternates a book of war with a romantic interlude for dramatic contrast, Steinbeck follows the violence of the first story with the tragic quiet of the second, with this same pattern repeated in the third and fourth sections. Where the first and third stories are about the violent deaths of horses, the second and fourth are about the twilight years of two old men.

The basic thematic rhythm unifying the four stories in *The Red Pony* is the life-death cycle. This organic theory of life ending in death which in turn produces new life is the major theme of Hemingway's "Indian Camp," where Nick Adams witnesses the Caesarean delivery of an Indian baby and the violent death of the father. It is the same cycle of life and death implicit in Whitman's image of the "cradle endlessly rocking."

In *The Red Pony* we see this rhythm in the cycle of the seasons, the buzzards flying overhead, the life and death of Jody's pony Galiban, the death of the buzzard Jody kills with his bare hands, the approaching death of the paisano Gitano and the old horse Easter (his very name suggesting life in death), and the two opposing sets of mountains: Galiban (jolly, populated, suggesting life) and the Great Ones (ominous, mysterious, suggesting death, a place where we must all go eventually), the little bird Jody kills with his slingshot and then beheads and dissects, the death of Nellie and the birth of her colt, and the approaching death of Jody's old grandfather, the old leader of the people, with the implication that Jody is to be the new one. All of these objects and incidents represent the never-ending rhythm of life and death to which Jody is continually exposed. The subtle expression of this theme can even be found at the beginning of **"The Leader of the People,"** when Billy Buck rakes the last of the old year's haystack, an action which implies the end of one season and the beginning of the next. In terms of the story, life is ending for the grandfather, but it is just beginning for Jody.

The most obvious example of Steinbeck's conscious effort to present this theme in *The Red Pony* is the sharp contrast he develops in **"The Promise"** between the black cy-

press tree by the bunkhouse and the water tub. Where the cypress is associated with death, the never-ending spring water piped into the old green tub is the symbol of the continuity of life. The two paragraphs where Steinbeck explains the effect these things have on Jody should be given in full:

> Jody traveled often to the brush line behind the house. A rusty iron pipe ran a thin stream of water into an old green tub. Where the water spilled over and sank into the ground there was a patch of perpetually green grass. Even when the hills were brown and baked in the summer that little patch was green. The water whined softly into the trough all the year round. This place had grown to be a center-point for Jody. When he had been punished the cool green grass and the singing water soothed him. When he had been mean the biting acid of meanness left him at the brush line. When he sat in the grass and listened to the purling stream, the barriers set up in his mind by the stern day went down to ruin.

> On the other hand, the black cypress tree by the bunkhouse was as repulsive as the water-tub was dear; for to this tree all the pigs came, sooner or later, to be slaughtered. Pig killing was fascinating, with the screaming and blood, but it made Jody's heart beat so fast that it hurt him. After the pigs were scalded in the big iron tripod kettle and their skins were scraped and white, Jody had to go to the water-tub to sit in the grass until his heart grew quiet. The water-tub and the black cypress were opposites and enemies.

As Jody daydreams about his colt, he finds himself under the black cypress and superstitiously moves over to the green grass near the trilling water. "As usual the water place eliminated time and distance."

Jody's communion with nature, a semi-mystical experience in which time and place are eliminated, is not very different from the withdrawal into the wilderness of Jim Casy in *The Grapes of Wrath*. Casy adds a religious dimension to the experience when he says, "There was the hills, an' there was me, an' we wasn't separate no more. We was one thing. An' that one thing was holy." The most explicit statement Steinbeck has made on this mystical feeling of oneness of the animate and inanimate is in *Sea of Cortez*, where he wrote:

> groups melt into ecological groups until the time when what we know as life meets and enters what we think of as non-life: barnacle and rock, rock and earth, earth and tree, tree and rain and air. And the units nestle into the whole and are inseparable from it . . . And it is a strange thing that most of the feeling we call religious, most of the mystical outcrying which is one of the most prized and used and desired reactions of our species, is really the understanding and the attempt to say that man is related to the whole thing, related inextricably to all reality, known and unknowable. This is a simple thing to say, but the profound feeling of it made a Jesus, a St. Augustine, a St. Francis, a Roger Bacon, a Charles Darwin, and an Einstein. Each of them in his own tempo and with his own voice discov-

ered and reaffirmed with astonishment the knowledge that all things are one thing and that one thing is all things.

Throughout his literary career John Steinbeck has attempted to render dramatically his passionate belief in the oneness of all life, and *The Red Pony* is no exception, as the life-death cycle and Jody's romantic communion with nature will attest. But there is one final example which should be mentioned because of its effective fusion of character, theme, and setting. It occurs in **"The Great Mountains."** To Jody, these mountains represent the mystery of the unknown, unlived life, but to the old man they stand for the mystery of death. Beyond them lies the sea— eternity. As Gitano rides off into the mountains, he carries a long rapier with a golden basket hilt, a family heirloom passed down to him by his father. This rapier adds just the right touch of myth and folklore to the ancient legend of an old man returning to his birthplace to die. It echoes the classic tradition of such weapons as the magical sword of King Arthur and Beowulf, the shield of Achilles, even the long rifle of Natty Bumppo. To Jody, Gitano is "mysterious like the mountains. There were ranges back as far as you could see, but behind the last range piled up against the sky there was a great unknown country. And Gitano was an old man, until you got to the dull dark eyes. And in behind them was some unknown thing." Thus the mountains are an extension of Gitano, and Gitano is an extension of the old horse with its ribs and hip-bones jutting out under its skin. All three objects blend into one as Jody watches them disappear in the distance, lying in the green grass near the water-tub, the symbol of timelessness:

> For a moment he thought he could see a black speck crawling up the farthest ridge. Jody thought of the rapier and Gitano. And he thought of the great mountains. A longing caressed him, and it was so sharp that he wanted to cry to get it out of his breast. He lay down in the green grass near the round tub at the brush line. He covered his eyes with his crossed arms and lay there a long time, and he was full of a nameless sorrow.

(pp. 391-94)

Arnold L. Goldsmith, "Thematic Rhythm in 'The Red Pony'," in College English, *Vol. 26, No. 5, February, 1965, pp. 391-94.*

Steinbeck in a 1933 letter to George Albee about "The Chrysanthemums":

I shall be interested to know what you think of ["**The Chrysanthemums**"]. . . . It is entirely different and is designed to strike without the reader's knowledge. I mean he reads it casually and after it is finished feels that something profound has happened to him although he does not know what nor how. It has had that effect on several people here. [My wife] thinks it is the best of all my stories.

John Steinbeck, in a 1933 letter to George Albee later collected in The True Adventures of John Steinbeck: Writer, *Viking Press, 1984.*

Elizabeth E. McMahan (essay date 1968-69)

[*In the essay below, McMahan explores the theme of sexual frustration in "The Chrysanthemums."*]

Virtually every critic who has considered John Steinbeck's short story **"The Chrysanthemums"** has agreed that its basic theme is a woman's frustration, but none has yet adequately explained the emotional reasons underlying that frustration. In fact, Kenneth Kempton would consider such an explanation impossible. He professes his inability to find any consistent motivation for Eliza's behavior, and declares the work "annoyingly arty, muddy, and unreal" [*Short Stories for Study*]. But most critics who have examined **"The Chrysanthemums"** admire the story and find it meaningful. Warren French, after identifying the theme of the story as frustration, suggests that the central action concerns "the manipulation of people's dreams for selfish purposes" [*John Steinbeck*]—an interesting and valid idea but one which fails to incorporate the obvious sexual overtones of the story. Another critic who overlooks the sexuality is Joseph Warren Beach. He sees the conflict in the story as a contest of wits between Eliza and the pot mender; frustration results from damage to her pride when she is outwitted [*American Fiction: 1920-1940*]. Ray B. West sees the story as "based on the assumed relationship between the fertile growth of plant life and physical violence and sexuality in human beings" [*The Short Story in America: 1900-1950*]. Peter Lisca explains Eliza's frustration as stemming from an unsuccessful "silent rebellion against the passive role required of her as a woman" [*The Wide World of John Steinbeck*]—an excellent idea but his treatment is too brief to account for all the elements of the story. F. W. Watt is on exactly the right track when he states that the story concerns Eliza's "struggle to express and fulfill desires which are ambiguously sexual and spiritual" [*John Steinbck*]. Unfortunately Watt, like Lisca, has not sufficient space in his book to give this story the thorough discussion that it deserves. The only such examination thus far is that of Mordecai Marcus ["The Lost Dream of Sex and Childbirth in 'The Chrysanthemums,'" *Modern Fiction Studies,* Spring 1965]. But his interesting and persuasive argument that Eliza's frustration results essentially from a longing for childbirth is not entirely satisfactory. Marcus encounters difficulties with the story which I think disappear if we do not equate sexual fulfillment with a yearning for motherhood. Eliza's need is definitely sexual, but it does not necessarily have anything to do with a longing for children.

In order to understand Eliza's emotions, we first should look closely at the relationship between her and her husband. Beach, somewhat surprisingly, observes that "Nothing is said about the relationship of this married pair, but everything shows that it is one of confidence and mutual respect." Partially true, certainly, but confidence and mutual respect are not the only qualities that Eliza Allen desires in her marriage. The evidence points to an outwardly passive, comfortable relationship between the two which satisfies Henry completely but leaves Eliza indefinably restless with excessive energy which she sublimates into the "over-eager" cultivation of her chrysanthemums, and the care of her "hard-swept looking little house with hard-polished windows." Henry is a good provider, we can be sure; he has just received a good price for thirty head of cattle. He is also thoughtful; he invites his wife to go into town that evening to celebrate the sale. A good provider, a thoughtful husband. But what else? There is a distinct lack of rapport between these two, despite all that mutual respect. And the confidence which Beach observes is an assurance of each other's capability; it is not a warm mutual confidence of things shared.

We see this lack of rapport demonstrated early in the story as Henry makes a suggestion for their evening's entertainment:

> Henry put on his joking tone. "There's fights tonight. How'd you like to go to the fights?"
>
> "Oh, no," she said breathlessly. "No, I wouldn't like fights."
>
> "Just fooling, Eliza. We'll go to a movie."

The fact that husband and wife do not share an interest in sports is not remarkable, but the fact that Eliza responds seriously to Henry's "joking tone" suggests either that she lacks a sense of humor or that for some reason she is not amused by Henry's teasing. We discover later that she has a ready sense of humor when talking to someone other than Henry. Unmistakably, Henry has no gift with words. When he compliments his wife on her chrysanthemums, he praises their size not their beauty and does so in the most prosaic terms. When he wants to compliment his wife on her appearance, he stammers, as if in surprise—and Eliza is hardly elated by the banal adjective:

> "Why—why, Eliza. You look so nice!"
>
> "Nice? You think I look nice? What do you mean by *nice*?"
>
> Henry blundered on. "I don't know. I mean you look different, strong and happy."

Henry's word choice here is particularly unfortunate since his wife has just devoted her entire attention to heightening her femininity. She has put on her "newest underclothing and her nicest stockings and the dress which was the symbol of her prettiness." "Strong" is the way she least wants to appear. But Henry manages to make matters even worse. Bewildered by Eliza's sharp retort, he is inspired to his only attempt at figurative language in hopes of making himself clear: " 'You look strong enough to break a calf over your knee, happy enough to eat it like a watermelon.' " It is hard to fancy the woman who would be pleased by Henry's agricultural comparison. Eliza is not amused.

We begin to sense the source of Eliza's discontent. She is a woman bored by her husband, bored by her isolated life on the farm. When the itinerant tinker arrives at Eliza's gate, we see that she is a woman who longs for what women's magazines vaguely call "romance." She wants, among other things, to be admired as a woman. The chrysanthemums that she cultivates so energetically produce great soft blossoms shaped like a woman's breasts. If one wishes to see the flowers as a symbol, they suggest the voluptuous softness of a sexually mature woman. There is no evidence to suggest that Eliza is a sex-starved female, that

her husband is perhaps impotent, as Kempton suggests. Henry's placidity would seem to indicate the contrary. But neither is Eliza a sexually satisfied woman. Something is lacking in her relationship with Henry, and this something has a great deal to do with sex, but it is not as simple as a need for the sex act alone. This undefined longing becomes more clear as we examine her reaction to the tinker.

Unlike Henry, who has trouble finding the right words to please his wife, the tinker seems to know them intuitively. His greeting to Eliza is a mildly humorous remark about his cowardly mongrel dog: " 'That's a bad dog in a fight when he gets started.' " Eliza gives no dead-pan response as she did to Henry's feeble joke. Instead, "Eliza laughed. 'I see he is. How soon does he generally get started?' The man caught up her laughter and echoed it heartily. 'Sometimes not for weeks and weeks,' he said." In contrast with Henry's uninspired comment on the size of her flowers, the tinker remembers that chrysanthemum blooms look " 'like a quick puff of colored smoke.' " Eliza is obviously pleased. " 'That's it. What a nice way to describe them,' " she says.

The man's physical appearance has little about it to warrant such a friendly response: "Eliza saw that he was a very big man. Although his hair and beard were greying, he did not look old." His clothes are grease-stained and disheveled, his hands are cracked and dirty. But there is one physical characteristic which would make the man appealing to Eliza: "His eyes were dark, and they were full of the brooding that gets in the eyes of teamsters and sailors." Obviously he lacks the honest, dependable virtues of Henry, the virtues a woman should cherish in a husband. But the important thing he has that Henry lacks is an aura of freedom, unpredictability, perhaps adventure, maybe even poetry, which his gypsy life produces. It has got to be this element of the man that attracts Eliza to him. His first reference to his wandering, carefree existence produces an unconscious feminine response from her. The tinker says, " 'I ain't in no hurry ma'am. I go from Seattle to San Diego and back every year. Takes all my time. About six months each way. I aim to follow nice weather.' " Eliza removes her unfeminine heavy leather gloves and "touched the under edge of her man's hat, searching for fugitive hairs. 'That sounds like a nice kind of a way to live,' she said." But instead of continuing to talk about his roving existence, the tinker begins giving her his sales pitch about mending pots and sharpening knives and scissors. Eliza becomes suddenly distant: "Her eyes hardened with resistance." She is fast losing patience with him when, in an inspired move, he inquires about her chrysanthemums. She warms towards him again almost at once: "The irritation and resistance melted from Eliza's face." After the man shrewdly asks her if he can take some sprouts to a customer down the road, she becomes enthusiastic. "Her eyes shone. She tore off the battered hat and shook out her dark pretty hair"—a movement entirely feminine and essentially seductive. She immediately invites him into the yard.

Eliza is now clearly excited. She scoops up the soil into a flower pot, presses the tender shoots into the damp sand, and describes for him how the plants must be cared for.

Salinas Valley in California where Steinbeck was born and raised. Many of the stories in The Red Pony *and* The Long Valley *are set in this area.*

"She looked deep into his eyes, searchingly. Her mouth opened a little, and she seemed to be listening." She tells him about her "planting hands," which pluck buds instinctively and unerringly. But the reader is aware that such emotion could scarcely be generated solely by an enthusiasm for the care and clipping of chrysanthemums. Eliza, kneeling now before the man, "looking up at him," appears to be experiencing sexual excitement. "Her breasts swelled passionately." Not breast, but breasts. Not heaved, but swelled. The man is suspicious of her strange behavior, perhaps embarrassed: his "eyes narrowed. He looked away self-consciously." She has asked him if he understands her feelings, and he begins a response so in keeping with Eliza's mood that she quite forgets herself.

> "Maybe I know," he said. "Sometimes in the night in the wagon there—"

> Eliza's voice grew husky. She broke in on him. "I've never lived as you do, but I know what you mean. When the night is dark—why, the stars are sharp-pointed, and there's quiet. Why, you rise up and up! Every pointed star gets driven into your body. It's like that. Hot and sharp and—lovely."

The sexual implications of her last four sentences are unmistakable, yet the sexual impact lies just beneath the surface level of meaning in the phallic imagery. Eliza is, more than likely, unaware of the sexual nature of her outburst, but her next action, while probably still unconsciously motivated, is quite overt. "Kneeling there, her hand went out toward his legs in the greasy black trousers. Her hesitant fingers almost touched the cloth. Then her hand dropped to the ground. She crouched low like a fawning dog." The tinker's matter-of-fact comment jolts her at once back to her state of natural reserve: " 'It's nice, just like you say. Only when you don't have no dinner it ain't.' " She is aware that he does not understand after all the feeling of erotic mysticism that she is trying to communicate. "She stood up then, very straight, and her face was ashamed. She held the flower pot out to him and placed it gently in his arms." To avoid further embarrassment, she goes at once to find some old saucepans for him to fix. After regaining her composure, she returns with the battered pots and chats with him as he works. She pays him for the repairs, and as he is leaving, calls out a reminder to keep the plants watered. She stands watching him go. "Her shoulders were straight, her head thrown back, her eyes half-closed, so that the scene came vaguely into them. Her lips moved silently, forming the words 'Good-bye—good-bye.' Then she whispered, 'That's a bright direction. There's a glowing there.' The sound of the whisper startled her. She shook herself free and looked about to see whether anyone had been listening. Only the dogs had heard."

After this the story returns to the portrayal of the relationship between Eliza and her husband, and in the final scenes her feelings toward Henry are clearly revealed. As the tinker's wagon moves out of sight, Eliza quickly returns to the house. The next scene portrays Eliza performing a purification ritual. She felt shame after her display of passion before the stranger. Now she cleanses herself before returning to her husband, the man to whom she should lawfully reach out in desire. "In the bathroom she tore off her soiled clothes and flung them into the corner. And then she scrubbed herself with a little block of pumice, legs and thighs, loins and chest and arms, until her skin was scratched and red." The abrasive action of the pumice suggests expiation for her imagined infidelity. Eliza then studies her naked body in a mirror: "She tightened her stomach and threw out her chest"—movements of a woman who wants to see her figure at its best, but also of a woman gathering resolution. The ceremonial preparation for her evening with Henry also has about it an element of resolve: "After a while she began to dress slowly. . . . She worked carefully on her hair, penciled her eyebrows and rouged her lips." She is steeling herself for the coming evening. "She heard the gate bang shut and *set* herself for Henry's arrival" (Italics mine). Eliza, ready early, goes out onto the porch and sits "primly and stiffly down" to wait for her husband. "Henry came banging out of the door, shoving his tie inside his vest as he came. Eliza stiffened and her face grew tight." There follows the passage examined earlier in which Eliza bridles at each of Henry's inept attempts to compliment her. The scene culminates in his ill-chosen simile describing her in her carefully chosen finery as looking strong enough to break a calf over her knee. "For a second she lost her rigidity. 'Henry! Don't talk like that. You didn't know what you said.' " She seems to lose heart, to wonder if she can abide this insensitive man, but her resolution returns: "She grew complete again. 'I'm strong,' she boasted. 'I never knew before how strong.' "

In the final scene we see this strength tested to the breaking point, finally giving way and dissolving into despair. As the two are driving into town for their festive evening of dinner and a movie, "far ahead on the road Eliza saw a dark speck. She knew." The tinker has discarded her chrysanthemums, symbol of the femininity which she hopes will inspire the excitement she longs for. But he has kept the pot—an insult on any level of interpretation, to discard her treasure and keep its utilitarian container.

This symbolic rejection produces a need for female revenge in Eliza. The idea of attending a prize fight which was repugnant to her a few hours earlier has its appeal now. She asks Henry whether "the men hurt each other very much" and speculates on "how they break noses, and blood runs down their chests." But as her anger cools, she realizes the futility of vicarious vengeance. It can do little to salve her damaged ego or save her dying dream. Henry has promised her wine with dinner, and she tries to console herself with this small romantic touch. " 'It will be enough if we can have wine. It will be plenty,' " she tells Henry. But she knows it will not really be enough. She knows that she will always have good, dull, dependable Henry, but how will she keep her mind from whispering. "There has got to be something more exciting, more beautiful in life than this"? No, wine will not be plenty. "She turned up her coat collar so he could not see that she was crying weakly—like an old woman"—like an old woman for whom all hope of romance is a thing of the past. (pp. 453-58)

> *Elizabeth E. McMahan, " 'The Chrysanthemums': Study of a Woman's Sexuality," in* Modern Fiction Studies, *Vol. XIV, No. 4, Winter, 1968-69, pp. 453-58.*

Bruce K. Martin   (essay date 1971)

[*In the essay below, Martin traces critical reaction to "The Leader of the People" and speculates whether Jody, the main character, changes or develops throughout the story.*]

Thirty years after its initial publication, **"The Leader of the People"** continues to be one of the most widely admired and frequently anthologized of John Steinbeck's writings. However, despite its evident appeal—as an example of Steinbeck's best writing, of typically "American" fiction, and of the peculiar art of the modern short story—it has received surprisingly little critical attention. The failure of critics to deal with **"The Leader of the People"** to the extent that many of Steinbeck's other works have been examined might be understandable but for the fact that the scant critical attention it has received reflects a large measure of disagreement over some rather basic questions. This disagreement, in turn, points to certain critical problems central to an understanding not only of

this story, but indeed of much of Steinbeck's writing and perhaps of modern fiction in general. If **"The Leader of the People"** deserves to be read—and its continuing popularity suggests in part that it does—then surely it deserves a correct reading.

Two very basic questions about the story upon which its critics have been unable to agree are the identity of the main character and the nature of the change or development, if any, which he undergoes. In his book on Steinbeck, Peter Lisca contends that while Jody is the central figure in the other three stories making up **The Red Pony,** in **"The Leader of the People"** the main center of interest is Grandfather, who sees his failure to adjust to the fact that the frontier cannot continue and his failure to communicate to the younger generation the real meaning of the frontier and "westering." According to Lisca, Grandfather's failures are pointed up by the contrasting behavior of the other characters in the story, who possess various but wiser attitudes toward the frontier past [*The Wide World of John Steinbeck*]. The story thus portrays the need for realism, exhibited in different ways by Jody, Carl, Carl's wife, and Billy Buck at the expense of foolish illusion, displayed by Grandfather. [Raymond Short and Richard B. Sewell] have supported Lisca's contention that Grandfather's experience and realization constitute the principal concern here, adding that the "chief impression" of the story is pity for the old man's plight, rather than simply the recognition of his errors and their significance [*A Manual for Teachers Using "Short Story for Study"*]. Alfred Grommon, attempting to determine "Who is the Leader of the People?", argues, however, that the story primarily shows Jody, in his concern for his grandfather, as truly heroic [*English Journal,* 1959]. Jody reveals himself to be a "non-teleological leader": like his grandfather in the past, he exhibits the ability to take command of a situation on the basis of the facts at hand. Grommon points out, though, that Jody's behavior involves no real growth on his part, that the time lapse in the story is too brief to make any basic maturing plausible. But, in contrast with Lisca, he sees Jody not only as the main character in his treatment of his grandfather, but as decidedly superior to the others around him, especially to his father.

There is, of course, much to be said for Grandfather's importance in the story. His arrival at the ranch precipitates at least indirectly all of the important subsequent action. Also, the nature of each of the other characters is in large part determined by his response to Grandfather, since the old man is the common object of interest for Jody, his parents, and Billy. Nor can there be any question but that Grandfather's remarks to Jody after overhearing Carl's outburst—the old man's longest and most formal statement in the entire story—constitute a climax to what precedes them. Grandfather's revelation of what the frontier meant to him and of his loneliness in the frontierless present represents an emotionally compelling end to a chain of action that began with his arrival at the ranch. Clearly the story, as Steinbeck has fashioned it, does not permit the reader to ignore Grandfather.

However, to regard his presence or what he experiences as the central concern of the story is to raise some serious problems. Certainly his moving confession suggests a change of mood in the old man, yet when his speech is set against his earlier behavior, the basis of his despair seems something less than the total realization which some readers would attribute to him. What he tells Jody is that the era of leadership he once knew is gone and that what he has been doing is merely telling stories about that era. "But they're not what I want to tell," he remarks ruefully: "I only know how I want people to feel when I tell them." That he has not mistaken his stories of the past for the reality of the present, that this realization of the frontier's passing has not come in the relatively short time spent at the Tiflin ranch, is suggested by the narrator's earlier description of Grandfather telling his stories as one who looked "as though he were not very interested in the story himself." As his confession indicates, he has been interested in the telling, in the affective value of the stories, not in the tales themselves as reality. And because Grandfather is established prior to the climax of the story as anything but a speedy reasoner, that he should grasp so quickly the rather sophisticated insight contained in his confession hardly seems probable. All that has happened since he was in what Steinbeck terms his "narrative groove" is that he has overheard Carl's disparaging remarks about the stories and concluded that no one wants to hear them. While he certainly regrets the passing of an era in which he was the leader of the people, he has conceived of his role in the present as that of a skilled storyteller, and at this point he regrets most of all his failure in that role. His sorrow for an irrecoverable past began long before the opening of the story. Here he bemoans primarily his inability even to create moving tales from his adventures.

This view of Grandfather's discovery, while closer to his actual experience in the story than the more profound realization sometimes claimed for him, hardly distinguishes him as a main character. His learning that he has lost his audience, or that he never had one, seems insignificant in light of the more epic issues raised in his dramatic outburst to Jody, since the questions of the frontier, of leadership, of communication, and of aging clearly appear in **"The Leader of the People."** Beside such questions his discovery pales.

Nor can his presence really explain or justify certain sections of the story, especially the relatively lengthy opening section before he arrives at the ranch or the final paragraphs, after his confession, when Jody goes inside to make lemonade. The beginning and the ending of the story—frequently of crucial importance in determining what a work of short fiction is principally about—are, of course, more readily related to the experience of Jody himself. And, like the beginning and the end, the middle of the story, when Grandfather is present, is narrated from the boy's point of view, with occasional accounts of sometimes appreciable length regarding Jody's thoughts away from his grandfather. In terms of the content of the story, then, Jody might appear a more plausible main character.

But to say that Jody seems more important or that certain parts of the story appear unrelated to Grandfather is not, of course, to demonstrate the boy's predominance in the story. To do that, it is necessary to establish precisely what Grandfather means to Jody, what exactly happens to Jody and what part Grandfather, obviously an important element in **"The Leader of the People,"** plays in moving the story to its conclusion. If it is difficult to see Grandfather undergoing the type of change demanded by the story's ideology, it is nevertheless necessary to show that Jody himself develops in a way worthy of the substantial concerns of the story.

One possibility is that Jody undergoes a basic change of character, moving away from an initial state of immaturity toward perceivably greater moral awareness. In this regard, Warren French contends that in the course of his encounters with Grandfather the boy acquires, among other things, a capacity for compassion. French sees the lemonade incident at the end of the story as evidence of such a change in Jody. To demonstrate such maturing one must show that Jody earlier in the story exhibits a deficiency of compassion. Grommon has argued rather forcibly, however, the superiority of Jody even initially to the other characters in terms of his capacity for sympathy. Pointing to the uncalled-for mistreatment of the boy throughout the story, he sees Jody as more interested than the others in easing the "snarl in human relationships" in the story.

A careful look at Steinbeck's narrative focusing further undercuts the idea of basic moral change in Jody. In the first dialogue between Jody and Billy Buck, the ranch hand answers the boy's request to hunt mice by advising him to ask his father. After Jody surmises that his father would not care, Steinbeck has Billy remark "ominously"—"You'd better ask him anyway. You know how he is."—and then moves the narrative into the mind of Jody, who mediates on how Carl "is," how he refuses to delegate authority on any matter "important or not." Even initially Steinbeck seems bent on portraying Carl as not only unsympathetic to Jody and everyone else, but irresponsible in his leadership of the ranch. What Grommon would see as mistreatment of Jody comes, of course, in the scene where Carl reproves his son for knowing about the letter from Grandfather, and Mrs. Tiflin concurs by calling Jody "Big-Britches" and noting his idleness. But even more than such mistreatment, Jody's compassionate behavior at the beginning of the story marks his character as good. For example, in the first exchange between Jody and his grandfather, the narrator notes Jody's primary concern with gratifying the old man. When grandfather suggests that the growing Jody may be turning to "pith and stalk," the boy quickly gauges Grandfather's face "to see whether his feelings *should* be hurt"—which suggests his willingness to appear hurt if Grandfather intends this—and, finding no malice in the old man's expression, he shifts his strategy of seeking-to-please to a potential source of more positive satisfaction for Grandfather, the killing of a pig. This same desire to appease the old man by whatever means necessary, which continues throughout the story, goes unrecognized by Jody's parents, as when Mrs. Tiflin miscalculates Jody's motives for including his grandfather in the promised mouse hunt by accusing him simply of desiring an accomplice in misbehavior. Perhaps the most striking indication of Jody's sympathetic nature comes in the showdown scene between Carl and Grandfather, when, while Carl is apologizing, the narrator describes

Jody's sharp surveillance of the situation and his empathetic awareness of Carl's agony: "It was an awful thing that he [Carl] was doing. He was tearing himself to pieces to talk like that. It was a terrible thing to him to retract a word, but to retract it in shame was infinitely worse." This keen feeling for the overly proud Carl precedes the climactic outburst of Grandfather to Jody and largely rules out the supposition that Jody lacks sympathy prior to the climax. Instead of pointing to a change of character in the boy, the lemonade incident at the end only further confirms the strong capacity for feeling that he exhibits earlier toward his antagonist. And, rather than signalling such a change, his mother's surprise at his wanting lemonade not for himself but for Grandfather only points up her belated recognition of the qualities in her son already abundantly evident to the reader.

If it is difficult to see Jody changing morally, it is equally difficult to ascribe certain other kinds of learning to him. Perhaps the simplest solution to the persisting problem of Grandfather's dramatic outburst and the response it produces in the boy is to say that at this point Jody learns from his mentor the disillusioning truth about the frontier. We have seen that the old man does not, or cannot, realize this himself in the short course covered by the story, but perhaps the boy—mentally sharper, less experienced and more curious—does. This hypothesis appears weak, however, in view of what Jody knows long before the climax. Early in the story, when the Tiflin family discuss Grandfather's impending visit, Carl observes the old man's obsession with a single topic of conversation, to which Jody answers excitedly, "Indians . . . Indians and crossing the plains." But that the boy cannot confuse the frontier with present reality, that he knows that Grandfather's stories are only stories about a dead past, is suggested by his overhearing, immediately after this scene, his mother tell Carl to tolerate her father's monomania because the object of his life is past: "It was a big thing to do, but it didn't last long. . . . You might be patient with him and pretend to listen." Jody's awareness of the frontier's demise is indicated further when the narrative follows him to bed that night, after Grandfather has arrived and begun extolling his adventures in characteristic fashion:

> Jody lay in his bed and thought of the impossible world of Indians and buffaloes, a world that had ceased to be forever. He wished he could have been living in the heroic time, but he was not of heroic timber. No one living now, save possible Billy Buck, was worthy to do the things that had been done. A race of giants had lived then, fearless men, men of a staunchness unknown in this day. Jody thought of the wide plains and of the wagons moving across like centipedes. He thought of Grandfather on a huge white horse, marshalling the people. Across his mind marched the great phantoms, and they marched off the earth and they were gone.
>
> He came back to the ranch for a moment, then. He heard the dull rushing sound that space and silence make. He heard one of the dogs, out in the doghouse, scratching a flea and bumping his elbow against the floor with every stroke. Then

the wind arose again and the black cypress groaned and Jody went to sleep.

Jody realizes the "impossibility" of what Grandfather has related to him; the contrast between the "race of giants" and the dog's scratching permeates his consciousness at this point.

But if he knows that the great age is gone, why, then, does he evidently share the old man's enthusiasm for "Indians and crossing the plains"? The explanation for his excitement lies, of course, in his situation, as Steinbeck describes it in the first section of the story. Initially Jody appears scuffling his shoes "in a way he had been told was destructive to good shoe-leather." and idly throwing stones: making gestures of uselessness and boredom. He views the prospect of hunting mice with relish: "They had grown smug in their security, over-bearing and fat. Now the time of disaster had come; they would not survive another day." As the narrator's paraphrase of the boy's state of mind suggests, he regards the mouse-hunt as an epic mission, a means to excitement and chance to assert leadership. His thinking about mice points up not the ridiculousness of Jody's vision, but the constraint of the situation forcing him into such a vision. All he can do is hunt mice and curse; ranch life surrounds him with an unvarying and undemanding routine.

With this in mind—and Steinbeck's ordering of materials in this early part of his story suggests his intention for the reader to have this in mind—the significance of Grandfather to the boy becomes clear. To Jody the frontier stories represent a welcome source of temporary escape from a dull existence. He values Grandfather as a producer of diversion through his entertaining stories. And the boy can be entertained by them because, unlike his parents, he has very little else to entertain him.

However, this is not to say that Jody's behavior toward Grandfather is motivated solely by a self-interested desire to avoid painful reality. Having learned from his mother the need for encouraging the old man, Jody first approaches his grandfather with dignity, in contrast with his "unseemly running" immediately before. In their dialogue about the mouse-hunt, he speaks of it as "just play" and readily admits the greater significance of hunting Indians. This deference turns to a careful defense of the old man's feelings once they arrive at the house. When Jody sees Grandfather repeating himself to Billy Buck, to confirm Carl's earlier accusation, the boy conceives of himself partly as a mediator between conflicting positions, but mostly as a protector of Grandfather. At the supper table Jody studies the responses of Grandfather and his parents very anxiously: Carl's moth-killing attempt to quiet the old man, his mother's anger at this, threatened lapses in the story-telling and Carl's remarking that he had heard the story before. At this point Jody "[rises] to heroism." by asking Grandfather to tell about the Indians, a request dictated by his increasing identification with the old man as victim of his father's tyranny. Noting the others' inattention to the tale which follows, and himself anticipating the words of the story, Jody nevertheless works to preserve what he considers to be the old man's unawareness of the reality to which Carl would tactlessly expose him.

Jody thus comes to regard the story-telling not so much as a way of solving his own problems but as a means of sheltering Grandfather, whom he loves and pities, from similar problems. His movement from self-concern to a concern with keeping up the old man's supposed illusions stems from the proneness to sympathy which he has exhibited initially, and represents not a basic change of character but only a shift of emphasis between two concerns which he has had from the beginning of the story.

And though the showdown between Carl and Grandfather threatens Jody's protective scheme, he seems hopeful of reviving the old man's spirits, as he asks him to tell some more stories, assuring him of his own interest in them. Jody's entire plan of protection has been based on the assumption that Grandfather lives in the past, that, unlike himself, Grandfather regards his stories as something more than tales of a dead frontier. He feels that by encouraging Grandfather to tell the stories, he can delude the old man into viewing the frontier as alive and real. What Jody thus learns from Grandfather's climactic outburst is that Grandfather already has realized that the past is dead and that his usefulness as a leader is gone. Jody now recognizes that he has not been promoting illusion in Grandfather, who has been fully aware of the facts. Like Jody, he has not confused fact with fiction. Jody learns that Grandfather too is trapped in present reality and that his plan to shelter Grandfather from painful truth was inherently futile. To the extent that Jody has patronized Grandfather initially, he might be said to suffer the moral discovery of his and Grandfather's "equality" as victims of reality. However, Steinbeck's characterization of the boy suggests nothing besides the desire to make happy someone whom he loves. In arguing with Grandfather that he (Jody) might lead the people in the future or that the frontier does not depend upon the mainland, Jody is attempting, futilely, to revive the old man's dream. The finality of Grandfather's reply—"It is finished"—causes Jody to recognize fully that Grandfather has lost this dream long ago, and that indeed Grandfather has discovered in his painful exchange with Jody's father not that the frontier is dead—this he's known for some time—but that no one cares to hear about it. In a sense, too, Jody suffers disappointment because he, a small boy, cannot please Grandfather in the way that adult attention might. Having turned from the "heroism" of the mouse-hunt to the greater challenge of instilling hope in his grandfather, Jody realizes more than before the constraint that his youth and status place upon him. Since he cannot shelter Grandfather from painful reality, all he can do is dull the pain slightly by offering lemonade. And, significantly, Steinbeck indicates the sort of "levelling" that life has imposed on Grandfather and Jody—the inescapable pressure of reality on all men—by reversing the relationship that the well-meaning Jody has envisioned earlier, for Grandfather ironically accepts the lemonade not to ease his own suffering but only to please the boy.

This reëxamination of **"The Leader of the People"** suggests, then, that what holds the story together is Jody Tiflin and his saddening discovery of how much his grandfather's plight parallels his own. Such a view certainly does not deny the significance of Grandfather; for though Jody

appears the more important character, the education that he undergoes is wholly contingent upon the old man's equally painful discovery during the story. Steinbeck carefully develops Grandfather's responses as a subplot, and a highly necessary one, to the final reactions of Jody. Nor does this reading question the centrality of what many critics have seen as the major "themes" of the story—the frontier, aging, communication, and leadership—for Jody in the moment when he seizes upon the totality of his grandfather's misery is confronted at once with the tremendous pain attending the assumption of leadership, the losing of power, and the passing of time, all of which make it impossible for Grandfather to sustain the illusions Jody mistakenly attributes to him. And though, as I have suggested, it is difficult to see Jody undergoing any drastic moral change—rather than becoming better ethically, he becomes more aware of the dilemma of adulthood—there is no question but that his earlier good intentions reflected somewhat naïve theorizing and that what he learns of Grandfather here will permit him in the future to apply his moral principles with more success. We have, then, Jody becoming better equipped, in terms of practical awareness, to serve as a "leader of the people" in his own age.

In the foregoing discussion I have attempted to answer two basic questions about the materials and order within the story. Lest a concern with identifying the main character and his experience seem pedestrian in light of what many perhaps would see as more important concerns, certain advantages of such an approach should be noted. For one thing, because the "themes" listed above apply to both Grandfather and Jody, a precise determination of which character's experience unifies the story permits one to speak more closely and accurately about economy and subtlety in Steinbeck's narrative. For example, when one sees that Jody is the main character, Jody's initial behavior takes on a dimension of importance beyond mere "preparation" for Grandfather. Second, because such "themes" relate to all of the **Red Pony** stories, this type of reading suggests more precisely the distinctive qualities of **"The Leader of the People."** And, conversely, it helps demonstrate the tightness of design in **The Red Pony,** for in all

---

Steinbeck on writing *The Red Pony*:

I have written five stories in the scene. It would be well now to start bending the thing into one piece. But how. I've thought of that often enough. Five stories have been written about Jody or in which Jody was the eyes. After the story of the ghost house, why not switch to Billy Buck—to Mrs. Tiflin, to Carl Tiflin. It wouldn't be a bad exercise to make a volume of short stories all about one family. I suppose it has been done. I can think of a number of books and series, but always the emphasis lay in the incidents—not in the family.

John Steinbeck, in a 1934 journal entry later collected in The True Adventures of John Steinbeck: Writer, *Viking Press, 1984.*

four stories we see Jody suffering often painful, but always valuable lessons in his quest for manhood. This is not to say that the approach employed here is the best or only approach, or that a more thematic approach does not yield equally meaningful insights, but simply that the question that I have considered here must be asked and must be answered for a total awareness of the artistry of **"The Leader of the People."** (pp. 423-32)

> Bruce K. Martin, " 'The Leader of the People' Reëxamined," in Studies in Short Fiction, Vol. VIII, No. 3, Summer, 1971, pp. 423-32.

Marilyn L. Mitchell   (essay date 1976)

[*In the following essay, Mitchell examines Steinbeck's treatment of women characters in "The Chrysanthemums" and "The White Quail."*]

Most writers of the first half of this century concentrated on characterizations of men and the problems and motivations of men. Perhaps that is because most writers of anything other than romantic novels or popular magazine stories were men. Two notable exceptions to the pattern were John Steinbeck and D. H. Lawrence, who tried to release woman from the pasteboard, shadowy role she generally assumed in fiction. Today, Lawrence's portraits of aggressive and often neurotic women have come under attack by certain feminist critics, while Steinbeck's contributions to American literature in any sense are ignored or dismissed. Mention of Steinbeck recalls only *The Grapes of Wrath*, a powerful social work but not his best literary achievement, nor the one in which he demonstrated greatest sensitivity to female characters. True, Ma Joad and Rosasharn are unforgettable women, but both clearly fall into the "earth-mother" category which is a stereotype, however flattering. Rather than in this novel or his others from the thirties, it is in his short stories that Steinbeck's understanding of his craft and of women is to be found.

Two of John Steinbeck's more intricate and memorable stories in *The Long Valley* are **"The Chrysanthemums"** and **"The White Quail."** Both examine the psychology and sexuality of strong women who must somehow express themselves meaningfully within the narrow possibilities open to women in a man's world. In each case the woman chooses a traditional feminine activity, gardening, as a creative outlet, yet the dedication with which each undertakes her project is of the sort traditionally considered masculine. It is the conflict between society's view of what constitutes masculinity and its view of what constitutes femininity as well as the conflict between the women and men depicted which carries the action and determines the development of character. In addition, Steinbeck reveals fundamental differences between the way women see themselves and the way they are viewed by men. For example, both husbands relate primarily to the physical attributes of their wives, making only meager attempts to comprehend their personalities. Consequently, a gulf of misunderstanding exists between the marriage partners which creates verbal as well as sexual blocks to communication. In each marriage at least one of the spouses is aware of some degree of sexual frustration, although dissatisfaction is never overtly articulated. Furthermore, the

propensity of the men to see their wives as dependent inferiors, while the women perceive themselves as being equal if not superior partners, creates a strain within the marriage which is partially responsible for the isolation of each of the characters.

Both Elisa Allen of **"The Chrysanthemums"** and Mary Teller in **"The White Quail"** display a strength of will usually identified with the male but which, in these cases, the husbands are not shown to have. Steinbeck's women, with their rather bisexual identities, naturally recall certain female characters created by D. H. Lawrence, notably Gudrun Brangwen in *Women in Love* and March in "The Fox." Critics Richard F. Peterson and Peter Lisca have also noted the similarity between Steinbeck and Lawrence in the "psychological portraits of frustrated females," but decline to draw parallels between specific characters. They imply, however, that such frustration is due to an incapacity for sexual response on the part of the women.

Elisa Allen demonstrates a very earthy sensuality in **"The Chrysanthemums,"** though not in the presence of her husband, indicating that their failure as a couple may be as much his fault as hers. Mary Teller, on the other hand, is frigid, yet she responds orgasmically to the sight of the white quail: "A shiver of pleasure, a bursting of pleasure swelled in Mary's breast. She held her breath. . . . A powerful ecstasy quivered in her body." But Mary's response is really triggered by the experience of seeing herself in another form and is therefore autoerotic:

> "Why," Mary cried to herself, "She's like me! . . . She's like the essence of me, an essence boiled down to utter purity. She must be the queen of the quail. She makes every lovely thing that ever happened to me one thing. . . . This is the me that was everything beautiful. This is the center of me, my heart."

Mary has a physical dimension, but she does not respond to that which is foreign to her, i.e., the male, her husband, who in turn tolerates her coldness, assuming that good women are naturally a bit repelled by sex. He understood that "there were things Mary didn't like to talk about. The lock on her bedroom door was an answer to a question, a clean, quick, decisive answer." Because he cannot force his will on her—she had married him for that reason—his frustration in the marriage will remain unvoiced, to be given expression only symbolically in his deliberate murder of her surrogate self, the white quail.

"The White Quail" is as fabulous and ethereal in dialogue and setting as **"The Chrysanthemums"** is naturalistic. Furthermore, Steinbeck has created in Elisa Allen a warm, three-dimensional character with whom the reader can identify, just as he has made Mary Teller a virtual caricature of the selfish, castrating female who inspires animosity. The only obvious connection one woman has with the other is the superficial but significant detail that Mary and Elisa are childless women who have transferred maternal impulses to a garden. In addition, however, both women are trapped between society's definition of the masculine and the feminine and are struggling against the limitations of the feminine. That struggle is more apparent in the life of Elisa Allen than in that of Mary Teller, who is more physically fragile. Yet Mary is one of the most ruthless and egotistical of all Steinbeck's characters, although outwardly she conforms to the stereotype of feminine weakness. Her mythic depiction in a story that is practically a fable in modern dress leads one to conclude that Steinbeck is using her to refute outmoded conceptions of what a woman should be. Mary is not Steinbeck's model of the wife; she is merely Elisa's opposite who serves to show the real human beauty beneath Elisa's rough and somewhat masculine exterior.

Steinbeck introduces the reader to the narrow world of Mary Teller's garden through a dormer window composed of leaded, diamond-shaped panes. The convex curvature of the window and the fragmentation of its space indicate that the vision of the person within, Mary Teller, is distorted. Having been thoroughly acquainted with the landscaping and contents of the garden, we are finally, in the third paragraph, introduced to Mary, "Mrs. Harry E. Teller, that is." In the last paragraph of Part 1, Steinbeck again uses Mary's name, followed by her husband's, to show that it is her vision which controls the story. For five years she had looked for the man who would construct the garden she had so meticulously planned. "When she met Harry Teller, the garden seemed to like him." Personification of the garden reveals that to Mary it is a "child" whose "step-father" she must carefully select with only a secondary interest in the man's desirability as a husband.

Harry, of course, has no understanding of Mary's personality or motivations, nor does he believe any is necessary. Just as she is attracted to him for his passivity and his income, so he is attracted to her for her apparent delicacy and beauty: "You're so pretty. You make me kind of—hungry." Her attractiveness will also make her an asset to his business: "He was proud of her when people came to dinner. She was so pretty, so cool and perfect." And since he does not expect a pretty girl to have any dimension but the physical, the firm determination with which she engineers the garden's construction comes as a surprise to him: "Who could tell that such a pretty girl could have so much efficiency." His misconception of women is largely responsible for Mary's success in completely dominating him, for she skillfully cloaks her aggressive manipulations in feminine frailty.

For her part, Mary is dedicated to the impossible task of creating something perfect, a beautiful reflection of herself which will remain forever unchanged. As the workmen finish landscaping, she says to her husband: "We won't ever change it, will we, Harry? If a bush dies, we'll put another one just like it in the same place. . . . If anything should be changed it would be like part of me being torn out." But neither the garden nor Mary's life can be completely perfect, because there are always dangers in the world waiting to destroy the beautiful. The threat to the garden comes from the wild foliage of the hill which would destroy its order and serenity were it not for the sturdy but exotic line of fuchsias, "little symbolic trees," obviously representing Mary. The hill too is a symbol—a symbol for everything which is not Mary. It, like Harry, opposes the irrationality of feeling and happenstance to her unemotional rationality.

Ironically perhaps, Mary's love for the garden does not imply a love of nature, for she reacts violently against the natural biological order which would alter her arrangement. Harry is appointed killer of the pests that come in the night to attack her garden, but, though he does not see it, she is the one who most relishes the slaughter:

> Mary held the flashlight while Harry did the actual killing, crushing the slugs and snails into oozy, bubbling masses. He knew it must be a disgusting business to her, but the light never wavered. "Brave girl," he thought. "She has a sturdiness in back of that fragile beauty." She made the hunts exciting too. "There's a big one, creeping and creeping," she would say. "He's after that big bloom. Kill him! Kill him quickly!" They came into the house after the hunts laughing happily.

Harry, however, declines to kill other animals for her sake. Although he meekly accepts her absolute refusal to let him own a dog which might "do things on the plants in her garden, or even dig in her flower beds," he will not set out poison for the cat which had crept from the hill into her garden and was threatening the birds. He argues that "animals suffer terribly when they get poison," and despite Mary's indifference to that argument, he insists that an air rifle will work as an effective deterrent once the cat has been stung by a pellet. Harry may realize subconsciously that the cat is symbolic of him just as the white quail is of Mary. It is evident that Mary, at least, sees the cat as a threat to her: "That white quail was *me,* the secret me that no one can ever get at, the me that's way inside. . . . Can't you see, dear? The cat was after me. It was going to kill me. That's why I want to poison it."

Throughout the story, Harry's threat as husband to Mary's perfection has been made obvious. She locks her bedroom door against his advances to prevent his getting at "the me that's way inside." Of course, the phrase also applies to her actual personality, which he is equally unable to penetrate. Mary does not like dirt, rust, disorder, and slimy things like the slugs, all of which she perceives as concomitants of the sex act. Since her range of emotional expression is circumscribed by the limitations of the self, Harry's person and that which emanates from him are beyond her appreciation. Harry is as much an outsider in her world as the animals and the hill. To her, sex is not a sharing of physical and emotional energy, but rather a price she must pay for the garden. Four times, in describing Mary's response to Harry's advances, Steinbeck writes that "she let him." The phrase is used three times describing their courtship, and only once following the wedding, after which the locked door is mentioned on two occasions. Furthermore, it is significant that "the lot was bought and the house was built, and they were married," in that order. Afterward, Harry is not invited into the garden except on those occasions when he is to protect it from harm. He may admire it but not enjoy it in the twilight hours which are "almost a sacred time" for her. "When Harry came home from the office, he stayed in the house and read his paper until she came in from the garden, star-eyed. It made her unhappy to be disturbed." How she in any way, in fact, functions as wife to Harry is unclear, because even their dinner is prepared by another person, a high-school girl.

Just as Mary, inside, perceives the garden through a distorted glass, so her perception of the home, and the marriage, is distorted when she is outside looking in. She sees the living room "like a picture, like the set of a play that was about to start," and having noticed Harry, in passing, reading the paper, she conjures a vision of herself sitting in the firelight's glow in quiet perfection:

> She could almost see herself sitting there. Her round arms and long fingers were resting on the chair. Her delicate, sensitive face was in profile, looking reflectively into the firelight. "What is she thinking about?" Mary whispered. "I wonder what's going on in her mind. Will she get up? No, she's just sitting there. The neck of that dress is too wide, see how it slips sideways over the shoulder. But that's rather pretty. It looks careless, but neat and pretty. Now—she's smiling. She must be thinking something nice."

Harry is but a financial necessity in Mary Teller's world. In begging him to poison the cat, which opposes her will, she is obliquely threatening him as well, and he responds to her challenge by deliberately, though surreptitiously, killing the white quail with which she so strongly identified. This act of destruction, F. W. Watt writes in his *Steinbeck* (1967), is the result of the "sexual and intellectual gulf between a husband and wife." Although Harry has temporarily forsaken his passive role for action, it is not a constructive one and will bring no resolution. His last words in the story are, "I'm lonely. . . . Oh, Lord, I'm so lonely." In a sense, he has become the white quail, a pitiful victim, while the garden, the cat, and Mary continue to survive.

In this story, as in **"The Chrysanthemums,"** Steinbeck proposes no solutions for the psychological conflicts which plague human interactions. There will always be predators and victims in life which is comprised of mere plateaus of contentment between joy and despair. Although Mary Teller, at story's end, is ignorant of the death of the quail, her period of happiness is nonetheless predestined to dissolution as are all the works of man. She cannot prevent the physical deterioration of her body or of the garden; then what will become of her self-admiration and her husband's love?

Elisa Allen of **"The Chrysanthemums,"** whom Joseph W. Beach calls "one of the most delicious characters ever transferred from life to the pages of a book," is a vastly more sympathetic figure than Harry Teller but more akin to him in her loneliness and frustration than to his wife, Mary. Still she, like Mary, "mothers" a garden, a chrysanthemum bed, and takes great pride in her ability to nurture life and beauty. She says of her flowers, as if they were children, that "it's" the budding that takes the most time." A similarity of setting is also notable. Elisa's house and garden, though not as spatially restricted as Mary Teller's, are proscribed areas of beauty and security which she maintains against the wilderness, yet without losing an appreciation for the wild beauty beyond her yard. Physically as well as emotionally, however, Elisa and Mary are almost complete opposites. Steinbeck continually refers to Mary as "pretty," but he describes Elisa's face as "eager and mature and handsome," interesting masculine adjectives. Mordecai Marcus is correct in saying in "The Lost Dream of Sex and Childbirth in 'The Chrysanthemums,' " that Elisa's "pervasive combination of femininity and masculinity" is an element "central to the story."

Another contrast is that, while Mary Teller's selfish refusal to compromise her ambitions recalls Gudrun Brangwen of *Women in Love,* who eventually destroyed her lover Gerald Crich, Elisa Allen's strength coupled with her vulnerability is reminiscent of March in "The Fox." This is Lawrence's description of March: "When she was out and about, in her puttees and breeches, her belted coat and her loose cap, she looked almost like some graceful, loose-balanced young man, for her shoulders were straight, and her movements easy and confident, even tinged with a little indifference, or irony." In his presentation of Elisa, Steinbeck's imagery is strikingly similar:

> She was thirty-five. Her face was lean and strong and her eyes were as clear as water. Her figure looked blocked and heavy in her gardening costume, a man's black hat pulled low over her eyes, clod-hopper shoes, a figured print dress almost completely covered by a big corduroy apron with four big pockets . . . her work with the scissors was over-eager, over-powerful. The chrysanthemum stems seemed too small and easy for her energy.

Of course it is mere speculation whether, or to what extent, Steinbeck was influenced by one or another of Lawrence's "masculine" women. What the women do share, and importantly so, is an intense strength of personality which sets them apart from so many of their retiring sisters in the literature of the twenties and thirties.

Elisa is essentially different from March, however, in the frustration she feels in her role as a rancher's wife; and part of Elisa's sense of frustration stems from the fact that her work, even the dirty work of gardening, remains "woman's work." When we first meet her she is tending the flower bed and watching her husband Henry discussing business with two men. "The three of them stood by the tractor shed, each man with one foot on the side of the little Fordson. They smoked cigarettes and studied the machine as they talked." Theirs is a sphere of money, tobacco, and machines from which she is deliberately excluded, although their conversation concerns the ranch and is therefore her affair as much as Henry's. Later, when Henry comes by to tell her about the transaction, he praises her for her gardening skills. "I wish you'd work out in the orchard and raise some apples that big," he comments; and she replies as to a challenge: "Maybe I could do it, too. I've got a gift with things, all right." But Henry obviously takes neither his remark nor her response seriously, for he says: "Well, it sure works with flowers." The fact that she strongly believes in her ability to perform paid work emerges again in her conversation with the itinerant pot-mender who boasts of his skill in the trade. She responds to this with a more positive challenge: "You might be surprised to have a rival some time. I can sharpen scissors, too. And I can beat the dents out of little pots.

I could show you what a woman might do." But he tells her that his life, which she views romantically, "ain't the right kind of life for a woman."

Elisa may know nothing of the world beyond her valley, but she believes in her talents and in the possibility of a life more rewarding than her own. As the man and his equipage move on down the road, she stands at the fence watching him: "Her lips moved silently, forming the words 'Good-bye—good-bye.' Then she whispered, 'That's a bright direction. There's a glowing there.' " At the conclusion, when the man's disregard for her and her work has been revealed by his callous disposal of her gift of the plants, she grasps at adventure on a smaller scale: wine with dinner. She acknowledges the fact that a man's freedom is denied her by agreeing with her husband that she would, after all, probably dislike the prizefights, saying: "It will be enough if we can have wine. It will be plenty."

Elisa's ambiguous combination of traditionally masculine and feminine traits, more apparent than Mary Teller's, has a great deal to do with making her a plausible character. It is also fully half the concern of the story. The second major theme of **"The Chrysanthemums"** is related to the first in its revelation of Elisa's sensuality and the apparent sexual frustration she experiences in her marriage. While she and her husband appear to be friends, there is a definite failure of communication between them in the exchange of ideas; therefore, it is reasonable to assume a similar malfunction of sexual communication. The exchange of dialogue following her meeting with the tinker and prior to the couple's evening in town is a typical example of Henry's capacity for understatement and his embarrassment in her presence. Elisa has just dressed in the garment "which was the symbol of her prettiness" and is waiting on the porch for Henry to appear. As he emerges from the house,

> Elisa stiffened and her face grew tight. Henry stopped short and looked at her. "Why—why, Elisa. You look so nice!"
>
> "Nice? You think I look nice? What do you mean by 'nice'?"
>
> Henry blundered on. "I don't know. I mean you look different, strong and happy."
>
> "I am strong? Yes, strong. What do you mean 'strong'?"
>
> He looked bewildered. "You're playing some kind of a game," he said helplessly. "It's a kind of a play."

In the tinker, though, Elisa finds a man whose strength seems to match hers, although she later discovers his emotional poverty. Their brief encounter reveals an aspect of Elisa which is not seen in her dealings with Henry—her erotic potential.

At first, she reacts to the tinker with firm sales resistance but is brought into sympathy with him by the interest he expresses in her flowers. At last he shatters her resistance by asking for a pot of the young shoots to give a customer of his who has no chrysanthemums. It is at this point that

Elisa begins to respond to him in a sexual fashion and shifts rapidly into the feminine, passive role. Steinbeck's imagery builds to Elisa's orgasmic speech to the tinker, then recedes in the afterglow of her bathing.

The first sign of change in Elisa is her desire to appear womanly for the man: "She tore off the battered hat and shook out her dark pretty hair." As she eagerly begins the transplanting, her gloves are discarded and she feels the rich earth between her bare fingers, an obviously sensual image. In the process she finds herself "kneeling on the ground looking up at him. Her breast swelled passionately." She is now below him in the traditional female position for intercourse. "Elisa's voice grew husky" as she tried to express for them both the feeling one has, alone, at night, beneath the stars:

> "Why, you rise up and up! Every pointed star gets driven into your body. It's like that. Hot and sharp and—lovely."
>
> Kneeling there, her hand went out toward his legs in the greasy black trousers. Her hesitant fingers almost touched the cloth. Then her hand dropped to the ground. She crouched low like a fawning dog.

Elisa is subconsciously contrasting him with her husband as a potential sexual partner. Ray B. West, Jr. says in *The Short Story in America, 1900-1950* (1952) that Elisa's vigorous bathing, following the tinker's departure, is an attempt on her part to maintain the physical vitality which he had aroused. It is equally probable that Elisa is attempting to wash away the taint of her own sensual approach to a stranger, whether or not he recognized her passion. The very idea that she might, even for a moment, have contemplated disloyalty toward the kind, if obtuse, Henry would impel her to scrub "legs and thighs, loins and chest and arms, until her skin was scratched and red." Steinbeck enumerates these parts of her body, the sexual ones, omitting mention of her face and hands which he had previously described as dirt-smudged. It is clear that he means this passage to be part of the story's sexual focus, and that he uses it as another detail which shows Elisa to be sexually repressed.

Despite whatever guilt Elisa feels as a result of the afternoon's experience, she also feels renewed confidence in her spiritual strength and in her physical attractiveness. Following the bath, she lingers awhile before the mirror appraising her body from different angles. Then she dresses slowly, luxuriously in her finest, newest clothing and expends a considerable amount of effort on her makeup.

Possibly because Elisa identifies so strongly with the male, at least in terms of a desire for adventure, she is vulnerable to the sexual appeal of a man. For whatever reasons, her husband does not stimulate her latent eroticism, so she has indulged herself in a fantasy involving a stranger. Her fantasy, however, is cruelly shattered by the tinker's deceit. She had believed they shared common emotions, that they actually communicated, but now she sees his talk as the salesman's trick that it was. In fact, he hadn't even the sensitivity to dump the plants furtively; he was too greedy to retain the pot. So she must see her small and broken flowers in the highway, a symbol of her broken dreams. Intuitively, she knows that her life will not change substantially, that the seasons will follow each other inexorably, and that only the birds will be migratory. Steinbeck says: "She turned up her coat collar so he [Henry] could not see that she was crying weakly—like an old woman." Indeed, part of the vision she must be seeing is herself as an old woman. Her dream of something in life beyond mere existence is crushed at this moment.

Henry is unaware of Elisa's suffering, nor could he offer effective consolation were he to notice her change of mood. Like the Tellers, the Allens are separated from one another by sexual, temperamental, and intellectual differences which they seem incapable of bridging. The women have certain needs of the spirit, the abstract nature of which keeps happiness forever elusive. The men are more practical, with greater involvement in physical concerns; but confronted by women whose malaise is partially due to a confusion of sexual identity, the men retreat from the masculine role of leadership, leaving the women to flounder between aggression and submission. Undoubtedly, part of the attraction the tinker holds for Elisa is his independence and the confidence of his manner which her husband apparently lacks. Likewise, Harry Teller, in his indulgence of Mary's whims, encourages her selfish dictation of their lives to the detriment of both partners. Steinbeck is not advocating that wives be submissive to their husbands; if his opinion on male-female relations can be interpreted at all from the two stories, it would seem to support a sharing of interests determined through real communication between people, so that none can say with Harry Teller: "Oh, Lord, I'm so lonely." (pp. 304-14)

> *Marilyn L. Mitchell, " 'Steinbeck's Strong Women': Feminine Identity in the Short Stories," in* Southwest Review, *Vol. 61, No. 3, Summer, 1976, pp. 304-15.*

Louis Owens   (essay date 1985)

[*In the following excerpt, taken from his* John Steinbeck's Re-Vision of America, *Owens examines the range of themes, symbols, and settings in* The Long Valley.]

In The Long Valley

The whole range of Steinbeck's symbolic topography is to be found in *The Long Valley,* Steinbeck's only collection of short stories, written over a period of several years and published in 1938. Because of the diversity of settings in this volume, the title is somewhat misleading, and Richard Astro is correct when he argues that "it is pointless to seek a unifying thematic thread connecting the eleven stories in *The Long Valley.*" Astro goes on, however, to assert incorrectly that "all but **'Saint Katy the Virgin'** are vignettes set in California's Salinas Valley." In actuality, only a few of the stories are set in the valley, and in this fact can be found the basis for the lack of thematic unity in the volume as a whole.

"Flight" and the stories that make up *The Red Pony* are set on the western and eastern slopes of the Santa Lucia

Mountains, and these mountains are the dominant symbols and thematic force in each of these stories. **"The Snake"** is set not in the valley but in Dr. Phillips's laboratory on Cannery Row in Monterey, and the sea with its strong symbolic ties to the unconscious is the major topographical force here, as it is in other Steinbeck writings set near the sea. . . . **"Breakfast,"** a fragment that is of interest primarily because it later found its way into *The Grapes of Wrath,* is of no thematic significance to this discussion and thus, along with the burlesque **"Saint Katy the Virgin"** has been omitted from discussion here. Of the remaining stories, it is possible to say that **"The Chrysanthemums," "The White Quail," "The Harness,"** and **"Johnny Bear"** are all very probably set in the "long valley" and take on thematic significance and unity because of this setting. **"The Murder"** is, like **"Flight"** and *The Red Pony* and *To A God Unknown,* set in the Santa Lucia Mountains, and this fact undoubtedly determined the central role death plays in the story. However, as Peter Lisca and Roy Simmonds have both shown, it is likely that this story was conceived originally as part of *The Pastures of Heaven,* another work with a valley setting, and to this intended setting can be attributed the strong thematic similarity between this story and the other stories set in the Salinas Valley. Because of this marked similarity, **"The Murder"** is discussed in this section. The settings for **"The Raid"** and **"The Vigilante"** are indeterminant and have little or no thematic significance in the stories. They may well be set in the valley, but thematically both stories look back toward the themes of group-man and commitment in *In Dubious Battle* and forward to the same themes in *The Grapes of Wrath.* These two stories contribute little to whatever thematic unity may be discovered in this volume, but because they do reflect the thematic concerns that engrossed Steinbeck in his major valley fiction—especially the central theme of commitment through sacrifice—they are also discussed here.

Warren French has found a unifying element in the theme of frustration running through several of the stories in *The Long Valley,* and Fontenrose has suggested that "Steinbeck's title indicates a topographical unity," and that "in *The Long Valley* the mythical theme of the garden is fused with the central theme of all mythologies, cosmos against chaos." Reloy Garcia has elaborated on the garden theme, suggesting that "there is a common context, the garden, and a common theme as well, which derives from the context and amplifies it. This theme is the brutal initiation into the world of disappointment, loneliness, manhood, knowledge, evil, and death; in short the world of man. . . . Over and against the painful awareness each initiation induces, character after character attempts to create a static, child's garden which walls out the chaotic world of man." While such readings are extremely helpful in understanding some of the stories in the volume, it is a mistake to attempt to harness the entire volume with a single thesis. It is with great difficulty, for example, that the theme of initiation can be made clear in such a story as **"The Chrysanthemums,"** or that *The Red Pony* can be understood as "cosmos against chaos." On the whole it is more useful to admit, as Fontenrose does elsewhere, that the volume is primarily "a series of unconnected stories," or to agree with Brian Barbour that "for the most part, the book's order seems random; stories do not comment on or deepen each other. . . . The book lacks a center.''

The exception to this apparent lack of unity can be found only in the group of stories unmistakably set in the valley for which the collection is named. If there is a thematic dominance in the volume, it is generated by the thematic continuity found in these stories. To attempt to impose a strict unity on the volume as a whole is to ignore the realities of the work—that it serves most obviously as a way for Steinbeck to capitalize on the fame he had suddenly begun to achieve with the publication of *Tortilla Flat, Of Mice and Men,* and *In Dubious Battle.* It is a patchwork volume, as such inclusions as **"Breakfast"** and **"Saint Katy"** should clearly illustrate.

"The Chrysanthemums": Waiting for Rain

Of the first story in **The Long Valley, "The Chrysanthe-mums,"** Steinbeck wrote: "It is entirely different and is designed to strike without the reader's knowledge. I mean he reads it casually and after it is finished feels that something profound has happened to him although he does not know what nor how." In light of the eagerness with which critics have rushed to praise this story, calling it "Steinbeck's most artistically successful story," and "one of the world's great short stories," it seems that most critics would agree that "something profound" happens in **"The Chrysanthemums."** And the great difficulty critics have encountered when trying to explain the "what" and "how" of this story suggests that Steinbeck's design has been very effective, has led, in fact, to what Roy Simmonds refers to as "a small critical industry" grown up around this story.

Like each of the stories in **The Long Valley** actually set in the valley, **"The Chrysanthemums"** is about the repression of powerful human impulses, the repression that would be necessary in any would-be Eden set in the fallen world of the valley. And like the subterranean current of the Salinas River that Steinbeck describes in *East of Eden,* these human urges throb just below the surface of everyday life and occasionally burst through to the surface in sudden floods. This theme of repression (which French labels "frustration") is introduced in the opening imagery of **"The Chrysanthemums"** when we are told that "the high grey-flannel fog of winter closed off the Salinas Valley from the sky and from all the rest of the world. On every side it sat like a lid on the mountains and made of the great valley a closed pot." In this fog-lidded valley, it is "a time of quiet and of waiting." We enter here the lifeless winter of T. S. Eliot's *The Waste Land,* and the fertilizing rain is not likely to come soon, for, as we are told, "fog and rain do not go together." Like the plowed earth which waits "to receive the rain deeply when it should come," Elisa Allen cultivates her flower garden in a kind of suspended life, awaiting the fertilizing imagination of the tinker.

The difficulty posed by the "what" and "how" of this story is indicated in the fact that most Steinbeck criticism has tended to touch only briefly upon the story in passing. French is satisfied to call Elisa Allen "the victim of an unscrupulous confidence man," but he fails to shed any significant light on the story. More recent and comprehensive

studies have been achieved in Mordecai Marcus's essay "The Lost Dream of Sex and Childbirth in 'The Chrysanthemums,'" Elizabeth McMahan's "'The Chrysanthemums': Study of a Woman's Sexuality," and William V. Miller's "Sexuality and Spiritual Ambiguity in 'The Chrysanthemums.'" As the titles suggest, each of these essays stresses the unmistakable significance in the story of Elisa's sexual frustration. The essays differ, however, about the importance of Elisa's frustrated maternal instinct. In a still more recent article, "The Original Manuscripts of Steinbeck's 'The Chrysanthemums,'" Roy Simmonds argues against the popular interpretation of Elisa's character, suggesting that "there is a case for suspecting that Elisa is the one who is unable or unwilling to satisfy her partner sexually."

According to Marcus's reading of the story, Elisa's unfulfilled yearning for children gives birth to the tremendous current of frustration running through the story. Marcus argues that when the tinker coldly discards the flowers, "her feminine self, her capacity for fructification and childbearing, the very offspring and representative of her body, have been thoughtlessly tossed aside." McMahan, arguing correctly that no critic "has yet adequately explained the emotional reasons underlying [Elisa's] frustration," contends that "Elisa's need is definitely sexual, but it does not necessarily have anything to do with a longing for children"; instead, McMahan proposes that Elisa is discontented: "She is a woman bored by her husband, bored by her isolated life on the farm." Miller, in a more comprehensive and persuasive approach, locates Elisa's dream of fulfillment on three levels: "the conventional, the sexual, and the 'romantic.'" Miller's reading would thus include the possibilities of sexual and maternal frustration (though Miller chooses to stress the former and to downplay the latter), while also accommodating McMahan's theory of "boredom." There is yet, however, a still more comprehensive basis for the tension and frustration which permeates this story, a basis involving once again the theme of commitment that runs in a steady current through Steinbeck's fiction.

It is obvious that these critics would all agree that "something profound has happened" in **"The Chrysanthemums,"** and just as obviously they would not agree precisely about what has happened or how it happened. To argue as McMahan and Miller do that Elisa's frustrated yearning for "fructification" does not play a very central role in this story is to ignore the full meaning and impact of the imagery of the story, imagery that introduces and reinforces the theme of procreation in the form of the ploughed land waiting for rain. Elisa, in middle age, is implicitly compared to the plowed furrows in winter, and to say that Elisa is simply bored with her life is to miss the force with which the opening paragraphs establish this parallel and the note of nearly hopeless expectancy dominating the story's atmosphere. At the same time, the theme of repression is very pronounced in the opening imagery and in Steinbeck's description of Elisa's "hard-swept looking little house" and her "over-eager, over-powerful" trimming of last year's flowers. Elisa's response to the tinker is violently sexual once he has made a connection between himself and the chrysanthemums, but only *after* he has made this vital link between himself and Elisa's "flower-children." The sexuality of Elisa's response to the tinker becomes unmistakable when she intones, "When the night is dark—why, the stars are sharp-pointed, and there's quiet. Why you rise up and up! Every pointed star gets driven into your body. It's like that. Hot and sharp and—lovely." Finally, Steinbeck has forced the sexual tension of the scene to such a pitch that Elisa becomes a parody of a bitch in heat: "She crouched low like a fawning dog."

While critics have been unanimous in recognizing the theme of repressed sexuality in this story, it is a mistake to attempt, as McMahan does, to limit the story's thematic significance to this alone. In Elisa the sexual and maternal impulses are blended into a single, frustrated urge, a longing for deep fulfillment. It is difficult not to see the "strong new crop" of flowers Elisa nurtures as surrogate children in her barren world. At the same time, the tinker's exotic life does symbolize a kind of escape for Elisa from the barrenness of the farm, an appeal to what Miller terms Elisa's "romantic" dream of fulfillment. All of these needs and urges come together, however, in the single powerful and unfulfilled yearning for the fertilizing potential inherent in deep human contact and commitment, the most significant symbols of which are sex, childbearing, and sacrifice. While the themes of sex and procreation are strong throughout the story, the theme of sacrifice is introduced in the story's conclusion.

After Elisa has seen the discarded flowers—evidence of the tinker's broken faith—she asks her husband, Henry, about the fights he has mentioned earlier. "I've read how they break noses," she says, "and blood runs down their chests. I've read how the fighting gloves get heavy and soggy with blood." Elisa's sudden interest in the fights which seemed to repulse her earlier has been seen as a rising desire for "vicarious vengeance" upon men, or simple "vindictiveness." Such readings seriously undervalue the complexity of the story, however, and of Elisa's emotional response to what has taken place. Although Elisa does ask, "Do the men hurt each other much?" the emphasis here is not upon simple vengeance upon mankind or vicariously upon the tinker; nor does it necessarily indicate Elisa's need for a "sense of dominance over the male" as Roy Simmonds suggests. Elisa's primary interest is in the blood. Coupled with her strong desire for wine at dinner, this imagery suggests another theme—that of commitment through sacrifice. Blood, as Mac knows well in *In Dubious Battle* and Joseph Wayne discovers in *To a God Unknown,* is the supreme symbol of commitment, and wine, of course, calls to mind the supreme Christian sacrifice. Elisa yearns here, in the wake of her abrupt awakening and disappointment, for a kind of futile sacrament—reacting to the arousal and frustration of her deepest needs, Elisa is seeking symbols of commitment in a world of physical, spiritual, and emotional isolation and sterility. Like so many of Steinbeck's characters, she is acting out of a profound loneliness.

"The Chrysanthemums" is Steinbeck's finest story precisely because he does not tell us the "what" or "how" and because the powerful imagery of the story is woven bril-liantly into a single fabric with theme and character. Elisa, on her isolated ranch in winter, waiting for the fructifying rain which is not likely to come, matched with a capable but not deeply sensitive husband, is cut off from fulfillment. In this story, the theme of human isolation and commitment central to *Of Mice and Men* is imbued with a strong current of repressed sexuality and maternity, and the result is the most emotionally forceful and subtly crafted of Steinbeck's stories.

"The White Quail": Inside the Garden

Perhaps the most unmistakable Eden in all of Steinbeck's writing is Mary Teller's garden in **"The White Quail,"** the second story in ***The Long Valley***. Unlike Elisa Allen's chrysanthemum garden, no powerful sexual current flows through Mary's Edenic garden, for Mary has willed her garden into being as a barrier between herself and all contact with the world outside. Mary's garden is an attempt to construct an unfallen Eden in a fallen world, a neurotic projection of Mary's self.

Mary's garden is cut off from the imperfections of the ordinary world of mankind by the fuchsias that wall out "the dark thickets of the hill," thickets which to Mary represent "the world that wants to get in, all rough and tangled and unkempt." Like the garden, Mary is, as her husband Harry says, "kind of untouchable." Harry tells her, "You're kind of like your own garden—fixed and just so." Joseph Fontenrose says, "Mary's garden is a Platonic heaven, changeless and eternal, a cosmos inhabited only by a creator, eternally admiring his (her) handiwork." "The hillside," Fontenrose adds, "represents the world, including human society. That is, our cosmos is Mary's chaos." Our world is, in fact, the actual fallen world, and Mary's garden is, like Elisa Allen's, very vulnerable to intrusions from that imperfect world regardless of the barriers she has willed into being.

Mary has been called "pathological," "narcissistic," and even a symbol of the Romantic artist "whose sublimination of all other values to her private vision is an act ultimately destructive of them." While each of these readings does provide some insight into Mary's character, the key to this character and the story may once again be found in the theme that dominates Steinbeck's writing during the thirties: the necessity for human commitment as a wasteland of human isolation and loneliness. Mary attempts to exclude sexuality, a vital aspect of human commitment (as was seen in **"The Chrysanthemums"**) and a symbol of imperfection in a perfect garden, from her make-believe Eden. We learn that, as a child, Mary was warned not to taste the "marvelous candy from Italy," because "it's prettier than it's good." Mary strives not to taste forbidden fruit, to keep experience out of the garden of her life; to achieve this end, she locks her door against Harry: "The lock was an answer to a question, a clean, quick, decisive answer. . . . It seemed to make him ashamed when he turned the knob and found the door locked."

As Fontenrose has suggested, Harry is one of the "devils" in Mary's paradise, a constant threat to the carefully crafted innocence of the garden. Like the threatening gray cat, Harry represents the real world that Mary cannot keep forever from her garden. When Harry deliberately shoots the white quail, he is intuitively attacking the very center of Mary's Edenic illusion, what she describes as "an essence boiled down to utter purity." Mary reacts angrily to Harry's suggestion that the quail is an albino with "no pigment in the feathers, something like that." "Albino" indicates the opposite of the perfection Mary seeks; it suggests a missing element, an incompleteness. The quail thus very accurately represents Mary's essence, for she too, like the much more diabolical Cathy of *East of Eden,* lacks completeness.

Like **"The Chrysanthemums," "The White Quail"** is a story about human isolation. Harry's poignant cry, "I'm lonely. . . . Oh, Lord, I'm so lonely," echoes Elisa's predicament and Doc Burton's lament in *In Dubious Battle.* It reiterates two central themes in Steinbeck's fiction: the futility of holding to the Eden myth—even the danger of the illusion—and the necessity for commitment. To see Mary as a symbol of the isolated artist does not conflict with this reading of the story, nor does it strain the thematic structure as Brian Barbour has suggested. That Steinbeck was very aware of and concerned with the role of the artist at this point in his career is obvious in his treatment of Doc in *In Dubious Battle;* that he felt that the artist must be actively committed to and a part of humanity is demonstrated by the increasingly subjective role of the author in *The Grapes of Wrath* and *East of Eden* and by the intense humanism of his Nobel speech.

"The White Quail" is a weaker story than **"The Chrysanthemums,"** and not as successful as other stories in *The Long Valley,* because Steinbeck too clearly left bare the "what" and "how" of his mechanism in this, his most mechanical Eden. Barbour is correct when he asserts that "the use of symbolism is heavy-handed, almost allegorical." He is less correct, however, when he claims that the shift in focus from Mary to the husband's frustration at the climax blurs the "force of the story." While there is no resolution, no sense that either the husband or the wife grasps the complexity of their predicament the way Elisa does in **"The Chrysanthemums,"** the story ends with a statement of the destructiveness of the Eden myth when it bars man from deep commitment to the world he inhabits, to "the one inseparable unit man plus his environment." Though Harry has brought the full force of imperfect reality to bear upon Mary's Eden the moment he has elected to kill the quail, the story ends with nothing truly changed. Though in his frustration Harry has struck at the heart of Mary's illusory garden, he finally permits her illusion to live on while taking upon himself the guilt for what he perceives to be a criminal act: "What a skunk I am . . . to kill a thing she loved so much." Harry is left lonely and ashamed, an exile from the unreal Eden which he has not the courage to destroy. Like **"The Chrysanthemums,"** this story offers a portrait of an emotional wasteland without any certain hope for fructification, spiritual or physical.

"The Harness": The Good, Fallen Man

The parallel themes of loneliness and illusion, which are central to both **"The Chrysanthemums"** and **"The White Quail,"** appear again in **"The Harness,"** another of the stories in this volume set in the valley. While Emma Randall has not tried to create an Edenic garden on the small farm she shares with her husband Peter, she has forced Peter to live within the strictures of an illusion she has willed into being. Peter is Emma's garden, and with the harness and girdle that she forces him to wear, Emma attempts to deny the reality of human imperfection or change.

Peter, who resembles both Elisa of **"The Chrysanthemums"** and Harry of **"The White Quail,"** is lonely and has an unfulfilled need for deeply felt human contact. His wife is cold and sickly, "a little skin-and-bones woman" who "was sick most of the time." Steinbeck describes the Randall house as being "as neat and restrained as its owners," and adds, "Emma had no children. The house was unscarred, uncarved, unchalked." It is a cold and barren existence in which Peter is cut off from warm human contact with his wife by her very nature and from the rest of the world by the illusion his wife forces him to maintain. Peter's deep sexual and spiritual starvation sends him on his annual trips to the "fancy houses" of San Francisco.

When Emma finally dies, Peter is freed of her strictures; he rips the harness and girdle off and declares, "I'm a natural fool! For twenty years I've been pretending I was a wise, good man—except for that one week a year." Peter's profound need for sensation, for color and warmth, is reflected in his immediate decision to plant the whole farm in sweet peas after his wife's death. As we learn near the end of the story, however, he has been unable to enjoy the sweet peas because the gamble with a delicate and unpredictable crop has worried him terribly the whole time. As Joseph Fontenrose has shown, the irony of this story lies in the fact that there is, after all, only one Peter Randall: Peter the respectable farmer who existed beneath Emma's harness. In the final scene of the story, we learn not only that Peter has not been able to enjoy the flowers, but also that he is once again "busting loose" in San Francisco and preparing to return home and do penance on the farm by putting in electric lights. "Emma always wanted electric lights," he says. Peter has not been able to change, and he attributes this fact to the belief that Emma is still controlling him. "She didn't die dead," he says, adding, "She won't let me do things." Peter's illusion prompts Fontenrose to suggest that Peter "needs Emma, alive or dead, to govern him, to save him from sinking into the chaos of instinct and sensual appetite." And Fontenrose adds, "Emma is a deity of a very Hebraic cosmos, and Peter is her faithful creature, subject, and servant." In actuality, there is never any danger that Peter would "sink into the chaos of instinct and sensual appetite." The real irony of the story is that Peter is the "wise, good man" he pretended to be. In trying to deny Peter's "natural" slouch, and in apparently denying any emotional or physical commitment between Peter and herself, Emma was attempting to deny the possibility that Peter could be both good and flawed, or fallen. The truly good Peter was denied in favor of an illusion of unfallen perfection. Even after Emma's death, Peter is unable to free himself from the trap of Emma's illusion and see himself for what he really is: the good, wise, "ordinary" farmer. Perpetually harnessed by Emma's illusion, Peter maintains the illusion that man cannot be both good and fallen.

"Johnny Bear": Artist as Recorder

The destructive force of the Eden myth is again at the center of **"Johnny Bear,"** still another of the stories in *The Long Valley* set in the Salinas Valley. In this story, the Hawkins sisters, Emalin and Amy, stand for spiritual and moral perfection in the midst of the "dirty little town" of Loma. The Hawkins sisters' aristocratic house, carefully walled in by a seemingly impenetrable cypress hedge, is the small town's unfallen garden, and the sisters bear the weight of this burden much as Peter Randall bore the harness of Emma's illusion. As it is in each of the other stories set in the valley, repression is again a key theme in **"Johnny Bear,"** and, as it was in **"The Chrysanthemums,"** this repression is symbolized by the fog that moves in upon the town from the "great black tule swamp" outside of town. The story is both about man's futile attempts to wall out reality in order to maintain an illusion of moral perfection and about the artist's role in laying bare the reality beneath the illusion.

Emalin and Amy Hawkins, we are told, are the town's "aristocrats, its family above reproach." They are "symbols" and "the community conscience." Of the sisters' role, the narrator says, "A place like Loma with its fogs, with its great swamp like a hideous sin, needed, really needed, the Hawkins women." Around the Hawkins house, the square "green barrier" of the cypress hedge appears "incredibly strong and thick." Appropriately, the narrator, slipping into the present tense, says, "There must be a small garden inside the square too." Like Mary Teller's little "symbolic trees"—the fuchsias—the hedge walls in the supposed Eden that serves to harness the town's symbols. Emalin and Amy are, above all, products of the town's need for the illusion—the town has willed them into being as much as Mary Teller willed into being her garden. The narrator suggests the painful repression of the sisters' lives when he sees them in their buggy and remarks, "It seemed to me that the check-rein was too short for such an old horse." The check-rein keeps the horse's neck arched, giving him the appearance of a young horse and maintaining an illusion of perfection that does not allow the old horse to fall into the posture dictated by age and nature. The check-rein is another version of Peter Randall's harness. Acting through the immediate presence of Emalin, the town serves as Amy's check-rein and eventually drives her to suicide. When Alex, the narrator's friend and the character who provides the necessary insight into the town's attitude toward the sisters, says, "There's something hanging over those people," he is inadvertently pointing to the force that the town's illusion brings to bear upon the women. Almost immediately, he adds, "They can't do anything bad. It wouldn't be good for any of us."

The fog, symbol of the pervasive repression, moves ominously in upon the town and the two women as the tragedy of Amy's suicide draws closer. When Alex stops the doctor's car and learns that something has happened to Amy, the narrator comments, "I was about to remark that the night was clear when, looking ahead, I saw the rags of fog creeping around the hill from the swamp side and climbing like slow snakes on the top of Loma." In this image, the fog represents both the repression forced upon the sisters and the serpent of experience, which coils about the town and finds its way into the Hawkins garden.

As Warren French has noted, **"Johnny Bear"** is one of Steinbeck's most haunting and least discussed stories. One of the first critics to deal with the story in any depth was Peter Lisca, who remarked perceptively that this story is "on one level an exploration of the artist's role in society," this role being to expose man's "hidden festers." Brian Barbour, in constrast, has argued that "no art literally holds the mirror up to nature. It doesn't reproduce the chaos of events. But Johnny Bear functions as little more than a super tape recorder, and attempts to show him as the artist revealing the community's secret soul to itself are not convincing." If we examine Johnny Bear closely, however, it appears that Barbour's objections are not valid. Johnny Bear's role is not merely to hold the mirror up to nature; his recording consciousness is informed and guided by what he is aware that his audience will pay for in whiskey. Thus, he reflects the need and desires of his audience, an audience which needs to know the reality behind the illusion even as it desires desperately to maintain the illusion. The narrator indicates as much when he says of Johnny Bear, "It's not his fault. . . . He's just a kind of recording and reproducing device, only you use a glass of whiskey instead of a nickel." Later, the narrator points out the real relationship between Johnny and his audience when he says, after having plied Johnny with whiskey, "I was really responsible." And again, the narrator defines Johnny's role when he says of those listening: "Now those men really wanted to know. They were ashamed of wanting to know, but their whole mental system required the knowledge." Thus, Johnny Bear, another Steinbeck natural, provides a necessary function, that of the artist whom society pays to tell it what it does not want to know about itself but must, in fact, know.

Johnny Bear is John Steinbeck, a writer who, while writing his most pessimistic novel, *In Dubious Battle,* thought of himself as merely a "recording consciousness," and who spent a large portion of his career holding his audience's illusions up to the light to show their falseness and their danger. Like Samuel Hamilton in *East of Eden,* Steinbeck's finest works hold man's illusions up to him—particularly the illusion of Edenic perfection in the New World—in order to show their "dirt and danger." **"Johnny Bear"** is one of those works.

"The Murder": Illusions of Chivalry

"The Murder" is undoubtedly the most difficult and perplexing of the stories collected in *The Long Valley.* As its inclusion as an O. Henry Prize Story for 1934 suggests, the story contains unmistakable power, but the "what" and "how" of this story are as difficult to discover as they are in **"The Chrysanthemums,"** the first story in *The Long Valley,* while the artistic fabric is much less successfully woven. Like Steinbeck's **"Flight,"** **"The Murder"** is set in the coastal mountains of north central California, in Cañon del Castillo, "one of those valleys in the Santa Lucia range which lies between its main spurs and ridges." And like **"Flight,"** this story is dominated by the theme of death. At the same time, **"The Murder"** clearly belongs with the other stories in *The Long Valley* in its incorporation of the themes of isolation and illusion, twin themes that form a continuous thread through **"The Chrysanthemums," "The White Quail," "The Harness,"** and **"Johnny Bear."**

As Katherine M. Morseberger and Robert E. Morseberger have stated, "Seen only as a narrative, the story makes little sense except in terms of suspense and erotic violence, and Steinbeck critics have accordingly ignored it almost entirely." In an interesting reading that stresses what they term the "folktale quality" of the story, the Morsebergers outline the ritualistic aspects of **"The Murder"** and suggest that Jelka "embodies primitive passions that tie man to his biological primordial past." These critics go on to see the story as "a testament that mysteriously primitive passions and past are still with us." While such a reading provides a fascinating perspective on the story's emotional force and is much superior to Warren French's suggestion that the story is "an illustration of racial superiority," or Brian Barbour's claim that the story is "absurd," it still deals with only one aspect of the story while ignoring others equally crucial.

Critics have consistently failed to examine very closely the theme of illusion which is introduced in the opening description of the "strange accident of time and water and erosion" that has created the illusion of a "tremendous stone castle, buttressed and towered like those strongholds the Crusaders put up in the path of their conquest." To Barbour, this description "sounds an opening note of the eerie and that is all . . . it is just window dressing." To the Morsebergers, the illusory castle merely reinforces the "folktale quality" of the story. America has produced no writer more acutely conscious of setting than Steinbeck. To assume that the carefully detailed introductory description in this story could be mere "window dressing" is to seriously misunderstand Steinbeck's method. To attribute the description somewhat vaguely to a desire for "folktale quality" is nearer to Steinbeck's method but seriously undervalues both technique and the importance of setting in Steinbeck's works.

As he does in other stories in this volume, Steinbeck introduces the theme of illusion in order to suggest man's failure to grasp a reality that conflicts with what he desires to believe. **"The Murder"** is heavily ironic because what Jim Moore wants to believe is that one should not beat one's wife, in spite of Jelka's father's advice that "he's not like a man that don't beat hell out of him." Jim's illusion consists of a kind of chivalry symbolized by the unreal castle—a chivalric code which dictates that it is barbarous and "foreign" to beat a wife even if the wife's culture has conditioned her to expect or even desire the beating. That the story embodies a conflict in cultural values has been pointed out by Roy Simmonds, who has shown that in the original draft of **"The Murder"** the protagonist was named Thomas Manuelo More, a name which was subsequently changed to Ernest More and finally to Jim Moore. As Simmonds states, the name More suggests "the intrin-

Steinbeck and his sister Mary on his "red pony," Jill.

230

sic theme of the story: the clash between the comparative mores of two racial communities." Because Jim refuses to recognize Jelka's foreignness, he cannot establish a deeply emotional or psychological commitment with her. The result is that there is "no companionship in her." His loneliness causes Jim to seek the noisy companionship of the girls in town and causes Jelka to seek that of one of her own people, her cousin. Jim Moore finds Jelka with the cousin; he ponders for a moment and then kills the cousin. Later, he beats Jelka severely with a bullwhip and establishes the emotional and psychological commitment that has been missing from the relationship.

In shooting the cousin, Jim acts accordingly to the accepted standards of chivalry for "Monterey County, in central California." The killing is condoned and even admired by Jim's neighbors and earns him respect in the nearby town. When Jim deliberately and dispassionately beats Jelka, he is bowing to what he now realizes are her expectations and needs, and when she asks expectantly, "Will you whip me any more—for this?" he replies carefully, "No, not anymore, for this." The implication is that the mores of Monterey County, which condone such a murder and even encourage it, are even more barbarous than those of Jelka's people, which require the beating of a wife. When he beats Jelka, Jim has fully accepted her difference. Katherine and Robert Morseberger make a very good point: "On a realistic level, the murder and the beating represent for Jelka the kind of absolute commitment she wants from Jim." On a symbolic level, the butchered calf that brings Jim back to the ranch, the pig's blood that he remembers his mother catching in a bucket, and the murder all represent sacrifices which, as throughout Steinbeck's fiction, are symbolic of commitment.

In the end, it is obvious that Jim Moore's mores and his illusion of chivalry were as false as the sandstone "castle" at the canyon's head. Once he can approach Jelka on her terms, the barrier between them is dissolved and for the first time her voice has a "resonance in it" and her eyes "dwelt warmly on him."

In finding a troublesome "indefinite overall conclusiveness" in **"The Murder,"** Roy Simmonds argues that the symbol of the illusory castle is "inadequately employed" and that "this carefully prepared ambiente is simply discarded." It should be clear, however, once we have recognized the central theme of this story—the theme of illusion—that the ambiente is not only carefully prepared but that it introduces very effectively and subtly the idea of an illusory chivalry that is central to an understanding of Steinbeck's story. In preparing his ambiente, Steinbeck is careful to associate the murder of Jelka's cousin with the sandstone castle: "Below the castle, on the nearly level floor of the canyon, stand the old ranch house, a weathered and mossy barn and a warped feeding-shed for cattle." Almost immediately following this description, we learn that imagination has turned the site of the murder into a place of awe, where "boys tramp through the rooms, peering into the empty closets and loudly defying the ghosts they deny." The imaginary castle casts an ironical light over the entire story. The castle establishes the perspective through which we are to view events in the story;

it informs the story and hovers over it as it does the abandoned farmhouse. Rather than being "simply discarded," the image of the castle is a highly effective device integral to the structural coherence of **"The Murder."**

However, in spite of Steinbeck's characteristically brilliant use of setting in this story, Simmonds is correct when he declares that " 'The Murder' is by no means one of Steinbeck's more successful stories." **"The Murder"** lacks the sense of precise control evident in such stories as **"The Chrysanthemums"** or **"Flight,"** a difficulty particularly evident in the role of the animal imagery in Steinbeck's characterization of Jelka. Simmonds suggests that the animal symbolism in this story is "somewhat overstressed, so that eventually, so unremittingly is it hammered home, it begins to defeat its own purpose." Throughout the story, Jelka is so closely and repeatedly associated with animal imagery as to become almost purely animal herself. At one point Steinbeck writes: "She was so much like an animal that sometimes Jim patted her head and neck under the same impulse that made him stroke a horse"; and when Jim looks for her after the murder, he unerringly goes to the barn and finds her in the hayloft. Jelka's close association with animals is intended to suggest her strong need for unconscious, physical, and sensual communication with Jim. Whereas Jim misses conversation, Jelka misses the physical contact her cultural background has supposedly taught her to need even in the form of beatings.

So heavy-handed is Steinbeck's association of Jelka with the animal imagery of the story that she comes closer than any other Steinbeck character with the exception of such "naturals" as Tularecito and Johnny Bear to fulfilling Edmund Wilson's myopic claim that *The Long Valley* deals "mostly with animals," and that "Mr. Steinbeck almost always in his fiction is dealing either with the lower animals or with humans so rudimentary that they are almost on the animal level." The flaw in Steinbeck's characterization of Jelka arises from the fact that Jelka is not a natural; her humanity is essential to the story's meaning. Like Lennie in *Of Mice and Men,* Jelka represents man's basic yearning for profound, unconscious commitment with his fellow man. While Lennie's animalism is carefully controlled, however, Jelka's becomes so overwhelming as to conflict awkwardly with her role as representative of a culture in conflict with the code of "Monterey County, in central California."

It is this uncertainty in Steinbeck's development of Jelka's character that pervades the story and causes it, in spite of its obvious power, to end on a disturbingly confused note. The unmistakable force of this story comes, however, not from characterization but from Steinbeck's painstaking integration of setting, symbol, and theme. From the first words of the story, and the description of the ominous "strange accident of time," Steinbeck introduces and underscores the theme of illusion, illusion that Jim Moore must transcend—even through murder—in order to realize a fundamental human commitment with Jelka. In spite of Steinbeck's apparent difficulties with Jelka's character, **"The Murder"** demonstrates an impressive structural coherence and power characteristic of the best of Steinbeck's stories in *The Long Valley.*

"The Raid": Commitment and Sacrifice

In contrast to the other stories discussed here, the valley setting plays no distinctive thematic role in **"The Raid,"** Steinbeck's story about two communist organizers who bear the brunt of a vigilante raid. As Peter Lisca has shown, this story, while tightly organized and projecting a remarkable tension, is of note primarily because it echoes important themes in *In Dubious Battle* and looks forward to *The Grapes of Wrath.* Lisca's well-supported contention that "the story was originally conceived as an episode in [*In Dubious Battle*] or as part of Steinbeck's biographical sketch which evolved into that novel" is persuasive. Thematically, the story parallels elements of both *In Dubious Battle* and *The Grapes of Wrath* in its emphasis on the theme of commitment expressed through self-sacrifice imbued with Christian overtones. Root's statement to the men who are beating him, "You don't know what you're doing." will be echoed almost verbatim by Jim Casy just before he is killed in *The Grapes of Wrath,* and his role as neophyte Party member who becomes quickly committed and is promptly "sacrificed" parallels that of Jim Nolan in *In Dubious Battle.* While the central theme of this story—commitment through sacrifice—is another expression of the primary theme of Steinbeck's fiction, **"The Raid"** is set apart from the other valley stories by the fact that there is no symbolic Eden and thus no illusion to be exposed and explored. **"The Raid"** appears, more than anything else, to be a valuable by-product of Steinbeck's strike novel.

"The Vigilante": Psychology of the Cell

In **"The Vigilante"** Steinbeck explores the psychology of the mob through the thoughts and emotions of one unit in that "phalanx." The story of Mike, who has just been part of a mob that has lynched a black man, reflects Steinbeck's acute interest during the thirties in the phenomenon of group-man. One of the "cells" of the mob, Mike knows that he has been part of something bigger than himself, but he cannot comprehend the thing: "Mike filled his eyes with the scene. He felt that he was dull. He wasn't seeing enough of it." As soon as Mike departs from the mob, he is not a part of the phalanx any longer and he feels cut off and lonely. When he meets the bartender, Welch, the two men instinctively group together in the loneliness that follows the breakup of the mob. They walk home together, seeking an ephemeral sense of commitment, but the sense of isolation deepens. In the end, after his wife accuses him of having been with a woman, Mike realizes that that is exactly how he feels. It isn't the lynching that has done this, however; it is the act of giving himself up to the larger whole—to the phalanx of the mob—that makes him feel this way.

"The Vigilante" explores the group-man theme of *In Dubious Battle* from the opposite perspective from that of Party leaders such as Mac and Jim. Acting again as merely a "recording consciousness," Steinbeck shows here the other side of the coin from **"The Raid"** and from the view of group-man we get in *The Grapes of Wrath.* It is Steinbeck's only attempt to delve into the mind of one of the common cells of the mob—recording without judging—and as such, it deals with a very different theme from the

other stories in *The Long Valley.* Only the theme of isolation, of apartness resulting from the breakup of the group, echoes the primary theme of the valley stories. The message, like that of *In Dubious Battle,* is that man has an urgent and unconscious need to belong to something larger than himself, a need to commit himself even if for only a moment to a cause as dubious as that of a lynch mob. (pp. 106-28)

> *Louis Owens, in his* John Steinbeck's Revision of America, *The University of Georgia Press, 1985, 225 p.*

Steinbeck on *The Red Pony*:

The Red Pony was written . . . when there was desolation in my family. The first death had occurred. And the family, which every child believes to be immortal, was shattered. Perhaps this is the first adulthood of any man or woman. The first tortured question of "why?" and the acceptance and the child becomes a man. *The Red Pony* was an attempt, an experiment if you wish, to set down this acceptance and growth.

> *John Steinbeck, in "My Short Novels,"* Wings, *1953.*

R. S. Hughes   (essay date 1987)

[*In the excerpt below, taken from his* Beyond the Red Pony: A Reader's Companion to Steinbeck's Complete Short Stories, *Hughes traces the thematic development of the stories in* The Long Valley.]

Even before *The Pastures of Heaven* came off the press in the autumn of 1932, Steinbeck had begun writing the first of fifteen stories collected in *The Long Valley* (1938). By 1934—his most prolific year in short fiction—he had composed a total of thirteen tales destined for that volume. By 1936, the two remaining pieces were completed. Before their publication in *The Long Valley,* however, most of these stories appeared in newspapers and magazines—sometimes not until three or four years after Steinbeck composed them. **"The Harness,"** for example, was written in summer, 1934, but not published until June, 1938. Similarly, **"The Chrysanthemums,"** composed in February, 1934, did not appear until October, 1937. This phenomenon, widespread among Steinbeck's *Long Valley* stories, is illustrated [below]:

Story	Composed	First Published
"Saint Katy the Virgin"	before May 1932	Dec. 1936
"The Gift"	ca. June 1933	Nov. 1933
"The Great Mountains"	ca. Summer 1933	Dec. 1933
"The Murder"	ca. Fall 1933	April 1934
"The Chrysanthemums"	February 1934	Oct. 1937
"The Promise"	Summer 1934	Aug.

		1937
"The Leader of the People"	Summer 1934	Aug. 1936
"The Raid"	Summer 1934	Oct. 1934
"The Harness"	Summer 1934	June 1938
"The White Quail"	Summer 1934	March 1935
"Flight"	Summer 1934	1938
"Johnny Bear"	Summer 1934	Sept. 1937
"The Vigilante"	Summer 1934	Oct. 1936
"The Snake"	ca. 1935	June 1935
"Breakfast"	ca. 1936	Nov. 1936

Until now the composition dates of several *Long Valley* stories have been unknown. Thus formerly it was not possible to determine the exact sequence in which Steinbeck wrote all fifteen selections, in order to gauge his development as a story writer. [The chart above] allows us for the first time to accomplish this; it also helps us to answer questions critics have raised about the milieu of these stories.

Joseph Fontenrose, for example, expresses concern that Steinbeck—"*the* socially conscious novelist" of the late 1930s—seldom alludes to "the depression and its problems" in *The Long Valley* [*Steinbeck's Unhappy Valley*]. [The chart] suggests why these problems rarely emerge in the stories: Steinbeck wrote all but two of them early in the decade, before his full attention had been turned to the Great Depression and its effects on California's agricultural valleys. Thus, only faint whisperings of troubled times can be detected. And while Steinbeck does deal directly with victims of the depression in the piece he composed last, **"Breakfast,"** this sketch is the exception rather than the rule. In other stories, such as **"The White Quail"** and **"The Raid,"** he merely hints at the impending malaise. Because of this, some critics expecting more political awareness from Steinbeck called *The Long Valley* ideologically aimless and inconclusive. As Eda Lou Walton in the *Nation* [October 1931] puts it: "These stories are clever, but they move toward nothing. . . . Nothing in the work seems resolved or progressing toward resolution."

The Long Valley's title has also raised eyebrows, since it somewhat misleadingly suggests that all stories are set—as in *The Pastures of Heaven*—in a single geographic area. Although this lends the collection an aura of unity, actually few of the tales take place in the Salinas "long" Valley. Louis Owens argues that probably only **"The Chrysanthemums,"** **"The White Quail,"** **"The Harness,"** and **"Johnny Bear"** can be definitely linked to this valley. **"Saint Katy the Virgin"** transpires in a markedly different time and place from that of the other stories in the volume. **"Flight"** occurs "on the wild coast" just north of Big Sur; **"The Snake"** is set on Cannery Row in Monterey; and **"The Murder"** takes place in the Santa Lucia range near "a tremendous stone castle," which in real life towers above the Corral de Tierra (i.e. *The Pastures of Heaven*). Nearby in these same mountains Steinbeck sets *The Red Pony* tales. **"Breakfast,"** later revised for inclusion in *The Grapes of Wrath* (1939), probably shares the novel's San

Joaquin or Sacramento Valley backdrop. Finally, as Owens points out, the settings in **"The Raid"** and **"The Vigilante"** are "indeterminant."

Why does such an obvious discrepancy exist between the selection of stories and the title of the volume? This question can be at least partially answered by reviewing the conditions under which *The Long Valley* was published. Steinbeck . . . had trouble selling his stories of the early 1930s. However, when the successes of *Tortilla Flat* (1935), *In Dubious Battle* (1936), and *Of Mice and Men* (1937) increased his fame, most of his unpublished stories of this decade were quickly snatched up by the nation's top magazines. Steinbeck finally had captured the public's attention, and his current publisher, Covici-Friede, intended to capitalize on his growing renown. Thus, by 1938 the climate seemed right to issue a volume of his collected stories. Although Steinbeck did not know it then, Covici-Friede was experiencing "financial difficulties" and, hence, they "needed another Steinbeck best-seller fast." Therefore, Pat Covici "pressed" the young author for the collection.

In a letter to Elizabeth Otis (May 2, 1938) Steinbeck expresses some surprise that his stories were to appear in a collected edition so quickly: "I didn't know that Pat was considering doing the short stories soon." *The Long Valley* was published in September, 1938, but even if it had enjoyed immediate popularity, the book's sales probably would not have saved Covici-Friede which declared bankruptcy later that summer.

The haste with which *The Long Valley* was rushed to press may account for some of its organizational flaws. Indications are that the collection might have been improved had Steinbeck given more time to selecting, revising, and arranging the stories. On the other hand, it can be argued that short of deleting such inappropriate tales as **"Saint Katy the Virgin,"** Steinbeck could have done little to enhance the volume. He included every complete story he had written during the 1930s, except **"How Edith McGillcuddy Met R.L.S."** and "Case History," both composed in summer, 1934. The former tale he had tried to publish earlier, but for reasons discussed below, he decided to withdraw it. The latter, which is actually more a philosophical disquisition than a story, was unsuitable for the collection. Therefore, Steinbeck had little choice but to include every publishable story of the decade, disparate though they were. Some observations about style and technique can be made, however, which apply to nearly all selections in *The Long Valley.*

Sometimes during his career as a story writer Steinbeck found it difficult to create unified, organic plots. Occasionally he placed characters in forced situations or he contrived action—particularly at the end of a story—to emphasize a preconceived symbol or theme. This fault crops up in *The Pastures of Heaven,* as we have seen, and also at times in *The Long Valley.* Peter Lisca calls the conclusion of **"Flight"** "theatrical," for instance, "because of its too perfect symbolic congruity." And in **"The White Quail"** and **"The Harness,"** the import of each story's central symbol seems too obvious. The effect of this, according to Brian Barbour, is a mechanical structure with symbolic meanings so fixed as to approach the condition of allegory. Steinbeck's plotting in such stories as **"The Gift"** and **"The Chrysanthemums,"** on the other hand, is superb. No tricks. No contrivances. Every element in these tales is smoothly connected and believable. Once Steinbeck learned to make his stories perfectly coherent in this way, he was capable of creating masterpieces.

Steinbeck's method of characterization in *The Long Valley* has occasioned considerable debate. Edmund Wilson calls his characters "rudimentary," conceived and presented in animal, rather than human terms. And Stanley Young argues that Steinbeck's protagonists simply "struggle with one primitive emotion after another." But in the same breath, Young praises Steinbeck's sensitivity and sympathy for human beings "on all levels of experience." Indeed, several characters emerging from these tales are unforgettable. Joseph Warren Beach calls Elisa Allen in **"The Chrysanthemums"** "delicious," saying, "She is much less simple than she seems."

Women characters, in general, play a more prominent role in Steinbeck's short stories than they do in his novels. In recent studies of Steinbeck's female characters, a disproportionately large number of the women discussed have come from the short fiction. These characters (as discussed above in reference to "Molly Morgan") are typically of two kinds: housewives and hookers. Most of the latter group turn up in the novels, while the short stories are usually peopled with the former. Male characters include cattle ranchers, farmers, blue-collar workers, nostalgic and lonely old men, and boys journeying through the sometimes elusive and difficult passage to "manhood."

Spare, crisp, and economical are the adjectives customarily used to describe Steinbeck's prose in *The Long Valley.* A master of the objective style, he often renders details with picture-like accuracy. While his prose is lean, it is also poetic. Images of color, light and darkness, plants, and animals abound, and seem at times so vivid as to tell the story themselves. Steinbeck's narrative point of view in *The Long Valley* stories is generally third person. In tales such as **"Flight,"** Steinbeck remains outside the mind of his protagonists. However, in **"The White Quail"** and others he does venture into the central character's thoughts. Two exceptions to Steinbeck's usual third-person point of view are **"Breakfast"** and **"Johnny Bear,"** both first-person narratives. After having difficulty with the first-person technique earlier in his career . . . , Steinbeck in *The Long Valley* handles it more successfully.

In his *Long Valley* stories, Steinbeck displays a wide variety of generic forms, including stories of initiation, sketches, parables, and even one beast fable. Though Brian Barbour argues that this variety is not "the product of experimentation" and therefore "reveals confusion of purpose," Steinbeck, on the contrary, enjoyed trying new forms. Once he was able to achieve his artistic aims in a given form, however, he frequently moved on. Thus, Steinbeck seldom repeated himself, even though repetition was exactly what many critics wanted from him. As Elmer Davis puts it, Steinbeck followed his own impulses, "instead of letting the expectations of his public push him into a groove."

Over the years scholars and critics have traditionally treated *The Long Valley* as if it comprised the entire canon of Steinbeck's short fiction. As we have seen, this is not the case. But although fewer than half of Steinbeck's stories are contained in the 1938 volume, it is easily accessible (while the uncollected and unpublished pieces are not), and is usually regarded as his finest performance as a writer of short fiction.

"The Chrysanthemums" is generally considered to be one of Steinbeck's finest short stories. According to Roy S. Simmonds, an early draft of the tale bears some likeness to **"The Harness,"** featuring a repressed husband and his shrewish, frustrated wife. That Henry Allen in the discarded draft (like Peter Randall in **"The Harness"**) intends to plant many "acres of sweet peas" represents a striking similarity between the two narratives. But Steinbeck apparently had misgivings about his early version of **"The Chrysanthemums"** and therefore rewrote the story. The finished tale, as Simmonds explains, proved to be a masterpiece:

> It is remarkable that Steinbeck could, after all the problems he had been encountering, produce in what appears to have been one flowing surge of creativity the short story which Andre Gide compared favorably with the best of Chehkov and which Mordecai Marcus unequivocally regards as "one of the world's great short stories."

"The Chrysanthemums" takes place at the Allen Ranch in the foothills of the Salinas Valley. A December fog blankets the fields as Elisa Allen, thirty-five, cuts down the old year's chrysanthemum stalks in her garden. Her husband, Henry, appears and suggests that they dine out that evening. After Henry leaves, a covered wagon drawn by an old bay horse and a burro pulls up to the house. The big, stubble-bearded driver asks Elisa if she has any pots to mend. Although Elisa at first resists him, her initial reluctance melts away when the tinker feigns interest in her garden. He tells her that a lady on his route wants some chrysanthemum seeds. Elisa excitedly gives him several sprouts in a red pot. Then she finds two saucepans which the tinker repairs for fifty cents. After the wagon pulls away, Elisa runs into the house, bathes, and dresses for the evening. Henry returns and marvels at how "strong" she looks. As the two are leaving for dinner in their roadster, Elisa sees the chrysanthemum sprouts lying in the road. The tinker has thrown them away, keeping the red pot. She begins to weep, but hides her tears from Henry.

Several critics have argued that it is the protagonist, Elisa Allen who makes **"The Chrysanthemums"** a great short story. Marilyn L. Mitchell, for example, calls Elisa one of Steinbeck's "strong women"—a woman who has "a strength of will usually identified" with men, as well as an "ambiguous combination of traditionally masculine and feminine traits." While these and other facets of Elisa's personality are no doubt responsible for much of the story's appeal, ultimately Steinbeck's well-crafted plot and his skillful use of symbol make the story great. As Brian Barbour puts it, Steinbeck "succeeds in organizing this story in a way he does nowhere else." **"The Chrysanthemums"** is a product, says Roy S. Simmonds, of "one flowing surge of creativity." That the author himself was more concerned with plot than character when he wrote the story is evident in his February 25, 1934 letter to George Albee:

> I shall be interested to know what you think of the story, the Chrysanthemums. It is entirely different [from **"The Murder"**] and is designed to strike without the reader's knowledge. I mean he reads it casually and after it is finished feels that something profound has happened to him although he does not know what nor how. It has had that effect on several people here.

The element of surprise Steinbeck alludes to underlies the difference in plot between **"The Chrysanthemums"** and his other stories of the 1930s. The surprise hinges on these few words: "Far ahead on the road Elisa saw a dark speck. She knew." A small clump of chrysanthemum sprouts tossed away by the tinker speaks silently but eloquently of his opportunism and insincerity. Specifically, it betrays his feigned interest in Elisa and her garden. In Aristotelian terms, Elisa's discovery constitutes a "recognition scene," in which she acquires vital knowledge previously withheld from her. In addition, it brings about a "reversal," or change of fortune, at least as far as her feelings are concerned. Elisa's rejuvenated strength and womanhood are instantly destroyed by the sight of her discarded chrysanthemum sprouts. The effect is one Steinbeck had attempted in other stories, but spoiled with contrived endings.

The magic of Elisa Allen's discovery is that it is genuinely surprising, yet developed organically from materials present in the story. It succeeds primarily because of Steinbeck's deft handling of the story's dominant symbol. Unlike in **"The White Quail,"** where Steinbeck directly equates a bird with the protagonist, Mary Teller, or in **"The Harness,"** where he identifies Peter Randall's shoulder brace and elastic belt with Randall's nagging wife, in **"The Chrysanthemums"** Steinbeck does not peg the dominant symbol to any single idea or thing. In fact, the symbol's power increases during the story precisely because of its ambiguity. Early in the narrative, for example, the chrysanthemum stalks seem to be phallic symbols, and Elisa's "over-eager" snipping of them suggests castration. Then in the "rooting" bed Elisa herself becomes masculine, inserting the "little crisp shoots" into open, receptive furrows. Later the sprouts become Elisa's children, when she explains lovingly to the tinker how to care for them as if they were leaving home for the first time. As a dominant symbol, Elisa's chrysanthemums are the very backbone of the plot. Just as the tinker's ability to use these plants in exploiting Elisa precipitates the rising action and climax of the story—when Elisa, at the height of her emotion, reaches out for the tinker's "greasy black trousers"—so too Elisa's recognition that he has tossed her chrysanthemum sprouts into the road brings about the catastrophe.

Although the story's greatness depends on this symbol and Steinbeck's superbly-crafted plot, Elisa Allen, her husband, and the tinker cannot be overlooked. Of these three characters, Henry Allen's role is the smallest. He utters only a few lines, but these few are significant in measuring changes in Elisa's feelings. The reader barely gets to know Henry, not only because he speaks so little, but

also because Steinbeck neglects to describe him in any detail. Henry's role is that of a regulator, or even a repressor, of Elisa's behavior. At one point he tells her that she is " 'playing some kind of a game.' " Then later he quips, " 'Now you're changed again.' " Henry is somewhat frightened when Elisa boasts, " 'I'm strong. . . . I never knew before how strong.' " The established order he represents seems to be in jeopardy because of Elisa's boldness, and consequently Henry almost loses his composure. But when he looks "down toward the tractor shed," and then brings "his eyes back to her, they [are] his own again. '*I'll* get the car,' " says Henry. Then he commands, " '*You* can put on *your* coat while *I'm* starting' " (italics added). Henry again exerts his authority. Yet the fact that Elisa purposely makes him wait while she dresses suggests that his authority does not go unquestioned.

The other male character, the itinerant pot mender, lives for his own pleasure. As he tells Elisa, " 'I ain't in any hurry ma'am. . . . I aim to follow nice weather.' " With his large body, stubble-beard, and nomadic lifestyle, he awakens Elisa's aboriginal energy. She becomes sexually excited ("Her breast swelled passionately. . . . Elisa's voice grew husky," and she reaches out to him with "hesitant fingers." Much of their conversation has sexual overtones, such as when Elisa says: " 'Every pointed star gets driven into your body.' " This contrasts to the bantering, formal dialogue between Elisa and her husband, Henry.

That the tinker has radically altered Elisa's behavior is obvious from her excitement upon his departure. Her shoulders "straight . . . head thrown back," she runs into the house, and with a burst of energy, tears "off her soiled clothes," flinging "them into the corner" of her room. Normally a neat and tidy housekeeper, Elisa now scatters her garments, caring little where they fall. Given this change in her behavior, Elisa is, in Freudian terms, an "ego figure"—attracted to the carefree tinker (representing her "id" or primal self) but then checked in this urge by her repressive husband (her "super ego" or civilized self). In this way she resembles Peter Randall, the repressed protagonist in **"The Harness."**

Although we have already considered some aspects of style, Steinbeck's point of view in this tale merits special attention. It is third-person objective—the narrative remaining outside the minds of the characters. This narrative stance requires self-restraint by the author, and is especially interesting since Steinbeck, nevertheless, is able to impute various qualities to Elisa Allen without revealing her inner-most thoughts. Much of the ambiguity—and the appeal—of Elisa Allen comes from the reader's never knowing precisely what she is thinking. (Compare Mary Teller in **"The White Quail,"** to whose ruminations the reader is privy.) Elisa remains a mystery because she seldom thinks out loud, and never reveals exactly what the chrysanthemums mean to her. The objective style insures the ambiguity of Elisa's character and helps to make **"The Chrysanthemums"** one of Steinbeck's finest short stories.

During 1934 when he was composing the bulk of his *Long Valley* stories, Steinbeck recorded feelings of severe loneliness despite his marriage of nearly five years. Although he rationalized that his desolation was making him more productive than he might otherwise have been, that it troubled him is suggested by the several lonely characters in *The Long Valley,* especially Harry Teller in **"The White Quail."** Another personal concern of Steinbeck's at this time was the fear of change. He "had experienced a profound sense of change in his life during the fatal illness of his mother and the wasting away of his father." His relationship with his sister, Mary, and with his wife had also altered sharply. After fighting his own perplexity over these changes, Steinbeck came to believe that "what was wrong with the world was that so many people irrationally feared and resisted the inevitability of change."

Steinbeck's feelings about these two obstacles to human happiness—loneliness and the fear of change—emerge through the two characters in **"The White Quail."** Mary Teller is a housewife whose garden is a model of perfection: lush cinerarias, a heart-shaped pool, and a wall of beautiful fuchsias. Mary had dreamt of this garden long before she met the man who made it possible—her husband, Harry Teller. Harry hires workmen to landscape the garden to Mary's specifications. She supervises them so closely that the garden emerges a floral reflection of herself—beautiful and changeless. Fear of change is implicit in Mary's question to her husband about the garden: " 'We won't ever change it, will we, Harry? If a bush dies, we'll put another one just like it in the same place.' " One afternoon when a white quail alights among her flowers, Mary believes the bird is the essence of herself. Suddenly a grey cat threatens the quail and Mary screams, scaring the feline away. Harry comforts his wife, and promises to shoot (but not kill) the cat early the next morning. After spending the night alone (Mary sleeps by herself in her own bedroom), Harry approaches the garden with his air rifle and shoots not the cat, but the white quail. He mutters to himself that he didn't mean to hurt the bird, but feels terribly alone.

The biographical nature of **"The White Quail"** may explain what Stanley Young calls its "unusual emotional province." A reflection of Steinbeck's life during this time, the narrative can be seen as a study of a failing marriage, which focuses first on the wife's fixation and aloofness from her husband, and then on the husband's consequent loneliness and resentment. Brian Barbour points out that such a shift in focus (from Mary to Harry Teller) diminishes the story's emotional power, for what begins as an expose of Mary's diseased imagination, culminates in a flash of violence when Harry kills the symbol of his wife's changeless purity—the white quail. The story ends without resolution. Harry, as a result of shooting the quail, feels remorse and increased loneliness. Mary remains unchanged.

Over the years, critics have suggested other themes for **"The White Quail."** The most unusual among them is Arthur L. Simpson's contention that Mary Teller constitutes Steinbeck's "Portrait of an Artist" (i.e., she is obsessed with her artistic creation [garden] to the exclusion of human warmth and compassion). Other critics have seen the story as the chronicle of a narcissist, the tale of a Platonic idealist, and a symbolic representation of sexual tension exploding into violence. But the themes of loneliness

and fear of change are particularly central, since each can be identified with one of the two characters, and both feelings are evidenced in the life of the author at this time.

The story's setting, like Mary Teller's garden, is unusually static. The scene never shifts from the Teller home and yard. The plot unfolds in six numbered sections, each indicating a change in time. Between sections one (Harry's proposal) and two (landscaping of the garden), the longest stretch of time elapses. Except when a cat threatens the white quail in section one and when Harry shoots the quail in section six, the story has little overt action. In addition to giving the story a generally static setting, Steinbeck omits details about the physical appearance of the characters. The reader may not notice this omission, though, since Mary's psyche is so thoroughly linked with her garden, and her "essence" with the white quail. Harry, on the other hand, is identified with the "grey cat" preying on Mary's quail. He not only refuses to poison the cat, but also kills the symbolic bird. Antoni Gajewski equates Harry with such other "enemies" as snails, dogs, and common garden pests that plague Mary.

The story's principal strength is neither in its plot nor its characters. Its distinctive quality can more accurately be called "lyric." Like a lyric poem, **"The White Quail"** is primarily an expression of the writer's emotions—loneliness and the fear of change, as we have seen. But, below the level of the author's consciousness, more sinister meanings surely lurk. The white quail represents beauty, purity, and helplessness, and is the crowning glory of Mary's private, ordered, and timeless garden. The cat is a predator, a threat to the symbol of Mary's inner self. Whether Harry realizes it or not, he has an affinity with the cat. And whether he wills it or not, he shoots quail, not cat.

When discussing Steinbeck's **"Flight"** in 1972, John M. Ditsky remarked that the story had "aroused surprising little critical comment." Today this statement no longer applies, since relative to all short stories in the Steinbeck canon, **"Flight"** has been perhaps the most popular subject for critical articles. One recent bibliography shows that only **"The Chrysanthemums"** and **"The Leader of the People"** rival **"Flight"** for this distinction.

Although **"Flight"** has provoked a flurry of criticism, the narrative is spare and can be quickly summarized: About fifteen miles south of Monterey, the Torres family farm clings to a sloping acreage above the Pacific Ocean. Nineteen-year-old Pepé, the oldest of three children, is sent to town for medicine by his mother. He wears the black hat and rides in the saddle of his deceased father. Once in Monterey, Pepé drinks too much wine, gets into a fight, and kills a man. Returning home, he saddles a fresh horse and flees into the Santa Lucia Mountains. Pepé rides for several days trying to outdistance the ominous "dark watchers" who pursue him. Although at first prepared with food, water, and a rifle, Pepé loses these, as well as his horse, on the trail. Before long he is fatigued and helpless—an easy prey for the bullets of the "dark watchers." Mortally wounded, Pepé tumbles from a mountaintop and starts a small avalanche which finally covers his head.

In his influential 1940 article, "The Californians: Storm and Steinbeck," Edmund Wilson singles out **"Flight"** as an example of what he calls Steinbeck's tendency to assimilate "human beings to animals." The "young Mexican boy," says Wilson, "is finally reduced to a state so close to that of the beasts that he is apparently mistaken by a mountain lion for another four-footed animal." Peter Lisca in *The Wide World of John Steinbeck* (1958) expands Wilson's literal reading in the story by demonstrating that **"Flight"** is a moral allegory operating on two levels: first, the physical level, which involves Pepé's literal "separation from civilized man and his reduction to the state of wild animal"; and second, the symbolic level (moving in the opposite direction), which shows "how man, even when stripped of all his civilized accoutrements . . . is still something more than an animal." On the symbolic level, Lisca contends that Pepé faces his doom "not with the headlong retreat or futile death struggle of an animal, but with the calm and stoicism required by the highest conception of manhood." By offering this broader interpretation of the story, Lisca opened the way for subsequent readings which went on to discuss Pepé's journey as the initiation of a child into the adult world.

In the typical initiation story the protagonist grows and changes until, through various rites of passage, he or she reaches maturity. **"Flight"** is somewhat more complex and ambiguous than this, however, since Pepé's initiation leads to his death. Consequently, M. R. Satyanarayana likens **"Flight"** to the Greek myth of Phaëthon, in which a son of Helios, when permitted to drive the chariot of the sun, is struck down with a thunderbolt by Zeus. Thus, in becoming a man, the boy dies. This tragic twist in Pepé's initiation can be seen as simply another element in the story, or as its governing principle. Viewing **"Flight"** according to the latter criterion, Warren French identifies Pepé's swift regression into a hunted animal as a naturalistic tragedy. Some confusion occurs, however, when we see Pepé as the protagonist of both a naturalistic tragedy and an initiation story. Brian Barbour, speaking of the instability caused by such a combination, contends that "the elements work against one another." According to Barbour, Steinbeck's marriage between these two forms is not a harmonious one.

Although his flight ends in death, as the protagonist of an initiation story Pepé is not one character, but two. At the beginning of the narrative he is a boy; at the conclusion, a man. Yet the point at which he is transformed from a boy to a man has been a matter of contention. Early in the tale Pepé is referred to as a lazy " 'peanut,' " a " 'coyote,' " and a " 'foolish chicken,' " yet he returns from his overnight journey to Monterey as a different person: "He was changed. The fragile quality seemed to have gone from his chin." From this description, Pepé's arrival into manhood is unequivocal. Yet some critics believe that the real test of his manliness, and hence the real proof he is a man, comes only at the story's end, when Pepé rises on a mountain top to greet his death heroically. One extreme view is that Pepé never attains manhood, since he is unequipped mentally to cope with the adult world. Throughout the narrative, however, Steinbeck takes pains

to present Pepé in the best possible light. For example, Steinbeck excludes the early scene in Monterey when Pepé kills a man to "avoid showing his protagonist acting senselessly, without thought, and fatefully." Pepé merely recalls the murder in summary form (the incident fills only one paragraph) to Mama Torres, so that the reader will understand the reason for his flight, while not losing interest in or sympathy for the youngster.

The Torres farm from which Pepé departs on his journey hangs precariously on a sloping cliff above the "hissing white waters of the ocean." The harsh hand of nature can be felt in the "rattling, rotting barn . . . grey-bitten with sea salt." A measure of pessimism imbues this landscape, as if Steinbeck intended to suggest that environmental factors govern the lives of the Torres family. And the dark, brooding coastal range into which Pepé flies is synonymous with death itself. Louis Owens says that along with Pepé, Joseph Wayne in *To a God Unknown* (1933), Gitano in **"The Great Mountains"** (1933), and several other Steinbeck characters trek into these same mountains to die. The moon, a stunning white orb when Pepé departs, follows him up the slopes, rising and descending during the several nights of his journey. Antoni Gajewski suggests that when the moon rises, Pepé is vigorous and strong; when it descends, his strength wanes. In addition, several animals suggest Pepé's condition as he proceeds into the mountains. A wildcat and eagle indicate power and perseverance. A rattlesnake and some lizards imply cunning and weakness. And "little birds" looking upon him without fear and buzzards circling above in search of carrion portend Pepé's doom. At other times, animals preying upon one another suggest by analogy the "dark watchers" in their pursuit of Pepé. Doves and quail run out to a spring, for example, but are soon encroached upon by a "spotted wildcat." This incident becomes a parable of Pepé's flight—the birds suggesting Pepé, and the wildcat, the dark watchers.

Steinbeck portrays this scene and others in the story with a style that is spare and economical. Peter Lisca says that this suggests a debt to Hemingway: "a crisp rendering of factual details which, while staying close to the actual object and action, avoids the myopic distortions of "realistic' writing." As in other artistically successful stories like **"The Chrysanthemums"** and **"The Gift,"** Steinbeck's point of view in **"Flight"** is third-person objective. The narrator remains outside the mind of his protagonist. Much of the mystery, ambiguity, and suspense in **"Flight"** stems from this objective stance. Steinbeck emphasizes external events—vivid physical action fills the story, and he refuses to translate this action into a clear-cut message or moral.

"I wrote the story just as it happened. . . . I don't know what it means." With these words, Steinbeck explains that his enigmatic tale, **"The Snake,"** recounts a real incident which occurred in the laboratory of his biologist friend, Ed Ricketts. As A. Grove Day, a friend of Steinbeck for many years, recalls the episode, once when he and Steinbeck were in Ricketts' laboratory a woman dropped and hurt a white mouse she had been playing with. Someone suggested they feed the mouse to a rattlesnake Ricketts' father had found on a golf course. All watched as a grotesquely funny thing happened. Upon swallowing the whole mouse except its tail, the snake with the thin protuberance from its jaws looked as if it were smoking a cigarette. In the story, Steinbeck substantially changes this incident, as Day remembers it. Ricketts, called "Dr. Phillips," arrives one morning at his laboratory on the cannery street in Monterey carrying a sack of starfish. With their sperm and ova, he begins a series of timed embryo experiments, when suddenly a tall, slim woman enters the laboratory. She waits for him momentarily, and then asks if she may buy a male rattlesnake. Once the purchase is arranged, she asks to see her snake eat. Dr. Phillips reluctantly agrees, placing a large white rat into the rattler's cage. As the snake poises to strike, Dr. Phillips notices that the woman duplicates exactly its movements. Her bizarre behavior so unnerves him, that he forgets one sequence of his embryo experiment. Angrily, he pours the ruined contents into the sink. Although the woman says she will return occasionally to visit her snake, Dr. Phillips never sees her again.

"The Snake" is one of the few short stories in which Steinbeck focuses on a single time, place, and action. The time elapsed is less than an hour. The sole setting, a laboratory, suggests the quasi-clinical conditions under which animal (and human) behavior can be observed. The plot focuses on one action. Events proceed chronologically, sometimes slowly, creating an aura of suspense. The incessant washing of waves against the laboratory pilings counterpoints and relieves the slow but steady progress of the narrative. These waves also evoke a primitive atmosphere, in keeping with the bizarre, primordial movements of the female visitor. On one occasion, Dr. Phillips cannot distinguish between the water's quiet splash among the piles and the woman's sigh.

Since Steinbeck clearly had Ed Ricketts in mind when he wrote **"The Snake,"** the author's attitude toward his friend becomes a key to understanding the fictional character, Dr. Phillips. In "About Ed Ricketts," Steinbeck affectionately calls Ricketts "half-Christ and half-goat," "an original," a "complex and many-faceted" man who thought in "mystical terms." Steinbeck tells us that Ricketts' tastes were catholic, running from cold beer to Gregorian chants to women of all types and dispositions. In the story Dr. Phillips reacts emotionally to the bizarre woman who disrupts his embryo experiment. According to Warren French, Steinbeck knows that "one's attitude can be simultaneously scientific and emotional." Thus, he characterizes Dr. Phillips as both a dispassionate observer of nature, as well as a sensitive, feeling human being.

The tall, slim woman who unexpectedly enters Dr. Phillips laboratory brings his character into high relief. Unable to divert his feelings toward her, Dr. Phillips becomes "piqued" because the woman shows no interest in his embryo experiment. Consequently, he tries to "arouse" and "shock" her by embalming a "limp dead cat," but she merely makes him more "nervous." Then, when she asks to buy a snake, he becomes "afraid" and later angry. Her attempt to reach into the snake's cage leaves Dr. Phillips "shaken" and a feeling of sorrow, and again anger, arises

in him when he puts the rodent into the cage. Finally, his emotions are wrought up to high pitch when the rattler prepares to strike. "He felt the blood drifting up in his body. . . . His veins were throbbing. . . ." " 'Perfect,' " he cries. " '[I]t was an emotional bath, wasn't it?' " The woman does not respond, and Dr. Phillips' anger boils again when he realizes that his embryo experiment has been ruined. Thus we witness the wide amplitude of Dr. Phillips' feelings.

French suggests that the central focus of the story is not so much the strange woman as it is "what she allows us to learn about another." "Another," of course, is Dr. Phillips. But the woman herself is quite an enigmatic character, probably one of the most bizarre in Steinbeck's fiction. Charles E. May characterizes her as a Jungian anima figure who has emerged from the primal, mythic world to jar Dr. Phillips out of what May calls his "scientific and therefore detached existence." Dr. Phillips, according to May, "has rejected the unconscious to such an extent that the instinctual forces [the woman] rise up in opposition." This argument, although debatable as it pertains to the biologist, marks a new approach to the puzzling woman, who had formerly been discussed by critics only in Freudian and biblical terms. Peter Lisca, for instance, contends that by watching the male rattler eat the white rat, the woman "objectifies her [sexual] frustration." And Joseph Fontenrose calls her a fascinated creature in a "zoological garden of Eden."

Steinbeck was apparently so enamored with this woman and her snake fixation that he recounted a variation of the incident in chapters 16 and 17 of *Sweet Thursday* (1954). In this latter rendition, the biologist's intruder, rather than a snake-like woman, is Suzy, a new "girl" at the Bear Flag Restaurant. This time what ruins the starfish embryo experiment is not a snake, but an argument between Suzy and the doctor, which shows him to be a lonely man deluding himself with dreams of writing what Suzy calls a " 'great big goddam highfalutin paper.' " Doc, admirably, realizes a true thing when he hears it, and begins to alleviate his loneliness by falling for Suzy. Although much of the suspense of the original story is lost in this retelling of **"The Snake,"** its inclusion in *Sweet Thursday* testifies to Steinbeck's enduring pleasure in the tale.

Like the story, **"The Snake," "Breakfast"** is another short work that Steinbeck incorporated into one of his novels. A revised version of this piece appears in Chapter 22 of *The Grapes of Wrath* (1939). But to call **"Breakfast"** a narrative fragment is misleading, since it was published some three years earlier than Steinbeck's famous novel. A more accurate term is "sketch," a "brief composition simply constructed and usually most unified in that it presents a single character, a single incident. It lacks a developed plot or very great characterization." On all counts, except perhaps for the arbitrary "single character," **"Breakfast"** fits this definition.

Steinbeck opens the sketch with a first-person narrator walking along a country road before sunrise. Ahead in the gathering light he sees a tent. Beside it a young woman, nursing a baby, cooks bacon and biscuits. Two stubble-bearded men in dungarees emerge from the tent, and the older one invites the passerby to join them for breakfast. He gladly accepts. The three men squat around a packing case, while the woman sets out a tin platter. They eat quickly. Afterwards, when the two male hosts stand and face the eastern dawn, the rising sun reflects brilliant light in the older man's eyes. They ask their guest to pick cotton with them that day, but he thanks them and walks off alone down the road.

Steinbeck's choosing an incident with an obvious beginning, middle, and end gives this sketch unity. **"Breakfast"** is unusually symmetrical: it opens with one paragraph addressed directly to the reader and closes in the same way. In both paragraphs, the narrator tries (but admits he is unable) to explain why the incident is memorable. The sun's journey from behind the eastern mountains across the sky also adds to the symmetry of the sketch. Its westward progress from dawn to sunrise frames the morning communion between the migrant family and the narrator. The faint illumination of the twilight brings the migrants' tent into the narrator's view. The sky continues to redden, as the nursing mother prepares biscuits and bacon. Once the family and guest sit down to share their repast, the sun climbs above the mountaintop with a "reddish gleam." Finally, when the two bearded men face east, the sunlight reflects in the older man's eyes.

The auroral splendor of daybreak helps to account for the warm "pleasure" and the "element of great beauty" the narrator feels in recalling the scene. The sunrise is majestic. Its brilliant scarlet light piercing through darkness lifts the narrator's spirits. The steaming hot biscuits, bacon, and coffee shared by the migrant family also inspire him. The meal becomes a feast for the narrator's senses. He is no doubt surprised at his hosts' generosity, considering they possess few of life's material comforts. Although they have little, they give a lot. Their humble repast becomes a ritual of holy communion, suggesting an indomitable faith in the brotherhood of man.

The first-person narrator's participation in the episode brings the reader close to the action and provides a unity of impression that is lost in the revised, third-person point of view sketch included in *The Grapes of Wrath*. In this latter rendition the austere beauty of the sunrise and the spiritual significance of the shared meal lose much of their impact. In addition, Steinbeck abandons his rigid principle of selection which makes **"Breakfast"** a spare, crisply focused narrative: he adds more dialogue—mainly small talk—and moves the migrants' lone tent from a quiet country road to a campground filled with other tents. Thus the solitude and serenity of the event is lost with the incursion of civilization. The atmosphere of the original lacking, the memorable sketch becomes an easily forgotten scene in the novel.

One of the few short stories in *The Long Valley* which ostensibly deals with topical issues of the 1930s is **"The Raid."** The story takes place one dark night in a California town. Two men emerge from a lunch wagon, Dick asking his younger companion, Root, if he has prepared his speech. The frightened youth answers in the affirmative, but worries about a possible raid. Walking toward the outskirts of town, they reach a deserted store and begin to prepare for an eight o'clock meeting. Root tacks up one poster portraying a man in harsh reds and blacks and a second bearing a large red symbol. Next he sets out a pile of leaflets and paper-bound books. At half past eight when no one has arrived, Root's fear intensifies. Then a man appears, warning that a raiding party is on the way. Dick encourages Root to stand firm. Suddenly a crowd of angry men rushes the building. Root begins his speech, but is knocked down by a flying two-by-four. The two men take a horrible beating. Sometime later, Dick and Root awaken bandaged in the hospital cell of a jail. Dick congratulates the younger man for not running under fire.

While **"The Raid"** concerns the plight of two communist organizers, many critics have found that their political ideology is less important than Steinbeck's psychological portrait of the younger man's grappling with fear. Steinbeck focuses on the novice party organizer, Root, and contrasts his behavior with that of a veteran, Dick. The essential difference between these two characters becomes the crux of the story. While both men are no doubt frightened by the raid, the seasoned activist, Dick, has learned to mask his fears under a facade of party slogans. The inexperienced Root, on the other hand, openly expresses his trepidation. Yet, when a swarm of angry vigilantes attack the two, Root proves himself. He stands alongside Dick, unflinching at flying fists and debris. Thus, **"The Raid"** has been correctly called an initiation story, for Root overcomes his dread and is initiated into the brotherhood of veteran activists. The victory recorded in the story, therefore, is not of communism over capitalism, or vice versa, but, in Antoni Gajewski's words, a "victory of a human being over human nature." Controling his fear regardless of the danger present is the lesson Root learns.

Dick and Root's stand against the vigilantes also has religious overtones. Peter Lisca notices a parallel between the two men and the martyrs of early Christianity. Even though Dick and Root have been tipped off about the raid, both men choose to face the onslaught with what amounts to religious zeal for the "cause" and for the portrait of the venerable man behind them. The human image on that poster becomes a god to the pair, and they are his disciples. Root, says Lisca, resembles Christ, for he undergoes a ritual death at the hands of the angry mob and is then reborn into a staunch, unwavering supporter of the party. Dick, as mentioned above, is a diehard party regular and already knows how to stand firm.

This brings up the essential difference between these two characters: while Dick is static, hardened into his opinions and behavior by party dogma, Root is dynamic and changes as the narrative progresses. Dick is Root's model for emulation, but perhaps because the older man obeys party orders unflinchingly, he is a somewhat less interesting character than Root. On the surface, Dick maintains a facade of unbending resolve which contrasts vividly with Root's apparent wavering. That Dick is not impervious to his subordinate's alarm, however, becomes evident when he warns Root: " 'Oh! Shut up, kid. You'll get my goat pretty soon.' " and " 'Keep still, will you? You'll drive me nuts.' " But, otherwise, Dick is the hardboiled activist. Even his peajacket suggests the tough, outer shell that

STEINBECK

such a man must don. And for the most part, his speech is laconic and curt, except when he elaborates on party doctrine. Thus, instead of expressing his own feelings, he quotes Marx. Dick's advice to Root betrays this fear of expressing feelings: " '[D]on't go opening up for everybody to show them how you feel.' "

In this respect, Root is the exact opposite of Dick. He cannot contain his fright, and lets it slip off his tongue in unchecked profusion. At first, Root behaves like a "cry-baby, a shrinking boy who lacks faith in his own strength." In fact, Root resembles a vulnerable infant from the beginning of the story. Unlike Dick who wears a hard outer shell (the peajacket), Root's apparel is a "blue turtle-neck sweater," suggesting softness. When Dick first accuses him of being scared, the young novice puts on his "toughest look," implying that Root is unsure of his toughness. And like a small boy, he speaks in a lonely, homesick voice when Dick questions him about his father. Once the raid is imminent, Root finally admits, " 'Yes, I'm scared. Maybe I won't be no good at this.' " Thus, Steinbeck clearly establishes that Root is untested.

Suspense, a key dramatic device in **"The Raid,"** increases as a result of Steinbeck's consistent focus on Root's fears. Root questions Dick: " '[Y]ou didn't hear nothing about no raid, did you?' " Out of nervousness, the young novice asks Dick on four separate occasions for the time. Dick's grudging replies set up the chronology of the story. Since the meeting is scheduled to begin at eight o'clock, each minute that elapses after eight increases the organizer's anxiety. On the last occasion when Root asks for the time, Dick replies: " 'Quarter-past nine.' " That the meeting participants are over an hour late signals danger.

Night sounds also add suspense. Rustling winds, barking dogs, and rumbling motor cars are heard outside the deserted store where Dick and Root prepare for the meeting. Steinbeck repeats variations on this motif six times. In the culminating sequence, he adds two new sounds, a train and an alarm clock. Some specific sounds: the wind rustling through the locust trees and the murmuring of automobiles—the mutter of engines, the squeal of brakes and the sound of horns—foreshadow the coming of the vigilantes. Just before the raiders arrive, Steinbeck ingeniously heightens the suspense with complete silence. The wind rushes fiercely and then dies away. Dogs stop barking, the thundering train disappears, the alarm clock falls silent.

"The Raid" is divided into four numbered sections which mark the progress of Root's initiation. M. R. Satyanarayana suggests that within these sections, Root goes through all the well-known rites of passage except change of name. These include: "(1) the hero's severance from the mother, (2) the revelation of the mystery of adult experience, (3) the ordeal, and (4) the symbolic death and rebirth." These sections form the infra-structure of the plot. The point of view is third-person omniscient, for the narrator imputes certain thoughts and feelings to Root which the reader would not learn of otherwise. The narrator's omniscience is crucial in depicting the psychological portrait of a young protagonist grappling with almost insurmountable fears. Thus, Root's victory over his fright is the focus of the story.

"The Harness" is a psychological study of Salinas Valley farmer and widower, Peter Randall. Upon the death of his wife, Randall becomes hysterical. To his friend Ed Chappell's surprise, Randall sheds his clothes revealing a shoulder harness and stomach belt—both of which he then removes. (They were Emma's idea.) He also confides that his annual "business trips" to San Francisco actually have been week-long orgies (to get away from Emma). Now with his wife gone, Randall vows to indulge himself daily, living without restraint. As a symbol of his liberation, he plants forty-five acres of sweet peas, a financially risky crop (Emma would have disapproved) which luckily pays off. Later in a San Francisco hotel, Ed Chappell encounters Randall returning on a drunken spree from the city's houses of prostitution. Randall hasn't changed. For a while he has shed the physical symbols—the harness and stomach belt—of his wife's domination, but he confesses that she continues to rule his mind.

Peter Randall is fifty, grave, and blue eyed, with a "carefully tended beard" and perfect posture. The telling feature of his personality, however, is the chained impulse within him, the "force held caged." In Jungian terms, Randall fails to achieve oneness, since the two sides of his personality remain at odds. The rejected, darker side (his "shadow") wars with the exemplary, public side (his "persona"). Thus, although Peter consciously advocates libidinous pleasures, the fact that he cannot integrate such pleasures into his everyday life means that he actually rejects them. When he runs off to San Francisco to indulge his senses, Peter merely allows himself to be "bad" temporarily. This signals no real change in his personality; Emma might as well still be alive.

When Emma dies and Randall plants forty-five acres of sweet peas, he appears to have completely shaken his wife's influence. The worried look upon his face seems understandable, considering the gamble Peter has taken. Therefore, except for a few hints in the narrative to the contrary, Randall appears to be liberated from Emma's domination. The blue and pink sea of sweet pea blossoms becomes a symbol of his liberation. One would expect, therefore, that Peter is free to live the libidinous life of his fantasies. But this is not the case. The new, liberated Peter turns out to be none other than the old, slavish Peter. His shoulder harness and stomach belt serve only to suggest his more significant psychological bondage. We do not discover this, however, until the story's conclusion.

Since Emma appears for only a short time in the narrative, Steinbeck characterizes her quickly, but with abundant details. She is a forty-five year old, "skin-and-bones," proud matron whose "face was as wrinkled and brown as that of an old, old woman." Steinbeck oddly compares her to a bird: This "little skinny bird of a woman" has "dark, sharp bird eyes." And like other wives in *The Long Valley,* Emma is childless. The Randall farmhouse is reflective of Emma: "clean and dusted," and "unscarred, uncarved, unchalked." Emma's house has the same "hard-swept" look as Elisa Allen's in **"The Chrysanthemums."** Similarly, each woman has a fenced yard, with a well-manicured garden, and their family farms are located "across the Salinas River, next to the foothills." The nearly identical setting in these two stories is no coincidence, for in the first manuscript version of **"The Chrysanthemums,"** as mentioned above, Henry Allen (like Peter Randall) intends to plant sweet peas and is also upbraided by his wife for tracking dirt into the house.

Ed Chappell, who like Emma appears infrequently, is instrumental in revealing three clues that Randall does not change after his wife's death. First, although claiming he will no longer wind the mantel clock whose "clack-clack-clack is too mournful," Randall keeps the clock running since its ticking suggests Emma's heartbeat. Second, despite his boast that he will "track dirt into the house" to trample upon his deceased wife's obsession with cleanliness, Randall continues to uphold her spick-and-span standards. And third, while he promises to hire a "big fat housekeeper"—his most rebellious plan, since Emma had adamantly "refused to hire a girl"—Randall never finds time to look for one. Ed Chappell carefully notes that none of these proposed changes is adopted. Each constitutes a hidden reminder of Emma's psychological domination over her husband.

Another minor character almost as important as Ed Chappell is expert farmer, Clark Dewitt. Although Dewitt never actually appears in the story, his pronouncements about the perils of growing sweet peas are given special weight because he, along with Peter Randall, is one of the valley's brightest farmers. Dewitt, like Chappell, is a device Steinbeck uses to place Randall in high relief. Without the opinions and observations of these minor characters, the third-person omniscient narrator would be left with the entire burden of characterizing the story's protagonist. Finally, **"The Harness"** is hardly the most artistically refined story in the collection, yet its surprising conclusion reveals a seemingly ordinary man to be psychologically complex, perhaps even profoundly disturbed.

During the mid-1930s, Steinbeck became fascinated with group or "mob" behavior. His interest in this phenomenon is especially evident in **"The Vigilante."** One night in a small, California town, a man named Mike joins some vigilantes who storm a jail and lynch a black prisoner. Afterward, as he walks from the dark scene towards a tavern, Mike is overcome by loneliness. He brags to the bartender, Welch, that he was the first into the jail and then displays a piece of blue denim torn from the victim's body. Welch offers to buy the souvenir, and pours Mike a free beer. Soon the two men close the bar and walk into a residential district. Arriving at his home, Mike is badgered by his suspicious wife, who accuses him of being with a woman. Rather than denying this, he simply tells her to read the morning paper. Nevertheless, when he looks in the mirror, Mike feels as if he has been unfaithful.

"The Vigilante" is a brief (only **"Breakfast"** is shorter) and a tightly-knit narrative. Although most critics contend that the story focuses on the aftermath of the lynching and Mike's reaction to it, Steinbeck devotes nearly one-half of the tale to describing the hanging itself. True, when the story opens, the black prisoner is already a dangling "bluish grey" corpse, yet how he comes to his demise is fully recounted in a series of flashbacks. First, Mike recalls struggling among the mob for a chance to pull the

execution rope. Second, he remembers an earlier moment when the vigilantes rushed the jail. Third, Mike retells the lynching incident in full to Welch, mentioning the sheriff's complicity and the gruesomeness of the prisoner's abduction. Finally, to complete this description of the events, Steinbeck has Mike speculate on how the sheriff will "cut the nigger down and clean up some."

Steinbeck devotes slightly more than half of the narrative to Mike's response to the lynching. At first, Mike feels heavy and unreal, and then ashamed. He slinks away from the hanging, pulling "his cap down over his eyes." But then his sense of human decency is aroused when the mob puts a torch to the dead man's dangling feet. "'That don't do no good,'" he says. Ironically, Mike who has put his body and soul into hanging a man, now quibbles over the treatment of his corpse. Mike must justify his participation, so he agrees with an onlooker that tax dollars have been saved by the gang-style murder. As soon as he leaves the crowd, Mike becomes desperately lonely and rushes for the nearest bar. Once the bar closes Mike becomes lonely again, and shies away when Welch asks him how the lynching made him feel. Mike merely replies that he feels "'satisfied . . . but tired and kind of sleepy.'" Thus, Mike responds to the hanging in different ways. He feels weary, satisfied, ashamed, indignant, lonely, and proud.

Images of light and darkness in the story echo Mike's feelings. Consistently, darkness to Mike means loneliness, and light, the escape from loneliness. Thus, when the vigilantes' torches are extinguished, Mike flees to a surer source of light, the "burning neon word BEER" on the nearby tavern. The illumination he finds there, however, is short-lived. Soon Welch switches off the "red neon sign and the house lights" and the two men step back into the darkness. As they approach Mike's house, he says, "'Look, there's light in the kitchen.'" Although the glow from his kitchen window is no cause for celebration, it represents to Mike a beacon guiding him out of the darkness. Each time he leaves an illuminated area, such as the lynching site or Welch's bar, loneliness overtakes him. Hence, he always moves toward light with a sense of urgency.

As a native of the small town where the lynching occurs, Mike speaks with defective grammar (e.g., "'That don't do no good'") and seems unable to think for himself. Upon hearing the catchy phrase "'sneaky lawyers,'" for instance, he repeats it over and over again. Mike's "thin, petulant" wife is suspicious, complaining, and apparently dissatisfied with her husband. And, like Elisa Allen and Mary Teller, she is childless. Welch, the bartender, is "small . . . like an aged mouse . . . unkempt and fearful". His furtive manner echoes that of the vigilantes who sneak silently away from the smoldering corpse. Curiously, Steinbeck describes the physical appearance of all the principal characters (even the corpse) except Mike, suggesting that he is an "average" man who behaves in this situation as any average man would. In fact, Mike (no last name) is the typical "unit man" Steinbeck has in mind when he explains the Phalanx Theory in his philosophical dialogue, "Case History."

Composed in the same copybook with **"The Vigilante"** and other short fiction of the 1930s, "Case History" is a

4,500-word narrative in which Steinbeck delivers perhaps his earliest and most comprehensive statement of the Phalanx, or "group-man," Theory. According to this theory, a group is an individual with desires, hungers, and strivings of its own, and actually controls the behavior of the unit men who comprise it. Preceding this explanation of the Phalanx Theory, Steinbeck depicts a lynching nearly identical to that in **"The Vigilante."** John Ramsy (counterpart of Mike) joins a furious mob that smashes through the door of the Salinas jail and lynches a suspected child murderer. Later Ramsy explains his actions to Will McKay (counterpart of Welch) and proves himself to be neither a bigot, nor a racist, nor even a violent man; he merely longs to become part of the group. These two elements of the narrative—the lynching scene and its explanation—make "Case History" an essential document for understanding **"The Vigilante."**

Over the years critics (without apparent knowledge of "Case History") have conjectured various reasons for Mike's behavior in **"The Vigilante"**: Warren French says that boredom and a suspicious wife precipitate Mike's violent actions; Franklin E. Court attributes the protagonist's behavior to the inescapable futility of his life; Brian Barbour suggests unrest of the soul and repressed sexual desire; Antoni Gajewski simply calls Mike the "average American racist." Peter Lisca believes that "The vigilante, like the grandfather in **'The Leader of the People,'** fully lives only for that time when he is part of the group"; and, similarly, Richard Astro contends that although lynching is "something unreal and foreign to his basic nature," Mike forgets himself and is swallowed up by the mob.

Steinbeck's explanation of Phalanx behavior in "Case History" parallels the arguments of Lisca and Astro on **"The Vigilante."** Through Ramsy, Steinbeck says that the unit man, regardless of his individual disposition, always yearns to join the group. Within him is a keying mechanism linked to the Phalanx. Consequently, when the group calls him, the unit man quickly responds. This, then, is the underlying reason why Mike becomes **"The Vigilante"**—not primarily because he is sexually frustrated, bored, or a racist, but because he longs to attach himself to the group.

Steinbeck's unusual short story, **"Johnny Bear,"** has less to do with its huge, moronic titular character, than with the village of Loma whose symbols of respectability he topples. Johnny Bear is an anthropoidal half-wit who begs whiskey from patrons at the Buffalo Bar. When anyone buys him a drink, he rewards his benefactor by mimicking voices he has overheard. One evening the narrator, a worker from a nearby dredging barge, hears Johnny Bear repeating the conversation of a man and a woman. The man's voice is that of the narrator himself, and the woman's, his date on a recent evening, Mae Romero. This performance embarrasses everyone in the bar, especially the narrator. To earn another whiskey, Johnny Bear then utters the voices of two women, one reprimanding the other for her unbridled passions. The words are those of Emalin and Amy Hawkins, the town's aristocrats. On a later night, Johnny Bear mimics the sisters' voices again, this time revealing that Amy has attempted to hang her-

self. Everyone in the bar is dumbstruck. After a few days, Johnny Bear discloses that Amy is pregnant by a Chinese man and has committed suicide. Buffalo Bar patrons are ashamed, for Loma's first ladies have been disgraced.

Peter Lisca rightly argues that the central focus of **"Johnny Bear"** is the fallen Hawkins sisters, rather than the strange cretin who reveals their unexpected behavior. Lisca contends that the tale exposes a "social group . . . and the conflict between its innate curiosity and its desire to perpetuate the symbols of its decorum." Although this may be the story's central interest, **"Johnny Bear"** contains several lesser, sometimes competing interests. The two most prominent are the swamp dredger with its crew, and the character, Johnny Bear.

The swamp dredger subplot in the story has its origin in Steinbeck's own experience. Nelson Valjean explains that Steinbeck once worked on a dredger "draining lakes and canals near Castroville," California. Castroville, today called by residents the artichoke capital of the world, was Steinbeck's model for the town of Loma. When employed on the dredger, Steinbeck frequently "ate at the little Bennett Hotel," the counterpart of Mrs. Ratz's house in the story. While his ability to particularize this setting lends the town an air of reality, Steinbeck's frequent references to the swamp dredger detract from the tale's artistic unity. The dredger's succession of cooks, its unfortunate spate of accidents—when one worker loses both legs and another develops blood poisoning—and the unabated (except Sundays) drone of its diesel engine, become random details cluttering the plot.

The second competing element in the story is Johnny Bear himself. The origins of this bizarre creature probably stem from an incident described by Steinbeck's Stanford classmate and friend, Webster Street:

> One day we were coming back from Palo Alto on the way to Salinas and we stopped for a beer at a bar just outside Castroville. We were sitting there talking, and suddenly we heard the bartender speaking to somebody wearing bib overalls. We listened for a while. The bartender said, "And then what did you do?" and the guy went through all sorts of motions. He didn't talk with his fingers as in sign language, rather he illustrated what he did. He was mute, he could hear but could not speak. I'm certain that John based the story of **"Johny Bear"** (sic) on that episode. As a matter of fact, on the way back he said, "Did you pay attention to that fella, the guy in the overalls? You know he could do a lot of harm, that guy."

Steinbeck keeps Johnny Bear so clearly in view during the narrative that Edmund Wilson has mistaken him for the protagonist. Called by the narrator, "just a kind of recording and reproducing device, only you use a glass of whiskey instead of a nickel," Johnny Bear is another of Steinbeck's "subnormal" characters, such as Lennie in *Of Mice and Men* (1937) and Tularecito in *Pastures of Heaven* (1932). But Johnny Bear has a distinctive gift: he can duplicate exactly the words and the voice of anyone he hears. That patrons of the Buffalo Bar will pay him in shots of whiskey if he repeats what he has heard is motivation enough for this hulking man. Silently he moves about Loma, eavesdropping on unsuspecting citizens. Peter Lisca equates his capacity as a recording device with "the artist's role in society. . . . Johnny Bear holds the mirror up to mankind and reveals through his mimetic talent the hidden festers of society." In this way, he embarrasses the story's narrator and exposes the secrets of the Hawkins family. Even given Johnny Bear's strange appearance and antics, he cannot function as a protagonist, as Wilson suggests, because he does not act; he only duplicates the words and actions of others, particularly the story's more likely protagonists—Amy and Emalin Hawkins.

Amy Hawkins' affair and Emalin's response to it actually provide enough material for a separate story. But Steinbeck uses this material in **"Johnny Bear"** to demonstrate how the fall of a "respectable" family can send shock waves through a narrow community like Loma. In Emalin and Amy, Steinbeck creates an early version of the Cain-Abel relationships (e.g., Charles-Adam, Cathy-Adam, Caleb-Aron, and Caleb-Abra) in *East of Eden* (1952). In these relationships one individual is usually soft, sensitive, warm, compassionate, and understanding, while the other is cold, stern, calculating, and sometimes diabolical. Thus, when Amy's mid-life passion is excited by a Chinese share-cropper, Emalin tells her sister that she would be better dead than to indulge it. When Amy inquires if her sister has ever felt such yearnings, Emalin replies, " 'if ever I had, I would cut that part of me away.' " Then after Amy's suicide, Emalin appeals to the doctor in a cold, controlled voice, " 'Can you make out a certificate without mentioning' " [Amy's pregnancy]? Emalin's concern for the family reputation blinds her to Amy's needs. In fact, the doctor even suggests Emalin's complicity in the suicide.

The Hawkins' horse and buggy provide an apt metaphor for Emalin's struggle to uphold rigid moral standards. The horse is harnessed in blinders and a "check-rein" that is entirely "too short for such an old horse." The blinders suggest narrow-mindedness. The short check-rein which prohibits the horse from lowering its neck implies the strict, even unhealthy rules of conduct Emalin applies to herself and Amy. Emalin expects Amy to remain fixed in a "respectable" moral posture—as Emma Randall expects of her husband in **"The Harness."** This forced compliance causes severe repercussions: Peter Randall becomes haunted and emotionally disturbed; Amy Hawkins commits suicide.

Steinbeck uses apt imagery to stress the moral murkiness of Loma. He notes "its fogs, with its great swamp like a hideous sin . . . ". This fog imagery recurs frequently: "nasty fog," "evil-smelling fog," "slow, squirming mist," and finally the narrator says, "It seemed to me that that fog was clinging to the cypress hedge of the Hawkins' house . . . fog balls were clustered about it and others were slowly moving in." Then he suggests the fog's meaning: "I smiled as I walked along at the way a man's thought can rearrange nature to fit his thoughts." In other words, he senses doom hanging over the Hawkins' house, the fog piling up upon their cypress hedge signifying this

doom, as well as the Hawkins sisters' attempt to conceal it.

In addition to the fog imagery, Steinbeck makes subtle comments about the Hawkins sisters and others in Loma through his descriptions of their dwellings. The most unusual feature of the Hawkins' house is its "incredibly thick and strong" hedge. The narrator calls it a high "green barrier" which suggests that the Hawkins sisters either desire exclusiveness or they have something to conceal. The story's surprise ending reveals that both assumptions are correct. Another curious feature about their home is its tan paint and dark brown trim, a color "combination favored for railroad stations and schools in California." Thus, even though concealed, the Hawkins' home assumes the aura of a public building, a public institution, or as Alex Hartnell calls it: " 'The safe thing . . . [t]he place where a girl can get reassurance.' "

Steinbeck's description of the village itself is most revealing. The Methodist church stands at the "highest place on the hill." This most visible edifice—its spire can be seen for miles—suggests the church's influence in the community. However, the influence Steinbeck seems to have in mind is not necessarily a good one. The populace of Loma lives in "small wooden houses" and the land owners live on "small yards usually enclosed by high walls of clipped cypress . . . ," suggesting narrow, cramped lives. Steinbeck says there is "nothing to do in Loma."

The only real communion that takes place occurs not in the Methodist Church or the Masonic Hall, but in the bar—" '[T]he Buffalo Bar is the mind of Loma.' " Here attitudes are molded and reinforced over shots of whiskey. "[P]osters and cards and pictures stuck to the wall" of the Buffalo Bar reflect the retarded consciousness of the community. These announcements contain appeals by political candidates, salesmen, and auctioneers, some of whom have been dead for years. The bar itself is an uncomfortable place with a "bare wood" floor and "hard and straight" chairs. Fat Carl, the bartender, utters his stock response to regulars and strangers alike: " 'What'll it be?' " His repetitive phrase illustrates the torpor that has stolen over Loma.

The story's surprise ending suggesting that Amy's liaison is doubly degrading since it involves a Chinese man—a "Chink"—does not represent the kind of thinking we like to remember Steinbeck for. Nor does the narrator's relationship with Mae Romero, the "pretty half-Mexican girl" with whom he has "scraped an acquaintance." When one night in the Buffalo Bar Johnny Bear recites the narrator's advances on Mae, he sighs, "I was cravenly glad Mae Romero had no brothers. What obvious, forced, ridiculous words had come from Johnny Bear." Alex Hartnell explains to his friend: " 'If you're worrying about Mae's reputation, don't. Johnny Bear has followed Mae before.' " Alex implies that Mae is disreputable, yet Buffalo Bar regulars find nothing wrong with the narrator's advances. By Loma's standards, a white male may seduce a non-white female with impunity. However, when a white woman (Amy Hawkins) has an affair with a Chinese share-cropper, she is thought a disgrace to the community. These rather unsavory attitudes, which may be more of a sign of the times than of Steinbeck's sensibility, make **"Johnny Bear"** one tale that does not entirely reflect well on its author.

Steinbeck's first short story to receive a national prize—the O. Henry Memorial Award of 1934—was **"The Murder."** In the tale California rancher Jim Moore marries a Yugoslavian girl whose ways are foreign to his own. Jelka Sepic becomes a dutiful wife, if not a good companion. Ignoring his father-in-law's admonition that Jelka will love only a man who beats her, Jim fails to develop a satisfying intimacy with her and instead begins to visit the Three Star brothel in Monterey. One Saturday evening on the trail to Monterey, a neighbor informs Jim that one of his calves has been killed by rustlers. Jim doubles back and arrives home to find Jelka in bed with her male cousin. After giving it a moment's thought, Jim aims his rifle between the cousin's eyes and fires. Once the murder charge is dismissed by a deputy sheriff, Jim flogs his wife bloody with a bull whip. Rather than revolt, Jelka smiles, becomes more personable, and lovingly fries her husband a breakfast of eggs and bacon.

As was his custom in stories written during the 1930s, Steinbeck begins **"The Murder"** with an extended description of the setting. The atmospheric details he emphasizes in most tales of the period bear on plot, theme, or character. In **"The Chrysanthemums,"** as we have seen, the fog which shrouds the Salinas Valley like a closed pot reflects Elisa Allen's spiritual frustration. The grey colors of winter, the absence of sunlight, and the cold air all suggest her condition and reinforce the story's theme. In such other *Long Valley* stories as **"The White Quail"** and **"Flight"**

Steinbeck in the early 1930s, the time in which he wrote most of his short stories.

the settings have similarly significant implications. In **"The Murder,"** however, this correspondence between setting and other elements in the narrative breaks down. Steinbeck painstakingly describes a "stone castle" and an old ranch house, creaking and rusting below it, but then never brings these back into the story again.

Roy S. Simmonds explains the reason for this incongruity between the setting and other formal qualities of the tale: "In the manuscript of **'The Murder'** Steinbeck initially set the story in the Corral de Tierra [fictional setting of *The Pastures of Heaven*] but subsequently, while the work was still in its primary manuscript stage, changed the setting to the Valle del Castillo. . . . " Even though Steinbeck tried to disguise the *Pastures* landscape, it emerges nevertheless. "At the head of the canyon there stands a tremendous stone castle. . . . " With these words Steinbeck describes a natural rock formation which towers above the old Moore ranch house abandoned when Jim Moore built a new home farther down the canyon. In real life this precipice stands over the Corral de Tierra and is called by local residents "the Castle."

In plot structure, as in setting, **"The Murder"** resembles several stories in *The Pastures of Heaven*—principally because of the surprise entrance of Moore's neighbor, George, who tips off Moore about a dead calf found with his brand on it. George's intrusion leading Jim to discover his wife with her lover is an obvious device reminiscent of the Munroe's interventions in *Pastures.* By encountering George on the trail to Monterey, Jim Moore's illusions about Jelka's fidelity are shattered, as is his mistaken assumption that he can treat his Yugoslavian wife like any American woman. Moore quickly recovers from his disillusionment and alters his behavior. He beats his wife, causing her to hold him in higher esteem. This beating solves both Jelka's problems and Jim's. Jelka now has a husband who treats her as (she thinks) a Yugoslavian wife should be treated. And with Jelka's new responsiveness to her husband, Jim may no longer need his weekly visits to the Three Star brothel in Monterey. The solution is as absurdly simply as it is unpalatable.

Jim Moore, who thrashes his wife and murders her cousin, is another of Steinbeck's nondescript male protagonists. Like Mike in **"The Vigilante"** and Peter Randall in **"The Harness,"** Moore's physical appearance remains shrouded. Nevertheless, Steinbeck's sketch of him evokes an aura of masculinity; his manly beard at age thirty and his purchase of a Guernsey bull contribute to this aura. Steinbeck describes Jelka, in contrast to Jim, with lavish detail. Sometimes she resembles an animal, with "eyes as large and questioning as a doe's eyes." She whimpers with pleasure at Jim's touch and whines like a puppy when he attacks her with a bull whip.

But it is not Jelka's apparent animal quality that separates her from Jim, (Jim realizes "that he could not get in touch with her in any way". Rather, culture and heritage divide the two. Only after Jim catches Jelka in an adulterous affair does he realize how wide this gap is, and then he quickly determines to narrow it. As a result, he alters what he considers the traditional role of a husband, and flogs Jelka. Robert Murray Davis suggests that Steinbeck focuses not on the physical action in the story, but on the psychological—specifically, "Jim's becoming a satisfactory husband and complete human being." In the end, Jim accepts principles foreign to his own—namely his father-in-law's counsel to physically abuse Jelka. Jim's changed behavior, though violent, suggests a certain humility and an understanding that his American way of doing things is not always the best. His slaying of her cousin, on the other hand, smacks of pure machismo.

Steinbeck's description of the shooting is remarkably graphic. With a few details he brings the scene into crisp focus: "Jim cocked the rifle. The steel click sounded through the house. . . . The front sight wavered a moment and then came to rest. . . . The gun crash tore the air. Jim, still looking down the barrel, saw the whole bed jolt under the blow." This passage illustrates the incarnation of a powerful emotion: the jealous husband's urge to kill his spouse's lover. The significance of the slaying is heightened since it seems to be Jim's way to vent his frustration over Jelka's foreignness. The cathartic effect of Jim's crime, therefore, is immense. No doubt judges for the O. Henry Memorial Award noticed this, and especially Steinbeck's breathtaking description of the crucial scene.

Generally recognized as an anomaly among Steinbeck's *Long Valley* stories, **"Saint Katy the Virgin"** represents a generic blend of the saint's life, beast fable, fabliau, and farce. Roark, a bad man who lives in the County of P—in the year 13—, tithes his depraved pig, Katy, to Brothers Paul and Colin. When Paul slips a cord through Katy's nose ring to lead her away, she takes a bite out of Colin's leg. Paul kicks Katy in the snout, increasing her ire. She chases both monks up a thorn tree, and waits underneath pacing back and forth. Paul soon lowers an iron crucifix and dangles it in front of her, which miraculously exorcises the devil from her. Upon arriving at the monastery with the redeemed pig, Paul and Colin are reprimanded by Father Benedict, since Katy—now a converted Christian—cannot be slaughtered. Katy's life henceforth becomes saintly. She heals the afflicted and blesses the multitudes, so that posthumously she is added to the Calendar of the Elect and her bones become holy relics able to cure female troubles and ringworm.

Most critics have questioned this odd addition to a collection of stories whose primary subject is purportedly the lives of Salinas Valley people during the 1930s. Among these tales which are homogeneous in milieu, a bawdy, farcical beast fable or saint's life does not seem to belong. Consequently, Joseph Fontenrose calls **"Saint Katy"** a "maverick in the collection." Brian Barbour, as noted above, says that the story's appearance in *The Long Valley* shows Steinbeck's "lack of critical judgment." And Warren French simply labels the tale "conspicuously different in content and tone." Why did Steinbeck include it? He did so, according to Sanford E. Marovitz, at the request of Pat Covici, then editor of Covici-Friede, the house slated to publish *The Long Valley.* Covici had no doubt been heartened by the rapid disappearance of the story's first edition printed privately as a monograph, "signed and limited to 199 copies." Since that monograph was so well

received, Steinbeck "willingly complied with his agent's request to bring the satirical tale back into print," a tale the author had "dashed off chiefly as an entertainment for himself."

Although Steinbeck placed **"Saint Katy the Virgin"** near the end of *The Long Valley,* he wrote it first (ca. May, 1932), more than a year before he composed his next story, **"The Gift"** (ca. June, 1933). Warren French suggests that **"Saint Katy"** may have existed even prior to 1932, "since it is written in the mannered, facetious style [Steinbeck] abandoned with the coming of the depression." Says French, the story also reflects an "attitude toward conventional religiosity" much like that expressed in *Cup of Gold* (1929) and *To a God Unknown* (1933). For like other Steinbeck stories whose title characters are animals, Katy (the pig) serves to point out the failings of humanity, especially religious hypocrisy. Through Katy, a profane, opportunistic side to monastic life shows through. Edmund Wilson underscores this point, saying that the result of the story "is not to dignify the animal . . . but to make human religion ridiculous."

The somewhat grotesque character, Roark, seems to be identified with this animal protagonist. Called by the narrator a "bad man," Roark transforms Katy from a docile piglet into a vicious sow. Both pig and master continue in their depraved ways until Katy's conversion, when Roark, too, is miraculously reformed: "From that day on, he was no longer a bad man; his whole life was changed in a moment." If Steinbeck meant anything by this identification between Roark and Katy, he neglected to develop it. Once Brothers Paul and Colin lead Katy to their monastery, Roark slips out of the story forever.

The brothers themselves are contrasting stereotypes of clergymen, a pairing to be found in Chaucer's *Canterbury Tales.* Paul (compare St. Paul) is an ascetic, idealized brother resembling the young clerk riding with Chaucer's pilgrims. Paul is a "thin, strong man, with a thin strong face and a sharp eye." Colin, fittingly, is a "short round man with a wide round face," who looks forward to "trying the graces of God" right here on earth. Like the identification between Roark and Katy, Steinbeck does no more than establish these contrasting traits between Paul and Colin. Marovitz suggests that Steinbeck may have changed "the emphasis and direction of his story as he wrote." This hypothesis, if correct, explains why seemingly important threads of the plot are introduced and then simply dropped—the Roark-Katy and Paul-Colin relationships, for example.

Marovitz offers three tentative allegorical readings of the tale: the first concerning topical issues in Monterey and Pacific Grove; the second national social and economic woes; and the third a veiled blast against organized religion. But whether the story is read as a beast fable or an allegory, or both, Steinbeck's satiric intent is clear. Institutionalism had been the target of his college satires, but in **"Saint Katy the Virgin"** he turns his attention from university administrators to the Christian clergy. Chief among his indictments is the clergy's tendency to ignore facts which contradict their view of reality. For instance, a "sow with a litter is nevertheless canonized as a virgin."

Even without the benefit of these thinly veiled jabs at the church, **"Saint Katy the Virgin"** is a humorous, earthy tale. Yet some readers have puzzled over the story, and found it irrelevant or even offensive. Speaking for them, Elmer Davis concludes: **"Saint Katy"** is a "burlesque hagiography which might better have been left in private circulation." (pp. 52-90)

> *R. S. Hughes, in his* Beyond the Red Pony: A Reader's Companion to Steinbeck's Complete Short Stories, *The Scarecrow Press, Inc., 1987, 164 p.*

Steinbeck on writing:

A man who writes a story is forced to put into it the best of his knowledge and the best of his feeling. The discipline of the written word punishes both stupidity and dishonesty. A writer lives in awe of words for they can be cruel or kind, and they can change their meanings right in front of you. They pick up flavors and odors like butter in a refrigerator. Of course, there are dishonest writers who go on for a little while, but not for long—not for long.

A writer out of loneliness is trying to communicate like a distant star sending signals. He isn't telling or teaching or ordering. Rather he seeks to establish a relationship of meaning, of feeling, of observing. We are lonesome animals. We spend all life trying to be less lonesome. One of our ancient methods is to tell a story begging the listener to say—and to feel—

"Yes, that's the way it is, or at least that's the way I feel it. You're not as alone as you thought."

Of course a writer rearranges life, shortens time intervals, sharpens events, and devises beginnings, middles and ends. We do have curtains—in a day, morning, noon and night, in a man, birth, growth and death. These are curtain rise and curtain fall, but the story goes on and nothing finishes.

To finish is sadness to a writer—a little death. He puts the last word down and it is done. But it isn't really done. The story goes on and leaves the writer behind, for no story is ever done.

> *John Steinbeck, in his "In Awe of Words," first published in* The Exonian *and later excerpted in* The Paris Review, *1969.*

John H. Timmerman (essay date 1990)

[*An American writer, critic, and educator, Timmerman has written extensively on Steinbeck's short stories. In the essay below, taken from his* The Dramatic Landscape of Steinbeck's Short Stories, *he provides an overview of Steinbeck's later and lesser-known short fiction.*]

Because Steinbeck expended such intense energy on short stories early in his career, one wonders why there are so few of them in the years that follow. However significant Steinbeck's short stories were for his development as an artist, critical attention has always focused primarily upon

his novels to the neglect of those stories. In retrospect, they may seem almost a literary diversion, a passing whimsy exercised with varying degrees of success over a short space of years and sporadically thereafter.

In actuality, of course, the stories were instrumental in his growth as an artist, and that fact by itself may explain the transition. It may also be argued that a number of the short stories, those collected in *The Pastures of Heaven* and those from 1934 inspired by the migrants, were either quasi-novelistic in conception or were anticipations of the novels. The stories may be seen, in this line of reasoning, as shorter manifestations of his essentially novelistic technique, a preparing ground for supposedly more fertile productions.

That response, however, is by itself insufficient. More satisfactory answers may be found, and they essentially respond to the fundamental question of why Steinbeck wrote the short stories in the first place.

One such reason was financial. His first two novels, *Cup of Gold* and *To A God Unknown*—assuming *The Pastures of Heaven* to be a collection of short stories rather than a novel—failed miserably as commercial ventures. Determined to make his way as a literary author, Steinbeck seemed nonetheless to face insuperable financial obstacles. Dependent to some degree upon his parents' stipend and Carol's meager income, money represented both artistic acceptance and independence for Steinbeck, and the sale of short stories seemed the likeliest avenue to a quick financial return. In 1934, Steinbeck entered a telling note in his ledger: "I must lay enough money aside so that the careful work can be done. And I must go on with these short stories for that purpose. There that's down. That must be followed."

When in later years he discovered large checks in his mail, the idea of the money in itself nearly overwhelmed him. In 1949 he dashed off **"His Father,"** and Elizabeth Otis immediately sold it to *Reader's Digest*. Steinbeck wrote her,

> You know darned well you done good with the little four page story. What a price! It is next best to Air Wick. Very good news.
>
> In the same mail with your letter, one from Ralph Henderson (Editor of *Reader's Digest*) assuring me that they bought the story because they liked it and not because of my name. Apparently you cut them deeply by asking for money as well as the honor of being published. In the light of this $2,500 for four pages—do you remember when you worked for months and finally got $90 for the longest story in the *Red Pony* series and forty for the shorter ones? I hardly made $1,000 on my first three novels.

But he never forgot the impoverished days. In 1949, he reflected, "I watched the postman with gleaming eyes this morning. Once long ago when a letter with a tiny check meant the difference between dinner and not, there was a long desert time and the postman got so ashamed that he walked on the other side of the street." One way to explain the transition from short stories to novels, then, lies in Steinbeck's growing financial independence, particularly with the startling sales of *Tortilla Flat.* Suddenly he had the financial freedom to consider longer works, to be written without the immediate pressure of financial need. The income introduced other problems, however. To George Albee, Steinbeck wrote of the crowds that had begun to harass him and the difficulty of finding quiet and leisure to write. Nonetheless, it should be clear that one reason Steinbeck wrote short stories was the prospect of quick remuneration, a reason obviated by the success of *Tortilla Flat* and subsequent novels.

Steinbeck had been writing, and telling, short stories since his youth. In one sense, the more focused work he started at Stanford University was a natural outgrowth of what he had been doing. But a second reason he turned his attention so intensely to short stories in the early 1930s was the prospect of recognition. As much as he lamented the publicity obtained by *Tortilla Flat,* it was something Steinbeck had deeply hungered for. The early years of obscurity and rejections seemed vindicated by that reception.

Short stories were indeed one way to garner recognition in the early 1930s. It is difficult for us in our age, when hundreds of little magazines struggle for survival, limping along on ever-dwindling pensions by universities and benefactors, to understand the immense popularity and prestige of the literary magazines of the 1930s. Short stories were the initiation rites into the fraternity of the famous, and popular acceptance assumed one's status as a genuine author.

Although he never experienced the financial rewards of some of his contemporaries writing short stories in the 1930s, Steinbeck did acquire recognition through them. Over the space of a year and a half, his stories appeared five times in the prestigious *North American Review.* **"The Murder"** was awarded the O. Henry Prize for 1934. Although he did not win it, he was considered for the Phelan Award in 1935.

Third, it is undeniable that the short stories were not artistic ends in themselves for Steinbeck, but part of a process of self-discovery. In them Steinbeck was solidifying his artistic aims, serving a kind of self-imposed apprenticeship. Those same aims—use of a recollected past, writing from experience, mastery of imagery patterns and narrative points of view—were, however, leading him beyond the short story into the world of the novel even as he mastered them. His deepening attraction to the labor unrest in mid-1934 could no longer find full expression in the short story. He needed a larger canvas to paint the needs and lives of these people. The work on *In Dubious Battle, Of Mice and Men,* and *The Grapes of Wrath* opened entirely new aesthetic arenas, and Steinbeck's athletic mind responded agilely to the challenge. In this respect, the training ground of the short stories served him well for the longer marathon of the novel.

We might also observe the fact that Steinbeck was a streaky writer, one easily consumed by a new project and quite willing to put behind him past efforts. He always seemed to have a new project in mind and dwelt little on projects once completed. Thus, while his interest was consumed by short stories for several years, it is not surprising

that he moved to another mode. The next great cycle was, of course, completed by *The Grapes of Wrath,* a work that drained every nervous and creative resource he had. In the journal he kept while working on *The Grapes of Wrath,* Steinbeck referred often to a "blind weariness" that limited his ability to work, or he would comment, "My nerves blew out a fuse and today I feel weak and powerless." In the white heat of writing, Steinbeck did not understand the word *moderation.*

The third great cycle culminated in *East of Eden,* a work begun far earlier than many have imagined. His interest in writing a history of his valley had been in his mind, really, since the early 1930s. In 1933, Steinbeck wrote Albee,

> I think I would like to write the story of this whole valley, of all the little towns and all the farms and the ranches in the wilder hills. I can see how I would like to do it so that it would be the valley of the world. But that will have to be sometime in the future. I would take so very long.

The essential trappings of *East of Eden,* the germ of the idea, may be found in that statement: to write a history of the valley, to have it represent a larger world, to spend a long period writing it. In 1944, Steinbeck announced his intentions to begin working on the novel: "Within a year or so I want to get to work on a very large book I've been thinking about for at least two years and a half. Everything else is kind of marking time." When he engaged the work on *East of Eden,* he often spoke of all his other work having been a kind of practice for this masterwork. The same idea appears in a 1946 letter to Carl Wilhelmson: "I'm working on a thing now that is giving me hell—a long novel. I want to take a long time with it. It seems to me that I have been rushing for five or six years, rushing as though I were trying to beat something." In 1948 Steinbeck was ready to do actual research for the novel. He wrote Paul Carswell, editor of the *Salinas-Californian,* for permission to consult his files. In April of 1948 he wrote Ed Ricketts of his growing excitement with the long project, and in 1949 he wrote Pascal Covici for "A Grey's [sic] Anatomy" and "a Pharmacopaea (can't even spell it)"— two of the works that were to be instrumental to the realistic and thematic details of the novel. Because of the combined effects of Ed Ricketts's death and the agonizing divorce from Gwyndolyn, his second wife, however, Steinbeck was unable to continue. Not until revitalized by his marriage to Elaine, his third wife, was he able to engage the work systematically, but the long progress of preparation, research, and writing demonstrate his complete absorption by a new project.

The fourth great cycle in Steinbeck's career centered upon his translation of *Morte D'Arthur.* In this case also, the project worked steadily, slowly, into every fiber of his nature until it became a consuming interest. Steinbeck announced his intentions in a November 1956 letter:

> I am taking on something I have always wanted to do. That is the reduction of Thomas Malory's Morte d'Arthur to simple readable prose without adding or taking away anything, simply to

put it into modern spelling and to translate the
obsolete words to modern ones and to straighten
out some of the more involved sentences. . . .

It was the very first book I knew and I have done
considerable research over the years as my work
will show. . . . I don't know any book save only
the Bible and perhaps Shakespeare which has
had more effect on our morals, our ethics and
our mores than this same Malory.

In one sense, *Travels with Charley in Search of America*
and *The Winter of Our Discontent* grew out of this central
interest. Both are studies of the moral character of the
present age, and Steinbeck often spoke of a wish to bring
the moral rigor of the Arthurian court to bear upon this
age.

In another sense, however, it can be argued that Steinbeck
never left off writing short stories. The six sections of *Of
Mice and Men,* so successfully adapted to the stage, may
be seen as six interlocking short stories. Each has an independent wholeness and unity. Similarly, many of the inter-
calary chapters of *The Grapes of Wrath* and *Sweet Thursday* may be seen as independent short stories, and in fact,
one outtake from *Cannery Row,* **"The Time the Wolves
Ate the Vice-Principal,"** was published independently as
a short story.

The story may have been well excised from the novel, for
even though the novel is surely one of the darkest in Steinbeck's canon, **"The Time the Wolves Ate the Vice-
Principal"** possesses a unmitigatedly violent and shocking
tone. *Cannery Row* is a novelistic probing of the dark, subconscious urges in humanity, based upon the metaphorical alliance with the sea and its violent subsurface world.
In the story, a pack of wolves appears in Salinas—not in
Monterey where the rest of the novel is set. They rampage
through the town, devouring what they can seize, including an old Airedale. They locate Mr. Hartley and rip him
to shreds on a woman's front porch, not even disturbing
her sleep. Here is a mob violence, enacted grimly and terribly while some local citizens merely sleep through it.

While this study will not consider those outtakes or inter-
chapters, designed as they were for the most part in connection with a larger novel, they do demonstrate a continuation of Steinbeck's ready facility for the short story.

This continued use of the short story in a larger context
may be most dramatically seen, however, in Steinbeck's
World War II journalism collected in *Once There Was a
War.* Constructed as a series of vignettes rather than as
straight journalism, the collection captures the lives of
characters in sharp, independent sketches much like his
short stories. Steinbeck's intention was to give the feeling,
the texture, of the war zone through stories. After recounting a sequence of little stories on the London bomb-
ings, he writes, "In all of the little stories it is the ordinary,
the commonplace thing or incident against the background of the bombing that leaves the indelible picture."
So too his task in this journalism: to give the stories that
leave an indelible imprint.

In 1943 Steinbeck was hired by the *New York Herald Tri-
bune* as a war correspondent, but prior to accreditation he
had to be cleared by the War and State departments. The
process was delayed considerably by charges of Steinbeck's sympathy to Marxist causes. Jackson Benson recounts the investigation at some length in *The True Adventures of John Steinbeck, Writer,* but one example, released under the Freedom of Information Act long after
Steinbeck's death, may indicate the difficulties Steinbeck
confronted:

In some ways the investigation was almost
funny. As John's widow commented after seeing
the report, "If John were only here to see this.
He would especially like the witness who reported that the 'subject' was usually badly dressed
and the agent who said he was a.k.a. Dr. Beck-
stein." But other aspects may have been ludicrous, though not very funny. Of the eight people interviewed, two didn't know him at all and
two had had barely any contact with him. In fact
the only really damaging personal report came
from one of those who had never met him, the
man who purchased the Los Gatos ranch. This
gentleman read Steinbeck's second-class mail
and found it "apparently communistic" and
"very radical." On the basis of the conditions in
the house when he bought it, the gentleman reported Steinbeck to be "very impulsive, eccentric, and unreliable socially."

Nonetheless, on June 3, 1943, Steinbeck departed on a
troop ship for England, the first stage of a remarkable adventure in his life and some remarkable, if overlooked,
writing collected in *Once There Was a War.* Sections of
this work have the immediacy and power of some of the
best war journalism:

The men slept in their pup tents and drew their
mosquito nets over them and scratched and
cursed all night until, after a time, they were too
tired to scratch and curse and they fell asleep the
moment they hit the blankets. Their minds and
their bodies became machine-like. They did not
talk about the war. They talked only of home
and of clean beds with white sheets and they
talked of ice water and ice cream and places that
did not smell of urine. Most of them let their
minds dwell on snow banks and the sharp winds
of Middle Western winter. But the red dust blew
over them and crusted their skins and after a
while they could not wash it all off any more.
The war had narrowed down to their own small
group of men and their own job. It would be a
lie to suggest that they liked being there. They
wish they were somewhere else.

Several of the pieces collected in *Once There Was a War*
have the narrative, thematic, and character unity that
would enable them to stand as independent short stories.
"The Cottage That Wasn't There" tells a tight little ghost
story through the mind and eyes of a weary sergeant. "A
Hand" provides a brief sketch of a wounded soldier with
a surprise ending. Big Train Mulligan appears several
times as a unifying character. And Mulligan serves as the
source for the one sketch published independently as a
short story under the title *The Crapshooter* in the Avon
publication *Various Temptations.*

Eddie the crapshooter always wins on Sunday, "a fact he

attributed to a clean and disinterested way of life." As he plays on the troopship, Eddie's pile grows steadily until he loses:

> "No," he said, "somepins wrong. I win on Sunday, always win on Sunday."
>
> A sergeant shuffled his feet uneasily. "Mister," he said. "Mister, you see, it ain't Sunday. We've went and crossed the date line. We lost Sunday."

Steinbeck concludes the story with a note, "Anyway, it's one of Mulligan's lies."

In the same way, other sketches might be considered short stories. For example, the delightful episode of McKnight's turkey in "Positano" could stand independently as a short story, as could "I Go Back to Ireland," a first-person account of Steinbeck's search for his ancestors, but told with the plotting and suspense of a short story. Another sketch commonly considered a short story is "Case of the Hotel Ghost—Or . . . What Are You Smoking in That Pipe, Mr. S?" Based upon a visit he and Elaine made to England in 1952, it was first published in the *Louisville Courier-Journal,* June 20, 1957, and later with some revisions in the London *Evening-Standard,* January 25, 1958. The story begins by comparing ghosts in England and Italy, and the narrator, who is Steinbeck speaking in the first person, undisguised by any narrative conventions, observes,

> Even I have—or had—my own shoddy ghost in London. It's an unlikely story, so preposterous on the face of it that I hesitate to put it down for an intelligent public. For my own peace of mind, I am glad my wife was with me when it happened. It gives one a feeling of mental security to know that someone else saw it too.

The narrative presence in the story tends to mark the piece as a journalistic document focusing upon a present experience rather than a short story evoking a fictional world. Actually it is a hybrid, with Steinbeck serving as undisguised narrator recounting journalistically a fictive event.

In the story the narrator and his wife return six years after the war to a hotel he stayed in as a correspondent before leaving to cover the Italian invasion. The narrator awakens at night dreaming of bombs. He tries to work in the morning but is distracted by his wife's increasing restlessness. They go to the White Tower for lunch, then walk back to the hotel to find "just a deep dark hole with rubble piled neatly around its edges." It is an effective little sketch, evoking well the disturbing emotional play of a postwar scene.

Story-like qualities mark this essentially journalistic piece, but good journalism will place a character in a setting, evoke a mood, have a plot of sorts. Nonetheless, the characters and place here are not fictional. The plot is a supposed event, but not a controlled sequence of events revealing a thematic purpose. The line between journalism and fiction is often a hazy one, meandering through gray areas that are not clearly defined. The safest judgment is that Steinbeck, as a fiction writer, wrote journalism that had many of the qualities of fiction.

It is also true, despite the very few short stories published after the *Long Valley* collection, that he wrote far more stories than he submitted for publication. He continued to write short stories, though several of them, as Jackson Benson noted, were "really just finger exercises" that underlined his frustration at times of acute stress in his life. Most intriguing of the short stories that failed to see publication is one that he wrote in the bleak time during his divorce from Gwyndolyn. Steinbeck wrote in an October 26, 1948, letter,

> Tonight I couldn't sleep and I wrote a little story that was so evil, so completely evil that when I finished it I burned it. It was effective, horribly effective. It would have made anyone who read it completely miserable. I don't mind evil if anything else is accomplished but this was unqualifiedly murderous and terrible. I wonder where it came from. It just seemed to creep in from under the door. I suppose the best thing was to write it and the next was to burn it.

Noting such facts as these—that the intensive period of early short-story writing achieved many of the ends Steinbeck wished, that he was indeed a streaky writer compelled by new projects, that there exists a story-like quality to nearly everything he wrote—one locates only a handful of short stories designed and written as such after *The Long Valley.* Nonetheless, written at a time when his artistic power was at its peak, they form an important part of Steinbeck's legacy.

[*The Forgotten Village* and **"The Miracle of Tepayac"**] seem at first entirely dissimilar works. *The Forgotten Village* was Steinbeck's first film script, a very slight work written quickly under pressure and finished on June 20, 1940. **"The Miracle of Tepayac"** is a retelling of the Image of Guadalupe story, its roots stretching back to 1531, written for the Christmas issue of *Collier's* in 1948. Nonetheless, fundamental similarities do exist. Furthermore, it is not improbable to label *The Forgotten Village* as a short story, if only in length. It is nearly the same length as any of Steinbeck's stories and only slightly longer than **"The Miracle of Tepayac."**

Although Steinbeck had visited Mexico during earlier years, his visits grew more frequent and his interest grew more intense during the 1940s. Mexico increasingly began to represent an escape and freedom for him. When he returned from his coverage of World War II in October 1943, he was physically and emotionally exhausted. However poor his condition, by January 11, 1944, he was on his way to Mexico again. He planned to work on *Cannery Row* and *The Pearl,* but work eluded him. The solace he was unable to find either in his work or in his marriage was sought in relentless travel, and over and over his travels led back to Mexico. The restlessness of spirit is mirrored in the relative shallowness of his work during this decade, in which he produced little that could be considered of major significance. Only *The Pearl,* thin volume that it is, can stake a fair claim to that significance.

Steinbeck's interest in Mexico during the 1940s is also reflected in his writing. Although *The Sea of Cortez* was a travel account of his voyage in the Gulf of California, loosely tied together with speculations on marine biology and the state of life, his first fictional piece with a Mexican setting was *The Forgotten Village*. It was an ill-fated filming venture, and by the time it was nearing completion Steinbeck had already distanced himself from it as much as he could. Although there were other Mexican works during the 1940s—*The Pearl, The Wayward Bus,* and *Viva Zapata!*—"**The Miracle of Tepayac**" closed the influence. The first work in many ways anticipates the last.

To say that *The Forgotten Village* is a story demonstrating the clash between ancient superstitions and spirituality versus technical knowledge and modern medicine is accurate, but also misleading. As he demonstrated in *Tortilla Flat*, Steinbeck was sensitive to the religious beliefs of people. While he loathed religion when it was used to keep a people under submission, Steinbeck considered it a warm and vital part of a people's way of life when it sprang naturally from their daily patterns of belief. The excessive superstition in *The Forgotten Village* is not there as the subject of satire or ridicule. This is the way people are, the way he found them.

The story opens with Juan Diego taking his pregnant wife, Esperanza, to the Wise Woman, Trini, who makes a prophecy about the child in exchange for a chicken. Trini's magic is severely tested, however, when the boy, Paco, suddenly becomes ill. According to Trini, the sickness is an evil in the air, and she tries to withdraw the evil spirit from Paco with an egg. But soon others in the village fall ill:

> Juan Diego went to see his friend the teacher, the only man in Santiago who had been to the outside world. And Juan Diego said, "You know many children are sick." "I know it," the teacher said. "They say it is in the air, the evil little spirits," Juan Diego said. "No, I think it is the water," the teacher said. "I think the germs are in the pueblo well. I can try to help, but I do not know enough. I can only try to help them." And he gathered his medicines and his books.

When the teacher confronts Trini, she exclaims, " 'What is this nonsense—these new things—these young men who tell their elders? You will kill the people with your new foolishness. This for your nonsense!' And she threw his medicines to the ground." Thus the essential conflict: the steadfast traditions rooted in a sense of superstition and magic and the introduction of knowledge and medicine.

But the teacher's practices are as ineffectual as Trini's. Paco dies during the night. Others, particularly the children, fall ill. When the possibility of a cure through inoculation is presented, the people protest: " 'We do not want horses' blood. Are we horses?' And another said, 'Truly, some of the children die and go to heaven. Perhaps it is intended that way. We do not like these new things.' " It falls upon Juan Diego, as the only believer in the efficacy of science to help his people, to take a letter to the authorities beseeching their aid. When the doctors do arrive to help, however, the people hide their children, refusing the help:

> The father was courteous, but he said, "We do not want horses' blood here." "But she will die

without the injection," the doctor warned. Ventura said, "Then she will die by God's will, not by horses' blood. You may not enter my house nor poison my children."

In desperation, the doctors treat the water at the village well, but Trini sees them doing so, and leads a revolt to have Juan Diego cast out of the village. Juan Diego returns to the doctor:

> "Do not worry about your sister—she will get well," the doctor said. "The teacher has medicine enough until our regular medical service truck gets back to the village. When the people see that your sister is well, they will accept the medicine. Do not blame them. It is the young people who will change them," the doctor said. "They come from the villages to learn, boys like you, Juan Diego, and girls. They learn not for themselves, but for their people. It will not be quick, Juan Diego; learning and teaching are slow, patient things."

The story tells of great loss, but also of great hope. A new generation will rise up to bring knowledge. The old ways will pass. Juan Diego of *The Forgotten Village,* then, is much the same as Juan Diego of "**The Miracle of Tepayac,**" as one who receives a great vision, is frustrated in fulfilling it, and ultimately perseveres.

"**The Miracle of Tepayac**" is based upon the legend of Our Lady of Guadalupe, in which the Virgin Mary's image was impressed upon a cloak to convince a bishop of her will. The image is still preserved today, kept behind bulletproof glass in the basilica of Our Lady of Guadalupe in Mexico City. Each year, approximately ten million pilgrims genuflect before the shrine, approaching to within twenty-five feet of the revered image. Jody Brant Smith describes the image in his historical study, *The Image of Guadalupe: Myth or Miracle?*:

> Her head is tilted to the right, her greenish eyes are cast downward in an expression of gentle concern. The mantle that covers her head and shoulders is of a deep turquoise, studded with gold stars and bordered in gold. Her hair is black, her complexion olive. She stands alone, her hands clasped in prayer, an angel at her feet.
>
> She is Our Lady of Guadalupe, a life-sized image of the Virgin Mary that appeared miraculously on the cactus-cloth tilma, or cape, of Juan Diego, an Aztec peasant, in 1531, a mere dozen years after Hernan Cortes conquered Mexico for the King of Spain. For four hundred and fifty years the colors of the portrait have remained as bright as if they were painted yesterday. The coarse-woven cactus cloth, which seldom lasts even twenty years, shows no signs of decay.

According to the earliest testimonies, preserved in the Aztec language, Juan Diego and his family were among the first converts to Christianity among the Aztecs. Steinbeck is faithful to the historical circumstance in the opening paragraphs of his story:

> The Spaniards came to Mexico with war and pestilence and ruin but they brought also the faith of Jesus Christ and his Mother Mary.

Many of the Indian people were baptized, and among the first of them Juan Diego and his wife Maria Lucia. They were humble people and they lived in the little town of Cuautilan, to the north of Mexico City.

For many years they had lived together in felicity. They had no children, so that their dependence on each other was very great. Their dwelling was a one-room hut of mud bricks, and they tended a garden and they were happy. Then one dawn Maria Lucia was feverish and at mid-morning her eyes were swollen and her breath labored. At noon she died.

According to the Aztec records, Juan Diego's first vision occurred on Saturday, December 9, 1531, as he left his village to hear mass celebrated in Santiago, which, incidentally, is also Juan Diego's home village in *The Forgotten Village*. While walking past the hill, Juan Diego hears his name called out of a bright light emanating from the top of the hill, a pattern in keeping with biblical theophanies in which God reveals himself in a vision of light and by calling the recipient's name.

Juan Diego is told by the Virgin that a temple should be erected at the hill of Tepayac. The implication is that religion belongs among the common people and is not the exclusive province of city officials. Juan Diego's beseeching of the bishop is rebuffed twice. The third time he brings a sign of the Virgin's will by carrying to the bishop a bouquet of roses of Castille, growing out of season, that he picked from the hill of Tepayac and carried in his cloak. When he unfurls the cloak, the roses are still fresh, and the Virgin's image appears in the weave of the cloth.

Although Steinbeck adds the fiction writer's touch to the legend by relaying the troubled emotions and the adamant persistence of Juan Diego in pursuing the Virgin's request, his rendition is completely loyal to the original. He refuses to pursue larger implications, ending the story with the character, Juan Diego, rather than the larger religious significance of the event:

> At Tepayac they raised a simple hermitage on the place where She had appeared, to serve until the temple could be fashioned. And Juan Diego built a new mud house near by and planted a garden. He swept out the chapel and cared for it until he died. He was very happy. And it is possible he did not know that through his heart Our Lady of Guadalupe had become the Holy Mother of his people.

In historical fact, the revelation was instrumental in the missionizing of Mexico. Jody Smith points out,

> News of the miraculous appearance of the Virgin's image on a peasant's cloak spread quickly throughout New Spain. Indians by the thousands, learning that the mother of the Christian God had appeared before one of their own and spoken to him in his native tongue, came from hundreds of miles away to see the image hung above the altar of the new church.
>
> The miraculous picture played a major role in advancing the Church's mission in Mexico. In just seven years, from 1532 to 1538, eight million

Indians were converted to Christianity. In one day alone, one thousand couples were married in the sacrament of matrimony.

Although the plots differ, a thematic parallel may be found between Steinbeck's first and last Mexican stories. Like Juan Diego of *The Forgotten Village*, Juan Diego in **"The Miracle of Tepayac"** receives a great vision—the one for the physical health of his people, the other for the spiritual health of his people. The first Juan Diego "walked through the village and he heard the talk at the well, heard how the children were sickening with the same pain as little Paco had. The women were frightened for the children." Responding to the suffering of his people, he engages his quest for help. The second Juan Diego's heart is also full with sorrow for the suffering of his people, and the Virgin tells him, "I wish that here on this bleak hill a temple may be built in witness of my love for your people. I have seen the suffering of your people and I have come to them through you." Both receive these visions from people in authority over them, and the authorities—the doctor and the Virgin—come from a great distance to direct the recipient. Both stories are thus predicated upon acts of grace. Both Juan Diegos must battle great odds and great skepticism of their visions to ultimately succor their people. Both persevere in the effort, overcoming the odds, and bring hope for the future.

It is interesting, furthermore, that both stories were written during periods when Steinbeck underwent intense periods of loss and bleakness. *The Forgotten Village* was written when the marriage to Carol was unraveling, **"The Miracle of Tepayac"** during the dissolution of his marriage to Gwyn. Both were written during periods of hectic busyness and personal depression. Both were written during periods of indirection in his artistry, when he was looking for a larger project that would satisfy his restlessness. Yet, both of them signal some larger hope, some elusive goal that at the time Steinbeck seemed capable of finding only in the fiction. And both locate that hope in the struggle of one man against an implacable universe. The stories were as much incarnations of Steinbeck's spirit as they were of Juan Diego's.

Steinbeck's acute disconsolation in the later 1940s grew out of and focused upon the dissolution of his marriage. To be sure, there were artistic concerns. His work of the 1940s had not been well received critically. *Cannery Row* especially had been devastated by reviewers. His editor and agents, moreover, were applying pressure for him to produce a "big book," another *The Grapes of Wrath*. Too much of his energy had been expended on quick writing and slight books. For a writer whose work was so closely allied with personal experience, feeling, and temperament, however, the artistic difficulties have to be linked with personal ones. In this case, the dissolution of the marriage with Gwyn was complicated by the fact that they had two children born of that marriage, sons Thom and John.

The final breakdown of the marriage, which had been unraveling almost from the beginning, occurred in a cruel combination of circumstances. On May 7, 1948, Ed Ricketts drove his old Packard down Cannery Row toward a blind railroad crossing and collided with the Del Monte

Express coming in from San Francisco. He died four days later, on May 11. After an agonizing flight to California, beset by long delays, Steinbeck arrived in Monterey shortly after his dearest friend died.

After the funeral and the deposition of certain personal items from the small estate, Steinbeck returned to New York. Jackson Benson reports,

> With the sense of timing that only someone with show-business experience could have developed, Gwyn confronted John upon his return from California and told him that she wanted a divorce. She gave familiar reasons: he was gone too much, and he was smothering her creativity. She added a new, more painful reason: she had not been in love with him for several years. The request for a divorce was not totally unexpected, but the combination of the two events together with the announcement that she had not loved him for years was devastating.

During the separation, Gwyn moved to Los Angeles with the children, and Steinbeck, once again, visited Mexico for much of the summer. Ostensibly he was to write about Zapata; in reality his life was a careening whirlpool of days clouded by alcohol and quick relationships. It was a self-destructive life, and one Steinbeck seemed to have little control over. From the romantic intensity of his love for Gwyn, he spun into a wasteland of unfettered passions. It was almost as if he were enacting Lancelot—losing his Guinevere, he went mad in the nightmare forests.

There is little reason to dwell on the peculiar cruelties of the divorce here, but the biographical details are essential to understanding the very brief short story, **"His Father."** It is a sketch that erupted viscerally from the reality of Steinbeck's life, especially his acute sense of failure as a father and the sense that he had abandoned his own sons.

Although Steinbeck was for the most part remarkably restrained about the situation in his letters to others, his concern for his children surfaces frequently. He could not, by any stretch of the imagination, have been considered a doting, careful parent to this point, but his love and concern for his boys was genuine. Now that too seemed threatened. Almost from the start of the marital breakdown, this large fear is present in his letters, and it intensifies whenever he thought about his periodic visits with them:

> My boys will be with me in another two weeks and I will be glad. I deeply resent their growing and me not there to see. That is the only thing I resent now. The rest is all gone. But imagine if you couldn't see your daughter for months at a time when every day is a change and growth and fascination.

For each visit, however, there was also the immediate prospect of renewed separation.

In one such letter, we are able to date the composition of **"His Father"** and observe it growing directly out of his life. To Bo Beskow on May 9, 1949, Steinbeck wrote,

> Three weeks ago I had a compulsion to go to New York to see my children and I did so think-

ing I was more well than I was. It struck me hard, all of the unhappiness arose again but it will not be very long before I am back where I was so that will be all right. My boys were well and healthy. I shall have them with me this summer and get to know them again.

> Coming home wrote three short stories and I don't know whether they are any good or not. It is long since I have worked in that form. I promptly tore up two of them because I am sure they were not very good and I don't have to put up with my own mediocrity any more.

The one short story he did not destroy was **"His Father,"** which two weeks later was purchased by *Reader's Digest* for $2,500.

The unnamed protagonist is a six-year-old boy identified only in the third person. (Thom Steinbeck was born August 2, 1944, and was not quite five when the story was written.) The narrator is omniscient, looking upon the boy's feelings as he wonders when his father will come home:

> He could feel Alvin [his chief tormentor] when he turned the corner two blocks away and a shuddering went over his skin. Alvin wouldn't say anything. None of the kids said anything, but it was in their eyes; it was always in their eyes looking out at him, and the look was shame, a burning, guilty shame. At first he had run away and stayed by himself, but you can't run away all the time and besides you get lonesome.

As his friends taunt him, excuses for his father flood his mind:

> "Where's your father?"

> What he should have said was, "He's away on a trip," but he didn't. The question caught him in the pit of his stomach up under his ribs. He could feel the question and he knew that it was pure cruelty. The kids weren't asking, they were telling, taunting, hurting, and that was the way they wanted it.

The jeers of the children rise to a tormenting chant: "Where's your father—where's your father—where's your father?" And the boy finally responds, "He's in the house. . . . He's in there working. He don't have to come out if he don't want to." This is the wish, that his father will be in the house. His emotions have shaped the reply, not reality.

The boy's anguish reaches a climax one day when he can no longer avoid Alvin. He sees him coming down the street and thinks of hitting him. But then, "There was a curious feeling—a strange explosive feeling in his chest. Something half noticed had caused it. He looked sharp right and it was true. His father had turned the corner and was walking rapidly toward him with his shoulders swinging the way they did." In this case, the father arrives at the right moment, a heroic deliverer. The boy screams out, *"He's here! You want to see him?"*

"His Father" is no more than a character sketch, but Steinbeck manages to penetrate the boy's yearning so deeply in so few words that the story also evokes a sense of profundity. The anguish is genuine, but relief over the father's return allays it. The boy dares outrage and defiance with his father beside him. He is no longer alone in the world. Totally missing from the story, its third person intimate point of view limiting our knowledge to the boy, is the father's reaction. One can't help wondering at his anguish as the boy screams out, "He's here! You want to see him?"

The turbulence of the 1940s, both personally and artistically, was laid to rest by Steinbeck's marriage to Elaine and his writing of *East of Eden.* Both were restorative for him. He had achieved the "big" book that he had been thinking of for much of his life, and his personal life achieved a measure of stability. That return to stability may also be seen in his lovely short story **"The Summer Before,"** with its evocation of youth and Salinas.

Steinbeck had by now irrevocably moved his home from California, and even though he realized that fact fully in *Travels with Charley,* it was impossible ever to fully remove it from his heart. This was the land that had birthed and nourished him, launched his career, and compelled so many stories. In a series of articles by famous authors on their home towns, *Holiday* published **"Always Something to Do in Salinas"** in June 1955. **"The Summer Before"** had been published the month prior, in the May 1955 issue of *Punch,* but there is a connection in tone and setting between the two pieces.

"Always Something to Do in Salinas" is one of those warm pieces of nostalgia, but one tempered here by Steinbeck's inveterate realism. He points out the darker side of life in Salinas as well as the bucolic:

> Salinas was never a pretty town. It took a darkness from the swamps. The high gray fog hung over it and the ceaseless wind blew up the valley, cold and with a kind of desolate monotony. The mountains on both sides of the valley were beautiful, but Salinas was not and we knew it.

As he did so often in his fiction, here too Steinbeck probed that darkness, which lay just out of sight beneath surface appearances:

> I wonder whether all towns have the blackness—the feeling of violence just below the surface.

> It was a blackness that seemed to rise out of the swamps, a kind of whispered brooding that never came into the open—a subsurface violence that bubbled silently like the decaying vegetation under the black water of the Tule Swamps.

Among the stories of Salinas demonstrating this subsurface violence is that of Andy, who gives the fourth-grade teacher whom he loves his severed ear as a present.

"The Summer Before" is also a probing reflection. It begins with the bright wanderings of children on long summer days but uncovers a mystery that confounds them for days to come. It is a sensitively told and very moving story with a genuinely startling ending. In it we find many bits and pieces of Steinbeck's own life. For example: "My pony Jill, who was only a pony by courtesy, being half shetland and half cayuse, had grown a raggedy coat and her forelock was so long that she peered through it, and she was fat from the spring grass so that we had hopes for a colt." The autobiographical nature of the story admits many of Steinbeck's boyhood friends—Glen Graves (who actually spelled his name *Glenn*), Jackie Berges, Ernie Wallet, Max Wagner. And then there is Willie Morton, the puzzling one, the son of a poor, single mother and the undeniable town bully.

It is a nice irony that the narrator's own champion in juvenile warfare is his kid sister Mary, for she has the gumption to tackle the narrator's antagonists and metes out to them a most unusual punishment:

> I had a secret weapon in my sister Mary who was younger and a girl. She was a rough little monkey with wild eyes looking out of tangled yellow hair. When I was very angry at a boy I would turn my sister Mary on him. She would then wait her chance, throw him down and kiss him, which cost him face and social position so that all he could do was to creep away until his shame evaporated.

The irony lies in the surprise ending, in which the tough little girl, Mary, is compared to the tough little boy, Willie Morton.

The commemorative nature of this semiautobiographical story gives many insights into Steinbeck's boyhood world. The recollection of those halcyon days of free and easy youth flows smoothly from the author's pen. It is the great temptation of an author to romanticize the past, particularly when, like Dylan Thomas, he has begun to understand,

> As I was young and easy in the mercy of his means,
>   Time held me green and dying
> Though I sang in my chains like the sea.

Under the wraps of this recollection, however, is the body of a potent short story—the revelation of Willie Morton, the toughest kid in town.

Willie has a reputation for being just plain mean, a true tough guy. It is nurtured in part by Willie's mother, a neurotic woman, we discover, who invests her lost husband in her child. The mother calls stridently from her doorway, "Willie—Oh! Willie, Where's my man?" The call cuts two ways: Where is her man who has forsaken her, and where is her man Willie? It is a trick of rhetoric, but also a cruel trick on Willie, as the story's ending reveals.

On one of the last days of summer the children plan a frankfurter roast by the river instead of their routine lunch of packed sandwiches. This is to be a day of freedom and frolic: "We knew we didn't have much more river time. We knew we had to go to school and suddenly we knew there were some good things about being a little kid. We'd always hated it before." Once at the river, the gang enjoys all the festivities of youthful indulgence: "Max got out a great big cigarette butt he had found and lighted it with a burning stick and passed it around. Everybody got a puff but Glen. He said it was a sin and he wouldn't do it. We knew then he was going to tell on us but we couldn't hit him until after he told." This a Mark Twain kind of reminiscence, sweetly calling forth the innocent evils of youth.

After a satisfying round of smoking, the gang decides on an end-of-season swim in the Salinas river: "We took our time getting our clothes off. Mary had to swim in her pants because she was a girl. Nobody told her she had to. She was just a girl and that's what they do." Willie, however, refuses to swim, watching from the bank as the boys tease him. Finally Willie jumps in with all his clothes on.

Under the river's calm surface, traps lurk. Old limbs of fallen trees still reach out to snag the unwary. One has to know the safe spots. Willie does not. The boys spot Willie underwater with the straps of his overalls snagged on a branch of sunken cottonwood. Mary climbs on the pony to get a Japanese farmer working nearby: "The Jap waded out and leaned down and pulled and yanked. Willie's overall strap broke and his pants came off. The Jap carried him out and laid him on the sand." Only then does the gang discover that Willie Morton, meanest boy in town, the one called "Willie, my man" by his mother is in fact a girl.

The revelation comes with a sharp kick of surprise because expectations have been so carefully prepared otherwise. But throughout the story, Steinbeck has laced clues:

> She called Willie her man—her only man. She would grab him and hug him and her face would be hungry and angry.

> She was crazy on the subject of toilets. Didn't want any two of us to go at once. She said it was dirty.

> We knew he was a poor kid and so we tolerated him perhaps more than we would have if he had been normal. But we knew he was strange just by the way he stood off and looked at us.

"The Summer Before" is a poignant little piece, wistfully evocative, touched by deft description and a fidelity to the child's point of view. It nicely captures Steinbeck's yearning for a simpler time now long past, receded into the well of memory. But those times, in retrospect, were really not so simple or sweet. Then too, there was anguish and turmoil. That realization is perfectly captured in the awful torment of Willie Morton, desperately playing a game his mother had designed for him.

Steinbeck's initial interest in the detective story was purely commercial. The year 1930 had placed him at artistic crossroads. One direction he took, albeit tentatively, was the hasty drafting of **"Murder at Full Moon by Peter Pym,"** a work assessed by Jackson Benson as "Jungian-flavored mumbo jumbo." Wavering unsteadily among the comic burlesque, the trappings of rational analysis of clues, and some fog-wrapped marshlands of the hypothetical Cone City, the work is a hodge-podge of formula fiction. But formula fiction needs some artistic control as well, and **"Murder at Full Moon"** has little. The experiment itself, however, was significant to Steinbeck. At least it steered him away from one direction this crossroads to his life may have pointed him. Henceforth he would write his own stories. Nonetheless, for nine days in late 1930,

and for a few months of attempted sales thereafter, the mystery story exercised a powerful tug on his imagination.

Steinbeck first announced the work, and his effort to write it to pay off a debt, in a December 1930 letter to Amasa Miller, who was informally acting as his agent. Observing the people "do not want to buy the things I have been writing," Steinbeck confesses that "to make the money I need, I must write the things they want to read." Steinbeck cautions Miller that the manuscript might make him sick and goes on to describe it:

> It was written complete in nine days. It is about sixty two or three thousand words long. It took two weeks to type. In it I have included all the cheap rackets I know of, and have tried to make it stand up by giving it a slightly burlesque tone. No one but my wife and my folks know that I have written it, and no one except you will know. I see no reason why a nom de plume should not be respected and maintained. The nom de plume I have chosen is Peter Pym.

> The story holds water better than most, and I think it has a fairish amount of mystery. The burlesqued bits, which were put in mostly to keep my stomach from turning every time I sat down at the typewriter, may come out.

Miller peddled the manuscript around, hoarding the rejections, which he would send to Steinbeck in a lot from time to time. By June Steinbeck was wondering about the fate of the manuscript: "On what grounds was the murder story rejected? Was it the sloppiness of it or just that it wasn't a good enough story? Do you think there is the least chance of selling it?" At the same time, Steinbeck was beginning contact with Mavis McIntosh for her to represent him. He listed **"Murder at Full Moon"** as one of the possible works for her to consider, adding, "The quicker I can forget the damned thing, the happier I shall be."

"Murder at Full Moon," however derogatorily Steinbeck himself spoke of it, represented more than a simple commercial effort to peddle a story. In the 1930s, detective stories experienced a heyday of popularity, rivaling westerns and romance confessionals for a share of a huge audience. It seemed an easy commercial ploy, this writing of a formula piece for a quick market. But Steinbeck left his own peculiar impress on the story, not allowing it to be pure detective, nor pure gothic, nor yet again pure burlesque. In January 1933, still with the idea of peddling **"Murder at Full Moon,"** he wrote Mavis McIntosh, "We live in the hills back of Los Angeles now and there are few people around. One of our neighbors loaned me three hundred detective magazines, and I have read a large part of them out of pure boredom. They are so utterly lousy that I wonder whether you have tried to peddle that thing I dashed off to any of them. It might mean a few dollars." Not long thereafter he crafted his short story, **"The Murder,"** which won the O. Henry Prize for 1934.

Perhaps the primary influence upon Steinbeck in composing **"Murder at Full Moon"** was not the 300 detective magazines he read, but the first master of the genre, Edgar Allan Poe. The pseudonym for the story is, of course, a combination of Dirk Peters and Arthur Gordon Pym, but beyond that there is something about the logic of the detective story, the cerebral triumph over emotional torment, that was deeply appealing to Steinbeck in the early 1930s and again in the 1950s. By 1920 Steinbeck had read several of Poe's works, including "The Murders in the Rue Morgue" and "The Purloined Letter." While it would be patently unfair to call Steinbeck a champion of the detective story, after the dismal experience of **"Murder at Full Moon"** and the decidedly low view of the genre he evidenced in later years, the influence resurges again in the construction of **"The Affair at 7, Rue de M———."**

"The Affair" was written in May 1954, when Steinbeck was living in Paris. France had by now replaced Mexico as his favorite retreat abroad, and he had decided to write for the French papers after they had demonstrated an avid interest in his work. In a May 27, 1954, letter he wrote of having "made a good start on my first short story of the series." and within two weeks wrote of having completed two pieces. **"The Affair,"** originally published as **"L'Affaire du l'avenue de M———"** in *Figaro* (August 28, 1954), was published under its present title in *Harper's Bazaar* (April 1955).

"The Affair" may be built on the foundation of a mystery, modeled as it is in tone upon Poe's "The Murders in the Rue Morgue," but it grows quickly into farce. Appropriately for the Poesque ratiocinative detective, the narrator is at first detached from the events: "I had hoped to withhold from public scrutiny those rather curious events which have given me some concern for the past month."

Steinbeck receiving the Nobel Prize in Stockholm, Sweden in 1962.

The narrator uses refined diction uncharacteristic of Steinbeck, punctuated by such French words as *arrondissement* and *bizarrerie.* With the dispassionate calm of the empiricist, the narrator says, "I shall set down the events as they happened without comment, thereby allowing the public to judge of the situation."

This detached, rational tone changes dramatically several paragraphs into the story. The sentence describing the narrator's son John is pure Steinbeck, both in the nature of the boy (John IV was born on June 12, 1946, and like the character was eight years old) and the language used to describe him: "If one must have an agency in this matter, I can find no alternative to placing not the blame but rather the authorship, albeit innocent, on my younger son John who has only recently attained his eighth year, a lively child of singular beauty and buck teeth." From this point on the narrator and Steinbeck seem to fuse; pretenses are for the most part set aside, and a slapstick plot abetted by puns and asides develops. The narrator happens to be a scholar working on an essay, "Sartre Resartus," a pun on Carlyle's *Sartor Resartus* and French existentialist Jean-Paul Sartre. When father and son examine the blob of bubble gum which is now chewing the boy, the narrator observes, "I regarded it with popping eyes."

The plot balloons into pure farce. The boy, who is inordinately fond of bubble gum, has to do without his addiction while living in France. However, a visiting friend brings a new supply, and once again, "The jaws were in constant motion, giving the face at best a look of agony while the eyes took on a glaze like those of a pig with a recently severed jugular." This particular wad takes on a life of its own. It lodges in John's mouth, not like an alien invader but like a friend come home, pulsating there like a primitive heartbeat. The subject of the detective's analysis is the remarkable life-form of this bubble gum:

> "I must think," I said. "This is something a little out of the ordinary, and I do not believe it should be passed over without some investigation."
>
> As I spoke a change came over the gum. It ceased to chew itself and seemed to rest for a while, and then with a flowing movement like those monocellular animals of the order Paramecium, the gum slid across the desk straight in the direction of my son.

To this task the narrator bends all of his considerable intellectual powers.

In the development of this farce, which as a genre is generally free from ethical investigation, one curious moral interpretation enters that has implications beyond the story. The narrator studies the blob under a microscope, examining it physically but also spiritually. In terms of Steinbeck's earlier distinction between nonteleological and teleological experience, the narrator is forced to consider the *why* and *how* of this phenomenon. He cannot remain the objective observer when the life of his son is threatened:

> The background I had been over hurriedly. It must be that from constant association with the lambent life which is my son, the magic of life had been created in the bubble gum. And with

life had come intelligence, not the manly open intelligence of the boy, but an evil calculating wiliness.

How could it be otherwise? Intelligence without the soul to balance it must of necessity be evil. The gum had not absorbed any part of John's soul.

The comment also applies to Cathy Ames of *East of Eden,* another soulless intelligence, and therefore evil.

The story does not linger over such speculations, however. Firing up his pipe in the manner of Poe's narrator in "The Murders in the Rue Morgue," this narrator also puffs his way to a conclusion. He glues the blob to a dish, where it dies a prolonged death, and then buries it in the garden:

I am now in the seventh day and I believe it is almost over. The gum is lying in the center of the plate. At intervals it heaves and subsides. Its color has turned to a nasty yellow. Once today when my son entered the room, it leaped up excitedly, then seemed to realize its hopelessness and collapsed on the plate. It will die tonight I think and only then will I dig a deep hole in the garden, and I will deposit the sealed bell jar and cover it up and plant geraniums over it.

"The Affair at 7 Rue de M———" is a delightfully farcical piece. It is in the pattern of *Sweet Thursday* and the novel written at this same time, *The Short Reign of Pippin IV.* Farce may indeed entertain serious matters, as *Sweet Thursday* does in the relentless loneliness of Doc. But for all its broken tone, cluttered structure, and narrative posturing, **"The Affair"** is simply a pleasant piece of diversionary reading—rather as detective stories were for Steinbeck.

His other quasi-mystery story, **"How Mr. Hogan Robbed a Bank,"** however, is quite a serious matter. This unusual story turns the expected trappings of the crime story upside down. That, in part, accounts for its peculiar charm and its salient moral theme. Steinbeck selects as protagonist an unassuming grocery store clerk, a man so plain and common that he blends easily into the background of the grocery shelves like one more piece in trade—which he is in a sense. But this unpretentious little man hatches a grand scheme to rob the bank next door. It is all so easy when planned carefully. Mr. Hogan's cardinal rule is, "To successfully rob a bank, forget all about hanky-panky."

That ordinariness of Mr. Hogan and his idea, right down to the split infinitive of his rule, is balanced artistically by close attention to detail. From the first sentence—"On the Saturday before Labor Day, 1955, at 9:04 ½ A.M., Mr. Hogan robbed a bank."—precision of detail marks the narrative. The opening paragraph describes the Hogan family like a fact sheet on the police blotter, where Mr. Hogan's name will never appear. Throughout the heist, detail governs every step. At the precise moment, Mr. Hogan prepares his mask, a ludicrous touch of Disneyland but a fitting one for the thematic development:

At ten minutes to nine, Mr. Hogan went to a shelf. He pushed a spaghetti box aside and took down a cereal box, which he emptied in the little closet toilet. Then, with a banana knife, he cut

out the Mickey Mouse mask that was on the back. The rest of the box he took to the toilet and tore up the cardboard and flushed it down. He went into the store then and yanked a piece of string loose and tied the ends through the side holes of the mask and then he looked at his watch—a large silver Hamilton with black hands. It was two minutes to nine.

This is a thoroughly ordinary person exercising an extraordinary plot.

Steinbeck supplies other details testifying to the precision of the exercise, for that is essentially what it is, somehow divested of moral significance: "Mr. Hogan opened the charge account drawer and took out the store pistol, a silver-colored Iver Johnson .38. He moved quickly to the storeroom, slipped off his apron, put on his coat, and stuck the revolver in his side pocket." The entire act is completed, Steinbeck tells us, by 9:07 ½. Only after the crime do the details begin to haze a bit: "It was 9:05, or :06, or :07, when he got back to the brown-shingle house at 215 East Maple." Mr. Hogan is back to his routine now; life slips into its informal way.

The story, however, leaves a jarring sense of moral dislocation. While Mr. Hogan's son John is winning honorable mention in the "I Love America" contest, Mr. Hogan executes his bank heist, untouched by any moral recrimination. The many stylistic parallels between **"How Mr. Hogan Robbed a Bank"** and *The Winter of Our Discontent* have been thoroughly analyzed, but it should also be clear that the moral concerns that sparked the novel are implicit in the short story. There is this important difference between the two: While Mr. Hogan snaps two five-dollar bills off his pile of $8,320 as gifts for his children, and thereby allows life to go its way, Ethan Hawley's moral debentures are called in at the expense of his life. For Mr. Hogan, we have no *why,* no motivation for the action. It can be done, so he does it. His is a thoroughly nonteleological action. Any moral speculation comes from the reader, not from the plot. For Ethan Hawley, however, the *why* becomes a roar of confusion. His life is a crooked path that wanders inevitably to the cave by the sea. The moral concern threads through every strand of the novel.

While living abroad, Steinbeck had placed himself in a unique perspective from which to view his own country. Once apart from it, he grew increasingly critical of it. The sense of America's moral failure becomes acute during his last decade and forms the artistic underpinnings of his late work. His letters too are increasingly marked by his concern. To Pascal Covici in July 1961, he wrote,

Through time, the nation has become a discontented land. I've sought for an out on this—saying it is my aging eyes seeing it, my waning energy feeling it, my warped vision that is distorting it, but it is only partly true. The thing I have described is really there. I did not create it. It's very well for me to write jokes and anecdotes but the haunting decay is there under it.

Well, there was once a man named Isaiah—and what he saw in his time was not unlike what I have seen, but he was shored up by a hard and durable prophecy that nothing could disturb. We have no prophecy now, nor any prophets.

What is merely implicit in **"How Mr. Hogan Robbed a Bank"** becomes increasingly explicit as Steinbeck donned the mantle of Isaiah and proclaimed a message of moral failure to his own nation.

That message is treated allegorically in his last pure short story, **"The Short-Short Story of Mankind: An Improbable Allegory of Human History Compressed for a Very Small Time Capsule."** Steinbeck believed that the nation had sunk into a quagmire through moral devolution: Values had been replaced by a rage for things; the bank vault had become the modern Bible; the aim of the church, as in *The Winter of Our Discontent,* had become power over humanity.

This devolution is traced allegorically in **"The Short-Short Story of Mankind."** As an allegory of humankind, it begins in the early age of humanity: "It was pretty drafty in the cave in the middle of the afternoon. There wasn't any fire—the last spark had gone out six months ago and the family wouldn't have any more fire until lightning struck another tree." In the cave a family quarrels over a chunk of mammoth meat. Here is the urge that can spin out of control: From the start humans have focused upon individual rather than corporate needs. Selfishness conflicts with the essential action of morality—the setting aside of self for the larger interests of the corporate body.

The cave dwellers see people move in down in the copse. They are fearful of and instinctively loathe these foreigners. Yet, the foreigners have some interesting attributes. For one thing, they eat better than the cave dwellers. Son Joe asks, "Pa, why don't we join up with those tree people? They've got a net kind of thing—catch all sorts of animals." And his father, old William, replies, "They're foreigners, that's why. They live in trees. We can't associate with savages. How'd you like your sister to marry a savage?" Joe responds, "She did!"

What begins as a battle of cravings and prejudices naturally develops into a religion in order to sanctify those very cravings and prejudices. The cave dwellers kill Elmer for being so different as to build a house, but when they move in and realize its advantages, they decide to make him a god: "Used to swear by him. Said he was the moon."

At this point the narrator steps in to comment, "You can see from this that things started going to pot right from the beginning. Things would be going along fine—law and order and all that and the leaders in charge—and then some smart aleck would invent something and spoil the whole business." The comment is redundant to the allegory itself, for the point is clear enough:

In time the people enter a new stage in human evolution and moral devolution. Wherever a group of people locate and begin to enjoy a time of prosperity, a leader of the people emerges. Here "Strong Arm Bugsy" takes over, a mix of ruthless dictator and 1920s gangster who ardently believes that might makes right. And the people are an easy mark for him: "By now the elders had confused protection with virtue because Bugsy passed out his surplus to the better people. The elders were pretty hard on anybody who complained. They said it was a sin." Thus the people have developed the religion of politics; the greased palm is raised to hail the leader. Any dissenting voice is drowned out by those proclaiming that dissent is a sin.

Bugsy turns any moral concept of ruling on its head. Instead of the leaders being responsible to the welfare of the people, the people become responsible to the welfare of the ruler. Bugsy insists that it is the task of the people to protect him. Perhaps no other political concern was so keen for Steinbeck as this conflict between public welfare and personal gain. It roots in his work among the migrants in the 1930s and flowers actively in his political involvement in the 1950s and 1960s. Louis Owens describes one case in point—Steinbeck's attitude toward Richard Nixon.

> Nixon would bring about his own downfall, Steinbeck prophesied, declaring, "Perhaps it is an accident that the names are the same—but the theme of *Richard III* will prove prophetic." It is surely a painful awareness of the political cynicism Steinbeck saw in both Nixon and Joseph McCarthy that informs the dark side of *The Short Reign of Pippin IV,* and just as surely when Steinbeck chose his title for *The Winter of Our Discontent* from the play featuring literature's most famous deep dissembler, he was thinking of Nixon.

But Steinbeck's contempt was not reserved for Nixon alone. Indeed, all of Washington seemed to have sunk into a murky world where the true values of government had been lost. Steinbeck's letters over a half-dozen years insistently announce his judgments. To Adlai Stevenson on November 5, 1959, he wrote,

> Back from Camelot, and, reading the papers not at all sure it was wise. Two first impressions. First a creeping, all-pervading, nerve-gas of immorality which starts in the nursery and does not stop before it reaches the highest offices, both corporate and governmental. Two, a nervous restlessness, a hunger, a thirst, a yearning for something unknown—perhaps morality.

And to James S. Pope on March 28, 1960, he wrote,

> Maybe the country has been in as bad a state before but the only times I can think of are the winter of Valley Forge and the glorious days of Warren Harding. The candidates are playing them so close that they have Ace marks on their shirt fronts. The mess in Washington now resembles a cat toilet in Rome.

Such concerns also surround the allegorical testament of **"The Short-Short Story of Mankind."** But what vindicates the moral dissolution in the mind of the people? The Gospel of Free Trade. So too in the story. A kind of free trade capitalism arises, but only after the man who thought of it is hanged head down over a fire. Bugsy himself assesses the reaction of the people: "Makes folks restless—why, it makes a man think he's as good as the ones that got it a couple of generations earlier." The essence of the Gospel of Free Trade is the belief in feeling good. If a deed, however dark, engenders prosperity, it must be good. Based upon this philosophy, the community expands to a nation predicated upon capitalism. The expansion is stopped by natural barriers, but missiles are invented to overcome those barriers. Once more the narrator, who cannot quite leave his allegory alone, intrudes:

> When people are finally forced with extinction, they have to do something about it. Now we've got the United Nations and the elders are right in there fighting it the way they fought coming out of caves. . . . It'd be kind of silly if we killed ourselves off after all this time. If we do, we're stupider than the cave people and I don't think we are. I think we're just exactly as stupid and that's pretty bright in the long run.

"The Short-Short Story of Mankind" is a rather bleak piece, the story of humankind viewed through a jaded eye. In an odd way, however, it may be seen as an outgrowth of Steinbeck's two quasi-detective stories. At its best, the detective story demonstrates the logical progression of human actions—even the most grisly and macabre, and the supersession of logic over emotions through the one who solves the case. **"The Short-Short Story of Mankind"** may well represent the logical consequence Steinbeck perceived of the emotional dispassion and the unflinching immorality in **"How Mr. Hogan Robbed a Bank."** Like the narrator in **"The Affair at 7 Rue d M———,"** Steinbeck examines the modern moral temperament and discovers that he can neither throw it away nor bottle it up and bury it. The little allegory here shows how immorality can possess a people, so that every step in humanity's evolution as a race is accompanied by a moral devolution in spirit. (pp. 245-80)

> *John H. Timmerman, in his* The Dramatic Landscape of Steinbeck's Short Stories, *University of Oklahoma Press, 1990, 333 p.*

FURTHER READING

Bibliography

Hayashi, Tetsumaro. *A New Steinbeck Bibliography: 1929-1971.* Metuchen, N.J.: Scarecrow Press, 1973, 225 p.
Standard bibliography of primary and secondary sources.

———. *A New Steinbeck Bibliography: 1971-1981.* Metuchen, N.J.: Scarecrow Press, 1983, 147 p.
Lists bibliographies, biographies, whole book studies, collections of criticism, doctoral dissertations, and journal articles.

Biography

Benson, Jackson J. *The True Adventures of John Steinbeck: Writer.* New York: Viking Press, 1984, 1116 p.
Definitive biography. The volume includes numerous illustrations, a list of notes and sources, and a comprehensive index.

O'Connor, Richard. *John Steinbeck.* New York: McGraw-Hill Book Co., 1970, 128 p.

Standard biography that includes selected primary and secondary bibliographies.

Criticism

Astro, Richard. "Something That Happened: A Non-Teleological Approach to 'The Leader of the People'." *Steinbeck Quarterly* VI, No. 1 (Winter 1973): 19-23.
Maintains that because the "The Leader of the People" was written from a non-teleological viewpoint, the story excites "feeling and compassion only as a means toward comprehension and never toward the establishment of precise value judgements."

Benton, Robert M. "Realism, Growth, and Contrast in 'The Gift'." *Steinbeck Quarterly* VI, No. 1 (Winter 1973): 3-9.
Analyzes "The Gift" as a bildungsroman.

Davis, Robert Murray. "Steinbeck's 'The Murder'." *Studies in Short Fiction* 14, No. 1 (Winter 1977): 63-8.
Asserts that in "The Murder" Steinbeck focused on the psychological development of his characters rather than on plot or action.

Fensch, Thomas, ed. *Conversations with John Steinbeck.* Literary Conversations Series, edited by Peggy Whitman Prenshaw. Jackson: University Press of Mississippi, 1988, 116 p.
Collects numerous interviews from the 1930s through the 1960s.

French, Warren. *John Steinbeck.* New York: Twayne Publishers, 1961, 190 p.
Examines the allegorical, non-teleological, and transcendental characteristics of Steinbeck's work so as to "get people to read as carefully as they should these deceptively lucid works and not to dismiss them with second-hand generalizations."

Hayashi, Tetsumaro, ed. *A Study Guide to Steinbeck: A Handbook to His Major Works.* Metuchen, N.J.: Scarecrow Press, 1974, 316 p.
Collects critical essays on Steinbeck's major works, including *The Pastures of Heaven* and *The Long Valley.*

Hayashi, Tetsumaro, and Moore, Thomas J., eds. *Steinbeck's "The Red Pony": Essays in Criticism.* Steinbeck Monograph Series, No. 13. Muncie, Ind.: Ball State University, 1988, 38 p.
Includes essays by Thomas M. Tammaro, Mimi R. Gladstein, Roy S. Simmonds, and Robert S. Hughes, Jr. on each of the four stories in *The Red Pony* as well as an introductory essay by Warren French.

Hughes, R. S. *John Steinbeck: A Study of the Short Fiction.* Boston: Twayne Publishers, 1989, 218 p.
Comprehensive overview of Steinbeck's short fiction. Includes "analyses of individual stories, observations on story writing by [Steinbeck] himself, and a sampling of previously published criticism."

Levant, Howard. "John Steinbeck's 'The Red Pony': A Study in Narrative Technique." *The Journal of Narrative Technique* 1, No. 2 (May 1971): 77-85.
Examines the narrative technique in *The Red Pony,* stating: "[This volume] is a very early and a completely successful instance of the organic relationship between structure and materials which distinguishes Steinbeck's most important fiction."

May, Charles E. "Myth and Mystery in Steinbeck's 'The

Snake': A Jungian View." *Criticism* XV, No. 4 (Fall 1973): 322-35.

> Examines the leading female character in "The Snake" as a "psychological archetype instead of a psychologically abnormal individual."

McCarthy, Paul. *John Steinbeck.* New York: Frederick Ungar Publishing Co., 1980, 163 p.

> Chronologically arranged critical survey of Steinbeck's career in which McCarthy attempts to identify the origins of Steinbeck's moral vision.

Modern Fiction Studies, Special Issue: John Steinbeck Number XI, No. 1 (Spring 1965): 1-104.

> Issue devoted to Steinbeck including essays on both his novels and short stories.

Osborne, William R. "The Texts of Steinbeck's 'The Chrysanthemums'." *Modern Fiction Studies* XII, No. 4 (Winter 1966-67): 479-84.

> Compares the differences in punctuation, tense, spelling, and phrasing between the magazine and book versions of "The Chrysanthemums."

Owens, Louis D. "Steinbeck's 'Flight': Into the Jaws of Death." *Steinbeck Quarterly* X, Nos. 3-4 (Summer-Fall 1977): 103-80.

> Analyzes Steinbeck's treatment of "the fine and intangible line" between life and death in this story.

———. "Steinbeck's 'The Murder': Illusions of Chivalry." *Steinbeck Quarterly* XVII, Nos. 1-2 (Winter-Spring 1984): 10-14.

> Discusses the themes of isolation and illusion in what the critic calls the most difficult and perplexing story collected in *The Long Valley.*

Pearce, Howard D. "Steinbeck's 'The Leader of the People': Dialectic and Symbol." *Papers on Language and Literature* VIII, No. 4 (Fall 1972): 415-26.

> Examines Steinbeck's use of symbolism and imagery in this story.

Pellow, C. Kenneth. " 'The Chrysanthemums' Revisited." *Steinbeck Quarterly* XXII, Nos. 1-2 (Winter-Spring 1989): 8-16.

> Focuses on the mechanical and animal imagery in "The Chrysanthemums."

Peterson, Richard F. "The Grail Legend and Steinbeck's 'The Great Mountains'." *Steinbeck Quarterly* VI, No. 1 (Winter 1973): 9-15.

> Maintains that "The Great Mountains," more than any other story in *The Red Pony,* evinces Jody's increasing spiritual and emotional maturity.

Piacentino, Edward J. "Patterns of Animal Imagery in Steinbeck's 'Flight'." *Studies in Short Fiction* 17, No. 4 (Fall 1980): 437-43.

> Examines Steinbeck's use of animal imagery in "Flight."

Renner, Stanley. "The Real Woman Inside the Fence in 'The Chrysanthemums'." *Modern Fiction Studies* 31, No. 2 (Summer 1985): 305-17.

> Discusses common critical interpretations of "The Chrysanthemums" as a story that evinces Steinbeck's awareness of feminist issues, concluding that this story was "informed far less by feminist sympathies than by traditional 'masculist' complaints."

Satyanarayana, M. R. " 'And Then the Child Becomes a Man': Three Initiation Stories of John Steinbeck." *Indian Journal of American Studies* 1, No. 4 (November 1971): 87-93.

> Discusses "The Raid," "The Red Pony," and "Flight" as stories of male initiation with mythic elements.

Shuman, R. Baird. "Initiation Rites in Steinbeck's *The Red Pony.*" *English Journal* 59, No. 9 (December 1970): 1252-55.

> Utilizes the terminology in Mircea Eliade's *Rites and Symbols of Initiation* (1958) to assert that "*The Red Pony* is the chronicle of a modern initiation rite in which the boy, Jody, passes from the natural mode to the cultural mode."

Simmonds, Roy S. "The Original Manuscripts of Steinbeck's 'The Chrysanthemums'." *Steinbeck Quarterly* VII, Nos. 3-4 (Summer-Fall 1974): 102-11.

> Discusses the magazine and book versions of "The Chrysanthemums," stating: "It is my purpose . . . to suggest that the long-accepted view of Elisa as a wholly sympathetic character may possibly be open to question [and] to contend that a textual study of the original manuscript of the final version of the story makes it patently obvious that Steinbeck was obliged to tone down some of the sexual implications in the work to mollify the editors of *Harper's Magazine.*"

———. "The First Publication of Steinbeck's 'The Leader of the People'." *Steinbeck Quarterly* VIII, No. 1 (Winter 1975): 13-18.

> Compares the textual variations between the 1936 publication of "The Leader of the People" in the British magazine *Argosy* and the version that appeared in *The Long Valley.*

Steinbeck Quarterly V, Nos. 3-4 (Summer-Fall 1972): 64-126.

> Includes section devoted to the short stories in *The Long Valley.*

Sullivan, Ernest W., II. "The Cur in 'The Chrysanthemums'." *Studies in Short Fiction* 16, No. 3 (Summer 1979): 215-17.

> Asserts that Steinbeck used dog imagery in "The Chrysanthemums," particularly "the repeated association of unpleasant canine characteristics with the otherwise attractive Elisa Allen," to elucidate social and sexual relationships between the story's characters.

Sweet, Charles A. "Ms. Elisa Allen and Steinbeck's 'The Chrysanthemums'." *Modern Fiction Studies* 20, No. 2 (Summer 1974): 210-14.

> Attempts to identify the emotional motivations underlying Elisa Allen's frustration in "The Chrysanthemums."

Timmerman, John H. "Dreams and Dreamers: The Short Stories." In his *John Steinbeck's Fiction: The Aesthetics of the Road Taken,* pp. 58-72. Norman: University of Oklahoma Press, 1986.

> Maintains that *The Pastures of Heaven* and *The Long Valley* evince Steinbeck's artistic maturity.

Vogel, Dan. "Steinbeck's 'Flight': The Myth of Manhood." *College English* 23, No. 3 (December 1961): 225-26.

> Analyzes Steinbeck's mythical treatment of the male rite of passage in "Flight."

West, Philip J. "Steinbeck's 'The Leader of the People': A

Crisis in Style." *Western American Literature* V, No. 2 (Summer 1970): 137-41.

> Examines how Steinbeck's emphasis on the theme of the passing of the frontier in "The Leader of the People" transforms the story from an epic to an elegy.

Woodward, Robert H. "Steinbeck's 'The Promise'." *Steinbeck Quarterly* VI, No. 1 (Winter 1973): 15-19.

> States that "The Promise" can be read "both as one event in the development of Jody Tiflin's growing awareness of the complexities of experience that make up the novelette and as a single story with its own structural and thematic unity."

Work, James C. "Coordinate Forces in 'The Leader of the People'." *Western American Literature* XVI, No. 4 (Winter 1982): 279-89.

> Analyzes "The Leader of the People" within the context of the other stories collected in *The Long Valley* and as a metaphor of the "American character" as defined by John Mason Peck and Frederick Jackson Turner.

Additional coverage of Steinbeck's life and works is contained in the following sources published by Gale Research: *Concise Dictionary of American Literary Biography: 1929-1941; Contemporary Authors,* **Volumes 1-4, 25-28, rev. eds. [obituary];** *Contemporary Authors New Revision Series,* **Volumes 1, 35;** *Contemporary Literary Criticism,* **Volumes 1, 5, 9, 13, 21, 34, 45, 59;** *Dictionary of Literary Biography,* **Volumes 7, 9;** *Dictionary of Literary Biography Documentary Series,* **Volume 2;** *Major 20th-Century Writers;* **and** *Something about the Author,* **Volume 9.**

Robert Louis Stevenson

1850-1894

(Full name Robert Lewis Balfour Stevenson) Scottish short story writer, novelist, poet, essayist, and playwright.

INTRODUCTION

Stevenson is the versatile and imaginative author of classic works in several genres. Renowned for the adventure novels *Treasure Island* and *Kidnapped,* he is additionally known as a travel writer and author of children's verse. Stevenson also wrote stories and short novels that, according to Charles Neider, display his "personal charm, optimism during much serious illness, romantic tastes, vigorous manner, fondness for medievalism . . . , powerful narrative, lively detail and a pliant, resonant and beautiful if sometimes high-blown style."

Stevenson was born in Edinburgh and attended Edinburgh University. Although he wanted to be a writer, his father insisted that Stevenson be trained in a more secure profession, and he took a law degree in 1875. He rarely practiced, however: a restless nature and poor health ensured that Stevenson spent much of his life in search of adventure and a congenial climate. His wanderings supplied the basis for travel essays and afforded him insight into a variety of cultures. He settled in Samoa in 1889, and the folklore of the indigenous peoples and his observations of the effects of foreign colonization form the background of several of his best stories. Stevenson died in Samoa at the age of forty-four from a cerebral hemorrhage.

Jeffrey Meyers identified the principal themes of Stevenson's short fiction as "romantic love, rivalry and vengeance, passion and renunciation, the supernatural and the macabre, the temptation of the forbidden, the torments of conscience, the strain of savagery beneath the veneer of civilization, the influence of ancestry, the conflict between fathers and sons, the double or alter ago and the dual nature of man." Stevenson pursued these themes in works that range widely in time and setting. The first story published under his name, "A Lodging for the Night," appeared in 1877. This account of a sordid episode in the life of medieval French poet François Villon is regarded as a masterpiece of characterization, if historically inaccurate. Stevenson subsequently set a number of works in distant historical epochs. The romantic adventure "The Sire de Malétroit's Door," for example, takes place in France during the Hundred Years' War. Featuring a dauntless soldier, secret doorway, beautiful maiden, and forced marriage, this story has been interpreted by Meyers as "Stevenson's ironic commentary on the chivalric ideal."

Several of Stevenson's most famous works feature the horrific and supernatural, including *The Strange Case of Dr. Jekyll and Mr. Hyde,* "The Body-Snatcher," and

"Markheim." Supposedly based on a nightmare brought on by fever and narcotic drugs, *Dr. Jekyll and Mr. Hyde* may also have derived from accounts of Deacon Brodie. A historical figure contemporaneous with Stevenson's childhood, Brodie was a carpenter by day and violent criminal by night. Tradition has it that an article of furniture in Stevenson's childhood bedroom was constructed by Brodie and that a family servant told him of Brodie's crimes. In Stevenson's novella, the basically decent scientist Jekyll compounds a drug that transforms him into the villainous Hyde. The transformations begin to occur randomly, and ultimately Jekyll kills himself to stop Hyde's predations. This story has been interpreted variously as an allegory of the twofold nature of man, a moralizing tale about good opposing evil, and a satire about what can happen when cultural forces require individuals to suppress natural urges. Often seen as a didactic Victorian cautionary tale about the dangers of abandoning oneself to base instincts, *Dr. Jekyll and Mr. Hyde* escapes sensationalism through its controlled narrative: gruesome events are described after the fact by different observers. *The Strange Case of Dr. Jekyll and Mr. Hyde* has been the subject of many stage and film adaptations, and the term "Jekyll and Hyde" has entered common parlance, denoting a split in personality. "The Body-Snatcher" is an account of super-natural retribution befalling two medical students who rob graves and commit murder to obtain cadavers for dissection. "Markheim" is a tale of psychological horror whose literary antecedents include Fedor Dostoevsky's *Crime and Punishment* and *Notes from the Underground,* and Edgar Allan Poe's "Imp of the Perverse" and "William Wilson." The protagonist commits an evidently premeditated murder and then encounters a stranger who seems to know everything about him, including his crime. The nature of the mysterious stranger is often discussed by critics, who generally concur that he represents Markheim's conscience.

Several of Stevenson's short stories follow in the Scottish literary tradition established by Sir Walter Scott. These include "Thrawn Janet," a ghost story written in Scots that draws on traditional folklore; "The Merry Men," a sea tale; and "The Pavilion on the Links" and "The Tale of Tod Lapraik," adventure stories with detailed historical backgrounds. Although Stevenson himself expressed concern that these stories were too topical to interest a general readership, they are commended for their evocation of place and for the skill with which Stevenson contrasted English and Scottish language and culture. The stories "The Bottle Imp" and "The Isle of Voices" draw from the folklore of the South Sea Islands. "The Beach at Falesá," which also has an island setting, is unusual for Stevenson in that it is a work of literary realism. Stevenson himself called it "the first realistic South Seas story; I mean with real South Sea character and details of life," and it has been hailed as the first work of fiction by an English author to indict British imperialism in the South Seas. In such stories as "Providence and the Guitar" and "The Story of a Life," Stevenson drew on his own vagabond youth, wryly detailing the posing and fakery that can accompany a bohemian way of life.

After Stevenson's untimely death, his family issued editions of his letters and approved an official biography, by Graham Balfour, designed to sustain popular perception of Stevenson as a brave, talented, and somewhat fey invalid whose life and works were above reproach. Many early twentieth-century commentators reacted to this veneration with largely negative assessments of Stevenson's character and work alike. *Treasure Island* and *Kidnapped,* and the poetry in *A Child's Garden of Verses* remain popular with young readers, however, and for many years Stevenson was regarded chiefly as an author for children. Beginning in 1927, however, with G. K. Chesterton's critical biography *Robert Louis Stevenson,* more balanced assessments of Stevenson's life and works have appeared. Recognition of his achievements has included acknowledgment that Stevenson produced a number of classic works of short fiction.

PRINCIPAL WORKS

SHORT FICTION

New Arabian Nights 1882

More New Arabian Nights: The Dynamiter [with Fanny Van de Grift Stevenson] 1885
The Strange Case of Dr. Jekyll and Mr. Hyde 1886
The Merry Men, and Other Tales and Fables 1887
Island Nights' Entertainments 1893
The Body-Snatcher 1895
The Strange Case of Dr. Jekyll and Mr. Hyde, with Other Fables 1896
Weir of Hermiston: An Unfinished Romance 1896
The Story of a Lie, and Other Tales 1904
The Works of Robert Louis Stevenson. 32 vols. (short stories, novels, poetry, essays, dramas, letters, and prayers) 1925

OTHER MAJOR WORKS

An Inland Voyage (essays) 1878
Edinburgh: Picturesque Notes, with Etchings (essays) 1879
Travels with a Donkey in the Cévennes (essays) 1879
Virginibus Puerisque, and Other Papers (essays) 1881
The Silverado Squatters (autobiography) 1883
Treasure Island (novel) 1883
Macaire (novel) 1885
Prince Otto (novel) 1885
A Child's Garden of Verses (poetry) 1885
Kidnapped (novel) 1886
Memories and Portraits (essays) 1887
The Black Arrow: A Tale of the Two Roses (novel) 1888
The Master of Ballantrae: A Winter's Tale (novel) 1889
The Wrong Box [with Lloyd Osbourne] (novel) 1889
A Footnote to History: Eight Years of Trouble in Samoa (history) 1892
Three Plays: Deacon Brodie, Beau Austin, Admiral Guinea [with W. E. Henley; first publication] (drama) 1892
The Wrecker [with Lloyd Osbourne] (novel) 1892
Catriona: A Sequel to "Kidnapped" (novel) 1893
In the South Seas (essays) 1896

CRITICISM

The Rock (essay date 1886)

[*The following anonymous review appeared in* The Rock, *a publication of the Unified Church of England and Ireland. The critic considers* Dr. Jekyll and Mr. Hyde *as an allegory based on the theory of "the two-fold nature of man" that posits the presence of both good and evil in every person.*]

A very remarkable book has lately been published, which has already passed through a second edition, called ***Strange Case of Dr. Jekyll and Mr. Hyde***. . . . It is an allegory based on the two-fold nature of man, a truth taught us by the Apostle PAUL in Romans vii., 'I find then a law that, when I would do good, evil is present with me.'

We have for some time wanted to review this little book, but we have refrained from so doing till the season of Lent had come, as the whole question of temptation is so much more appropriately considered at this period of the Christian year, when the thoughts of so many are directed to the temptations of our Lord.

Our readers, however, must not understand us to mean that this is a religious book. The name of CHRIST we do not remember to have seen, and the name of GOD, we think, only appears once. As for texts, or quotations from the Word of GOD, such are conspicuous by their absence. Nevertheless, the book is calculated to do a great deal of good, not only to those who profess and call themselves Christians, but to those who are, in every sense of the word, true believers. Though there is nothing distinctively Christian about it, we hope none will suppose that we mean to imply that there is anything antagonistic to Christianity. The truth taught us by the Apostle, to which we have referred above, is one recognised by those outside Christian Churches. Every thoughtful Hindoo, Mahommedan, Buddhist, or Parsee recognises the fact of the dual nature of his composition—the higher and the lower. Among the heathen in all ages have ever been found some who, like one well-known classical writer, confessed that he approved of that which is good, though he followed that which was evil.

In the allegory with which we are dealing we are introduced to a Dr. JEKYLL, who was a well-to-do medical man of a very respectable type, pleasant and genial, but somewhat weak and yielding. Of the best of men it can always be said that there is about them an element of evil, whereas with the worst of men there is, if we can only discover it, an element of good—doubtless a relic of primitive man 'made in the image of God' before the fall of our ancestors. Dr. JEKYLL is no exception to the general rule, and he finds that mixed up with much that was good there was in his character a certain amount of evil. He discovers a medicine which is capable of separating his two natures into two distinct identities. By taking one dose he completely throws off all traces of his better self, and his lower nature asserts itself without any of the constraining influences of his higher nature being left. Not only was this the case with regard to his moral nature, but even his very appearance became so changed that no one could possibly recognise him. Consequently he assumes another name when the evil nature predominated, and called himself Mr. HYDE. Even the worst of men have something good in them, and consequently they do not appear to us so repulsive as Mr. HYDE, who had not a single trace of the better nature.

The allegory is good. How many men live out two distinct characters? To the outer world they are the honourable, upright men, with a good professional name, holding a respectable position in society, looked up to and spoken well of by all their neighbours. Within, however, the inner sanctum of their own hearts they are conscious of another self, a very different character. So far this is more or less common to all. It is a result of the Fall of Man that we have ever present a lower nature struggling to get the mastery. So conscious was the Apostle of this second self that

he cried out, 'O wretched man that I am! Who shall deliver me from the body of this death?' The metaphor here, is, doubtless, borrowed from an ancient cruel custom of binding together a living captive with a corpse. The dead body must of necessity be repugnant to the living man, and to the living Christian the very existence of the lower nature must be abhorrent. Unfortunately, however, some act the part played by Dr. JEKYLL. They live the respectable life 'to be seen of men,' and then, when away from the public gaze, they give way to the lower nature. Our SAVIOUR says of them, 'For every one that doeth evil hateth the light, neither cometh to the light, lest his deeds should be reproved.'

There are two strange scenes brought before us in the allegory. The first is, Mr. HYDE trampling over the body of a child in the street, treading down, as it were, innocence. In the second scene, Mr. HYDE commits a murder. Both scenes take place at night, both bring a penalty. The first one was comparatively easily atoned for, as the child, no thanks to Mr. HYDE, was not permanently injured. The second scene, however, results in a price being set on the head of the murderer, which finally leads to his committing suicide. Immediately after the crime of murder, however, Mr. HYDE takes his dose of chemicals, and he becomes again Dr. JEKYLL, the respectable member of a scientific profession, about the last man in the town to be suspected of such a crime. We need hardly say that, though no one could recognise in Dr. JEKYLL the foul villain who had trampled down innocence and committed a murder, his memory was keenly alive and his sorrow was intense. In the words of the author 'the pangs of transformation' had not done tearing him, before HENRY JEKYLL, with streaming tears of gratitude and remorse, had fallen upon his knees and lifted his clasped hands to GOD. The veil of self-indulgence was rent from head to foot, 'I saw my life as a whole; I followed it up from the days of childhood, when I walked with my father's hand, and through the self-denying toils of my professional life, to arrive again and again, with the same sense of unreality, at the damned horrors of the evening. I could have screamed aloud; I sought with tears and prayers to smother down the crowd of hideous images and sounds with which my memory swarmed against me; and still, between the petitions, the ugly face of my iniquity stared into my soul. . . . But I was still cursed with my duality of purpose, and, as the first edge of my penitence wore off, the lower side of me, so long indulged, so recently chained down, began to growl for licence. Not that I dreamt of resuscitating HYDE, the bare idea of that would startle me to frenzy; no, it was in my own person that I was once more tempted to trifle with my conscience, and it was as an *ordinary secret sinner* that I at last fell before the assaults of temptation.'

We regret that our limited space prevents us going more into the details of the book which we are considering. The most thrilling part is that in which Dr. JEKYLL, to his horror, discovers that from having so frequently assumed the form of Mr. HYDE, that nature gradually begins to assert itself in him. To such an extent is this the case that, though he retires to rest at night as Dr. JEKYLL, he finds that when he wakes up in the morning he is Mr. HYDE. At first this discovery does not trouble him so much, as a dose of his chemicals effects a transformation back again. But, by degrees, he finds that from frequent interchange of character the chemicals lose their power. He doubles the strength of the ingredients, but all to no avail. The better man has gone, the lower and the viler nature gains the ascendancy. Mr. HYDE is the murderer—he, if discovered, will be hanged—so that the conviction grows on his mind that the day of reckoning is coming, the penalty will, sooner or later, have to be paid. After a very graphic description of the appalling horrors of his position, we find Dr. JEKYLL has disappeared, but that Mr. HYDE has taken his place and, with a view to escape his impending fate, dies by his own hand.

How many there may be who will read this book, and, if they rightly understand it, will recall the words of NATHAN the prophet to DAVID the King, 'Thou art the man.' At first they trifle with their lower nature, always conscious that they can, at any time, reassume their better self. By degrees, however, the unfortunate victim finds that he is losing his better self, and that the lower nature acquires more and more power. The jovial man does not mean to become a drunkard, though he yields now and then in secret. The man whose passions are strong has no intentions of becoming a sensualist, though he, too, gives way to the fascinating power of temptation. The fashionable lady of the world does not mean to become insincere, though she, too, with a view of pleasing those around her, does not always strictly adhere to the path of truth. We might enumerate many other different forms of sin. But enough: *ex une omne discit.* The appalling truth bursts on the victim that the will, which once was so powerful, has lost its strength, and that the lower nature, which every one should seek to bring into subjection, has gained the ascendancy. That which has hitherto been done in secret is at last proclaimed upon the housetops; all restraints are

---

An excerpt from *The Strange Case of Dr. Jekyll and Mr. Hyde*

Mr. Hyde was pale and dwarfish; he gave an impression of deformity without any nameable malformation; he had a displeasing smile; he had borne himself to the lawyer with a sort of murderous mixture of timidity and boldness; and he spoke with a husky, whispering, and somewhat broken voice—all these were points against him. But not all of these together could explain the hitherto unknown disgust, loathing, and fear with which Mr. Utterson regarded him. "There must be something else," said the perplexed gentleman. "There *is* something more, if I could find a name for it. God bless me, the man seems hardly human! Something troglodytic, shall we say? or can it be the old story of Dr. Fell? or is it the mere radiance of a foul soul that thus transpires through, and transfigures, its clay continent? The last, I think; for, O my poor old Harry Jekyll, if ever I read Satan's signature upon a face, it is on that of your new friend."

Robert Louis Stevenson, in his The Strange Case of Dr. Jekyll and Mr. Hyde, *1886. Reprint. Scholastic Book Services, 1963.*

---

thrown aside. May GOD grant that this book may be a warning to many who are trifling with sin, unconscious of its awful power to drag them down to the lowest depths of hell. We need hardly say even to the most guilty, even to those who have sunk lowest, that we believe that there is a Divine power in CHRIST to enable us to become more than conquerors through Him that loved us, and washed us in His own most precious blood. (pp. 224-27)

In an excerpt in Robert Louis Stevenson: The Critical Heritage, *edited by Paul Maixner, Routledge & Kegan Paul, 1981, pp. 224-27.*

Arthur Symons (essay date 1894)

[*An English poet, dramatist, short story writer, and critic, Symons gained initial notoriety during the 1890s as one of the leading figures of the Decadent movement in England, eventually establishing himself as an important critic of the modern era. In the following obituary tribute, he commends the romantic, whimsical, and fantastic elements in Stevenson's work.*]

The death of Robert Louis Stevenson deprived English literature of the most charming and sympathetic writer of the present day. He was a fastidious craftsman, caring, we might almost say pre-eminently, for style; yet he was popular. He was most widely known as the writer of boys' books of adventure; yet he was the favourite reading of those who care only for the most literary aspects of literature. Within a few days after the news of his death reached England, English newspapers vied with each other in comparing him with Montaigne, with Lamb, with Scott, with Defoe; and he has been not merely compared, but preferred. Uncritical praise is the most unfriendly service a man can render to his friend; but here, where so much praise is due, may one not try to examine a little closely just what those qualities are which call for praise, and just what measure of praise they seem to call for?

Stevenson somewhere describes certain of his own essays as being "but the readings of a literary vagrant." And, in truth, he was always that, a literary vagrant; it is the secret of much of his charm, and of much of his weakness. He wandered, a literary vagrant, over the world, across life, and across literature, an adventurous figure, with all the irresponsible and irresistible charm of the vagabond. To read him is to be for ever setting out on a fresh journey, along a white, beckoning road, on a blithe spring morning. Anything may happen, or nothing; the air is full of the gaiety of possible chances. And in this exhilaration of the blood, unreasoning, unreasonable, as it is, all the philosophies merge themselves into those two narrow lines which the *Child's Garden of Verses* piously encloses for us:

> The world is so full of a number of things,
> I am sure we should all be as happy as kings.

It is the holiday mood of life that Stevenson expresses, and no one has ever expressed it with a happier abandonment to the charm of natural things. In its exquisite exaggeration, it is the optimism of the invalid, due to his painful consciousness that health, and the delights of health, are what really matter in life. Most of those who have written captivatingly of the open air, of what are called natural, healthy things, have been invalids: Thoreau, Richard Jefferies, Stevenson. The strong man has leisure to occupy his thoughts with other things; he can indulge in abstract thinking without a twinge of the brain, can pursue the moral issues of conduct impersonally; he is not condemned to the bare elements of existence. And, in his calm acceptance of the privileges of ordinary health, he finds no place for that lyric rapture of thanksgiving which a bright day, a restful night, wakens in the invalid. The actual fever and languor in the blood: that counts for something in Stevenson's work, and lies at the root of some of its fascination.

His art, in all those essays and extravagant tales into which he put his real self, is a romantic art, alike in the essay on "Walking Tours" and in the **"Story of the Young Man with the Cream Tarts."** Stevenson was passionately interested in people; but there was something a trifle elvish and uncanny about him, as of a bewitched being who was not actually human, had not actually a human soul, and whose keen interest in the fortunes of his fellows was really a vivid curiosity, from one not quite of the same nature as those about him. He saw life as the most absorbing, the most amusing, game; or, as a masquerade, in which he liked to glance behind a mask, now and again, on the winding and coloured way he made for himself through the midst of the pageant. It was only in his latest period that he came to think about truth to human nature; and even then it was with the picturesqueness of character, with its adaptability to the humorous freaks of incident, that he was chiefly concerned.

It was for the accidents and curiosities of life that he cared, for life as a strange picture, for its fortunate confusions, its whimsical distresses, its unlikely strokes of luck, its cruelties, sometimes, and the touch of madness that comes into it at moments.

—*Arthur Symons*

He was never really himself except when he was in some fantastic disguise. From **"The Pavilion on the Links"** to *Dr Jekyll and Mr Hyde,* he played with men and women as a child plays with a kaleidoscope; using them freakishly, wantonly, as colours, sometimes as symbols. In some wonderful, artificial way, like a wizard who raises, not living men from the dead, but the shadows of men who had once died, he calls up certain terrifying, but not ungracious, phantoms, who frisk it among the mere beings of flesh and blood, bringing with them the strangest "airs from heaven or blasts from hell." No; in the phrase of Beddoes, Stevenson was "tired of being merely human." Thus there are no women in his books, no lovers; only the lure of hidden treasures and the passion of adventure. It was for the accidents and curiosities of life that he cared, for life as a strange picture, for its fortunate confusions, its

whimsical distresses, its unlikely strokes of luck, its cruelties, sometimes, and the touch of madness that comes into it at moments. For reality, for the endeavour to see things as they are, to represent them as they are, he had an impatient disregard. These matters did not interest him.

But it is by style, largely, we are told, that Stevenson is to live, and the names of Lamb and of Montaigne are called up on equal terms. Style, with Stevenson, was certainly a constant preoccupation, and he has told us how, as a lad, he trained himself in the use of language; how, in his significant phrase, he "lived with words"; by "playing the sedulous ape to Hazlitt, to Lamb, to Wordsworth, to Sir Thomas Browne, to Defoe, to Hawthorne, to Montaigne, to Baudelaire, and to Obermann." He was resolved from the first to reject the ready-made in language, to combine words for himself, as if no one had ever used them before; and, with labour and luck, he formed for his use a singularly engaging manner of writing, full of charm, freshness, and flexibility, and with a certain human warmth in the words. But it is impossible to consider style in the abstract without taking into account also what it expresses; for true style is not the dress, but the very flesh, of the informing thought. Stevenson's tendency, like that of his admirers, was rather to the forgetfulness of this plain and sometimes uncongenial fact. But, in comparing him with the great names of literature, we cannot but feel all the difference, and all the meaning of the difference, between a great intellect and a bright intelligence. The lofty and familiar homeliness of Montaigne, the subtle and tragic humour of Lamb, are both on a far higher plane than the gentle and attractive and whimsical confidences of Stevenson. And, underlying what may seem trifling in both, there is a large intellectual force, a breadth of wisdom, which makes these two charming writers not merely charming, but great. Stevenson remains charming; his personality, individual and exquisite as it was, had not the strength and depth of greatness. And, such as it was, it gave itself to us completely; there was no sense, as there is with the really great writers, of reserve power, of infinite riches to draw upon. Quite by himself in a certain seductiveness of manner, he ranks, really, with Borrow and Thoreau, with the men of secondary order in literature, who appeal to us with more instinctive fascination than the very greatest; as a certain wayward and gipsy grace in a woman thrills to the blood, often enough, more intimately and immediately than the august perfection of classic beauty. He is one of those writers who speak to us on easy terms, with whom we may exchange affections. We cannot lose our heart to Shakespeare, to Balzac; nay, even to Montaigne, because of the height and depth, the ardour and dignity, of the wisdom in his "smiling" pages (to use Stevenson's own word). But George Borrow makes every one who comes under his charm a little unfit for civilisation, a little discontented with drawing-rooms; Thoreau leads his willing victim into the ardent austerity of the woods; and Stevenson awakens something of the eternal romance in the bosom even of the conventional. It is a surprising, a marvellous thing to have done; and to afford such delights, to call forth such responsive emotions, is a boon that we accept with warmer rejoicing than many more solid gifts. (pp. 77-81)

Arthur Symons, "Robert Louis Stevenson," in

his Studies in Prose and Verse, *J. M. Dent & Co., 1904, pp. 77-82.*

Kenneth Payson Kempton   (essay date 1947)

[*In the following excerpt, Kempton identifies the principal theme of "Markheim" and discusses Stevenson's handling of three problematic narrative elements: the plausibility of the sequence of events that the story presents, the apparently supernatural nature of the mysterious visitant, and the protagonist's seemingly sudden repentance.*]

In Stevenson's **"Markheim"** a young man enters an antique jewelry shop on a dark Christmas afternoon ostensibly to buy a gift for his fiancée. Talking with the "little pale, round-shouldered dealer," Markheim remarks that he has "done well on the Stock Exchange" and is, happily, about to marry wealth. But his manner belies his words. He seems ill at ease, rejects a hand glass almost with horror; and then, while the old man is fumbling under the counter for another offering, Markheim suddenly stabs and kills him. Taking the dealer's keys despite the terror and guilt that now nearly paralyze him, Markheim shuts the shop door and goes upstairs to find the old man's money. He closes the drawing-room door and feels safe. Whereupon, although alone in the house except for the corpse, Markheim hears a step on the stairs. The knob turns, the lock clicks, and the door opens.

> Fear held Markheim in a vice. What to expect he knew not, whether the dead man walking, or the official ministers of human justice, or some chance witness blindly stumbling in to consign him to the gallows. But when a face was thrust into the aperture, glanced round the room, looked at him, nodded and smiled as if in friendly recognition, and then withdrew again, and the door closed behind it, his fear broke loose from his control in a hoarse cry. At the sound of this the visitant returned.

> "Did you call me?" he asked, pleasantly, and with that he entered the room and closed the door behind him.

The theme is very simple: conquest of man by his conscience. The outcome is ironic: Markheim, who had planned his crime with care and intelligence and executed it with skill to escape detection, is betrayed by himself—first by his fear, then by his awakened sense of sin. The telling method is for the most part objective; perhaps a thousand words only, between the murder of the dealer and the arrival of the "visitant," with Markheim alone on scene, necessarily being analysis of sense impressions, thoughts and emotions; and a single sentence at the end, when he is again alone, interpreting thoughts and action. Published in 1885, the story antedated stream of experience, which might seem its natural medium, by at least thirty years.

But one can't be sure that Stevenson would have used stream of experience even if the medium had been known to him. If so written, from the death of the dealer on—more than four fifths of its length—the story would have represented Markheim alone and talking to himself. The "visitant," who knows him well and likes him and has

often tried to "help" Markheim, whom Markheim takes to be the devil and whom a piously minded reader might take to be his guardian angel, is really only himself, one side—the better side—of himself. In stream of experience much of the story might have been dull. But as Robert Louis Stevenson wrote it, must it face a more serious charge? Is it plausible at all? Can it be fair for a writer to say that somebody enters a room, talks with his protagonist and persuades him to a course of action, when he means that no second person is there?

Turn back to the beginning of the story and note the literal facts Stevenson used and the preparation for agreement with his astounding fiction he undertook through preliminary, unobtrusive reference to traits in people, details of place, and coming action. To gain agreement, preparation had to surmount three hurdles: motivation of the murder, appearance of the "visitant," and Markheim's surrender.

"Some [customers] are dishonest," the dealer says at the start, holding up a candle to scrutinize Markheim (the shop is shuttered), "and in that case I profit by my virtue." Markheim blinks and cannot meet the dealer's gaze. No matter how reasonable the young man's story, from here on his motive is suspect; but the touch is very deft, Markheim has just come in off the street, the blinking might be normal reflex; this is the first unobtrusive reference, slipped in for post-operative recall. Others follow. We learn that Markheim had prepared what he would tell the dealer, and once he is launched on this line he seems more at ease. When the dealer stoops to draw an object from the showcase, leaving himself unprotected, Markheim's emotional reaction is suggestive; it is when the old man repeats the movement to withdraw another object that the knife is to fall. Markheim snatches the hand mirror and confronts the dealer with it; the dealer starts back at this threatening gesture, but "perceiving there was nothing worse [than a mirror] on hand," chuckles and goes on. So much as preparation for murder, a mere physical act resulting from motives preceding the story, and, itself, coming early; thus the easiest of Stevenson's three problems in plausibility.

The second, the appearance of the "visitant," was difficult enough in 1885, though "Saki," Lord Dunsany, Walter de la Mare, and others were soon to make mysticism and fantasy welcome in England; it might well have proved insuperably hard in our hard-boiled American twenties; since Kafka, Katherine Anne Porter, John Collier, and Ben Hecht, however, such material has become only moderately difficult again. Stevenson's efforts to prepare for this apparently supernatural event can be traced through his portrayal and step-by-step embodiment of young Markheim's fear. They begin with the story: Markheim's blinking in the candlelight, his failure to meet the dealer's gaze, his unease—all bits of behavior suggesting fear. They soon become more explicit as Markheim stalls for time, describes the hand glass as a conscience, and after the murder sees himself reflected in many mirrors, thinks his own steps are those of pursuers, takes the sound of rain to be footsteps or whispers—his terrors becoming more and more incarnate, hallucinations merging with reality so that he (and we, equally important) can hardly tell which is which, and "one portion of his mind was alert and cunning, another trembled on the brink of lunacy." The final preparations are the jovial gentleman beating on the outside door and calling the dead man by name, Markheim's palpably false sense of security upstairs, and the comfort wrought in him by the sound of innocent children outside singing a carol. Then comes the "visitant," cool and friendly. To Markheim he was an utterly real person. Though sharing his hysteria, one side of the reader's mind, too, has been carefully kept "alert and cunning," and he knows that Markheim has been hearing and seeing things that weren't there. And the reader knows now what Markheim does not know: that the "visitant" also is not there, except in Markheim's frantic imagination. The success of the author's handiwork is attested by the fact that nobody will question or worry about what becomes of the "visitant" at the end of the story. He never visibly or audibly leaves as he came in; Markheim is simply alone again; neither he nor the reader notices or misses the departure of the "visitant," because there is no departure. In fact Markheim has been alone (with his conscience) from the murder to the entrance of the servant at the close of the story. The apparently supernatural is thus solidly grounded on reality.

The third problem, repentance and its active result, surrender, was the most difficult of all. Strong passions, deep emotion, and, especially, deep emotional change—these things in real life take time, and the short story has no representative space to spare. Will a man who could cold-bloodedly murder with intent to rob repent the act, give himself to the gallows, and find peace, in an hour or so? Offhand, hardly; yet by the time he opens the door to the servant Markheim's change seems natural enough, the only thing to do. To discover Stevenson's ways and means of motivation, we must go back once again to the beginning of the story and pick up the clues he laid down to work upon us unawares. At the start Markheim's manner is engaging, though we know there is something fishy about it; the dealer's ironical reference to the uncle's cabinet (as the source of objects Markheim has previously come to sell) and Markheim's straightforward denial call for sympathy; we feel that the dealer is the stronger of the two men. This is important, for a logical outcome depends on sympathy for Markheim; the reader must not be led to think that Markheim is a hardened criminal or a capricious fool. In a pause, the ticking of many clocks in the shop may be a symbol of the passage of needed (for plausibility) time that the storyteller is not going to be able to recount literally. Markheim's interpretation of the mirror as a conscience before the murder is, after the act, emphasized by his seeing his reflection in dozens of mirrors— "his face repeated and repeated, as it were an army of spies; his own eyes met and detected him." (A lead.) The voices begin: the clocks ticking, a boy's feet running outside, all the town clocks striking three. And the moving candle flame makes the shop a jungle of swaying shadows, into which the slit of daylight from the shop door ajar peers and points "like a pointing finger." The act accomplished, time again looms over Markheim; time stopped for the dead man, time (to escape?) beginning for him. He sees flaws in what he has planned so carefully; he feels the constable's hand on his shoulder, sees "the dock, the pris-

on, the gallows, and the black coffin." Turning over the body of his victim, he remembers his horror as a child at finding famous crimes pictured at a fair. "The thumping of the drums" and "a bar of that day's music" bring "a qualm . . . a breath of nausea, a sudden weakness of the joints, which he must instantly resist and conquer." He forces himself to look at the dead face, remain unmoved. Penitence? "Not a tremor." (This is a strong lead.) But the rain brings voices again. He has a growing feeling that he is not alone in the house, and upstairs at last, goes to pieces again. Weird tricks of nature revealing his crime occur to him: "the hands of God reached forth against sin. But about God himself he was at ease; his act was doubtless exceptional, but so were his excuses, which God knew; it was there, and not among men, that he felt sure of justice." (A remarkable lead.) Then the sense of security with the drawing-room door closed, and the children's singing voices reminding him again of his childhood, now happily—"back again to church, and the somnolence of summer Sundays, and the high genteel voice of the parson . . . and the painted Jacobean tombs, and the dim lettering of the Ten Commandments in the chancel." (Gently reared, after all. An echo of the appealing personality suggested at the start.) All this time we have suffered with Markheim; from the entrance of the "visitant" to the act of repentance an even stronger pull on our sympathy is exerted. For the "visitant" argues contrariwise, his proffered "help" is to get the money, murder the servant, and slip away. Markheim stoutly refuses, disavows baseness, insists his first crime is to be his last.

> "And are my vices only to direct my life [he cries], and my virtues to lie without effect, like some passive lumber of the mind? Not so; good, also, is a spring of acts."

The "visitant" remarks coldly that Markheim's past life promises no great change. Then the doorbell rings, the maid returning. The "visitant" makes a last quick plea, showing the way to escape. But the young man, awakened, desperate, resolved at last, is ready.

> Markheim steadily regarded his counsellor. "If I be condemned to evil acts," he said, "there is still one door of freedom open—I can cease from action. If my life be an ill thing, I can lay it down . . . "

And we, too, are completely ready for his simple, courageous words to the servant: "You had better go for the police. I have killed your master." (pp. 180-85)

> *Kenneth Payson Kempton, "Plausibility," in his* The Short Story, *Cambridge, Mass.: Harvard University Press, 1947, pp. 172-88.*

David Daiches   (essay date 1947)

[*Daiches is a prominent English scholar and critic who has written extensively on English and American literature. In the following excerpt, he asserts that Stevenson's characteristic "combination of romantic adventure with optimistic morality" is especially evident in his short stories.*]

The peculiar qualities of the Stevensonian romance are

perhaps best studied by taking a general view of Stevenson's short stories. For—if we except *Treasure Island* and that piece of "tushery" *The Black Arrow*—in his longer works the pure vein of romance is never to be found alone; other intentions are intermingled; the claims of psychology, history, topography and autobiography assert themselves, and the adventure story changes as it proceeds, to become something more complicated and sometimes less adequately integrated. It is not, of course, true, that Stevenson was simply or even essentially a romancer; to diagnose his artistic character thus would be to ignore not only his preoccupations with style, but also certain less definable but extremely important aspects of his art which emerge in the first part of *The Master of Ballantrae* and, triumphantly, in the unfinished **Weir of Hermiston.** But romance, in the simple old-fashioned sense of "a rattling good yarn," was certainly one important element in Stevenson's literary character and ambitions. The exciting world of make-believe had been one (but only one) of the factors responsible for his choosing the career of author: ever since he had discovered "the Eldorado of romantic comedy" in Skelt's toy-theatre as a six-year-old boy, ever since as a sick child he had discovered the contrast between physical inaction and the adventurous world of the imagination, one of the main functions of literature had always been for him the escapist and compensatory one of presenting a thrilling, exciting, yet essentially moral life to writer and reader. In this respect, literature for him was but an extension of those childhood games of romantic make-believe that he has described so vividly in his autobiographical essays.

It is this combination of romantic adventure with optimistic morality that we see so clearly in Stevenson's short stories. As these stories are admittedly intended as pleasing wish-fulfilments and substitutes for actual inactivity, there can be no suggestion of the triumph of evil, or of death finally overtaking the hero, in such works. The morality is of the breeziest kind: people are punished and rewarded according to their intentions rather than their acts: it is, indeed, the morality of Fielding and Robert Burns and the sentimental Deists of the eighteenth century. The good heart is all. And there is hardly a single story in which Stevenson is not present, either in an ideal projection (Prince Florizel) or in a semiautobiographical reminiscence (John Nicholson).

The short stories collectively entitled **The New Arabian Nights** are of particular interest in this connection, and throw some light on Stevenson's underlying personal ambitions. Prince Florizel, almost a parody of a romantic hero, possesses both rank and power and great personal charm. Everyone is deferential to him; he accepts this deference as of right with an easy yet condescending grace. And not only is he high-born, handsome and influential; he is also supremely competent. He is, indeed, the complete feudal hero, and heads a social hierarchy in virtue both of his birth and his ability.

Florizel is not, of course, a wholly serious character. He is drawn with a half-humorous—indeed, a half-satirical—touch. Stevenson is laughing a little at himself. But it is himself that he is laughing at, his own romantic and feudal

ideal. And the fact that he could laugh at it—that he could recognize its incongruity in the modern world—did not mean that he was prepared to abandon it. When, like Scott at Abbotsford, he set himself up as a feudal landowner at Vailima, he was only putting into practice a theory of living which emerges time and again from his writing. (pp. 3-5)

The element of childhood reminiscence that plays so important a part in Stevenson's work is continually modified by a quite different adult strain which manifests itself sometimes by irony and sometimes in purely stylistic devices. The adult strain is more consistently visible in his short stories than in his novels. *Treasure Island* and *The Black Arrow* were written primarily for boys, and the main tone derives from his recollection of what had appealed most to his imagination as a boy. In his short stories he is largely concerned with the studied turn of phrase, the well cadenced paragraph, the mannered style. **The New Arabian Nights** is an adult work in which the adventures appropriate to a boy's imagination are cleverly embedded in an atmosphere of irony, and the author, while sacrificing none of the exciting properties of the adventure story, manages to parade himself, a knowing and worldly figure, before the sophisticated reader.

But not all Stevenson's short stories are careful combinations of the adolescent and the sophisticated. Often they are pure allegories, where the action is strictly subordinated to the allegorical intention and is of little interest in itself. This is true of **"Will o' the Mill,"** in which the generalised nature of the allegory gives Stevenson a certain latitude to indulge in careful picturesque description as the story moves slowly forward. A remarkable sense of atmosphere is achieved in this story, but it is an uneconomical achievement in that its contribution to the allegory is, if not superfluous, at least ambiguous. The charm of the situation interested Stevenson as much as its meaning, with the result that the picture of rustic living is filled out in idyllic detail until the shape of the allegory is almost lost.

Stevenson was always interested in the presentation of atmosphere, but it took him a long time before he could put his gift for creating atmosphere to its most effective literary purpose. **"Thrawn Janet,"** for example, a short story which has been much overpraised, possesses an atmosphere disproportionate, in its nature and intensity, to the action, which is simple and even mechanical, in the conventional supernatural tradition. **"The Pavilion on the Links"** and **"The Merry Men"** are stories written to illustrate Stevenson's feeling about the atmosphere of certain parts of the Scottish coast: this is particularly true of the latter, where the action is almost purely symbolic: in the former there is not altogether successful attempt to use a flamboyant and melodramatic episode as a means of suggesting the quality of the Scottish east coast near North Berwick. As a result, the effective handling of realistic detail in the first part of the **"Pavilion"** loses part of its force in the face of an action which is on a wholly different level of probability.

Dr. Jekyll and Mr. Hyde, **"Markheim,"** **"The Bottle Imp"** and **"The Treasure of Franchard"** are all allegories, but very different both from **"Will o' the Mill"** and from each other. **Dr. Jekyll and Mr. Hyde** owes its popularity to the striking nature of its theme and the picturesque boldness with which it is treated. As an allegory it does not stand up very well to detailed examination, but this is unimportant beside the fact that the ringing strokes employed by Stevenson in fashioning the story give it an extraordinary vigor; it is a rough hewn and crude piece of work, but as narrative it is extremely well managed. **"Markheim"** is the kind of melodramatic allegory so beloved of Dickens: it might almost have been one of the manuscripts read in bed on a windy night by Mr. Pickwick. It possesses the great merit of concentration, and, unlike **"Will o' the Mill,"** it consistently uses the atmosphere to reinforce the meaning of the allegory. **"The Treasure of Franchard"** is the most like **"Will o' the Mill"** of all these stories, not in theme but in treatment, for here, too, the details of the narrative go beyond what are necessary to present the allegorical meaning effectively, so that the allegory fades out as we read the story, and more and more we read it as a rather charming study of French provincial life at its most attractive, saved from sentimentality by a generous sprinkling of good natured irony. **"The Bottle Imp,"** written for a Polynesian audience, is simple fable, told with an appropriate simplicity of style.

That Stevenson sometimes used the short story form to try out his hand simply at the creation of atmosphere is made clear by **"A Lodging for the Night,"** an attempt to give substance to his impressions of the background of Villon. Like its companion piece **"The Sire de Malétroit's Door,"** but more effectively, it reads like a sketch for a scene in a novel: indeed, a great deal of Stevenson's essays and short stories which have for their primary function the building up of atmosphere read like lost chapters from novels—backgrounds lacking an appropriate foreground. It was not until he came to write the early part of *The Master of Ballantrae* that Stevenson showed that he could use "organically" his gift for creating atmosphere; and in the unfinished *Weir of Hermiston* he demonstrated conclusively that he had learned how to use both description and narrative to their best mutual advantage.

The three short stories which must head any list of Stevenson's work in this field are **"Thrawn Janet,"** the **"Pavilion on the Links"** and **"The Beach of Falesa."** In the first two, magnificent though they are in parts, the relation of action to background and atmosphere is disproportionate. **"The Beach of Falesa"** is the one short story in which Stevenson is wholly successful in plotting an action that follows easily and naturally the line laid down by the atmosphere. It is the best integrated of all Stevenson's short stories. The atmosphere of shabby intrigue spiced with danger, that is so much a part of trading life in the islands of the South Seas, is not only perfectly comprehended and recorded: the action at every point at once illustrates and makes inevitable the mood suggested by all the background description. The adventure story is here refined to a high degree of social and psychological subtlety without losing its quality as adventure story, a feat which, of Stevenson's contemporaries, only Conrad could emulate and surpass. **"The Beach of Falesa"** stands with *Weir of Hermiston* as a sign showing the way Stevenson could have developed had he lived: he was moving towards the final reconcilia-

tion of the two major strains which had run through all his work, the adolescent and the adult, action and atmosphere, adventure story and essay. This reconciliation had been attempted earlier in other ways—notably through the mixture of adventure and irony in **The New Arabian Nights**—but it was with the final solution that Stevenson found his real stature as a writer.

When Stevenson tried romance without irony in a short story he made a bad mess of it: **"Olalla,"** with its cardboard Spanish setting and preposterously artificial action, humorless, wooden and conventional, is a complete failure, and shows very clearly what happened when Stevenson took a theme from the schoolboy side of his talent and inflated it with an eye on an adult audience. Stevenson as a pure romancer, the Stevenson of *Treasure Island*, did best when writing in terms of a young audience, just as Stevenson the stylist and ironist could only operate in a "pure" state when writing essays for adults. The romancer could only sublimate his narrative talents if he combined them with the products of the other side of his genius—his sense of character and atmosphere, of "local colour" and history, which eventually was to become senior partner in the curious literary firm of Robert Louis Stevenson and Son.

Stevenson's short stories are of particular interest to anyone concerned with the relation between the two distinct sides of his talent, as they show the various attempts he made to reconcile the two, and the final, successful form which that reconciliation took. All of Stevenson's short stories can be fitted into a discussion of this problem—except **"The Body Snatcher,"** that rather low piece of pure sensationalism, the two pieces written for a Polynesian audience (**"The Bottle Imp"** and **"The Isle of Voices"**), and those two somewhat low-pressured comedies, the **"Misadventures of John Nicholson"** and **"The Story of a Lie."** (pp. 11-16)

> *David Daiches, in his* Robert Louis Stevenson, *New Directions Books, 1947, 196 p.*

Sean O'Faolain   (essay date 1951)

[*O'Faolain was an Irish short story writer, novelist, and critic. In the following excerpt, he finds* "The Sire de Malétroit's Door" *exemplary of Stevenson's characteristic method of constructing a short story around a central image or idea.*]

Let us look over the shoulder of a writer of short-stories after he has chosen his subject; after he has started with his idea. The word 'idea' is not a good word but it will have to do. It may . . . be a prepossession of some kind, some scene or character that excites him, something which, in a manner inexplicable to himself, has an almost symbolical significance in his mind . . . [One of Stevenson's prepossessions is] The Closed Door. Let us watch him at work on **"The Sire de Malétroit's Door."** He has got to the point where a soldier, fleeing from his pursuers, presses his back against a great oaken door and feels it, on oiled hinges, open silently and as silently close behind him, holding him imprisoned in an unknown darkness.

An excerpt from "The Body-Snatcher"

The Resurrection Man—to use a by-name of the period—was not to be deterred by any of the sanctities of customary piety. It was part of his trade to despise and desecrate the scrolls and trumpets of old tombs, the paths worn by the feet of worshippers and mourners, and the offerings and the inscriptions of bereaved affection. To rustic neighbourhoods, where love is more than commonly tenacious, and where some bonds of blood or fellowship unite the entire society of a parish, the body-snatcher, far from being repelled by natural respect, was attracted by the ease and safety of the task. To bodies that had been laid in earth, in joyful expectation of a far different awakening, there came that hasty, lamplit, terror-haunted resurrection of the spade and mattock. The coffin was forced, the cerements torn, and the melancholy relics, clad in sackcloth, after being rattled for hours on moonless byways, were at length exposed to uttermost indignities before a class of gaping boys.

Robert Louis Stevenson, in his "The Body-Snatcher,"
1884. Reprint. The Body Snatcher, and Other Stories,
New American Library, 1988.

Let us watch Stevenson mould his principle about this image; by which I mean mould his idea of Life, as he himself has defined it, or made one of his characters in *The New Arabian Nights* define it:—'By Life I do not mean Thackeray's novels but the crimes and secret possibilities of our society and the principles of wise conduct among exceptional events.' It is the definition of a particular kind of romantic, or realist-romantic, but it is not very different to the ideas of other writers. It is mainly not a new idea but another literary vocabulary; for in 'exceptional events' we find 'incident' and in 'principles of wise conduct' we find that assertion of permanent 'human values,' or that adumbration of a civilised idea of society to which Balzac or Chekov would have subscribed in other words but with like sense.

But, first, I must make one point quite clear. I have said 'mould his story . . . ' I borrow that phrase from one of Stevenson's critics, Marcel Schwob. He said, 'As the smelter casts his bronze about the core of clay, Stevenson casts his story about the image he has called up.' This is an excellent phrase to describe the close construction of the short story, because it means that the tale clings to the original idea. (pp. 193-94)

We may now come back to Stevenson's story **"The Sire de Malétroit's Door."** The young soldier has meanwhile been hesitating in the hallway behind the door. What next? Stevenson makes him explore the house, and in the first room that he enters he finds, to his amazement, an old man, who is the Sire de Malétroit, sitting waiting patiently for him. Now, this strikes us as both astonishing and absolutely right, because if the door was prepared it must have been prepared for some purpose, by somebody, and somebody astute and cunning enough to do it. True, the question uppermost in our minds is, 'How did the Sire de Malétroit know that, by chance, the young man would come

at that very hour to that door of all doors in the town?' Therefore the tale must cling to this conundrum. The Sire de Malétroit, an unpleasantly leering old gentleman, tells the young man that *the* young lady is waiting for him, and presently she is introduced. The young man is further told that he must marry the lady before dawn—or die. The Sire de Malétroit retires and the young woman explains. She has been kept in that house as closely as if she were in a convent, but she has managed nevertheless to gain the attention and affection of a young officer in the town whom she had first seen at church. The unfortunate young hero of the story has been so unlucky as to come upon the door hitherto used nightly by this unknown lover. Her uncle has decided that she has disgraced him and that she shall marry her officer. A coincidence has been boldly foisted on us.

Stevenson has now got his characters into a first-class romantic situation. As we watch him proceed from this point we know that every step is crucial. One false note will wreck the story. But how is he to proceed? How is he to get his hero and this young woman out of the dilemma into which he has put them? First of all, the young soldier is the instrument. Secondly, the key-note is Romance. Thirdly, the atmosphere is Danger. The 'principle,' by implication, is Honour and Happiness. For this story is a prologue-story, as I venture to call all romantic stories, as compared with the epilogue-story, which I apply as a convenient term to all tragic stories. This story does not end somebody's illusions. It begins them. We may, however, rely on Stevenson. He had, as somebody said, a great art of embroidery. His stories weave themselves into a tapestry of purple and scarlet and marigold. If it were only on style alone he is certain to carry it off.

But let us keep our eyes glued on the construction. The night passes. These two young people are alone. To save the lady's honour the young man has decided to refuse to marry her, which is highly romantic though rather inconvenient for everybody, not excluding Stevenson. Then, as both he and she look at the great cliff outside and think of the armed men waiting in the ante-rooms, their hearts are stirred towards one another, towards life, towards a great admiration on her part, and a great pity on his. There comes, just when it is emotionally due, the first touch of dawn—one of the most delicate descriptions of dawn in literature (and Stevenson was always excellent at natural description, and as it comes, the two young people are drawn irresistibly towards one another. By their love the problem is solved in honour and in happiness.

There is no need to examine the tale more closely here, but it is well worth the reader's while to examine it at his leisure, and when he does re-read it he will see how closely the tale clings to the line of its original image. It moves from darkness to morning, from danger to salvation, from storm to calm, in tune throughout with its own impulse and the expectation that it arouses, as logical as a sonnet whose opening theme dictates its end, never divagating from its own character, and though it is not a closely compacted story—for that was not Stevenson's way—it is in every part wholly relevant to the original mood.

As to what final 'principles of wise conduct' emerge from

this highly exceptional event I think it would be straining a point to extract them explicitly. What we get, rather, is a feeling of elevation such as we always get when we live vicariously through some gallant enterprise in which a man carries himself bravely. A fresh and happy light has been flung across the face of life. A bright wash of colour has been drawn over the landscape of experience. Human nature seems a little nobler. But we must not strain the point, and it is no more really than happens when we read any romantic tale, such as one of Scott's, or any story in which the sight of men acting and doing is always invigorating. The point is that there is some point, and that the story is built up, or constructed, to carry it like a pennant, and that without it **"The Sire de Malétroit's Door"** would be merely a film-romance.

So much for the analysis, admittedly sketchy, of Stevenson's treatment of this subject. So analysed it looks straightforward and simple. 'Anybody could do it.' If he could think of it. But of what did Stevenson think? That we cannot know. What was the subject in the crudest alloy before Stevenson refined it to this perfection? That is the essential question about the construction of stories; not how a writer handles what one reads but what matter it was that he handled. What angle did the writer adopt to that matter? What line, what simplification, compression or distillation was it that made the subject fit into the mould of the short-story and so become a short-story? Perhaps the only answer is that given by Stevenson himself in *Memories and Portraits,* an answer which is sybilline but suggestive. (I italicise the parts which seem to me the more suggestive):—

> The threads of a story *come from time to time together and make a picture* in the web; the characters fall from time to time into *some attitude to each other or to nature,* which stamps the story home *like an illustration.* Crusoe recoiling from the footprint, Achilles shouting over against the Trojans, Ulysses bending the great bow, Christian running with his fingers in his ears—these are each *culminating moments in the legend* and each has been printed on the mind's eye for ever. . . . This, then, is the plastic part of literature: *to embody character, thought or emotion in some act or attitude* that shall be remarkably striking to the mind's eye.

Sybilline, to us, because we would know what moment, which attitude, and which picture allured him in this tale, if, indeed, it 'came off' as he foresaw, and was not (as so often happens) replaced by some other arrangement which 'came together' or happily 'fell' into position, unplanned. At least, however, we see the dramatic approach, and the compactness that resulted, as distinct from the discursive way of, say, Henry James. It would seem, in fact, that because of this approach Stevenson might be considered a better writer of episodes than of novels, as James was certainly a better writer of novels than of episodes. (pp. 195-99)

Sean O'Faolain, "On Construction," in his The Short Story, *The Devin-Adair Company, 1951, pp. 193-216.*

Eric LaGuardia   (essay date 1958)

[In the following essay, the critic explores the implicit eroticism of "The Sire de Malétroit's Door."]

The most striking quality of [**"Sire de Maletroit's Door"**] is its rhythm: there is a continuous and repetitious movement from the safe to the dangerous, the dangerous to the safe. Denis de Beaulieu is at first confident and happy; his life becomes endangered; he retreats to safety; he finds himself in danger again; and again he attempts to escape, only to involve himself in more danger. Finally he is relieved of all threats, and the reader is released from the tensions of this rhythmic narrative. This tension, this rhythm, is, in a sense, the true theme of the story; and thus the final union of Blanche and Denis is insignificant. It is, rather, the apprehension for and with Denis, the anticipation of his ultimate well-being which excites us, which has the most meaning for us. It is only these flights into danger and retreats to safety that make the ending possible at all; the pleasure of Denis' union with Blanche results from the anticipation of that very pleasure. If this is true for the reader, it is certainly true for Denis, a young man whose final happiness is prepared by the danger he becomes involved in, and the union with Blanche made pleasurable by its contrast with the preceding danger.

In addition to this safety-danger anxiety, there is another impressive quality to this story—that of unreality. The setting, of course, is remote in time and space; but also the descriptions of the nocturnal scene provide the story with an air of mystery and foreboding. And the most unreal aspect is the exaggerated nature of the characters: the derring-do, the cavalier, the chivalrous bearing of young Denis; the evilness of Maletroit; and the beauty and purity of Blanche. These are all highly Romantic characteristics, but they are also the characteristics of phantasy, of the dream. If this story is Romantic and phantastic, then whose phantasy is it? It may be that it is Stevenson's projected into Denis de Beaulieu; but whether we believe it to be the author's or not, it is clear that it is Denis' phantasy—a phantasy of dire threats countered with safety, and more threats countered with safety until he reaches a kind of total "safeness." It is important, I think, to realize that Denis is never, during the story, allowed to remain safe for very long, except at the end. The danger is always mounting, multiplying, until the anticipation of his union with Blanche becomes the sole effect of the narrative. It is important because, if we are to understand this story as a phantasy, we must be aware that this is Denis' emotion too. The image-making power is not only Stevenson's, it is also Denis'; the adventure in which he is involved is purely the product of his imagination.

Denis has constructed a phantasy in which he puts himself in danger and then out of danger, in again then out, and so on. This pattern clearly produces, in Denis, strong feelings of suspense and anticipation; and since the pleasures of anticipation increase as suffering increases, we may suppose that this young man relishes the humiliations and threats which precede his embrace with Blanche. The implication here is that this phantasy has an erotic quality; and if, in addition, the details of description and dialogue in the story are examined, it becomes evident that **"Sire** de Maletroit's Door" can be, even should be, analyzed in terms of Denis de Beaulieu's sexual-psychology.

The problem at the moment is to understand the relevance of this safety-danger-safety pattern to Denis' personality. The psychologist has always been interested in man's seemingly peculiar desire to humiliate himself, to imagine himself as helpless and weak; and he characterizes this desire as the masochistic instinct. Freud theorizes that this is a normal instinct in the sexual development of man, and is closely connected with the desire for sexual gratification. The wishes for sexual pleasure are, in childhood, countered by reproaches and warnings from the parents—most strongly for the male child from the father. As a result, the child, in the later stages of his development, tends to associate these humiliations with his drive for normal, adult sexual pleasure. The father, however, is not only a figure to be feared, but also one to be admired because of his masculine success. In adolescence, the stage at which the task of successful sexual expression is full upon the individual, anxiety may arise. This anxiety can be caused by fear and doubt concerning sexual gratification, stemming from the reproaches and warnings of the father, in opposition to the strong desire for this gratification. As a result, the individual wavers between sensations of discomfort and shame, and anticipation of sexual pleasure. This vacillation is commonly called the masochistic suspense. In addition, since the individual is not aware of the nature of his anxiety, and it therefore must be rooted in his unconscious, he is not able to differentiate between the discomfort and the pleasure; in fact the one is a necessary prelude to the other, and the greater the humiliation experienced, the greater the pleasure anticipated. He finds it necessary to construct phantasy adventures for himself in which he experiences humiliations and threats, in order that he may look forward to sexual fulfillment within his phantasy.

These phantasies, unfortunately, by their very phantastic nature, merely reproduce the anxiety of the individual and do not constitute a real sexual satisfaction, although they are always gratifying at the moment—they replace normal sexual expression. In other words we should not assume that the occurrence of this kind of phantasy is in any way a permanent resolution of the personality problem; its only therapeutic value rests in the temporary relaxation of the anxiety through the unconscious and thus frank recreation of it. These imaginations can occur in day or night dreams, the difference being that in one a certain amount of control can be exerted over the details of the phantasy. The disturbance, however, which produces the dream is identical in both cases.

It is appropriate now to return to young Denis de Beaulieu. It seems to me that his personality exemplifies the one I have outlined, and the story itself is his own unconscious construction of a phantasy through the process of a nocturnal dream. The dream arises to temporarily alleviate his anxiety by reflecting his conflict between the desire for sexual fulfillment and feelings of incapability and fear, and is presented in a pattern of masochistic suspense. To facilitate a discussion of the story from this position, I have divided Denis' dream into three major sections. First: the entry into the dream world with feelings of pleasure and

safety; the subsequent introduction of a danger; and the temporary retreat to safety again. In this section we learn a good deal about Denis' character, we observe his night visit to his friend's house, we see his life threatened by a round of troops, and we accompany him in his retreat to safety behind Sire de Maletroit's door. Second: the double repetition of the safety-danger pattern; the meeting with Blanche, the sexual object; and the crucial humiliation and threat imposed by Sire de Maletroit. In this section Denis loses his feeling of safeness again, and charges up the staircase to confront whatever the danger may be, only to discover a brightly lit apartment with the coat of arms of a noble family on the wall. This sense of well-being is short-lived as he learns more of his position, is introduced to Blanche, and suffers the discomfort of the old Sire's threat. Third: the agonies of indecision, and the final gratification of desire. In this last section Denis torments himself with the alternatives of death and love; and the discomfort of the threat of death renders the final embrace with Blanche overwhelmingly ecstatic for him.

Before I begin a more detailed examination of these three sections, I would like to re-emphasize two important considerations. First, that all the aspects of the story—the description, the narration, the characters, the dialogue—are Denis' own construction; it is his dream, and an erotic one at that. Second, that this phantasy builds itself in his unconscious for two reasons: to relax his fear of attaining sexual gratification by admitting it to himself; and to prepare himself, in his dream, by the only means he can, for a phantasy fulfillment of his desire.

Part I—The entry into the dream world with feelings of pleasure and safety; the subsequent introduction of a danger; and the temporary retreat to safety again.

We learn at the outset that Denis is twenty-one, but "he counted himself a grown man, and a very accomplished cavalier . . . " We also discover that "lads are early formed in that . . . epoch," that one becomes manly through "pitched battle," and that we should excuse Denis' swagger. These details concerning manliness and the test of manliness, together with the fact that Denis merely *thought* himself a man and therefore swaggered, are the first indications that he may have a conflict within himself—a conflict between the wanting to be manly and the inability to be.

As Denis sets out on his visit in the "grey of the evening," he is in an "agreeable frame of mind." His entry into the night, however, "was not a very wise proceeding . . . the town was full of troops;" and "though Denis was there on safe-conduct, his safe-conduct was like to serve him little on a chance encounter." It is the depths of the dream world that Denis is entering; it is a peaceful, pleasant, nocturnal state, but it also holds a potential of danger. The setting of his dream world is eerie and foreboding; it is windy, rainy, leaves are flying along the streets. The sounds of merry-making are "swallowed up and carried away by the wind." The sky is a "tumultuous, leaden chaos." The scene increases in tension as the pleasure he gains from his visit with his friend is combined with the black and deathly quality of the night. His pleasant visit has been transformed into a terrifying and confusing jour-

Vailima, the house at Apia, Samoa, where Stevenson spent the last years of his life.

ney through the ominous and enveloping darkness of the mind—the unconscious. He is now at the full mercy of his unconscious, and what it pictures for him is a scene in which he is lost and must find his way; a scene which is strange and discomforting. Denis' desire for manhood, or, sexual fulfillment, is countered by feelings of terror and doubt; and therefore the nocturnal scene becomes, for him, figured with symbols of his central preoccupation—sexual intercourse. He was not acquainted with "the intricate lanes" of the town, he knew he must keep "mounting the hill' for his inn was "up at the head, under the great church spire." For Denis it is "an eerie and mysterious position to be thus submerged in opaque blackness in an almost unknown town. The silence is terrifying in its possibilities." he now enters a narrow lane and comes upon the house in which he is about to have his most significant dream adventures, and it represents itself to him with a wealth of phallic symbolism: It has pinnacles and turret-tops, the round stern of a chapel, flying buttresses, gargoyles, tapers within the chapel, a peaked roof. And, as he gazes at this house, it reminds him of his own; he compares its inhabitants to his own family.

The danger makes itself evident now in the form of a round of troops. Denis attracts their attention and, faced with the task of asserting himself against these soldiers, re-

treats to the door of the house, which opens and engulfs him in safety. The progression of these events—the phantasy construction of forces that outnumber him, the ostensibly accidental attraction of their attention, and finally the retreat—indicates that Denis has provided a danger for himself in order that he may escape it, and in this way prolong the moment when he must face the task before him. It is this pattern that is repeated throughout the dream.

Denis becomes aware that the inner surface of this "black interior" behind the door is "quite smooth, not a handle, not a moulding, not a projection of any sort." The symbolic characteristics of a womb are obvious here, and justifiable if we conceive of Denis retreating to the safety of pre-birth, to a place where he can not be called on to demonstrate his manhood. He draws his sword (another phallic symbol) immediately before being engulfed by the womb; no doubt a last moment and ineffectual exertion of his maleness. As he stands safely behind the door he hears the round of troops still searching for him, and a lance (still another phallic symbol) rattles on the door demanding, so to speak, that Denis come out and "be a man."

Thus far in his dream Denis has exhibited his strong preoccupation with the problem of attaining sexual gratification, and a masochistic personality in which this problem is manifest. The suspense of the narrative is really Denis' own insistence on masochistic suspense. His "flight forward" toward ultimate sexual pleasure is hindered by the appearance of danger, and later by mental humiliation and threats.

Part II—The double repetition of the danger-safety pattern; the meeting with Blanche, the sexual object; and the crucial humiliation and threat imposed by Maletroit.

He senses a certain danger now in his position, but he is not yet able to accept the feeling: "It looked like a snare; yet who could suppose a snare in such a quiet by-street and in a house of so prosperous and even noble exterior? And yet—snare or no snare, intentionally or unintentionally—here he was, prettily trapped; and for the life of him he could see no way out of it again." This threat suddenly becomes more concrete for him and "the idea went to his vitals with a shock." He whirls around "as if to defend his life." He has again transformed safety into danger. The comfort of the womb denies the object of his dream journey—sexual expression. It is necessary, therefore, that he remove himself from this womb and face the danger that he has constructed. The means of exit from the womb describes itself to him in the most vivid symbolism, again, of sexual intercourse—indicative of his ultimate goal. He becomes aware of a flight of stairs and a shining handrail ascending to "a vertical thread of light, widening towards the bottom . . . What could be more natural than to mount the staircase, lift the curtain, and confront his difficulty."

Through this erotic sensation he has taken an additional "flight forward" toward ultimate pleasure. His excitation by the promise of danger, however, falters immediately. He returns to a state of well-being as he reacts to the familiarity of the apartment, and is gratified to discover the coat of arms of a noble family. Slowly, though, he again begins to build an uncomfortable situation. The sight of Maletroit fills him with disgust; but this old man is, for Denis, an ambiguous figure. His face is strongly masculine, and there is a suggestion of greed and brutality and danger about him. He has, also, the white hair of a saint, venerable sweetness, and, to climax the impression he makes, his hands are sensuous and folded in his lap like a virgin martyr's. The fact that Denis associates this house with his own, and that he felt "in good hands" or at home, suggests that the figure of Sire de Maletroit is an unconscious representation of his own father; and the ambivalence of Denis' reaction to him indicates that he both fears and admires his father.

He is somehow wary of the possibilities of this confrontation, and informs Maletroit, "nothing could be more contrary to my wishes—than this intrusion." The old man is not put off by this and calmly tells Denis that their "little affairs" will be arranged presently, adding: "By your own account, you were not desirous of making my acquaintance. We old people look for such reluctance now and then; and when it touches our honors, we cast about until we find some way of overcoming it." He is sure the figure of Maletroit is a threat to him; he is convinced the man is a lunatic, and feels he is being humiliated. He asserts

himself and demands to be released, threatening to hack the door to pieces with the phallic sword. The door is now a symbol of the authority of the father figure, a restriction of Denis' quest for sexual fulfillment in his dream.

Hostility between the two becomes more evident as Maletroit refers to Denis as his "dear nephew" (an unconscious indication of their blood relationship), and Denis replies, "you lie in your throat." The old man is incensed at this remark; and with a sudden, harsh voice informs Denis that he has a choice, a choice which is symbolic of Denis' conflict between the desire for sexual success and the fear of it. If he surrenders to Maletroit's humiliations he will remain "a free young buck;" but if he refuses he will be "bound hand and foot" until his "bones ache." He chooses, of course, to remain a free young buck, for only in this way will he be able to attain his goal. To be bound hand and foot is to terminate his quest, to destroy his manhood, to castrate him. He is, nevertheless, a prisoner of the old Sire; and Denis no longer sees him as a madman. He is now boiling with anger and chilled with apprehension. He builds the tension within himself as he approaches the climax of his phantasy, as he is about to be introduced to the object of his desire. Culmination is at hand, but how will he face it, "what countenance was he to assume?"

As Denis approaches his most significant phantasy experiences, it is understandable that his eroticism should become more clearly defined; and, thus, as the arras is pulled aside, the chapel in which he discovers Blanche is seen as a mass of symbols of male and female sexuality. "A light groining sprang from six stout columns, and hung down in two rich pendants from the centre of the vault. The place terminated behind the altar in a round end, embossed and honeycombed with a superfluity of ornament in relief, and pierced by many little windows, shaped like stars, trefoils and wheels . . . The tapers, of which there must have been half a hundred burning on the altar, were unmercifully blown about; and the light went through many different phases of brilliancy and semi-eclipse." When Denis perceives that Blanche is dressed as a bride, a chill settles over him and he "fought with desparate energy against the conclusion that was being thrust upon his mind; it could not—it should not—be as he feared." His incapabilities are reflected in this passage, and as Blanche rejects him as the wrong person they become even more evident. "Their eyes met; shame gave place to horror and terror in her looks; the blood left her lips; with a piercing scream she covered her face with her hands and sank upon the chapel floor."

Maletroit now explains to Denis that he expects him to marry Blanche. Denis attempts to extricate himself from this discomfort with a simple refusal, but the Sire makes it quite clear that he must choose between marriage and death. The final danger is upon him; he must either renounce his manhood or express it.

In this section of the phantasy, Denis imposes even more discomfort and danger upon himself; danger that is, for him, represented by the image of his father. In his father he not only recognizes the success of masculinity, but also threats and reproaches concerning sexuality. The father is imagined as forcing Denis on toward sexual gratification with Blanche and at the same time making it as uncomfortable as possible. This is a symbolization of Denis' mixed feelings about his father; he is a man who both encourages and restrains his son's impulses. Fatherly authority is both the eternal symbol of the gratification of the flesh and the cause of childhood sexual fear. It is because of this tension within himself that Denis constructs the ambiguous Maletroit, a man who is evil and beautiful and manly, and who controls Denis' future by his threat of marriage or death. As a result of his fear of sex, Denis has conducted himself through a dangerous and phantastic world, a world in which his fear will be ultimately dispelled by repeated fearful adventures.

Part III—The agonies of indecision and the final gratification of desire.

After Maletroit leaves the chapel the girl turns on Denis with flashing eyes. "And what sir," she demands, "may be the meaning of all this?" "God knows." answers Denis, "I am prisoner in this house, which seems full of mad people. More I know not; and nothing do I understand." "And pray how came you here?" she asks; and after telling her as briefly as he can, Denis adds, "For the rest perhaps you will follow my example, and tell me the answer to all these riddles, and what, in God's name, is like to be the end of it." Blanche gives him the details of the circumstance, and Denis, in a great show of honor to hide his fear, leads the girl back to Maletroit in the apartment without, and refuses to marry her, all the while insisting on her beauty and purity. Here again Denis is retreating from the humiliation of Maletroit because of his fear of the sexual act, but one senses that he is aware of the imminence of the crucial choice; and his protest is only a mockery of himself. His fear even leads him to challenge Maletroit to a duel; one manhood against the other, an attempt to destroy his father and relieve himself of the demands upon him. He relapses quickly, of course, into the depths of the needed humiliation as Maletroit makes even more vivid the dangers that await him. With a bow the old man leaves the young couple alone to decide whether to become married or not.

Blanche now exhibits an attraction and sympathy for Denis: "You shall not die, you shall marry me after all," she cries. She is asking to be taken, but Denis refuses: "I am afraid that you underrate the difficulty, madam. What you may be too generous to refuse, I may be too proud to accept." At these words Blanche bursts into tears, and Denis, thrown into acute discomfort, sits "playing with the guard of his rapier," examining his maleness, wondering what to do with it. They remain silent for a long interval, during which Denis takes notice of certain details in the apartment. "There were such wide spaces between furniture . . . the light fell so badly and cheerlessly over all . . . he had never seen a church so vast, nor a tomb so melancholy . . . He stared into shadowy corners until he imagined they were swarming with horrible animals; and every now and again he awoke with a start, to remember that his last two hours were running, and death was on the march."

These details of his fear and the danger he is in are in contrast with his reaction to Blanche. He begins to notice her

more and more now, and she is, for him, "so plump and yet so fine, with a warm brown skin, and the most beautiful hair . . . " Her hands "looked infinitely caressing." The death alternative would certainly remove the task before him, but his desire for Blanche is increasing and about to replace the desire for death. However, he is still fearful of his acceptance by Blanche, still fearful that he is incapable of taking her. His long speech to her rationalizes his position; he insists the pleasures of the world are illusory, that no matter what one achieves in life, death will erase all success forever. Denis is attempting to justify his fears by denying the importance of manly accomplishments. "When a man is in a fair way and sees all life open in front of him, he seems to himself to make a very important figure in the world. His horse whinnies to him; the trumpets blow and the girls look out of the window as he rides into the town before his company; he receives many assurances of trust and regard—sometimes by express in a letter—sometimes face to face, with persons of great consequence falling on his neck. It is not wonderful if his head is turned for a time. But once he is dead, were he as brave as Hercules or as wise as Solomon, he is soon forgotten . . . death is a dark and dusty corner, where a man gets into his tomb and has the door shut after him till the judgment day."

This passage is also remarkable as a kind of analog to Denis' personality conflict as it has been revealed so far in his dream. Strangely enough, his surname can be translated as "in a fair way," and he does have all life open in front of him. We learned earlier that Denis swaggers, and this characteristic is echoed here as, "he seems to himself to make a very important figure in the world." His head is turned by the desire to express his manliness with Blanche, but he is about to get into his tomb and have the door shut after him.

Blanche now openly expresses her desire for him, but adds, ". . . if you should go back from your word already given, I would no more marry you than I would marry my uncle's groom." Denis has put himself in a most uncomfortable situation, a situation in which the object of his instincts both wants and rejects him, in which he both wants and refuses her. Denis constructs this discomfort in order to achieve the purpose of his phantasy. The more difficult his task becomes, the greater the pleasure anticipated will be. His masochistic instinct is identical with his sexual instinct. The pleasure of physical fulfillment can only occur as a result of sufferings.

The predicament is resolved irrationally, suddenly, orgastically. "The daylight kept flooding insensibly out of the east, which was soon to grow incandescent and cast up that red-hot cannon-ball, the rising sun." "With a swift, uncertain, passionate utterance," Denis says, "Blanche, you have seen whether I fear death. You must know well enough that I would as gladly leap out of that window into the empty air as to lay a finger on you with out your free and full consent." And in the final, orgastic moment of the dream Denis takes "her supple body in his arms," and covers "her wet face with kisses."

The erotic nature of this story is further attested by the coincidence between certain particulars of Denis' problem and the translations of the names of the characters. We have already noticed the occurrence of the English equivalent of Denis' surname. He is "in a fair way," he is at the stage when his self, his maleness demands to be expressed. The name of Denis' rival, or more appropriately his "other self," Florimond de Champdivers, can be translated loosely as a "flourishing, worldly man of many opportunities or careers." It is this kind of personality that Denis desires, and thus he substitutes himself in his dream for Florimond de Champdivers. Sire, of course, means lord or master; and one of the many possible translations of Maletroit is "evilly strict". As a father figure for Denis in his dream, the old man clearly exercises mastery over Denis; a mastery that is, for him, both evil and strict. However, Maletroit can also be translated as "difficultly tight;" and the obvious erotic connotation of this phrase can be applied to Denis' feelings about Blanche de Maletroit. And, finally, I should hardly need to mention, at this point, the similarity between our young hero's Christian name and the organ of male sexuality. (pp. 411-23)

> *Eric LaGuardia, in a review of "Sire de Maletroit's Door," in* American Imago, *Vol. 15, No. 3, Fall, 1958, pp. 411-23.*

Henry James on *The Strange Case of Dr. Jekyll and Mr. Hyde*:

Is *Doctor Jekyll and Mr Hyde* a work of high philosophic intention, or simply the most ingenious and irresponsible of fictions? It has the stamp of a really imaginative production, that we may take it in different ways; but I suppose it would be called the most serious of the author's tales. It deals with the relation of the baser parts of man to his nobler, of the capacity for evil that exists in the most generous natures; and it expresses these things in a fable which is a wonderfully happy invention. The subject is endlessly interesting, and rich in all sorts of provocation, and Mr Stevenson is to be congratulated on having touched the core of it. I may do him injustice, but it is, however, here, not the profundity of the idea which strikes me so much as the art of the presentation—the extremely successful form. There is a genuine feeling for the perpetual moral question, a fresh sense of the difficulty of being good and the brutishness of being bad; but what there is above all is a singular ability in holding the interest. I confess that that, to my sense, is the most edifying thing in the short, rapid, concentrated story, which is really a masterpiece of concision.

> *Henry James, in his* The House of Fiction, *London, Rupert Hart-Davis, 1957.*

Joseph J. Egan (essay date 1966)

[*In the following excerpt, the critic considers "Markheim" as a moral fable, the action of which is largely symbolic.*]

Stevenson's intention in **"Markheim"** was to present not a short story as such, but a moral fable in the form of an exploration of his main character's mind. The entire atmosphere of the tale is presented as remote and preternatural in order to reduce the elements of realism in the story to a functional minimum. The movement of **"Markheim"** is thus to a large degree symbolic, and, as we shall see, the setting of the story gradually becomes the central character's own mind.

It is significant that the pawnbroker's shop in which the entire tale takes place contains "many rich mirrors" that hold a strange kind of terror for Markheim: "He saw his face repeated and repeated, as it were an army of spies; his own eyes met and detected him." The mirrors seem to accuse Markheim of his evil and become suggestive of the many depths and facets within his own soul. Though he savagely plunges a dagger into the back of the shopkeeper, Markheim can still find meaning in the remembrance of childhood innocence: "How fresh the youthful voices! Markheim gave ear to it smilingly . . . and his mind was thronged with answerable ideas and images; churchgoing children and the pealing of the high organ; children afield, bathers by the brookside, ramblers on the brambly common." It is because Markheim yet shows an attachment to goodness that the reflections in the mirrors can seem so horrible to him; if evil had gained complete control over his life, the voice of his conscience would have been silenced forever. The mirrors which so mercilessly reveal Markheim's spiritual decay to his own anguished eyes are thus the means by which Stevenson prepares us for the conclusion of the tale where Markheim's conscience, the better self in his soul, appears to him and persuades him to forego evil.

The pawnbroker himself is closely associated with the mirrors in his shop, and indeed he offers the fifteenth-century hand glass to Markheim: " 'I ask you,' said Markheim, 'for a Christmas present, and you give me this—this damned reminder of years, and sins and follies—this hand-conscience!' " Like the mirrors that he buys and sells, the pawnbroker, too, becomes a reflection of the evil within Markheim's own soul, as is suggested by the strange conversation in which the two men engage:

> The dealer looked closely at his companion. It was very odd, Markheim did not appear to be laughing; there was something in his face like an eager sparkle of hope, but nothing of mirth.
>
> "What are you driving at?" the dealer asked.
>
> "Not charitable?" returned the other, gloomily. "Not charitable; not pious; not scrupulous; unloving, unbeloved; a hand to get money, a safe to keep it. Is that all? Dear God, man, is that all?"

Immediately before this exchange, we were given an early glimpse of Markheim's attempt to rationalize his situation. He knows that he has done wrong, but he has deluded himself into thinking that his evil is not really an essential part of him and that he is as one with the pawnbroker, whom he tries to depict as being "in secret a very charitable man." But when the dealer shows his disdain for goodness and human sentiments by labelling them " 'nonsense'," an awareness of the way in which he himself has continually chosen evil over the good is brought home to Markheim: " 'Every second is a cliff, if you think upon it—a cliff a mile high—high enough, if we fall, to dash us out of every feature of humanity'." It is important to our understanding of Stevenson's tale to realize why Markheim " 'cannot look [the dealer] in the eye'." Markheim has spent his life "pawning" his soul with good resolutions he had never intended to keep, but he will not admit the extent of his evil even to himself, and his murdering the pawnbroker is symbolic of his refusal to face the truth about his life.

In addition to his being the reflection of Markheim's own evil, the pawnbroker also functions to suggest the whole course of spiritual ruination which the murderer's life has taken. He is described as "the little pale, round-shouldered dealer" to call attention to the "sickly" nature of Markheim's soul, and he continually talks in terms of "time" to indicate that Markheim's spiritual condition is the result of a lifetime of self-delusion and neglect of humane values: " 'You will have to pay for my loss of time. . . . I in love! I never had the time, nor have I the time to-day for all this nonsense'." In fact, the dealer lives in "the house of time," for his shop is filled with clocks and time pieces of various centuries: "Time had some score of small voices in that shop, some stately and slow as was becoming to their great age; others garrulous and hurried. All these told out the seconds in an intricate chorus of tickings." The idea that Markheim sees in the pawnbroker the summation of the degradation of his whole life is given further emphasis when the contemplation of his victim's corpse carries the murderer back in time to a day in his boyhood on which he beheld in a fair booth reproductions of famous murder scenes:

> The thing was as clear as an illusion; he was once again that little boy; he was looking once again, and with the same sense of physical revolt, at these vile pictures; he was still stunned by the thumping of the drums. A bar of that day's music returned upon his memory; and at that, for the first time, a qualm came over him, a breath of nausea, a sudden weakness of the joints, which he must instantly resist and conquer.

Markheim has not been successful in his attempt to shut out guilt, for at this point the awareness of his evil is beginning to break in upon his thoughts and his salvation now becomes possible. And yet we are told that "the same heart which had shuddered before the painted effigies of crime, looked on its reality unmoved": "At best, he felt a gleam of pity for one who had been endowed in vain with all those faculties that can make the world a garden of enchantment, one who had never lived and who was now dead. But of penitence, no, not a tremour." The irony of this passage lies in our realization that Markheim is looking upon the image of his own soul's dissolution; and the murderer's lack of penitence indicates that he will have to pass a severe test before he can overcome the inhumanity which has been flourishing in his heart for a lifetime.

Although Markheim constantly fears that someone will discover the pawnbroker's body while he is searching for his money, these fears are really but an extension of the accusation of his own conscience. From the dark corners of Markheim's soul arises the terrible realization of his wickedness and guilt, and this realization haunts his thoughts:

He looked about him awfully. The candle stood on the counter, its flame solemnly wagging in a draught; and by that inconsiderable movement, the whole room was filled with noiseless bustle and kept heaving like a sea: the tall shadows nodding, the gross blots of darkness swelling and dwindling as with respiration, the faces of the portraits and the china gods changing and wavering like images in water. The inner door stood ajar, and peered into that leaguer of shadows with a long slit of daylight like a pointing finger.

The pawnbroker's house, then, becomes at once both the image and exterior reflection of Markheim's troubled mind, and as we follow the tormented murderer from chamber to chamber in this place of "mingled shine and darkness", we penetrate ever further into the depths of his psyche. It is in relationship to this interpretation of the significance of the dealer's house that the hero's name takes on symbolic overtones, for *Markheim* (*Mark* = German, essence; *heim* = German, house) may be translated as the *essential house,* that is, the house of the soul.

The strange movement of time now adds to the horror of this psychological journey into Markheim's mind, as the fleeting moments which are told off by the multitude of clocks in the dealer's shop become symbolic of the murderer's entire passage through life: "Outside, it had begun to rain smartly; and the sound of the shower upon the roof had banished silence. Like some dripping cavern, the chambers of the house were haunted by an incessant echoing, which filled the ear and mingled with the ticking of the clocks." The relentless raindrops become alternates to clock ticks, and the phrase "to plunge into a bath of London multitudes" suggests forgetfulness of time through a dissolution of individual identity and the sense of guilt: "Here was a broad hint to hurry what remained to be done, to get forth from this accusing neighbourhood, to plunge into a bath of London multitudes, and to reach, on the other side of day, that haven of safety and apparent innocence—his bed." Markheim's desire for his bed, his desire to "sleep," symbolizes his wish to drive out all thoughts of his wasted life by putting an end to time through death, the eternal sleep. The twenty-four steps to the first story of the pawnbroker's dwelling, which we are told "were four-and-twenty agonies" for Markheim, are suggestive of the twenty-four hours of the day and reinforce the time-movement motif of the story, which concentrates a lifetime of evil and guilt into minutes, as Markheim wanders alone in the dark passages of his own soul. Time seems to be closing in on the haunted murderer, and the phantom steps which dog his flight and the mysterious shadow that retreats before him herald the approach of the moment when Markheim will have to face his own conscience and make the final and irrevocable choice between good and evil: "He glanced over his shoulder at the open door, where the shadow was still lingering and shivering . . . and as he began with a great effort to mount the stairs, feet fled quietly before him and followed stealthily behind."

The upper drawing-room of the dealer's house symbolizes the innermost depths of Markheim's consciousness; he can go no further now but must answer the demands of conscience. The confused state of the drawing-room mirrors the disorder within the murderer's soul: "The room was quite dismantled, uncarpeted besides, and strewn with packing-cases and incongruous furniture." We are told that "the windows [of the room] opened to the floor; but by great good fortune the lower part of the shutters had been closed, and this concealed him from the neighbours." Of course, the fact that the shutters conceal Markheim from the observation of others is ironic, for they also "shut" him in to the dreadful scrutiny of his own conscience. Significantly, like the ground floor shop, the drawing-room, too, contains "several great pier-glasses, in which he beheld himself at various angles, like an actor on a stage."

"**Markheim**" is the first of Stevenson's tales in which the alter-ego appears as a distinct personality, and the mysterious visitor who enters the door of the drawing-room is thus the figure of Markheim's better self come to confront the evil in his soul. It is important to see that the better self appears at precisely the moment that Markheim hears "the music of a hymn, and the voices of many children" from "the other side" of the partition and begins to think back on past moments of goodness: "And then, at another cadence of the hymn, back again to church, and the somnolence of summer Sundays, and the high genteel voice of the parson (which he smiled a little to recall) . . . and the dim lettering of the Ten Commandments in the chancel." The other side of the partition symbolizes "the other side" of Markheim's life—the past goodness from which his evil has now separated him; and his generous response to these memories of innocence represents the first step in the murderer's spiritual and psychological salvation, for it brings on the flow of his better emotions, as signified by the appearance of the alter-ego.

The voice of Markheim's conscience now becomes another self which assumes the role of a demon tormentor in order to draw forth the last vestiges of goodness from the murderer's heart. At first Markheim continues his rationalizing and desperately tries to pass himself off as a kind of Byronic hero who has a strange secret hidden in his soul which drives him on to evil: " 'My life is but a travesty and slander on myself. I have lived to belie my nature . . . I am worse than most; my self is more overlaid; my excuse is known to me and God'." But the excuses and self-deception which the murderer advances in defense of his wicked deeds all fall in their turn before the relentless exposé of the alter-ego. The visitor finally forces Markheim to admit that there is not one thing in which he has improved but that he has steadily withdrawn himself from all goodness: " 'No,' he added, with despair, 'in none! I have gone down in all'." In the closing passages of "**Markheim**," Stevenson seems to anticipate the methods of modern psychiatry since Markheim is capable of declaring for goodness only after he acknowledges his evil and honestly confesses it to his better self without attempting to hide any part of his guilt: " 'It is true,' said Markheim; 'and I see clearly what remains for me by way of duty. I thank you for these lessons from my soul; my eyes are opened, and I behold myself at last for what I am'."

By disguising himself as the vile agent of evil, the visitor is able to summon up all of Markheim's hatred and loathing for the wickedness in his soul. Stevenson's use of irony in the debate between Markheim and his alter-ego gives a subtle emphasis and an additional artistic dimension to the meaning of the story. The better self taunts Markheim with the idea that " 'you will never change . . . the words of your part on this stage are irrevocably written down'," and Markheim becomes convinced that his tormentor is correct: " 'My love of good is damned to barrenness; it may, and let it be! But I have still my hatred of evil; and from that, to your galling disappointment, you shall see that I can draw both energy and courage'." Though Markheim believes that he is no longer capable of doing good, his better self has been so successful in calling forth the murderer's hatred of evil that Markheim is actually spurred on to an objectively good act. Thus when the pawnbroker's maid returns to her employer's shop, the visitor urges Markheim to kill her and thereby free himself from the danger of arrest for his crime. But the alter-ego has counted on Markheim's not complying with his promptings; and when he says to him, " 'Up, friend; your life hangs trembling in the scales! up, and act!' " it is for the "life" of his soul that he wishes Markheim to act. Markheim's hatred of the evil which he has allowed to flourish in his soul moves him to tell the shopkeeper's maid to call the police, and as he does so, "the features of the visitor began to undergo a wonderful and lovely change: they brightened and softened with a tender triumph; and, even as they brightened, faded and dislimned."

The Christmas Day setting of "**Markheim**" suggests that Stevenson wanted us to see that the alter-ego enters the winter twilight of the drawing-room as the savior of the hero's soul. The visitor has helped Markheim restore his soul to a measure of order by making him admit his spiritual degradation to himself. This confession of guilt moves from an interior to an exterior level of consciousness and the realistic mood of the story is reinstated when Markheim opens the door of the dealer's shop to the returning maid. His subsequent request for the police represents the murderer's removal of the mask of self-deception and false goodness under which he had sought to conceal his evil from society. In admitting to the public crime of murder, Markheim openly acknowledges his "crime" against his own soul and his willingness to accept the consequences of his accumulated evils. (pp. 377-84)

> *Joseph J. Egan, " 'Markheim': A Drama of Moral Psychology," in* Nineteenth-Century Fiction, *Vol. 20, No. 4, March, 1966, pp. 377-84.*

Charles Neider (essay date 1969)

[In the following excerpt, Neider surveys Stevenson's stories and short novels.]

[Stevenson's short stories and short novels] reflect surprisingly well those aspects of his "bright, particular genius," as Henry James called it—personal charm, optimism during much serious illness, romantic tastes, vigorous manner, fondness for medievalism (which he shared with Wal-

---

An excerpt from *The Strange Case of Dr. Jekyll and Mr. Hyde*

He put the glass to his lips and drank at one gulp. A cry followed; he reeled, staggered, clutched at the table, and held on, staring with injected eyes, gasping with open mouth; and as I looked, there came, I thought, a change—he seemed to swell—his face became suddenly black, and the features seemed to melt and alter—and the next moment I had sprung to my feet and leaped back against the wall, my arm raised to shield me from that prodigy, my mind submerged in terror.

"O God!" I screamed, and "O God!" again and again; for there before my eyes—pale and shaken, and half-fainting, and groping before him with his hands, like a man restored from death—there stood Henry Jekyll!

Robert Louis Stevenson, in his The Strange Case of Dr. Jekyll and Mr. Hyde, *1886. Reprint. Scholastic Book Services, 1963.*

---

ter Scott), powerful narrative, lively detail and a pliant, resonant and beautiful if sometimes high-blown style—for which he came to be known through his book-length works.

He began his career as a fictionist with the publication of **"A Lodging for the Night"** in 1877, a month before he turned twenty-seven. Prior to this he had published a number of essays which had given him a circumscribed fame for their originality and style. From that year on, his fiction gradually superseded his essays. The story immediately strikes the notes for which he became famous in most of his novels: a swashbuckling manner, a cloak and dagger mode, and a time remote from his own cloddish Victorian one, a time of personal danger, feudal loyalty and knightly honor. Stevenson, the frustrated soldier (as he believed), often indulged a martial strain when he wrote. With this first fictive publication he achieved what many readers believe to be a masterpiece. Not surprisingly, **"A Lodging for the Night,"** like **"Markheim," "The Sire de Malétroit's Door," "Thrawn Janet"** and **"The Beach of Falesá,"** has been anthologized many times. It is a tale brilliantly told with much suspense, color and with a sense of the special human brutality of François Villon's time. The story is well *seen* and excellently projected, the vocabulary rich, the language vivid. Despite Villon's unpleasant adventure and the mood of menace surrounding him, Stevenson's almost compulsive optimism, shared by many tuberculars (he was one), pervades the text. Stevenson's particular optimism came from a determination to take the rosiest view regardless of personal circumstances—the more desperate his illness the rosier his manner; the more bedridden he was the more athletic were the projections of his imagination. But I do not mean to suggest that his response was programmatic and lacking in self-doubt and great personal courage.

Published in October of the year, the tale followed an essay on Villon which appeared in August, "François Villon, Student, Poet and House-breaker." Many of the story's details—for example, the murder of Thevenin Pensete by Montigny—are based on facts which Stevenson obtained from a new biography of the poet by Longnon, which he reviewed in the essay. In the essay, as fortunately not in the story, he employed a moralizing tone concerning Villon's "low" way of life, his "low" companions and his apparent lack of moral ideals, then indulged himself in admiring anecdotes about the poet's life and times and spoke of Villon's greatness as a poet before concluding with a few choice caustic sentences about his "low" nature. Although the high-dudgeon tone is less muted in the Villon essay than in later ones it is fairly typical of Stevenson's point of view: he is fascinated by irregular, "low" lives but is unable to resist censuring them in print for the then fashionable purposes of moral uplift. The latter, it seemed to him (as to many of his fellow Victorians), was an indispensable part of the baggage of a good writer. In his essay "The Morality of the Profession of Letters"—the very title is from a seemingly ancient era—he wrote, "To treat all subjects in the highest, the most honourable, and the pluckiest spirit, consistent with the fact, is the first duty of a writer." Did he not ask himself privately if it was for him to state universally what the first duty of a writer was? Might there not be a writer, perhaps in France, who would insist that the first duty of a writer was to be true to his self no matter how evil?

Stevenson, despite his love of velvet jackets, unkempt long hair, exotic, piquant manners, despite his grumblings about the dullness of a mercantile empire, was a Presbyterian product of the Scottish variety and in his infancy and childhood he had been nursed by a woman who had stringent notions about damnation and hell, which she had no inhibition about imparting to her charge. In his "Memoirs of Himself" he spoke of the "high-strung religious ecstasies and terrors of his childhood," telling about how he would lie awake and weep for Jesus, fearing that if he fell asleep he would be unaccepted at the gates of judgment and would slip into eternal ruin. In his childhood he often had nightmares about Hell and in the daytime had a habit of adding "If I am spared" to things he said, in the hope of disarming fate. Under the tutelage of his nurse, Cummy, he worried about the spiritual condition of his parents (he was an only child) because they gave dinner parties and played cards. In later years he confided to his step-son, Lloyd Osbourne, that one of his most vivid memories "was finding himself clutched to Cummy's breast, both convulsed with emotion and streaming tears while she called on God" to save his parents from the pit, probably because they were playing after-dinner whist. His wife, Fanny Van de Grift, an American, wrote after his death, "Cummy's piety was her strongest recommendation, but her convictions and consequent teachings, believing as she did in a literal hell along with the other tenets of her church, were rather strong meat for the mental digestion of an imaginative, nervous child. My husband has told me of the terrors of the night, when he dared not go to sleep lest he should awake amid the flames of eternal torment, and how he would be taken from his bed in the morning unrefreshed, feverish, and ill, but rejoicing that he had gained at least a respite from what he believed to be his just doom; Cummy, the kindly soul, never dreaming of the dire effect of her religious training." Still, Stevenson, in childhood and in the years of his maturity, had nothing but love for his Cummy (Alison Cunningham), whom he sometimes styled his second mother.

His moral strictures on Villon's character and way of life were too strongly felt and stated in the essay, and when the latter became part of a book, *Familiar Studies of Men and Books,* he tried to make amends in a preface. "I am tempted to regret that I ever wrote on this subject, not merely because the paper strikes me as too picturesque by half, but because I regarded Villon as a bad fellow. Others still think well of him, and can find beautiful and human traits where I saw nothing but artistic evil; and by the principle of the art, those should have written of the man, and not I. Where you see no good, silence is the best. Though this penitence comes too late, it may be well, at least, to give it expression."

If we are to trust Lloyd Osbourne's memory Stevenson did not regard *The New Arabian Nights* tales highly. "Although Stevenson enjoyed them hugely he attached no importance to them; it was enough that they filled a few empty columns of *London,* and brought in a few pounds. They attracted no notice whatever, and in the bottom of his heart I believe R. L. S. was just a little ashamed of them. I know at least that when it was suggested a few years later to publish them in book-form he emphatically demurred on the ground that it might hurt his reputation." Fanny's recollections, written before Lloyd's, did not exactly match the latter's. "For some five or six years the *New Arabian Nights* lay hidden between the covers of a defunct journal [*London,* edited by Stevenson's friend and later his malicious enemy, W. E. Henley]. Mr. Kegan Paul [a London publisher] advised against their republication, thinking the tales too fantastic, and likely to injure the reputation of their author. There was not a single story, poem, article, or novel written by my husband that was not similarly condemned by some one of his friends and literary advisers."

From the foregoing one might expect to find the tales absurd and badly written but they are neither. They are not serious fiction but they are very entertaining, evidence much literary virtuosity and verbal economy, the dialogues are often spritely, intelligent, graceful and amusing, there's a fair amount of suspense, and the characters though simple are vivid. This is a pretty fair score, taken in the round, for a writer who was still shaping his abilities. It is obvious that Stevenson enjoyed writing the tales; his enjoyment of them is infectious. Occasionally one encounters badly managed, even mawkish things—"The Prince threw himself upon the Colonel's neck in a passion of relief" (the neck in Stevenson's more fervent scenes is a stronger part of the human anatomy than the modern reader is likely to have experienced it)—and it is true that such touches tend to trivialize a tale, but they are not too frequent. Actually (and surprisingly) the tales are better on a second reading than on the first. At times one may wish that the dialogues were less formal and more true to life. A Paris detective speaks with the elegance of Prince Florizel himself—"Your Highness returns good for evil. To an act of presumption he replies by the most amiable

condescension." But then it's all a fantasy and part of the fun is in the graceful elevated speech.

"*The New Arabian Nights* offer us, as the title indicates, the wonderful in the frankest, most delectable form," wrote Henry James. "Partly extravagant and partly very specious, they are the result of a very happy idea, that of placing a series of adventures which are pure adventures in the setting of contemporary English life, and relating them in the placidly ingenuous tone of Scheherezade. . . . In this line '**The Suicide Club**' is Mr. Stevenson's greatest success, and the first two pages of it, not to mention others, live in the memory." Not that we need allow ourselves to be entirely convinced by James, who although a great craftsman and wonderful critic had certain flaws in his ability to judge literary masters: he was not one to appreciate Tolstoy, for example, and he disliked *Crime and Punishment* because the protagonist was not objectively portrayed enough (a point which would have been beside the point for Dostoyevsky). James no doubt enjoyed *The New Arabian Nights* because he believed that Stevenson's originality lay in his passion for youth and for literary style. "This combination," he stated in 1887, "is the keynote to Mr. Stevenson's faculty and the explanation of his perversities."

Do the perversities outweigh the faculties in these fanciful tales? Is Stevenson "deliberately resolved," as William Archer claimed in 1885, that his readers "shall look first to his manner, and only in the second place to his matter?" Deliberately resolved seems rather strong, for perhaps Stevenson is wearing the literary garments which nature, his training and his illness gave him. If he is overclothed (at a time when overfurnishing of houses and canvases and ships and novels was in fashion) it may be because it is more natural to him, as it is to James. James said, "he is conspicuously one of the draped: he would never, if I may be allowed the expression, pose for the nude," adding, "There are writers who present themselves before the critic with just the amount of drapery that is necessary for decency; but Mr. Stevenson is not one of these—he makes his appearance in an amplitude of costume. . . . Before all things he is a writer with a style—a model with a complexity of curious and picturesque garments." Which is a pretty close description of James himself.

"**Providence and the Guitar,**" a farce with much good detail, was based on a story told to Stevenson by a strolling French actor and his Bulgarian wife. It is a tale of the artist as a burlesqued type: the mediocre bohemian insulted by the burgesses, not without some reason inasmuch as he is nomadic and part mountebank by nature and inclination. Stevenson's perspective is ambiguous. He is ironic about the "artist," possibly a bit revolted by him, but he is also increasingly sympathetic. Stevenson was a "gentleman" in manner and held to the gentlemanly ideal, going so far at times as to believe it to be of importance in making or ruining a work of literature. "**Providence**" contains a certain home-grown sympathy inasmuch as Stevenson himself had had at least one run-in with the village police in France because, happening to be very casually, almost vagrantly, dressed, he was taken to belong to a class considerably lower than his own. Although he liked to behave fluidly in a striated society he was not without class-consciousness. The scene of the player, his wife and the English student given shelter by the quarrelling mediocrity of a painter and his wife could be out of a countrified *La Bohème*. The moral is plain: birds of a feather stick together, and bohemians are more generous, certainly to their own kind and possibly to mankind in general, than the callous, xenophobic burgesses.

Another farce dealing with the theme of artist-as-phony is **"The Story of a Lie,"** written largely in a second-class cabin during a voyage to the United States in August 1879, a voyage which was probably Stevenson's symbolic liberation from Great Britain and his parents. It was one he took in pursuit of Fanny, whom he married in San Francisco in May of the following year. He described the writing of the story as occurring "in a slantindicular cabin, with the table playing bob-cherry with the ink-bottle." Between stints of composition he made visits to the steerage, whose conditions and passengers appalled and fascinated him. He carefully put down his impressions of steerage life in the journal which was to be the basis of *The Amateur Emigrant* but he was unable, apparently, to bring himself to view life as he encountered it as the subject of his fiction. The mood and scene of **"The Story of a Lie"** are at times lovely and the Admiral is a very funny character. The details are often extremely good, as they are in the description of the Admiral when drunk: "The appearance of the Admiral . . . was rosy, and flabby, and moist; his jowl hung over his shirt collar, his smile was loose and wandering, and he had so far relaxed the natural control of his eyes, that one of them was aimed inward, as if to catch the growth of the carbuncle [on his nose]."

"The Sire de Malétroit's Door," once again a romance of medieval times, is set some quarter century earlier than the Villon story. It is very romantic. The dialogues between Denis and Blanche are too perfumed, too courtly-knightly for my taste. Nor am I taken with **"The Pavilion on the Links"** (a short novel . . .), which at times reads like a parody of *Wuthering Heights*. Can Stevenson have believed with the narrator that Clara Huddlestone is a lovely name or that the relations between the narrator and Clara, reminding one of some of the sentimental excesses of pre-Raphaelite paintings, are real? The final chapter, unless I am mistaken, is absurd with its phony gestures, actions, sentiments and speeches. While I am being negative I may as well add that the point of the bloated **"Treasure of Franchard"** . . . largely escapes me—what Stevenson needed was some of Mark Twain's frontier humor to make it work. Am I suggesting that Stevenson sometimes nodded? It would have been a miracle if he hadn't. He was too prolific, too driven to earn money, too assailed by spells of dangerous illness, too committed to the publishing conventions of his time and too attentive to an idolizing claque whose literary tastes contained much that was provincial and immature.

Having said this, perhaps unfairly, it is a relief to turn to stories for which I have great admiration—**"Will o' the Mill,"** for instance, with its beautiful nature descriptions, its fine articulateness in dealing with a largely inarticulate character, and its vividness. It is a moving and beautiful

story delicately and gracefully told. James said that in it "there is something exceedingly rare, poetical and unexpected, with that most fascinating quality a work of imagination can have—a dash of alternative mystery as to its meaning, an air (the air of life itself), of half inviting, half defying you to interpret. . . . The story is in the happiest key and suggests all kinds of things: but what does it in particular represent? The advantage of waiting, perhaps—the valuable truth that, one by one, we tide over our impatiences."

Stevenson, his wife and his parents spent the summer of 1881 in a rented cottage in the highlands near Pitlochry in Scotland. The idea was that Stevenson would get plenty of sunshine and fresh air. But the weather was mostly cold, wet and windy and consequently he was cooped up much of the time in a small, stuffy sitting room. In an effort to alleviate boredom he and Fanny wrote stories and read them to each other. It was in these circumstances that **"Thrawn Janet,"** which James called "a masterpiece in thirteen pages," was born. After her husband's death Fanny recalled the evening when he first read the ghost story to her. "That evening is as clear in my memory as though it were yesterday,—the dim light of our one candle, with the acrid smell of a wick we forgot to snuff, the shadows in the corners of the 'lang, laigh, mirk chalmer, perishing cauld,' the driving rain on the roof close above our heads, and the gusts of wind that shook our windows. . . . By the time the tale was finished my husband had fairly frightened himself, and we crept down the stairs clinging hand in hand like two scared children."

Stevenson told Fanny, "I doubt if this is good enough for my father to hear." He had a great respect for his civil engineer father's literary opinions and even permitted *The Amateur Emigrant,* already sold to a publisher, to be repurchased by his father and suppressed because the father did not think its publication would be good for the son's reputation. This was a mistake, for *The Amateur Emigrant,* much underrated among Stevenson's books, is a marvellously vivid, simply written, intelligently observed work. It did not appear until after his death. The probable truth is that the book's subject seemed to the gloomy, Calvinistic father not sufficiently uplifting, and possibly a degrading influence on the son's sensibility and style. Also, he may have guessed that it represented the crucial moment when the only child left parents and country behind him in headlong, empty-pocket and sick pursuit of an older and married woman. But the father enjoyed the tale of Scottish life and superstition, causing the son to take it more seriously. In later years Stevenson wrote, " **'Thrawn Janet'** has two defects; it is true only historically, true for a hill parish in Scotland in the old days, not true for mankind and the world. Poor Mr. Soukis's faults we may equally recognise as virtues; and feel that by his conversion he was merely coarsened; and this, although the story carries me away every time I read it, leaves a painful feeling on the mind. I hope I should admire **'Will o' the Mill'** and **'Markheim'** as much as if they had been written by someone else; but I am glad no one else wrote them."

"The Merry Men" was composed the same summer. Fanny reported, "The story itself, overshadowed by its surroundings, did not come so easily as **'Thrawn Janet,'** and never quite satisfied its author, who believed that he had succeeded in giving the terror of the sea [the sea is the tale's hero], but had failed to get a real grip on his story." When the tale was half finished Stevenson wrote to a friend, "It is a fantastic sonata about the sea and wrecks; and I like it much above all my other attempts at story-telling; I think it is strange; if ever I shall make a hit, I have the line now, I think." The story is very powerful and its marvellous language brings pungently to the reader the island and its bubbling waters. It was not for nothing that Stevenson had taught himself to be a writer of travel books like *An Inland Voyage* and *Travels with a Donkey,* in which brilliant descriptions of nature, aided by pencil sketches made on the spot, abounded. In its vividness and sobriety **"The Merry Men"** seems to me as good as the beginning of the unfinished, posthumously published novel, *Weir of Hermiston.* As though suddenly, Stevenson saw that he could do the spring-water, Scottish mood wonderfully well. Here there is no cloak and dagger child's play, no saccharine dialogues between frustrated lovers. The materials are those Stevenson is familiar with: moors, gales, the northern sun: a "dark" world like that of **"Thrawn Janet."**

"The Body-Snatcher," like **"Thrawn Janet,"** is a ghost story but its style and detail are not as simple and genuine as those of the earlier story. Sidney Colvin, a close friend and admirer of Stevenson, said that it "was advertised in the streets of London by sandwich-men carrying posters so horrific that they were suppressed, if I remember right, by the police." Of **"Olalla"** Stevenson wrote, "The trouble with [it] is that it somehow sounds false. . . . 'Markheim' is true; 'Olalla' false; and I don't know why, nor did I feel it while I worked at them; indeed I had more inspiration with 'Olalla,' as the style shows." But the style does not show it, unfortunately. And the story itself is too romantical from beginning to end, with its mountain setting, the degeneracy of family blood, the officer's super-infatuation with the idealized Olalla, and the arch dialogues. (pp. xi-xxii)

[**"The Misadventures of John Nicholson"**] is a comedy of errors which was originally subtitled "A Christmas Story" and which first appeared in *Yule-Tide,* Cassell's Christmas Annual for 1887. In a letter to James, Stevenson called it "a silly Xmas story (with some larks in it)" and in a letter of 1891 to H. B. Baildon he said, "Did you see a silly tale, **'John Nicholson's Predicament,'** or some such name, in which I made free with your home at Murrayfield? There is precious little sense in it, but it might amuse. Cassell's published it in a thing called *Yule-Tide* years ago, and nobody that ever I heard of read or has seen *Yule-Tide.* It is addressed to a class we never met—readers of Cassell's series and that class of conscientious chaff, and my tale was dull, though I don't recall that it was conscientious. Only there's a house at Murrayfield and a dead body in it."

Of *Dr. Jekyll and Mr. Hyde* it is fair to say that both its conception and execution were remarkable. Stevenson was living in Bournemouth, England, in a house which his father had given Fanny as a gift, together with some money

to furnish it. Bournemouth was fashionable then as a seaside health resort where well-cushioned admirals and upper civil servants spent their retirement years. The house was pleasant enough, with pleasant gardens and pleasant company (including occasionally Henry James) but there were times when Stevenson was not nearly so well in it as he had been in many less healthful places. He was collaborating with Henley on some plays by which he hoped to make a fortune—this was largely under Henley's prodding—and Henley's ebullience, vigor and drive (Henley was living with the Stevensons at the time) had made him ill with over-excitement and over-work. Then he had a hemorrhage of the lungs, followed by a fever. It was in these circumstances that he dreamed the story of Dr. Jekyll up to the transformation scene. The dream was a nightmare, complete with Stevenson's cries. But when Fanny woke him he was indignant. "I was dreaming a fine bogey tale," he said. At daybreak he began to work at the tale, the first draft of which he finished in three days. Elated, he read it to Fanny and Lloyd. Fanny's judgment was that he had missed the allegorical point, without which the story was little better than a bit of brilliant sensationalism. Although he was furious for a while, that same day he admitted that she was right and, according to Lloyd, threw the manuscript into the fire to avoid being tempted by it. In the following three days he rewrote the story and, by Lloyd's account, looked more refreshed after this amazing stint than he had in some time.

Although most of *Dr. Jekyll* had come to him in a dream, Stevenson had not made it of whole cloth. He had already written **"Markheim,"** a story of a schizoid murderer which owed a debt to Dostoyevsky's Raskolnikov of *Crime and Punishment* (which Stevenson read in a French translation). Perhaps he had also read "Notes from Underground," Dostoyevsky's supreme projection of a split personality who is enchanted by human abysses. He had read much of Poe, including Poe's brief but extremely perceptive, incisive and sensitive story, "The Imp of the Perverse," which prefigured Dostoyevksy's efforts to illuminate the self-destructive, perverse side of man's nature. (In Poe's tale the narrator says, "I am not more certain that I breathe, than that the assurance of the wrong or error of any action is often the one unconquerable *force* which impels us to its prosecution. Nor will this overwhelming tendency to do wrong for the wrong's sake, admit of analysis, or resolution into ulterior elements. It is a radical, a primitive impulse—elementary.") In addition, when Stevenson was a child in Edinburgh his room contained a bookcase and a chest of drawers made by one Deacon Brodie, who led a double life, being an artisan by day and a thief at night. And finally, Stevenson had read a paper in a French scientific journal on "subconsciousness," which according to Fanny had much impressed him and which, again according to her, had, together with the memory of Deacon Brodie's career, caused him to dream the story of Dr. Jekyll.

Technically there is no question that *Dr. Jekyll* is masterly and that Stevenson's genius as a story-teller is at its zenith. There is nothing fuzzy or uncertain; everything is cleanly handled and carefully controlled despite the great speed with which the tale was composed. There is a surprising amount of "mind" at play in it, for example in Jekyll's final statement, in which he explores the themes of moral ambiguity, of the double, and of identity in detail, at length and with surprising subtlety. The shortcoming of the tale, in my view, is that, especially by comparison with Dostoyevsky's work in a similar vein, it reveals for us so little humanly; it remains, despite its display of genius, a fantasy, a horror story, a thriller. Although Stevenson is said to have been empathetic in his relations with living people his fictive work too often seems brilliantly cold. Nor does the story contain any suggestion of the ambiguity of morality and neurosis: Hyde is evil plain and simple. A more subtle treatment (but Stevenson is not a subtle psychologist although at times he is a strangely, unexpectedly good one) would have had Hyde predominantly evil but with a part of him good. Such distinctions were on the whole foreign to Stevenson's broad-sword fictive side and were not in vogue during the Victorian era, which was more inclined to focus on the glaring poles of good and evil than on the twilit way-stops between them. Absorbing as the story is while one is immersed in it, it loses resonance when one is away from it.

James thought highly of it although he had his reservations. "Is *Dr. Jekyll and Mr. Hyde* a work of high philosophic intention," he inquired,

> or simply the most ingenious and irresponsible of fictions? It has the stamp of a really imaginative production, that we may take it in different ways; but I suppose it would generally be called the most serious of the author's tales. It deals with the relation of the baser parts of man to his nobler, of the capacity for evil that exists in the most generous natures; and it expresses these things in a fable which is a wonderfully happy invention. The subject is endlessly interesting, and rich in all sorts of provocation, and Mr. Stevenson is to be congratulated on having touched the core of it. I may do him injustice, but it is, however, here, not the profundity of the idea which strikes me so much as the art of presentation—the extremely successful form. There is a genuine feeling for the perpetual moral question, a fresh sense of the difficulty of being good and the brutishness of being bad; but what there is above all is a singular ability in holding the interest. I confess that that, to my sense, is the most edifying thing in the short, rapid, concentrated story, which is really a masterpiece of concision.

What troubled James was the magic powders. "I have some difficulty in accepting the business of the powders, which seems to me too explicit and explanatory. The powders constitute the machinery of the transformation, and it will probably have struck many readers that this uncanny process would be more conceivable (so far as one may speak of the conceivable in such a case), if the author had not made it so definite." This is a curious and not well taken cavil. Why object to the powders and not to the physical changes which take place in Jekyll as he becomes Hyde—changes of his size and very skeleton, changes ungrounded in fact? (It was well known that the taking of drugs could cause profound psychic changes.) "If the author had not made it so definite"—it has a haunting ring coming from the master of the indefinite, of the not explic-

it, the not explanatory. Are we going too far in suspecting that James would have preferred that Stevenson had written the tale more in the Jamesian manner?

In his last years, when he had settled in Samoa, Stevenson published three South Sea tales, two of them, **"The Isle of Voices"** and **"The Bottle Imp,"** fair work and the third, **"The Beach of Falesá,"** a masterpiece. Stevenson at times insisted that he admired **"The Bottle Imp,"** the idea for which he obtained indirectly from German folklore. To Colvin he claimed (January 1893), "You always had an idea that I depreciated the **'B. I.';** I can't think wherefore; I always particularly liked it—one of my best works, and ill to equal." But to A. Conan Doyle he wrote in August, "I . . . have had the indiscretion to perpetrate a trifling piece of fiction entitled **'The Bottle Imp.'** " After being published in English the story was translated into Samoan. "We wondered," Fanny recalled, "why so many of our native visitors demanded a view of the large safe in Vailima, and were puzzled by the expression of disappointment that crossed their faces when they were shown its interior and saw that it contained a little money. We afterwards discovered there was a popular belief that Tusitala [Stevenson] still possessed the magic bottle, and the great iron safe had been placed in Vailima solely for its protection. . . . I do not understand what civilising effect the story of **'The Bottle Imp'** was supposed to have on the natives, but I cannot think it quite fulfilled the expectations of the missionary who translated it."

"The Beach of Falesá," written in a somewhat vernacular style (a refreshing change from Stevenson's usual highfalutin language) is one of the most successful of his shorter fictions. One seems to detect the influence of Mark Twain's vernacular in it, particularly as exemplified in *Huckleberry Finn.* Its vernacular mode is not its only link with *Huckleberry Finn;* the first-person stance and the unstylish sympathy with the Kanakas or natives (recalling Huck's sympathy with the Negro's plight through the figure of Jim) also recall Clemens's great if badly flawed novel. Stevenson read the novel shortly after its first publication. In a letter to John Addington Symonds of February 1885 he said, "Have you read *Huckleberry Finn?* It contains many excellent things; above all, the whole story of a healthy boy's dealings with his conscience, incredibly well done."

Regarding **"The Beach of Falesá"** Stevenson wrote to Colvin in September 1891,

> It is the first realistic South Seas story; I mean with real South Sea character and details of life. Everybody else who has tried, that I have seen, got carried away by the romance, and ended in a kind of sugar candy sham epic, and the whole effect was lost—there was no etching, no human grin, consequently no conviction. Now I have got the smell and look of the thing a good deal. You will know more about the South Seas after you have read my little tale than if you had read a library. As to whether any one else will read it, I have no guess. I am in an off time, but there is just the possibility it might make a hit; for the yarn is good and melodramatic, and there is quite a love affair—for me; and Mr. Wiltshire

(the narrator) is a huge lark, though I say it. But there is always the exotic question, and everything, the life, the place, the dialects—trader's talk, which is a strange conglomerate of literary expressions in English and American slang, and Beach de Mar, or native English,—the very trades and hopes and fears of the characters, are all novel, and may be found unwelcome to that great, hulking, bullering whale, the public.

But it was not the great bullering whale that constituted a road block; the public was to prove more genial than he feared. It was London editors and publishers, exemplars and guardians of Victorian interests, manners and tastes. The marriage contract in the story was fraudulent, therefore Wiltshire and his Kanaka wife were living in sin. Such a tale, an affront to the British family, was unsuitable for a family magazine. Poor Stevenson, who had believed for a while that he had escaped from English narrowness as well as from the wretched British climate. Living in a bare-breasted culture, he learned that an English magazine had published the tale without the marriage contract, giving the impression that the marriage was genuine. He was forewarned regarding book publication; also somewhat shaken. " **'The Beach of Falesá'** I still think well of, but it seems it's immoral and there's a to-do, and financially it may prove a heavy disappointment," he wrote to Colvin in January 1892. "The plaintive request sent to me, to make the young folks married properly 'that night,' I refused; you will see what would be left of the yarn, had I consented. This is a poison bad world for the romancer, this Anglo-Saxon world; I usually get out of it by not having any women in it at all; but when I remember I had **'The Treasure of Franchard'** refused as unfit for a family magazine, I feel despair weigh upon my wrists."

Not that Colvin needed to be informed about the difficulties the story was encountering. Colvin was in London, at the heart of British publishing, not thousands of miles away on a half-savage island in the South Seas. Colvin, who was acting as a sort of literary agent for his friend, had seen what the magazine had done and had not had the heart to send a copy to Stevenson. (Stevenson had come upon one anyhow.) Stevenson's stated reason for leaving women out of his fictional world might have impressed Colvin, who idolized him and his work, but it needn't blind a modern reader to the fact that he probably had a more compelling one: he was unable almost throughout his career to give them sufficient fictional life, perhaps because the company of men so clearly fascinated him more than that of women. For women who were his exact contemporaries he seemed to have no great regard. Fanny was eleven years his senior; he always remained profoundly attached to his nurse Cummy, whom as we have noted he called his second mother; and to his first he had bonds which were perhaps stronger than usual, not least because he and she had shared the experience of precarious health from the time of his earliest memories.

In the tale as we know it the fraudulent contract is supposed to be in effect for a week. This was one of Stevenson's necessary compromises with a society-righteous publisher. Writing to Colvin in May, he said, "Well, well, if the dears prefer a week, why, I'll give them ten days, but

the real document, from which I have scarcely varied, ran for one night." That Stevenson was depressed by all this there is no doubt. Lloyd Osbourne remembered an observation Stevenson made to him near the end of his life:

> How the French misuse their freedom; see nothing worth writing about save the eternal triangle; while we, who are muzzled like dogs, but who are infinitely wider in our outlook, are condemned to avoid half the life that passes us by. What books Dickens could have written had he been permitted! Think of Thackeray as unfettered as Flaubert or Balzac! What books I might have written myself! But they give us a little box of toys, and say to us, "You mustn't play with anything but these."

Stevenson's pleasure in the story, however, was not altogether flattened by the stiff backs it encountered in the London world. In August he informed Colvin, "I have now received all **'Falesá,'** and my admiration for that tale rises; I believe it is in some ways my best work; I am pretty sure, at least, I have never done anything better than Wiltshire. . . . Since the **'Beach,'** I know nothing, except that men are fools and hypocrites, and I know less of them than I was fond enough to fancy." (pp. xxii-xxx)

> *Charles Neider, in an introduction to* The Complete Short Stories of Robert Louis Stevenson, *edited by Charles Neider, Doubleday & Company, Inc., 1969, pp. xi-xxx.*

Joseph J. Egan   (essay date 1970)

[*In the following excerpt, Egan examines Stevenson's presentation of Renaissance poet François Villon in "A Lodging for the Night."*]

Although historically inaccurate, [Stevenson's] interpretation of Villon transcended the pathetic and admirable figure of the fifteenth century; Stevenson was interested in the "Vagabond Poet" primarily as one who, because of his unwillingness to take the blame for his failures and to continue to strive against evil, became for him an archetype of human degradation:

> Somehow or other, though he does not know what goodness is, he must try to be good; somehow or other, though he cannot tell what will do it, he must try to give happiness to others.

> . . . . .

> Nor will he complain at the summons which calls a defeated soldier from the field: defeated, ay, if he were Paul or Marcus Aurelius!—but if there is still one inch of fight in his old spirit, undishonoured. ("A Christmas Sermon")

For Stevenson the human task is commitment to life, and only through generous fellow-feeling can man gain the knowledge and courage to fulfill that commitment.

From the outset of **"A Lodging for the Night,"** the fundamental irony in Villon's position is implicit: as a poet he dwells in the world of the spirit, but as a man he lives in the most sordid of material worlds, where he elects to waste his sensibilities in the company of desperate rogues.

The miserable physical condition to which the poet-thief has fallen externalizes his spiritual and psychological decay, the animal imagery suggesting the dehumanizing nature of the life Villon has chosen: "The poet was a rag of a man, dark, little, and lean, with hollow cheeks and thin black locks. He carried his four-and-twenty years with feverish animation. Greed had made folds about his eyes, evil smiles had puckered his mouth. The wolf and pig struggled together in his face. It was an eloquent, sharp, ugly, earthly countenance. His hands were small and prehensile, with fingers knotted like a cord." Villon's destitution of soul is further reflected in the bleak, snow-covered atmosphere of Paris in late November when "flake after flake descended out of the black night air, silent, circuitous, interminable." In fact, setting is artistically purposeful throughout **"A Lodging for the Night"**; and the wintry landscape, dismal cemetery, and deserted, foreboding streets reinforce the concern of the story with death in its various contexts.

Villon's flight from the dimly-lit hut, the scene of Montigny's slaying of Pensete, to the home of the seigneur de Brisetout, his final "lodging for the night," takes on the character of a psychological journey in which fear is his constant companion: "Wherever he went he must weave, with his own plodding feet, the rope that bound him to the crime and would bind him to the gallows . . . and he kept quickening his pace as if he could escape from unpleasant thoughts by mere fleetness of foot." When he stumbles on the corpse of a dead harlot in an abandoned hotel that he enters for fear of a passing patrol, Villon's increasing psychic dissolution is evident: "His heart gave a leap, and he sprang two steps back and stared dreadfully at the obstacle. Then he gave a little laugh of relief. It was only a woman, and she dead." The sight of the frozen woman whose "cheeks had been heavily rouged that same afternoon" does generate a modicum of pity in Villon's heart; he calls her "poor jade" and is "moved with a deep sense of pathos that she should have died before she had spent her money." Nonetheless, Villon's odd sense of "relief" and his genuine but singularly misdirected feelings of compassion indicate that he has lost most of the human emotions he once had and that the few remaining have become eccentric.

This scene, in which the poet confronts the dead prostitute in the porch of the empty hotel, still another of his temporary "lodgings for the night," is central to the spiritual-psychological revelation. The "half-ruinous" porch is suggestive of Villon's moral deterioration; as the poet leaves the open starlight of the November evening and passes into the darkness of this enclosure, he seems to enter the hidden "lodging" of his own heart, where he is offered a belated opportunity to redeem a portion of his humanity. When he discovers that someone has stolen his purse and in his ensuing rage kicks at the frozen corpse before him, we understand that it is beginning to be too late for Master Francis on his "night's" journey: "Villon stood and cursed . . . he shook his fist at heaven; he stamped, and was not horrified to find himself trampling the poor corpse." In the context of the psychical discovery of the tale, the dead prostitute whom he abuses symbolizes the vestiges of Villon's ruined humanity and the projection of

his now dead, "harlotized" spirit, which has been "frozen" by repeated acts of lovelessness. Ironically, Villon can see in the tragedy of the dead whore only the foreshadowing of his possible fate if he cannot find a place of shelter: "The idea of the dead woman popped into his imagination, and gave him a hearty fright; what had happened to her in the early night might very well happen to him before morning." The poet's critical lack of awareness is vividly portrayed here, for he fears only bodily death and is insensible to the spiritual decline that threatens him. Throughout, Stevenson places special emphasis on the fact that Villon is a bankrupt, his impoverished condition supplying an effective intimation of his soul-state. He is thus unprotected amid the winter wind and frost, and his plea that " 'the cold lies at my heart' " calls attention to the "cold," naked quality of his isolation from human values. Appropriately, on the way to the lord of Brisetout's home, his last hope for the night, Villon's mind is oppressed by the thought of "ravening" wolves, a thought that evokes for the Christian reader a traditional image of evil: "He passed a street corner, where, not so long before, a woman and her child had been devoured by wolves. . . . He stopped and looked upon the place with an unpleasant interest . . . and held his breath to listen, lest he should detect some galloping black things on the snow or hear the sound of howling between him and the river."

[In "The Villon Cult in England," *Comparative Literature*, 1966, Glen] Omans maintains that in the duologue between Villon and the seigneur de Brisetout, Stevenson presents the retired knight as "the essence of bourgeois respectability." If this statement is valid, it is so chiefly in relationship to the more abstract portion of their debate, that part that is concerned with whether the soldier or the thief is the worse depredator and in which, as might be expected, Villon makes some telling points. It is only when the argument comes down to the fundamental issues of their own lives, however, that the words of the two men take on real significance. The seigneur sympathizes with his guest's claim that the poor must steal in order to stay alive, but realizes that Villon, once having satisfied the basic wants of the body, fails to attend to the needs of the soul:

> You speak of food and wine, and I know very well that hunger is a difficult trial to endure; but you do not speak of other wants; you say nothing of honour, of faith to God and other men, of courtesy, of love without reproach. It may be that I am not very wise—and yet I think I am— but you seem to me like one who has lost his way and made a great error in life. You are attending to little wants, and you have totally forgotten the great and only real ones, like a man who should be doctoring toothache on the Judgment Day. For such things as honour and love and faith are not only nobler than food and drink, but indeed I think we desire them more, and suffer more sharply for their absence.

These words, though debatable in particular points, touch upon an essential truth that Villon has perhaps always felt, but never quite admitted even to himself—his lack of honor. The poet becomes enraged at this home-thrust and immediately seeks self-vindication: " 'I would have you to know I've an honour of my own, as good as yours. . . . There are your damned goblets, as safe as in a church; there are you, with your heart ticking as good as new'." Stevenson has prepared us to judge this speech fairly, since on entering his host's dwelling, Villon revealed his true code of "honor": " 'Seven pieces of plate. . . . If there had been ten, I would have risked it. A fine house, and a fine old master, so help me all the saints!' " The colloquy, then, points up a persistent Stevensonian idea, namely, that it is his intention, his will to do good which measure a person's human dignity: ". . . if I could show you these men and women, all the world over, in every stage of history, under every abuse of error, under every circumstance of failure, without hope, without help, without thanks, still obscurely fighting the lost fight of virtue, still clinging, in the brothel or on the scaffold, to some rag of honour, the poor jewel of their souls! . . . all their lives long, the desire of good is at their heels, the implacable hunter" ("Pulvis Et Umbra"). Brisetout showed pity for the shivering poet and, after taking him in and literally saving his life, prepared a meal for him with his own hands. Despite this evident hospitality, which demands at least a passing sentiment of gratitude, a sentiment that would have cost him nothing but perhaps gained him much, Villon has thoughts only of robbery and thus discloses his degree of moral insensitivity.

The juxtaposition of the nimble-minded, cunning poet and the generous soldier with a face "honourable rather than intelligent" creates a pointed psychological contrast. It is in relationship to Villon's alleged honor that the host's designation *Brisetout* (French, he who *breaks everything*) takes on symbolic overtones, for in his rough, sometimes blundering way he has "broken" all of Villon's perverse attempts at rationalization and self-justification. The past disposition of his mind gives the lie to the poet's claim to essential human feelings, and, tragically, he has benefited not at all from his night with the seigneur de Brisetout, the last hope of his soul:

> The door closed behind him. The dawn was breaking over the white roofs. A chill, uncomfortable morning ushered in the day. Villon stood and heartily stretched himself in the middle of the road. "A very dull old gentleman," he thought. "I wonder what his goblets may be worth."

The phrase *the door closed behind him* implies the moral fate of Villon. Stevenson tells us that in the house Villon has just left "some smart tapestry hung upon the wall, representing the crucifixion of our Lord in one piece, and in another a scene of shepherds and shepherdesses by a running stream." The religious imagery here is functional: the Crucifixion is a reminder that even Christ himself met with earthly defeat and that no man has a right to despair; the sheep in the pastoral offer a salutary alternative to the previous wolf image; and the running stream is suggestive of the waters of spiritual rebirth associated with the baptismal graces gained by the redemptive death of Our Lord. In turning his back to this symbolic "lodging," Villon, though physically restored, has "closed the door" on the life of his soul; it is indeed an "uncomfortable morning" that is dawning for the poet-thief.

In **"A Lodging for the Night"** the careful dramatization of a single night in the life of Villon becomes subtly connotative of the course of his earthly existence; even his age of "four-and-twenty years," evocative of the twenty-four hours of the day, reinforces the lifetime-movement motif of the story. This is far less the tale of a Renaissance poet than a vivid chronicle of the inevitable tragedy of a soul that, endowed though it is with the loftiest powers of mind and imagination, so gravely lacks fidelity to principles of human decency that the gifts are perverted; and instead of life and growth, their fruit is self-injury and self-degradation. Stevenson's Villon, who wanders alone in a cold world, unloved and at last incapable of love (his image of woman being a dead whore whom he tramples) is a figure whose erstwhile possibilities for noble intention make more pitiful his having sunk beneath the recognition of his own evil into an existence less than human. (pp. 403-08)

> Joseph J. Egan, "Dark in the Poet's Corner: Stevenson's 'A Lodging for the Night'," in Studies in Short Fiction, Vol. VII, No. 3, Summer, 1970, pp. 402-08.

The correct pronounciation of "Jekyll":

Stevenson's attempt to convince people that Jekyll is pronounced with a long "e" may be ranked with his unsuccessful efforts to withstand Hyde's equation with sexuality.

Irving S. Saposnik, in his "The Anatomy of Dr. Jekyll and Mr. Hyde," Studies in English Literature, *1971.*

Walter Allen (essay date 1981)

[*Allen is an English novelist, historian, and critic. In the following excerpt, he pronounces "The Beach of Falesá" Stevenson's best short story and asserts that this work introduced the theme of interaction between Western Europeans and Pacific Islanders into English fiction.*]

Stevenson's place in English writing is a strange one. He was not a great novelist, except perhaps in *Weir of Hermiston,* which was unfinished at his death (at the age of forty-four), or a great poet, and he was a great short-story writer only once or twice. Yet it is difficult not to see him as a great writer. He brought even to his lightest works the scrupulousness of treatment and seriousness of execution that other writers have generally reserved for their most considered works. It is this that gives *Treasure Island,* for example, its classic status, its particular and altogether special eminence as a book for children. It was, it seems to me, his romantic temperament, his response to the past and antipathy to the prosaic present that prevented his being, except occasionally, a great writer of the modern short story, which is concerned very much with the immediate. Yet towards the end of his relatively short life he was ready and able to embrace the immediate; as is made manifest in his greatest short story, **'The Beach at Falesa'.**

It brought a new theme into English fiction, one we associate both with Conrad and with Maugham, the interaction between the exotic, more precisely, the Pacific scene and its peoples, and the Western European. Stevenson wrote it on Samoa in 1891 and he knew exactly what he had done. It was, he wrote in a letter, 'the first realistic South Sea story',

> . . . I mean with real South Sea characters and details of life. Everybody else who has tried that I have seen, got carried away by the romance, and ended with a kind of sugar candy sham epic, and the whole effect was lost—there was no etching, no human grin, consequently no conviction. Now I have got the smell, and the look of the thing a good deal. You will know more about the South Seas after you have read my little tale than if you had read a library.

In other words, it is a work of realism, containing, among other things, a sexual frankness we find nowhere else in Stevenson and uncommon anywhere in English writing of the time. And, more than this, he expresses the contemporary world as it were through the speaking voice of that world. **'The Beach at Falesa'** is a triumph of writing in the vernacular; or, rather, Stevenson most cunningly suggests the vernacular, for the story is told by a Mr Wiltshire, a trader who aims at making enough money to enable him to return to England and keep a pub.

Wiltshire goes to Falesa to manage the store there for his company. Before he disembarks he learns that all his predecessors have died mysteriously. Later, he meets Mr Case, the other white trader on the island, and through him a native girl, Uma, whom he marries against all his notions of proper behaviour by white men in the South Seas. Then he finds himself under a mysterious tabu; his trade is non-existent; and Case, who professes to fear the consequences of association with him, shuns him. In time, Wiltshire finds out that Case exercises a reign of terror over the natives in order to maintain his monopoly of the copra crop. The source of the man's power, he discovers, is that he is worshipped as a devil. He demolishes Case's 'shrine' with dynamite and kills him.

The story ends:

> My public house? Not a bit of it, nor ever likely. I'm stuck here, I fancy. I don't like to leave the kids, you see; and—there's no use talking— they're better off here than they would be in a white man's country; though Ben took the eldest up to Auckland, where he's being schooled with the best. But what bothers me is the girls. They're only half-castes, of course; I know that as well as you do, and there's nobody thinks less of half-castes than I do; but they're mine, and about all I've got. I can't reconcile my mind to their taking up with Kanakas, and I'd like to know where I'm to find the whites?

What emerges from Wiltshire's self-told story is the portrait of a man uneducated, prejudiced, and ignobly decent, one of the first representations, as V. S. Pritchett has observed in his introduction to the Pilot Press's 1945 edition of *Novels and Stories* by Robert Louis Stevenson, 'of the very common, common man who has since become quite a figure; and has succeeded the gentleman'. As a story of

colonial exploitation and its effects on exploited and exploiters alike, **'The Beach at Falesa'** has links with stories by Kipling and Conrad. In the character of Mr Case, Stevenson anticipates villains in Conrad such as Jones and Ricardo and even Kurtz. Rather more than fifty pages in length, **'The Beach at Falesa'** is sometimes referred to as a short novel. It seems to me without question a short story: it has a double unity, that of theme, for everything is subordinated to the account of Wiltshire's defeat of Case, and that of tone, the speaking voice of Wiltshire. (pp. 16-18)

> *Walter Allen, "The Modern Story: Origins, Background, Affinities: Scott, Dickens, Hardy, Stevenson," in his* The Short Story in English, *Oxford at the Clarendon Press, 1981, pp. 3-23.*

Vladimir Nabokov on the origin and currency of the term derived from Stevenson's famous story:

"Dr. Jekyll and Mr. Hyde," as a phrase, has entered the language for just the reason of its epoch-making scene, the impression of which cannot be effaced. The scene is, of course, the narrative of Jekyll's transformation into Mr. Hyde which, curiously, has the more impact in that it comes as the explanation contained in two letters after the chronological narrative has come to an end, when Utterson—alerted by Poole that it is someone other than the doctor who for days has immured himself in the laboratory—breaks down the door and finds Hyde in Jekyll's too-large clothes, dead on the floor and with the reek of the cyanide capsule he has just crushed in his teeth.

> *Vladimir Nabokov, in his* Lectures on Literature, *Harcourt Brace Jovanovich, 1980.*

Daniel V. Fraustino   (essay date 1982)

[*In the following essay, the critic examines the process whereby two major secondary characters in* The Strange Case of Dr. Jekyll and Mr. Hyde, *Dr. Hastie Lanyon and the lawyer Gabriel John Utterson, overcome the distorting and deceptive effects of language and social forms to discover that Henry Jekyll and Edward Hyde are the same person.*]

Since Robert Louis Stevenson first published **Dr. Jekyll and Mr. Hyde** almost a century ago, critics have generally regarded the work as moral allegory, a dramatization of the conflicts between Jekyll and Hyde, good and evil, split parts of a dual personality. Recent scholarship, however, disputes this reading approach, focusing on the contradictions within Jekyll's own personality, which eliminate him as a symbol of pure respectability, and on the importance of secondary characters. While Edwin Eigner [in *Robert Louis Stevenson and the Romantic Tradition*] notes that Utterson and Enfield are the first doppelgängers encountered in the novel, Masao Miyashi states that Jekyll is not really committed to goodness but to mere respectability. Miyashi further suggests that the secondary characters, formerly thought to contrast and intensify Jekyll's downfall, are in reality all "barren of ideas," "joyless," and inherently corrupt ["Dr. Jekyll and the Emergence of Mr. Hyde," *College English,* 27, 1966].

While Jekyll and Hyde are obviously disparate segments of the human personality, they are still integral parts of the whole, and Lanyon's and Utterson's failure to recognize this fact figures importantly in the novel. In *Novelists in a Changing World* Donald Stone states that there is a "buried theme" in **Jekyll and Hyde,** its key lying in the secondary characters, who are unable "to deal with the 'monster' Hyde in a normal manner." In keeping with Eigner's, Miyashi's, and Stone's revisionist focus on secondary characters, my purpose in the following paragraphs will be to discuss the novel's presentation of the two major secondary characters, Lanyon and Utterson, as they confront the truth of Jekyll and Hyde's single identity. For Stevenson's penetrating examination into his characters constitutes one of the novel's major themes: the formative and often distorting effects of language and society on man's perception of himself and his world.

Dr. Hastie Lanyon is described by Jekyll as "long . . . bound to the most narrow and material views," and Stevenson seems to have selected his first name to suggest this defect. A "hide-bound pedant," Stevenson puns, Lanyon's clear intention is to block out the bimorphous reality of Hyde—the dual nature of man—so as to preserve his own social sense of man as inherently perfectible. For Lanyon man's social character is synonomous with man's essential self, hence he views Dr. Jekyll's excursion into Faustian metaphysics as a sign of moral perversion. Significantly, Lanyon is the only character in the novel who has no knowledge of Hyde's existence prior to his one fatal encounter. In a sense, Lanyon has completely alienated himself from the Hyde within him, hence his life is shaken "to its roots" when he witnesses Hyde's metamorphosis and realizes the latter's source in Jekyll. Ironically, Lanyon's ignorance culminates in his own destruction.

Like its literary heir *Heart of Darkness,* **Dr. Jekyll and Mr. Hyde** suggests that society purposely cultivates self-deceit in obscuring from its Lanyons the truth about themselves. But Stevenson implies, again like Conrad, that life is not redeemable without its illusions. After his fatal encounter with Hyde, when he finally recognizes the real duality of man, Lanyon states: "I have had a shock . . . and I shall never recover. It is a question of weeks. Well, life has been pleasant; I liked it; yes, sir, I used to like it. I sometimes think that if we knew all, we should be more glad to get away."

Like his friend Lanyon, Utterson is a kind of guardian of orthodox knowledge. As a lawyer he has specialized knowledge of the laws by which society operates and exists. But unlike Lanyon, Utterson's recognition of Jekyll and Hyde's single identity is more gradual and narrated in greater detail. When he first hears Enfield's account of the trampling incident, Utterson becomes obsessed with seeing Hyde's face. His first response to Enfield's story is to ask, "What sort of man is he to see?" This incipient mania is described at length:

> And still the figure had no *face* by which he might know it; even in his dreams, it had no *face,*

or one that baffled him and melted before his eyes; and thus it was that there sprang up and grew apace in the lawyer's mind a singularly strong, almost an inordinate, curiosity to behold the features of the real Mr. Hyde. If he could but once set eyes on him, he thought the mystery would lighten and perhaps roll altogether away, as was the habit of mysterious things when well examined. He might see a reason for his friend's strange preference or bondage (call it what you please) and even for the startling clause of the will. At least it would be a *face* worth seeing: the *face* of a man who was without bowels of mercy: a *face* which had but to show itself to raise up, in the mind of the unimpressionable Enfield, a spirit of enduring hatred. (emphasis supplied)

Utterson's obsession derives from his assumption that reality can be known by its outward form, an assumption perhaps rooted in his belief in the credibility of social appearances. Accordingly, after staking out Hyde's doorway, Utterson first asks to "let me see your face." In view of Hyde's bimorphous nature, Utterson's query is ironic, and his statement that he will now "know" Hyde somewhat absurd. In the dualistic world of Jekyll and Hyde nothing can be known for sure, appearances being often misleading.

Unable to understand the enigma with which he is confronted, Utterson attempts to arbitrate reality by means of language, an act as perennial as art and as primitive as magic formula. Accordingly, Utterson's initial response to Enfield's narrative about the trampling is to "ask the name of that man who walked over the child." And this same preoccupation with definition underlies his need to find a *name* for Hyde's vague deformity. The lawyer is therefore in great "mental perplexity" because Hyde's strange physical "impression" created on onlookers is not a "nameable malformation." He ponders: "There *is* something more if I could find a name for it." Although Utterson suffers from a common human need to name and thereby control, his linguistic obsession is chronic, and, as in the case of Hastie Lanyon, his name suggests his proclivity. Perhaps used to the changeless regularity of legal language, Utterson may have forgotten that there is no value to words other than their arbitrary man-made one. Thus, pledging to search out Hyde, Utterson says, "If he be Mr. Hyde . . . I shall be Mr. Seek." Similarly, he dubs Jekyll "Dr. Fell" and declares to Poole, "let our name be vengeance." Finally, the lawyer's obsession with words is underlined by his concern for Hyde's lack of "fitting language" at their first interview.

For Utterson, the purely social man, words are surrogates for reality, manipulation of the former representing control of the latter. While the use of language in this way is common enough, Utterson chronically fails to discriminate between the symbol and the reality. Hence, in his utter confusion over the perplexing relationship between the respectable Dr. Jekyll and the sinister Mr. Hyde, Utterson with great wonderment reads: "Henry Jekyll, M.D., D.C.L., LL.D., F.R.S., etc." To Utterson, the words encompass the total reality, and in these symbols there is clearly no room for Hyde. But Stevenson clearly implies that words cannot satisfactorily communicate reality and that reality is not answerable to language. Thus Lanyon declares after his fatal encounter with Hyde, "I have brought on myself a punishment and a danger that I cannot name," Jekyll states that his "affairs cannot be mended by talking," and he writes in his suicide note that his situation is "nameless." Finally, prior to killing the eminent Sir Danvers, Hyde appropriately says "never a word."

Implicitly, the reality of Hyde and his relationship with Jekyll are beyond the scope of Utterson's language. If it does anything, language, a man-made apparatus, obfuscates reality rather than clarifies it. Though man's linguistic attempts to understand and control constitute an artistic activity with sources deep in the human unconscious, man deceives himself when rendering in the artificial constructs of language that which is essentially chaotic. The impossibility of the purely "social" man ever coming to grips with life's formless diversity and illogic is comically paradigmed by Utterson's ineffectual explanation to Poole of how the man behind the door writing in Jekyll's hand could be both Jekyll and someone else. The impeccable logic which Utterson uses to explain erroneously the enigma of the familiar hand and strange voice (an argument made even more farcical by the convincing repetition of *hence*) satirizes his methodology and ultimately his basic grasp of reality:

> "These are all very strange circumstances," said Mr. Utterson, "but I think I begin to see daylight. Your master, Poole, is plainly seized with one of those maladies that both torture and deform the sufferer; hence, for aught I know, the alteration of his voice; hence the mask and the avoidance of his friends; hence his eagerness to find this drug, by means of which the poor soul retains some hope of ultimate recovery—God grant that he be not deceived! There is my explanation; it is sad enough, Poole, ay, and appalling to consider; but it is plain and natural, hangs well together, and delivers us from all exorbitant alarms."

Utterson's attempt to place experience within the narrow confines of a world artificially ordered by language is what underlies his concern that his explanation be "plain," "natural," hang "well together," and deliver him from "all exorbitant alarms." Poole's reply to this last grasp at order and sanity is even more absurd in its complete lack of sophistication, yet it is not basically different from Utterson's tendency to interpret reality in the narrow terms in which he has been conditioned to think: " 'O, sir,' cried Poole. . . . 'Do you think I do not know where his head comes to in the cabinet door, where I saw him every morning of my life?' " Clearly, if truth can be known it is not found by the same measure which defines the external limits of a cabinet door. Here, Stevenson's satire on man's proclivity for concretion and hence distortion may be unmerciful but is probably directed at himself as well.

Perhaps Stevenson suggests that, unlike his early ancestors, modern man suffers from an ever-widening split in his consciousness, and we are all Lanyons, Uttersons, and Jekylls who have repressed, alienated, or otherwise estranged the Hyde within us—acts which doom us to in-

habit the outskirts of reality as well as those of our own personalities. However, even this seems too optimisitic for those of us who regard ***Dr. Jekyll and Mr. Hyde*** as Stevenson's dim statement on man's perpetual unfitness for life. An artist by nature, man is chiefly an imaginative animal who will always filter his experience through his symbols, impotently manipulating these out of a primitive impulse to control, perceiving structure where there is only the illusion of structure, and meaning where there is only fact. (pp. 235-40)

> *Daniel V. Fraustino, " 'Dr. Jekyll and Mr. Hyde': Anatomy of Misperception," in* Arizona Quarterly, *Vol. 38, No. 3, Autumn, 1982, pp. 235-40.*

James B. Twitchell   (essay date 1985)

[*Twitchell is an American educator and critic who has written extensively on horror literature. In the following excerpt from his critical study* Dreadful Pleasures: An Anatomy of Modern Horror, *he considers the central theme of* The Strange Case of Dr. Jekyll and Mr. Hyde *to be the Victorian notion of conflict between warring elements within the self. An unexcerpted portion of the chapter from which this excerpt is drawn offers close analysis of major film adaptations of* Jekyll and Hyde.]

Like so many clichés in intellectual and cultural history, the current interpretation of the late nineteenth century as marking the onset of modern schizophrenia is not without basis. The breakdown of the belief in a uniform consciousness, with the subsequent acknowledgment of the divided self were, however, a long time coming. Superficially, we can chart the dissociation of sensibilities from the Cartesian assertion that a soul/flesh division was natural through the Neoclassical observation that absolute mind/body unity was impossible anyway, because we were only "touched" by God, to the romantic acceptance, gleeful at times, of our animal nature, to the disinterested but clearly frightful Victorian observation that man was indeed perpetually trapped between the beast and the angel. Now, thanks to developments in psychology, we not only accept multiple personalities or roles, but many analysts like R. D. Laing even contend such schizophrenia is the basis of normalcy. In retrospect, we can see by the innovations in the doppelgänger motif that this move toward diversity of selves was well under way before the rise of modern horror. What is interesting is not that Victorian man was divided, but that he was so passionately divided against himself. Matthew Arnold had contended that modern man was caught between worlds, "one dead and the other powerless to be born." Robert Louis Stevenson knew better: there was a "war," he contended, "among the members," hostilities *within* the self. So what we often see in the doubles of *fin-de-siècle* fiction are monsters, not as externally independent projections of repression, like the vampire or the Frankenstein monster, but as internally unfolded aberrations like Dorian Gray or Mr. Hyde. These new secret sharers come from within and never even pretend independence from their parental host.

There was a precedent for this kind of fiend in folklore, not in English lore but in ancient Irish and continental legends of the werewolf. For the werewolf literally turns his skin inside out as the transformation from man to wolf is effected. This beast is a "versipellis," literally a skin changer, a pagan turncoat who did for generations of Europeans what Mr. Hyde does for us: he provided first the frisson of a metamorphosis gone awry, and then the shock of ensuing bestial aggression. (pp. 204-05)

Essentially, the Dr. Jekyll/Mr. Hyde saga has reversed the mythic dispersion of the Wolfman by refocusing attention on the family. In so doing, Jekyll/Hyde has become one of the central horror sequences of our time, itself fostering such variants as the Jekyllesque doctor of *The Invisible Ray* (1933), the out-of-Hyding slasher of *Silent Scream* (1980), and the amusing and morbid tale of Duane and his nasty sidekick Belial in *Basket Case* (1982). If you ask a teenager to tell you the "whole" Jekyll/Hyde story he will usually start by attributing a werewolfesque causality into Jekyll's behavior. Dr. Jekyll is not cursed like the vampire, but instead initially *wants* to transform and then, once transformed into Hyde, he is powerless to re-create Jekyll. As Hyde, Jekyll now disturbs women, usually at least two women, one of whom he supposedly loves. Your adolescent informer may also tell you that Hyde kills the father of Jekyll's intended bride, that Hyde is finally caught, killed, and that the story ends with Jekyll's visage once again asserting itself through Hyde's hide.

This story begins to answer questions raised by the werewolf-Wolfman scenario. For instance, who is Jekyll, the candidate for transformation into beast? As the story now goes, Jekyll is a good but fussy scientist who concocts a potion that allows him safe passage into the atavistic Mr. Hyde. But why Jekyll should want this brew in the first place has to be explained to the modern audience; it is not enough to just want to be a werewolf. Often Jekyll is a good man who wants to help mankind; he wants to separate the evil animal part and cast it out. He wants natural goodness to prevail. Rarely, if ever, is he just curious about evil—his acts are always tinged with brittle altruism. And so is his medical sub-specialty: sometimes he is a charity doctor, sometimes a psychiatrist, sometimes a social worker, sometimes a professor of medical science; always his initial desires are for the improvement of us all.

Along with his altruism he is very sensitive. When he is handed any setback he literally falls apart, and the setback in the saga occurs when the woman he intends to marry is temporarily kept from him by her father. The "mother" in this story is rarely seen and never does anything important. Jekyll always (that I know of) drinks the brew right after the marriage ceremony is postponed. Jekyll is "beside himself" with anxiety, goes into the backroom lab, gulps down the id-emetic, and part of him comes loose. Hyde is not a monster yet, but it is clear *he* is not going to waste any time moping over Jekyll's lost love. Hyde is off for a night on the town. Let Jekyll still love the young lady; Hyde knows where the excitement is, and is soon courting a young wench. Could there be a more Victorian solution to a more Victorian problem: the double standard is taken literally.

In our modern version, culled from hundreds of movies and television shows, things initially go well. But then Hyde turns nasty; he brutalizes the "other woman." In fact, he is a Wolfman to her. It is no accident that Hyde is actually pictured as lupine in such movies as *Daughter of Dr. Jekyll* (1957), *Abbott and Costello Meet Dr. Jekyll and Mr. Hyde* (1953), or, better yet, the Spanish *Dr. Jekyll and the Werewolf* (1971), in which Hyde is clearly portrayed as a Wolfman. Interestingly, in the first major werewolf/Wolfman movie, *Werewolf of London* (1935), Henry Hull is pure Dr. Jekyll and his wolf pure Mr. Hyde. But what separates the young man/wolf and Jekyll/Hyde is that, by the time Jekyll's inamorata is finally allowed to marry him, it is too late: Hyde has taken control and is brutalizing the street woman just for the fun of it. Jekyll's "wolf," now in control, goes to the house of the forbidden lady and kills, not her, but her father. He is then pursued until death by the police and changes, too late, back into Jekyll. Is he unhappy in death? No, rather like the vampire, he has probably had a better life as a monster than he would have had as a man. But he has to die for it.

There have been many renditions of this story, all of which exaggerate various aspects: the altruism of Jekyll, the prohibited love, the transformation, the "other woman," the sadism of Hyde, the pursuit and destruction. But the one aspect that has made them all interesting to students of modern horror is that they have not just strayed from the printed text, they have positively overturned it. When we look at Robert Louis Stevenson's ***The Strange Case of Dr. Jekyll and Mr. Hyde*** (1886), we find not two women, but one little eight-year-old girl. We see no father-in-law but a doddering old Sir Danvers Carew, whose only link with Jekyll is that they have the same lawyer, and we follow no linear development of narrative but are cocooned inside pockets of narratives so that we are often getting the tale third-hand. What we find in the printed text is "a strange case," indeed a case more in keeping with the detective story than with a gothic horror story. But a gothic horror story is surely what it has become; one genre has cannibalized the story line of another.

To understand how and why Jekyll/Hyde has joined the ranks of Dracula and Frankenstein we return momentarily to the Victorian context. Carlyle, who understood so well the achievement of the early nineteenth century, said that what made romanticism so revolutionary was the acknowledgment of states of consciousness. The romantics, moreover, were interested not in consciousness per se but in its extremes: in transcendent consciousness, the sublime, on one hand, and the subverbal, the dream, on the other. To the nineteenth-century artist man was still, as Pope had said in *An Essay on Man*, in a middle state: "With too much knowledge for the Sceptic side / With too much weakness for the Stoic's pride / He hangs between; in doubt to act, or rest; / In doubt to deem himself a God, or Beast" (Epistle II, 5-8). Man was divided within the self as well: there was the urge to soar and the urge to sink, the urge to multiply and the urge to divide; as Blake said, the urge of the Prolific and the urge of the Devourer. Christianity had initially tried to separate consciousness in order to glorify the transcendent, the "good thoughts," the Prolific, but the romantics realized that the bestial, the Devourer, could not only not be discharged, but that it was instead a source of tremendous natural energy. One need only look at animal paintings early in the century, paintings by Goya, Delacroix, Géricault, Stubbs, and Blake, to see the new enthusiasm for the beast.

In a sense, a simple awareness of consciousness itself implies division. For to be aware of the self means that there are at least two parties, the observed and the observing. The dispassionate observer may well condemn the erotic and passionate self as brutish, but without this self the "higher" self is barren. This ironic observation of the self in which the thinking ego comments on the feeling ego represents a logical development of one aspect of romanticism—what has been called "negative romanticism"—and is at the epistemological heart of so much of modern horror. Indeed, it is the basis of late gothic, the Victorian horrors.

What the neoclassicist attempted to reconcile and the romantic acknowledged, the mid-Victorian tried to repress and the late Victorian delighted in, or at least pretended to. In this sense modern horror can be said to begin with the late eighteenth century rediscovery of Milton's Satan, the feral double of Christ, for clearly at the beginning of *Paradise Lost* Milton is more than willing to give the devil his due. The beast is there and it is trite but true to say that he is more interesting than his ariel counterparts. This is a development not lost in the gothic novel, for one finds the same doubling, or in reverse, the same splitting, in the protagonist/antagonist in *Castle of Otranto, Vathek, Caleb Williams, The Italian, The Monk, Melmoth the Wanderer,* and many others. In each, a case can be made for the fatal attraction of the satanic second self. So it should come as no surprise that James Hogg's *Confessions of a Justified Sinner* was Robert Louis Stevenson's confessed model for **The Strange Case of Dr. Jekyll and Mr. Hyde,** nor is it any wonder that Hyde *in print* is a strangely sympathetic figure.

What characterizes Victorian schizophrenia is not that the nasty shadow gets loose—the Victorians all acknowledge that is almost inevitable—but that, once outside, the second self is often rather appealing. Far more unattractive is the attempt to repress the split. Tennyson's Ulysses sublimates with conquest, Arnold's Merman with denial, Browning's Lippi with artifice, but somehow the beasts manage to get out: in *Maud,* in *The Buried Life,* in *The Ring and the Book.* It is splendid for Carlyle to say "Work" or Newman to say "Study" or Arnold to say "Search"; in the dark night of the soul the creatures will have out, and, as Thompson, Rossetti, and Pater found out, nothing can contain them.

Had *Dracula* been written in 1810 it would be now hailed as a great romantic novel, but had **Dr. Jekyll and Mr. Hyde** also appeared then it would have been forgotten. **Dr. Jekyll and Mr. Hyde** was a stunning success in the 1890s precisely because of what had happened in the 1860s and 1870s. Although no one would compare it to *Jude the Obscure* or *Our Mutual Friend* or even *The Picture of Dorian Gray,* which are in many ways rather similar, its influence, especially in popular culture, is far more profound. Masao Miyoshi makes the case in *The Divided Self: A Perspective on the Literature of the Victorians* (1969) that *Jekyll and Hyde* was at the epicenter of the literature of the 1890s—

in fact, the masterpiece of the gothic revival. John Fowles, in *The French Lieutenant's Woman* (1969), goes even further:

> This—the fact that every Victorian had two minds—is the one piece of equipment we must always take with us in our travels back into the nineteenth century. It is a schizophrenia seen at its clearest, its most notorious, in the poets . . . Tennyson, Clough, Arnold, Hardy; but scarcely less clearly in the extraordinary political veerings from Right to Left and back again of men like the younger Mill and Gladstone; in the ubiquitous neuroses and psychosomatic illnesses of intellectuals otherwise as different as Charles Kingsley and Darwin, in the execration at first poured on the Pre-Raphaelites, who tried—or seemed to be trying—to be one-minded about both art and life; in the endless tug-of-war between Liberty and Restraint, Excess and Moderation, Propriety and Conviction, between the principled man's cry for Universal Education and his terror of Universal Suffrage; transparent also in the mania for editing and revising, so that if we want to know the real Mill or the real Hardy we can learn far more from the deletions and alterations of their autobiographies than from the published versions—more from correspondences that somehow escaped burning, from private diaries, from the petty detritus of the concealment operation. Never was the record so completely confused, never a public facade so successfully passed off as the truth on a gullible posterity; and this, I think, makes the best guidebook to the age very possibly **Dr. Jekyll and Mr. Hyde.** Behind its latterday Gothic lies a very profound and epoch-revealing truth.

I also think one of the reasons for this short work's long influence has to do with the refreshing surprise of modern schizophrenia. For buried under all the blankets of narrative is a figure of forbidden attractiveness, a figure who has since become one of the central archetypes of modern horror—Mr. Hyde. Hyde is part of us all and reminds us what we have repressed or grown out of, namely, early adolescence. Far more than the vampire or the Frankenstein monster, Hyde is the monster of latency.

That is the Hyde of the literary text; the Hyde we now know, thanks to film, is remarkably different. Once again, as with Dracula and Frankenstein, Jekyll and Hyde were profoundly changed as they leapt from medium to medium. What Peggy Webling did for *Frankenstein* and John Balderston did for *Dracula,* Thomas Sullivan did for **Dr. Jekyll and Mr. Hyde.** The stage play made the story part of popular culture; it straightened out the plot, it provided causality, it made sexual interactions clear, it excised all narrative sophistication, and it profoundly transformed the monster. By the time these adaptations of Victorian horror in prose had made it to film, the stage plays had already made them myths. To understand how this transformation took place with **Jekyll and Hyde,** let us go back to the text.

According to academic lore (no scholar has been able to document the whole of this story) the idea of Jekyll/Hyde came to Stevenson in a dream. As in the works of Mary

Shelley and Bram Stoker, a specific, recorded nightmare seems to lie at the heart of their stories as well. In 1885 Stevenson was living on the coast at Bournemouth without money, without much hope of success, with a wife about whom he felt sexually ill at ease, and with a mother who was still a dominant force. He was sick, suffering the initial onslaught of tuberculosis, and he was taking narcotic painkillers. Stevenson's dream, so he reported, was brought to him by his "little helpers, the brownies"—the muse—but it may have been helped on by drugs. It was a brief dream as he reported:

> For two days I went about racking my brains for a plot of any sort, and on the second night I dreamed the scene at the window, and a scene afterwards split in two, in which Hyde, pursued for some crime, took the powder and underwent the change in the presence of his pursuers. All the rest was made awake, and consciously, although I can trace in much of it the manner of my Brownies. The meaning of the tale is therefore mine, and had long pre-existed in my garden of Adonis, and tried one body after another in vain; indeed, I do most of the morality, worse luck! and my Brownies have not a rudiment of what we call a conscience. Mine, too, is the setting, mine the characters. All that was given me was the matter of the three scenes, and the central idea of a voluntary change becoming involuntary. (*On Dreams*)

This is not much dream-stuff to analyze (although this scene appears as the "Incident at the Window" in the text), but we know it made him so uneasy that he screamed. Stevenson was awakened by Fanny, his wife, for he was, she said, shrieking. Stevenson knew the dream was ripe with unexplored excitement—he was, remember, "racking [his] brains for a plot of any sort" and complained to Fanny that she had disturbed "a fine bogey tale." In retrospect, however, she may have done him a service, for at least the images did not slip away unrecovered. During the next three days Stevenson tried to recreate the scene in prose, but succeeded in writing only a tale of supernatural terror—his wife called it a "crawler, a shilling shocker." Fanny said the story should be written as an allegory. In a fit of bravado, the kind loved by compilers of literary anecdotes, Stevenson threw the first draft of some forty thousand words into the fire, turned on his heel, and stomped upstairs. Four weeks later he had the text ready for publication.

This story, doubtless exaggerated in many respects, does more than buttress the romantic myth of inspirational composition. It shows instead that Stevenson was finally forming a context for a subject that had been of continuing interest: "doubling" as a literary theme and device. In the years before the composition of *Jekyll* he had collaborated with William Ernest Henley on *Deacon Brodie; or, The Double Life,* a play about a mild-mannered carpenter by day, a violent burglar by night, as well as finishing **"Markheim,"** which dealt with the transformation of selves. Whether it was this dream that gave Stevenson the inspiration for the doubling motif, or the fact that he himself was taking powerful drugs, quite possibly opiates, we will never know. But the personality-splitting draft was a

stroke of original genius—a fact now obscured because it has become such a donnée of modern renditions that it is never omitted. While Henry James found it "too explicit and explanatory," we still, thanks no doubt to our own pharmacological culture, find the device necessary.

However, the real excitement in the story is not so much the potation or the transposition of selves, but the fact that the double is not an animal like the werewolf, but in fact another human, an antagonist who is physically, mentally, and spiritually of the same protoplasmic stuff as Jekyll. We may have some trouble believing this because all but the most recent films have made Hyde, not metaphorically, but actually, bestial. Hyde is a tarantula in the Barrymore version, an ape in the March version, and a wolf in numerous other ones. While we may find much to criticize in the Spencer Tracy version (namely, the acting of Spencer Tracy), at least the truth of the printed text comes through: Hyde is Jekyll first and a beast second. As G. K. Chesterton observed long ago in *Robert Louis Stevenson* (1928),

> The real stab of the story is not in the discovery that the one man is two men; but in the discovery that the two men are one man. After all the diverse wandering and warring of those two incompatible beings, there was still one man born and only one man buried. . . . The point of the story is not that a man *can* cut himself off from his conscience, but that he cannot. The surgical operation is fatal in the story. It is an amputation of which both the parts die.

Stevenson clearly had technical troubles with this transformation that was not literally a clean split. Metamorphosis, from classical myth to German fairy tale to English lore, has involved significant shape-shifting. From Ovid to Kafka the human structure usually had to be regressive, but Stevenson shoved it—at least initially—sideways. In the printed text Hyde is apish, to be sure, or better yet troglodytic, but he is always sentient and fully conscious and, until the very end, very human. In fact, the irony is that he may well be far more sentient and conscious than Jekyll. Hyde is not all glands and Jekyll all mind. This is not originally a "blow the lid off the id" tale or a Manichean tale, even though it has often been told in those ways.

To observe Hyde's humanity we may have to burrow back into the text. And "burrow" is not an inappropriate trope, for Stevenson has delivered the story with so much narrative complexity that we find ourselves led from one cul-de-sac into another. This is, of course, exactly how *Frankenstein* and *Dracula* were constructed. We are continually distanced from the horror until, too late, we find ourselves at the top of the stairs and the attic door is opening before us. We must be taken level by level to the monster, from Walton to Frankenstein to the creature, from Harker to Seward to Van Helsing to Count Dracula, or in this case from Utterson to Enfield to Layton to Jekyll to Hyde.

As with the other modern horror stories, *The Strange Case* is told to us by the kindest of gentlemen: in this case two doctors, one lawyer, and a "man about town." Each takes a little different narrative stance, and we pass by two first-person points of view, then an impersonal report, followed by a third-person narration based on first-and second-hand information. The printed text of **Dr. Jekyll** is thus a tilted house of mirrors, each interdependent and all concealing/revealing the central lore, the explosive shock, those brief appearances of Hyde. Since this shock is so well disguised, we might do well to see how each of the gentlemen reacts to Hyde, for if such controlled men of reason cannot stanch the horror, how can we expect to survive?

The first man to actually observe the monster is Mr. Richard Enfield, a jovial, fun-loving bon vivant. He sees Hyde knock down and run over a young girl. "It was like some damned Juggernaut," he initially reports, and later adds yet more obfuscation to this already dim image:

> He is not easy to describe. There is something wrong with his appearance, something displeasing, something down-right detestable. I never saw a man I so disliked, and yet I scarce know why. He must be deformed somewhere; he gives a strong feeling of deformity, although I couldn't possibly specify the point. He's an extraordinary looking man, and yet I really can name nothing out of the way. No, sir; I can make no hand of it; I can't describe him. And it's not want of memory; for I declare I can see him this moment.

The next person to describe Hyde is Gabriel John Utterson, a witness who needs some introduction. Although "Gabriel John" is the center of the narrative consciousness, and although his first two names are biblical terms for "justice" and "mercy" and his surname "Utterson" implies that his utterances are to be believed (after all, with names like Hyde, "hide" in both the sense of "out of sight" and integument, and Jekyll, the French "I" and "kill," it is hard for the reader not to make puns on all the names), we may well conclude that he is going to be an accurate observer. He is, in addition, a lawyer, a man of acute powers of observation. But from the very first page there are hints that work against his credibility. We may well suspect his brittleness; in fact, we may well conclude that he is really a Jekyll manqué. We are told on the first page by an omniscient narrator: "[Mr. Utterson] was austere with himself; drank gin when he was alone, to mortify a taste for vintages; and though he enjoyed the theater, had not crossed the doors of one for twenty years." The good lawyer may well be incubating his own repressed demon. Utterson's response to Hyde is first excitement ("If he be Mr. Hyde . . . I shall be Mr. Seek") and then nausea. He is horribly nauseated when he sees the "faceless" monster. But if both Enfield and Utterson are repulsed by Hyde, observe the reaction of Hastie Lanyon, a Scottish doctor like Jekyll who is also morally fussy. After seeing Hyde,

> The rosy man had grown pale; his flesh had fallen away; he was visibly balder and older and yet it was not so much these tokens of a swift physical decay that arrested the lawyer's notice, as a look in the eye and quality of manner that seemed to testify to some deep-seated terror of the mind.

Lanyon dies from the awful sight of the Jekyll-Hyde transformation. In his own words now,

My life is shaken to its roots; sleep has left me; the deadliest terror sits by me at all hours of the day and night; and I feel that my days are numbered, and that I must die; and yet I shall die incredulous. As for the moral turpitude that man unveiled to me, even with tears of penitence, I cannot, even in memory, dwell on it without a start of horror. I will say one thing, Utterson, and that (if you can bring your mind to credit it) will be more than enough. The creature who crept into my house that night was, on Jekyll's own confession, known by the name of Hyde. . . .

What can be so bad, so horrible, that it causes one grown man to be unable to describe it, another to vomit, and a third to die? First, let us see what Hyde really looks like and then what he actually does. We all think we know what he looks like—his face is on the cover of every paperback edition of the text. He looks like Fredric March in Rouben Mamoulian's 1931 film version. He is a buck-toothed Neanderthal. This image is not quite true to the text. Certainly it is truer than a spider or a wolf, and certainly it is more literal than our current folk images of Dracula and the Frankenstein monster, but it is not interpretatively helpful. March's Hyde is too old and too big, much too old and much too big. As we will see, this makes a difference in how we have come to understand Jekyll/Hyde, for the price of having the filmic story become a "star vehicle" is that Hyde is forever physically the same as Jekyll. In the text this is initially not so: Hyde is played off against Jekyll. Jekyll is fiftyish, suave, well-dressed, and large, while Hyde is twentyish, apelike, feral, and small. One of the few common characteristics of eyewitness accounts is that Dr. Jekyll's clothes are far too big for Hyde and that Hyde moves not like a juggernaut, but like an ape. He is a dwarfish Jekyll, a miniature, yet, as Utterson reminds us, with something "troglodytic" about him.

In a crucial sense, a sense long since absent in our current renditions, Hyde is almost Jekyll as a teenager, the "Jekyll" that Dr. Jekyll has had to repress in order to become, like Utterson, a man of property, a man of means. Utterson keeps his "Hyde" hidden when he abstains from "vintages" or stays away from the theater. Perhaps this is why Utterson makes the proper diagnosis:

> [Jekyll] was wild when he was young; a long while ago to be sure; but in the law of God, there is no statute of limitations. Ay, it must be that; the ghost of some old sin, the cancer of some concealed disgrace: punishment coming, *pede claudo,* years after memory has forgotten and self-love condoned the fault.

He concludes this line of thought by suggesting that Hyde might even be Jekyll's illegitimate son come back to torture him. This conclusion may be wrong, but not inappropriate. Just look at the youthful vigor of Hyde as he comes bounding forth after Jekyll's first encounter with the forbidden vintages. In Jekyll's words,

> The most racking pangs succeeded: a grinding in the bones, deadly nausea, and a horror of the spirit that cannot be exceeded at the hour of birth or death. Then these agonies began swiftly to subside, and I came to myself as if out of a

great sickness. There was something strange in my sensations, something indescribably new and, from its very novelty, incredibly sweet. I felt younger, lighter, happier in body; within I was conscious of a heady recklessness, a current of disordered sensual images running like a mill-race in my fancy, a solution of the bonds of obligation, an unknown but not an innocent freedom of the soul. I knew myself at the first breath of this new life, to be more wicked, tenfold more wicked, sold a slave to my original evil; and the thought, in that moment, braced and delighted me like wine. I stretched out my hands, exulting in the freshness of these sensations; and in the act, I was suddenly aware that I had lost in stature.

A loss of stature, yes, but what exaltation of sensation, what a return to youth! Jekyll's fascination continues:

> And yet when I looked upon that ugly idol in the glass, I was conscious of no repugnance, rather of a leap of welcome. This, too, was myself. It seemed natural and human. In my eyes it bore a livelier image of the spirit, it seemed more express and single, than the imperfect and divided countenance I had been hitherto accustomed to call mine. And in so far I was doubtless right. I have observed that when I wore the semblance of Edward Hyde, none could come near to me at first without a visible misgiving of the flesh.

Yet, Hyde becomes evil to Jekyll; evil in the way the vampire is evil to his victim, in the way the Frankenstein monster is evil to his creator. It is a malevolence emanating from "desire with loathing strangely mix'd." Hyde is evil not because he attacks Jekyll, but because he acts out Jekyll's own base desires and gets away with it. Jekyll knows he is supposed to abominate his savage Hyde, but he secretly is fond of him, at least until it is too late. Jekyll rationalizes:

> Men have before hired bravos to transact their crimes, while their own person and reputation sat under shelter. I was the first that ever did so for his pleasures. I was the first that could plod in the public eye with a load of genial respectability, and in a moment like a schoolboy, strip off these lendings and spring headlong into the sea of liberty. But for me, in my impenetrable mantle, the safety was complete.

. . . . .

> When I would come back from these excursions, I was often plunged into a kind of wonder at my vicarious depravity. This familiar that I called out of my own soul, and sent forth alone to do his good pleasure, was a being inherently malign and villainous; his every act and thought centered on self; drinking pleasure with bestial avidity from any degree of torture to another; relentless like a man of stone. Henry Jekyll stood at times aghast before the acts of Edward Hyde; but the situation was apart from ordinary laws, and insidiously relaxed the grasp of conscience. It was Hyde, after all, and Hyde alone, that was guilty. Jekyll was no worse; he woke again to his good qualities seemingly unimpaired. . . .

Consider what this adolescent Hyde does for his mentor, look at what this son, so to speak, does for his father. First, he wantonly runs down a young girl, "tramples" her, Utterson says, and demands that the paternal Jekyll pay the damages. Next, he carouses in Soho and thrashes what seems a supernumerary on the London scene, Sir Danvers Carew (who will become the father-in-law figure in the film versions), just for the lusty thrill of killing. All we ever know about Carew is that he was Jekyll's elder by a good many years, that he was a pillar of established society, and that Hyde pummeled him mercilessly.

What we begin to see is that Hyde is not so much Jekyll's double, his id, but instead, as the transactional analysts would say, his repressed "child." Hyde is the "child" that Jekyll, the single and celibate parent, has had to push aside. As long as these two aspects are in conflict, Jekyll will never be simply "adult." Jekyll almost says as much in his concluding "Full Statement": "[I] had more than a father's interest; Hyde had more than a son's indifference." He then proceeds to condense his own family history:

> I saw my life as a whole: I followed it up from the days of childhood, when I had walked with my father's hand, and through the self-denying toils of my professional life, to arrive again and again, with the same sense of unreality, at the damned horrors of the evening.

Toward the end Hyde has become such an obstreperous child that he threatens to destroy the parental Jekyll. So Jekyll abstains from the brew for two months, but to no avail. While resting in Regent's Park, Hyde bursts forth without pharmacological help, and, although Jekyll tries desperately to repress him, Hyde clearly now is in control. And what does Hyde do to torment his parental host? He makes still bigger messes. Jekyll reports:

> Hence the ape-like tricks that he would play me, scrawling in my own hand blasphemies on the pages of my books, burning the letters and destroying the portrait of my father; and indeed, had it not been for his fear of death, he would long ago have ruined himself in order to involve me in the ruin. But his love of life is wonderful; I go further: I, who sicken and freeze at the mere thought of him, when I recall the abjection and passion of this attachment, and when I know how he fears my power to cut him off by suicide, I find it in my heart to pity him.

Surely, it is important that Hyde's enemies are Jekyll's books (Utterson had been reported earlier as being "amazed" to find Hyde's "blasphemous annotations" in one of Jekyll's "pious" works and this, along with the destruction of the image of Jekyll's father, is tantalizing to speculate about. Hyde is, after all, like the Frankenstein monster, going to clear a path for Jekyll, a path Jekyll could only dream of clearing for himself. Hyde is Jekyll's self-confessed "bravo." Yet, one of Jekyll's utterances says more of Hyde: "He, I say—I cannot say, I." But Hyde will clear Jekyll a path to where, to what? The answer is that this is simply not in the printed text, or, if it is there, it is only by exclusion. Women are the one important element so prevalent in the movie and stage and television versions of ***Dr. Jekyll and Mr. Hyde,*** yet are almost totally missing in the novella. There are really no women characters in Stevenson's text, only a maid, a match girl, and that nameless waif who is out late at night, that little girl whom Hyde tramples.

Stevenson's "bogey tale" has been made one of the central horror myths of our time not because of literary or artistic merit, but because it was clearly telling the werewolf story right—or almost right. Let Protestant ministers like Joseph Jacobs claim that ***"Dr. Jekyll and Mr. Hyde*** stands beside *Pilgrim's Progress* and *Gulliver's Travels* as one of the three great allegories in English" (*Literary Studies*); anyone who has read the first two might do well to pass it by. The attraction of Dr. Jekyll is not that it is a cautionary tale lauding Calvinist repression, but that it is a sensational playing-out of buried desire. It is an allegory, yes, or rather it has been made allegorical in the manner of pornography—it projects repressed desire *not* to censure it, but to experience it. The censure comes later, and has been softened by the contritional death scene.

The achievement of Thomas R. Sullivan's stage adaptation is that it started to exploit all the excitement and cast away the narrative slag, that is to say, the "art." The most obvious "art" to be deleted (and this invariably troubles literary critics who mourn the "coarsening" of almost any work when it changes medium) is the china-box structure. Here, for instance, is Professor Edwin M. Eigner in *Robert Louis Stevenson and Romantic Tradition* (1966): "After Sullivan's play, there were three successful movie versions . . . each one did its bit to coarsen Stevenson's ideas." Eigner's response is typical, but in the transition from print to celluloid certain changes are inevitable, and certainly the most important is how the story can be told. Sophisticated shifts in point of view as with Enfield to Utterson to Lanyon to Jekyll simply cannot be achieved on the stage or on film. The novel can *enfold*, but the stage play and movie are most efficient when *unfolding*, when they essentially unreel before our eyes. Sullivan's 1887 adaptation does just that. It starts at the beginning, goes to the middle, and ends where it ought to, with the death of Hyde. In the third act Hyde transforms into Jekyll; in the last act Jekyll transforms into Hyde.

In retrospect, Sullivan's most important contribution was not the untangling of narrative sequences, but the provision of family connections for Jekyll. Here they are as developed through the plot. Sir Danvers Carew, a widower, has a daughter Agnes who is being courted by the eligible Dr. Jekyll. As the play opens Danvers is entertaining friends, Utterson and Lanyon, and the subject of Hyde comes up. A nasty man if ever there was one, all agree, just as pale Jekyll comes on the scene. Carew is fond of Jekyll and the subject changes to Jekyll's experiments or, in Carew's words, Jekyll's "scientific balderdash." If only the young doctor would abstain, things would improve and maybe Carew would soften. But Jekyll is committed and we overhear him telling Agnes that he is about to discover the "duplicity of man." Alas, however, just as he is expounding on the Janus-like nature of man, he feels a change coming on and must abruptly leave. "My God! I feel the change approaching. I must go at once to my cabi-

net." A skulking malevolent next appears at the window and asks Sir Danvers to fetch his daughter, and when the old man refuses, he is choked to death by the shadowy thing.

No sophistication here: boy loves girl, intended father-in-law disapproves, boy turns bestial and kills older man. The die is cast; Jekyll may struggle against Hyde, but in vain. We next see Hyde in his Soho apartment perversely toasting the ghost of Sir Danvers. It is a scene straight out of Elizabethan blood-and-thunder drama. Hyde is an evil and conniving marplot gloating over his victory: the damsel will soon be his! But wait, here come the police, so first a quick change—back into Jekyll. As Jekyll he soon beseeches Lanyon to bring Agnes to his window so he may explain all. Lanyon does; Jekyll confesses, but halfway through his plaint the change overcomes him. Heroically, Jekyll poisons Hyde before he can attack Agnes. Jekyll succeeds; he dies. The curtain falls.

Sullivan's play found the audience for ***Dr. Jekyll,*** an audience that is still very much in place: it is not a literary or sophisticated audience; it is an audience eager to be thrilled. Sullivan was not without imitators; in fact, at least two other full-length dramas were performed that season, as a result of improper copyright protection, but Sullivan's version prevailed. It had the pièce de résistance: Richard Mansfield. Mansfield's virtuosity in the dual role set the standard for all future performances—the actor who plays Jekyll must be a master of the art, for he has to unlock Hyde in full audience view. Ironically, Mansfield, aptly referred to as "jack of all trades, master of one," perfected the transformation that has done the original text the most damage. Thanks to Mansfield's on-stage virtuosity, Jekyll and Hyde will continue to be played by the same actor, and this almost mandates what we see in the photograph [of Mansfield in the title role]: Jekyll saintly and Hyde demonic. Hyde will never be small enough and young enough to do justice to the text, and Jekyll will always be too saintly and heaven-searching. It would now be almost impossible to play the parts with two actors because the audience has been conditioned to expect a dramatic triumph of one actor. So, from the very first, ***Jekyll and Hyde*** has been a "star vehicle," and most of the movie versions are known not for the playwright or screenwriter but for the actor. So it was first the "Mansfield *Jekyll*," then the "Barrymore," then "Tracy," "Palance," "Michael Rennie," "Kirk Douglas," "Oliver Reed," and, most recently, the "David Hemmings *Jekyll*." The only exception to this rule is that the Fredric March rendition (ironically the best acted, at least according to the Academy of Motion Picture Sciences, which awarded March the only Oscar ever for a horror performance) is usually referred to as the "Mamoulian *Jekyll*," a tribute to Rouben Mamoulian's important contribution, not just to the story, but to filmmaking in general.

Dr. Jekyll has provided an almost countless number of renditions; arguably, the "divided personality" has provided the most popular subject of horror movies, maybe of all movies. From the 1908 Selig Polyscope Company's *The Modern Dr. Jekyll* to the Ken Russell/Arthur Penn/Paddy Chayefsky *Altered States* (1980), the idea has proved the basis of modern man's favorite stories. I am not so much interested in what this myth may say about the schizophrenic quality of modern life as I am in how the filmic versions have built, often unconsciously, on each other to produce a saga so prevalent that it is known to us before we enter the movie house. We get to know this story early, about the same time that we learn about Dracula and Frankenstein, and we never forget it. In addition, many of us know the movie versions even though we have never seen them flickering before our eyes. S. S. Prawer perceptively claimed in *Caligari's Children: The Film as Tale of Terror* (1980) that this adventure was almost made for film; that there is an almost perspicacious relationship between print and celluloid renditions already embedded in the novella. He reminds us that the "cinematic image existed well before the cinema" by citing this revealing passage from the text:

> Six o'clock struck on the bells of the church that was so conveniently near to Mr. Utterson's dwelling, and still he was digging at the problem. Hitherto it had touched him on the intellectual side alone; but now his imagination also was engaged, or rather enslaved; and as he lay and tossed in the gross darkness of the night and the curtained room, Mr. Enfield's tale went by before his mind *in a scroll of lighted pictures* [Prawer's italics]. He would be aware of the great field of lamps of a nocturnal city; then of the figure of a man walking swiftly; then of a child running from the doctor's; and then these met, and that human Juggernaut trod the child down and passed on regardless of her screams. Or else he would see a room in a rich house, where his friend lay asleep, dreaming and smiling at his dreams; and then the door of that room would be opened, the curtains of the bed plucked apart, the sleeper recalled, and lo! there would stand by his side a figure to whom power was given, and even at that dead hour, he must rise and do its bidding. The figure in these two phases haunted the lawyer all night; and if at any time he dozed over, it was but to see it glide more stealthily through sleeping houses, or move the more swiftly and still the more swiftly, even to dizziness, through wider labyrinths of lamp-lighted city, and at every street corner crush a child and leave her screaming. And still the figure had no face by which he might know it; even in his dreams, it had no face, or one that baffled him and melted before his eyes; and thus it was that there sprang up and grew apace in the lawyer's mind a singularly strong, almost an inordinate, curiosity to behold the features of the real Mr. Hyde.

Prawer is correct, of course. This description *is* cinematic, not because Stevenson was anticipating film, but because film takes its inspiration from the same source as the horror story—dream-life. Movies are indeed, as the surrealists loved to say, "dreaming with the eyes open," the cinéma vérité of the unconscious. We may not need Suzanne Langer to remind us what everyone since George Méliès has known, but it helps to be reminded: films are dreams. (pp. 228-45)

James B. Twitchell, "Dr. Jekyll and Mr. Wolf-man," in his Dreadful Pleasures: An Anatomy of Modern Horror, *Oxford University Press, 1985, pp. 204-57.*

Jeffrey Meyers   (essay date 1988)

[*In the following excerpt, Meyers surveys themes, styles, and plots of Stevenson's short stories.*]

Robert Louis Stevenson, who came from a repressive Calvinistic background and spent his adult life as a restless invalid in search of health, was born in Edinburgh in 1850 and died in Samoa in 1894. His great themes are romantic love, rivalry and vengeance, passion and renunciation, the supernatural and the macabre, the temptation of the forbidden, the torments of conscience, the strain of savagery beneath the veneer of civilization, the influence of ancestry, the conflict between fathers and sons, the double or alter ego and the dual nature of man.

He is excellent at evoking the setting—in a few vivid paragraphs—of London and Edinburgh, the Scottish moorlands and highlands, France and Spain, Hawaii and Samoa. He writes in many genres: black comedies, historical fables, moral allegories and folk tales. His stories, an odd mixture of the adolescent and the sophisticated, combine atmosphere and action, adventure and morality. Many of them take place in nocturnal darkness or crepuscular light. He employs an archaic style to evoke the past, and is stronger at inventing than concluding his ingenious plots.

His dashing and decent heroes fall instantly in love, usually in lonely landscapes. Most of his women, compromised in some strange fashion, are noble, beautiful and boring. In **"The Sire de Malétroit's Door"** the protagonist chooses marriage over death; in **"The Pavilion on the Links"** he defeats a vicious rival in love; in **"Olalla"** he renounces his love for an attractive lady in a bestial family; in **"The Bottle Imp"** he overcomes adversity and is reunited with his devoted wife; in **"The Beach at Falesá"** he accepts domesticity with a native woman; in the unfinished **"Weir of Hermiston"** he is destined to be rescued from prison and escape to America with his beloved after killing a friend who had seduced her.

The subtly controlled tone, perfect diction and grim ironic humor make **"The Body-Snatcher"** a minor masterpiece. A frame story (or story within a story)—in which Fettes confronts and accuses Macfarlane, his old confederate in an unnatural occupation that runs counter to funerary convention—leads into the fictional equivalent of Rembrandt's *Anatomy Lesson*. Fettes' pathological duty in the Edinburgh school of medicine had been "to supply, receive, and divide the various subjects" who "supplied the table" in the anatomy class. He frequently noticed "the singular freshness of the bodies" and, when a personal acquaintance is delivered in a sack, is forced to admit that almost all his corpses had been murdered.

Macfarlane encourages his progressive immersion in evil by urging Fettes to suppress and ignore the truth. When Macfarlane produces a corpse he himself has murdered, forces Fettes to conceal the crime ("The more things are wrong the more we must act as if all were right") and briskly announces: "Richardson may have the head," Fettes realizes the thin partition between life and death, the gruesome contrast between the physical and spiritual aspects of man: "To bodies that had been laid in earth, in joyful expectation of a far different awakening, there came that hasty, lamp-lit, terror-haunted resurrection of the spade and mattock," which exposed the body "to uttermost indignities before a class of gaping boys." Fettes' exclamation at the beginning of the story, "I wished to know if, after all, there were a God; I know now that there is none," illuminates the meaning of the supernatural transformation at the end. If there is no God, then the devil is free to do evil.

A historical romance set in France in 1429 during the Hundred Years' War, **"The Sire de Malétroit's Door"** opens as Denis de Beaulieu, feeling his way through the darkness ("the touch of cold window-bars . . . startles the man like the touch of a toad"), is pursued by hostile men-at-arms and finds refuge through a door that suddenly opens behind him. Malétroit's character is revealed in his countenance: "equivocal and wheedling . . . greedy, brutal, and dangerous." Their dialogue begins with a misconception ("I have been expecting you all the evening") and ends with Beaulieu's realization that he has been mistakenly snared for an impromptu marriage.

Malétroit's niece Blanche, whose name, "white," suggests her innocence, explains that her recent flirtation with a young captain, which Malétroit feels has dishonored their ancient family, has led Beaulieu into the trap set for her lover. Forced to choose between hanging and nuptials, Beaulieu at first feels honor-bound to refuse matrimonial coercion. They debate the niceties of the situation during the two hours allowed by her wicked uncle and, as dawn breaks, Beaulieu does the decent thing and opts for life rather than for "a dark and dusty corner, where a man gets into his tomb and has the door shut after him till the Judgment Day." "Though I will die for you blithely," he confides to Blanche, "it would be like all the joys of Paradise to live on and spend my life in your service." The wildly improbable plot can be read as Stevenson's ironic commentary on the chivalric ideal.

"The Pavilion on the Links" is as thrilling and intriguing as **"The Sire de Malétroit's Door"** is pleasantly absurd. For the former contains all the romantic elements: a remote setting, keen suspense, mysterious strangers, hidden crimes, fatal quicksands, dangerous attacks, a passionate love triangle, a destructive conflagration and a rescue ship that arrives too late to help.

Cassilis, after nine years of wandering, returns to the links ("a Scottish name for sand which has ceased drifting and become more or less solidly covered with turf") where he had once spent a lonely winter and then quarreled with his friend, Northmour. A puzzling misogynist and lover, Northmour is both handsome and repulsive, brave and cowardly, and "combined the vivacity of the south with the sustained and deadly hatreds of the north." On the links, Cassilis witnesses a number of enigmatic events and asks: "Why was the pavilion secretly prepared? Why had Northmour landed with his guests at dead of night? . . .

Why had he sought to kill me? . . . How had he come to have a dagger ready in his hand?"

Cassilis saves the beautiful Clara from the quicksands and falls in love with her. As their courtship develops, she elucidates the baffling incidents. Her father, Bernard Huddlestone, a dishonest and ruined banker, is fleeing from his enemies. In return for marrying his daughter to his savior, he is about to escape to the South Seas in Northmour's yacht. In a neighboring village, Cassilis discovers three Italians in pursuit of Huddlestone. Ominous seagulls—who "wheeled over his sepulchre with their usual melancholy piping" and continue to hover and circulate throughout the story—indicate that one of the Italians has fallen into the deadly sands. Northmour is enraged when he discovers Cassilis embracing Clara. He reveals that Huddlestone had gambled away a huge sum of money deposited in his bank by a group of Italian revolutionaries who have now come to Scotland to murder him. For Clara's sake, the two suitors agree to suspend hostilities and to risk their lives in defense of the thieving banker. The Italians move in to attack the fortified pavilion, call for the blood of the traitor Huddlestone and promise to spare the others if they will hand him over.

There are some surprising and perverse sexual moments, swirling beneath the conventional romance of the novel, which excite the men and reinforce their bond at the expense of the passive girl. Northmour, realizing that he has lost Clara to Cassilis and will probably be killed, declares: "By God, I'll have a kiss!" He rudely and repeatedly embraces the woman as Cassilis looks on impotently, and then urges his rival to take a kiss himself to square accounts. When Cassilis contemptuously refuses, Northmour justly exclaims: "You've been a prig in life; a prig you'll die." After they have been driven out of the house by the fire and Huddlestone rushes into the avengers' bullets to save the others, Clara faints. The next moment, as Cassilis cries "Shame!" Northmour, still eager for sexual compensation, "was straining Clara to his heart and covering her unconscious hands and face with his caresses." Not to be outdone by his passionate rival, and also taking advantage of his beloved's unconsciousness (though under the guise of assisting her), Cassilis, in a wonderful phrase, "loosened, as well as I was able, her dress and corset." Though Northmour warns him to keep his hands off the girl, he again falls to his knees and plants a chaste kiss on her brow. Cassilis' comparative restraint takes the wind out of Northmour's sails. Defeated in love, he atones for gross lechery by sacrificing himself for the cause of Italian freedom. Years later, he is killed in the Austrian Tyrol, fighting under the patriotic colors of Giuseppe Garibaldi.

"Markheim," influenced by Poe's theme of the double self and by the murder of the old pawnbroker in Dostoyevsky's *Crime and Punishment,* is Stevenson's macabre contribution to the genre of the Christmas story. Markheim (whose German name makes him seem more sinister) enters a London curio shop and rejects a mirror, or hand-conscience, as a Christmas gift. He then anticipates the "double" theme by observing his reflection in a series of mirrors and in several large pier glasses. He muses that life is short and insecure and, in an unmotivated and gratuitous act, kills the dealer with a dagger. Staring at the body of his victim, "where it lay both humped and sprawling," he notices that it looks "incredibly small and strangely meaner than in life."

After the murder the story moves inside the tortured mind of Markheim with considerable psychological penetration. The sense that he was not alone "grew upon him to the verge of madness." He is confronted by his alter ego or evil conscience in the form of a commonplace yet odd devil-figure, who says he lives for evil and debates the meaning of the murder. He urges Markheim to steal the dealer's money and to stab his maid, and offers to help him escape. Yet Markheim, with a resurgence of moral awareness in his corroded heart, rejects this advice. He moves from justifying his evil deed—"about God Himself he was at ease; his act was doubtless exceptional, but so were his excuses, which God knew; it was there, and not among men, that he felt sure of justice"—to an acceptance of his guilt. Though he does not admit responsibility and repent at the end of the story, he struggles with his conscience and decides to resist evil: "If I be condemned to evil acts . . . there is still one door of freedom open—I can cease from action." Knowing the consequences of his crime—the dock, the prison, the gallows and the black coffin—he has the moral courage to spare the maid and tell her: "You had better go for the police. . . . I have killed your master."

The opening of the vastly underrated **"Olalla"** anticipates the beginning of D. H. Lawrence's story, "Sun," and has strikingly Lawrencean themes: sun worship, primitivism, "blood-consciousness" and the ghastliness of Catholic iconography (as in Lawrence's essay, "Christs in Tirol"). Stevenson's "Lawrencean" belief, expressed in a letter to his cousin Bob, suggests the theme of the story, for he wrote that man should "honour sex more religiously. THE DAMNED THING of our [puritanical] education is that Christianity does not recognize and hallow sex."

The English hero of the story is sent to recover from a war wound in the salubrious mountain residence of an ancient but decayed Spanish family. Stevenson recreates the Spanish landscape (perhaps the Sierra de Guadarrama north of Madrid), which he had never seen, with consummate skill. Before leaving for the mountains, the hero learns that the wild mother of the family broke with all tradition and married (or perhaps never bothered to marry) a muleteer or smuggler. Her half-witted son Felipe—still a common type, whom Spanish villagers today call *mental* and treat with unusual sympathy—conveys the hero to the decayed mansion and is chastised by him for torturing a squirrel.

The mother's nearly mute and exceptionally hedonistic behavior is subtly portrayed. She spends her days brushing her hair and lolling in the sun with "an expression of almost imbecile good-humor and contentment," her vacuous face "a moral blank expressing literally naught." Her beauty and stupidity soothe and amuse the hero, though she is bored by him, yawns in his face and falls asleep while he is conversing with her: "She lived in her body; and her consciousness was all sunk into and disseminated through her members." When the scirocco blows in from Africa, everyone in the house becomes tense and de-

pressed. Late at night, the hero is shocked to hear an outbreak of atavistic cries of pain and rage, but he is unable to discover where they came from or what caused them.

The hero is introduced to the elusive and mysterious daughter, Olalla (whose name echoes the disturbing ululations), through her books and poetry that present a complete contrast to the rest of the feral family. The first words she speaks to him are an order to go away, and the rest of the story explains why he must unwillingly obey her command. The good soldier immediately responds that he "would gladly forswear my country, my language, and my friends, to live forever by her side." The deeper vision of Tolstoy's realistic *Anna Karenina* shows how the romantic love of Anna and Vronksy is destroyed by precisely these sacrifices.

In an extraordinary brutal scene, the hero (perhaps punishing himself, seeking a nurse or searching for a reason to remain) slashes his wrist on a casement window. (Both Stevenson and Lawrence were obsessed by blood, which recalled their nearly fatal tubercular hemorrhages.) When he shows his bloody wound to the bestial mother, she thrusts his hand in her mouth, bites it to the bone, utters the monstrous cries that had awakened him on the night of the hot wind and is pinned to the floor by Felipe. Her screams, the hero realizes, "were the death-cry of my love. . . . This savage and bestial strain ran not only through the whole behaviour of her family, but found a place in the very foundations and story of our love."

Olalla believes that she can end her cursed inheritance ("the hands of the dead . . . guide me") only by refusing to propagate her race. Though she is the great exception in the degenerate family, she persuades the hero to accept her Christ-like renunciation: "We must all bear and expiate a past which was not ours." Unlike the muleteer who damned himself with her mother, the hero—guided by the Christian precept that pleasure is "not an end, but an accident"—abandons love, marriage, sex, procreation and the concept of earthly happiness.

A fable and folk tale, written with engaging simplicity for a Polynesian audience in Hawaii, **"The Bottle Imp"** is fired by Stevenson's Calvinistic sense of damnation and incites the fears instilled in the islanders by hellfire missionaries. The gentle hero Keawe—who wanders between San Francisco, Honolulu and Tahiti—buys the "round-bellied bottle with a long neck; the glass of it was white like milk, with changing rainbow colours in the grain. Within-sides something obscurely moved, like a shadow and a fire." Though the bottle imp grants every wish at once, there are two conditions: The bottle must always be sold at a loss, and if a man dies before he sells it, he must burn in hell forever.

The bottle is sold five times in the story. Keawe, having fulfilled his desire for a magnificent house, sells it to a friend who wants to own a schooner. After falling in love with a beautiful maiden, Kokua, Keawe discovers he has leprosy and buys back the bottle to rid himself of the disease. But he fears he will not be able to sell it for less than one cent and imagines the fire burning him in the bottomless pit. He marries Kokua, tells her that he dared hell in order to possess her and is overjoyed by her suggestion that he sell it for French centimes. But he does not want to save himself by the eternal ruin of another man. Kokua repeats Keawe's sacrificial act by buying the bottle back from an old man who has bought it from her. Stevenson invites the reader to anticipate, rather than merely read about, a satisfactory solution that would enable Keawe to achieve a happy ending. The story suggests not only that a man's character is revealed by his material desires and that human greed finds it impossible to resist the temptation of unlimited and immediately gratified desires, but also that crass materialism can be transcended by noble altruism.

The two longer and more substantial stories, **"The Beach at Falesá"** and **"Weir of Hermiston,"** show a considerable advance in realism, depth of characterization and narrative skill, and show Stevenson working at the height of his powers at the end of his tragically curtailed career. **"The Beach at Falesá,"** a South Seas *Heart of Darkness,* helped to create the image of the innocent and degenerate tropical islands that is also found in the work of Melville, Gauguin and Maugham. (The story was transformed into a film script by Dylan Thomas.) The opening paragraph of the salty first-person narrative instantly evokes the fresh and exotic setting and brings the hero, John Wiltshire, to an atmosphere heavy with menace and to a place where white men die suddenly. Like Conrad, Stevenson exposes the corruption of the white man's colonialism—Wiltshire exclaims: "It would be a strange thing if we came all this way and couldn't do what we pleased"—and his crude exploitation of the gentle island people.

Though he learns about the disastrous fate of his predecessor and sees in the drunken Captain Randall (who has "gone native") a warning of his future fate, Wiltshire clings to his optimistic expectations. He naively accepts the lies of Case, a rival trader, who provides a wife, Uma, a bogus marriage contract and false reassurance that everyone is honest in Falesá. In the course of the story, Wiltshire moves from passive persecution by Case to a decision to retaliate, from exploitation of the native woman to a recognition of her generosity and appreciation of her love.

Though Wiltshire pours his case of gin over the edge of the verandah in order to make himself worthy of his new wife, things immediately begin to go wrong. Valuable stock is stolen; the natives gather in a circle to stare at him; they refuse to buy anything in his store; he learns that Case has poisoned a previous trader, Johnny Adams; the native pastor is terrified of Wiltshire's appearance; and he is taboo for mysterious reasons. Case, who can speak the local language, offers to help; but Wiltshire finally realizes that Case has turned the people against him. Uma then reveals that she has been jilted by her suitor and rejected by the village, and that she too is responsible for the taboo. Nevertheless, Wiltshire's love for Uma grows, and he is properly remarried by a missionary. The missionary tells Wiltshire that Case has also corrupted the native pastor, driven one trader off the island and buried a second one alive.

In order to defend himself against Case's evil, Wiltshire seeks Case's devilish shrine—the source of his power over

the natives, who are caught in the uneasy transition between paganism and Christianity. In the bush, Wiltshire finds eerie noises made by Aeolian (he calls them "Tyrolean") wind-harps that Case placed in the trees and demonic idols burnished with luminous paint. When Wiltshire exposes Case's fraud to the young chief Maea, Case's rival in love, Maea lifts the taboo and buys from Wiltshire's shop.

To complete the destruction of his enemy, Wiltshire returns to the bush to blow up the shrine with dynamite. As he passes through the jungle, "the light of the lantern, striking among all these trunks and forked branches and twisted rope-ends of lianas, made the whole place, or all that you could see of it, a kind of puzzle of turning shadows." Uma follows him to warn him of danger, they are both wounded by Case and Wiltshire stabs him to death—taking considerable sadistic pleasure from the extinction of evil: "His body kicked under me like a spring sofa; he gave a dreadful kind of a long moan, and lay still. . . . The blood came over my hands, I remember, hot as tea."

At the end of the story, Captain Randall dies after his hand is accidentally blown off and Black Jack (who had performed the bogus wedding ceremony) is eaten by cannibals. Wiltshire finally restores to the island the simplicity and innocence he had originally hoped to find there. He abandons his plan to return to England and open a pub, and remains loyal to his wife and children: "There's nobody thinks less of half-castes than I do; but they're mine, and about all I've got."

Stevenson was dictating **"Weir of Hermiston"** on the day he died of a cerebral hemorrhage. But his notes and conversation anticipate the conclusion of the novel. Adam Weir, the father of the hero, is based on a notorious eighteenth-century hanging judge, though the bitter quarrels with his son Archie reflect the young Stevenson's arguments with his father. There are four Elliott brothers in the story, three Weirs, two Kirsties (aunt and niece) and one rival for young Kirstie's love, Frank Innes.

The marriage of Archie's parents is an unnatural union of opposites: the father coarse and cruel, the mother refined and religious. The father is hostile to the son, the mother adores him. In a finely wrought, almost Shakesperean scene, the older Kirstie is forced to announce the wife's death to the husband:

> "The Lord peety ye, Hermiston! the Lord prepare ye!," she keened out. "Weary upon me, that I should have to tell it." . . .
>
> "Has the French landit?" cried he. . . .
>
> "Is onybody deid?" says his lordship. "It's no Erchie?" . . .
>
> "It's the mistress, my lord; she just fair flittit before my e'en." . . .
>
> "Weel, it's something of the suddenest," said he. "But she was a dwaibly [infirm] body from the first."

Adam begins to decline after his wife's death—"he became less formidable and infinitely more disgusting"—

and, as the animosity between father and son increases, Archie seeks out the wise and sympathetic Lord Glenalmond as a substitute parent.

Archie attends a trial at which his father pronounces the death sentence—"the loathsomeness of Duncan Jopp enveloped and infected the image of his judge," publicly denounces "this God-defying murder" and also condemns capital punishment at a university debating society. (It is a great pity that Stevenson, unlike Orwell, did not give a detailed description of the hanging.) Archie's subsequent interview with his father, which parallels the talk with Lord Glenalmond and shows Adam in a more favorable light, is the high point of the fragment. Instead of defending his principles, Archie, overawed by his father's personality, admits he has made a fool of himself and promises filial obedience. Outraged by his son's disloyalty, Adam disqualifies him from the bar and sends him to manage their country estate at Hermiston. This concludes the first part of the story.

Archie's ephemeral opposition to his father leads to independence as laird of Hermiston, a complete contrast to Adam's house in Edinburgh, and allows him to fulfill his emotional destiny. His wooing of the young Kirstie is strikingly different from his parents' courtship. He finds in her the qualities of his dead mother; she discovers in him the gentleness so notably absent in her four brothers. Though they come from different social classes, Kirstie's father, like Archie's, "had never been loved, but he had been feared in honour." The brothers' honorable vengeance of their father's murder—one "rode his horse to and fro upon the human remnant" of the attacker—foreshadows Archie's projected vengeance on Kirstie's seducer, Frank Innes.

Archie and Kirstie first see each other in church and are immediately attracted, though the torn page in her psalm book warns of their danger. Their fate is hastened by the arrival of the mephistophelean Frank Innes, a casual university friend who sponges off Archie when he runs out of money. He resents Archie's indifference to his visit, quarrels with his friend, slanders him and discovers his secret courtship of Kirstie. Old Kirstie, who had established a satisfying friendship with her master before he met her niece, repeats—for equally selfish motives—Frank's criticism of Archie's love for Kirstie. Both Frank and old Kirstie resent the loss of his favor and both are emotionally frustrated. In a final interview with Kirstie, before the story breaks off, Archie rejects her embraces and pedantically warns her that they must not risk scandal by their supposedly secret meetings. Archie's rather priggish lecture will provoke Kirstie's desire to punish him and lead to her tragic involvement with Frank Innes.

The bleak moorland setting of **"Weir of Hermiston"** is very different from the lush tropics of Samoa, where he wrote the story; yet the contrast stimulated Stevenson to recall the memories of his Scottish childhood. (pp. vii-xviii)

> *Jeffrey Meyers, in an introduction to* The Body Snatcher and Other Stories: Robert Louis Stevenson, *edited by Jeffrey Meyers, New American Library, 1988, pp. vii-xviii.*

Richard Mansfield in the leading role of the 1887-1888 stage adaptation of Dr. Jekyll and Mr. Hyde.

Joyce Carol Oates   (essay date 1988)

[*Oates is an American fiction writer and critic. In the following essay, she considers* The Strange Case of Dr. Jekyll and Mr. Hyde *illustrative of the characteristic Victorian belief in an absolute dichotomy between good and evil.*]

Like such mythopoetic figures as Frankenstein, Dracula, and, even, Alice ("in Wonderland"), Dr.-Jekyll-and-Mr.-Hyde has become, in the century following the publication of Robert Louis Stevenson's famous novella, what might be called an autonomous creation. That is, people who have never read the novella—people who do not in fact "read" at all—know by way of popular culture who Jekyll-Hyde is. (Though they are apt to speak of him, not altogether accurately, as two disparate beings: *Dr.* Jekyll, *Mr.* Hyde.) A character out of prose fiction, Jekyll-Hyde seems nonetheless autogenetic in the way that vampires and werewolves and (more benignly) fairies seem autogenetic: surely he has always existed in the collective imagination, or, like Jack the Ripper, in actual history? (As "Dracula" is both the specific creation of the novelist Bram Stoker and a nightmare figure out of middle European history.) It is ironic that, in being so effaced, Robert Louis Stevenson has become immortalized by way of his private fantasy—which came to him, by his own testimony, unbidden, in a dream.

The Strange Case of Dr. Jekyll and Mr. Hyde (1886) will strike contemporary readers as a characteristically Victorian moral parable, not nearly so sensational (nor so piously lurid) as Stoker's *Dracula;* in the tradition, perhaps, of Mary Shelley's *Frankenstein,* in which a horrific tale is conscientiously subordinated to the author's didactic intention. Though melodramatic in conception it is not melodramatic in execution since virtually all its scenes are narrated and summarized after the fact. There is no ironic ambiguity, no Wildean subtlety, in the doomed Dr. Jekyll's confession: he presents himself to the reader as a congenital "double dealer" who has nonetheless "an almost morbid sense of shame" and who, in typically Victorian middle-class fashion, must act to dissociate "himself" (i.e., his reputation as a highly regarded physician) from his baser instincts. He can no longer bear to suppress them and it is impossible to eradicate them. His discovery that "Man is not truly one, but two" is seen to be a scientific fact, not a cause for despair. (And, in time, it may be revealed that man is "a mere polity of multifarious, incongruous and independent denizens"—which is to say that the ego contains multitudes: multiple personalities inhabit us all. It cannot be incidental that Robert Louis Stevenson was himself a man enamoured of consciously playing roles and assuming personae: his friend Arthur Symons said of him that he was "never really himself except when he was in some fantastic disguise.")

Thus Dr. Jekyll's uncivilized self, to which he gives the symbolic name Hyde, is at once the consequence of a scientific experiment (as the creation of Frankenstein's monster was a scientific experiment) and a shameless indulgence of appetites that cannot be assimilated into the propriety of everyday Victorian life. There is a sense in which Hyde, for all his monstrosity, is but an addiction like alcohol, nicotine, drugs: "The moment I choose," Dr. Jekyll says, "I can be rid of him." Hyde must be hidden not simply because he is wicked but because Dr. Jekyll is a willfully good man—an example to others, like the much-admired lawyer Mr. Utterson who is "lean, long, dusty, dreary and yet somehow [improbably?] lovable." Had the Victorian ideal been less hypocritically ideal or had Dr. Jekyll been content with a less perfect public reputation his tragedy would not have occurred. (As Wilde's Basil Hallward says in *The Picture of Dorian Gray:* "We in our madness have separated the two [body and soul] and have invented a realism that is vulgar, and an ideality that is void." The key term here is surely "madness.")

Dr. Jekyll's initial experience, however, approaches ecstasy as if he were, indeed, discovering the Kingdom of God that lies within. The magic drug causes nausea and a grinding in the bones and a "horror of the spirit that cannot be exceeded at the hour of birth or death." Then:

> I came to myself as if out of a great sickness. There was something strange in my sensations, something indescribably new and, from its very novelty, incredibly sweet. I felt younger, lighter, happier in body; within I was conscious of a heady recklessness, a current of disordered sensual images running like a mill race in my fancy,

> a solution of the bonds of obligation, an unknown but not an innocent freedom of the soul. I knew myself, at the first breath of this new life, to be more wicked, tenfold more wicked, sold a slave to my original evil; and the thought, in that moment, braced and delighted in me like wine.

Unlike Frankenstein's monster, who is nearly twice the size of an average man, Jekyll's monster is dwarfed: "less robust and less developed" than the good self since Jekyll's rigorously suppressed life has been the consequence of unrelenting "effort, virtue and control." (Stevenson's anatomy of the human psyche is as grim as Freud's—virtually all a "good" man's waking energies are required in beating back and denying the "badness" in him!) That Hyde's frenzied pleasures are even in part specifically sexual is never confirmed, given the Victorian cast of the narrative itself, but, to extrapolate from an incident recounted by an eyewitness, one is led to suspect they are: Hyde is observed running down a ten-year-old girl in the street and calmly trampling over her body. Much is made subsequently of the girl's "screaming"; and of the fact that money is paid to her family as recompense for her violation.

Viewed from without Hyde is detestable in the abstract: "I never saw a man I so disliked," the lawyer Enfield says, "and yet I scarce know why. He must be deformed somewhere. . . ." Another witness testifies to his mysteriously intangible deformity "without any nameable malformation." But when Jekyll looks in the mirror he is conscious of no repugnance, "rather of a leap of welcome. This, too, was myself. It seemed natural and human." When Jekyll returns to himself after having been Hyde he is plunged into wonder rather than remorse at his "vicarious depravity." The creature summoned out of his soul and sent forth to do his pleasure is a being "inherently malign and villainous; his every act and thought centered on self; drinking pleasure with bestial avidity from any degree of torture to another; relentless like a man of stone." Yet Hyde is safely *other*—"It was Hyde, after all, and Hyde alone, that was guilty."

Oscar Wilde's equally didactic but far more suggestive and poetic *The Picture of Dorian Gray* (1890) makes the disturbing point that Dorian Gray, the *unblemished* paragon of evil, "is the type of which the age is searching for, and what it is afraid it has found." (Just as Wilde's Lord Henry defends insincerity "as a method by which we can multiply our personalities.") By contrast Jekyll's Hyde is a very nearly Bosch-like creature, proclaiming his wickedness to the naked eye as if, in Utterson's words, he is a "troglodyte . . . the mere radiance of a foul soul that thus transpires through, and transfigures, its clay continent." One is reminded of nineteenth-century theories of criminology advanced by C. S. Lombroso and Henry Maudsley, among others, who argued that outward physical defects and deformities are the visible signs of inward and invisible faults: the criminal is a type that can be easily identified by experts. Dr. Jekyll is the more reprehensible in his infatuation with Hyde in that, as a well-trained physician, he should have recognized at once the telltale symptoms of mental and moral degeneracy in his alter ego's very face.

By degrees, like any addict, Jekyll surrenders his autonomy. His ego ceases being "I" and splits into two distinct and eventually warring selves, which share memory as they share a common body. Only after Hyde commits murder does Jekyll make the effort to regain control; but by this time, of course, it is too late. What had been "Jekyll"—that precarious cuticle of a self, that field of tensions in perpetual opposition to desire—has irrevocably split. It is significant that the narrator of Jekyll's confession speaks of both Jekyll and Hyde as if from the outside. And with a passionate eloquence otherwise absent from Stevenson's prose:

> The powers of Hyde seemed to have grown with the sickliness of Jekyll. And certainly the hate that now divided them was equal on each side. With Jekyll, it was a thing of vital instinct. He had now seen the full deformity of that creature that shared with him some of the phenomena of consciousness, and was co-heir with him to death: and beyond these links of community, which in themselves made the most poignant part of his distress, he thought of Hyde, for all his energy of life, as of something not only hellish but inorganic. This was the shocking thing; that the slime of the pit seemed to utter cries and voices; that the amorphous dust gesticulated and sinned; that what was dead, and had no shape, should usurp the offices of life. And this again, that that insurgent horror was knit to him closer than a wife, closer than an eye; lay caged in his flesh, where he heard it mutter and felt it struggle to be born; and at every hour of weakness, and in the confidence of slumber, prevailed against him, and deposed him out of life.

"Think of it," Jekyll had gloated at the start, "—I did not even exist!" And the purely metaphorical becomes literally true.

The Strange Case of Dr. Jekyll and Mr. Hyde, though stimulated by a dream, is not without its literary antecedents: among them Edgar Allan Poe's "William Wilson" (1839), in which, paradoxically, the "evil" self is the narrator and the "good" self, or conscience, the double; and Charles Dickens' uncompleted *The Mystery of Edwin Drood* (1870), in which the Choirmaster Jack Jasper, an opium addict, oscillates between "good" and "evil" impulses in his personality with an anguish so convincingly calibrated as to suggest that, had Dickens lived to complete the novel, it would have been one of his masterpieces—and would have made *The Strange Case of Dr. Jekyll and Mr. Hyde* redundant. Cautionary tales of malevolent, often diabolical doubles abound in folklore and oral tradition, and in Plato's *Symposium* it was whimsically suggested that each human being has a double to whom he was once *physically* attached—a bond of Eros that constituted in fact a third, and higher, sex in which male and female were conjoined.

The visionary starkness of *The Strange Case of Dr. Jekyll and Mr. Hyde* anticipates that of Freud in such late melancholy meditations as *Civilization and Its Discontents* (1929-30): there is a split in man's psyche between ego and instinct, between civilization and "nature," and the split can never be healed. Freud saw ethics as a reluctant concession of the individual to the group, veneer of a sort overlaid upon an unregenerate primordial self. The various stratagems of culture—including, not incidentally, the "sublimation" of raw aggression by way of art and science—are ultimately powerless to contain the discontent, which must erupt at certain periodic times, on a collective scale, as war. Stevenson's quintessentially Victorian parable is unique in that the protagonist initiates his tragedy of doubleness out of a fully lucid sensibility—one might say a scientific sensibility. Dr. Jekyll knows what he is doing, and why he is doing it, though he cannot, of course, know how it will turn out. What is unquestioned throughout the narrative, by either Jekyll or his circle of friends, is mankind's fallen nature: sin is *original,* and *irremediable.* For Hyde, though hidden, will not remain so. And when Jekyll finally destroys him he must destroy Jekyll too. (pp. 603-08)

> Joyce Carol Oates, "Jekyll/Hyde," in The Hudson Review, *Vol. XL, No. 4, Winter, 1988, pp. 603-08.*

An excerpt from *The Strange Case of Dr. Jekyll and Mr. Hyde*

I was coming home from some place at the end of the world, about three o'clock of a black winter morning, and my way lay through a part of town where there was literally nothing to be seen but lamps. Street after street, and all the folks asleep—street after street, all lighted up as if for a procession, and all as empty as a church—till at last I got into that state of mind when a man listens and listens, and begins to long for the sight of a policeman. All at once I saw two figures: one a little man who was stumping along eastward at a good walk, and the other a girl of maybe eight or ten who was running as hard as she was able down a cross street. Well, sir, the two ran into one another naturally enough at the corner; and then came the horrible part of the thing; for the man trampled calmly over the child's body and left her screaming on the ground. It sounds nothing to hear, but it was hellish to see. It wasn't like a man; it was like some damned Juggernaut.

> *Robert Louis Stevenson, in his* The Strange Case of Dr. Jekyll and Mr. Hyde, *1886. Reprint. Scholastic Book Services, 1963.*

Kenneth Gelder   (essay date 1989)

[*In the following excerpt, Gelder considers Stevenson's reputation as a Scottish writer and examines principal literary influences on Stevenson's Scottish stories.*]

Stevenson's reputation as a Scottish writer, among earlier twentieth century critics especially, has not been good. C. M. Grieve (Hugh MacDiarmid) launched a passing attack on Stevenson while praising Sir Walter Scott's 'Wandering Willie's Tale' from *Redgauntlet* (1824)—'a masterpiece of prose . . . which one must go back to the seventeenth century to parallel'—and Carlyle's 'struggle' between his native Scots and the dominance of the English language. Yet Stevenson also shows symptoms of that 'struggle', as will be suggested below: in some of the Scottish stories he *did* write, Stevenson drew attention to the differences between Scots and English, linguistically and culturally. Moreover, Stevenson's **'The Tale of Tod Lapraik'** directly alludes to and is comparable in many ways to Scott's 'Wandering Willie's Tale'; it is not impossible to see Stevenson as operating *within* a tradition of writing in Scots established by the Scott MacDiarmid had praised. More importantly, this story and others by Stevenson return for their inspiration *to* the 17th century, so highly regarded by MacDiarmid, as will also be shown below.

Stevenson's reputation as a Scottish writer has also been attacked by less actively nationalist critics. In his revised *The Scots Literary Tradition,* the Leavisite critic John Speirs remarks on the 'inconsistency' of including George Douglas Brown's *The House with the Green Shutters* (1901) while omitting altogether the novels of Scott. Although he too admires 'Wandering Willie's Tale', he argues that a 'Scott and Stevenson phase' must be grown out of; and he notes somewhat dismissively that he first wrote *The Scots Literary Tradition* 'at a time when Stevenson (not to speak of Barrie and John Buchan) continued to be overestimated as representing "the line of Scott" with the added attraction of "style" '. Certainly Stevenson *was* operating very much within a literary tradition prescribed by Scott, for better or worse. But like Scott again, his stories in Scots and some of his Scottish characters complicate the issue and call for some kind of reassessment of Stevenson's own Scottishness. (pp. 1-2)

For Speirs, 'the line of Scott' seems to have more or less described how certain nineteenth-century Scottish novels, under Scott's influence, had slipped into the somewhat 'debased' or juvenile literary mode of romance. Certain novels by Stevenson, *Catriona* (1893) in particular, were very much a part of the romance mode as Scott had presented it. In Stevenson's well-known essay 'A Gossip on Romance', Scott's novels are discussed at some length, and Stevenson calls him 'out and away the king of the romantics' (*Memories and Portraits*). Of course, Stevenson was influenced by other writers using the romance mode elsewhere, especially in France. Alexandre Dumas, *père,* was a particular favourite and Stevenson had also written an essay on Dumas's romantic novel *Vicomte de Bragelonne* (1843), 'A Gossip on a Novel of Dumas's'. But Scott was certainly the dominant influence on Stevenson's *Scottish* fiction in terms of his use of the romance mode. Shorter Scottish stories by Stevenson like **'The Pavilion on the Links'** and **'The Merry Men'** clearly owe much to Scott. They are, loosely, romantic adventure stories told by narrators who, in temperament and background, are very much like the narrators of, say, *Rob Roy* (1817) or *Redgauntlet.* Frank Cassilis in **'The Pavilion on the Links'** is in rivalry against a character called Northmour in a way that recalls the Lowlander/Highlander juxtaposition common to Scott's novels. Both Cassilis and Charles Darnaway, the narrator of **'The Merry Men',** are solitary, drifting, yet moralising and somewhat bland young men who fall in love with romanticised heroines—again very much like Scott's 'mediocre heroes', as George Lukács called them in his seminal study of Scott.

Of course as Lukács pointed out, Scott's protagonists, for all their mediocrity, are nevertheless implicated in history and historical struggle. However, in Stevenson's **'The Pavilion on the Links'** and **'The Merry Men'**—his most Scott-like stories in many ways—history by contrast seems to be more or less absent; the characters seem, even, removed from history, with events taking place in isolated parts of Scotland. Here, history is now replaced by a much less ambitious and more private context, the family. For Stevenson in these stories, the protagonist's family now becomes the primary site for struggle and opposition. And there is at least one difference between the family in Stevenson's Scott-like stories and the family as Scott had represented it in his novels. In Scott's novels, the narrators generally speak fondly of their fathers and uphold the patriarchy (Alan Fairford follows his father's profession in *Redgauntlet;* even the Whig Darsie Latimer comes to admire his Jacobite uncle in this novel); but in Stevenson's **'The Pavilion on the Links'** and **'The Merry Men'**, the patriarchy is always shown to be in decay, both physically and morally. Cassilis's father-in-law or 'uncle' is a swindler, while Darnaway's uncle Gordon is corrupted by the treasures from sunken ships which he hoards on his islands. In both stories, the father-figures are subjected to the criticism and moral upbraiding of the younger narrators, and eventually come to grief as victims of their own degraded lives. The stories end by severing the two generations from one another, even to the extent in **'The Pavilion on the Links'** of erasing the father-figure completely from the narrative: just after Mr Huddlestone is killed, there is literally 'no sign of him, nor so much as a trace of blood'.

In Stevenson's **'The Misadventures of John Nicholson',** the patriarchy is again severely criticised; but as a comic Christmas story, it offers a final scene of reconciliation between father and son that is more akin to Scott. Old Mr Nicholson is an Edinburgh patriarch from, probably, the mid-1840s. In the story, his intransigence and conservatism are linked to his position as an upholder of the newly-formed Free Church of Scotland. Through Mr Nicholson, the story attacks the Free Church's rigid position on Sabbath-breaking and intemperance and shows the old man as, for a while, incapable of the Christian act of forgiveness. And here, Stevenson's involvement with Scottish cultural history begins to deepen. For old Mr Nicholson, the formation of the Free Church and the events of the Disruption of 1843 are specific to what the story calls the 'tight little theological kingdom of Scotland', incomprehensible to the English beyond the border; indeed, they confirm and secure his position *within* the specifics of Scottish cultural history. His house in stately Randolph Crescent becomes an emblem of that secure position, an emblem of Scotland itself: 'Here, at least, was a citadel unassailable by right-hand defections or left-hand extremes'.

This description of old Mr Nicholson's house is important to notice: Stevenson is in fact paraphrasing a passage from the Convenanter historian Patrick Walker's well-known complaint about 'dissenters' in his *Biographia Presbyteriana* (1827). The Covenanter allusion is significant, since as Drummond and Bulloch note, the newly-formed Free Church actually saw itself as 'the Church of the Reformers and Covenanters, in her rightful freedom'. Old Mr

Nicholson's Walker-like position, however, is one that disallows 'Dissenters'; indeed, he fortifies himself in his 'citadel' at Randolph Crescent *against* dissension. Of course, the 'Dissenter' in this story is Mr Nicholson's son John, and the story goes on to show the split between the older generation with its Covenanting traditions and a younger generation for whom those traditions allow no room. In a way, Stevenson may be remarking on his own position in Scotland here, and there are in fact close parallels between his own movements (especially his trip to California) and the 'misadventures' John experiences. The Free Church of Scotland, with the support of patriarchs like old Mr Nicholson, revives a specifically Scottish tradition with Covenanting origins; such a tradition, intransigent and conservative, is ultimately unable to accommodate (or it actually resists accommodating) 'Dissenters' like, perhaps, Stevenson himself.

In his two stories written in Scots, **'Thrawn Janet'** and **'The Tale of Tod Lapraik',** Stevenson brought the specifics of history back into his writing by actually turning *to* the days of the Covenanters, and it is his fascination with them (partly admiring, partly critical) that seems to me to lie at the base of Stevenson's own Scottishness. In this context, the suggestion that he merely operated in 'the line of Scott' is now too reductive and too dismissive; interestingly, in these two stories in Scots, Stevenson also turned his back on the romance mode that had otherwise dominated his fiction. These stories are now implicated in a specific moment of Scottish history. Stevenson drew on Patrick Walker again for his account of the 'outed' Covenanter minister and prophet Alexander Peden, prisoner on the Bass Rock in **'The Tale of Tod Lapraik';** while in **'Thrawn Janet',** the days of the Persecution in the late 17th century provide an invisible yet still potent historical site for events that take place some thirty years later. Stevenson wrote **'Thrawn Janet'** in mid-1881, but there is evidence that he had worked on the story as early as 1868, when he was seventeen, for inclusion in a projected 'Covenanting Story-Book'. By this time, Stevenson had already written his essay 'The Pentland Rising', a bicentennial account of the Pentland insurrection of November 1666 when a small Covenanter army was defeated by the notorious persecutor Sir Thomas Dalyell. Stevenson's biographer J. C. Furnas has noted in passing that the essay consists of 'extracts from . . . Patrick Walker'; in fact, Walker was not a source for this essay at all, but many other Covenanter historians were, and 'The Pentland Rising' testifies to the depth of Stevenson's interest even at such a young age in the turbulent events at this time. His [early story **'The Plague-Cellar'**] . . . follows on from those events in 'The Pentland Rising', set as it is in Edinburgh in early January 1667 'with the blood of five of the Pentland insurgents' still fresh on the scaffold. The story is sensationalist, but it is important to remember that the Convenanter histories Stevenson drew upon (and immersed himself in) were themselves sensationalist narratives, speaking always from the position of oppressed visionaries at a time when the 'true Kirk' was seen to be at its most persecuted.

It might be useful to provide a brief summary of the background to events in the so-called days of the Persecution. When the Stuart Charles II was restored to the throne in 1660, Presbyterianism in Scotland soon came under attack. As J. M. Reid summarises, 'By its Act Rescissory of 1661 the Scottish Parliament swept away all legislation passed since 1633, when Scotland had Charles I's bishops'. The Act meant a return to episcopacy and in 1662 bishops were formally restored. James Sharp, minister of Crail at this time, was sent down to London to negotiate for Presbyterian uniformity in Scotland, but he returned as the Archbishop of St Andrews and came to preside over the executions of the Pentland Convenanters in Edinburgh in December 1666: Stevenson refers to him a number of times in his Scottish essays, and the mad Covenanter Ravenswood in **'The Plague-Cellar'** rightly calls him an 'apostate'. Episcopacy soon dominated. As Reid continues,

> patronage was restored and the settling of a minister in his parish had to be approved not by the presbytery but by the bishop. Ministers appointed since 1649 had none of these qualifications. On October 1st, 1662, the Scottish Privy Council, in a drunken session at Glasgow, ordered that ministers in this position who failed to find the backing of a patron and of their bishop during the next month should leave their churches. To the surprise of the Government 274 refused to apply for a bishop's collation and were expelled. Most of them were in the south-western shires where the Protestors, who held most firmly to the Covenants, were strong.

These ministers were 'outed', their places taken by 'curates' who gave an oath of allegiance to the King and had the support of a bishop. However, when more and more parishioners in some areas began to attend the secret conventicles held by their 'outed' ministers, the government raised an army under Sir Thomas Dalyell and the days of the Persecution began in force. Stevenson describes the kinds of harassment to which parishioners in the southwest were subjected in 'The Pentland Rising'; it was sufficient to incite an insurrection, resulting in the Covenanter defeat at Rullion Green in November 1666. There were other famous Covenanter battles throughout the 1670s and 1680s against commanders like Dalyell and John Graham of Claverhouse, but this turbulent time at last came to an end when James II and the Stuart line was overthrown, and in 1689 the Dutchman William of Orange was crowned King. On 7 June 1690 the Presbyterian Kirk of Scotland was again fully established by law, marking the climax of this long-awaited Glorious Revolution.

As indicated already, the Covenanter historians who documented events at this time wrote from the position of an oppressed, outlawed and radical minority. Their rhetoric was forceful and figurative, and in their accounts of persecutions and martyrdom they constructed a rich and vivid mythology. Stevenson's favourite Covenanter sources included Patrick Walker, Robert Wodrow and James Kirkton. Kirkton was an especial favourite and, like Stevenson's Ephraim Martext in **'The Plague-Cellar',** he was an 'outed' Presbyterian minister: he had refused the acts of the Council in 1662, and was outlawed by the Council in 1674 for holding conventicles at Cramond, preaching in secret to those of his own persuasion. The purity of this position contrasted with those ministers like James Sharp who had embraced episcopacy, and Kirkton in his *The Secret and True History of the Church of Scotland, from the restoration to the year 1678* told a number of stories about the grisly fates that befell such 'apostates' who betrayed or compromised the Presbyterian church during the days of the Persecution (his history also contained James Russell's account of Sharp's murder in May 1679). One story involves Edward Thomson, the son of a devout Presbyterian minister. Thomson tries to follow the true Kirk, as his father had, but he later wearies of a life of non-conformity and becomes the 'curate' of Anstruther Easter. Stevenson takes up Kirkton's story of 'curat Thomson' in his essay 'The Coast of Fife': one night, while coming home, the devil passes by him, and soon after (so the mythology surrounding Thomson's death goes) he is taken by the devil for his apostacy. Kirkton's story, paraphrased by Stevenson, shows late 17th century Presbyterian ideology transformed into a basic and effective narrative structure: those who ignore or betray the true cause of Presbyterianism can expect, sooner or later, to be overtaken by the real Enemy of the Kirk himself. This narrative structure is put into practice in Stevenson's two stories written in Scots, **'Thrawn Janet'** and **'The Tale of Tod Lapraik'**.

In Summer 1871, when he was twenty, Stevenson wrote in a letter to Mrs Churchill Babington about just why he was so interested in the Covenanters and their 'secret histories' and narratives:

> It is a pet idea of mine that one gets more real truth out of one avowed partisan than out of a dozen of your sham impartialists—wolves in sheep's clothing—simpering honesty as they suppress documents. After all what one wants to know is not what people did, but why they did it—or rather, why they *thought* they did it; and to learn that, you should go to the men themselves. Their very falsehood is often more than another man's truth.

His attraction to Covenanter histories is an attraction to 'partisan' writing, writing that mythologises its radical ideology, its faith and convictions, through narrative. His two stories in Scots show this process at work, and seem to support his claim in a letter to J. M. Barrie in December 1893, 'My style is from the Covenanting writers'. They are both in fact narrated by 'partisans', supporters of the Kirk and Covenant. Although **'Thrawn Janet'** is set in 1712, well after the Glorious Revolution (and after the Union of 1707), the narrator looks longingly back at the 'outed' ministers who preached in secret during the days of the Persecution 'wi' a Bible under their oxter an' a spirit o' prayer in their heart'. Later, he speaks figuratively of the moment 'the blessed licht shone upon the kingdom', the Glorious Revolution of 1689 that returned Presbyterianism to the country. Black Andie Dale, the narrator of **'The Tale of Tod Lapraik',** is described by David Balfour (the narrator of *Catriona,* in which the tale appears) as 'a good Whig and Presbyterian; read daily in a pocket Bible, and . . . both eager and able to converse seriously on religion, leaning more than a little towards the Cameronian extremes'. Andie's 'partisan' character fundamentally colours the tale he tells. It is about the fortunes of two of King Charles' soldiers employed to guard Covenanter prisoners

on the Bass Rock in the mid-1670s, in the midst of the days of the Persecution. One soldier, Tam Dale, is so influenced by the Covenanter Alexander Peden that he refuses ever more to 'lift arms against the cause o' Christ': he is, in other words, converted to the Covenanter position, realising at last the error of his ways. The other soldier, Tod Lapraik, undergoes no such conversion. His history as a persecutor of the true Kirk catches up with him, and he suffers an extraordinary and diabolical fate.

Stevenson seems to have been particularly pleased with the Scottishness of, and his use of Scots in, these two stories: as he wrote to Sidney Colvin in April 1893, 'he who can't read Scots can *never* enjoy **'Tod Lapraik'** . . . '**Tod Lapraik'** is a piece of living Scots; if I had never writ anything but that and **'Thrawn Janet'**, still I'd have been a writer'. Certainly the 'partisan' positions of the narrators of these two stories produce a kind of writing (though both stories are actually spoken) that is recognisably located within a 'living' Scottish Covenanting tradition. Indeed, one of the points of both stories is to show that this tradition *is* still very much alive. Both stories show the lingering effects of the bygone days of the Persecution in the late 17th century on characters who may otherwise have forgotten about them or dismissed them. In **'Thrawn Janet'**, the naive young Rev. Mr Murdoch Soulis comes to Balweary parish fresh from 'booklearnin' at Edinburgh University. He considers the days of the Persecution well and truly over, and this upsets the 'auld, concerned, serious men and women' in the parish who still clearly remember those turbulent times. These older folk (the narrator is one of them) consider the new minister to have 'nae *leevin'* experience in religion' (my italics), and, like a kind of cautionary tale, the story provides him with just such a 'leevin' experience' by resurrecting the horrors of those days gone by.

The effects of this on Soulis are quite profound. He changes from a liberal and progressive young minister to 'the man ye ken the day', a 'severe, bleak-faced old man, dreadful to his hearers' who now frightens 'the younger sort' away with his vivid, fundamentalist sermons. He has become, in other words, like the Covenanter ministers he had earlier dismissed. The account of what Soulis is now like is given in English fifty years after the events told in Scots by the old narrator, and the juxtaposition in time and in language produces an ambivalence about Soulis's fate. From the older Covenanter position, the naive young minister has deserved a lesson in Scottish religious 'living' history. But the English introduction suggests that the lesson has a tragic effect, among other things alienating the minister from a younger generation still keen to come to church. From this English position, a progressive post-Union liberal minister has been restrained by a tradition (recalling the description in **'The Misadventures of John Nicholson'**) specific to the 'tight little theological kingdom of Scotland': a young 'Dissenter' has, in other words, been made to conform to the Scottish traditions of an older generation. And here is a version of the 'struggle' between two cultures, poignantly represented through the clash between old and young, traditional and progressive; and through the use of two opposing languages, Scots ('living Scots') and English.

The partisan representation of historically-based events in the two stories in Scots certainly contrasts with Stevenson's other Scottish stories, **'The Pavilion on the Links'** and **'The Merry Men'** especially. Here, the narrators, as 'mediocre heroes' with romantic inclinations, operate very much within the romance mode mentioned earlier; they may in this sense be in 'the line of Scott', though not the Scott of 'Wandering Willie's Tale'. But as already noted, these stories are also less historically specific, less historically implicated than Scott's novels. The stories dissociate themselves from history just as their protagonists dissociate themselves from Scots. In **'The Merry Men'**, Charles Darnaway is more or less totally Anglicised, educated at Edinburgh University: he only breaks into Scots once, in a moment of distress when declaring his love for Mary. The story contrasts him with his uncle Gordon who has a Cameronian background, and in fact Charles distances himself from his uncle and his uncle's generation by showing him to be overtaken by a Cameronian-infused self-consuming insanity. But even Charles is momentarily affected by his uncle's Cameronian superstitions, as is shown when he dives for the sunken Armada treasures (one of the reasons he visits his uncle on the island in the first place); even here, the younger generation isn't entirely free from its own history. Indeed, **'The Merry Men'** seems to me to express the very tension arising from this generational and cultural-linguistic division through its own uncertain literary form. Unlike **'The Pavilion on the Links'**, it is not properly *in* the romance mode: the relationship between Charles and Mary is hardly central to the story and, in fact, is more or less forgotten as the story goes on. What replaces it is an account of uncle Gordon's reactions to the 'black man' from the shipwreck, reactions firmly located within his own Scottishness and the superstitions it has generated. As a consequence, the story turns away from the romance mode and towards the kind of Scottish tragedy evoked more succinctly in **'Thrawn Janet'** and **'The Tale of Tod Lapraik'**. The earlier part of the story seems less historically related but, finally, history catches up and dominates **'The Merry Men'**.

'The Merry Men' is actually quite literally in 'the line of Scott', drawing on Scott's descriptions of Sumburgh Roost in *The Pirate* (1822) in its own descriptions of Aros Roost and the ships that come to grief there; Stevenson may even have lifted the title of his story from Scott's introduction to the novel. For Stevenson, *The Pirate* was a particular favourite not least because it had evolved out of Scott's famous tour of the northern islands in late Summer 1814 with the lighthouse commissioners, one of whom was Stevenson's grandfather Robert Stevenson. In 1893, Stevenson wrote a short introduction to his grandfather's account of the tour: . . . and like Stevenson's 'Memoirs of an Islet' it is useful to read alongside **'The Merry Men'**.

Indeed, all the Scottish essays . . . are worth reading alongside the stories, often linking up with them quite specifically. As already noted, Stevenson (like Scott) blurred the boundaries between fiction and fact in his stories. Some of his Covenanter sources have been remarked upon above, and of course the Covenanter historians themselves were adept at fictionalising or mythologising the factual. Stevenson had often planned stories *about* actual Cove-

nanters: he mentions his early attempts at writing a novel on David Hackston of Rathillet, one of James Sharp's murderers, in his essay 'The Coast of Fife'. Other stories turned to different sources. **'The Body Snatcher'** draws on the actual confession of William Burke printed in the *Edinburgh Evening Courant*, 21 January 1829: this is certainly a very different Scottish Christmas story from his later comic effort, **'The Misadventures of John Nicholson'**. (pp. 2-11)

> *Kenneth Gelder, in an introduction to* Robert Louis Stevenson: The Scottish Stories and Essays, *edited by Kenneth Gelder, Edinburgh University Press, 1989, pp. 1-14.*

FURTHER READING

Bibliography

Prideaux, W. F. *A Bibliography of the Works of Robert Louis Stevenson.* New York: Charles Scribner's Sons, 1903, 300 p.
  Lists first editions, juvenilia, privately printed verse, and contributions to books and periodicals.

Swearingen, Roger G. *The Prose Writings of Robert Louis Stevenson: A Guide.* Hamden, Conn.: Archon Books, 1980, 217 p.
  Extensively researched primary bibliography excluding Stevenson's poetry.

Biography

Balfour, Graham. *The Life of Robert Louis Stevenson.* Rev. ed. New York: Charles Scribner's Sons, 1915, 364 p.
  The official biography, approved by Stevenson's family and first published in 1901, offering an idealized portrait.

Calder, Jenni. *Robert Louis Stevenson: A Life Study.* New York: Oxford University Press, 1980, 362 p.
  Focuses on those portions of Stevenson's life that bear on his literary career.

Carre, Jean Marie. *The Frail Warrior: A Life of Robert Louis Stevenson.* New York: Coward-McCann, 1930, 297 p.
  Biography intended to counter the "legend," established after Stevenson's death, that he was a "charming, delicate dreamer of an elegant and brilliant imagination, floating through life like a sprite, writing pretty children's stories." Carre, however, covers little new biographical ground other than acknowledging that Stevenson probably had youthful love-affairs and describing him as "a Bohemian, almost an adventurer."

Elwin, Malcolm. *The Strange Case of Robert Louis Stevenson.* London: Macdonald, 1950, 256 p.
  Biography exploring aspects of Stevenson's life and character suppressed or overlooked by earlier biographers. Elwin focuses in particular on the effects of Stevenson's marriage on his life and works.

Furnas, J. C. *Voyage to Windward: The Life of Robert Louis Stevenson.* New York: William Sloan Associates, 1951, 566 p.

Balanced biography with some commentary on Stevenson's career.

Hellman, George S. *The True Stevenson: A Study in Clarification.* Boston: Little, Brown, and Co., 1925, 253 p.
Account of Stevenson's life based on unpublished poems, letters, and essays previously unexamined by biographers.

Pope–Hennessy, James. *Robert Louis Stevenson.* London: Jonathan Cape, 1974, 276 p.
Biography based largely on Stevenson's letters and diaries. Possibly intended as a revision of Pope–Hennessy's earlier *Stevenson* and as a reassessment and revaluation of Stevenson's literary reputation, this volume was not in final form when Pope–Hennessy died.

Criticism

Beach, Joseph Warren. "The Sources of Stevenson's 'Bottle Imp'." *Modern Language Notes* XXV, No. 1 (January 1910): 12-18.
Suggests that Stevenson derived his 1891 story from the German folktale "Das Galgemännlen" by Friedrich de la Motte Fouqué, translated and adapted for the English stage in about 1828.

Brantlinger, Patrick. "From *Dawn Island* to *Heart of Darkness*" and "Imperial Gothic: Atavism and the Occult in the British Adventure Novel, 1880-1914." In his *Rule of Darkness: British Literature and Imperialism, 1830-1914*, pp. 19-46; 227-54. Ithaca: Cornell University Press, 1988, 309 p.
Includes discussion of "The Beach at Falesá" in an examination of British Victorian literature expressing criticism or skepticism about the benefits of imperialism. The second chapter cited discusses *The Strange Case of Dr. Jekyll and Mr. Hyde* as an "imperial Gothic fantasy," equating Hyde's actions with the degenerate behavior of colonials who "go native."

Calder, Jenni, ed. *Robert Louis Stevenson: A Critical Celebration.* Totowa, N.J.: Barnes & Noble Books, 1980, 104.
Critical and reminiscential essays by J. M. Barrie, Sidney Colvin, J. C. Furnas, Edmund Gosse, W. E. Henley, Henry James, and Will Low. Several of the pieces are excerpted from longer works.

——, ed. *Stevenson and Victorian Scotland.* Edinburgh: Edinburgh University Press, 1981, 141 p.
Critical essays by Michael Balfour, David Daiches, J. C. Furnas, Douglas Gifford, Christopher Harvie, W. W. Robson, and Trevor Royle examining Stevenson's Scottish literary heritage.

Campbell, James. "A Stevenson Discovery." *The Times Literary Supplement,* No. 4,167 (11 February 1983): 140.
Describes Stevenson scholar Richard Swearingen's identification of Stevenson as the author of the anonymously published short story "An Old Song."

Chesterton, G. K. *Robert Louis Stevenson.* New York: Dodd, Mead, & Co., 1928, 211 p.
Critical biography.

Doane, Janice, and Hodges, Devon. "Demonic Disturbances of Sexual Identity: The Strange Case of Dr. Jekyll and Mr/s Hyde." *Novel* 23, No. 1 (Fall 1989): 63-74.
Relates the theme of a demonic "other" in *Dr. Jekyll and Mr. Hyde* to Victorian concerns about shifts in traditional gender roles, in particular those precipitated by the aggressive and independent "New Woman," who was actively seeking social and political parity with men.

Egan, Joseph J. "The Relationship of Theme and Art in *The Strange Case of Dr. Jekyll and Mr. Hyde.*" *English Literature in Transition* 10 (1967): 28-32.
Suggests that the artistic design or structure of the story supports its central theme: "that Dr. Jekyll himself is both good and evil."

Gaughan, Richard T. "Mr. Hyde and Mr. Seek: Utterson's Antidote." *The Journal of Narrative Technique* 17, No. 2 (Spring 1987): 184-97.
Discusses the central role of Gabriel Utterson, a character similar in nature and social standing to Henry Jekyll, whose greater tolerance, kindness, and perceptiveness alert him to the "discrepancy between appearances and reality" that is central to the narrative.

Geduld, Harry M., ed. *The Definitive "Dr. Jekyll and Mr. Hyde" Companion.* New York: Garland Publishing, 1983, 219 p.
Reprints the text and criticism of the story, pastiches and parodies, and essays on stage and film adaptations. Appendices list principal editions, parodies, sequels, and film, radio, and television adaptations.

Gelder, Kenneth. "Stevenson and the Covenanters: 'Black Andie's Tale of Tod Lapraik' and 'Thrawn Janet'." *Scottish Literary Journal* 11, No. 2 (December 1984): 56-70.
Examines two of Stevenson's stories that feature the activities of the Fife Covenanters, Scottish Presbyterians who rebelled against an edict by England's Charles I that imposed Anglican liturgy.

Girling, H. K. "The Strange Case of Dr. James and Mr. Stevenson." *Wascana Review* 3, No. 1 (1968): 65-76.
Suggests that *Dr. Jekyll and Mr. Hyde*—which is "obviously a moral allegory about the duality of good and evil in a single soul"—may also be interpreted as an allegory about the two principal modes of narrative, the realistic and the romantic, open to novelists of Stevenson's age. Girling finds that this duality may be represented by contrasting the work of Henry James with that of Stevenson.

Going, William T. "Stevenson's 'A Lodging for the Night'." *The Explicator* VIII, No. 5 (March 1950): item 41.
Identifies the central theme of this story as the revelation of François Villon as a poet and not as a thief.

Gossman, Ann. "On the Knocking at the Gate in 'Markheim'." *Nineteenth-Century Fiction* 17, No. 1 (June 1962): 73-6.
Asserts that the episode of the customer seeking to enter the shop after Markheim has murdered the owner illustrates Stevenson's ability to effectively convey character, thought, or emotion through his presentation of a character's response to a brief, striking incident.

Heath, Stephen. "Psychopathis Sexualis: Stevenson's *Strange Case.*" *Critical Quarterly* 28, Nos. 1 and 2 (Spring-Summer 1986): 93-108.
Suggests that Hyde's incidents of random violence function as substitutions for sexual attacks, which would have been unacceptable in fiction of the period.

James, Henry. "Robert Louis Stevenson." In his *Partial Por-*

traits, pp. 137-74. Ann Arbor: University of Michigan Press, 1970.

>   Approbatory critical essay originally published in 1887 that especially commends Stevenson's originality, complex and picturesque narrative style, and his wide range of themes.

Linehan, Katherine Bailey. "Taking Up with Kanakas: Stevenson's Complex Social Criticism in 'The Beach at Falesá'." *English Literature in Transition 1880-1920* 33, No. 4 (1990): 407-22.

>   Assesses Stevenson's 1892 South Sea island tale as "a fascinatingly complex reflection of and commentary on late Victorian attitudes towards race, Empire, and sexuality."

MacAndrew, Elizabeth. "The Victorian Hall of Mirrors." In her *The Gothic Tradition in Fiction,* pp. 151-239. New York: Columbia University Press, 1979.

>   Considers *Dr. Jekyll and Mr. Hyde* exemplary of the late-nineteenth-century integration of Gothic effects into social novels.

Maixner, Paul, ed. *Robert Louis Stevenson: The Critical Heritage.* London: Routledge & Kegan Paul, 1981, 532 p.

>   Collects significant early reviews and commentary on Stevenson's principal works. The editor includes an introduction surveying Stevenson's critical reception as well as a selected bibliography of primary and secondary sources.

Manlove, Colin. " 'Closer Than an Eye': The Interconnection of Stevenson's *Dr. Jekyll and Mr. Hyde.*" *Studies in English Literature* XXIII (1988): 87-103.

>   Identifies as the central theme of *Dr. Jekyll and Mr. Hyde* the fact that intimate relationships exist between seemingly isolated events and individuals.

Martin, Valerie. *Mary Reilly.* New York: Doubleday, 1990, 263 p.

>   Novel recounting the events of *Dr. Jekyll and Mr. Hyde* in first-person narrative from the point of view of a servant in the Jekyll household.

Massie, Irving. "The Third Self: *Dracula, Jekyll and Hyde,* 'Lokis'." In his *The Gaping Pig: Literature and Metamorphosis,* pp. 98-114. Berkeley: University of California Press, 1976.

>   Suggests that the action of *Dr. Jekyll and Mr. Hyde* derives from the unity rather than the duality of the central character, who in tampering with his own unified nature, incorporating both good and evil, allowed only evil to remain.

McAlpin, Edwin A. "Sin and Its Consequences." In his *Old and New Books as Life Teachers,* pp. 36-49. Garden City, N.Y.: Doubleday, Doran, and Co., 1928.

>   Asserts that *Dr. Jekyll and Mr. Hyde* demonstrates that indulgence in sin will destroy the ability to distinguish between right and wrong. The critic concludes that "under its strange fantasies *Dr. Jekyll and Mr. Hyde* is a good account of the dual elements in personality."

Menikoff, Barry, ed. *Robert Louis Stevenson and "The Beach of Falesa": A Study in Victorian Publishing.* Stanford, Calif.: Stanford University Press, 1984, 199 p.

>   Provides a publication history of "The Beach of Falesá," critical discussion of the story, and reprints the text of the story as well as illustrations from different editions. The editor also includes portions of Stevenson's correspondence pertaining to this story.

Miyoshi, Masao. "Masks in the Mirror: The Eighteen-Nineties." In his *The Divided Self: A Perspective on the Literature of the Victorians,* pp. 289-340. New York: New York University Press, 1969.

>   Includes discussion of *The Strange Case of Dr. Jekyll and Mr. Hyde* in an examination of the theme of the double or secret self in Victorian literature.

Moore, John Robert. "Stevenson's Sources for 'The Merry Men'." *Philological Quarterly* XXIII, No. 2 (April 1944): 135-40.

>   Suggests that the story "The *Santa Trinidada:* A Tale of the Hebrides," by William E. Aytoun, an account of a sunken Spanish treasure-ship published in 1842, may have inspired Stevenson's story "The Merry Men."

Noble, Andrew, ed. *Robert Louis Stevenson,* London: Vision, 1983, 229 p.

>   Collection of critical essays, several of which include discussion of Stevenson's short fiction.

Omans, Glen. "The Villon Cult in England." *Comparative Literature* XVIII, No. 1 (Winter 1966): 16-35.

>   Asserts that Stevenson's depiction of François Villon in the essay "François Villon, Student, Poet, and Housebreaker" and the story "A Lodging for the Night" is biased and unfair.

Parsons, Coleman O. "Stevenson's Use of Witchcraft in 'Thrawn Janet'." *Studies in Philology* XLIII, No. 3 (July 1946): 551-71.

>   Appraises Stevenson's familiarity with Scottish literature concerning witchcraft and distinguishes between incidents adapted from existing literature and those he wholly invented for the story cited.

Prawer, S. S. "Book into Film I: Mamoulian's *Dr. Jekyll and Mr. Hyde.*" In his *Caligari's Children: The Film as Tale of Terror,* pp. 85-107. Oxford: Oxford University Press, 1980.

>   Examines director Rouben Mamoulian's adaptation of Stevenson's novella into his 1931 film of the same name.

Punter, David. "Gothic and Decadence." In his *The Literature of Terror: A History of Gothic Fictions from 1765 to the Present Day,* pp. 239-67. London: Longman, 1980.

>   Considers *The Strange Case of Dr. Jekyll and Mr. Hyde* "one of the most potent of modern literary myths" to arise from the "decadent Gothic" literature of the 1890s.

Saposnik, Irving S. "Stevenson's 'Markheim': A Fictional 'Christmas Sermon'." *Nineteenth-Century Fiction* 21, No. 1 (June 1966): 277-82.

>   Suggests that Stevenson probably intended the mysterious visitant to represent Markheim's conscience or unconscious.

——. "A Single Glimpse, A Few Sharp Sounds" and "The Anatomy of *Dr. Jekyll and Mr. Hyde.*" In his *Robert Louis Stevenson,* pp. 60-87, 88-101. Boston: Twayne, 1974.

>   Overview of Stevenson's short stories. The second chapter cited offers a close examination of *Dr. Jekyll and Mr. Hyde.*

Shearer, Tom. "A Strange Judgment of God's? Stevenson's

'The Merry Men'." *Studies in Scottish Fiction* XX (1985): 71-87.

> Examines the use of first-person narration in "The Merry Men," maintaining that "interpretation of events depends to a large extent on understanding the personality of the narrator."

Swearingen, Roger G., ed. *A Newly Discovered Long Story, "An Old Song," and a Previously Unpublished Short Story, "Edifying Letters of the Rutherford Family," by Robert Louis Stevenson.* Hamden, Conn.: Archon Books, 1982, 102 p.

> Recounts Swearingen's discovery and indentification of two previously unknown Stevenson stories. The editor also provides and extensively annotates the texts of the stories.

Thomas, Ronald R. "In the Company of Strangers: Absent Voices in Stevenson's *Dr. Jekyll and Mr. Hyde* and Beckett's *Company*." *Modern Fiction Studies* 32, No. 2 (Summer 1986): 157-72.

> Compares Stevenson's conclusion of *Dr. Jekyll and Mr. Hyde* in a "narrative impasse" with Samuel Beckett's similar construction of *Company*.

Veeder, William, and Hirsch, Gordon. *Dr. Jekyll and Mr. Hyde after One Hundred Years.* Chicago: University of Chicago Press, 1988, 312 p.

Includes critical essays by the editors and by Patrick Brantlinger and Richard Boyle, Peter K. Garrett, Jerrold E. Hogle, Donald Lawler, Ronald R. Thomas, and Virginia Wright Wexman.

Warner, Fred B., Jr. "Stevenson's First Scottish Story." *Nineteenth-Century Fiction* 24, No. 3 (December 1969): 335-44.

> Finds "Thrawn Janet" an early example of Stevenson's effective use of Scottish dialect, history, and culture in his fiction.

————. "The Significance of Stevenson's 'Providence and the Guitar'." *English Literature in Transition 1880-1920* 14, No. 2 (1971): 103-14.

> Examines the possible autobiographical basis of the story "Providence and the Guitar."

Wilstach, Paul. "Chapter Twelve (1887-1888)." In his *Richard Mansfield: The Man and the Actor,* pp. 143-57. New York: Charles Scribner's Sons, 1908.

> Includes an account of Thomas R. Sullivan's stage adaptation of *Dr. Jekyll and Mr. Hyde* and discusses Mansfield's conception of the dual leading role and his portrayal of the part.

Additional coverage of Stevenson's life and career is contained in the following sources published by Gale Research: *Children's Literature Review,* **Volumes 10, 11;** *Dictionary of Literary Biography,* **Volumes 18, 57;** *Nineteenth-Century Literature Criticism,* **Volumes 5, 14; and** *Yesterday's Authors of Books for Children,* **Volume 2.**

Miguel de Unamuno

1864-1936

(Full name Miguel de Unamuno y Jugo) Spanish short story and novella writer, poet, essayist, novelist, playwright, and journalist.

INTRODUCTION

A pioneer of existentialism, Unamuno was one of the most influential Spanish writers and thinkers of his era. Best known for his novels, essays, and poetry that primarily treat Spain's search for renewal and world recognition, Unamuno is also noted for short stories and novellas that explore the individual's struggle for purpose and immortality. While enlarging the scope of traditional Spanish literature with his existential perspectives, Unamuno remained preoccupied with such timeless polarities as immortality versus death, faith versus doubt, and illusion versus reality.

Spain's political tension and unrest, particularly the Carlist siege of Unamuno's home city, Bilbao, stirred in him a desire to fight for freedom and against injustice. In 1891, Unamuno was appointed professor of Greek at the University of Salamanca, where he spent most of his life, apart from a period of political exile from 1924 to 1930. Unamuno was well-read in Western literature and philosophy, and his first two novels—*Paz en la guerra* and *Amor y pedagogía*—exhibit the influence of G. W. F. Hegel's theory of dialectic synthesis, according to which a concept is encompassed, preserved, and fulfilled by its opposite. After experiencing a religious crisis in 1897, during which he lost orthodox faith in God, Unamuno abandoned Hegel's theories and adopted those of Søren Kierkegaard, Henri Bergson, and William James. These thinkers favored humanism over Hegel's objective philosophy, and held that a life directed by religion, replete with suffering, leads to the highest freedom. Unamuno's resulting philosophy of salvation through anguish was shaped over several years, resolving at last in the novella *San Manuel Bueno, mártir* (*Saint Emmanuel the Good, Martyr*). In this work, Unamuno demonstrated the incompatibility of faith and reason, as represented by philosophy or religion and science. Acknowledging the inability of science to give meaning to life, Unamuno called for humanity to live according to religiously based ethical values, although he believed them to be ultimately invalid. For this idealistic alternative to spiritual inertia, Unamuno's name is often linked to that of his literary hero, Don Quixote de la Mancha. Unamuno is also noted as a leader of the Generation of 1898, a group of Spanish intellectuals that wished to revive a distinctively Spanish culture and reject what they perceived as the inauthentic foreign culture popular with Spain's urban sophisticates. Because of his opposition to both factions dur-

ing the Spanish Civil War, Unamuno was confined by military order to his house, where he died in 1936.

Although many of Unamuno's works of short fiction—including *Abel Sánchez* and *La tía Tula*—are commonly referred to as novels, their structure and length distinguish them as novellas. Reluctant to force his unique works of fiction into established categories, however, Unamuno created the *nivola*, a subgenre of the novel which L. Livingstone characterized as "an attempt to transfer to the technique of the novel the mystic's desire to free himself from the bonds of the material world, which is an illusion, and become identified with the source of true reality." In *El espejo de la muerte*, a collection of his early short stories, Unamuno's primary themes are unjust death and the tasks that one must complete in preparation for a death free from fear or regret. In "La beca," the lazy Don Augustín and his wife cause their son's death by forcing him to work excessively for their gain. They seem to feel no guilt when he dies, merely mourning the loss of their benefactor. In "Cruce de caminos," an old man dies peacefully only after his adopted granddaughter finds love, and in "El amor que asalta" a couple's decision to act on their feelings of love for each other after years of inaction results in their deaths. In both stories, the protagonists find meaning in their lives through fulfillment of love, and this allows them to die without dread or remorse.

Displays of the strength of human will, for both evil and benevolent purposes, pervade Unamuno's short fiction. In the collection *Tres novelas ejemplares y un prólogo* (*Three Exemplary Novels and a Prologue*), the novellas *Dos madres* and *El marqués de Lumbría* depict two ruthless women who, through deception and manipulation, contrive to adopt children to satisfy maternal desires thwarted by their infertility. In the novella *Nada menos que todo un hombre,* a man's overweening pride and thirst for power lead him to destroy the only woman he has ever truly loved, a sentiment he recognizes only after she has died. In *Abel Sánchez,* which is based on the biblical story of Cain and Abel, Unamuno portrayed a man whose jealousy makes him unable to stop hating his best friend even when faced with his own death; the protagonist dies with the realization that his hatred is directed toward himself. The plot of *La tía Tula* revolves around a woman who abstains from physical pleasures and forgoes marrying the man she loves in order to act as spiritual mother to the children he has with her sister and another woman. The protagonist of *Saint Emmanuel the Good, Martyr,* a priest who does not believe in eternal life, also longs for spirituality. Uncertain whether to preach that which he believes to be true or that which he has been taught is true, the priest decides that it is morally responsible to encourage his parishioners to trust that immortality exists, since it is possible that it does. The protagonists of *La tía Tula* and *Saint Emmanuel the Good, Martyr* both benefit others by denying themselves full self-expression, through the sheer determination and manipulation of their own will.

Because of its complexity, idealism, rationality, and depth, Unamuno's work has inspired much scholarly study during the twentieth century. Unamuno provided few details of space and time in his fiction, depicting instead spiritually centered characters whose essence is defined by what Salvador de Madariaga has called "conflicts of souls." Some commentators argue that this renders Unamuno's characters lifeless symbols in morality plays. Others, however, maintain that Unamuno's portrayal of characters' inner lives makes them more fully realized, and thus more accessible to the reader. *Saint Emmanuel the Good, Martyr* is widely considered Unamuno's best fictional work in terms of the intricacy with which emotion and logic are synthesized in the character of Don Manuel, who, because of his combination of passion and wisdom, has been compared to the Grand Inquisitor in Fedor Dostoevski's *The Brothers Karamazov.* Unamuno is particularly praised for incorporating philosophical discourse into his fictional narratives, which he utilized to depict the manifestation of ideas in the lives of ordinary people.

PRINCIPAL WORKS

SHORT FICTION

El espejo de la muerte   1913

Abel Sánchez   1917
   [*Abel Sánchez,* 1947]
Tres novelas ejemplares y un prólogo   1920
   [*Three Exemplary Novels and a Prologue,* 1930]
La tía Tula   1921
   [*Tía Tula* published in *Ficciones,* 1976]
San Manuel Bueno, mártir, y tres historias más   1933
   [*Saint Emmanuel the Good, Martyr* published in *Abel Sánchez, and Other Stories,* 1956]
Abel Sánchez, and Other Stories   1956

OTHER MAJOR WORKS

Paz en la guerra   (novel)   1897
Amor y pedagogia   (novel)   1902
El torno al casticismo   (essays)   1902
Paisajes   (essays)   1902
Vida de Don Quijote y Sancho   (essay)   1905
   [*The Life of Don Quixote and Sancho,* 1927]
Poesias   (poetry)   1907
La esfinge   (drama)   1909
La difunta   (drama)   1910
Rosario de sonetos líricos   (poetry)   1911
Del sentimiento trágico de la vida en los hombres y en los pueblos   (essay)   1913
   [*The Tragic Sense of Life in Men and in Peoples,* 1921]
Niebla (Nivola)   (novel)   1914
   [*Mist (Niebla),* 1928]
Fedra   (drama)   1918
El Cristo de Velázquez   (poetry)   1920
   [*The Christ of Velázques,* 1951]
La venda   (drama)   1921
El pasado que vuelve   (drama)   1923
Rimas de dentro   (poetry)   1923
Teresa   (poetry)   1924
L'agonie du christianisme   (essay)   1925; also published as *La agonía del Christianismo,*   1931
Raquel encadenada   (drama)   1926
Cómo se hace una novela   (essay)   1927
Sombras de sueño   (drama)   1930
El otro   (drama)   1932
   [*The Other* published in *Ficciones,* 1976]
El hermano Juan; o, El mundo es teatro [first publication]   (drama)   1934
Obras completas. 15 vols.   (novels, essays, poetry, dramas, and novellas)   1950-63
Ensayos. 7 vols.   (essays)   1951
Poems   (poetry)   1952
Cancionero, Diario poético   (poetry)   1953
Soledad   (drama)   1953
The Last Poems of Miguel de Unamuno   (poetry)   1974

CRITICISM

Mario J. Valdés   (essay date 1964)

[*An American critic, educator, and editor, Valdés has*

written several scholarly works on Spanish literature and has served as editor of the periodical Revista Canadiense de Estudios Hispánicos. *In the following excerpt, he examines Unamuno's treatment of death in* El espejo de la muerte *and* Tres novelas ejemplares y un prólogo.]

The twenty-seven short stories that comprise [*El espejo de la muerte*] were all written earlier and published in the Hispanic press. Among these narratives there are ten which are the further development of [Unamuno's] second literary attitude: the personal *yo* [roughly, authentic self] before his world and his death. The earlier creations (1891-1900) are the negative rejection of the unauthentic man who has no realization of his individuality nor of death. In **"La beca," ".Viva la introyección!," ",Por qué ser asi?," "El diamante de Villasola,"** and **"Juan Manso,"** Unamuno creates the empty man of the *no querer ser* and the *no querer no ser*. Even when death comes to others who are near this man, he is oblivious, for he has neither will nor individuality. Consequently, death is never known by these negative men. Death is a reality only to the authentic man; thus, in this first phase it is a meaningless event seen in others. In the case of **"Juan Manso,"** which is subtitled "Cuento de muertos," because it depicts the living dead, Unamuno turns the focus on a little man. He appears to be timid only because he hates everyone and is empty inside. This is a *yo* who has only a shell existence. Other narratives—**"Una vista al viejo poeta"** and **"El abejorro"**—move toward the authentic self-realization of the *yo*. However, the last three representative narratives treated here, all of 1912, give the positive expression of the attitude: **"El sencillo don Rafael, cazador y tresillista," "Cruce de caminos," "El amor que asalta."**

In **"La beca"** (n.d.) Unamuno creates one of his *abúlicos* who has no awareness of himself nor of those around him as personal *yos*. Don Agustin rationalizes to himself: " 'Pero ¿por qué seré así, Dios mío?', se preguntaba, y seguía siendo así, como era, ya que sólo de tal modo podía ser él el que era." He was a man who met failure at every turn due to his almost entire lack of will. After every defeat he planned new projects, but the time was never right for them or he simply did not have the will to put them into reality. Thus, he and his wife put all their expectations into one hope—a scholarship for their son on which they could all live: "Es nuestra única esperanza—decía la madre."

The son is burdened with the responsibilities of the family and he receives the scholarship, but only at the cost of his health. The situation continues from day to day; the boy needs rest and fresh air, but the demands of the family force him to continue:

> —¡Dejar los libros!—exclamó don Agustin.
> ¿Y con qué comemos?
> —Trabaje usted [dijo el médico].
> —Pues si busco y no encuentro; si . . .
> —Pues si se les muere, por su cuenta . . .
> . . . Y se lo comieron, con ayuda de la tisis.

After the son's death the mother could only feel the loss of a provider for the family. And don Agustin gave this epitaph to his son: "—Sí, muy triste—murmuró el padre, pensando que en una temporada no podría ir al café."

The narrator ends the short story with the pessimistic tone that humanity is composed of these will-less *mansos,* who consider themselves to be without any voice in their life and therefore must depend on someone else, be it the government or, as in this case, their children.

The same type of negative attack is launched in **".Viva la introyección!,"** where the mass-man who follows like a sheep is depicted.

The negative focus of **"La beca"** is used again in **",Por qué ser asi?"** (1898) which was first part of a longer story, **"Nerón tiple o el calvario de un inglés"** (1890):

> Pero, ¡Dios mío!—se decía—, ¿por qué soy así? ¿Por qué soy como soy? Todo se me vuelven propósitos de energia que se me disipan en nieblas así que afronto la realidad.

"El diamante de Villasola" (1898) has the theme of *Amor y pedagogia* without the sarcastic humor. The *maestro* is probably the first characterization of what will later be don Avito Carrascal in the novel. The teacher of the town considers his students only as means to an end: the abstraction of the system itself. When a brilliant student finally comes his way, he can only think of the system: "¡Aquél sí que era ejemplar para sus ensayos y para poner a prueba su destreza!."

The result in this narrative is not suicide, as with Apolodoro, but rather frustration and disillusionment as the boy encounters life treating his fellow men as things.

"Juan Manso," which is subtitled *cuento de muertos* (1892), is the clearest example of this phase of Unamuno's literary creation. Juan is the man who does not want to differ in the slightest manner from the social group. He is the *yo que no quiere ser*.

> —Yo no soy nada. . . .
>
> No le valió, sin embargo, su mansedumbre y al cabo se murió, que fué el único acto comprometedor que efectuó en su vida.

From this extreme of the unauthentic man, the first step toward an authentic awareness of the *yo* and his world is to question the "why" of human activity. In **"Una visita al viejo poeta"** (1899), Unamuno takes this first step into the character of the old poet. At the height of his fame the poet had retired from public life. Now, in an interview, he recalls his secluded life:

> He renunciado a aquel yo ficticio y abstracto que me sumía en la soledad de mi propio vacio. Busqué a Dios a través de él; pero como ese mi yo era una idea abstracta, un yo frio y difuso, de rechazo, jamás di con más Dios que con su proyección al infinito, con una niebla fria y difusa también; con un Dios lógico, mudo, ciego y sordo.

The poet has not found the key to an authentic way of life; he has fled from the unauthentic but he has not found the authentic.

Again in **"El abejorro,"** 1900, there is the feeling of anguish before the question: to what end is human behavior directed? What is good and what is bad? "Sin esa pregunta, nadie creería en la muerte."

In 1912 Unamuno wrote **"El sencillo don Rafael, cazador y tresillista."** Don Rafael is a strong-willed character who has felt the necessity of having faith in order to live and who has accepted the approach of death as the source of meaning to life. Don Rafael lived alone, having lost his family years before; his life was empty, but it was his life and he was aware of it. To this man was left a newborn child—abandoned on his doorstep. He responded with decision and firmness. He would adopt the child and give him a home. His doctor was able to get a wet nurse for the infant; she was an unwed mother whose child had been born dead. In response to the objections of the housekeeper about appearances, don Rafael answered with an expression of the freedom of will of the protagonist of **Nada menos que todo un hombre:** "Soy libre. . . . No me cabe la culpa de que haya nacido, pero tendré el mérito de hacerle vivir." The young girl nursed the child and don Rafael accepted her as an individual, with no prejudice because of her past. After an illness of the child during which he obliged the nurse to remain with them in his house, he proposed marriage to her. She accepted, and that night they began the continuation of the family.

By giving chance a place, don Rafael accepts his position of being free to accept or reject what it might bring; thus, in essence, he, the man don Rafael, is the maker of his destiny.

Two other stories of 1912 which had appeared as "Don Rafael . . . ," with the subtitle *cuentos del azar,* also bring out the freedom of the will of the *yo.* In **"Cruce de caminos"** and **"El amor que asalta"** the characters are brought together by pure chance, but they consciously choose each other from that moment unto death. Death comes to the old man in **"Cruce de caminos"** when his adopted granddaughter finds a love to fill her life—all the man awaited before death. In **"El amor que asalta"** the fulfillment of love, which the man and woman choose, brings death from a heart attack. Thus, in both stories the characters choose love which gives life meaning and purpose before death. (pp. 83-7)

. . . . .

Contained in the publication of **Tres novelas ejemplares** (1920) are the two short novels **Dos madres** and **El marqués de Lumbría,** which present the theme of motherhood once more. In **Dos madres,** Raquel, who was tormented because she had never had children, found a way to overcome the frustration by acting as the *celestina* between her own lover, Juan, and her candidate for motherhood, Berta. She controlled every step of the procreation of the child, and, once born, had Juan name the infant girl Raquel. The helpless Juan was torn between the two mothers—the spiritual one and the physical bearer—and had no other way out but to die. After his death Raquel easily bought the right of adoption from Berta and her parents. Thus, the frustrated mother not only caused the birth of the child but gave her her own name and therefore achieved a measure of re-creation of herself.

Carolina, the eldest daughter of **El marqués de Lumbría,**

is another Unamunian woman with the furor of maternity. She completely dominates her lover, who later marries her younger sister. She is more than the bearer of the child; she is the will that begets the child and later claims and wins his birthright as the future Marqués. Carolina tells Tristán:

> —¡Fuí yo quien te seduje! ¡Yo! . . . Yo quise ser la madre del marqués. . . . Tú despertaste mi carne y con ella mi orgullo de mayorazga. . . . Y cuando entraste aquí te hice sentir que la mujer era yo, yo, y no mi hermana . . . ¿Quieres que te recuerde la caída?.

The *yo*-will of the mother has been passed on to her son, who not only is her flesh and blood but also the heir of the family name as the *Marqués.*

The novel **La tía Tula,** which was started in 1902 but was not completed until 1921, is the Unamunian narration of the longest gestation. The plot itself was already established in 1902, as can be seen from Unamuno's letter of that year to the Catalan poet Juan Maragall:

> Ahora ando metido en una nueva novela, **La tía,** historia de una joven que rechazando novios se queda soltera para cuidar a unos sobrinos, hijos de una hermana que se le muere. Vive con el cuñado, a quien rechaza para marido, pues no quiere *manchar* con el débito conyugal el recinto en que respiran aire de castidad sus *hijos.* Satisfecho el instinto de maternidad, ¿para qué ha de perder su virginidad? Es virgen madre.

What Unamuno adds to this initial outline is the intimate convent atmosphere which the spiritual mother, Tula, instills in the household after the death of the physical mother, Rosa. Unamuno wrote in the prologue that he was not aware of this mother superior rôle which was adopted by Tula until he reread it after its completion in 1921. It is clear that the influence of Santa Teresa enters into the novel slowly and is not marked until the later chapters. In the review of the world of this novel, its own development will be followed so that the multiple factors of the re-creation of the *yo* can be seen in the novel's own trajectory.

The basic drive behind Tula, manifested from the opening lines, is an overwhelming desire for maternity. For Tula the only end in life is to have children and thus to create and re-create the personal *yo.* This iron-willed woman, like Raquel of **Dos madres,** precipitates the marriage of Rosa to Ramiro, who is the first suitor to approach her. She remains aloof from the married couple until their first child is about to be born; at this time Tula moves in to direct and safeguard the birth of the child, who is more important to her than her sister. After assisting the doctor in delivering the child, she declares: "Y en cuanto a éste—y al decirlo apretábalo contra su seno palpitante—, corre ya de mi cuenta, y o poco he de poder o haré de él un hombre." Unamuno does not let the image of maternity slip from the forceful Tula as he adds: "La casa le daba vueltas en derredor a Ramiro. Y del fondo de su alma salíale una voz diciendo: '¿Cuál es la madre?' " And when she takes the child into the room of the exhausted mother, Tula whispers in her ear: "Este se llamará Ramiro, como su padre . . . y la otra, porque la siguiente será niña, Gertrudis, como yo."

Tula takes over the complete care of the child and insists that her sister devote herself to her husband and to the procreation of the next child. As Tula gives her entire energy to the care of the child, she is careful to keep him well separated from the spirit of the physical love of the parents:

> Era como una preocupación en la tía la de ir sustrayendo al niño, ya desde su más tierna edad de inconciencia, de conocer, ni en las más leves y remotas señales, el amor de que había brotado. Colgóle al cuello, desde luego, una medalla de la Santísima Virgen, de la Virgen Madre, con su Niño en brazos.

Thus, from the beginning of her life in the house, Tula establishes in her own mind her status of the virgin mother. Her designs pay dividends as Rosa has a second child and then a third. By this time, the division of labor that she had established from the start makes her conscious of her rôle as the worker bee whose mission is the care and upbringing of the brood of the queen bee. It must be mentioned that the various symbols that characterize Tula's changing rôle in the household are not a mere narrative descriptive technique; they are conscious states of mind that Tula accepts.

Rosa dies after the birth of the third child, and once more in Unamuno's literature the Leopardi verses of the proximity of love and death are recalled. Now Ramiro, the widower, turns to his sister-in-law, seeking to make her his wife as well as the spiritual mother of his children, but she refuses him: "No insistas; ya te tengo dicho que no debo casarme ni contigo ni con otro menos."

Slowly Tula takes on the new status of the mother superior of the convent-like house: "En la ciudad estaba su convento, su hogar, y en él su celda. Allí adormecería mejor a su cuñado. . . . Gertrudis leia mucho a Santa Teresa." It is during this period that the moon symbol of the Matriarch goddess is applied to Tula, for she is not only the unquestioned ruler of the house but is now becoming a household divinity.

When she discovers that Ramiro has found sexual satisfaction with the young maid, she forces him into marriage for the second time. Two more children are added to the three of Rosa, and all five are equally the children of Tula, the virgin mother. Ramiro dies shortly before the last child is born. In his last words he speaks to Tula: "La madre de mis hijos eres tú, tú, tú." Then he asks her if she thinks he will be reunited with Rosa beyond death, but Tula can only reassure him with this inner confession of her maternal drive: "Piensa en vivir, en tus hijos." Shortly after Ramiro's death, the maid, the last concubine for the virgin mother, dies in childbirth. Tula is now alone with her convent of children. Her prayer to the Blessed Virgin that she might also become a mother without having to know man is now granted.

Unamuno describes the passage of time in these words: "Corrieron unos años apacibles y serenos. La orfandad daba a aquel hogar, en el que de nada de bienestar se carecía, una íntima luz espiritual de serena calma."

Finally, when the oldest son, Ramiro, reaches manhood, Tula moves him into marriage with Caridad, another fecund partner for the creation of men and the re-creation of Tula. The young bride immediately becomes part of the family group and is soon pregnant. But before this last child can be born, the Matriarch Tula dies. Unamuno then writes:

> ¿Murió la tía Tula? No, sino que empezó a vivir en la familia, e irradiando de ella, con una nueva vida más entrañada y más vivifica, con la vida eterna de la familiaridad inmortal. Ahora era ya para sus hijos, sus sobrinos, la Tía, no más que la Tía, ni *madre* ya ni *mamá,* ni aún tía Tula, sino sólo la Tía. Fué este nombre de invocación, de verdadera invocación religiosa, como el canonizamiento doméstico de una santidad de hogar.

The re-creation of the *yo* in others, which in this section has been examined from the point of view of heredity, both physical and spiritual, has been developed by Unamuno from the ridiculous logical abstractions of *Amor y pedagogia* to the sublime emotional drive of **La tía Tula.** However, the need for the re-creation has dominated in this exposition, for although frustrations have been felt by the characters, there has been no agonizing doubt as to the effectiveness of the re-creation for the continued existence of the personal *yo.* This type of destructive doubt is an agony of the inner thoughts of the *yo* which has been seen in the second attitude. (pp. 129-33)

> *Mario J. Valdés, in his* Death in the Literature of Unamuno, *1964. Reprint by University of Illinois Press, 1966, 173 p.*

Julián Marías   (essay date 1966)

[*A Spanish critic, educator, translator, and editor, Marías has written numerous studies on Spanish literature. In the excerpt below, he analyzes Unamuno's approach to personal existentialism in* Abel Sánchez *and shared existentialism in* La tía Tula.]

[In **Abel Sánchez,** Unamuno] tries for the first time to descend to the profoundest depths of the person, to what he called "the depths of the soul," to capture the secret of existence and even of personality. Of individual and naked existence, of course; none of Unamuno's stories—except **Nada menos que todo un hombre,** which has such a profound affinity with this one—carries so far the bareness, the lack of reference to a world or a setting. Not even a social world, for the relations among the few characters are strictly interindividual, man to man—or woman—and all are seen from the viewpoint of the tormented soul of Joaquín Monegro, whose confession constitutes the nucleus of the story.

Starting from a situation—hate or envy—Unamuno attempts to penetrate the innermost recesses of the character and possess himself of his intimate substance. Hatred is, in a certain sense, the principal character. When Unamuno reedited the book, he wondered if it would have been better to subtitle it "History of a passion"; but that would not be accurate, for the hatred is not per se, as passion, the theme of the story; rather the theme is the dimension in which it is revealed, in which it consists, in Joaquín's soul. The terrifying descriptions in this novel are not psychological but existential. At the end of chapter III the initial atmosphere, charged with tension, thickens, and hatred appears under its own name, that is, made patent or real. "I began to hate Abel with all my soul and at the same time I resolved to hide that hatred, to fertilize it, to nurse it, to foster it in the darkest places of the depths of my soul. Hatred? I was not yet willing to give it its true name, I didn't want to admit that I was born, predestined, with the bulk and the seed of it inside me. That night I was born to the hell of my life." And then, in chapter V, when he speaks of the wedding of his adored cousin Helena to Abel, his intimate friend whom he simultaneously loves and hates, the two emotions closely intertwined, he describes his passion and is described in it. "In the days that followed that on which he told me they were getting married," Joaquí wrote in his Confession,

> I felt as if my whole soul were freezing. And the ice pressed in on my heart. It was like flames made of ice. I could hardly breathe. Hate for Helena, and especially for Abel, because it was hate, cold hate whose roots choked my spirit, that had turned me to stone. It wasn't a weed, it was like a sheet of ice that had pierced my soul; rather, my whole soul was frozen by that hatred. And the ice was so transparent that I could see everything through it with perfect clarity.

And later,

> As the fatal moment came closer, I counted the seconds. 'Soon,' I said, 'everything will be over for me!' I think my heart stopped. I heard the two 'I do's,' his and hers, clearly and distinctly. She looked at me as she said it. And I felt colder than ever, without a qualm, without a tremor, as if I had heard nothing that affected me. And that very fact filled me with a diabolical terror of myself. I felt worse than a monster; I felt as if I did not exist, as if I were nothing but a piece of ice, as if I would be one forever. I even touched my skin, pinched myself, and took my pulse. I said to myself, 'But am I alive? Is this really I?'

Note the way in which Unamuno approaches the specific theme of the lover who witnesses his beloved's wedding and is present at the consummation of his despair. One might expect that Joaquín would think of his memories, of his past hopes, of Helena, of the now-closed horizon of his future life and of the imaginary boundary which once had meant hope to him, of what might have been. One might perhaps have expected him to show the bitterness or the grief or the animosity that filled his soul. But there is nothing of this. Joaquín keenly describes his own reality; it is this that concerns him, not so much his hatred, his passion of hating, but the fact that he sees himself as turned into hate, petrified, frozen in hate. It is something that concerns his own self, and he feels terror and anguish at himself, not at what has just happened outside him. For, in the last analysis, what crushes and shocks him is not the

external event of another's wedding, nor even the loss of his hopes, but the transformation which is produced in him by the event. Strictly speaking, what Joaquín is witnessing is his own perdition, the horrifying alienation of himself, of his own personality. Joaquín will no longer be himself, Joaquín; he will be *the man who hates Abel,* and, consequently, the man who needs Abel in order to exist, the man who is not himself nor master of himself, the man who has lost his own selfhood. On the other hand, he writes this conclusive word about his friend Abel, "He didn't even know how to hate, he was so full of himself."

Therefore, when in the following chapter Unamuno tells of Abel's illness, and how Joaquín takes care of him, and how he dreams that his friend might die and that Helena might realize that she had always loved him, he adds: " 'But he won't die!,' he said to himself. 'I won't let him die, I mustn't, my honor is involved, and anyway . . . I need to have him live!' And when he said, 'I need to have him live!,' his whole soul trembled, as the leaves of an oak tree tremble when a hurricane shakes it." From then on Joaquín Monegro lives on his hate, consists of it, and needs it; he needs it and its object in order to be—to be who he is, of course. So he recognizes clearly that any cure for his hatred will have to be, strictly speaking, a conversion, a becoming someone else, and at the same time a liberation, when he would stop being alienated and return to himself.

This situation dominates Joaquín and determines his whole life. When he marries Antonia, the daughter of the woman whom as a doctor he has treated until her death, his relationship with her is affected by the hate that fills his soul. "Antonia felt that between her and her Joaquín," Unamuno writes in chapter IX,

> there was a sort of invisible wall, a glassy, transparent wall of ice. That man could not belong to his wife because he did not belong to himself. He was not his own master, for he was at once alienated and possessed. In the most intimate transports of conjugal relations, a sinister invisible shadow fell between them. Her husband's kisses seemed to her to be stolen kisses, when they were not kisses of rage.

Then, in chapter XII, after he has read Lord Byron's *Cain,* which makes such a tremendous impression on him, Joaquín thinks of a possible cure or solution through love.

> But did I truly come to love my Antonia? Ah, if I had been capable of loving her, I would have been saved. For me she was only another instrument of vengeance. I wanted her as the mother of a son or a daughter who would avenge me. Though I did think, wretch that I am, that being a father would cure me of all that. But did I not perhaps marry to create other hateful beings like myself, to transmit my hate, to immortalize it?

Joaquín always fluctuates between two extremes: the desire to be cured, to free himself from his hate, and his profound attachment to it, the deep-seated bond which ties him to the passion that devours him. And this reveals that he feels his hatred to be his own reality, like an ontological moment which makes up his essence. Unamuno sees clearly that it is not a question of a feeling, but of a determination of the being; Joaquín *is* hateful, and because of that urge to persevere in one's being which Spinoza talked about, he clings to his being as a hater. He would only wish to escape from it in the name of another possible being of his, a deeper one perhaps, the one he would be if he had an authentic love, for his wife or for a child, that is, another ontological determination of the opposite sign.

Joaquín feels ever more deeply the metaphysical reality of his hatred and its undying character, written inexorably on his soul. "Until I read and reread Byron's *Cain,*" he says,

> I, who had seen so many men suffer and die, hadn't thought about death, hadn't discovered it. And then I wondered if when I died I would die with my hate, whether it would die with me or survive me; I wondered if hatred survives the haters, if it is something substantial and can be transmitted, whether it is the soul, the very essence of the soul.

And, a little further on:

> I saw that that immortal hatred was my soul. I felt as if that hatred must have existed before my birth and would survive my death. And I shuddered with terror at the thought of living forever in order to hate forever. That would indeed be Hell. And I had laughed so at belief in it! It was Hell!

The theological allusion was inevitable; Unamuno, who thinks of this hatred as something existing in and of itself, as a constituent element of the reality of the later, is obliged to pose the problem of its survival. And, since life passes but *I* remain, one must also consider that hate or love do not die but survive and endure. Since Unamuno's view is of love and hate as ontological moments of man, not as mere psychic affections, he reaches a point of view from which the anthropology latent in all Christian eschatology becomes comprehensible. Man's reality delivers him to death, and death to survival; and in that reality itself he finds immediately postulated eternal love or unending hate, Heaven or Hell. The attempt to penetrate the last redoubt of human personality leads Unamuno to the horizon of Last Things.

This situation of hatred—or envy: "All hatred is envy," Unamuno says—for Abel continues to mold Joaquín's life. He envies all his friend's success: his marriage, his son, his fame as a painter, his easy charm, his ultimate indifference to himself, Joaquín. He feels the necessity of delivering himself from his anguish; but two opposing ways lie before him, in a new choice which tears him to pieces: to cure his envy with envy, or with love—with charity, it might be said.

> This idea that they didn't even think about me, that they didn't hate me, tortured me even more than the other. If he had hated me with a hatred like the one I had for him, that would have been something, and might even have been my salvation.

And later he analyzes this inclusion of the hater and this yearning—parallel to that of love—to achieve, a hatred that would be returned, to feel himself to exist in the other, for in the last instance that is what we are dealing with; it is a mode of returning, in a certain sense, to oneself, of escaping from that situation which Unamuno accurately describes as being at one and the same time "alienated and possessed."

> In solitude he never managed to be alone, for the other was always there. The other! He even caught himself talking with him, supplying the other's words for him. And the other, in these solitary dialogues, these dialogued monologues, would say unimportant or pleasant things, and never showed him any rancor. "My God, why doesn't he hate me!," Joaquín would say to himself. "Why doesn't he hate me?"

> And one day he caught himself on the point of asking God, in a shameful, diabolical prayer, to infiltrate Abel's soul with hatred for himself, Joaquín. And again, "Oh, if only he would envy me . . . if he envied me!" And at this idea, which crossed the shadows of his embittered spirit like a livid flash of lightning, he felt a melting joy, a joy that made him tremble to the shivering marrow of his soul. To be envied! To be envied!

Finally, Joaquín discovers the ultimate root of his hatefulness in the lack of love for himself, in the radical inversion of his person which makes him hate and envy himself. " 'But isn't it,' he said, 'that I hate, I envy myself?' " He went to the door, locked it, looked all around, and when he saw he was alone he fell on his knees, murmuring with scalding tears in his voice, 'Lord, Lord! You told me: love thy neighbor as thyself! And I don't love my neighbor, I can't love him, because I don't love myself. I don't know how, I can't love myself. What have you done to me, Lord?' " And, in the final pages of the book, when he is about to die, surrounded by his wife, Antonia, his daughter, his son-in-law, Abel, the son of his now-dead friend and enemy, and Abelín, the grandson of the two of them, he asks himself again:

> "Why have I been so envious, so evil? What did I do to be like this? What milk did I suck? Was it a poisonous draught of hate? Has my blood been poison too? Why was I born in a land of hate? In a land where the precept seemed to be: Hate thy neighbor as thyself. Because I have lived hating myself; for here below we all live hating ourselves." And he says to his wife, "I never loved you. If I had loved you I would have been cured. I didn't love you. And now it hurts me that I didn't. If only we could begin all over again . . . "

He cannot begin over, he cannot because death is already upon him; he even feels that if he were to live longer he still could not stop hating in this life. But Joaquín dies with his hate overcome, at least possessed and recognized to its very root. So far Unamuno goes. But one could keep on asking, pursue more deeply still this murky exploration of the depths of the soul, perhaps to emerge and *riveder le stelle*. In the first place, where does the man who hates himself hate from, or better still, from whom? Who is the deeper *I* that turns against his other, separated I? What ontological problem is posed by this strange possibility of love or hate for oneself? And, in the second place, what is the root of that hatred of oneself and of others? All hate is envy, says Unamuno; but then what is the sense of hatred toward oneself? It would not be difficult to find in it a root of pride, of hatred for limitation, for finitude, for the unaccepted necessity of dying; at bottom it might be said to be a satanic envy of God, an *odium Dei,* the absolute inversion of charity. From this inversion of charity in its primary meaning as *amor Dei* inevitably flows the destruction of charity as love for one's neighbor. And sometimes the concrete origin of the hatred for God and of the most profound despair is hate for His image, for man. So the circle closes. As St. John says, if a man say, I love God, and hateth his brother, he is a liar; for he that loveth not his brother whom he hath seen, how can he love God whom he hath not seen? *Si quis dixerit quoniam diligo Deum, et fratrem suum oderit, mendax est. Qui enim non diligit fratrem suum quem videt, Deum quem non videt quomodo potest diligere?* We see, therefore, how far this attempt to penetrate the secret of the human soul can carry us. (pp. 94-101)

. . . . .

In his novel *La tía Tula,* written in 1920, Unamuno maintained his plan of a novel without a setting, without scenery or realisms. At first glance it is a narrative of the same type as [*Abel Sánchez*], or like the three he called *Novelas ejemplares.* However, if we probe into the matter a little, we can find appreciable differences. In the first place, the narrative itself has more consistency than the others; it is not a mere pretext to show off the characters and bare their souls. Or, rather, they are bared by reason of the drama as it happens to them, as it develops, and form themselves within it as it proceeds. In the second place, there is a plurality of characters, in a very different sense from that which we find in *Niebla,* on the one hand, and *Abel Sánchez,* on the other. In the first of these novels it was a question of creating a multitude of fictional beings, of watching this living world of secondary creatures proliferate, and of weaving a web of relationships between them which formed an ambiance, a misty atmosphere in which they lived. In the second they are characters who play a necessary role, each in respect to others, and thus define the very structure of the drama: the man who envies, the man who is envied, the origin of the envy, the children who prolong the story. In *La tía Tula,* on the other hand, the plurality is the basis of a higher unity within which the life of each one of the characters takes place; they are together, all exist for the others and each for the family group. There are not merely several characters, then, nor even relationships between them—these exist already by themselves—but a living together, a common life, so that what each of them *is* comes to pass only within their unity. And Gertrudis, Tía Tula, is precisely the foundation of that unity, a foundation, as we shall see, of a strictly personal kind.

Gertrudis appears from the start as a strongly emphasized personality, but she is shown, not in isolation but in union—first to her sister Rosa, then to Rosa's entire family, which is to become even more truly her own.

"It was Rosa and not her sister Gertrudis," Unamuno begins the story,

> who always went out with her, who attracted those anxious glances Ramiro used to send in their direction. Or at least that was what both Rosa and Ramiro thought when they first felt attracted to each other.
>
> The two sisters, always together, but for all that not always united in feeling, formed an apparently indissoluble pair and were always thought of as a single unit. At first it was Rosa's splendid and somewhat provocative beauty, her blooming flesh that seemed to open to heaven and light and wind, which drew people's eyes to the pair; but then it was Gertrudis' magnetic eyes which both attracted and kept at a distance the eyes that rested on hers.
>
> When you looked at them carefully and at close range, it was Gertrudis who aroused desire. While her sister Rosa opened splendidly to all the winds and all the light the flower of her living flesh, Gertrudis was like a closed and sealed coffer which hinted at a treasure of love and secret delights.
>
> But Ramiro, who wore his soul in his eyes, thought he saw only Rosa, and Rosa was the one to whom he was attracted from the beginning.

This defines the general situation of the novel. Ramiro, approaching Rosa, sees Gertrudis at close range and is attracted to her, as she is silently attracted to him. But Gertrudis, noticing Ramiro's hesitation, without letting him speak or explain himself, urges him with all the weight of her quiet gravity, her "great black mourning eyes," to marry Rosa quickly. "If you love her," she tells him, "marry her, and if you don't love her there's no room for you in this house." And Unamuno adds, "Her heart seemed to stop as these words came out of her cold lips. An icy silence followed them; meanwhile the blood, repressed before and now set free, rose to the sister's cheek. And then, in the pregnant silence, the racing, trembling beat of her heart could be heard."

Gertrudis, Tula, continues to accompany her sister, though from afar, and as the latter begins to have children—eventually three—she enters more and more into the life of the house and dedicates herself with total devotion to the care and love of the children: she is turning into Tía Tula. Ramiro, though he always remembers the enthralling impression of Gertrudis, becomes deeply attached to his wife, and when she dies he feels that he recognizes all the deep bonds which tied him to Rosa, all the powerful reality of their life together. It is then that he has an inkling of the meaning of everyday life, but within the strictly individual picture, not the collective one as in *Paz en la guerra,* where each man's daily existence emerged from the common depths of the life of Bilbao. Ramiro feels that his own life has been interwoven little by little with that of his wife, that the two of them have made one single life between them in the continuity of many days that were all alike; and that when Rosa, a member of this single life, died, the apparently paradoxical truth was that he had also died in part, but that Rosa lived again in the mutilated life of her husband.

> Now, only now that he was a widower, Ramiro realized how much he had loved his wife Rosa without even suspecting it. The greatest of his consolations was to shut himself in that bedroom where they had lived and loved so much, and to live over his married life.
>
> First their engagement, an engagement which, though it was not very long, was slow and quiet, in which it seemed that Rosa was stealing his soul away, almost as though he did not have one, making him believe that he would not know her until she was his once and for all; that quiet and reserved engagement, under the gaze of Gertrudis, who was all soul . . .
>
> Then came the wedding and the intoxication of the first months, the honeymoon; Rosa opened her spirit to him by degrees, but it was a spirit so simple, so transparent, that Ramiro realized she had not concealed or withheld anything from him. His wife lived with her heart in her hand and held out that hand in an offering gesture, with the innermost part of her spirit laid open to the air of the world, totally given over to the concern of the moment, like the roses of the field and the larks in the heavens. And at the same time Rosa's spirit was a reflection of her sister's, like running water in the sun, while the other's was like the closed spring from which it rose . . .
>
> She was like daily bread, like homemade everyday bread . . . Her glance, which bestowed peace, her smile, the impression of life she gave were the expression of a quiet, peaceful, and domestic spirit . . . There was something plantlike in that hidden but powerful strength with which she continually, moment after moment, sucked in the essence of the depths of everyday life, and in the sweet naturalness with which she opened her perfumed petals.

And that common life is the life that survives in the form of deprivation, better still, of mutilation, for Ramiro; not only does it survive in him, but also in that reality which is the home, into which Unamuno brings us with great skill, and which will be jealously preserved and maintained by Tula. "But did Rosa actually die? Did she really die? How could she have died while he, Ramiro, still lived? No, during the now-solitary nights, while he slept alone in that bed of death and life and love, he could feel beside him the rhythm of her breathing, her gentle warmth, though it brought him an agonizing sense of emptiness. And he would stretch out his hand and run it over the other half of the bed, pressing it sometimes." "No, Rosa, his Rosa, had not died; it was not possible that she had died; his wife was there, as alive as ever and radiating life all around her; his wife could not die."

This form of everyday life—which is constantly maintained even after Rosa dies—is sharply cut in two by her death. Death puts life to the question, especially daily life, for death is the unaccustomed factor, the one which does not admit of repetition, and when death is not a mere ceas-

ing to exist, it places us in the authenticity of life, which possesses itself in its ending and at the same time becomes problematical. "During the choking spells her eyes looked into the eyes of her Ramiro from the edge of eternity. And that look seemed to be a supreme and despairing question, as if, on the point of departing never more to return to earth, she were asking him what the hidden meaning of life was. Those looks of quiet sorrow, of sorrowful quietness, seemed to say, 'You, you who are my life; you, who with me have brought new human souls into the world; you, who have had three lives from me; you, my man, tell me: what is this?' It was an abysmal afternoon." Once again Unamuno looks for the secret of life in the creation of new lives; the man who is able to produce them is able, in a certain sense, to divine life's mystery; and this, which Unamuno applies directly to spiritual creatures, to fictitious personages, here refers to fatherhood and motherhood. Then he adds this profound metaphoric description—it cannot be described except metaphorically—of Rosa's death, which clearly tries to reproduce the radical anguish of that unique and irrevocable moment.

> At last the supreme moment came upon her, the moment of transition, and it seemed as though, on the threshold of the eternal shades, suspended over the abyss, she clung to him, to her man, who trembled as he felt drawn in too. The poor creature tried to tear open her throat with her nails; she looked at him terrified, her eyes begging him for air; then, with her eyes seeming to plumb the depths of his soul, she let go of his hand and fell back on the bed where she had conceived and borne her three children."

Unamuno speaks of the abyss, of the eternal shades, of a fall, but he takes good care to call death a transition. It is indeed a question of falling into an abyss, into the depths of oneself, into an unknown death; of falling, of something happening, not that nothing happens. Unamuno shows death as a reality, as something that one accomplishes, or at least that is accomplished in oneself. Man dies; he does not simply cease to exist.

This death divides the novel, as it does the life of its characters, into two parts; now, in the home of Ramiro the widower, it is Tula who is everything. She is the spiritual mother of the children, whom she feels to be her own, more than her own since they are not children of the flesh, and Gertrudis has a constant obsession with purity. With the passage of time Ramiro feels more strongly than ever the attraction for Tula which has always been alive in him, though concealed by Rosa's authentic everyday love. Her brother-in-law's love, in the last instance returned by her, galls Gertrudis; she rejects it because she is reluctant to succeed her own sister, in spite of her deathbed request, for fear that children of her own would affect the love she feels for those who are only children of the spirit, and because of that exacerbated need for absolute purity which dominates her in spite of herself. "If I married Ramiro . . . then I would really be a stepmother," Gertrudis says, "and even more so if he gave me children of my own flesh and blood . . ." Unamuno adds: "And the thought of children of her flesh made the very marrow of Gertrudis' soul shake with sacred terror, for she was all motherhood, but spiritual motherhood." At bottom this is again a problem of personality. Tula is in anguish, less for what she may do than for what she will *be* (we often forget that some of our actions turn us into other persons, and that is why we feel seized with terror when we contemplate them). She is in love with Ramiro, but she wants to be Tía Tula, always virginal, the spiritual mother of Rosa's and Ramiro's children and even of Rosa and Ramiro, the foundation of their home, keystone of a common existence which she has created and to which she has dedicated herself. What is to become of those things? I repeat, it is not a question of a trivial conflict between opposing appetites, or between desires and duties or supposed duties, but of a problem of personality which affects the very being. This is why Unamuno says, "And certainly, in Gertrudis's closed-up soul a great storm was brewing. Her head battled with her heart, and both head and heart battled in her with something even more deeply buried, more private, more intimate, with something that was like the marrowbones of her spirit." This something is no other than what Unamuno called the depths of the soul and which I prefer to call the basis of the person, the "who" that each one of us is.

When Ramiro insists, Gertrudis, softened in her loving uncertainty through pity for him, gives him the space of a year to decide at the end of that time whether they should marry. But during that period Ramiro, overcome by the temptations of the flesh, falls into sin with the maid of the house, Manuela, "a nineteen-year-old girl from the orphanage, sickly and pale, with a feverish gleam in her eyes, of gentle, submissive manners, of few words, almost always sad." When Gertrudis finds out about it she feels great pity for her brother-in-law, and at the same time suspects that her own virtue may have caused him to sin, that she may have been inhuman. But, simply and imperiously she makes Ramiro marry the girl so that his new child can have a father and mother, and Tula can be spiritual mother of them all. When the orphan is about to have her second child, which will be a girl, Ramiro falls ill and dies. Shortly before, in a moving dialogue between brother- and sister-in-law, Tula bares her soul to him and Ramiro dies holding her hand. Gertrudis, "broken by a long exhaustion, the fatigue of years, pressed her mouth for one moment to Ramiro's cold mouth and relived their lives, which had been one life." Gertrudis renounces nothing; those who have departed survive in her, she tries to make them go on living in the house. This is the decisive point: she embodies all their sense of coexistence, which she nurtures with memories. When Manuela dies giving birth to her daughter, Tula is left alone with the five children, all of whom she thinks of as equally her children; and year after year she makes them live in intimate communion with the three dead parents, and even with the ancestors one step removed from them whom they have never known: Tía Tula's dead. She devotes herself particularly to Manolita, the youngest, the one who would not have been born had she not obliged Ramiro to marry the orphan girl, the one who never had a mother, the one she will form in her image and who will be Tula's successor in the family.

During this time, in which Gertrudis relives all her memo-

ries, in the serene seriousness of her maternal life, the meaning of the unity she has formed and defends at all costs becomes clear to her, as does her mistake in regard to Ramiro. " 'Do I love him or not?' she had asked herself sometimes when he was alive. 'Isn't that pride? Isn't it like the sad, lonely passion of the ermine, who won't jump into the mire to save his fellow for fear of getting dirty? I don't know . . . I don't know . . .' " And when she is about to die, after she has left her nieces and nephews, who are all really her children, grown up and united in the house of which she has been the soul, she tells them as a final piece of advice:

> Think well, very, very well about what you are going to do, think very well . . . so that you'll never have to repent of doing something, and still less for not having done it . . . And if you see that the one you love has fallen into a pool of mire, a cesspool even, a sewer, jump in to save him . . . don't let him drown there . . . or drown together . . . in the sewer . . . No, we don't have wings, or if we do they're only chicken's wings . . . we are not angels . . . we will be in the other life . . . where there is no mire and no blood! Filth there is in Purgatory, flaming mire that burns and cleanses . . . This is the last thing I can tell you: don't be afraid of filth . . . Pray for me, and may the Virgin forgive me.'

At last, after Gertrudis has died, her meaning as founder of the family's coexistence is made most clearly apparent. In the prologue Unamuno alludes explicitly to St. Theresa, and says that he did not notice the deep and hidden similarities to the saint until after he had written the novel. Tula is the founder of a domestic community which survives her; her life, her strong personality, is not destined to feed on itself but to realize itself in the common life of the house. Perhaps it is for this reason that Gertrudis' ultimate loneliness is so stressed, that loneliness from which she draws the intimacy necessary for the common life of the others.

"Did Tía Tula die?" Unamuno asks at the beginning of chapter XXIV. "No, instead she began to live in the family, with a new sort of life that was more inward and more life-giving than ever, with the eternal life of immortal family spirit. Tía Tula was the foundation and the rooftree of that home." And Manolita, the youngest girl, is the continuator of Tula's spirit.

> She kept the other's archive and her treasure; she had the key of the secret hiding places of her who in flesh and blood was no more; she kept, with the doll she had had as a child, Tula's childhood doll, and some letters and the prayer book and Don Primitivo's breviary. She was the one in the family who knew the sayings and doings of the forebears still within memory: of Don Primitivo, who was no blood relation of hers; of the elder Ramiro's mother; of Rosa; of her own mother Manuela—no sayings or doings here, only silence and passions. She was the domestic history; the spiritual eternity of the family was continued in her.

(pp. 104-112)

Julián Marías, in his Miguel de Unamuno,

translated by Frances M. López-Morillas, Cambridge, Mass.: Harvard University Press, 1966, 224 p.

J. F. Tull, Jr.   (essay date 1970)

[*In the excerpt below, Tull explores the themes of psychological and metaphysical alienation in* Nada menos que todo un hombre *and* San Manuel Bueno, mártir.]

Spanish authors of the last two centuries, like many of their counterparts in other Western countries, have been dealing with the themes of both psychological and metaphysical alienation while, generally, not attempting to label them as such. . . .

But it was in the social, political and spiritual crisis of Spain at the turn of the century that writers came to the fore who spoke, in the clearest terms, of the intimately related concepts of psychological and metaphysical estrangement. (p. 27)

[It was] for Unamuno, a figure who transcends the notion of generations and who speaks, at one and the same time, as both modern and universal man, to synthesize and spell out in his poetry, essays and, especially, in his "nivolas" the dilemma of the individual "of flesh and bones," as he was fond of saying, alienated both psychologically and metaphysically in the twentieth century. In this study, I should like to single out, as examples of this synthesis, three characters in the three "nivolas," *Niebla,* ("*Film*" [that dims the sight]), **Nada menos que todo un hombre,** (*Every Inch a Man*), and **San Manuel Bueno mártir,** (**Saint Immanuel the Good, Martyr**). (p. 28)

Julia Yáñez, in [**Nada menos que todo un hombre**], combines the same aspects of psychological and metaphysical alienation found in *Niebla,* in a slightly different form. For her father, Don Victorino, "a person of very dubious moral background" she and her beauty were the key to his hopes of economic redemption. (pp. 29-30)

Then came her suitors: first, Enrique, "an incipient Don Juan," who sought a way to end his relationship with Julia "once he succeeded in making it known in all of Renada that its sacred regional beauty had admitted him to her window." Next it was Pedro "more stout-hearted" than Enrique, who exclaimed that Julia was mad when she suggested the idea of a mutual suicide pact, an act that would put an end to the maneuverings of her father toward her. . . . Julia believed that her father was capable of selling her favors to [the wealthy landowner] Don Alberto, that, for him, it would not seem a bad idea.

At this point, the *indiano,* Alejandro Gómez, arrived on the scene. He is described by Unamuno as "very willful and very stubborn and very self-centered." He courted Julia and won her hand in marriage. . . . Nevertheless, like her father, he made no display of affection toward her, regarded her as a possession and caused her to ask herself repeatedly "Does he love *me,* or is it only that he wants to show off my beauty?"

Unquestionably, the exclamation "your beauty will cause your ruin!," a thought which obsessed Julia at the begin-

ning of the story, seems to be the key to the understanding of her state of constant emotional and spiritual crisis throughout the work. Like Pedro, Alejandro views Julia as "neurasthenic," and Unamuno confirms the idea of acute psychological stress when he comments, shortly before her death, "All these tortures of her spirit destroyed Julia's life, and she became gravely ill, mentally ill." This mental illness caused her death, a psychic suicide comparable to that of Augusto in *Niebla.* The enigma of Julia's pathological state and consequent death is not clarified by Unamuno and must rest upon interpretation.

At first glance it would seem that Julia's beauty "caused her ruin" and death because of the cruelty and avarice of her father, a sense of betrayal by her suitors, Alejandro's hermetic nature, in other words, because of her relationship with the men she regarded as most important in her life.

There is, however, another interpretation which explains more profoundly Julia's spiritual crisis, her psychic suicide. "This interpretation has to do not only with her beauty, but with her concept of beauty, with her concept of her own being. As has been pointed out, Julia constantly asked herself whether Alejandro loves her or her beauty. And, in similar fashion, when Enrique abandons her, she exclaims, "And he said he loved me! No, he didn't love me, he loved my beauty." After Pedro leaves her, she thinks to herself: "He didn't love me either, he didn't either. They fall in love with my beauty, not with me."

This thorough identification with an internal "ego" separated from her body seems to indicate that Julia suffered from a dualistic alienation between her psyche and her external appearance. She despised her body. . . . In fact, we might conclude that there is not one Julia, complete and integrated, but a woman split in two by an illusory dualism between inward personality and outward physical appearance. Julia is both psychologically and metaphysically alienated because she has not understood and accepted the fusion of corporeal elements and psychic aspects which constitute the totality of every individual and, consequently, she dies.

Spanish criticism of the "Christian atheist," Don Manuel, in **San Manuel Bueno, mártir** has seen in him "the most complete personification of the tormented incredulity of [the work's] author," Unamuno. It has also recognized that Don Manuel's consolation was "to console myself by consoling others, even though the consolation I give them may not be mine." This body of criticism recognizes, moreover, the existential base of Don Manuel's metaphysical anxiety and alienation and his search "to do! to do!," to flee from "idle thoughts, alone," and that, for him, "the truth . . . is perhaps something terrible, something intolerable, something mortal; simple folk could not live with it." The most recent criticism that suggests that Unamuno, with this statement, had repented rather belatedly "for having agitated others with his own religious doubts and anxieties" has been that of Marín, in his introduction to **San Manuel** in *Literatura española, selección.* (pp. 30-1)

I should like to expound, at this point, the hypothesis that both creator and fictional character sensed in this late fruit of Unamuno's literary output intuitive glimpses of the possibility of a resolution of the "tortured incredulity" of both. I make reference, specifically, to the curious juxtaposition of three incidents in the very heart of the story, quoted by Lázaro, brother of the narrator and confidante of Don Manuel.

The first episode that Lázaro relates is a sense at the edge of the omnipresent lake when Don Manuel comments: "This is my greatest temptation." He continues by describing his perpetual combat against a suicidal impyulse. The second incident, immediately following, is the scene of the shepherdess, in which Don Manuel says: "Look, it seems as if time had come to an end, as if this shepherdess had been there always, and just as she is, and singing as she is, and as if she were going to continue being there always, as she was before my consciousness began, as she will be when it ends. That shepherdess forms a part, with the rocks, the clouds, the trees, the water, of nature and not history". The juxtaposition of episodes ends with Lázaro's commentary on the day of the snow storm when Don Manuel said: "Have you ever seen, Lázaro, a mystery greater than that of the snow falling in the lake and dying in it . . . "

To me, these three incidents represent three phases in the process of spiritual maturation, intuitive at first, which occur to many individuals, in different cultures and different times, tormented like Don Manuel by incredulity before the meaning of their own existence. In the first episode, I do not believe, with Marín, that the lake represents "the death and oblivion in which men are interred," but rather Don Manuel's intuitive aspiration toward a sublimation—a "suicide," if you will—of his conscious ego, imprisoned until now by his alienation, his doubts and anxieties, into a wider vision of human existence, manifested, as will be seen, in the scene of the shepherdess. The rest which Don Manuel aspires to achieve in his last hours (once again, as *Niebla* and **Nada menos,** a physically motivated death) is not the rest of oblivion with physical death, but rather the spiritual rest after the individual's conscious ego sees itself not as an isolated object, alienated from a foreign and impersonal universe, but as an integral part of a process which both incorporates and transcends its individual existence.

Unamuno—Don Manuel intuits this interpretation of existence in the moments of the shepherdess and the snow storm. The shepherdess—the man freed from his metaphysical alienation—is outside of history, or of the conventional, linear concept we hold of history and life in general. The shepherdess lives in an eternal present, "as if time had come to an end," in intimate contact with her environment. This is precisely the sensation of existence that Don Manuel has intuited, but has not experienced. It might be added that his constant "via negativa," his "neti neti," the negation which he embraces in his interpretation of life, has led many individuals, paradoxically, to an affirmation of life not as an occasion to "console others", but as an experience which we shall now examine in the incident of the snow storm.

In the storm, the last phase of spiritual development, the snowflake, the individual, senses that he is fused as an inte-

gral part of the cosmos. His alienation and incredulity end, not with respect to the convention of a life after death, but rather with respect to the intimate and sometimes ecstatic relationship that exists between the individual and his universe.

We may thus conclude that Unamuno intuited in these three key incidents the possibility of a concept, a feeling of existence, that is immensely wider for the individual alienated from the rest of nature by his incredulity. Yet Unamuno, like Don Manuel, never achieved the full sensation of this vision of the world simply because he could never completely "let go," in the words of the French psychiatrist, Hubert Benoit; he could not go beyond his concept of human personality as an ego imprisoned and alienated. He did not recognize totally the abandonment of this ego in a "suicide" which, again, paradoxically, results in a sense of the eternal present and an awareness of man's fusion with the "lake" which is the cosmos.

Unamuno on the Spanish Revolution and the spirit of the Spaniard:

Today, as yesterday, I believe that the well-being of the people can be secured only by profound reforms. But it is necessary to ascertain who is capable of effecting these reforms. . . . Those whom I followed in the beginning have not succeeded. I had hoped to aid them by helping in the elaboration of their doctrines. I came to acquire, as you know, the reputation of being a great thinker, of which reputation I do not (in confidence) feel proud.

All these efforts were in vain. And it is this that has decided me to join myself with those whom I had not ceased fighting up to now. Could it be inconstancy on my part?

Perhaps one could pick out many faults which I really have, but I maintain that this one, inconstancy, would never forgive my having betrayed the spiritual friendship, so to speak, which unites us, and this is the real reason why I continue to call you very sincerely "My dear friend". I am certain that upon reading this letter you will see it proved once again that two hearts can continue beating in unison even when the minds have ceased to be in accord.

Perhaps this statement about two hearts may make you smile. But we Spaniards, even under the austere gown of the professor or the savant, remain men of feeling. We do not know what it is to be one of those calloused individuals who suppress their feelings, and we retain within ourselves a reserve of emotion which at times can draw forth tears. Yes, I wish to confess it; I have wept.

I have wept, because a great tragedy has overtaken my country. Spain is becoming red, and blood is flowing; and do you know what this means? It means that in every Spanish home there dwells pain and anguish. And I, who believed that I was working for the good of my people, I too bear responsibility for this catastrophe. I was one of those who wanted to save mankind without knowing man.

Miguel de Unamuno, in a letter in Spanish Liberals Speak on the Counter-Revolution in Spain, *translated and edited by the Spanish Relief Committee, 1987.*

Unamuno, in [**Nada menos que todo un hombre** and **San Manual Bueno, mártir**], wrote of modern man's psychological alienation and universal man's metaphysical alienation because he had experienced both to the depths of his being. In fact, as may be seen from this study, it is very difficult to draw the line between the two aspects of alienation, the best solution possibly being to recognise that they are conventional distinctions made by an intellect that is habituated to categorizing and defining. In any event, . . . while alienation as a term is in danger of abuse, as a literary theme in the hands of an author with the creative powers of an Unamuno, it can strike us with particular force that this is the way that many men "of flesh and bones" live and have lived. (pp. 31-2)

> *J. F. Tull, Jr., "Alienation, Psychological and Metaphysical, in Three 'Nivolas' of Unamuno," in* The Humanities Association Bulletin, *Vol. XXI, No. 1, Winter, 1970, pp. 27-33.*

Victor Ouimette   (essay date 1974)

[*Ouimette is a Canadian critic and educator. In the following excerpt, he discusses the female antiheroes of* Tres novelas ejemplares y un prólogo *and Don Manuel's victory over doubt in* San Manuel Bueno, mártir.]

The theme of believing while doubting is a constant throughout Unamuno's writings and received its fullest theoretical treatment in 1925 with the publication of *La agonía del cristianismo*. He gave it life and new dimensions in **San Manuel Bueno, mártir,** written in 1930 and one of his most concrete works. In the latter there is no abstraction of the ego, nor is the protagonist an incarnation of a monomania, as is the case in most of the other novels. Don Manuel represents creative doubt. He lives with death throughout his life. It is not terror of death specifically that corrodes his strength, but rather the feeling that earthly life may have no purpose if there is no immortality. This is indeed a heroic concern, but, as has been said, Unamuno felt that such a sense of despair could possibly be alleviated by fame, as it was in part for Don Quixote, or by physical descendants.

Neither of these choices is open to don Manuel, however, because he is a priest whose mission is to show the significance of eternal resurrection. He cannot compromise with mere fame, nor can he count on children to re-create him through time: he can create disciples, but they will be followers of what he himself does not believe in and they cannot perpetuate his intimate being, but only an image of him. Therefore, don Manuel's only hope of salvation lies in the hero's polarization—here, between the priest and his parishioners. They need him to teach them about and give them faith in eternal life, while he needs them to help him to believe, since he is incapable of believing on his own. Just as Don Quixote's flagging faith was restored by the encouragement of Sancho, so don Manuel looks for the same support from the people of Valverde de Lucerna.

The novel is yet another treatment of the problem (or what at this time Unamuno was calling the "mystery") of personality. "The other one" in this case is the parish. In don Manuel, there is not a true conflict between reason and emotion, since he has no faith and that is what the parishioners provide: they are his faith and he is their reason. They complement each other; but just as the hero cannot exist without his audience, so don Manuel finds himself on the brink of oblivion and annihilation throughout his life. He saves his parishioners from despair through his reason, but because theirs is the "collier's faith," they do not depend on him for existence in the way that he needs them for justification. Specifically, he doubts his own immortality but searches for peace for his flock.

Although he has lost his faith, he has tried to replace it with his sense of ethical responsibility. That is, he tries to fulfill his mission as he sees it even though he questions its validity. This is his weakness, of course, for if the hero must constantly re-evaluate his course of action and its relevance to his personal frame of reference, why does don Manuel continue what he feels is a lost cause? The answer is one we have already examined: that it is no more certain that there is *not* a chance for immortality than it is that there *is* a chance, and don Manuel decides that while he personally doubts, there is no reason to destroy his flock by robbing them of their simple hope. Rather than insist constantly on his own beliefs in the hope of converting someone to his cause, he has chosen to champion his followers' cause in the hope that he will be able to convert himself.

Don Manuel's position is ambivalent because he seems to equivocate in his teachings and this could be unjust, as Unamuno points out; but don Manuel feels that if there is a God and immortality, his duty is to lead his flock toward them. Don Quixote released the galley slaves because he felt that, although it was not right in secular terms, it was acceptable from the superior point of view of divine justice. Don Manuel echoes this sentiment when he says: "Human justice does not concern me." Just as his mission is to indoctrinate his parishioners as if there were a God, he himself must try to live in accordance with this possibility too. He must devote himself entirely to the salvation of the town, as his entire existence will become illusory and irrelevant without the immortality that can be his only through the success of these efforts.

For this reason he almost never allows himself to be alone with his fears: the people sustain him, give him justification, and are his polarization, and he admits: "I must not live alone; I must not die alone. I must live for my people, die for my people. How am I going to save my soul if I do not save my people's soul?" He creates faith in the people so that they may live heroically, for without it, they could lack the strength to live at all. Manuel Bueno is a hero whose mission is inconsistent with his personality, but this is also the source of his heroism: to the best of his ability he tries to rise above this limitation and fulfill his purpose.

There is another obstacle to the total honesty of don Manuel: the town would not have believed in his lack of faith in any case. Heroism is deeds, and those of don Manuel carried far more weight than any protestations regarding his beliefs: "They would have believed in his works and not in his words, because words do not serve to support works, but rather the works are enough in themselves." He was not making an intellectual or rational appeal to his parishioners, but an emotional one. They were not, and would not have been, interested in his theology because the deep spiritual crises through which he passed would have been meaningless to them. Reality is what makes people work and this is the basis of the people's belief in don Manuel's faith. They could see its positive results in their daily lives, and whether or not these good works to which he devoted himself had their basis in hypocrisy would be of no importance to them.

Obviously, this lays open the entire question of the truth of the religion that don Manuel was teaching, but he said that human justice did not concern him and he clearly felt that the religion he gave them was the most relevant to their lives: "True religion? All religions are true, as long as they cause the people who profess them to live spiritually, as long as they comfort them for having to be born in order to die; and for each people the truest religion is their own, the one that has made them. And mine? Mine is to comfort myself by comforting others, even though the comfort that I give them may not be my own." Religion is man's support, but not his master. Don Manuel may be providing a placebo, a fiction for his parishioners, but it enriches them and makes life more meaningful for them. This makes it truth and, as Unamuno says, don Manuel's main characteristic is "heroic saintliness," while Lázaro refers to don Manuel's "saintly cause."

If don Manuel's actions had led him to faith, both in himself and in the hope of immortality, he would indeed have been a true hero; but his rational being defeated his will, or as Lázaro says, "he is too intelligent to believe everything that he has to teach." He cannot, then, pass his lifetime in contemplation because that is what has weakened him: "His life was active and not contemplative, as he fled as much as he could from having nothing to do." Through his charitable activities and his complete dedication to the welfare and faith of his people, he could avoid excessive reflection on the danger of annihilation. These activities were also a possible source of faith in the sense that they brought him closer to those who did believe and might have given him some of their faith, but did not.

There are many circumstantial similarities between don Manuel, Don Quixote, and Christ. Like Don Quixote, don Manuel refused to believe in anyone's evil intentions, and like both of them, he left none of his teachings in writing. These are superficial points of contact, to be sure, but they do create a certain parallelism with other heroic figures, and Unamuno thus leads us to wonder how many others who seemed to have unshakable faith were indeed racked by doubts and fears. On his deathbed, Don Quixote renounced his faith, just as in his last mass don Manuel renounces his hope of heroism and says, "There is no eternal life other than this one." After having given up all hope of faith he, too, dies; but just as Unamuno hopes for the resurrection of Don Quixote, so the townspeople hope for that of don Manuel.

Don Manuel's Sancho is Lázaro, the progressive atheist who becomes a devoted disciple of Manuel's creative doubt in a deep spiritual union. Lázaro is his real triumph, much more so than the town itself, because Manuel brings him from negation and atheism to doubt and belief in a possibility. Lázaro is his spiritual son and will carry on after his death in a similar state of dynamism and tension, very much alive and very active. If Manuel managed to satisfy the town by means of a well-intentioned deceit, this was not possible with Lázaro, whom he could convert only by means of a more rationally based truth. He believed in Lázaro and put him on the road to the absolutes that he himself never found, but not by means of the blind faith of Valverde or Blas, the village idiot who mechanically repeats the things he hears, much as the parishioners do. If Blas and Valverde represent don Manuel as seen from without, Lázaro and, to a certain extent, Angela, reveal him from within. Angela is to don Manuel what Paul was to Christ and what Cervantes was to Don Quixote. She, too, eventually enters into a state of creative doubt, as she evolves within her own narrative and begins to see both sides of don Manuel's heroism: that which changed the parishioners as well as that darker side which changed Lázaro but destroyed don Manuel. (pp. 163-67)

One of Unamuno's most distinctive types of protagonist is the person who shows signs of a well-defined personality at the service of a misguided mission. These characters direct and control the personalities of others in such a way that the dominated character cannot develop. The degree to which the aim is false varies greatly, but it is this poor choice of motive that deprives the protagonist of his true greatness and often makes him a negative influence. Many of these are women whose fanaticism about motherhood causes them to destroy those in their path and to use others as instruments for their own fulfillment.

In 1920, the volume *Tres novelas ejemplares y un prólogo* was published, containing two novels in which this type of person appears: *Dos madres* and *El marqués de Lumbria.* The cunning Raquel of the first gave much besides her name to the protagonist of the play *Raquel encadenada,* but she is a far less altruistic person, although no less real for being so. She is the only strength that her lover, don Juan, has, and their relationship works, says Unamuno, only because "don Juan needed a will to make up for the one he was lacking." This is to say that he lacks personality because of Raquel, or at least that any he might have had has been crushed under the weight of her strong will. There is no real question of love, and certainly none of polarization, since don Juan seems incapable of doing anything on his own initiative: "Was he, don Juan, in love with Raquel? No, rather absorbed by her, submerged in her, lost in the woman and in her widowhood." Just as Cosme was nothing without Damián, so is don Juan insignificant without the will of Raquel to which he so readily responds. He is a man whose weakness as an individual extends even to his thoughts of immortality. He has no interest in children, either spiritual or physical because his sense of defeat does not let him imagine that they could be any stronger than he: "But he had no appetite for fatherhood! . . . Why should he leave in the world another one like himself?" This is a sound point, but it is of no concern to Raquel, whose only interest is in having children, regardless of whom they resemble or what their character may be. If they were to be similar in spirit to Juan, they would be more compliant with her wishes.

Juan is not stupid, however, and it is this awareness of his plight that gives pathos to his character and emphasizes the strength of character in Raquel. Juan knows full well what part he plays in his mistress's life, but has been so emasculated that he is unable to resist: "He felt that for Raquel he was just an instrument, a means. A means for what? For satisfying an excessive hunger for motherhood? Or rather a strange vengeance, a vengeance from other worlds?" There is a parallel to be drawn between Juan and the Raquel of *Raquel encadenada*. Both of them are victimized in similar ways, but whereas Raquel sacrifices everything to free herself from her chains and devote herself to children, Juan permits himself the complacency that Unamuno so often railed against. Even when he agrees to marry Berta, it is with the secret hope that she will give him the will to rebel; that becomes impossible, however, when Berta, in her way, falls as much under the domination of Raquel as Juan: "The one with whom Berta was madly in love was Raquel, Raquel was her idol." By allowing Raquel to take over her children with no moral justification whatsoever, she too becomes enslaved. No one believes that it is possible to succeed against Raquel's wishes and no effort is made—either by Juan, or by the parents of Berta, or by Berta herself, who possibly benefits from the situation more than anyone besides Raquel herself because she learns what her own weakness is through her relationship with the woman: "And she let herself be absorbed by Juan's mistress and kept discovering herself through the other woman." In fact, all the secondary characters learn of their ineptness as individuals through their dealings with and defeat by Raquel.

Unamuno does more to give Raquel depth by describing those who wallow in her wake than he does by describing her directly. She does know her own mind and is capable of exerting her will so that she may be herself and be all— but she is tyrannical. The closer she comes to motherhood, however apparential it may be, the more despotic she becomes. Like the other characters in this category, she is something of a monomaniac, with her own benefit as her only goal. She is defeated in her ambition to have a child only by her sterility. Her strength of character and determination are basically heroic, but she spurs no one on to greater fulfillment.

The situation presented in *El marqués de Lumbria,* is not dissimilar. Carolina, with her iron will, conquers and annihilates Tristán, a weak man throughout, and becomes a mother by dint of that will. Like Raquel, she allows herself to be stopped by nothing. Her character makes her capable of anything, but again her goal is beneficial only to herself and is unjust for all.

The most complete development of the theme is to be found in the novel *La Tía Tula,* published only one year later, in 1921. The central motivation, however, is slightly different. Rather than concentrate merely on the business of acquiring a child, Unamuno shows in this work what could be called the essence of being a mother. *Dos madres* and *El marqués de Lumbría* deal with creating a concrete mother-child relationship through whatever means seem

necessary; but in this novel he goes one step further, as he examines how a woman can impose herself on her "children" in a truly spiritual sense. These are the psychological aspects of maternity.

The hero must fulfill a need; he must show or prove the possibility of greater development by bringing to the fore the inherent weaknesses in one's character. Tula, however, weakens her audience (Ramiro and the children) first and then fills the need she has created. In many ways she resembles Alejandro Gómez (*Nada menos que todo un hombre*) in this; for her heroism, if it may momentarily be called that, is false in that it has its greatest effect where it should have been least necessary. There is something frightful about Tula and her methods. She lacks the purity of purpose that we saw in Manuel Bueno, for example, but is not as nefarious as Raquel (*Dos madres*) or Carolina. She shows, however, no respect for anyone else's will. On the surface she is the model of motherhood and purity, but as Ramiro realizes: " 'You're a saint, Gertrudis,' Ramiro told her, 'but a saint who has made sinners.' " There is a perversion in her efforts and in her view of purposes. Only when Manuela dies does Tula finally begin to feel some of the guilt that is rightfully hers. Devoting herself almost entirely to the children of Manuela and Ramiro, she cries: "They are the children of my sin! Yes, of my sin!" She is the founder of a family that eventually becomes a community representing her personal fulfillment and immortality. It has been formed, however, through a dedication to the principle of broadening her own position as spiritual mother. There is a lack of evolution in her personality, as her function as mother is never threatened, and is indeed reinforced, by these people who seem born to live together, subject to her domination, and participating as members of the family group.

The remarkable thing about this community, aside from its cohesiveness, is its solitude. Virtually no interpenetration of characters is possible in the novel, since each person lives in almost complete isolation. The justification for their existence as a group is a kind of spiritual inbreeding in which each member gives meaning to the mother. The children give Tula her fulfillment as a mother, and she in turn emasculates and eliminates Ramiro. He is the producer of children in any woman not worried, as Tula is, by the preservation of her virginity; then, like Raquel, she takes control of the fruit of this union. She is necessary to Ramiro because she is his refuge and continuity, not as an individual woman but symbolically. Like most of Unamuno's women, she represents the intrahistory of man. The importance to her of the children's attitude toward her is evidenced by her eagerness to be called "mother" and reluctance to be referred to as "step-mother," and thus be relegated to a secondary position in their ill-defined personalities. This is a deliberate technique used by Unamuno to show the children's individuality but lack of inner development at Tula's hand. The only one who emerges is Manolita, since she is designated as Tula's follower, her Sancho. What we have learned about Tula is assumed to apply to Manolita as well: "through her, the spiritual eternity of the family continued. She inherited the family's soul, rendered spiritual in the Aunt." Tula succeeds in achieving some degree of immortality, even though it is done through shadows instead of personalities. She has felt a sense of mission throughout her life and has resolved to die with the thought that she must have completed that mission. Like all heroes, she vacillates and entertains certain doubts about herself—"But do I understand myself? Do I understand myself?"—but she does not interrupt the continuity of her course of action. Her entire life has been centered around an activity limited to her immediate family: "But she had passed through the world outside the world." The blame must be shared, however, with Ramiro, who resigned himself to the situation. He alone could have prevented it, but his reaction was somewhat like that of Juan in *Dos madres.* For example, after his marriage to Manuela he abandons himself completely: "Ramiro lived deep in resigned despair and more subjected than ever to Gertrudis's will." Tula only accepted the opportunities that she caused to come about. Her actions were destructive to many, but no one had the stronger will necessary to stop her, and she believed that her motives were just.

One of the most direct representations of the effects of a despotic personality is the theatrical novella **Nada menos que todo un hombre** (1916), in which the protagonist has a brutal will dominated completely by the image it has formed of itself. Alejandro Gómez is scarcely human, nor is he intended to be; yet he dominates Julia with every breath. There is something intentionally grotesque about him, and his absurd attempts at Nietzschean heroism show him to be without substance or viable motivation. His sense of mission is limited to the perpetuation of him-

self through the son whom he claims he inevitably had to father; yet beneath the image there is the destructive void of a desperate will without justification beyond that which he demands from others. His barbarity is mitigated only at the end when he sinks into a realization of his crimes and of his true love for Julia.

His influence is not heroic in any sense of the word since it is founded on fear and not on exemplary conduct: he is pure egotism and wants to better himself at the cost of his wife. His vaunting is false and his claims that he is unlike others are tricks sustained by his lack of a past. Like Don Quixote and Julio Macedo, he claims to be reborn, but he does not reinforce this rebirth with new vital content. His wife thus becomes an object, an instrument to give him a justification that he cannot achieve alone. When she finally discovers the truth about him, he is without force and the outcome of the story is inevitable. He finishes without having transcended himself at all, since he did not follow up his claims and declarations of uniqueness with authentic actions. He is essentially as Eugenio de Nora pictures him: "No, Alejandro is not, strictly speaking, a man, not even a *being;* he is a blind *wanting,* an exclusive and brutal will projected on his surroundings." He is designed to reveal the necessary authenticity of the heroic ego and the self-destruction incurred by deception. The house built on sand must inevitably fall under the weight of its own superstructure. (pp. 199-205)

> *Victor Ouimette, in his* Reason Aflame: Unamuno and the Heroic Will, *Yale University Press, 1974, 237 p.*

Frances Wyers   (essay date 1976)

[*In the excerpt below, Wyers illustrates Unamuno's treatment of the division between body and soul in* La tía Tula.]

In the prologue to **La tía Tula** Unamuno compared the novel to **Abel Sánchez** because both delve into the dark "cellars and hiding places of the heart, catacombs of the soul". The readers who found that novel inhuman will find this one so also, he says. **Abel Sánchez** is about "fraternal" relations—and Unamuno reminds us that the first fraternal act was Cain's—and **La tía Tula** is about "sororal" ones. For Unamuno the sibling tie invariably suggests two linked themes—psychological splitting and the goal of total self-sufficiency that lies behind it. **La tía Tula** focuses on the second, though aspects of the first are naturally a part of the protagonist's characterization.

The novel opens with contrasting portraits of two sisters, Rosa and Gertrudis (Tula) who are, Unamuno says, like two halves of a sundered whole. This initial opposition sets up a physical and psychological duality that will be resolved by the destruction or absorption of one by the other. Unamuno's description evokes the dichotomy of inner and outer, spirit and flesh: Rosa opens to the world "the flower of her flesh", whereas Tula is like "a locked and sealed coffer in which one divines a treasure of tenderness and secret pleasure". Rosa's beauty attracts but Tula's "tenacious eyes" capture. If Gertrudis represents the invisible inner substance (the inner self), the novel, on

Unamuno in 1883, when he was a university student in Madrid.

one level, dramatizes the war between body and soul as the protagonist tries to affirm her spirit and assure its continuity through the creation of new beings. Like Raquel, Tula aims at a purely spiritual maternity.

Her characterization is wholly in terms of the exaltation of spirit over matter; she hates sensuality; she hates the flesh. Because she would like to be a disembodied will, she scrupulously avoids any compromise with the body. When Rosa's suitor, Ramiro, begins to notice her, she quickly arranges a marriage that will free her for what she describes as her vocation to be an aunt, that is, a spiritual mother. Like Raquel, Tula uses another to conceive and bear for her so that the child can be the uncontaminated offspring of her will. Although she is, as Unamuno says, "all soul", she seeks incarnation in another as if her spirit were trying, in a circuitous way, to reunite itself with the body through the creation of a child who would be, in spite of its real parentage, hers. This "spiritual maternity" entails, of course, a complete disregard for the physical parents; when Rosa almost dies in childbirth, Tula does not allow the doctor to risk the child's life in order to save the mother who, being flesh and not spirit, is dispensable.

The plot is linear and simple, tracing Tula's ever-growing control over her sister's household and the constancy of a virginity that is more than physical. When Rosa dies after the birth of her third child, Ramiro tries to persuade Tula to marry him, but she is repelled by his "brutishness", she esteems herself too highly to serve as the "remedy" for some man's sensuality. Besides, married to Ramiro she would be the stepmother of his children and she prefers to be the "spiritual" mother. "The idea of children of her own flesh made the marrow of her soul's bones tremble with sacred terror, for Gertrudis was all maternity, but spiritual maternity." Ramiro, desiring Tula, gets a servant girl pregnant and Tula forces them to marry, thus turning him into her obedient child and reducing the maid to reproductive servitude. The girl bears two children for Tula and dies during her second delivery. Ramiro dies shortly afterwards and Tula is left in undisputed control of a family forged by her will, a "pure" family of innocent children and a virgin mother.

Tula seeks to recreate the home in which she and her sister grew up. Orphaned early, they lived with an uncle, a pious old priest who brought them up "with the cult of the Virgin Mother and the cult of their mother and their grandmother". Her ideal is a succession through parthenogenesis, a community of untainted spirits (women and children) who live free from the flesh and ignorant of it. She wants a chaste home where "no door ever has to be closed, a home without mysteries".

The division of the sexes is, for Tula, a figuration of the struggle between body and spirit—and spirit must triumph since men are "all flesh and very brutish". Yet Tula sees the world teeming with evidence of a frightening and despicable sensuality. During a country vacation, she worries that the sight of farm animals, "serpents in paradise", might corrupt the children. The sea alone appears to be clean, lifeless, sterile, though even the salt air brings a "dangerous tingling". The earth itself is an affront to chastity; she refuses to sit on the ground next to Ramiro and

"in front of the children". Purity exists only "in the cell, the cloister, the city". The city, which is a monastery of solitary people, isolates, whereas nature brings them together and couples them. We remember that for Unamuno the monastery is the incubator of envy. Solitude and envy, which are the concomitants of purity, are only hinted at in this novel; they barely emerge as almost hidden themes.

Tula is repelled by life because it is limited and mortal and she longs for absolute dominion. Her idea of virtue is, she says "inhuman", that is, beyond the human. She aims at spiritual impregnability, or rather at the spirit's power to conceive itself. All signs of the body's vulnerability, such as blood and vomit, fill her with "unspeakable disgust", though her need to make the spirit flesh in "her" children leads to copious blood-letting. The novel's gory scenes of childbirth and death, which twice coincide, speak of a fascination that ties together murder and procreation, death and copulation, at once repugnant and alluring. Tula keeps herself free from the flesh by destroying that of others.

Freedom means freedom from all forms of dependence. Tula imagines herself as "an orphan loaded with children", and her passion for maternity excludes any filial feeling ("is this not pride?" she asks). She wants to derive from herself alone, be her own creator and the sole founder of the family (she does not need the collaboration of the male because hers is a spiritual family). The life of the bees intrigues her because their art and tradition, wax and hive, are the work of "aunts" who have no part in the reproductive process. This is the kind of tradition she would like to hand down to "her" children. Yet the need for perfect autonomy means that even the children can exist only as instruments of her will. She calls them her "works", and they themselves come to accept this designation, forgetting their real parents and imagining that they are a "creation of hers". Tula, like Berta and Raquel, would bring forth the world and others in her image.

Playing god means the subjection of others; Tula's last years are filled with remorse and self-accusation. She tells her confessor that her life has been "a lie, a mistake, a failure". She charges herself with having used and abused all those around her, for having treated them, as she says on her deathbed, like puppets—"dolls all of them!" At the end she repents of her grandiose and demonic dreams, yet she does not reconcile herself to the human world. She blames herself for rejecting Ramiro and thus precipitating his "fall" into sensuality. Before her death she tells the children, "If you see that someone you love has fallen into a sea of mud—throw yourself in, even at the risk of drowning . . . and if you should die amidst mud and filth? It does not matter . . . we do not have wings—we are not angels . . . we will be in the next life—where there is no mire—no blood!" She veers from the arrogance of total spiritual control to a willed debasement of the flesh. But it is clear that such debasement is really a roundabout way of winning control, a self-punishing detour to perfect saintliness; the person who throws himself in the mud earns thereby the right to a purified existence in the next world. In either case she aims at something beyond this world. Tula refuses to live here and with others; to the end she is faithful to her divided vision, longing for the pure world of angels where there is no mire, no blood, no sex.

The rest of the novel describes the family that Tula has founded and the reverence in which her memory is held. The children turn her into the patron saint of a self-contained community, cut off from the society that surrounds it (the lack of references to the outside world heightens the closeted and stifling feel of the novel). The youngest daughter becomes Tula's representative, reproducing her style, gestures, and maxims. Through her, says Unamuno, the "spiritual eternity" of the family was perpetuated. "She had inherited its soul, spiritualized in the Aunt." Since none of the children remembers anything of Tula but her devotion, tenderness, and self-abnegation, the conclusion of the novel seems to signify the fulfillment of her goal—self-duplication. When the youngest says, in the book's final words, that Aunt Tula must forgive and unite them all, it looks as if her life has not been, after all, "a lie, a mistake".

The narrative seems to have shifted gears entirely; one would think that the last pages refer to a different character altogether—Tula as she thought she was and not the rapacious and devouring person revealed by her actions. And there is nothing in the text to indicate that this shift in portrayal is ironic. Unamuno is not contrasting the delusion of the children with the reality of Tula's behaviour.

This duplicity is not really new, however. The reader might have noticed it earlier when, for example, Unamuno said that Tula was "all maternity, but spiritual maternity", because that phrase, with all the associations the word "spirit" has in his works, takes on a glow of righteousness. He is not there referring to the devastating consequences of the quest for spiritual purity, any more than when he talked about the self that is underneath the self that acts, he was referring to the tormenting dissociation that springs from that concept. As always, Unamuno manages to keep his ideal separate from the violent gestures needed to maintain it. The formal characteristics of his novels—rapid development of plot, reduction of description to a bare minimum, highly-charged dialogue that propels events in a swift staccato while giving a sudden, lightning-like illumination to motives and character—facilitate this separation, for they allow him to dramatize the implications of a character's aims and acts without colouring them through the narrator's language. Thus the impressive and almost startling objectivity of his novels frequently conceals Unamuno's contradictory treatment of characters and situations. But then his double-mindedness is revealed, all the more surprisingly, in certain incidental and explanatory comments and, in some novels, in the final turn of the plot. *La tía Tula* first traces the destruction wrought by Tula's passion for purity and control and then redeems that passion in the piety of the conclusion.

In the prologue Unamuno compares Tula to Don Quixote and St. Theresa (in her role of founder of new communities) and contrasts the hazardous competitiveness of "masculine" civilization with the comforting shelter of "feminine" domesticity. If we take these observations as evidence of Unamuno's personal assessment of his character, we might again conclude that he endorses her endeav-

ors. Or does he mean to suggest that just as civilization begins with the murder of the brother, domesticity begins with the murder of the sister? Is he trying to show that good works can be rooted in murderous passions? Yet he seems unaware of the reversal and of the ambivalent presentation of character. The prologue, like the novel itself, presents a puzzling and apparently unrecognized ambiguity that is the textual counterpart of Unamuno's divided aspiration. He does not so much portray the undeniable link between cruelty and kindness (their evolutionary tie in the life of the emotions) as mask the first by the second. The movement is familiar to us from the essays; an impulse becomes its opposite but the author seems to "forget" the connection and presents first one, then the other, as if each were the only reality. The destructiveness of the "creative will," fully exposed in *Dos madres,* is obscured by the wishful endings of *Nada menos que todo un hombre* and *La tía Tula.* (pp. 78-81)

Frances Wyers, in her Miguel De Unamuno: The Contrary Self, *Tamesis Books Limited, 1976, 124 p.*

C. A. Longhurst   (essay date 1981)

[*In the following excerpt, Longhurst explains how Unamuno's narrative strategy in* San Manuel Bueno, mártir *obscures specific theological or philosophical meaning in the work.*]

Unamuno's *San Manuel Bueno, mártir* has often been called the most perfect, most satisfying of Unamuno's novels, and more than one critic has described it as a prose poem. Yet almost the entire critical debate on this novel has revolved around the mainly theological or philosophical question of whether the protagonist exemplifies religious scepticism or uncertainty or an unusual kind of faith. There are indeed a whole host of questions about the nature of Don Manuel's beliefs which the work poses, questions which have understandably, if inconclusively, aroused a good deal of critical interest. But in pursuing these questions which have to do with finding the meaning *of* the work, other questions more specifically directed to finding meaning *in* the work have largely been ignored. Why did Unamuno employ a personalized narrator? Why did he choose a female narrator? Why should Angela want to write down Don Manuel's story anyway? (p. 582)

The following proposition will serve as my basic premise: there is no way we can get to know the truth about Don Manuel because we do not see Don Manuel directly; all we see is Angela's reconstruction of him. We get absolutely no other view of Don Manuel, not even Lázaro's, because Lázaro's account of him is given through Angela. The only objective knowledge we possess of Don Manuel (objective within the fiction, of course) is that he had a reputation for sanctity and that because of this reputation the bishop of the diocese is promoting the process of beatification. Indeed the reader learns this fact (i.e., the promotion of the beatification process) in the very first sentence of Angela's narrative: it stands out as a significant fact. Obviously for beatification to take place the Church will require not only sanctity but also orthodoxy: it is not going to beatify someone who does not believe in the resurrection of Christ. The bishop and the villagers appear to have no doubts about Don Manuel's orthodoxy. Now suppose that Angela's memoir fell into the hands of the bishop and the ecclesiastical court considering Don Manuel's beatification: how would they react to it? This, after all, is exactly the position the reader of Angela's account is in at the start of the novel. Like the bishop and the ecclesiastical court of inquiry the reader will want to establish the truth about Don Manuel. The bishop and other members of the court of inquiry, then (and by analogy the reader), if they were honest and conscientious, would want to consider two questions in connexion with Angela's account: (1) Is there any external evidence to support Angela's view of Don Manuel? (2) What sort of a person is the writer of this document: is she a completely reliable witness, reliable enough for what she says to be taken literally? The answer to the first question must be no; Angela has not a single supporting witness upon whom to call. Lázaro, who might have shed further light, is by now dead (and the notes which he left behind appear to contain Don Manuel's teachings, not evidence of his disbelief—Angela never actually quotes from these notes). The answer to the second question is of course crucial to the interpretation of the novel. (pp. 582-83)

Angela's personal re-creation of Don Manuel is an equivocal and contradictory one, governed by her own ambiguous relationship with him. It is a portrayal of Don Manuel in which the overt aim of presenting him in a saintly light is undermined by a covert reprobation which has no very clear cause but which reflects her lonely and unhappy situation at the time of writing. If speculation about a fictitious character's real motives were not such a debatable exercise one might conjecture that she is suffering from a suppressed resentment caused by rebuff or frustration. But in any case what emerges perfectly clearly without any need to speculate is her mental confusion and disorientation, her bewilderment and even perturbation. This is not merely implicit in her ambivalent portrayal of Don Manuel but is explicitly recognized by her at the end of her story: she confesses that she can no longer tell truth from falsehood, reality from imagination; she wonders whether what she relates actually happened the way she relates it. Curiously she brings in the idea of conscience . . . , suggesting that writing down her memoir has some therapeutic or cathartic value. Angela had forged a relationship with Don Manuel which, on her side, clearly went further than the normal one between confessor and penitent or between priest and acolyte. For Angela, Don Manuel became a father-figure with a latent sexual role. Just as a nun entering a convent and taking her vows becomes 'the bride of Christ', so Angela on entering her own convent of Valverde de Lucerna (as she herself calls it) becomes in her own imagination the bride of Don Manuel. Psychologically this ties in perfectly with what we learn of Angela's childhood. The loss of her own father when very young provokes a search for a surrogate father, and given her mother's devotion to Don Manuel, the child's attention is drawn towards the priest. This initial conditioning is reinforced by Angela coming under the tutelage of the priest at a particularly impressionable age: sixteen. On returning to the village from school she immediately becomes emo-

tionally involved (as is evident from her first encounter with Don Manuel) with the figure of the priest whom her mother has for so long held up to her as a father-figure; the surrogate father becomes a surrogate husband. What is recognized by developmental psychology as being only a passing phase in female adolescence becomes, in Angela's case, a permanent state of affairs; indeed this possibility has already been adumbrated by the early reference in the text to the lure of the convent and the visions of romantic and matrimonial adventures all in the same breath. Angela *qua* narrator and Angela *qua* character are thus beautifully consistent.

This view of Angela not only appears to fit the facts of her life-story, but also goes some way towards explaining why she writes. For her, Don Manuel has been at the centre of her life. When he dies, she still has Lázaro to help maintain alive the image of the priest and to act as a link with her past. . . . Lázaro's death signifies a break in Angela's life, and this break, exacerbated by the bishop's insistent questioning and by his decision to write a book about Don Manuel thus threatening to take over from Angela the creative function of keeping alive the image of the priest, precipitates a crisis that leads directly to her memoir. (Angela's references to the present, that is the time of narration, indicate that she writes not long after Lázaro's death and at the time of the ecclesiastical inquiry into Don Manuel's life.) For Angela, now old and lonely ('desolada', 'envejecida'), the memoir is a life-support: it enables her to relive in fantasy her association with Don Manuel, to try and find meaning and consolation in the past as she searches for some sense of purpose in the present. As she consciously consigns her memories to paper she also subconsciously betrays feelings of perplexity and regret at having given her life to Don Manuel's spiritual cause only to find herself in the end sad, lonely, and confused. It is evident that Angela's reconstruction of Don Manuel's life, her revelation of his 'secreto trágico' or of his 'piadoso fraude', represents a reply and a challenge to the orthodox biography that the bishop is preparing. Angela, who has been a doubting Thomas all her life, from the time she started reading her father's books to the moment of writing her memoir, makes an even greater one of Don Manuel. This 'togetherness in doubt' compensates for the simple fact that she never succeeded in being as close to Don Manuel as Lázaro and Blasillo: she did not enjoy the affection of Don Manuel as the village idiot did, nor did she enjoy the confidence of Don Manuel as her brother did. The unconscious recognition that Don Manuel did not fully reciprocate her infatuation leads her to write a double-edged account of the priest's life, encomiastic yet subtly critical. But the memoir allows us to infer much more about Angela herself than about the priest: *she* is the real doubter. The only real truth in the novel is the truth of the narrator herself; the real Don Manuel, hidden behind the impenetrable barrier of Angela's personality, uncertainties, and emotions, is inaccessible. One could in theory go further and put forward the view that the entire memoir was conceived by the novelist as a mere piece of fantasy on the part of the fictional narrator, with no basis in reality (fictional reality, that is). But such an explanation, though perfectly admissible in the case of certain stories by Poe, Borges, and others, seems to me unhelpful in this particular case. The theme and tone of the story suggest that what Unamuno had in mind was not a stark true/false alternative but an exploration of the nature of perception and belief, that is, of an individual's own intimate reasons, motivations, or pressures for accepting or not accepting something as true and real. At any rate we can be fairly certain that one of the reasons why Unamuno chose a personalized narrator, and a very particular one at that, was in order to eschew the 'truth' or the 'reality' within the fiction, in other words to provide us, the readers, with sufficient grounds on which to question the exactitude of Angela's account. One of the aims of Unamuno in **San Manuel Bueno, mártir**—at any rate one of the results of the technique he employs—is to raise the question of narrative authority, in which he was deeply interested, with special reference to the Gospels. Narratives, whether historical or fictitious, speak in hidden and personal ways and cannot simply be taken as mere records of facts. Just as the Gospels of Christ written by Matthew, Mark, Luke, and John were described by Unamuno (both in this work and elsewhere) as novels and not history, so the gospel of San Manuel written by Angela is her novel: not a record of a life but a personal interpretation of it, the work of Angela's imagination and fantasy having only partial links with an external reality, as she herself comes close to recognizing at the end. If we were to examine Angela's memoir from the point of view of its documentary value, several levels of factualness would be clearly distinguished, ranging from the totally factual to the non-factual. These levels could be schematized briefly as follows:

Totally factual

The basic elements of Angela's story: her family circumstances and certain events in her life; the existence of Don Manuel, his reputation for sanctity, the process of beatification; Lázaro's public conversion.

Semi-factual

A good deal of information about Don Manuel: Angela's anecdotes about him (she was not present), her impressions, recollections, reminiscences and reconstruction of distant events and conversations, all of which merge in her memory to give the account its oft-noticed dreamlike and poetic qualities.

Uncertain

The motives behind Lázaro's conversion and his relationship with Don Manuel: did Don Manuel tell Lázaro the complete truth about himself?; did Lázaro tell Angela the complete truth about Don Manuel?; did he tell her the truth about his own motives? A certain amount of critical information about Don Manuel is allegedly obtained through Lázaro; but Lázaro is not a neutral witness: according to Angela he is an atheist who thinks Don Manuel 'demasiado inteligente para creer todo lo que tiene que enseñar' ['too intelligent to believe everything he teaches'.] . . . Has Angela been unduly influenced by her brother? Or is Lázaro the excuse for her subtle denunciation of the priest?

Non-factual

Angela's personal interpretation of Don Manuel's reli-gious ideology; her constant insinuations in the direction of unbelief.

Unconscious

Angela's self-portrayal: certain anecdotes about herself and her use of particular words and phrases in the account of Don Manuel which betray the submerged and unconfessed nature of her attachment to the priest and her ambivalent attitude towards him.

In giving his novel a structure based on levels of factualness or truth, Unamuno is moving away from an extra-literary reality and towards the fictive form itself. Indeed it is not even enough to talk conventionally of structure in this particular instance; it is the novel's *infrastructure* that gives it its special quality and ambiguity. But this ambiguity is not that of a capricious writer who merely seeks to mystify his readers or deviously to defend his own personal ideology; it is not the obfuscation and the 'aesthetic ambiguity' denounced by Frances Wyers . . . ; for while the work is certainly ambiguous, this ambiguity has its own internal justification: it is more than just a cheap attempt at fashionable obscurity; it is an integral part of the story, an essential dimension without which this particular novel would collapse. Another kind of narrator would write quite another kind of work. Angela's history, her personality, her circumstances, create the fiction. On this level the work is perfectly meaningful and intelligible and there is no need to resort to Unamuno's own biography in search of the rosetta stone with which to decipher his novelistic hieroglyphics. (pp. 592-96)

I should like to conclude this article by briefly considering the relevance of part of Unamuno's authorial interpolation to Angela's account.

Having first acknowledged the creative role of the narrator, that is, the crucial nature of her intervention, Unamuno goes on to insert a short paragraph which is both obscure and at the same time potentially decisive in any attempt to infer the author's attitude towards his fictional narrator. The paragraph ends with . . . a phrase of biblical origin which functions as an invitation to look beyond the surface for the deeper implication of the speaker's words. In this cryptic paragraph, on the face of it rather superfluous, Unamuno, quoting the epistle of St Jude, verse 9, reminds us of St Michael the Archangel's reproof to the Devil, who was claiming Moses's body: 'El Señor te reprenda' ['The Lord rebuke you']. There are three entities involved in this biblical anecdote: Moses, St Michael and the Devil. Since (1) Don Manuel has earlier been explicitly associated with Moses, since (2) Unamuno is explicitly identifying with St Michael (he reminds us that St Michael is his patron saint), and since (3) the only other person responsible for transmitting the story is Angela (as Unamuno has just reminded us in the immediately preceding paragraph), the clear possibility arises that Angela is being associated with the Devil (the association of angels with devils occurs in St Jude's epistle too), and that the dispute between St Michael and the Devil over who was to have jurisdiction over the body of Moses is meant to represent a divergence of views between Unamuno and his narrator. But why, one might well ask, should Unamuno choose this strange way of giving an authorial nod to the reader? Why should he cast Angela in the role of the Devil? The answer to this is beautifully simple and says a great deal for Unamuno's artistry, for the explanation is contained in the circumstances of composition of the life-story of Don Manuel. What prompts Angela to write her memoir is the beatification process initiated by the bishop of the diocese (this is mentioned twice by Angela, at the beginning and at the end of her memoir). Don Manuel is now the subject of an inquiry by an ecclesiastical court that will have to sit in judgement and decide whether he is a worthy candidate for beatification. In such a court of inquiry the Church always appoints a prosecutor (technically *promotor fidei* but more widely referred to as *advocatus diavoli*) whose function it is to oppose the promoters of the beatification process by questioning the evidence put forward for beatification and by looking for contrary evidence. In the case of Don Manuel it is the bishop (in accordance with canonical procedure) who is promoting the process of beatification and who is writing his life as an example of perfect priestliness. Contrariwise Angela, in her testimony, is presenting Don Manuel as a man lacking in faith, and is consequently hitting at the very heart of the case for beatification. In the context of a canonical beatification process (the starting-point for Angela's story), Angela and the bishop are antagonists. It follows that Angela is cast in the role of *advocatus diavoli.* There is further evidence that this is indeed what Unamuno was getting at, for in the very same paragraph he includes, at first sight gratuitously, a definition of the Devil which fits in exactly with the role of Angela as *advocatus diavoli:* ['the devil means accuser, prosecutor']. (pp. 596-97)

Having given us what amounts to a cryptic but intelligible warning not to take Angela's account of Don Manuel at face value, Unamuno ends his interpolation by claiming the superiority of imaginative literature over historiography, of *novela* over *cronicón,* and he goes on to say that his *relato* is not history because in it nothing happens: ['but I hope that in it everything remains, as lakes and mountains do remain'.] . . . If these symbols of permanence are going to attain their full value, it will be only by virtue of the opportunity that imaginative literature gives to the reader to respond to and keep alive the creative consciousness not of the individual, for that is lost forever, but of the artist. An approach to Unamuno's fiction based on a theological, philosophical, or biographical search for the meaning or the message is unlikely to get to the hub of Unamuno's art. Most novelists after all do not write novels to voice meanings; they turn to novels in order to construct artefacts out of language. In Western fiction of the post-realist mode, of which Unamuno is a prime example, the clear tendency was to allow the narrative to speak with its own voice. The meaning or the message was banished as something extra-literary; but what remained had its own kind of truth, its poem-like structure, its internal justification for existing. In *San Manuel Bueno, mártir* Unamuno has given us an artistic 'document', as he calls it, which invites the reader to search for the truth within the story. But the skilful arrangement of the narrative—with its subtle use of personalized narration and of Janus-like symbols and suggestive language—keeps the truth tantalizingly beyond our reach. The fact that ultimately there can be no truth, no reality, except that of the story itself, the fact that we the readers can never hope to be in possession of the truth about Don Manuel, is but a reflection on one level of man's limited access to knowledge of others and on another of the potential that literature has for creating self-contained worlds that are ever-beckoning but ever-mysterious. Angela will have one view of reality, we may have another one; but the truth itself must always elude us. (p. 597)

C. A. Longhurst, "The Problem of Truth in 'San Manuel Bueno, Mártir'," in The Modern Language Review, *Vol. 76, No. 3, July, 1981, pp. 581-97.*

Gonzalo Navajas   (essay date 1985)

[*In the essay below, Navajas offers a close examination of the protagonist of* La tía Tula.]

A considerable number of critics of Unamuno have found it difficult to interpret *La tía Tula* in a way that would account for the fundamental contradiction that determines the character and the conduct of the protagonist, Tula. Faced with the opposition between Tula's nobility and courage, on the one hand, and with her selfishness and cruelty, on the other, those critics tend to circumvent this apparently intractable conflict by making a moral reduction of Tula and passing unequivocal judgments on her. The critics evaluate Tula's personality precisely, but they do not elucidate it sufficiently by studying it within an interpretive framework that explains Tula's essential conflict. The main purpose of my paper is to furnish such a framework and propose an interpretation of Tula that situates her meaningfully in relation to some of the central trends of modern thought.

It is possible to read *La tía Tula* in a literal or heuristic manner, accepting the semantic value of Tula's numerous and explicit assertions as they appear on the surface of the discourse. In this type of reading, Tula stands out as a heartless and manipulative person, firmly in control of herself and intent on achieving the absolute domination of those around her. If we read *La tía Tula* in this manner, Tula, as Ricardo Gullón has pointed out, becomes an inhuman figure, a monster, worthy only of our rejection. But, although this reading is perhaps necessary, it is insufficient. Another kind of reading is required to complete and at the same time transcend the literal one. In it, the text is subjected to a hermeneutic interpretation that, putting aside the apparent traits of the characters' actions, attempts to uncover the factors determining their fundamental nature. In this second reading, Tula is revealed not as a master of her environment but as a victim of it, paying dearly for her subjugation. In addition to this, I shall consider the fact that Tula's greatness, which is one of the issues most extensively treated in the text, is paradoxically derived not from her independence of a constraining environment but from her subordination to it.

In my interpretation of Tula I shall make use of two categories that have been analyzed by Jacques Lacan in his studies on human psychology. The first one is the Imaginary, which basically corresponds to the inner, intuitive life of the subject. The second one is the Symbolic, which is the order of values imposed on the individual from outside. This order can also be figuratively called the Law. Most subjects are able to find a reasonable balance between the Imaginary and the Symbolic and can accordingly lead normal lives. I shall propose that in Tula this balance does not exist since her life has been overpowered by the Symbolic. In her, the Symbolic originates in a restrictive cultural environment that prevents the natural development of human relations. Its most important manifestation is the denial of physical and intimate love because it entails the surrender of the self and the abandonment of the subject's beliefs. This abnormal denial has significant effects on Tula's personality, contributing to shape it in a distinctive manner.

In place of a real and personal form of love, Tula uses delusive abstractions, such as the belief in a chaste, nonphysical notion of motherhood, and tries to persuade herself that those abstractions are more real than natural impulses and feelings. In order to accomplish this difficult substitution of the Imaginary by the Symbolic, Tula needs to apply the uncommon strength of her will power to the suppression of the drives of her body and the incitements of the other. Thus Tula becomes a unidimensional subject, bent on negating the inclinations of her self. In addition to this, since the persons around her do not share to the same extent her allegiance to the Symbolic and therefore are a danger to it, she attempts to negate their effectiveness by exerting total domination over them. Consequently, the implementation of the order of the Symbolic transforms Tula into a dominator of the other. Since her world is narrowly provincial, the other, in her case, is limited to her family and a few friends.

Tula is intent on domination, but she knows that being a woman is a hindrance to the attainment of her purpose. She is aware that womanhood, within the traditional Spanish cultural milieu, is linked to subservience to man. In order to counter this unfavorable situation, she adopts some of the most evident traits of the behavior that she perceives as being associated with man—such as desire for power and emotional self-control—, and strives to make them absolutely her own. Tula is not the only feminine character in Unamuno's work who, rejecting any manifestation of frailty and insecurity in her personality, makes herself stronger and more self-assured than the men in the text. Raquel and Carolina, in *Tres novelas ejemplares y un prólogo,* are similar to Tula in their personal strength and independence. What is distinctive in Tula is that her attempt is presented as more profound and systematic than those of other feminine figures of Unamuno, although, as will be seen later, it is not unattended by feelings of uncertainty.

Tula is impelled towards absolute control of the other, especially of those who may most directly threaten the precarious stability of her life, a stability painfully achieved through the repression of her Imaginary. This is why she wants to dominate Rosa and Ramiro in particular, without being deterred by the fact that they are her sister and brother-in-law. For Tula, Rosa and Ramiro are unmistakable signs of the existence of the Imaginary, of the power-

ful affirmation of the body that Tula, under the influence of the stifling values of the Symbolic, wishes to deny. Rosa is beautiful and open to others. Ramiro is a reminder of the possibility of passion. Tula, in contrast, is introverted and not especially attractive, and determined to avert what she considers would be the loss of herself through the experience of desire. Although she is strongly attracted to Ramiro and knows that he and Rosa are not in love, she convinces them to marry, silencing the doubts that both have about doing so. In order to persuade Ramiro that he should proceed with his marriage to Rosa, Tula puts forth questionable justifications and when these prove insufficient she does not hesitate to resort to intimidations and threats. This can be seen in the following dialogue between Tula and Ramiro about the approaching marriage. Ramiro, secretly in love with Tula, dares to offer objections to her arguments. Her harsh response makes Ramiro yield to her wishes:

> —¡Pues bien, Gertrudis, quiero decirte toda la verdad!
> —No tienes que decirme más verdad—le atajó severamente—; me has dicho que quieres a Rosa y que estás resuelto a casarte con ella; todo lo demás de la verdad es a ella a quien se lo tienes que decir luego que os caséis.
> —Pero hay cosas . . .
> —No, no hay cosas que no se deban decir a la mujer . . .
> —¡Pero, Tula!
> —Nada de Tula, te he dicho. Si la quieres, a casarte con ella, y si no la quieres, estás de más en esta casa . . .
> Al día siguiente se fijaba el de la boda.

Believing more in the fixed and solid structure of external laws than in the unpredictability of her feelings, Tula needs to see the realization of what for her is the immutable law of marriage to assure her that the Symbolic order is not destroyed through Ramiro's intervention in her life. Tula's obsession with the continued prevalence of the Symbolic makes her disregard any possible concerns that she might have had about the consequences of her sister's marriage to Ramiro. After Rosa and Ramiro marry and it becomes evident that their relation is not a happy one, Tula is not at all troubled by thoughts of her responsibility for their unhappiness. Her urge for self-preservation is her only motive. Therefore it is consistent with her thinking that, when Rosa dies and Ramiro becomes once more a threat to her, she promptly arranges another marriage for him, this time with Manuela the housemaid. Ramiro resists this imposition but, in the end, succumbs to the weight of Tula's forcefully expressed opinions.

Tula uses her skill in logical thinking and her remarkable command of language as the main instruments to implement her domination of the other. On other occasions, she resorts to different means of control because she considers them more effective. Her intense gaze is one of those means. With Ramiro, she uses it to remind him silently of her permanent control and influence over him. For example, immediately after Rosa's first dangerous labor, Tula insists that her sister should have another child soon. By articulating her points through a series of questions, she appears to allow for other points of view. However, the possible uncertainty contained in Tula's words is instantly overcome by the semantic precision of her gaze, directly aimed at Ramiro and transmitting explicitly her intention to him: "—¿Y qué hacer?—replicó ella—; ¿para qué se han casado, si no? ¿No es así, Ramiro?—y le clavó los ojos." The fear that Tula's gaze instills in Ramiro is a significant factor that determines his decision to have another child despite his strong resistance to the idea.

Tula needs to possess the other, make it permanently and unquestionably her own. Consequently, it is understandable that, for her, love is conceived merely as an extension of her drive for domination. After Rosa's death, she has the opportunity to have a life in common with Ramiro and bear her own children. She could thus abandon her proud but barren solitude and lead a more satisfying life. She thinks persistently about that possibility, knowing that Ramiro is eagerly in favor of it. Nevertheless, her overpowering impulse to make of the other an indisputable personal possession prevails, and she rejects an appealing marriage to Ramiro because he had previously been "possessed" by her sister: "¿De otra? ¡No! ¡De otra, no! ¡Ni después de mi muerte! ¡Ni de mi hermana! . . . ¡De otra, no! No se puede ser más que de una. . . ."

Tula is especially afraid of the thought of having to share Ramiro's body with Rosa even after her sister's death: "Porque cuando él estuviese a mi lado, arrimado a mí, carne a carne, ¿quién me dice que no estuviese pensando en ella?" This fear is increased by the fact that she knows that she would be giving her body—that part of herself that is alien to her, that is not mastered by her—to someone who might elude her influence in the future. In that case, Tula would experience a double failure: on the one hand, she would have to accept the dominance of the Imaginary over the Symbolic (since her senses would rule over her soul), and, on the other, she would be subjected to the supremacy of the other over her. Faced with the choice between a real and complete relationship, which could escape her power, and her sterile but self-sufficient inner world, Tula chooses the latter. Thus, although she longs for motherhood and considers it the highest value in life, she chooses to raise only "spiritual" children, those of her sister and Manuela.

Because of its deficiencies, the order of the Symbolic can only survive through the establishment of rigid norms that regulate all aspects of life potentially threatening to the subject. These norms will apply to Tula's life but also to the life of the family members who live under her influence. Consequently, it is not surprising that, even though she has never experienced a love relation, Tula does not hesitate to give precise instructions to her nephew regarding his dealings with women. In this instance, as in others, her norms are characterized by inflexibility and a complete incapacity for innovation: "No, nada de pruebas, nada de noviazgos; nada de eso de 'hablo con Fulana'. Todo seriamente. . . ." Likewise, the implementation of these norms demands an authoritarian attitude that Tula adopts without reservation.

Tula's authority over her family, which she exercises to prevent the free development of the Imaginary, is not challenged. In fact, her domination of others outlives her.

After she dies, Manuela, the orphan whom she has trained according to her wishes, assumes her place and loyally carries on Tula's order, bringing about her glorification and raising her to an unassailable moral plane. Thus, within the realm of her family, not only does Tula's power perpetuate itself, but its self-serving motives are masked under seemingly noble aims. The order of the Symbolic, unmistakably born of Tula's limitations and frustrations, becomes securely established in her family, conditioning permanently the lives of its members. Manuela's final words are revealing of the total domination of Aunt Tula over the other: "¡Es la Tía, la tía Tula, la que tiene que perdonaros y unirnos y guiarnos a todos!."

Despite some apparent benefits, the imposition of the Symbolic is not free of unfavorable consequences for the subject. Undoubtedly, Tula fulfills a considerable number of her expectations thanks to the rigid suppression of her most intimate desires and to the implantation of her order over others. For all intents and purposes, she becomes the mother of Rosa's and Manuela's children, who love her more than they love their real mothers. In addition to this, she achieves a high degree of self-esteem due to the respect that she enjoys among her friends and relatives. Tula is the admired leader of her family and her decisions command undisputed acceptance. However, Tula's external accomplishments are in contrast with her troubled conscience, which experiences a *Spaltung,* a violent division between the self and the ego, produced by the imposition of the Symbolic.

I shall make a distinction between self and ego, two notions that are often mistakenly considered interchangeable. The self is the true identity of the subject, that part of him that conforms to a genuine mode of existence. The ego, on the other hand, is a falsified configuration of the self. It is a *persona,* a mask worn by the subject to supplant his real self and conceal or deny the unsolved conflicts that rend his conscience. According to Lacan, the ego "opposes its irreducible inertia of pretenses and misunderstandings to the concrete problematic of realization of the subject." The nature of the ego is a result of the subject's identification with external Imagos that do not reflect his real identity. Instead, these Imagos are in accordance with the expectations of the other or with the delusions harbored by the subject in relation to himself. In most cases, the subject is not aware of his internal division and denies its existence, believing that his ego constitutes his only identity. *Spaltung* and its denial by the subject inevitably have a traumatic effect on the subject's psyche.

Tula's personality and behavior respond to the fragmentation of her conscience and its subsequent denial by her. Tula finds the source of her ego formation in the Imago of sainthood. For others, Tula is an exceptional individual totally committed to the well-being of her family. Her capacity for self-sacrifice and her dedication to the needs of others are boundless. She apparently lives for and by others, totally oblivious of her own needs or desires. Her life overlaps so precisely with that of others that she seems to realize herself in them. Tula's renunciation of herself and her absolute generosity develop around her an image of superiority and perfection that is corroborated by other characters, who consider her a saint. The text itself confirms extensively this image and, in the preface to the novel, Tula is associated with Saint Theresa and several fictive figures, such as Antigone and Don Quixote, who are mentioned for their exceptional qualities and their capacity to devote themselves to extraordinary causes.

The environment of sainthood that Tula has striven to create around her becomes self-sustaining, and in time it evolves into a solid ideological structure that provides security for her. Nevertheless, since this structure is built on false premises and does not correspond to the genuine nature of her character, it becomes her prison. Initiated as an impulse—albeit misguided—towards self-realization, the Imago of sainthood is the ultimate instrument of Tula's alienation. Tula's presumed sainthood is a distancing mechanism, a way to avoid her inner reality. This brings about the impossibility of her ever finding her true identity, which would open the path to self-knowledge and would arrest the fragmentation of her conscience. At the same time, it effects a final and insurmountable separation between her and the others, who are always made conscious of Tula's superiority over them. Thus Tula's sainthood can be considered as an extension of her will to power, as it constitutes the most effective form of domination over her family. It is especially suitable to her purposes because it is held in high esteem by all those surrounding her. Sainthood is, however, beyond the reach of anyone except herself and consequently it makes unchallengeable her dominant position within the family hierarchy.

As Nietzsche and some modern critics inspired by him, such as Paul de Man, have pointed out, the human mind functions not in a neutral vacuum, in accordance with strictly logical principles, but following the nonobjective and rhetorical modes of language. Opposing a view of knowledge influenced by positivism, these critics maintain that man develops his thinking through the use of tropological devices. We think by analogy, through metaphors and metonymies, by an oblique approximation to reality instead of by apprehending it *in toto,* defining it with exactitude. This general characteristic of the mind is reflected in Tula. Her impulse towards sainthood is a configuration of metonymic desire, a movement of displacement of the real aims of her self. Tula desires Ramiro and wants to be the mother of his children. Since she can attain neither of these two goals because of the restrictions of the Symbolic, she single-mindedly applies herself to the achievement of a substitute for her desire. Her passion for Ramiro is changed into devotion for his children and an unmitigated dedication to her self-imposed duties.

In order to bring about the displacement of her desire, Tula emphasizes the need for the denial of the body, whose inciting impulses she dismisses in the name of the superior designs of her spirit and her family obligations. Her rejection of the body leads her, in turn, to despise nature, since nature, by providing a context in which the body finds numerous stimuli, reminds her of the unmistakable existence of that which she denies. This is why, soon after the beginning of an excursion that she and Ramiro take to the countryside, she decides to return

quickly home because the country is an unwanted excitement to her senses that could create instability within her Symbolic system. For its preservation, Tula's sainthood requires the confining and tedious environment of the city: "No, la pureza no es del campo; la pureza es celda, de claustro y de cuidad; . . . la ciudad es monasterio, convento de solitarios; aquí la tierra, sobre que casi se acuestan, los une y los animales son otras tantas serpientes del paraíso . . . ¡A la cuidad, a la cuidad!"

Tula's notion of marriage reflects a similar negation of the physical and a reduction of love and feelings to a severe discipline of the senses. Her stern warning to Rosa that her love for Ramiro should become an inescapable obligation is a consequence of this conception. Likewise, her advice to both her sister and her husband as to the real aim of marriage responds to her limited view of human relations: "El matrimonio se instituyó para casar, para dar gracia a los casados y que críen hijos para el cielo."

The displacement of desire has detrimental effects for the subject, who is compelled to devote a large amount of his energy to oppose his natural drives. The hidden conflicts of the self eventually surface as symptoms, which function as metaphors of the forbidden desire. In Tula, we find several symptoms of her traumatized self. Her obsession with cleanliness is one of them. She identifies the body with dirt, and dirt in general with confusion and disorder, with aspects of reality that could dominate her. Consequently, she compulsively strives for the elimination of dirt and disorder, an act that she considers equivalent to the elimination of the body.

This compulsion becomes an automatic reflex in her, uncontrollable even in cases when uncleanliness is associated with one of her beloved children. In the following passage, it is Manolita, her niece, who provokes her defensive reaction: "Alguna vez la criatura se vomitó sobre aquella cama, limpia siempre hasta entonces como una patena, y de pronto sintió Gertrudis la punzada de la mancha. Su pasión *morbosa* por la pureza, de que procedía su culto *místico* a la limpieza, sufrió entonces, y tuvo que esforzarse por dominarse." (Italics mine). In this instance, the narrator himself clears the hermeneutic path for the reader. On the one hand, he affirms the spiritual excellence of Tula's attitude ("culto místico') whereas, on the other, he explicitly indicates its subliminal nature ("pasión morbosa").

Tula's aversion to blood is another metaphoric manifestation of her incapacity to accept her body. From a semiological perspective, blood is a cultural seme that connotes emotional effervescence, excitement of the senses, the unrestricted flux of the inner self. In accordance with this, Tula perceives in blood a sign of the spontaneity and freedom of the Imaginary. Faced with what she considers is a direct confrontation to her beliefs, Tula reacts to the sight of blood in an extreme manner, as can be seen when she assists Manuela during the birth of Manuelita:

> La niña misma nació envuelta en sangre. Y
> Gertrudis tuvo que vencer la repugnancia que la
> sangre, sobre todo la negra y cuajada, le producía: siempre le costó una terrible brega consigo
> misma el vencer este asco. Cuando una vez, poco
> antes de morir, su hermana Rosa tuvo un vómi-

to, Gertrudis huyó de elia despavorida. Y no era
miedo, no; era, sobre todo, asco.

The excess of Tula's reaction, rather than demonstrating
a physiological revulsion towards blood, has a figurative
value, revealing the strain produced by the conflict between the Symbolic and the Imaginary in her. During
Manuelita's birth, this conflict takes the form of an opposition between Tula's chastity and her desire for motherhood, and it is manifested when Tula, despite her efforts,
cannot prevent the indirect emergence of her anguish and
dissatisfaction.

Some of Gertrudis's personal preferences can be included
within the symptomatological pattern just alluded to. Her
love of geometry is an example. This science is not merely
a superficial interest. For her, it is a symbol of her values.
Thus the opposition that she establishes between geometry, on the one hand, and anatomy and physiology, on the
other, is not accidental but responds to a basic motivation
in her. In geometry, she sees a reflection of her inclinations, a confirmation of her *Weltanschauung:* "Y es que
en aquellas demostraciones de la geometría, ciencia árida
y fría al sentir de los más, encontraba Gertrudis un no
sabía qué de luminosidad y de pureza." On the contrary,
the sciences of the body are to be shunned because of their
indeterminate and uncontrollable character: "Esas son
porquerías—decía—y en que nada se sabe de cierto ni de
claro."

The disproportionate character of Tula's rejection of Don
Juan's overtures is another manifestation of the substitutions that take place in her conscience. Her response stems
from fear of yielding to the call of the senses rather than
from scorn of her obliging suitor. When Don Juan timidly
asks her to marry him, her reply is unnecessarily cruel:
" . . . Y no vuelva a poner los pies en esta casa./ ¿Por qué,
Gertrudis?/ [asks Don Juan]. Y así se despidieron para
siempre." Thus Don Juan is made into another victim of
Tula's power and becomes merely an instrument for the
affirmation of her axiological system.

The subordination of the subject to the Symbolic can be
related to a post-Freudian conception of the death instinct. According to Lacan, death should be understood
not only in a biological sense, as it is mostly in Freud, but
in a psychological sense as well. For Lacan, the subject
causes the death of his true self by asserting himself in society through the acceptance of the social and cultural system of the other. This notion of the death instinct can be
verified in Tula, who sacrifices her self to the attainment
of a falsified form of sainthood, thus bringing about her
inner death. The sign of death indelibly marks Tula, wrest-
ing the life from her words and her actions, depriving
them of truth. It also spreads by contiguity to the members of her family, who live in a state close to death, unable
to free themselves from her domination. It is not surprising, then, that several death scenes are included in the text.
Physical extinction can be read as the ultimate form of the
untruthful condition of the self. Furthermore, the intensity with which the deaths of Gertrudis, Ramiro and Manuela are presented underscores the novel's semantic orientation that equates death and falsification of the self.

Despite man's impulse towards sublimation, towards the

identification with the Symbolic, his nature leads him to
find an accommodation with other registers of his life, incorporating in some way what his conscience strives to
deny. Although the imposition of the Symbolic is accepted
in the end by most men, their adjustment to it is never
complete. At times, episodes of defiance occur, due to the
subject's desire to recover parcels of his self that had been
condemned to a secondary function or to oblivion. On
those occasions, the subject, in search of a more genuine
configuration of the self, attempts to see through the different personifications that his ego has adopted. This takes
place more intensely in individuals who, like Tula, have
a strong inclination to discover the truth about themselves.

Her appearance of self-confidence notwithstanding, Tula
does not feel at one with herself. I have already mentioned
some of the symptoms in which her inner conflicts are revealed. Tula makes great efforts to unify her conscience,
to produce the precise overlap of self and ego. But the
rents in her conscience are evident to her. Inevitably she
must face moments of truth when she can no longer disregard her doubts and dissatisfaction with her assumed role.
In a psychoanalytic context, these are the moments when
the subject finds the opportunity to take command of his
life and to become the originator of his circumstances
rather than a victim of them. Even though Tula is never
freed from the imposition of the Symbolic, she acquires,
thanks to her personal revelations, a substantial degree of
real consciousness that puts her in contact with the most
authentic aspects of herself.

The majority of these revelatory moments in Tula's life
occur not in the isolation of her conscience but in a dialog-
ic context in which she manifests her intimate feelings to
a witness. These moments bear considerable resemblance
to a psychoanalytical encounter. Tula's witnesses are not
impartial, as is conventionally to be expected of the analyst in the psychoanalytic process. They are her relatives
or close friends. However, rather like the analyst, they
function as mediators who help to elicit the real content
of the subject's conscience. I shall consider two of these
enlightening occurrences in which a witness is present,
among the several that can be found in the text.

In the first such occurrence, the mediating witness is
Ramiro. During a conversation that takes place between
him and Tula, he is the agent who facilitates Tula's honest
revelation of herself when he suggests that her sainthood
may have had unfavorable consequences: "Eres una santa,
Gertrudis—le decía Ramiro—; pero una santa que ha
hecho pecadores." To which she replies: "No digas eso;
soy una pecadora que me esfuerzo en hacer santos. . . ."
Ramiro, who always remains under Tula's spell, has no
doubts about the excellence of his sister-in-law. For him,
she is still undeniably a saint. But Tula takes advantage
of the lead given to her by Ramiro's questioning remark
to rectify his belief about her and redefine her image for
him and above all for herself.

It is no accident that Tula's most intimate revelatory
searches take place in the presence of another subject. Her
Imago of sainthood is constructed as much by the other
as by her. She is a saint, to a great extent, because the oth-

ers make her one, building for her a reputation that in time supplants her real personality. Therefore, she requires the presence and participation of the other to try to reverse her false image. She needs to confess to the other and, through him, to relieve herself of the burden of a greatness that in her conscience she knows she does not deserve. The other is expected to perform the role of judge in her life, and take the responsibility of dispossessing her of her sainthood in the same way that he had previously invested her with it.

The function of the other as the recipient of a confession can be seen with special clarity in my second example, in which the witness of Tula's revelation is her confessor, Father Alvarez. The close association of truth with confession is the reason why Tula chooses him to manifest her real self with utmost openness and perceptivity. The exchange does not happen in the process of a formal confession, but it reproduces faithfully the dialectic of guilt that is characteristic of that act. In this case, though, the role of Father Alvarez is paradoxical. It consists in reassuring Tula of the validity of her supposedly wrong actions, trying to convince her that her guilt is unjustified and that she should persist in her behavior, living up to the image of her ego that others have made for her. This can be verified in the most significant passage of the conversation between Father Alvarez and Tula:

> —. . . Sea la que es . . . , la tía Tula que todos conocemos y veneramos y admiramos . . . ; sí, ¡admiramos! . . .
> —¡No, padre, no! ¡Usted lo sabe! Por dentro soy otra . . .
> —Pero hay que ocultarlo . . .
> —Sí, hay que ocultarlo, sí; pero hay días en que siento ganas de reunir a mis hijos, a mis hijos . . .
> —¡Sí, suyos, de usted!
> —¡Sí, yo madre, como usted . . . padre!
> —Deje eso, señora; deje eso . . .
> —Sí, reunirles y decirles que toda mi vida ha sido una mentira, una equivocación, un fracaso . . .
> —Usted se calumnia, señora. Esa no es usted, usted es la otra . . . , la que todos conocemos . . . , la tía Tula.
> —Yo le hice [a Ramiro] desgraciado, padre . . . Y fue por soberbia!

The dichotomy between self and ego is clearly established by Tula ("Por dentro soy otra"), in face of the opposition of Father Alvarez, who emphasizes the unity of Tula's self, the identity of the I for oneself and the I for the other. Tula is seeking an accurate definition of herself, and the conviction with which she presents her search is so strong that for a moment she wins the complicity of the priest, when she makes him admit that her real identity is unknown to others. This acknowledgment of the truth is short-lived in Father Alvarez, as the intimidating power of the voice of the other prevails in him ("Esa no es usted, usted es la otra . . . , la que todos conocemos . . ."). Tula, on the other hand, proclaims the double nature of her actions and the debased origin of her sainthood.

It is in the disavowal of her sainthood—and not in its affirmation, as the text seems to imply—that Tula achieves her

greatness. She reaches excellence when she is able to resist the opinion of the community, disregarding her personal interest. Her sainthood is attained precisely in the absence of sainthood, when she fathoms the real essence of her identity. In this sense, her association with Antigone, Don Quixote, and other paragons of human behavior is not inappropriate. In a way similar to them, she is capable of following her personal truth even in the face of unfavorable circumstances. However, the analogy between Tula and those figures is only partly correct, since, unlike them, Tula is not entirely faithful to herself and her search does not culminate in an act of final commitment. She arrests the movement towards the consolidation of her true identity because she cannot face the consequences of knowledge. As she herself asserts: "Quiero irme de este mundo sin saber muchas cosas. Porque hay cosas que el saberlas mancha. . . ." Despite the fact that the fundamental limitations of her purity are known to Tula, she prefers that purity, which is protected by the authority of the other, to the uncertainty of the impulses of her isolated self, to actions analogous to those of Antigone, defiant and "anarchical," and so highly praised in the preface to *La tía Tula*.

This partial approach to the self is manifest in Tula's attitude towards womanhood. In a manner which is not customary in other feminine characters of Spanish literature, Tula is a woman whose intelligence and strength are clearly shown to be far superior to those of the men in the text. She is proud of being a woman and considers women to be free of many of the weaknesses and defects of men. In her relations with Ramiro, for example, she is the one who makes the important decisions and, on one occasion, she consoles him when he cries over some of the difficulties that easily overwhelm him. Tula assumes her femininity and makes of it a mode of self-assertion. Her independence can be viewed as an act of rebellion against the traditional subordination of women to men in Spanish society, and, for this reason, she could be considered an advocate of feminism *avant la lettre*. Nevertheless, in this aspect of her life as in others, the force of the Symbolic proves to be more powerful than her will to revolt.

In Tula's references to womanhood, the Symbolic is identified with the doctrinal code of Christianity. Often, Tula does not approve of this code and acknowledges in her conscience that Christianity does not favor the improvement of the condition of women. However, she does not dare defy the Christian religion in a fundamental way. At times at the risk of becoming a heretic, she even contemplates the possibility of openly opposing some aspects of her religion, which she sees as favoring man's dominance. For instance, she denounces the unequal treatment that Christianity gives women, and she maintains that Christianity has not actively incorporated women into the core of its life. Tula realizes that the Christian Symbolic, instilled in her life since childhood, is a man's order that assigns a subordinate position to women:

> 'El cristianismo, al fin, y a pesar de la Magdalena, es religión de hombres—se decía Gertrudis—; masculinos el Padre, el Hijo y el Espíritu Santo! . . .' Pero, ¿y la Madre? La religión de la Madre está en: 'He aquí la criada del Señor, hágase en mí según tu palabra' . . ..

Tula's thinking on this issue is clear. Had she followed her conscience and pursued the path of rebellion envisioned by her self, she could have become a more fully realized subject. Instead, she prefers to resort once more to repressing her self: "'¡No, no lo volveré a pensar!,'" she commands herself as a means of suppressing the unorthodox thoughts that endanger the balance of her conscience.

In order to make the silencing of her self more effective, Tula pretends that her disagreements with Christianity are induced by the devil, thus making them easier to renounce. The Imaginary is, in this case, linked with an evil force to which Tula can attribute her religious doubts. Hence what was an unsettling intellectual struggle in Tula's spirit becomes a moral issue in which she must opt between two distinct opponents: Christianity and the devil. Her choice is an easy one. For example, when she refers to the Gospel episode of the wedding at Cana, Tula notices the brusqueness with which Jesus addresses his mother. Her self does not fail to register the abrupt treatment given to the foremost feminine figure in the Christian religion. She quickly dismisses the critical bent of her thinking, however, considering it invalid due to the intervention of the devil. Tula first reacts unfavorably to the answer given by Jesus to his mother: "'¿Qué tengo yo que ver contigo, mujer? Aún no ha venido mi hora.'" "*Y llamarle mujer y no madre . . .*" [thinks Tula]. (Italics mine). But, alarmed by her thoughts, she promptly retreats into the safe fortress of the Symbolic: " . . . Y volvió a santiguarse, esta vez con verdadero temblor. Y es que el demonio de su guarda—así creía ella—le susurró: ¡Hombre al fin!'" With his parenthetical observation ("así creía ella"), the narrator unequivocally indicates the split that exists between Tula's self, which acknowledges reality ("Hombre al fin"), and her ego, which disguises it ("El demonio de su guarda"). The narrator's aim is to underscore for the reader the real state of Tula's conscience in the face of her self-deceiving attempts to accommodate its two opposite components.

Tula differs from other feminine characters in the text (Rosa and Manuela, for instance) in that she questions the hierarchy that rigidly determines the relations between men and women. Unlike Rosa and Manuela, who conform to the wishes of the men in their lives, Tula presents forcefully her views to men and is able to persuade them of their validity. But these acts prove to be sporadic and without significant consequences. Tula never questions the traditional social structure that creates the inequitable situation of women. In fact, at times, she is one of its most ardent advocates, favoring a strict adherence to conventional roles. For example, when Manuela mentions to Tula her inability to find worthy goals in her life, Tula readily provides them for her. She defines them around the concept of woman's total dedication to her conventional function within the family: " . . . las muchachas deben vivir . . . para casarse . . . , para criar familia . . . ." Thus Tula betrays a noticeable disparity between some of her personal ideas and behavior and statements such as the above. The former correspond to those of a woman interested in zealously pursuing her individual goals, in disregard of preestablished principles about womanhood, whereas the latter assert the superiority of those principles. In this instance, the conflict between self and ego is manifested in the *décalage* between language and mind. Tula's exact, self-controlled language is a reflection of her repressed conscience, while some of her more spontaneous and unrestricted ideas (later materialized in actions) are connected with the free flow of her unconscious.

Tula's final words before her death cancel any possible uncertainty or ambiguity that might have existed in her past. It is as though, in her last moments, she would like to establish a perfect match between self and ego, a precise coincidence of her discourse and her praxis. This unity is founded in the incontrovertible affirmation of the Symbolic. Tula asserts the definitive supremacy of the Symbolic with her reference to the afterlife, where she aspires to obtain the absolute certainty that has escaped her in her real life: " . . . seremos [ángeles] en la otra vida." Tula's last words together with the perpetuation of her principles in Manuela provide a strong indication that the Symbolic is the prevailing force in Tula and that, in the end, her self is clearly overcome by her ego. Therefore it could be concluded that Tula's most genuine source of sainthood, which, as I have maintained, is found in her pursuit of her true identity against the opposition of the other, is ultimately invalidated. However, it is not impossible to find a more valid source of Tula's greatness.

In psychoanalytical thinking, sublimation or the Symbolic, despite their repressive nature, can be viewed as necessary forces for social and cultural advancement, because they provide a constructive orientation for what would otherwise be purely uncontrolled instinctive energy. It is this orientation that leads to the realization of productive works beneficial to humanity. The Symbolic restricts the subject, but this restriction is, in turn, the origin of the achievements that transcend the narrow boundaries of the self. By abandoning himself to the other, man realizes himself in a more diverse and complete manner. From this perspective, the case for Tula's sainthood could be argued. Tula's self-sacrifice, her total dedication to the care of Rosa's and Manuela's children are essential for the preservation of her family. Without her, her family would probably have disintegrated, leading to painful consequences for its members. As has been shown, Tula's sainthood is in many respects a pretext, a false Imago to justify her incapacity for a meaningful sharing of her life with others. Nevertheless, her sainthood is also real and legitimate because it is motivated by her desire to save her family even when at times she may be the main agent of the family's troubles. Thus the well-established paradigm of the relations of self and other is reenacted in Tula. The other destroys her, making her a victim of an arbitrary law. At the same time, through her identification with the Symbolic and her relentless defense of it, she is able to raise herself above the mediocrity of her environment, achieving in this manner uniqueness and uncommon excellence. (pp. 117-35)

Gonzalo Navajas, "The Self and the Symbolic in Unamuno's 'La tia Tula'," in Revista de Estudios Hispánicos, *Vol. 19, No. 3, October, 1985, pp. 117-37.*

Rose Marie Marcone   (essay date 1986)

[*In the essay below, Marcone explores the relationship between Abel and Joaquín and their quest for self-knowledge in* Abel Sánchez.]

Abel Sánchez is not only an existential work but is written existentially. Unamuno employs a technique to create a work which will function according to existential principles. The device is the novel of confessions which produces a text that does not simply contain but also illustrates an existential theme. The subject is the mystery of the personality, and the purpose of the confessions is to assert the principle that self-understanding depends on one's observation of his behavior. From the outset it is apparent that Joaquín's quest is to realize his self and the confessions are the vehicle through which he assesses his subjective experiences. In fact, his first entry in the confessions relates to the issue of self-knowledge. He comments "Ya desde entonces era él simpático, no sabía por qué, y antipático yo, sin que se me alcanzara mejor la causa de ello . . . ." But the novelistic structure illustrates more than Joaquín's endeavor because it focuses on Unamuno's mistrust of the confessions to carry out their intended purpose. And the reason for this mistrust returns us to the problem of the personality which can never be fully understood. If Joaquín obtained some knowledge of his self, it is limited. If this knowledge illuminates, it simultaneously provokes bewilderment, as we shall see.

However, the confessions serve still another purpose. Through the confession, dialogues and monologues, Unamuno reintroduces a familiar personage or the autonomous character. The memoirs complete the central narrative as Unuamuno becomes, imperceptibly, the voice of Joaquín in the character's dual role as author and commentator. In this way, Unamuno removes himself from the text and relies, for the most part, on the diverse relationships of the central characters to create their personalities free from their author. The relationship of Joaquín to Abel is important to the process of personality formation, but it is the thesis of this paper that this exterior psychological movement is preceded by the unique struggle each one contains within himself . . . These inner struggles initiated and made possible by the confessions, constitute a dimension of the novel which is crucial to the understanding of any and all other relationships, especially that of the main characters, and for this reason internal conflict will be the focus of this study.

Abel and Joaquín have been interpreted as examples of conflicting elements within the *yo* which questions its authentic self in the other or in the *yo* of another individual, or as independent representations of a split personality. However, in all these cases, internal conflict is not self-contained. Rather, it is extended to include association with the *yo* of another individual who becomes part of the self as the self assimilates the other into its being and personal struggle. But the problem should be refocused to include another dimension of *desdoblamiento* or *the splitting of the self*: it is a dimension in which the *yo* with its conflicts remains distinct from all other personalities. The confessions establish the internal level of of the self as the focus of the work and the locus of the struggle because

they are the instrument with which Joaquín splits or duplicates himself as he confronts his irrational self, or his double, which his intellectual ego analyzes in the memoirs. In this paper the double will be defined and discussed as the irrational aspect of the self in contradistinction to the rational level of the *yo*. It is this division within the self which creates the split personality, which serves as the impetus of all conflict, and which generates the inner tension each character encounters as the rational and irrational levels of his being coëxist in altering and disparate relationships. Consequently, the confrontation between Joaquín and Abel originates separately within each character and in no association with the other. *Abel Sánchez* enacts a version of the Cain-and-Abel story in order to emphasize irrationality as an element of the personality, and let us recall that the work appropriately carries the subtitle, *"Una historia de pasión"*.

As readers, we witness conflict within the *yo* and, above all, we experience a state of mind, or Joaquín's and Abel's anxieties which become, in fact, their ambience and that of the text. Accordingly, Abel and Joaquín are not one-sided psychological representations or separate halfs of a single *yo*, as they have been described, because the phenomenon of the doubled self is acted out by each one within his own being. Abel and Joaquín enact two separate struggles and two psychological developments. And in the process, Unamuno lays bare the irrational origins of behavior which he attempts to explain rationally. If rationalization, or Joaquín's confessions, fail to provide such an explanation, the failure is calculated, perhaps, to demonstrate the ineffectiveness of rationalism to master life and the tragic nature of the *yo* which remains undeterminable and antagonistic.

A study of the text appropriately begins with a separate discussion of Joaquín and Abel, and a consideration of Joaquín, author of the confessions, is a logical point of departure. Joaquín is an existential hero. For all practical purposes, he feels alone and unique with his envy: "Me sentí peor que un monstruo, me sentí como si no existiera, como si no fuese nada más que un pedazo de hielo." He has no confidence that his intelligence reflects anything absolute, and he lacks assurance that he fits into any specific scheme. His task is to create his identity and his lifelong sequence of of activities to cast vengeance on Abel is a testimonial to his freedom to act. When he has done all that he can do, he may be able to say what he is, as we shall see.

In the course of the novel, he observes, suffers his inadequacies and feels within him an uncontrollable force. If he is free to act, his actions fail to free him from the hate he feels, and he declares himself condemned to the hell of hate, or the irrational aspect of his self:

> . . . empecé a odiat a Abel con toda mi alma
> y a proponerme a la vez ocultar ese odio . . .
> ¿Odio? Aún no quería darle su nombre, ni quería
> reconocer que nací, predestinado, con su masa
> y con su semilla. Aquella noche nací al infierno
> de mi vida.

But we must qualify Joaquín's sense of predestination and his negation of free will. If Joaquín felt truly condemned, then there is little chance that he would struggle to be free or to overcome what would be impossible. The fact that he struggled is an assertion of his will and of his existential quest to control his personality. The measure of his will to be is the efforts he exerted and not the success of these efforts. The apparent paradox between freedom and condemnation is resolved when one considers the fact that the irrational self cannot be avoided. It is our double and part of our being but it is only one aspect of the total self. If Joaquín feels condemned, the condemnation is to his irrational self which dominates his being, and he fights for his freedom by attempting to achieve a balance within his personality.

With this objective in mind, Joaquín begins the process, or the writing of the confessions, which initiates the novel, *Abel Sánchez.* The purpose of the confessions is to reveal his irrational or inner self and the narration is described as "el relato óa su lucha íntima con la pasión que fué su vida, con aquel demonio con quien peleó . . . ." The memoirs are an unburdening of the self, or "un desahogo," in which Joaquín attempts to objectify himself so that he may order his *yo*. In this sense, the activity of writing can be considered the greatest existential act Joaquín ever undertook, because if his relationship with Abel, or his actions on the exterior level, failed to provide him with a sense of freedom and superiority, his confessions, written after the fact or experience, allow him the chance to know himself. And his self-knowledge should lead to his self-possession because to know himself better than Abel claimed to know him is to save himself from Abel. The writing of the confessions can also be the expression of pride as Joaquín flaunts his pain which he considers to be "la señal de los grandes predestinados."

The motives for the confessions are various, as indicated by the text, and I have not exhausted the list inasmuch as as they can be reduced to one basic cause. Whether the reason is self-defense, counter-accusation, confession of faults, or narration of obsessions, one thing is certain. The confessions originate in an existential wish to assert the self and to examine the personality. Although Joaquín never successfully controlled his irrational self, he did acquire self-knowledge. Through the confessions he realizes that his rational and irrational selves comprise two antagonistic principles which constitute his life, govern his behavior, and cause the conflict he experiences. As he illustrates, one side temporarily expresses itself, and the other side remains passive and ineffective. On several occasions, as the author of the confessions, Joaquín describes his self as divided and not reduced to the single passion usually attributed to him. He becomes more than a symbol of hate. He is a vital being who is caught between reason and passion, although his passion is, indeed, the dominant side of his personality. After commenting on the anguish he experienced upon learning of Abel's and Helena's pending marriage, he concludes: "Fué una tempestad de malos deseos . . . de rabia. Con el día y el cansancio de tanto sufrir volvióme la reflexión, comprendi que no tenía derecho alguno a Helena . . . ."

On another occasion, Joaquín recalls his inner struggle as he decided whether to let Abel live or die. He describes his interior torment as a struggle with madness which was ultimately conquered, if only temporarily, when reason took control: " . . . estaba comprometida mi salud mental, mi razón. Comprendí que me agitaba bajo las garras de la locura; vi el espectro de la dementia haciendo sombra a mi corazón. Y venci." With the recognition of the dual nature of his personality, Joaquín implies the question that seems to dominate the novel: To what degree are reason and intelligence possible? Unamuno provides no solutions. Only realizations are possible, even if some of those realizations are unanswerable questions. The confessions serve to underscore irrationality. They do not provide a rationale for its existence and it remains the inexplicable demon.

Abel appears to be a less dramatic character. He seems rational, sure of himself, and respected. Above all, he seems to know from the outset who he is. But such an initial impression is not without qualification and, from the beginning of the text, the reader may very well have suspicions about Abel. We cannot help but note his withdrawal from the rational process of self-inquiry in a novel in which self-interrogation is the framework. This reaction is atypical of one who appears to be such a reasonable individual. Also, we recall that the novel contains Abel's name as the title and not Joaquín's though he is the author of the confessions. These observations are significant for an understanding of Abel's nature. He is, in a sense, an agent of change because he is the external factor which causes Joaquín to move inside of himself. And it is this movement inward that initiates Joaquín's personal struggle and self-analysis which precede all exterior confrontations and assessments of his relationships with Abel and others.

But Abel is more than a catalyst. He becomes a master of deceit and of changing possibilities. He, too, is in motion as he masterfully conceals the irrational aspect of his self, or his double. If Joaquín seeks to reveal, Abel strives to conceal. In fact, concealment is Abel's central motive in the novel and it is this gesture that defines his *yo*. He is at all times careful not to disclose his envy of Joaquín's sensitivity. Yet the situation changes for Abel. Chapter XIV, containing Joaquín's banquet speech, is pivotal in the tale because it reveals the depths of Joaquín's emotions and Abel's admission of his limitation: "Joaquín, lo que acabas de decir vale más que mi cuadro . . . Eso, eso es una obra de arte y de corazón. Yo no sabía lo que he hecho hasta que te he oído. ¡Tú, y no yo, has hecho mi cuadro, tú!." Abel has been properly called a "potential Cain" because he feared possible rivals, whether they be Joaquín as a rival for his grandson's love or Abelín as a competitor in art.

Joaquín's accusations which label Abel as unfeeling and calculating are no longer invidious remarks but become truth. We see Abel for what he is, and he is less than the ideal personality. Yet he retains control of his reason and justifies his limitation by almost converting it into a unique capacity worthy of his profession: "No nos metamos al fondo. Soy pintor y no pinto los fondos de las personas . . . todo hombre lleva fuera todo lo que tiene dentro . . . ." Abel is content with surfaces and mirror images. The reason for his withdrawal from self-inquiry is now clear. The truth of the matter is that he is incapable of such an undertaking. He is, indeed, a less heroic character than Joaquín because he seeks no positive change nor shows concern for the quality of his being. However, his behavior does change with the revelation of his flaw. He more readily moves outside of himself in his own defense as the victim of the envy which he contains within his being. Until his limitation was revealed he could exhibit a sense of superiority because he felt unchallenged and his envy could be kept in control. The situation has changed as Joaquín becomes a more apparent rival, outwardly affecting Abel's professional and personal image.

With the disclosure of Abel's irrational self, we see duality as an aspect of personality. Clearly, Joaquín is not unique for the bifurcated character that he contains. Both characters experience inner struggles, and this observation relates to a "villain/victim identification" in terms of the Abel-and-Cain story associated with the tale. Both Abel and Joaquín emerge as Cains, and this correlation emphasizes their mutual envy and irrationality. The other is not the source of conflict and Joaquín confirms this fact when he admits that Abel's death will not destroy his envy. Rather, the cause resides within each individual and is his property as the creation of his personality or as the product of the irrational aspect of his self. Envy, as one form of internal conflict, is "la herencia de Cain" and is part of the human condition. It cannot be explained further, and this is the point of *Abel Sánchez:* Rational man lives irrationally at times, and this paradoxical fact cannot be rationalized. Unamuno illustrates the limits of knowledge because the self cannot be understood completely.

If the novel offers no solutions, then one wonders where Joaquín's writings leave him. At best, he is aware of the human tragedy, and he states: " . . . todo hombre es . . . hijo de contradicción." With these words Joaquín realizes his limitation, and Unamuno defines the personality: the *yo* is described as unascertainable because the individual contains within him the dynamism which creates everchanging states of being and with them, anxieties. In the final chapter, Joaquín confronts his limitation, and as a consequence he wills not to continue struggling or, by extention, he wills not to continue living. He ends an existential hero as he began. He assumed responsibility for his life.

With *Abel Sánchez,* once again Unamuno discloses the complex human personality which, by its very nature, is divided against itself. The theme of the double is employed not so much to engage in a psychoanalytic study in which predetermined psychological ideologies are applied to lend imagery to a universal problem: the relationship of the self to the self. Revelation of the double affirms the irrational self as the vital center of the being and as the source of all passion. The work is a self-reflexive device for Joaquín and for anyone like him who realizes the *yo* to be an enigma and who is aware of the integral personality instead of the rational fragment. (pp. 54-6)

> *Rose Marie Marcone, "Internal Conflict in 'Abel Sánchez',"* in The USF Language Quarterly, *Vol. XXV, Nos. 1-2, Fall-Winter, 1986, pp. 54-6.*

> **His sense of the interpenetration of body and soul is so deep that he does not for one moment let us forget how bodily his 'souls' are, and how pregnant with spiritual significance is every one of their words and gestures. No. These characters are not arguments on legs. They truly are men and women of 'flesh and bones', human, terribly human.**
>
> **—*Salvador de Madariaga, in his introduction to* The Tragic Sense of Life in Men and Peoples by Miguel de Unamuno, *1921.***

Colbert I. Nepaulsingh   (essay date 1987)

[*In following excerpt, Nepaulsingh establishes* San Manuel Bueno, mártir *within a tradition of Spanish evangelical literature.*]

Unamuno's *San Manuel Bueno, mártir* provides an unusually fruitful opportunity for literary critics to begin to discuss the best ways to apply positivistic details to arrive at an understanding of a literary text. Let us take, for example, the following sentence, which Hippolyte Taine himself might have considered a model for positivistic criticism: "El escenario de la obra es español [*race*], y ésta refleja las circunstancias políticas de España [*milieu*] en la época en que escribió [*moment*], así como la reacción de Unamuno ante ellas." Unamuno himself admits that these details are all true—that the work's setting was suggested by a visit he made, on June 1, 1930, to a lake and villages in Spain, and that these villages, like others in Spain, were dying partly for political reasons such as the rights a certain landowner claimed to have inherited from the monks of San Martín de Castañeda:

> Escenario hay en *San Manuel Bueno, mártir,* sugerido por el marvilloso y tan sugestivo lago de San Martín de Castañeda, en Sanabria, al pie de las ruinas de un convento de bernardos y donde vive la leyenda de una ciudad, Valverde de Lucerna, que yace en el fondo de las aguas del lago, Y voy a estampar aquí dos poesías que escribí a raíz de haber visitado por primera vez ese lago el día primero de junio de 1930.

> . . . . .

> En efecto, la trágica y miserabilísima aldea de Riba de Lago, a la orilla del de San Martín de Castañeda, agoniza y cabe decir que se está muriendo. Es de una desolación tan grande como la de las alquerías, ya famosas, de las Hurdes. En aquellos pobrísimos tugurios, casuchas de armazón de madera recubierto de adobes y barro, se hacina un pueblo al que ni le es permitido pescar las ricas truchas en que abunda el lago y sobre las que una supuesta señora creía haber hereda-

do el monopolio que tenían los monjes bernardos de San Martín de Castañeda.

But Unamuno also informs the reader that these details, though true, are not the whole truth, that in fact they cannot serve as a key or as a model for an adequate understanding of his work:

> Pero ni Riba de Lago, ni San Martín de Castañeda, ni Galende, el otro pobladillo más cercano al Lago de Sanabria—éste mejor acomodado—, ninguno de los tres puede ser ni fue el modelo de mi Valverde de Lucerna. El escenario de la obra de mi Don Manuel Bueno y Lázaro Carballino supone un desarrollo mayor de vida pública, por pobre y humilde que ésta sea, que la vida de esas pobrísimas y humildísimas aldeas.

While not denying the immediate sources for the setting of the work, Unamuno also directs the reader to a much wider, perhaps universal, tradition to which the setting belongs: "el escenario de la obra . . . supone un desarrollo mayor de vida pública." Hugo Rodríguez Alcalá has attempted to identify this larger tradition for the setting as biblical: "Entonces, la montañna de Valverde de Lucerna *tiene un no sé qué* de la del Sermón de Cristo; el lago de la aldea, por otra parte, cobra también *un no sé qué* del lago o mar de Galilea. Y algo parejo acontece con los personajes de la novela cuya *semejanza* con figuras de la Biblia se sugiere y muestra más de una vez. El resultado de esto es lo que he llamado la palestinización . . . del escenario." And Mario Valdés has succeeded in adding precisión to the symbolic equivalents which Rodríguez Alcalá left as *"no sé qué"* For Valdés it is not merely a question of what Rodríguez Alcalá called the "palestinización . . . del escenario," but rather, the setting symbolizes humanity (aldea/Valverde de Lucerna) struggling on a cross between faith (montaña) and doubt (lago):

> El lugar-ambiente en esta novela no es descriptivo, aunque tenga el fondo implícito del León de los *Paisajes*. El espacio narrativo en este texto es simbólico. Hay una aldea remota situada entre montaña y el lago. Aldea, montaña y lago representan los tres símbolos de la novela . . . El sistema creativo de Unamuno se basa en tres tropos tradicionales empleados en el contexto de estos tres símbolos.
>
>   . . . . .
>
> Valverde de Lucerna se extiende, por uso de metonimia, a identificar el lugar con la población para elevarlo al significado de la humanidad en la *intrahistoria*. En cambio, con lago y montaña, Unamuno emplea el símil y la metáfora para crear el significado más profundo de su obra: la dictomía entre la fe y la duda y su personificación en el protagonista Manuel-Cristo
>
>   . . . . .
>
> Don Manuel personifica la cruz del nacimiento al estar situado entre la fe y la duda de su pueblo. Esta personificación le hace no solamente santo, sino mártir, porque toma la duda y la sufre por todos.

One conclusion that emerges from the above juxtaposition of commentaries on the setting of *San Manuel Bueno, mártir,* is that it is not sufficient to know the sources in order to understand Unamuno's work; one must also know the tradition in which Unamuno chose to place his work, and more importantly, one must know how Unamuno reinterprets the language and the texts of that tradition. In *San Manuel Bueno, mártir,* every word of the title belongs to the biblical tradition in which Unamuno chose to write, but he re-interprets, redefines every word of the title in order to recreate the traditional texts of stories that tell of leaders who suffer for humanity's sake.

The failure to distinguish clearly between source and tradition has led to some confusion in the criticism of *San Manuel Bueno, mártir:* Sánchez Barbudo implied with the title of his article that Rousseau's *El vicario Saboyano* is a source and that Unamuno follows the French tradition of Chateauabriand and Senancour; Eleanor K. Paucker thought she found "A possible source in Spanish American literature;" John V. Falconieri listed eight possible sources and concluded in despair that "in this instance the search for sources has led some critics into worlds never envisaged by the author with the pernicious result that values, concepts and intentions are attributed to him that may very well prove detrimental to his art and even falsify it;" Manuel García Blanco noted that there are antecedents of Manuel Bueno in Unamuno's own work: "Yo me permito sugerir este otro precedente, tomado de sus propios escritos, y que ya aduje en alguna ocasión. Lo encuentro en unos titulados 'Diálogos del escritor y el político' que don Miguel publicó en . . . 1908;" Ciriaco Morón Arroyo demonstrated that *San Manuel* is a sort of *summa* of Unamuno's own ideas, that the circumstances that define don Manuel Bueno

> tienen como fuente primaria la obra misma de Unamuno. Esta novela constituye un fenómeno de 'total recall:' las ideas madres del autor expuestas por vez primera en 1894 o en 1897, se refrescan para 'quedar' en 1933 incorporadas en *San Manuel.* La novela resulta así un inventario de las ideas de Unamuno.

One way out of this confusion between Unamuno's original ideas and similar ideas found in a host of other works written in the same tradition (some of which Unamuno read) would be to acknowledge that the central theme of *San Manuel Bueno* is commonplace: the theme of the leader who is himself led by his followers (in this case into the Promised Land) is not only one of the oldest stories known to mankind, but it is also as trite as the formula "the carpenter whose house is crooked," "the cobbler whose shoe needs mending," "the plumber whose pipes leak," "the physician who must heal herself," "the savior who cannot save himself," et cetera. With ideas as commonplace as these, polygenesis is at least as frequent as direct influence, especially with writers, like Unmauno, who think dialectically, in terms of opposites.

One of the first Unamuno critics to begin to shed light on the confusion between source and tradition was Mario Valdés. Valdés refused to be engaged in discussions based on false premises about originality and the influence on a writer of direct sources; rather he demonstrates clearly that what a writer reads does not necessarily therefore become a direct source for what that writer later composes; in Unamuno's case we know that before he wrote **San Manuel Bueno,** he marked and annotated two editions of the works of William Blake which he received as gifts in 1907 and 1920, and yet Valdés demonstrates "that William Blake's 'Jerusalem' was not a direct 'source' for **San Manuel Bueno, mártir,** and that Blake's poem gave Unamuno a profound reaffirmation in the development of his symbolism—which can be traced to the last decade of the nineteenth century." In an earlier article Valdés had shown that a Korean writer, who had not read Unamuno's **San Manuel Bueno,** published a novel with a strikingly similar narrative theme of faith and despair. This is not to say that Valdés regards source study as futile; he admits that "the close reader of literature might magnanimously grant to the poet's sources a limited function in the analysis of the poem, but the key to this type of commentary must be recognizable in the poem itself." And in 1973 he published, together with Maria Elena de Valdés, *An Unamuno Source Book,* which is destined to become a model for works of its kind, and an indispensable tool for all source studies of Unamuno's writings.

What Mario Valdés has done for the aesthetic relationships between Unamuno and Blake has been paralleled recently by the article of a political philosopher, Michael Weinstein, for Unamuno and Dostoevsky. Weinstein compares "the Grand Inquisitor and San Manuel" without attempting to establish that Dostoevsky's *The Brothers Karamazov* is a source for **San Manuel.** Indeed, since Weinstein makes no reference to Valdés' *An Unamuno Source Book,* he seems to be unaware that Unamuno owned an English and Spanish translation of *The Brothers Karamazov,* both of which he marked extensively, presumably before the composition of **San Manuel Bueno.** It is inconceivable to me that the following passage from *The Brothers Karamazov* (not cited by Weinstein) would not have moved Unamuno deeply as he read it: "Why can there not be among them one martyr oppressed by great sorrow and loving humanity? . . . What if he doesn't believe in God! At last you have guessed it. It's perfectly true that that's the whole secret. But isn't that suffering, at least for a man like that, who has wasted his whole life in the desert and yet could not shake off his incurable love of humanity?" The similarities between Dostoevsky's Grand Inquisitor and Unamuno's San Manuel are clear, and so are the differences. If, for example, both characters are described as priests and martyrs who do not believe what they preach, it is also clear that their secret disbeliefs are different: the Grand Inquisitor is an atheist who does not believe in God; San Manuel, on the other hand, has no problem expressing belief in God, but his silence betrays his struggle to believe in "the resurrection of the body" and in "life everlasting:"

> Había un santo ejercicio que introdujo en el culto popular y es que, reuniendo en el templo a todo el pueblo, hombres y mujeres, vijos y niños, unas mil personas, recitábamos al unísono, en una sola voz, el Credo: "Creo en Dios Padre Todopoderoso Creador del Cielo y de la Tierra . . ." y lo que sigue. Y no era un coro, sino una sola voz, una voz simple y unida, fundidas todas en una y haciendo como una montaña,

cuya cumbre perdida a las veces en nubes, era Manuel. Y al llegar a lo de "creo en la resurrección de la carne y la vida perdurable" la voz de don Manuel se zambullía, como en un lago, en la del pueblo todo, y era que él se callaba.

Dostoevsky, like Blake, does not provide a source of ideas new to Unamuno; rather, Unamuno discovers reaffirmation of his own ideas as he reads a passage in Dostoevsky that is written in the same biblical tradition that Unamuno too has chosen to recreate.

If one were writing, therefore, a certain kind of history of world literature, one would be obligated to find ways of comparing Unamuno's work with others in a tradition shared also by writers like Rousseau, Chateaubriand, Senancour, Milton, Blake, Dostoevsky, Santiago Pérez Triana, Richard Kim, and so on. But if one were writing another kind of history of *Spanish* literature, other writers would have to be considered, for Unamuno's **San Manuel Bueno** is not the only Spanish masterpiece of its kind.

There is in Spanish literature before **San Manuel Bueno, mártir** a tradition of composing literary texts according to well-known biblical patterns in such a way that the new literary text seeks to recreate, reinterpret or substitute the sacred text. (pp. 315-20)

What Cervantes does to the tradition . . . , is to shift the blasphemous love from the woman to the text itself. Don Quijote's madness derives not so much from his love of Dulcinea . . . , but especially from his blasphemous faith

Self-caricature by Unamuno.

in chivalric texts like the *Amadís de Gaula,* a faith which causes him to live a life *imitatio Amadis* instead of *imitatio Christi.* On his deathbed don Quijote denounces the profane texts which he had treated as if they were sacred, and he expresses regret that little time is left to him to recompense by reading sacred texts:

Yo tengo juicio ya libre y claro sin las sombras caliginosas de la ignorancia que sobre el me pusieron su amarga y continua leyenda de los detestables libros de las caballerías. Ya conozco sus disparates y sus embelecos y no me pesa sino que este desengaño ha llegado tan tarde, que no me deja tiempo para hacer alguna recompensa leyendo otros que sean luz del alma . . .—Dadme albricias, buenos señores, de que ya yo no soy don Quijote de la Mancha, sino Alsonso Quijano, a quien mis costumbres me dieron renombre de *Bueno.* Ya soy enemigo de Amadís de Gaula y de toda la infinita caterva de su linaje; ya me son odiosas todas las historias de la andante caballería; ya conozco mi necedad y el peligro en que me pusieron haberlas leído.

When Miguel de Unamuno comments on the above passage from the *Quijote,* it becomes clear that his *San Manuel Bueno, mártir* belongs, with *Cárcel de Amor, Celestina,* and the *Quijote* to the evangelical tradition of Spanish literature in which this article places it. Unamuno expresses delight in the type of Cervantine word-play which he and Diego de San Pedro and Fernando de Rojas mastered ("renombre" in Cervantes' text means both "renown" and "re-naming"); and more importantly, in terms of the evangelical tradition, Unamuno links the passage by Cervantes to its prototype in the New Testament where someone called Jesus, "Good Master" and he replied, "Why callest thou me good? There is none good but one, that is, God."

Llamó Don Quijote a sus buenos amigos el cura, el bachiller Sansón Carrasco y a maese Nicholás el barbero, y pidió confesarse y hacer testamento. Y apenas vio entrar a los tres, les dijo: "Dadme albricias, buenos señores, de que ya no soy Don Quijote de la Mancha, sino Alonso Quijano, a quien mis costumbres me dieron renombre de bueno." Pocos días hace que hablando con don Alvaro de Tarfe y al llamarle éste bueno, le dijo: "yo no sé si soy bueno, pero sé decir que no soy el malo," tal vez recordando aquello del Evangelio: "¿por qué me llamas bueno? Ninguno es bueno sino uno: Dios" (Mat, XIX, 17) y ahora a pique de morir y por la luz de la muerte alumbrado, dice que sus costumbres le dieron "renombre de bueno." ¡Renombre! ¡Renombre!, y ¡cuán dura de arrancar es, Don Quijote mío, la raíz de la locura de tu vida! ¡Renombre de bueno!, ¡renombre de bueno! ¡renombre!

In his evangelical commentary on Cervantes' use of the word, Unamuno also explains the use of *bueno* in his title *San Manuel Bueno, mártir,* and, in his prologue to *San Manuel Bueno,* Unamuno refers to the connection he sees between don Quijote and San Manuel: "Y no quiero aquí comentar ya más ni el martirio de Don Quijote ni el de Don Manuel Bueno, martirios quijotescos los dos." But *San Manuel Bueno* is not the first *evangelio de amor* com-

posed by Unamuno. It is clear that Unamuno believed that his version of the life of Don Quijote is a better *evangelio de amor* than Cervantes'—citing Acts 28:20 and comparing himself to St. Paul, Unamuno writes in a sonnet composed in exile in 1924: "Tu evangelio, mi señnor Don Quijote, / al pecho de tu pueblo, cual venablo / lancé . . . / . . . me vuelvo a los gentiles y les hablo / tus hazañas, haciendo de San Pablo / de tu fe, . . . / . . . / y llevando tu bautismo / de burlas de pasión a gente extraña / forjaré universal el quijotismo." Unamuno encountered Cervantes' text of the *Quijote* and he recreated and reinterpreted it; he probably would have finished differently the first act of *Celestina* that Rojas found. (pp. 321-23)

Thus *Cárcel de Amor, Celestina,* and the *Quijote* are not sources for *San Manuel Bueno, mártir,* they are antecedents in a tradition in which Unamuno chose to compose, and as such they can help us understand his *San Manuel Bueno.* But the major themes of this tradition are so universally commonplace that it would be well to begin to define some major elements of the tradition so that other works that belong to it can be more easily identified. A text that could be studied fruitfully within the evangelical tradition in Spanish literature should deal with, or add to, variants of the following elements, at least.

First, there should be functional, not superficial, use of the evangelical idea "to die for love" in some sense comparable to how Jesus Christ is said to have died for love of humanity. By superficial I mean the type of commonplace courtly usage described aptly by Alicia de Colombí-Monguió: "El amante . . . que piensa en 'morir de amor,' y que expresa su egocéntrica locura en hipérboles sacroprofanas, es el enamorado universal, común a la literatura de Europa, aquenda y allende los Pirineos. Nada de lo que él dice sale de lo común." By functional, I mean an elaboration of the Christian idea "to die for love" in such a way that it becomes a special cornerstone of the text. For example, in *Cárcel de Amor,* Leriano's passion has been correctly compared with the passion of Christ; likewise the garden in which Calisto worships his God parodies the Garden of Gethsemane where Jesus prayed to God and from which he was led away to his death; Calisto's religion, of which Celestina is a sort of high priestess, is a parody of Christianity based on a curious admixture of sacred and profane texts; likewise, Don Quijote admits the similarities between the texts he worships and the New Testament when he says that St. Paul was a "caballero andante por la vida, y santo a pie quedo por la muerte . . . porque estos santos y caballeros profesaron lo que yo profeso, que es el ejercicio de las armas . . . Ellos conquistaron el cielo a fuerza de brazos porque el cielo padece fuerza" (cf. Matthew 11:12); and Unamuno changed the epigraph for *San Manuel Bueno, mártir* from one text of the New Testament (John 11:35) to another (I Corinthians 15:19), thus leaving no doubt about the functional significance of the Gospels to his work.

Second, there should be, in addition to important use of the New Testament idea of dying for love, a functional (not superficial) tension between Old Testament ideas and New Testament ideas. For example, in *Cárcel de Amor,* many of the laws by which the fictitious kingdom of Macedonia is governed are Old Testament laws, so that it becomes impossible to decide whether the Macedonia of the text is a Jewish or a Christian country; likewise, in *Celestina,* Calisto disobeys the most fundamental Old Testament law, the first commandment against idolatry, and he goes "whoring after other gods" as prohibited throughout the Old Testament (cf. Exodus 34:12, 16); *Celestina* was, apparently, a popular work among Jews—it was translated into Hebrew in Italy; for Jews, Melibea in her *hortus conclusus* would be a type for the Virgin Mary, and Calisto's worship of her as the Virgin Mary would be idolatrous; in the *Quijote,* the Old versus New Testament tension is generated by Sancho's repeated description of himself as Old Christian and of Don Quijote's possible New Christian status hinted at, for example, in his Saturday meal of "duelos y quebrantos;" but Cervantes also adds the Moorish dimension to the Jewish Christian question as, for example, in the story of Zoraida/Leila Marien; already in *Celestina* there was a tendency to amplify the Jewish/Christian debate, for example, when Sempronio says that about the evils of women "gentiles, judíos, cristianos e moros, todos en esta concordia están," or when Pleberio says that love's flame destroys the body and soul of all human beings, "no sólo de christianos; mas de gentiles e judíos e todo en pago de buenos servicios;" in the case of **San Manuel Bueno, mártir,** the Old versus New Testament tension is highly functional: San Manuel's patron saint is Jesus Christ himself, but he also compares himself fundamentally to Moses; also, the verse repeated throughout the text as among the last words of Jesus ("¡Dios mío, Dios mío!, ¿por qué me has abandonado?") belongs both to the Old and the New Testament, since Jesus was actually chanting a Psalm (Psalm 22) that Jews recite in moments of deepest despair.

Third, as a result partly of the tension between Old and New Testament ideas described briefly in the preceding paragraph, texts composed in the evangelical tradition are inherently and irresolvably ambiguous. Diego de San Pedro and Fernando de Rojas succeeded in composing ambivalent "converso" texts that could be interpreted differently by Jewish and Christian readers, just like early Spanish printers published the same biblical texts in two different editions—one with notes for Christian readers and another annotated for Jewish readers . . . In the case of the *Quijote* the text is not merely ambivalent but plurivalent, a phenomenon critics have described as perspectivism. Likewise, it is impossible and unwise to decide whether San Manuel is indeed a sinner or a saint, a martyr or a hypocrite, whether Leriano, Calisto, and Don Quijote are heroes or fools, New Testament Christians or Old.

Fourth, texts composed in the evangelical tradition should have a positivistic relationship with contemporary politics; just as the political question of treason under Roman law functions in the New Testament where Jesus is described as King of the Jews, so too contemporary politics functions in *Cárcel de Amor* and *Celestina* where the Goddess Fortuna and her Wheel of Fortune are used as political metaphors for those who rise and fall from power, and for those who suffer on wheels of torture. In the *Quijote* Fortuna is no longer much of a political symbol, she functions mainly as chance ("ventura") that propels the action

from adventure to adventure; but, the idea of the inquisition is kept alive in the auto-da-fe for Don Quijote's books; and, one burning political question in the *Quijote* is the expulsion of the "moriscos." In **San Manuel Bueno,** Fortuna is not "chance" but wealth in the sense of fortunes to be amassed in the New World by people like Angela's brother, Lázaro; and the idea of the Inquisition is kept alive when San Manuel, obviously commenting on contemporary Spain, gives his verdict on Marxism: "Y en cuanto a eso del sindicato, es en ti [Lázaro] un resabio de tu época de progresismo . . . Opio sí. Démosle opio, y que duerma y sueñe;" later, Lázaro told Angela;

> El me curó de mi progresismo. Porque hay, Angela, dos clases de hombres peligrosos y nocivos: los que convencidos de la vida de ultratumba, de la resurrección de la carne, atormentan, como inquisidores que son, a los demás . . . y los que no creyendo más que en este mundo esperan no sé qué sociedad futura y se esfuerzan en negarle al pueblo el consuelo de creer en otro.

Fifth, there should be in an evangelical text, at least as a minor theme, some variant of the idea of sleep and its relationship to dreams, visions, and death. In *Cárcel de Amor* the first scenes take place as in a dream; the apparition ("estraña visión") of the Wild Man who leads Leriano captive, and the fact that Leriano asks someone to come over (into Macedonia) and help, are reminiscent of the "vision" that "appeared to Paul in the night;" "a man of Macedonia was standing beseeching him and saying, 'Come over to Macedonia and help us' " (Acts 16:9). In *Celestina,* Melibea and Lucrecia in the garden sing to the stars to awake the lover if he is asleep, so that Melibea, as God, prays to heaven while Calisto as disciple might be asleep, a variation of Christ praying in the garden of Gethsemane while his disciples slept; more significantly, Calisto cannot decide whether his meeting with Melibea was a dream or real: "¡O dichoso e bienandante Calisto, si verdad es que no ha sido sueño lo pasado! ¿Soñélo o no? ¿Fue fantaseado o passó en verdad?"; earlier he had confessed to Celestina that he dreamt of Melibea many nights: "en sueños la veo tantas noches." Don Quijote's madness is closely linked to his lack of sleep from reading, and he sleeps a deep, long, curative sleep between parts 1 and 2, and before he dies; the relationship between dreams and reality functions constantly in Don Quijote's world. In **San Manuel Bueno,** Unamuno cites Calderón (La vida es sueño) and intensifies the relationship between dreams and reality, between life and death.

Sixth, one of the most important elements of the evangelical tradition is the mysterious nature of the transmission of the text, and of the insertion by the author of himself into the text. In *Cárcel de Amor,* the text is transmitted by a narrator who witnessed the events and was a carrier of the letters he transcribes; yet it is a mystery that this narrator is able to transcribe verbatim even the letters that Leriano tore up and swallowed when he died; the texts of *Celestina, Quijote,* and *San Manuel* also reach the reader in mysterious ways. Diego de San Pedro inserts himself into his text in more than one way—in an epistolary prologue he refers to the similarity between the work and his other writings: "Podré ser reprehendido si en lo que agora escrivo tornare a dezir algunas razones de las que en otras cosas he dicho;" this compares remarkably well with Fernando de Rojas' acrostic reference to himself in one of the prologues to *Celestina,* with Cervantes' reference to the author of *La Galatea* and *El curiso impertinente,* and especially with Unamuno's statement that the text of San Manuel "se parece mucho a otras cosas que he escrito." Diego de San Pedro also inserts himself into his text more subtly by making artistic use of his apostolic surname: the prison of love on which Calisto founds his faith is described so as to coincide with the description of St. Peter as the rock on which the Christian Church is founded. This is to be compared with Rojas' identification of himself as the person who finished a blasphemous text he found, and especially with his appeal to the reader to judge him fairly: "Y así no me juzgues por esso liviano; / Mas antes zeloso de limpio bivir / . . . / Sacando muy limpio d'entr'ellas al grano." It should also be compared with Cervantes' reference to "un tal de Saavedra" in the captive's tale in Part I, and with this reference in the prologue to Part II to the soldier's wounds: "las que el soldado muestra en el rostro y en los pechos, estrellas son que guían a los demás al cielo de la honra." It is especially to be compared with how Unamuno, like Diego de San Pedro, makes use of his name at the end of *San Manuel Bueno:* "lo que hace un nombre / —, donde se nos dice como mi celestial patrón, San Miguel Arcángel—Miguel quiere decir ¿Quién como Dios? / y arcángel, archimensajero—, disputó con el Diablo."

Of course, it would take a booklength study to document fully the six elements I list above as common to *Cárcel de Amor, Celestina,* the *Quijote,* and *San Manuel Bueno, mártir;* this is why I claim in this article only to begin to search for a tradition for *San Manuel Bueno.* I hope only to persuade the reader that Unamuno himself might have agreed with my placing his work in the evangelical tradition, since he wrote at the end of it his own comparison of it with the Gospels: "Bien sé que en lo que se cuenta en este relato, si se quiere novelesco—y la novela es la más íntima historia, la más verdadera, por lo que no me explico que haya quien se indigne de que se llame novela al Evangelio . . . ."(pp. 324-28)

> *Colbert I. Nepaulsingh, "In Search of a Tradition, Not a Source, for 'San Manuel Bueno, Mártir'," in* Revista Canadiense de Estudios Hispánicos, *Vol. XI, No. 2, Winter, 1987, pp. 315-30.*

Geoffrey Ribbans   (essay date 1987)

[In the essay below, Ribbans outlines and accounts for contradictory elements in La tía Tula's *protagonist.]*

One of the strangest features of the very sparse criticism devoted to *La tía Tula* is the extraordinary variety of responses its eponymous heroine has provoked. One source of difficulty is what has been seen as a contradiction between the "official" statements, favourable and supportive as they are, made by Unamuno about his creation, particularly in the *Prólogo,* and the actions of the protagonist revealed in the narrative. While such scholars as Juan Rof

Carballo and Ricardo Gullón roundly deny that Gertrudis can be compared with St Theresa, Don Quixote, Antigone or Abishag the Shunammite, David G. Turner points out that normally Unamuno's prologues bear a close relationship with the text of the novels they precede and indicates his view that "the type of woman outlined [in the Prologue] and Tula are basically the same, although this does not exhaust Tula who is a more complex character than the former." For Frances Wyers [Weber], in one of the most perceptive and forthright analyses of the novel, it is the unrecognized ambiguity in the prologues which gives rise to the many "bizarre" interpretations of the novel. Similarly, the most recent critic to discuss the novel, Gonzalo Navajas, starts off by indicating that a "considerable number of critics of Unamuno have found it difficult to interpret *La tía Tula* in a way which would account for the fundamental contradiction that determines the character and conduct of the protagonist, Tula."

As a consequence critics tend to line up into those who, following Unamuno's lead, basically admire Gertrudis' attitude and those who deplore it. Among the former is Julián Marías who in an influential study dating from 1943 speaks of her as the "fundadora de una comunidad doméstica, que se prolonga después de ella; su vida, de tan fuerte personalidad, no está destinada a nutrirse de sí misma, sino a realizarse en la convivencia de la casa." Turner, too, emphasises Gertrudis' role as an apostle of a spiritual cult of domesticity. Though "the fundamentally good intentions of the author and his protagonist may lead to undesirable results," her "altruistic maternity" is "an extremely important aspect of her personality . . . for which the author felt real admiration." According to another scholar, Antonio Sánchez Barbudo, Tula is "generosa, abnegada, dispuesta siempre a contribuir a la felicidad de los otros, olvidando la suya propia."

By contrast, a second group of critics are unequivocally severe in their judgement. Ricardo Gullón, in particular, in an important study, calls her a "monstruo" and speaks of the Mr. Hyde behind "este doctor Jekill [sic] con faldas." Turner quotes Segundo Serrano Poncela as viewing her as "an existentially inauthentic woman because she chokes her natural instincts towards reproduction and love with a personal and specifically sexual morality which is false." Others are clear that negative qualities constitute at least one facet of her personality. Thus Frances Wyers refers to "the rapacious and devouring person revealed by her actions," in apparent contradiction with the awe felt by other characters and the approval of Unamuno himself. Gonzalo Navajas observes acutely that in a literal or heuristic reading, which he finds "perhaps necessary but insufficient," "Tula stands out as a heartless and manipulative person, firmly in control of herself and intent on achieving the absolute domination of those around her."

Since the 1920 Prologue is at the centre of the dispute, we should take a closer look at it. The sub-title "(que puede saltar el lector de novelas)," although typical of Unamuno's style, may perhaps indicate that it is not of great direct relevance to the text. More decisive is the assertion made emphatically and repetitively that the parallels established with St Teresa and Don Quixote are *a posteriori,* discovered after the novel was written:

> No crea el lector, por lo que precede, que el rela-to que se sigue y va a leer es, en modo alguno, un comentario a la vida de la Santa española. ¡No, nada de esto! Ni pensábamos en Teresa de Jesús al emprenderlo y desarrollarlo; ni en Don Quijote. Ha sido después de haberlo terminado cuando aun para nuestro ánimo, que lo concibió, resultó una novedad este parangón, cuando hemos descubierto las raíces de este relato no-velesco. Nos fue oculto su más hondo sentido al emprenderlo. No hemos visto sino después, al hacer sobre él examen de conciencia de autor, sus raíces teresianas y quijotescas. Que son una misma raíz.

It may likewise be assumed that the comparisons with An-tigone and Abishag did not form part of the original con-scious plan either.

As it happens, we have some objective confirmation of the lateness of the published prologue and so, perhaps, of its lack of immediate relevance. Added to the early first un-finished draft of the novel is the sketch of another "Prólo-go," the first lines of which refer directly to *La tía Tula:*

> Añado una novela más a la lista de mis desgra-ciadas. Nivolas y no novelas. No imaginación. Abstracciones. El hombre es la idea, la idea hombre. Pasión. El de *Niebla.* Las notas de esta novela y trozo de ella, cap. [?] hace años dur-miendo, incubándose. Entre tanto *Amor y ped., Niebla,* **Nada menos,** etc., **Abel Sánchez.**

This *"Prólogo"* gives the impression of having been writ-ten after the draft of the novel was complete. In any case since it refers to **Abel Sánchez** it must be later than 1917, but presumably before *Tres novelas ejemplares* was con-ceived as a book in 1920.

It is significant that Unamuno here links his latest novel with its predecessors, accepts the term "nivola" and sees the characteristics of all of them as abstract rather than imaginative, with the characters as personifications of ideas and as representing passion. It is curious to note that the rest of the prologue links the composition of the novel with a very different if equally characteristic impulse of the author's: a lyrical evocation of the wild and imposing landscape of La Peña de Francia. It appears that Unamu-no completely rejected this rapprochement of his charac-ter to nature to adopt an entirely new approach incorpo-rating the comparisons we have just discussed. In view of this the final prologue, to which I shall return later, loses some of its puzzling nature.

As is well known, *La tía Tula* is a work which had a long gestation. The genesis of the story is found in a letter of November 1902 to Juan Maragall in which he describes a young woman who combines a disgust at sexual relations with a strong maternal instinct. Unamuno's story starts therefore with two preconditions, one negative, rejection of sexual relations, the other positive, yearning for chil-dren: two roles in life which are in natural terms complete-ly incompatible. The only exception, for Christians, is the unique case of the Virgin Mary, where the contradiction

is miraculously transcended. The potential for the eventu-al parallel established between Tula and the Virgin is thus present from the beginning. What is unclear at this stage is whether Unamuno saw the virgin-mother combination as resulting from a conscious decision or from fortuitous circumstances, as it presumably was for the real-life model.

A slightly later stage is revealed in the incomplete auto-graph I have published and discussed in a recent article. The starting point is Ramiro at the moment of losing his wife, corresponding essentially to Chapter VII of the com-pleted novel. When Tula is introduced, we are told explic-itly, in a passage omitted from the final version, that "desde mozuela había sentido la brutalidad y la petulancia del hombre." The most significant thing however is that we do not witness her actions during the courtship of Ramiro and Rosa which allow her to construct her life firmly around her devotion to "aunthood." It is not sur-prising therefore that Unamuno concluded, in a note added to the top of the autograph, "Hay que empezar antes." The six first chapters before the autograph begins thus deserve close scrutiny.

The opening paragraph of the novel is remarkable both for its contents and its admirable directness:

> Era a Rosa y no a su hermana Gertrudis, que siempre salía de casa con ella, a quien ceñían aquellas ansiosas miradas que les enderezaba Ramiro. *O, por lo menos, así lo creían ambos, Ramiro y Rosa, al atraerse el uno al otro.* (my italics)

Ramiro and Rosa believe that he is attracted just by her; but the narrator, with that tell-tale *por lo menos,* implies doubts, and Gertrudis is not mentioned as holding this view. As the narration continues, it is implied that the two sisters have a complementary nature; as in the beehive, as we shall see, there is a strict division of labour. While Rosa's beauty, "algún tanto provocativa," is immediately more appealing, Gertrudis' "ojos tenaces," the key to the "cofre cerrado y sellado" of her hidden charms, has more to offer. Thus Ramiro, following his superficial nature ("llevaba el alma toda a flor de los ojos"), *"no creyó* ver más que a Rosa" (my italics once more) and proposes to her.

The conversation which follows between the two sisters reveals a marked difference: on Rosa's part, a completely conventional attitude; she likes Ramiro, wants a *novio,* but feels inclined to stall for a time ("hacerse valer") so as not to appear too eager. Gertrudis' attitude is at total variance; she refuses to express ignorance or surprise at the news of Ramiro's letter or to give, as both irrelevant and unseem-ly, her own opinion of Ramiro's looks and character; she disapproves of what she calls coquettishness and advises her to accept him without more ado. The important thing for them to do is to get on with the essential job of produc-ing children. Different considerations evidently apply to Gertrudis. Marriage is not as yet excluded but, by her own account, she would scrutinize very closely indeed any po-tential *novio.* She has no illusions about the normal options open to women ("el matrimonio o el convento") but she begins to formulate one which is different from either: "ser tía," which she hastens to elucidate: "ser tía de tus hijos." Finally, the narrator informs us that "Lo [Rosa's engagement] que empezó a cuajar la soledad de Gertrudis." It is important to realise that this isolation is entered upon quite voluntarily. It is of course to be a spiritual isolation, not a physical one; full of activity on behalf of others, but with no dependency on others, like "una huérfana cargada de hijos."

Immediately afterwards, we are told all that we are going to know about Gertrudis' and Rosa's background. Orphans since early childhood, they have an adequate pension (Unamuno excludes all socio-economic problems) and are brought up in an atmosphere of naive innocence by their maternal uncle, a priest, Don Primitivo. The resemblance between Gertrudis and her aunt, Don Primitivo's sister, and her grandmother, his mother, is emphasised; there is evidently a hereditary trait involved here in the female line which contrasts with the complete and deliberate absence of the other factors—temporal or environmental—of the positivist criterion represented by Taine. It is to be noted that good, if schematic, logical and psychological reasons for Tula's attitude are provided, but this does not detract from the emphasis placed on her personal decision. For the rest, only the barest of information is supplied: except in the case of Ramiro (his surname is Cuadrado, his mother is Doña Venancia), no personal data are given. We do not know Gertrudis' or Rosa's surname, place of residence, education, interests, or the date of the actions; even physical description, with the exception of Tula's eyes, is severely limited.

Fearful of men's constancy, she advocates a speedy marriage and when, in the second chapter, it is clear that Ramiro's love for Rosa is not as ardent as it should be, she rides roughshod over his growing attachment for her, expressed forcibly and characteristically in physical terms: "Desmudósele el semblante y se le vio vacilar. La serenidad de aquellos serenos ojazos de luto le concentró la sangre toda en su corazón." Repeatedly, she refuses to allow him to call her Tula (for the protagonist a sign of excessive intimacy). She insists on his declaring once more his love for Rosa and refuses to listen to what is evidently about to be a confession of his love for her. Instead, she delivers an ultimatum, prohibiting him from exercising his will to change his allegiance: "Si la quieres, a casarte con ella, y si no la quieres, estás de más en esta casa."

The suppression of her feelings for Ramiro costs her great anguish, just as she had experienced earlier when the thought occurred to her that Rosa might change her mind, but she voluntarily endures the distress in the interests of her scheme. Characteristically, this emotional strain is expressed in stark physical terms: "se le paraba el corazón . . . un silencio de hielo . . . la sangre, antes represada y ahora suelta, le encendió la cara . . . podía oírsele el galope trepidante del corazón."

From all this it is evident that the marriage is Gertrudis' deliberate making, as she later admitted to Ramiro and to his son. La tía Tula not only took over her sister's household on her death, combining the roles of spinster and mother, as in the kernel of the story. By imposing her will on others, she actively pursued a course of action which would achieve this end and so evade the problem of the two equally unacceptable options—matrimony or the convent—we have seen as open to Spanish women.

After the marriage she proceeds to direct its course further, by persuading them to abandon frivolities—to give away their dog, to put aside Rosa's doll—though she keeps away in order not to "disturb" the couple, i.e. to interfere with their procreative function. Once Rosa becomes pregnant, she visits them more frequently. When the question arises of whether both mother and baby could survive the difficult confinement her priorities are clear. Her unexpressed thought in answer to the doctor that not only could the surviving mother have other children but that there were other mothers is a first indication of how unswerving and ruthless the criterion she was now following was. Similarly, her encouragement of the couple to have more children—which awakened a protest even from Don Primitivo—can only have one result: Rosa's premature death, a consequence she appears to accept with equanimity. Thus we reach Chapter VII, where the draft autograph began. With her rejection of Ricardo (less abrupt in the manuscript version, for Ricardo visits Ramiro's home and plays with the children), Gertrudis has found her solitary chosen path and has confirmed it by exerting her will on others. Her reign as virgin-mother now commences.

I shall not attempt to trace in detail the tactics Gertrudis adopts to avoid sexual involvement while retaining her function as surrogate mother of Rosa's children and later of Manuela's as well. My essential views on the subject have already been outlined in a previous study, so that I shall confine myself here to a few additional comments. First, Gertrudis overcomes the claims of both her head and her heart, for both reason and affection, though fundamentally inimical, would lead her to accept Ramiro, in favour of another impulse which is described as "algo más ahincado, más entrañado, más intimo, con algo que era como el tuétano de los huesos de su espíritu," with that characteristic fusion of physical and spiritual terms which is repeated more than once. These terms can only mean the exercise of will reflecting her deepest instinctive urges: "el que uno quiere ser . . . *en su seno,* el creador . . . el real de verdad" (my italics), according to a text I shall return to later. Second, Gertrudis persuades herself of the truth of an evident falsification of Rosa's dying request ("no tendrán madrastra"); for her own purposes she takes it as a prohibition for her to marry Ramiro, which it is not, but has no compunction later in obliging him to marry Manuela, which is directly against Rosa's desires. Similarly, she erects herself into the interpreter of Rosa's wishes, claiming to have consulted her beyond the grave. And third, her devotion to the Virgin Mary leads her to request the Virgin to accomplish miracles: to give her breast milk to suckle Ramirín, and later to save Manuela's life at the expense of her own. These form part of a constant defiance of the laws of nature, constantly called into question by her insistence in being named mother of the children. Thus Manolita's eyes come to resemble Tula's, though she has no blood relationship with her: she is "su obra" by dint of will power. She speculates on having some physical tie with young Ramiro if his father was thinking of her, Tula, rather than Rosa when he was conceived. Conversely, she shudders at the thought that, were she to marry him, Ramiro might be thinking of Rosa while making love to her. The question of breast-feeding, for her an acceptable form of physical contact, greatly worries her. Unable to provide milk herself, she objects to hired wet-nurses and eventually takes a religious pride in artificial feeding which has the same fusion of maternal care and spurious motherhood as her role as aunt-mother. A similar physical function which brings her close to reproduction without sexual contact is midwifery: "es usted comadrona de nacimiento."

What critical attitude should be taken towards this novel in which the protagonist is portrayed as so self-assertive as completely to dominate the action? First, it must be reiterated that it is entirely inappropriate to apply the criteria of the realist novel to *La tía Tula* and its protagonist. Even the blanket approval or disapproval of her conduct discussed earlier is not altogether apposite to a novel which in the words of the suppressed prologue deals with abstractions and personified ideas, not social interaction. Indeed, if we were to consider the novel from the viewpoint of normal social relations, we might expect Tula's rigid rules on conduct, the meticulous exclusion of sex from the existence, half hive-like, half-conventual, of her household, to produce some violent reaction: an explosion of frustrated sexuality from her or from other characters, an attempt at independence from the children or at least some resentment of the restrictions imposed on them: something, say, of what occurs in Lorca's *La casa de Bernarda Alba.* On the contrary, Tula evokes admiration and emulation, and the novel ends on a note of continuity: the example of *la tía,* whatever her own doubts, continues into the next generation.

Yet many scholars are unable to forego inappropriate realistic or everyday presuppositions. Antonio Sánchez Barbudo, for instance, emphasizes Tula's real-life qualities, in exaggerated contrast with the fictionalized ideas which make up the protagonists of *Abel Sánchez, Dos madres* or *Raquel, encadenada:*

> A la tía Tula, en cambio, su pasión, la frustrada maternidad, que es la esencia de su ser, no le resta en modo alguno naturalidad, vida, verdad. Y es que ella, a pesar de lo que suele decirse al tratar de esta novela, no es un mero símbolo, no es una simple encarnación del "hambre" de maternidad . . . es un personaje vivo, *de carne y hueso* . . .

Other critics, more cautiously, stress her clearly defined personality, in contrast with the supine qualities of other characters, and several hanker after the denser social context of the realist tradition or else convince themselves, somewhat erroneously, that such a context is present."

The worst examples of the false application of realist criteria concern Tula's motivation. Thus Sánchez Barbudo without justification rewrites the story, giving it a Romantic twist of his imagining:

> Un amor "perfecto", "único." Esa idea romántica sin duda fue el sueño de la joven Gertrudis . . . Lo extraordinario es que ella se mantuviera siempre, aun después de todas sus

experiencias, aun en su madurez, firmemente aferrada a esa fantasía. La causa original del fracaso primero fue sin duda la timidez, la falta de voluntad de Ramiro. Y la desilusión hizo que ella se encerrara en sí.

From this he deduces a non-existent "resentimiento y encerramiento en sí misma, soledad al ver frustrado el sueño de un amor 'perfecto' y su ardiente deseo de ser madre" and that "no vivió contenta: no satisfizo nunca del todo su 'instinto de maternidad' ni se sintió tampoco muy feliz con su virginidad." In my view none of this is compatible with the existentialist tenor of Tula's story. Equally unjustifiable is Juan Rof Carballo's definition of the novel, "pese a la equivoca opinión de su propio autor(!)," as "la novela de la envidia femenina." This he explains by asserting that she is "varona por despecho amoroso, por haber sido su hermana y no ella la elegida." Even Ricardo Gullón falls into the trap of considering Tula resentful and vindictive: "No puede perdonar a Ramiro que prefiriese (siquiera un momento) a Rosa: y les hará pagar el pasajero hechizo."

David Turner has pointed out that Unamuno has written a clear "¡No!" in the margin of his copy of Julián Balseiro's *El vigía,* in which the writer declared that "A la tía Tula le impulsaba un sentimiento de venganza contra Ramiro." It is important in my view to establish that she is neither resentful of Rosa, nor desirous to marry Ramiro, nor frustrated by the circumstances of her life. Unamuno has deliberately set up a story in which external appearances create this impression, but we should be wary about being taken in in the same way as the characters are. Tula has in fact chosen her own path with the utmost deliberation and has imposed her own will systematically upon others: her doubts and her anguish, when they appear, are not about what others, individuals or society, have done to her but about the choice she herself has made. They are not in the least dependent on other people.

One of the most eloquent signs of the degree to which Tula is a supreme individualist, a loner, is the extraordinary degree of misunderstanding to which she is subject by other characters. These misunderstandings embrace all the significant characters of the novel except Don Primitivo, who is so overwhelmed by his niece's perception and intelligence that he does not even try to understand her. A few examples: when she plans to broach the subject of the date of the wedding with Ramiro . . . she anticipates two conventional misinterpretations (both of them "disparates") of her motives: "Dirá, si quiere, que es a mí a quien me conviene que tú te cases para facilitar así el que se me pretenda o para quedarme a mandar aquí sola." Her cheerfulness at the wedding gives rise to some surprise and criticism, which again reflect misunderstanding of her personality. Ricardo, the doctor Don Juan and the priest Padre Alvarez all signally fail to understand her motives, attributing to her designs on her brother-in-law (Ricardo and Don Juan) or resentment of Rosa and bruised pride (Padre Alvarez), while those nearest to her, Rosa and Ramiro, are equally incapable of penetrating fully into her psychology.

All these false interpretations of Tula's mentality link her with social or environmental forces rather than with an assertion of will. Only Ricardo Gullón has squarely faced the issue that Tula made at various stages a conscious, if painful, decision to pursue the course she did. She thus exemplifies two of Unamuno's most important pronouncements on the roots of human conduct. The first is his famous call in *Del sentimiento trágico* for every individual to strive to deserve immortality by making himself *insustituible:*

> Y el sentimiento de hacernos insustituibles, de no merecer la muerte, de hacer que nuestra aniquilación, si es que nos está reservada, sea una injusticia, no sólo debe llevarnos a cumplir religiosamente, por amor a Dios y a nuestra eternidad y eternización nuestro propio oficio, sino a cumplirlo apasionadamente, trágicamente, si se quiere. Debe llevarnos a esforzarnos por sellar a los demás con nuestro sello, por perpetuarnos en ellos y en sus hijos dominándoles, por dejar en todo imperecedera nuestra cifra. La más fecunda moral es la moral de la imposición mutua.

The second comes from the *Prólogo* to *Tres novelas ejemplares y un prólogo,* which is Unamuno's most forceful denunciation of realism and its effects on novel-writing. It is his adaptation of Oliver Wendell Holmes' comment in *The Autocrat at the Breakfast Table:*

> Y digo que, además del que uno es para Dios—si para Dios es uno alguien—y del que es para los otros y del que se cree ser, hay el que quisiera ser. Y que éste, el que uno quiere ser, es en él, en su seno, el creador, y es el real de verdad. Y por el que hayamos querido ser, no por el que hayamos sido, nos salvaremos o perderemos. Dios le premiará o castigará a uno a que sea por toda la eternidad lo que quiso ser.

La tía Tula is the supreme example of a woman who makes herself *insustituible* and imposes her will, consciously and consistently on herself and on her acquired family, in the name of a quasi-religious conviction.

"Her strong passion for maternity and aversion to men" may be, as Turner claims, "irremovable characteristics" or in the repeated words of the text "el tuétano de los huesos del alma," but they only determine her conduct to the extent she wills them to do so. Far from being an inevitable process ("No-one [and this includes Tula . . .] can avoid being what he or she is in the deepest part of his being"), Tula's self-willed itinerary through life (*el que hayamos querido ser*), whatever its real import (*el que hayamos sido*) will determine her salvation.

Will also determines length of life. Once a sense of purpose or mission is over death ensues. Don Primitivo fulfilled his mission and died. Rosa accomplished hers with her fertility and Tula herself suddenly deteriorates physically once her spiritual succession—Manolita—and the physical continuity of Ramiro's line—by Carita's pregnancy—are assured.

In his interesting recent article, Gonzalo Navajas is fully conscious of the role Tula's will plays in her decisions, as well as of the ambiguity of her conduct, but in my view he unnecessarily and misleadingly associates her contra-dictory impulses with the Lacanian categories of the Imaginary and the Symbolic. While one may readily concede that Tula suppresses the "Imaginary," the inner, intuitive life of the subject, in the interest of a different order of values, the latter does not seem to me to correspond to Lacan's Symbolic category, imposed on the individual from the outside, which may be figuratively called the Law. The second category is rather, as I see it, the rigid application of a conscious decision to follow her inbuilt urges; her will power, acknowledged by Navajas, is not a means to an end, but an end in itself.

On the other hand, the distinction Navajas makes, again following Lacan, between self and ego, seems to me a valid one:

> The self is the true identity of the subject, that part of him that conforms to a genuine mode of existence. The ego, on the other hand, is a falsified configuration of the self. It is a *persona,* a mask worn by the subject to supplant his real self, and conceal or deny the unsolved conflicts that rend his conscience.

As we shall see, Tula is seeking to determine and follow her authentic self, but she is wracked by doubts that she is simply adopting a false *persona.*

There is no doubt about the heroic and even saintly qualities towards which Tula's assertion of will drives her. This is accentuated by the astonishing subservience and admiration demonstrated by the other characters, Don Primitivo, Rosa, Ramiro and Manuela; instead of asserting themselves in any way, they are all abjectly grateful to her for her sacrificial virtues or forceful intelligence. She creates a household on a monastic ideal, "a religion of domesticity" as Turner calls it, with its strictly imposed cult of purity. Its essential feature therefore is the absolute equation of sexual activity—and, by extension all bodily secretions—with sin and filth. Thus the community she envisages is a peculiarly distorted one. It has certain curious feminist traits, in that she is determined to impose an aggressive view of women's priorities as she sees them upon her immediate, ostensibly male-dominated society. In her ideology, men have an unjustifiably dominant position despite their frivolity regarding the sole purpose of existence: procreation. They either play at life ("os jugáis al matrimonio") or they are *machista* ("de carne y muy brutos") mistaking the means—sex—for the end—reproduction. Priests like Don Primitivo and Father Alvarez and even Jesus himself share male prejudices. Not that women (with the exception of Tula herself and her designated successor) fare any better. They are allotted no function save procreation, and reduced to an almost vegetable existence, with no remission from child-bearing except death. In this world, all hint of sexual activity must be excluded; only within marriage is it encouraged, even at the expense of the couple's health. Otherwise, all effort must be made to avoid sexual commitment. Hence Tula's postponing of any decision on marrying Ramiro—crucial both to the action of the novel and to her psychology—her outrage at Father Alvarez's proposal of her being a Pauline remedy against sensuality and her contemptuous rejection of the harmless Don Juan. Children, however young, must see no sign of their parents' physical affection; any indication of Ramiro's attraction for Gertrudis is prohibited; Ramiro must beg his wife's pardon when his first child is born; Manuela's pregnancy must be concealed. The country, for Gertrudis, proves to be dangerous and provocative; she will not sit on the ground; the animals, even the sea breeze, may arouse carnal thoughts.

The model Unamuno proposes, of course, is the bee-hive, where according to an article written in 1920: "hay una [abeja] que los hombres llamamos reina, a la que un batallón de zánganos corteja para fecundarle y a la que mantienen y crían y educan las obreras, que son unas tías estériles, solteronas que trabajan y pican."

Bees are also referred to in similar terms in the text of the novel. Gertrudis commands that they should not be harmed:

> —Sé lo que son las abejas estas, las que pican y
> hacen la miel; sé lo que es la reina y sé también
> lo que son los zánganos.
> —Los zánganos somos nosotros, los hombres
> [adds Ramiro].
> —Claro está.

In this analogy where the men are drones and the mass of women queen bees, conditioned to the one task of childbearing, the active and aggressive force is that of the worker-bees, *tías estériles, solteronas que trabajan y pican,* like, of course, *la tía Tula.*

The fullest working out of the parallel of the hive comes later at a crucial moment of the story when Manolita's inheritance of Tula's spiritual authority is discussed.

> ¿Herencia? Se transmite por herencia en una colmena el espíritu de las abejas, la tradición abejil, el arte de la melificación y de la fábrica del panal, la *abejidad,* no se transmite, sin embargo, por carne y por jugos de ella. La carnalidad se perpetúa por zánganos y por reinas . . . La tradición del arte de las abejas . . . no de transmisión de carne, sino de espíritu . . . débese a las tías, a las abejas que ni fecundan huevecillos ni los ponen. Y todo esto lo sabía Manolita, a quien se lo había enseñado la Tía . . .

Here the distinction between carnal inheritance through queen bees and drones and spiritual inheritance which derives from the *abejidad* of the worker-bees, is clear-cut. Thus Tula is able to transmit her spirit to a weakling child who has none of her blood: a supreme defiance of natural laws. The parallel is an apposite one, though it is worth noting that it breaks down on two points. First, on the question of numbers: in the natural world, there is one queen bee or breeder to hordes of sterile workers: by contrast, in Tula's world, there is only one worker-bee at a time and an unlimited supply—we have only two in the story, but more are available—of queen bees. Second, only the literary parallel Unamuno is establishing can justify calling worker-bees *tías.* And Tula resents the insinuation, from Don Juan, that she herself might be thought of as sterile, except by her own volition.

How far can Tula's example be extended into a wider context? In the *Prólogo* specially, as the identification with the spiritual values, at once homely and Quixotic, of St There-

sa and that of such self-sacrificing heroines as Antigone and Abishag, indicate, the potentiality is there, though it is not realized in the novel itself where neither of the latter two figures are mentioned. Unamuno seems to have a future project, not fully carried out, in mind. In the case of Antigone, indeed, a female order of priorities—religious domesticity versus purely civic virtues, anarchist individualism versus official tyranny: what Unamuno calls *matria* and *sororidad* as opposed to *patria* and *fraternidad*—is outlined which goes well beyond Tula's domestic religion, capable of enduring after her death, appeasing the children's divisions and strife in the interests of spiritual continuity. It is depicted, moreover, as superior to the traditional masculine cult of aggression, envy and *machismo* exemplified by Cain's murder of his brother. It would be unwise, however, in my view to take this as representing Unamuno's considered opinion of the role of women in society. Rather it should be noted that it is only one of many possible extreme positions taken up momentarily. As *Abel Sánchez* demonstrates, the apparently antithetical masculine principle—creative fraternal strife—is, equally paradoxically, applauded. The important thing is that both are assertions of the naked will and it is the pushing of these assertions to extremes, not the underlying doctrine, which is held up for admiration.

Although such self-projection is given apparently favoured treatment, its negative features are also implied, as well as being openly voiced in Tula's doubts. The two sides of the problem are shown in the key phrase of Ramiro's, uttered after the birth of Manuela's first child and reiterated by Tula on his deathbed: "Eres una santa, Gertrudis— pero una santa que ha hecho pecadores . . .." Sanctity, then, achieved at the expense of others? or, as Tula herself adds, "Acaso he tenido una idea inhumana de la virtud." Yet her next riposte on the first occasion: "Soy una pecadora que me esfuerzo por hacer santos; santos a tus hijos, a ti y a tu mujer" offers another alternative: a sinner who sacrifices herself for others. As such, it is strikingly similar to a possible formulation of Don Manuel Bueno's situation: "un ateo que ha hecho sanos y fieles a sus feligreses," though Don Manuel can certainly not be said to have "una idea inhumana de la virtud."

Tula certainly had a decisive effect on the children, Ramiro and Rosa, forcing them to follow a traditional code of values, but without independence of judgement. In what way, though, was her conduct sinful? This is a subject which she dwells on increasingly, . . . linking her solitude with the culpable effects of proud isolation: "¿No es soberdia esto? ¿No es la triste pasión del armiño que por no mancharse no se echa a nado en un lodazal a salvar a su compañero?" According to this viewpoint, pride, the sin of self-assertion against God's will in the form of an aloof cult of purity, would replace sexual involvement, still considered besmirched, as the real sin. In the course of the narrative her doubts increase and culminate in her denunciation of her cult of purity and all it implies in her deathbed harangue:

> . . . pensadlo muy bien . . . que nunca tengáis
> que arrepentiros de haber hecho algo y menos de
> no haberlo hecho . . . Y si veis que el que
> queréis se ha caído en una laguna de fango y aun-

que sea en un pozo negro, en un albañal, echaos a salvarle, aun a riesgo de ahogaros, . . . servidle de remedio, sí, de remedio . . . ¿que morís entre légamo y porquerías?, no importa . . . Es lo último que os digo, no tengáis miedo a la podredumbre.

What are we to make of this? Within the novel, Father Alvarez thinks she is prematurely senile, *chocha.* Frances Wyers sees it as a further twist in her self-centred thinking: "such debasement is really a roundabout way of winning control, a self-punishing detour to perfect saintliness." Accordingly, she perceives it within the structure of the novel as an example of the "strange cross purposes and apparent reversals" she discerns in the novels as a whole: a shifting of gears a duplicity, a double-mindedness which is part of a "divided aspiration" and which obscures the destructiveness of the "creative will" in a wishful ending.

Wyers has also done much to explain Unamuno's technique of opposites, describing him as "a person who veers ceaselessly between mutually exclusive and ultimately self-defeating aims," but the last phrase reveals that perhaps she does not fully appreciate that Unamuno seeks no resolution of his contradictions. Within her well-reasoned arguments there is an assumption that such a reconciliation is possible or desirable, whereas in fact Unamuno's incomplete dialectic is of a permanent and irreconcilable confrontation of opposites, with no attempt at all at a synthesis. Clearly, it is quite legitimate to criticise Unamuno for this characteristic, which no doubt accounts, understandably, for the critical tone of her book, but it is important to realise that this was deliberate policy on Unamuno's part: the ending is ambiguous rather than wishful.

Finally, a second line of thought which obsesses the dying Tula should be indicated. Her evil thought, which she calls "un susurro diabólico," is that all the children (all her family perhaps) are like the doll she has retained from her childhood: "¡Muñecas todos!" As has been pointed out, this exclamation reveals that she is conscious that she has been reducing them to the level of playthings, without freewill; but more important are the ontological implications, linked with her declaration on her deathbed (is she *chocha?*) that she does not really exist and never has. If Unamuno's conviction that human beings act singlemindedly in such a way as to deserve immortality does not hold, then they, and Tula with them, are reduced to a state of predetermined puppets, lacking freewill, with no authentic existence, like Augusto Pérez in *Niebla,* at least according to his creator and his own inner despair. Tula's doubts about the course of action on which she had built her life thus bring in their train distrust of the very existence of meaningful life. The alternative possibility, that of despair, that the assertive individual, be he Alejandro Gómez, Joaquín Montenegro or Unamuno himself, is after all playing a role, as an *histrión,* that immortality is a vain aspiration, represents the duality present in all Unamuno's fiction and is essential for the structure of the work.

Is Tula initially right, then, in rejecting a conventional life by marrying Ramiro and imposing her individualist concept of existence so unequivocally on all around her? Or

> *La tía* Tula is therefore a figure who . . . has to be judged . . . as a character who within a given human or psychological context is working out a particular aspect of those problems of existence, belief and conduct which obsessed Unamuno. Tula's character may and no doubt does arouse the most diverse reactions on the readers of her story, irritating, astonishing or disturbing them, but it represents in an oblique but forceful fashion Unamuno's own very considerable capacity and desire to irritate, astonish and disturb.
>
> —*Geoffrey Ribbans*

are her final denunciations of her actions as examples of sinful pride and exclusiveness valid? The question is left undetermined just as Unamuno remained in agonised uncertainty about survival after death. The whole novel is based essentially on this ambivalence: the inbuilt contradiction or paradox at the centre of his existence reflected in the parallel paradox at the centre of that of his created character. Since his public stance is of strident and provocative assertion of the irrational and the impossible, he appears to hold up *la tía* Tula as a model of resolution, imposition of positive values, a female proponent of domestic virtue; yet her doubts about her distinctive exclusivist role correspond to Unamuno's own. Just as Gertrudis aspired to a world in which motherhood could be had without sexual intercourse, but comes to doubt the validity of her own exclusiveness, so Unamuno yearns for a world in which death does not mean annihilation, but finds himself obliged at times to resign himself despairingly to mortality as other men do.

La tía Tula is therefore a figure who, like all Unamuno's protagonists or *agonistas,* has to be judged, not in relation with conventional notions of realism, verisimilitude or social representativeness, but as a character who within a given human or psychological context is working out a particular aspect of those problems of existence, belief and conduct which obsessed Unamuno. Tula's character may and no doubt does arouse the most diverse reactions on the readers of her story, irritating, astonishing or disturbing them, but it represents in an oblique but forceful fashion Unamuno's own very considerable capacity and desire to irritate, astonish and disturb. (pp. 403-18)

> *Geoffrey Ribbans, "A New Look at 'La tía Tula',"* in Revista Canadiense de Estudios Hispánicos, *Vol. XI, No. 2, Winter, 1987, pp. 403-20.*

Rose Marie Marcone (essay date 1987)

[*In the following essay, Marcone defines and discusses the role of the impostor in* San Manuel Bueno, mártir, Nada menos que todo un hombre, *and* Abel Sánchez.]

Much discussion centers on Unamuno's use of doubles and fragmentation as attempts to analyze the relationship of the self to the other and to the self. But Unamuno's motif of the divided self serves still another purpose: to display human error. Seen in this light, his characters are not suffering, introspective persons searching for the truth, but, instead, are calculating individuals trying to manipulate and to adjust to their circumstances. In this context, they are not to be viewed as victims of uncontrollable events, but as individuals contributing to their situations.

If Unamuno destroys the notion of a fixed human identity, his characters must do something to deal with their situation. Their attempts to cope constitute the story of the "nivolas" and relate a moral message as well: Unamuno reveals the frail, egotistical, and ineffective human personality as an impostor responsible for any misfortune which befalls him. Clearly, Unamuno's characters are involved in role playing as they enact the essential cause of their tragedy: the erroneous belief that man can order his own being. This postulate, which dominates the characters behavior, illustrates the misuse of reason or the tragic flaw which leads to their demise. The "nivolas" demonstrate the futile efforts to control the "yo" and become, in effect, one pattern unifying this prose.

Unamuno is emblematic of the introspective mind obsessed with its individuality and powerlessness. His tragic view of man shows him absorbed by the dissolution of his image while attempting to design some way to give meaning to his life and identity. The result is a fragmented self-vision which is the only logical consequence of the ruse or game in which Unamuno's characters are involved.

And the words "game" and "ruse" are appropriate terms, indeed, to describe the characters' engagement with life. Illusions are the fabric of which Unamuno's novels are made, for in this fiction we encounter characters whose intent is to exist in the imagination of others. In this way, the characters are recreated through the ideals of a fiction or the false vision they project of the self. Against visible facts, doubts and suspicions, Unamuno's protagonists strive to initiate and preserve the illusion that the others have of them. And to accomplish this task, the characters assume a posture which fits the form of the illusion. It is only fair to say that Unamuno's protagonists are caught up in a world of acting. The recreated "yo" as the image of the other functions like a marionette as the author creates characters with removable facades or obvious deceptions. The facade is, in a sense, a mask or concealed face which is the instrument used to create and to perpetuate the image. This gesture emanates from the characters' yearning for a singleness of vision in which appearance and reality coincide since in this capacity the "yo" can control the self and is saved from the intervention and interpretation by the other. However, inspite of all efforts, their wish remains distinct from their reality as the individuals witness discrepancy as the rule which governs their behavior and not the longed for complementarity. The novelistic tension consists of the creation and subsequent shattering of the illusion of a unified self-vision or what will be called in this study, the ruse of the mask. The

movement from illusion to truth is the movement from mask to face as the protagonists exchange fiction for life, tragic as it may be, with their unmasking. The psychic malaise generated by this failure to control the paradoxical self, or the way it is and the way it appears, results in the anxiety of frustrated efforts and unrealized ideals.

Unamuno's novels enact the dialectic of the mask or the story of characters who fail to live up to the unrealistic dreams they impose. They conclude with the destruction of the desired image and even with the unauthenticity of their identity. Unamuno has set out to reveal strategies and to strip away artifices since he believes that everyone has chosen the gesture which would permit him to dodge himself, others, and all painful truths, if only temporarily. The process of masking and unmasking is Unamuno's narrative design and the thematic nucleus which will be examined in three "nivolas"; *San Manuel Bueno, mártir, Nada menos que todo un hombre,* and *Abel Sánchez.*

San Manuel Bueno, mártir is more than a study of a religious struggle and the conflicting relationships of man and God. We must consider the novel in terms of the tragic circumstances precipitated by the misuse of reason in an individual who is in conflict with his self and his society. Manuel is an active agent contributing to his dilemma. If we consider that what happened to him is unavoidable, we are in error. The core of Manuel's tragic situation lies in the fact that long before the novel opens, he confronted a choice: whether to confess his doubt or to play the role of a faithful priest, the mask he assumes. His position that the truth of doubt would be too heavy a burden for the people to bear is, in part, a rationalization to relieve his anxieties. Clearly, Manuel had the possibility of choice which he did indeed exercise. His wrong choice is to assume an unauthentic posture which fails to unite the aspects of his self just as it fails to unite him with the society that he attempts to console. His interaction with his congregation causes anxiety and guilt, and this combination adds to his despair and loneliness. We can, in this light, interpret much of Manuel's characterization as an attempt to cope with these conflicting forces while at the same time trying to establish human relationships. His association with Ángela and Lázaro relieves the feeling of separation since he shares with them the secret of the disbelief that initiated his tragic circumstance: "Oíd: cuidad de estas pobres ovejas, que se consuelen de vivir, que crean lo que yo no he podido creer." These words, and other statements spoken by Manuel in moments of truth, constitute his unmasking. Ángela and Lázaro are aware of the miscarriage of reason which comprises Manuel's deception or "piadoso fraude" and which causes his departure from the world where his authentic self could be established and function.

Manuel's retreat from truthful and meaningful relationships, caused by his ruse, symbolizes, in a sense, his avoidance of life which his admissions reverse as they engage him fully with his complex self. Unamuno comments on the crisis of moral values which leads to a temporary loss of self. As Manuel demonstrates, one must be true to himself in the final analysis. The novel becomes the narration of confessions which allow Manuel to free his complete self and which permit the reader to make a moral judgment. On the one hand, we can sympathize with the suffering priest. But on the other, we note his egocentricity. As a priest, he attempted to uphold the ideals of sanctity which allowed him to escape the unholy humanity and egocentric will of a doubter. Manuel's facade removed him, if only partially, from the world of doubt and misery in order to be venerated. He knew enough about people and their weaknesses to know that his ruse would bring him heroism in their eyes. He would be their model teaching them how to die well.

In *Nada menos que todo un hombre,* the ruse of the mask is enacted, above all, by Alejandro. The novel leads us through a maze woven of paradoxes and conflicts in which the unifying thread seems to be the belief that the greatest illusion of all is to believe that illusions can solve one's dilemma. Once again, as in *San Manuel Bueno, mártir,* appearance contradicts reality as we witness the perplexing relationships of the self to the other and consequently, the self to the self. The seemingly self-assured Alejandro, convinced that the posture he assumes will be his strength, effectively hides his insecurities and gradually assumes authority over Julia. The novel is one of revelation. The story evolves from the character of Alejandro who, unlike Manuel, could never engage in the narration of confessions nor acknowledge the truth about himself. In fact, Alejandro's misuse of reason is his decision to hide the truth. He does everything to avoid actions or events that will result in suspicions or admissions. His attempts to misrepresent the self accelerate the dissolution of his relationship with his wife and forces Julia to extramarital flirtation. But Alejandro pays for his error and for his wrong belief that he could control the paradoxial self.

Part of Alejandro's problem relates to the matter of love. The love that Julia bore for him is made of understanding and forgiveness. Alejandro, weak and truly without a clear identity of which we are aware, finds such sentiment incomprehensible and even intolerable. His references to love are demeaning. He responds to Julia's declaration of love: "Bueno, ya te he dicho que no me gustan frases de novelas sentimentales. Cuanto menos se diga que se le quiere a uno, mejor." And so he remains indifferent to affection perhaps because he fears that the expression of love will lead to self-revelation or because he does not know how to love another or how to deal with his emotive self. Whatever the case may be, his inability to return love is a major source of his anxiety. His failure to love underscores Alejandro's feeling of helplessness which he successfully conceals until the end of the novel at which time his weakness is magnified and leads to his self-destruction. He is haunted by the ruse and fictions that he created. He is unable to bear the loathsome reminder of his misdirection and is unmasked. Without Julia, there is nothing to give his life security and meaning. His previously strong self-affirmations are reversed in the confession he makes to Julia: "Yo? Nada más que tu hombre . . ., el que tú me has hecho." The tables are turned as we see Alejandro for what he is: less than heroic and nothing more than an egotist.

The characters, Abel and Joaquín, in *Abel Sánchez* present interesting studies of "yoismo". With raw egocentricity, each sees the other as an extension of himself and something which he must master. They represent, in different ways, the basic drives for power and pleasure. As a consequence, they become destructive when their drives are either frustrated or threatened. Since these moments occur at different times in the novel and mark the dramatic tension of the prose, we witness an alternating pattern of role-playing as one or the other gains the superior position in the ruse of masks.

Although admittedly a novel of confession, *Abel Sánchez* is, more accurately, a novel of interrogation: that is, a novel of self-interrogation and interrogation of the other. We note that the structure differs from the confessions which constitute *San Manuel Bueno, mártir.* If Manuel's words, through Ángela's transcription, are an admission of failures and weakness, Joaquín's observations are an inquiry into the motives for failures and weakness. And Joaquín's interrogation produces a response. That response is envy. The motive is most directly stated when Joaquin and Abel confront each other as rivals for Helena's affection. As Helena is the object over which to wield power and to give Joaquin pleasure, Abel, in the influence he exerts on Helena, is a serious threat to Joaquín as he has always been. Joaquín must respond to that threat and does so in the only way he knows: by consuming himself and the other with envy. However, the novel contains a unique variation on the use of masks. Unlike Manuel and Alejandro, the main character, Joaquín, begins unmasked, revealing himself with all his weakness and interrogating himself for the causes. It is not until the banquet speech that Joaquín assumes the mask of self-control and overshadows his life-long enemy, Abel. At this moment, Abel, who role-played throughout the novel, is unmasked and admits his inferiority to Joaquín, his envied rival: "Joaquín, lo que acabas de decir vale más, mucho más, que mi cuadro, más que todos los cuadros que he pintado, más que todos los que pintaré . . ., Eso, eso es una obra de arte y de corazón. Yo no sabía lo que he hecho hasta que te he oído. Tú, y no yo, has hecho mi cuadro, tú!"

As the novel progresses, we note that the interchange between the two characters has one constant theme: one is a continued threat to the other. Each is a potential conquest which will affect the other's development. And, in effect, the characters' development can be understood in their attempts to overcome the other. Each is an image of total self-absorption which nurtures his selfishness and insecurity. This portrayal of the two characters reveals human misery and with it, the ruse or game enacted in the novel: at best, a test of endurance to overcome and to overshadow the other. In fact, the reason for their existence is to conquer the other. As the characters move closer to moments of truth, their will to live wanes, as evidenced by their failing health. The masks are permanently removed: Abel and Joaquín reveal their mutual weakness as victims of envy, the real illness which plagued them all their life. Without masks, they cannot live for they cannot suffer the truth of their existence. Joaquín well summarizes the agony of life unmasked: "¿Salvarme? Y a qué llamas salvarse? . . . ¿Para qué? ¿Para llegar a viejo? . . . No, no quiero llegar a viejo. Reñiría con los nietos por celos . . ., ¡les odiaría! . . . No, no . . .; ¡basta de odio!"

But if Joaquín admits his sins, one wonders in what resides his misuse of reason. Like Abel, his error is to subjugate reason to passion. His castigation of fate as the cause of his situation is a poor excuse for what he should have been able to control. With his confessions, Joaquín is free to disclose the passion consuming him. But Unamuno does not give Joaquín freedom from hate. We must not misconstrue Unamuno's message. He gives Joaquín freedom for self-realization. The path does not necessarily lead to control of self or cure of affliction but to knowledge of self. And it is this self-knowledge that causes Joaquín, unmasked, to end his futile attempts to order his being. This conclusion deserves a bit more discussion since it relates to Unamuno's tragic view of humanity.

In reality, Joaquín can do nothing to change himself. He is unable to do so, and the responsibility is his. Likewise, Abel cannot change himself and feels no urgency to make such an attempt so long as pretense and satisfying false images of himself exist to nourish his "yo". But Abel is finally revealed as are Manuel, Alejandro, and Joaquín, and these relevations are, indeed, significant. The sense of emptiness and isolation expressed by each of these characters is no longer a unique condition but becomes a more general experience as Unamuno implies the case of a egocentric generation absorbed by self-love and possessing no belief in the need for divine retribution. Man has appointed himself his only guardian and redeemer. He has no aspiration to heaven and is here in this world trying to work things out for himself, even if his efforts are marked by deception and end in futility. Although Unamuno reveals the limits of human intelligence which can be ensnared with its own ideas and designs, he recognizes the vital function of this intelligence to analyze subjective reality. And with this realization, Unamuno proposes the secular idea that man is responsible to and for himself, imperfect as he may be. Whatever he learns about his self will be sought in this existence and will be uncovered through his own efforts. Unamuno attempts to convince the reader that the best one can do in this life is to cope with one's circumstance, and for this reason, this prose probes the asperities of existence.

These observations suggest a definition of Unamuno's humanism which can be labeled a philosophy of resistance. In fact, this ideology underscores the conflicts which occur in the "nivolas". Each protagonist asserts his independence from established structures, systems of belief, and behavior which would insure effective communication and socialization. Each character is an emblem of existential will which places the individual's destiny within his own control as he assumes sole responsibility for his existence, no matter what the cost may be. But Unamuno remains realistic inspite of the ambitious goal that he sets for his characters as he views the ensuing tragedy each will encounter: given this scenario of one against the world, his protagonists can only fail, be culpable for their mistakes, and face the consequences alone. They are the victims of their own machinations. (pp. 66-71)

Rose Marie Marcone, "Unamuno's Impostors: An Approach to the 'Nivolas'," in Neophilologus, *Vol. LXXI, No. 1, January, 1987, pp. 66-71.*

Phillip Williams   (essay date 1989)

[*In the following excerpt, Williams illustrates how Unamuno combines male and female attributes in the protagonist of* Saint Emmanuel the Good, Martyr.]

Miguel de Unamuno's reputation in the English-speaking world rests primarily on his discursive religious writing, owing to the disproportionate—and perhaps unjustified—influence of his *Tragic Sense of Life.* Unamuno himself exalted his novelistic production, exemplified by *Mist,* above his essays, viewing the former as his most universalized work. Unamuno poured so much of his personality into his fictional worlds that his thought, *always* oriented toward religious problems, finds its most sustained expression in the fictional arena. The depth of Unamuno's contribution to modern theological discourse can only be sounded by taking into account the central role of his philosophic novel as a form (for him, *the* privileged form) of theological thought.

Unamuno's last and perhaps greatest novel, **Saint Emmanuel the Good, Martyr** (1933), recapitulates his fictional enterprise from an angle not previously explored in his long and productive career. This novel has been almost universally praised for its literary qualities. What has not yet been recognized is the way in which **Saint Emmanuel** enables Unamuno to see a new relationship between gender and the "problem of personality," the central issue—encompassing questions of identity and perdurance—preoccupying all his novels. From this last fictional vista, Unamuno both alludes to and radically questions the theological strategies of the previous novels. The present study will consider the breakthrough in Unamuno's religious thought that **Saint Emmanuel** involves, through the advancement of a different, partially discontinuous narrative model designed to explore the nature of human personality. In this final reworking of the metaphysical problems that had preoccupied him since he began to write, Unamuno goes beyond Don Quixote, the figure of religious transcendence that had captivated him earlier, coming instead to find in the maternal role—paradoxically exemplified by the Christ-like Emmanuel—a model of action.

In the prologue to the 1933 collection of his final novellas, among which appears **Saint Emmanuel,** Unamuno reveals what he considers to be the crux of his novelistic thought. He writes, concerning the fictional beings of his imagination: "What poisoned them all was the awesome problem of personality, if one *is,* and will continue to be, what one is." It is, in other words, the age-old question of being itself and the related problem of human continuity that quickens his fictional characters. But Unamuno confesses that this is precisely the same problem that has haunted him throughout the years. He links the dilemma of these latest novelistic children to the same idée fixe that has inspired him to create almost all his fictional personages:

> It is not a question of a special state of mind which seized me upon writing, in a little over two months, these three novellas, but rather a general state of mind in which I have persisted since I began to write. That problem, that torment, better said, of the consciousness of one's

own personality, an anguished state of mind sometimes tragic and at other times comic, is what has inspired me for the creation of almost all my fictional characters.

In order to exemplify this anguished state of mind, Unamuno turns immediately to the case of Emmanuel, the priest described in the title novella of the collection, whose tragic longing for immortality parallels Unamuno's own. Since Emmanuel cannot believe in the Christian doctrine of the resurrection of the dead, he can count only on his exemplary life of charity to assure him a kind of immortality in the communal memory of the village of Valverde de Lucerna.

Unamuno, in this same passage, goes on, finally, to note the appearance of this problem of personality in the work of other authors, singling out Cervantes and the seventeenth-century Spanish dramatist Calderón de la Barca in particular. Writing near the end of a long and productive literary career that included novels, poetry, dramas, and religious and philosophic essays, Unamuno in this introduction to his last fictional works makes the phrase "problem of personality" function as a kind of metonymic summa for his own life in language (i.e., *his* personality). In this late formulation, coming near the end of his life, of the religious gestalt that has shaped his own fictional quests as well as his readings of other authors, Unamuno continues to emphasize the longing for immortality as an essential component of personality, while viewing it within a broader context of search for identity. The "unpacking" of the development of this issue in Unamuno's fiction appears virtually indistinguishable from an analysis of the problem in the life of Unamuno; both of these levels converge in *Saint Emmanuel* as the issue of gender identity comes to the forefront.

If Unamuno himself is at pains to emphasize similarity, placing Emmanuel on a continuum of questers drawn from Unamuno's other fiction as well as the works of other Spanish authors, it is perhaps the discontinuities that reveal most about the nature of Unamuno's novelistic achievement in this work. Emmanuel proves radically dissimilar from all of Unamuno's other fictional protagonists because of a deeper apprehension, on the part of character and author, of the maternal dimension in life, art, and religion.

One's mode of self-definition differs radically for men and women in the Unamunian novel. The final mediation of these gender-dependent differences in *Saint Emmanuel* produces Unamuno's most articulated novelistic treatment of the "anguished and glorious problem of personality," as Unamuno succeeds in moving beyond the model originally furnished by Cervantes's Don Quixote to a new synthesis, an image of a maternal Christ. Unamuno's wholesale adoption of a quixotic persona in his own life and work is all too well known. His choice of Don Quixote, one of the most beloved of all Spanish fictional characters, as mediator was *not* esoteric. In his idiosyncratic interpretations of Don Quixote, Unamuno had already anticipated, in a certain measure, the theological breakthrough of *Saint Emmanuel* with his reading of Cervantes's novel *au rebours,* sketching in, in numerous essays

and in *Our Lord Don Quixote,* a whole tragic background where virtually none existed in the comic Cervantine landscape. It is only with *Saint Emmanuel,* however, that Unamuno takes the final, definitive step in his radical reworking of Western narrative models, making an explicit connection between the feminine and the story of the life of Christ. If we regard Don Quixote as the key paradigmatic myth of the life of Unamuno, in a fashion similar to Lévi-Strauss's discovery of the central generating myth of the Bororo Indians, then *Saint Emmanuel* must be understood as the narrative moment of discontinuity, of rupture. In this final novel, Unamuno breaks with his quixotic mentor. As the culmination of Unamuno's fictional thought, Emmanuel marks the passage from the Cervantine Don Quixote as spiritual monad to a new cultural hero who unites Christ and the divine Androgyne, a male figure who paradoxically embodies the role of Mother, a paternal womb/wound open to the world.

Women in the fiction of Unamuno possess a privileged status that sets them apart from men. They rarely fabricate words, they seldom become famous, but because they have the potential, through their role as mothers, for creating life physically and spiritually, women most often develop a sense of identity and find a kind of personal salvation de facto through maternity. The meaning of "maternity" in Unamuno's novels does not remain static, to be sure. The concept expands from the limited, and sometimes limiting, female role of childbearing and child rearing to the embrace, in *Saint Emmanuel,* by both sexes, of the universal Christian concept of *caritas,* which involves a kind of spiritual maternity, the playing of the part of the mother to any suffering person.

Unamuno, for most of his career, tends, like Freud, to write from the viewpoint of the male in his assaying of religious and philosophic issues. Whereas a woman most often discovers her identity preestablished in the maternal role (as a sizable portion of Unamuno's fiction on mothers and motherhood attests), the male in Unamuno's fiction is characteristically a quester, a kind of Don Quixote who attempts to save his personality eternally through fame. In his lifelong fascination with the Don Quixote myth, Unamuno himself often appears emblematic of the Western tradition's emphasis on heroic deeds in the individual's quest for glory (the writer's apotheosis). It is essentially the male quest, the masculine striving to mitigate, on some level, the finality of death through children of the flesh, through children of the spirit, that preoccupies Unamuno for much of his career. In this respect, he stands in a long tradition of male seekers, from Homer to Melville to Mishima. History from such a perspective remains essentially a male domain, the public arena of masculine deeds in which men define their identities. Unamuno's essentially masculinist view of reality successively converts immortality, religion, life itself into metaphorical battles to be aggressively engaged in and won.

In tension with this view, there also develops from Unamuno's earliest writings a strong countertextual vein that calls into question this dominant theme of self-definition through spiritual dominion. This other voice reveals itself both in Unamuno's fascination with the psychological and metaphysical life of women, evidenced above all in his narrative portrayal of their maternal role, and in the concept of *intro-historia,* "inner history," the unconscious, routine daily activities of life beneath or within the surface drama of historical events.

These two countertextual elements, furthermore, prove intimately linked. The balancing of history with *intra-historia,* of man with woman, in Unamuno's writings up until **Saint Emmanuel,** sometimes involves the classic stereotypical view of woman as foil, mollifier, or complement to man's essentially aggressive nature. Eugenia del Arco of *Mist* represents the comic inversion of this ideal, of course. She is strong; she earns a living; she is violent. With **Saint Emmanuel,** Unamuno reaches the end of his trajectory of male voyaging, turning away from quests and metaquests in a way comparable to Prospero's breaking his staff and burying his book at the end of *The Tempest* or Lévi-Strauss's fond farewell to savages at the conclusion of his autobiographical *Tristes Tropiques.* Unlike the other male protagonists of Unamuno's novels, Emmanuel has given up all desire to exist in the heroic public arena; this renunciation takes place before the novel opens. Focusing his ministry on the daily life of a backwater Spanish village, Emmanuel lives in *intra-historia.* In the first paragraph of the novel, Angela paradoxically identifies him as "that matriarchal man," for Emmanuel has entered the domain of the feminine.

If woman most characteristically finds her own self-identity through maternal love in Unamuno's fiction, it is obviously not the way Don Quixote of *Our Lord Don Quixote* and Augusto Pérez of *Mist* consciously seek their identities. Paradoxically, identity through maternal love is perhaps the most important aspect of how Emmanuel searches for resolution to his metaphysical anguish. Why does this transformation come about in Unamuno's last novel?

Certainly, the image of maternal love arises from the ashes of Unamuno's fondest hope for some form of supernatural transcendence of death. The key issue of personality in Unamuno's thought, an issue encompassing the related problems of identity and perdurance, comes to hinge, in this final novelistic rethinking, upon the maternal, apparently out of despair over both the Christian "solution" to eternal life and the shadowy immortality of name and fame. The role of the mother (not the flesh-and-blood mother but the spiritual mother, who may paradoxically be a father) in **Saint Emmanuel** provides a biological or "natural" analogue of eternity, in Unamuno's turning away from the hero's *askesis* within a Greek, male-oriented view of the heroic quest for immortality. The mystic perception of eternity *in* time that permeates the fictional realm of **Saint Emmanuel** engages a whole other order of thought and imagery than that typified by Saint Paul's characterization of the active Christian life in the metaphors of battle and race. Personality still appears as an ongoing historical project that only death finalizes (in the sense of both ending and completion), but the emphasis has shifted from the pursuit of immortality through public, heroic deeds to an infinite valuation of "women's work." In virtually Unamuno's final word on the subject,

this latter type of immortality, born of a maternal compassion for the sufferings of others who, in turn, preserve one's personality after death in memory, proves more real, more satisfying, than the heroic name and fame of a Don Quixote.

A biological male who performs what traditional Western society characterizes as the role of the female, Emmanuel succors the sick, salvages wrecked marriages, takes an interest in maternity cases and the care of children, looks after his deceased sister's children, finds a stepfather for an illegitimate child, reconciles parents to their children, provides for the poor, helps the village teacher, plays with the children, consoles the embittered and the weary in spirit, watches over the village idiot, and helps everyone to die well. Whereas Augusto Pérez in *Mist* is linked unconsciously with the feminine, Emmanuel by contrast actively chooses to identify himself with the feminine role, a choice charged not only with psychological and social but religious implications as well.

> The question of life after death almost always presupposes that only the life of ego, the life of the individual self, is worth considering. Spiritual quixotism, the egocentric quest for immortality, gives way in [*Saint Emmanuel the Good, Martyr*] to a more tranquil vision of the eternal realm as a dimension of this life in which the individual participates but which ultimately transcends ego.
>
> —*Phillip Williams*

In the exchange of one view of immortality for another, time and eternity in **Saint Emmanuel** appear fused (or better, perhaps, time appears as the temporal unfolding of eternity). Through the image of the mother, Unamuno negotiates this radical shift. The mother, through her attachment to blood, to soil, is more firmly rooted in the natural world than her male counterpart. An immanentist view of divinity or eternity in the novel seems inescapably linked to the image of the mother, in contrast to the transcendent father. By converging seeming opposites in the figure of the "matriarchal man" Emmanuel, Unamuno symbolically recovers the pre-Judeo-Christian fascination with both the powerful, eternal feminine and the role of nature in the image of divinity.

In Unamuno's symbolist novel, the relation between names and things does not appear arbitrary as it does in the realist novel (and in conventional language usage outside a fictional context). Emmanuel bears one of the names of Christ—one which Unamuno has obviously chosen with care because of its maternal connotations—and he embodies its meaning, which signifies not transcendence but *presence* ("God with us"). In a manner parallel to Christ's mediating role in the gospel narratives, Emmanuel as novelistic symbol balances the polarities of doubt and faith, life and death, time and eternity, and, Unamuno would have us consider, male and female. Incarnating both psychosexual roles, Emmanuel significantly gives precedence to the feminine. He represents the structural inverse of that Christ of the Gospel of the Egyptians who declares: "I have come to destroy the works of the female." The exchange of the model of the extroverted personality typified by the knight errant for the introverted androgynous saint in this novel involves a structure of plottable transformations, perhaps the most important of which consists of the repositioning of the feminine in the place of the divine.

The question of life after death almost always presupposes that only the life of ego, the life of the individual self, is worth considering. Spiritual quixotism, the egocentric quest for immortality, gives way in Unamuno's last novel to a more tranquil vision of the eternal realm as a dimension of this life in which the individual participates but which ultimately transcends ego. The eternal becomes equated in Unamuno with history which has recognized *intra-historia* as its most truthful inner depths, in the shift of focus from the heroic posture to a Zen-like appreciation of the smallest details of daily existence. True history as the manifestation of human consciousness involves the temporal process of transformation of the personal, the individual, the determinate, into the universal. Like the ancient Homeric heroes, Emmanuel is assured survival in the heaven of communal memory that pronounces his name blessed instead of cursed. Unlike them, his beatitude springs from his devotion to *caritas* in its most idealized Christian expression of self-sacrifice for others.

Clearly, from Emmanuel's example, one's uniqueness alone does not, in the final analysis, hold out the possibility of transcendence of death. Not through one's isolated idiosyncrasies but through one's commonalities with others does one remain a part of some tradition—the historical bearer of personalities—in Unamuno's understanding of tradition as whatever passes from one to another (i.e., what is exchangeable or communicable or consumable) but does not pass away. Emmanuel's uniqueness is not so impenetrable that it cannot be subsumed under certain familiar *topoi*. His life endures under two seemingly contradictory rubrics, "life of Christ" and "divine mother." Unamuno is at pains to show that these organizing models prove, beneath the surface, not to be antithetical at all, in his fictional elaboration of yet another variant of the most beloved *mythos* of Western culture, the life of Christ. The ancient world, of course, venerated the divine mother under various guises as well as the male figure that played the role of the female (the Androgyne). Through his fiction, Unamuno restores these repressed images. The essence of Christ-likeness is revealed to be identical with the essence of maternal love, his narrative suggests.

What shows itself as most universal in his thought, going against the grain of his own consciously willed, lifelong promotion of quixotism, is not the frenetic search for individual fame exemplified by the mad Knight. Unamuno's script modulates in the course of his career from one emphasizing individual values to one that must finally come

to grips with those timeless, communal models of self-sacrifice, Christ and the all-loving mother. In *Saint Emmanuel,* Unamuno for the first time collapses both gender roles, heretofore bifurcated, in one person. With this novel, we find a new synthesis of the agonic and the contemplative, the male and the female. This novel, which, according to Unamuno's own admission, completes the trilogy begun with *The Tragic Sense of Life* (1913) and continued with *The Agony of Christianity* (1925), perhaps helps to explain why the latter was written, as a revision of *The Tragic Sense of Life* at last fully acknowledging a perspective implicit but undeveloped in the earlier work.

While in the novel [*La tía Tula*] (1921) Unamuno begins to separate spiritual and blood relations, to view blood kinship as an imperfect reflection of a higher form of kinship in which one can play any gender role, he does not really liberate this idea until he finally sees that his male characters can also be maternal, the "mother" understood not as an external object of desire for the male (Freud) but, in its deepest metaphysical sense, as a potential internalized role within man himself.

When Emmanuel dies, Angela resurrects him through her personal and secret confession. She conjectures that he died a believer; in her testimony to church officials, she protects his interior life from the scrutiny of the ecclesiastical authorities who are considering his canonization. She carefully selects which facts to reveal or conceal so as to assure that his saintly legend will live on. In this respect, she is similar to the other women in Unamuno's writings who play maternal roles, from [tía Tula] to the two Rachaels, one of the short story *Two Mothers* and the other found in the drama [*Raquel encadenada*] Angela has in Emmanuel a spiritual "child" whom she cares for, and she attempts to save his personality. Unlike these other fictional women, however, Angela's maternal concern involves her in the act of authoring, an activity traditionally identified closely with the male.

No explanation of why Angela writes her confession appears in the novel, and she herself admits her inability to justify the motivation of her composition. One possible explanation consonant with the novel is that her love, seeking to express itself in some form, responds to Emmanuel's personality in a way which best realizes his irreducible dream of eternal life. Angela's confession, the verbal recreation of Emmanuel's life, provides him one powerful form of the immortality for which he longs. By assuming the role of author, Angela appropriates aspects of the male gender role, just as Emmanuel appropriates the female. Each inverts the role that tradition assigns. This "transvestism" goes beyond a mere exchange of certain gender-defined gestures and roles. Angela radically redefines the role of authoring, suffusing it with her own values, just as Emmanuel provides fresh insight into the metaphysical nature of maternity quite apart from its biological incidents. Whereas Emmanuel sublimates his desire for immortality through lineage and deeds in the maternal role, Angela, a kind of female father (like Saint Teresa of Avila, as Unamuno understood her), appears as both his spiritual child and progenitor. As the spiritual midwife of Emmanuel's soul, she allows key aspects of his personality to live

Miguel de Unamuno.

on through the novel. Other potentially competing authors appear in the narrative, for example, those ecclesiastical authorities who are in the process of composing their own, official version of Emmanuel's life. Angela's expressed fear of all authorities, even ecclesiastical ones, mandates a rejection of the institution of authorship in the traditional sense. The charitable care that she lavishes on Emmanuel in life and death compels a new understanding of what it means to author. Angela's novel supplants the old model of creation by a transcendent god, which the ecclesiastical authorities, after their ersatz fashion, are imitating. In the ironic reversals and paradoxical reverberations of the narrative, Emmanuel, a priest and hence a sexually neuter being in the eyes of the church, first teaches Angela how to mother. A male mother who cares for his spiritual children, including Angela, Emmanuel is unique among Unamuno's male protagonists. Angela, in turn, perpetuates the same model of charity through her carrying on the ministry of Emmanuel after his death as well as through her shaping the novel, the form of which has traditionally been a vehicle of the will to bourgeois (male) power.

It might be objected that Emmanuel's teaching to Angela the role of the mother in the novel represents another at-

tempt to divest women of their rights and prerogatives. Such an interpretation points up the danger of applying feminine religious imagery to males. Unamuno does not suggest, however, that the maternal role promoted in the novel originates with Emmanuel. Emmanuel's models consist of the scriptures and the monastic tradition, especially that connected with Saint Bernard of Clairvaux, who, perhaps more than any other monastic except Julian of Norwich, dramatized the feminine aspects of God. By bringing into sharp focus a very minor medieval tradition of viewing Christ as mother, Bernard himself was recovering an even more ancient tradition. While a single passage in the New Testament explicitly applies a maternal image to Christ (Matt. 23:37, repeated in Luke 13:34), this paucity of precedent did not stop a number of early church fathers from viewing maternity as one aspect of the nature of Christ. Interestingly, the suppression of "mother" as one of the titles for Christ by the Latin translator of the Acts of Peter has a very revealing modern parallel in the suppression of the key phrase, "matriarchal man," to describe Emmanuel at the outset of Unamuno's novel: the words have been altered, whether consciously or unconsciously, to read "patriarchal man" by at least one Spanish editor of the work!

Certainly, as Caroline Walker Bynum has argued, the Bernadine tradition of viewing Christ as mother sometimes involved the enhancement of the male image at the expense of actual females. Any element of this cannibalizing of real women has been expunged from the idealized fictional world of Unamuno, however. It is clearly the accidents of age and sex that place Emmanuel in a privileged position at first with respect to Angela. He is older, a priest. Moreover, the image of the divine mother that he excavates from the Christian tradition soon proves corrosive of all such hierarchical arrangements. In the Christian society created by Emmanuel in the novel, every man and woman becomes Christ. While Emmanuel first plays the role of mother to Angela, she will later reciprocate in a spiritual kinship system in which anyone who assumes the burden of compassion impersonates Christ himself.

Unamuno has presented in *Saint Emmanuel* a revision of the nature of God, and in so doing, he prefigures in his fiction certain key elements of the current theological debate over the role of gender and ideology in the formation of religious language. While the question of the necessity of a feminine component in the Christian conception of divinity is posed very powerfully in *The Tragic Sense of Life,* Unamuno significantly does not rest in this observation until he has given it narrative life in the form of the cosmological drama that Emmanuel enacts upon the stage of the village of Valverde de Lucerna. The "God with us" to whom both Angela and Emmanuel, martyrs, bear witness is a maternal "man" (his manhood transcending all biological accidents) who finds his/her identity and transcendence of mortality in caring for others as a mother cares.

The problem of personality as viewed within the framework of *Saint Emmanuel* may be expressed in terms of the cross-reference between the individual and the species. While each person develops in his or her own way through suffering, it is that same suffering that unites all men and women in Christ. Unamuno would evidently extend the concept of personality beyond the "lower" forms of life to that which we normally regard as inanimate in his desire to attribute to every corner of the universe a consciousness like his own, a consciousness that anguishes over the knowledge of death. Once we bring to bear on *Saint Emmanuel* Unamuno's insights about Christianity as a form of life based upon the eternal principle of love for others, which is a mystery of suffering in time coterminous with eternity, it is clear that Unamuno's views on this subject have too often been misrepresented. In Unamuno's complex conceptual system, it is not, as much critical thought would have us believe, agnosticism or atheism that essentially characterizes Emmanuel or Unamuno, but Christianity, its agonic love. Through the religious symbolism of the novel, Emmanuel and Angela come to form a composite image, that of the Mother-and-Son-in-Agony, upon which Unamuno imposes his own voice in the epilogue. That image, which paradoxically points to another, that of the absent father Unamuno, encompasses three persons. This triune relationship, unlike the Christian Trinity, is heavily weighted toward the feminine, containing a biological female, Angela, a maternal son, and an author who is in the very process of renouncing all claim to authority. Only within the context of that inner life of ceaseless suffering, that psychic martyrdom that ultimately engenders charity for the whole universe, do Emmanuel and Angela (and, by implication, Unamuno and the "beloved reader" as fellow sufferers) become persons, those who experience peace through war (a metaphysical war synonymous with spiritual struggle), faith through doubt, eternal life through death, God through the feminine.

To anticipate one important criticism that might be leveled at Unamuno's novelistic linkage of the maternal role with a religious model of personality sharply differing from the traditional one in Western culture and in the previous work of Unamuno, does not Unamuno reduce the myriad potential roles that women play to one? Rather than seeing maternity as a fixed role that should define woman's place in the world, in this last major novel Unamuno views maternity as a role that, more than any other, has the potential for expanding human awareness, one which both men and women should aspire to. And in this elevation of the maternal role, it must be reiterated that Unamuno is not dealing with physical maternity at all, the actual production of flesh-and-blood children. It is instead a spiritual kinship not bound by ties of blood, a spiritual maternity, that preoccupies him. The trajectory of his fiction has traced the problem of the male quest for eternal life; in *Saint Emmanuel,* Unamuno opens a new door, reintegrating the maternal subtext in the agonic hero in the final twist of his novelistic thought.

This male incorporation of the feminine is at the opposite pole from that of the Greek myths. A classic case of such "identification" is that of Zeus's quite literal appropriation of female procreativity, his devouring of his wife in the *mythos,* followed by his subsequent giving birth—through his head (or from his thigh in a variant version of the story)—to Athena, goddess of war. In *Saint Emmanuel,* the male mother does not devour the female; Angela, the narrator of the novel, performs, with complete symmetry and reciprocity, the same spiritually active, maternal role for Emmanuel that he performs for her.

In a world in which a system of patriarchy that values power, domination, conviction, and control has been closely linked with and validated by religion, we find in the last major novel of Unamuno a final, definitive turning away from the politics of power engendered by such a sexist view of the cosmos. This revolution in Unamuno's thought, which Unamuno himself cannot be said finally to control since the epilogue to *Saint Emmanuel* places in doubt all forms of authority—including Unamuno's own—is both surprising and not totally unprepared for. Placed within the broader context of his philosophic sympathies, this illuminating discontinuity appears as the logical outgrowth of his religious thought, which from the beginning recognized the monstrosity of any conceptual system that does not possess a built-in structural component of self-doubt and self-negation. The advent of imperialism, the origin of logical positivism, the rise of fascism, the genesis of the modern police state: each deformed birth recapitulates the same fatal flaw, the lack of a self-regulating mechanism that preserves the voice of the Other.

We may use the term "machismo" to characterize that completely self-assured male posturing that goes on generating a whole way of life, a politics, a cosmology, a theology. In its more virulent as well as in its more innocuous forms, it always manifests itself as the repression of all ετεροδ in the name of ομοιοδ. Unamuno prophetically seizes upon doubt as the essential element that keeps religious faith vital, recognizing the nature of human personality not only in its goal but also in all those elements, myriad harbingers of death, that place it in jeopardy. Absent the obstacle, no dialectic and no real narrative history of the self is possible. The person is destined to become a persona, a mask, to be sure, in the narrative translation of the individual into a role, a pattern that can be narratized. The name appears as the revealing site of personality (a site in our chirographic culture at once spatial and temporal), for it indicates, on the one hand, to self and others, that human stories do merit singling out through a noun that distinguishes one from the other. The complete objectification of that name and that story with the death of the individual allows that name and that story to live on, independent of their bearer, in the memory of others. Modern cemeteries, with their tombstones inscribed with the names of the deceased, reflect this age-old human connection between naming and burying.

Like Feuerbach, like Heidegger (a confessed reader and admirer of Unamuno), Unamuno discovers the salutary role of death in human life as the first and fundamental Other that makes us persons, conscious of our limits, who are all involved, willy-nilly, in anguished attempts to transcend mortality. Unamuno subsequently decreed to the existential movement a way of seeing that must be described as "religious" even if it proceeds from the most radical atheism, because it recognizes the key functions of contingency, dependency, and relatedness in shaping human personality. By dramatically highlighting the role of the feminine in relation to the masculine world at large, he called attention to all those often hidden, essential dependencies that underlie our myths of autonomy and autochthonous creation, from our theologies to our living arrangements. From the peripheral position of the feminine in the social and religious order, Unamuno derived his last and perhaps most compelling metaphor of human personality. From the paradox of seeing man, in the generic sense, as a being-toward-immortality, he passes to the paradox of understanding man as a male manqué, whose machismo must be subverted. In the specific case of Emmanuel, the sacrifice of his male ego is a self-inflicted wound that paradoxically makes him whole.

Within the Western theological context, the concept of the transcendent father, resting upon the blinding discovery of the male's role in procreation, established, in its two most definitive forms in the Greek theogonies and the Hebrew Scriptures, the frame for virtually all Western thought and discourse. From this metaphysical presupposition emerges not only the occidental theological order rooted in God but also, at a much later date, those author-centered fictional forms, chief among which figures the classic novel. If distance and control, those two quintessential prerequisites of paternal creation, find their fullest artistic expression in the novel of a Cervantes or a Flaubert, the Unamunian novel, by contrast, surrenders these values and their metaphysical "support systems," placing

in doubt the patriarchal conceptual framework that upholds them. In so doing, Unamuno allies himself with all those repressed elements of the Western narrative tradition seen in its broadest scope, encompassing philosophical and theological discourses as well as the fictions of man. In a life-long effort to salvage human personality from the deformations of every ideology, whether theological, scientific, or artistic, Unamuno recalls us to the roots of the person in life and language and the way in which every true discourse, be it historical or fictional—the distinction for him, as for Jorge Luis Borges, appears meaningless—must fully acknowledge the vitalizing role of the alien, the eccentric, the other. (pp. 344-58)

> *Phillip Williams, "Beyond Don Quixote: Rethinking the 'Problem of Personality' in Light of Changing Gender Roles in Unamuno's 'Saint Emmanuel the Good, Martyr',"* in The Journal of Religion, *Vol. 69, No. 3, July, 1989, pp. 344-58.*

FURTHER READING

Biography

Rudd, Margaret Thomas. *The Lone Heretic: A Biography of Miguel de Unamuno y Jugo.* Austin: University of Texas Press, 1963, 349 p.

   A comprehensive biography.

Criticism

Baker, Armand F. "Unamuno and the Religion of Uncertainty." *Hispanic Review* 58, No. 1 (Winter 1990): 37-56.

   Discusses Unamuno's belief in the educative possibilities of imagination and intuition over those of logic and how this is reflected in his works.

Barcía, José Rubia, and Zeitlin, M. A., eds. *Unamuno: Creator and Creation.* Berkeley: University of California Press, 1967, 253 p.

   Reprints fourteen scholarly essays presented to the symposium "Unamuno: The Man and His Work," from 22 October through 6 November 1964.

Glannon, Walter. "Unamuno's *San Manuel Bueno, mártir:* Ethics through Fiction." *MLN* 102, No. 2 (March 1987): 316-33.

   Illustrates how Unamuno's prose style in *San Manuel Bueno, mártir* illuminates his ethical stance.

Gordon, M. "The Elusive Self: Narrative Method and Its Implications in *San Manuel Bueno, mártir.*" *Hispanic Review* 54, No. 2 (Spring 1986): 147-61.

   Examines Unamuno's narrative approach to self-division in *San Manuel Bueno, mártir.*

Huertas-Jourda, José. *The Existentialism of Miguel de Unamuno.* University of Florida Monographs: Humanities, no. 13. Gainesville: University of Florida Press, 1963, 70 p.

   Explores Unamuno's quixotic vision and its expression in his work.

Ilie, Paul. "Language and Cognition in Unamuno." *Revista Canadiense De Estudios Hispánicos* XI, No. 2 (Winter 1987): 289-314.

>   Outlines how language determines meaning in Unamuno's works.

Kerrigan, Anthony. Introduction to *Abel Sánchez and Other Stories,* by Miguel de Unamuno, translated by Anthony Kerrigan, pp. vii-xvii. South Bend, Ind.: Gateway Editions, Ltd., 1956.

>   Places the stories in *Abel Sanchez, and Other Stories* within the context of events in Unamuno's life.

King, Shirley. "*San Manuel Bueno* and Unamuno's Reading of Hauptmann." *Revista de Estudios Hispanicos* 19, No. 1 (January 1985): 39-54.

>   Explores Unamuno's use of Gerhart Hauptmann's *Der ketzer von Soana* (1919, *The Heretic of Soana*) as a source for *San Manuel Bueno, mártir.*

Lacy, Allen. *Miguel de Unamuno: The Rhetoric of Existence.* Studies in Philosophy, vol. XII. The Hague: Mouton & Co., 1967, 289 p.

>   An introductory study of Unamuno and his works.

Marcone, Rose Marie. "Self and Self-Creation: Conflict in the *Nivolas.*" *The USF Language Quarterly* 26, Nos. 3-4 (Spring-Summer 1988): 35, 39.

>   Explores the divided nature of characters in *San Manuel Bueno, mártir, Nada menos que todo un hombre,* and *Abel Sánchez.*

Olson, Paul R. "Unamuno's Break with the Nineteenth Century: Invention of the *Nivola* and the Linguistic Turn." *MLN* 102, No. 2 (March 1987): 307-15.

>   Discusses Unamuno's *nivolas* and their role in viewing reality in terms of language.

Valdés, Mario J. and Valdés, María Elena de. *An Unamuno Source Book: A Catalogue of Readings and Acquisitions with an Introductory Essay on Unamuno's Dialectical Enquiry.* Toronto: University of Toronto Press, 1973, 305 p.

>   A comprehensive catalogue of Unamuno's personal library, with an informative critical introduction.

Additional coverage of Unamuno's life and career is contained in the following sources published by Gale Research: *Contemporary Authors,* Volumes 104, 131; *Dictionary of Literary Biography,* Volume 108; *Hispanic Writers; Major 20th-Century Writers;* and *Twentieth-Century Literary Criticism,* Volumes 2, 9.

Oscar Wilde

1854-1900

(Born Oscar Fingal O'Flahertie Wills Wilde) Anglo-Irish playwright, novelist, essayist, short story writer, and critic.

INTRODUCTION

Wilde was one of the most prominent figures of late nineteenth-century literary Decadence, a movement whose members adhered to the doctrine of "art for art's sake" and sought to eliminate moral, political, and social concerns from their art. While his poetry, plays, and novel *The Picture of Dorian Gray* are among the most characteristic works of literary Decadence, Wilde deviated from the aesthetic tradition in his short fiction by incorporating a strong moral element. In these works Wilde utilized traditional short story structures to explore the themes of guilt, suffering, and love and to address such ethical and religious questions as the nature of good and evil, the meaning of Christianity, and the cruelty and artificiality of human institutions in comparison to the simplicity of the natural world.

Wilde was born and raised in Dublin, Ireland. As a student at Dublin's Trinity College and later at Oxford University in London, he was influenced by the writings of Walter Pater, who, in his *Studies in the History of the Renaissance* (1873), urged indulgence of the senses and stylistic perfection in art. Wilde adopted aestheticism as a way of life, cultivating an extravagant persona that was burlesqued in the popular press, copied by other youthful iconoclasts, and indulged by the avant-garde literary and artistic circles of London. Following a lecture tour of the United States in 1882 and 1883, Wilde returned to Dublin and married Constance Mary Lloyd, with whom he later had two sons. It is speculated that a number of Wilde's fairy tales have their origins in stories he made up and told his children. During the mid-1880s Wilde published reviews in such journals as the *Pall Mall Gazette* and the *Dramatic Review,* and in 1887 became editor in chief of *Lady's World.* Renamed *Woman's World* under Wilde's editorship, the magazine became a leading publication of fiction, criticism, and articles on art, fashion, and modern life. Most of Wilde's short stories were written between 1887 and 1891; they are among the last of his works published in periodicals before he established himself as one of the foremost playwrights of his age. During this time Wilde also became active in London's homosexual subculture; many commentators suggest that his immersion in this way of life may have been the impetus for the explorations of good and evil that dominate his short fiction. Wilde's trial and subsequent conviction on charges of "gross indecency between male persons" in 1895 led to ignominy for the author and obscurity for his works. At the

time of his death in 1900 the scandal associated with him led most commentators to discuss Wilde diffidently, if at all.

"The Canterville Ghost: A Hylo-Idealistic Romance," the first of Wilde's short stories to appear in print, was published in *Court and Society* in February 1887. This was the first of four short stories—including "A Model Millionaire: A Note of Admiration," "The Sphinx without a Secret: An Etching," and "Lord Arthur Savile's Crime: A Study of Duty"—that appeared in various London magazines that same year and were later collected in *Lord Arthur Savile's Crime, and Other Stories.* In these early stories, generally described as social satires, Wilde parodied what he considered American naïveté as well as the cultural and social snobbery associated with the British aristocracy. "The Canterville Ghost" is a story about an American family who rents a haunted castle in England but steadfastly refuses to believe in the increasingly indignant ghost. Often dismissed as simplistic and melodramatic, this story nonetheless evinces Wilde's fascination with the supernatural and the dark side of human nature. Wilde further explored these themes in "Lord Arthur Savile's Crime." In this story, Lord Arthur, who is soon to be married, meets a palm reader who predicts that he will soon commit murder. Because Arthur believes in predestination, he feels obligated to fulfill the prophesy before allowing himself to marry. Like the family in "The Canterville Ghost," Arthur is unable to acknowledge or accept the existence of evil in himself and in others. At the end of the story, after killing the palm reader by throwing him in the Thames, he heaves a "deep sigh of relief" before happily marrying his fiancée.

The fairy tales collected in *The Happy Prince, and Other Tales* and *A House of Pomegranates* are often described as fantastic due to their exotic characters and settings, but critics generally agree that they are thematically more complex than Wilde's earlier stories. The characters in these tales take responsibility for their actions, are conscious of the suffering of those around them, and are capable of generosity and forgiveness as well as selfishness and cruelty. In "The Happy Prince," for example, one of Wilde's most popular and well-known fairy tales, a jewel-encrusted and gold-plated statue asks a swallow to remove its valuable adornments to help feed the poor people of the surrounding village. Once reduced to its lead armature, however, the statue is deemed useless and is discarded because it is no longer beautiful. Wilde also explored the selfishness, pain, and disillusionment associated with love in such stories as "The Nightingale and the Rose." In this tale, a young woman promises to dance with a student who has fallen in love with her if he brings her a perfect red rose. A nightingale overhears the request and offers up his life to obtain such a rose. The young woman scornfully rejects the gift, however, because it "does not go with her dress" as do the jewels given to her by another man. Oblivious to the nightingale's sacrifice, the student throws the rose in the gutter and proclaims that love is a "silly thing" and "not half as useful as Logic."

Initial critical reaction to Wilde's short stories and fairy tales was mixed. Some reviewers considered them unsuitable for children due to their elaborate descriptions and sometimes disturbing subject matter, while others commended Wilde for addressing the consequences of greed and self-indulgence. Wilde himself explained that his fairy tales were "an attempt to mirror modern life in a form remote from reality—to deal with modern problems in a mode that is ideal and not imitative . . . they are of course, slight and fanciful, and written, not for children, but for childlike people from eighteen to eighty!" Contemporary studies of Wilde's short fiction can be divided into biographical criticism and academic criticism; the first relates Wilde's short stories to his homosexuality and decadent life-style, and the latter focuses on Wilde's sophisticated use of symbolism and allegory. While Wilde's short stories have been periodically described as wordy, mawkish, and pedantic, most twentieth-century commentators recognize the complexity and diversity of Wilde's canon and include discussion of Wilde's short fiction in appraisals of his literary accomplishments as a whole.

PRINCIPAL WORKS

SHORT FICTION

The Happy Prince, and Other Tales   1888

A House of Pomegranates   1891
Lord Arthur Savile's Crime, and Other Stories   1891

OTHER MAJOR WORKS

Vera; or, The Nihilists: A Drama in Four Acts   (drama) 1880
Poems   (poetry)   1881
The Duchess of Padua: A Tragedy of the XVI Century (drama)   1883; also published as *The Duchess of Padua: A Play by Oscar Wilde,*   1908
Intentions   (essays)   1891
The Picture of Dorian Gray   (novel)   1891
Lady Windermere's Fan: A Play about a Good Woman (drama)   1892
Salomé: Drame en un acte   (drama)   1893
   [*Salome: A Tragedy in One Act,*   1894]
A Woman of No Importance   (drama)   1893
The Sphinx   (drama)   1894
The Importance of Being Earnest: A Trivial Comedy for Serious People   (drama)   1895
The Soul of Man under Socialism   (essay)   1895
The Ballad of Reading Gaol   (poetry)   1898
An Ideal Husband   (drama)   1899
*De Profundis   (letter)   1905
The First Collected Edition of the Works of Oscar Wilde.   15 vols.   (poetry, essays, short stories, novel, dramas, and criticism)   1908-1922
The Letters of Oscar Wilde   (letters)   1962

*This work was not published in its entirety until 1949.

CRITICISM

William Sharp   (essay date 1891)

[*Sharp was a Scottish short story writer, poet, and playwright who wrote under the pseudonym Fiona Macleod. In the following excerpt, he castigates the stories in* Lord Arthur Savile's Crime, and Other Stories *for their banality and lack of wit.*]

"Lord Arthur Savile's Crime" and its three companion stories, will not add to their author's reputation. Mr. Oscar Wilde's previous book, [*A House of Pomegranates*], though in style florid to excess, and in sentiment shallow, had at least a certain cleverness; this quality, however, is singularly absent in at least the first three of these tales. Much the best of the series is the fourth, the short sketch entitled **"A Model Millionaire,"** though even this brief tale is spoilt by such commonplace would-be witticisms as "the poor should be practical and prosaic," "it is better to have a permanent income than to be fascinating." There is much more of this commonplace padding in the story that gives its name to the book, *e.g.,* "actors can choose whether they will appear in tragedy or comedy," &c., "but in real life it is different. Most men and women are forced to perform parts for which they have no qualifications," and so on, and so on, even to the painfully hackneyed "the world is a stage, but the play is badly cast." This story is an attempt to follow in the footsteps of the author of *New*

Arabian Nights. Unfortunately for Mr. Wilde's ambition, Mr. Stevenson is a literary artist of rare originality. Such a story as this is nothing if not wrought with scrupulous delicacy of touch. It is, unfortunately, dull as well as derivative. **"The Sphinx without a Secret"** is better. **"The Canterville Ghost"** is, as a story, better still, though much the same kind of thing has already been far better done by Mr. Andrew Lang; but it is disfigured by some stupid vulgarisms. "We have really everything in common with America nowadays, except, of course, language." "And manners," an American may be prompted to add. A single example may suffice:

> The subjects discussed were merely such as form the ordinary conversation of cultured Americans of the better class, such as the immense superiority of Miss Fanny Davenport over Sara Bernhardt as an actress; the difficulty of obtaining green corn, buckwheat cakes, and hominy, even in the best English houses . . . and the sweetness of the New York accent as compared to the London drawl.

It is the perpetration of banalities of this kind which disgusts Englishmen as well as "cultured Americans." One should not judge the society of a nation by that of a parish; the company of the elect by the sinners of one's own acquaintance. Mr. Wilde's verbal missiles will serve merely to assure those whom he ridicules that another not very redoubtable warrior has bestirred himself in the camps of Philistia.

> *William Sharp, in a review of "Lord Arthur Savile's Crime," in* The Academy, *Vol. XL, No. 1009, September 5, 1891, p. 194.*

Pall Mall Gazette   (essay date 1891)

[*In the excerpt below, the critic states that* A House of Pomegranates *is not suitable for children and praises the work's descriptions and social concerns.*]

Is *A House of Pomegranates* intended for a child's book? We confess that we do not exactly know. The ultra-aestheticism of the pictures seems unsuitable for children—as also the rather 'fleshly' style of Mr. Wilde's writing. The stories are somewhat after the manner of Hans Andersen—and have pretty poetic and imaginative flights like his; but then again they wander off too often into something between a 'Sinburnian' ecstasy and the catalogue of a high art furniture dealer. Children may be very much attached to *bric-à-brac* (though of this we have our doubts), but the more natural among them would certainly prefer Hansel and Grethel's sugar-house to any amount of Mr. Wilde's 'rich tapestries' and 'velvet canopies'. Would they not probably yawn over the following?—

> The walls were hung with rich tapestries representing the Triumph of Beauty. A large press, inlaid with agate and lapis-lazuli, filled one corner, and facing the window stood a curiously wrought cabinet with lacquer panels of powdered and mosaiced gold, on which were placed some delicate goblets of Venetian glass, and a cup of dark-veined onyx.

The Countess d'Aulnoy's charming tales, it is true, abounded in sumptuary detail, but with her it formed the stage-scenery for her dwarfs and fairies. Again, Mr. Wilde's diction seems to us hardly suitable to children. Joys are 'fierce and fiery-coloured'; the King, watching his little daughter at play, thinks of her dead and embalmed mother, and (this unpleasant suggestion reminds us of *Dorian Gray*) 'the odours of strange spices, spices such as embalmers use, seemed to taint—or was it fancy?—the clear morning air.' Eyes are of all kinds: 'dark woodland eyes', 'mauve-amethyst eyes', 'eyes of bossy gold'. A young boy spends a whole night 'in noting the effect of the moonlight on a silver statue of Endymion.' But all Mr. Wilde's stories, whether intended for children or not, have a deep meaning which 'he who runs may read'. This underlying allegory is their chief beauty. **'The Young King'** touches on Socialistic economics; **'The Birthday of the Infanta'** has a masterly touch of pathos; while **'The Fisherman and his Soul'** is perhaps the most far-reaching and most elaborate effort. In this latter there are capital descriptions of the wonders of the sea, as good as some of those in Kingsley. (pp. 113-14)

> *In an excerpt in* Oscar Wilde: The Critical Heritage, *edited by Karl Beckson, Barnes & Noble, Inc., 1970, pp. 113-14.*

The Athenaeum   (essay date 1892)

[*The following review was written in response to a letter Wilde wrote to the editor of the* Athenaeum *in which he stated, "In building this* House of Pomegranates *I had about as much intention of pleasing the British child as I had of pleasing the British public. . . . No artist recognizes any standard of beauty but which is suggested by his own temperament."*]

Mr. Oscar Wilde has been good enough to explain, since the publication of [*A House of Pomegranates*], that it was intended neither for the "British Child" nor for the "British Public," but for the cultured few who can appreciate its subtle charms. The same exiguous but admiring band will doubtless comprehend why a volume of allegories should be described as *A House of Pomegranates,* which we must confess is not apparent to our perverse and blunted intellect. It consists of four storeys (we mean stories), **'The Young King,' 'The Birthday of the Infanta,' 'The Fisherman and his Soul,'** and **'The Star-Child,'** each dedicated to a lady of Mr. Wilde's acquaintance, and all characterized by the peculiar faults and virtues of his highly artificial style. The allegory, as we have had occasion to remark on former occasions, when discussing the work of Lady Dilke and Miss Olive Schreiner in this particular field, is one of the most difficult of literary forms. In Mr. Wilde's *House of Pomegranates* there is too much straining after effect and too many wordy descriptions; but at the same time there is a good deal of forcible and poetic writing scattered through its pages, and its scenes have more colour and consistence than those which we criticized in 'Dreams' and 'The Shrine of Love.' Mr. Wilde resembles the modern manager who crowds his stage with æsthetic upholstery and *bric-à-brac* until the characters have scarcely room to walk about. Take this inventory of the contents of a chamber in the young king's palace, which reads for all the world like an extract from a catalogue at Christie's:—

> After some time he rose from his seat, and leaning against the carved penthouse of the chimney looked round at the dimly-lit room. The walls were hung with rich tapestries representing the Triumph of Beauty. A large press, inlaid with agate and lapis-lazuli, filled one corner, and facing the window stood a curiously wrought cabinet with lacquer panels of powdered and mosaiced gold, on which were placed some delicate goblets of Venetian glass and a cup of dark-veined onyx. Pale poppies were broidered on the silk coverlet of the bed, as though they had fallen from the tired hands of Sleep, and tall reeds of fluted ivory bare up the velvet canopy, from which great tufts of ostrich plumes sprang, like white foam, to the pallid silver of the fretted ceiling. A laughing Narcissus in green bronze held a polished mirror above its head. On the table stood a flat bowl of amethyst.

The adornment of these "beautiful tales," as Mr. Wilde modestly calls them, has been entrusted to Messrs. C. Ri-

---

Wilde responds to a negative review of *A House of Pomegranates*:

Sir, I have just had sent to me from London a copy of the *Pall Mall Gazette* containing a review of my book *A House of Pomegranates.* The writer of this review makes a certain suggestion about my book which I beg you will allow me to correct at once.

He starts by asking an extremely silly question, and that is, whether or not I have written this book for the purpose of giving pleasure to the British child. Having expressed grave doubts on this subject, a subject on which I cannot conceive any fairly-educated person having any doubts at all, he proceeds, apparently quite seriously, to make the extremely limited vocabulary at the disposal of the British child the standard by which the prose or an artist is to be judged! Now in building this *House of Pomegranates* I had about as much intention of pleasing the British child as I had of pleasing the British public. Mamilius is as entirely delightful as Caliban is entirely detestable, but neither the standard of Mamilius nor the standard of Caliban is my standard. No artist recognises any standard of beauty but that which is suggested by his own temperament. The artist seeks to realise in a certain material his immaterial idea of beauty, and thus to transform an idea into an ideal. That is the way an artist makes things. That is why an artist makes things. The artist has no other object in making things. Does your reviewer imagine that Mr Shannon, for instance, whose delicate and lovely illustrations he confesses himself quite unable to see, draws for the purpose of giving information to the blind?

I remain, sir, your obedient servant,

OSCAR WILDE

Oscar Wilde, in a letter to the editor of the Pall Mall Gazette, *11 December 1891.*

---

cketts and C. H. Shannon, and for combined ugliness and obscurity it would be hard, we imagine, to beat them. The full-page illustrations are so indistinctly printed that whatever excellence they may possess is lost to view, while the grotesque black-and-white woodcuts are hideous to behold. It is, perhaps, as well that the book is not meant for the "British Child"; for it would certainly make him scream, according to his disposition, with terror or amusement. (pp. 176-77)

> *A review of "A House of Pomegranates," in* The Athenaeum, *No. 3354, February 6, 1892, p. 177.*

The Saturday Review (essay date 1892)

[*The following is a laudatory review of* A House of Pomegranates.]

We fear that Mr. Oscar Wilde's enemies (supposing him to be capable of possessing any) must have seen in this handsome book a deliberate provocation to the *bourgeois au front glabre.* Amid the pomegranates and other trimmings on the cover, there is a back view of a peacock which looks for all the world like that of an elderly spinster with her hands behind her back, and her profile turned towards the beholder. [The illustrators] Mr. Shannon and Mr. Ricketts have sprinkled the pages with devices rare and strange in the latest and straitest school of Neo-Preraphaelitism, and the chief illustrations in the book are of a most absolute fancy. Mr. Wilde has, we observe, protested in the public press against the judgment that they are invisible, and, strictly speaking, they are not. But being printed in very faint grisaille on very deeply cream-tinted plate paper, they put on about as much invisibility as is possible to things visible, and as they are arranged, neither facing letterpress nor with the usual tissue guard, but with a blank sheet of paper of the same tint and substance opposite them, a hasty person might really open the leaves and wonder which side the illustration was. Nevertheless, we rather like them, for when you can see them, they are by no means uncomely, and they suit their text—a compliment which we are frequently unable to pay to much more commonplace instances of the art of book illustration.

In the case of the text, also, hasty judgment is likely to be unduly harsh judgment. The pomegranates that compose the house—the grains that make up the pomegranate would have been a better metaphor—are four in number, and are all tales of the *Märchen* order, though one is something even more of a *fabliau* than of a *Märchen*. This is called **"The Birthday of the Infanta,"** and tells, to put it very shortly, how a certain little Spanish princess had an ugly dwarf who loved her, and died of a broken heart when he found out, not only how ugly he himself was, but how his beloved mistress thought of him as nothing but a fantastic toy. 'Tis an ower true tale. But we are not sure that Mr. Wilde's manner of telling it is quite the right one. The first and the last of the four, **"The Young King,"** and **"The Star Child,"** are pretty enough moralities; the first of half-mediæval, half-modern Socialist strain. The other tells how a child was cured of cruelty, partly by some metaphysical aid, partly (we do not know whether Mr. Wilde intended to draw this part of the moral, but he has) by sound beatings and a not excessive allowance of bread and water.

But the third piece, **"The Fisherman and his Soul,"** is much longer, as long, indeed, as any two of them, and to our fancy a good deal better. It tells how a fisherman fell in love with a mermaid, and, to gain her, consented to part with, but not in the ordinary fashion to sell; his soul; how after a time he grew weary of his happiness, went to look after his soul, and found her, divorced as she was from his or any heart, a rather unpleasant, not to say immoral, companion; how he in vain endeavoured to return once more to his mermaid and only found her dead, when he and she and the soul were reunited once for all; and how, when the dead bodies of the pair were found and buried in unhallowed ground, there came a miracle converting to charity the heart of the parish priest who had cast them out. The separate ingredients of the piece are, of course, not very novel; but, to tell the truth, the separate ingredients of a story of this kind hardly can be, and Mr. Wilde has put them together with considerable skill, and communicated to the whole an agreeable character. The little mermaid is very nice, both when she is caught literally napping, and when she sings, and when she explains the necessity of her lover parting with his soul if he will have her. Also the young witch (to whom, when the parish priest has, not unnaturally, declined to unsoul him, the fisherman goes) is pleasing. She had red hair, and in gold tissue embroidered with peacock's eyes and a little green velvet cap she must have looked very well. The Sabbath, too, is good (there are too few Sabbaths in English), though the gentlemanly Satan is not new. Good, too, is the business-like manner in which the fisherman separates his soul from him by a device not impossibly suggested by one Adelbert von Chamisso, a person of ability. The adventures of the discarded and heartless soul are of merit, and it is a very good touch to make the fisherman's final, and hardly conscious, desertion of his mermaid-love turn on nothing more than a sudden fancy to dance, and the remembrance that she had no feet and could not dance with him. It is particularly satisfactory to learn that the mermaid's tail was of pearl-and-silver. There has been an impression in many circles that mermaids' tails are green, and we have always thought that it would be unpleasant to embrace a person with a green tail. But pearl-and-silver is *quite* different.

A review of "A House of Pomegranates," in The Saturday Review, *London, Vol. 73, No. 1893, February 6, 1892, p. 160.*

W. B. Yeats (essay date 1923)

[*Yeats was the leading figure of the Irish Renaissance and a major twentieth-century poet. In the following excerpt, he asserts that Wilde's most successful short stories are those that most closely resemble his conversation.*]

When I was lecturing in Boston a little before the War an Arab refugee told me that Oscar Wilde's works had been translated into Arabian and that his ***Happy Prince and Other Tales*** had been the most popular:—'They are our own literature,' he said. I had already heard that 'The Soul of Man under Socialism' was much read in the Young China party; and for long after I found myself meditating upon the strange destiny of certain books. My mind went back to the late eighties when I was but just arrived in London with the manuscript of my first book of poems, and when nothing of Wilde's had been published except his poems and ***The Happy Prince.*** I remember the reviews were generally very hostile to his work, for Wilde's aesthetic movement was a recent event and London journalists were still in a rage with his knee breeches, his pose—and it may be with his bitter speeches about themselves; while men of letters saw nothing in his prose but imitations of Walter Pater or in his verse but imitations of Swinburne and Rossetti. Never did any man seem to write more deliberately for the smallest possible audience or in a style more artificial, and that audience contained nobody it seemed but a few women of fashion who invited guests to listen to his conversation and two or three young painters who continued the tradition of Rossetti. And then in the midst of my meditation it was as though I heard him saying with that slow precise, rhythmical elocution of his, 'I have a vast public in Samarkand.' Perhaps they do not speak Arabian in Samarkand, but whatever name he had chosen he would have chosen it for its sound and for its suggestion of romance. His vogue in China would have touched him even more nearly, and I can almost hear his voice speaking of jade and powdered lacquer. Indeed, when I remember him with pleasure it is always the talker I remember, either as I have heard him at W. E. Henley's or in his own house or in some passage in a play, where there is some stroke of wit which had first come to him in conversation or might so have come. He was certainly the greatest talker of his time. 'We Irish', he had said to me, 'are too poetical to be poets, we are a nation of brilliant failures, but we are the greatest talkers since the Greeks.' He talked as good Irish talkers always do—though with a manner and music that he had learnt from Pater or Flaubert—and as no good English talker has ever talked. He had no practical interest, no cause to defend, no information to give, nor was he the gay jester whose very practical purpose is our pleasure. Behind his words was the whole power of his intellect, but that intellect had given itself to pure contemplation. (pp. 396-97)

The further Wilde goes in his writings from the method of speech, from improvisation, from sympathy with some especial audience the less original he is, the less accomplished. I think 'The Soul of Man under Socialism' is sometimes profound because there are so many quotations in it from his conversation; and that ***The Happy Prince and Other Tales*** is charming and amusing because he told its stories, (his children were still young at that time) and that ***A House of Pomegranates*** is over-decorated and seldom amusing because he wrote its stories; and because when he wrote, except when he wrote for actors, he no longer thought of a special audience. In '**The Happy Prince**' or '**The Selfish Giant**' or '**The Remarkable Rocket**' there is nothing that does not help the story, nothing indeed that is not story; but in '**The Birthday of the Infanta**' there is hardly any story worth the telling. '**The Fisher-**

man and his Soul', from the same book, has indeed so good a story that I am certain that he told it many times; and, that I may enjoy it, I try to imagine it as it must have been when he spoke it, half consciously watching that he might not bore by a repeated effect or an unnecessary description, some child or some little company of young painters or writers. Only when I so imagine it do I discover that the incident of the young fisherman's dissatisfaction with his mermaid mistress, upon hearing a description of a girl dancing with bare feet was witty, charming and characteristic. The young fisherman had resisted many great temptations, but never before had he seen so plainly that she had no feet. In the written story that incident is so lost in decorations that we let it pass unnoticed at a first reading, yet it is the crisis of the tale. To enjoy it I must hear his voice once more, and listen once more to that incomparable talker. (pp. 397-98)

> *W. B. Yeats, in a review of "The Happy Prince, and Other Tales," in* Oscar Wilde: The Critical Heritage, *edited by Karl Beckson, Routledge & Kegan Paul, 1970, pp. 396-99.*

[The stories in *The Happy Prince, and Other Tales*] are studies in prose, put for Romance's sake into a fanciful form: meant partly for children, and partly for those who have kept the child-like faculties of wonder and joy, and who find in simplicity a subtle strangeness.

—Oscar Wilde, in an 1888 letter later collected in The Letters of Oscar Wilde, *Harcourt, Brace and World, 1962.*

Christopher S. Nassaar (essay date 1974)

[*Nassaar is a Lebanese critic and educator who has written numerous works on Wilde and whose chief aim as a critic "is to establish Oscar Wilde as a major literary figure and to show the importance of the Rossetti-Pater-Wilde line in nineteenth-century literature." In the following excerpt, taken from his* Into the Demon Universe: A Literary Exploration of Oscar Wilde, *Nassaar divides Wilde's literary career into two distinct stages, stating that fairy tales belong to the second stage, during which Wilde began to engage in homosexual activities, and reflect the author's increasing mastery of such themes as sin, crime, and innocence.*]

1886—in that year Oscar Wilde died and was born anew. Shelley, in *Adonais,* speaks of "the contagion of the world's slow stain," and for Wilde this contagion began at the age of thirty-two, when he was seduced into homosexual practices by Robert Ross. Richard Ellmann rightly treats this event as pivotal both for Wilde the man and Wilde the artist. Suddenly, and at a remarkably late age, Oscar Wilde became seriously aware of the dark side of life, and suddenly the second-rate, highly imitative writer

disappeared and Wilde began to produce original literature with a claim to immortality. To read his works chronologically is to discover that Wilde's vision darkened almost without interruption until it ended in despair.

> We poets in our youth begin in gladness;
> But thereof come in the end despondency and
> madness,

wrote Wordsworth in "Resolution and Independence," thereby summarizing in two lines a central problem in Romantic experience.

Wilde, the last of the nineteenth-century Romantics, faced this problem in his own way, and failed entirely to solve it. The process of age, of growing up, is one that opens the Romantic to the world's slow stain and immerses him in a black and soul-destroying universe. Wilde's literary productions during and after 1886 evince a deepening if jagged exploration of the demonic and a final shocked cry of despair. The life and the works reflect each other, but it is my purpose in this study to focus on Wilde's works and to keep his life in the background, insofar as this is possible. There are many biographies of Wilde. What is needed is an adequate study of the literature he produced.

"Lord Arthur Savile's Crime" is the first work to emerge out of what Richard Ellmann calls "the new Wilde"—the Wilde who had succumbed to the homosexual impulse and had become interested in sin and crime. It is also Wilde's first important literary production and one of the most delightfully hilarious things he ever wrote. Much of the story's charm, however, lies in its rich, cleverly camouflaged intellectual content. The theme of the tale is foreshadowed in the very first paragraph:

> It was Lady Windermere's last reception before Easter, and Bentinck House was even more crowded than usual. Six Cabinet Ministers had come on from the Speaker's Levée in their stars and ribands, all the pretty women wore their smartest dresses, and at the end of the picture-gallery stood the Princess Sophia of Carlsrühe, a heavy Tartar-looking lady, with tiny black eyes and wonderful emeralds, talking bad French at the very top of her voice, and laughing immoderately at everything that was said to her. It was certainly a wonderful medley of people. Gorgeous peeresses chatted affably to violent Radicals, popular preachers brushed coat-tails with eminent sceptics, a perfect bevy of bishops kept following a stout prima-donna from room to room, on the staircase stood several Royal Academicians, disguised as artists, and it was said that at one time the supper-room was absolutely crammed with geniuses. In fact, it was one of Lady Windermere's best nights, and the Princess stayed till nearly half-past eleven.

The paragraph is a collection of opposites, wonderfully held in balance, but unnaturally so. Lady Windermere's reception cannot last forever, and with its end the delicate balance of opposites will collapse and hostilities will resume between the gorgeous peeresses and the violent radicals, the geniuses and the demands of the stomach. The Princess Sophia is particularly worthy of notice. As a princess from a foreign land, wearing wonderful emeralds at a charming reception, she suggests the beautiful, pure, and angelic. However, there is clearly something savage and demonic about her. She looks like a Tartar, has tiny black eyes, and behaves in an uncivilized manner, talking bad French and laughing immoderately. The Princess Sophia is particularly important because she combines within herself two opposing strains, one pure and the other demonic. In a possible allusion to Cinderella, Wilde has her leave the reception shortly before midnight. Subtly and unobtrusively, Wilde has suggested the main theme of his story in the first paragraph.

We never learn what happens to Princess Sophia, but Lord Arthur Savile also possesses two opposing strains in his character. The pure strain is reflected in his name. In the last decades of the nineteenth century, *The Idylls of the King* was an extremely well-known and very popular work, and the name Arthur in a literary work tended to associate its possessor with Tennyson's noble and totally pure King Arthur. Wilde makes this association more explicit by elevating his Arthur to the rank of lord. Lord Arthur's high-sounding surname, moreover, connects him with the earls of Savile and also suggests George Savile, who succeeded his father, Sir William, as fourth baronet in 1644. A famous English politician, George Savile was elevated to the peerage in 1668 as Baron Savile of Eland and Viscount Halifax. In 1679, he was created earl of Halifax and finally, in 1682, he became the first marquess of Halifax. He died in 1695 and was succeeded by his son, with whose death the peerage became extinct. Savile also suggests Savile Row, an extremely fashionable London street known for its tailor shops frequented by the aristocracy. Lord Arthur Savile's impressive name, then, connects its tall, handsome possessor with a realm that is pure, elevated, and exclusive. Apparently, he is destined to exist in a world above and separate from the ugly, evil things in life.

There is latent in Arthur, however, a strain that is quite base. **"Lord Arthur Savile's Crime"** is about the coming-of-age of Arthur. "I am not a child," he insists, and indeed he is engaged to be married. Marriage is a symbol of the transition from boyhood to manhood, but this transition involves for him the destruction of boyish innocence and the consequent unpleasant confrontation with evil. In an amused, ironic tone, Wilde reports Arthur's reaction as he first confronts the palm-reader Podgers:

> He had lived the delicate and luxurious life of a young man of birth and fortune, a life exquisite in its freedom from sordid care, its beautiful boyish insouciance; and now for the first time he had become conscious of the terrible mystery of Destiny, of the awful meaning of Doom.

Sybil, Arthur's beautiful fiancée, is a symbol incarnate of all that is pure within Arthur, and his devotion to her is a symbolic devotion to an ideal of purity within himself. "Sybil was to him a symbol of all that is good and noble," Wilde informs us, and later on we are told that Arthur "stopped at a florist's, and sent Sybil a beautiful basket of narcissus." The fat and coarse Podgers, on the other hand—a groveler at the feet of the aristocracy—is a symbol of all that is base and corrupt within Arthur. The evi-

dence for this statement is, I feel, strong. When Podgers reads Lord Arthur's palm, he finds there not only Lord Arthur's future but his own as well. The streak of blood he finds embedded in Arthur's palm is Podger's own blood. The only conceivable reason, moreover, why Lord Arthur cannot marry Sybil until he has murdered Podgers is because Podgers exists within Arthur and will destroy the marriage if it occurs: the principle of good cannot be totally possessed until the principle of evil is faced and destroyed within the self. The murder will be a form of self-purification for Arthur, and Podgers is well aware that he is to be the victim. Consider the following quotation:

> For a moment Lord Arthur had been tempted to play the coward's part, to write to Lady Clementina for the [poisoned] pill, and to let the marriage go on as if there was no such person as Mr. Podgers in the world. His better nature, however, soon asserted itself, and even when Sybil flung herself weeping into his arms, he did not falter. The beauty that stirred his senses had touched his conscience also. He felt that to wreck so fair a life for the sake of a few months' pleasure would be a wrong thing to do.

Lord Arthur's baser nature tempts him cowardly to destroy Sybil "for the sake of a few months' pleasure," but "his better nature" soon asserts itself and he decides not to. As long as there is such a person as Mr. Podgers in the world, Arthur cannot marry Sybil without destroying her. The reason is that Podgers is an embodiment of Arthur's baser nature, existing within as well as outside him, though Arthur, at this stage, is too thoroughly innocent to recognize the fact. As Wilde reminds us at one point, "He was still very young."

But Arthur will destroy Podgers, as Podgers realizes at once upon seeing Lord Arthur's palm:

> When Mr. Podgers saw Lord Arthur's hand he grew curiously pale, and said nothing. A shudder seemed to pass through him, and his great bushy eyebrows twitched convulsively, in an odd, irritating way they had when he was puzzled. Then some huge beads of perspiration broke out on his yellow forehead, like a poisonous dew, and his fat fingers grew cold and clammy.

Podgers, cornered, reveals all to Lord Arthur except the fact that it is he Arthur is destined to murder. "It will take a little time" for Arthur to discover this, and Podgers, "playing nervously with a flash watch-chain," knows this and finally manages to smile at Arthur's impatience.

Podgers's revelation plunges Lord Arthur into a terrible world, black and hideous:

> The night was bitter cold, and the gas-lamps round the square flared and flickered in the keen wind; but his hands were hot with fever, and his forehead burned like fire. . . . A policeman looked curiously at him as he passed, and a beggar, who slouched from an archway to ask for alms, grew frightened, seeing misery greater than his own. . . .
>
> Then he wandered across Oxford street into nar-

row, shameful alleys. Two women with painted faces mocked at him as he went by. From a dark courtyard came a sound of oaths and blows, followed by shrill screams, and, huddled upon a damp door-step, he saw the crooked-backed forms of poverty and eld.

Arthur does not remain long in this demonic underworld, however. As the dawn breaks, he sees a group of rustics coming into London, and "rude as they were, with their heavy, hobnailed shoes, and their awkward gait, they brought a little of Arcady with them." Lord Arthur then goes home, sleeps, and wakes to a new world:

> Never had life seemed lovelier to him, never had the things of evil seemed more remote.
>
> Then his valet brought him a cup of chocolate on a tray. After he had drunk it, he drew aside a heavy *portière* of peach-coloured plush, and passed into the bathroom. The light stole softly from above, through thin slabs of transparent onyx, and the water in the marble tank glimmered like a moonstone. He plunged hastily in, till the cool ripples touched throat and hair, and then dipped his head right under, as though he would have wiped away the stain of some shameful memory. When he stepped out he felt almost at peace. The exquisite physical conditions of the moment had dominated him, as indeed often happens in the case of very finely-wrought natures, for the senses, like fire, can purify as well as destroy.

Lord Arthur's bath is a symbolic baptism, an entry into a world of beauty and purity higher than the one from which he had fallen—"Never had life seemed lovelier to him, never had the things of evil seemed more remote." He emerges from the bath purified and "almost at peace." He is not totally at peace, however, because he has not yet attained the highest state of purification, the state that will allow him to marry Sybil. He has faced Podgers and escaped from his world, but Podgers still lives.

The rest of the story is largely a satire on the Victorian sense of duty—indeed the story is subtitled "A Study of Duty." Since Podgers is able to predict the future—and there is no question about that—the future is obviously predetermined and nothing can be done to alter it. Arthur never once doubts the truth of Podgers's prediction of murder. Lord Arthur's chief fault, however, is his extreme impatience. "Be quick," he twice orders Podgers, causing the doomed man to smile, and after learning that he has successfully murdered Podgers, he dashes at full speed to Sybil:

> "My dear Sybil," cried Lord Arthur, "let us be married tomorrow."
>
> "You foolish boy! Why, the cake is not even ordered!" said Sybil, laughing through her tears.
>
> When the wedding took place, some three weeks later. . . .

One cannot rush Providence, but Lord Arthur solemnly decides it is his duty to Sybil to do precisely that and commit murder as soon as possible. Carlyle, in *Sartor Resartus* and *The French Revolution,* had stated that the Divine

Will unfolds itself in time and that it is man's duty to assist it. Of all the Victorians, it was Carlyle who spoke the loudest of man's duty. It is quite possible, then, that Wilde had Carlyle specifically in mind when he wrote **"Lord Arthur Savile's Crime,"** and this is supported by Jane Percy's letter in the story. She is the dean of Chichester's daughter, and one sentence in her letter reads as follows: "Papa says Liberty was invented at the time of the French Revolution. How awful it seems!" Is the reference to the revolution itself or to Carlyle's *The French Revolution?*

At the risk of straining the reader's credence, I would like to suggest that it is probably the latter. Indeed, much of the letter—it appears to me—seems to be a series of suppressed comic jabs at Carlyle. For instance: "Thank you so much for the flannel for the Dorcas Society, and also for the gingham. I quite agree with you that it is nonsense their wanting to wear pretty things, but everybody is so Radical and irreligious nowadays, that it is difficult to make them see that they should not try and dress like the upper classes. I am sure I don't know what we are coming to." And again: "How true, dear aunt, your idea is, that in their rank of life they should wear what is unbecoming. I must say it is absurd, their anxiety about dress, when there are so many more important things in this world, and in the next. I am so glad your flowered poplin turned out so well, and that your lace was not torn." And Jane goes on to talk about frills and bows and satins, as Wilde playfully retailors *Sartor Resartus* along dandiacal lines.

Lord Arthur, in pursuing what he considers to be his duty, only succeeds in tempting Providence, for he does not realize it is Podgers he must murder. This is the result of his listening to a false prophet, and therefore receiving the truth incomplete. As Lady Windermere observes, however, "Surely Providence can resist temptation by this time." Luckily for Arthur, it can, and Lady Clementina dies a natural death despite his efforts. Arthur then sends an explosive clock to the dean of Chichester, but it blows up harmlessly, only knocking over the carving of the goddess of liberty, causing it to fall flat on its face and break its nose. Finally, Arthur despairs of success and comes to thoroughly identify destiny with doom, as he has been doing more or less throughout the tale. "We live in an age of unbelief," preaches the dean of Chichester, and Arthur is indeed an excellent example of the age in this respect. At any rate, he decides on total passivity:

> He had made up his mind not to try any more experiments. Then he wandered down to the Thames Embankment, and sat for hours by the river. The moon peered through a mane of tawny clouds, as if it were a lion's eye, and innumerable stars spangled the hollow purple dome. Now and then a barge swung out into the turbid stream, and floated away with the tide, and the railway signals changed from green to scarlet as the trains ran shrieking across the bridge. After some time, twelve o'clock boomed from the tall tower at Westminster, and at each stroke of the sonorous bell the night seemed to tremble. Then the railway lights went out, one solitary lamp left gleaming like a large ruby on a giant mast, and the roar of the city became fainter.

> At two o'clock he got up, and strolled towards Blackfriars. How unreal everything looked! How like a strange dream! The houses on the other side of the river seemed built out of darkness. One would have said that silver and shadow had fashioned the world anew. The huge dome of St. Paul's loomed like a bubble through the dusky air.

The first point to note about this passage is the emphasis on time. The story is shot through with references to time and clocks and watches. Now we have Big Ben itself announcing the end of a day and the beginning of a new one. Before 12:00 P.M., Arthur's world is a beautiful but tainted one. It is dominated by the moon and an exquisite, star-spangled "hollow purple dome"; but it also contains such disturbingly unaesthetic elements as barges, a turbid stream, and shrieking trains. After 12:00 P.M., this world begins to fade away—lights go out, the roar of the city grows faint—and an entirely fabulous dreamworld of silver and shadow emerges, wrapped in the religious aura of the huge, lofty dome of St. Paul's. The time for his salvation has come: Arthur accidentally stumbles across Podgers, the only remaining blot on the scene, and quickly flings him into the Thames. "At last he seemed to have realised the decree of destiny. He heaved a deep sigh of relief, and Sybil's name came to his lips."

Finally, **"Lord Arthur Savile's Crime"** is also about two forms of art. Podgers is an artist-figure, and he practices the art of reading palms. He is at Lady Windermere's to perform, and she associates him with other artists. Lady Windermere complains that Podgers does not look "a bit like a cheiromantist," then adds, "All my pianists look exactly like poets; and all my poets look exactly like pianists." Podgers's "art" is called a science, however, and he pursues it with great objectivity, to the point of using a small magnifying glass to study Lord Arthur's palm. Podgers's art, furthermore, deals with the dark, fallen side of life, and he makes his living by revealing people's sins and vices. All this suggests the naturalist artist—Zola, perhaps, or George Moore, whose novel *A Mummer's Wife* (1885) was "the first completely Naturalistic novel in English." Podgers is the type of the fallen artist who deals with the fallen world.

Sybil counterbalances Podgers; she represents a pure, beautiful art that stands in opposition to naturalistic art, and is utterly untainted by the fallen world. Lord Arthur's devotion to her as a symbol of the highest spiritual state suggests the aesthetic artist—Rossetti, Poe, and others. In the 1880s Oscar Wilde was a prominent aesthete, and his story is a celebration of aestheticism and aesthetic art. In Greek mythology Sybil is Apollo's handmaiden, and Apollo is mainly the god of prophecy and the patron god of art. Though Wilde's Sybil has no prophetic powers, she does suggest aesthetic art in this tale, and the mythic roots of her name reinforce her connection with art. That Wilde was fully aware of the connotations of the name becomes clear when we read what he wrote about Elizabeth Barrett Browning in "English Poetesses," an article published in 1888: "She was a Sybil delivering a message to the world, sometimes through stammering lips, and once at least with blinded eyes, yet always with the true fire and fervour

of a lofty and unshaken faith, always with the great raptures of a spiritual nature, the high ardours of an impassioned soul. As we read her best poems we feel that, though Apollo's shrine be empty and the bronze tripod overthrown, and the vale of Delphi desolate, still the Pythia is not dead."

Sybil, then, is like the song of pure art, and to marry her is to enter a sparkling world of romance, entirely beautiful and untainted:

> Never for a single moment did Lord Arthur regret all that he had suffered for Sybil's sake, while she, on her side, gave him the best things a woman can give to any man—worship, tenderness, and love. For them romance was not killed by reality. They always felt young.

This is pure fairy tale, the world that Rossetti sought and never found, the world that Poe longed for and could have reached in the symbolic Lenore. Lord Arthur attains it. It is the higher innocence, which can be attained only after the child's world of innocence has been destroyed and the problem of evil faced and solved.

"The Fisherman and His Soul" is one of Wilde's later fairy tales. It again deals with the fall from the world of innocence and the attainment of a higher innocence, but it counterpoints **"Lord Arthur Savile's Crime"** in its treatment of the demonic. Lord Arthur reaches a state of higher innocence by destroying Podgers, but the young fisherman attains it only after his heart grows large enough to include in love both the beautiful mermaid and his evil soul. The story is a humorless and puzzling one, but is worthy of detailed analysis because it shows the development of Wilde's attitude toward the demonic in the fairy tales and also reveals how extremely symbolic he could be in his thinking.

Essentially, we have two worlds in **"The Fisherman and His Soul"**: the beautiful underwater world of the mermaid and the demonic world of dry land, a world of evil and suffering. This split is indicated at the very opening of the story:

> Every morning the young Fisherman went out upon the sea, and threw his nets into the water.
>
> When the wind blew from the land he caught nothing, or but little at best, for it was a bitter and black-winged wind, and rough waves rose up to meet it. But when the wind blew to the shore, the fish came in from the deep, and swam into the meshes of his nets, and he took them to the market-place and sold them.

The fisherman belongs on dry land, but he is drawn to the sea, as his occupation clearly indicates. The two worlds are separate and apparently irreconcilable, however. When the fisherman catches a stunningly beautiful mermaid in his net, he finds that he cannot marry her:

> And one evening he called to her and said: "Little Mermaid, little Mermaid, I love thee. Take me for thy bridegroom, for I love thee."
>
> But the Mermaid shook her head. "Thou hast a human soul," she answered. "If only thou

wouldst send away thy soul, then could I love thee."

The mermaid is a concentrated symbol of the beautiful, dazzling undersea world, and she refuses to come into contact with anything that is ugly or that belongs to the demonic dry land. She is not human, however. She helps the fisherman only in his capacity as fisherman, and is willing to love him only if he abandons the human part of himself, his soul, for "the Sea-folk have no souls." The fisherman, being young, exists in a boyish, carefree world of innocence, is insulated from any knowledge of evil, and yearns to unite only with what is beautiful. "Of what use is my soul to me?" he asks himself. "I cannot see it. I may not touch it. I do not know it. Surely I will send it away from me, and much gladness shall be mine."

In order to get rid of his soul, the fisherman first goes to a priest, but the priest informs him that the soul is infinitely valuable and curses the sea-folk as soulless. The merchants, on the other hand, refuse to buy his soul because it has no value whatsoever. He finally goes to a red-haired witch, who takes him to a Witches' Sabbath and introduces him to a proud, well-dressed gentleman, the Devil himself. It is a measure of the young fisherman's innocence at this point that he does not realize the danger he is in. Nor does he recognize the well-dressed gentleman. The Devil exudes such an aura of evil, though, that the fisherman, on approaching him, involuntarily makes the sign of the cross and calls on God's name. The witches shriek and fly away, and the Devil sadly withdraws, but the fisherman captures the red-haired witch and forces her to tell him how to cast off his soul.

It is the fisherman's heart, not his soul, that occupies the position of highest importance in this tale, for love is seen as the supreme value and the road to salvation. The soul's problem is that the fisherman's love is exclusive—his heart belongs to the mermaid alone. Consequently, the soul is cast off without a heart:

> And his Soul said to him, "If indeed thou must drive me from thee, send me not forth without a heart. The world is cruel, give me thy heart to take with me."
>
> He tossed his head and smiled. "With what should I love my love if I gave thee my heart?" he cried.
>
> "Nay, but be merciful," said his Soul: "Give me thy heart, for the world is very cruel, and I am afraid."
>
> "My heart is my love's," he answered, "therefore tarry not, but get thee gone."
>
> "Should I not love also?" asked his Soul.
>
> "Get thee gone, for I have no need of thee," cried the young Fisherman.

Exiled to the demon universe of dry land, the soul, cast off without a heart, becomes thoroughly evil. The fisherman, on the other hand, is now able to reject the dry land completely and live in an underwater world of innocence with the mermaid. The fisherman opens his heart only to the beautiful mermaid and allows the mermaid to occupy

it. The mermaid unites with the fisherman—"nor shall our lives be divided"—and dwells within his heart while the soul is banished altogether from his body.

The fisherman's state of innocence cannot last forever, though, which is indicated by the fact that he obviously cannot consummate his relationship with the mermaid. The fisherman's world of innocence, moreover, exists through an unnatural fragmentation, a destruction of the unity of body and soul that renders the fisherman inhuman. The soul carries the full burden of this fragmentation, and it yearns to reunite with its body. The soul now exists as the opposite of the mermaid, a concentrated symbol of the evil and suffering that constitute the dry land. Once each year it tempts the fisherman to take it back. The first year it tempts him with a lying offer of total wisdom:

> "Do but suffer me to enter into thee again and be thy servant, and thou shalt be wiser than all the wise men, and Wisdom shall be thine. Suffer me to enter into thee, and none will be as wise as thou."
>
> But the young Fisherman laughed. "Love is better than Wisdom," he cried, "and the little Mermaid loves me."
>
> "Nay, but there is nothing better than Wisdom," said the Soul.
>
> "Love is better," answered the young Fisherman, and he plunged into the deep, and the Soul went weeping away over the marshes.

The second year, the evil soul tempts the fisherman with a lying offer of great wealth, but he again rejects the offer in favor of love. The third year, however, the soul tempts the fisherman with a more beautiful lover than the mermaid:

> "Her face was veiled with a veil of gauze, but her feet were naked. Naked were her feet, and they moved over the carpet like little white pigeons. Never have I seen anything so marvellous, and the city in which she dances is but a day's journey from this place."
>
> Now when the young Fisherman heard the words of his Soul, he remembered that the little Mermaid had no feet and could not dance. And a great desire came over him, and he said to himself, "It is but a day's journey, and I can return to my love," and he laughed, and stood up in the shallow water, and strode towards the shore.

The fisherman's motive for leaving the mermaid is a deep love for what is beautiful. Also, the fisherman is coming of age—he now wants a human lover, not one whose lower half is a fish's tail. The new lover's face is veiled, and it is her lower limbs that attract him. There is little beauty on the dry land, however, as he finds when he takes his soul back. The soul leads the fisherman to commit acts of evil, but the fisherman soon rebels and tries to cast out his soul again. He discovers that the act can only be performed once. Symbolically, what this means is that the world of innocence, once abandoned, can never be re-entered.

Evil is no longer an external and banished part of the fisherman, it is now a vital part of his nature, one he is intensely aware of, and he must either deal with it effectively or remain forever trapped in the demon universe into which he has stepped. The fisherman refuses to remain in the demon universe, so he returns to the seashore and calls to his beloved mermaid. But the mermaid does not answer, nor can he plunge beneath the waves to seek her anymore—the undersea world is closed to him. For three years he remains by the seashore, motivated by the power of love, calling to the mermaid every morning, noon, and evening.

The soul, wishing the fisherman to return to the dry land, tempts him first with evil, hoping to destroy the love in his heart:

> And ever did his Soul tempt him with evil, and whisper of terrible things. Yet did it not prevail against him, so great was the power of his love.

Then it tempts him with good:

> So he spake to the young Fisherman and said, "I have told thee of the joy of the world, and thou hast turned a deaf ear to me. Suffer me now to tell thee of the world's pain, and it may be that thou wilt hearken. . . . To and fro over the fens go the lepers, and they are cruel to each other. The beggars go up and down on the highways, and their wallets are empty. Through the streets of the cities walks Famine, and the Plague sits at their gates. Come, let us go forth and mend these things, and make them not to be. Wherefore shouldst thou tarry here calling to thy love, seeing she comes not to thy call? And what is love, that thou shouldst set this high store upon it?"

> But the young Fisherman answered it not, so great was the power of his love.

Finally the soul despairs, yields to the power of love, and asks to be purified—a request it would never have made had it been sold to the Devil:

> "Lo! now I have tempted thee with evil, and I have tempted thee with good, and thy love is stronger than I am. Wherefore will I tempt thee no longer, but I pray thee to suffer me to enter thy heart, that I may be one with thee even as before."

> "Surely thou mayest enter," said the young Fisherman, "for in the days when with no heart thou didst go through the world thou must have much suffered."

> "Alas!" cried his Soul, "I can find no place of entrance, so compassed about with love is this heart of thine."

> "Yet I would that I could help thee," said the young Fisherman.

The fisherman is now ready to attain a state of higher innocence. His desire to help and love his demonic soul is a genuine one, and it deals a final blow to the beautiful, exclusive world of innocence:

> And as he spake there came a great cry of mourning from the sea, even the cry that men hear when one of the Sea-folk is dead. And the

young Fisherman leapt up, and left his wattled house, and ran down to the shore. And the black waves came hurrying to the shore, bearing with them a burden that was whiter than silver. White as the surf it was, and like a flower it tossed on the waves. And the surf took it from the waves, and the foam took it from the surf, and the shore received it, and lying at his feet the young Fisherman saw the body of the little Mermaid. Dead at his feet it was lying.

The mermaid exists within the fisherman's heart as something very beautiful and fragile, something that cannot come into contact with evil and survive. As soon as the fisherman begins to open his heart to his soul, the mermaid dies.

The late nineteenth century was fascinated with the Jekyll-Hyde character. In **"Lord Arthur Savile's Crime,"** Sybil and Podgers are projections of the Jekyll-Hyde split within the protagonist. In **"The Fisherman and His Soul,"** the mermaid and the soul are the same projections. Sybil, unlike the mermaid, suggests a higher innocence distinct from Arthur's initial world of careless, boyish insouciance, but both Podgers and the soul embody the demonic, which is at once inside and outside the protagonist. Arthur attains a state of higher innocence by destroying Podgers and loving and marrying Sybil. For the fisherman, the road is a very different one indeed:

Illustration from "The Remarkable Rocket" by artist Charles Robinson.

> The black sea came nearer, and the white foam moaned like a leper. With white claws of foam the sea grabbed at the shore. . . .
>
> And his Soul besought him to depart, but he would not, so great was his love. And the sea came nearer, and sought to cover him with its waves, and when he knew that the end was at hand he kissed with mad lips the cold lips of the Mermaid, and the heart that was within him brake. And as through the fulness of his love his heart did break, the Soul found an entrance and entered in, and was one with him even as before. And the sea covered the young Fisherman with its waves.

The fisherman dies, but he has attained a state of higher innocence and his place is now in heaven. His heart embraces in love both the mermaid and the soul at exactly the same time that distinctions between sea and dry land are swept away. By following the road of love, he finally manages to put an end to fragmentation within a framework of total purity. The mermaid acquires a soul—the fisherman's—the soul acquires a heart and is purified, and the fisherman reconciles the warring aspects of himself. The initial world of innocence was one of love, but a private, exclusive love limited to the beautiful mermaid. The higher innocence is again a world of love, but one that is all-encompassing. It is the lesson of total love that the priest learns in the end, as flowers burst from the barren soil over the fisherman's grave. He had earlier cursed the dead fisherman, the mermaid, the sea, and the sea-folk as godless, and had ordered the fisherman and the mermaid to be buried in barren ground. The grave blooms, however, and the flowers cause a strange transformation in the priest. The tale ends with the priest preaching God's love and blessing all of God's creatures and works:

> And in the morning, while it was still dawn, he went forth with the monks and the musicians, and the candle-bearers and the swingers of censers, and a great company, and came to the shore of the sea, and [blessed] all the wild things that are in it. The Fauns also he blessed, and the little things that dance in the woodland, and the bright-eyed things that peer through the leaves. All the things in God's world he blessed, and the people were filled with joy and wonder.

No one and nothing is excluded.

This fall from the world of innocence and subsequent attainment of a higher innocence is the governing principle of Wilde's fairy tales. Not all the tales reproduce this pattern in its entirety: some begin with the higher innocence, such as **"The Nightingale and the Rose"**; some never go beyond the child's world of innocence, as for example **"The Birthday of the Infanta"**; but the pulsing heart of the fairy tales, the thread that runs through all of them and ties them together, is this theme of the fall and the discovery of a higher innocence.

In brief, the world of innocence is a beautiful world that is blissfully unaware of the other, demonic side of existence. The demonic side of life is a universe of suffering or evil or both, and it may be internal, external, or both. The child begins in the world of innocence, but the process of maturing inevitably shatters this world and forces him to confront the demonic in life. The third stage, as in Blake, is the attainment of a higher innocence. This is total spiritual purity, and the road to it is love. It can only be reached after the world of innocence has been destroyed and the demon universe faced and dealt with effectively.

"The Canterville Ghost"—perhaps Wilde's most famous fairy tale—is somewhat marred because of its unfortunate attempt to reproduce this entire pattern. The story begins in the world of innocence, and here Wilde is brilliant. Practically every British child knows the story of the American family that rented a haunted castle in England, refused at first to believe that it was haunted, then tried to chase the ghost away with pesticides, and finally laughed it into a nervous breakdown.

There is a serious point to all this, though. The ghost is evil—it recalls its past crimes with glee—but the innocent American family refuses to recognize the demonic or to treat it seriously. Virginia, however, a virgin who is just coming of age, finally takes pity on the neurotic ghost and agrees to help it die. As a result, she opens herself to the full experience of the demonic, disappears into a vast dark hole, and emerges a while later with a box of indescribably valuable jewels given to her by the grateful ghost.

The jewels symbolize Virginia's attainment of a higher innocence. Her ability to love and pity the ghost has led to her total purification. She has developed a heart large enough to include everyone—even the British aristocracy, which her republican father continues to attack until the end. Unfortunately, however, the world of innocence Wilde portrays is so delightful that the story does not survive its loss. Virginia's development beyond this world is pale and uninteresting.

"The Happy Prince" also reproduces the entire fairy-tale pattern. The prince begins as a blissful boy who, after his death, becomes a beautiful statue high above the city and is happy because of his beauty. His cocoonlike world of beauty is soon shattered, however, for he realizes that a great deal of suffering exists in the city. Bit by bit, he strips himself of his beautiful jewels and gold leaf and gives them to the poor. Finally all his beauty is gone, and his lead heart breaks when the swallow who had been helping him dies, after undergoing a similar pattern of development. The story ends thus:

> "Bring me the two most precious things in the city," said God to one of His angels; and the angel brought Him the leaden heart and the dead bird.
>
> "You have rightly chosen," said God, "for in my garden of Paradise this little bird shall sing for evermore, and in my city of gold the Happy Prince shall praise me."

The higher innocence—far more beautiful than the first world of innocence—has been reached. Totally pure, their hearts overflowing with love, the prince and the swallow enter heaven forever.

"The Selfish Giant" is another variation on the same theme. The giant's castle and garden are beautiful, but he selfishly excludes a group of children from the garden and builds a wall to keep them out. The children suffer, but the giant does not care. The giant, having become aware of human suffering and refusing to feel love and pity, finds his beautiful private world shattered. A perpetual winter—the symbol of his fallen nature—descends upon his castle and garden, until the children manage to creep back in through a crack in the wall. They bring the spring with them, and the giant rushes out to meet them. They all run away, however, except for one tiny child whose eyes are so full of tears that he does not see the giant coming. "And the Giant's heart melted" at the child's suffering; he helps him, then knocks the wall down. The children, seeing that the giant has changed, return to the garden and come there daily after that. When the giant is old and ready to die, Christ personally comes and takes him to heaven, appearing in the form of the child the giant had helped many years before. But the giant, of course, had really entered heaven many years earlier, when his heart melted for the little child.

"The Young King" again reproduces the entire pattern of the fall from innocence and the achievement of a higher innocence. It is a story worthy of special notice, however, because the Christian ethos of the fairy tales is at its most intense here, and because **"The Young King"** will later prove helpful in understanding *De Profundis.* The tale begins with the cruel murder of a pure white princess and a beautiful aesthetic artist by order of the diabolical old king. The princess and the artist had married in secret. Their newly born son, the young king, is disowned and given to a goatherd to be raised. Realizing on his deathbed that he has no heir, however, the old king sends for his disowned grandson and names him as the heir. "From the first moment of his recognition," Wilde tells us, the young king "had shown signs of that strange passion for beauty that was destined to have so great an influence over his life." The son of aesthetes, he reacts aesthetically to his surroundings:

> The wonderful palace—*Joyeuse,* as they called it—of which he now found himself lord, seemed to him to be a new world fresh-fashioned for his delight; and as soon as he could escape from the council-board or audience-chamber, he would run down the great staircase with its lions of gilt bronze and its steps of bright porphyry, and wander from room to room, and from corridor to corridor, like one who was seeking an anodyne from pain, a sort of restoration from sickness.

> Upon these journeys of discovery, as he would call them—and indeed, they were to him real voyages through a marvellous land, he would sometimes be accompanied by the slim, fair-haired Court pages, with their floating mantles, and gay fluttering ribands; but more often he would be alone, feeling through a certain quick instinct which was almost a divination, that the secrets of art are best learned in secret, and that Beauty, like Wisdom, loves the lonely worshipper.

I have quoted at length because this is an extremely important passage. The young king's journeys of discovery are

journeys of self-discovery. His nature had been suppressed in peasant surroundings, but he has now found a new world whose beauty is the external manifestation of the "marvellous land" within. It is the world of his parents, whose nature he has inherited and is now exploring. The young king's world of innocence is not devoid of evil, however. This is symbolized by the fact that, though his parents were a pure white princess and a beautiful foreign artist, the young king's grandfather was the old king. The council-boards and audience-chambers are associated with the old king, and they create in the young king a spiritual pain that can be cured only by the beauty of art. As in "The Palace of Art," however, the young king's art world is private and therefore selfish: he excludes from it even the innocent "slim, fair-haired Court pages."

"The Young King" is about the coming-of-age of the young king. When found, "he was only a lad, being but sixteen years of age." In **"Lord Arthur Savile's Crime,"** marriage symbolizes the transition from boyhood to manhood. Here the symbol is the assumption of the authorities and responsibilities of kingship, and it is on the night before his coronation that the young king fully confronts the demonic element hitherto latent within himself.

Of all the beautiful art objects in the palace, most of them brought there by him, the young king finds his coronation robe of tissued gold, his ruby-studded crown, and his pearl-decorated scepter to be the most artistically pleasing. In three successive dreams, however—the first beginning at midnight—he comes to a vivid realization of the huge amount of evil and suffering that went into the making of the robe and the procuring of the rubies and pearls. Sleep is a state of mind where conscious thoughts are laid to rest and thoughts that lie beneath the surface emerge. The young king is now forced to explore a different aspect of his nature. What he was only subconsciously aware of when he gave the orders to fashion the robe, crown, and scepter, he now becomes terrifyingly aware of:

> Then the diver came up for the last time, and the pearl that he brought with him was fairer than all the pearls of Ormuz, for it was shaped like the full moon, and whiter than the morning star. But his face was strangely pale, and as he fell upon the deck the blood gushed from his ears and nostrils. He quivered a little, and then he was still. The negroes shrugged their shoulders, and threw the body overboard.

> And the master of the galley laughed, and, reaching out, he took the pearl, and when he saw it he pressed it to his forehead and bowed. "It shall be," he said, "for the sceptre of the young king."

The result is that guilt destroys the young king's enjoyment of an art world founded on evil and suffering:

> "Take these things away, and hide them from me. Though it be the day of my coronation, I will not wear them. For on the loom of Sorrow, and by the white hands of Pain, has this robe been woven. There is Blood in the heart of the ruby, and Death in the heart of the pearl."

The young king's three dreams constitute a fall into the

demon universe. His enclosed world of artistic beauty is shattered, and he becomes irreversibly and unbearably aware of the pain of others and his complicity in causing this pain. Instead of accepting his position and becoming a carbon copy of the old king, however, the young king's nature propels him to purge himself of evil and enter a state of complete purity. Christ is the symbol of the higher innocence the young king seeks. Motivated by a deep love for suffering humanity, he dons a beggar's robe and a crown of thorns and goes to his coronation.

His attempt to assume a Christ-like stature, however, is opposed by the realm. The whole kingdom—nobles, workers, clergy—makes a concerted effort to keep the young king in the demon universe. All argue in favor of a fragmented society in which men are not brothers. The last and subtlest argument comes from the bishop, who sincerely contends that evil is an integral part of the world and that man cannot alter this: "In the salt-marshes live the lepers; they have houses of wattled reed, and none may come nigh them. The beggars wander through the cities, and eat their food with the dogs. Canst thou make these things not to be? Wilt thou take the leper for thy bedfellow, and set the beggar at thy board? Shall the lion do thy bidding, and the wild boar obey thee?" The young king, however, refuses to be seduced by this argument and insists on following the path of love to its ultimate destination. Earlier, in the world of innocence, he had worshiped a picture from Venice and had spent a whole night contemplating a statue of Endymion. Now he stands before a different statue:

> He stood before the image of Christ, and on his right hand and on his left were the marvellous vessels of gold, the chalice with the yellow wine, and the vial with the holy oil. He knelt before the image of Christ, and the great candles burned brightly by the jewelled shrine, and the smoke of the incense curled in thin blue wreaths through the dome.

It should be stressed that Christ is connected with beautiful art objects. Wilde, in this tale, dissolves all differences between Christ and the highest manifestation of the artistic impulse, and identifies Christ with the highest and most beautiful art. The young king prays, then rises and faces the nobles who have entered the cathedral to slay him. But a strange thing happens:

> And lo! through the painted windows came the sunlight streaming upon him, and the sun-beams wove round him a tissued robe that was fairer than the robe that had been fashioned for his pleasure. The dead staff blossomed, and bare lilies that were whiter than pearls. The dry thorn blossomed, and bare roses that were redder than rubies. Whiter than fine pearls were the lilies, and their stems were of bright silver. Redder than male rubies were the roses, and their leaves were of beaten gold. . . . He stood there in a king's raiment, and the Glory of God filled the place, and the saints in their carven niches seemed to move.

God, in crowning the young king and elevating him to the stature of Christ, simultaneously creates for him a world of art that is far purer and more beautiful than the old world that had its roots in human suffering. The young king receives a new robe, a new scepter, and a new crown, far superior to the ones he had rejected and refused to wear. These new objects, moreover, are completely pure: they are straight from God and have no connection with human suffering. They are also public, symbols of the new reign that is about to commence, a reign of love and forgiveness for all. The young king, in attaining the higher innocence, becomes a second Christ, reconciles all fragmentation within a framework of love, and simultaneously enters the highest and most beautiful possible world of art.

"The Star-Child" again follows the entire fairy-tale pattern. The star-child begins, quite literally, in a cocoonlike world of beauty—enfolded in "a cloak of golden tissue, curiously wrought with stars, and wrapped in many folds." Although he comes to the world seemingly as a gift from the stars, he is brought up by a woodcutter's family. As he grows physically more beautiful each year, he also becomes proud and disdainful, despising the ugly and the poor and actually inflicting pain upon them. He becomes progressively more evil until he loses his symbolic star-parentage and acquires a new symbolic parent—a ragged, ugly, bleeding beggar-woman, who reveals herself as his mother. Though he rejects her disdainfully, the sparkling world of his star-parents vanishes: he loses his beauty and turns into a scaly monster. When the star-child's world of beauty is shattered, he finds himself a hideous part of the universe of pain and ugliness. After many severe trials and humiliations, he acquires a heart, purges himself of evil, and reaches a state of higher innocence. The symbols of the higher innocence are the regaining of his physical beauty, his new parents—a king and queen—and his new status as king. As an adolescent, he led a group of village boys in evil deeds, but he now leads a kingdom in love. Interestingly, though, the star-child dies within three years, for his sufferings have been too terrible and searing. If one's fall from the world of innocence is not cushioned, it seems, one may remain scarred for life or be utterly destroyed by the demon universe.

The other fairy tales do not fully reproduce a person's fall from the world of innocence and the attainment of a higher innocence, but they are nevertheless governed, in varying degrees, by this pattern. In **"The Birthday of the Infanta,"** for instance, the Infanta remains in the world of innocence from beginning to end, but the tale is a clear appeal to the reader to recognize human suffering, develop a heart, and attain a state of higher innocence. The dwarf whose act amuses the Infanta so much falls in love with her. He stalks into the palace to declare his love, but catches sight of himself in a mirror, recognizes that he is ugly and misshapen, and dies of a broken heart. The Infanta finds the dwarf's inert body and insists that he dance for her once more:

> "*Mi bella Princesa*, your funny little dwarf will never dance again. It is a pity, for he is so ugly that he might have made the king smile."

> "But why will he not dance again?" asked the Infanta, laughing.

"Because his heart is broken," answered the Chamberlain.

And the Infanta frowned, and her dainty rose-leaf lips curled in pretty disdain. "For the future let those who come to play with me have no hearts," she cried, and she ran out into the garden.

The tale clearly does not endorse the Infanta's heartlessness, but rather appeals to the reader to develop beyond it.

In **"The Nightingale and the Rose,"** we have a student who exists in the fallen world and a nightingale who is already approaching the highest state of love. The student—who diligently pursues the disciplines of logic, philosophy, and metaphysics—is downcast because he cannot find a red rose for his love. The nightingale tries to find him a rose, but discovers that the price she must pay for it is her own life. The rose-tree sadly informs her that "if you want a red rose, . . . you must build it out of music by moonlight, and stain it with your own heart's-blood." The nightingale does this:

> The nightingale pressed closer against the thorn, and the thorn touched her heart, and a fierce pang of pain shot through her. Bitter, bitter was the pain, and wilder and wilder grew her song, for she sang of the Love that is perfected by Death, of the Love that dies not in the tomb.

The nightingale dies, but her love—like Christ's—is "the Love that dies not in the tomb." And indeed, the thorn does suggest that the nightingale has attained a Christ-like stature. The student, on the other hand, is rejected by his love because the rose does not go with her dress and because he is not rich enough. Cynically, he tosses the rose away, declares that love is silly and not half as useful as logic, and returns to his room to read a dusty book. It turns out that the student is hopelessly lost in the fallen world and knows nothing of love. Because of him, however, the nightingale has attained utter spiritual purity through a self-sacrificial act of love, and she goes, one assumes, straight to heaven, where she will join the happy prince and the swallow.

"The Devoted Friend" is about two friends, little Hans and big Hugh the miller. Big Hugh is entirely selfish and befriends Hans simply because of what Hans can do for him. Big Hugh is rich, and he lives with his family in a beautiful home from which he excludes all that suffers or is ugly. Little Hans, on the other hand, is poor and "not distinguished at all, except for his kind heart." Hans, motivated by friendship, continually does favors for big Hugh until the last favor costs him his life. Because of friendship and love, Hans endangers his life to get a doctor for big Hugh's boy, and he dies in a storm. But Hans's act of love, like that of the nightingale, is really the attainment of complete spiritual purity, and his place is now in heaven.

"The Remarkable Rocket" is an entirely comic study in selfishness. The remarkable rocket is totally self-centered and makes the following statement to the other fireworks: "I am always thinking about myself, and I expect everybody else to do the same. That is what is called sympa-

thy." He outlines his virtues in great detail to the other fireworks, insists that he should be admired, and actually cries in order to prove his sympathetic nature. The rocket's tears so dampen his powder, however, that he fails to go off at the appointed time—the celebration of the prince's wedding—and is therefore discarded and tossed into a mudpile. Finally, two boys use him for firewood and he does go off. The spectacle is quite beautiful, but the remarkable rocket is the only one around to admire it—even the two boys are asleep. Since the rocket is completely selfish, his beautiful world remains private and his need for admiration is frustrated. And his beautiful world is ephemeral: the unseen spectacle soon ends, and the rocket falls back to the earth, a burnt-out stick. The world of innocence cannot last forever, though the rocket, to the end, does not realize that he must develop beyond this world and become truly sympathetic. Consequently, once the world of innocence is shattered, the rocket gasps and dies.

If one reads Wilde's fairy tales in the order of their composition, one notices that the demonic element in them grows steadily more sinister until it threatens to break out of the fairy-tale mold and destroy it. The movement from **"Lord Arthur Savile's Crime"** through *The Happy Prince and Other Tales* to the tales of *A House of Pomegranates* is toward an increasing awareness of the demonic and a corresponding inability to control and contain it. In the earlier tales, Wilde usually presents the demonic in a light-hearted way. For example, in **"The Selfish Giant,"** Wilde's presentation of the demonic is playful:

> The Snow covered up the grass with her great white cloak, and the Frost painted all the trees silver. Then they invited the North Wind to stay with them, and he came. He was wrapped in furs, and he roared all day about the garden, and blew the chimney-pots down. "This is a delightful spot," he said; "we must ask the Hail on a visit." So the Hail came. Every day for three hours he rattled on the roof of the castle till he broke most of the slates, and then he ran round and round the garden as fast as he could go. He was dressed in gray, and his breath was like ice.

The late fairy tale, **"The Young King,"** however, uses the same method of personification to give us a relatively sinister picture of the demonic:

> And Death laughed again, and he whistled through his fingers, and a woman came flying through the air. Plague was written upon her forehead, and a crowd of lean vultures wheeled round her. She covered the valley with her wings, and no man was left alive.
>
> And Avarice fled shrieking through the forest, and Death leaped upon his red horse and galloped away, and his galloping was faster than the wind.
>
> And out of the slime at the bottom of the valley crept dragons and horrible things with scales, and the jackals came trotting along the sand, sniffing up the air with their nostrils.

Examples of this change in mood abound. In the early

"The Remarkable Rocket," the selfish assertion of superiority is presented in a harmless way:

> "My father was a rocket like myself, and of French extraction. He flew so high that the people were afraid that he would never come down again. He did, though, for he was of a kindly disposition, and he made a most brilliant descent in a shower of golden rain. The newspapers wrote about his performance in very flattering terms. Indeed, the Court Gazette called him a triumph of Pylotechnic art."
>
> "Pyrotechnic, Pyrotechnic, you mean," said a Bengal Light; "I know it is Pyrotechnic, for I saw it on my own canister."
>
> "Well, I said Pylotechnic," answered the Rocket, in a severe tone of voice, and the Bengal Light felt so crushed that he began at once to bully the little squibs in order to show that he was still a person of some importance.

In the later **"The Star-Child,"** the selfish assertion of superiority is presented differently:

> And his companions followed him, for he was fair, and fleet of foot, and could dance, and pipe, and make music. And wherever the Star-Child led them they followed, and whatever the Star-Child bade them do, that did they. And when he pierced with a sharp reed the dim eyes of the mole, they laughed, and when he cast stones at the leper they laughed also.

We have moved from a rocket bullying a Bengal light to a beautiful young boy piercing a harmless animal's eyes with a sharp reed.

Along with the increasingly sinister presentation of the demonic element, the movement of Wilde's fairy tales shows a steady lessening of the comic element. The two trends are inextricable and interdependent. As the demonic element becomes more central and disturbing, it ceases to be funny and can no longer be treated comically. **"Lord Arthur Savile's Crime"** is comic from beginning to end. Even Arthur's exploration of the fallen world remains comic, for there is no objective correlative between Podger's reading of Arthur's palm and Arthur's reaction to the reading. The early fairy tale **"The Devoted Friend"** is also comic from beginning to end, despite its grim theme of what amounts to the murder of little Hans by big Hugh.

The tales of *The Happy Prince* collection, however—of which **"The Devoted Friend"** is a part—are not entirely comic. Two of the five tales, **"The Devoted Friend"** and **"The Remarkable Rocket,"** are comic all the way through, but **"The Selfish Giant"** is rather touching as the giant attains the higher innocence and is finally claimed by Christ. **"The Nightingale and the Rose"** mixes the comic and the serious. The nightingale's self-sacrifice is moving, but the student's experience with the girl he thinks he loves is comic—or at any rate has comic elements. **"The Happy Prince"** is largely serious, except in its amusing presentation of utilitarian attitudes.

The tales of *A House of Pomegranates,* on the other hand, are almost entirely lacking in humor. There is no humor

in **"The Young King,"** except for a single joke in the opening paragraph. In **"The Birthday of the Infanta,"** the tone is quite serious, though the Infanta remains in the world of innocence from beginning to end. **"The Fisherman and His Soul"** is not comic. **"The Star-Child"** begins comically, but that element disappears after the opening paragraphs and never appears again. The movement of Wilde's fairy tales, then, is toward the elimination of the comic element.

In the later fairy tales, moreover, it is not enough to become aware of the demonic element—one must incorporate it within an all-inclusive framework of love. This becomes especially clear when we compare **"Lord Arthur Savile's Crime"** and **"The Fisherman and His Soul."** As has already been indicated, in the earlier tale Arthur becomes aware of Podgers but tosses him into the Thames and attains a state of higher innocence by loving and marrying Sybil; he never feels any love or pity for Podgers. In the later tale, however, the fisherman attains the higher innocence only when his heart becomes large enough to include both the beautiful mermaid and his own demonic soul. Podgers and his fallen world are destroyed, but the soul and its evil, agonized world of dry land are loved and purified. These two tales stand at opposite ends of the spectrum, but a movement is discernible in the fairy tales away from Arthur's inability to love and pity the demonic.

The early **"The Canterville Ghost"**—written very shortly after **"Lord Arthur Savile's Crime"**—may be seen as transitional in this respect: the ghost, though sent to its grave, is pitied and loved by Virginia. This movement is again inextricable from the growing concern with the demonic in the fairy tales. As the demonic element becomes more sinister and difficult to control, it can no longer be flipped into the Thames or sent to its grave, but has to be dealt with more realistically. When the young king reaches a state of higher innocence, he acquires a Christ-like stature and a heart large enough to embrace an entire realm, and so does the star-child. For the star-child, the higher innocence unites the beauty of the world of innocence with a deep love for all that suffers and is ugly. In the later fairy tales, then, the demonic element becomes more sinister but is still contained within an all-inclusive framework of love.

And these tales are, after all, fairy tales—a genre that admits the demonic only to neutralize and defeat it. In *The Decay of Lying,* written early during the fairy-tale period, Wilde's main thesis is that the imagination gives meaning to the forms and shapes of the outside world. The pure imagination creates a beautiful world and a Romantic literature, while the fallen imagination produces a Darwinian universe and Zola-like, naturalistic literature. Wilde playfully uses the vocabulary of the fallen imagination throughout the essay, referring to the fallen universe as real, factual, scientific, and to the pure universe as unreal, a dream, a lie. Wilde's view of art at this stage is compactly stated by his character, Vivian:

> *Vivian* (reading). "Art begins with decoration, with purely imaginative and pleasurable work dealing with what is unreal and non-existent. This is the first stage. Then Life becomes fasci-

nated with this new wonder, and asks to be admitted into the charmed circle. Art takes life as part of her rough material, recreates it, and refashions it in fresh forms, is absolutely indifferent to fact, invents, imagines, dreams, and keeps between herself and reality the impenetrable barrier of beautiful style, of decorative or ideal treatment. The third stage is when Life gets the upper hand, and drives Art out into the wilderness. This is the true decadence, and it is from this that we are now suffering."

The fairy tales belong to the second stage. They admit Life—that is, the fallen world—into their charmed circle, but they refashion and recreate it and never allow it to get the upper hand. They are an assertion of childlike purity. As Wilde wrote of *The Happy Prince and Other Tales* in 1888: "They are studies in prose, put for Romance's sake into a fanciful form: meant partly for children, and partly for those who have kept the child-like faculties of wonder and joy, and who find in simplicity a subtle strangeness." In this respect, the fairy tales are very much like Blake's *Songs of Innocence,* and may be read as Wilde's *Songs of Innocence.* Meant to capture a childlike state of the mind, they are for those who have not yet crossed the threshold from innocence into experience. Their great paradox is that, though their genre places them firmly in the world of innocence, their main theme is the fall from innocence and the attainment of a higher innocence. What Wilde seems to be saying is that one can become aware of the stages beyond innocence without actually being claimed by them—can absorb, as it were, the entire Blakean pattern and contain it within the realm of childlike innocence.

A biographer might read the fairy tales as Wilde's attempt to assert the primacy of his family life and to reject the siren call of homosexuality. **"Lord Arthur Savile's Crime"** revolves around a marriage that cannot succeed until the coarse Podgers—Robert Ross?—is destroyed within the self. As for the other tales, they are probably Wilde's attempt to remain within the charmed circle of his children, innocent and safe from evil. Cyril and Vyvyan, Wilde's two boys, were very young during this period, and Wilde was very attached to both of them—especially Cyril. As the fairy tales insist, however—both in their theme and in their progressively darker vision of the demonic—the movement from innocence to experience is inevitable and must be made.

In *The Picture of Dorian Gray,* Wilde crosses the threshold. Some years later, in 1892, he wrote to Coulson Kernahan, who had sent him a fairy tale, "The Garden of God": "Your strength lies not in such fanciful, winsome work. You must deal directly with Life—modern terrible Life—wrestle with it, and force it to yield you its secret. You have the power and the pen. You know what passion is, what passions are; you can give them their red raiment, and make them move before us. You can fashion puppets with bodies of flesh, and souls of turmoil: and so, you must sit down, and do a great thing." (pp. 1-36)

> *Christopher S. Nassaar, "The Fairy Tales," in his* Into the Demon Universe: A Literary Exploration of Oscar Wilde, *Yale University Press, 1974, pp. 1-36.*

> **[*The Happy Prince, and Other Tales*] is a volume of as pretty fairy tales as our generation has seen.**
>
> **—William Butler Yeats, in a review published in** United Ireland, *26 September 1891.*

Mary Walker   (essay date 1976)

[*Walker was an American educator, critic, and author of children's books. In the excerpt below, she provides a thematic and stylistic overview of Wilde's fairy tales.*]

> It is the duty of every father to write fairy tales for his children, but the mind of a child is a great mystery. It is incalculable, and who shall divine it, or bring to it its own peculiar delights? You humbly spread before it the treasures of your imagination, and they are as dross.
>
> [Oscar Wilde]

In trying to delve into this mystery, Wilde has given us a collection [of fairy tales] which has thrown most of his critics into various states of confusion, while at the same time confirming, to some degree at least, Pearson's theory that 'like all who have expressed themselves in stories or plays for children, from Hans Andersen to James Barrie, he was emotionally undeveloped' [*The Life of Oscar Wilde,* 1946]. By now, Wilde's comment that 'I had about as much intention of pleasing the British child as I had of pleasing the British public' has become common knowledge. Pearson's corollary, 'True; but he had thoroughly pleased an Irish child: himself', provides an interesting critical atmosphere for reviewing [Wilde's two volumes of tales, *The Happy Prince, and Other Tales* (1888) and *A House of Pomegranates* (1891)]. (p. 30)

"The Happy Prince" is the story of a statue who, although 'gilded all over with thin leaves of fine gold', with eyes of bright sapphires, and a 'large red ruby' on his sword hilt, is unhappy because, despite admiration from the people, he can see, from his position of grandeur above the city, all the ugliness and misery within it. His leaden heart is sore, and tears fall from his bejewelled eyes on to a migrant swallow. This swallow unselfishly postpones his trip to Egypt to become the prince's messenger. First the prince bids him to remove the jewels to cure a child's fever, a writer's hunger, and to save a little match girl from her father's wrath. Stripped of his jewels, the prince is blind, but still there is misery and poverty in the city, which he perceives through the eyes of the swallow. He makes an irrevocable and drastic decision: 'I am covered with fine gold, . . . you must take it off, leaf by leaf, and give it to my poor; the living always think that gold can make them happy'. As the good work progresses, so does the year, and soon the snow and frost begin to weaken the sparrow—'but he would not leave the Prince, he loved him too well'.

Finally the end comes for the sparrow, and after kissing the prince on the lips, falls dead at his feet. 'At that moment a curious crack sounded inside the statue, as if something had broken. The fact is that the leaden heart had snapped right in two.' The prince now looks forlornly shabby, and even worse, there is a dead bird lying at his feet; he is sent to the furnace where the amazing discovery that his heart will not melt causes it to be thrown, in disgust, on the dust heap. So the prince and the little swallow, who is also lying on the dust heap, are united in death, and their reward is a place in paradise.

'No child will sympathise at all . . . when he [the prince] is melted down . . . in obedience to the dictum of the art professor that since "he is no longer beautiful, he is no longer useful".' [Alexander Galt Ross in *The Saturday Review*, 1888]. This may be true; it certainly points to one important flaw in **"The Happy Prince"** and all the other tales—the overuse of crude irony and epigram which, when written, is very artificial and hence subject to criticism. On the other hand, Ransome's comment [in his *Oscar Wilde: A Critical Study*] that these are 'very married stories' is a valuable one. It is not difficult to imagine how children could be captivated by the idea that 'the eyes of the Happy Prince were filled with tears, and tears were running down his golden cheeks', or the swallow's reaction to the prince's lead heart: ' "What! Is he not solid gold?" he said to himself. He was too polite to make any personal remarks out loud'. These are humourous asides and if they were to come from a master story-teller with a benign twinkle in his eye, they would assuredly delight the audience, just as they delighted Pater who found them a consolation while he was in bed suffering from gout!

In print, **"The Happy Prince"** displays many undesirable characteristics. The diction, although modern, is often stilted: ' "How cool I feel!" said the boy, "I must be getting better." ' This hardly sounds like the language of a child in a fever—even if he is being fanned by a swallow's wings. Similarly, it is difficult to visualize children, their faces becoming rosier, playing in the streets and shouting 'We have bread now'. It is unnatural, and what is worse, mundanely so. Fairy tales should not have to state the obvious. In contrast, the swallow's descriptions are too 'aesthetic', too wildly unreal. He tells of 'the King in his painted coffin', 'wrapped in yellow linen, and embalmed with spices'; and the chain of 'pale green jade' and his hands 'like withered leaves' are the fantastic details of death.

The irony, like the diction, lacks subtlety. Wilde frequently seemed to have found difficulty in leaving things unsaid. We know the poor mother is 'thin and worn, and she has coarse red hands, all pricked by the needle'; we know that she is desperately trying to complete the maid-of-honour's ball gown. Wilde's determination to emphasize the Socialist orientation results in his changing the scene to a balcony where a beautiful girl is languidly musing, 'I hope my dress will be ready. . . . I have ordered passion flowers to be embroidered on it; but the seamstresses are so lazy'. The irony here is unnecessarily overt.

Woodcock speaks of 'the theme of the misery of the people and the callousness of rulers' in **"The Happy Prince"** [in his *The Paradox of Oscar Wilde*]. Although Wilde was apparently becoming more aware of the plight of the poor and downtrodden, I think that Woodcock is wrong to stress this awareness as a theme. Pearson calls **"The Happy Prince"** a 'sermon in practical Christianity', and here is the more telling point. Wilde certainly was becoming more and more interested in the personality of Jesus Christ, 'an interest that increased every year until at length he almost identified himself with Christ and often spoke in parables'. This, one of the most significant features of the fairy tales, is demonstrated clearly in God's request at the end of **"The Happy Prince"**:

> 'Bring me the two most precious things in the city,' said God to one of His Angels; and the Angel brought Him the leaden heart and the dead bird. 'You have rightly chosen,' said God, 'for in my garden of Paradise this little bird shall sing for evermore, and in my city of gold the Happy Prince shall praise me.'

Clearly their deaths are not in vain; although paradoxically, they are rejected by their fellow men, they are received into the bosom of God. Salvation is their reward for doing good works, a moral which is, [according to Ransome], 'a little too obvious even for grown-up people'.

"The Nightingale and the Rose" is a far more successful story, even if its many unsubtle epigrams seem to serve little purpose. It is a more romantic tale than **"The Happy Prince"**, and here we begin to see some of the 'charming fancies and quaint humour' referred to by one of the many critics of the time who were not prepared to reveal their identity. The story tells of how a nightingale overhears the wail of a true lover who is spurned because he cannot find a red rose to give his love; without this, she will not dance with him, and since his garden is barren, he is in despair. He is a student; his 'hair is dark as the hyacinth blossom, and his lips are red as the rose of his desire; but passion has made his face like pale ivory, and sorrow has set her seal upon his brow'.

The nightingale resolves to relieve his misery by presenting him with the red rose he needs. Each rose bush she tries in vain—they are all of less important colours—but at last she comes to a bush whose roses are 'as red as the feet of the dove and redder than the great fans of coral that wave and wave in the ocean cavern'. But the winter's frost and wind have wreaked destruction on this sad rose bush, and she will bear no roses at all. There is only one terrible way that a red rose can be got—so terrible that when asked, the poor tree hesitates to tell. It must be 'built out of music by moonlight' and 'stained with your own heart's blood'. Nothing is too much to sacrifice for Love, so the nightingale sadly prepares for death. All night she sings while the thorn pierces her heart. Next morning the student opens his window and plucks the beautiful, perfect rose. His delight is to be short-lived: the girl heartlessly rejects his attentions. The rose will not go with her dress, and besides, 'jewels are better than flowers', Sadder and wiser, the student returns to his room, pulls out a 'great dusty book', and buries his sorrows in intellectual pursuits.

In this simple story of self-sacrifice, Wilde combines some of his best descriptive powers with an amazingly tight construction. This is a real fairy tale, not a Christian sermon. There is no happy ending; the nightingale's sufferings and death are totally futile. In keeping with this stronger concept, the imagery and tempo are more forceful. 'What I sing of, he suffers: what is joy to me, to him is pain'. This counterbalance of emotion sets the rhythmic pattern for the tale. It has an interesting progression, a sort-of question and answer technique which finally becomes reality with the nightingale's pleas to the rose trees. Their roses are 'white as the foam of the sea, and whiter than the snow upon the mountain', 'yellow as the hair of the mermaiden who sits upon an amber throne, and yellower than the daffodil that blooms in the meadow'. The balance is maintained with the red rose's reply, already quoted. From this rhythmical balance the story moves to a more powerful rhythm—the macabre song of the bird as she presses against the thorn, driving it deeper and deeper into her. The images astound by their simple beauty: 'on the topmost spray . . . there blossomed a marvellous rose, petal following petal, as song followed song'. The tension builds up steadily: 'pale was it, at first as the mist that hangs over the river—pale as the feet of the morning, and silver as the wings of the dawn'.

A deeply emotional, almost sexual tone develops as 'the nightingale pressed closer against the thorn, and louder and louder grew her song, for she sang of the birth of passion in the soul of man and a maid'. Not until *The Ballad of Reading Gaol* is Wilde to use repetition to such effect again. The sexual image continues as 'the thorn touched her heart, and a fierce pang of pain shot through her. Bitter, bitter was the pain, and wilder and wilder grew her song . . . and the marvellous rose became crimson . . . crimson was the girdle of petals, and crimson as a ruby was the heart . . . then she gave one last burst of music. . . . the red rose heard it, and it trembled all over with ecstasy and opened its petals'.

'Wilde's sense of beauty was uncertain, his technique came and went' [wrote Arthur Symons in the *Athenaeum* in 1908]. In this ebb and flow of talent, which shows again his mental confusion, his attempts to be humorous often have detrimental effects on his work. In **"The Nightingale and the Rose"**, the linking of powerful, macabre imagery with tongue-in-cheek witticisms brings this tale down to the level of **"The Happy Prince"** at times. The contrasts are bizarre in a completely unacceptable way; the student faithfully mouths some Wildean pet theory when he sagely decides that the girl 'is like most artists; she is all style without any sincerity'. Too often there is a remark which 'plays to the audience' and does nothing for the story.

The final comment, that 'Love is not half so useful as Logic. . . . in fact it is quite unpractical, and as in this age to be practical is everything, I shall go back to Philosophy and study Metaphysics', shows Wilde at his worst.

"The Selfish Giant" [the story Ransome called] a 'delightful essay in Christian legend', tells of how a giant returns from a visit to a Cornish ogre to find his beautiful garden full of children happily playing. Shouting 'My own garden is my own garden . . . and I will allow nobody to play in it but myself', he immediately banishes all the children, erects a high wall, and puts up a 'Trespassers will be Prosecuted' notice. Such an unnatural act of selfishness draws a similar response from Nature. The season abruptly changes to Winter, and when Spring tries to return to the world, a little flower pops up, sees the notice and, her heart sad for the children, sinks back at once into the ground to sleep. A long time passes, the giant despairs of ever seeing Spring again, or of having fruit or flowers in his garden; but one day he looks out to see a miraculous transformation. All the trees but one are bedecked with blossoms and leaves, and in each tree sits a child. They have crept through a hole in the wall. Under the solitary bare tree where the winter wind still howls stands a little boy crying bitterly, too tiny to climb up. At once the giant's heart melts: 'How selfish I have been! . . . now I know why the Spring would not come'. As he lifts the little child into the branches, the tree bursts into flower. The boy kisses the giant, who resolves to remove the wicked wall with its selfish notice; but in spite of this, the little boy never returns.

Many years later, it is Winter again, winter in the giant's life too, for he is old and feeble now. As the old man looks out into the farthest corner of his sleeping garden, another miraculous sight meets his incredulous gaze—the tree 'covered with lovely white blossoms', its golden branches hanging with silver fruit, is sheltering 'the little boy he loved'. The giant notices in horror the terrible prints of the nails on the child's feet and hands, and for a moment his old noisy wrath returns. But his rage is cut short with the sudden realisation that the child is divine. And with the realization of this divinity, he dies.

One again recalls Pearson's comment on Wilde's increasing interest in the Christ figure, and his growing tendency to speak in parables. This tale, non-tragic in the end, as the emblem of Christ predominates, is unfortunately another example of what Gide refers to as a 'masterpiece manqué'. It is not necessary for the boy to say, Biblically, 'today you shall come with me to my garden, which is Paradise', as if Wilde felt the moral required explanation. Similarly lacking in feeling is the cry of the children: 'How happy we were there!' Such a prosaic analysis of situation is not normal in children's conversation.

In contrast to these stodgy moments, there are many appealing flights of fancy; the reciprocal action of Nature's withdrawal in the face of human meanness is delightful. 'Once a beautiful flower put its head out from the grass, but when it saw the notice board . . . it slipped back into the ground again and went off to sleep.' This clever technical device is accompanied by skilful images which complement the structure. 'The Snow covered up the grass with her great white cloak, and the Frost painted all the trees silver'; the North wind thought the garden 'a delightful spot' and endeavoured to 'break all the slates on the roof by inviting Hail for a visit'. The image is one of a real fairy land, where the elements and the seasons are capable of discrimination. The giant, too, is a rough diamond, and his conversion is painlessly and lovingly achieved. Pater, referring to its 'beauty and tenderness', describes [in an 1888 letter to Wilde] **"The Selfish Giant"** as 'perfect in its kind'. Here Wilde shows his fondness for magical moments where dramatic events occur as if inspired by the legendary wand. The moment of vision, the powerful insight into truth which kills the giant, brings out the most gently moving passage in the tale: 'the children . . . found the Giant lying dead under the tree, all covered with white blossoms'.

Wilde's next offering, **"The Devoted Friend"**, has been described, in complete contrast to the other tales, as 'the cleverest and least agreeable in the volume' [Ross]. Clever it most certainly is, as there is a doubt as to who the devoted friend actually is—Hans, a timid little creature, or big Hugh, the miller. The latter, we are told ironically, is Hans's most devoted friend because he engineers situations so that Hans is always doing tasks for him, to the detriment of his own interests.

Hugh keeps Hans in feudal submission by promising to give him an old wheelbarrow—which never materializes. This happy state of affairs (for Hugh) continues throughout the summer. Hans is left to his own devices during winter 'for when people are in trouble they should be left alone and not bothered by visitors'; and indeed, Hans is the first to tell his neighbours how indebted he is to the miller. The end comes when Hans is caught in a fierce storm and drowns on his way to fetch a doctor for Hugh's son.

Numerous comparisons to Hans Christian Andersen have been made by critics of Wilde's fairy tales. In most of the stories, frequent touches of pathos and similarity of situation (in **"The Happy Prince"** there is a poor little match girl, for example) make this a reasonable comparison, although Harold Child's remark that 'they would never have been written but for Hans Anderson [sic]' is farfetched. **"The Devoted Friend"** seems to embody much of what is similar to Andersen's style, while bringing to the fore Wilde's own comic spirit and sense of the absurd. First, as in Andersen's "The Fir Tree", this is a tale within a tale. The story of Hans is told by a Linnet to his friends in the river, amid much laughter and somewhat unsubtle wit, very much in Hans Andersen vein. The Water-rat scorns the anxious Duck who is having difficulty with her children: 'you will never be in the best society unless you can stand on your heads', she cries. The ducklings are so young that 'they did not know what an advantage it is to be in society at all'. Andersen's 'The Mole fell in love with her . . . but he said nothing at the time, for he was a very discreet person' displays a similar sense of humour. In Wilde's story, the rat's remark that 'Love is all very well in its way, but friendship is much higher' prompts the sad saga of little Hans.

Throughout the tale a topsy-turvey humour is always present; paradoxes and witticisms are sprinkled generously, sometimes slightly cynically. 'How well you talk! . . . really I feel quite drowsy. It is just like being in church', is Mrs Hugh's admiring remark to her husband. Warming to his subject, he continues: ' . . . lots of people act well . . . but very few people talk well, which shows that talking is much the more difficult thing of the two, and much the finer thing also'. Wilde seems to be sticking his tongue out at his critics here, an attitude which persists as he tells us this peculiar story whose moral (a 'dangerous thing to do', he admits) can only convince us that he is laughing at the moral tale as an art form. The double stan-

dard of satire thus presented eliminates, or lessens, the 'quality of bitterness' said to predominate in the stories. The focal point of this double standard is our hero, Hans. Wilde creates here a hero as ludicrous and pathetic as the Emperor with his new clothes. Hans is a gullible fool, not a serious figure in any sense. It is tempting to say he deserves his miserable downfall. Certainly it is almost impossible to sympathize with him. Similarly, the miller is not really an evil character, in the Iago way; he is merely selfish, thoughtless, bombastic and vain. Crudely depicted as 'the villain of the piece', he is actually only taking advantage of a character less forceful than himself, and he does not have to put much effort into his conquest. There is no question of persuasion, no element of tension whatsoever. Admittedly there are a few transparently ironic remarks, which delude Hans, not the reader; but in effect, the miller tells Hans what to do, and he obeys. I raise these points as a reminder that in Wilde's concept of 'plot' classical tragic elements persist. The potential is never realized—he probably never intended it to be—and with these tales, particularly **"The Devoted Friend"**, the positions of tragedy and comedy are becoming inverted. It is possible to see a situation developing where, as the comic gains the ascendancy, Wilde gives himself more and more opportunities to try out witty dialogue, possibly establishing a pattern for his later work.

"The Remarkable Rocket", despite the 'piquant touch of contemporary satire which differentiates Mr Wilde from the teller of pure fairy tales', is, in fact, a real fairy tale. The plot is simple, the characters delightfully unreal (the tale is told by fire works and concerns their progression to fame and success on the occasion of the Prince's wedding), the language typical of Wilde's cleverest gently satirical style. The Catherine Wheel is 'one of those people who think that, if you say the same thing over and over a great many times, it becomes true in the end'. The Roman Candle cracks jokes and the Cracker 'nearly explodes with laughter'. The Bengal Light bullies the squibs to cover up his embarrassment at being insulted by the Rocket who, being tall, supercilious and superior to his fellows in every way, suffers acutely when he is accidentally left out of the firework display. He consoles himself as best he can, but his spirits are soon dampened as he finds himself thrown into a ditch with only frogs and ducks for company. His 'public life' has suddenly ended, and his downfall is complete when he is used for kindling. The moral of the story, what Pater calls its 'wise wit', is that vanity is evil.

If plot is novel, the manner of telling the tale is not. Yet **"The Remarkable Rocket"** is designed to please, and that it does. The wit succeeds in its child-like freshness and gaiety. The characters are created to be obtuse, so the heavy-handed humour, the unsubtle irony, the carefully engineered pun are all equally acceptable. There is little in this tale that can give offence, unless the over-use of humorous satire could be so considered. The language is certainly pleasing in its simplicity. For once, Wilde has managed to avoid the pitfall of useless ornamentation. With this mixture of wit and paradox, the first book of fairy tales comes to an end.

The further Wilde goes in his writings from the method of speech, from improvisation, from sympathy with some especial audience the less original he is, the less accomplished . . . *The Happy Prince and Other Tales* is charming and amusing because he told its stories, . . . and *A House of Pomegranates* is over-decorated and seldom amusing because he wrote its stories.

[W. B. Yeats, in his introduction to *The Complete Works of Oscar Wilde,* 1923]

This comment is amply demonstrated in **"The Young King"**, which tells of a prince who, after a 'classical' up-bringing by peasants, is suddenly acknowledged as the heir to the throne. In his new environment, he 'cultivates that strange passion for beauty that was destined to have so great an influence over his life'; immature and unsophisticated, 'rather like Wilde himself, he sets out with a naïve and thoughtless pleasure to enjoy the beautiful life based on wealth and power'.

Eventually the old king dies; the young prince has the awful burden of monarchy to face, and elaborate preparations are made for the coronation. On the eve of the great day, however, the prince has three dream-visions which show in horrific detail the misery and suffering caused by his imminent coronation. The first dream takes him to 'a long, low attic, amidst the whir and clatter of many looms. The meagre daylight . . . showed him the gaunt figures of the weavers . . . pale, sickly-looking children . . . their faces pinched with famine'. The young king, subdued and chastened by what he sees, hears from one of the weavers: 'we must work to live, and they give us such mean wages that we die'. In a sudden flash the youth realizes that the cloth of gold they are weaving is for his own coronation robe, and with a cry of horror he wakes.

He has two other visions, in which he sees the gruesome and agonizing conditions in which men toil, sacrificing their lives for pearls and other jewels for his robes and trappings. He is incredulous, but eventually full awareness of the truth sets his course. He refuses to wear the robes that have been woven with so much misery, or the precious stones that have been got by so many deaths.

Clad again in his 'leathern tunic and rough sheepskin coat', he goes sadly from the palace to the cathedral, amid jeering from the crowds, hostility from his nobles and amazement from the bishop. In a miraculous spontaneous transformation, as he stands at the altar he is clothed in divinely regal raiment, crowned with light, and his rough staff breaks into flower.

Altogether, **"The Young King"** is too forced, too contrived, and completely lacking in subtlety. As a character, the prince himself moves from one extreme of behaviour to another; the conflicting pagan and Christian themes are embodied in him. He starts off life with somewhat shady origins—he is not illegitimate, but his mother sealed her own damnation by marrying one 'much beneath her in station'. Upon arrival at the court, the prince becomes a truly pagan figure, an undeniably 'aesthetic' youth who is described as lying on his embroidered couch 'wild-eyed and open-mouthed, like a brown woodland Faun'. He leans delicately against the carved penthouse of the chimney and contemplates beauty while languidly admiring the *objets d'art* surrounding him. In the midst of all this languid splendour the ghastly visions occur. The change in the young king's attitude to life is instant and dramatic. In his Christ-like abandonment of wordly, material things, he even goes so far as to make a crown of thorns to wear.

In keeping with this Christian-moral atmosphere, Wilde's diction is Biblical and archaic. [Rupert Croft-Cooke in his *Feasting With Panthers*], refers to many of the personalities who posed their way through this period of 'faked decadence' as 'precious'. It is an excellent description of the young king. One can imagine the delight of Wilde in putting platitudes such as 'shall joy wear what grief has fashioned?' into the mouth of his little woodland faun. The bishop, too, sounds like a rambling biblical extract: 'will thou take the leper for thy bedfellow, and set the beggar at thy board? Shall the lion do thy bidding, and the wild boar obey thee?' The weaver's speech in the vision is similarly stilted. 'Why art thou watching me? Art thou a spy?' seems to link two irreconcilable ideas—the down-to-earth idea of spying does not seem to fit with the language of 'arts' and 'thous'. Any possibility of spiritual enrichment is destroyed by the triteness of the diction.

The concept of the three dreams, or visions, is by no means new; unfortunately, Wilde chose one of the most difficult of literary techniques—the allegory—but his tale lacks the simplicity and force of the true Christian parable. 'The stories . . . have pretty poetic and imaginative flights . . . but then again they wander off too often into something between a "Swinburnian" ecstacy and the catalogue of a high art furniture dealer.' The reference [published in an unsigned 1891 review in the *Pall Mall Gazette*], is particularly to the extensive list of bric-a-brac in the young king's chamber, which includes a press 'inlaid with lapis lazuli', rich tapestries, a 'curiously wrought cabinet with lacquer panels of powdered and mosaiced gold', a cup of 'dark veined onyx', and a 'laughing Narcissus in green bronze'. The chamber is a complement to the young king who, with his 'dark woodland eyes', 'a smile lingering around his boyish lips', and face framed with dark curls, seems the emblem of the decadent era. The obvious pleasure in gruesome description, each horrible detail of the dreams laboriously recounted, shows Wilde still in the grip of a literary standard which thrives upon the macabre.

In the third dream, Wilde uses an almost mediaeval style of allegory. On a plain, like William's vision of Piers the Plowman, the young king sees the battle for supremacy between Ague, Avarice and Death:

> Death laughed and took up a black stone, and threw it into the forest . . . and out came Fever in a robe of flame. She passed through the multitude . . . and each man that she touched died. The grass withered beneath her feet as she walked.

The tempo of the tale grows more and more intense, causing [what James Gibbons Huneker in a 1914 edition of *Puck*, called] a sort-of 'hot-house atmosphere'. The detail becomes stifling, the tone oppressive.

The intensity of atmosphere is heightened by the heavily

dramatic ending. Once again, the imagery relies upon often-used vocabulary, the emotion is cloying, with definite sexual undertones:

> And lo! . . . the dead staff blossomed, and bare lilies that were whiter than pearls. . . . Redder than male rubies were the roses, and their leaves were of beaten gold. . . . the gates of the jewelled shrine flew open and from the crystal of the many-rayed monstrance shone a marvellous and mystical light.

Not satisfied, Wilde adds: 'The Bishop's face grew pale and his hands trembled. "A greater than I hath crowned thee", he cried'. From a conversation between Wilde and Richard Le Gallienne comes an unintentional criticism of **"The Young King"**. I quote at length, as it sums up quite remarkably the main stylistic defects. Wilde recounts a conversation with his son, Cyril:

> Then I, believing of course that something picturesque would be expected of me, spoke of magnificent things. 'What do I dream of ? . . . dragons with gold and silver scales, . . . eagles with eyes made of diamonds . . . elephants! . . . so I laboured on with my fancy, till observing that Cyril was entirely unimpressed, and indeed quite undisguisedly bored, I came to a humiliating stop, and, turning to him, I said: 'But tell me, what do you dream of, Cyril?' His answer was like a divine revelation. 'I dream of PIGS,' he said.

As [what Woodcock calls] a 'parable on the capitalist system of industrial exploitation . . . exposing the evils of monarchy, capitalism and imperialism', **"The Young King"** fails. It has, naturally, a strong Socialist strain (Wilde thought Socialism a good idea at the time) but it lacks all the simplicity which could give it effectiveness; in addition, there is a Dickensian overtness which reminds one of Tiny Tim and the Ghost of Christmas Yet to Come. A 'pretty enough morality' is perhaps a more realistic comment, although the sharp contrast between the Christian elements and the mediaeval macabre shows that the conflict in Wilde's own mind was still obviously hampering his literary expression.

As in **"The Young King"**, the dramatic effects of self-knowledge, the awareness of reality when applied to oneself, form the basis for **"The Birthday of the Infanta"**. The little princess, a spoilt girl, has assembled a variety of marvellous acts to entertain her and her guests at her birthday party. Although all the acts are good, the last is undoubtedly superior: the dancing of the little Dwarf. 'When he stumbled into the arena, waddling on his crooked legs and wagging his huge misshapen head from side to side, the children went off into a loud shout of delight.' Later, the Dwarf, who has immediately fallen in love with the princess, searches throughout the palace for a glimpse of her. At last he enters the most beautiful chamber of all but notices a peculiar small figure watching him from the other end of the room. As he approaches, he sees that it is a horrible little monster. His fear grows as the monster imitates his every move. Appalled, he suddenly apprehends the truth; he knows who the monster really is and, in despair, sinks sobbing to the floor. When the princess and her

friends arrive, laughing at his grief-stricken antics, and begging him to continue his dance, he realizes, all too clearly, that his grotesque ugliness is a bizarre novelty, and that his beloved princess regards him purely as a fantastic toy. His heart breaks—to the disgust of the Infanta, who cries in disdain: 'For the future let those who come to play with me have no hearts'.

In that self-realization leads to ruin, to the total destruction of the Dwarf's happiness and finally to Death, this tale is tragic. The climax, pointing definitely to a situation more fully exploited in *The Picture of Dorian Gray,* shows Wilde's ability to create an image of horror: 'He struck at it, and it returned blow for blow. He loathed it, and it made hideous faces at him'. Yet this hero is anti-tragic in his comical grotesqueness. The position of hero is twisted to reveal a figure so degraded, so foul, that identification with it is impossible; nevertheless, there is a 'masterly touch of pathos' which removes it from the stodginess of merely 'exemplifying the theme of the wicked carelessness of people in power to those below them'. It does do that, but again, I do not think Wilde's motives (or his inclinations) were ever truly Socialistic. The Grand Inquisitor and Don Pedro, the Infanta's uncle, are moved almost to tears by a puppet play, and it is not surprising that Wilde should have included this as a contrast to their later behaviour. They react to the Dwarf's agonized lifelessness at the end with the words, 'A whipping master should be sent for', and simply shrug their shoulders when they discover that he is dead. The irony is too transparent to be taken really seriously. A more credible example of cruelty is the account of the Dwarf's discovery in the forest by nobles who, knowing the Spanish Court's 'cultivated passion for the horrible', present him as a gift to the Infanta. This incident, revealing the concept of human beings being given as gifts, shows more of the evils of power than do the acts of obvious cruelty.

With his descriptions of the Dwarf, Wilde brings out much of the pathos in the story. 'Perhaps the most amusing thing about him was his complete unconsciousness of his own grotesque appearance.' The strain of pathos is heightened by the fact that the Dwarf falls in love with the princess the moment he sees her, so when she jestingly throws him a rose 'he takes the whole matter quite seriously, and pressing the flower to his coarse lips, he put his hand upon his heart, and sank on one knee before her, grinning from ear to ear, and with his little bright eyes sparkling with pleasure'. The effectiveness of the emotion is sealed by the use of very plain language. One recalls here the tale Wilde told of 'poor Aunt Jane', the proud old Wildean relative in County Tipperary who, upon realizing how proud and selfish she had been, resolved to give a huge ball for the whole county, the cost of which she would bear—if it took the rest of her life to repay. There is a dramatic sadness in the picture of the grand dame alone in the midst of all the splendid preparations, and quietly dying of sorrow at the absence of her guests; 'and not for some considerable time after her death was it discovered that Aunt Jane had quite forgotten to send out any invitations'.

In style, Wilde seems to have considered **"The Birthday**

Illustration from "The Selfish Giant" by artist Walter Crane.

of the Infanta" his best story. 'He gravely told some friends that he had conceived it "in black and silver", but that, when translated into French, it had come out "pink and blue". The fairy-tale Infanta is certainly a good example of a jumbled Anglo-French ensemble:

> Her robe was of grey satin . . . heavily embroidered with silver . . . studded with rows of fine pearls. Two tiny slippers with big pink rosettes peeped out . . . pink and pearl was her great gauze fan, and in her hair, which like an aureole of faded gold stood out stiffly from her pale little face, she had a beautiful white rose.

Many descriptions in [what Woodcock describes as] this 'heavily jewelled fantasy' demonstrate 'the growing addiction to the use of words merely for the sake of their sounds from which Wilde apparently derived a sensuous pleasure. The over-long ornate lists have by now a familiar ring about them, particularly the view of the rooms in the palace, which [according to an unsigned 1892 review in *The Athenaeum*], 'reads like an extract from a catalogue at Christie's'.

In fairness, it must be said that occasionally, Wilde produced a masterpiece of imaginative writing; the trouble was, that, like the little girl in the nursery rhyme, 'when he was good, he was very, very good . . . '. For example, the image of Nature paying homage to the Infanta is superbly portrayed:

> Even the pale yellow lemons, that hung in such profusion from the mouldering trellis and along the dim arcades, seemed to have caught a richer

colour from the wonderful sunlight, and the magnolia trees opened their great glove-like blossoms of folded ivory, and filled the air with a sweet heavy perfume.

Like many of his contemporaries, Wilde was aware that 'there were certain colour-forces in English, a power of rendering gloom', which he carefully uses in the somewhat pointless 'subplot' in **"The Birthday of the Infanta"** by frequent contrasting of light and dark. The Infanta's mother, who died within six months of giving birth, is embalmed and laid in the 'black marble' chapel. The king, 'wrapped in a dark cloak', clutches at the 'pale jewelled hands' of his dead wife in a 'wild agony of grief', trying in vain to 'wake by his mad kisses the cold painted face'. His married life, 'with its fierce, fiery-coloured joys' (with these sort of images Wilde leaves Andersen far behind), seems a bit out of place in the story, yet Wilde devotes nearly two pages to this gloomy and macabre man who prefers the chapel 'where the sun was never allowed to enter' to his daughter's birthday party. This concession to the *Decadence,* the desire to astonish with images [that H. Jackson, in his *The Eighteen Nineties,* calls] 'not always mystical, or even symbolical; in the majority of cases . . . frankly sensuous', can only stress the relevance of the comment that these are 'written' stories, written moreover for a particular audience.

The third story, **"The Fisherman and His Soul"**, is a good deal longer than the others. It tells of a fisherman who, to gain the love of a beautiful mermaid with 'mauve-amethyst eyes', sells, or rather, by means of sorcery, pawns his soul. The soul, heartless (since the mermaid has the heart), wanders far and wide, attaining new heights of wisdom, discovering the magic formula for untold wealth, and generally becomes degenerate. Eventually the soul returns to the fisherman in the hope of seducing him away from his love, and thus become whole again. After two years, the soul succeeds in tempting the fisherman with the promise of immoral and unknown delights. Although he succumbs to the soul's persuasive promises, the fisherman soon realizes his mistake; he sees the ugliness of his soul, the depravity of its pleasures. In desperation he tries to cut it from him again, but now it is too late, for once a soul has been received back, it can never be cast off.

Sadly he makes a little wattle hut, intending to live as a hermit, ever hoping that his dear mermaid will return to him, but years pass, and his hopes are never fulfilled. Then one day there is a great cry from the sea, and the waves wash the mermaid's body up on to the shore. As the fisherman's heart breaks in a frenzy of longing, the soul finds an entrance. The fisherman is reunited with his love—and with his soul—and where they are buried, strangely beautiful flowers grow. So magnificently aethereal are they, that the cynical priest is shaken into regretting his harsh sermonizing about the evil of the sea folk, and by a miracle his heart is converted to charity.

In a review written in 1891, this story was described as 'the most far-reaching and elaborate effort' of all the tales in the volume. To question this statement, apart from its apparent meaninglessness, raises several valid points. Why, first, does the critic see this story as 'far-reaching'? Possibly because he could think of nothing better to say; but perhaps, unconsciously, he touched on an important flaw: it combines so many loose strands, drags in so vast and varied a selection of moral sources that in spite of its general 'fairy-tale' background, it is decidedly not a fairy-tale. Most children would give up in despair or disgust after the tenth long-winded page—and there are twenty five. Thematically, it is far-reaching; the Faustian idea of selling one's soul straight away strikes a note of seriousness. The queer witch with her red hair, her dress embroidered with peacocks' eyes and her little cap of green velvet, is a slightly off-key symbol of evil. Her repetitious diction and ridiculous oaths—'by the hoofs of the goat I swear it'—reduce her potency, yet she is the instrument of evil, the escapist route to abandonment of earthly temptation as real as anything in *Faust*.

Finally, it is the knowledge of what he really is that brings the fisherman's ruin; while he lives in blissful oblivion with the mermaid, he ignores the temptations of the soul. It is simply non-existent for him. When the soul returns, disaster befalls him. Here is the opposite moral, if there is a moral as such, from that in **"The Young King"** where the experiences lead to salvation. Both the tales are a sort of Pilgrim's Progress, but the fisherman's ordeals end in death. If there is a heaven, the fisherman goes to it with the pagan mermaid. The only person who appears to obtain a Christian benefit is the miserable priest.

[Arthur Symons wrote in *The Athenaeum* in 1908 that] 'Wilde's style is constantly changing. . . . it is only at intervals that it ceases to be artificial, imitative or pretentious. The attempt to write constantly in a beautiful way leads to a vast amount of grandiloquence which is never convincing because it is evidently not sincere'. Because of this erratic quality in Wilde's work, **"The Fisherman and His Soul"** contains some of the most powerful passages of dramatic writing he ever did, some excruciating moments of action, and flung in alongside them, some hopelessly over-burdened 'aesthetic' meanderings. The soul's journeys, for example, strike one as being aimless, and forced into an ornate mould; they are functional as 'fillers', but do not really have value to the story, not even in heightening the illusion.

In contrast, the scene where the witches dance in the moonlight on top of the mountain, where, 'like a targe of polished metal the round sea lay at his feet, . . . a great owl, with yellow sulphurous eyes, calls to him', brings into focus the excitement of ancient alchemy and the terror of witchcraft. The evil which is born of frenzied ritual, the sterile loathsomeness of the persona of Satan, is present in:

> Round and round they whirled, and the young Witch jumped so high that he could see the scarlet heels of her shoes. Then right across the dancers came the sound of the galloping of a horse, but no horse was to be seen, and he felt afraid.
>
> 'Faster,' cried the Witch, and she threw her arms about his neck, and her breath was hot upon his face. 'Faster, faster!' she cried, and the earth seemed to spin beneath his feet, and his brain grew troubled, and a great terror fell on

him, as of some evil thing that was watching him. . . .

> It was a man dressed in a suit of black velvet . . . his face was strangely pale, but his lips were like a proud red flower . . . heavy eyelids drooped over his eyes.

The rhythmic climax shows a profoundly dramatic spirit, bringing to mind Tam O'Shanter urging his mare over the brig in terror of his life. The only note of bathos comes when the fisherman feels compelled to make the sign of the Cross and call upon the 'holy name'; then his diction becomes 'Biblical', and remains unnatural throughout.

As Wilde's sense of beauty came and went, so did his sense of the bizarre. The fisherman's love for the mermaid hinges on a basically comic idea. He is tempted to abandon her by the image of a dancing girl whose naked feet move over the carpet 'like little white pigeons'. The realism of his reaction makes it the more absurd: 'He remembered that the little Mermaid had no feet and could not dance'. Surely Wilde was not serious. Strangely, and yet not completely unexpected, the idea of the dancing girl is one of sensuality, and the fisherman's reaction to it stems from a decadent emotion, as does his behaviour with the mermaid's body on the sea shore:

> He kissed the cold red of the mouth, and toyed with the wet amber of the hair. . . . in his brown arms he held it to his breast. . . . into the shells of its ears he poured the harsh wine of his tale. He put the little hands round his neck, and with his fingers he touched the thin reed of the throat.

At the same time there is much of beauty, much forcible writing in the story. There is the tension of the cutting off of the soul, and the dallying courtship of evil. There is strength of expression in the description of the mermaid, whose 'hair was as a wet fleece of gold, . . . her body was as white as ivory and her tail was of silver and pearl. Silver and pearl was her tail and the green weeds of the sea coiled round it'. Economy of adjectives and controlled use of repetition enhances the dramatic effect of the images, which sometimes attain a vividness reminiscent of parts of the Ancient Mariner's tale. Completely different are the Wildean touches of the ridiculous—the heartless soul, and the mermaid who cannot dance because she has no feet. In the end, it is not a unified whole; the crisis of the tale is so 'lost in decorations' that 'we let it pass unnoticed at a first reading'; [Symons] the themes are jumbled and tangled, and the long, apparently purposeless passages make it frankly boring.

The last of the stories in **"A House of Pomegranates"** conforms to the vague allegorical pattern of the others. **"The Star Child"** concerns a child who literally falls from heaven in a bright flash of gold, to land in the path of a woodcutter who brings him up as his own. Growing up, he becomes increasingly beautiful, and sadly, increasingly cruel and vain. It seems as if he is to go the way of many a foolish Narcissus, but he is saved, for as Fate had dropped him from the heavens, so she drops his salvation, namely his mother, who has assumed the personage of a foul hag. The youth's initial rejection of his mother—symbolizing the

world's poor and deprived—causes him to undergo a severe trial, a long pilgrimage in which, as a toad-like creature, repulsive and covered with scales, he has to serve
penance for his misdeeds. Rejected by Nature and humanity alike, he at last arrives at the point of truth; he is given
three almost impossible tasks by a magician—he has to
find three different pieces of gold, and failure to return
with them holds the promise of the most horrifying punishment. Freeing a hare from a trap enables him to remake
a bond between himself and Nature, which in turn gives
him the courage to risk giving the gold to a poor leper who
is begging at the city gate. On his third sortie, the miracle
happens: as he gives the gold to the leper, he is transformed into a beautiful youth again, and the leper and the
beggar-woman are transformed into his handsome parents. At once he repents of all his earlier sins, and accordingly, miracle follows miracle—his parents are the King
and Queen, who set him up as ruler. His brief but glorious
reign, based on mercy and justice ends after only three
years, and paradoxically, 'he who came after him ruled
evilly'.

The irony of the last line sounds a note of despair for the
salvation of mankind. The Socialist ideal of government
in brotherhood and love appears to be disqualified by
Wilde's irony and his obvious confusion about the destiny
of humanity. The star-child himself, when confronted by
choices at the beginning, makes the wrong decision—
wrong in Christian terms, that is, which is interesting
since the child's life seems to be pagan-oriented in its dramatic start. Fate throws this child upon the woodcutter,
whose charitable act in adopting him allows him to get on
the path to salvation. Fate intervenes again, as the boy's
mother simply pops into the story at a crucial point in his
road to ruin. The *deus ex machina* performs its last function by throwing the boy into the magician's hands and
stationing the leper at the gate (a Biblical touch here, in
keeping with the Biblical diction).

The pilgrimage of penance—the boy literally wanders far
and wide—described by Wilde as 'the bitter fire of his testing', has much in common with the mediaeval morality
sagas. I am thinking particularly of something like *Sir Ga-
wain and the Green Knight,* where the blend of Christian
and pagan hangs upon similar points of importance, the
most notable perhaps being the significant intervention of
Fate and the use of Nature to symbolize humility, maturity or sterility. The repetition of question and denial from
the animal kingdom is similar to the rhythmical repetition
in **"The Young King"**, where the device lends an air of expectation. The mediaeval love of repetition is evident in
the use of numbers, too. Here the number three is imbued
with special significance; the three-year journey is repeated in the performance of the three tasks set by the magician. In these ways, this tale has an element of romance,
a cyclic movement apparently, from despair and sorrow
to a new generation of hope and love, rather like the structure of *A Winter's Tale,* where the actions of the children
go full circle to make the parents whole again.

[B. H. Clark wrote in his *European Theories of The Drama*
that] 'Insistence upon the rank of the tragic hero, or the
so-called nobility of his character, is really but a clinging

to the outward forms of tragedy.' These outward forms,
the least important elements after all, were buried deep in
Wilde's soul, but in the Fairy Tales he failed to create tragedy, and ended up in sentimentality. The allegory is one
of the most demanding of literary devices, but with his inevitable excesses in decoration and, more damaging, his
lopsided sense of realism, Wilde was never able to achieve
the simplicity required by that form. Finally, Bosman, [in
his *A Boer Rip Van Winkel*], sums up neatly the greatest
area of failure: 'I don't mind writing a story in which the
plot is vague. But when the atmosphere isn't there—the
background and the psychology and the interplay of situation and character—then what is left isn't my idea of a
story'. (pp. 30-41)

> *Mary Walker, "Wilde's Fairy Tales," in* Unisa
> English Studies, *Vol. XIV, Nos. 2 & 3, Septem-
> ber, 1976, pp. 30-41.*

John Allen Quintus　(essay date 1977)

[*Quintus is an American educator and critic. In the following essay, he examines the moral dimension of
Wilde's fairy tales.*]

A curious strategy common to most studies of Oscar
Wilde is the omission of his fairy tales, prose poems, and,
more often than not, his criticism. The avoidance of these
stories and articles suggests an unwillingness to treat material which is *prima facie* more serious and more moral
than the amoral hedonism, the "studied trivialty" so long
associated with both Wilde's life and his art. Even a recent
book, Christopher Nassaar's *Into the Demon Universe*
(1974), characterizes Wilde's literary art as demonic, or,
at best, as an exploration of the latent evil impulses which
reside in all of us. Wilde's consistent indictment of selfishness, his celebration of love, his compassion for suffering—all evident both in well-known and unsung works—
rarely receive attention today, just as they did not (for the
most part) during Wilde's lifetime.

To be sure, several scholars have noted a moral intent in
Wilde's art. Holbrook Jackson, Edouard Roditi, George
Woodcock, Epifanio San Juan, and Hesketh Pearson,
Wilde's English biographer, at least mention this moral dimension, even if they consider it an anomaly in view of
Wilde's personal habits. But largely critics have emphasized aestheticism, Satanism, decadence, and degeneration
in Wilde's work and have hesitated to allow that the real
Oscar, underneath the masks and poses, was a Victorian
gentleman who could not altogether escape a Victorian
predilection to preach—indeed, to be moralistic.

It is too great a task here to cover Wilde's entire canon,
underscoring all the while the moral argument of individual works. Rather, I would like to review the unheralded
fairy tales, and claim that the moral direction so obvious
in them is analogous to the morality Wilde espouses
throughout his art, from the early poetry to his *Epistola*
to Alfred Douglas (popularly known as *De Profundis*).
Further, some of the tales reflect significant personal tensions regarding art and morality or art appreciation and
religious obligation which also appear throughout the
range of Wilde's work. These tensions reveal a critical in-

stinct that goes beyond clever aphorisms and self-indulgent paradoxes. They also illustrate a moral dimension in Wilde that is generally unexamined.

Wilde published two collections of tales: *The Happy Prince and Other Tales* in 1888 and *A House of Pomegranates* in 1891. The tales did not create the sensation that the novel (*The Picture of Dorian Gray,* 1890) or the subsequent plays did, although the tales were reviewed favorably by *The Saturday Review, The Athenaeum,* and the *Pall Mall Gazette.* Wilde himself said little of the two books, but a passing remark of his about one of the tales could be applied to all of them and to *Dorian Gray* as well: **"The Happy Prince,"** he wrote in a letter, "is an attempt to treat a tragic modern problem in a form that aims at delicacy and imaginative treatment; it is a reaction against the purely imitative character of modern art." The "form" Wilde chooses is fantasy, which he clearly prefers to realism or the "purely imitative character of modern art": Wilde can treat a tragic problem even in a fairy tale that is unconcerned with sordid details or with a fidelity to everyday occurrences. Wilde also said that the tales were not intended for children.

The tales examine a number of vices and virtues. Most of the tales expose and criticize selfishness and insensitivity. The Selfish Giant will not permit children to play in his beautiful garden. The Star-Child rejects "inferiors" as well as his own mother. The Infanta makes fun of a deformed dwarf who dances for the Infanta's pleasure on her birthday. Big Hugh the Miller, ironically styled in **"The Devoted Friend,"** hypocritically steals from his neighbor, little Hans. The Young King embraces an unaccustomed life of luxury and lives entirely for pleasure. The Roman Rocket in **"The Remarkable Rocket"** considers himself inexpressibly superior to lesser fireworks.

In a few of the tales, the main character recognizes his error, is repentant, and achieves something like a state of grace. This process occurs in **"The Selfish Giant," "The Young King,"** and **"The Star-Child."** In other tales, characters like Big Hugh, the Infanta, and the Remarkable Rocket remain blinded by their conceit and consequently unregenerate. Two of the tales, **"The Happy Prince"** and **"The Nightingale and the Rose,"** deal with self-sacrifice and love and portray, unlike the other stories, virtues rather than vices. **"The Fisherman and His Soul,"** the most intricate of the tales, is another treatment of the doppelgänger theme in which the body and soul are separated, as they are in *The Picture of Dorian Gray.*

Some of the tales have been labeled "lessons in practical Christianity" by Pearson, but I suspect that Wilde would rather say "imaginative treatment" than Christian lesson, however Christian the moral of a particular tale might be. Indeed, Wilde warns his readers (and himself) against making the moral of the tale too blatant or sententious. At the end of **"The Devoted Friend,"** when the Waterrat leaves in a huff after hearing the Linnet's account of Big Hugh's abuse of little Hans, the Linnet muses:

"I told him a story with a moral."

"Ah! That is always a very dangerous thing to do," said the Duck. And [the narrator adds] I quite agree with her.

Dangerous or not, Wilde still makes moral affirmations in his fairy tales, perhaps even at the expense of imaginative treatment. Generally, like Aesop's fables, the tales reveal levels of human folly and wisdom while they also uphold virtuous behavior. Wilde's tales are not, however, designed to encourage faith or advocate Christianity. Rather, in simple terms, they propose decency and generosity in human relations. Hence their moral dimension, and hence Wilde's fear that the moral of the tale intruded, at least potentially, on the art of the tale.

"The Devoted Friend" is not the only example of Wilde's self-consciousness in the tales. **"The Remarkable Rocket"** can easily be read as a self-parody, although no one, at least in print, has done so. The Rocket, the *ne plus ultra* of pyrotechnics, brags of his parentage and superiority before a group of fireworks. He even tries to prove that he can wet his powder and still go off. But alas, he fails to ignite and is summarily thrown into a ditch, where he encounters a frog, a dragon fly, and later a duck, none of whom is impressed by his claims to fiery artifice. He observes, incidentally, that a person of his position is never useful. When two boys toss him into a fire he lights up, shrieks, "What a success I am!" and finally explodes. Unfortunately, no one sees him. He falls, a burnt shaft, upon a goose's back. "Good heavens! It is going to rain sticks," says the goose in dismay. "I knew I should create a great sensation," gasps the Rocket and then goes out.

The Rocket bears a striking resemblance to Wilde, the aesthete, the braggadocio, the sensation of the season, the preëminent artificer, who is aware of his posing and of the unlikelihood of his affecting anyone; and who is also capable of making fun of himself. There are, to be sure, a number of warnings or adumbrations of failure in Wilde's work dating from the publication of his book of poems in 1881. **"The Remarkable Rocket"** is by far the most comic of them. Significantly, it comes at the end of the second collection, and because *A House of Pomegranates* was published when Wilde's fame (or notoriety) was pronounced, the comparison between the Rocket and Wilde is most inviting.

"The Young King" also seems to refer at least obliquely to Wilde, for the principal character becomes so enamored of artifice he turns his back on human suffering until a dream vision shows him the misery his subjects must endure for his sake. He then forswears his kingly pomp and demonstrates to his subjects the importance of spiritual integrity. It is typical of Wilde to play the instinct of aggrandizement against the instinct of religious sensibility. The narrator of **"The Sphinx"** (1894), for example, turns in horror from his sexual fantasies to bow before his pallid crucifix. In his own experience, Wilde shuttled regularly between the salon and the cathedral. But in his art if not always in his life, Wilde denigrates materialism while he extols the spiritual realm of human experience and constantly reminds his audience of the importance of the soul.

The tales of sacrifice and love, **"The Happy Prince"** and **"The Nightingale and the Rose,"** depict characters who give their lives for others, in the former instance for the poor and in the latter for love. The world takes little note of these sacrifices, for it is indifferent if not hostile to self-lessness. The Prince and his helper, the Swallow, are nevertheless carried off to heaven as a reward for their efforts.

"The Nightingale and the Rose" closes more bitterly. The Nightingale kills herself by crushing her breast against a thorn so that a rose, nourished by her blood, will grow, and a young student will have a flower to give to the girl he loves. But the girl rejects the rose because it will not go with her dress, and the young man, now spurned by what was once the object of his romantic ardor, sighs, "What a silly thing Love is," and returns to his dusty studies.

The Nightingale, who sings magnificently as she dies, is clearly the superior artist to the Roman Rocket, whose artistry is only self-serving. The Nightingale may be the image of the artist Wilde would like to aspire to, while the Rocket seems to be the poseur he fears he might never rise above. Regrettably, unlike the Prince and the Swallow, the Nightingale is not wafted up to heaven or in any way canonized, and so the conclusion of the tale leaves one with the feeling that it was all for naught. Wilde no doubt harbored that fear, too. Perhaps the true artist suffers more than the false one, and though both are vulnerable, the Nightingale's vulnerability renders her situation tragic, while the Rocket's is farcical.

The most interesting of the tales is **"The Fisherman and His Soul."** It is told in a manner reminiscent of the Holy Bible and *The Arabian Nights*. The language is rich with sensuous imagery, and the episodes of the tale are both mysterious and arcane. The diction is archaic, that is, Elizabethan, and the repetition of words and adventures (things happen thrice, as they do elsewhere in Wilde's tales and almost generically in folklore) affords the tale a stylized ambience which is less easily penetrated than that of the other tales, especially because of the puzzling richness of detail. Indeed, the story borders on the abstruse, although its moral remains accessible.

In the tale, a young fisherman elicits the help of the nether-world to separate his soul from his body, for he has fallen in love with a mermaid and cannot join her and her Sea-Folk unless he is, like them, soulless. He is forewarned by the local priest, who cautions that the Sea-Folk "are as beasts of the field that know not good from evil." The priest adds that the "love of the body is vile." Nevertheless, the fisherman decides to join the beautiful mermaid, and so he goes through a Satanic ritual, cuts his soul from his body, and joins his underwater beauty. The soul, however, is thoroughly distraught. It wanders about for three years gaining wisdom, riches, and an appreciation of sensuality in three separate and highly allegorical adventures; and it returns at the end of each year to tempt the fisherman with its acquisitions. The soul wants to reenter the heart of the fisherman, but none of its temptations proves captivating save the last: a dazzling dancing girl. Since mermaids cannot by nature dance, the fisherman is intrigued and accompanies his soul to see the girl.

During their search, the soul entices the fisherman to steal, to strike a child, and to murder a merchant: the man and his soul are now bound to each other by the commission of evil deeds. But the fisherman experiences terrible remorse over the crimes he commits, and so the soul tempts him to perform good deeds. Anything is preferable so far as the soul is concerned to the fisherman's returning to the mermaid. But the young man is determined to be with his love once more.

In the meantime, the mermaid dies of loneliness and despair. The fisherman leaps into the sea in a frantic effort to rejoin her, but he is no longer innocent (that is, he now knows both good and evil through experience), and therefore he cannot live underwater. His heart breaks, and at the last moment his soul gains entry into his broken heart. The bodies of the fisherman and the mermaid wash onto the beach and are buried without benefit of clergy in an obscure corner of a field. Eventually, though, much to everyone's amazement, gorgeous white flowers spring from the unmarked grave. The flowers are displayed upon the local church's altar, and the priest, learning of their origin, undergoes a radical change of heart. His transformation is recorded in an appropriately biblical fashion:

> And in the morning, while it was still dawn, he went forth with the monks and the musicians, and the candlebearers and the swingers of censers, and a great company, and came to the shore of the sea, and blessed the sea, and all the wild things that are in it. The Fauns also he blessed, and the little things that dance in the woodland, and the bright-eyed things that peer through the leaves. All the things in God's world he blessed, and the people were filled with joy and wonder.

The priest's sternness has given way to Christian mercy, much as the New Testament, to Christians, fulfills and supersedes the Old. The priest "spake not of the wrath of God, but of the God whose name is Love."

The story differs from *The Picture of Dorian Gray* in that the soul brings the body to ruin rather than *vice versa*. But the common ground between the novel and the tale is the tale's implication that the body cannot live or exist in a blissful state without the assistance or balance of a soul. Wilde usually held that the body and soul must live in harmony with one another, or, more precisely, that one's soul is finally the unity of one's mind and body. In separating himself from his soul the fisherman makes life with the Sea-Folk possible, but he becomes soulless as well as incapable of experiencing sin and repentance. Through his commission of sin and subsequent suffering, he not only regains his soul but God's mercy as well. And foremost, the fisherman and the mermaid, through their sacrifice for each other's love, soften otherwise hard hearts. Love triumphs (albeit in death) despite society's disapproval. The white flowers that bloom on the couple's grave signify the innocence of their love while they demonstrate God's sanction. Though the priest would not forgive the fisherman for joining the mermaid and indulging in "the love of the body," God celebrates the fisherman's love by adorning his grave. This act of divine mercy effects a transformation of cold human hearts, and all of God's world receives a blessing.

A miracle effected by divine compassion is not unique to **"The Fisherman and His Soul."** White blossoms cover the

Selfish Giant's dead body after he has been invited by the boy-Christ to accompany the boy to his garden, "which is Paradise." The poet of *The Ballad of Reading Gaol* (1898) envisions red and white roses blooming above the unhallowed grave of the executed murderer. Again, the priests (as representatives of institutionalized religion) will not sanctify the grave of a sinner:

> The Chaplain would not kneel to pray
>   By his dishonoured grave:
> Nor mark it with that blessed Cross
>   That Christ for sinners gave,
> Because the man was one of those
>   Whom Christ came down to save.

Perhaps it is not surprising in view of his life style that the Tannhäuser motif and the theological concept of a *felix culpa* had a strong hold on Wilde's imagination. He once joked that he expected his umbrella to sprout flowers during a visit to St. Peter's. Perhaps he even sincerely hoped a sign of forgiveness would be shown to him. In any event, some critics have suggested that Wilde's personal guilt prompted the definition of morality Wilde offers in his confessional *Epistola* to Douglas: Christ's "morality is all sympathy, just what morality should be." But Wilde championed sympathy long before he was incarcerated or involved in any public scandal. The strategy of sin and redemption occurs in several of the tales and in many other pre-Reading Gaol works as well.

Similarly, a movement from harsh judgment to empathetic tolerance characterizes another common strategy in Wilde's art. At the close of *A Woman of No Importance* (1893), the puritanical Hester announces that "God's law is only love." She too has been transformed; she has abandoned an inflexible moral system. Arthur Goring, the dandy of *An Ideal Husband* (1895), informs his friend Lady Chiltern that "It is love, and not German philosophy, that is the true explanation for this world, whatever may be the explanation of the next." Lady Chiltern eventually embraces Goring's position and "forgives" her errant husband, Sir Robert. Lady Windermere also recognizes the necessity of charity in *Lady Windermere's Fan* (1892), and love unites the principals of *The Importance of Being Earnest* (1895) in the traditional symbol of worldly harmony: marriage. It is further significant that *Salome* (1896), Wilde's most important tragedy, achieves its tragic catharsis through the absence of love and the overwhelming presence of debauchery.

A more complex example of the moral dimensions expressed in several of the fairy tales is Wilde's famous essay "The Soul of Man under Socialism" (1890). Here, in probably his least disguised literary voice, Wilde chastens the rich for their indifference to suffering and their inattentiveness to the spiritual (emotional, aesthetic) spheres of human life. "The Soul of Man" is clearly a moral tract from start to finish. Its criticism of the wealthy and powerful stung many of Wilde's admirers. Its invitation to selfhood and its advocacy of individualism and aesthetic sensibility evince a strong moral tone designed not only to pique Wilde's readers but ultimately to improve his country's attitude toward the downtrodden. And, in juxtaposition with the moral prerogatives found in Wilde's fiction

and drama, the essay can hardly be considered an anomaly. Nor should Wilde's sentiments be regarded as insincere just because Oscar loved absinthe and boys. That is an old and tiresome argument; it deserves shelving.

Illustrations of Wilde's moral prerogative are indeed manifold, but I promised I would not try to cover everything. Still, I must observe that many critics have done Oscar Wilde a disservice by omitting the abundant evidence of his interest in compassion, generosity, and love. He decried Victorian ethics and intransigent moral positions but not moral truths, truths of the human heart. In an 1882 letter to Charles Godfrey Leland regarding Leland's son's education, Wilde indicates the connection between "morals" and art which Wilde could proclaim without hesitation at the age of 28.

> . . . a lad who learns any simple art learns honesty, and truthtelling, and simplicity, in the most practical school of simple morals in the world, the school of art, learns too to love nature . . . to be kind to animals and all living things . . . to wonder and worship at God's works more.

Wilde did not alter his opinion on the subject as he grew older, although he rarely stated it so openly. Instead, he made the connection between art and "simple morals" through his own creative genius while he directly and indirectly formulated a new morality, or, if you will, a new attitude toward 19th-century morality. And he accomplished this end by telling a story with a moral, even if that is a "very dangerous thing to do." (pp. 708-17)

> *John Allen Quintus, "The Moral Prerogative in Oscar Wilde: A Look at the Fairy Tales," in* The Virginia Quarterly Review, *Vol. 53, No. 4, Autumn, 1977, pp. 708-17.*

Walter Pater, in a letter to Wilde about *The Happy Prince, and Other Tales:*

My dear Wilde,

I am confined to my room with gout, but have been consoling myself with **The Happy Prince,** and feel it would be ungrateful not to send a line to tell you how delightful I have found him and his companions. I hardly know whether to admire more the wise wit of **"The Wonderful [Remarkable] Rocket,"** or the beauty and tenderness of **"The Selfish Giant":** the latter certainly is perfect in its kind. Your genuine 'little poems in prose,' those at the top of pages 10 and 14, for instance, are gems, and the whole, too brief, book abounds with delicate touches and pure English. . . .

   Ever

   Very sincerely yours

   WALTER PATER

Walter Pater, in a 1888 letter to Oscar Wilde later collected in The Letters of Oscar Wilde, *Harcourt, Brace and World, 1962.*

Robert K. Martin   (essay date 1979)

[*An American educator and critic, Martin has written works on American literature and the English homosexual literary tradition. In the essay below, he asserts that it was only through the fairy tale genre that Wilde was able to express his homosexuality.*]

Oscar Wilde's fairy tales have been little considered, and, when discussed, frequently misunderstood. And yet the fairy tale was important for Wilde, enabling him to express his own inner development in a form free from social scrutiny. Wilde used the fairy tale to express some of his deepest concerns and to record his own growing commitments, including one to homosexual love, in a way which would have been impossible without the protection offered by the conventions of fantasy.

"The Happy Prince," probably his best-known and most successful tale, conveys a change of heart, a rejection of hedonism and aestheticism and an acceptance of involvement in the human condition of suffering, brought about through love. For, as Wilde points out clearly in his tale, it is Eros which lies at the heart of Agape.

The change of heart is conveyed by the symbolic transformation of the Prince's heart. Now that it is lead, ironically, it displays far more sympathy than when it was human. The weeping Prince informs the swallow, "When I was alive and had a human heart, I did not know what tears were . . . now that I am dead . . . and though my heart is made of lead yet I cannot choose but weep." The Prince's transformation has already occurred; it remains but for him to realize that transformation by carrying out the acts of self-sacrifice which form the basis of the tale. The swallow is not yet transformed, however, and it is the Prince who will lead the swallow along the path to spiritual regeneration through love. Thus, at the end, each arrives at a perfected spiritual state, and they are able to share a state of bliss.

The Prince specifically rejects his former state, in terms which cannot fail to remind us of Wilde's own life and reputation: "I lived in the Palace of Sans-Souci, where sorrow is not allowed to enter . . . My courtiers called me the Happy Prince, and happy indeed I was, if pleasure be happiness." Wilde's distinction between pleasure and happiness points to his rejection of a pure aestheticism which ignores the problems of the real world and which substitutes physical gratification for spiritual enrichment. This element of renunciation in the tale, combined with its composition in the years immediately following Wilde's marriage (in 1884) and the birth of his sons, has led many critics to see this tale and others as statements of an attempt to reject homosexuality. One writes, for instance, "A biographer might read the fairy tales as Wilde's attempt to assert the primacy of his family life and to reject the siren call of homosexuality, . . . [The tales] are probably Wilde's attempt to remain within the charmed circle of his children, innocent and safe from evil." In fact, the opposite is true: **"The Happy Prince"** announces the beauty and value of homosexual love in contrast to heterosexual love, and specifically uses homosexual love as a model of selfless love and heterosexual love as a model of selfish love. In **"The Happy Prince"** (written about 1886) Wilde depicted the superiority of homosexuality over the heterosexual life he had lived before—precisely because the heterosexuality depicted in **"The Happy Prince"** is loveless.

Although the Swallow has not yet reached the state of transformation of the Prince, his situation is analogous. The Swallow's Egypt represents a symbolic state not unlike that of the Prince's Sans-Souci: it is characterized by forgetfulness ("large lotus-flowers"), sleep, and death. It stands for the death of the soul, in a world of comfort which ignores suffering. The Swallow's willingness to stay one night with the Prince is the first postponement of his desires, the first recognition of the possibility of a higher claim, a claim which unites personal love (the Swallow's for the Prince) with impersonal (the Prince's for his people).

The Swallow's first mission for the Prince gives him, in passing, an illustration of the vanity of women. Whilst on his way to bring the Prince's ruby to the poor seamstress who is embroidering passion-flowers on a gown for a maid-of-honour, he passes over the beautiful girl who remarks to her romantic lover: "I hope my dress will be ready in time for the State-ball; I have ordered passion-flowers to be embroidered on it, but the seamstresses are so lazy." The episode offers an illustration of the indifference of the maid-of-honour, her inability to understand the lives of those who work for her, and, not insignificantly, her lover's inevitable deception at the hands of so unworthy a beloved (a theme developed more fully in **"The Nightingale and the Rose"**). The Swallow has already had his own experience of heterosexual love, with the Reed. Attracted by "her slender waist," he soon discovers that "She has no conversation" and is too "domestic." A good deal of Oscar's experience with Constance undoubtedly went into that passage: she, although attractive, was hardly literary and was intellectually incapable of sharing her husband's life.

As the Swallow performs the three tasks asked of him by the Prince, his love for the Prince grows. He even abandons his plan to go to Egypt, declaring to the Prince no longer, "I will stay with you for one night," but, "I will stay with you always." This decision means his death, of course, since he cannot support the cold, but first his love for the Prince must be consummated. When he asks to kiss the Prince's hand, the Prince responds, "I am glad that you are going to Egypt at last, little Swallow, you have stayed too long here; but you must kiss me on the lips, for I love you." The dynamics of the fairy tale allow Wilde to present two men kissing on the lips, a taboo relationship which would be "inconceivable" in serious fiction; ironically, such forbidden love can only be portrayed in the world of children's literature, where nothing is "real." What is more, although both the Prince and the Swallow must "die," they are not to go unrewarded; nor is their love to perish. In the next world, they are to be reunited and in God's "garden of Paradise this little bird shall sing for evermore." The restored Paradise is a world of friendship, caring, and love—unlike the real world.

Readers have often misunderstood Wilde's tale because they have tended to identify aestheticism and homosexuality in his work. In fact, this is merely the application to literary criticism of a more general social attitude, in which homosexuality is linked to a concern for beauty at the expense of larger social concerns. Since Wilde is well-known as a homosexual and as an exponent of aestheticism, it is convenient to suppose that the two are linked in his work. But **"The Happy Prince"** specifically condemns the Aesthetic Movement through the character of the Art Professor, who maintains of the Happy Prince, "As he is no longer beautiful he is no longer useful." Wilde, who had made his reputation as a spokesman for the Aesthetic Movement, was developing into the second major stage of his career, which would see the publication of "The Soul of Man Under Socialism" as well as his biting satiric dramas of upper-class life (and marriage in particular) and of course his own arrest and imprisonment. As G. Wilson Knight has pointed out, Wilde's arrest and conviction were due not only to his homosexuality but more importantly to his consorting with lower-class boys, what Knight has termed his "sexual ratification of human unity." His homosexuality had offered him a way out of the narrow confines of the world of aesthetic theory and social graces and into a world of greater caring.

In the fairy tale Wilde dramatizes himself as the Happy Prince, a man who renounces the Palace of Sans-Souci, who gives up his worldly wealth, in order to share his goods with the poor and to share his happiness with his beloved Swallow. The tale reveals that Wilde yearned for a lover whom he could teach to love selflessly and who would come to share with him in acts of self-abnegation and spiritual development. Alfred Douglas, alas, was hardly that ideal Swallow. Nonetheless, **"The Happy Prince"** remains an important inner journal, an account of the way in which for Wilde the recognition and acceptance of his homosexuality coincided with the rejection of his previously held Aestheticism. Far from being the cause of frivolity and his Aesthetic Camp, Wilde's homosexuality led to a deepening of the human capacity for love and the willingness to sacrifice all for a beloved. The only literary form in which he could record this change of heart was the fairy tale. Wilde's legacy to his sons was the journal of his own heart. (pp. 74-7)

Robert K. Martin, "Oscar Wilde and the Fairy Tale: 'The Happy Prince' as Self-Dramatization," in Studies in Short Fiction, Vol. 16, No. 1, Winter, 1979, pp. 74-7.

Michael C. Kotzin   (essay date 1979)

[*Kotzin is an American educator and critic. In the essay below, he asserts that "The Selfish Giant" is an example of the nineteenth-century literary fairy tale, which he defines as a retelling of a traditional or classic fairy tale with an additional artistic or didactic purpose.*]

The stories in Oscar Wilde's *The Happy Prince and Other Tales* have delighted children and adults alike since the collection first appeared in 1888, and **"The Selfish Giant"** has been a particular favorite for many readers. Soon after the book appeared Walter Pater wrote Wilde to tell him "how delightful" he had found the Happy Prince "and his companions." He continued: "I hardly know whether to

admire more the wise wit of **'The Wonderful [Remarkable] Rocket,'** or the beauty and tenderness of **'The Selfish Giant'**: the latter certainly is perfect in its kind." Yeats has described the collection as "charming and amusing," and Auden fairly recently singled it out as an example of Wilde's nondramatic prose which "we can still read . . . with great pleasure." But despite the continued exposure and prestigious acclaim that the stories have received, they have been granted little critical attention (**"The Selfish Giant,"** very little), and when criticism has appeared it usually has been in the form of comments relating the stories to broader concerns about Wilde's writings in general. It is time, then, for **"The Selfish Giant"** to be approached more fully and more directly than it yet has been, as can be done with particular profit if it is looked at as an instance of its "kind," that is, a nineteenth-century literary fairy tale.

The literary fairy tale can be defined as an "original" story similar but not necessarily identical to the anonymous traditional fairy tales of folk culture. The author of a literary fairy tale is aware of the conventions which make the traditional fairy tale a very characteristic type of story. He often reveals considerable self-consciousness in his use of those conventions. Yet he is not bound by them. His purpose is usually not to create a new fairy tale which one might mistake for a folk tale. Rather, he wants to produce a work with clear ties to the fairy-tale tradition but which also has an apparent artfullness; thus the German Romantics, who to a certain extent invented the form, called it the *"Kunstmärchen."* (There is no such standard term in English, and of the alternatives I prefer "literary fairy tale"; "art fairy tale" has other connotations, I think.) Furthermore, the author of the literary fairy tale is not as much of a "mere" storyteller as was the teller of folk fairy tales. He usually also has a purpose in mind which he wants to use the tale to accomplish, and this is so whether the tale is clearly aimed at an adult audience or whether it is ostensibly a "children's" story. The fairy tale thus becomes a vehicle for the investigation of human psychology, the criticism of social behavior, the portrayal of a Christian doctrine, the teaching of a moral lesson, or the expression of an aspect of Romantic philosophy. Though there were literary treatments of fairy tales before the Romantic period, the coming of Romanticism notably stimulated the development of the literary fairy tale. The Romantic respectful appreciation of folk fairy tales drew men of letters toward them, and Romantic tastes led authors to want to create literature which in some ways resembled fairy tales. Then, following the early Romantics, a long list of nineteenth-century writers throughout Europe, including England, produced a series of instances of the literary fairy tale. And Oscar Wilde was one of them.

Of all the conventions of traditional folk fairy tales, two aspects of the tales stand out as most central in characterizing them: they follow typical sorts of narrative patterns in which typical character types participate (thus structuralists find them a particularly rich field for study); and they move in a characteristic unreal world, defined by the presence of a special kind of magic (and it is this aspect of them which is especially emphasized and appreciated by J. R. R. Tolkien). **"The Selfish Giant"** is built around the kind of narrative structure typical of fairy tales and it is rich in fairy-tale fantasy. In it a group of children, playing the part usually filled by one or two children, face the opposition of a fairy-tale villain, a giant who deprives them of happiness by driving them out of his garden, where they had played during the seven years he was away visiting an ogre. In describing the effects of this expulsion Wilde makes use of animism, a device found in traditional fairy tales which was highly favored by Hans Christian Andersen, Wilde's major precursor as a writer of literary fairy tales, and which was also used by Wilde's personal mentor John Ruskin in his lone instance of the genre, "The King of the Golden River." Like Andersen and Ruskin, Wilde personifies objects in nature, giving them human feelings and describing them as acting in accordance with those feelings. It was spring elsewhere, but

> in the garden of the Selfish Giant it was still winter. The birds did not care to sing in it as there were no children, and the trees forgot to blossom. Once a beautiful flower put its head out from the grass, but when it saw the notice-board [forbidding trespassing] it was so sorry for the children that it slipped back into the ground again, and went off to sleep. The only people who were pleased were the Snow and the Frost. . . . The Snow covered up the grass with her great white cloak, and the Frost painted all the trees silver. Then they invited the North Wind to stay with them, and he came. He was wrapped in furs, and he roared all day about the garden, and blew the chimney-pots down. "This is a delightful spot," he said, "we must ask the Hail on a visit." So the Hail came. Every day for three hours he rattled on the roof of the castle till he broke most of the slates, and then he ran round and round the garden as fast as he could go. He was dressed in grey, and his breath was like ice.

As in most fairy tales, the fortunes of the children ultimately undergo a radical change for the better. A year later, the children creep into the garden through a hole in the wall. The giant, looking out of his bedroom window, sees them in its trees and he sees that the spring too has returned, except in one corner of the garden where there stands a crying boy too small to reach the branches of the tree near him. Again objects in nature are personified: "The poor tree was still quite covered with frost and snow, and the North Wind was blowing and roaring above it. 'Climb up! little boy,' said the Tree, and it bent its branches down as low as it could; but the boy was too tiny." And then the turning point in the story comes, marked by a simple metaphoric touch which is indeed, to use Pater's words, beautiful, tender, and perfect. "And the Giant's heart melted as he looked out" at the boy, Wilde writes, endowing a cliché with new power in this story about a year-long winter which suddenly thaws. " 'How selfish I have been!' " says the giant, who now changes his ways as well as his attitudes. He comes down into the garden to put the boy into the tree and to knock down the wall and open the garden to the children " 'for ever and ever.' " At first the children are frightened by him and run away, but when they see how kind he is to the little boy they come "running back, and with them [comes] the Spring." The

giant is no longer a threat and the children's permanent happiness is assured.

In the remaining part of the story we discover that the children, like the central characters of many fairy tales, achieved their final happiness thanks to outside, supernatural assistance. However, by the time we make that discovery the focus of the story has shifted from the children to the giant. The giant, who plays in the garden with the children, becomes sad because the little boy never returns with the others and they don't know where he is. A note of pathetic sentimentality is sounded, reminiscent of the tone of some of Andersen's stories, as the giant's feelings of loss are described. Years pass and at last, as the moment of his death approaches, the giant is reunited with the child. Magic pervades the scene. Though it is winter, "in the farthest corner of the garden was a tree quite covered with lovely white blossoms. Its branches were golden, and silver fruit hung down from them, and underneath it stood the little boy." He has "the prints of two nails" on his hands and his feet and he tells the giant that they " 'are the wounds of Love.' " " 'Who art thou?' " asks the giant, who is moved to feel "a strange awe" by these revelations and kneels. The child answers that " 'You let me play once in your garden, to-day you shall come with me to my garden, which is Paradise.' " The child, we realize, is Christ, who came as a child and later was crucified. In stimulating the giant's heart to melt, Christ the child had not only helped the innocent children to remain in the garden, thus aiding them the way a good fairy might help children in a fairy tale; he also had served the giant, making him worthy of gaining happiness in the garden during the balance of his life and in heaven after his death, which now comes. "When the children ran in [to the garden] that afternoon, they found the Giant lying dead under the tree, all covered with white blossoms." The child's wounds are the wounds of Love in that he allowed himself to suffer them because he loved sinners like the giant, and so that through love of him such men could be saved. **"The Selfish Giant"** is not just a fairy tale about the children's victory over the giant. It is also a Christian parable about the salvation of the giant, salvation which he gains by loving Christ.

It is not altogether rare for a fairy tale to have a Christian dimension, and Iona and Peter Opie point out that "a curious parallel to the Christ story is apparent" particularly in fairy tales which describe spells and releases from them. "The man of perfect heart, living in the guise of a poor carpenter's son [in our case as a weak child], has to be accepted in his lowly state. . . . Had Christ been shown in his full glory, recognition of his virtues, whether by pauper or by prince, would have been valueless. On the face of it the message of the fairy tales is that transformation to a state of bliss is effected not by magic, but by the perfect love of one person for another." In the stories discussed by the Opies, such as "Beauty and the Beast," the Christ-like figure is helped and loved and then, transformed, he reveals his true identity and the glory that is his, and brings happiness to his helper. Similarly, Wilde's child, helped and loved by the giant, reappears to reveal himself as not only wounded but also with magical powers and the ability to bring the giant to Paradise.

In Wilde's story, as we have noticed, the Christian meaning is not submerged the way that it is in most of those traditional folk fairy tales where it can be found. Here the Christian meaning is quite explicit, as it is in many literary fairy tales and particularly in ones by Andersen and by George MacDonald, a British Victorian writer who, along with Andersen and Ruskin, was a possible influence on Wilde as an author of fairy tales. Famous stories like Andersen's "The Little Mermaid" and "The Red Shoes" and MacDonald's *At the Back of the North Wind* are obvious exempla for Christian sermons. Like **"The Selfish Giant"** they are versions of the Everyman story in which it is shown that the reward for proper Christian behavior is a happiness which comes after death. In these and in other, similar stories by Andersen and MacDonald the introduction of such meaning can strike one as the injection of an alien element into the fairy-tale context. Characters no longer dwell in the timeless realm of fairy tales. Instead, they live in a world of time where time is worthless in reference to eternity. Happiness is not available to them in fairyland or on earth but only in heaven. Despite his Christian meanings, Wilde is able to keep his story closer to the fairy-tale context than Andersen and MacDonald do. He does that by making it, in effect, two stories: the "pure" fairy tale about the children whose final status in the garden is intended to last "for ever and ever" (and indeed, we never hear about their growing old), and the fairy tale with obvious Christian implications about the giant who does grow "very old and feeble" and finally dies and goes to heaven. The ending of the children's story, which we had been prepared to respond to as though it were something final, thus also becomes but one stage in the giant's story, which has its own major climax later. This introduces a structural awkwardness which I think deprives the story as a whole of the perfection which Pater claimed for it. But nevertheless Wilde here is quite successful in having things both ways, for despite the presence of the Christian elements the story remains dominated by its fairy-tale ambience, thanks to the presence within it of the children's "pure" fairy tale and of the fairy-tale elements in the giant's story, particularly the workings of its plot.

As fairy tale the giant's story has parallels with tales of the "Toads and Diamonds" type in which a person confronts a strange creature who often is later discovered to have supernatural powers: if the person responds to the creature in a selfish way then he is punished, as is the sister from whose mouth toads fall, but if he is generous and kind then he gains a reward, as does the other sister, who produces diamonds. This motif, repeated, provides the major narrative pattern of Ruskin's "The King of the Golden River." In its first chapter a strange man is treated cruelly by Hans and Schwartz, two "black brothers" who refuse to share shelter or food with him on a stormy night. As a result the man, who really is the Southwest wind, punishes them by blowing off the roof of their house and inundating it with water, and by turning their fertile valley into a wasteland. A third brother, Gluck, had responded to the man differently from them. His "heart [had] melted" and he had wanted to help him, but his brothers had interfered. He therefore is spared some of the direct suffering brought by the Southwest wind the night of the storm and he gets a

full reward later in the story. His kindness was witnessed by the King of the Golden River who, because of enchantment, was in the form of a mug and who, when freed from enchantment, provides Gluck with the secret of how to turn into gold the river which he has high on a mountain. He also helps Gluck fulfill this task after the boy, on his way up to the river, once again in contrast to his brothers shows further kindness and generosity toward an old man, a child, and a dog (who reveals himself to be the King, as perhaps the others were too). Instead of becoming actual gold for Gluck though, the river instead is rechanneled so that it flows into the valley, which is revived: "the Treasure Valley became a garden again," and Gluck's reward is a good Victorian Puritan one, requiring him to continue to work.

In Wilde's version of this type of fairy tale the giant's selfish expulsion of the children from his garden brings it perpetual winter and then, after his heart has melted and he has acted kindly toward one child, the garden is rejuvenated and he is rewarded. However, **"The Selfish Giant"** differs from standard fairy tales of this type because the giant in effect plays the part of all of the brothers, both the selfish ones who are punished and the kind one who is rewarded. In fairy tales a person who would perform a good action will do so every chance that he has to, whereas a person who acts wrongly, as the giant does, is simply punished, even destroyed. As the Opies put it: "In fairy tales there is no saving of the wicked in heart. Their fate is to have inflicted on them the evil they would inflict on others." Gluck's two brothers try before he does to fulfill the task and be rewarded by the river, but they have learned nothing from their earlier experience, continue to be cruel and selfish, and end up transformed into the black stones which they metaphorically resemble. The giant, unlike them and unlike the conventional villains of fairy tales whom he resembles by being the enemy of the children in the first part of the story, is not destroyed but converted.

Though it does not deal with outright villains, there is one kind of fairy tale which does portray a character's conversion to virtue, and it is to it that we can turn for further parallels with **"The Selfish Giant."** In stories of the "King Thrushbeard" type proud princesses are humbled and learn to love the seemingly-poor men they have been forced to marry, who are really wealthy royalty. MacDonald's "The Light Princess" is a variant on this type of tale. In it a princess suffers from the curse of being light physically and of not being able to take anything seriously; by falling in love with a prince who, Christ-like, is sacrificing himself to save her and the community she is able to acquire physical gravity and to learn about the importance of being earnest. The giant, then, can be regarded as similar to these princesses who must replace false values with true ones; he does so after being deprived (cf. "King Thrushbeard") and after feeling love for a Christ figure (cf. "The Light Princess").

Most traditional fairy tales have at least a moral thrust, but the types of fairy tales which we have seen the giant's story most closely resemble are ones with very obvious didactic implications. Indeed, the potential didacticism of fairy tales provided one of the main bases for their acceptance as suitable children's literature during the Victorian period and was exploited by most of the period's authors of original fairy tales, and Wilde, albeit a spokesman of the doctrine of "art for art's sake," was no exception. Ruskin underlines the lesson of his story by saying that "the inheritance, which had been lost by cruelty, was regained by love," and Wilde makes his rather similar lesson equally explicit in **"The Selfish Giant,"** drawing a reader's attention to it even in the title of the story. Selfishness, the vice attacked by the story, is exemplified by the giant, who says " 'My own garden is my own garden' " when he drives the children out. "He was a very selfish Giant," we are told. Then we are shown how he is punished for his selfishness. Neither spring, summer, nor fruit-bearing autumn come to his garden. " 'He is too selfish,' " says autumn. Finally, discovering the sad little boy among the happy other children in his garden, the giant, moved to sympathy, recognizes the error of his ways. " 'How selfish I have been!' he said; 'now I know why the Spring would not come here. I will put that poor little boy on the top of the tree, and then I will knock down the wall, and my garden shall be the children's playground for ever and ever.' He was really very sorry for what he had done." Properly motivated, he now acts properly as well, and just as his vice was punished so his virtue is rewarded; in acting to make the child happy he brings himself happiness too, temporal and, ultimately, eternal.

The ending of the story can leave us with a final speculation about it, strengthened by the observation that fairy tales, saturated by fantasy, can lend themselves to the expression of their authors' dreams (and so "The Ugly Duckling," for example, can be seen in the light of Andersen's biography), and additionally provoked by the fact that we inevitably come to all of Wilde's writings with his life in mind more than for almost any other writer. **"The Selfish Giant"** turns out to be about a sinner who is forgiven, as Wilde the sinner hoped that he himself would be. Richard Ellmann points out that Wilde provided this happy fate for many of his characters. "In self-abasement they are usually rescued with fairy-tale speed and indulgence. Wilde cancelled his nightmare of being found out with lighthearted dreams of pardon and transfiguration. . . . The fairy tale was a natural form for him to choose to write in, and perhaps all his creative work belongs to this genre." Wilde may have identified himself with the giant particularly strongly, since he himself was a person of considerable size; in fact, after claiming that Wilde's mother was the victim of a disease that made her hands and feet abnormally large, Shaw said: "I have always maintained that Oscar was a giant in the pathological sense." The forgiveness which Wilde dreamed of for himself is thus dramatically rendered in his portrayal of the selfish giant achieving salvation. But, ironically, the giant qualified for salvation thanks to his act of love toward a boy, a "little boy [who] stretched out his two arms and flung them round the Giant's neck, and kissed him" and whom "the Giant loved . . . the best [of all the children] because he had kissed him." As elsewhere, Wilde wants to eat his cake and have it too. The giant's act of expiation, his loving and being kissed by the boy, resembles the very "sin" that Wilde would want to be forgiven for committing in his life, which tragically would not imi-

tate all of the developments in his art. Even the crucified Christ, whom the giant loves and who loves the giant, appears in the form of a boy, and though he and the giant were separated in life they are reunited for eternity as Wilde ends his fairy tale with what can be regarded as his version of the marriage of the redeemer and the redeemed.

Like **"The Nightingale and the Rose,"** of which Wilde said "I like to fancy that there may be many meanings in the tale, for in writing it I did not start with an idea and clothe it in form, but began with a form and strove to make it beautiful enough to have many secrets and many answers," **"The Selfish Giant"** resonates with "many meanings, . . . many secrets and many answers." Soon after he published *The Happy Prince* Wilde wrote Ruskin that "there is in you something of prophet, of priest, and of poet," naming the roles that he himself had been filling in addition to that of storyteller as he composed works like the literary fairy tale **"The Selfish Giant,"** which is at once a children's story, a Christian allegory, a moral exemplum, and a personal dream. (pp. 301-09)

> *Michael C. Kotzin, " 'The Selfish Giant' as Literary Fairy Tale," in* Studies in Short Fiction, *Vol. 16, No. 4, Fall, 1979, pp. 301-09.*

Wilde in response to an anonymous 1888 review of *The Happy Prince, and Other Tales*:

No doubt there will always be critics who, like a certain writer in the *Saturday Review,* will gravely censure the teller of fairy-tales for his defective knowledge of natural history, who will measure imaginative work by their own lack of any imaginative faculty, and will hold up their ink-stained hands in horror if some honest gentleman, who has never been farther than the yew-trees of his own garden, pens a fascinating book of travels like Sir John Mandeville, or, like great Raleigh, writes a whole history of the world, without knowing anything whatsoever about the past.

Oscar Wilde, in his "The Decay of Lying," Nineteenth Century, January 1889.

Norbert Kohl   (essay date 1980)

[*Kohl is a German educator and critic. In the following excerpt, originally published in German, he identifies Wilde's fairy tales as a turning point in the author's career and analyzes their form and narrative style.*]

The publication in May 1888 of Wilde's first collection of fairy-tales, *The Happy Prince and other Tales,* must have come as a surprise to all those who had known him only as the notorious figurehead of aestheticism and the author of epigonic poems and sentimental dramas. The little book was dedicated to Carlos Blacker and illustrated by Walter Crane and Jacomb Hood, and the critics gave it a favourable reception. The *Athenaeum* said it contained 'charming fancies and quaint humour', while the *Saturday Review* detected an underlying current of satire. The author was sufficiently encouraged to send copies to friends and such prominent figures as Gladstone, Ruskin and Pater. He had the satisfaction of soon receiving a letter from his revered teacher at Brasenose College, Oxford, to say how 'delightful' he had found the stories. Heartened by these positive reactions, Wilde published a second collection three years later, in November 1891, under the title *A House of Pomegranates,* illustrated by Charles Ricketts and C. H. Shannon and dedicated to his wife. These tales, of which **'The Young King'** and **'The Birthday of the Infanta'** had already appeared separately, were each dedicated to ladies of high society—a gesture not unconnected with his work as editor of the magazine *The Woman's World* from 1887 to 1889. Unlike the first collection, *A House of Pomegranates* attracted little attention initially. The relatively high price (one guinea) may well have been a deterrent, and the unsatisfactory reproduction of the illustrations, which according to Stuart Mason was due to a technical fault in the printing process, had a damaging effect on the appearance of the book.

Along with *The Picture of Dorian Gray* and the comedies, Wilde's fairy-tales are probably the works with which most people would link his name most readily. In German-speaking countries alone the two collections (or at least one of them) appeared—often together with *Lord Arthur Savile's Crime and other Stories*—in more than twenty different translations between 1902 and 1976. . . . It is impossible to calculate exactly how many copies of Wilde's tales have been sold on the German market, but the extent of their popularity may perhaps be gauged from the fact that the Insel paperback edition first published in 1972 had by 1987 sold some 180,000 copies. A part of this success is certainly due to the tales being a particular favourite in schools, and if the countless school editions are added to the total, the sales in German-speaking countries must amount to hundreds of thousands.

Critics have not paid a great deal of attention to these stories, but when occasionally they have asked what led Wilde to write them, the usual answer has been along biographical lines. Hesketh Pearson thought Wilde was 'emotionally undeveloped', but this explanation, though it might perhaps help us to understand certain weaknesses in the comedies as regards plot and characterisation, is perhaps a little too facile, especially since it ignores the time at which Wilde decided to embrace the genre. In this respect, Robert Merle's observations are rather more helpful, for he draws attention to Wilde's situation as husband and father of two children, as well as to his homosexual tendencies. The first collection of tales reveals Wilde as 'apaisé, détendu, heureux autant qu'il pouvait l'être' (calm, relaxed, as happy as he could ever be), while *A House of Pomegranates* is a symbolic expression of his sexual ambivalence. Within this psychological frame of reference Merle, together with Léon Lemonnier, interprets the fisherman's relationship with a creature half-woman and half-fish (**'The Fisherman and his Soul'**) as symbolising renunciation of 'normal' sexual behaviour; similarly the ugliness of the dwarf (**'The Birthday of the Infanta'**) and of **'The Star-Child'** represents a physical image of the 'disgrâce de l'inverti' (disgrace of the invert) of which he was all too aware, since his homosexuality was a taboo subject in the society of his day. Against this back-

ground, the autoeroticism of the star-child takes on added significance, for Freud maintained that male homosexuality is characterised by a strong element of narcissism. Merle considers that Wilde's cruel rejection of his mother may be seen in conjunction with his growing estrangement from his wife, 'l'épouse que deux maternités successives avaient déformée'.

Reading the tales like a psychoanalyst deciphering his patient's dreams may be fascinating, but it is also risky, for no one really knows for sure when Wilde's homosexuality first began to dominate his sexual leanings, and in any case the psychological, psychoanalytical approach to literature is fraught with methodological difficulties. Apart from [what Theodor W. Adorno called] its indisputable merit of: 'Kunst aus dem Bann des absoluten Geistes herauszuholen' (releasing art from the power of the absolute spirit) and offering 'Glieder konkreter Vermittlung zwischen der Struktur von Gebilden und der gesellschaftlichen' (elements of concrete mediation between the structure of [artistic] creations and society), its ahistorical reductionism constantly runs the inherent risk of cutting down origin, themes and structure to the mere dimensions of objective correlatives of the author's psychological experiences, thus completely ignoring, for instance, the effects of literary traditions and the conventions of his chosen genre. The fantastic transformation of the star-child from a beautiful boy into an ugly one, seen by Merle as a reference to Wilde's relationship with his wife, is a commonplace motif in fairy-tales and, in Vladimir Propp's terms, is one of the conventional and indeed basic functions of protagonists in this genre. However interesting and sometimes revealing it may be to interpret literary texts as reflections of their author's subconscious mind, the critic's first line of argument must surely concern the author's artistic development, as he describes the form, content and effect of a text, analysing and evaluating it, as well as setting it in the context of the author's work as a whole.

Wilde himself made various comments on the tales, and these show how close was the link between their artistic conception and his general ideas about aesthetics. It is well worth remembering that shortly after the publication of *The Happy Prince* etc., he published one of his most important essays, 'The Decay of Lying'. There he emphatically denounced the emergence of an all too factual naturalism in nineteenth-century literature, declaring the true aim of the artist to be 'the telling of beautiful untrue things'. Art begins with 'purely imaginative and pleasurable work dealing with what is unreal and non-existent'. These theoretical utterances run parallel to the comments he made about the tales. In a letter to G. H. Kersley he calls them 'studies in prose, put for Romance's sake into a fanciful form', and of **'The Happy Prince'** he writes:

> The story is an attempt to treat a magic modern problem in a form that aims at delicacy and imaginative treatment: it is a reaction against the purely imitative character of modern art—and now that literature has taken to blowing loud trumpets I cannot but be pleased that some ear has cared to listen to the low music of a little reed.

Illustration from "The Happy Prince" by artist Walter Crane.

It is clear from these remarks that the tales did not owe their existence merely to the chance circumstances of his personal or family life, but that they were the product of a deliberate artistic decision: their fantastic form resulted from his anti-realistic concept of art being put into creative practice. The fact that he chose the genre of the fairy-tale may be due in part to its attraction of magic and a heightened unreality, but also to the dynamic, almost mythical force that drove him into story-telling. From this point of view even *The Picture of Dorian Gray*— at least as far as its main theme is concerned—contains elements of a modern fairy-tale.

In neither *Dorian Gray* nor the tales, however, is the link between aesthetic theory and narrative practice as tight as it may at first appear. Primarily the gaps are due not to any shortcomings in textual structure or thematic motivation, but to unresolved problems in Wilde's aesthetic theory. He proclaimed the autonomy of art, preferring the imaginative to the imitative ideal and separating art from life and from all moral purposes, but paradoxically it was even more difficult for him to conform to these principles in the tales than it was in the novel. For in spite of their apparent detachment from the real world, they are inevitably imbued with their own special imagery which refers back to the reader's experience of reality, and indeed can only take on its meaning through such reference. Wilde's awareness of the problem was evident during the controversy over *Dorian Gray*, which he described as 'a story with a moral'. Similarly, at the end of **'The Devoted Friend'** the linnet confesses to having told a 'story with a

moral', to which the duck replies: ' . . . that is always a very dangerous thing to do'—an observation confirmed by the authorial narrator: 'And I quite agree with her.'

Structures, themes and style of the tales

Despite the variety of their themes, the tales—apart from **'The Fisherman and his Soul'**, the scope and complexity of which make it exceptional—have several structural features in common, and these are well worth analysing. They all have as their starting-point some kind of deficiency, which may be manifested in one of two ways: either the characters have no proper understanding of themselves and their surroundings, or they are lacking in love and consideration for their fellow creatures. In both cases, tensions arise between asocial egotism and social responsibility, between selfishness and thought for others, and it is these tensions that give the action its springboard and its direction. At first the (un)happy prince and the young king know nothing of the people's suffering, the ugly dwarf mistakes amusement for admiration, the student does not understand the nightingale's sacrifice, the supercilious rocket talks only about himself and regards his companions merely as a background for his own self-display, the selfish giant drives the children out of his garden and builds a wall round it, the narcissistic star-child pitilessly sends his weeping mother away, and the egotistical miller exploits poor Hans with false promises. The development of the action in all these stories depends on whether the initial moral defect or lack of insight is overcome—thus leading to a change in the character's behaviour—or continued to the end. Thus there are two types of dénouement: if the character passes his test and the fault is corrected, the ending is positive, in the form of a reward—often through some kind of Christian transformation, as in **'The Happy Prince'**, **'The Young King'**, and **'The Star-Child'**; if the character persists in his self-deception and egotism, the ending is negative—a kind of unreconciled fade-out, as in **'The Remarkable Rocket'**, **'The Nightingale and the Rose'**, and **'The Devoted Friend'**. In the tales with a positive ending, love of one's fellows, sympathy and self-sacrifice are rewarded, but in those with a negative ending the unenlightened or unpurified hero is punished: little Hans must die because he does not realise that he is only an object of exploitation for the miller; the rocket explodes unnoticed; the sacrifice of the nightingale, which presses its breast against the thorn of a rosebush so that its blood will be absorbed and bring forth a red rose, is senseless because the world around her, especially the student, does not appreciate it. Little Hans, the supercilious rocket, and the self-sacrificing nightingale have remained trapped in their illusions, unaware of the true nature of themselves or of others. An exception, though, is the ending of **'The Birthday of the Infanta'**, where the dwarf's insight into himself brings about his death. In view of these different categories of ending, it is hard to subscribe to Christopher S. Nassaar's thesis that: 'The fall from the world of innocence and subsequent attainment of a higher innocence is the governing principle of Wilde's fairy tales.'

Moral purification, in the form of the change from selfish to selfless conduct—as manifested in the tales with a positive ending—requires both insight and a readiness for self-sacrifice. The prince—who is only happy in the eyes of the mayor and town councillors—has no pangs of conscience until he learns from his exalted position about ugliness and misery. So long as he remained inside the palace of Sans-Souci, which was cut off from the world by a high wall, he had no idea what went on outside. Now he is ready to give up his gold so that he and his friend, the helpful swallow, may relieve the suffering of the poor and needy. When God asks his angel to bring the two most precious things in the city, these turn out to be the leaden heart of the prince, and the dead bird. There is a similar situation in 'The Young King'. There the king has three dreams, in which he sees three different people who are living in misery and have to slave away in order to supply the robes and jewels for his coronation, and only then does he become aware of the suffering that exists outside his resplendent palace Joyeuse. At once he renounces his royal pomp, takes his old worn-out clothes from the chest, puts a crown of briar on his head and rides off, despite the mockery of the courtiers and the people, to the coronation in the cathedral. It is not the bishop who places upon him the insignia of his earthly power, but God Himself, miraculously transforming him and dressing him in 'the raiment of a king'. In both tales, the hero's change of attitude is stimulated by insight into the suffering around him and is rewarded by divine intervention.

It is, however, dangerous to draw premature conclusions from the social implications of these two stories as, for example, George Woodcock does with reference to 'The Young King':

> This ['The Young King'] is a parable on the capitalist system of exploitation as severe as anything in William Morris, and it can stand beside the grimmest passages of Marx as an indictment of the kind of horrors which, Wilde was fully aware, were inflicted on the toilers in this world for the benefit of the people he satirised in his plays.

To set Wilde beside Morris and Marx is surely going a little too far, and the socialism inherent in his gentle fairy-tale seems far more geared to aesthetic effect than to political propaganda. If these tales are indeed 'wry pieces of social and moral commentary', as one critic suggests, then it must be said that the commentary contains little insight into or analysis of the social causes and effects of poverty. Instead, there is a series of snapshots: in 'The Happy Prince' we have the worn-out seamstress with her sick son, the starving writers, the weeping matchgirl; in 'The Young King' we see the gaunt weavers in their attic, the exploited galley-slave, and the toilers searching the dried-up river bed for rubies. This is poverty seen from outside—the scenery against which the main characters are to perform their actions. Beside the severity of Morris and the grimness of Marx, their tone is rather that of a 'modischen Sozialsentimentalismus' (fashionable social sentimentalism) such as emerged from the organised philanthropy of the many charities that sprang up during the nineteenth century.

In 'The Happy Prince' and 'The Young King', the ignorant heroes are purified by their new awareness of social misery; in 'The Selfish Giant' and 'The Star-Child', the egotistic heroes are transformed under somewhat different circumstances. The giant drives the children out of his garden, which then suffers continual winter until one day the children come back through a hole in the wall. Then the trees blossom, the grass grows, the birds twitter, and it is spring again. The giant realizes that the prolonged winter had been caused by his selfishness, and so he repents and resolves to tear down the wall and make his garden into a children's playground for ever. He helps a child to climb the one frost-covered tree, which blossoms at once. In this story, the conflict and the solution are clear: the giant's asocial egotism, symbolised by the winter cold, is overcome by an act of unselfishness and love. The initial impetus for this transformation, however, comes from outside: the rhythm of nature is broken, and is only restored when the children return to play. The process is similar in 'The Star-Child', where the hero is transformed supernaturally from Narcissus-like beauty to toad-like ugliness, and only then becomes aware of his own cruelty to his mother:

> I have been cruel to my mother, and as a punishment has this evil been sent to me. Wherefore I must go hence, and wander through the world till I find her, and she gives me forgiveness.

For three years he wanders in search of his mother, until he is finally sold as a slave to a magician, who on three successive days sends him to look for three pieces of gold in a wood. He is helped in this task by a little hare, but each time, in spite of the fact that the magician will beat him, he gives the gold to a leper who would otherwise starve to death. When, after his last good deed, he walks through the city gate, his original beauty is restored, he finds his mother, and he is made king. The structure of the tale is similar to that of 'The Selfish Giant': selfish behaviour, of which the character is made aware by supernatural events, leads through different tests to insight and a new attitude. In 'The Happy Prince' and 'The Young King', the scenes of poverty and suffering indicate a disturbance in the social order, whereas in 'The Selfish Giant' and 'The Star-Child' there are strange and discomforting changes in nature—endless winter in the giant's garden, and the child's beauty transformed to ugliness—which function as external manifestations of a disturbed moral order. In all four tales, the relief of suffering and the restoration of the natural order are not ends in themselves, but serve to change the characters' moral values. The problems and their solutions are individual, though they have social implications.

In form and structure, Wilde's fairy-tales are very much in the tradition of European folk-tales. The characters are one-dimensional, without psychological motivation, and generally they are simply the nameless bearers of particular qualities and functions: the happy prince, the selfish giant, the remarkable rocket. There is little or no description of their personal, social or historical background, and the story has no specific geographical or historical setting. On those occasions when Wilde does give some detailed description—for example in 'The Young King', 'The Birthday of the Infanta', and 'The Fisherman and his Soul'—the intention seems to be less a matter of directing the reader towards a precise setting than of the author indulging his predilection for lavish décor. The reduction of character to function and the general renunciation of any fixed time or place lead to a corresponding lack of complexity in the action itself. For the most part the problems and conflicts are limited to simple aesthetic, social or moral contrasts: beautiful/ugly, poor/rich, selfish/considerate. Changes of attitude or situation are not gradual, but, in nearly all cases, sudden and complete, often through the intervention of some supernatural agent. There are miraculous transformations rather than psychological developments.

In all the stories there is a single plot centred upon a single character, though the action may develop between two or even three figures whose relation to the hero is often contrastive or complementary. Little Hans' goodwill, extended to the point of self-sacrifice, stands in contrast to the miller's ruthless pragmatism; the happy prince and the star-child, on the other hand, are helped and befriended by the swallow and the hare. The active participation of talking animals and objects, incidentally, is as commonplace in Wilde as in so many folk-tales. There is also a tendency for the narrative to be divided up in patterns, as is most evident in the frequent use of triple themes: the young king's three dreams, the three good deeds of the swallow and the star-child, the soul's three journeys in **'The Fisherman and his Soul'**. Unlike many folk-tales, however, Wilde's stories do not make use of any set formulae for the beginning or the end. According to Lutz Röhrich: 'Der Märchenausgang ist stereotyp: die Liebenden werden ein Paar; der Arme wird reich' (the fairy-tale ending is stereotyped: the lovers become a pair; the poor man becomes rich), but this principle does not apply to Wilde's tales. Indeed some of them leave behind a rather bitter taste. Even the star-child who becomes king after passing all his tests, reigns for only three years: 'And he who came after him ruled evilly'. The death of the fisherman and of the mermaid, and the broken heart of the dwarf in **'The Birthday of the Infanta'**, endow these tales with a note of gloom which is far from the conventional happy ending.

The style of the narrative is not always as simple as one might expect from such subjects, and the incorporation of archaic, even biblical turns of phrase, together with personifications and ornate descriptions are all indicative of a highly artistic use of language. This deliberate stiltedness of expression reinforces the sense of other-worldliness and, at the same time, uses its extra emotional values—derived from the reader's own recollection of the Authorized Version—to imbue the action with a sort of magic amounting in some cases to Christian exaltation. The manner in which the star-child addresses his mother after the long search shows no spontaneous joy of reunion, but sounds like the repentant sinner's plea for absolution:

> 'Mother, I denied thee in the hour of my pride. Accept me in the hour of my humility. Mother, I gave thee hatred. Do thou give me love. Mother, I rejected thee. Receive thy child now.'

The archaic pronouns, and parallel sentences containing emotional contrasts such as pride/humility, hatred/love, are rhythmically reminiscent of biblical cadences, while

their content is redolent of sin and forgiveness, guilt and expiation. Thus the situation is detached from the real world and set in an idealised Christian frame of reference. The use of allegory and personification reinforces the unrealistic tenor of the tales already effected by the nameless generality of the characters, the vagueness of space and time, and the simplicity of the plot. It is interesting to note how Wilde uses this particular artifice. In **'The Young King'**, for instance, the misery of the weavers and the ruby-seekers is at first described realistically, but then this description suddenly breaks off and is continued on an allegorical level: 'Death' and 'Avarice' look at the workers and quarrel over the booty. 'Ague', 'Fever' and 'Plague' appear as Death's mighty allies, and thus an all too realistic atmosphere is palliated by abstraction, and we are once more distanced from the ugliness of the everyday world.

The same escapist tendency is apparent in the descriptions of decorative settings, where the lure of the colourful, rare and costly is depicted [as what Volker Klotz calls] 'mit verdichteter Sinnlichkeit' (concentrated sensuality). Assembled here is everything that has—in an industrialised, standardised and utilitarian world—become ever rarer and ever more expensive. For Wilde's *goût du précieux* does not confine itself to the stylised expression of an aesthetic philosophy of life, but it also mirrors his aristocratic predilection for the select, the exclusive, the elite. The young king, for instance, is in a room which sounds almost like the catalogue of a museum of arts and crafts listing the contents of some extraordinary interior:

> The walls were hung with rich tapestries representing the Triumph of Beauty. A large press, inlaid with agate and lapis lazuli, filled one corner, and facing the window stood a curiously wrought cabinet with lacquer panels of powdered and mosaiced gold, on which were placed some delicate goblets of Venetian glass, and a cup of dark-veined onyx. Pale poppies were broidered on the silk coverlet of the bed, as though they had fallen from the tired hands of sleep, and tall reeds of fluted ivory bore up the velvet canopy, from which great tufts of ostrich plumes sprang, like white foam, to the pallid silver of the fretted ceiling. A laughing Narcissus in green bronze held a polished mirror above its head. On the table stood a flat bowl of amethyst.

Frequently this *goût du précieux* is combined with a *nostalgie de l'étranger,* as in **'The Fisherman and his Soul'**, where the depiction of oriental splendour conveys an extra atmospheric charm. But the reader will search in vain for the intellectual edge, the wit and the paradox of the comedies, for these would not have fitted in at all with the predominantly moral tone of the tales. Nevertheless a different and perhaps disturbing discrepancy does arise between, on the one hand, the style with its mixture of simplicity, biblical and archaic expression, and decoratively aesthetic idiom, and on the other the content with its Christian and humanitarian sentiments. Even though Wilde did for the most part conform to the given conventions of the genre, he could not bring himself to renounce the formal trappings of his art and his well-known propensity for gems.

The literary conventions of the fairy-tale are not to be found in handbooks on poetics, but they manifest themselves variously in individual works. If a nineteenth-century English author had been asked for a classic representative of the genre, he would most certainly have come up with a single name: Hans Christian Andersen. The writings of Denmark's national poet, which had been available in numerous English translations since 1846, were widely read and immensely popular. Dickens had a very high regard for him, having first met him in 1847, and they became good friends, although their relations gradually cooled in later years. Interest in Andersen was enhanced by the fact that England had no real tradition of her own in this genre, with the single exception of *Alice's Adventures in Wonderland* (1865). Dickens, Thackeray and Ruskin all failed to achieve a breakthrough with their tales, and so it was only natural that Wilde should follow the European tradition. One of the very first reviews of **House of Pomegranates** notes the impression that the stories are written 'somewhat after the manner of Hans Andersen'. This vague feeling does not, however, become any more precise when one compares the work of the Irishman with the work of the Dane. The vanity of the remarkable rocket, and its adventures up until the unnoticed explosion, bear a certain similarity to Andersen's story of the proud darning-needle: 'who thought herself so fine that she fancied she must be fit for embroidery'. After its flight, nothing of the rocket remains except its stick, which falls on the back of a goose, while the ambitious needle finishes up under a cart. Little Hans—could he be an allusion to Hans Christian Andersen?—in **'The Devoted Friend'** reminds one of little Claus in 'Little Claus and Big Claus', but any initial similarity disappears entirely in the course of the story.

The clearest thematic links are to be found between **'The Fisherman and his Soul'** and Andersen's 'The Little Mermaid'. Both tales deal with the relationship between a human being and a mermaid. In Andersen's story the latter wishes to be rid of her tail so that she can become human and be close to the prince whom she loves and whose life—unbeknown to him—she once saved. Only if he marries her can she gain an immortal soul. If the prince gives his love to another—as happens towards the end of the story—then the mermaid must die. In **'Fisherman'** Wilde takes up the same theme, but turns it the other way round: his fisherman falls in love with the mermaid. In order to win her love, he must rid himself of his soul, which eventually he does—following the instructions of a witch—by standing in the moonlight and cutting his shadow away from his body. Every year the wandering soul returns from distant lands to the sea where the fisherman lives, in order to tell him about its many adventures. Only in the third year, when the soul tells of a veiled dancer with feet like 'little white pigeons', does the fisherman finally give way to the temptation and rejoin his spiritual companion. His soul, however, makes him commit wicked deeds because it had wandered the world for so long without a heart and had seen so much evil. The fisherman continues to love the mermaid, until one day he gives in to the soul's plea to enter his heart. Then the mermaid dies, and he himself, overcome by grief, dies as well.

The two main themes of this tale—the love between man and mermaid, and the separation of soul and body—are already to be found in Andersen's 'Little Mermaid' and also in 'Shadow', but both are of romantic origin. They are variations on the Undine theme in Friedrich de la Motte Fouqué's tale 'Undine' (1811) and the Schlemihl theme in Adelbert von Chamisso's novella *Peter Schlemihl's wundersame Geschichte* (1814). But the style, plot and outcome of Wilde's **'Fisherman'** and Andersen's 'Little Mermaid' show how very differently these two authors regarded both their art and the world. Andersen tended towards a poetic transfiguration of the everyday world, lingering reflectively on homely, domestic realities to which he gave idyllic form in such narrative gems as 'The Brave Tin Soldier', 'The Darning-Needle', 'The Shirt-Collar', and 'The Ugly Duckling'. There is nothing like this in Wilde. And indeed how could one expect common ground between the shoemaker's son from Odense, whose parents owned just so much as 'to live from day to day', and the snobbish Oxford graduate with his love of blue Chinese porcelain? The contrasting treatment of the Undine motif is certainly no coincidence. The little mermaid's longing to become human, to have an immortal soul and to share in human suffering springs directly from Andersen's love of the familiar and of that which is accessible to human experience. Wilde's **'Fisherman'** is the direct opposite, for in his love there is none of the self-sacrifice that characterises Andersen's mermaid. His love is, rather, a mixture of aesthetic sensuality and the thrill of the abnormal, the unnatural inherent in this hybrid creature—it is far more the offshoot of her strange beauty than the outpouring of the fisherman's own emotions.

> Her hair was a wet fleece of gold, and each separate hair as a thread of fine gold in a cup of glass. Her body was as white ivory, and her tail was of silver and pearl. Silver and pearl was her tail, and the green weeds of the sea coiled round it; and like seashells were her ears, and her lips were like sea-corals. The cold waves dashed over her cold breasts, and the salt glistened upon her eyelids.

In two respects, this mermaid seems unnatural: the combination of woman and fish is a perversion of nature, giving rise to an extraordinary hybrid, whilst the aesthetic stylisation endows this monster with a seductive, almost mythical charm. While Andersen seeks familiar emotions and experiences in the trivia of his fairy-tale world, Wilde favours the exotic and the extraordinary. The journeys of the soul into distant lands, whose oriental splendours burst open the domestic confines of the reading public's predominantly insular imagination, reflect Wilde's own desire to penetrate into the unexplored regions of fantasy, to savour each new sensation to the full, and thus to escape from the worn-out world of the present. Wilde's mermaid does not symbolise a return to nature, but she represents total otherness, the anomaly that stands in absolute contrast to the normality and routine of everyday human relations—indeed she may even stand for what the psychologically orientated critics of Wilde have assumed to be the 'deviance' of the homosexual. What lures the fisherman away from the sprite is the feet of a woman—in other words: 'une femme complète . . . l'amour normal'. But the search for such a woman, to whom his soul is supposed to lead him, is—as we learn from the tale itself—in vain.

'The Fisherman and his Soul' is strikingly different from the other tales in its scale, its complexity, and its decorative style. More than all the others it reveals motifs, thematic patterns and forms of expression that Wilde was to use again in subsequent works, particularly *The Picture of Dorian Gray.* The fisherman's separation from his soul anticipates Dorian's split identity, and the aesthetic attractions of the mermaid foreshadow Dorian's love for Sibyl Vane, whose acting talents fascinate him far more than her character. The relationship between a human being and a soulless hybrid opens up poetic possibilities that Wilde does not fully exploit in **'The Fisherman'**, but it is a theme to which he returns in his poem 'The Sphinx.' The mixture of lust and fatal cruelty, which characterises the 'sensibilità erotica' of this composite creature and of Salomé, plays no part in **'Fisherman'**, but one can already sense the incipient form of the *femme fatale,* the symbol of female demonry. As for the elaborate depiction of precious objects and an exotic ambience, this too has its later echo in *Dorian Gray,* particularly Chapter 11, and in *Salomé* and the 'Sainte Courtisane'.

These thematic and stylistic links between the tales and Wilde's later works are not confined to **'The Fisherman and his Soul'**. The dwarf gazing into the mirror at a deformed monster has its parallel in Dorian Gray's unveiling of the portrait which shows his bloodstained image, the painted likeness of his soul. Both are moments of revelation and self-knowledge which are shattering for the characters concerned. In **'The Birthday of the Infanta'**, the dwarf's illusion is destroyed by the reality of his appearance, while in *Dorian Gray* the beautiful and eternally youthful appearance of the protagonist cannot continue to mask the reality of his depraved soul. The structure of the two stories, however, is quite different. Dorian takes the opposite course from that of the dwarf, sacrificing his soul in order to preserve his youth and beauty. This contrary path also leads to a contrary end: instead of Christian transfiguration, the outcome is suicide—a psychological solution instead of a supernatural one.

In the tales, the simple plots are motivated by the basic contrasts between good and evil, beauty and ugliness, illusion and awareness, egotism and unselfishness; in Wilde's later fiction and drama, these contrasts are woven into more complex forms—for instance, the tension between aesthetic conduct and moral awareness in *Dorian Gray,* and the conflict between personal identity and social integration in the comedies. The thematic shifts of emphasis are unmistakable, and are only partly due to the fact that Wilde used different literary forms with different conventions. The blatant egotism of the rocket, for example: 'I am always thinking about myself, and I expect everybody else to do the same', recurs later in the maxims of dandyism, but is charmingly refurbished: 'To love oneself is the beginning of a life-long romance.'

The idealistic endings and the moral tone of many of the tales certainly suggest an underlying conformity to given conventions of the genre. At the same time, it is worth noting that despite his pose as the amoral *provocateur,* Wilde also remains true to conventional morality in his later works, with evil being punished and good rewarded: Dorian Gray stabs himself in front of his grotesque portrait, the 'good women' maintain the upper hand over the 'women with a past', Salomé is crushed between the shields of the soldiers, and the student in *The Sphinx* resists the charms of the seductive monster by looking at the crucifix. In the tales, Wilde was unburdened by the role the public expected him to play, and also by his own need to present himself as a wit and a clever but amoral outsider, and so he was quite free to tell his stories and to reveal another side of his character, that is, his conventional morality. The Basil Hallward in his personality had no need here of a Lord Henry at his side to counterbalance the moral norms with dazzling epigrams and smart philosophy.

The stories

In the fairy-tales, Wilde experimented with themes, structures and solutions within a comparatively simple framework; at about the same time he was writing a number of short stories which were published as a collection in 1891: **'Lord Arthur Savile's Crime: A Study of Duty', 'The Canterville Ghost: A Hylo-idealistic Romance', 'The Sphinx without a Secret: An Etching'**, and **'The Model Millionaire: A Note of Admiration'**. In these stories, where he was not bound by the same rigid conventions of the fairy-tale genre, he begins to test out those literary techniques and strategies of presentation which in *Dorian Gray* and the comedies were to become his favourite forms of expression: irony, paradox, and the complete reversal of situations into their opposites. The title story begins with a vivid description of a reception held by Lady Windermere in Bentinck House for an illustrious assembly of aristocrats, clergy, artists and politicians. One cannot help feeling that such an account of a *grande soirée* could only be written by an author with first-hand experience:

> It was certainly a wonderful medley of people. Gorgeous peeresses chatted affably to violent Radicals, popular preachers brushed coat-tails with eminent sceptics, a perfect bevy of bishops kept following a stout primadonna from room to room, on the staircase stood several Royal Academicians, disguised as artists, and it was said that at one time the supper-room was absolutely crammed with geniuses. In fact, it was one of Lady Windermere's best nights.

The hostess, who has developed an interest in palmistry, introduces some of her guests to Mr Podgers, a 'chiromantist'—not a 'chiropodist', as the Duchess of Paisley mistakenly calls him. His attention roused by some remarkable proofs of the man's ability, Lord Arthur Savile asks Mr Podgers to read his future for him. What the chiromantist sees in Lord Arthur's palm and—after much hesitation, repeated refusals, and a discreet discussion of the fee—is at last prepared to divulge, causes Savile to rush away from the party: 'Murder! that is what the chiromantist had seen there. Murder!' Not that any shady characters were aiming to take the life of this rich idler, but, on the contrary, he himself would one day be driven by Fate to commit such a crime.

Tormented by fear, Lord Arthur rushes through the London night, in a confusion of thoughts similar to those of Dorian Gray when he leaves Sibyl Vane and hurries through the maze of streets. But despite this initial agitation, Lord Arthur retains his commonsense and his awareness of the immediate future. Is it not his duty to commit this deed and fulfil the prophecy before he marries Sybil Merton, so that their marriage cannot be tainted by such a crime? This situation demands courage and selfless action, not a passive and cowardly attendance on Fate. After due consideration, he chooses his victim: Lady Clementina Beauchamp, an elderly lady with heart trouble, second cousin on his mother's side; his method is to be a fast-working pill, which he selects after careful study of toxicology. But all his efforts are in vain, because Lady Clem proceeds to die a natural death. Lord Arthur does not give up, but tries again, this time putting dynamite in a little French clock with a detonator installed by a helpful German anarchist named Winckelkopf; this he sends as an anonymous gift to the Dean of Chichester, a collector of antique clocks. But this attempt also fails miserably: 'a little puff of smoke came from the pedestal of the figure, and the goddess of Liberty fell off, and broke her nose on the fender'. Lord Arthur is in despair. Then one night, when he is walking along the Thames Embankment, he sees a figure leaning over the railing and, in the light of a street lantern, he recognizes him as Mr Podgers, the palmist. On the spur of the moment he grasps the man's legs and throws him into the river. Thus the prophecy is fulfilled, the long-postponed wedding can take place, and Lord Arthur Savile and his wife Sybil Merton can enter a clear future.

It is evident from this gem of black humour how far Wilde has moved away from the thematic structure, style and tone of the fairy-tales. The description of the *soirée,* the upper-class names of the ladies—Windermere, Jedburgh, Plymdale, all of which recur in the comedies—the pointed, epigrammatic dialogue of the characters, these all belong to the world of *Dorian Gray* and the social plays. Basically **'Lord Arthur Savile's Crime'** is a parody on contemporary detective stories: instead of a search for the criminal, we have the character's search for the crime; his problem is to *become* a criminal, not to catch one. Ironically it is the prophet of the deed who unwittingly fulfils his own prophecy by becoming the victim. The narrative strategy aims at a kind of double snub to the readers. First, Lord Arthur makes himself the executor of a destiny which the reader might have expected him to suffer only passively; he takes the prophecy for an inevitable fate, when for all we know it might just as easily be a lot of hocus-pocus. Secondly, the prophecy does not relate to a happy event that one might look forward to, but to a murder, which Lord Arthur appears to regard—against all the expectations of common sense—as an act of duty, indeed of self-sacrifice, and which must be performed in order to leave the way clear for his marriage. His justification for this somewhat perverse interpretation runs along the following lines:

> Many men in his position would have preferred the primrose path of dalliance to the steep heights of duty; but Lord Arthur was too consci-

entious to set pleasure above principle. There was more than mere passion in his love; and Sybil was to him a symbol of all that is good and noble. For a moment he had a natural repugnance against what he was asked to do, but it soon passed away. His heart told him that it was not a sin, but a sacrifice; his reason reminded him that there was no other course open. He had to choose between living for himself and living for others, and terrible though the task laid upon him undoubtedly was, yet he knew that he must not suffer selfishness to triumph over love.

This paradoxical argument, in which concepts such as 'duty', 'sacrifice' and 'love' are used to justify a totally immoral deed, depends on the deed being beyond the scope of moral law. Once it is released from such conventional restrictions, it becomes in itself a morally neutral action, and thus only the performance of it is associated with values—it is then a task to be fulfilled as expeditiously as possible, without fear of recriminations from the conscience. By thus hollowing out the substance of the above-mentioned concepts, it becomes perfectly easy to use them in vindication of that which they should diametrically oppose: in actual fact, it is not his duty that Lord Arthur is fulfilling, but a flagrant violation of it; he is driven, not by the courage of self-sacrifice, but by the cold-blooded search for an unknown victim; and no reader will believe that this is a matter of love triumphing over selfishness. The ethical code of the fairy-tales is turned upside down in this story. But at the same time it is more than just a piece of farcical comedy. Just as in *The Importance of Being Earnest* Wilde ridicules the earnestness of Victorian life by playing with the name Ernest, so too in this 'study of duty', behind the mask of satire and black humour, he shows how the concept of duty can be misused if it is loosened from the bonds of what Kant called the 'categorical imperative'.

'Lord Arthur Savile's Crime' is a humorous treatment of a serious theme, but at times it becomes positively macabre, whereas **'The Canterville Ghost: A Hylo-idealistic Romance'**, despite an abundance of gruesome details, maintains its cheerful tone throughout and is much more in the vein of the fairy-tales. Mr Hiram B. Otis, an American minister, comes to England and buys Canterville Chase, a haunted castle, ignoring the dire admonitions of the previous owner, Lord Canterville. He tells Mr Otis about the ghost of Sir Simon de Canterville, who murdered his wife Eleonore in 1575. The down-to-earth American, however, has no time for ghosts, and he and his family soon move into their new residence. A mysterious bloodstain in the salon is energetically removed with 'Champion Stain Remover and Paragon Detergent', but inexplicably reappears every day. After a few days, the master of the house is rudely awakened by steps in the corridor and the rattle of chains, thereby losing for ever his doubts about the existence of the ghost. But Mr Otis does not in any way allow these events to disturb his peace of mind; he simply offers his unusual guest a bottle of 'Tammany Rising Sun Lubricator', with the remark that he should oil his chains.

This is the start of a tough time for Sir Simon. Despite his wonderful powers of transformation—sometimes he appears as 'Black Isaac, or the Huntsman of Hogley Woods', sometimes as 'Reckless Rupert, or the Headless Earl'—he simply cannot impress the Otis family, let alone scare them. On the contrary: during his nightly tours of the castle, he stumbles over cunningly hidden trip-wires, when he enters a room a jug of water falls on his head, and once he is struck rigid with terror as he is suddenly confronted by a ghost—not, of course, a colleague, but a figure cobbled together out of a bed-curtain, a sweeping-brush, a kitchen cleaver, and a turnip. Once again they have played a nasty trick on him. Broken by all these unnerving experiences, Sir Simon is one day sitting downcast and depressed in the 'Tapestry Chamber' when Virginia, the minister's daughter, comes in and apologises to him for the rude behaviour of her brothers. In the course of the conversation, the ghost tells her that he longs for a peaceful death, but this he can only have if she weeps for his past sins and prays for the salvation of his soul. She does as he asks, and after centuries of restless haunting, Sir Simon at last takes a well-earned rest.

'The Canterville Ghost' is a delightful parody of the traditional ghost story. Instead of the spirit terrifying the occupants of the castle, he himself becomes the victim. The reversal of the conventional situation is accompanied by a reversal of the narrative perspective, because for most of the time the reader views events through the eyes of the tormented Sir Simon. What gives the story a special flavour is the fact that it also satirises the American way of life, which Wilde had experienced during his lecture tour in 1882. Among the features that seem to him typical of the American character are materialism, a predominantly pragmatic way of thinking, no sense of aesthetics, no sense of history, and generally no sense of culture. Everything can be bought, nearly everything can be made, and there is nothing that can resist the creative power of common sense. 'I reckon that if there was such a thing as a ghost in Europe, we'd have it at home in a very short time in one of our public museums, or on the road as a show.' For mysterious bloodstains, there is the 'Champion Stain Remover' etc., rusted chains require lubricating oil, and the best medicine for indigestion is Dr Dobell's tincture. There could be no greater contrast than that between Mr Otis—the puritanically raised and republically minded representative of the New World, cherishing his 'republican simplicity' and dismissing Sir Simon's family heirlooms as the 'appurtenances of idle luxury'—and the discreet, conservative Lord Canterville, who can trace his family back to the sixteenth century and can even include a castle ghost among his ancestors. Wilde's delightful 'hylo-idealistic romance' in addition to parodying the ghost story, thus offers an additional and highly entertaining commentary on the different mentalities of two nations, although perhaps the difference is not always as great as it may appear. For he writes of Mrs Otis:

> Indeed, in many respects, she was quite English, and was an excellent example of the fact that we have really everything in common with America nowadays, except, of course, language.

Beside 'The Canterville Ghost' and 'Lord Arthur Savile's Crime', the remaining two stories in the collection of 1891—'The Sphinx without a Secret: An Etching' and 'The Model Millionaire: A Note of Admiration'—are of less interest. They are *feuilleton* anecdotes, once more structured on the principle of reversal, with a character finally turning out to be the opposite of what he or she had at first appeared to be. In 'The Sphinx without a Secret', the strange behaviour of the widowed Lady Alroy suggests to Lord Murchison that she has a secret to hide. During a party, for instance, she speaks on even the most banal topics with a hushed voice as if she is afraid of being overheard; letters must not be sent to her private address in Park Lane, but must be sent 'care of Whittaker's Library'. By chance, Lord Murchison one day sees her hurrying through an area of ill repute and entering a boarding-house to which she has the key. In answer to the question whom she met there, she replies abruptly: 'I went to meet no one.' And strange as it may seem, this is the truth. As the landlady reports, the veiled lady simply sat in a room, read books, and had an occasional cup of tea. The narrator tells us at the end:

> Lady Alroy was simply a woman with a mania for mystery. She took these rooms for the pleasure of going there with her veil down, and imagining she was a heroine. She had a passion for secrecy, but she herself was merely a Sphinx without a secret.

A surprise, albeit a more pleasant one, also awaits Hughie Erskine in 'The Model Millionaire'. This good-looking but penniless young man needs exactly £10,000 to marry his beloved Laura Merton, 'the daughter of a retired Colonel who had lost his temper and his digestion in India, and had never found either of them again'. One day Erskine is visiting his friend, the painter Alan Trevor, who is busy painting the portrait of an old, shabby beggar. Erskine is so touched by the sight of the beggar's sad face that he gives him a sovereign, even though this means that he won't be able to afford a carriage ride for the next fortnight. The reward for this noble deed follows immediately. The beggar is not a beggar: beneath the ragged clothes is concealed one of the richest men in Europe. Erskine promptly receives a cheque for £10,000, and so he can go ahead and marry Laura. Indeed millionaire models may be rare, but model millionaires are even rarer.

Adeline R. Tintner has pointed out that this story may have been based on an anecdote that was going around concerning Baron James Mayer de Rothschild. The painter Delacroix suggested that the Baron should pose as a beggar, and in due course this eccentric financier, from the French side of the Rothschild family, arrived at the artist's studio where Delacroix's assistant, not knowing the real identity of the shabby-looking visitor, slipped him a one-franc piece. The following day the kind-hearted young man received a cheque for 10,000 francs, signed by James de Rothschild. This tale is told in two biographies of Rothschild, and the similarity between it and Wilde's story is surely too great to be mere coincidence.

Although in the fairy-tales and stories Wilde was still experimenting with existing forms, there is no doubt that here, for the first time, he was speaking with his own voice. He was now well on the way to establishing his own literary identity. The epigonic style of the early poems and dramas had been overcome, even if he still had not found the perfect form to express his fantasy. After 1891 he wrote no more fairy-tales or short stories. Indeed, at this stage of his career, it was not clear whether his leanings were more towards literature or criticism. While his talent for story-telling had blossomed at social gatherings and had taken on permanent form in the tales and stories, at the same time his reviews were developing into critical essays. The late 1880s were a period of professional and artistic orientation, after he had set up house in Tite Street, following his marriage to Constance Lloyd in 1884 and the subsequent birth of his sons Cyril and Vyvyan. The family needed a regular income, and so Wilde took on the post of editor of *The Woman's World*—a strange job for a man who many biographers have suggested was already indulging in secret homosexual relationships as early as 1886. Certainly family life soon began to bore him as much as the daily routine of going to the office. His creative and critical spirit, and also his need to assume a prominent position in London's cultural scene, demanded new outlets which he sought beyond the confines of home and office. What, then, could be more natural than that his imagination should dream up stories where the extraordinary became possible, dreams could come true, and restrictions could magically be lifted. If the fairy-tales are still predominantly coloured by conventional Christian morality—'Wilde is preaching not what he believes in, but what he feels he ought to believe in' [Edward Lucie-Smith]—a story like **'Lord Arthur Savile's Crime'** shows that he is already exploring an alternative world. The moral defects that were taken seriously and expiated in the tales are here turned satirically on their heads. The ethic of 'Love thy neighbour' is given its ultimate twist in *The Soul of Man under Socialism:* 'One should sympathise with the entirety of life, not with life's sores and maladies merely, but with life's joy and beauty and energy and health and freedom.' Selfless behaviour is no longer a form of social sympathy, but becomes an expression of aesthetic self-fulfilment. The tension between moral idealism and aesthetic individualism—which runs through Wilde's entire work—begins to take on recognisable form in the tales and stories, becomes personalised in the main characters of *Dorian Gray,* and determines the two poles of dandyism and respectability in the social comedies. (pp. 49-67)

> *Norbert Kohl, in his* Oscar Wilde: The Works of a Conformist Rebel, *translated by David Henry Wilson, Cambridge University Press, 1989, 439 p.*

Guy Willoughby (essay date 1988)

[In the excerpt below, Willoughby analyzes how Wilde equates Christ with the artist in "The Nightingale and the Rose."]

"One always thinks of him", wrote Oscar Wilde of Jesus in his famous *apologia* [*De Profundis*], "as a lover for whose love the whole world was too small." The nature and extent of that awe-inspiring example is a recurring theme in Wilde's mature fiction and essays, one which allows us also to grasp the full import of the writer's aesthetics; and with this in mind, I consider in this article the first

mature allusions to Christ, those found in *The Happy Prince and Other Tales* (1888). In three of these decorative fables—**"The Happy Prince"**, **"The Nightingale and the Rose"**, and **"The Selfish Giant"**—the pattern of references establishes Jesus as a compelling ethical ideal for the central characters, as they battle to win community in a sadly divided and fractious world. In particular, the parable Wilde constructs in **"The Nightingale and the Rose"** invites the reader to conflate Jesus with the artist in a manner that anticipates Wilde's major Christological studies, *The Soul of Man Under Socialism* (1891) and *De Profundis* (1897). This tale is therefore the focus of my article. Before we can examine the story in the context of the volume, however, it is necessary to relate the writer's activity in *The Happy Prince* to the rephrased Platonic theories of his concurrent dialogue, "The Decay of Lying".

To begin with, Wilde's generic choice in *The Happy Prince* is ironically apt, given his themes—and his audience. Fairy tale, and fairy-tale conventions, had become a convenient and popular Victorian means of presenting urgent moral problems without reference to Naturalistic demands; for Wilde, whose stories satirize the very notion of a mutually understood moral problem, the associative resonance of the genre nevertheless ensures a readership. Wilde's elegant tales of mutual misunderstanding reflect his awareness, imbibed most noticeably from Walter Pater's *The Renaissance,* of the fracturing and relativist world that science, psychology and social dislocation were exposing at the end of the 1880s.

Paradoxically, the fairy-tale genre of *The Happy Prince* enables the author to depict the post-Paterian universe of partisan visions, "each mind keeping as a solitary prisoner its own dream of a world", as the writer of *The Renaissance* hauntingly describes it, in a popular and accessible form. Moreover, at the same time that the dangerously solipsistic intellectual climate of the age is dramatically rendered, the style and structure of each tale triumphantly exemplifies Wilde's mature aesthetic theory. At the time of publication he wrote that the stories are "an attempt to mirror modern life in a form remote from reality—to deal with modern problems in a mode that is ideal and not imitative", and this brief statement of intention relates the book to the author's wider intellectual concerns.

This germ of theory is elaborated in the first of Wilde's critical dialogues published in *The Nineteenth Century* for January 1889, in which Vivian proposes to Cyril that the "decay of lying" in English letters signals a dangerous misunderstanding of the true relations of art and life, and of the role of the art work in offering to a sceptical era new, outlandish and regenerative modes of action; in a phrase, that "Life imitates Art far more than Art imitates Life."

What follows is a sustained and witty attack on the notions of sincerity and verisimilitude so dear to the Victorian reader—an attack, according to certain later readers, that presages the new aesthetic directions of the early twentieth century. Those very "lies" which Plato feared would sully and distort ideal forms, become—in an age without belief in enduring verities—vitally important:

> Remote from reality, and with her eyes turned
> away from the shadows of the cave, Art reveals

her own perfection, and the wondering crowd that watches the opening of the marvellous, many-petalled rose fancies that it is its own history that is being told it, its own spirit that is finding expression in a new form. But it is not so . . . Art develops purely on her own lines. She is not symbolic of her own age. It is the ages that are her symbols.

Wilde's reference to Plato's metaphor of the cave emphasizes his view that in the 1880s there are no longer any absolute values for the artist to advance or distort. Art is likewise detached from "reality" (a word which in *The Republic* signifies the a priori world), and "turned away from . . . the cave" in which Plato's spectators gaze at dim reflections of those perfect forms. Describing "her own perfection", art exists in no facile relation with either a dubious ideality or with everyday life; but in her perfection, existing without immediate reference to her surroundings, a new ideal may yet be figured forth for humanity to follow. Those who gaze at the "marvellous, many-petalled rose" will discover in its abstract perfection their own unconscious desires, and may thus be encouraged to enact them in life. The energy of life, Vivian states earlier, is "simply the desire for expression", and art provides the forms whereby this may be achieved.

Wilde's *magister* goes on to stress art's independence of current issues, for "the more abstract, the more ideal an art is, the more it reveals to us the temper of the age." The art that combines thematic suggestiveness and formal congruity can most successfully bear the burden of the *Zeitgeist;* in the terms of Wilde's teasing transposition, "It is the ages that are her symbols", because art will inspire the spectator to transfer that unconscious "desire for expression" into life.

Whatever the flaws in his argument, Wilde's proclamation of the non-representational and innovative aspect of art is one important reaction to the severe assaults that Romantic notions of individual integrity were currently undergoing. Certainly, Wilde is trying to find a way to graft the wider social role of art—as prescribed by his mentors Ruskin and Arnold—on to the truly contemporary problems of aesthetics and the individual consciousness that he found expressed in Pater and the French Decadents. Art is the ultimate statement of defiance against mechanistic philosophy, against "Mr. Herbert Spencer, scientific historians, and the compilers of statistics in general," a spirited protest that individuality will not wither, but consolidate. If "self-perfection", the Hellenic dream that Wilde shares with Arnold and Pater, is to be realized, the role of art in offering individual consciousness a model of complex integrity will be crucial. This is the kind of model the storyteller offers in *The Happy Prince.*

In these tales the conflicting claims of self and community are proved to be indissoluble aspects of that true self-perfection that haunts the writer's work; the narrowly egotistical characters like the Rocket and the Water-Rat who reject others may survive in smug myopia, but they are clearly shut out from the greater self-knowledge of their selfless counterparts.

Only those characters who imitate Jesus' unconditional love can attain a genuine self-completion. Thus the Happy Prince, aided by his beloved disciple, the little Swallow, redistributes the gold leaf of his statue until he is no longer recognizable, "little more than a beggar", but is dazzlingly reconstituted out of nature—like Yeats's golden bird—in God's "City of Gold." Similarly, the Selfish Giant, initially a grasping misanthrope, throws open his garden to nature and the neighbouring children, and dies at last "all covered with white blossoms", transfigured by love and bound for paradise. For each of these figures the example of Jesus is instrumental: in **"The Happy Prince"** a subtle pattern of allusion confirms the hero's Christ-like status once the extent of human suffering, "the ugliness and misery of my city", has been revealed to him after death. The Giant's change of heart is initiated by Christ directly, when he appears as a tiny child "so small that he could not reach up to the branches of the tree", and inspires the title-figure's dormant compassion. Christian discipleship, in spite of societal hostility or incomprehension, becomes the warrant of a wonderful perfection, paradoxically achieved after death by a commitment to others that effaces self.

But in **"The Nightingale and the Rose"** the "perfection" attained by the songbird through sacrifice is realized, not in heaven, but in a work of art. Through her assumption of the lovesick young Student's burden she exemplifies that which Wilde would say in *De Profundis* of Christ: " . . . he realised in the entire sphere of human relations that imaginative sympathy which in the sphere of art is the sole secret of creation."

That "imaginative sympathy" is crucial to the Nightingale's accomplishment, for she represents the Romantic artist, who—as Wilde had earlier declared in a sonnet on his favourite poet Keats—is martyred by a hostile society which fails to comprehend the value of her art. In "The English Renaissance of Art" (1882), the most extended of his early lectures on aesthetics, Wilde first makes this connection between the artist's experience, the completed art work, and audience response. His remarks illuminate the artistic parable in **"The Nightingale and the Rose"**:

> . . . while the incomplete lives of ordinary men bring no healing power with them, the thorn-crown of the poet will blossom into roses for our pleasure: for our delight his despair will gild its own thorns, and his pain, like Adonis, be beautiful in its agony: and when the poet's heart breaks it will break in music.

In this sonorous passage, the necessary relationship between pain and great art is explicit: the artist's "despair" will be his audiences' "delight", his "pain" will be "beautiful" to his viewers. The reference to Adonis, the martyred fertility god who is the subject of the first Greek idyllic poetry, suggests that the artist's creation becomes his elegy, a beautiful monument to his own sacrifice. This is encapsulated in the figure of roses blooming from the symbolically resonant "thorn-crown". More than this, Wilde asserts here that, in creating fine work out of his suffering, an artist perfects himself—his despair "will gild its own thorns"—and, in so doing, he will bring a "healing power" to those "incomplete lives of ordinary men".

Wilde's story of the Nightingale is an allegory for the all-consuming love and commitment required of Christ's most notable imitator, the artist. In literal terms, the "thorn-crown" of her agony will blossom into a red rose, venerable symbol of love, beauty and perfection, which represents the art work in whose symmetry and formal coherence the martyrdom of its creator is incarnate.

The rose includes in the reverberance of its literary associations an image of Heaven itself, and therefore of divine love, as used by Dante in *Il Paradiso*. The nightingale, of course, has been celebrated throughout European literature for the power and quality of its song, and is therefore an apposite emblem for the artist. In **"The Nightingale and the Rose"** the wonderful power of the bird's song becomes, as we shall see, a potent image for the transformation of experience of which art, according to the arguments of "The Decay of Lying", is capable.

The story begins with the Student's stagey protestations of unrequited passion, which place him in that long line of ardent and mellifluous suitors that we trace back to Petrarch and the medieval conventions of courtly love. In the responses of the Nightingale, listening intently from the holm-oak tree, the vital idealizing power of the artist is emphasized:

> "Here at last is a true lover," said the Nightingale. "Night after night have I sung of him, though I knew him not; night after night have I told his story to the stars, and now I see him."

The post-Platonic artist, as viewed by Vivian in "The Decay of Lying", always figures forth an ideal, a beautiful "lie" which in turn will be embodied in life. In this story, the Nightingale's "true lover" appears to personify the convention itself.

In a sense, then, the Student seems to be the Nightingale's creation, the ideal lover that she and her predecessors—Petrarch, Sydney, Spenser and the rest—have embodied in song. This explains her excitement: it is the excitement of recognition, proof positive that the images of art may become concrete. This excitement is reinforced in her second reflection, which deliberately echoes the first:

> "Here, indeed, is the true lover," said the Nightingale. "What I sing of, he suffers; what is joy to me, to him is pain. Surely love is a wonderful thing."

Moved by the Student's plight, the sympathetic Nightingale decides to do all she can to create the "red rose" needed by the young man to win his beloved's hand. Her life is at stake, for the bird must press her breast against the thorn of the barren Rose-tree—a venerable device, whereby the author skilfully combines a variety of literary and mythic conventions to emphasize the magnitude of the Nightingale's sacrifice. Traditionally, the red rose was believed to be infused with the songbird's blood, for by piercing itself against the thorn the nightingale is able to sing by night, and so to resist falling asleep and becoming prey to its traditional enemy, the snake.

This connection between the quality of the bird's song and the rose that is infused with its blood acquires a richer meaning, one central to the connection Wilde is making, when we recall the medieval myth that Christ's blood turned the white rose red at the time of his crucifixion. In the image of the rose deepening in colour as the life of the nightingale ebbs away, Wilde is creating a resonant symbol for the Christlike totality of sacrifice that art requires of its practitioners. That this symbol of perfection is to be "built" from the bird's music by "moonlight", and nourished with its "own heart's blood", powerfully represents the artist's commitment and her method.

It is the business of art, says Vivian in "The Decay of Lying", to help life express itself in a new form; and the Nightingale's relationship with the Rose-tree, who " 'shall have no roses at all this year' " without the bird's help, accords with this Aristotelian prescription. Only the artist-Nightingale can help nature realize that triumphant new form; she must submit herself to the Rose-tree's invitation, that " 'the thorn must pierce your heart, and your life-blood must flow into my veins, and become mine.' " If art represents a brilliant refinement of nature, the bird's agonies allegorize the terrible toll exacted of the artist who creates that new form.

It is important in terms of the parable Wilde is constructing that the Nightingale understand fully the extent of her sacrifice. She signals an acute anticipatory sense of loss that culminates in a moving assertion:

> "Death is a great price to pay for a red rose," cried the Nightingale, "and life is very dear to all . . . Yet love is better than life, and what is the heart of a bird compared to the heart of a man?"

The Nightingale's touching attempts to communicate with the young Student, and his brusque refusal to take her seriously, is a suggestive figure for the author's acute sense of the current divide between art and its audience. The bird's attempts to reassure the weeping Student—" 'Be happy!' cried the Nightingale, 'be happy, you shall have your red rose . . .!' "—meet with complete incomprehension. The artist and her subject, who is also her audience, do not share a common language, even though the latter is susceptible to her influence:

> The Student looked up from the grass, and listened, but he could not understand what the Nightingale was saying to him, for he only knew the things that are written down in books.

The artist and her audience in this story are literally of different species, and in the Student's terms the bird cannot "speak"; accordingly, the true value of her work will be unrecognized, and her sacrifice unseen.

The Student's reflection on the Nightingale's requiem for the holm-oak tree underlines this complete divorcement of understanding. Like Mr Bright, the representative Philistine in Arnold's *Culture and Anarchy,* he demands of art some practical use. Pulling "a note-book and a lead pencil out of his pocket", he vividly typifies the Victorian middle-class position on aesthetics:

> "She has form . . . but has she got feeling? I am afraid not. In fact, she is like most artists; she is all style without any sincerity. She would not

Oscar Wilde in the United States, 1882.

sacrifice herself for others. She thinks merely of music, and everybody knows the arts are selfish. Still, it must be admitted that she has some beautiful notes in her voice. What a pity it is that they do not mean anything, or do any practical good!"

Here Wilde satirizes the prevailing assumptions—so ably expressed in the pages of *Punch*—about the Aesthetic Movement in particular, and artistic endeavour in general. The clear remove the Student espies between art and life— " 'She thinks merely of music, and everybody knows the arts are selfish' "—is a kind of popular parody of the ideas of a Whistler or a Pater. But in presenting a disjunction between stylistic or formal coherence and the "sincerity" or otherwise of the artist, the Student describes only his inability to understand the real demands of the creative process; indeed, only his own self-absorption is revealed. Of the kind of imaginative engagement with art that Wilde is inviting, the Philistine student knows nothing. His own limited vision is made plain in that final exclamation: " 'What a pity they do not mean anything, or do any practical good!' "

The artist's actual commitment to her audience, and thereby to her creation, will in fact be powerfully demonstrated while the Student is asleep on his pallet-bed. She will literally pour herself into her work, and so will cele-

brate, in the perfect rose, the love the true artist feels for her subjects:

> She sang first of the birth of love in the heart of a boy and a girl. And on the topmost spray of the Rose-tree there blossomed a marvellous rose, petal following petal, as song followed song.

The blossoming rose will, in short, be an objective correlative for the evolution of love, and this is signified in the deepening colour of the flower. The artist-bird achieves this representation by exercising her "imaginative sympathy", and literally assuming the burden of pain her subject experiences; she "pressed closer against the thorn, and louder and louder grew her song, for she sang of the birth of passion in the soul of a man and a maid."

It is only when the artist apprehends the nature of a love that transcends the limits of her immediate situation, however, that the art work is perfected. Such apprehension is obtainable only when she achieves a total transference of being from herself to her creation:

> But the thorn had not reached her heart, so the rose's heart remained white, for only a Nightingale's heart's-blood can crimson the heart of a rose.

And the Tree cried to the Nightingale to press closer against the thorn.

With the climax of the process, the bird celebrates in the rose a love that in its intensity defies physical life. At this triumphant moment the epoch-making sacrifice of Jesus is directly recalled, so that the author can invest the Nightingale-artist with the same awesome power of imaginative assumption:

> So the Nightingale pressed closer against the thorn, and the thorn touched her heart, and a fierce pang of pain shot through her. Bitter, bitter was the pain, and wilder and wilder grew her song, for she sang of the love that is perfected by death, of the love that dies not in the tomb.
>
> And the marvellous rose became crimson, like the rose of the eastern sky.

The sacrifice calls forth a magnificent correlative, a rose whose symmetry represents the love that Christ embodied in his life and death, and which the artist, in her turn, may similarly realize in her work.

There is a further crucial dimension to the parable, one that brings us back to the issue of the audience's response. In **"The Happy Prince"** the hero's altruism is completely unperceived, not only by a myopic and complacent governing clique, but by its very recipients; in **"The Nightingale and the Rose"** the Student and his beloved are incapable of truly valuing the lovely flower. They are both the offspring of modern book-learning—he is a student, and she the coquettish daughter of a Professor—and the exchange between them reveals that they have been corrupted by a Utilitarian scale of values. In the young woman fashion has combined with acquisitiveness to make her rejection of the Student's offering especially callous:

> "I am afraid it will not go with my dress," she answered; "and, besides, the Chamberlain's nephew has sent me some real jewels, and everybody knows that jewels cost far more than flowers."

In the terms of the fable, neither this young woman nor her suitor can realize any beautiful suggestion from the rose, because they lack the imaginative sympathy to see beyond their prejudices. Discussing the story in a letter to an interested reader, Wilde made this point in forthright terms:

> I am afraid I don't think as much of the young Student as you do. He seems to me a rather shallow young man, and almost as bad as the girl he thinks he loves. The Nightingale is the true lover, if there is one. She, at least, is Romance, and the Student and the girl are, like most of us, unworthy of Romance.

Not only are the Student and the Professor's daughter too selfish to love each other, but they are also too selfish to respond to abstract beauty. Only those with compassion have the true aesthetic instinct, the denouement here suggests; and that is why the Nightingale-artist is the true disciple of Christ.

The Student's petulant reaction to the girl's rejection—he tosses the rose into the street, where "a cartwheel went over it"—indicates that he clearly has as little appreciation for the flower as the girl. Being a more intellectual Utilitarian, he will seek consolation in his studies; and his final reflections are a fine parody of the Benthamite notion of utility which the British middle classes had appropriated. It is the perspective of a Mr Gradgrind that we recognize—the Gradgrind of the opening scenes of *Hard Times*:

> "What a silly thing love is!" said the Student as he walked away. "It is not half as useful as Logic, for it does not prove anything, and is always telling one of things that are not going to happen, and making one believe things that are not true. In fact, it is quite unpractical, and, as in this age to be practical is everything, I shall go back to Philosophy and study Metaphysics."

The irony of Wilde's story is, of course, that whereas in *Hard Times* the representative Utilitarian learns, through experience, that without love his philosophy is worthless, in **"The Nightingale and the Rose"** the Student arrives at the opposite conclusion; he begins as an ardent romantic, and concludes as an advocate of computable knowledge. This ironic reversal of what had become a familiar thematic structure in nineteenth-century English fiction highlights Wilde's profound pessimism about the real capacity of an audience to 'learn', in a didactic sense, from art: on the contrary, such a tale points to a widening divide between artist and spectator, of a manifest failure of the latter to grasp either the artist's intention or achievement.

And yet, in the last analysis, the validity of the bird's sacrifice, like that of the Happy Prince or the little Swallow, is unaffected. Even though the beautiful rose is crushed in the street, the Nightingale has realized herself in an awe-inspiring act of self-denial. If the beautiful creation which embodies that perfection has been obliterated at the hands of an insensitive and materialistic audience, her achievement remains undiminished.

Although the story evokes the collapse of communication between the artist and her spectators, we must remember that, in its readability, it becomes—like the rose—the bird's record and its monument. In composing such a parable its writer assumes, and invites, an audience, and accordingly supposes that at least some coherent reading may be possible.

In **"The Nightingale and the Rose"** the bird's *imitatio Christi* is perfected in a beautiful correlative, the peerless work of art, which Vivian had similarly characterized as a "marvellous many-petalled rose" in which the "wondering crowd" discovers a host of meanings. This delicately couched tale dramatically identifies Christ with the artist, exemplifying in the Nightingale's passion and death the author's later thesis in *De Profundis* that artistic endeavour is, in essence, a mode of love.

To conclude, we find in these brief but suggestive tales a fascinating variation on the meaning of Christ in a fluid and arbitrary world. Christ personifies a commitment to community, and **"The Happy Prince"** is a shining allegory for the individual completion that will follow such commitment; **"The Nightingale and the Rose"** is Wilde's definitive representation of the suffering witness to imaginative sympathy that artists enact. The story-teller is trying to formulate a model personality that incorporates ethics within the canons of aesthetics. As these tales suggest, that model will be increasingly identified with the figure of Christ. (pp. 107-15)

> *Guy Willoughby, "The Marvellous Rose: Christ and the Meaning of Art in 'The Nightingale and the Rose',"* in English Studies in Africa, *Vol. 31, No. 2, 1988, pp. 107-17.*

W. B. Yeats on the unpredictable Irish spirit of Wilde's short stories:

[*Lord Arthur Savile's Crime, and Other Stories*] disappoints me a little, I must confess. The story it takes its name from is amusing enough in all conscience. **'The Sphinx without a Secret'** has a quaint if rather meagre charm; but **'The Canterville Ghost'** with its supernatural horse-play, and **'The Model Millionaire',** with its conventional motive, are quite unworthy of more than a passing interest. . . .

Surely we have in this story something of the same spirit that filled Ireland once with gallant, irresponsible ill-doing, but now it is in its right place making merry among the things of the mind, and laughing gaily at our most firm fixed convictions. In one other Londoner, the socialist, Mr. Bernard Shaw, I recognize the same spirit. His account of how the old Adam gradually changed into the great political economist Adam Smith is like Oscar Wilde in every way. These two men, together with Mr. Whistler, the painter—half an Irishman also, I believe—keep literary London continually agog to know what they will say next.

W. B. Yeats, in United Ireland, *26 September 1891.*

Maria Edelson   (essay date 1988)

[*In the following essay, Edelson examines Wilde's use of allegory in his fairy tales.*]

Oscar Wilde believed that literature should not try to imitate life because "realism is always spoiling the subject matter of art" and in accordance with this conviction he seldom used the realistic method of writing. When he did use it, his attempts were artistic failures; he was much more successful in creating artificial word-made worlds which gave him more possibilities to express his own ideas, attitudes and visions.

Since Wilde's fairy-tales contained in *The Happy Prince* (1888) and *A House of Pomegranates* (1891) owe their existence solely to the writer's imagination unrestricted by requirements of realism, they provide a useful source of information about his creative impulse and method.

Imaginary worlds usually originate in certain concepts and because of this fact they easily fall into the category of allegorical creation. The allegorical character of Wilde's tales is often emphasized by his critics and reviewers; they refer to the stories as "moralities" or "parables" and, at other times, call them "artistic apologues" or "allegories". Among them is Arthur Symons, for instance, who discusses Wilde's tales in a review and assures us that "Every narrative is an allegory".

There is ample evidence in the stories which proves the validity of such views. As Maureen Quilligan reminds us in her book *The Language of Allegory*, "the key to the story's meaning lies in the text's language" and, indeed, the language used by Oscar Wilde in his tales is that of allegory.

Like most writers of traditional allegory Wilde often resorts to the device of personified abstractions. In **"The Happy Prince"**, for example, the little Swallow says: "I am going to the House of Death. Death is the brother of Sleep, is he not?", and the weaver in **"The Young King"** describes his life in the following way: "Through our sunless lanes creeps Poverty with her hungry eyes, and Sin with his sodden face follows close behind her. Misery wakes us in the morning, and Shame sits with us at night." The description is a miniature allegory in itself. The story has another, more elaborate personification allegory in its narrative: the Young King sees in his dream Death and Avarice quarrelling about who should get more of the men gathering rubies for the King; Death sends first Ague, then Fever, and finally Plague to have them all killed and thus to possess them.

A different method of personification is used when Wilde endows flowers, animals, inanimate objects (in **"The Devoted Friend"**, **"The Nightingale and the Rose"**, **"The Birthday of the Infanta"**, **"The Remarkable Rocket"**) with the human ability to speak. The device is a characteristic feature of numerous fairy-tales, beast-fables and, of course, allegories. The allegorical character of Wilde's tales is strengthened by the use of significant names given to places such as the palace *Joyeuse* in which the Young King lives or the Palace of Sans-Souci of the Happy Prince. Palaces, as well as castles, strong-walled cities, gates, roads, gardens, valleys, mountains, seas and ships belong to conventional allegorical setting. Quite a number of these elements will be found in Wilde's stories, especially the ones which contain the quest-journey motif. When the Soul of the Fisherman says: "At dawn we rose and knocked at the gate of the city," or when the Star-Child "came to the gate of a strong-walled city by the river, and weary and footsore though he was, he made to enter in," the author signals important experiences of symbolic value in which his characters will get involved. Also objects with allegorical associations frequently appear in Wilde's tales. In **"The Fisherman and His Soul"**, for example, the Mirror of Wisdom and the Ring of Riches are offered to the Soul, and in **"The Nightingale and the Rose"** the red rose of love becomes the story's central symbol.

With the exception of little Hans in **"The Devoted Friend"**, characters created by Wilde have no proper names. They are known as the Happy Prince, the Young King, the Giant, the Student, the Fisherman, or the Infanta. This device places distance on them and is, according to Mary Doyle Springer, one of a number of signals which suggest the "possibility of apologue as the unifying principle" [*Forms of the Modern Novella*].

Unspecified time and place in Wilde's tales constitute yet another signal of allegory. More evidence of its presence will be found in the author's generalizing, often moralizing, comments, in the structuring of the narratives round a revealing situation, in the selection of significant events and characters and in use of the dream-vision device (**"The Young King"**).

The devices used by Oscar Wilde belong to the long established allegorical tradition and the writer does not prove original when he follows its conventions. Neither are his moral teachings strikingly original; his stories, so far as their didacticism is concerned, "would satisfy the most exacting moralist". The messages, ideas and structures of Wilde's fairy-tales often resemble those by Hans Andersen. Their imitative quality is so obvious that it makes a reviewer remark that they "would never have been written but for Hans Andersen".

In spite of the conventionality of the allegorical framework and morality and the imitativeness of the tone and concept, the stories in *The Happy Prince* and *A House of Pomegranates* have unmistakable features of Oscar Wilde's writings. The originality of the tales lies in the "peculiar clothing" of the allegories, in the way in which they are told, in their imagery.

The language of Oscar Wilde's tales has had about as many admirers as hostile critics. Those who praise the tales believe them to be delicate, charming, witty, imaginative "poems in prose"; those who dislike them, find the stories artificial, pretentious, dishonest and even vulgar. There is, indeed, something in the stories that, in spite of their ostensibly moral tone, makes some readers feel uneasy and unsure of their value and taste. St. John Ervine, the author of *Oscar Wilde: A Present Time Appraisal*, blames the weakness of the stories on the influence of the writer's homosexual relationships:

> Something had happened to Wilde. He met Mr. Robert Baldwin Ross.
>
> The effect of this unfortunate encounter is to be seen in Wilde's work during the period under discussion. . . . *The Happy Prince* appeared in 1888; and was followed up to the year 1891, when Wilde made his second unfortunate friendship, with Lord Alfred Douglas, by *The House of Pomegranates*. . . . There is nothing here for exultation.

This is an exaggerated, but by no means isolated opinion. Other critics also suggest, however indirectly, that the stories are not quite healthy morally. The unsigned review in the *Pall Mall Gazette* expresses the following view of the language of *A House of Pomegranates*: "The ultra-aestheticism of the pictures seems unsuitable for children—as also the rather 'fleshy' style of Mr. Wilde's writing."

One of the reasons why Wilde's tales may evoke such responses lies in the fact that nearly all of them have endings in which the main characters die and the descriptions of these deaths often produce pleasurable effects. **"The Fisherman and His Soul"**, for example, ends in the death of the young man and his beloved mermaid. The bodies of the lovers are buried together and on their grave strange, white flowers of "curious beauty" grow. The title charac-

ter in **"The Selfish Giant"**, who had not allowed children to play in his garden, ceased to be selfish when he saw that his egoism had caused an unending winter. He was happy to see spring and children in his garden again. The Giant was rewarded for his kindness: when he died, he was taken to the garden of Paradise. The story ends with the sentence: "And when the children ran in that afternoon, they found the Giant lying dead under the tree, all covered with white blossoms." **"The Happy Prince"** ends on a similar note. When the statue of the Prince is left without its gold and jewels, which have been given to the poor, it becomes unattractive and the Town Councillors decide to get rid of it. The heart of the statue, which would not melt, is thrown on a dust-heap where the Swallow, the Prince's little friend and helper, now dead, is also lying. The leaden heart and the dead bird are taken to God as the most precious things in the city.

Wilde seems compelled to conclude his stories with deaths even if such endings are quite unnecessary in the construction of the tales. The title character of **"The Star-Child"** changes into a good boy after his bitter experiences, he becomes a dutiful son and is rewarded with a kingdom to rule. An ordinary fairy-tale would probably end at this point, but Wilde's tale has as its conclusion the following paragraph:

> Yet ruled he not long, so great had been his suffering, and so bitter the fire of his testing, for after a space of three years he died. And he who came after him ruled evilly.

Bruno Bettelheim argues in *The Uses of Enchantment: The Meaning and Importance of Fairy Tales* that happy endings of traditional fairy-tales satisfy children's deep need to be reassured about the possibility of overcoming obstacles and attaining happiness; the possibility is often suggested by the typical last sentence of a fairy-story "They lived happily ever after". There are fairy-tales with sad endings, too. Oscar Wilde's stories, however, tend to have closures which are not only sad, but often also bitterly pessimistic or satiric and cynical. The ironic tale **"The Devoted Friend"**, in which the rich hypocritical Miller exploits poor little Hans, taking advantage of his good nature, closes with the funeral of the good man. "Everybody went to little Hans' funeral, as he was so popular and the Miller was the chief mourner." The comments made by the mourners as well as the remarks made by the animals of the framework of the tale, provide a satiric view of human greed, callousness and selfishness which go unpunished. Bitter satire and death conclude also **"The Birthday of the Infanta"** and **"The Nightingale and the Rose"**. Even the lightest of all the tales **"The Remarkable Rocket"** ends in a kind of death. The Rocket cannot go off during a display of fireworks because he gets wet with his tears of self-pity. When he finally does go off there is nobody to impress except a goose. This, however, does not change the high notion the Rocket has of himself. His life ends with a self-congratulatory remark: " 'I knew I should create a great sensation', gasped the Rocket, and he went out."

It is not only in the conclusions of the stories that Wilde turns his thoughts to death. An interesting example of his preoccupation with death will be found in **"The Birthday**

of the Infanta". The Infanta's father lost his wife twelve years earlier:

> So great had been his love for her that he had not suffered even the grave to hide her from him. She had been embalmed by a Moorish physician . . . and her body was still lying on its tapestries bier in the black marble chapel of the palace. . . . Once every month the King . . . went in and knelt by her side . . . he would clutch at the pale jewelled hands in a wild agony of grief, and try to wake by his mad kisses the cold painted face.

The same kind of fascination with death marks the long description of the scene in which the Nightingale dies pressing her body against a rosebush in order to colour a rose with her own blood. Here is a sample of the language of the description:

> So the Nightingale pressed closer against the thorn, and the thorn touched her heart, and a fierce pang of pain shot through her. Bitter, bitter was the pain, and wilder, wilder grew her song of the Love that is perfected by Death, of the Love that dies not in the tomb.

Death is thus made attractive because of its sentimental sadness and its aesthetic appeal.

The interest in the beauty of what is lifeless rather than in living things can be noticed also in Wilde's tendency to find artifacts more attractive than natural phenomena. His descriptions of beautiful scenes do make mentions of birds, flowers and trees sometimes, but it is basically jewelry, furniture, draperies, and other objects like these that get Wilde's loving attention. He seems to derive pleasure from the mere naming of things like "porphyry staircase", "vessels of gold", "crosses of gold", "silver armour", "wonderful white statues on their jasper pedestals", "richly embroidered curtains", "palace of amber", "pavement of bright pearl", "doors of powdered lacquer", "silver bracelets embossed all over with creamy turquoise stones," "a gate of wrought ivory".

The most notable concentration of such evocative expressions occurs in **"The Young King", "The Birthday of the Infanta",** and **"The Fisherman and His Soul".** In the passage quoted below, the Soul uses this kind of richly adorned description in order to impress the Fisherman with tales of remote places and thus make the young man leave his mermaid and join his soul:

> Thou couldst not believe how marvellous a place it was. There were huge tortoise-shells full of pearls, and hollowed moonstones of great size piled up with red rubies. The gold was stored in coffers of elephant-hide, and the gold-dust in leather bottles. There were opals and sapphires, the former in cups of crystal, and the latter in cups of jade. Round green emeralds were ranged in order upon thin plates of ivory, and in one corner were silk bags filled, some with turquoise-stones, and others with beryls. The ivory horns were heaped with purple amethysts, and the horns of brass with chalcedonies and sards. The pillars, which were of cedar, were hung with strings of yellow lynx-stones.

Perhaps, as one of Wilde's critics notes, the tales are spoiled by "too much straining after effect and too many wordy descriptions. . . . Mr. Wilde resembles the modern manager who crowds his stage with aesthetic upholstery". The critic admits, however, that there is poetry and subtle charm in Wilde's stories. There is also passionate fascination with the beautiful which is in sharp contrast with beauty's cold lifelessness. This contrast is best represented by the Young King who had a "strange passion for beauty" and "who had been seen, so the tale ran, pressing his warm lips to the marble brow of an antique statue."

Like the characters of his fairy-tales the Young King and the Star-Child, Wilde was "enamoured of beauty" of art and it made him look at life in terms of beautiful artifacts. Living creatures, human beings, are often presented in his stories as if they were pictures, statues or other objects of art. The Mermaid in **"The Fisherman and His Soul"**, for example, is described in the following way:

> Her hair was a wet fleece of gold, and each separate hair as a thread of fine gold in a cup of glass. Her body was as white as ivory, and her tail was of silver and pearl . . . and like sea-shells were her ears, and her lips were like sea-coral.

A similar method is used to present the Fisherman. When the Fisherman drew his net into his boat, "like lines of blue enamel round a vase of bronze, the long veins rose up on his arms." He is compared to a statue in another scene: "bronze-limbed and well-knit, like a statue wrought by a Grecian, he stood on the sand . . . ". In **"The Nightingale and the Rose"** the Student's face is "like pale ivory"; several characters' hair is compared to gold ("the pale gold of her hair," "hair was like fine gold," and sometimes to amber ("wet amber of her hair").

Nature seems to be reduced to decorative functions in expressions like the following: "birds made of silver," "gold snake," "slim reed of crystal," "a frog with bright jewelled eyes," and in comparisons of peacock's tails to "disks of ivory," earth to "a flower of silver" and the moon to "a flower of gold" as well as in sentences like "Its branches were golden, and silver fruit hung down from them". . . .

"The Remarkable Rocket" and **"The Devoted Friend"** deal with more down-to-earth matters and are therefore more lifelike and have less of the "aesthetic upholstery" in them, but in other stories Wilde's peculiar style petrifies life as art and strengthens the impression that Wilde's tales negate life. His language certainly proves that beauty and art are of supreme importance in Oscar Wilde's tales. One should not be deceived by the fact that the Young King, the Happy Prince, the Star-Child and also the Giant give up their beautiful treasures for the sake of the needy; their sacrifice is rewarded by an even greater kind of beauty—the beauty of the garden of Paradise, the aesthetic heaven.

The morality of the stories is certainly dominated by aestheticism, but Wilde does not reject it altogether; he obeys moral conventions even if it is only lip-service that he pays to them and often yields to the temptation to introduce some "exquisite poison" into his writing. The "clash between pagan appetite and Christian morality", which Epifanio San Juan finds responsible for the sense of doubt and dread in Wilde's writing, results also in the uneasy combination of the professed moral values with the aesthetic needs of the tales.

Thus the language of allegory in Oscar Wilde's tales, their imagery and, implied by it, thematic motifs point to a third level of their meaning: the tales are not mere "pretty enough moralities", stories with disguised didacticism, they are also about the relation between art and life. If we are inclined to dismiss Oscar Wilde's remark that "Life imitates Art far more than Art imitates Life" as one that is clever but not to be taken seriously, his tales prove that the source of this seemingly flippant statement is in the writer's deeply felt inclinations and needs, and remind us that also in dealing with paradoxes it is important to be earnest. (pp. 165-71)

> Maria Edelson, "The Language of Allegory in Oscar Wilde's Tales," in Anglo-Irish and Irish Literature—Aspects of Language and Culture: Proceedings of the Ninth International Association for the Study of Anglo-Irish Literature, edited by B. Bramsbäck and M. Croghan, Acta Univ. Ups.: Studia Anglistica Upsaliensia, Vol. II, 1988, pp. 165-71.

FURTHER READING

Bibliography

Mikhail, E. H. *Oscar Wilde: An Annotated Bibliography of Criticism.* Totowa, N.J.: Rowman & Littlefield, 1978, 249 p.
　　Lists book and play reviews, earlier bibliographies of criticism, and whole and partial books of criticism on Wilde. The work also includes author and subject indexes and a brief primary bibliography.

Biography

Ellmann, Richard. *Oscar Wilde.* New York: Alfred A. Knopf, 1988, 680 p.
　　Standard biography.

Hyde, H. Montgomery. *Oscar Wilde: A Biography.* New York: Farrar, Straus & Giroux, 1975, 410 p.
　　Excellent biography.

Criticism

Cohen, Philip K. "Marriages and Murders: 'Lord Arthur Savile's Crime' and 'The Canterville Ghost'." In his *The*

Moral Vision of Oscar Wilde, pp. 53-70. Cranbury, N.J.: Associated University Presses, 1978.
　　Examines Wilde's use of realism and romance in these two stories.

Erickson, Donald H. "The Stories." In his *Oscar Wilde,* pp. 53-72. Boston: Twayne, 1977.
　　Provides plot summaries and discussion of principal themes of Wilde's short fiction.

Griswold, Jerome. "Sacrifice and Mercy in Wilde's 'The Happy Prince'." *Children's Literature* 3 (1974): 103-06.
　　Asserts that "a clear understanding of the idea of sacrifice as a kind of self-discipline that provides for future rewards" is essential to a critical reading of Wilde's "The Happy Prince."

Miller, Robert Keith. "Mannered Morality: *The Happy Prince* and *A House of Pomegranates*." In his *Oscar Wilde,* pp. 90-115. New York: Frederick Ungar Publishing, 1982.
　　Provides plot summaries and analyses of the stories collected in *The Happy Prince, and Other Tales* and *A House of Pomegranates,* maintaining it is "readily apparent that these stories advocate a consistently moral point of view."

Murray, Isobel. Introduction to *The Writings of Oscar Wilde,* by Oscar Wilde, edited by Isobel Murray, pp. vii-xix. Oxford: Oxford University Press, 1989.
　　Critical overview and revaluation that includes discussion of the exquisite irony with which Wilde, in the short story "Lord Arthur Savile's Crime," debunked characteristic Victorian concerns with sincerity and earnestness.

Raby, Peter. "Stories." In his *Oscar Wilde,* pp. 49-66. Cambridge: Cambridge University Press, 1988.
　　Provides a thematic and stylistic analysis of Wilde's short stories and fairy tales.

Ross, Alexander Galt. Review of *The Happy Prince, and Other Tales. The Saturday Review* 66, No. 1721 (20 October 1888): 472.
　　States that while some of the stories in this volume are entertaining, others are overly sentimental.

Wilburn, Lydia Reineck. "Oscar Wilde's 'The Canterville Ghost': The Power of an Audience." *Papers on Language and Literature* 23, No. 1 (Winter 1987): 41-55.
　　Examines Wilde's treatment of the relationship between artist and audience as evinced in "The Canterville Ghost," a story later adapted to theater. Wilburn states: "The conflicting notions of the audience's role preoccupied Wilde throughout his career, and they have preoccupied his critics, who continue to search for a resolution to these contradictions."

Additional coverage of Wilde's life and career is contained in the following sources published by Gale Research: *Contemporary Authors,* Vols. 104, 119; *Concise Dictionary of British Literary Biography, 1890-1914; Dictionary of Literary Biography,* Vols. 10, 19, 34, 57; *Something about the Author,* Vol. 24; *Twentieth-Century Literary Criticism,* Vols. 1, 8, 23, 41; and *World Literature Criticism.*

Appendix:

Select Bibliography of General Sources on Short Fiction

BOOKS OF CRITICISM

Allen, Walter. *The Short Story in English.* New York: Oxford University Press, 1981, 413 p.

Aycock, Wendell M., ed. *The Teller and the Tale: Aspects of the Short Story* (Proceedings of the Comparative Literature Symposium, Texas Tech University, Volume XIII). Lubbock: Texas Tech Press, 1982, 156 p.

Averill, Deborah. *The Irish Short Story from George Moore to Frank O'Connor.* Washington, D.C.: University Press of America, 1982, 329 p.

Bates, H. E. *The Modern Short Story: A Critical Survey.* Boston: Writer, 1941, 231 p.

Bayley, John. *The Short Story: Henry James to Elizabeth Bowen.* Great Britain: The Harvester Press Limited, 1988, 197 p.

Bennett, E. K. *A History of the German Novelle: From Goethe to Thomas Mann.* Cambridge: At the University Press, 1934, 296 p.

Bone, Robert. *Down Home: A History of Afro-American Short Fiction from Its Beginning to the End of the Harlem Renaissance.* Rev. ed. New York: Columbia University Press, 1988, 350 p.

Bruck, Peter. *The Black American Short Story in the Twentieth Century: A Collection of Critical Essays.* Amsterdam: B. R. Grüner Publishing Co., 1977, 209 p.

Burnett, Whit, and Burnett, Hallie. *The Modern Short Story in the Making.* New York: Hawthorn Books, 1964, 405 p.

Canby, Henry Seidel. *The Short Story in English.* New York: Henry Holt and Co., 1909, 386 p.

Current-García, Eugene. *The American Short Story before 1850: A Critical History.* Twayne's Critical History of the Short Story, edited by William Peden. Boston: Twayne Publishers, 1985, 168 p.

Flora, Joseph M., ed. *The English Short Story, 1880-1945: A Critical History.* Twayne's Critical History of the Short Story, edited by William Peden. Boston: Twayne Publishers, 1985, 215 p.

Foster, David William. *Studies in the Contemporary Spanish-American Short Story.* Columbia, Mo.: University of Missouri Press, 1979, 126 p.

George, Albert J. *Short Fiction in France, 1800-1850.* Syracuse, N.Y.: Syracuse University Press, 1964, 245 p.

Gerlach, John. *Toward an End: Closure and Structure in the American Short Story.* University, Ala.: The University of Alabama Press, 1985, 193 p.

Hankin, Cherry, ed. *Critical Essays on the New Zealand Short Story.* Auckland: Heinemann Publishers, 1982, 186 p.

Hanson, Clare, ed. *Re-Reading the Short Story.* London: MacMillan Press, 1989, 137 p.

Harris, Wendell V. *British Short Fiction in the Nineteenth Century.* Detroit: Wayne State University Press, 1979, 209 p.

Huntington, John. *Rationalizing Genius: Idealogical Strategies in the Classic American Science Fiction Short Story.* New Brunswick: Rutgers University Press, 1989, 216 p.

Kilroy, James F., ed. *The Irish Short Story: A Critical History.* Twayne's Critical History of the Short Story, edited by William Peden. Boston: Twayne Publishers, 1984, 251 p.

Lee, A. Robert. *The Nineteenth-Century American Short Story.* Totowa, N. J.: Vision / Barnes & Noble, 1986, 196 p.

Leibowitz, Judith. *Narrative Purpose in the Novella.* The Hague: Mouton, 1974, 137 p.

Lohafer, Susan. *Coming to Terms with the Short Story.* Baton Rouge: Louisiana State University Press, 1983, 171 p.

Lohafer, Susan, and Clarey, Jo Ellyn. *Short Story Theory at a Crossroads.* Baton Rouge: Louisiana State University Press, 1989, 352 p.

Mann, Susan Garland. *The Short Story Cycle: A Genre Companion and Reference Guide.* New York: Greenwood Press, 1989, 228 p.

Matthews, Brander. *The Philosophy of the Short Story.* New York: Longmans, Green and Co., 1901, 83 p.

May, Charles E., ed. *Short Story Theories.* Athens, Oh.: Ohio University Press, 1976, 251 p.

McClave, Heather, ed. *Women Writers of the Short Story: A Collection of Critical Essays.* Englewood Cliffs, N. J.: Prentice-Hall, 1980, 171 p.

Moser, Charles, ed. *The Russian Short Story: A Critical History.* Twayne's Critical History of the Short Story, edited by William Peden. Boston: Twayne Publishers, 1986, 232 p.

New, W. H. *Dreams of Speech and Violence: The Art of the Short Story in Canada and New Zealand.* Toronto: The University of Toronto Press, 1987, 302 p.

Newman, Frances. *The Short Story's Mutations: From Petronius to Paul Morand.* New York: B. W. Huebsch, 1925, 332 p.

O'Connor, Frank. *The Lonely Voice: A Study of the Short Story.* Cleveland: World Publishing Co., 1963, 220 p.

O'Faolain, Sean. *The Short Story.* New York: Devin-Adair Co., 1951, 370 p.

Orel, Harold. *The Victorian Short Story: Development and Triumph of a Literary Genre.* Cambridge: Cambridge University Press, 1986, 213 p.

O'Toole, L. Michael. *Structure, Style and Interpretation in the Russian Short Story.* New Haven: Yale University Press, 1982, 272 p.

Pattee, Fred Lewis. *The Development of the American Short Story: An Historical Survey.* New York: Harper and Brothers Publishers, 1923, 388 p.

Peden, Margaret Sayers, ed. *The Latin American Short Story: A Critical History.* Twayne's Critical History of the Short Story, edited by William Peden. Boston: Twayne Publishers, 1983, 160 p.

Peden, William. *The American Short Story: Continuity and Change, 1940-1975.* Rev. ed. Boston: Houghton Mifflin Co., 1975, 215 p.

Reid, Ian. *The Short Story.* The Critical Idiom, edited by John D. Jump. London: Methuen and Co., 1977, 76 p.

Rhode, Robert D. *Setting in the American Short Story of Local Color, 1865-1900.* The Hague: Mouton, 1975, 189 p.

Rohrberger, Mary. *Hawthorne and the Modern Short Story: A Study in Genre.* The Hague: Mouton and Co., 1966, 148 p.

Shaw, Valerie, *The Short Story: A Critical Introduction.* London: Longman, 1983, 294 p.

Stephens, Michael. *The Dramaturgy of Style: Voice in Short Fiction.* Carbondale, Ill.: Southern Illinois University Press, 1986, 281 p.

Stevick, Philip, ed. *The American Short Story, 1900-1945: A Critical History.* Twayne's Critical History of the Short Story, edited by William Peden, Boston: Twayne Publishers, 1984, 209 p.

Summers, Hollis, ed. *Discussion of the Short Story.* Boston: D. C. Heath and Co., 1963, 118 p.

Vannatta, Dennis, ed. *The English Short Story, 1945-1980: A Critical History.* Twayne's Critical History of the Short Story, edited by William Peden. Boston: Twayne Publishers, 1985, 206 p.

Voss, Arthur. *The American Short Story: A Critical Survey.* Norman, Okla.: University of Oklahoma Press, 1973, 399 p.

Ward, Alfred C. *Aspects of the Modern Short Story: English and American.* London: University of London Press, 1924, 307 p.

Weaver, Gordon, ed. *The American Short Story, 1945-1980: A Critical History.* Twayne's Critical History of the Short Story, edited by William Peden. Boston: Twayne Publishers, 1983, 150 p.

West, Ray B., Jr. *The Short Story in America, 1900-1950.* Chicago: Henry Regnery Co., 1952, 147 p.

Williams, Blanche Colton. *Our Short Story Writers.* New York: Moffat, Yard and Co., 1920, 357 p.

Wright, Austin McGiffert. *The American Short Story in the Twenties.* Chicago: University of Chicago Press, 1961, 425 p.

CRITICAL ANTHOLOGIES

Atkinson, W. Patterson, ed. *The Short-Story.* Boston: Allyn and Bacon, 1923, 317 p.

Baldwin, Charles Sears, ed. *American Short Stories.* New York: Longmans, Green and Co., 1904, 333 p.

Charters, Ann, ed. *The Story and Its Writer: An Introduction to Short Fiction.* New York: St. Martin's Press, 1983, 1239 p.

Current-García, Eugene, and Patrick, Walton R., eds. *American Short Stories: 1820 to the Present.* Key Editions, edited by John C. Gerber. Chicago: Scott, Foresman and Co., 1952, 633 p.

Fagin, N. Bryllion, ed. *America through the Short Story.* Boston: Little, Brown, and Co., 1936, 508 p.

Frakes, James R., and Traschen, Isadore, eds. *Short Fiction: A Critical Collection.* Prentice-Hall English Literature Series, edited by Maynard Mack. Englewood Cliffs, N.J.: Prentice-Hall, 1959, 459 p.

Gifford, Douglas, ed. *Scottish Short Stories, 1800-1900.* The Scottish Library, edited by Alexander Scott. London: Calder and Boyars, 1971, 350 p.

Gordon, Caroline, and Tate, Allen, eds. *The House of Fiction: An Anthology of the Short Story with Commentary.* Rev. ed. New York: Charles Scribner's Sons, 1960, 469 p.

Greet, T. Y., et. al. *The Worlds of Fiction: Stories in Context.* Boston: Houghton Mifflin Co., 1964, 429 p.

Gullason, Thomas A., and Caspar, Leonard, eds. *The World of Short Fiction: An International Collection.* New York: Harper and Row, 1962, 548 p.

Havighurst, Walter, ed. *Masters of the Modern Short Story.* New York: Harcourt, Brace and Co., 1945, 538 p.

Litz, A. Walton, ed. *Major American Short Stories.* New York: Oxford University Press, 1975, 823 p.

Matthews, Brander, ed. *The Short-Story: Specimens Illustrating Its Development.* New York: American Book Co., 1907, 399 p.

Menton, Seymour, ed. *The Spanish American Short Story: A Critical Anthology.* Berkeley and Los Angeles: University of California Press, 1980, 496 p.

Mzamane, Mbulelo Vizikhungo, ed. *Hungry Flames, and Other Black South African Short Stories.* Longman African Classics. Essex: Longman, 1986, 162 p.

Schorer, Mark, ed. *The Short Story: A Critical Anthology*. Rev. ed. Prentice-Hall English Literature Series, edited by Maynard Mack. Englewood Cliffs, N. J.: Prentice-Hall, 1967, 459 p.

Simpson, Claude M., ed. *The Local Colorists: American Short Stories, 1857-1900*. New York: Harper and Brothers Publishers, 1960, 340 p.

Stanton, Robert, ed. *The Short Story and the Reader*. New York: Henry Holt and Co., 1960, 557 p.

West, Ray B., Jr., ed. *American Short Stories*. New York: Thomas Y. Crowell Co., 1959, 267 p.

Short Story Criticism Indexes

Literary Criticism Series
Cumulative Author Index

SSC Cumulative Nationality Index
SSC Cumulative Title Index

This Index Includes References to Entries in These Gale Series

Black Literature Criticism provides excerpts from criticism of the most significant works of black authors of all nationalities over the past 200 years. Complete in three volumes.

Concise Dictionary of American Literary Biography contains illustrated entries on major American authors selected and updated from the *Dictionary of Literary Biography.*

Contemporary Literary Criticism presents excerpts of criticism on the works of novelists, poets, dramatists, short story writers, scriptwriters, and other creative writers who are now living or who have died since 1960.

Twentieth-Century Literary Criticism contains critical excerpts by the most significant commentators on poets, novelists, short story writers, dramatists, and philosophers who died between 1900 and 1960.

Nineteenth-Century Literature Criticism offers significant passages from criticism on authors who died between 1800 and 1899.

Literature Criticism from 1400 to 1800 compiles significant passages from the most noteworthy criticism on authors of the fifteenth through eighteenth centuries.

Classical and Medieval Literature Criticism offers excerpts of criticism on the works of world authors from classical antiquity through the fourteenth century.

Short Story Criticism compiles excerpts of criticism on short fiction by writers of all eras and nationalities.

Poetry Criticism presents excerpts of criticism on the works of poets from all eras, movements, and nationalities.

Drama Criticism contains excerpts of criticism on dramatists of all nationalities and periods of literary history.

Children's Literature Review includes excerpts from reviews, criticism, and commentary on works of authors and illustrators who create books for children.

Contemporary Authors Series encompasses five related series. *Contemporary Authors* provides biographical and bibliographical information on more than 97,000 writers of fiction and nonfiction. *Contemporary Authors New Revision Series* provides completely updated information on authors covered in *CA. Contemporary Authors Permanent Series* consists of listings for deceased and inactive authors. *Contemporary Authors Autobiography Series* presents specially commissioned autobiographies by leading contemporary writers. *Contemporary Authors Bibliographical Series* contains primary and secondary bibliographies as well as analytical bibliographical essays by authorities on major modern authors.

Dictionary of Literary Biography encompasses four related series. *Dictionary of Literary Biography* furnishes illustrated overviews of authors' lives and works. *Dictionary of Literary Biography Documentary Series* illuminates the careers of major figures through a selection of literary documents, including letters, interviews, and photographs. *Dictionary of Literary Biography Yearbook* summarizes the past year's literary activity and includes updated entries on individual authors. *Concise Dictionary of American Literary Biography* comprises six volumes of revised and updated sketches on major American authors that were originally presented in *Dictionary of Literary Biography.*

Major 20th-Century Writers contains in four volumes both newly written and completely updated *CA* sketches on over one thousand of the most influential authors of our time.

Something about the Author Series encompasses three related series. *Something about the Author* contains well-illustrated biographical sketches on juvenile and young adult authors and illustrators from all eras. *Something about the Author Autobiography Series* presents specially commissioned autobiographies by prominent authors and illustrators of books for children and young adults. *Authors & Artists for Young Adults* provides high school and junior high school students with profiles of their favorite creative artists.

Yesterday's Authors of Books for Children contains heavily illustrated entries on children's writers who died before 1961. Complete in two volumes.

Literary Criticism Series
Cumulative Author Index

A. E. . . . . TCLC **3, 10**
  See also Russell, George William
  See also DLB 19

A. M.
  See Megged, Aharon

Abasiyanik, Sait Faik 1906-1954
  See Sait Faik
  See also CA 123

Abbey, Edward 1927-1989 . . . . . . CLC **36, 59**
  See also CA 45-48; 128; CANR 2

Abbott, Lee K(ittredge) 1947- . . . . . . CLC **48**
  See also CA 124

Abe Kobo 1924- . . . . CLC **8, 22, 53**
  See also CA 65-68; CANR 24; MTCW

Abell, Kjeld 1901-1961 . . . . CLC **15**
  See also CA 111

Abish, Walter 1931- . . . . CLC **22**
  See also CA 101; CANR 37

Abrahams, Peter (Henry) 1919- . . . . . CLC **4**
  See also BW; CA 57-60; CANR 26;
  DLB 117; MTCW

Abrams, M(eyer) H(oward) 1912-. . . CLC **24**
  See also CA 57-60; CANR 13, 33; DLB 67

Abse, Dannie 1923-. . . . . CLC **7, 29**
  See also CA 53-56; CAAS 1; CANR 4;
  DLB 27

Achebe, (Albert) Chinua(lumogu)
  1930- . . . . CLC **1, 3, 5, 7, 11, 26, 51**
  See also BLC 1; BW; CA 1-4R; CANR 6,
  26; CLR 20; DLB 117; MAICYA;
  MTCW; SATA 38, 40; WLC

Acker, Kathy 1948- . . . . CLC **45**
  See also CA 117; 122

Ackroyd, Peter 1949-. . . . . CLC **34, 52**
  See also CA 123; 127

Acorn, Milton 1923-. . . . . CLC **15**
  See also CA 103; DLB 53

Adamov, Arthur 1908-1970 . . . . . . CLC **4, 25**
  See also CA 17-18; 25-28R; CAP 2; MTCW

Adams, Alice (Boyd) 1926- . . . CLC **6, 13, 46**
  See also CA 81-84; CANR 26; DLBY 86;
  MTCW

Adams, Douglas (Noel) 1952- . . . CLC **27, 60**
  See also AAYA 4; BEST 89:3; CA 106;
  CANR 34; DLBY 83

Adams, Francis 1862-1893. . . . . . . NCLC **33**

Adams, Henry (Brooks)
  1838-1918 . . . . TCLC **4**
  See also CA 104; 133; DLB 12, 47

Adams, Richard (George)
  1920- . . . . CLC **4, 5, 18**
  See also AITN 1, 2; CA 49-52; CANR 3,
  35; CLR 20; MAICYA; MTCW;
  SATA 7, 69

Adamson, Joy(-Friederike Victoria)
  1910-1980 . . . . CLC **17**
  See also CA 69-72; 93-96; CANR 22;
  MTCW; SATA 11, 22

Adcock, Fleur 1934- . . . . CLC **41**
  See also CA 25-28R; CANR 11, 34;
  DLB 40

Addams, Charles (Samuel)
  1912-1988 . . . . CLC **30**
  See also CA 61-64; 126; CANR 12

Addison, Joseph 1672-1719 . . . . LC **18**
  See also CDBLB 1660-1789; DLB 101

Adler, C(arole) S(chwerdtfeger)
  1932- . . . . CLC **35**
  See also AAYA 4; CA 89-92; CANR 19;
  MAICYA; SATA 26, 63

Adler, Renata 1938- . . . . CLC **8, 31**
  See also CA 49-52; CANR 5, 22; MTCW

Ady, Endre 1877-1919 . . . . TCLC **11**
  See also CA 107

Afton, Effie
  See Harper, Frances Ellen Watkins

Agapida, Fray Antonio
  See Irving, Washington

Agee, James (Rufus)
  1909-1955 . . . . TCLC **1, 19**
  See also AITN 1; CA 108;
  CDALB 1941-1968; DLB 2, 26

Aghill, Gordon
  See Silverberg, Robert

Agnon, S(hmuel) Y(osef Halevi)
  1888-1970 . . . . CLC **4, 8, 14**
  See also CA 17-18; 25-28R; CAP 2; MTCW

Aherne, Owen
  See Cassill, R(onald) V(erlin)

Ai 1947-. . . . . CLC **4, 14, 69**
  See also CA 85-88; CAAS 13; DLB 120

Aickman, Robert (Fordyce)
  1914-1981 . . . . CLC **57**
  See also CA 5-8R; CANR 3

Aiken, Conrad (Potter)
  1889-1973 . . . CLC **1, 3, 5, 10, 52; SSC 9**
  See also CA 5-8R; 45-48; CANR 4;
  CDALB 1929-1941; DLB 9, 45, 102;
  MTCW; SATA 3, 30

Aiken, Joan (Delano) 1924-. . . . . . . CLC **35**
  See also AAYA 1; CA 9-12R; CANR 4, 23,
  34; CLR 1, 19; MAICYA; MTCW;
  SAAS 1; SATA 2, 30

Ainsworth, William Harrison
  1805-1882 . . . . NCLC **13**
  See also DLB 21; SATA 24

Aitmatov, Chingiz (Torekulovich)
  1928- . . . . CLC **71**
  See also CA 103; CANR 38; MTCW;
  SATA 56

Akers, Floyd
  See Baum, L(yman) Frank

Akhmadulina, Bella Akhatovna
  1937- . . . . CLC **53**
  See also CA 65-68

Akhmatova, Anna
  1888-1966 . . . . CLC **11, 25, 64; PC 2**
  See also CA 19-20; 25-28R; CANR 35;
  CAP 1; MTCW

Aksakov, Sergei Timofeyvich
  1791-1859 . . . . NCLC **2**

Aksenov, Vassily . . . . CLC **22**
  See also Aksyonov, Vassily (Pavlovich)

Aksyonov, Vassily (Pavlovich)
  1932- . . . . CLC **37**
  See also Aksenov, Vassily
  See also CA 53-56; CANR 12

Akutagawa Ryunosuke
  1892-1927 . . . . TCLC **16**
  See also CA 117

Alain 1868-1951 . . . . TCLC **41**

Alain-Fournier. . . . . TCLC **6**
  See also Fournier, Henri Alban
  See also DLB 65

Alarcon, Pedro Antonio de
  1833-1891 . . . . NCLC **1**

Alas (y Urena), Leopoldo (Enrique Garcia)
  1852-1901 . . . . TCLC **29**
  See also CA 113; 131; HW

Albee, Edward (Franklin III)
  1928- . . . CLC **1, 2, 3, 5, 9, 11, 13, 25, 53**
  See also AITN 1; CA 5-8R; CABS 3;
  CANR 8; CDALB 1941-1968; DLB 7;
  MTCW; WLC

Alberti, Rafael 1902- . . . . CLC **7**
  See also CA 85-88; DLB 108

Alcala-Galiano, Juan Valera y
  See Valera y Alcala-Galiano, Juan

Alcott, Amos Bronson 1799-1888 . . NCLC **1**
  See also DLB 1

Alcott, Louisa May 1832-1888 . . . . NCLC **6**
  See also CDALB 1865-1917; CLR 1;
  DLB 1, 42, 79; MAICYA; WLC;
  YABC 1

Aldanov, M. A.
  See Aldanov, Mark (Alexandrovich)

Aldanov, Mark (Alexandrovich)
  1886(?)-1957 . . . . TCLC **23**
  See also CA 118

Aldington, Richard 1892-1962. . . . . . CLC **49**
  See also CA 85-88; DLB 20, 36, 100

Aldiss, Brian W(ilson)
  1925- . . . . CLC **5, 14, 40**
  See also CA 5-8R; CAAS 2; CANR 5, 28;
  DLB 14; MTCW; SATA 34

Alegria, Fernando 1918-. . . . . CLC **57**
  See also CA 9-12R; CANR 5, 32; HW

Aleichem, Sholom . . . . TCLC **1, 35**
  See also Rabinovitch, Sholem

Aleixandre, Vicente 1898-1984 . . . **CLC 9, 36**
See also CA 85-88; 114; CANR 26;
DLB 108; HW; MTCW

Alepoudelis, Odysseus
See Elytis, Odysseus

Aleshkovsky, Joseph 1929-
See Aleshkovsky, Yuz
See also CA 121; 128

Aleshkovsky, Yuz . . . . **CLC 44**
See also Aleshkovsky, Joseph

Alexander, Lloyd (Chudley) 1924- . . **CLC 35**
See also AAYA 1; CA 1-4R; CANR 1, 24,
38; CLR 1, 5; DLB 52; MAICYA;
MTCW; SATA 3, 49

Alfau, Felipe 1902-. . . . . **CLC 66**
See also CA 137

Alger, Horatio Jr. 1832-1899 . . . . . **NCLC 8**
See also DLB 42; SATA 16

Algren, Nelson 1909-1981 . . . . **CLC 4, 10, 33**
See also CA 13-16R; 103; CANR 20;
CDALB 1941-1968; DLB 9; DLBY 81,
82; MTCW

Ali, Ahmed 1910- . . . . **CLC 69**
See also CA 25-28R; CANR 15, 34

Alighieri, Dante 1265-1321 . . . . **CMLC 3**

Allan, John B.
See Westlake, Donald E(dwin)

Allen, Edward 1948-. . . . . **CLC 59**

Allen, Roland
See Ayckbourn, Alan

Allen, Woody 1935- . . . . **CLC 16, 52**
See also CA 33-36R; CANR 27, 38;
DLB 44; MTCW

Allende, Isabel 1942- . . . . **CLC 39, 57**
See also CA 125; 130; HW; MTCW

Alleyn, Ellen
See Rossetti, Christina (Georgina)

Allingham, Margery (Louise)
1904-1966 . . . . **CLC 19**
See also CA 5-8R; 25-28R; CANR 4;
DLB 77; MTCW

Allingham, William 1824-1889 . . . **NCLC 25**
See also DLB 35

Allston, Washington 1779-1843. . . . **NCLC 2**
See also DLB 1

Almedingen, E. M. . . . . **CLC 12**
See also Almedingen, Martha Edith von
See also SATA 3

Almedingen, Martha Edith von 1898-1971
See Almedingen, E. M.
See also CA 1-4R; CANR 1

Alonso, Damaso 1898-1990 . . . . **CLC 14**
See also CA 110; 131; 130; DLB 108; HW

Alta 1942-. . . . . **CLC 19**
See also CA 57-60

Alter, Robert B(ernard) 1935-. . . . . . **CLC 34**
See also CA 49-52; CANR 1

Alther, Lisa 1944-. . . . . **CLC 7, 41**
See also CA 65-68; CANR 12, 30; MTCW

Altman, Robert 1925-. . . . . **CLC 16**
See also CA 73-76

Alvarez, A(lfred) 1929-. . . . . **CLC 5, 13**
See also CA 1-4R; CANR 3, 33; DLB 14,
40

Alvarez, Alejandro Rodriguez 1903-1965
See Casona, Alejandro
See also CA 131; 93-96; HW

Amado, Jorge 1912-. . . . . **CLC 13, 40**
See also CA 77-80; CANR 35; DLB 113;
MTCW

Ambler, Eric 1909-. . . . . **CLC 4, 6, 9**
See also CA 9-12R; CANR 7, 38; DLB 77;
MTCW

Amichai, Yehuda 1924- . . . . . . **CLC 9, 22, 57**
See also CA 85-88; MTCW

Amiel, Henri Frederic 1821-1881 . . **NCLC 4**

Amis, Kingsley (William)
1922- . . . . . . **CLC 1, 2, 3, 5, 8, 13, 40, 44**
See also AITN 2; CA 9-12R; CANR 8, 28;
CDBLB 1945-1960; DLB 15, 27, 100;
MTCW

Amis, Martin (Louis)
1949-. . . . . **CLC 4, 9, 38, 62**
See also BEST 90:3; CA 65-68; CANR 8,
27; DLB 14

Ammons, A(rchie) R(andolph)
1926- . . . . **CLC 2, 3, 5, 8, 9, 25, 57**
See also AITN 1; CA 9-12R; CANR 6, 36;
DLB 5; MTCW

Amo, Tauraatua i
See Adams, Henry (Brooks)

Anand, Mulk Raj 1905-. . . . . **CLC 23**
See also CA 65-68; CANR 32; MTCW

Anatol
See Schnitzler, Arthur

Anaya, Rudolfo A(lfonso) 1937- . . . . **CLC 23**
See also CA 45-48; CAAS 4; CANR 1, 32;
DLB 82; HW; MTCW

Andersen, Hans Christian
1805-1875 . . . . **NCLC 7; SSC 6**
See also CLR 6; MAICYA; WLC; YABC 1

Anderson, C. Farley
See Mencken, H(enry) L(ouis); Nathan,
George Jean

Anderson, Jessica (Margaret) Queale
. . . . **CLC 37**
See also CA 9-12R; CANR 4

Anderson, Jon (Victor) 1940- . . . . . . **CLC 9**
See also CA 25-28R; CANR 20

Anderson, Lindsay (Gordon)
1923-. . . . . **CLC 20**
See also CA 125; 128

Anderson, Maxwell 1888-1959 . . . . . **TCLC 2**
See also CA 105; DLB 7

Anderson, Poul (William) 1926-. . . . **CLC 15**
See also AAYA 5; CA 1-4R; CAAS 2;
CANR 2, 15, 34; DLB 8; MTCW;
SATA 39

Anderson, Robert (Woodruff)
1917-. . . . . **CLC 23**
See also AITN 1; CA 21-24R; CANR 32;
DLB 7

Anderson, Sherwood
1876-1941 . . . . . . **TCLC 1, 10, 24; SSC 1**
See also CA 104; 121; CDALB 1917-1929;
DLB 4, 9, 86; DLBD 1; MTCW; WLC

Andouard
See Giraudoux, (Hippolyte) Jean

Andrade, Carlos Drummond de . . . . . . **CLC 18**
See also Drummond de Andrade, Carlos

Andrade, Mario de 1893-1945. . . . . **TCLC 43**

Andrewes, Lancelot 1555-1626 . . . . **LC 5**

Andrews, Cicily Fairfield
See West, Rebecca

Andrews, Elton V.
See Pohl, Frederik

Andreyev, Leonid (Nikolaevich)
1871-1919 . . . . **TCLC 3**
See also CA 104

Andric, Ivo 1892-1975 . . . . **CLC 8**
See also CA 81-84; 57-60; MTCW

Angelique, Pierre
See Bataille, Georges

Angell, Roger 1920-. . . . . **CLC 26**
See also CA 57-60; CANR 13

Angelou, Maya 1928-. . . . . **CLC 12, 35, 64**
See also AAYA 7; BLC 1; BW; CA 65-68;
CANR 19; DLB 38; MTCW; SATA 49

Annensky, Innokenty Fyodorovich
1856-1909 . . . . **TCLC 14**
See also CA 110

Anon, Charles Robert
See Pessoa, Fernando (Antonio Nogueira)

Anouilh, Jean (Marie Lucien Pierre)
1910-1987 . . . . . . **CLC 1, 3, 8, 13, 40, 50**
See also CA 17-20R; 123; CANR 32;
MTCW

Anthony, Florence
See Ai

Anthony, John
See Ciardi, John (Anthony)

Anthony, Peter
See Shaffer, Anthony (Joshua); Shaffer,
Peter (Levin)

Anthony, Piers 1934-. . . . . **CLC 35**
See also CA 21-24R; CANR 28; DLB 8;
MTCW

Antoine, Marc
See Proust,
(Valentin-Louis-George-Eugene-)Marcel

Antoninus, Brother
See Everson, William (Oliver)

Antonioni, Michelangelo 1912-. . . . . **CLC 20**
See also CA 73-76

Antschel, Paul 1920-1970. . . . . . . **CLC 10, 19**
See also Celan, Paul
See also CA 85-88; CANR 33; MTCW

Anwar, Chairil 1922-1949 . . . . **TCLC 22**
See also CA 121

Apollinaire, Guillaume . . . . **TCLC 3, 8**
See also Kostrowitzki, Wilhelm Apollinaris
de

Appelfeld, Aharon 1932- . . . . **CLC 23, 47**
See also CA 112; 133

Apple, Max (Isaac) 1941-. . . . . **CLC 9, 33**
See also CA 81-84; CANR 19

Appleman, Philip (Dean) 1926-. . . . . **CLC 51**
See also CA 13-16R; CANR 6, 29

Appleton, Lawrence
See Lovecraft, H(oward) P(hillips)

Apuleius, (Lucius Madaurensis)
125(?)-175(?) . . . . **CMLC 1**

Aquin, Hubert 1929-1977. . . . . **CLC 15**
See also CA 105; DLB 53

Aragon, Louis 1897-1982. . . . . **CLC 3, 22**
See also CA 69-72; 108; CANR 28;
DLB 72; MTCW

Arany, Janos 1817-1882. . . . . **NCLC 34**

Arbuthnot, John 1667-1735 . . . . **LC 1**
See also DLB 101

Archer, Herbert Winslow
See Mencken, H(enry) L(ouis)

Archer, Jeffrey (Howard) 1940- . . . . **CLC 28**
See also BEST 89:3; CA 77-80; CANR 22

Archer, Jules 1915- . . . . **CLC 12**
See also CA 9-12R; CANR 6; SAAS 5;
SATA 4

Archer, Lee
See Ellison, Harlan

Arden, John 1930- . . . . **CLC 6, 13, 15**
See also CA 13-16R; CAAS 4; CANR 31;
DLB 13; MTCW

Arenas, Reinaldo 1943-1990 . . . . **CLC 41**
See also CA 124; 128; 133; HW

Arendt, Hannah 1906-1975 . . . . **CLC 66**
See also CA 17-20R; 61-64; CANR 26;
MTCW

Aretino, Pietro 1492-1556 . . . . **LC 12**

Arguedas, Jose Maria
1911-1969 . . . . **CLC 10, 18**
See also CA 89-92; DLB 113; HW

Argueta, Manlio 1936- . . . . **CLC 31**
See also CA 131; HW

Ariosto, Ludovico 1474-1533 . . . . **LC 6**

Aristides
See Epstein, Joseph

Aristophanes
450B.C.-385B.C. . . . . **CMLC 4; DC 2**

Arlt, Roberto (Godofredo Christophersen)
1900-1942 . . . . **TCLC 29**
See also CA 123; 131; HW

Armah, Ayi Kwei 1939- . . . . **CLC 5, 33**
See also BLC 1; BW; CA 61-64; CANR 21;
DLB 117; MTCW

Armatrading, Joan 1950- . . . . **CLC 17**
See also CA 114

Arnette, Robert
See Silverberg, Robert

Arnim, Achim von (Ludwig Joachim von
Arnim) 1781-1831 . . . . **NCLC 5**
See also DLB 90

Arnim, Bettina von 1785-1859. . . . **NCLC 38**
See also DLB 90

Arnold, Matthew
1822-1888 . . . . **NCLC 6, 29; PC 5**
See also CDBLB 1832-1890; DLB 32, 57;
WLC

Arnold, Thomas 1795-1842 . . . . . . **NCLC 18**
See also DLB 55

Arnow, Harriette (Louisa) Simpson
1908-1986 . . . . **CLC 2, 7, 18**
See also CA 9-12R; 118; CANR 14; DLB 6;
MTCW; SATA 42, 47

Arp, Hans
See Arp, Jean

Arp, Jean 1887-1966. . . . . **CLC 5**
See also CA 81-84; 25-28R

Arrabal. . . . . **CLC 2, 9, 18**
See also Arrabal, Fernando

Arrabal, Fernando 1932- . . . . **CLC 58**
See also Arrabal
See also CA 9-12R; CANR 15

Arrick, Fran. . . . . **CLC 30**

Artaud, Antonin 1896-1948 . . . . . **TCLC 3, 36**
See also CA 104

Arthur, Ruth M(abel) 1905-1979. . . . **CLC 12**
See also CA 9-12R; 85-88; CANR 4;
SATA 7, 26

Artsybashev, Mikhail (Petrovich)
1878-1927 . . . . **TCLC 31**

Arundel, Honor (Morfydd)
1919-1973 . . . . **CLC 17**
See also CA 21-22; 41-44R; CAP 2;
SATA 4, 24

Asch, Sholem 1880-1957 . . . . **TCLC 3**
See also CA 105

Ash, Shalom
See Asch, Sholem

Ashbery, John (Lawrence)
1927- . . . **CLC 2, 3, 4, 6, 9, 13, 15, 25, 41**
See also CA 5-8R; CANR 9, 37; DLB 5;
DLBY 81; MTCW

Ashdown, Clifford
See Freeman, R(ichard) Austin

Ashe, Gordon
See Creasey, John

Ashton-Warner, Sylvia (Constance)
1908-1984 . . . . **CLC 19**
See also CA 69-72; 112; CANR 29; MTCW

Asimov, Isaac
1920-1992 . . . . **CLC 1, 3, 9, 19, 26**
See also BEST 90:2; CA 1-4R; 137;
CANR 2, 19, 36; CLR 12; DLB 8;
MAICYA; MTCW; SATA 1, 26

Astley, Thea (Beatrice May)
1925- . . . . **CLC 41**
See also CA 65-68; CANR 11

Aston, James
See White, T(erence) H(anbury)

Asturias, Miguel Angel
1899-1974 . . . . **CLC 3, 8, 13**
See also CA 25-28; 49-52; CANR 32;
CAP 2; DLB 113; HW; MTCW

Atares, Carlos Saura
See Saura (Atares), Carlos

Atheling, William
See Pound, Ezra (Weston Loomis)

Atheling, William Jr.
See Blish, James (Benjamin)

Atherton, Gertrude (Franklin Horn)
1857-1948 . . . . **TCLC 2**
See also CA 104; DLB 9, 78

Atherton, Lucius
See Masters, Edgar Lee

Atkins, Jack
See Harris, Mark

Atticus
See Fleming, Ian (Lancaster)

Atwood, Margaret (Eleanor)
1939- . . . . **CLC 2, 3, 4, 8, 13, 15, 25, 44;**
SSC 2
See also BEST 89:2; CA 49-52; CANR 3,
24, 33; DLB 53; MTCW; SATA 50; WLC

Aubigny, Pierre d'
See Mencken, H(enry) L(ouis)

Aubin, Penelope 1685-1731(?) . . . . **LC 9**
See also DLB 39

Auchincloss, Louis (Stanton)
1917- . . . . **CLC 4, 6, 9, 18, 45**
See also CA 1-4R; CANR 6, 29; DLB 2;
DLBY 80; MTCW

Auden, W(ystan) H(ugh)
1907-1973 . . . . . **CLC 1, 2, 3, 4, 6, 9, 11,**
14, 43; PC 1
See also CA 9-12R; 45-48; CANR 5;
CDBLB 1914-1945; DLB 10, 20; MTCW;
WLC

Audiberti, Jacques 1900-1965 . . . . . . **CLC 38**
See also CA 25-28R

Auel, Jean M(arie) 1936-. . . . . **CLC 31**
See also AAYA 7; BEST 90:4; CA 103;
CANR 21

Auerbach, Erich 1892-1957 . . . . . . **TCLC 43**
See also CA 118

Augier, Emile 1820-1889 . . . . **NCLC 31**

August, John
See De Voto, Bernard (Augustine)

Augustine, St. 354-430 . . . . **CMLC 6**

Aurelius
See Bourne, Randolph S(illiman)

Austen, Jane
1775-1817 . . . . **NCLC 1, 13, 19, 33**
See also CDBLB 1789-1832; DLB 116;
WLC

Auster, Paul 1947-. . . . . **CLC 47**
See also CA 69-72; CANR 23

Austin, Mary (Hunter)
1868-1934 . . . . **TCLC 25**
See also CA 109; DLB 9, 78

Autran Dourado, Waldomiro
See Dourado, (Waldomiro Freitas) Autran

Averroes 1126-1198 . . . . **CMLC 7**
See also DLB 115

Avison, Margaret 1918-. . . . . **CLC 2, 4**
See also CA 17-20R; DLB 53; MTCW

Ayckbourn, Alan 1939- . . . . **CLC 5, 8, 18, 33**
See also CA 21-24R; CANR 31; DLB 13;
MTCW

Aydy, Catherine
See Tennant, Emma (Christina)

Ayme, Marcel (Andre) 1902-1967. . . **CLC 11**
See also CA 89-92; CLR 25; DLB 72

Ayrton, Michael 1921-1975. . . . . **CLC 7**
See also CA 5-8R; 61-64; CANR 9, 21

Azorin. . . . . **CLC 11**
See also Martinez Ruiz, Jose

Azuela, Mariano 1873-1952. . . . . . . **TCLC 3**
See also CA 104; 131; HW; MTCW

Baastad, Babbis Friis
See Friis-Baastad, Babbis Ellinor

Barthelme, Donald
    1931-1989 . . . . . **CLC 1, 2, 3, 5, 6, 8, 13,
                            23, 46, 59; SSC 2**
    See also CA 21-24R; 129; CANR 20;
    DLB 2; DLBY 80, 89; MTCW; SATA 7,
    62

Barthelme, Frederick 1943-. . . . . . . **CLC 36**
    See also CA 114; 122; DLBY 85

Barthes, Roland (Gerard)
    1915-1980 . . . . **CLC 24**
    See also CA 130; 97-100; MTCW

Barzun, Jacques (Martin) 1907- . . . . **CLC 51**
    See also CA 61-64; CANR 22

Bashevis, Isaac
    See Singer, Isaac Bashevis

Bashkirtseff, Marie 1859-1884 . . . **NCLC 27**

Basho
    See Matsuo Basho

Bass, Kingsley B. Jr.
    See Bullins, Ed

Bassani, Giorgio 1916-. . . . . **CLC 9**
    See also CA 65-68; CANR 33; MTCW

Bastos, Augusto (Antonio) Roa
    See Roa Bastos, Augusto (Antonio)

Bataille, Georges 1897-1962 . . . . **CLC 29**
    See also CA 101; 89-92

Bates, H(erbert) E(rnest)
    1905-1974 . . . . **CLC 46; SSC 10**
    See also CA 93-96; 45-48; CANR 34;
    MTCW

Bauchart
    See Camus, Albert

Baudelaire, Charles
    1821-1867 . . . . **NCLC 6, 29; PC 1**
    See also WLC

Baudrillard, Jean 1929- . . . . **CLC 60**

Baum, L(yman) Frank 1856-1919 . . . **TCLC 7**
    See also CA 108; 133; CLR 15; DLB 22;
    MAICYA; MTCW; SATA 18

Baum, Louis F.
    See Baum, L(yman) Frank

Baumbach, Jonathan 1933- . . . . . . **CLC 6, 23**
    See also CA 13-16R; CAAS 5; CANR 12;
    DLBY 80; MTCW

Bausch, Richard (Carl) 1945- . . . . . . **CLC 51**
    See also CA 101; CAAS 14

Baxter, Charles 1947-. . . . . **CLC 45**
    See also CA 57-60

Baxter, James K(eir) 1926-1972 . . . . **CLC 14**
    See also CA 77-80

Baxter, John
    See Hunt, E(verette) Howard Jr.

Bayer, Sylvia
    See Glassco, John

Beagle, Peter S(oyer) 1939-. . . . . **CLC 7**
    See also CA 9-12R; CANR 4; DLBY 80;
    SATA 60

Bean, Normal
    See Burroughs, Edgar Rice

Beard, Charles A(ustin)
    1874-1948 . . . . **TCLC 15**
    See also CA 115; DLB 17; SATA 18

Beardsley, Aubrey 1872-1898 . . . . . **NCLC 6**

Beattie, Ann
    1947- . . . . **CLC 8, 13, 18, 40, 63; SSC 11**
    See also BEST 90:2; CA 81-84; DLBY 82;
    MTCW

Beattie, James 1735-1803 . . . . . . **NCLC 25**
    See also DLB 109

Beauchamp, Kathleen Mansfield 1888-1923
    See Mansfield, Katherine
    See also CA 104; 134

**Beauvoir, Simone (Lucie Ernestine Marie
    Bertrand) de**
    1908-1986 . . . **CLC 1, 2, 4, 8, 14, 31, 44,
                            50, 71**
    See also CA 9-12R; 118; CANR 28;
    DLB 72; DLBY 86; MTCW; WLC

Becker, Jurek 1937-. . . . . **CLC 7, 19**
    See also CA 85-88; DLB 75

Becker, Walter 1950-. . . . . **CLC 26**

Beckett, Samuel (Barclay)
    1906-1989 . . . . . **CLC 1, 2, 3, 4, 6, 9, 10,
                            11, 14, 18, 29, 57, 59**
    See also CA 5-8R; 130; CANR 33;
    CDBLB 1945-1960; DLB 13, 15;
    DLBY 90; MTCW; WLC

Beckford, William 1760-1844 . . . . **NCLC 16**
    See also DLB 39

Beckman, Gunnel 1910-. . . . . **CLC 26**
    See also CA 33-36R; CANR 15; CLR 25;
    MAICYA; SAAS 9; SATA 6

Becque, Henri 1837-1899. . . . . **NCLC 3**

Beddoes, Thomas Lovell
    1803-1849 . . . . **NCLC 3**
    See also DLB 96

Bedford, Donald F.
    See Fearing, Kenneth (Flexner)

Beecher, Catharine Esther
    1800-1878 . . . . **NCLC 30**
    See also DLB 1

Beecher, John 1904-1980. . . . . **CLC 6**
    See also AITN 1; CA 5-8R; 105; CANR 8

Beer, Johann 1655-1700. . . . . **LC 5**

Beer, Patricia 1924-. . . . . **CLC 58**
    See also CA 61-64; CANR 13; DLB 40

Beerbohm, Henry Maximilian
    1872-1956 . . . . **TCLC 1, 24**
    See also CA 104; DLB 34, 100

Begiebing, Robert J(ohn) 1946-. . . . . **CLC 70**
    See also CA 122

Behan, Brendan
    1923-1964 . . . . **CLC 1, 8, 11, 15**
    See also CA 73-76; CANR 33;
    CDBLB 1945-1960; DLB 13; MTCW

Behn, Aphra 1640(?)-1689 . . . . **LC 1**
    See also DLB 39, 80; WLC

Behrman, S(amuel) N(athaniel)
    1893-1973 . . . . **CLC 40**
    See also CA 13-16; 45-48; CAP 1; DLB 7,
    44

Belasco, David 1853-1931 . . . . **TCLC 3**
    See also CA 104; DLB 7

Belcheva, Elisaveta 1893- . . . . **CLC 10**

Beldone, Phil "Cheech"
    See Ellison, Harlan

Beleno
    See Azuela, Mariano

Belinski, Vissarion Grigoryevich
    1811-1848 . . . . **NCLC 5**

Belitt, Ben 1911-. . . . . **CLC 22**
    See also CA 13-16R; CAAS 4; CANR 7;
    DLB 5

Bell, James Madison 1826-1902 . . . **TCLC 43**
    See also BLC 1; BW; CA 122; 124; DLB 50

Bell, Madison (Smartt) 1957- . . . . . . **CLC 41**
    See also CA 111; CANR 28

Bell, Marvin (Hartley) 1937-. . . . . **CLC 8, 31**
    See also CA 21-24R; CAAS 14; DLB 5;
    MTCW

Bell, W. L. D.
    See Mencken, H(enry) L(ouis)

Bellamy, Atwood C.
    See Mencken, H(enry) L(ouis)

Bellamy, Edward 1850-1898 . . . . . . **NCLC 4**
    See also DLB 12

Bellin, Edward J.
    See Kuttner, Henry

Belloc, (Joseph) Hilaire (Pierre)
    1870-1953 . . . . **TCLC 7, 18**
    See also CA 106; DLB 19, 100; YABC 1

Belloc, Joseph Peter Rene Hilaire
    See Belloc, (Joseph) Hilaire (Pierre)

Belloc, Joseph Pierre Hilaire
    See Belloc, (Joseph) Hilaire (Pierre)

Belloc, M. A.
    See Lowndes, Marie Adelaide (Belloc)

Bellow, Saul
    1915- . . . . . **CLC 1, 2, 3, 6, 8, 10, 13, 15,
                            25, 33, 34, 63**
    See also AITN 2; BEST 89:3; CA 5-8R;
    CABS 1; CANR 29; CDALB 1941-1968;
    DLB 2, 28; DLBD 3; DLBY 82; MTCW;
    WLC

Belser, Reimond Karel Maria de
    1929- . . . . **CLC 14**

Bely, Andrey . . . . **TCLC 7**
    See also Bugayev, Boris Nikolayevich

Benary, Margot
    See Benary-Isbert, Margot

Benary-Isbert, Margot 1889-1979 . . . **CLC 12**
    See also CA 5-8R; 89-92; CANR 4;
    CLR 12; MAICYA; SATA 2, 21

Benavente (y Martinez), Jacinto
    1866-1954 . . . . **TCLC 3**
    See also CA 106; 131; HW; MTCW

Benchley, Peter (Bradford)
    1940- . . . . **CLC 4, 8**
    See also AITN 2; CA 17-20R; CANR 12,
    35; MTCW; SATA 3

Benchley, Robert (Charles)
    1889-1945 . . . . **TCLC 1**
    See also CA 105; DLB 11

Benedikt, Michael 1935- . . . . **CLC 4, 14**
    See also CA 13-16R; CANR 7; DLB 5

Benet, Juan 1927-. . . . . **CLC 28**

Benet, Stephen Vincent
    1898-1943 . . . . **TCLC 7; SSC 10**
    See also CA 104; DLB 4, 48, 102; YABC 1

Benet, William Rose   1886-1950 ... **TCLC 28**
See also CA 118; DLB 45

Benford, Gregory (Albert)   1941-.... **CLC 52**
See also CA 69-72; CANR 12, 24;
DLBY 82

Benjamin, Lois
See Gould, Lois

Benjamin, Walter   1892-1940..... **TCLC 39**

Benn, Gottfried   1886-1956........ **TCLC 3**
See also CA 106; DLB 56

Bennett, Alan   1934-.............. **CLC 45**
See also CA 103; CANR 35; MTCW

Bennett, (Enoch) Arnold
1867-1931 .... **TCLC 5, 20**
See also CA 106; CDBLB 1890-1914;
DLB 10, 34, 98

Bennett, Elizabeth
See Mitchell, Margaret (Munnerlyn)

Bennett, George Harold   1930-
See Bennett, Hal
See also BW; CA 97-100

Bennett, Hal .... **CLC 5**
See also Bennett, George Harold
See also DLB 33

Bennett, Jay   1912-.............. **CLC 35**
See also CA 69-72; CANR 11; SAAS 4;
SATA 27, 41

Bennett, Louise (Simone)   1919-..... **CLC 28**
See also BLC 1; DLB 117

Benson, E(dward) F(rederic)
1867-1940 .... **TCLC 27**
See also CA 114

Benson, Jackson J.   1930-......... **CLC 34**
See also CA 25-28R; DLB 111

Benson, Sally   1900-1972 .... **CLC 17**
See also CA 19-20; 37-40R; CAP 1;
SATA 1, 27, 35

Benson, Stella   1892-1933........ **TCLC 17**
See also CA 117; DLB 36

Bentham, Jeremy   1748-1832 ..... **NCLC 38**
See also DLB 107

Bentley, E(dmund) C(lerihew)
1875-1956 .... **TCLC 12**
See also CA 108; DLB 70

Bentley, Eric (Russell)   1916-....... **CLC 24**
See also CA 5-8R; CANR 6

Beranger, Pierre Jean de
1780-1857 .... **NCLC 34**

Berger, Colonel
See Malraux, (Georges-)Andre

Berger, John (Peter)   1926- ..... **CLC 2, 19**
See also CA 81-84; DLB 14

Berger, Melvin H.   1927- .... **CLC 12**
See also CA 5-8R; CANR 4; SAAS 2;
SATA 5

Berger, Thomas (Louis)
1924- .... **CLC 3, 5, 8, 11, 18, 38**
See also CA 1-4R; CANR 5, 28; DLB 2;
DLBY 80; MTCW

Bergman, (Ernst) Ingmar
1918- .... **CLC 16, 72**
See also CA 81-84; CANR 33

Bergson, Henri   1859-1941 .... **TCLC 32**

Bergstein, Eleanor   1938-.......... **CLC 4**
See also CA 53-56; CANR 5

Berkoff, Steven   1937-............. **CLC 56**
See also CA 104

Bermant, Chaim (Icyk)   1929- ...... **CLC 40**
See also CA 57-60; CANR 6, 31

Bernanos, (Paul Louis) Georges
1888-1948 .... **TCLC 3**
See also CA 104; 130; DLB 72

Bernard, April   1956- .... **CLC 59**
See also CA 131

Bernhard, Thomas
1931-1989 ....**CLC 3, 32, 61**
See also CA 85-88; 127; CANR 32;
DLB 85; MTCW

Berrigan, Daniel   1921-........... **CLC 4**
See also CA 33-36R; CAAS 1; CANR 11;
DLB 5

Berrigan, Edmund Joseph Michael Jr.
1934-1983
See Berrigan, Ted
See also CA 61-64; 110; CANR 14

Berrigan, Ted................... **CLC 37**
See also Berrigan, Edmund Joseph Michael
Jr.
See also DLB 5

Berry, Charles Edward Anderson   1931-
See Berry, Chuck
See also CA 115

Berry, Chuck..................... **CLC 17**
See also Berry, Charles Edward Anderson

Berry, Jonas
See Ashbery, John (Lawrence)

Berry, Wendell (Erdman)
1934- .... **CLC 4, 6, 8, 27, 46**
See also AITN 1; CA 73-76; DLB 5, 6

Berryman, John
1914-1972 ..... **CLC 1, 2, 3, 4, 6, 8, 10,
13, 25, 62**
See also CA 13-16; 33-36R; CABS 2;
CANR 35; CAP 1; CDALB 1941-1968;
DLB 48; MTCW

Bertolucci, Bernardo   1940- .... **CLC 16**
See also CA 106

Bertrand, Aloysius   1807-1841 .... **NCLC 31**

Bertran de Born   c. 1140-1215..... **CMLC 5**

Besant, Annie (Wood)   1847-1933 ... **TCLC 9**
See also CA 105

Bessie, Alvah   1904-1985.......... **CLC 23**
See also CA 5-8R; 116; CANR 2; DLB 26

Bethlen, T. D.
See Silverberg, Robert

Beti, Mongo.................... **CLC 27**
See also Biyidi, Alexandre
See also BLC 1

Betjeman, John
1906-1984 .... **CLC 2, 6, 10, 34, 43**
See also CA 9-12R; 112; CANR 33;
CDBLB 1945-1960; DLB 20; DLBY 84;
MTCW

Betti, Ugo   1892-1953............. **TCLC 5**
See also CA 104

Betts, Doris (Waugh)   1932-.... **CLC 3, 6, 28**
See also CA 13-16R; CANR 9; DLBY 82

Bevan, Alistair
See Roberts, Keith (John Kingston)

Beynon, John
See Harris, John (Wyndham Parkes Lucas)
Beynon

Bialik, Chaim Nachman
1873-1934 .... **TCLC 25**

Bickerstaff, Isaac
See Swift, Jonathan

Bidart, Frank   19(?)-.............. **CLC 33**

Bienek, Horst   1930-............ **CLC 7, 11**
See also CA 73-76; DLB 75

Bierce, Ambrose (Gwinett)
1842-1914(?) ..... **TCLC 1, 7, 44; SSC 9**
See also CA 104; CDALB 1865-1917;
DLB 11, 12, 23, 71, 74; WLC

Billings, Josh
See Shaw, Henry Wheeler

Billington, Rachel   1942-.......... **CLC 43**
See also AITN 2; CA 33-36R

Binyon, T(imothy) J(ohn)   1936- .... **CLC 34**
See also CA 111; CANR 28

Bioy Casares, Adolfo   1914-.... **CLC 4, 8, 13**
See also CA 29-32R; CANR 19; DLB 113;
HW; MTCW

Bird, C.
See Ellison, Harlan

Bird, Cordwainer
See Ellison, Harlan

Bird, Robert Montgomery
1806-1854 .... **NCLC 1**

Birney, (Alfred) Earle
1904- ....**CLC 1, 4, 6, 11**
See also CA 1-4R; CANR 5, 20; DLB 88;
MTCW

Bishop, Elizabeth
1911-1979 ..... **CLC 1, 4, 9, 13, 15, 32;
PC 3**
See also CA 5-8R; 89-92; CABS 2;
CANR 26; CDALB 1968-1988; DLB 5;
MTCW; SATA 24

Bishop, John   1935-.............. **CLC 10**
See also CA 105

bissett, bill   1939- .... **CLC 18**
See also CA 69-72; CANR 15; DLB 53;
MTCW

Bitov, Andrei (Georgievich)   1937-... **CLC 57**

Biyidi, Alexandre   1932-
See Beti, Mongo
See also BW; CA 114; 124; MTCW

Bjarme, Brynjolf
See Ibsen, Henrik (Johan)

Bjoernson, Bjoernstjerne (Martinius)
1832-1910 .... **TCLC 7**
See also Bjornson, Bjornstjerne; Bjornson,
Bjornstjerne (Martinius)
See also CA 104

Bjornson, Bjornstjerne .... **TCLC 37**
See also Bjoernson, Bjoernstjerne
(Martinius)

Bjornson, Bjornstjerne (Martinius) ... **TCLC 7**
See also Bjoernson, Bjoernstjerne
(Martinius)

Black, Robert
See Holdstock, Robert P.

Blackburn, Paul 1926-1971 ..... **CLC 9, 43**
See also CA 81-84; 33-36R; CANR 34;
DLB 16; DLBY 81

Black Elk 1863-1950 .... **TCLC 33**

Black Hobart
See Sanders, (James) Ed(ward)

Blacklin, Malcolm
See Chambers, Aidan

Blackmore, R(ichard) D(oddridge)
1825-1900 .... **TCLC 27**
See also CA 120; DLB 18

Blackmur, R(ichard) P(almer)
1904-1965 .... **CLC 2, 24**
See also CA 11-12; 25-28R; CAP 1; DLB 63

Black Tarantula, The
See Acker, Kathy

Blackwood, Algernon (Henry)
1869-1951 .... **TCLC 5**
See also CA 105

Blackwood, Caroline 1931- .... **CLC 6, 9**
See also CA 85-88; CANR 32; DLB 14;
MTCW

Blade, Alexander
See Hamilton, Edmond; Silverberg, Robert

Blair, Eric (Arthur) 1903-1950
See Orwell, George
See also CA 104; 132; MTCW; SATA 29

Blais, Marie-Claire
1939- .... **CLC 2, 4, 6, 13, 22**
See also CA 21-24R; CAAS 4; CANR 38;
DLB 53; MTCW

Blaise, Clark 1940- .... **CLC 29**
See also AITN 2; CA 53-56; CAAS 3;
CANR 5; DLB 53

Blake, Nicholas
See Day Lewis, C(ecil)
See also DLB 77

Blake, William 1757-1827 .... **NCLC 13**
See also CDBLB 1789-1832; DLB 93;
MAICYA; SATA 30; WLC

Blasco Ibanez, Vicente
1867-1928 .... **TCLC 12**
See also CA 110; 131; HW; MTCW

Blatty, William Peter 1928-........ **CLC 2**
See also CA 5-8R; CANR 9

Bleeck, Oliver
See Thomas, Ross (Elmore)

Blessing, Lee 1949-.............. **CLC 54**

Blish, James (Benjamin)
1921-1975 .... **CLC 14**
See also CA 1-4R; 57-60; CANR 3; DLB 8;
MTCW; SATA 66

Bliss, Reginald
See Wells, H(erbert) G(eorge)

Blixen, Karen (Christentze Dinesen)
1885-1962
See Dinesen, Isak
See also CA 25-28; CANR 22; CAP 2;
MTCW; SATA 44

Bloch, Robert (Albert) 1917-....... **CLC 33**
See also CA 5-8R; CANR 5; DLB 44;
SATA 12

Blok, Alexander (Alexandrovich)
1880-1921 .... **TCLC 5**
See also CA 104

Blom, Jan
See Breytenbach, Breyten

Bloom, Harold 1930- .... **CLC 24**
See also CA 13-16R; CANR 39; DLB 67

Bloomfield, Aurelius
See Bourne, Randolph S(illiman)

Blount, Roy (Alton) Jr. 1941-...... **CLC 38**
See also CA 53-56; CANR 10, 28; MTCW

Bloy, Leon 1846-1917............ **TCLC 22**
See also CA 121

Blume, Judy (Sussman) 1938-... **CLC 12, 30**
See also AAYA 3; CA 29-32R; CANR 13,
37; CLR 2, 15; DLB 52; MAICYA;
MTCW; SATA 2, 31

Blunden, Edmund (Charles)
1896-1974 .... **CLC 2, 56**
See also CA 17-18; 45-48; CAP 2; DLB 20,
100; MTCW

Bly, Robert (Elwood)
1926- .... **CLC 1, 2, 5, 10, 15, 38**
See also CA 5-8R; DLB 5; MTCW

Bobette
See Simenon, Georges (Jacques Christian)

Boccaccio, Giovanni 1313-1375
See also SSC 10

Bochco, Steven 1943-............. **CLC 35**
See also CA 124; 138

Bodenheim, Maxwell 1892-1954 ... **TCLC 44**
See also CA 110; DLB 9, 45

Bodker, Cecil 1927- .... **CLC 21**
See also CA 73-76; CANR 13; CLR 23;
MAICYA; SATA 14

Boell, Heinrich (Theodor)
1917-1985 ... **CLC 2, 3, 6, 9, 11, 15, 27,
39**
See also Boll, Heinrich (Theodor)
See also CA 21-24R; 116; CANR 24;
DLB 69; DLBY 85; MTCW

Bogan, Louise 1897-1970..... **CLC 4, 39, 46**
See also CA 73-76; 25-28R; CANR 33;
DLB 45; MTCW

Bogarde, Dirk .... **CLC 19**
See also Van Den Bogarde, Derek Jules
Gaspard Ulric Niven
See also DLB 14

Bogosian, Eric 1953- .... **CLC 45**
See also CA 138

Bograd, Larry 1953-.............. **CLC 35**
See also CA 93-96; SATA 33

Boiardo, Matteo Maria 1441-1494 .... **LC 6**

Boileau-Despreaux, Nicolas
1636-1711 .... **LC 3**

Boland, Eavan 1944-.......... **CLC 40, 67**
See also DLB 40

Boll, Heinrich (Theodor)
1917-1985 ... **CLC 2, 3, 6, 9, 11, 15, 27,
39, 72**
See also Boell, Heinrich (Theodor)
See also DLB 69; DLBY 85; WLC

Bolt, Robert (Oxton) 1924-........ **CLC 14**
See also CA 17-20R; CANR 35; DLB 13;
MTCW

Bomkauf
See Kaufman, Bob (Garnell)

Bonaventura.................. **NCLC 35**
See also DLB 90

Bond, Edward 1934-....... **CLC 4, 6, 13, 23**
See also CA 25-28R; CANR 38; DLB 13;
MTCW

Bonham, Frank 1914-1989......... **CLC 12**
See also AAYA 1; CA 9-12R; CANR 4, 36;
MAICYA; SAAS 3; SATA 1, 49, 62

Bonnefoy, Yves 1923-........ **CLC 9, 15, 58**
See also CA 85-88; CANR 33; MTCW

Bontemps, Arna(ud Wendell)
1902-1973 .... **CLC 1, 18**
See also BLC 1; BW; CA 1-4R; 41-44R;
CANR 4, 35; CLR 6; DLB 48, 51;
MAICYA; MTCW; SATA 2, 24, 44

Booth, Martin 1944-............. **CLC 13**
See also CA 93-96; CAAS 2

Booth, Philip 1925-............... **CLC 23**
See also CA 5-8R; CANR 5; DLBY 82

Booth, Wayne C(layson) 1921- ..... **CLC 24**
See also CA 1-4R; CAAS 5; CANR 3;
DLB 67

Borchert, Wolfgang 1921-1947 ..... **TCLC 5**
See also CA 104; DLB 69

Borges, Jorge Luis
1899-1986 ... **CLC 1, 2, 3, 4, 6, 8, 9, 10,
13, 19, 44, 48; SSC 4**
See also CA 21-24R; CANR 19, 33;
DLB 113; DLBY 86; HW; MTCW; WLC

Borowski, Tadeusz 1922-1951 ...... **TCLC 9**
See also CA 106

Borrow, George (Henry)
1803-1881 .... **NCLC 9**
See also DLB 21, 55

Bosschere, Jean de 1878(?)-1953... **TCLC 19**
See also CA 115

Boswell, James 1740-1795.......... **LC 4**
See also CDBLB 1660-1789; DLB 104;
WLC

Bottoms, David 1949-............. **CLC 53**
See also CA 105; CANR 22; DLB 120;
DLBY 83

Boucolon, Maryse 1937-
See Conde, Maryse
See also CA 110; CANR 30

Bourget, Paul (Charles Joseph)
1852-1935 .... **TCLC 12**
See also CA 107

Bourjaily, Vance (Nye) 1922- .... **CLC 8, 62**
See also CA 1-4R; CAAS 1; CANR 2;
DLB 2

Bourne, Randolph S(illiman)
1886-1918 .... **TCLC 16**
See also CA 117; DLB 63

Bova, Ben(jamin William) 1932-.... **CLC 45**
See also CA 5-8R; CANR 11; CLR 3;
DLBY 81; MAICYA; MTCW; SATA 6,
68

Bowen, Elizabeth (Dorothea Cole)
   1899-1973 .... **CLC 1, 3, 6, 11, 15, 22;
      SSC 3**
   See also CA 17-18; 41-44R; CANR 35;
   CAP 2; CDBLB 1945-1960; DLB 15;
   MTCW

Bowering, George   1935- .... **CLC 15, 47**
   See also CA 21-24R; CAAS 16; CANR 10;
   DLB 53

Bowering, Marilyn R(uthe)   1949- ... **CLC 32**
   See also CA 101

Bowers, Edgar   1924- .... **CLC 9**
   See also CA 5-8R; CANR 24; DLB 5

Bowie, David .... **CLC 17**
   See also Jones, David Robert

Bowles, Jane (Sydney)
   1917-1973 .... **CLC 3, 68**
   See also CA 19-20; 41-44R; CAP 2

Bowles, Paul (Frederick)
   1910- .... **CLC 1, 2, 19, 53; SSC 3**
   See also CA 1-4R; CAAS 1; CANR 1, 19;
   DLB 5, 6; MTCW

Box, Edgar
   See Vidal, Gore

Boyd, Nancy
   See Millay, Edna St. Vincent

Boyd, William   1952- .... **CLC 28, 53, 70**
   See also CA 114; 120

Boyle, Kay   1902- .. **CLC 1, 5, 19, 58; SSC 5**
   See also CA 13-16R; CAAS 1; CANR 29;
   DLB 4, 9, 48, 86; MTCW

Boyle, Mark
   See Kienzle, William X(avier)

Boyle, Patrick   1905-1982......... **CLC 19**
   See also CA 127

Boyle, T. Coraghessan   1948- ... **CLC 36, 55**
   See also BEST 90:4; CA 120; DLBY 86

Brackenridge, Hugh Henry
   1748-1816 .... **NCLC 7**
   See also DLB 11, 37

Bradbury, Edward P.
   See Moorcock, Michael (John)

Bradbury, Malcolm (Stanley)
   1932- .... **CLC 32, 61**
   See also CA 1-4R; CANR 1, 33; DLB 14;
   MTCW

Bradbury, Ray (Douglas)
   1920- .... **CLC 1, 3, 10, 15, 42**
   See also AITN 1, 2; CA 1-4R; CANR 2, 30;
   CDALB 1968-1988; DLB 2, 8; MTCW;
   SATA 11, 64; WLC

Bradford, Gamaliel   1863-1932..... **TCLC 36**
   See also DLB 17

Bradley, David (Henry Jr.)   1950- ... **CLC 23**
   See also BLC 1; BW; CA 104; CANR 26;
   DLB 33

Bradley, John Ed   1959- .... **CLC 55**

Bradley, Marion Zimmer   1930- ..... **CLC 30**
   See also AAYA 9; CA 57-60; CAAS 10;
   CANR 7, 31; DLB 8; MTCW

Bradstreet, Anne   1612(?)-1672 .... **LC 4**
   See also CDALB 1640-1865; DLB 24

Bragg, Melvyn   1939- .... **CLC 10**
   See also BEST 89:3; CA 57-60; CANR 10;
   DLB 14

Braine, John (Gerard)
   1922-1986 .... **CLC 1, 3, 41**
   See also CA 1-4R; 120; CANR 1, 33;
   CDBLB 1945-1960; DLB 15; DLBY 86;
   MTCW

Brammer, William   1930(?)-1978 .... **CLC 31**
   See also CA 77-80

Brancati, Vitaliano   1907-1954..... **TCLC 12**
   See also CA 109

Brancato, Robin F(idler)   1936- ..... **CLC 35**
   See also AAYA 9; CA 69-72; CANR 11;
   SAAS 9; SATA 23

Brand, Millen   1906-1980.......... **CLC 7**
   See also CA 21-24R; 97-100

Branden, Barbara .... **CLC 44**

Brandes, Georg (Morris Cohen)
   1842-1927 .... **TCLC 10**
   See also CA 105

Brandys, Kazimierz   1916- .... **CLC 62**

Branley, Franklyn M(ansfield)
   1915- .... **CLC 21**
   See also CA 33-36R; CANR 14, 39;
   CLR 13; MAICYA; SATA 4, 68

Brathwaite, Edward (Kamau)
   1930- .... **CLC 11**
   See also BW; CA 25-28R; CANR 11, 26

Brautigan, Richard (Gary)
   1935-1984 .... **CLC 1, 3, 5, 9, 12, 34, 42**
   See also CA 53-56; 113; CANR 34; DLB 2,
   5; DLBY 80, 84; MTCW; SATA 56

Braverman, Kate   1950- .... **CLC 67**
   See also CA 89-92

Brecht, Bertolt
   1898-1956 .... **TCLC 1, 6, 13, 35**
   See also CA 104; 133; DLB 56; MTCW;
   WLC

Brecht, Eugen Berthold Friedrich
   See Brecht, Bertolt

Bremer, Fredrika   1801-1865 ..... **NCLC 11**

Brennan, Christopher John
   1870-1932 .... **TCLC 17**
   See also CA 117

Brennan, Maeve   1917- .... **CLC 5**
   See also CA 81-84

Brentano, Clemens (Maria)
   1778-1842 .... **NCLC 1**

Brent of Bin Bin
   See Franklin, (Stella Maraia Sarah) Miles

Brenton, Howard   1942- .... **CLC 31**
   See also CA 69-72; CANR 33; DLB 13;
   MTCW

Breslin, James   1930-
   See Breslin, Jimmy
   See also CA 73-76; CANR 31; MTCW

Breslin, Jimmy .... **CLC 4, 43**
   See also Breslin, James
   See also AITN 1

Bresson, Robert   1907- .... **CLC 16**
   See also CA 110

Breton, Andre   1896-1966... **CLC 2, 9, 15, 54**
   See also CA 19-20; 25-28R; CAP 2;
   DLB 65; MTCW

Breytenbach, Breyten   1939(?)- .. **CLC 23, 37**
   See also CA 113; 129

Bridgers, Sue Ellen   1942- .... **CLC 26**
   See also AAYA 8; CA 65-68; CANR 11,
   36; CLR 18; DLB 52; MAICYA;
   SAAS 1; SATA 22

Bridges, Robert (Seymour)
   1844-1930 .... **TCLC 1**
   See also CA 104; CDBLB 1890-1914;
   DLB 19, 98

Bridie, James .... **TCLC 3**
   See also Mavor, Osborne Henry
   See also DLB 10

Brin, David   1950- .... **CLC 34**
   See also CA 102; CANR 24; SATA 65

Brink, Andre (Philippus)
   1935- .... **CLC 18, 36**
   See also CA 104; CANR 39; MTCW

Brinsmead, H(esba) F(ay)   1922- .... **CLC 21**
   See also CA 21-24R; CANR 10; MAICYA;
   SAAS 5; SATA 18

Brittain, Vera (Mary)
   1893(?)-1970 .... **CLC 23**
   See also CA 13-16; 25-28R; CAP 1; MTCW

Broch, Hermann   1886-1951....... **TCLC 20**
   See also CA 117; DLB 85

Brock, Rose
   See Hansen, Joseph

Brodkey, Harold   1930-.......... **CLC 56**
   See also CA 111

Brodsky, Iosif Alexandrovich   1940-
   See Brodsky, Joseph
   See also AITN 1; CA 41-44R; CANR 37;
   MTCW

Brodsky, Joseph .... **CLC 4, 6, 13, 36, 50**
   See also Brodsky, Iosif Alexandrovich

Brodsky, Michael Mark   1948- ..... **CLC 19**
   See also CA 102; CANR 18

Bromell, Henry   1947-............ **CLC 5**
   See also CA 53-56; CANR 9

Bromfield, Louis (Brucker)
   1896-1956 .... **TCLC 11**
   See also CA 107; DLB 4, 9, 86

Broner, E(sther) M(asserman)
   1930- .... **CLC 19**
   See also CA 17-20R; CANR 8, 25; DLB 28

Bronk, William   1918-............ **CLC 10**
   See also CA 89-92; CANR 23

Bronstein, Lev Davidovich
   See Trotsky, Leon

Bronte, Anne   1820-1849.......... **NCLC 4**
   See also DLB 21

Bronte, Charlotte
   1816-1855 .... **NCLC 3, 8, 33**
   See also CDBLB 1832-1890; DLB 21; WLC

Bronte, (Jane) Emily
   1818-1848 .... **NCLC 16, 35**
   See also CDBLB 1832-1890; DLB 21, 32;
   WLC

Brooke, Frances   1724-1789 .... **LC 6**
   See also DLB 39, 99

Brooke, Henry   1703(?)-1783 .... **LC 1**
   See also DLB 39

Brooke, Rupert (Chawner)
   1887-1915 .... **TCLC 2, 7**
   See also CA 104; 132; CDBLB 1914-1945;
   DLB 19; MTCW; WLC

Brooke-Haven, P.
See Wodehouse, P(elham) G(renville)

Brooke-Rose, Christine 1926- ...... **CLC 40**
See also CA 13-16R; DLB 14

Brookner, Anita 1928- ...... **CLC 32, 34, 51**
See also CA 114; 120; CANR 37; DLBY 87;
MTCW

Brooks, Cleanth 1906- .... **CLC 24**
See also CA 17-20R; CANR 33, 35;
DLB 63; MTCW

Brooks, George
See Baum, L(yman) Frank

Brooks, Gwendolyn
1917- .... **CLC 1, 2, 4, 5, 15, 49**
See also AITN 1; BLC 1; BW; CA 1-4R;
CANR 1, 27; CDALB 1941-1968;
CLR 27; DLB 5, 76; MTCW; SATA 6;
WLC

Brooks, Mel .... **CLC 12**
See also Kaminsky, Melvin
See also DLB 26

Brooks, Peter 1938- .... **CLC 34**
See also CA 45-48; CANR 1

Brooks, Van Wyck 1886-1963 ...... **CLC 29**
See also CA 1-4R; CANR 6; DLB 45, 63,
103

Brophy, Brigid (Antonia)
1929- .... **CLC 6, 11, 29**
See also CA 5-8R; CAAS 4; CANR 25;
DLB 14; MTCW

Brosman, Catharine Savage 1934- .... **CLC 9**
See also CA 61-64; CANR 21

Brother Antoninus
See Everson, William (Oliver)

Broughton, T(homas) Alan 1936- ... **CLC 19**
See also CA 45-48; CANR 2, 23

Broumas, Olga 1949- .... **CLC 10**
See also CA 85-88; CANR 20

Brown, Charles Brockden
1771-1810 .... **NCLC 22**
See also CDALB 1640-1865; DLB 37, 59,
73

Brown, Christy 1932-1981 .... **CLC 63**
See also CA 105; 104; DLB 14

Brown, Claude 1937- .... **CLC 30**
See also AAYA 7; BLC 1; BW; CA 73-76

Brown, Dee (Alexander) 1908- .. **CLC 18, 47**
See also CA 13-16R; CAAS 6; CANR 11;
DLBY 80; MTCW; SATA 5

Brown, George
See Wertmueller, Lina

Brown, George Douglas
1869-1902 .... **TCLC 28**

Brown, George Mackay 1921- .... **CLC 5, 48**
See also CA 21-24R; CAAS 6; CANR 12,
37; DLB 14, 27; MTCW; SATA 35

Brown, Moses
See Barrett, William (Christopher)

Brown, Rita Mae 1944- .... **CLC 18, 43**
See also CA 45-48; CANR 2, 11, 35;
MTCW

Brown, Roderick (Langmere) Haig-
See Haig-Brown, Roderick (Langmere)

Brown, Rosellen 1939- .... **CLC 32**
See also CA 77-80; CAAS 10; CANR 14

Brown, Sterling Allen
1901-1989 .... **CLC 1, 23, 59**
See also BLC 1; BW; CA 85-88; 127;
CANR 26; DLB 48, 51, 63; MTCW

Brown, Will
See Ainsworth, William Harrison

Brown, William Wells
1813-1884 .... **NCLC 2; DC 1**
See also BLC 1; DLB 3, 50

Browne, (Clyde) Jackson 1948(?)-... **CLC 21**
See also CA 120

Browning, Elizabeth Barrett
1806-1861 .... **NCLC 1, 16**
See also CDBLB 1832-1890; DLB 32; WLC

Browning, Robert
1812-1889 .... **NCLC 19; PC 2**
See also CDBLB 1832-1890; DLB 32;
YABC 1

Browning, Tod 1882-1962 .... **CLC 16**
See also CA 117

Bruccoli, Matthew J(oseph) 1931- .. **CLC 34**
See also CA 9-12R; CANR 7; DLB 103

Bruce, Lenny .... **CLC 21**
See also Schneider, Leonard Alfred

Bruin, John
See Brutus, Dennis

Brulls, Christian
See Simenon, Georges (Jacques Christian)

Brunner, John (Kilian Houston)
1934- .... **CLC 8, 10**
See also CA 1-4R; CAAS 8; CANR 2, 37;
MTCW

Brutus, Dennis 1924- .... **CLC 43**
See also BLC 1; BW; CA 49-52; CAAS 14;
CANR 2, 27; DLB 117

Bryan, C(ourtlandt) D(ixon) B(arnes)
1936- .... **CLC 29**
See also CA 73-76; CANR 13

Bryan, Michael
See Moore, Brian

Bryant, William Cullen
1794-1878 .... **NCLC 6**
See also CDALB 1640-1865; DLB 3, 43, 59

Bryusov, Valery Yakovlevich
1873-1924 .... **TCLC 10**
See also CA 107

Buchan, John 1875-1940 .... **TCLC 41**
See also CA 108; DLB 34, 70; YABC 2

Buchanan, George 1506-1582 .... **LC 4**

Buchheim, Lothar-Guenther 1918- ... **CLC 6**
See also CA 85-88

Buchner, (Karl) Georg
1813-1837 .... **NCLC 26**

Buchwald, Art(hur) 1925- .... **CLC 33**
See also AITN 1; CA 5-8R; CANR 21;
MTCW; SATA 10

Buck, Pearl S(ydenstricker)
1892-1973 .... **CLC 7, 11, 18**
See also AITN 1; CA 1-4R; 41-44R;
CANR 1, 34; DLB 9, 102; MTCW;
SATA 1, 25

Buckler, Ernest 1908-1984 .... **CLC 13**
See also CA 11-12; 114; CAP 1; DLB 68;
SATA 47

Buckley, Vincent (Thomas)
1925-1988 .... **CLC 57**
See also CA 101

Buckley, William F(rank) Jr.
1925- .... **CLC 7, 18, 37**
See also AITN 1; CA 1-4R; CANR 1, 24;
DLBY 80; MTCW

Buechner, (Carl) Frederick
1926- .... **CLC 2, 4, 6, 9**
See also CA 13-16R; CANR 11, 39;
DLBY 80; MTCW

Buell, John (Edward) 1927- .... **CLC 10**
See also CA 1-4R; DLB 53

Buero Vallejo, Antonio 1916- ... **CLC 15, 46**
See also CA 106; CANR 24; HW; MTCW

Bugayev, Boris Nikolayevich 1880-1934
See Bely, Andrey
See also CA 104

Bukowski, Charles 1920- .... **CLC 2, 5, 9, 41**
See also CA 17-20R; DLB 5; MTCW

Bulgakov, Mikhail (Afanas'evich)
1891-1940 .... **TCLC 2, 16**
See also CA 105

Bullins, Ed 1935- .... **CLC 1, 5, 7**
See also BLC 1; BW; CA 49-52; CAAS 16;
CANR 24; DLB 7, 38; MTCW

Bulwer-Lytton, Edward (George Earle Lytton)
1803-1873 .... **NCLC 1**
See also DLB 21

Bunin, Ivan Alexeyevich
1870-1953 .... **TCLC 6; SSC 5**
See also CA 104

Bunting, Basil 1900-1985 .... **CLC 10, 39, 47**
See also CA 53-56; 115; CANR 7; DLB 20

Bunuel, Luis 1900-1983 .... **CLC 16**
See also CA 101; 110; CANR 32; HW

Bunyan, John 1628-1688 .... **LC 4**
See also CDBLB 1660-1789; DLB 39; WLC

Burford, Eleanor
See Hibbert, Eleanor Burford

Burgess, Anthony
.. **CLC 1, 2, 4, 5, 8, 10, 13, 15, 22, 40, 62**
See also Wilson, John (Anthony) Burgess
See also AITN 1; CDBLB 1960 to Present;
DLB 14

Burke, Edmund 1729(?)-1797 .... **LC 7**
See also DLB 104; WLC

Burke, Kenneth (Duva) 1897- .... **CLC 2, 24**
See also CA 5-8R; CANR 39; DLB 45, 63;
MTCW

Burke, Leda
See Garnett, David

Burke, Ralph
See Silverberg, Robert

Burney, Fanny 1752-1840 .... **NCLC 12**
See also DLB 39

Burns, Robert 1759-1796 .... **LC 3**
See also CDBLB 1789-1832; DLB 109;
WLC

Burns, Tex
See L'Amour, Louis (Dearborn)

Burnshaw, Stanley 1906- . . . . . **CLC 3, 13, 44**
See also CA 9-12R; DLB 48

Burr, Anne 1937- . . . . **CLC 6**
See also CA 25-28R

Burroughs, Edgar Rice
1875-1950 . . . . **TCLC 2, 32**
See also CA 104; 132; DLB 8; MTCW;
SATA 41

Burroughs, William S(eward)
1914- . . . . **CLC 1, 2, 5, 15, 22, 42**
See also AITN 2; CA 9-12R; CANR 20;
DLB 2, 8, 16; DLBY 81; MTCW; WLC

Busch, Frederick 1941- . . . **CLC 7, 10, 18, 47**
See also CA 33-36R; CAAS 1; DLB 6

Bush, Ronald 1946- . . . . **CLC 34**
See also CA 136

Bustos, F(rancisco)
See Borges, Jorge Luis

Bustos Domecq, H(onorio)
See Bioy Casares, Adolfo; Borges, Jorge
Luis

Bustos Domecq, H(onrio)
See Borges, Jorge Luis

Butler, Octavia E(stelle) 1947- . . . . . **CLC 38**
See also BW; CA 73-76; CANR 12, 24, 38;
DLB 33; MTCW

Butler, Samuel 1612-1680 . . . . **LC 16**
See also DLB 101

Butler, Samuel 1835-1902 . . . . . . **TCLC 1, 33**
See also CA 104; CDBLB 1890-1914;
DLB 18, 57; WLC

Butor, Michel (Marie Francois)
1926- . . . . **CLC 1, 3, 8, 11, 15**
See also CA 9-12R; CANR 33; DLB 83;
MTCW

Buzo, Alexander (John) 1944- . . . . . . **CLC 61**
See also CA 97-100; CANR 17, 39

Buzzati, Dino 1906-1972 . . . . **CLC 36**
See also CA 33-36R

Byars, Betsy (Cromer) 1928- . . . . **CLC 35**
See also CA 33-36R; CANR 18, 36; CLR 1,
16; DLB 52; MAICYA; MTCW; SAAS 1;
SATA 4, 46

Byatt, A(ntonia) S(usan Drabble)
1936- . . . . **CLC 19, 65**
See also CA 13-16R; CANR 13, 33;
DLB 14; MTCW

Byrne, David 1952- . . . . **CLC 26**
See also CA 127

Byrne, John Keyes 1926- . . . . **CLC 19**
See also Leonard, Hugh
See also CA 102

Byron, George Gordon (Noel)
1788-1824 . . . . **NCLC 2, 12**
See also CDBLB 1789-1832; DLB 96, 110;
WLC

C.3.3.
See Wilde, Oscar (Fingal O'Flahertie Wills)

Caballero, Fernan 1796-1877 . . . . . **NCLC 10**

Cabell, James Branch 1879-1958 . . . **TCLC 6**
See also CA 105; DLB 9, 78

Cable, George Washington
1844-1925 . . . . **TCLC 4; SSC 4**
See also CA 104; DLB 12, 74

Cabrera Infante, G(uillermo)
1929- . . . . **CLC 5, 25, 45**
See also CA 85-88; CANR 29; DLB 113;
HW; MTCW

Cade, Toni
See Bambara, Toni Cade

Cadmus
See Buchan, John

Caedmon fl. 658-680 . . . . **CMLC 7**

Caeiro, Alberto
See Pessoa, Fernando (Antonio Nogueira)

Cage, John (Milton Jr.) 1912- . . . . . . **CLC 41**
See also CA 13-16R; CANR 9

Cain, G.
See Cabrera Infante, G(uillermo)

Cain, Guillermo
See Cabrera Infante, G(uillermo)

Cain, James M(allahan)
1892-1977 . . . . **CLC 3, 11, 28**
See also AITN 1; CA 17-20R; 73-76;
CANR 8, 34; MTCW

Caine, Mark
See Raphael, Frederic (Michael)

Caldwell, Erskine (Preston)
1903-1987 . . . . **CLC 1, 8, 14, 50, 60**
See also AITN 1; CA 1-4R; 121; CAAS 1;
CANR 2, 33; DLB 9, 86; MTCW

Caldwell, (Janet Miriam) Taylor (Holland)
1900-1985 . . . . **CLC 2, 28, 39**
See also CA 5-8R; 116; CANR 5

Calhoun, John Caldwell
1782-1850 . . . . **NCLC 15**
See also DLB 3

Calisher, Hortense 1911- . . . **CLC 2, 4, 8, 38**
See also CA 1-4R; CANR 1, 22; DLB 2;
MTCW

Callaghan, Morley Edward
1903-1990 . . . . **CLC 3, 14, 41, 65**
See also CA 9-12R; 132; CANR 33;
DLB 68; MTCW

Calvino, Italo
1923-1985 . . . . **CLC 5, 8, 11, 22, 33, 39;
SSC 3**
See also CA 85-88; 116; CANR 23; MTCW

Cameron, Carey 1952- . . . . **CLC 59**
See also CA 135

Cameron, Peter 1959- . . . . **CLC 44**
See also CA 125

Campana, Dino 1885-1932 . . . . **TCLC 20**
See also CA 117; DLB 114

Campbell, John W(ood Jr.)
1910-1971 . . . . **CLC 32**
See also CA 21-22; 29-32R; CANR 34;
CAP 2; DLB 8; MTCW

Campbell, Joseph 1904-1987 . . . . **CLC 69**
See also AAYA 3; BEST 89:2; CA 1-4R;
124; CANR 3, 28; MTCW

Campbell, (John) Ramsey 1946- . . . . **CLC 42**
See also CA 57-60; CANR 7

Campbell, (Ignatius) Roy (Dunnachie)
1901-1957 . . . . **TCLC 5**
See also CA 104; DLB 20

Campbell, Thomas 1777-1844 . . . . **NCLC 19**
See also DLB 93

Campbell, Wilfred . . . . **TCLC 9**
See also Campbell, William

Campbell, William 1858(?)-1918
See Campbell, Wilfred
See also CA 106; DLB 92

Campos, Alvaro de
See Pessoa, Fernando (Antonio Nogueira)

Camus, Albert
1913-1960 . . . **CLC 1, 2, 4, 9, 11, 14, 32,
63, 69; DC 2; SSC 9**
See also CA 89-92; DLB 72; MTCW; WLC

Canby, Vincent 1924- . . . . **CLC 13**
See also CA 81-84

Cancale
See Desnos, Robert

Canetti, Elias 1905- . . . . **CLC 3, 14, 25**
See also CA 21-24R; CANR 23; DLB 85;
MTCW

Canin, Ethan 1960- . . . . **CLC 55**
See also CA 131; 135

Cannon, Curt
See Hunter, Evan

Cape, Judith
See Page, P(atricia) K(athleen)

Capek, Karel
1890-1938 . . . . **TCLC 6, 37; DC 1**
See also CA 104; WLC

Capote, Truman
1924-1984 . . . . . **CLC 1, 3, 8, 13, 19, 34,
38, 58; SSC 2**
See also CA 5-8R; 113; CANR 18;
CDALB 1941-1968; DLB 2; DLBY 80,
84; MTCW; WLC

Capra, Frank 1897-1991 . . . . **CLC 16**
See also CA 61-64; 135

Caputo, Philip 1941- . . . . **CLC 32**
See also CA 73-76

Card, Orson Scott 1951- . . . . **CLC 44, 47, 50**
See also CA 102; CANR 27; MTCW

Cardenal (Martinez), Ernesto
1925- . . . . **CLC 31**
See also CA 49-52; CANR 2, 32; HW;
MTCW

Carducci, Giosue 1835-1907 . . . . **TCLC 32**

Carew, Thomas 1595(?)-1640 . . . . **LC 13**

Carey, Ernestine Gilbreth 1908- . . . . **CLC 17**
See also CA 5-8R; SATA 2

Carey, Peter 1943- . . . . **CLC 40, 55**
See also CA 123; 127; MTCW

Carleton, William 1794-1869 . . . . . . **NCLC 3**

Carlisle, Henry (Coffin) 1926- . . . . . . **CLC 33**
See also CA 13-16R; CANR 15

Carlsen, Chris
See Holdstock, Robert P.

Carlson, Ron(ald F.) 1947- . . . . **CLC 54**
See also CA 105; CANR 27

Carlyle, Thomas 1795-1881 . . . . . . **NCLC 22**
See also CDBLB 1789-1832; DLB 55

Carman, (William) Bliss
1861-1929 . . . . **TCLC 7**
See also CA 104; DLB 92

Carpenter, Don(ald Richard)
1931- . . . . **CLC 41**
See also CA 45-48; CANR 1

Carpentier (y Valmont), Alejo
1904-1980 . . . . **CLC 8, 11, 38**
See also CA 65-68; 97-100; CANR 11;
DLB 113; HW

Carr, Emily 1871-1945 . . . . **TCLC 32**
See also DLB 68

Carr, John Dickson 1906-1977 . . . . . . **CLC 3**
See also CA 49-52; 69-72; CANR 3, 33;
MTCW

Carr, Philippa
See Hibbert, Eleanor Burford

Carr, Virginia Spencer 1929- . . . . . . **CLC 34**
See also CA 61-64; DLB 111

Carrier, Roch 1937- . . . . **CLC 13**
See also CA 130; DLB 53

Carroll, James P. 1943(?)- . . . . **CLC 38**
See also CA 81-84

Carroll, Jim 1951- . . . . **CLC 35**
See also CA 45-48

Carroll, Lewis . . . . **NCLC 2**
See also Dodgson, Charles Lutwidge
See also CDBLB 1832-1890; CLR 2, 18;
DLB 18; WLC

Carroll, Paul Vincent 1900-1968 . . . . **CLC 10**
See also CA 9-12R; 25-28R; DLB 10

Carruth, Hayden 1921- . . . . **CLC 4, 7, 10, 18**
See also CA 9-12R; CANR 4, 38; DLB 5;
MTCW; SATA 47

Carson, Rachel Louise 1907-1964 . . . **CLC 71**
See also CA 77-80; CANR 35; MTCW;
SATA 23

Carter, Angela (Olive)
1940-1991 . . . . **CLC 5, 41**
See also CA 53-56; 136; CANR 12, 36;
DLB 14; MTCW; SATA 66; SATO 70

Carter, Nick
See Smith, Martin Cruz

Carver, Raymond
1938-1988 . . . **CLC 22, 36, 53, 55; SSC 8**
See also CA 33-36R; 126; CANR 17, 34;
DLBY 84, 88; MTCW

Cary, (Arthur) Joyce (Lunel)
1888-1957 . . . . **TCLC 1, 29**
See also CA 104; CDBLB 1914-1945;
DLB 15, 100

Casanova de Seingalt, Giovanni Jacopo
1725-1798 . . . . **LC 13**

Casares, Adolfo Bioy
See Bioy Casares, Adolfo

Casely-Hayford, J(oseph) E(phraim)
1866-1930 . . . . **TCLC 24**
See also BLC 1; CA 123

Casey, John (Dudley) 1939- . . . . **CLC 59**
See also BEST 90:2; CA 69-72; CANR 23

Casey, Michael 1947- . . . . **CLC 2**
See also CA 65-68; DLB 5

Casey, Patrick
See Thurman, Wallace (Henry)

Casey, Warren (Peter) 1935-1988 . . . **CLC 12**
See also CA 101; 127

Casona, Alejandro . . . . **CLC 49**
See also Alvarez, Alejandro Rodriguez

Cassavetes, John 1929-1989 . . . . **CLC 20**
See also CA 85-88; 127

Cassill, R(onald) V(erlin) 1919- . . . **CLC 4, 23**
See also CA 9-12R; CAAS 1; CANR 7;
DLB 6

Cassity, (Allen) Turner 1929- . . . . **CLC 6, 42**
See also CA 17-20R; CAAS 8; CANR 11;
DLB 105

Castaneda, Carlos 1931(?)- . . . . **CLC 12**
See also CA 25-28R; CANR 32; HW;
MTCW

Castedo, Elena 1937- . . . . **CLC 65**
See also CA 132

Castedo-Ellerman, Elena
See Castedo, Elena

Castellanos, Rosario 1925-1974 . . . . . **CLC 66**
See also CA 131; 53-56; DLB 113; HW

Castelvetro, Lodovico 1505-1571 . . . . . **LC 12**

Castiglione, Baldassare 1478-1529 . . . **LC 12**

Castle, Robert
See Hamilton, Edmond

Castro, Guillen de 1569-1631 . . . . **LC 19**

Castro, Rosalia de 1837-1885 . . . . . **NCLC 3**

Cather, Willa
See Cather, Willa Sibert

Cather, Willa Sibert
1873-1947 . . . . . . **TCLC 1, 11, 31; SSC 2**
See also CA 104; 128; CDALB 1865-1917;
DLB 9, 54, 78; DLBD 1; MTCW;
SATA 30; WLC

Catton, (Charles) Bruce
1899-1978 . . . . **CLC 35**
See also AITN 1; CA 5-8R; 81-84;
CANR 7; DLB 17; SATA 2, 24

Cauldwell, Frank
See King, Francis (Henry)

Caunitz, William J. 1933- . . . . **CLC 34**
See also BEST 89:3; CA 125; 130

Causley, Charles (Stanley) 1917- . . . . . **CLC 7**
See also CA 9-12R; CANR 5, 35; DLB 27;
MTCW; SATA 3, 66

Caute, David 1936- . . . . **CLC 29**
See also CA 1-4R; CAAS 4; CANR 1, 33;
DLB 14

Cavafy, C(onstantine) P(eter) . . . . . . **TCLC 2, 7**
See also Kavafis, Konstantinos Petrou

Cavallo, Evelyn
See Spark, Muriel (Sarah)

Cavanna, Betty . . . . **CLC 12**
See also Harrison, Elizabeth Cavanna
See also MAICYA; SAAS 4; SATA 1, 30

Caxton, William 1421(?)-1491(?) . . . . . **LC 17**

Cayrol, Jean 1911- . . . . **CLC 11**
See also CA 89-92; DLB 83

Cela, Camilo Jose 1916- . . . . . . **CLC 4, 13, 59**
See also BEST 90:2; CA 21-24R; CAAS 10;
CANR 21, 32; DLBY 89; HW; MTCW

Celan, Paul . . . . **CLC 53**
See also Antschel, Paul
See also DLB 69

Celine, Louis-Ferdinand
. . . . **CLC 1, 3, 4, 7, 9, 15, 47**
See also Destouches, Louis-Ferdinand
See also DLB 72

Cellini, Benvenuto 1500-1571 . . . . **LC 7**

Cendrars, Blaise
See Sauser-Hall, Frederic

Cernuda (y Bidon), Luis
1902-1963 . . . . **CLC 54**
See also CA 131; 89-92; HW

Cervantes (Saavedra), Miguel de
1547-1616 . . . . **LC 6**
See also WLC

Cesaire, Aime (Fernand) 1913- . . **CLC 19, 32**
See also BLC 1; BW; CA 65-68; CANR 24;
MTCW

Chabon, Michael 1965(?)- . . . . **CLC 55**

Chabrol, Claude 1930- . . . . **CLC 16**
See also CA 110

Challans, Mary 1905-1983
See Renault, Mary
See also CA 81-84; 111; SATA 23, 36

Chambers, Aidan 1934- . . . . **CLC 35**
See also CA 25-28R; CANR 12, 31;
MAICYA; SAAS 12; SATA 1, 69

Chambers, James 1948-
See Cliff, Jimmy
See also CA 124

Chambers, Jessie
See Lawrence, D(avid) H(erbert Richards)

Chambers, Robert W. 1865-1933 . . . **TCLC 41**

Chandler, Raymond (Thornton)
1888-1959 . . . . **TCLC 1, 7**
See also CA 104; 129; CDALB 1929-1941;
DLBD 6; MTCW

Chang, Jung 1952- . . . . **CLC 71**

Channing, William Ellery
1780-1842 . . . . **NCLC 17**
See also DLB 1, 59

Chaplin, Charles Spencer
1889-1977 . . . . **CLC 16**
See also Chaplin, Charlie
See also CA 81-84; 73-76

Chaplin, Charlie
See Chaplin, Charles Spencer
See also DLB 44

Chapman, Graham 1941-1989 . . . . . . **CLC 21**
See also Monty Python
See also CA 116; 129; CANR 35

Chapman, John Jay 1862-1933 . . . . . **TCLC 7**
See also CA 104

Chapman, Walker
See Silverberg, Robert

Chappell, Fred (Davis) 1936- . . . . **CLC 40**
See also CA 5-8R; CAAS 4; CANR 8, 33;
DLB 6, 105

Char, Rene(-Emile)
1907-1988 . . . . **CLC 9, 11, 14, 55**
See also CA 13-16R; 124; CANR 32;
MTCW

Charby, Jay
See Ellison, Harlan

Chardin, Pierre Teilhard de
See Teilhard de Chardin, (Marie Joseph)
Pierre

Charles I 1600-1649 . . . . **LC 13**

Charyn, Jerome 1937- . . . . **CLC 5, 8, 18**
See also CA 5-8R; CAAS 1; CANR 7;
DLBY 83; MTCW

Chase, Mary (Coyle) 1907-1981 ...... **DC 1**
See also CA 77-80; 105; SATA 17, 29

Chase, Mary Ellen 1887-1973 .... **CLC 2**
See also CA 13-16; 41-44R; CAP 1;
SATA 10

Chase, Nicholas
See Hyde, Anthony

Chateaubriand, Francois Rene de
1768-1848 .... **NCLC 3**
See also DLB 119

Chatterje, Sarat Chandra 1876-1936(?)
See Chatterji, Saratchandra
See also CA 109

Chatterji, Bankim Chandra
1838-1894 .... **NCLC 19**

Chatterji, Saratchandra .... **TCLC 13**
See also Chatterje, Sarat Chandra

Chatterton, Thomas 1752-1770 .... **LC 3**
See also DLB 109

Chatwin, (Charles) Bruce
1940-1989 .... **CLC 28, 57, 59**
See also AAYA 4; BEST 90:1; CA 85-88;
127

Chaucer, Daniel
See Ford, Ford Madox

Chaucer, Geoffrey 1340(?)-1400 ..... **LC 17**
See also CDBLB Before 1660

Chaviaras, Strates 1935-
See Haviaras, Stratis
See also CA 105

Chayefsky, Paddy .... **CLC 23**
See also Chayefsky, Sidney
See also DLB 7, 44; DLBY 81

Chayefsky, Sidney 1923-1981
See Chayefsky, Paddy
See also CA 9-12R; 104; CANR 18

Chedid, Andree 1920- .... **CLC 47**

Cheever, John
1912-1982 ..... **CLC 3, 7, 8, 11, 15, 25,
64; SSC 1**
See also CA 5-8R; 106; CABS 1; CANR 5,
27; CDALB 1941-1968; DLB 2, 102;
DLBY 80, 82; MTCW; WLC

Cheever, Susan 1943- .... **CLC 18, 48**
See also CA 103; CANR 27; DLBY 82

Chekhonte, Antosha
See Chekhov, Anton (Pavlovich)

Chekhov, Anton (Pavlovich)
1860-1904 ...... **TCLC 3, 10, 31; SSC 2**
See also CA 104; 124; WLC

Chernyshevsky, Nikolay Gavrilovich
1828-1889 .... **NCLC 1**

Cherry, Carolyn Janice 1942-
See Cherryh, C. J.
See also CA 65-68; CANR 10

Cherryh, C. J. .... **CLC 35**
See also Cherry, Carolyn Janice
See also DLBY 80

Chesnutt, Charles W(addell)
1858-1932 .... **TCLC 5, 39; SSC 7**
See also BLC 1; BW; CA 106; 125; DLB 12,
50, 78; MTCW

Chester, Alfred 1929(?)-1971 .... **CLC 49**
See also CA 33-36R

Chesterton, G(ilbert) K(eith)
1874-1936 .... **TCLC 1, 6; SSC 1**
See also CA 104; 132; CDBLB 1914-1945;
DLB 10, 19, 34, 70, 98; MTCW;
SATA 27

Chiang Pin-chin 1904-1986
See Ding Ling
See also CA 118

Ch'ien Chung-shu 1910- .... **CLC 22**
See also CA 130; MTCW

Child, L. Maria
See Child, Lydia Maria

Child, Lydia Maria 1802-1880 .... **NCLC 6**
See also DLB 1, 74; SATA 67

Child, Mrs.
See Child, Lydia Maria

Child, Philip 1898-1978 .... **CLC 19, 68**
See also CA 13-14; CAP 1; SATA 47

Childress, Alice 1920-.......... **CLC 12, 15**
See also AAYA 8; BLC 1; BW; CA 45-48;
CANR 3, 27; CLR 14; DLB 7, 38;
MAICYA; MTCW; SATA 7, 48

Chislett, (Margaret) Anne 1943-.... **CLC 34**

Chitty, Thomas Willes 1926-....... **CLC 11**
See also Hinde, Thomas
See also CA 5-8R

Chomette, Rene Lucien 1898-1981 .. **CLC 20**
See also Clair, Rene
See also CA 103

Chopin, Kate .... **TCLC 5, 14; SSC 8**
See also Chopin, Katherine
See also CDALB 1865-1917; DLB 12, 78

Chopin, Katherine 1851-1904
See Chopin, Kate
See also CA 104; 122

Christie
See Ichikawa, Kon

Christie, Agatha (Mary Clarissa)
1890-1976 ...... **CLC 1, 6, 8, 12, 39, 48**
See also AAYA 9; AITN 1, 2; CA 17-20R;
61-64; CANR 10, 37; CDBLB 1914-1945;
DLB 13, 77; MTCW; SATA 36

Christie, (Ann) Philippa
See Pearce, Philippa
See also CA 5-8R; CANR 4

Christine de Pizan 1365(?)-1431(?) .... **LC 9**

Chubb, Elmer
See Masters, Edgar Lee

Chulkov, Mikhail Dmitrievich
1743-1792 .... **LC 2**

Churchill, Caryl 1938- .... **CLC 31, 55**
See also CA 102; CANR 22; DLB 13;
MTCW

Churchill, Charles 1731-1764........ **LC 3**
See also DLB 109

Chute, Carolyn 1947- .... **CLC 39**
See also CA 123

Ciardi, John (Anthony)
1916-1986 .... **CLC 10, 40, 44**
See also CA 5-8R; 118; CAAS 2; CANR 5,
33; CLR 19; DLB 5; DLBY 86;
MAICYA; MTCW; SATA 1, 46, 65

Cicero, Marcus Tullius
106B.C.-43B.C............... **CMLC 3**

Cimino, Michael 1943-............ **CLC 16**
See also CA 105

Cioran, E(mil) M. 1911-........... **CLC 64**
See also CA 25-28R

Cisneros, Sandra 1954-........... **CLC 69**
See also AAYA 9; CA 131; HW

Clair, Rene...................... **CLC 20**
See also Chomette, Rene Lucien

Clampitt, Amy 1920- .... **CLC 32**
See also CA 110; CANR 29; DLB 105

Clancy, Thomas L. Jr. 1947-
See Clancy, Tom
See also CA 125; 131; MTCW

Clancy, Tom...................... **CLC 45**
See also Clancy, Thomas L. Jr.
See also AAYA 9; BEST 89:1, 90:1

Clare, John 1793-1864........... **NCLC 9**
See also DLB 55, 96

Clarin
See Alas (y Urena), Leopoldo (Enrique
Garcia)

Clark, (Robert) Brian 1932-........ **CLC 29**
See also CA 41-44R

Clark, Eleanor 1913- .... **CLC 5, 19**
See also CA 9-12R; DLB 6

Clark, J. P.
See Clark, John Pepper
See also DLB 117

Clark, John Pepper 1935- .... **CLC 38**
See also Clark, J. P.
See also BLC 1; BW; CA 65-68; CANR 16

Clark, M. R.
See Clark, Mavis Thorpe

Clark, Mavis Thorpe 1909-........ **CLC 12**
See also CA 57-60; CANR 8, 37; MAICYA;
SAAS 5; SATA 8

Clark, Walter Van Tilburg
1909-1971 .... **CLC 28**
See also CA 9-12R; 33-36R; DLB 9;
SATA 8

Clarke, Arthur C(harles)
1917- ...... **CLC 1, 4, 13, 18, 35; SSC 3**
See also AAYA 4; CA 1-4R; CANR 2, 28;
MAICYA; MTCW; SATA 13, 70

Clarke, Austin C(hesterfield)
1934-..................... **CLC 8, 53**
See also BLC 1; BW; CA 25-28R;
CAAS 16; CANR 14, 32; DLB 53

Clarke, Austin 1896-1974........ **CLC 6, 9**
See also CA 29-32; 49-52; CAP 2; DLB 10,
20

Clarke, Gillian 1937- .... **CLC 61**
See also CA 106; DLB 40

Clarke, Marcus (Andrew Hislop)
1846-1881 .... **NCLC 19**

Clarke, Shirley 1925-............. **CLC 16**

.... **CLC 30**
See also Headon, (Nicky) Topper; Jones,
Mick; Simonon, Paul; Strummer, Joe

Claudel, Paul (Louis Charles Marie)
1868-1955 .... **TCLC 2, 10**
See also CA 104

Cudlip, David 1933- . . . . **CLC 34**

Cullen, Countee 1903-1946 . . . . . **TCLC 4, 37**
See also BLC 1; BW; CA 108; 124;
CDALB 1917-1929; DLB 4, 48, 51;
MTCW; SATA 18

Cum, R.
See Crumb, R(obert)

Cummings, Bruce F(rederick) 1889-1919
See Barbellion, W. N. P.
See also CA 123

Cummings, E(dward) E(stlin)
1894-1962 . . . . . **CLC 1, 3, 8, 12, 15, 68;**
PC 5
See also CA 73-76; CANR 31;
CDALB 1929-1941; DLB 4, 48; MTCW;
WLC 2

Cunha, Euclides (Rodrigues Pimenta) da
1866-1909 . . . . **TCLC 24**
See also CA 123

Cunningham, E. V.
See Fast, Howard (Melvin)

Cunningham, J(ames) V(incent)
1911-1985 . . . . **CLC 3, 31**
See also CA 1-4R; 115; CANR 1; DLB 5

Cunningham, Julia (Woolfolk)
1916- . . . . **CLC 12**
See also CA 9-12R; CANR 4, 19, 36;
MAICYA; SAAS 2; SATA 1, 26

Cunningham, Michael 1952- . . . . **CLC 34**
See also CA 136

Cunninghame Graham, R(obert) B(ontine)
1852-1936 . . . . **TCLC 19**
See also Graham, R(obert) B(ontine)
Cunninghame
See also CA 119; DLB 98

Currie, Ellen 19(?)- . . . . **CLC 44**

Curtin, Philip
See Lowndes, Marie Adelaide (Belloc)

Curtis, Price
See Ellison, Harlan

Czaczkes, Shmuel Yosef
See Agnon, S(hmuel) Y(osef Halevi)

D. P.
See Wells, H(erbert) G(eorge)

Dabrowska, Maria (Szumska)
1889-1965 . . . . **CLC 15**
See also CA 106

Dabydeen, David 1955- . . . . **CLC 34**
See also BW; CA 125

Dacey, Philip 1939- . . . . **CLC 51**
See also CA 37-40R; CANR 14, 32;
DLB 105

Dagerman, Stig (Halvard)
1923-1954 . . . . **TCLC 17**
See also CA 117

Dahl, Roald 1916-1990 . . . . **CLC 1, 6, 18**
See also CA 1-4R; 133; CANR 6, 32, 37;
CLR 1, 7; MAICYA; MTCW; SATA 1,
26; SATO 65

Dahlberg, Edward 1900-1977 . . . **CLC 1, 7, 14**
See also CA 9-12R; 69-72; CANR 31;
DLB 48; MTCW

Dale, Colin . . . . **TCLC 18**
See also Lawrence, T(homas) E(dward)

Dale, George E.
See Asimov, Isaac

Daly, Elizabeth 1878-1967 . . . . **CLC 52**
See also CA 23-24; 25-28R; CAP 2

Daly, Maureen 1921- . . . . **CLC 17**
See also AAYA 5; CANR 37; MAICYA;
SAAS 1; SATA 2

Daniels, Brett
See Adler, Renata

Dannay, Frederic 1905-1982 . . . . **CLC 11**
See also Queen, Ellery
See also CA 1-4R; 107; CANR 1, 39;
MTCW

D'Annunzio, Gabriele
1863-1938 . . . . **TCLC 6, 40**
See also CA 104

d'Antibes, Germain
See Simenon, Georges (Jacques Christian)

Danvers, Dennis 1947- . . . . **CLC 70**

Danziger, Paula 1944- . . . . **CLC 21**
See also AAYA 4; CA 112; 115; CANR 37;
CLR 20; MAICYA; SATA 30, 36, 63

Dario, Ruben . . . . **TCLC 4**
See also Sarmiento, Felix Ruben Garcia

Darley, George 1795-1846 . . . . **NCLC 2**
See also DLB 96

Daryush, Elizabeth 1887-1977 . . . . **CLC 6, 19**
See also CA 49-52; CANR 3; DLB 20

Daudet, (Louis Marie) Alphonse
1840-1897 . . . . **NCLC 1**

Daumal, Rene 1908-1944 . . . . **TCLC 14**
See also CA 114

Davenport, Guy (Mattison Jr.)
1927- . . . . **CLC 6, 14, 38**
See also CA 33-36R; CANR 23

Davidson, Avram 1923-
See Queen, Ellery
See also CA 101; CANR 26; DLB 8

Davidson, Donald (Grady)
1893-1968 . . . . **CLC 2, 13, 19**
See also CA 5-8R; 25-28R; CANR 4;
DLB 45

Davidson, Hugh
See Hamilton, Edmond

Davidson, John 1857-1909 . . . . **TCLC 24**
See also CA 118; DLB 19

Davidson, Sara 1943- . . . . **CLC 9**
See also CA 81-84

Davie, Donald (Alfred)
1922- . . . . **CLC 5, 8, 10, 31**
See also CA 1-4R; CAAS 3; CANR 1;
DLB 27; MTCW

Davies, Ray(mond Douglas) 1944- . . **CLC 21**
See also CA 116

Davies, Rhys 1903-1978 . . . . **CLC 23**
See also CA 9-12R; 81-84; CANR 4

Davies, (William) Robertson
1913- . . . . **CLC 2, 7, 13, 25, 42**
See also BEST 89:2; CA 33-36R; CANR 17;
DLB 68; MTCW; WLC

Davies, W(illiam) H(enry)
1871-1940 . . . . **TCLC 5**
See also CA 104; DLB 19

Davies, Walter C.
See Kornbluth, C(yril) M.

Davis, B. Lynch
See Bioy Casares, Adolfo; Borges, Jorge
Luis

Davis, Gordon
See Hunt, E(verette) Howard Jr.

Davis, Harold Lenoir 1896-1960 . . . . **CLC 49**
See also CA 89-92; DLB 9

Davis, Rebecca (Blaine) Harding
1831-1910 . . . . **TCLC 6**
See also CA 104; DLB 74

Davis, Richard Harding
1864-1916 . . . . **TCLC 24**
See also CA 114; DLB 12, 23, 78, 79

Davison, Frank Dalby 1893-1970 . . . **CLC 15**
See also CA 116

Davison, Lawrence H.
See Lawrence, D(avid) H(erbert Richards)

Davison, Peter 1928- . . . . **CLC 28**
See also CA 9-12R; CAAS 4; CANR 3;
DLB 5

Davys, Mary 1674-1732 . . . . **LC 1**
See also DLB 39

Dawson, Fielding 1930- . . . . **CLC 6**
See also CA 85-88

Day, Clarence (Shepard Jr.)
1874-1935 . . . . **TCLC 25**
See also CA 108; DLB 11

Day, Thomas 1748-1789 . . . . **LC 1**
See also DLB 39; YABC 1

Day Lewis, C(ecil)
1904-1972 . . . . **CLC 1, 6, 10**
See also Blake, Nicholas
See also CA 13-16; 33-36R; CANR 34;
CAP 1; DLB 15, 20; MTCW

Dazai, Osamu . . . . **TCLC 11**
See also Tsushima, Shuji

de Andrade, Carlos Drummond
See Drummond de Andrade, Carlos

Deane, Norman
See Creasey, John

de Beauvoir, Simone (Lucie Ernestine Marie Bertrand)
See Beauvoir, Simone (Lucie Ernestine
Marie Bertrand) de

de Brissac, Malcolm
See Dickinson, Peter (Malcolm)

de Chardin, Pierre Teilhard
See Teilhard de Chardin, (Marie Joseph)
Pierre

Dee, John 1527-1608 . . . . **LC 20**

Deer, Sandra 1940- . . . . **CLC 45**

De Ferrari, Gabriella . . . . **CLC 65**

Defoe, Daniel 1660(?)-1731 . . . . **LC 1**
See also CDBLB 1660-1789; DLB 39, 95,
101; MAICYA; SATA 22; WLC

de Gourmont, Remy
See Gourmont, Remy de

de Hartog, Jan 1914- . . . . **CLC 19**
See also CA 1-4R; CANR 1

de Hostos, E. M.
See Hostos (y Bonilla), Eugenio Maria de

Fisher, Roy 1930-................ **CLC 25**
See also CA 81-84; CAAS 10; CANR 16;
DLB 40

Fisher, Rudolph 1897-1934 .... **TCLC 11**
See also BLC 2; BW; CA 107; 124; DLB 51,
102

Fisher, Vardis (Alvero) 1895-1968.... **CLC 7**
See also CA 5-8R; 25-28R; DLB 9

Fiske, Tarleton
See Bloch, Robert (Albert)

Fitch, Clarke
See Sinclair, Upton (Beall)

Fitch, John IV
See Cormier, Robert (Edmund)

Fitgerald, Penelope 1916- .... **CLC 61**

Fitzgerald, Captain Hugh
See Baum, L(yman) Frank

FitzGerald, Edward 1809-1883 .... **NCLC 9**
See also DLB 32

Fitzgerald, F(rancis) Scott (Key)
1896-1940 .... **TCLC 1, 6, 14, 28; SSC 6**
See also AITN 1; CA 110; 123;
CDALB 1917-1929; DLB 4, 9, 86;
DLBD 1; DLBY 81; MTCW; WLC

Fitzgerald, Penelope 1916-...... **CLC 19, 51**
See also CA 85-88; CAAS 10; DLB 14

FitzGerald, Robert D(avid)
1902-1987 .... **CLC 19**
See also CA 17-20R

Fitzgerald, Robert (Stuart)
1910-1985 .... **CLC 39**
See also CA 1-4R; 114; CANR 1; DLBY 80

Flanagan, Thomas (James Bonner)
1923- .... **CLC 25, 52**
See also CA 108; DLBY 80; MTCW

Flaubert, Gustave
1821-1880 ..... **NCLC 2, 10, 19; SSC 11**
See also DLB 119; WLC

Flecker, (Herman) James Elroy
1884-1915 .... **TCLC 43**
See also CA 109; DLB 10, 19

Fleming, Ian (Lancaster)
1908-1964 .... **CLC 3, 30**
See also CA 5-8R; CDBLB 1945-1960;
DLB 87; MTCW; SATA 9

Fleming, Thomas (James) 1927- .... **CLC 37**
See also CA 5-8R; CANR 10; SATA 8

Fletcher, John Gould 1886-1950... **TCLC 35**
See also CA 107; DLB 4, 45

Fleur, Paul
See Pohl, Frederik

Flying Officer X
See Bates, H(erbert) E(rnest)

Fo, Dario 1926-.................. **CLC 32**
See also CA 116; 128; MTCW

Fogarty, Jonathan Titulescu Esq.
See Farrell, James T(homas)

Folke, Will
See Bloch, Robert (Albert)

Follett, Ken(neth Martin) 1949- .... **CLC 18**
See also AAYA 6; BEST 89:4; CA 81-84;
CANR 13, 33; DLB 87; DLBY 81;
MTCW

Fontane, Theodor 1819-1898 ..... **NCLC 26**

Foote, Horton 1916-............. **CLC 51**
See also CA 73-76; CANR 34; DLB 26

Forbes, Esther 1891-1967......... **CLC 12**
See also CA 13-14; 25-28R; CAP 1;
CLR 27; DLB 22; MAICYA; SATA 2

Forche, Carolyn (Louise) 1950-..... **CLC 25**
See also CA 109; 117; DLB 5

Ford, Elbur
See Hibbert, Eleanor Burford

Ford, Ford Madox
1873-1939 .... **TCLC 1, 15, 39**
See also CA 104; 132; CDBLB 1914-1945;
DLB 34, 98; MTCW

Ford, John 1895-1973............. **CLC 16**
See also CA 45-48

Ford, Richard 1944-............. **CLC 46**
See also CA 69-72; CANR 11

Ford, Webster
See Masters, Edgar Lee

Foreman, Richard 1937-.......... **CLC 50**
See also CA 65-68; CANR 32

Forester, C(ecil) S(cott)
1899-1966 .... **CLC 35**
See also CA 73-76; 25-28R; SATA 13

Forez
See Mauriac, Francois (Charles)

Forman, James Douglas 1932-..... **CLC 21**
See also CA 9-12R; CANR 4, 19;
MAICYA; SATA 8, 70

Fornes, Maria Irene 1930-...... **CLC 39, 61**
See also CA 25-28R; CANR 28; DLB 7;
HW; MTCW

Forrest, Leon 1937- .... **CLC 4**
See also BW; CA 89-92; CAAS 7;
CANR 25; DLB 33

Forster, E(dward) M(organ)
1879-1970 .... **CLC 1, 2, 3, 4, 9, 10, 13,
15, 22, 45**
See also AAYA 2; CA 13-14; 25-28R;
CAP 1; CDBLB 1914-1945; DLB 34, 98;
MTCW; SATA 57; WLC

Forster, John 1812-1876 .... **NCLC 11**

Forsyth, Frederick 1938-...... **CLC 2, 5, 36**
See also BEST 89:4; CA 85-88; CANR 38;
DLB 87; MTCW

Forten, Charlotte L.............. TCLC 16
See also Grimke, Charlotte L(ottie) Forten
See also BLC 2; DLB 50

Foscolo, Ugo 1778-1827......... **NCLC 8**

Fosse, Bob .... **CLC 20**
See also Fosse, Robert Louis

Fosse, Robert Louis 1927-1987
See Fosse, Bob
See also CA 110; 123

Foster, Stephen Collins
1826-1864 .... **NCLC 26**

Foucault, Michel
1926-1984 .... **CLC 31, 34, 69**
See also CA 105; 113; CANR 34; MTCW

Fouque, Friedrich Heinrich Karl) de la Motte
1777-1843 .... **NCLC 2**
See also DLB 90

Fournier, Henri Alban 1886-1914
See Alain-Fournier
See also CA 104

Fournier, Pierre 1916-........... **CLC 11**
See also Gascar, Pierre
See also CA 89-92; CANR 16

Fowles, John
1926- .... **CLC 1, 2, 3, 4, 6, 9, 10, 15, 33**
See also CA 5-8R; CANR 25; CDBLB 1960
to Present; DLB 14; MTCW; SATA 22

Fox, Paula 1923-................ **CLC 2, 8**
See also AAYA 3; CA 73-76; CANR 20,
36; CLR 1; DLB 52; MAICYA; MTCW;
SATA 17, 60

Fox, William Price (Jr.) 1926- ..... **CLC 22**
See also CA 17-20R; CANR 11; DLB 2;
DLBY 81

Foxe, John 1516(?)-1587 .... **LC 14**

Frame, Janet ...... **CLC 2, 3, 6, 22, 66**
See also Clutha, Janet Paterson Frame

France, Anatole.................. **TCLC 9**
See also Thibault, Jacques Anatole Francois

Francis, Claude 19(?)- .... **CLC 50**

Francis, Dick 1920- .... **CLC 2, 22, 42**
See also AAYA 5; BEST 89:3; CA 5-8R;
CANR 9; CDBLB 1960 to Present;
DLB 87; MTCW

Francis, Robert (Churchill)
1901-1987 .... **CLC 15**
See also CA 1-4R; 123; CANR 1

Frank, Anne(lies Marie)
1929-1945 .... **TCLC 17**
See also CA 113; 133; MTCW; SATA 42;
WLC

Frank, Elizabeth 1945-........... **CLC 39**
See also CA 121; 126

Franklin, Benjamin
See Hasek, Jaroslav (Matej Frantisek)

Franklin, (Stella Maraia Sarah) Miles
1879-1954 .... **TCLC 7**
See also CA 104

Fraser, Antonia (Pakenham)
1932- .... **CLC 32**
See also CA 85-88; MTCW; SATA 32

Fraser, George MacDonald 1925-.... **CLC 7**
See also CA 45-48; CANR 2

Fraser, Sylvia 1935-............. **CLC 64**
See also CA 45-48; CANR 1, 16

Frayn, Michael 1933-...... **CLC 3, 7, 31, 47**
See also CA 5-8R; CANR 30; DLB 13, 14;
MTCW

Fraze, Candida (Merrill) 1945-..... **CLC 50**
See also CA 126

Frazer, J(ames) G(eorge)
1854-1941 .... **TCLC 32**
See also CA 118

Frazer, Robert Caine
See Creasey, John

Frazer, Sir James George
See Frazer, J(ames) G(eorge)

Frazier, Ian 1951-................ **CLC 46**
See also CA 130

Frederic, Harold 1856-1898...... **NCLC 10**
See also DLB 12, 23

Frederick the Great 1712-1786 ...... **LC 14**

Fredro, Aleksander 1793-1876..... **NCLC 8**

Freeling, Nicolas 1927- .... **CLC 38**
See also CA 49-52; CAAS 12; CANR 1, 17;
DLB 87

Freeman, Douglas Southall
1886-1953 .... **TCLC 11**
See also CA 109; DLB 17

Freeman, Judith 1946- .... **CLC 55**

Freeman, Mary Eleanor Wilkins
1852-1930 .... **TCLC 9; SSC 1**
See also CA 106; DLB 12, 78

Freeman, R(ichard) Austin
1862-1943 .... **TCLC 21**
See also CA 113; DLB 70

French, Marilyn 1929- ...... **CLC 10, 18, 60**
See also CA 69-72; CANR 3, 31; MTCW

French, Paul
See Asimov, Isaac

Freneau, Philip Morin 1752-1832.. **NCLC 1**
See also DLB 37, 43

Friedman, B(ernard) H(arper)
1926- .... **CLC 7**
See also CA 1-4R; CANR 3

Friedman, Bruce Jay 1930-.... **CLC 3, 5, 56**
See also CA 9-12R; CANR 25; DLB 2, 28

Friel, Brian 1929-........... **CLC 5, 42, 59**
See also CA 21-24R; CANR 33; DLB 13;
MTCW

Friis-Baastad, Babbis Ellinor
1921-1970 .... **CLC 12**
See also CA 17-20R; 134; SATA 7

Frisch, Max (Rudolf)
1911-1991 ..... **CLC 3, 9, 14, 18, 32, 44**
See also CA 85-88; 134; CANR 32;
DLB 69; MTCW

Fromentin, Eugene (Samuel Auguste)
1820-1876 .... **NCLC 10**

Frost, Robert (Lee)
1874-1963 ... **CLC 1, 3, 4, 9, 10, 13, 15,
26, 34, 44; PC 1**
See also CA 89-92; CANR 33;
CDALB 1917-1929; DLB 54; DLBD 7;
MTCW; SATA 14; WLC

Froy, Herald
See Waterhouse, Keith (Spencer)

Fry, Christopher 1907-....... **CLC 2, 10, 14**
See also CA 17-20R; CANR 9, 30; DLB 13;
MTCW; SATA 66

Frye, (Herman) Northrop
1912-1991 .... **CLC 24, 70**
See also CA 5-8R; 133; CANR 8, 37;
DLB 67, 68; MTCW

Fuchs, Daniel 1909- .... **CLC 8, 22**
See also CA 81-84; CAAS 5; DLB 9, 26, 28

Fuchs, Daniel 1934- .... **CLC 34**
See also CA 37-40R; CANR 14

Fuentes, Carlos
1928- ...... **CLC 3, 8, 10, 13, 22, 41, 60**
See also AAYA 4; AITN 2; CA 69-72;
CANR 10, 32; DLB 113; HW; MTCW;
WLC

Fuentes, Gregorio Lopez y
See Lopez y Fuentes, Gregorio

Fugard, (Harold) Athol
1932- .... **CLC 5, 9, 14, 25, 40**
See also CA 85-88; CANR 32; MTCW

Fugard, Sheila 1932- .... **CLC 48**
See also CA 125

Fuller, Charles (H. Jr.)
1939- .... **CLC 25; DC 1**
See also BLC 2; BW; CA 108; 112; DLB 38;
MTCW

Fuller, John (Leopold) 1937-...... **CLC 62**
See also CA 21-24R; CANR 9; DLB 40

Fuller, Margaret .... **NCLC 5**
See also Ossoli, Sarah Margaret (Fuller
marchesa d')

Fuller, Roy (Broadbent)
1912-1991 .... **CLC 4, 28**
See also CA 5-8R; 135; CAAS 10; DLB 15,
20

Fulton, Alice 1952-............... **CLC 52**
See also CA 116

Furphy, Joseph 1843-1912....... **TCLC 25**

Futabatei, Shimei 1864-1909 ..... **TCLC 44**

Futrelle, Jacques 1875-1912 ..... **TCLC 19**
See also CA 113

G. B. S.
See Shaw, George Bernard

Gaboriau, Emile 1835-1873 ...... **NCLC 14**

Gadda, Carlo Emilio 1893-1973 .... **CLC 11**
See also CA 89-92

Gaddis, William
1922- .... **CLC 1, 3, 6, 8, 10, 19, 43**
See also CA 17-20R; CANR 21; DLB 2;
MTCW

Gaines, Ernest J(ames)
1933- .... **CLC 3, 11, 18**
See also AITN 1; BLC 2; BW; CA 9-12R;
CANR 6, 24; CDALB 1968-1988; DLB 2,
33; DLBY 80; MTCW

Gaitskill, Mary 1954-............. **CLC 69**
See also CA 128

Galdos, Benito Perez
See Perez Galdos, Benito

Gale, Zona 1874-1938 .... **TCLC 7**
See also CA 105; DLB 9, 78

Galeano, Eduardo (Hughes) 1940-... **CLC 72**
See also CA 29-32R; CANR 13, 32; HW

Galiano, Juan Valera y Alcala
See Valera y Alcala-Galiano, Juan

Gallagher, Tess 1943-......... **CLC 18, 63**
See also CA 106; DLB 120

Gallant, Mavis
1922- .... **CLC 7, 18, 38; SSC 5**
See also CA 69-72; CANR 29; DLB 53;
MTCW

Gallant, Roy A(rthur) 1924- .... **CLC 17**
See also CA 5-8R; CANR 4, 29; MAICYA;
SATA 4, 68

Gallico, Paul (William) 1897-1976 ... **CLC 2**
See also AITN 1; CA 5-8R; 69-72;
CANR 23; DLB 9; MAICYA; SATA 13

Gallup, Ralph
See Whitemore, Hugh (John)

Galsworthy, John 1867-1933 .... **TCLC 1, 45**
See also CA 104; CDBLB 1890-1914;
DLB 10, 34, 98; WLC 2

Galt, John 1779-1839 .... **NCLC 1**
See also DLB 99, 116

Galvin, James 1951-.............. **CLC 38**
See also CA 108; CANR 26

Gamboa, Federico 1864-1939...... **TCLC 36**

Gann, Ernest Kellogg 1910-1991.... **CLC 23**
See also AITN 1; CA 1-4R; 136; CANR 1

Garcia Lorca, Federico
1898-1936 ..... **TCLC 1, 7; DC 2; PC 3**
See also CA 104; 131; DLB 108; HW;
MTCW; WLC

Garcia Marquez, Gabriel (Jose)
1928- ... **CLC 2, 3, 8, 10, 15, 27, 47, 55;
SSC 8**
See also Marquez, Gabriel (Jose) Garcia
See also AAYA 3; BEST 89:1, 90:4;
CA 33-36R; CANR 10, 28; DLB 113;
HW; MTCW; WLC

Gard, Janice
See Latham, Jean Lee

Gard, Roger Martin du
See Martin du Gard, Roger

Gardam, Jane 1928-.............. **CLC 43**
See also CA 49-52; CANR 2, 18, 33;
CLR 12; DLB 14; MAICYA; MTCW;
SAAS 9; SATA 28, 39

Gardner, Herb.................... **CLC 44**

Gardner, John (Champlin) Jr.
1933-1982 .... **CLC 2, 3, 5, 7, 8, 10, 18,
28, 34; SSC 7**
See also AITN 1; CA 65-68; 107;
CANR 33; DLB 2; DLBY 82; MTCW;
SATA 31, 40

Gardner, John (Edmund) 1926-..... **CLC 30**
See also CA 103; CANR 15; MTCW

Gardner, Noel
See Kuttner, Henry

Gardons, S. S.
See Snodgrass, William D(e Witt)

Garfield, Leon 1921-.............. **CLC 12**
See also AAYA 8; CA 17-20R; CANR 38;
CLR 21; MAICYA; SATA 1, 32

Garland, (Hannibal) Hamlin
1860-1940 .... **TCLC 3**
See also CA 104; DLB 12, 71, 78

Garneau, (Hector de) Saint-Denys
1912-1943 .... **TCLC 13**
See also CA 111; DLB 88

Garner, Alan 1934-............... **CLC 17**
See also CA 73-76; CANR 15; CLR 20;
MAICYA; MTCW; SATA 18, 69

Garner, Hugh 1913-1979 .... **CLC 13**
See also CA 69-72; CANR 31; DLB 68

Garnett, David 1892-1981 .... **CLC 3**
See also CA 5-8R; 103; CANR 17; DLB 34

Garos, Stephanie
See Katz, Steve

Garrett, George (Palmer)
1929- .... **CLC 3, 11, 51**
See also CA 1-4R; CAAS 5; CANR 1;
DLB 2, 5; DLBY 83

Grayson, Richard (A.) 1951- .... CLC 38
See also CA 85-88; CANR 14, 31

Greeley, Andrew M(oran) 1928- .... CLC 28
See also CA 5-8R; CAAS 7; CANR 7;
MTCW

Green, Brian
See Card, Orson Scott

Green, Hannah
See Greenberg, Joanne (Goldenberg)

Green, Hannah .... CLC 3
See also CA 73-76

Green, Henry .... CLC 2, 13
See also Yorke, Henry Vincent
See also DLB 15

Green, Julian (Hartridge)
1900- .... CLC 3, 11
See also CA 21-24R; CANR 33; DLB 4, 72;
MTCW

Green, Julien
See Green, Julian (Hartridge)

Green, Paul (Eliot) 1894-1981 ...... CLC 25
See also AITN 1; CA 5-8R; 103; CANR 3;
DLB 7, 9; DLBY 81

Greenberg, Ivan 1908-1973
See Rahv, Philip
See also CA 85-88

Greenberg, Joanne (Goldenberg)
1932- .... CLC 7, 30
See also CA 5-8R; CANR 14, 32; SATA 25

Greenberg, Richard 1959(?)- .... CLC 57
See also CA 138

Greene, Bette 1934- .... CLC 30
See also AAYA 7; CA 53-56; CANR 4;
CLR 2; MAICYA; SATA 8

Greene, Gael .... CLC 8
See also CA 13-16R; CANR 10

Greene, Graham (Henry)
1904-1991 ... CLC 1, 3, 6, 9, 14, 18, 27,
37, 70, 72
See also AITN 2; CA 13-16R; 133;
CANR 35; CDBLB 1945-1960; DLB 13,
15, 77, 100; DLBY 91; MTCW;
SATA 20; WLC

Greer, Richard
See Silverberg, Robert

Greer, Richard
See Silverberg, Robert

Gregor, Arthur 1923- .... CLC 9
See also CA 25-28R; CAAS 10; CANR 11;
SATA 36

Gregor, Lee
See Pohl, Frederik

Gregory, Isabella Augusta (Persse)
1852-1932 .... TCLC 1
See also CA 104; DLB 10

Gregory, J. Dennis
See Williams, John A(lfred)

Grendon, Stephen
See Derleth, August (William)

Grenville, Kate 1950- .... CLC 61
See also CA 118

Grenville, Pelham
See Wodehouse, P(elham) G(renville)

Greve, Felix Paul (Berthold Friedrich)
1879-1948
See Grove, Frederick Philip
See also CA 104

Grey, Zane 1872-1939 .... TCLC 6
See also CA 104; 132; DLB 9; MTCW

Grieg, (Johan) Nordahl (Brun)
1902-1943 .... TCLC 10
See also CA 107

Grieve, C(hristopher) M(urray)
1892-1978 .... CLC 11, 19
See also MacDiarmid, Hugh
See also CA 5-8R; 85-88; CANR 33;
MTCW

Griffin, Gerald 1803-1840 .... NCLC 7

Griffin, John Howard 1920-1980.... CLC 68
See also AITN 1; CA 1-4R; 101; CANR 2

Griffin, Peter .... CLC 39

Griffiths, Trevor 1935- .... CLC 13, 52
See also CA 97-100; DLB 13

Grigson, Geoffrey (Edward Harvey)
1905-1985 .... CLC 7, 39
See also CA 25-28R; 118; CANR 20, 33;
DLB 27; MTCW

Grillparzer, Franz 1791-1872...... NCLC 1

Grimble, Reverend Charles James
See Eliot, T(homas) S(tearns)

Grimke, Charlotte L(ottie) Forten
1837(?)-1914
See Forten, Charlotte L.
See also BW; CA 117; 124

Grimm, Jacob Ludwig Karl
1785-1863 .... NCLC 3
See also DLB 90; MAICYA; SATA 22

Grimm, Wilhelm Karl 1786-1859 .. NCLC 3
See also DLB 90; MAICYA; SATA 22

Grimmelshausen, Johann Jakob Christoffel
von 1621-1676 .... LC 6

Grindel, Eugene 1895-1952
See Eluard, Paul
See also CA 104

Grossman, David .... CLC 67
See also CA 138

Grossman, Vasily (Semenovich)
1905-1964 .... CLC 41
See also CA 124; 130; MTCW

Grove, Frederick Philip .... TCLC 4
See also Greve, Felix Paul (Berthold
Friedrich)
See also DLB 92

Grubb
See Crumb, R(obert)

Grumbach, Doris (Isaac)
1918- .... CLC 13, 22, 64
See also CA 5-8R; CAAS 2; CANR 9

Grundtvig, Nicolai Frederik Severin
1783-1872 .... NCLC 1

Grunge
See Crumb, R(obert)

Grunwald, Lisa 1959- .... CLC 44
See also CA 120

Guare, John 1938- .... CLC 8, 14, 29, 67
See also CA 73-76; CANR 21; DLB 7;
MTCW

Gudjonsson, Halldor Kiljan 1902-
See Laxness, Halldor
See also CA 103

Guenter, Erich
See Eich, Guenter

Guest, Barbara 1920- .... CLC 34
See also CA 25-28R; CANR 11; DLB 5

Guest, Judith (Ann) 1936- .... CLC 8, 30
See also AAYA 7; CA 77-80; CANR 15;
MTCW

Guild, Nicholas M. 1944-......... CLC 33
See also CA 93-96

Guillemin, Jacques
See Sartre, Jean-Paul

Guillen, Jorge 1893-1984.......... CLC 11
See also CA 89-92; 112; DLB 108; HW

Guillen (y Batista), Nicolas (Cristobal)
1902-1989 .... CLC 48
See also BLC 2; BW; CA 116; 125; 129;
HW

Guillevic, (Eugene) 1907-.......... CLC 33
See also CA 93-96

Guillois
See Desnos, Robert

Guiney, Louise Imogen
1861-1920 .... TCLC 41
See also DLB 54

Guiraldes, Ricardo (Guillermo)
1886-1927 .... TCLC 39
See also CA 131; HW; MTCW

Gunn, Bill .... CLC 5
See also Gunn, William Harrison
See also DLB 38

Gunn, Thom(son William)
1929- .... CLC 3, 6, 18, 32
See also CA 17-20R; CANR 9, 33;
CDBLB 1960 to Present; DLB 27;
MTCW

Gunn, William Harrison 1934(?)-1989
See Gunn, Bill
See also AITN 1; BW; CA 13-16R; 128;
CANR 12, 25

Gunnars, Kristjana 1948-.......... CLC 69
See also CA 113; DLB 60

Gurganus, Allan 1947- .... CLC 70
See also BEST 90:1; CA 135

Gurney, A(lbert) R(amsdell) Jr.
1930- .... CLC 32, 50, 54
See also CA 77-80; CANR 32

Gurney, Ivor (Bertie) 1890-1937... TCLC 33

Gurney, Peter
See Gurney, A(lbert) R(amsdell) Jr.

Gustafson, Ralph (Barker) 1909-.... CLC 36
See also CA 21-24R; CANR 8; DLB 88

Gut, Gom
See Simenon, Georges (Jacques Christian)

Guthrie, A(lfred) B(ertram) Jr.
1901-1991 .... CLC 23
See also CA 57-60; 134; CANR 24; DLB 6;
SATA 62; SATO 67

Guthrie, Isobel
See Grieve, C(hristopher) M(urray)

Harrison, James (Thomas) 1937-
See Harrison, Jim
See also CA 13-16R; CANR 8

Harrison, Jim . . . . **CLC 6, 14, 33, 66**
See also Harrison, James (Thomas)
See also DLBY 82

Harrison, Kathryn 1961- . . . . **CLC 70**

Harrison, Tony 1937- . . . . **CLC 43**
See also CA 65-68; DLB 40; MTCW

Harriss, Will(ard Irvin) 1922- . . . . . . **CLC 34**
See also CA 111

Harson, Sley
See Ellison, Harlan

Hart, Ellis
See Ellison, Harlan

Hart, Josephine 1942(?)- . . . . **CLC 70**
See also CA 138

Hart, Moss 1904-1961 . . . . **CLC 66**
See also CA 109; 89-92; DLB 7

Harte, (Francis) Bret(t)
1836(?)-1902 . . . . **TCLC 1, 25; SSC 8**
See also CA 104; CDALB 1865-1917;
DLB 12, 64, 74, 79; SATA 26; WLC

Hartley, L(eslie) P(oles)
1895-1972 . . . . **CLC 2, 22**
See also CA 45-48; 37-40R; CANR 33;
DLB 15; MTCW

Hartman, Geoffrey H. 1929- . . . . **CLC 27**
See also CA 117; 125; DLB 67

Haruf, Kent 19(?)- . . . . **CLC 34**

Harwood, Ronald 1934- . . . . **CLC 32**
See also CA 1-4R; CANR 4; DLB 13

Hasek, Jaroslav (Matej Frantisek)
1883-1923 . . . . **TCLC 4**
See also CA 104; 129; MTCW

Hass, Robert 1941- . . . . **CLC 18, 39**
See also CA 111; CANR 30; DLB 105

Hastings, Hudson
See Kuttner, Henry

Hastings, Selina . . . . **CLC 44**

Hatteras, Amelia
See Mencken, H(enry) L(ouis)

Hatteras, Owen
See Mencken, H(enry) L(ouis)

Hatteras, Owen . . . . **TCLC 18**
See also Nathan, George Jean

Hauptmann, Gerhart (Johann Robert)
1862-1946 . . . . **TCLC 4**
See also CA 104; DLB 66, 118

Havel, Vaclav 1936- . . . . **CLC 25, 58, 65**
See also CA 104; CANR 36; MTCW

Haviaras, Stratis . . . . **CLC 33**
See also Chaviaras, Strates

Hawes, Stephen 1475(?)-1523(?) . . . . . **LC 17**

Hawkes, John (Clendennin Burne Jr.)
1925- . . . . . . **CLC 1, 2, 3, 4, 7, 9, 14, 15,
27, 49**
See also CA 1-4R; CANR 2; DLB 2, 7;
DLBY 80; MTCW

Hawking, S. W.
See Hawking, Stephen W(illiam)

Hawking, Stephen W(illiam)
1942- . . . . **CLC 63**
See also BEST 89:1; CA 126; 129

Hawthorne, Julian 1846-1934 . . . . . **TCLC 25**

Hawthorne, Nathaniel
1804-1864 . . . **NCLC 2, 10, 17, 23; SSC 3**
See also CDALB 1640-1865; DLB 1, 74;
WLC; YABC 2

Hayaseca y Eizaguirre, Jorge
See Echegaray (y Eizaguirre), Jose (Maria
Waldo)

Hayashi Fumiko 1904-1951 . . . . . . **TCLC 27**

Haycraft, Anna
See Ellis, Alice Thomas
See also CA 122

Hayden, Robert E(arl)
1913-1980 . . . . **CLC 5, 9, 14, 37**
See also BLC 2; BW; CA 69-72; 97-100;
CABS 2; CANR 24; CDALB 1941-1968;
DLB 5, 76; MTCW; SATA 19, 26

Hayford, J(oseph) E(phraim) Casely
See Casely-Hayford, J(oseph) E(phraim)

Hayman, Ronald 1932- . . . . **CLC 44**
See also CA 25-28R; CANR 18

Haywood, Eliza (Fowler)
1693(?)-1756 . . . . **LC 1**

Hazlitt, William 1778-1830 . . . . . . **NCLC 29**
See also DLB 110

Hazzard, Shirley 1931- . . . . **CLC 18**
See also CA 9-12R; CANR 4; DLBY 82;
MTCW

Head, Bessie 1937-1986 . . . . **CLC 25, 67**
See also BLC 2; BW; CA 29-32R; 119;
CANR 25; DLB 117; MTCW

Headon, (Nicky) Topper 1956(?)- . . . **CLC 30**
See also The Clash

Heaney, Seamus (Justin)
1939- . . . . **CLC 5, 7, 14, 25, 37**
See also CA 85-88; CANR 25;
CDBLB 1960 to Present; DLB 40;
MTCW

Hearn, (Patricio) Lafcadio (Tessima Carlos)
1850-1904 . . . . **TCLC 9**
See also CA 105; DLB 12, 78

Hearne, Vicki 1946- . . . . **CLC 56**

Hearon, Shelby 1931- . . . . **CLC 63**
See also AITN 2; CA 25-28R; CANR 18

Heat-Moon, William Least . . . . **CLC 29**
See also Trogdon, William (Lewis)
See also AAYA 9

Hebert, Anne 1916- . . . . **CLC 4, 13, 29**
See also CA 85-88; DLB 68; MTCW

Hecht, Anthony (Evan)
1923- . . . . **CLC 8, 13, 19**
See also CA 9-12R; CANR 6; DLB 5

Hecht, Ben 1894-1964 . . . . **CLC 8**
See also CA 85-88; DLB 7, 9, 25, 26, 28, 86

Hedayat, Sadeq 1903-1951 . . . . **TCLC 21**
See also CA 120

Heidegger, Martin 1889-1976 . . . . . . **CLC 24**
See also CA 81-84; 65-68; CANR 34;
MTCW

Heidenstam, (Carl Gustaf) Verner von
1859-1940 . . . . **TCLC 5**
See also CA 104

Heifner, Jack 1946- . . . . **CLC 11**
See also CA 105

Heijermans, Herman 1864-1924 . . . **TCLC 24**
See also CA 123

Heilbrun, Carolyn G(old) 1926- . . . . . **CLC 25**
See also CA 45-48; CANR 1, 28

Heine, Heinrich 1797-1856 . . . . **NCLC 4**
See also DLB 90

Heinemann, Larry (Curtiss) 1944- . . **CLC 50**
See also CA 110; CANR 31; DLBD 9

Heiney, Donald (William) 1921- . . . . . **CLC 9**
See also CA 1-4R; CANR 3

Heinlein, Robert A(nson)
1907-1988 . . . . . . **CLC 1, 3, 8, 14, 26, 55**
See also CA 1-4R; 125; CANR 1, 20;
DLB 8; MAICYA; MTCW; SATA 9, 56,
69

Helforth, John
See Doolittle, Hilda

Hellenhofferu, Vojtech Kapristian z
See Hasek, Jaroslav (Matej Frantisek)

Heller, Joseph
1923- . . . . **CLC 1, 3, 5, 8, 11, 36, 63**
See also AITN 1; CA 5-8R; CABS 1;
CANR 8; DLB 2, 28; DLBY 80; MTCW;
WLC

Hellman, Lillian (Florence)
1906-1984 . . . . . **CLC 2, 4, 8, 14, 18, 34,
44, 52; DC 1**
See also AITN 1, 2; CA 13-16R; 112;
CANR 33; DLB 7; DLBY 84; MTCW

Helprin, Mark 1947- . . . . . **CLC 7, 10, 22, 32**
See also CA 81-84; DLBY 85; MTCW

Helyar, Jane Penelope Josephine 1933-
See Poole, Josephine
See also CA 21-24R; CANR 10, 26

Hemans, Felicia 1793-1835 . . . . . . **NCLC 29**
See also DLB 96

Hemingway, Ernest (Miller)
1899-1961 . . . **CLC 1, 3, 6, 8, 10, 13, 19,
30, 34, 39, 41, 44, 50, 61; SSC 1**
See also CA 77-80; CANR 34;
CDALB 1917-1929; DLB 4, 9, 102;
DLBD 1; DLBY 81, 87; MTCW; WLC

Hempel, Amy 1951- . . . . **CLC 39**
See also CA 118; 137

Henderson, F. C.
See Mencken, H(enry) L(ouis)

Henderson, Sylvia
See Ashton-Warner, Sylvia (Constance)

Henley, Beth . . . . **CLC 23**
See also Henley, Elizabeth Becker
See also CABS 3; DLBY 86

Henley, Elizabeth Becker 1952-
See Henley, Beth
See also CA 107; CANR 32; MTCW

Henley, William Ernest
1849-1903 . . . . **TCLC 8**
See also CA 105; DLB 19

Hennissart, Martha
See Lathen, Emma
See also CA 85-88

Henry, O.............. **TCLC 1, 19; SSC 5**
See also Porter, William Sydney
See also WLC

Henryson, Robert 1430(?)-1506(?).... **LC 20**

Henry VIII 1491-1547............ **LC 10**

Henschke, Alfred
See Klabund

Hentoff, Nat(han Irving) 1925-..... **CLC 26**
See also AAYA 4; CA 1-4R; CAAS 6;
CANR 5, 25; CLR 1; MAICYA;
SATA 27, 42, 69

Heppenstall, (John) Rayner
1911-1981 .... **CLC 10**
See also CA 1-4R; 103; CANR 29

Herbert, Frank (Patrick)
1920-1986 .... **CLC 12, 23, 35, 44**
See also CA 53-56; 118; CANR 5; DLB 8;
MTCW; SATA 9, 37, 47

Herbert, George 1593-1633......... **PC 4**
See also CDBLB Before 1660

Herbert, Zbigniew 1924- .... **CLC 9, 43**
See also CA 89-92; CANR 36; MTCW

Herbst, Josephine (Frey)
1897-1969 .... **CLC 34**
See also CA 5-8R; 25-28R; DLB 9

Hergesheimer, Joseph
1880-1954 .... **TCLC 11**
See also CA 109; DLB 102, 9

Herlihy, James Leo 1927-......... **CLC 6**
See also CA 1-4R; CANR 2

Hermogenes fl. c. 175-.......... **CMLC 6**

Hernandez, Jose 1834-1886...... **NCLC 17**

Herrick, Robert 1591-1674 .... **LC 13**

Herriot, James.................... **CLC 12**
See also Wight, James Alfred
See also AAYA 1

Herrmann, Dorothy 1941-........ **CLC 44**
See also CA 107

Herrmann, Taffy
See Herrmann, Dorothy

Hersey, John (Richard)
1914- .... **CLC 1, 2, 7, 9, 40**
See also CA 17-20R; CANR 33; DLB 6;
MTCW; SATA 25

Herzen, Aleksandr Ivanovich
1812-1870 .... **NCLC 10**

Herzl, Theodor 1860-1904....... **TCLC 36**

Herzog, Werner 1942-............ **CLC 16**
See also CA 89-92

Hesiod c. 8th cent. B.C.-......... **CMLC 5**

Hesse, Hermann
1877-1962 ... **CLC 1, 2, 3, 6, 11, 17, 25,
69; SSC 9**
See also CA 17-18; CAP 2; DLB 66;
MTCW; SATA 50; WLC

Hewes, Cady
See De Voto, Bernard (Augustine)

Heyen, William 1940- .... **CLC 13, 18**
See also CA 33-36R; CAAS 9; DLB 5

Heyerdahl, Thor 1914-............ **CLC 26**
See also CA 5-8R; CANR 5, 22; MTCW;
SATA 2, 52

Heym, Georg (Theodor Franz Arthur)
1887-1912 .... **TCLC 9**
See also CA 106

Heym, Stefan 1913-.............. **CLC 41**
See also CA 9-12R; CANR 4; DLB 69

Heyse, Paul (Johann Ludwig von)
1830-1914 .... **TCLC 8**
See also CA 104

Hibbert, Eleanor Burford 1906-..... **CLC 7**
See also BEST 90:4; CA 17-20R; CANR 9,
28; SATA 2

Higgins, George V(incent)
1939-............... **CLC 4, 7, 10, 18**
See also CA 77-80; CAAS 5; CANR 17;
DLB 2; DLBY 81; MTCW

Higginson, Thomas Wentworth
1823-1911 .... **TCLC 36**
See also DLB 1, 64

Highet, Helen
See MacInnes, Helen (Clark)

Highsmith, (Mary) Patricia
1921-............**CLC 2, 4, 14, 42**
See also CA 1-4R; CANR 1, 20; MTCW

Highwater, Jamake (Mamake)
1942(?)-..................... **CLC 12**
See also AAYA 7; CA 65-68; CAAS 7;
CANR 10, 34; CLR 17; DLB 52;
DLBY 85; MAICYA; SATA 30, 32, 69

Hijuelos, Oscar 1951- .... **CLC 65**
See also BEST 90:1; CA 123; HW

Hikmet, Nazim 1902-1963........ **CLC 40**
See also CA 93-96

Hildesheimer, Wolfgang
1916-1991 .... **CLC 49**
See also CA 101; 135; DLB 69

Hill, Geoffrey (William)
1932-............... **CLC 5, 8, 18, 45**
See also CA 81-84; CANR 21;
CDBLB 1960 to Present; DLB 40;
MTCW

Hill, George Roy 1921- .... **CLC 26**
See also CA 110; 122

Hill, Susan (Elizabeth) 1942- .... **CLC 4**
See also CA 33-36R; CANR 29; DLB 14;
MTCW

Hillerman, Tony 1925-........... **CLC 62**
See also AAYA 6; BEST 89:1; CA 29-32R;
CANR 21; SATA 6

Hilliard, Noel (Harvey) 1929-...... **CLC 15**
See also CA 9-12R; CANR 7

Hillis, Rick 1956-................ **CLC 66**
See also CA 134

Hilton, James 1900-1954........ **TCLC 21**
See also CA 108; DLB 34, 77; SATA 34

Himes, Chester (Bomar)
1909-1984 .... **CLC 2, 4, 7, 18, 58**
See also BLC 2; BW; CA 25-28R; 114;
CANR 22; DLB 2, 76; MTCW

Hinde, Thomas .... **CLC 6, 11**
See also Chitty, Thomas Willes

Hindin, Nathan
See Bloch, Robert (Albert)

Hine, (William) Daryl 1936-....... **CLC 15**
See also CA 1-4R; CAAS 15; CANR 1, 20;
DLB 60

Hinkson, Katharine Tynan
See Tynan, Katharine

Hinton, S(usan) E(loise) 1950- ..... **CLC 30**
See also AAYA 2; CA 81-84; CANR 32;
CLR 3, 23; MAICYA; MTCW;
SATA 19, 58

Hippius, Zinaida .... **TCLC 9**
See also Gippius, Zinaida (Nikolayevna)

Hiraoka, Kimitake 1925-1970
See Mishima, Yukio
See also CA 97-100; 29-32R; MTCW

Hirsch, Edward 1950- .... **CLC 31, 50**
See also CA 104; CANR 20; DLB 120

Hitchcock, Alfred (Joseph)
1899-1980 .... **CLC 16**
See also CA 97-100; SATA 24, 27

Hoagland, Edward 1932-......... **CLC 28**
See also CA 1-4R; CANR 2, 31; DLB 6;
SATA 51

Hoban, Russell (Conwell) 1925- .. **CLC 7, 25**
See also CA 5-8R; CANR 23, 37; CLR 3;
DLB 52; MAICYA; MTCW; SATA 1, 40

Hobbs, Perry
See Blackmur, R(ichard) P(almer)

Hobson, Laura Z(ametkin)
1900-1986 .... **CLC 7, 25**
See also CA 17-20R; 118; DLB 28;
SATA 52

Hochhuth, Rolf 1931-........ **CLC 4, 11, 18**
See also CA 5-8R; CANR 33; MTCW

Hochman, Sandra 1936-......... **CLC 3, 8**
See also CA 5-8R; DLB 5

Hochwaelder, Fritz 1911-1986...... **CLC 36**
See also Hochwalder, Fritz
See also CA 29-32R; 120; MTCW

Hochwalder, Fritz................. **CLC 36**
See also Hochwaelder, Fritz

Hocking, Mary (Eunice) 1921-..... **CLC 13**
See also CA 101; CANR 18

Hodgins, Jack 1938-............. **CLC 23**
See also CA 93-96; DLB 60

Hodgson, William Hope
1877(?)-1918 .... **TCLC 13**
See also CA 111; DLB 70

Hoffman, Alice 1952-............ **CLC 51**
See also CA 77-80; CANR 34; MTCW

Hoffman, Daniel (Gerard)
1923- .... **CLC 6, 13, 23**
See also CA 1-4R; CANR 4; DLB 5

Hoffman, Stanley 1944-........... **CLC 5**
See also CA 77-80

Hoffman, William M(oses) 1939-... **CLC 40**
See also CA 57-60; CANR 11

Hoffmann, E(rnst) T(heodor) A(madeus)
1776-1822 .... **NCLC 2**
See also DLB 90; SATA 27

Hofmann, Gert 1931-............ **CLC 54**
See also CA 128

Hofmannsthal, Hugo von
1874-1929 .... **TCLC 11**
See also CA 106; DLB 81, 118

Hogarth, Charles
See Creasey, John

Hogg, James 1770-1835 . . . . **NCLC 4**
See also DLB 93, 116

Holbach, Paul Henri Thiry Baron
1723-1789 . . . . **LC 14**

Holberg, Ludvig 1684-1754 . . . . **LC 6**

Holden, Ursula 1921- . . . . **CLC 18**
See also CA 101; CAAS 8; CANR 22

Holderlin, (Johann Christian) Friedrich
1770-1843 . . . . **NCLC 16; PC 4**

Holdstock, Robert
See Holdstock, Robert P.

Holdstock, Robert P. 1948- . . . . **CLC 39**
See also CA 131

Holland, Isabelle 1920- . . . . **CLC 21**
See also CA 21-24R; CANR 10, 25;
MAICYA; SATA 8, 70

Holland, Marcus
See Caldwell, (Janet Miriam) Taylor
(Holland)

Hollander, John 1929- . . . . . . **CLC 2, 5, 8, 14**
See also CA 1-4R; CANR 1; DLB 5;
SATA 13

Hollander, Paul
See Silverberg, Robert

Holleran, Andrew 1943(?)- . . . . **CLC 38**

Hollinghurst, Alan 1954- . . . . **CLC 55**
See also CA 114

Hollis, Jim
See Summers, Hollis (Spurgeon Jr.)

Holmes, John
See Souster, (Holmes) Raymond

Holmes, John Clellon 1926-1988 . . . . **CLC 56**
See also CA 9-12R; 125; CANR 4; DLB 16

Holmes, Oliver Wendell
1809-1894 . . . . **NCLC 14**
See also CDALB 1640-1865; DLB 1;
SATA 34

Holmes, Raymond
See Souster, (Holmes) Raymond

Holt, Victoria
See Hibbert, Eleanor Burford

Holub, Miroslav 1923- . . . . **CLC 4**
See also CA 21-24R; CANR 10

Homer c. 8th cent. B.C.- . . . . **CMLC 1**

Honig, Edwin 1919- . . . . **CLC 33**
See also CA 5-8R; CAAS 8; CANR 4;
DLB 5

Hood, Hugh (John Blagdon)
1928- . . . . **CLC 15, 28**
See also CA 49-52; CANR 1, 33; DLB 53

Hood, Thomas 1799-1845 . . . . **NCLC 16**
See also DLB 96

Hooker, (Peter) Jeremy 1941- . . . . . . **CLC 43**
See also CA 77-80; CANR 22; DLB 40

Hope, A(lec) D(erwent) 1907- . . . . **CLC 3, 51**
See also CA 21-24R; CANR 33; MTCW

Hope, Brian
See Creasey, John

Hope, Christopher (David Tully)
1944- . . . . **CLC 52**
See also CA 106; SATA 62

Hopkins, Gerard Manley
1844-1889 . . . . **NCLC 17**
See also CDBLB 1890-1914; DLB 35, 57;
WLC

Hopkins, John (Richard) 1931- . . . . . . **CLC 4**
See also CA 85-88

Hopkins, Pauline Elizabeth
1859-1930 . . . . **TCLC 28**
See also BLC 2; DLB 50

Horatio
See Proust,
(Valentin-Louis-George-Eugene-)Marcel

Horgan, Paul 1903- . . . . **CLC 9, 53**
See also CA 13-16R; CANR 9, 35;
DLB 102; DLBY 85; MTCW; SATA 13

Horn, Peter
See Kuttner, Henry

Horovitz, Israel 1939- . . . . **CLC 56**
See also CA 33-36R; DLB 7

Horvath, Odon von
See Horvath, Oedoen von
See also DLB 85

Horvath, Oedoen von 1901-1938 . . . **TCLC 45**
See also Horvath, Odon von
See also CA 118

Horwitz, Julius 1920-1986 . . . . **CLC 14**
See also CA 9-12R; 119; CANR 12

Hospital, Janette Turner 1942- . . . . . **CLC 42**
See also CA 108

Hostos, E. M. de
See Hostos (y Bonilla), Eugenio Maria de

Hostos, Eugenio M. de
See Hostos (y Bonilla), Eugenio Maria de

Hostos, Eugenio Maria
See Hostos (y Bonilla), Eugenio Maria de

Hostos (y Bonilla), Eugenio Maria de
1839-1903 . . . . **TCLC 24**
See also CA 123; 131; HW

Houdini
See Lovecraft, H(oward) P(hillips)

Hougan, Carolyn 19(?)- . . . . **CLC 34**

Household, Geoffrey (Edward West)
1900-1988 . . . . **CLC 11**
See also CA 77-80; 126; DLB 87; SATA 14,
59

Housman, A(lfred) E(dward)
1859-1936 . . . . **TCLC 1, 10; PC 2**
See also CA 104; 125; DLB 19; MTCW

Housman, Laurence 1865-1959 . . . . . **TCLC 7**
See also CA 106; DLB 10; SATA 25

Howard, Elizabeth Jane 1923- . . . **CLC 7, 29**
See also CA 5-8R; CANR 8

Howard, Maureen 1930- . . . . . **CLC 5, 14, 46**
See also CA 53-56; CANR 31; DLBY 83;
MTCW

Howard, Richard 1929- . . . . . . **CLC 7, 10, 47**
See also AITN 1; CA 85-88; CANR 25;
DLB 5

Howard, Robert Ervin 1906-1936 . . . **TCLC 8**
See also CA 105

Howard, Warren F.
See Pohl, Frederik

Howe, Fanny 1940- . . . . **CLC 47**
See also CA 117; SATA 52

Howe, Julia Ward 1819-1910 . . . . . **TCLC 21**
See also CA 117; DLB 1

Howe, Susan 1937- . . . . **CLC 72**
See also DLB 120

Howe, Tina 1937- . . . . **CLC 48**
See also CA 109

Howell, James 1594(?)-1666 . . . . **LC 13**

Howells, W. D.
See Howells, William Dean

Howells, William D.
See Howells, William Dean

Howells, William Dean
1837-1920 . . . . **TCLC 41, 7, 17**
See also CA 104; 134; CDALB 1865-1917;
DLB 12, 64, 74, 79

Howes, Barbara 1914- . . . . **CLC 15**
See also CA 9-12R; CAAS 3; SATA 5

Hrabal, Bohumil 1914- . . . . **CLC 13, 67**
See also CA 106; CAAS 12

Hsun, Lu . . . . **TCLC 3**
See also Shu-Jen, Chou

Hubbard, L(afayette) Ron(ald)
1911-1986 . . . . **CLC 43**
See also CA 77-80; 118; CANR 22

Huch, Ricarda (Octavia)
1864-1947 . . . . **TCLC 13**
See also CA 111; DLB 66

Huddle, David 1942- . . . . **CLC 49**
See also CA 57-60

Hudson, Jeffery
See Crichton, (John) Michael

Hudson, W(illiam) H(enry)
1841-1922 . . . . **TCLC 29**
See also CA 115; DLB 98; SATA 35

Hueffer, Ford Madox
See Ford, Ford Madox

Hughart, Barry . . . . **CLC 39**
See also CA 137

Hughes, Colin
See Creasey, John

Hughes, David (John) 1930- . . . . **CLC 48**
See also CA 116; 129; DLB 14

Hughes, (James) Langston
1902-1967 . . . . **CLC 1, 5, 10, 15, 35, 44;
PC 1; SSC 6**
See also BLC 2; BW; CA 1-4R; 25-28R;
CANR 1, 34; CDALB 1929-1941;
CLR 4, 7, 48, 51, 86; MAICYA;
MTCW; SATA 4, 33; WLC

Hughes, Richard (Arthur Warren)
1900-1976 . . . . **CLC 1, 11**
See also CA 5-8R; 65-68; CANR 4;
DLB 15; MTCW; SATA 8, 25

Hughes, Ted 1930- . . . . . **CLC 2, 4, 9, 14, 37**
See also CA 1-4R; CANR 1, 33; CLR 3;
DLB 40; MAICYA; MTCW; SATA 27,
49

Hugo, Richard F(ranklin)
1923-1982 . . . . **CLC 6, 18, 32**
See also CA 49-52; 108; CANR 3; DLB 5

Hugo, Victor (Marie)
1802-1885 . . . . **NCLC 3, 10, 21**
See also DLB 119; SATA 47; WLC

James, Daniel (Lewis)   1911-1988
See Santiago, Danny
See also CA 125

James, Dynely
See Mayne, William (James Carter)

James, Henry
    1843-1916 .... **TCLC 2, 11, 24, 40, 47;**
                                          SSC 8
See also CA 104; 132; CDALB 1865-1917;
DLB 12, 71, 74; MTCW; WLC

James, Montague (Rhodes)
    1862-1936 .... **TCLC 6**
See also CA 104

James, P. D. .... **CLC 18, 46**
See also White, Phyllis Dorothy James
See also BEST 90:2; CDBLB 1960 to
Present; DLB 87

James, Philip
See Moorcock, Michael (John)

James, William   1842-1910..... **TCLC 15, 32**
See also CA 109

James I   1394-1437 .... **LC 20**

Jami, Nur al-Din 'Abd al-Rahman
    1414-1492 .... **LC 9**

Jandl, Ernst   1925- .... **CLC 34**

Janowitz, Tama   1957- .... **CLC 43**
See also CA 106

Jarrell, Randall
    1914-1965 .... **CLC 1, 2, 6, 9, 13, 49**
See also CA 5-8R; 25-28R; CABS 2;
CANR 6, 34; CDALB 1941-1968; CLR 6;
DLB 48, 52; MAICYA; MTCW; SATA 7

Jarry, Alfred   1873-1907........ **TCLC 2, 14**
See also CA 104

Jarvis, E. K.
See Bloch, Robert (Albert); Ellison, Harlan;
Silverberg, Robert

Jeake, Samuel Jr.
See Aiken, Conrad (Potter)

Jean Paul   1763-1825 .... **NCLC 7**

Jeffers, (John) Robinson
    1887-1962 .... **CLC 2, 3, 11, 15, 54**
See also CA 85-88; CANR 35;
CDALB 1917-1929; DLB 45; MTCW;
WLC

Jefferson, Janet
See Mencken, H(enry) L(ouis)

Jefferson, Thomas   1743-1826 .... **NCLC 11**
See also CDALB 1640-1865; DLB 31

Jeffrey, Francis   1773-1850....... **NCLC 33**
See also DLB 107

Jelakowitch, Ivan
See Heijermans, Herman

Jellicoe, (Patricia) Ann   1927- ...... **CLC 27**
See also CA 85-88; DLB 13

Jen, Gish .... **CLC 70**
See also Jen, Lillian

Jen, Lillian   1956(?)-
See Jen, Gish
See also CA 135

Jenkins, (John) Robin   1912- .... **CLC 52**
See also CA 1-4R; CANR 1; DLB 14

Jennings, Elizabeth (Joan)
    1926- .... **CLC 5, 14**
See also CA 61-64; CAAS 5; CANR 8, 39;
DLB 27; MTCW; SATA 66

Jennings, Waylon   1937-.......... **CLC 21**

Jensen, Johannes V.   1873-1950.... **TCLC 41**

Jensen, Laura (Linnea)   1948- ...... **CLC 37**
See also CA 103

Jerome, Jerome K(lapka)
    1859-1927 .... **TCLC 23**
See also CA 119; DLB 10, 34

Jerrold, Douglas William
    1803-1857 .... **NCLC 2**

Jewett, (Theodora) Sarah Orne
    1849-1909 .... **TCLC 1, 22; SSC 6**
See also CA 108; 127; DLB 12, 74;
SATA 15

Jewsbury, Geraldine (Endsor)
    1812-1880 .... **NCLC 22**
See also DLB 21

Jhabvala, Ruth Prawer
    1927- .... **CLC 4, 8, 29**
See also CA 1-4R; CANR 2, 29; MTCW

Jiles, Paulette   1943-........... **CLC 13, 58**
See also CA 101

Jimenez (Mantecon), Juan Ramon
    1881-1958 .... **TCLC 4**
See also CA 104; 131; HW; MTCW

Jimenez, Ramon
See Jimenez (Mantecon), Juan Ramon

Jimenez Mantecon, Juan
See Jimenez (Mantecon), Juan Ramon

Joel, Billy .... **CLC 26**
See also Joel, William Martin

Joel, William Martin   1949-
See Joel, Billy
See also CA 108

John of the Cross, St.   1542-1591 .... **LC 18**

Johnson, B(ryan) S(tanley William)
    1933-1973 .... **CLC 6, 9**
See also CA 9-12R; 53-56; CANR 9;
DLB 14, 40

Johnson, Charles (Richard)
    1948- .... **CLC 7, 51, 65**
See also BLC 2; BW; CA 116; DLB 33

Johnson, Denis   1949-........... **CLC 52**
See also CA 117; 121; DLB 120

Johnson, Diane (Lain)
    1934- .... **CLC 5, 13, 48**
See also CA 41-44R; CANR 17; DLBY 80;
MTCW

Johnson, Eyvind (Olof Verner)
    1900-1976 .... **CLC 14**
See also CA 73-76; 69-72; CANR 34

Johnson, J. R.
See James, C(yril) L(ionel) R(obert)

Johnson, James Weldon
    1871-1938 .... **TCLC 3, 19**
See also BLC 2; BW; CA 104; 125;
CDALB 1917-1929; DLB 51; MTCW;
SATA 31

Johnson, Joyce   1935-............ **CLC 58**
See also CA 125; 129

Johnson, Lionel (Pigot)
    1867-1902 .... **TCLC 19**
See also CA 117; DLB 19

Johnson, Mel
See Malzberg, Barry N(athaniel)

Johnson, Pamela Hansford
    1912-1981 .... **CLC 1, 7, 27**
See also CA 1-4R; 104; CANR 2, 28;
DLB 15; MTCW

Johnson, Samuel   1709-1784........ **LC 15**
See also CDBLB 1660-1789; DLB 39, 95,
104; WLC

Johnson, Uwe
    1934-1984 .... **CLC 5, 10, 15, 40**
See also CA 1-4R; 112; CANR 1, 39;
DLB 75; MTCW

Johnston, George (Benson)   1913- ... **CLC 51**
See also CA 1-4R; CANR 5, 20; DLB 88

Johnston, Jennifer   1930-.......... **CLC 7**
See also CA 85-88; DLB 14

Jolley, (Monica) Elizabeth   1923- ... **CLC 46**
See also CA 127; CAAS 13

Jones, Arthur Llewellyn   1863-1947
See Machen, Arthur
See also CA 104

Jones, D(ouglas) G(ordon)   1929-.... **CLC 10**
See also CA 29-32R; CANR 13; DLB 53

Jones, David (Michael)
    1895-1974 .... **CLC 2, 4, 7, 13, 42**
See also CA 9-12R; 53-56; CANR 28;
CDBLB 1945-1960; DLB 20, 100; MTCW

Jones, David Robert   1947-
See Bowie, David
See also CA 103

Jones, Diana Wynne   1934- .... **CLC 26**
See also CA 49-52; CANR 4, 26; CLR 23;
MAICYA; SAAS 7; SATA 9, 70

Jones, Gayl   1949-............... **CLC 6, 9**
See also BLC 2; BW; CA 77-80; CANR 27;
DLB 33; MTCW

Jones, James   1921-1977.... **CLC 1, 3, 10, 39**
See also AITN 1, 2; CA 1-4R; 69-72;
CANR 6; DLB 2; MTCW

Jones, John J.
See Lovecraft, H(oward) P(hillips)

Jones, LeRoi .... **CLC 1, 2, 3, 5, 10, 14**
See also Baraka, Amiri

Jones, Louis B. .... **CLC 65**

Jones, Madison (Percy Jr.)   1925-.... **CLC 4**
See also CA 13-16R; CAAS 11; CANR 7

Jones, Mervyn   1922- .... **CLC 10, 52**
See also CA 45-48; CAAS 5; CANR 1;
MTCW

Jones, Mick   1956(?)- .... **CLC 30**
See also The Clash

Jones, Nettie (Pearl)   1941- .... **CLC 34**
See also CA 137

Jones, Preston   1936-1979 .... **CLC 10**
See also CA 73-76; 89-92; DLB 7

Jones, Robert F(rancis)   1934-....... **CLC 7**
See also CA 49-52; CANR 2

Jones, Rod   1953- .... **CLC 50**
See also CA 128

Jones, Terence Graham Parry
 1942- .... CLC 21
 See also Jones, Terry; Monty Python
 See also CA 112; 116; CANR 35; SATA 51

Jones, Terry
 See Jones, Terence Graham Parry
 See also SATA 67

Jong, Erica 1942- .... CLC 4, 6, 8, 18
 See also AITN 1; BEST 90:2; CA 73-76;
 CANR 26; DLB 2, 5, 28; MTCW

Jonson, Ben(jamin) 1572(?)-1637..... LC 6
 See also CDBLB Before 1660; DLB 62, 121;
 WLC

Jordan, June 1936- .... CLC 5, 11, 23
 See also AAYA 2; BW; CA 33-36R;
 CANR 25; CLR 10; DLB 38; MAICYA;
 MTCW; SATA 4

Jordan, Pat(rick M.) 1941- .... CLC 37
 See also CA 33-36R

Jorgensen, Ivar
 See Ellison, Harlan

Jorgenson, Ivar
 See Silverberg, Robert

Josipovici, Gabriel 1940- .... CLC 6, 43
 See also CA 37-40R; CAAS 8; DLB 14

Joubert, Joseph 1754-1824 .... NCLC 9

Jouve, Pierre Jean 1887-1976..... CLC 47
 See also CA 65-68

Joyce, James (Augustine Aloysius)
 1882-1941 ...... TCLC 3, 8, 16, 35; SSC 3
 See also CA 104; 126; CDBLB 1914-1945;
 DLB 10, 19, 36; MTCW; WLC

Jozsef, Attila 1905-1937......... TCLC 22
 See also CA 116

Juana Ines de la Cruz 1651(?)-1695 ... LC 5

Judd, Cyril
 See Kornbluth, C(yril) M.; Pohl, Frederik

Julian of Norwich 1342(?)-1416(?) .... LC 6

Just, Ward (Swift) 1935- .... CLC 4, 27
 See also CA 25-28R; CANR 32

Justice, Donald (Rodney) 1925- .. CLC 6, 19
 See also CA 5-8R; CANR 26; DLBY 83

Juvenal c. 55-c. 127 .... CMLC 8

Juvenis
 See Bourne, Randolph S(illiman)

Kacew, Romain 1914-1980
 See Gary, Romain
 See also CA 108; 102

Kadare, Ismail 1936- .... CLC 52

Kadohata, Cynthia................. CLC 59

Kafka, Franz
 1883-1924 ...... TCLC 2, 6, 13, 29, 47;
                                        SSC 5
 See also CA 105; 126; DLB 81; MTCW;
 WLC

Kahn, Roger 1927- .... CLC 30
 See also CA 25-28R; SATA 37

Kain, Saul
 See Sassoon, Siegfried (Lorraine)

Kaiser, Georg 1878-1945 .... TCLC 9
 See also CA 106

Kaletski, Alexander 1946- .... CLC 39
 See also CA 118

Kalidasa fl. c. 400- .... CMLC 9

Kallman, Chester (Simon)
 1921-1975 .... CLC 2
 See also CA 45-48; 53-56; CANR 3

Kaminsky, Melvin 1926-
 See Brooks, Mel
 See also CA 65-68; CANR 16

Kaminsky, Stuart M(elvin) 1934- ... CLC 59
 See also CA 73-76; CANR 29

Kane, Paul
 See Simon, Paul

Kane, Wilson
 See Bloch, Robert (Albert)

Kanin, Garson 1912-.............. CLC 22
 See also AITN 1; CA 5-8R; CANR 7;
 DLB 7

Kaniuk, Yoram 1930-............. CLC 19
 See also CA 134

Kant, Immanuel 1724-1804 ...... NCLC 27
 See also DLB 94

Kantor, MacKinlay 1904-1977 ...... CLC 7
 See also CA 61-64; 73-76; DLB 9, 102

Kaplan, David Michael 1946- ...... CLC 50

Kaplan, James 1951- .... CLC 59
 See also CA 135

Karageorge, Michael
 See Anderson, Poul (William)

Karamzin, Nikolai Mikhailovich
 1766-1826 .... NCLC 3

Karapanou, Margarita 1946-....... CLC 13
 See also CA 101

Karinthy, Frigyes 1887-1938...... TCLC 47

Karl, Frederick R(obert) 1927-..... CLC 34
 See also CA 5-8R; CANR 3

Kastel, Warren
 See Silverberg, Robert

Kataev, Evgeny Petrovich 1903-1942
 See Petrov, Evgeny
 See also CA 120

Kataphusin
 See Ruskin, John

Katz, Steve 1935-................ CLC 47
 See also CA 25-28R; CAAS 14; CANR 12;
 DLBY 83

Kauffman, Janet 1945-............ CLC 42
 See also CA 117; DLBY 86

Kaufman, Bob (Garnell)
 1925-1986 .... CLC 49
 See also BW; CA 41-44R; 118; CANR 22;
 DLB 16, 41

Kaufman, George S. 1889-1961..... CLC 38
 See also CA 108; 93-96; DLB 7

Kaufman, Sue .... CLC 3, 8
 See also Barondess, Sue K(aufman)

Kavafis, Konstantinos Petrou 1863-1933
 See Cavafy, C(onstantine) P(eter)
 See also CA 104

Kavan, Anna 1901-1968........ CLC 5, 13
 See also CA 5-8R; CANR 6; MTCW

Kavanagh, Dan
 See Barnes, Julian

Kavanagh, Patrick (Joseph)
 1904-1967 .... CLC 22
 See also CA 123; 25-28R; DLB 15, 20;
 MTCW

Kawabata, Yasunari
 1899-1972 .... CLC 2, 5, 9, 18
 See also CA 93-96; 33-36R

Kaye, M(ary) M(argaret) 1909-..... CLC 28
 See also CA 89-92; CANR 24; MTCW;
 SATA 62

Kaye, Mollie
 See Kaye, M(ary) M(argaret)

Kaye-Smith, Sheila 1887-1956..... TCLC 20
 See also CA 118; DLB 36

Kaymor, Patrice Maguilene
 See Senghor, Leopold Sedar

Kazan, Elia 1909-.......... CLC 6, 16, 63
 See also CA 21-24R; CANR 32

Kazantzakis, Nikos
 1883(?)-1957 .... TCLC 2, 5, 33
 See also CA 105; 132; MTCW

Kazin, Alfred 1915- .... CLC 34, 38
 See also CA 1-4R; CAAS 7; CANR 1;
 DLB 67

Keane, Mary Nesta (Skrine) 1904-
 See Keane, Molly
 See also CA 108; 114

Keane, Molly..................... CLC 31
 See also Keane, Mary Nesta (Skrine)

Keates, Jonathan 19(?)-........... CLC 34

Keaton, Buster 1895-1966 .... CLC 20

Keats, John 1795-1821...... NCLC 8; PC 1
 See also CDBLB 1789-1832; DLB 96, 110;
 WLC

Keene, Donald 1922- .... CLC 34
 See also CA 1-4R; CANR 5

Keillor, Garrison .... CLC 40
 See also Keillor, Gary (Edward)
 See also AAYA 2; BEST 89:3; DLBY 87;
 SATA 58

Keillor, Gary (Edward) 1942-
 See Keillor, Garrison
 See also CA 111; 117; CANR 36; MTCW

Keith, Michael
 See Hubbard, L(afayette) Ron(ald)

Kell, Joseph
 See Wilson, John (Anthony) Burgess

Keller, Gottfried 1819-1890....... NCLC 2

Kellerman, Jonathan 1949- .... CLC 44
 See also BEST 90:1; CA 106; CANR 29

Kelley, William Melvin 1937-...... CLC 22
 See also BW; CA 77-80; CANR 27; DLB 33

Kellogg, Marjorie 1922-............ CLC 2
 See also CA 81-84

Kellow, Kathleen
 See Hibbert, Eleanor Burford

Kelly, M(ilton) T(erry) 1947-....... CLC 55
 See also CA 97-100; CANR 19

Kelman, James 1946-............. CLC 58

Kemal, Yashar 1923- .... CLC 14, 29
 See also CA 89-92

Kemble, Fanny 1809-1893 .... NCLC 18
 See also DLB 32

Kemelman, Harry 1908-............ **CLC 2**
See also AITN 1; CA 9-12R; CANR 6;
DLB 28

Kempe, Margery 1373(?)-1440(?) ..... **LC 6**

Kempis, Thomas a 1380-1471 ...... **LC 11**

Kendall, Henry 1839-1882....... **NCLC 12**

Keneally, Thomas (Michael)
1935- ..... **CLC 5, 8, 10, 14, 19, 27, 43**
See also CA 85-88; CANR 10; MTCW

Kennedy, Adrienne (Lita) 1931- .... **CLC 66**
See also BLC 2; BW; CA 103; CABS 3;
CANR 26; DLB 38

Kennedy, John Pendleton
1795-1870 .... **NCLC 2**
See also DLB 3

Kennedy, Joseph Charles 1929-...... **CLC 8**
See also Kennedy, X. J.
See also CA 1-4R; CANR 4, 30; SATA 14

Kennedy, William 1928-... **CLC 6, 28, 34, 53**
See also AAYA 1; CA 85-88; CANR 14,
31; DLBY 85; MTCW; SATA 57

Kennedy, X. J.................... **CLC 42**
See also Kennedy, Joseph Charles
See also CAAS 9; CLR 27; DLB 5

Kent, Kelvin
See Kuttner, Henry

Kenton, Maxwell
See Southern, Terry

Kenyon, Robert O.
See Kuttner, Henry

Kerouac, Jack ..... **CLC 1, 2, 3, 5, 14, 29, 61**
See also Kerouac, Jean-Louis Lebris de
See also CDALB 1941-1968; DLB 2, 16;
DLBD 3

Kerouac, Jean-Louis Lebris de 1922-1969
See Kerouac, Jack
See also AITN 1; CA 5-8R; 25-28R;
CANR 26; MTCW; WLC

Kerr, Jean 1923-................. **CLC 22**
See also CA 5-8R; CANR 7

Kerr, M. E. .... **CLC 12, 35**
See also Meaker, Marijane (Agnes)
See also AAYA 2; SAAS 1

Kerr, Robert .... **CLC 55**

Kerrigan, (Thomas) Anthony
1918- .... **CLC 4, 6**
See also CA 49-52; CAAS 11; CANR 4

Kerry, Lois
See Duncan, Lois

Kesey, Ken (Elton)
1935-......... **CLC 1, 3, 6, 11, 46, 64**
See also CA 1-4R; CANR 22, 38;
CDALB 1968-1988; DLB 2, 16; MTCW;
SATA 66; WLC

Kesselring, Joseph (Otto)
1902-1967 .... **CLC 45**

Kessler, Jascha (Frederick) 1929-.... **CLC 4**
See also CA 17-20R; CANR 8

Kettelkamp, Larry (Dale) 1933- .... **CLC 12**
See also CA 29-32R; CANR 16; SAAS 3;
SATA 2

Kherdian, David 1931-........... **CLC 6, 9**
See also CA 21-24R; CAAS 2; CANR 39;
CLR 24; MAICYA; SATA 16

Khlebnikov, Velimir .... **TCLC 20**
See also Khlebnikov, Viktor Vladimirovich

Khlebnikov, Viktor Vladimirovich 1885-1922
See Khlebnikov, Velimir
See also CA 117

Khodasevich, Vladislav (Felitsianovich)
1886-1939 .... **TCLC 15**
See also CA 115

Kielland, Alexander Lange
1849-1906 .... **TCLC 5**
See also CA 104

Kiely, Benedict 1919-......... **CLC 23, 43**
See also CA 1-4R; CANR 2; DLB 15

Kienzle, William X(avier) 1928- .... **CLC 25**
See also CA 93-96; CAAS 1; CANR 9, 31;
MTCW

Kierkegaard, Soeren 1813-1855... **NCLC 34**

Kierkegaard, Soren 1813-1855.... **NCLC 34**

Killens, John Oliver 1916-1987..... **CLC 10**
See also BW; CA 77-80; 123; CAAS 2;
CANR 26; DLB 33

Killigrew, Anne 1660-1685.......... **LC 4**

Kim
See Simenon, Georges (Jacques Christian)

Kincaid, Jamaica 1949-........ **CLC 43, 68**
See also BLC 2; BW; CA 125

King, Francis (Henry) 1923-..... **CLC 8, 53**
See also CA 1-4R; CANR 1, 33; DLB 15;
MTCW

King, Stephen (Edwin)
1947-............. **CLC 12, 26, 37, 61**
See also AAYA 1; BEST 90:1; CA 61-64;
CANR 1, 30; DLBY 80; MTCW;
SATA 9, 55

King, Steve
See King, Stephen (Edwin)

Kingman, Lee.................... **CLC 17**
See also Natti, (Mary) Lee
See also SAAS 3; SATA 1, 67

Kingsley, Charles 1819-1875 ..... **NCLC 35**
See also DLB 21, 32; YABC 2

Kingsley, Sidney 1906-........... **CLC 44**
See also CA 85-88; DLB 7

Kingsolver, Barbara 1955-........ **CLC 55**
See also CA 129; 134

Kingston, Maxine (Ting Ting) Hong
1940- .... **CLC 12, 19, 58**
See also AAYA 8; CA 69-72; CANR 13,
38; DLBY 80; MTCW; SATA 53

Kinnell, Galway
1927-........... **CLC 1, 2, 3, 5, 13, 29**
See also CA 9-12R; CANR 10, 34; DLB 5;
DLBY 87; MTCW

Kinsella, Thomas 1928- .... **CLC 4, 19**
See also CA 17-20R; CANR 15; DLB 27;
MTCW

Kinsella, W(illiam) P(atrick)
1935-.................... **CLC 27, 43**
See also AAYA 7; CA 97-100; CAAS 7;
CANR 21, 35; MTCW

Kipling, (Joseph) Rudyard
1865-1936 .... **TCLC 8, 17; PC 3; SSC 5**
See also CA 105; 120; CANR 33;
CDBLB 1890-1914; DLB 19, 34;
MAICYA; MTCW; WLC; YABC 2

Kirkup, James 1918- .... **CLC 1**
See also CA 1-4R; CAAS 4; CANR 2;
DLB 27; SATA 12

Kirkwood, James 1930(?)-1989 ...... **CLC 9**
See also AITN 2; CA 1-4R; 128; CANR 6

Kis, Danilo 1935-1989 .... **CLC 57**
See also CA 109; 118; 129; MTCW

Kivi, Aleksis 1834-1872......... **NCLC 30**

Kizer, Carolyn (Ashley) 1925-... **CLC 15, 39**
See also CA 65-68; CAAS 5; CANR 24;
DLB 5

Klabund 1890-1928.............. **TCLC 44**
See also DLB 66

Klappert, Peter 1942-............. **CLC 57**
See also CA 33-36R; DLB 5

Klein, A(braham) M(oses)
1909-1972 .... **CLC 19**
See also CA 101; 37-40R; DLB 68

Klein, Norma 1938-1989 .... **CLC 30**
See also AAYA 2; CA 41-44R; 128;
CANR 15, 37; CLR 2, 19; MAICYA;
SAAS 1; SATA 7, 57

Klein, T(heodore) E(ibon) D(onald)
1947- .... **CLC 34**
See also CA 119

Kleist, Heinrich von 1777-1811.... **NCLC 2**
See also DLB 90

Klima, Ivan 1931-................ **CLC 56**
See also CA 25-28R; CANR 17

Klimentov, Andrei Platonovich 1899-1951
See Platonov, Andrei
See also CA 108

Klinger, Friedrich Maximilian von
1752-1831 .... **NCLC 1**
See also DLB 94

Klopstock, Friedrich Gottlieb
1724-1803 .... **NCLC 11**
See also DLB 97

Knebel, Fletcher 1911-............ **CLC 14**
See also AITN 1; CA 1-4R; CAAS 3;
CANR 1, 36; SATA 36

Knickerbocker, Diedrich
See Irving, Washington

Knight, Etheridge 1931-1991....... **CLC 40**
See also BLC 2; BW; CA 21-24R; 133;
CANR 23; DLB 41

Knight, Sarah Kemble 1666-1727 ..... **LC 7**
See also DLB 24

Knowles, John 1926- ...... **CLC 1, 4, 10, 26**
See also CA 17-20R; CDALB 1968-1988;
DLB 6; MTCW; SATA 8

Knox, Calvin M.
See Silverberg, Robert

Knye, Cassandra
See Disch, Thomas M(ichael)

Koch, C(hristopher) J(ohn) 1932- ... **CLC 42**
See also CA 127

Koch, Christopher
See Koch, C(hristopher) J(ohn)

Koch, Kenneth 1925- .... **CLC 5, 8, 44**
See also CA 1-4R; CANR 6, 36; DLB 5;
SATA 65

Kochanowski, Jan 1530-1584....... **LC 10**

Lancaster, Bruce 1896-1963........ **CLC 36**
See also CA 9-10; CAP 1; SATA 9

Landau, Mark Alexandrovich
See Aldanov, Mark (Alexandrovich)

Landau-Aldanov, Mark Alexandrovich
See Aldanov, Mark (Alexandrovich)

Landis, John 1950-.............. **CLC 26**
See also CA 112; 122

Landolfi, Tommaso 1908-1979... **CLC 11, 49**
See also CA 127; 117

Landon, Letitia Elizabeth
1802-1838 .... **NCLC 15**
See also DLB 96

Landor, Walter Savage
1775-1864 .... **NCLC 14**
See also DLB 93, 107

Landwirth, Heinz 1927-
See Lind, Jakov
See also CA 9-12R; CANR 7

Lane, Patrick 1939- .... **CLC 25**
See also CA 97-100; DLB 53

Lang, Andrew 1844-1912........ **TCLC 16**
See also CA 114; 137; DLB 98; MAICYA;
SATA 16

Lang, Fritz 1890-1976 .... **CLC 20**
See also CA 77-80; 69-72; CANR 30

Lange, John
See Crichton, (John) Michael

Langer, Elinor 1939- .... **CLC 34**
See also CA 121

Langland, William 1330(?)-1400(?)... **LC 19**

Langstaff, Launcelot
See Irving, Washington

Lanier, Sidney 1842-1881 .... **NCLC 6**
See also DLB 64; MAICYA; SATA 18

Lanyer, Aemilia 1569-1645 .... **LC 10**

Lao Tzu .... **CMLC 7**

Lapine, James (Elliot) 1949- .... **CLC 39**
See also CA 123; 130

Larbaud, Valery (Nicolas)
1881-1957 .... **TCLC 9**
See also CA 106

Lardner, Ring
See Lardner, Ring(gold) W(ilmer)

Lardner, Ring W. Jr.
See Lardner, Ring(gold) W(ilmer)

Lardner, Ring(gold) W(ilmer)
1885-1933 .... **TCLC 2, 14**
See also CA 104; 131; CDALB 1917-1929;
DLB 11, 25, 86; MTCW

Laredo, Betty
See Codrescu, Andrei

Larkin, Maia
See Wojciechowska, Maia (Teresa)

Larkin, Philip (Arthur)
1922-1985 ... **CLC 3, 5, 8, 9, 13, 18, 33,**
39, 64
See also CA 5-8R; 117; CANR 24;
CDBLB 1960 to Present; DLB 27;
MTCW

Larra (y Sanchez de Castro), Mariano Jose de
1809-1837 .... **NCLC 17**

Larsen, Eric 1941- .... **CLC 55**
See also CA 132

Larsen, Nella 1891-1964 .... **CLC 37**
See also BLC 2; BW; CA 125; DLB 51

Larson, Charles R(aymond) 1938-... **CLC 31**
See also CA 53-56; CANR 4

Latham, Jean Lee 1902-......... **CLC 12**
See also AITN 1; CA 5-8R; CANR 7;
MAICYA; SATA 2, 68

Latham, Mavis
See Clark, Mavis Thorpe

Lathen, Emma .... **CLC 2**
See also Hennissart, Martha; Latsis, Mary
J(ane)

Lathrop, Francis
See Leiber, Fritz (Reuter Jr.)

Latsis, Mary J(ane)
See Lathen, Emma
See also CA 85-88

Lattimore, Richmond (Alexander)
1906-1984 .... **CLC 3**
See also CA 1-4R; 112; CANR 1

Laughlin, James 1914- .... **CLC 49**
See also CA 21-24R; CANR 9; DLB 48

Laurence, (Jean) Margaret (Wemyss)
1926-1987 .. **CLC 3, 6, 13, 50, 62; SSC 7**
See also CA 5-8R; 121; CANR 33; DLB 53;
MTCW; SATA 50

Laurent, Antoine 1952- .... **CLC 50**

Lauscher, Hermann
See Hesse, Hermann

Lautreamont, Comte de
1846-1870 .... **NCLC 12**

Laverty, Donald
See Blish, James (Benjamin)

Lavin, Mary 1912-...... **CLC 4, 18; SSC 4**
See also CA 9-12R; CANR 33; DLB 15;
MTCW

Lavond, Paul Dennis
See Kornbluth, C(yril) M.; Pohl, Frederik

Lawler, Raymond Evenor 1922- .... **CLC 58**
See also CA 103

Lawrence, D(avid) H(erbert Richards)
1885-1930 ... **TCLC 2, 9, 16, 33; SSC 4**
See also CA 104; 121; CDBLB 1914-1945;
DLB 10, 19, 36, 98; MTCW; WLC

Lawrence, T(homas) E(dward)
1888-1935 .... **TCLC 18**
See also Dale, Colin
See also CA 115

Lawrence Of Arabia
See Lawrence, T(homas) E(dward)

Lawson, Henry (Archibald Hertzberg)
1867-1922 .... **TCLC 27**
See also CA 120

Laxness, Halldor .... **CLC 25**
See also Gudjonsson, Halldor Kiljan

Laye, Camara 1928-1980 .... **CLC 4, 38**
See also BLC 2; BW; CA 85-88; 97-100;
CANR 25; MTCW

Layton, Irving (Peter) 1912- ..... **CLC 2, 15**
See also CA 1-4R; CANR 2, 33; DLB 88;
MTCW

Lazarus, Emma 1849-1887 .... **NCLC 8**

Lazarus, Felix
See Cable, George Washington

Lea, Joan
See Neufeld, John (Arthur)

Leacock, Stephen (Butler)
1869-1944 .... **TCLC 2**
See also CA 104; DLB 92

Lear, Edward 1812-1888 .... **NCLC 3**
See also CLR 1; DLB 32; MAICYA;
SATA 18

Lear, Norman (Milton) 1922- ...... **CLC 12**
See also CA 73-76

Leavis, F(rank) R(aymond)
1895-1978 .... **CLC 24**
See also CA 21-24R; 77-80; MTCW

Leavitt, David 1961-.............. **CLC 34**
See also CA 116; 122

Lebowitz, Fran(ces Ann)
1951(?)- .... **CLC 11, 36**
See also CA 81-84; CANR 14; MTCW

le Carre, John .... **CLC 3, 5, 9, 15, 28**
See also Cornwell, David (John Moore)
See also BEST 89:4; CDBLB 1960 to
Present; DLB 87

Le Clezio, J(ean) M(arie) G(ustave)
1940- .... **CLC 31**
See also CA 116; 128; DLB 83

Leconte de Lisle, Charles-Marie-Rene
1818-1894 .... **NCLC 29**

Le Coq, Monsieur
See Simenon, Georges (Jacques Christian)

Leduc, Violette 1907-1972........ **CLC 22**
See also CA 13-14; 33-36R; CAP 1

Ledwidge, Francis 1887(?)-1917 ... **TCLC 23**
See also CA 123; DLB 20

Lee, Andrea 1953- .... **CLC 36**
See also BLC 2; BW; CA 125

Lee, Andrew
See Auchincloss, Louis (Stanton)

Lee, Don L. .... **CLC 2**
See also Madhubuti, Haki R.

Lee, George W(ashington)
1894-1976 .... **CLC 52**
See also BLC 2; BW; CA 125; DLB 51

Lee, (Nelle) Harper 1926-...... **CLC 12, 60**
See also CA 13-16R; CDALB 1941-1968;
DLB 6; MTCW; SATA 11; WLC

Lee, Julian
See Latham, Jean Lee

Lee, Lawrence 1903- .... **CLC 34**
See also CA 25-28R

Lee, Manfred B(ennington)
1905-1971 .... **CLC 11**
See also Queen, Ellery
See also CA 1-4R; 29-32R; CANR 2

Lee, Stan 1922-................... **CLC 17**
See also AAYA 5; CA 108; 111

Lee, Tanith 1947-................. **CLC 46**
See also CA 37-40R; SATA 8

Lee, Vernon .... **TCLC 5**
See also Paget, Violet
See also DLB 57

Lee, William
See Burroughs, William S(eward)

Liliencron, (Friedrich Adolf Axel) Detlev von
1844-1909 . . . . **TCLC 18**
See also CA 117

Lima, Jose Lezama
See Lezama Lima, Jose

Lima Barreto, Afonso Henrique de
1881-1922 . . . . **TCLC 23**
See also CA 117

Limonov, Eduard . . . . **CLC 67**

Lin, Frank
See Atherton, Gertrude (Franklin Horn)

Lincoln, Abraham 1809-1865 . . . . . **NCLC 18**

Lind, Jakov . . . . **CLC 1, 2, 4, 27**
See also Landwirth, Heinz
See also CAAS 4

Lindsay, David 1878-1945 . . . . **TCLC 15**
See also CA 113

Lindsay, (Nicholas) Vachel
1879-1931 . . . . **TCLC 17**
See also CA 114; 135; CDALB 1865-1917;
DLB 54; SATA 40; WLC

Linke-Poot
See Doeblin, Alfred

Linney, Romulus 1930- . . . . **CLC 51**
See also CA 1-4R

Li Po 701-763 . . . . **CMLC 2**

Lipsius, Justus 1547-1606 . . . . **LC 16**

Lipsyte, Robert (Michael) 1938- . . . . **CLC 21**
See also AAYA 7; CA 17-20R; CANR 8;
CLR 23; MAICYA; SATA 5, 68

Lish, Gordon (Jay) 1934- . . . . **CLC 45**
See also CA 113; 117

Lispector, Clarice 1925-1977 . . . . . . **CLC 43**
See also CA 116; DLB 113

Littell, Robert 1935(?)- . . . . **CLC 42**
See also CA 109; 112

Littlewit, Humphrey Gent.
See Lovecraft, H(oward) P(hillips)

Litwos
See Sienkiewicz, Henryk (Adam Alexander
Pius)

Liu E 1857-1909 . . . . **TCLC 15**
See also CA 115

Lively, Penelope (Margaret)
1933- . . . . **CLC 32, 50**
See also CA 41-44R; CANR 29; CLR 7;
DLB 14; MAICYA; MTCW; SATA 7, 60

Livesay, Dorothy (Kathleen)
1909- . . . . **CLC 4, 15**
See also AITN 2; CA 25-28R; CAAS 8;
CANR 36; DLB 68; MTCW

Lizardi, Jose Joaquin Fernandez de
1776-1827 . . . . **NCLC 30**

Llewellyn, Richard . . . . **CLC 7**
See also Llewellyn Lloyd, Richard Dafydd
Vivian
See also DLB 15

Llewellyn Lloyd, Richard Dafydd Vivian
1906-1983
See Llewellyn, Richard
See also CA 53-56; 111; CANR 7;
SATA 11, 37

Llosa, (Jorge) Mario (Pedro) Vargas
See Vargas Llosa, (Jorge) Mario (Pedro)

Lloyd Webber, Andrew 1948-
See Webber, Andrew Lloyd
See also AAYA 1; CA 116; SATA 56

Locke, Alain (Le Roy)
1886-1954 . . . . **TCLC 43**
See also BW; CA 106; 124; DLB 51

Locke, John 1632-1704 . . . . **LC 7**
See also DLB 101

Locke-Elliott, Sumner
See Elliott, Sumner Locke

Lockhart, John Gibson
1794-1854 . . . . **NCLC 6**
See also DLB 110, 116

Lodge, David (John) 1935- . . . . **CLC 36**
See also BEST 90:1; CA 17-20R; CANR 19;
DLB 14; MTCW

Loennbohm, Armas Eino Leopold 1878-1926
See Leino, Eino
See also CA 123

Loewinsohn, Ron(ald William)
1937- . . . . **CLC 52**
See also CA 25-28R

Logan, Jake
See Smith, Martin Cruz

Logan, John (Burton) 1923-1987 . . . . . **CLC 5**
See also CA 77-80; 124; DLB 5

Lo Kuan-chung 1330(?)-1400(?) . . . . . . **LC 12**

Lombard, Nap
See Johnson, Pamela Hansford

London, Jack . . . . **TCLC 9, 15, 39; SSC 4**
See also London, John Griffith
See also AITN 2; CDALB 1865-1917;
DLB 8, 12, 78; SATA 18; WLC

London, John Griffith 1876-1916
See London, Jack
See also CA 110; 119; MAICYA; MTCW

Long, Emmett
See Leonard, Elmore (John Jr.)

Longbaugh, Harry
See Goldman, William (W.)

Longfellow, Henry Wadsworth
1807-1882 . . . . **NCLC 2**
See also CDALB 1640-1865; DLB 1, 59;
SATA 19

Longley, Michael 1939- . . . . **CLC 29**
See also CA 102; DLB 40

Longus fl. c. 2nd cent. - . . . . **CMLC 7**

Longway, A. Hugh
See Lang, Andrew

Lopate, Phillip 1943- . . . . **CLC 29**
See also CA 97-100; DLBY 80

Lopez Portillo (y Pacheco), Jose
1920- . . . . **CLC 46**
See also CA 129; HW

Lopez y Fuentes, Gregorio
1897(?)-1966 . . . . **CLC 32**
See also CA 131; HW

Lorca, Federico Garcia
See Garcia Lorca, Federico

Lord, Bette Bao 1938- . . . . **CLC 23**
See also BEST 90:3; CA 107; SATA 58

Lord Auch
See Bataille, Georges

Lord Byron
See Byron, George Gordon (Noel)

Lord Dunsany . . . . **TCLC 2**
See also Dunsany, Edward John Moreton
Drax Plunkett

Lorde, Audre (Geraldine)
1934- . . . . **CLC 18, 71**
See also BLC 2; BW; CA 25-28R;
CANR 16, 26; DLB 41; MTCW

Lord Jeffrey
See Jeffrey, Francis

Lorenzo, Heberto Padilla
See Padilla (Lorenzo), Heberto

Loris
See Hofmannsthal, Hugo von

Loti, Pierre . . . . **TCLC 11**
See also Viaud, (Louis Marie) Julien

Louie, David Wong 1954- . . . . **CLC 70**

Louis, Father M.
See Merton, Thomas

Lovecraft, H(oward) P(hillips)
1890-1937 . . . . **TCLC 4, 22; SSC 3**
See also CA 104; 133; MTCW

Lovelace, Earl 1935- . . . . **CLC 51**
See also CA 77-80; MTCW

Lowell, Amy 1874-1925 . . . . **TCLC 1, 8**
See also CA 104; DLB 54

Lowell, James Russell 1819-1891 . . **NCLC 2**
See also CDALB 1640-1865; DLB 1, 11, 64,
79

Lowell, Robert (Traill Spence Jr.)
1917-1977 . . . **CLC 1, 2, 3, 4, 5, 8, 9, 11,
15, 37; PC 3**
See also CA 9-12R; 73-76; CABS 2;
CANR 26; DLB 5; MTCW; WLC

Lowndes, Marie Adelaide (Belloc)
1868-1947 . . . . **TCLC 12**
See also CA 107; DLB 70

Lowry, (Clarence) Malcolm
1909-1957 . . . . **TCLC 6, 40**
See also CA 105; 131; CDBLB 1945-1960;
DLB 15; MTCW

Lowry, Mina Gertrude 1882-1966
See Loy, Mina
See also CA 113

Loxsmith, John
See Brunner, John (Kilian Houston)

Loy, Mina . . . . **CLC 28**
See also Lowry, Mina Gertrude
See also DLB 4, 54

Loyson-Bridet
See Schwob, (Mayer Andre) Marcel

Lucas, Craig 1951- . . . . **CLC 64**
See also CA 137

Lucas, George 1944- . . . . **CLC 16**
See also AAYA 1; CA 77-80; CANR 30;
SATA 56

Lucas, Hans
See Godard, Jean-Luc

Lucas, Victoria
See Plath, Sylvia

Ludlam, Charles 1943-1987 . . . . . **CLC 46, 50**
See also CA 85-88; 122

Ludlum, Robert 1927- .... **CLC 22, 43**
See also BEST 89:1, 90:3; CA 33-36R;
CANR 25; DLBY 82; MTCW

Ludwig, Ken .... **CLC 60**

Ludwig, Otto 1813-1865 .... **NCLC 4**

Lugones, Leopoldo 1874-1938 ..... **TCLC 15**
See also CA 116; 131; HW

Lu Hsun 1881-1936 .... **TCLC 3**

Lukacs, George .... **CLC 24**
See also Lukacs, Gyorgy (Szegeny von)

Lukacs, Gyorgy (Szegeny von) 1885-1971
See Lukacs, George
See also CA 101; 29-32R

Luke, Peter (Ambrose Cyprian)
1919- .... **CLC 38**
See also CA 81-84; DLB 13

Lunar, Dennis
See Mungo, Raymond

Lurie, Alison 1926- .... **CLC 4, 5, 18, 39**
See also CA 1-4R; CANR 2, 17; DLB 2;
MTCW; SATA 46

Lustig, Arnost 1926- .... **CLC 56**
See also AAYA 3; CA 69-72; SATA 56

Luther, Martin 1483-1546 .... **LC 9**

Luzi, Mario 1914- .... **CLC 13**
See also CA 61-64; CANR 9

Lynch, B. Suarez
See Bioy Casares, Adolfo; Borges, Jorge
Luis

Lynch, David (K.) 1946- .... **CLC 66**
See also CA 124; 129

Lynch, James
See Andreyev, Leonid (Nikolaevich)

Lynch Davis, B.
See Bioy Casares, Adolfo; Borges, Jorge
Luis

Lyndsay, Sir David 1490-1555 .... **LC 20**

Lynn, Kenneth S(chuyler) 1923- .... **CLC 50**
See also CA 1-4R; CANR 3, 27

Lynx
See West, Rebecca

Lyons, Marcus
See Blish, James (Benjamin)

Lyre, Pinchbeck
See Sassoon, Siegfried (Lorraine)

Lytle, Andrew (Nelson) 1902- ...... **CLC 22**
See also CA 9-12R; DLB 6

Lyttelton, George 1709-1773 .... **LC 10**

Maas, Peter 1929- .... **CLC 29**
See also CA 93-96

Macaulay, Rose 1881-1958 ..... **TCLC 7, 44**
See also CA 104; DLB 36

MacBeth, George (Mann)
1932-1992 .... **CLC 2, 5, 9**
See also CA 25-28R; 136; DLB 40; MTCW;
SATA 4; SATO 70

MacCaig, Norman (Alexander)
1910- .... **CLC 36**
See also CA 9-12R; CANR 3, 34; DLB 27

MacCarthy, (Sir Charles Otto) Desmond
1877-1952 .... **TCLC 36**

MacDiarmid, Hugh ..... **CLC 2, 4, 11, 19, 63**
See also Grieve, C(hristopher) M(urray)
See also CDBLB 1945-1960; DLB 20

MacDonald, Anson
See Heinlein, Robert A(nson)

Macdonald, Cynthia 1928- ..... **CLC 13, 19**
See also CA 49-52; CANR 4; DLB 105

MacDonald, George 1824-1905 ..... **TCLC 9**
See also CA 106; 137; DLB 18; MAICYA;
SATA 33

Macdonald, John
See Millar, Kenneth

MacDonald, John D(ann)
1916-1986 .... **CLC 3, 27, 44**
See also CA 1-4R; 121; CANR 1, 19;
DLB 8; DLBY 86; MTCW

Macdonald, John Ross
See Millar, Kenneth

Macdonald, Ross ..... **CLC 1, 2, 3, 14, 34, 41**
See also Millar, Kenneth
See also DLBD 6

MacDougal, John
See Blish, James (Benjamin)

MacEwen, Gwendolyn (Margaret)
1941-1987 .... **CLC 13, 55**
See also CA 9-12R; 124; CANR 7, 22;
DLB 53; SATA 50, 55

Machado (y Ruiz), Antonio
1875-1939 .... **TCLC 3**
See also CA 104; DLB 108

Machado de Assis, Joaquim Maria
1839-1908 .... **TCLC 10**
See also BLC 2; CA 107

Machen, Arthur .... **TCLC 4**
See also Jones, Arthur Llewellyn
See also DLB 36

Machiavelli, Niccolo 1469-1527 ...... **LC 8**

MacInnes, Colin 1914-1976 ...... **CLC 4, 23**
See also CA 69-72; 65-68; CANR 21;
DLB 14; MTCW

MacInnes, Helen (Clark)
1907-1985 .... **CLC 27, 39**
See also CA 1-4R; 117; CANR 1, 28;
DLB 87; MTCW; SATA 22, 44

Mackenzie, Compton (Edward Montague)
1883-1972 .... **CLC 18**
See also CA 21-22; 37-40R; CAP 2;
DLB 34, 100

Mackintosh, Elizabeth 1896(?)-1952
See Tey, Josephine
See also CA 110

MacLaren, James
See Grieve, C(hristopher) M(urray)

Mac Laverty, Bernard 1942- .... **CLC 31**
See also CA 116; 118

MacLean, Alistair (Stuart)
1922-1987 .... **CLC 3, 13, 50, 63**
See also CA 57-60; 121; CANR 28; MTCW;
SATA 23, 50

MacLeish, Archibald
1892-1982 .... **CLC 3, 8, 14, 68**
See also CA 9-12R; 106; CANR 33; DLB 4,
7, 45; DLBY 82; MTCW

MacLennan, (John) Hugh
1907- .... **CLC 2, 14**
See also CA 5-8R; CANR 33; DLB 68;
MTCW

MacLeod, Alistair 1936- .... **CLC 56**
See also CA 123; DLB 60

MacNeice, (Frederick) Louis
1907-1963 .... **CLC 1, 4, 10, 53**
See also CA 85-88; DLB 10, 20; MTCW

MacNeill, Dand
See Fraser, George MacDonald

Macpherson, (Jean) Jay 1931- ...... **CLC 14**
See also CA 5-8R; DLB 53

MacShane, Frank 1927- .... **CLC 39**
See also CA 9-12R; CANR 3, 33; DLB 111

Macumber, Mari
See Sandoz, Mari(e Susette)

Madach, Imre 1823-1864 .... **NCLC 19**

Madden, (Jerry) David 1933- .... **CLC 5, 15**
See also CA 1-4R; CAAS 3; CANR 4;
DLB 6; MTCW

Maddern, Al(an)
See Ellison, Harlan

Madhubuti, Haki R. 1942- .... **CLC 6; PC 5**
See also Lee, Don L.
See also BLC 2; BW; CA 73-76; CANR 24;
DLB 5, 41; DLBD 8

Madow, Pauline (Reichberg) .... **CLC 1**
See also CA 9-12R

Maepenn, Hugh
See Kuttner, Henry

Maepenn, K. H.
See Kuttner, Henry

Maeterlinck, Maurice 1862-1949 ... **TCLC 3**
See also CA 104; 136; SATA 66

Maginn, William 1794-1842 .... **NCLC 8**
See also DLB 110

Mahapatra, Jayanta 1928- .... **CLC 33**
See also CA 73-76; CAAS 9; CANR 15, 33

Mahfouz, Naguib (Abdel Aziz Al-Sabilgi)
1911(?)-
See Mahfuz, Najib
See also BEST 89:2; CA 128; MTCW

Mahfuz, Najib .... **CLC 52, 55**
See also Mahfouz, Naguib (Abdel Aziz
Al-Sabilgi)
See also DLBY 88

Mahon, Derek 1941- .... **CLC 27**
See also CA 113; 128; DLB 40

Mailer, Norman
1923- ...... **CLC 1, 2, 3, 4, 5, 8, 11, 14,**
28, 39
See also AITN 2; CA 9-12R; CABS 1;
CANR 28; CDALB 1968-1988; DLB 2,
16, 28; DLBD 3; DLBY 80, 83; MTCW

Maillet, Antonine 1929- .... **CLC 54**
See also CA 115; 120; DLB 60

Mais, Roger 1905-1955 .... **TCLC 8**
See also BW; CA 105; 124; MTCW

Maitland, Sara (Louise) 1950- ...... **CLC 49**
See also CA 69-72; CANR 13

Major, Clarence 1936- .... **CLC 3, 19, 48**
See also BLC 2; BW; CA 21-24R; CAAS 6;
CANR 13, 25; DLB 33

Major, Kevin (Gerald) 1949- . . . . . . **CLC 26**
See also CA 97-100; CANR 21, 38;
CLR 11; DLB 60; MAICYA; SATA 32

Maki, James
See Ozu, Yasujiro

Malabaila, Damiano
See Levi, Primo

Malamud, Bernard
1914-1986 . . . . . **CLC 1, 2, 3, 5, 8, 9, 11,
18, 27, 44**
See also CA 5-8R; 118; CABS 1; CANR 28;
CDALB 1941-1968; DLB 2, 28;
DLBY 80, 86; MTCW; WLC

Malcolm, Dan
See Silverberg, Robert

Malherbe, Francois de 1555-1628 . . . . . **LC 5**

Mallarme, Stephane
1842-1898 . . . . **NCLC 4; PC 4**

Mallet-Joris, Francoise 1930- . . . . . . **CLC 11**
See also CA 65-68; CANR 17; DLB 83

Malley, Ern
See McAuley, James Phillip

Mallowan, Agatha Christie
See Christie, Agatha (Mary Clarissa)

Maloff, Saul 1922- . . . . **CLC 5**
See also CA 33-36R

Malone, Louis
See MacNeice, (Frederick) Louis

Malone, Michael (Christopher)
1942- . . . . **CLC 43**
See also CA 77-80; CANR 14, 32

Malory, (Sir) Thomas
1410(?)-1471(?) . . . . **LC 11**
See also CDBLB Before 1660; SATA 33, 59

Malouf, (George Joseph) David
1934- . . . . **CLC 28**
See also CA 124

Malraux, (Georges-)Andre
1901-1976 . . . . . . **CLC 1, 4, 9, 13, 15, 57**
See also CA 21-22; 69-72; CANR 34;
CAP 2; DLB 72; MTCW

Malzberg, Barry N(athaniel) 1939- . . . **CLC 7**
See also CA 61-64; CAAS 4; CANR 16;
DLB 8

Mamet, David (Alan)
1947- . . . . **CLC 9, 15, 34, 46**
See also AAYA 3; CA 81-84; CABS 3;
CANR 15; DLB 7; MTCW

Mamoulian, Rouben (Zachary)
1897-1987 . . . . **CLC 16**
See also CA 25-28R; 124

Mandelstam, Osip (Emilievich)
1891(?)-1938(?) . . . . **TCLC 2, 6**
See also CA 104

Mander, (Mary) Jane 1877-1949 . . . **TCLC 31**

Mandiargues, Andre Pieyre de . . . . . . **CLC 41**
See also Pieyre de Mandiargues, Andre
See also DLB 83

Mandrake, Ethel Belle
See Thurman, Wallace (Henry)

Mangan, James Clarence
1803-1849 . . . . **NCLC 27**

Maniere, J.-E.
See Giraudoux, (Hippolyte) Jean

Manley, (Mary) Delariviere
1672(?)-1724 . . . . **LC 1**
See also DLB 39, 80

Mann, Abel
See Creasey, John

Mann, (Luiz) Heinrich 1871-1950 . . . **TCLC 9**
See also CA 106; DLB 66

Mann, (Paul) Thomas
1875-1955 . . . **TCLC 2, 8, 14, 21, 35, 44;
SSC 5**
See also CA 104; 128; DLB 66; MTCW;
WLC

Manning, Frederic 1887(?)-1935 . . . **TCLC 25**
See also CA 124

Manning, Olivia 1915-1980 . . . . . . **CLC 5, 19**
See also CA 5-8R; 101; CANR 29; MTCW

Mano, D. Keith 1942- . . . . **CLC 2, 10**
See also CA 25-28R; CAAS 6; CANR 26;
DLB 6

Mansfield, Katherine . . . **TCLC 2, 8, 39; SSC 9**
See also Beauchamp, Kathleen Mansfield
See also WLC

Manso, Peter 1940- . . . . **CLC 39**
See also CA 29-32R

Mantecon, Juan Jimenez
See Jimenez (Mantecon), Juan Ramon

Manton, Peter
See Creasey, John

Man Without a Spleen, A
See Chekhov, Anton (Pavlovich)

Manzoni, Alessandro 1785-1873 . . **NCLC 29**

Mapu, Abraham (ben Jekutiel)
1808-1867 . . . . **NCLC 18**

Mara, Sally
See Queneau, Raymond

Marat, Jean Paul 1743-1793 . . . . **LC 10**

Marcel, Gabriel Honore
1889-1973 . . . . **CLC 15**
See also CA 102; 45-48; MTCW

Marchbanks, Samuel
See Davies, (William) Robertson

Marchi, Giacomo
See Bassani, Giorgio

Marie de France c. 12th cent. - . . . . **CMLC 8**

Marie de l'Incarnation 1599-1672 . . . . **LC 10**

Mariner, Scott
See Pohl, Frederik

Marinetti, Filippo Tommaso
1876-1944 . . . . **TCLC 10**
See also CA 107; DLB 114

Marivaux, Pierre Carlet de Chamblain de
1688-1763 . . . . **LC 4**

Markandaya, Kamala . . . . **CLC 8, 38**
See also Taylor, Kamala (Purnaiya)

Markfield, Wallace 1926- . . . . **CLC 8**
See also CA 69-72; CAAS 3; DLB 2, 28

Markham, Edwin 1852-1940 . . . . . . **TCLC 47**
See also DLB 54

Markham, Robert
See Amis, Kingsley (William)

Marks, J
See Highwater, Jamake (Mamake)

Marks-Highwater, J
See Highwater, Jamake (Mamake)

Markson, David M(errill) 1927- . . . . **CLC 67**
See also CA 49-52; CANR 1

Marley, Bob . . . . **CLC 17**
See also Marley, Robert Nesta

Marley, Robert Nesta 1945-1981
See Marley, Bob
See also CA 107; 103

Marlowe, Christopher 1564-1593 . . . . . **DC 1**
See also CDBLB Before 1660; DLB 62;
WLC

Marmontel, Jean-Francois
1723-1799 . . . . **LC 2**

Marquand, John P(hillips)
1893-1960 . . . . **CLC 2, 10**
See also CA 85-88; DLB 9, 102

Marquez, Gabriel (Jose) Garcia . . . . . . **CLC 68**
See also Garcia Marquez, Gabriel (Jose)

Marquis, Don(ald Robert Perry)
1878-1937 . . . . **TCLC 7**
See also CA 104; DLB 11, 25

Marric, J. J.
See Creasey, John

Marrow, Bernard
See Moore, Brian

Marryat, Frederick 1792-1848 . . . . **NCLC 3**
See also DLB 21

Marsden, James
See Creasey, John

Marsh, (Edith) Ngaio
1899-1982 . . . . **CLC 7, 53**
See also CA 9-12R; CANR 6; DLB 77;
MTCW

Marshall, Garry 1934- . . . . **CLC 17**
See also AAYA 3; CA 111; SATA 60

Marshall, Paule 1929- . . **CLC 27, 72; SSC 3**
See also BLC 3; BW; CA 77-80; CANR 25;
DLB 33; MTCW

Marsten, Richard
See Hunter, Evan

Martha, Henry
See Harris, Mark

Martin, Ken
See Hubbard, L(afayette) Ron(ald)

Martin, Richard
See Creasey, John

Martin, Steve 1945- . . . . **CLC 30**
See also CA 97-100; CANR 30; MTCW

Martin, Webber
See Silverberg, Robert

Martin du Gard, Roger
1881-1958 . . . . **TCLC 24**
See also CA 118; DLB 65

Martineau, Harriet 1802-1876 . . . . **NCLC 26**
See also DLB 21, 55; YABC 2

Martines, Julia
See O'Faolain, Julia

Martinez, Jacinto Benavente y
See Benavente (y Martinez), Jacinto

Martinez Ruiz, Jose 1873-1967
See Azorin; Ruiz, Jose Martinez
See also CA 93-96; HW

McGinley, Phyllis 1905-1978 ...... **CLC 14**
See also CA 9-12R; 77-80; CANR 19;
DLB 11, 48; SATA 2, 24, 44

McGinniss, Joe 1942- .... **CLC 32**
See also AITN 2; BEST 89:2; CA 25-28R;
CANR 26

McGivern, Maureen Daly
See Daly, Maureen

McGrath, Patrick 1950- .... **CLC 55**
See also CA 136

McGrath, Thomas (Matthew)
1916-1990 .... **CLC 28, 59**
See also CA 9-12R; 132; CANR 6, 33;
MTCW; SATA 41; SATO 66

McGuane, Thomas (Francis III)
1939- .... **CLC 3, 7, 18, 45**
See also AITN 2; CA 49-52; CANR 5, 24;
DLB 2; DLBY 80; MTCW

McGuckian, Medbh 1950- .... **CLC 48**
See also DLB 40

McHale, Tom 1942(?)-1982 ...... **CLC 3, 5**
See also AITN 1; CA 77-80; 106

McIlvanney, William 1936- ...... **CLC 42**
See also CA 25-28R; DLB 14

McIlwraith, Maureen Mollie Hunter
See Hunter, Mollie
See also SATA 2

McInerney, Jay 1955- .... **CLC 34**
See also CA 116; 123

McIntyre, Vonda N(eel) 1948- ..... **CLC 18**
See also CA 81-84; CANR 17, 34; MTCW

McKay, Claude .... **TCLC 7, 41; PC 2**
See also McKay, Festus Claudius
See also BLC 3; DLB 4, 45, 51, 117

McKay, Festus Claudius 1889-1948
See McKay, Claude
See also BW; CA 104; 124; MTCW; WLC

McKuen, Rod 1933- .... **CLC 1, 3**
See also AITN 1; CA 41-44R

McLoughlin, R. B.
See Mencken, H(enry) L(ouis)

McLuhan, (Herbert) Marshall
1911-1980 .... **CLC 37**
See also CA 9-12R; 102; CANR 12, 34;
DLB 88; MTCW

McMillan, Terry 1951- .... **CLC 50, 61**

McMurtry, Larry (Jeff)
1936- .... **CLC 2, 3, 7, 11, 27, 44**
See also AITN 2; BEST 89:2; CA 5-8R;
CANR 19; CDALB 1968-1988; DLB 2;
DLBY 80, 87; MTCW

McNally, Terrence 1939- ...... **CLC 4, 7, 41**
See also CA 45-48; CANR 2; DLB 7

McNamer, Deirdre 1950- .... **CLC 70**

McNeile, Herman Cyril 1888-1937
See Sapper
See also DLB 77

McPhee, John (Angus) 1931- ...... **CLC 36**
See also BEST 90:1; CA 65-68; CANR 20;
MTCW

McPherson, James Alan 1943- ..... **CLC 19**
See also BW; CA 25-28R; CANR 24;
DLB 38; MTCW

McPherson, William (Alexander)
1933- .... **CLC 34**
See also CA 69-72; CANR 28

McSweeney, Kerry .... **CLC 34**

Mead, Margaret 1901-1978 .... **CLC 37**
See also AITN 1; CA 1-4R; 81-84;
CANR 4; MTCW; SATA 20

Meaker, Marijane (Agnes) 1927-
See Kerr, M. E.
See also CA 107; CANR 37; MAICYA;
MTCW; SATA 20, 61

Medoff, Mark (Howard) 1940- ... **CLC 6, 23**
See also AITN 1; CA 53-56; CANR 5;
DLB 7

Meged, Aharon
See Megged, Aharon

Meged, Aron
See Megged, Aharon

Megged, Aharon 1920- .... **CLC 9**
See also CA 49-52; CAAS 13; CANR 1

Mehta, Ved (Parkash) 1934- .... **CLC 37**
See also CA 1-4R; CANR 2, 23; MTCW

Melanter
See Blackmore, R(ichard) D(oddridge)

Melikow, Loris
See Hofmannsthal, Hugo von

Melmoth, Sebastian
See Wilde, Oscar (Fingal O'Flahertie Wills)

Meltzer, Milton 1915- .... **CLC 26**
See also AAYA 8; CA 13-16R; CANR 38;
CLR 13; DLB 61; MAICYA; SAAS 1;
SATA 1, 50

Melville, Herman
1819-1891 ...... **NCLC 3, 12, 29; SSC 1**
See also CDALB 1640-1865; DLB 3, 74;
SATA 59; WLC

Menander c. 342B.C.-c. 292B.C.... **CMLC 9**

Mencken, H(enry) L(ouis)
1880-1956 .... **TCLC 13**
See also CA 105; 125; CDALB 1917-1929;
DLB 11, 29, 63; MTCW

Mercer, David 1928-1980 .... **CLC 5**
See also CA 9-12R; 102; CANR 23;
DLB 13; MTCW

Merchant, Paul
See Ellison, Harlan

Meredith, George 1828-1909 ... **TCLC 17, 43**
See also CA 117; CDBLB 1832-1890;
DLB 18, 35, 57

Meredith, William (Morris)
1919- .... **CLC 4, 13, 22, 55**
See also CA 9-12R; CAAS 14; CANR 6;
DLB 5

Merezhkovsky, Dmitry Sergeyevich
1865-1941 .... **TCLC 29**

Merimee, Prosper
1803-1870 .... **NCLC 6; SSC 7**
See also DLB 119

Merkin, Daphne 1954- .... **CLC 44**
See also CA 123

Merlin, Arthur
See Blish, James (Benjamin)

Merrill, James (Ingram)
1926- .... **CLC 2, 3, 6, 8, 13, 18, 34**
See also CA 13-16R; CANR 10; DLB 5;
DLBY 85; MTCW

Merriman, Alex
See Silverberg, Robert

Merritt, E. B.
See Waddington, Miriam

Merton, Thomas
1915-1968 .... **CLC 1, 3, 11, 34**
See also CA 5-8R; 25-28R; CANR 22;
DLB 48; DLBY 81; MTCW

Merwin, W(illiam) S(tanley)
1927- ...... **CLC 1, 2, 3, 5, 8, 13, 18, 45**
See also CA 13-16R; CANR 15; DLB 5;
MTCW

Metcalf, John 1938- .... **CLC 37**
See also CA 113; DLB 60

Metcalf, Suzanne
See Baum, L(yman) Frank

Mew, Charlotte (Mary)
1870-1928 .... **TCLC 8**
See also CA 105; DLB 19

Mewshaw, Michael 1943- .... **CLC 9**
See also CA 53-56; CANR 7; DLBY 80

Meyer, June
See Jordan, June

Meyer-Meyrink, Gustav 1868-1932
See Meyrink, Gustav
See also CA 117

Meyers, Jeffrey 1939- .... **CLC 39**
See also CA 73-76; DLB 111

Meynell, Alice (Christina Gertrude Thompson)
1847-1922 .... **TCLC 6**
See also CA 104; DLB 19, 98

Meyrink, Gustav .... **TCLC 21**
See also Meyer-Meyrink, Gustav
See also DLB 81

Michaels, Leonard 1933- .... **CLC 6, 25**
See also CA 61-64; CANR 21; MTCW

Michaux, Henri 1899-1984 ...... **CLC 8, 19**
See also CA 85-88; 114

Michelangelo 1475-1564 .... **LC 12**

Michelet, Jules 1798-1874 .... **NCLC 31**

Michener, James A(lbert)
1907(?)- .... **CLC 1, 5, 11, 29, 60**
See also AITN 1; BEST 90:1; CA 5-8R;
CANR 21; DLB 6; MTCW

Mickiewicz, Adam 1798-1855 ..... **NCLC 3**

Middleton, Christopher 1926- ...... **CLC 13**
See also CA 13-16R; CANR 29; DLB 40

Middleton, Stanley 1919- .... **CLC 7, 38**
See also CA 25-28R; CANR 21; DLB 14

Migueis, Jose Rodrigues 1901- ..... **CLC 10**

Mikszath, Kalman 1847-1910 ..... **TCLC 31**

Miles, Josephine
1911-1985 .... **CLC 1, 2, 14, 34, 39**
See also CA 1-4R; 116; CANR 2; DLB 48

Militant
See Sandburg, Carl (August)

Mill, John Stuart 1806-1873 ..... **NCLC 11**
See also CDBLB 1832-1890; DLB 55

Millar, Kenneth 1915-1983 . . . . **CLC 14**
See also Macdonald, Ross
See also CA 9-12R; 110; CANR 16; DLB 2;
DLBD 6; DLBY 83; MTCW

Millay, E. Vincent
See Millay, Edna St. Vincent

Millay, Edna St. Vincent
1892-1950 . . . . **TCLC 4**
See also CA 104; 130; CDALB 1917-1929;
DLB 45; MTCW

Miller, Arthur
1915- . . . . . . **CLC 1, 2, 6, 10, 15, 26, 47;**
DC 1
See also AITN 1; CA 1-4R; CABS 3;
CANR 2, 30; CDALB 1941-1968; DLB 7;
MTCW; WLC

Miller, Henry (Valentine)
1891-1980 . . . . **CLC 1, 2, 4, 9, 14, 43**
See also CA 9-12R; 97-100; CANR 33;
CDALB 1929-1941; DLB 4, 9; DLBY 80;
MTCW; WLC

Miller, Jason 1939(?)- . . . . **CLC 2**
See also AITN 1; CA 73-76; DLB 7

Miller, Sue 19(?)- . . . . **CLC 44**
See also BEST 90:3

Miller, Walter M(ichael Jr.)
1923- . . . . **CLC 4, 30**
See also CA 85-88; DLB 8

Millett, Kate 1934- . . . . **CLC 67**
See also AITN 1; CA 73-76; CANR 32;
MTCW

Millhauser, Steven 1943- . . . . **CLC 21, 54**
See also CA 110; 111; DLB 2

Millin, Sarah Gertrude 1889-1968 . . **CLC 49**
See also CA 102; 93-96

Milne, A(lan) A(lexander)
1882-1956 . . . . **TCLC 6**
See also CA 104; 133; CLR 1, 26; DLB 10,
77, 100; MAICYA; MTCW; YABC 1

Milner, Ron(ald) 1938- . . . . **CLC 56**
See also AITN 1; BLC 3; BW; CA 73-76;
CANR 24; DLB 38; MTCW

Milosz, Czeslaw
1911- . . . . **CLC 5, 11, 22, 31, 56**
See also CA 81-84; CANR 23; MTCW

Milton, John 1608-1674 . . . . **LC 9**
See also CDBLB 1660-1789; WLC

Minehaha, Cornelius
See Wedekind, (Benjamin) Frank(lin)

Miner, Valerie 1947- . . . . **CLC 40**
See also CA 97-100

Minimo, Duca
See D'Annunzio, Gabriele

Minot, Susan 1956- . . . . **CLC 44**
See also CA 134

Minus, Ed 1938- . . . . **CLC 39**

Miranda, Javier
See Bioy Casares, Adolfo

Miro (Ferrer), Gabriel (Francisco Victor)
1879-1930 . . . . **TCLC 5**
See also CA 104

Mishima, Yukio
. . . . **CLC 2, 4, 6, 9, 27; DC 1; SSC 4**
See also Hiraoka, Kimitake

Mistral, Gabriela . . . . **TCLC 2**
See also Godoy Alcayaga, Lucila

Mistry, Rohinton 1952- . . . . **CLC 71**

Mitchell, Clyde
See Ellison, Harlan; Silverberg, Robert

Mitchell, James Leslie 1901-1935
See Gibbon, Lewis Grassic
See also CA 104; DLB 15

Mitchell, Joni 1943- . . . . **CLC 12**
See also CA 112

Mitchell, Margaret (Munnerlyn)
1900-1949 . . . . **TCLC 11**
See also CA 109; 125; DLB 9; MTCW

Mitchell, Peggy
See Mitchell, Margaret (Munnerlyn)

Mitchell, S(ilas) Weir 1829-1914 . . **TCLC 36**

Mitchell, W(illiam) O(rmond)
1914- . . . . **CLC 25**
See also CA 77-80; CANR 15; DLB 88

Mitford, Mary Russell 1787-1855 . . **NCLC 4**
See also DLB 110, 116

Mitford, Nancy 1904-1973 . . . . **CLC 44**
See also CA 9-12R

Miyamoto, Yuriko 1899-1951 . . . . . **TCLC 37**

Mo, Timothy (Peter) 1950(?)- . . . . . . **CLC 46**
See also CA 117; MTCW

Modarressi, Taghi (M.) 1931- . . . . . . **CLC 44**
See also CA 121; 134

Modiano, Patrick (Jean) 1945- . . . . **CLC 18**
See also CA 85-88; CANR 17; DLB 83

Moerck, Paal
See Roelvaag, O(le) E(dvart)

Mofolo, Thomas (Mokopu)
1875(?)-1948 . . . . **TCLC 22**
See also BLC 3; CA 121

Mohr, Nicholasa 1935- . . . . **CLC 12**
See also AAYA 8; CA 49-52; CANR 1, 32;
CLR 22; HW; SAAS 8; SATA 8

Mojtabai, A(nn) G(race)
1938- . . . . **CLC 5, 9, 15, 29**
See also CA 85-88

Moliere 1622-1673 . . . . **LC 10**
See also WLC

Molin, Charles
See Mayne, William (James Carter)

Molnar, Ferenc 1878-1952 . . . . **TCLC 20**
See also CA 109

Momaday, N(avarre) Scott
1934- . . . . **CLC 2, 19**
See also CA 25-28R; CANR 14, 34;
MTCW; SATA 30, 48

Monroe, Harriet 1860-1936 . . . . **TCLC 12**
See also CA 109; DLB 54, 91

Monroe, Lyle
See Heinlein, Robert A(nson)

Montagu, Elizabeth 1917- . . . . **NCLC 7**
See also CA 9-12R

Montagu, Mary (Pierrepont) Wortley
1689-1762 . . . . **LC 9**
See also DLB 95, 101

Montague, John (Patrick)
1929- . . . . **CLC 13, 46**
See also CA 9-12R; CANR 9; DLB 40;
MTCW

Montaigne, Michel (Eyquem) de
1533-1592 . . . . **LC 8**
See also WLC

Montale, Eugenio 1896-1981 . . . **CLC 7, 9, 18**
See also CA 17-20R; 104; CANR 30;
DLB 114; MTCW

Montesquieu, Charles-Louis de Secondat
1689-1755 . . . . **LC 7**

Montgomery, (Robert) Bruce 1921-1978
See Crispin, Edmund
See also CA 104

Montgomery, Marion H. Jr. 1925- . . . **CLC 7**
See also AITN 1; CA 1-4R; CANR 3;
DLB 6

Montgomery, Max
See Davenport, Guy (Mattison Jr.)

Montherlant, Henry (Milon) de
1896-1972 . . . . **CLC 8, 19**
See also CA 85-88; 37-40R; DLB 72;
MTCW

Python . . . . **CLC 21**
See also Chapman, Graham; Cleese, John
(Marwood); Gilliam, Terry (Vance); Idle,
Eric; Jones, Terence Graham Parry; Palin,
Michael (Edward)
See also AAYA 7

Moodie, Susanna (Strickland)
1803-1885 . . . . **NCLC 14**
See also DLB 99

Mooney, Edward 1951- . . . . **CLC 25**
See also CA 130

Mooney, Ted
See Mooney, Edward

Moorcock, Michael (John)
1939- . . . . **CLC 5, 27, 58**
See also CA 45-48; CAAS 5; CANR 2, 17,
38; DLB 14; MTCW

Moore, Brian
1921- . . . . **CLC 1, 3, 5, 7, 8, 19, 32**
See also CA 1-4R; CANR 1, 25; MTCW

Moore, Edward
See Muir, Edwin

Moore, George Augustus
1852-1933 . . . . **TCLC 7**
See also CA 104; DLB 10, 18, 57

Moore, Lorrie . . . . **CLC 39, 45, 68**
See also Moore, Marie Lorena

Moore, Marianne (Craig)
1887-1972 . . . **CLC 1, 2, 4, 8, 10, 13, 19,**
47; PC 4
See also CA 1-4R; 33-36R; CANR 3;
CDALB 1929-1941; DLB 45; DLBD 7;
MTCW; SATA 20

Moore, Marie Lorena 1957-
See Moore, Lorrie
See also CA 116; CANR 39

Moore, Thomas 1779-1852 . . . . **NCLC 6**
See also DLB 96

Morand, Paul 1888-1976 . . . . **CLC 41**
See also CA 69-72; DLB 65

Morante, Elsa 1918-1985....... **CLC 8, 47**
See also CA 85-88; 117; CANR 35; MTCW

Moravia, Alberto...... **CLC 2, 7, 11, 27, 46**
See also Pincherle, Alberto

More, Hannah 1745-1833 .... **NCLC 27**
See also DLB 107, 109, 116

More, Henry 1614-1687............ **LC 9**

More, Sir Thomas 1478-1535 .... **LC 10**

Moreas, Jean.................... **TCLC 18**
See also Papadiamantopoulos, Johannes

Morgan, Berry 1919- .... **CLC 6**
See also CA 49-52; DLB 6

Morgan, Claire
See Highsmith, (Mary) Patricia

Morgan, Edwin (George) 1920-..... **CLC 31**
See also CA 5-8R; CANR 3; DLB 27

Morgan, (George) Frederick
1922-...................... **CLC 23**
See also CA 17-20R; CANR 21

Morgan, Harriet
See Mencken, H(enry) L(ouis)

Morgan, Jane
See Cooper, James Fenimore

Morgan, Janet 1945- .... **CLC 39**
See also CA 65-68

Morgan, Lady 1776(?)-1859...... **NCLC 29**
See also DLB 116

Morgan, Robin 1941-.............. **CLC 2**
See also CA 69-72; CANR 29; MTCW

Morgan, Scott
See Kuttner, Henry

Morgan, Seth 1949(?)-1990 .... **CLC 65**
See also CA 132

Morgenstern, Christian
1871-1914 .... **TCLC 8**
See also CA 105

Morgenstern, S.
See Goldman, William (W.)

Moricz, Zsigmond 1879-1942 ..... **TCLC 33**

Morike, Eduard (Friedrich)
1804-1875 .... **NCLC 10**

Mori Ogai .... **TCLC 14**
See also Mori Rintaro

Mori Rintaro 1862-1922
See Mori Ogai
See also CA 110

Moritz, Karl Philipp 1756-1793 ...... **LC 2**
See also DLB 94

Morren, Theophil
See Hofmannsthal, Hugo von

Morris, Julian
See West, Morris L(anglo)

Morris, Steveland Judkins 1950(?)-
See Wonder, Stevie
See also CA 111

Morris, William 1834-1896 .... **NCLC 4**
See also CDBLB 1832-1890; DLB 18, 35, 57

Morris, Wright 1910-... **CLC 1, 3, 7, 18, 37**
See also CA 9-12R; CANR 21; DLB 2;
DLBY 81; MTCW

Morrison, Chloe Anthony Wofford
See Morrison, Toni

Morrison, James Douglas 1943-1971
See Morrison, Jim
See also CA 73-76

Morrison, Jim .... **CLC 17**
See also Morrison, James Douglas

Morrison, Toni 1931-..... **CLC 4, 10, 22, 55**
See also AAYA 1; BLC 3; BW; CA 29-32R;
CANR 27; CDALB 1968-1988; DLB 6,
33; DLBY 81; MTCW; SATA 57

Morrison, Van 1945- .... **CLC 21**
See also CA 116

Mortimer, John (Clifford)
1923-.................... **CLC 28, 43**
See also CA 13-16R; CANR 21;
CDBLB 1960 to Present; DLB 13;
MTCW

Mortimer, Penelope (Ruth) 1918-.... **CLC 5**
See also CA 57-60

Morton, Anthony
See Creasey, John

Mosher, Howard Frank .... **CLC 62**

Mosley, Nicholas 1923-........ **CLC 43, 70**
See also CA 69-72; DLB 14

Moss, Howard
1922-1987 .... **CLC 7, 14, 45, 50**
See also CA 1-4R; 123; CANR 1; DLB 5

Motion, Andrew 1952-............ **CLC 47**
See also DLB 40

Motley, Willard (Francis)
1912-1965 .... **CLC 18**
See also BW; CA 117; 106; DLB 76

Mott, Michael (Charles Alston)
1930-.................... **CLC 15, 34**
See also CA 5-8R; CAAS 7; CANR 7, 29

Mowat, Farley (McGill) 1921- ..... **CLC 26**
See also AAYA 1; CA 1-4R; CANR 4, 24;
CLR 20; DLB 68; MAICYA; MTCW;
SATA 3, 55

Mphahlele, Es'kia
See Mphahlele, Ezekiel

Mphahlele, Ezekiel 1919-......... **CLC 25**
See also BLC 3; BW; CA 81-84; CANR 26

Mqhayi, S(amuel) E(dward) K(rune Loliwe)
1875-1945 .... **TCLC 25**
See also BLC 3

Mr. Martin
See Burroughs, William S(eward)

Mrozek, Slawomir 1930-........ **CLC 3, 13**
See also CA 13-16R; CAAS 10; CANR 29;
MTCW

Mrs. Belloc-Lowndes
See Lowndes, Marie Adelaide (Belloc)

Mtwa, Percy (?)-................ **CLC 47**

Mueller, Lisel 1924-........... **CLC 13, 51**
See also CA 93-96; DLB 105

Muir, Edwin 1887-1959 .... **TCLC 2**
See also CA 104; DLB 20, 100

Muir, John 1838-1914 .... **TCLC 28**

Mujica Lainez, Manuel
1910-1984 .... **CLC 31**
See also Lainez, Manuel Mujica
See also CA 81-84; 112; CANR 32; HW

Mukherjee, Bharati 1940-......... **CLC 53**
See also BEST 89:2; CA 107; DLB 60;
MTCW

Muldoon, Paul 1951-.......... **CLC 32, 72**
See also CA 113; 129; DLB 40

Mulisch, Harry 1927-............. **CLC 42**
See also CA 9-12R; CANR 6, 26

Mull, Martin 1943-.............. **CLC 17**
See also CA 105

Mulock, Dinah Maria
See Craik, Dinah Maria (Mulock)

Munford, Robert 1737(?)-1783 .... **LC 5**
See also DLB 31

Mungo, Raymond 1946-.......... **CLC 72**
See also CA 49-52; CANR 2

Munro, Alice
1931- .... **CLC 6, 10, 19, 50; SSC 3**
See also AITN 2; CA 33-36R; CANR 33;
DLB 53; MTCW; SATA 29

Munro, H(ector) H(ugh) 1870-1916
See Saki
See also CA 104; 130; CDBLB 1890-1914;
DLB 34; MTCW; WLC

Murasaki, Lady.................. **CMLC 1**

Murdoch, (Jean) Iris
1919-...... **CLC 1, 2, 3, 4, 6, 8, 11, 15,
22, 31, 51**
See also CA 13-16R; CANR 8;
CDBLB 1960 to Present; DLB 14;
MTCW

Murphy, Richard 1927-.......... **CLC 41**
See also CA 29-32R; DLB 40

Murphy, Sylvia 1937-............. **CLC 34**
See also CA 121

Murphy, Thomas (Bernard) 1935-... **CLC 51**
See also CA 101

Murray, Les(lie) A(llan) 1938- ..... **CLC 40**
See also CA 21-24R; CANR 11, 27

Murry, J. Middleton
See Murry, John Middleton

Murry, John Middleton
1889-1957 .... **TCLC 16**
See also CA 118

Musgrave, Susan 1951- .... **CLC 13, 54**
See also CA 69-72

Musil, Robert (Edler von)
1880-1942 .... **TCLC 12**
See also CA 109; DLB 81

Musset, (Louis Charles) Alfred de
1810-1857 .... **NCLC 7**

My Brother's Brother
See Chekhov, Anton (Pavlovich)

Myers, Walter Dean 1937- .... **CLC 35**
See also AAYA 4; BLC 3; BW; CA 33-36R;
CANR 20; CLR 4, 16; DLB 33;
MAICYA; SAAS 2; SATA 27, 41, 70, 71

Myers, Walter M.
See Myers, Walter Dean

Myles, Symon
See Follett, Ken(neth Martin)

Ossoli, Sarah Margaret (Fuller marchesa d')
1810-1850
See Fuller, Margaret
See also SATA 25

Ostrovsky, Alexander
1823-1886 . . . . NCLC **30**

Otero, Blas de 1916- . . . . CLC **11**
See also CA 89-92

Otto, Whitney 1955-. . . . . CLC **70**

Ouida . . . . TCLC **43**
See also De La Ramee, (Marie) Louise
See also DLB 18

Ousmane, Sembene 1923- . . . . CLC **66**
See also BLC 3; BW; CA 117; 125; MTCW

Ovid 43B.C.-18th cent. (?). . . CMLC **7**; PC **2**

Owen, Wilfred 1893-1918 . . . . . TCLC **5, 27**
See also CA 104; CDBLB 1914-1945;
DLB 20; WLC

Owens, Rochelle 1936-. . . . . CLC **8**
See also CA 17-20R; CAAS 2; CANR 39

Oz, Amos 1939- . . . CLC **5, 8, 11, 27, 33, 54**
See also CA 53-56; CANR 27; MTCW

Ozick, Cynthia 1928-. . . . . . CLC **3, 7, 28, 62**
See also BEST 90:1; CA 17-20R; CANR 23;
DLB 28; DLBY 82; MTCW

Ozu, Yasujiro 1903-1963 . . . . CLC **16**
See also CA 112

Pacheco, C.
See Pessoa, Fernando (Antonio Nogueira)

Pa Chin
See Li Fei-kan

Pack, Robert 1929-. . . . . CLC **13**
See also CA 1-4R; CANR 3; DLB 5

Padgett, Lewis
See Kuttner, Henry

Padilla (Lorenzo), Heberto 1932- . . . CLC **38**
See also AITN 1; CA 123; 131; HW

Page, Jimmy 1944-. . . . . CLC **12**

Page, Louise 1955-. . . . . CLC **40**

Page, P(atricia) K(athleen)
1916-. CLC **7, 18**
See also CA 53-56; CANR 4, 22; DLB 68;
MTCW

Paget, Violet 1856-1935
See Lee, Vernon
See also CA 104

Paget-Lowe, Henry
See Lovecraft, H(oward) P(hillips)

Paglia, Camille 1947-. . . . . CLC **68**

Pakenham, Antonia
See Fraser, Antonia (Pakenham)

Palamas, Kostes 1859-1943 . . . . TCLC **5**
See also CA 105

Palazzeschi, Aldo 1885-1974 . . . . CLC **11**
See also CA 89-92; 53-56; DLB 114

Paley, Grace 1922-. . . . CLC **4, 6, 37**; SSC **8**
See also CA 25-28R; CANR 13; DLB 28;
MTCW

Palin, Michael (Edward) 1943- . . . . . CLC **21**
See also Monty Python
See also CA 107; CANR 35; SATA 67

Palliser, Charles 1947-. . . . . CLC **65**
See also CA 136

Palma, Ricardo 1833-1919. . . . . . . TCLC **29**

Pancake, Breece Dexter 1952-1979
See Pancake, Breece D'J
See also CA 123; 109

Pancake, Breece D'J. . . . . CLC **29**
See also Pancake, Breece Dexter

Papadiamantis, Alexandros
1851-1911 . . . . TCLC **29**

Papadiamantopoulos, Johannes 1856-1910
See Moreas, Jean
See also CA 117

Papini, Giovanni 1881-1956. . . . . . . TCLC **22**
See also CA 121

Paracelsus 1493-1541. . . . . LC **14**

Parasol, Peter
See Stevens, Wallace

Parfenie, Maria
See Codrescu, Andrei

Parini, Jay (Lee) 1948- . . . . CLC **54**
See also CA 97-100; CAAS 16; CANR 32

Park, Jordan
See Kornbluth, C(yril) M.; Pohl, Frederik

Parker, Bert
See Ellison, Harlan

Parker, Dorothy (Rothschild)
1893-1967 . . . . CLC **15, 68**; SSC **2**
See also CA 19-20; 25-28R; CAP 2;
DLB 11, 45, 86; MTCW

Parker, Robert B(rown) 1932-. . . . . . CLC **27**
See also BEST 89:4; CA 49-52; CANR 1,
26; MTCW

Parkes, Lucas
See Harris, John (Wyndham Parkes Lucas)
Beynon

Parkin, Frank 1940-. . . . . CLC **43**

Parkman, Francis Jr. 1823-1893. . NCLC **12**
See also DLB 1, 30

Parks, Gordon (Alexander Buchanan)
1912-. CLC **1, 16**
See also AITN 2; BLC 3; BW; CA 41-44R;
CANR 26; DLB 33; SATA 8

Parnell, Thomas 1679-1718. . . . . LC **3**
See also DLB 94

Parra, Nicanor 1914-. . . . . CLC **2**
See also CA 85-88; CANR 32; HW; MTCW

Parson Lot
See Kingsley, Charles

Partridge, Anthony
See Oppenheim, E(dward) Phillips

Pascoli, Giovanni 1855-1912 . . . . . . TCLC **45**

Pasolini, Pier Paolo
1922-1975 . . . . CLC **20, 37**
See also CA 93-96; 61-64; MTCW

Pasquini
See Silone, Ignazio

Pastan, Linda (Olenik) 1932- . . . . . . CLC **27**
See also CA 61-64; CANR 18; DLB 5

Pasternak, Boris (Leonidovich)
1890-1960 . . . . CLC **7, 10, 18, 63**
See also CA 127; 116; MTCW; WLC

Patchen, Kenneth 1911-1972. . . CLC **1, 2, 18**
See also CA 1-4R; 33-36R; CANR 3, 35;
DLB 16, 48; MTCW

Pater, Walter (Horatio)
1839-1894 . . . . NCLC **7**
See also CDBLB 1832-1890; DLB 57

Paterson, A(ndrew) B(arton)
1864-1941 . . . . TCLC **32**

Paterson, Katherine (Womeldorf)
1932-. . . . . CLC **12, 30**
See also AAYA 1; CA 21-24R; CANR 28;
CLR 7; DLB 52; MAICYA; MTCW;
SATA 13, 53

Patmore, Coventry Kersey Dighton
1823-1896 . . . . NCLC **9**
See also DLB 35, 98

Paton, Alan (Stewart)
1903-1988. . . . . . . CLC **4, 10, 25, 55**
See also CA 13-16; 125; CANR 22; CAP 1;
MTCW; SATA 11, 56; WLC

Paton Walsh, Gillian 1939-
See Walsh, Jill Paton
See also CANR 38; MAICYA; SAAS 3;
SATA 4

Paulding, James Kirke 1778-1860. . NCLC **2**
See also DLB 3, 59, 74

Paulin, Thomas Neilson 1949-
See Paulin, Tom
See also CA 123; 128

Paulin, Tom. . . . . CLC **37**
See also Paulin, Thomas Neilson
See also DLB 40

Paustovsky, Konstantin (Georgievich)
1892-1968 . . . . CLC **40**
See also CA 93-96; 25-28R

Pavese, Cesare 1908-1950 . . . . TCLC **3**
See also CA 104

Pavic, Milorad 1929-. . . . . CLC **60**
See also CA 136

Payne, Alan
See Jakes, John (William)

Paz, Gil
See Lugones, Leopoldo

Paz, Octavio
1914- . . . . . . CLC **3, 4, 6, 10, 19, 51, 65**;
PC **1**
See also CA 73-76; CANR 32; DLBY 90;
HW; MTCW; WLC

Peacock, Molly 1947-. . . . . CLC **60**
See also CA 103; DLB 120

Peacock, Thomas Love
1785-1866 . . . . NCLC **22**
See also DLB 96, 116

Peake, Mervyn 1911-1968. . . . . . . CLC **7, 54**
See also CA 5-8R; 25-28R; CANR 3;
DLB 15; MTCW; SATA 23

Pearce, Philippa . . . . CLC **21**
See also Christie, (Ann) Philippa
See also CLR 9; MAICYA; SATA 1, 67

Pearl, Eric
See Elman, Richard

Pearson, T(homas) R(eid) 1956- . . . . CLC **39**
See also CA 120; 130

Peck, John 1941- . . . . CLC **3**
See also CA 49-52; CANR 3

Peck, Richard (Wayne) 1934-. . . . . . CLC **21**
See also AAYA 1; CA 85-88; CANR 19,
38; MAICYA; SAAS 2; SATA 18, 55

Poe, Edgar Allan
1809-1849 ... **NCLC 1, 16; PC 1; SSC 1**
See also CDALB 1640-1865; DLB 3, 59, 73, 74; SATA 23; WLC

Poet of Titchfield Street, The
See Pound, Ezra (Weston Loomis)

Pohl, Frederik 1919- .... **CLC 18**
See also CA 61-64; CAAS 1; CANR 11, 37; DLB 8; MTCW; SATA 24

Poirier, Louis 1910-
See Gracq, Julien
See also CA 122; 126

Poitier, Sidney 1927-............. **CLC 26**
See also BW; CA 117

Polanski, Roman 1933- .... **CLC 16**
See also CA 77-80

Poliakoff, Stephen 1952- .... **CLC 38**
See also CA 106; DLB 13

.... **CLC 26**
See also Copeland, Stewart (Armstrong); Summers, Andrew James; Sumner, Gordon Matthew

Pollitt, Katha 1949- .... **CLC 28**
See also CA 120; 122; MTCW

Pollock, Sharon 1936- .... **CLC 50**
See also DLB 60

Pomerance, Bernard 1940-........ **CLC 13**
See also CA 101

Ponge, Francis (Jean Gaston Alfred)
1899-1988 .... **CLC 6, 18**
See also CA 85-88; 126

Pontoppidan, Henrik 1857-1943 ... **TCLC 29**

Poole, Josephine .... **CLC 17**
See also Helyar, Jane Penelope Josephine
See also SAAS 2; SATA 5

Popa, Vasko 1922- .... **CLC 19**
See also CA 112

Pope, Alexander 1688-1744.......... **LC 3**
See also CDBLB 1660-1789; DLB 95, 101; WLC

Porter, Connie 1960- .... **CLC 70**

Porter, Gene(va Grace) Stratton
1863(?)-1924 .... **TCLC 21**
See also CA 112

Porter, Katherine Anne
1890-1980 ..... **CLC 1, 3, 7, 10, 13, 15, 27; SSC 4**
See also AITN 2; CA 1-4R; 101; CANR 1; DLB 4, 9, 102; DLBY 80; MTCW; SATA 23, 39

Porter, Peter (Neville Frederick)
1929- .... **CLC 5, 13, 33**
See also CA 85-88; DLB 40

Porter, William Sydney 1862-1910
See Henry, O.
See also CA 104; 131; CDALB 1865-1917; DLB 12, 78, 79; MTCW; YABC 2

Portillo (y Pacheco), Jose Lopez
See Lopez Portillo (y Pacheco), Jose

Post, Melville Davisson
1869-1930 .... **TCLC 39**
See also CA 110

Potok, Chaim 1929- .... **CLC 2, 7, 14, 26**
See also AITN 1, 2; CA 17-20R; CANR 19, 35; DLB 28; MTCW; SATA 33

Potter, Beatrice
See Webb, (Martha) Beatrice (Potter)
See also MAICYA

Potter, Dennis (Christopher George)
1935- .... **CLC 58**
See also CA 107; CANR 33; MTCW

Pound, Ezra (Weston Loomis)
1885-1972 ..... **CLC 1, 2, 3, 4, 5, 7, 10, 13, 18, 34, 48, 50; PC 4**
See also CA 5-8R; 37-40R; CDALB 1917-1929; DLB 4, 45, 63; MTCW; WLC

Povod, Reinaldo 1959-............ **CLC 44**
See also CA 136

Powell, Anthony (Dymoke)
1905- .... **CLC 1, 3, 7, 9, 10, 31**
See also CA 1-4R; CANR 1, 32; CDBLB 1945-1960; DLB 15; MTCW

Powell, Dawn 1897-1965 .... **CLC 66**
See also CA 5-8R

Powell, Padgett 1952-............. **CLC 34**
See also CA 126

Powers, J(ames) F(arl)
1917- .... **CLC 1, 4, 8, 57; SSC 4**
See also CA 1-4R; CANR 2; MTCW

Powers, John J(ames) 1945-
See Powers, John R.
See also CA 69-72

Powers, John R. .... **CLC 66**
See also Powers, John J(ames)

Pownall, David 1938-............ **CLC 10**
See also CA 89-92; DLB 14

Powys, John Cowper
1872-1963 .... **CLC 7, 9, 15, 46**
See also CA 85-88; DLB 15; MTCW

Powys, T(heodore) F(rancis)
1875-1953 .... **TCLC 9**
See also CA 106; DLB 36

Prager, Emily 1952-.............. **CLC 56**

Pratt, Edwin John 1883-1964 ...... **CLC 19**
See also CA 93-96; DLB 92

Premchand .... **TCLC 21**
See also Srivastava, Dhanpat Rai

Preussler, Otfried 1923-........... **CLC 17**
See also CA 77-80; SATA 24

Prevert, Jacques (Henri Marie)
1900-1977 .... **CLC 15**
See also CA 77-80; 69-72; CANR 29; MTCW; SATA 30

Prevost, Abbe (Antoine Francois)
1697-1763 .... **LC 1**

Price, (Edward) Reynolds
1933- .... **CLC 3, 6, 13, 43, 50, 63**
See also CA 1-4R; CANR 1, 37; DLB 2

Price, Richard 1949- .... **CLC 6, 12**
See also CA 49-52; CANR 3; DLBY 81

Prichard, Katharine Susannah
1883-1969 .... **CLC 46**
See also CA 11-12; CANR 33; CAP 1; MTCW; SATA 66

Priestley, J(ohn) B(oynton)
1894-1984 ....**CLC 2, 5, 9, 34**
See also CA 9-12R; 113; CANR 33; CDBLB 1914-1945; DLB 10, 34, 77, 100; DLBY 84; MTCW

Prince, F(rank) T(empleton) 1912- .. **CLC 22**
See also CA 101; DLB 20

Prince 1958(?)- .... **CLC 35**

Prince Kropotkin
See Kropotkin, Peter (Aleksieevich)

Prior, Matthew 1664-1721.......... **LC 4**
See also DLB 95

Pritchard, William H(arrison)
1932- .... **CLC 34**
See also CA 65-68; CANR 23; DLB 111

Pritchett, V(ictor) S(awdon)
1900- .... **CLC 5, 13, 15, 41**
See also CA 61-64; CANR 31; DLB 15; MTCW

Private 19022
See Manning, Frederic

Probst, Mark 1925- .... **CLC 59**
See also CA 130

Prokosch, Frederic 1908-1989.... **CLC 4, 48**
See also CA 73-76; 128; DLB 48

Prophet, The
See Dreiser, Theodore (Herman Albert)

Prose, Francine 1947-............. **CLC 45**
See also CA 109; 112

Proudhon
See Cunha, Euclides (Rodrigues Pimenta) da

Proust,
(Valentin-Louis-George-Eugene-)Marcel
1871-1922 .... **TCLC 7, 13, 33**
See also CA 104; 120; DLB 65; MTCW; WLC

Prowler, Harley
See Masters, Edgar Lee

Pryor, Richard (Franklin Lenox Thomas)
1940- .... **CLC 26**
See also CA 122

Przybyszewski, Stanislaw
1868-1927 .... **TCLC 36**
See also DLB 66

Pteleon
See Grieve, C(hristopher) M(urray)

Puckett, Lute
See Masters, Edgar Lee

Puig, Manuel
1932-1990 .... **CLC 3, 5, 10, 28, 65**
See also CA 45-48; CANR 2, 32; DLB 113; HW; MTCW

Purdy, A(lfred) W(ellington)
1918- ....**CLC 3, 6, 14, 50**
See also Purdy, Al
See also CA 81-84

Purdy, Al
See Purdy, A(lfred) W(ellington)
See also DLB 88

Purdy, James (Amos)
1923- .... **CLC 2, 4, 10, 28, 52**
See also CA 33-36R; CAAS 1; CANR 19; DLB 2; MTCW

Pure, Simon
See Swinnerton, Frank Arthur

Pushkin, Alexander (Sergeyevich)
1799-1837 .... **NCLC 3, 27**
See also SATA 61; WLC

P'u Sung-ling 1640-1715 .... **LC 3**

Reiner, Max
See Caldwell, (Janet Miriam) Taylor (Holland)

Reis, Ricardo
See Pessoa, Fernando (Antonio Nogueira)

Remarque, Erich Maria
1898-1970 . . . . **CLC 21**
See also CA 77-80; 29-32R; DLB 56; MTCW

Remizov, A.
See Remizov, Aleksei (Mikhailovich)

Remizov, A. M.
See Remizov, Aleksei (Mikhailovich)

Remizov, Aleksei (Mikhailovich)
1877-1957 . . . . **TCLC 27**
See also CA 125; 133

Renan, Joseph Ernest
1823-1892 . . . . **NCLC 26**

Renard, Jules 1864-1910 . . . . **TCLC 17**
See also CA 117

Renault, Mary . . . . **CLC 3, 11, 17**
See also Challans, Mary
See also DLBY 83

Rendell, Ruth (Barbara) 1930- . . **CLC 28, 48**
See also Vine, Barbara
See also CA 109; CANR 32; DLB 87; MTCW

Renoir, Jean 1894-1979 . . . . **CLC 20**
See also CA 129; 85-88

Resnais, Alain 1922- . . . . **CLC 16**

Reverdy, Pierre 1889-1960 . . . . **CLC 53**
See also CA 97-100; 89-92

Rexroth, Kenneth
1905-1982 . . . . . . **CLC 1, 2, 6, 11, 22, 49**
See also CA 5-8R; 107; CANR 14, 34; CDALB 1941-1968; DLB 16, 48; DLBY 82; MTCW

Reyes, Alfonso 1889-1959 . . . . **TCLC 33**
See also CA 131; HW

Reyes y Basoalto, Ricardo Eliecer Neftali
See Neruda, Pablo

Reymont, Wladyslaw (Stanislaw)
1868(?)-1925 . . . . **TCLC 5**
See also CA 104

Reynolds, Jonathan 1942- . . . . **CLC 6, 38**
See also CA 65-68; CANR 28

Reynolds, Joshua 1723-1792 . . . . **LC 15**
See also DLB 104

Reynolds, Michael Shane 1937- . . . . **CLC 44**
See also CA 65-68; CANR 9

Reznikoff, Charles 1894-1976 . . . . **CLC 9**
See also CA 33-36; 61-64; CAP 2; DLB 28, 45

Rezzori (d'Arezzo), Gregor von
1914- . . . . **CLC 25**
See also CA 122; 136

Rhine, Richard
See Silverstein, Alvin

Rhys, Jean
1890(?)-1979 . . . . **CLC 2, 4, 6, 14, 19, 51**
See also CA 25-28R; 85-88; CANR 35; CDBLB 1945-1960; DLB 36, 117; MTCW

Ribeiro, Darcy 1922- . . . . **CLC 34**
See also CA 33-36R

Ribeiro, Joao Ubaldo (Osorio Pimentel)
1941- . . . . **CLC 10, 67**
See also CA 81-84

Ribman, Ronald (Burt) 1932- . . . . . . **CLC 7**
See also CA 21-24R

Ricci, Nino 1959- . . . . **CLC 70**
See also CA 137

Rice, Anne 1941- . . . . **CLC 41**
See also AAYA 9; BEST 89:2; CA 65-68; CANR 12, 36

Rice, Elmer (Leopold)
1892-1967 . . . . **CLC 7, 49**
See also CA 21-22; 25-28R; CAP 2; DLB 4, 7; MTCW

Rice, Tim 1944- . . . . **CLC 21**
See also CA 103

Rich, Adrienne (Cecile)
1929- . . . . . **CLC 3, 6, 7, 11, 18, 36; PC 5**
See also CA 9-12R; CANR 20; DLB 5, 67; MTCW

Rich, Barbara
See Graves, Robert (von Ranke)

Rich, Robert
See Trumbo, Dalton

Richards, David Adams 1950- . . . . . . **CLC 59**
See also CA 93-96; DLB 53

Richards, I(vor) A(rmstrong)
1893-1979 . . . . **CLC 14, 24**
See also CA 41-44R; 89-92; CANR 34; DLB 27

Richardson, Anne
See Roiphe, Anne Richardson

Richardson, Dorothy Miller
1873-1957 . . . . **TCLC 3**
See also CA 104; DLB 36

Richardson, Ethel Florence (Lindesay)
1870-1946
See Richardson, Henry Handel
See also CA 105

Richardson, Henry Handel . . . . **TCLC 4**
See also Richardson, Ethel Florence (Lindesay)

Richardson, Samuel 1689-1761 . . . . **LC 1**
See also CDBLB 1660-1789; DLB 39; WLC

Richler, Mordecai
1931- . . . . **CLC 3, 5, 9, 13, 18, 46, 70**
See also AITN 1; CA 65-68; CANR 31; CLR 17; DLB 53; MAICYA; MTCW; SATA 27, 44

Richter, Conrad (Michael)
1890-1968 . . . . **CLC 30**
See also CA 5-8R; 25-28R; CANR 23; DLB 9; MTCW; SATA 3

Riddell, J. H. 1832-1906 . . . . **TCLC 40**

Riding, Laura . . . . **CLC 3, 7**
See also Jackson, Laura (Riding)

Riefenstahl, Berta Helene Amalia 1902-
See Riefenstahl, Leni
See also CA 108

Riefenstahl, Leni . . . . **CLC 16**
See also Riefenstahl, Berta Helene Amalia

Riffe, Ernest
See Bergman, (Ernst) Ingmar

Riley, Tex
See Creasey, John

Rilke, Rainer Maria
1875-1926 . . . . **TCLC 1, 6, 19; PC 2**
See also CA 104; 132; DLB 81; MTCW

Rimbaud, (Jean Nicolas) Arthur
1854-1891 . . . . **NCLC 4, 35; PC 3**
See also WLC

Ringmaster, The
See Mencken, H(enry) L(ouis)

Ringwood, Gwen(dolyn Margaret) Pharis
1910-1984 . . . . **CLC 48**
See also CA 112; DLB 88

Rio, Michel 19(?)- . . . . **CLC 43**

Ritsos, Giannes
See Ritsos, Yannis

Ritsos, Yannis 1909-1990 . . . . . **CLC 6, 13, 31**
See also CA 77-80; 133; CANR 39; MTCW

Ritter, Erika 1948(?)- . . . . **CLC 52**

Rivera, Jose Eustasio 1889-1928 . . . **TCLC 35**
See also HW

Rivers, Conrad Kent 1933-1968 . . . . . . **CLC 1**
See also BW; CA 85-88; DLB 41

Rivers, Elfrida
See Bradley, Marion Zimmer

Riverside, John
See Heinlein, Robert A(nson)

Rizal, Jose 1861-1896 . . . . **NCLC 27**

Roa Bastos, Augusto (Antonio)
1917- . . . . **CLC 45**
See also CA 131; DLB 113; HW

Robbe-Grillet, Alain
1922- . . . . . . **CLC 1, 2, 4, 6, 8, 10, 14, 43**
See also CA 9-12R; CANR 33; DLB 83; MTCW

Robbins, Harold 1916- . . . . **CLC 5**
See also CA 73-76; CANR 26; MTCW

Robbins, Thomas Eugene 1936-
See Robbins, Tom
See also CA 81-84; CANR 29; MTCW

Robbins, Tom . . . . **CLC 9, 32, 64**
See also Robbins, Thomas Eugene
See also BEST 90:3; DLBY 80

Robbins, Trina 1938- . . . . **CLC 21**
See also CA 128

Roberts, Charles G(eorge) D(ouglas)
1860-1943 . . . . **TCLC 8**
See also CA 105; DLB 92; SATA 29

Roberts, Kate 1891-1985 . . . . **CLC 15**
See also CA 107; 116

Roberts, Keith (John Kingston)
1935- . . . . **CLC 14**
See also CA 25-28R

Roberts, Kenneth (Lewis)
1885-1957 . . . . **TCLC 23**
See also CA 109; DLB 9

Roberts, Michele (B.) 1949- . . . . **CLC 48**
See also CA 115

Robertson, Ellis
See Ellison, Harlan; Silverberg, Robert

Robertson, Thomas William
1829-1871 . . . . **NCLC 35**

Robinson, Edwin Arlington
1869-1935 . . . . **TCLC 5; PC 1**
See also CA 104; 133; CDALB 1865-1917; DLB 54; MTCW

Robinson, Henry Crabb
1775-1867 . . . . NCLC **15**
See also DLB 107

Robinson, Jill 1936- . . . . CLC **10**
See also CA 102

Robinson, Kim Stanley 1952- . . . . . . CLC **34**
See also CA 126

Robinson, Lloyd
See Silverberg, Robert

Robinson, Marilynne 1944- . . . . CLC **25**
See also CA 116

Robinson, Smokey . . . . CLC **21**
See also Robinson, William Jr.

Robinson, William Jr. 1940-
See Robinson, Smokey
See also CA 116

Robison, Mary 1949- . . . . CLC **42**
See also CA 113; 116

Roddenberry, Eugene Wesley 1921-1991
See Roddenberry, Gene
See also CA 110; 135; CANR 37; SATA 45

Roddenberry, Gene . . . . CLC **17**
See also Roddenberry, Eugene Wesley
See also AAYA 5; SATO 69

Rodgers, Mary 1931- . . . . CLC **12**
See also CA 49-52; CANR 8; CLR 20;
MAICYA; SATA 8

Rodgers, W(illiam) R(obert)
1909-1969 . . . . CLC **7**
See also CA 85-88; DLB 20

Rodman, Eric
See Silverberg, Robert

Rodman, Howard 1920(?)-1985 . . . . . CLC **65**
See also CA 118

Rodman, Maia
See Wojciechowska, Maia (Teresa)

Rodriguez, Claudio 1934- . . . . CLC **10**

Roelvaag, O(le) E(dvart)
1876-1931 . . . . TCLC **17**
See also CA 117; DLB 9

Roethke, Theodore (Huebner)
1908-1963 . . . . . . CLC **1, 3, 8, 11, 19, 46**
See also CA 81-84; CABS 2;
CDALB 1941-1968; DLB 5; MTCW

Rogers, Thomas Hunton 1927- . . . . . CLC **57**
See also CA 89-92

Rogers, Will(iam Penn Adair)
1879-1935 . . . . TCLC **8**
See also CA 105; DLB 11

Rogin, Gilbert 1929- . . . . CLC **18**
See also CA 65-68; CANR 15

Rohan, Koda . . . . TCLC **22**
See also Koda Shigeyuki

Rohmer, Eric . . . . CLC **16**
See also Scherer, Jean-Marie Maurice

Rohmer, Sax . . . . TCLC **28**
See also Ward, Arthur Henry Sarsfield
See also DLB 70

Roiphe, Anne Richardson 1935- . . . CLC **3, 9**
See also CA 89-92; DLBY 80

**Rolfe, Frederick (William Serafino Austin
Lewis Mary)** 1860-1913 . . . . . . TCLC **12**
See also CA 107; DLB 34

Rolland, Romain 1866-1944 . . . . . . TCLC **23**
See also CA 118; DLB 65

Rolvaag, O(le) E(dvart)
See Roelvaag, O(le) E(dvart)

Romain Arnaud, Saint
See Aragon, Louis

Romains, Jules 1885-1972 . . . . CLC **7**
See also CA 85-88; CANR 34; DLB 65;
MTCW

Romero, Jose Ruben 1890-1952 . . . TCLC **14**
See also CA 114; 131; HW

Ronsard, Pierre de 1524-1585 . . . . LC **6**

Rooke, Leon 1934- . . . . CLC **25, 34**
See also CA 25-28R; CANR 23

Roper, William 1498-1578 . . . . LC **10**

Roquelaure, A. N.
See Rice, Anne

Rosa, Joao Guimaraes 1908-1967 . . . CLC **23**
See also CA 89-92; DLB 113

Rosen, Richard (Dean) 1949- . . . . . . CLC **39**
See also CA 77-80

Rosenberg, Isaac 1890-1918 . . . . . . TCLC **12**
See also CA 107; DLB 20

Rosenblatt, Joe . . . . CLC **15**
See also Rosenblatt, Joseph

Rosenblatt, Joseph 1933-
See Rosenblatt, Joe
See also CA 89-92

Rosenfeld, Samuel 1896-1963
See Tzara, Tristan
See also CA 89-92

Rosenthal, M(acha) L(ouis) 1917- . . . CLC **28**
See also CA 1-4R; CAAS 6; CANR 4;
DLB 5; SATA 59

Ross, Barnaby
See Dannay, Frederic

Ross, Bernard L.
See Follett, Ken(neth Martin)

Ross, J. H.
See Lawrence, T(homas) E(dward)

Ross, (James) Sinclair 1908- . . . . CLC **13**
See also CA 73-76; DLB 88

Rossetti, Christina (Georgina)
1830-1894 . . . . NCLC **2**
See also DLB 35; MAICYA; SATA 20;
WLC

Rossetti, Dante Gabriel
1828-1882 . . . . NCLC **4**
See also CDBLB 1832-1890; DLB 35; WLC

Rossner, Judith (Perelman)
1935- . . . . CLC **6, 9, 29**
See also AITN 2; BEST 90:3; CA 17-20R;
CANR 18; DLB 6; MTCW

Rostand, Edmond (Eugene Alexis)
1868-1918 . . . . TCLC **6, 37**
See also CA 104; 126; MTCW

Roth, Henry 1906- . . . . CLC **2, 6, 11**
See also CA 11-12; CANR 38; CAP 1;
DLB 28; MTCW

Roth, Joseph 1894-1939 . . . . TCLC **33**
See also DLB 85

Roth, Philip (Milton)
1933- . . . . . . CLC **1, 2, 3, 4, 6, 9, 15, 22,
31, 47, 66**
See also BEST 90:3; CA 1-4R; CANR 1, 22,
36; CDALB 1968-1988; DLB 2, 28;
DLBY 82; MTCW; WLC

Rothenberg, Jerome 1931- . . . . CLC **6, 57**
See also CA 45-48; CANR 1; DLB 5

Roumain, Jacques (Jean Baptiste)
1907-1944 . . . . TCLC **19**
See also BLC 3; BW; CA 117; 125

Rourke, Constance (Mayfield)
1885-1941 . . . . TCLC **12**
See also CA 107; YABC 1

Rousseau, Jean-Baptiste 1671-1741 . . . LC **9**

Rousseau, Jean-Jacques 1712-1778 . . . LC **14**
See also WLC

Roussel, Raymond 1877-1933 . . . . . TCLC **20**
See also CA 117

Rovit, Earl (Herbert) 1927- . . . . CLC **7**
See also CA 5-8R; CANR 12

Rowe, Nicholas 1674-1718 . . . . LC **8**
See also DLB 84

Rowley, Ames Dorrance
See Lovecraft, H(oward) P(hillips)

Rowson, Susanna Haswell
1762(?)-1824 . . . . NCLC **5**
See also DLB 37

Roy, Gabrielle 1909-1983 . . . . CLC **10, 14**
See also CA 53-56; 110; CANR 5; DLB 68;
MTCW

Rozewicz, Tadeusz 1921- . . . . CLC **9, 23**
See also CA 108; CANR 36; MTCW

Ruark, Gibbons 1941- . . . . CLC **3**
See also CA 33-36R; CANR 14, 31;
DLB 120

Rubens, Bernice (Ruth) 1923- . . . CLC **19, 31**
See also CA 25-28R; CANR 33; DLB 14;
MTCW

Rudkin, (James) David 1936- . . . . . . CLC **14**
See also CA 89-92; DLB 13

Rudnik, Raphael 1933- . . . . CLC **7**
See also CA 29-32R

Ruffian, M.
See Hasek, Jaroslav (Matej Frantisek)

Ruiz, Jose Martinez . . . . CLC **11**
See also Martinez Ruiz, Jose

Rukeyser, Muriel
1913-1980 . . . . CLC **6, 10, 15, 27**
See also CA 5-8R; 93-96; CANR 26;
DLB 48; MTCW; SATA 22

Rule, Jane (Vance) 1931- . . . . CLC **27**
See also CA 25-28R; CANR 12; DLB 60

Rulfo, Juan 1918-1986 . . . . CLC **8**
See also CA 85-88; 118; CANR 26;
DLB 113; HW; MTCW

Runyon, (Alfred) Damon
1884(?)-1946 . . . . TCLC **10**
See also CA 107; DLB 11, 86

Rush, Norman 1933- . . . . CLC **44**
See also CA 121; 126

Sarton, (Eleanor) May
  1912- .... **CLC 4, 14, 49**
  See also CA 1-4R; CANR 1, 34; DLB 48;
  DLBY 81; MTCW; SATA 36

Sartre, Jean-Paul
  1905-1980 ... **CLC 1, 4, 7, 9, 13, 18, 24,**
  44, 50, 52
  See also CA 9-12R; 97-100; CANR 21;
  DLB 72; MTCW; WLC

Sassoon, Siegfried (Lorraine)
  1886-1967 .... **CLC 36**
  See also CA 104; 25-28R; CANR 36;
  DLB 20; MTCW

Satterfield, Charles
  See Pohl, Frederik

Saul, John (W. III) 1942- .... **CLC 46**
  See also BEST 90:4; CA 81-84; CANR 16

Saunders, Caleb
  See Heinlein, Robert A(nson)

Saura (Atares), Carlos 1932-....... **CLC 20**
  See also CA 114; 131; HW

Sauser-Hall, Frederic 1887-1961.... **CLC 18**
  See also CA 102; 93-96; CANR 36; MTCW

Savage, Catharine
  See Brosman, Catharine Savage

Savage, Thomas 1915- .... **CLC 40**
  See also CA 126; 132; CAAS 15

Savan, Glenn .... **CLC 50**

Saven, Glenn 19(?)- .... **CLC 50**

Sayers, Dorothy L(eigh)
  1893-1957 .... **TCLC 2, 15**
  See also CA 104; 119; CDBLB 1914-1945;
  DLB 10, 36, 77, 100; MTCW

Sayers, Valerie 1952-............. **CLC 50**
  See also CA 134

Sayles, John Thomas 1950-... **CLC 7, 10, 14**
  See also CA 57-60; DLB 44

Scammell, Michael .... **CLC 34**

Scannell, Vernon 1922- .... **CLC 49**
  See also CA 5-8R; CANR 8, 24; DLB 27;
  SATA 59

Scarlett, Susan
  See Streatfeild, (Mary) Noel

Schaeffer, Susan Fromberg
  1941- .... **CLC 6, 11, 22**
  See also CA 49-52; CANR 18; DLB 28;
  MTCW; SATA 22

Schary, Jill
  See Robinson, Jill

Schell, Jonathan 1943-........... **CLC 35**
  See also CA 73-76; CANR 12

Schelling, Friedrich Wilhelm Joseph von
  1775-1854 .... **NCLC 30**
  See also DLB 90

Scherer, Jean-Marie Maurice 1920-
  See Rohmer, Eric
  See also CA 110

Schevill, James (Erwin) 1920-...... **CLC 7**
  See also CA 5-8R; CAAS 12

Schisgal, Murray (Joseph) 1926-..... **CLC 6**
  See also CA 21-24R

Schlee, Ann 1934-................ **CLC 35**
  See also CA 101; CANR 29; SATA 36, 44

Schlegel, August Wilhelm von
  1767-1845 .... **NCLC 15**
  See also DLB 94

Schlegel, Johann Elias (von)
  1719(?)-1749 .... **LC 5**

Schmidt, Arno (Otto) 1914-1979.... **CLC 56**
  See also CA 128; 109; DLB 69

Schmitz, Aron Hector 1861-1928
  See Svevo, Italo
  See also CA 104; 122; MTCW

Schnackenberg, Gjertrud 1953-..... **CLC 40**
  See also CA 116; DLB 120

Schneider, Leonard Alfred 1925-1966
  See Bruce, Lenny
  See also CA 89-92

Schnitzler, Arthur 1862-1931 ...... **TCLC 4**
  See also CA 104; DLB 81, 118

Schor, Sandra (M.) 1932(?)-1990 ... **CLC 65**
  See also CA 132

Schorer, Mark 1908-1977 .... **CLC 9**
  See also CA 5-8R; 73-76; CANR 7;
  DLB 103

Schrader, Paul Joseph 1946-....... **CLC 26**
  See also CA 37-40R; DLB 44

Schreiner, Olive (Emilie Albertina)
  1855-1920 .... **TCLC 9**
  See also CA 105; DLB 18

Schulberg, Budd (Wilson)
  1914- .... **CLC 7, 48**
  See also CA 25-28R; CANR 19; DLB 6, 26,
  28; DLBY 81

Schulz, Bruno 1892-1942......... **TCLC 5**
  See also CA 115; 123

Schulz, Charles M(onroe) 1922-.... **CLC 12**
  See also CA 9-12R; CANR 6; SATA 10

Schuyler, James Marcus
  1923-1991 .... **CLC 5, 23**
  See also CA 101; 134; DLB 5

Schwartz, Delmore (David)
  1913-1966 .... **CLC 2, 4, 10, 45**
  See also CA 17-18; 25-28R; CANR 35;
  CAP 2; DLB 28, 48; MTCW

Schwartz, Ernst
  See Ozu, Yasujiro

Schwartz, John Burnham 1965- .... **CLC 59**
  See also CA 132

Schwartz, Lynne Sharon 1939-..... **CLC 31**
  See also CA 103

Schwartz, Muriel A.
  See Eliot, T(homas) S(tearns)

Schwarz-Bart, Andre 1928-....... **CLC 2, 4**
  See also CA 89-92

Schwarz-Bart, Simone 1938-....... **CLC 7**
  See also CA 97-100

Schwob, (Mayer Andre) Marcel
  1867-1905 .... **TCLC 20**
  See also CA 117

Sciascia, Leonardo
  1921-1989 .... **CLC 8, 9, 41**
  See also CA 85-88; 130; CANR 35; MTCW

Scoppettone, Sandra 1936-........ **CLC 26**
  See also CA 5-8R; SATA 9

Scorsese, Martin 1942- .... **CLC 20**
  See also CA 110; 114

Scotland, Jay
  See Jakes, John (William)

Scott, Duncan Campbell
  1862-1947 .... **TCLC 6**
  See also CA 104; DLB 92

Scott, Evelyn 1893-1963.......... **CLC 43**
  See also CA 104; 112; DLB 9, 48

Scott, F(rancis) R(eginald)
  1899-1985 .... **CLC 22**
  See also CA 101; 114; DLB 88

Scott, Frank
  See Scott, F(rancis) R(eginald)

Scott, Joanna 1960- .... **CLC 50**
  See also CA 126

Scott, Paul (Mark) 1920-1978.... **CLC 9, 60**
  See also CA 81-84; 77-80; CANR 33;
  DLB 14; MTCW

Scott, Walter 1771-1832......... **NCLC 15**
  See also CDBLB 1789-1832; DLB 93, 107,
  116; WLC; YABC 2

Scribe, (Augustin) Eugene
  1791-1861 .... **NCLC 16**

Scrum, R.
  See Crumb, R(obert)

Scudery, Madeleine de 1607-1701..... **LC 2**

Scum
  See Crumb, R(obert)

Scumbag, Little Bobby
  See Crumb, R(obert)

Seabrook, John
  See Hubbard, L(afayette) Ron(ald)

Sealy, I. Allan 1951- .... **CLC 55**

Search, Alexander
  See Pessoa, Fernando (Antonio Nogueira)

Sebastian, Lee
  See Silverberg, Robert

Sebastian Owl
  See Thompson, Hunter S(tockton)

Sebestyen, Ouida 1924-........... **CLC 30**
  See also AAYA 8; CA 107; CLR 17;
  MAICYA; SAAS 10; SATA 39

Sedges, John
  See Buck, Pearl S(ydenstricker)

Sedgwick, Catharine Maria
  1789-1867 .... **NCLC 19**
  See also DLB 1, 74

Seelye, John 1931-............... **CLC 7**

Seferiades, Giorgos Stylianou 1900-1971
  See Seferis, George
  See also CA 5-8R; 33-36R; CANR 5, 36;
  MTCW

Seferis, George .... **CLC 5, 11**
  See also Seferiades, Giorgos Stylianou

Segal, Erich (Wolf) 1937- .... **CLC 3, 10**
  See also BEST 89:1; CA 25-28R; CANR 20,
  36; DLBY 86; MTCW

Seger, Bob 1945-................. **CLC 35**

Seghers, Anna .... **CLC 7**
  See also Radvanyi, Netty
  See also DLB 69

Seidel, Frederick (Lewis) 1936-..... **CLC 18**
  See also CA 13-16R; CANR 8; DLBY 84

Smith, David (Jeddie) 1942-
See Smith, Dave
See also CA 49-52; CANR 1

Smith, Florence Margaret
1902-1971 .... CLC **8**
See also Smith, Stevie
See also CA 17-18; 29-32R; CANR 35;
CAP 2; MTCW

Smith, Iain Crichton 1928- .... CLC **64**
See also CA 21-24R; DLB 40

Smith, John 1580(?)-1631 .... LC **9**

Smith, Johnston
See Crane, Stephen (Townley)

Smith, Lee 1944-................ CLC **25**
See also CA 114; 119; DLBY 83

Smith, Martin
See Smith, Martin Cruz

Smith, Martin Cruz 1942-......... CLC **25**
See also BEST 89:4; CA 85-88; CANR 6, 23

Smith, Mary-Ann Tirone 1944-..... CLC **39**
See also CA 118; 136

Smith, Patti 1946- .... CLC **12**
See also CA 93-96

Smith, Pauline (Urmson)
1882-1959 .... TCLC **25**

Smith, Rosamond
See Oates, Joyce Carol

Smith, Sheila Kaye
See Kaye-Smith, Sheila

Smith, Stevie............. CLC **3, 8, 25, 44**
See also Smith, Florence Margaret
See also DLB 20

Smith, Wilbur A(ddison) 1933-..... CLC **33**
See also CA 13-16R; CANR 7; MTCW

Smith, William Jay 1918- .... CLC **6**
See also CA 5-8R; DLB 5; MAICYA;
SATA 2, 68

Smith, Woodrow Wilson
See Kuttner, Henry

Smolenskin, Peretz 1842-1885.... NCLC **30**

Smollett, Tobias (George) 1721-1771 .. LC **2**
See also CDBLB 1660-1789; DLB 39, 104

Snodgrass, William D(e Witt)
1926- .... CLC **2, 6, 10, 18, 68**
See also CA 1-4R; CANR 6, 36; DLB 5;
MTCW

Snow, C(harles) P(ercy)
1905-1980 .... CLC **1, 4, 6, 9, 13, 19**
See also CA 5-8R; 101; CANR 28;
CDBLB 1945-1960; DLB 15, 77; MTCW

Snow, Frances Compton
See Adams, Henry (Brooks)

Snyder, Gary (Sherman)
1930- .... CLC **1, 2, 5, 9, 32**
See also CA 17-20R; CANR 30; DLB 5, 16

Snyder, Zilpha Keatley 1927-...... CLC **17**
See also CA 9-12R; CANR 38; MAICYA;
SAAS 2; SATA 1, 28

Soares, Bernardo
See Pessoa, Fernando (Antonio Nogueira)

Sobh, A.
See Shamlu, Ahmad

Sobol, Joshua................... CLC **60**

Soderberg, Hjalmar 1869-1941 .... TCLC **39**

Sodergran, Edith (Irene)
See Soedergran, Edith (Irene)

Soedergran, Edith (Irene)
1892-1923 .... TCLC **31**

Softly, Edgar
See Lovecraft, H(oward) P(hillips)

Softly, Edward
See Lovecraft, H(oward) P(hillips)

Sokolov, Raymond 1941-........... CLC **7**
See also CA 85-88

Solo, Jay
See Ellison, Harlan

Sologub, Fyodor .... TCLC **9**
See also Teternikov, Fyodor Kuzmich

Solomons, Ikey Esquir
See Thackeray, William Makepeace

Solomos, Dionysios 1798-1857 ... NCLC **15**

Solwoska, Mara
See French, Marilyn

Solzhenitsyn, Aleksandr I(sayevich)
1918- .. CLC **1, 2, 4, 7, 9, 10, 18, 26, 34**
See also AITN 1; CA 69-72; MTCW; WLC

Somers, Jane
See Lessing, Doris (May)

Sommer, Scott 1951- .... CLC **25**
See also CA 106

Sondheim, Stephen (Joshua)
1930- .... CLC **30, 39**
See also CA 103

Sontag, Susan 1933-... CLC **1, 2, 10, 13, 31**
See also CA 17-20R; CANR 25; DLB 2, 67;
MTCW

Sophocles
496(?)B.C.-406(?)B.C.... CMLC **2; DC 1**

Sorel, Julia
See Drexler, Rosalyn

Sorrentino, Gilbert
1929- .... CLC **3, 7, 14, 22, 40**
See also CA 77-80; CANR 14, 33; DLB 5;
DLBY 80

Soto, Gary 1952-................. CLC **32**
See also CA 119; 125; DLB 82; HW

Soupault, Philippe 1897-1990 ...... CLC **68**
See also CA 116; 131

Souster, (Holmes) Raymond
1921-.................... CLC **5, 14**
See also CA 13-16R; CAAS 14; CANR 13,
29; DLB 88; SATA 63

Southern, Terry 1926- .... CLC **7**
See also CA 1-4R; CANR 1; DLB 2

Southey, Robert 1774-1843 .... NCLC **8**
See also DLB 93, 107; SATA 54

Southworth, Emma Dorothy Eliza Nevitte
1819-1899 .... NCLC **26**

Souza, Ernest
See Scott, Evelyn

Soyinka, Wole
1934- .... CLC **3, 5, 14, 36, 44; DC 2**
See also BLC 3; BW; CA 13-16R;
CANR 27, 39; MTCW; WLC

Spackman, W(illiam) M(ode)
1905-1990 .... CLC **46**
See also CA 81-84; 132

Spacks, Barry 1931-.............. CLC **14**
See also CA 29-32R; CANR 33; DLB 105

Spanidou, Irini 1946-............. CLC **44**

Spark, Muriel (Sarah)
1918- .... CLC **2, 3, 5, 8, 13, 18, 40;
SSC 10**
See also CA 5-8R; CANR 12, 36;
CDBLB 1945-1960; DLB 15; MTCW

Spaulding, Douglas
See Bradbury, Ray (Douglas)

Spaulding, Leonard
See Bradbury, Ray (Douglas)

Spence, J. A. D.
See Eliot, T(homas) S(tearns)

Spencer, Elizabeth 1921-.......... CLC **22**
See also CA 13-16R; CANR 32; DLB 6;
MTCW; SATA 14

Spencer, Leonard G.
See Silverberg, Robert

Spencer, Scott 1945-.............. CLC **30**
See also CA 113; DLBY 86

Spender, Stephen (Harold)
1909- .... CLC **1, 2, 5, 10, 41**
See also CA 9-12R; CANR 31;
CDBLB 1945-1960; DLB 20; MTCW

Spengler, Oswald (Arnold Gottfried)
1880-1936 .... TCLC **25**
See also CA 118

Spenser, Edmund 1552(?)-1599 .... LC **5**
See also CDBLB Before 1660; WLC

Spicer, Jack 1925-1965 ...... CLC **8, 18, 72**
See also CA 85-88; DLB 5, 16

Spielberg, Peter 1929- .... CLC **6**
See also CA 5-8R; CANR 4; DLBY 81

Spielberg, Steven 1947- .... CLC **20**
See also AAYA 8; CA 77-80; CANR 32;
SATA 32

Spillane, Frank Morrison 1918-
See Spillane, Mickey
See also CA 25-28R; CANR 28; MTCW;
SATA 66

Spillane, Mickey................ CLC **3, 13**
See also Spillane, Frank Morrison

Spinoza, Benedictus de 1632-1677 .... LC **9**

Spinrad, Norman (Richard) 1940-... CLC **46**
See also CA 37-40R; CANR 20; DLB 8

Spitteler, Carl (Friedrich Georg)
1845-1924 .... TCLC **12**
See also CA 109

Spivack, Kathleen (Romola Drucker)
1938- .... CLC **6**
See also CA 49-52

Spoto, Donald 1941-.............. CLC **39**
See also CA 65-68; CANR 11

Springsteen, Bruce (F.) 1949- ...... CLC **17**
See also CA 111

Spurling, Hilary 1940-........... CLC **34**
See also CA 104; CANR 25

Squires, Radcliffe 1917-.......... CLC **51**
See also CA 1-4R; CANR 6, 21

Srivastava, Dhanpat Rai 1880(?)-1936
See Premchand
See also CA 118

Stacy, Donald
See Pohl, Frederik

Stael, Germaine de
See Stael-Holstein, Anne Louise Germaine
Necker Baronn
See also DLB 119

Stael-Holstein, Anne Louise Germaine Necker
Baronn 1766-1817 . . . . **NCLC 3**
See also Stael, Germaine de

Stafford, Jean 1915-1979 . . . **CLC 4, 7, 19, 68**
See also CA 1-4R; 85-88; CANR 3; DLB 2;
MTCW; SATA 22

Stafford, William (Edgar)
1914- . . . . **CLC 4, 7, 29**
See also CA 5-8R; CAAS 3; CANR 5, 22;
DLB 5

Staines, Trevor
See Brunner, John (Kilian Houston)

Stairs, Gordon
See Austin, Mary (Hunter)

Stannard, Martin . . . . **CLC 44**

Stanton, Maura 1946- . . . . **CLC 9**
See also CA 89-92; CANR 15; DLB 120

Stanton, Schuyler
See Baum, L(yman) Frank

Stapledon, (William) Olaf
1886-1950 . . . . **TCLC 22**
See also CA 111; DLB 15

Starbuck, George (Edwin) 1931- . . . . **CLC 53**
See also CA 21-24R; CANR 23

Stark, Richard
See Westlake, Donald E(dwin)

Staunton, Schuyler
See Baum, L(yman) Frank

Stead, Christina (Ellen)
1902-1983 . . . . **CLC 2, 5, 8, 32**
See also CA 13-16R; 109; CANR 33;
MTCW

Steele, Richard 1672-1729 . . . . **LC 18**
See also CDBLB 1660-1789; DLB 84, 101

Steele, Timothy (Reid) 1948- . . . . **CLC 45**
See also CA 93-96; CANR 16; DLB 120

Steffens, (Joseph) Lincoln
1866-1936 . . . . **TCLC 20**
See also CA 117

Stegner, Wallace (Earle) 1909- . . . **CLC 9, 49**
See also AITN 1; BEST 90:3; CA 1-4R;
CAAS 9; CANR 1, 21; DLB 9; MTCW

Stein, Gertrude 1874-1946 . . . **TCLC 1, 6, 28**
See also CA 104; 132; CDALB 1917-1929;
DLB 4, 54, 86; MTCW; WLC

Steinbeck, John (Ernst)
1902-1968 . . . . . **CLC 1, 5, 9, 13, 21, 34,**
45; SSC 11
See also CA 1-4R; 25-28R; CANR 1, 35;
CDALB 1929-1941; DLB 7, 9; DLBD 2;
MTCW; SATA 9; WLC

Steinem, Gloria 1934- . . . . **CLC 63**
See also CA 53-56; CANR 28; MTCW

Steiner, George 1929- . . . . **CLC 24**
See also CA 73-76; CANR 31; DLB 67;
MTCW; SATA 62

Steiner, Rudolf 1861-1925 . . . . **TCLC 13**
See also CA 107

Stendhal 1783-1842 . . . . **NCLC 23**
See also DLB 119; WLC

Stephen, Leslie 1832-1904 . . . . **TCLC 23**
See also CA 123; DLB 57

Stephen, Sir Leslie
See Stephen, Leslie

Stephen, Virginia
See Woolf, (Adeline) Virginia

Stephens, James 1882(?)-1950 . . . . . . **TCLC 4**
See also CA 104; DLB 19

Stephens, Reed
See Donaldson, Stephen R.

Steptoe, Lydia
See Barnes, Djuna

Sterchi, Beat 1949- . . . . **CLC 65**

Sterling, Brett
See Bradbury, Ray (Douglas); Hamilton,
Edmond

Sterling, Bruce 1954- . . . . **CLC 72**
See also CA 119

Sterling, George 1869-1926 . . . . **TCLC 20**
See also CA 117; DLB 54

Stern, Gerald 1925- . . . . **CLC 40**
See also CA 81-84; CANR 28; DLB 105

Stern, Richard (Gustave) 1928- . . . **CLC 4, 39**
See also CA 1-4R; CANR 1, 25; DLBY 87

Sternberg, Josef von 1894-1969 . . . . . **CLC 20**
See also CA 81-84

Sterne, Laurence 1713-1768 . . . . **LC 2**
See also CDBLB 1660-1789; DLB 39; WLC

Sternheim, (William Adolf) Carl
1878-1942 . . . . **TCLC 8**
See also CA 105; DLB 56, 118

Stevens, Mark 1951- . . . . **CLC 34**
See also CA 122

Stevens, Wallace
1879-1955 . . . . **TCLC 3, 12, 45**
See also CA 104; 124; CDALB 1929-1941;
DLB 54; MTCW; WLC

Stevenson, Anne (Katharine)
1933- . . . . **CLC 7, 33**
See also CA 17-20R; CAAS 9; CANR 9, 33;
DLB 40; MTCW

Stevenson, Robert Louis (Balfour)
1850-1894 . . . . **NCLC 5, 14; SSC 11**
See also CDBLB 1890-1914; CLR 10, 11;
DLB 18, 57; MAICYA; WLC; YABC 2

Stewart, J(ohn) I(nnes) M(ackintosh)
1906- . . . . **CLC 7, 14, 32**
See also CA 85-88; CAAS 3; MTCW

Stewart, Mary (Florence Elinor)
1916- . . . . **CLC 7, 35**
See also CA 1-4R; CANR 1; SATA 12

Stewart, Mary Rainbow
See Stewart, Mary (Florence Elinor)

Still, James 1906- . . . . **CLC 49**
See also CA 65-68; CANR 10, 26; DLB 9;
SATA 29

Sting
See Sumner, Gordon Matthew

Stirling, Arthur
See Sinclair, Upton (Beall)

Stitt, Milan 1941- . . . . **CLC 29**
See also CA 69-72

Stockton, Francis Richard 1834-1902
See Stockton, Frank R.
See also CA 108; 137; MAICYA; SATA 44

Stockton, Frank R. . . . . **TCLC 47**
See also Stockton, Francis Richard
See also DLB 42, 74; SATA 32

Stoddard, Charles
See Kuttner, Henry

Stoker, Abraham 1847-1912
See Stoker, Bram
See also CA 105; SATA 29

Stoker, Bram . . . . **TCLC 8**
See also Stoker, Abraham
See also CDBLB 1890-1914; DLB 36, 70;
WLC

Stolz, Mary (Slattery) 1920- . . . . **CLC 12**
See also AAYA 8; AITN 1; CA 5-8R;
CANR 13; MAICYA; SAAS 3;
SATA 10, 70, 71

Stone, Irving 1903-1989 . . . . **CLC 7**
See also AITN 1; CA 1-4R; 129; CAAS 3;
CANR 1, 23; MTCW; SATA 3; SATO 64

Stone, Robert (Anthony)
1937- . . . . **CLC 5, 23, 42**
See also CA 85-88; CANR 23; MTCW

Stone, Zachary
See Follett, Ken(neth Martin)

Stoppard, Tom
1937- . . . **CLC 1, 3, 4, 5, 8, 15, 29, 34, 63**
See also CA 81-84; CANR 39;
CDBLB 1960 to Present; DLB 13;
DLBY 85; MTCW; WLC

Storey, David (Malcolm)
1933- . . . . **CLC 2, 4, 5, 8**
See also CA 81-84; CANR 36; DLB 13, 14;
MTCW

Storm, Hyemeyohsts 1935- . . . . **CLC 3**
See also CA 81-84

Storm, (Hans) Theodor (Woldsen)
1817-1888 . . . . **NCLC 1**

Storni, Alfonsina 1892-1938 . . . . **TCLC 5**
See also CA 104; 131; HW

Stout, Rex (Todhunter) 1886-1975 . . . **CLC 3**
See also AITN 2; CA 61-64

Stow, (Julian) Randolph 1935- . . **CLC 23, 48**
See also CA 13-16R; CANR 33; MTCW

Stowe, Harriet (Elizabeth) Beecher
1811-1896 . . . . **NCLC 3**
See also CDALB 1865-1917; DLB 1, 12, 42,
74; MAICYA; WLC; YABC 1

Strachey, (Giles) Lytton
1880-1932 . . . . **TCLC 12**
See also CA 110

Strand, Mark 1934- . . . . . . **CLC 6, 18, 41, 71**
See also CA 21-24R; DLB 5; SATA 41

Straub, Peter (Francis) 1943- . . . . . . **CLC 28**
See also BEST 89:1; CA 85-88; CANR 28;
DLBY 84; MTCW

Strauss, Botho 1944- . . . . **CLC 22**

Streatfeild, (Mary) Noel
1895(?)-1986 . . . . **CLC 21**
See also CA 81-84; 120; CANR 31;
CLR 17; MAICYA; SATA 20, 48

Tolson, Melvin B(eaunorus)
1898(?)-1966 . . . . **CLC 36**
See also BLC 3; BW; CA 124; 89-92;
DLB 48, 76

Tolstoi, Aleksei Nikolaevich
See Tolstoy, Alexey Nikolaevich

Tolstoy, Alexey Nikolaevich
1882-1945 . . . . **TCLC 18**
See also CA 107

Tolstoy, Count Leo
See Tolstoy, Leo (Nikolaevich)

Tolstoy, Leo (Nikolaevich)
1828-1910 . . . . . **TCLC 4, 11, 17, 28, 44;**
SSC 9
See also CA 104; 123; SATA 26; WLC

Tomasi di Lampedusa, Giuseppe 1896-1957
See Lampedusa, Giuseppe (Tomasi) di
See also CA 111

Tomlin, Lily . . . . **CLC 17**
See also Tomlin, Mary Jean

Tomlin, Mary Jean 1939(?)-
See Tomlin, Lily
See also CA 117

Tomlinson, (Alfred) Charles
1927- . . . . **CLC 2, 4, 6, 13, 45**
See also CA 5-8R; CANR 33; DLB 40

Tonson, Jacob
See Bennett, (Enoch) Arnold

Toole, John Kennedy
1937-1969 . . . . **CLC 19, 64**
See also CA 104; DLBY 81

Toomer, Jean
1894-1967 . . . . . **CLC 1, 4, 13, 22; SSC 1**
See also BLC 3; BW; CA 85-88;
CDALB 1917-1929; DLB 45, 51; MTCW

Torley, Luke
See Blish, James (Benjamin)

Tornimparte, Alessandra
See Ginzburg, Natalia

Torre, Raoul della
See Mencken, H(enry) L(ouis)

Torrey, E(dwin) Fuller 1937- . . . . **CLC 34**
See also CA 119

Torsvan, Ben Traven
See Traven, B.

Torsvan, Benno Traven
See Traven, B.

Torsvan, Berick Traven
See Traven, B.

Torsvan, Berwick Traven
See Traven, B.

Torsvan, Bruno Traven
See Traven, B.

Torsvan, Traven
See Traven, B.

Tournier, Michel (Edouard)
1924- . . . . **CLC 6, 23, 36**
See also CA 49-52; CANR 3, 36; DLB 83;
MTCW; SATA 23

Tournimparte, Alessandra
See Ginzburg, Natalia

Towers, Ivar
See Kornbluth, C(yril) M.

Townsend, Sue 1946- . . . . **CLC 61**
See also CA 119; 127; MTCW; SATA 48,
55

Townshend, Peter (Dennis Blandford)
1945- . . . . **CLC 17, 42**
See also CA 107

Tozzi, Federigo 1883-1920 . . . . **TCLC 31**

Traill, Catharine Parr
1802-1899 . . . . **NCLC 31**
See also DLB 99

Trakl, Georg 1887-1914 . . . . **TCLC 5**
See also CA 104

Transtroemer, Tomas (Goesta)
1931- . . . . **CLC 52, 65**
See also CA 117; 129

Transtromer, Tomas Gosta
See Transtroemer, Tomas (Goesta)

Traven, B. (?)-1969 . . . . **CLC 8, 11**
See also CA 19-20; 25-28R; CAP 2; DLB 9,
56; MTCW

Treitel, Jonathan 1959- . . . . **CLC 70**

Tremain, Rose 1943- . . . . **CLC 42**
See also CA 97-100; DLB 14

Tremblay, Michel 1942- . . . . **CLC 29**
See also CA 116; 128; DLB 60; MTCW

Trevanian (a pseudonym) 1930(?)- . . . **CLC 29**
See also CA 108

Trevor, Glen
See Hilton, James

Trevor, William
1928- . . . . **CLC 7, 9, 14, 25, 71**
See also Cox, William Trevor
See also DLB 14

Trifonov, Yuri (Valentinovich)
1925-1981 . . . . **CLC 45**
See also CA 126; 103; MTCW

Trilling, Lionel 1905-1975 . . . . **CLC 9, 11, 24**
See also CA 9-12R; 61-64; CANR 10;
DLB 28, 63; MTCW

Trimball, W. H.
See Mencken, H(enry) L(ouis)

Tristan
See Gomez de la Serna, Ramon

Tristram
See Housman, A(lfred) E(dward)

Trogdon, William (Lewis) 1939-
See Heat-Moon, William Least
See also CA 115; 119

Trollope, Anthony 1815-1882 . . **NCLC 6, 33**
See also CDBLB 1832-1890; DLB 21, 57;
SATA 22; WLC

Trollope, Frances 1779-1863 . . . . . **NCLC 30**
See also DLB 21

Trotsky, Leon 1879-1940 . . . . **TCLC 22**
See also CA 118

Trotter (Cockburn), Catharine
1679-1749 . . . . **LC 8**
See also DLB 84

Trout, Kilgore
See Farmer, Philip Jose

Trow, George W. S. 1943- . . . . **CLC 52**
See also CA 126

Troyat, Henri 1911- . . . . **CLC 23**
See also CA 45-48; CANR 2, 33; MTCW

Trudeau, G(arretson) B(eekman) 1948-
See Trudeau, Garry B.
See also CA 81-84; CANR 31; SATA 35

Trudeau, Garry B. . . . . **CLC 12**
See also Trudeau, G(arretson) B(eekman)
See also AITN 2

Truffaut, Francois 1932-1984 . . . . . . **CLC 20**
See also CA 81-84; 113; CANR 34

Trumbo, Dalton 1905-1976 . . . . **CLC 19**
See also CA 21-24R; 69-72; CANR 10;
DLB 26

Trumbull, John 1750-1831 . . . . . . **NCLC 30**
See also DLB 31

Trundlett, Helen B.
See Eliot, T(homas) S(tearns)

Tryon, Thomas 1926-1991 . . . . **CLC 3, 11**
See also AITN 1; CA 29-32R; 135;
CANR 32; MTCW

Tryon, Tom
See Tryon, Thomas

Ts'ao Hsueh-ch'in 1715(?)-1763 . . . . . . **LC 1**

Tsushima, Shuji 1909-1948
See Dazai, Osamu
See also CA 107

Tsvetaeva (Efron), Marina (Ivanovna)
1892-1941 . . . . **TCLC 7, 35**
See also CA 104; 128; MTCW

Tuck, Lily 1938- . . . . **CLC 70**

Tunis, John R(oberts) 1889-1975 . . . **CLC 12**
See also CA 61-64; DLB 22; MAICYA;
SATA 30, 37

Tuohy, Frank . . . . **CLC 37**
See also Tuohy, John Francis
See also DLB 14

Tuohy, John Francis 1925-
See Tuohy, Frank
See also CA 5-8R; CANR 3

Turco, Lewis (Putnam) 1934- . . . **CLC 11, 63**
See also CA 13-16R; CANR 24; DLBY 84

Turgenev, Ivan
1818-1883 . . . . **NCLC 21; SSC 7**
See also WLC

Turner, Frederick 1943- . . . . **CLC 48**
See also CA 73-76; CAAS 10; CANR 12,
30; DLB 40

Tusan, Stan 1936- . . . . **CLC 22**
See also CA 105

Tutuola, Amos 1920- . . . . **CLC 5, 14, 29**
See also BLC 3; BW; CA 9-12R; CANR 27;
MTCW

Twain, Mark . . . . . **TCLC 6, 12, 19, 36; SSC 6**
See also Clemens, Samuel Langhorne
See also DLB 11, 12, 23, 64, 74; WLC

Tyler, Anne
1941- . . . . **CLC 7, 11, 18, 28, 44, 59**
See also BEST 89:1; CA 9-12R; CANR 11,
33; DLB 6; DLBY 82; MTCW; SATA 7

Tyler, Royall 1757-1826 . . . . **NCLC 3**
See also DLB 37

Tynan, Katharine 1861-1931 . . . . **TCLC 3**
See also CA 104

Tytell, John 1939- . . . . **CLC 50**
See also CA 29-32R

Tyutchev, Fyodor 1803-1873 . . . . . **NCLC 34**

Tzara, Tristan .... **CLC 47**
See also Rosenfeld, Samuel

Uhry, Alfred 1936- .... **CLC 55**
See also CA 127; 133

Ulf, Haerved
See Strindberg, (Johan) August

Ulf, Harved
See Strindberg, (Johan) August

Unamuno (y Jugo), Miguel de
1864-1936 .... **TCLC 2, 9; SSC 11**
See also CA 104; 131; DLB 108; HW;
MTCW

Undercliffe, Errol
See Campbell, (John) Ramsey

Underwood, Miles
See Glassco, John

Undset, Sigrid 1882-1949 .... **TCLC 3**
See also CA 104; 129; MTCW; WLC

Ungaretti, Giuseppe
1888-1970 .... **CLC 7, 11, 15**
See also CA 19-20; 25-28R; CAP 2;
DLB 114

Unger, Douglas 1952- .... **CLC 34**
See also CA 130

Updike, John (Hoyer)
1932- ...... **CLC 1, 2, 3, 5, 7, 9, 13, 15,**
23, 34, 43, 70
See also CA 1-4R; CABS 1; CANR 4, 33;
CDALB 1968-1988; DLB 2, 5; DLBD 3;
DLBY 80, 82; MTCW; WLC

Upshaw, Margaret Mitchell
See Mitchell, Margaret (Munnerlyn)

Upton, Mark
See Sanders, Lawrence

Urdang, Constance (Henriette)
1922- .... **CLC 47**
See also CA 21-24R; CANR 9, 24

Uris, Leon (Marcus) 1924- ...... **CLC 7, 32**
See also AITN 1, 2; BEST 89:2; CA 1-4R;
CANR 1; MTCW; SATA 49

Urmuz
See Codrescu, Andrei

Ustinov, Peter (Alexander) 1921- .... **CLC 1**
See also AITN 1; CA 13-16R; CANR 25;
DLB 13

V
See Chekhov, Anton (Pavlovich)

Vaculik, Ludvik 1926- .... **CLC 7**
See also CA 53-56

Valenzuela, Luisa 1938- .... **CLC 31**
See also CA 101; CANR 32; DLB 113; HW

Valera y Alcala-Galiano, Juan
1824-1905 .... **TCLC 10**
See also CA 106

Valery, (Ambroise) Paul (Toussaint Jules)
1871-1945 .... **TCLC 4, 15**
See also CA 104; 122; MTCW

Valle-Inclan, Ramon (Maria) del
1866-1936 .... **TCLC 5**
See also CA 106

Vallejo, Antonio Buero
See Buero Vallejo, Antonio

Vallejo, Cesar (Abraham)
1892-1938 .... **TCLC 3**
See also CA 105; HW

Valle Y Pena, Ramon del
See Valle-Inclan, Ramon (Maria) del

Van Ash, Cay 1918- .... **CLC 34**

Vanbrugh, Sir John 1664-1726 ...... **LC 21**
See also DLB 80

Van Campen, Karl
See Campbell, John W(ood Jr.)

Vance, Gerald
See Silverberg, Robert

Vance, Jack .... **CLC 35**
See also Vance, John Holbrook
See also DLB 8

Vance, John Holbrook 1916-
See Queen, Ellery; Vance, Jack
See also CA 29-32R; CANR 17; MTCW

Van Den Bogarde, Derek Jules Gaspard Ulric
Niven 1921-
See Bogarde, Dirk
See also CA 77-80

Vandenburgh, Jane .... **CLC 59**

Vanderhaeghe, Guy 1951- .... **CLC 41**
See also CA 113

van der Post, Laurens (Jan) 1906- ... **CLC 5**
See also CA 5-8R; CANR 35

van de Wetering, Janwillem 1931- .. **CLC 47**
See also CA 49-52; CANR 4

Van Dine, S. S. .... **TCLC 23**
See also Wright, Willard Huntington

Van Doren, Carl (Clinton)
1885-1950 .... **TCLC 18**
See also CA 111

Van Doren, Mark 1894-1972 ..... **CLC 6, 10**
See also CA 1-4R; 37-40R; CANR 3;
DLB 45; MTCW

Van Druten, John (William)
1901-1957 .... **TCLC 2**
See also CA 104; DLB 10

Van Duyn, Mona (Jane)
1921- .... **CLC 3, 7, 63**
See also CA 9-12R; CANR 7, 38; DLB 5

Van Dyne, Edith
See Baum, L(yman) Frank

van Itallie, Jean-Claude 1936- ...... **CLC 3**
See also CA 45-48; CAAS 2; CANR 1;
DLB 7

van Ostaijen, Paul 1896-1928 ..... **TCLC 33**

Van Peebles, Melvin 1932- ...... **CLC 2, 20**
See also BW; CA 85-88; CANR 27

Vansittart, Peter 1920- .... **CLC 42**
See also CA 1-4R; CANR 3

Van Vechten, Carl 1880-1964 ...... **CLC 33**
See also CA 89-92; DLB 4, 9, 51

Van Vogt, A(lfred) E(lton) 1912- ..... **CLC 1**
See also CA 21-24R; CANR 28; DLB 8;
SATA 14

Vara, Madeleine
See Jackson, Laura (Riding)

Varda, Agnes 1928- .... **CLC 16**
See also CA 116; 122

Vargas Llosa, (Jorge) Mario (Pedro)
1936- ...... **CLC 3, 6, 9, 10, 15, 31, 42**
See also CA 73-76; CANR 18, 32; HW;
MTCW

Vasiliu, Gheorghe 1881-1957
See Bacovia, George
See also CA 123

Vassa, Gustavus
See Equiano, Olaudah

Vassilikos, Vassilis 1933- .... **CLC 4, 8**
See also CA 81-84

Vaughn, Stephanie .... **CLC 62**

Vazov, Ivan (Minchov)
1850-1921 .... **TCLC 25**
See also CA 121

Veblen, Thorstein (Bunde)
1857-1929 .... **TCLC 31**
See also CA 115

Venison, Alfred
See Pound, Ezra (Weston Loomis)

Verdi, Marie de
See Mencken, H(enry) L(ouis)

Verdu, Matilde
See Cela, Camilo Jose

Verga, Giovanni (Carmelo)
1840-1922 .... **TCLC 3**
See also CA 104; 123

Vergil 70B.C.-19B.C. .... **CMLC 9**

Verhaeren, Emile (Adolphe Gustave)
1855-1916 .... **TCLC 12**
See also CA 109

Verlaine, Paul (Marie)
1844-1896 .... **NCLC 2; PC 2**

Verne, Jules (Gabriel) 1828-1905 ... **TCLC 6**
See also CA 110; 131; MAICYA; SATA 21

Very, Jones 1813-1880 .... **NCLC 9**
See also DLB 1

Vesaas, Tarjei 1897-1970 .... **CLC 48**
See also CA 29-32R

Vialis, Gaston
See Simenon, Georges (Jacques Christian)

Vian, Boris 1920-1959 .... **TCLC 9**
See also CA 106; DLB 72

Viaud, (Louis Marie) Julien 1850-1923
See Loti, Pierre
See also CA 107

Vicar, Henry
See Felsen, Henry Gregor

Vicker, Angus
See Felsen, Henry Gregor

Vidal, Gore
1925- ..... **CLC 2, 4, 6, 8, 10, 22, 33, 72**
See also AITN 1; BEST 90:2; CA 5-8R;
CANR 13; DLB 6; MTCW

Viereck, Peter (Robert Edwin)
1916- .... **CLC 4**
See also CA 1-4R; CANR 1; DLB 5

Vigny, Alfred (Victor) de
1797-1863 .... **NCLC 7**
See also DLB 119

Vilakazi, Benedict Wallet
1906-1947 .... **TCLC 37**

Warner, Sylvia Townsend
1893-1978 .... **CLC 7, 19**
See also CA 61-64; 77-80; CANR 16;
DLB 34; MTCW

Warren, Mercy Otis 1728-1814... **NCLC 13**
See also DLB 31

Warren, Robert Penn
1905-1989 ... **CLC 1, 4, 6, 8, 10, 13, 18,
39, 53, 59; SSC 4**
See also AITN 1; CA 13-16R; 129;
CANR 10; CDALB 1968-1988; DLB 2,
48; DLBY 80, 89; MTCW; SATA 46, 63;
WLC

Warshofsky, Isaac
See Singer, Isaac Bashevis

Warton, Thomas 1728-1790........ **LC 15**
See also DLB 104, 109

Waruk, Kona
See Harris, (Theodore) Wilson

Warung, Price 1855-1911........ **TCLC 45**

Warwick, Jarvis
See Garner, Hugh

Washington, Alex
See Harris, Mark

Washington, Booker T(aliaferro)
1856-1915 .... **TCLC 10**
See also BLC 3; BW; CA 114; 125;
SATA 28

Wassermann, (Karl) Jakob
1873-1934 .... **TCLC 6**
See also CA 104; DLB 66

Wasserstein, Wendy 1950-...... **CLC 32, 59**
See also CA 121; 129; CABS 3

Waterhouse, Keith (Spencer)
1929- .... **CLC 47**
See also CA 5-8R; CANR 38; DLB 13, 15;
MTCW

Waters, Roger 1944-.............. **CLC 35**
See also Pink Floyd

Watkins, Frances Ellen
See Harper, Frances Ellen Watkins

Watkins, Gerrold
See Malzberg, Barry N(athaniel)

Watkins, Paul 1964-............. **CLC 55**
See also CA 132

Watkins, Vernon Phillips
1906-1967 .... **CLC 43**
See also CA 9-10; 25-28R; CAP 1; DLB 20

Watson, Irving S.
See Mencken, H(enry) L(ouis)

Watson, John H.
See Farmer, Philip Jose

Watson, Richard F.
See Silverberg, Robert

Waugh, Auberon (Alexander) 1939-.. **CLC 7**
See also CA 45-48; CANR 6, 22; DLB 14

Waugh, Evelyn (Arthur St. John)
1903-1966 ... **CLC 1, 3, 8, 13, 19, 27, 44**
See also CA 85-88; 25-28R; CANR 22;
CDBLB 1914-1945; DLB 15; MTCW;
WLC

Waugh, Harriet 1944- .... **CLC 6**
See also CA 85-88; CANR 22

Ways, C. R.
See Blount, Roy (Alton) Jr.

Waystaff, Simon
See Swift, Jonathan

Webb, (Martha) Beatrice (Potter)
1858-1943 .... **TCLC 22**
See also Potter, Beatrice
See also CA 117

Webb, Charles (Richard) 1939-...... **CLC 7**
See also CA 25-28R

Webb, James H(enry) Jr. 1946- .... **CLC 22**
See also CA 81-84

Webb, Mary (Gladys Meredith)
1881-1927 .... **TCLC 24**
See also CA 123; DLB 34

Webb, Mrs. Sidney
See Webb, (Martha) Beatrice (Potter)

Webb, Phyllis 1927-.............. **CLC 18**
See also CA 104; CANR 23; DLB 53

Webb, Sidney (James)
1859-1947 .... **TCLC 22**
See also CA 117

Webber, Andrew Lloyd............ CLC 21
See also Lloyd Webber, Andrew

Weber, Lenora Mattingly
1895-1971 .... **CLC 12**
See also CA 19-20; 29-32R; CAP 1;
SATA 2, 26

Webster, John 1579(?)-1634(?) .... **DC 2**
See also CDBLB Before 1660; DLB 58;
WLC

Webster, Noah 1758-1843 .... **NCLC 30**

Wedekind, (Benjamin) Frank(lin)
1864-1918 .... **TCLC 7**
See also CA 104; DLB 118

Weidman, Jerome 1913-........... **CLC 7**
See also AITN 2; CA 1-4R; CANR 1;
DLB 28

Weil, Simone (Adolphine)
1909-1943 .... **TCLC 23**
See also CA 117

Weinstein, Nathan
See West, Nathanael

Weinstein, Nathan von Wallenstein
See West, Nathanael

Weir, Peter (Lindsay) 1944- .... **CLC 20**
See also CA 113; 123

Weiss, Peter (Ulrich)
1916-1982 .... **CLC 3, 15, 51**
See also CA 45-48; 106; CANR 3; DLB 69

Weiss, Theodore (Russell)
1916- .... **CLC 3, 8, 14**
See also CA 9-12R; CAAS 2; DLB 5

Welch, (Maurice) Denton
1915-1948 .... **TCLC 22**
See also CA 121

Welch, James 1940-........ **CLC 6, 14, 52**
See also CA 85-88

Weldon, Fay
1933(?)- .... **CLC 6, 9, 11, 19, 36, 59**
See also CA 21-24R; CANR 16;
CDBLB 1960 to Present; DLB 14;
MTCW

Wellek, Rene 1903- .... **CLC 28**
See also CA 5-8R; CAAS 7; CANR 8;
DLB 63

Weller, Michael 1942-........ **CLC 10, 53**
See also CA 85-88

Weller, Paul 1958- .... **CLC 26**

Wellershoff, Dieter 1925-......... **CLC 46**
See also CA 89-92; CANR 16, 37

Welles, (George) Orson
1915-1985 .... **CLC 20**
See also CA 93-96; 117

Wellman, Mac 1945- .... **CLC 65**

Wellman, Manly Wade 1903-1986 .. **CLC 49**
See also CA 1-4R; 118; CANR 6, 16;
SATA 6, 47

Wells, Carolyn 1869(?)-1942 ...... **TCLC 35**
See also CA 113; DLB 11

Wells, H(erbert) G(eorge)
1866-1946 ...... **TCLC 6, 12, 19; SSC 6**
See also CA 110; 121; CDBLB 1914-1945;
DLB 34, 70; MTCW; SATA 20; WLC

Wells, Rosemary 1943-........... **CLC 12**
See also CA 85-88; CLR 16; MAICYA;
SAAS 1; SATA 18, 69

Welty, Eudora
1909- .... **CLC 1, 2, 5, 14, 22, 33; SSC 1**
See also CA 9-12R; CABS 1; CANR 32;
CDALB 1941-1968; DLB 2, 102;
DLBY 87; MTCW; WLC

Wen I-to 1899-1946 .... **TCLC 28**

Wentworth, Robert
See Hamilton, Edmond

Werfel, Franz (V.) 1890-1945 ...... **TCLC 8**
See also CA 104; DLB 81

Wergeland, Henrik Arnold
1808-1845 .... **NCLC 5**

Wersba, Barbara 1932-........... **CLC 30**
See also AAYA 2; CA 29-32R; CANR 16,
38; CLR 3; DLB 52; MAICYA; SAAS 2;
SATA 1, 58

Wertmueller, Lina 1928- .... **CLC 16**
See also CA 97-100; CANR 39

Wescott, Glenway 1901-1987....... **CLC 13**
See also CA 13-16R; 121; CANR 23;
DLB 4, 9, 102

Wesker, Arnold 1932- .... **CLC 3, 5, 42**
See also CA 1-4R; CAAS 7; CANR 1, 33;
CDBLB 1960 to Present; DLB 13;
MTCW

Wesley, Richard (Errol) 1945-....... **CLC 7**
See also BW; CA 57-60; DLB 38

Wessel, Johan Herman 1742-1785 .... **LC 7**

West, Anthony (Panther)
1914-1987 .... **CLC 50**
See also CA 45-48; 124; CANR 3, 19;
DLB 15

West, C. P.
See Wodehouse, P(elham) G(renville)

West, (Mary) Jessamyn
1902-1984 .... **CLC 7, 17**
See also CA 9-12R; 112; CANR 27; DLB 6;
DLBY 84; MTCW; SATA 37

West, Morris L(anglo) 1916-..... **CLC 6, 33**
See also CA 5-8R; CANR 24; MTCW

West, Nathanael
1903-1940 . . . . **TCLC 1, 14, 44**
See also CA 104; 125; CDALB 1929-1941;
DLB 4, 9, 28; MTCW

West, Paul 1930- . . . . **CLC 7, 14**
See also CA 13-16R; CAAS 7; CANR 22;
DLB 14

West, Rebecca 1892-1983 . . **CLC 7, 9, 31, 50**
See also CA 5-8R; 109; CANR 19; DLB 36;
DLBY 83; MTCW

Westall, Robert (Atkinson) 1929- . . . **CLC 17**
See also CA 69-72; CANR 18; CLR 13;
MAICYA; SAAS 2; SATA 23, 69

Westlake, Donald E(dwin)
1933- . . . . **CLC 7, 33**
See also CA 17-20R; CAAS 13; CANR 16

Westmacott, Mary
See Christie, Agatha (Mary Clarissa)

Weston, Allen
See Norton, Andre

Wetcheek, J. L.
See Feuchtwanger, Lion

Wetering, Janwillem van de
See van de Wetering, Janwillem

Wetherell, Elizabeth
See Warner, Susan (Bogert)

Whalen, Philip 1923- . . . . **CLC 6, 29**
See also CA 9-12R; CANR 5, 39; DLB 16

Wharton, Edith (Newbold Jones)
1862-1937 . . . . **TCLC 3, 9, 27; SSC 6**
See also CA 104; 132; CDALB 1865-1917;
DLB 4, 9, 12, 78; MTCW; WLC

Wharton, James
See Mencken, H(enry) L(ouis)

Wharton, William (a pseudonym)
. . . . **CLC 18, 37**
See also CA 93-96; DLBY 80

Wheatley (Peters), Phillis
1754(?)-1784 . . . . **LC 3; PC 3**
See also BLC 3; CDALB 1640-1865;
DLB 31, 50; WLC

Wheelock, John Hall 1886-1978 . . . . **CLC 14**
See also CA 13-16R; 77-80; CANR 14;
DLB 45

White, E(lwyn) B(rooks)
1899-1985 . . . . **CLC 10, 34, 39**
See also AITN 2; CA 13-16R; 116;
CANR 16, 37; CLR 1, 21; DLB 11, 22;
MAICYA; MTCW; SATA 2, 29, 44

White, Edmund (Valentine III)
1940- . . . . **CLC 27**
See also AAYA 7; CA 45-48; CANR 3, 19,
36; MTCW

White, Patrick (Victor Martindale)
1912-1990 . . **CLC 3, 4, 5, 7, 9, 18, 65, 69**
See also CA 81-84; 132; MTCW

White, Phyllis Dorothy James 1920-
See James, P. D.
See also CA 21-24R; CANR 17; MTCW

White, T(erence) H(anbury)
1906-1964 . . . . **CLC 30**
See also CA 73-76; CANR 37; MAICYA;
SATA 12

White, Terence de Vere 1912- . . . . . . **CLC 49**
See also CA 49-52; CANR 3

White, Walter
See White, Walter F(rancis)
See also BLC 3

White, Walter F(rancis)
1893-1955 . . . . **TCLC 15**
See also White, Walter
See also CA 115; 124; DLB 51

White, William Hale 1831-1913
See Rutherford, Mark
See also CA 121

Whitehead, E(dward) A(nthony)
1933- . . . . **CLC 5**
See also CA 65-68

Whitemore, Hugh (John) 1936- . . . . . **CLC 37**
See also CA 132

Whitman, Sarah Helen (Power)
1803-1878 . . . . **NCLC 19**
See also DLB 1

Whitman, Walt(er)
1819-1892 . . . . **NCLC 4, 31; PC 3**
See also CDALB 1640-1865; DLB 3, 64;
SATA 20; WLC

Whitney, Phyllis A(yame) 1903- . . . . **CLC 42**
See also AITN 2; BEST 90:3; CA 1-4R;
CANR 3, 25, 38; MAICYA; SATA 1, 30

Whittemore, (Edward) Reed (Jr.)
1919- . . . . **CLC 4**
See also CA 9-12R; CAAS 8; CANR 4;
DLB 5

Whittier, John Greenleaf
1807-1892 . . . . **NCLC 8**
See also CDALB 1640-1865; DLB 1

Whittlebot, Hernia
See Coward, Noel (Peirce)

Wicker, Thomas Grey 1926-
See Wicker, Tom
See also CA 65-68; CANR 21

Wicker, Tom . . . . **CLC 7**
See also Wicker, Thomas Grey

Wideman, John Edgar
1941- . . . . **CLC 5, 34, 36, 67**
See also BLC 3; BW; CA 85-88; CANR 14;
DLB 33

Wiebe, Rudy (H.) 1934- . . . . . . **CLC 6, 11, 14**
See also CA 37-40R; DLB 60

Wieland, Christoph Martin
1733-1813 . . . . **NCLC 17**
See also DLB 97

Wieners, John 1934- . . . . **CLC 7**
See also CA 13-16R; DLB 16

Wiesel, Elie(zer) 1928- . . . . . **CLC 3, 5, 11, 37**
See also AAYA 7; AITN 1; CA 5-8R;
CAAS 4; CANR 8; DLB 83; DLBY 87;
MTCW; SATA 56

Wiggins, Marianne 1947- . . . . **CLC 57**
See also BEST 89:3; CA 130

Wight, James Alfred 1916-
See Herriot, James
See also CA 77-80; SATA 44, 55

Wilbur, Richard (Purdy)
1921- . . . . **CLC 3, 6, 9, 14, 53**
See also CA 1-4R; CABS 2; CANR 2, 29;
DLB 5; MTCW; SATA 9

Wild, Peter 1940- . . . . **CLC 14**
See also CA 37-40R; DLB 5

Wilde, Oscar (Fingal O'Flahertie Wills)
1854(?)-1900 . . . . . . **TCLC 1, 8, 23, 41;**
SSC 11
See also CA 104; 119; CDBLB 1890-1914;
DLB 10, 19, 34, 57; SATA 24; WLC

Wilder, Billy . . . . **CLC 20**
See also Wilder, Samuel
See also DLB 26

Wilder, Samuel 1906-
See Wilder, Billy
See also CA 89-92

Wilder, Thornton (Niven)
1897-1975 . . . . . **CLC 1, 5, 6, 10, 15, 35;**
DC 1
See also AITN 2; CA 13-16R; 61-64;
DLB 4, 7, 9; MTCW; WLC

Wiley, Richard 1944- . . . . **CLC 44**
See also CA 121; 129

Wilhelm, Kate . . . . **CLC 7**
See also Wilhelm, Katie Gertrude
See also CAAS 5; DLB 8

Wilhelm, Katie Gertrude 1928-
See Wilhelm, Kate
See also CA 37-40R; CANR 17, 36; MTCW

Wilkins, Mary
See Freeman, Mary Eleanor Wilkins

Willard, Nancy 1936- . . . . **CLC 7, 37**
See also CA 89-92; CANR 10, 39; CLR 5;
DLB 5, 52; MAICYA; MTCW;
SATA 30, 37, 71

Williams, C(harles) K(enneth)
1936- . . . . **CLC 33, 56**
See also CA 37-40R; DLB 5

Williams, Charles
See Collier, James L(incoln)

Williams, Charles (Walter Stansby)
1886-1945 . . . . **TCLC 1, 11**
See also CA 104; DLB 100

Williams, (George) Emlyn
1905-1987 . . . . **CLC 15**
See also CA 104; 123; CANR 36; DLB 10,
77; MTCW

Williams, Hugo 1942- . . . . **CLC 42**
See also CA 17-20R; DLB 40

Williams, J. Walker
See Wodehouse, P(elham) G(renville)

Williams, John A(lfred) 1925- . . . . **CLC 5, 13**
See also BLC 3; BW; CA 53-56; CAAS 3;
CANR 6, 26; DLB 2, 33

Williams, Jonathan (Chamberlain)
1929- . . . . **CLC 13**
See also CA 9-12R; CAAS 12; CANR 8;
DLB 5

Williams, Joy 1944- . . . . **CLC 31**
See also CA 41-44R; CANR 22

Williams, Norman 1952- . . . . **CLC 39**
See also CA 118

Williams, Tennessee
1911-1983 . . . . **CLC 1, 2, 5, 7, 8, 11, 15,**
19, 30, 39, 45, 71
See also AITN 1, 2; CA 5-8R; 108;
CABS 3; CANR 31; CDALB 1941-1968;
DLB 7; DLBD 4; DLBY 83; MTCW;
WLC

Wright, Rick 1945-.............. **CLC 35**
See also Pink Floyd

Wright, Rowland
See Wells, Carolyn

Wright, Stephen 1946-............ **CLC 33**

Wright, Willard Huntington 1888-1939
See Van Dine, S. S.
See also CA 115

Wright, William 1930-............ **CLC 44**
See also CA 53-56; CANR 7, 23

Wu Ch'eng-en 1500(?)-1582(?)....... **LC 7**

Wu Ching-tzu 1701-1754............ **LC 2**

Wurlitzer, Rudolph 1938(?)- ... **CLC 2, 4, 15**
See also CA 85-88

Wycherley, William 1641-1715.... **LC 8, 21**
See also CDBLB 1660-1789; DLB 80

Wylie, Elinor (Morton Hoyt)
1885-1928 .... **TCLC 8**
See also CA 105; DLB 9, 45

Wylie, Philip (Gordon) 1902-1971... **CLC 43**
See also CA 21-22; 33-36R; CAP 2; DLB 9

Wyndham, John
See Harris, John (Wyndham Parkes Lucas)
Beynon

Wyss, Johann David Von
1743-1818 .... **NCLC 10**
See also MAICYA; SATA 27, 29

Yakumo Koizumi
See Hearn, (Patricio) Lafcadio (Tessima
Carlos)

Yanez, Jose Donoso
See Donoso (Yanez), Jose

Yanovsky, Basile S.
See Yanovsky, V(assily) S(emenovich)

Yanovsky, V(assily) S(emenovich)
1906-1989 .... **CLC 2, 18**
See also CA 97-100; 129

Yates, Richard 1926-......... **CLC 7, 8, 23**
See also CA 5-8R; CANR 10; DLB 2;
DLBY 81

Yeats, W. B.
See Yeats, William Butler

Yeats, William Butler
1865-1939 .... **TCLC 1, 11, 18, 31**
See also CA 104; 127; CDBLB 1890-1914;
DLB 10, 19, 98; MTCW; WLC

Yehoshua, Abraham B. 1936- ... **CLC 13, 31**
See also CA 33-36R

Yep, Laurence Michael 1948-...... **CLC 35**
See also AAYA 5; CA 49-52; CANR 1;
CLR 3, 17; DLB 52; MAICYA; SATA 7,
69

Yerby, Frank G(arvin)
1916-1991 .... **CLC 1, 7, 22**
See also BLC 3; BW; CA 9-12R; 136;
CANR 16; DLB 76; MTCW

Yesenin, Sergei Alexandrovich
See Esenin, Sergei (Alexandrovich)

Yevtushenko, Yevgeny (Alexandrovich)
1933- .... **CLC 1, 3, 13, 26, 51**
See also CA 81-84; CANR 33; MTCW

Yezierska, Anzia 1885(?)-1970 ..... **CLC 46**
See also CA 126; 89-92; DLB 28; MTCW

Yglesias, Helen 1915-.......... **CLC 7, 22**
See also CA 37-40R; CANR 15; MTCW

Yokomitsu Riichi 1898-1947 ..... **TCLC 47**

York, Jeremy
See Creasey, John

York, Simon
See Heinlein, Robert A(nson)

Yorke, Henry Vincent 1905-1974 ... **CLC 13**
See also Green, Henry
See also CA 85-88; 49-52

Young, Al(bert James) 1939-....... **CLC 19**
See also BLC 3; BW; CA 29-32R;
CANR 26; DLB 33

Young, Andrew (John) 1885-1971.... **CLC 5**
See also CA 5-8R; CANR 7, 29

Young, Collier
See Bloch, Robert (Albert)

Young, Edward 1683-1765........... **LC 3**
See also DLB 95

Young, Neil 1945-................ **CLC 17**
See also CA 110

Yourcenar, Marguerite
1903-1987 .... **CLC 19, 38, 50**
See also CA 69-72; CANR 23; DLB 72;
DLBY 88; MTCW

Yurick, Sol 1925-................ **CLC 6**
See also CA 13-16R; CANR 25

Zamiatin, Yevgenii
See Zamyatin, Evgeny Ivanovich

Zamyatin, Evgeny Ivanovich
1884-1937 .... **TCLC 8, 37**
See also CA 105

Zangwill, Israel 1864-1926....... **TCLC 16**
See also CA 109; DLB 10

Zappa, Francis Vincent Jr. 1940-
See Zappa, Frank
See also CA 108

Zappa, Frank.................... **CLC 17**
See also Zappa, Francis Vincent Jr.

Zaturenska, Marya 1902-1982.... **CLC 6, 11**
See also CA 13-16R; 105; CANR 22

Zelazny, Roger (Joseph) 1937- ..... **CLC 21**
See also AAYA 7; CA 21-24R; CANR 26;
DLB 8; MTCW; SATA 39, 57

Zhdanov, Andrei A(lexandrovich)
1896-1948 .... **TCLC 18**
See also CA 117

Zhukovsky, Vasily 1783-1852 .... **NCLC 35**

Ziegenhagen, Eric .... **CLC 55**

Zimmer, Jill Schary
See Robinson, Jill

Zimmerman, Robert
See Dylan, Bob

Zindel, Paul 1936- .... **CLC 6, 26**
See also AAYA 2; CA 73-76; CANR 31;
CLR 3; DLB 7, 52; MAICYA; MTCW;
SATA 16, 58

Zinov'Ev, A. A.
See Zinoviev, Alexander (Aleksandrovich)

Zinoviev, Alexander (Aleksandrovich)
1922- .... **CLC 19**
See also CA 116; 133; CAAS 10

Zoilus
See Lovecraft, H(oward) P(hillips)

Zola, Emile 1840-1902... **TCLC 1, 6, 21, 41**
See also CA 104; WLC

Zoline, Pamela 1941-............. **CLC 62**

Zorrilla y Moral, Jose 1817-1893.. **NCLC 6**

Zoshchenko, Mikhail (Mikhailovich)
1895-1958 .... **TCLC 15**
See also CA 115

Zuckmayer, Carl 1896-1977........ **CLC 18**
See also CA 69-72; DLB 56

Zuk, Georges
See Skelton, Robin

Zukofsky, Louis
1904-1978 .... **CLC 1, 2, 4, 7, 11, 18**
See also CA 9-12R; 77-80; CANR 39;
DLB 5; MTCW

Zweig, Paul 1935-1984........ **CLC 34, 42**
See also CA 85-88; 113

Zweig, Stefan 1881-1942 .... **TCLC 17**
See also CA 112; DLB 81, 118

SSC Cumulative Nationality Index

SSC Cumulative Title Index

Title Index

Title Index

"The Elm-Tree Mother" (Andersen)
See "The Elder-Tree Mother"

"An Eloquence of Grief" (Crane) 7:130

"Elsie in New York" (Henry) 5:194

"The Embarkment for Cythera" (Cheever)
1:93

"An Embarrassing Situation" (Chopin) 8:72

"Emelyan and the Empty Drum" (Tolstoy)
See "The Empty Drum"

"Emma Zunz" (Borges) 4:16, 18-19, 23, 37,
39, 40

"Emotional Bankruptcy" (Fitzgerald) 6:50

"The Emperor's New Clothes" (Andersen)
6:10-11, 13, 16, 18, 26, 30

"The Empire of the Ants" (Wells) 6:361, 365,
382, 391-92, 403

"The Empty Amulet" (Bowles) 3:76

"The Empty Drum" ("Emelyan and the
Empty Drum") (Tolstoy) 9:377, 380, 388

"An Empty Purse" (Jewett) 6:156

"En famille" (Maupassant) 1:259-60, 263,
272, 274, 278

"En voyage" (Maupassant) 1:280

"En wagon" (Maupassant) 1:263

"The Enamored Youth" (Hesse) 9:243

"The Encantadas; or, The Enchanted Isles"
(Melville) 1:293, 297-99, 303-04, 308, 310-
11, 321-22, 329

"The Enchanted Bluff" (Cather) 2:97, 102,
104-05, 108

"An Enchanted Garden" (Calvino)
See "Un giardino incantato"

"The Enchanted Kiss" (Henry) 5:159, 163

"The Enchanted Sea-Wilderness" (Twain)
6:337

"The Enchantress" (Bates) 10:123

The Enchantress, and Other Stories (Bates)
10:123

"An Encounter" (Joyce) 3:201, 205, 208,
217-18, 225-26, 230, 232, 234, 237, 247

"Encounter at Dawn" (Clarke) 3:127, 135,
143

"Encounter with Evil" (Cortazar)
See "Encuentro con el mal"

Encounters (Bowen) 3:29, 40

"Encuentro con el mal" ("Encounter with
Evil") (Cortazar) 7:94

"The End" (Borges) 4:10

"The End of Something" (Hemingway)
1:208, 234, 244-45

"The End of the Duel" (Borges) 4:20, 33-4

End of the Game (Cortazar)
See *Final del juego*

"The End of the Passage" (Kipling)
See "At the End of the Passage"

"The End of the Story" (London) 4:256

"The End of the Tether" (Conrad) 9:140-41,
143, 145

"The End of the World" (Turgenev) 7:335

The End of the World, and Other Stories
(Gallant) 5:130

"The End of Wisdom" (Chesterton) 1:140

"Endicott and the Red Cross" (Hawthorne)
See "Endicott of the Red Cross"

"Endicott of the Red Cross" ("Endicott and
the Red Cross") (Hawthorne) 3:175-76

"L'endormeuse" (Maupassant) 1:284

"The Enduring Chill" (O'Connor) 1:342-43,
356, 365

"Enemies" (Chekhov) 2:158

"The Enemies" (Thomas) 3:407-09

"The Enemies to Each Other" (Kipling)
5:283

"L'enfant malade" (Colette) 10:274-76

"Engineer-Private Paul Klee Misplaces an
Aircraft between Milbertschofen and
Cambrai, March 1916" (Barthelme) 2:49,
54

"England, My England" (Lawrence) 4:212-
13, 229, 231-32, 235

England, My England, and Other Stories
(Lawrence) 4:202, 230-31, 233-37

"England versus England" (Lessing) 6:199,
218

"English Writers on America" (Irving) 2:244,
254

"L'enlèvement de la rédoute" ("The Taking of
the Redoubt") (Merimee) 7:278, 280-81,
283, 287-89

"The Enlightenments of Pagett, M. P."
(Kipling) 5:261

"Enormous Changes at the Last Minute"
(Paley) 8:391-92, 397, 407-08, 410-11, 415

"The Enormous Radio" (Cheever) 1:106, 109

The Enormous Radio, and Other Stories
(Cheever) 1:89, 92, 95, 98-100

"Enough" (Turgenev) 7:323, 325, 336

"Enragée" (Maupassant) 1:274

"Enter a Dragoon" (Hardy) 2:215

"The Entomologist" (Cable) 4:50

L'entrada en guerra (Calvino) 3:97, 116

L'entrave (*The Shackle*) (Colette) 10:257, 272

L'envers du music-hall (Colette) 10:291

"EPICAC" (Vonnegut) 8:429

"Epilogue: The Photographer" (Munro)
3:332, 338, 340, 343

"Les epingles" (Maupassant) 1:263, 286

"Episode" (Maugham) 8:380

"Episode in the Life of an Ancestor" (Boyle)
5:54, 70

"An Episode of War" (Crane) 7:104, 109-10

"Epitaph" (O'Brien) 10:345, 347

"Eric Hermannson's Soul" (Cather) 2:96,
100-01, 105, 107

"Ermolai and the Miller's Wife" (Turgenev)
See "Yermolai and the Miller's Wife"

"Ernst in Civilian Clothes" (Gallant) 5:133,
138

"Errand" (Carver) 8:43

"Error" (Singer) 3:377

"An Error in Chemistry" (Faulkner) 1:179

"Esarhaddon, King of Assyria" (Tolstoy)
9:380, 388

"The Escape" (Mansfield) 9:293

The Escaped Cock (Lawrence)
See *The Man Who Died*

"Escapement" (Ballard) 1:68

"La escritura del Dios" ("The God's Script")
(Borges) 4:7, 23, 28-9

"La escuela de noche" ("The School by
Night") (Cortazar) 7:91

"Eskimo" (Munro) 3:347

El espejo de la muerte (Unamuno) 11:312

"La espera" (Borges) 4:16

"Estación de la mano" ("Season of the Hand")
(Cortazar) 7:94

"Esther" (Toomer) 1:445, 450-51, 457, 459

"Esther Kreindel the Second" (Singer) 3:363

"Eterna" (Lavin) 4:184, 189

The Eternal Husband (Dostoevsky)
See *Vechny muzh*

"The Eternity of Forms" (London) 4:255-56,
295

"Ethan Brand" (Hawthorne) 3:159, 179-80,
182

Ethan Frome (Wharton) 6:415-17, 419, 422,
438-39

"The Ethics of Pig" (Henry) 5:166

"Etude de femme" (Balzac) 5:31

Etudes analytiques (*Analytical Studies*) (Balzac)
5:8-9, 31

Études de moeurs au XIXe siècle (Balzac) 5:3

Etudes philosophiques (*Philosophic Studies*)
(Balzac) 5:8-9, 12, 31, 48

"Eugénie Grandet" (Barthelme) 2:40

"Euphrasie" (Chopin) 8:69-70

"Eva está dentro de su gato" ("Eva Inside Her
Cat") (Garcia Marquez) 8:154-55

"Eva Inside Her Cat" (Garcia Marquez)
See "Eva está dentro de su gato"

"Eveline" (Joyce) 3:205, 226, 231, 234, 247-
48

"Evening at Home" (Boyle) 5:63-4

"An Evening with Dr. Faust" (Hesse) 9:230,
236

"The Evening's at Seven" (Thurber) 1:417,
425

Evenings on a Farm near Dikanka (Gogol)
See *Vechera ná khutore bliz Dikanki*

"Events of That Easter" (Cheever) 1:93

Eventyr, fortalte for børn (*Fairy Tales; New
Stories; Stories; Stories Told for Children;
Wonder Stories Told for Children; Wonder
Tales; Wonder Tales for Children*)
(Andersen) 6:8, 12, 15, 22, 30

"An Every-Day Girl" (Jewett) 6:156-59

"Everybody Was Very Nice" (Benet) 10:142,
144, 153

"Everyday Use" (Walker) 5:402-03, 406, 416-
17

"Everything in Its Right Place" (Andersen)
6:4, 22-3

"Everything Stuck to Him" (Carver)
See "Distance"

"Everything That Rises Must Converge"
(O'Connor) 1:341, 363

Everything That Rises Must Converge
(O'Connor) 1:341-43

"Eve's Diary" (Twain) 6:295

"The Eviction" (O'Flaherty) 6:277, 280

"Evil Allures, but Good Endures" (Tolstoy)
9:388

"Excellent People" (Chekhov) 2:155

"The Executor" (Spark) 10:362, 366, 368,
370

L'éxil et le royaume (*Exile and the Kingdom*)
(Camus) 9:103-05, 108-11, 118, 122, 125-
26, 131, 134

Exile and the Kingdom (Camus)
See *L'éxil et le royaume*

"Exile of Eons" (Clarke) 3:144

"Expedition to Earth" (Clarke) 3:150

Expedition to Earth (Clarke) 3:124, 135, 149-
50

"Experiment in Luxury" (Crane) 7:136, 138

"An Experiment in Misery" (Crane) 7:102,
108-09, 129, 136, 138, 145

"The Explanation" (Barthelme) 2:35, 40-1, 55

*Extracts from Captain Stormfield's Visit to
Heaven* (Twain) 6:295, 303, 339

"Extraordinary Little Cough" (Thomas)
3:394, 403, 406, 411-12

"Extricating Young Gussie" (Wodehouse)
2:342

"The Eye" (Bowles) 3:75, 80

Title Index

Title Index

Title Index

Title Index

ISBN 0-8103-7953-8

90000

9 780810 379534